D0085911

Erika L. Rosenberg

©Erika Rosenberg

Erika L. Rosenberg is an emotions researcher, health psychologist, and teacher of meditation. Dr. Rosenberg received her PhD in Psychology from the University of California, San Francisco, where she studied with Paul Ekman. Dr. Rosenberg served on the faculties at the University of Delaware and the College of William & Mary. Erika is a Senior Investigator at the Center for Mind and Brain at the University of California, Davis, Senior Teacher at the Center for Compassion and Altruism Research and Education (CCARE) at Stanford University, Faculty at Nyingma Institute of Tibetan Studies, in Berkeley, CA, and Founding Faculty at The Compassion Institute, a new nonprofit devoted to the promotion of compassion worldwide.

Dr. Rosenberg is a world-renowned expert in facial expression of emotion, who trains and consults on facial measurement using the Facial Action Coding System (FACS). She teaches FACS workshops worldwide and consults on facial expression with academic, corporate, and entertainment industry clients worldwide, including digital effects and animators in major computer game and film production companies. From 2009–2011 she served as Scientific Consultant on the Fox TV show *Lie to Me*.

Erika's work with meditation encompasses both teaching and personal practice and spans nearly three decades. As a senior teacher at Stanford University's CCARE, she co-authored the Compassion Cultivation Training (CCT) program with Thupten Jinpa and others in 2009. In 2010, she personally presented the CCT program to His Holiness the Dalai Lama. Erika Rosenberg has taught meditation in diverse international venues such as Google Inc., Lerab Ling Monastery, Upaya Zen Center, Kripalu Yoga Center, The Telluride Institute, and Burning Man.

In addition to McGraw-Hill's *Psychology: Perspectives and Connections*, 4e, Erika is co-editor of *What the Face Reveals* (with Paul Ekman), now in press in its 3rd edition, and author of numerous scientific articles and chapters on facial expression, emotion, and meditation.

Formerly married, now amicably divorced and forever colleagues, Erika and Greg have two sons, Jerry and Evan, and live in Oakland, California.

Brief Contents

PSYCHOLOGY
PERSPECTIVES AND CONNECTIONS

Gregory J. Feist

San Jose State University

Erika L. Rosenberg

University of California, Davis

Mc
Graw
Hill
Education

PSYCHOLOGY: PERSPECTIVES AND CONNECTIONS, FOURTH EDITION

4 5 6 7 8 9 QVS 22 21 20 19 18

Looseleaf ISBN: 978-1-259-67697-0
MHID: 1-259-67697-8

Bound ISBN: 978-1-260-39703-1
MHID: 1-260-39703-3

Portfolio Manager: *Nancy Welcher*
Product Developers: *Sara Gordus, Dawn Groundwater*
Content Project Managers: *Melissa M. Leick, Sandy Wille; Jodi Banowetz*
Buyer: *Laura Fuller*
Designer: *Matt Backhaus*
Content Licensing Specialist: *Lori Slattery*
Cover Image: *© Ann and Steve Toon/Getty Images*
Compositor: *MPS Limited*

Library of Congress Cataloging-in-Publication Data

Feist, Gregory J., author. | Rosenberg, Erika L., author.
  Psychology : perspectives and connections / Gregory J. Feist, San Jose State University, Erika L. Rosenberg, University of California, Davis.
  Fourth edition. | New York, NY : McGraw-Hill Education, [2019]
  LCCN 2017026157 | ISBN 9781259676970 (alk. paper)
  LCSH: Psychology.
  LCC BF121 .F32 2019 | DDC 150—dc23 LC record available at
  https://lccn.loc.gov/2017026157

mheducation.com/highered

To our most precious collaborative work,

Jerry and Evan

About the Authors

Gregory J. Feist

©Gregory Feist

Gregory J. Feist is Professor of Psychology in Personality and Adult Development at San Jose State University. He has also taught at the College of William & Mary and the University of California, Davis. He received his PhD from the University of California, Berkeley, and his undergraduate degree from the University of Massachusetts–Amherst.

Dr. Feist is widely published in the psychology of creativity, the psychology of science, personality, and the development of scientific talent. One of his major goals is establishing the psychology of science as a healthy and independent study of science, along the lines of history, philosophy, and sociology of science. Toward this end, Dr. Feist has published a book titled *Psychology of Science and the Origins of the Scientific Mind* (2006, Yale University Press), which was awarded the 2007 William James Book Prize by the Division of General Psychology, American Psychological Association (APA). In addition, he is the founding president of the International Society for the Psychology of Science and Technology.

A second major focus for Dr. Feist is the identification and development of scientific talent, as seen in finalists of the Westinghouse and Intel Science Talent Search. His paper (co-authored with Frank Barron) "Predicting Creativity from Early to Late Adulthood: Intellect, Potential, and Personality" won Article of the Year for 2003 in the *Journal of Research in Personality* and *Psychology of Aesthetics, Creativity and the Arts*. His teaching efforts have been recognized by outstanding teaching awards at both UC Berkeley and UC Davis. Dr. Feist is also co-author with his late father, Jess Feist (and Tomi-Ann Roberts), of the undergraduate text *Theories of Personality*. In his spare time, Dr. Feist enjoys cycling, camping, hiking, and skiing.

Contents

©michaeljung/iStock/Getty Images RF

©Jane Underwood/My.Third.Eye Photography/Moment Select/Getty Images

3 The Biology of Behavior 74

©Gage/Getty Images

©Güldenhaupt/Moment/Getty Images RF

©Tom Merton/Getty Images RF

5 Human Development 162

©Andrea Golden/Getty Images RF

©Eternity in an Instant/The Image Bank/Getty Images

©Dave Fimbres Photography/ Getty Images RF

©Jade/Getty Images RF

©Westend61/Getty Images RF

©Daly and Newton/Getty Images RF

Foreword by Paul Ekman

Perhaps it was because I had never taken Introductory Psychology that I became a psychologist—or so I used to quip at the start of undergraduate lectures. Fifty years ago the textbooks for introductory courses were a turn-off. Most were dry and segmented. The only reason to read them was to pass Introductory Psychology in order to get to the higher-level courses you really wanted to take. It was an obstacle you had to jump over. Things have changed!

This textbook—I hesitate to use the word—is fun to read, enlightening, useful, and provocative. I recommend it to anyone—not just undergraduates—who wants a contemporary overview of psychology. In fact, people with no intentions of studying psychology will find this book engaging and interesting and useful to their life. Wow.

Make no mistake—this is not a how-to book. It is not going to tell you how to get rid of whatever bothers you or find a mate or choose a career or become the most charming person in the world. But it will fascinate you; in each chapter, you will learn about the cutting edge of knowledge, how science is done, what it means, and why it is important to understand that most complex of all subjects—why we do what we do and when and how we do it.

My own specialty for 40 years has been the study of facial expressions, and in the last decade or so I have reached out to develop a theory about emotion itself and how to lead a better emotional life. So I was surprised to find that when I read the chapter "Motivation and Emotion," I learned something new. This is a comprehensive book; the coverage, even from a specialist's view, is amazing. And in each chapter the reader learns about both the breakthrough discoveries that have fundamentally altered the field of psychology and those scientists responsible for them.

I still find it a bit amazing that I should be ending a foreword to a textbook with the phrase "have fun."

Psychology: Perspectives

Just because we "think" something doesn't make it true. *Psychology: Perspectives and Connections* guides students in moving beyond what may seem obvious, to reevaluating the thoughts and beliefs they bring to the course. Students will learn to challenge their assumptions, understand the elements of scientific research, and recognize that in psychology, *no one perspective tells the whole story.*

CHALLENGING ASSUMPTIONS

Questioning assumptions is the first step in thinking scientifically. While building a foundation in the concepts and principles of psychology, our goal as teachers and authors has always been to encourage students to examine their preconceptions (as well as those held by others) and understand that there is often more than one plausible explanation for a given phenomenon.

> **Challenge Your Assumptions**
> **True or False?** Genetic influence on our thoughts and actions is set at birth and can't be changed.
> **False:** Experience can and does change how and when genes get expressed.

Each chapter opens with **Challenge Your Assumptions**, a list of common assumptions for students to consider.

THINKING SCIENTIFICALLY

Throughout the *Psychology: Perspectives and Connections* program, we model critical thinking and offer multiple opportunities for students to practice this skill. In "Introduction to Psychology," we define the discipline, analyze major ways of thinking about the human experience, and present a framework for analyzing research and testing assumptions against real world observation. At the end of each chapter, **Bringing It All Together: Making Connections** integrates the major ideas covered in the chapter, shows their application to a common problem, and highlights connections across the various subfields of psychology.

We focus on high-interest topics including obsessive-compulsive disorder (OCD) and anxiety disorders (Treatment of Psychological Disorders) and how people of different genders and cultures experience the world (Sensing and Perceiving Our World), to

Bringing It All Together
Making Connections in Psychology
Studying Electronic Social Interactions

There are nearly a dozen ways a person can interact with others electronically—via email, blogs, phone calls, chat rooms, texting, instant messaging, audio or video chats, gaming (either solo or multiplayer), videos, photos, bulletin boards, and social network sites (SNSs). Humans have taken to electronic forms of interaction like fish to water. As a form of behavior that is evolving at a rapid pace, electronic social interaction holds great interest for psychologists in all of the subfields you read about in this chapter. Let's consider how psychologists from some of these areas might study electronic communication and its effects on human behavior and thought.

Cognitive Psychology
Cognitive scientists typically are interested in how we learn, speak, remember, think, and reason. They are also interested in attention. The widespread use of mobile devices has sparked a number of research questions. The

©Alejandro Rivera/Getty Images RF

How does technology change how we learn, think, feel, and behave with others?

emphasize how psychological science uses systematic investigation to address important questions about the human experience.

Another key goal is helping students to understand the theoretical perspectives and learn to apply them in a variety of settings—hence, the presence of the term *perspectives* in the title. We call attention to the influence of theoretical perspectives on advances in psychology, as well as in the different subfields of psychology. For example, we include a section comparing theoretical perspectives on intelligence (Intelligence, Problem Solving, and Creativity), and we invite students to explore the influences of nature and nurture on personality development, along with the theoretical perspectives that have inspired personality researchers (Personality: The Uniqueness of the Individual). By understanding that it's possible to study behavior through different lenses, students learn to look for underlying points of view.

Psychology: Perspectives and Connections also encourages students to consider the diverse approaches to the study of human thought and behavior. **Connection** annotations appear throughout the text, emphasizing the interrelatedness of subfields of psychology.

> **Connection**
> How do psychologists tease apart the question of how much of a trait is due to genetics and how much is due to environment? A common approach is to study twins (both identical and fraternal) who are reared apart or reared together.
>
> See "The Relative Effects of Genes and Environment Can Be Teased Apart," in the chapter "The Biology of Behavior". (p. 79)
>
> **rationalism**
> The view that using logic and reason is the way to understand how the world works.

and Connections

MAKING SCIENCE ACCESSIBLE

Psychology: Perspectives and Connections approaches the science of psychology in a straightforward, approachable manner to help students develop scientific literacy. Beginning with the question "What is science?" in the "Introduction to Psychology" chapter, we stress that psychology shares with the natural and physical sciences a way of thinking about the world that separates what we *believe* from what is *real*. A strong focus on research and the scientific method in the "Conducting Research in Psychology" chapter lays the foundation for subsequent science-based chapters on neuroscience and genetics and on sensation and perception, which are challenging topics for many students. Throughout the program, we describe classic and contemporary research in depth to familiarize students with the scientific approach to collecting and analyzing data and sharing the results to advance knowledge. Moreover, this edition reflects the latest thinking, based on current research, in all areas of psychology.

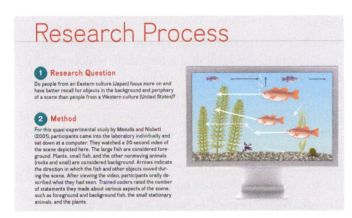

Overcoming preconceptions about the research process may be one of the biggest challenges students face in Introductory Psychology. **Research Process** features, appearing in Chapters 2 through 16, demystify research by providing a step-by-step visual approach to the scientific method.

Using the basic structure of a contemporary study to exemplify scientific thinking, we walk through the "story" of how the research was conducted. In the chapter "Sensing and Perceiving Our World," for example, this feature illustrates the methodology chosen by a researcher to answer the question, "Do people from an Eastern culture (Japan) focus more on and have better recall for objects in the background and periphery of a scene than people from a Western culture (United States)?"

Most chapters in the fourth edition feature expanded coverage on technology and social media and how they affect thought and behavior. For example, in the "Social Behavior" chapter, we address the concept of groupthink in social media as well as the rise of "fake news" sites.

APPLYING PSYCHOLOGY TO EVERYDAY LIFE

One of the perennially difficult tasks we face as instructors is to connect course material to students' lives and interests. In *Psychology: Perspectives and Connections*, we demonstrate the relevance of psychology in multiple ways in both the text and digital programs.

Psychology in the Real World features show how psychological research can directly affect people's lives. For instance, how musical training changes the brain ("Human Development"), and whether Internet use can become an addiction ("Psychological Disorders").

Additional examples in the text make psychological principles and concepts more concrete by connecting them to current, real-world experiences; for instance, in the chapter "Consciousness", the limits of *attention* are underscored with the example of how texting during class prevents attention to the lecture, and graphics in the chapter "Learning" use student-relevant examples of classical and operant conditioning to make these difficult concepts accessible.

IMPROVING READING AND STUDY

 McGraw-Hill Connect© is a highly reliable, easy-to-use homework and learning management solution that utilizes learning science and award-winning adaptive tools to improve student results.

- Connect assignments help students contextualize what they've learned through application, so they can better understand the material and think critically.
- Connect will create a personalized study path customized to individual student needs through SmartBook®.
- SmartBook helps students study more efficiently by delivering an interactive reading experience through adaptive highlighting and review.
- The Connect eBook makes it easy for students to access their reading material on smartphones and tablets. They can study on the go and don't need Internet access to use it as a reference, with full functionality.

PROVIDING POWERFUL REPORTING

Whether a class is face-to-face, hybrid, or entirely online, McGraw-Hill Connect provides the tools needed to reduce the amount of time and energy instructors spend administering their courses. Easy-to-use course management tools allow instructors to spend less time administering and more time teaching, while reports allow students to monitor their progress and optimize their study time.

- The **At-Risk Student Report** provides instructors with one-click access to a dashboard that identifies students who are at risk of dropping out of the course due to low engagement levels
- The **Category Analysis Report** details student performance relative to specific learning objectives and goals, including APA learning goals and outcomes and levels of Bloom's taxonomy
- **Connect Insight** is a one-of-a-kind visual analytics dashboard—now available for both instructors and students—that provides at-a-glance information regarding student performance
- The **LearnSmart Reports** allow instructors and students to easily monitor progress and pinpoint areas of weakness, giving each student a personalized study plan to achieve success.

REVISING WITH STUDENT DATA

Step 1. Over the course of three years, data points showing concepts that caused students the most difficulty were anonymously collected from the Connect **SmartBook** for *Psychology: Perspectives and Connections*, 3/e.

Step 2. The data from **SmartBook** was provided to the authors in the form of a **Heat Map**, which graphically illustrated "hot spots" in the text that impacted student learning.

Step 3. Greg Feist and Erika Rosenberg used the Heat Map data to refine the content and reinforce student comprehension in the new edition. Additional quiz questions and assignable activities were created for use in Connect to further support student success.

Result: With empirically based feedback at the paragraph and even sentence level, the authors developed the new edition using precise student data to pinpoint concepts that caused students to struggle.

INFORMING AND ENGAGING STUDENTS

At the Remember and Understand levels of Bloom's taxonomy, **Concept Clips** help students break down key themes and difficult concepts in psychology. Using easy-to-understand analogies, visual cues,

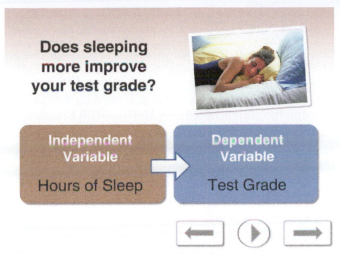

audio, and colorful animation, Concept Clips make psychology meaningful to everyday life.

New Concept Clips in the fourth edition include: Hypothesis and Theories; Forgetting; The Meaning of Dreams; The Four Phases of the Human Sexual Response; Sensation and Perception of Touch; Sex and Gender; Aggression, Conformity, and Obedience; Routes of Persuasion; Stereotypes/Prejudice/Discrimination; Social Facilitation, Replication of Research, Interpersonal Attraction, Learned Gender Roles, and more.

At the Understand and Apply levels of Bloom's taxonomy, **Interactivities**, assignable through Connect, engage students with content through experiential activities. New and updated activities include: Perspectives in Psychology; Correlations; Neurons; The Brain and Drugs; The Stages of Sleep; Levels of Processing; Maslow's Hierarchy of Needs; Naturalistic Observation; Observational Learning; Defense Mechanisms, Stereotypes and Prejudice, Heuristics, Personality Assessment, and First Impressions and Attraction.

At the Understand and Apply levels of Bloom's taxonomy, **NewsFlash** exercises, powered by Connect, tie current news stories to key psychological principles and learning objectives. After interacting with a contemporary news story, students are assessed on their ability to make the connection between real life and research findings. Cases are revisited across chapters, encouraging students to consider multiple perspectives.

At the Apply and Analyze levels of Bloom's taxonomy, **Scientific Reasoning Activities** offer in-depth arguments to sharpen students' critical thinking skills and prepare them to be more discerning consumers of psychology in their everyday lives. For each chapter, there are multiple sets of arguments accompanied by auto-graded assessments requiring students to think critically about claims presented as facts. These exercises can also be used in Connect as group activities or for discussion.

New! Anatomy and Physiology REVEALED® for Psychology McGraw-Hill Education presents an interactive tool that encourages the exploration of biological structures related to psychology. Lab Activity assignments in Connect walk students through virtual nervous system and cell dissection experiences, including views of CT scans, x-ray imaging and histology, and include illustrated animations that link anatomy to the biology of behavior.

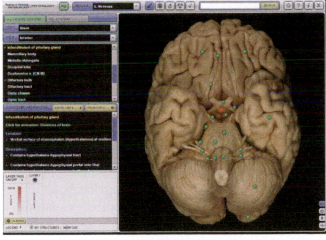

Touring the Brain and Touring the Senses Two digital components, **Touring the Brain and Nervous System** and **Touring the Senses,** offer detailed digital overlays of key structures. These tours provide students with practice in grasping key biological structures and processes that are essential to an appreciation of the role of science in psychology and success in the course.

New! Power of Process, now available in McGraw-Hill Connect™, guides students through the process of critical reading, analysis, and writing. Faculty can select or upload their own content, such as journal articles, and assign analysis strategies to gain insight into students' application of the scientific method. For students, Power of Process offers a guided visual approach to exercising critical thinking strategies to apply before, during, and after reading published research.

Psychology at Work videos, assignable and assessable within McGraw-Hill Connect™, highlight nine careers in which knowledge of psychology is beneficial. Each video introduces a person at work in his or her job, who specifies how knowledge gained from taking introductory psychology in college is applied to the work environment.

SUPPORTING INSTRUCTORS WITH TECHNOLOGY

With McGraw-Hill Education, you can develop and tailor the course you want to teach.

 Use a different learning management system. **McGraw-Hill Campus** (www.mhcampus.com) provides faculty with true single sign-on access to all of McGraw-Hill's course content, digital tools, and other high-quality learning resources from any learning management system. McGraw-Hill Campus includes access to McGraw-Hill's entire content library, including eBooks, assessment tools, presentation slides, and multimedia content, among other resources, providing faculty open, unlimited access to prepare for class, create tests/quizzes, develop lecture material, integrate interactive content, and more.

 With **Tegrity**, you can capture lessons and lectures in a searchable format and use them in traditional, hybrid, "flipped classes," and online courses. With Tegrity's personalized learning features, you can make study time efficient. Its ability to affordably scale brings this benefit to every student on campus. Patented search technology and real-time learning management system (LMS) integrations make Tegrity the market-leading solution and service.

 Easily rearrange chapters, combine material from other content sources, and quickly upload content you have written, such as your course syllabus or teaching notes, using McGraw-Hill Education's **Create**. Find the content you need by searching through thousands of leading McGraw-Hill Education textbooks. Arrange your book to fit your teaching style. Create even allows you to personalize your book's appearance by selecting the cover and adding your name, school, and course information. Order a Create book, and you will receive a complimentary print review copy in three to five business days or a complimentary electronic review copy via email in about an hour. Experience how McGraw-Hill Education empowers you to teach *your* students *your* way. **http://create.mheducation.com**

TRUSTED SERVICE AND SUPPORT

Connect offers comprehensive service, support, and training throughout every phase of your implementation. If you're looking for some guidance on how to use Connect, or want to learn tips and tricks from super users, you can find tutorials as you work. Our Digital Faculty Consultants and Student Ambassadors offer insight into how to achieve the results you want with Connect.

INTEGRATION WITH YOUR LEARNING MANAGEMENT SYSTEM

McGraw-Hill integrates your digital products from McGraw-Hill Education with your school LMS for quick and easy access to best-in-class content and learning tools. Build an effective digital course, enroll students with ease and discover how powerful digital teaching can be.

Available with Connect, integration is a pairing between an institution's learning management system (LMS) and Connect at the assignment level. It shares assignment information, grades and calendar items from Connect into the LMS automatically, creating an easy to manage course for instructors and simple navigation for students. Our assignment-level integration is available with **Blackboard Learn**, **Canvas by Instructure**, and **Brightspace by D2L**, giving you access to registration, attendance, assignments, grades, and course resources in real time, in one location.

INSTRUCTOR SUPPLEMENTS

Instructor's Manual   The instructor's manual provides a wide variety of tools and resources for presenting the course, including learning objectives, and ideas for lectures and discussions.

Test Bank   By increasing the rigor of the test bank development process, McGraw-Hill Education has raised the bar for student assessment. A coordinated team of subject-matter experts methodically vetted each question and set of possible answers for accuracy, clarity, effectiveness, and accessibility; each question has been annotated for level of difficulty, Bloom's taxonomy, APA learning outcomes, and corresponding coverage in the text. Organized by chapter, the questions are designed to test factual, conceptual, and applied understanding. All test questions are available within Test-Gen™ software and as Word documents.

PowerPoint Presentations   The PowerPoint presentations, available in a dynamic lecture-ready format and a WCAG-compliant version, highlight the key points of the chapter and include supporting visuals. All of the slides can be modified to meet individual needs.

Image Gallery   The Image Gallery features the complete set of downloadable figures and tables from the text. These can be easily embedded by instructors into their own PowerPoint slides.

CHAPTER-BY-CHAPTER CHANGES

In addition to global updates based on anonymous student Heat Map data across all chapters, chapter-by-chapter changes are listed below.

Chapter 1: Introduction to Psychology

- Moved section on critical thinking from Chapter 9 to Chapter 1 so students are introduced to it right up front and to better set the stage for challenging assumptions
- Added a Perspectives section, outlining and summarizing the 7 major theoretical perspectives in psychology
- Updated research throughout the text

Chapter 2: Conducting Research in Psychology

- New coverage of the logic of twin adoption designs
- New section on longitudinal design
- New material on scientific misconduct
- New material on replication movement in psychology
- New material on big data
- New key terms, including qualitative and quantitative design
- Revised discussion of surveys
- New Bringing It All Together on how social media affects thought and behavior

Chapter 3: The Biology of Behavior

- Updated research throughout chapter
- New material on genetics and epigenetics; genetics section condensed
- New brain imaging techniques
- New research on neuroprosthetics

Chapter 4: Sensing and Perceiving Our World

- Revised coverage of the gateway theory of pain
- Added literature and new discussion on individual differences in absolute and JND thresholds
- Updated coverage on why some are born with no pain receptors
- Added new material on the gustatory cortex
- Updated the section on hearing loss
- New research on neuroplasticity in deaf people
- Restructured vision section

Chapter 5: Human Development

- New material on the "Marshmallow Test"
- Revised discussion of intellectual disability
- New and revised coverage of gender identity with a focus on transgender identity
- Updated research on adolescent personality development

- Revised coverage of technology across lifespan
- Updated discussion of Piaget's theory, including critique and limitations
- Revised coverage of attachment

Chapter 6: Consciousness

- Major updating of sections on attention and multitasking
- Major update to "Real World" section on distracted driving
- Updated sleep staging
- Extensive updates to the section on drugs

Chapter 7: Memory

- New chapter opening on cases dealing with super autobiographical memory, extreme number recall, implicit memory, and faulty eyewitness testimony
- Restructured the entire chapter to match current perspectives on memory with main sections now being:
  - Forming Memories
  - Types of Memory
  - Memory and the Brain
  - Memory Reconstruction and Distortion
  - Forgetting and Memory Loss
- Additional new material was added on eyewitness testimony and the case of Jennifer Thompson and Ronald Cotton

Chapter 8: Learning

- Updated examples on the effects of violence in movies and video games
- Updated coverage of the Little Albert story
- Updated coverage on how nature and nurture work together in learning
- Updated research on operant conditioning

Chapter 9: Language and Thought

- New chapter opening on becoming bilingual and thinking differently
- New research on advantages of being bilingual, chimp language, and culture, language and thought
- New material on fake news and critical thinking
- Updated graphic on concept hierarchy
- Updated research throughout chapter
- New key term "base-rate"

Chapter 10: Intelligence, Problem Solving, and Creativity

- New research on the greater connectivity between hemispheres and creative people
- New coverage on savants
- Revised coverage of fluid/crystalized intelligence and familial-cultural intellectual disability
- Updated research throughout the chapter
- New coverage of developmental changes in different aspects of intelligence

- Added coverage of assessing multiple intelligence
- New coverage of the brain's connectome and intelligence
- New coverage of default mode network: boredom, walking, and daydreaming

Chapter 11: Motivation and Emotion

- New meaningful graphic on weight loss maintenance
- Updated research throughout the chapter
- New connections across motivation and emotion
- Additional coverage of emotion and culture
- Expanded coverage of emotion and gender differences
- Revised and expanded coverage of eating disorders

Chapter 12: Stress and Health

- New chapter opener on the connection between stress and health
- New section on the gut-brain axis
- Updated research throughout chapter
- New coverage of current research on telomere length/telomerase and stress
- Revised coverage on good stress versus bad stress

Chapter 13: Personality: The Uniqueness of the Individual

- Updated research throughout chapter
- New research and examples on animal personality
- New research on personality and social media
- New chapter opener on five new (Big Five) personality vignettes/case studies
- New key terms, including "by-product" and "psychological mechanism"
- New section on evolutionary personality theory
- Updated table on perspectives on personality
- Revised discussion on perspectives on personality
- New meaningful graphic on the biology of introversion/extroversion
- Revised coverage of id, ego, superego, archetypes, the biological basis of introversion/extroversion, and face validity
- Revised coverage of situational consistency, twin studies, shared and unshared environments
- Revised discussion of the origins of personality

Chapter 14: Social Behavior

- Updated coverage of technology/social media and social cognition
- Revised coverage of groupthink to include 2016 research on fake news sites.
- Updated chapter opener
- Updated research on mere exposure effect
- New research on racism
- Major research updates about social networks to include contemporary U.S. and Asian research
- New glossary term of "dehumanization"

- New 2017 research conducted during the 2016 presidential campaign on prejudice toward Mexicans and anti-Muslim sentiment
- Added new research on cross-cultural findings and social perception

Chapter 15: Psychological Disorders

- Revised coverage of biological theories of depression
- Expanded discussion of the connection between schizophrenia and infection
- New section on gut microbes and the brain
- Updated coverage of Internet addiction
- Updated research throughout the chapter
- New section on connecting "learned helplessness" to the causes of depression
- Expanded discussion on the possible causes of obsessive-compulsive disorder

Chapter 16: Treatment of Psychological Disorders

- New chapter opener on microdosing for major depression
- Updated research throughout chapter, particularly in the areas of technology-based, biomedical, and emerging therapies
- New research on the shortcomings of SSRIs
- Revised coverage of deep brain stimulation for obsessive-compulsive disorder
- New coverage on electronic treatment of disorders, including virtual reality and therapy apps
- New section on psychedelic medicine

REVIEWERS

Lana Andrean, Bridge Valley Community and Technical College

Clarissa Arms-Chavez, Auburn University at Montgomery

Sheryl Attig, Tri-County Technical College

Amy Mitchell Bechtol, Catawba Valley Community College

John Biondo, Community College of Allegheny Country: Boyce Campus

Stephen Blessing, The University of Tampa

Carla Bluhm, College of Coastal Georgia

Terry Booth, Horry Georgetown Technical College

Leanne Boucher, Nova Southeastern University

Erin Boyd, The University of Texas at Arlington

Gerald Braasch, McHenry County College

Jennifer Meehan Brennom, Kirkwood Community College

Mary Elizabeth Bridges, The University of Louisiana at Monroe

Brenya Buchalski, The University of Texas at San Antonio

Randi Burton, Eastern Florida State College

Netali Chopra, College of DuPage

James R. Clopton, Texas Tech University

Gary Creasey, Old Dominion University

Carmen Culotta, Wright State University

Christie Cunningham, Pellissippi State Community College

Myra Darty, North Idaho College

Lisa Davies, Nashville State Community College

Elizabeth Dose, Georgia Highlands College

Ernestine A. W. Duncan, Norfolk State University

Mike Drysdale, Vincennes University

Jennifer Engler, York College of Pennsylvania

Fay Evans-Martin, Gainesville State College

Annette Flugstad, Kirkwood Community College

Tony Fowler, Florence-Darlington Technical College

Nathalie Franco, Broward College

Desiree Franks, Northeast Wisconsin Technical College

Malinda Freitag, The University of Utah

Perry Fuchs, The University of Texas at Arlington

Pam Garverick, Wright State University

Joanna Greene, Indian River State College

Christine Grela, McHenry County College

Joshua Halonen, The University of Tampa

Deletha Hardin, The University of Tampa

Rickye Heffner, The University of Toledo

Jessica C. Hill, Utah Valley University

Brooke Hindman, Greenville Technical College

Debra Hope, The University of Nebraska–Lincoln

Becky Howell, Forsyth Technical Community College

Juan Hu, Oregon State University

Michael Huff, College of the Canyons

Kara Janowski, United States Air Force Academy

Joan Jensen, Central Piedmont Community College

Brian Johnson, The University of Tennessee at Martin

Luanne Kea, Midlands Technical College

Donna Kearns, The University of Central Oklahoma

Kevin Keating, Broward College

Chad Keller, Lewis and Clark Community College

Fahad Khan, College of DuPage

Lynnel Kiely, Harold Washington College

Caleb Lack, The University of Central Oklahoma

Eric Kim, Lane Community College

Kristina T. Klassen, North Idaho College

Rachel L. Laimon, Mott Community College

Eric Lance, Forsyth Technical Community College

Juliet Lee, Cape Fear Community College

Brian Littleton, Mott Community College

Laura Mars, Johnston Community College

Robert Martinez, University of the Incarnate Word

Elaine Mawhinney, Horry Georgetown Technical College

Melissa McCeney, Montgomery College

Michael Jason McCoy, Cape Fear Community College

Tai McMiller, York Technical College

Renee Miranda, Georgia Highlands College

Tracy Morgan, Eastern Florida State College

Suzanne Morrow, Old Dominion University

Courtney Mozo, Old Dominion University

Craig Nagoshi, The University of Texas at Arlington

Katy Neidhardt, Cuesta College

John B. Nezlek, College of William and Mary

Rui Ni, Wichita State University

Rebecca Noble, Northeast Wisconsin Technical College

Gina O'Neal-Moffitt, Florida State University

Maria Ortega, Washtenaw Community College

Amy Osmon, Daytona State College

Brian Parry, Colorado Mesa University

Shirley A. Pavone, Sacred Heart University

Jennifer Pemberton, The Community College of Baltimore County

Marion Perlmutter, University of Michigan

Leigh Alison Phillips, Iowa State University

Andrea Phronebarger, York Technical College

Jason Piccone, Nova Southeastern University

Eileen R. Price, Midlands Technical College

Jamie A. Quattlebaum, Wichita State University

Laura Rambarose, Broward College

Sarah K. Rankin, Lewis and Clark Community College

Timothy Razza, Nova Southeastern University

Michael Reiter, Nova Southeastern University

Heather Rice, Washington University in St. Louis

Darla Rocha, San Jacinto College North Campus

Joshua S. Rodefer, Valdosta State University

James Rodgers, Hawkeye Community College

Josephine Laquis Rodriguez, Broward College

Lisa Rosen, Texas Woman's University

Peggy Russell, Indian River State College

Lawrence J. Ryan, Oregon State University

Edie Sample, Metropolitan Community College

Anna Schwartz, College of Staten Island

Joseph Sclafani, The University of Tampa

Teresa Segelken, Coastal Carolina Community College

Randi Shedlosky, York College of Pennsylvania

Will Shelstad, Wichita State University

Rebecca Shepherd, College of the Canyons

Aya Shigeto, Nova Southeastern University

Brett Silverstein, City College of New York

Michelle Smith, Wright State University

Stephanie Smith, Indiana University Northwest

Carla Strassle, York College of Pennsylvania

Barry Stennett, University of North Georgia

Weylin Sternglanz, Nova Southeastern University

Eli Stav, Broward College

Cari Stevenson, Kankakee Community College

Don Sweeney, College of DuPage

Anita Tam, Greenville Technical College

Khia Thomas, Broward College

Geneene Thompson, Greenville Technical College

Linda Eagleheart Thomas, The University of Montana

Joseph Vielbig, Arizona Western College

Jovana Vukovic, Broward College

Berta Ward, Pellissippi State Community College

David Wasieleski, Valdosta State University

Brady Wiggins, Brigham Young University–Idaho

Glenda S. Williams, Lone Star College–North Harris

Manda J. Williamson, The University of Nebraska–Lincoln

Melissa Wright, Northwest Vista College

Stephanie M. Wright, Georgia Highlands College

Judith Wrightman, Kirkwood Community College

Ryan Yoder, Indiana University–Purdue University Fort Wayne

Christi Young, Southwestern Michigan College

Acknowledgments

Writing *Psychology: Perspectives and Connections* has been an enormous undertaking of hard work and love. We have felt privileged by the opportunity to delve into the literature of so many areas of psychology in depth, something for which career academics rarely have time. We have also been fortunate to have had the commitment of a vast team of collaborators, to whom we offer our profound gratitude. We thank the wonderful professionals at McGraw-Hill Education who have had utter confidence in this project from day one: Nancy Welcher, brand manager for psychology, jump-started our vision for this edition and shepherded it through the intense revision schedule. Judith Kromm, our first product developer, who early on acted as a third author in crafting text, interpreting reviews, and helping us learn that strong substance can co-exist with simple and clear writing. Sara Gordus is the product developer who took us to the finish line. She has been amazing at keeping us on task and bringing the final version of the 4th edition to completion. Dawn Groundwater, lead product developer, was instrumental in keeping the project on task and developing new ideas for how to best package the unique qualities of the book. Thank you also to A. J. Laferrera and Ann Helgerson, marketing managers, and Suzie Flores, senior market development manager, who have their fingers on the pulse of the people for whom we wrote the book—instructors and students. As mid-career authors, we sometimes forget how 19- and 20-year-old students think and will respond to the information we are presenting.

Our thanks also go to the Editing, Design, and Production team: Sandy Wille, who guided us through the copyediting and composition stages of production; designer Matt Backhaus; and Content Licensing Specialist Lori Slattery. We also must thank copyeditor Julie Kennedy who offered invaluable advice in helping craft the language and clarify text. We also have been honored to have the invaluable input of our friends and colleagues—all experts in their fields—on various topics in the book. In particular, we are grateful to Paul Ekman, Elissa Epel, Jess Feist, David Galin, Mary Gomes, Lee Huntington, Allen Kanner, Alan Kaufman, James Kaufman, Lee Kirkpatrick, Katherine MacLean, Clifford Saron, Valerie Stone, and especially Mary True, who contributed her developmental expertise to important revisions in Chapter 5 on both the second and third editions of this book.

We have also benefited from having research support from our students Sarah Greene, Adam Larson, Spencer James, and Yvette Szabo. Yvette wrote a wonderful new piece for Chapter 1 on what Introduction to Psychology has meant for her. Our colleague Rebecca Jedel also caught some inaccuracies in the chapters on Learning and Personality in the previous edition, and we are thankful for that feedback. Sarah Butler helped us flesh out some of the research on sexuality. We extend our thanks also to Dean Simonton, who pointed out historical inaccuracies in the two-string problem discussion and graphic. We also thank our parents—Sandra Rosenberg and the late Jess and Mary Jo Feist—for their love and unending support throughout the writing of previous editions. We also want to give our special and heartfelt thanks to our two wonderful boys, Jerry and Evan. They have been real troopers throughout our work on all the editions. We owe Jerry an extra thanks for helping with some of the research for the 4th edition.

Erika would like to extend a very heartfelt "THANKS!" to every single student she has ever taught, in every class, who have been her greatest teachers in life. She is grateful to Stanley Marshall for his kindness and support throughout the writing of this edition. Erika would also like to thank her favorite local café, Bica Coffeehouse, for their superb coffees and lovely space that served as her primary office during her writing of the second, third, and fourth editions. Finally, Erika is also grateful to Phil and Jill Lesh for their Terrapin Crossroads—an enriching community of music and love—that has kept Erika sane and happy during both the difficult and easy times and has reinforced her faith in the power of community.

Greg would like to thank his thousands of Introductory Psychology students over the years who—with their questions and fresh interest—keep him on his toes and who constantly remind him of the fun and joy in learning how fascinating and perplexing human thought and behavior is and can be.

Finally, we were married 24 years and started this project when our children were young. Although we are no longer married, we remain deeply grateful to each other as co-authors and co-parents. We share an eternal personal and professional history, and are indebted to each other for the long-term collaboration on a book as complex as this one is—now entering its 4th edition and almost 15 years after we began work on the 1st edition. We have learned how to play off each other's strengths, balance viewpoints and expertise, and compromise. With a collaboration like this one, we are ready for another 15 years!

1 Introduction to Psychology

Chapter Outline

Challenge Your Assumptions

True or False?

- If you are a psychologist you diagnose and treat mental disorders. (see page 5)

- Psychology is made up of many different subfields. (see page 9)

- Genetic influence on our thoughts and actions is set at birth and can't be changed. (see page 18)

- Psychologists agree that most of human thought and behavior cannot be explained by one perspective. (see page 27)

- Critical thinking involves seeing only the weaknesses and flaws in ideas. (see page 27)

ver the last few years in the United States, numerous videos of police officers shooting African American males have been posted on various social media websites. Although these events all differ in circumstance and explanation, the videos have often led to protests of police behavior. These protests have even spilled over into professional sports, most notably when the football player Colin Kaepernick refused to stand during the playing of the national anthem. Whatever position one may take on the explanation and cause of these events, there is no doubt that the universal ownership of cell phones with cameras and widespread use of social media outlets have changed the dynamic between police and civilians and begun a full-blown debate about race and justice in the United States.

These examples give just a small hint of the wide-ranging ways that online technologies have changed social interaction and human behavior. Here are some others:

- Millions of people have free or very inexpensive access to online learning through massive open online courses (MOOCs), such as Udacity and Coursera.

- We can immediately be in contact with friends and family via texting and email, and with wider circles of people via Twitter, Facebook, Tumblr, and Reddit, to name a few.

- Online psychotherapies have helped many individuals and couples dealing with mental illness and broken relationships.

- Sexting photos have had traumatic effects on people's lives and even ruined politicians' careers.

- A baby died of malnutrition and neglect by a couple in South Korea who were spending 14–16 hours a day raising a virtual baby on the online site Prius Online.

- Distracted driving (much of which involves mobile device use) kills more than 3,000 Americans a year (more than 10 each day; *Distracted driving*, 2013).

In many ways, people behave online much the way they do in everyday life, but with the capacity to affect more people, both known and unknown, and potentially with more widespread impact. What happens to social interactions when they become primarily electronic? Do the depths of our friendships increase or decrease through social media? Does technology make our attention scattered, or does it improve our ability to do more than one thing at a time? These are important questions; our interactions and social connections, or *networks*, can influence everything from opinion to eating patterns to one's likelihood of quitting smoking (Christakis & Fowler, 2007, 2008). For example, socially isolated people are more prone to illness and even early death (Kim et al., 2016). Do Facebook and other social networks operate in ways that resemble real-world networks? What are the consequences of electronic interaction for our social lives? Each of these questions centers on understanding the effects of technology on thought, feeling, and behavior.

You might assume that social networks only enhance social life. The surprise from psychological science is that social networking both improves and impairs our relationships (Garrett & Danziger, 2008; Lundy & Drouin, 2016). People use "friending" on social networks to widen their social circles, which can translate into real-life social benefits (Lange, 2008). These media help us reach people we might not otherwise communicate with at all (such as long-lost cousins). Yet social networking can also reduce interactions with close friends to short electronic statements and lessen the amount of face-to-face time. In addition, technology in general increases our likelihood to multitask, which makes it harder for us to engage in any one task deeply (Bowman et al., 2010; Foerde, Knowlton, & Poldrack, 2006; Werner, Cades, & Boehm-Davis, 2015). As psychology begins to identify the pros and cons of this overlap between real and virtual worlds, the ways to navigate this realm in a healthy manner become clearer.

You may be wondering why we are opening a text about psychology with a discussion of people's use of technology. The answer is that technology involves people thinking, behaving, and interacting, which is what psychology is all about.

WHAT IS PSYCHOLOGY?

In one sense, you have been a psychologist for most of your life. Every time you ponder why you think and feel in particular ways, you are thinking psychologically. Every time you try to explain what someone else is doing—and why—you are thinking psychologically. You do it when you say your friend dominates conversations because he is self-absorbed. You also do it when you conclude that your big sister is bossy because she is older and always gets what she wants. We think and live psychology every day.

Psychology Defined

Many fields of study aim to understand people's thoughts and actions. Literature helps us understand people through storytelling, character exploration, development of setting, and use of imagery. History helps us understand people through description and analysis of past events and artifacts. Anthropology is the study of human culture and origins. Sociology seeks to understand people in terms of large-scale social forces and group membership rather than individuals. Psychology is unique in that it is the *science* of understanding individuals—animals as well as people. Formally defined, **psychology** is the scientific study of thought and behavior. The root word *psyche* comes from the Greek for "mind," but modern psychology is as likely to study the brain and behavior as it is the "mind."

psychology
The scientific study of thought and behavior.

You might be thinking, Don't psychologists treat people with mental illness or try to help us figure out how our parents messed us up? Yes, they do these things too. Some professional psychologists practice, or *apply*, psychology to diagnose and treat problems of thought and behavior. In fact, psychology is both a clinical practice and a science. The clinical practice side encompasses the services provided in therapists' offices, schools, hospitals, and businesses. Without fail, when we (the authors of this text) tell people that we are psychologists, they immediately think we are clinical psychologists and are analyzing their every move, looking for hidden meaning in everything they do.

You can also find popular psychology in homes, on radio talk shows, on Internet news sites, and in TV news reports. What sets scientific psychology apart from popular psychology—known as *pop psychology*—are the methods used in each. As you will see in the chapter "Conducting Research in Psychology" and again in the chapter "Treatment of Psychological Disorders", the methods of scientific and clinical psychologists are quite different from people in general, who sometimes draw from an unreliable body of knowledge known as *common sense*.

Challenge Your Assumptions

True or False? If you are a psychologist, you diagnose and treat mental disorders.

False: Some psychologists diagnose and treat mental illness but others conduct scientific studies on human thought and behavior. Psychology is both a practice and a science.

Psychology in the Real World

Why Psychology Is Important to My Life

Yvette Szabo, *University of Louisville*

For me, studying psychology has meant so much more than learning concepts for an exam. Every day I see how it applies to my life. Material from class and the textbook come alive in my daily encounters. For instance, I now understand what affects my own productivity and what increases my motivation. I know that stress sometimes serves as a major stimulant for me and activates me to work, but it also wears down my immune system. Also, too much stress impairs the quality of my work. From Intro Psych, I learned that these experiences are consistent with what research on motivation, stress, and health tells us.

I have also noticed how patterns of behavior repeat themselves within families or groups of friends. When I learned about the effects of birth order on personality, for example, I was able to connect the concept to my sister and me. I am the younger sister, and I am more rebellious and open to new ideas. In contrast, my elder sister is more agreeable and has a more cautious personality. When I learned in Intro Psych that younger-born children are "born to rebel" [see the chapter "Personality: The Uniqueness of the Individual"], I was amazed to discover that the pattern I see with my sister and me is a common one. This has helped put my own life in a larger context of human behavior.

As a curious student, I always enjoy understanding something new. One thing I appreciated with this class is how all of the fields of psychology overlap and interconnect. For example: Different people see and perceive events differently. In other words, social and personality psychology are closely connected to memory, sensation, and perception. What we perceive and remember overlaps with our social environment and our personality. Perceiving and remembering is almost like a camera lens, but the lens has filters—your personality and previous experiences filter what you take in, what sense you make of it, and what you recall.

Additionally, for me, connections between the subfields are clearer when I look at an area that interests me—diagnoses and treatments for depression. In order to understand both the causes of and treatments for depression, you need to appreciate how the biological origins of depression, such as hormones and neurotransmitters, are affected by life experiences, such as stress and trauma. If we don't integrate the biological and social approaches to understanding disorders, then we won't be very successful at diagnosing and treating them.

Moreover, psychology often explores the roles of nature and nurture in shaping behavior and personality. This book in particular does a great job of emphasizing how nature and nurture work together to create who we are and who we become. I have seen this firsthand. My cousin, adopted by my uncle and his wife, developed mannerisms similar to those of her family members. And yet, I've also learned in class that twins separated at birth will likely

---

Perhaps because of the ubiquity of popular psychology, most people you talk to on the street don't think of psychology as a science; rather, they probably think of it only as a clinical practice. The editors of *Scientific American*, for instance, commented that "whenever we run articles on social topics, some readers protest that we should stick to 'real science' " ("The peculiar institution," 2002, p. 8).

As we will see throughout this text, not only is psychology a science, but it is also considered a core science, along with medicine, earth science, chemistry, physics, and math (Boyack, Klavans, & Börner, 2005). Core sciences are those that have many other disciplines organized around them.

Why Should You Study Psychology?

Reasons for studying psychology vary from person to person. Maybe your adviser suggested it would be a good course to take, or maybe you're taking the course because it satisfies a general education requirement. Psychology is considered part of a good general education because its content is useful to many fields. It is also relevant to your life.

Adopting a scientific perspective on human behavior helps you develop a curiosity for how behavior works. It also fosters an appreciation for how much of

have similar interests and characteristics. These examples both show that nature and nurture are intertwined.

My knowledge of psychology provides constant explanations for the kinds of relationships I see all around me. For example, as I learned in my psychology courses, research shows that children who were bullied at home will be more likely to befriend someone meek so they can achieve dominance. Sure enough, a close friend of mine recently admitted she was a bully in grade school because it was the one place she was tougher than those around her. At home she was picked on, and so she wanted to dominate when she could at school. Psychology allowed me to better understand this not-so-desirable behavior in my friend. Similarly, I learned that people who do not receive much human contact and were not held as children will likely have difficulty forming bonds and close attachments as adults. I have seen this play out among numerous friends and acquaintances. Both of these cases show the importance of caregiving behavior in the formation of social relationships.

By turning what I learn in my classes outward, I can better understand the actions of others. I am more effective at motivating others and myself, because I better understand individual differences and different types of motivation that stem from internal and environmental sources. I am more conscious about what motivates me. Sometimes I am more motivated by an internal source, such as when I participate in a sport because I enjoy the game. Other times, I am more motivated by external sources, such as when I work to earn a high grade in a class.

Most importantly, the things I learned in Introductory Psychology have laid a foundation for all my future studies in psychology and even other courses. As I have studied more about the clinical applications of psychology, I have become more conscious of the role of a listener and speaker and have greatly improved my listening skills. Psychology has taught me techniques for learning, like scheduling study time over several days, getting a good night's sleep, rehearsing material, and making information personal and relevant. Intro Psych can help you not only to understand other people but also to do well in college.

Psychology has helped me so much in my everyday life that I want to continue to take as many psychology classes as I can and then pursue a doctoral degree in psychology. My motivation to learn more than what is required originated from the sampling of fields covered in introductory psychology. It is only in Intro Psychology where you learn about everything in psychology—from the brain and genetics to learning, memory, and perception; from development and aging to social groups and disorders of the mind. Intro Psych has been a wonderful foundation for understanding my own and other people's thought and behavior—and after all, isn't that what psychology is all about?

Yvette Szabo, University of Louisville. Used by permission.

---

human thought and behavior cannot be explained from one perspective. As you move through this text, you will find that many of the concepts you learn, such as memory, have several definitions depending on how you look at them. *Memory,* for instance, can refer either to a specific recalled event (such as your memory of last summer's vacation) or to the process by which we recall such information.

Studying psychology not only makes you more aware of how people work in general, but it also makes you more aware of how *you* work—very practical knowledge to have in many settings. Understanding others' thoughts, feelings, and motives—as well as your own—may help you be a more effective doctor, lawyer, businessperson, or friend. Understanding how children learn, think, reason, and play will help you if you become a parent or a teacher. To learn how one recent college graduate has applied her knowledge of psychology in her life, read the "Psychology in the Real World" feature.

The study of psychology is as old as the human species. Before people wondered about the stars, rocks, and planets, no doubt they tried to figure out themselves and others.

©Ben Curtis/AP Images

They did, after all, form relationships, have children, and protect their families. Human babies could not survive without others to care for them. Perhaps that is why people fascinate us. From our very first days, we humans are inherently interested in other humans—for survival. Newborns prefer faces to almost any other object. Our very existence is social, and as you will learn, our brains have evolved mechanisms and structures that allow us to understand others in a remarkably complex way (Dunbar, 1996; Frith & Frith, 2010).

As you begin your study of psychology, you will learn just how broad the field is. You may even find a subfield that dovetails with another interest you have already developed.

Quick Quiz 1: What Is Psychology?

1. Psychology is best defined as the scientific study of
   a. human behavior.
   b. mental illness.
   c. neuroses.
   d. human thought and behavior.

2. As a field, psychology is
   a. a social science.
   b. the practice of diagnosing and treating mental illness.
   c. a biological science.
   d. all of the above.

3. How does psychology differ from the related field of sociology?
   a. Psychology studies systems; sociology studies cultures.
   b. Psychology studies cultures; sociology studies people.
   c. Psychology studies individuals; sociology studies groups.
   d. Psychology studies groups and cultures; sociology studies human behavior.

Answers can be found at the end of the chapter.

SUBDISCIPLINES OF PSYCHOLOGY

As a science and a practice, psychology is divided into various areas of investigation. Just as this book consists of chapters on different topics in psychology, the field of psychology is divided into more than 25 distinct, but increasingly interrelated, subdisciplines. Figure 1 gives a breakdown of the percentages of doctorates awarded in 2014 in each of the major subdisciplines we discuss (Doctorate Recipients, 2016). It is noteworthy, that 71% of all PhDs in psychology in 2014 were earned by women. Each subdiscipline in psychology had more than 50% women PhDs, and the only two subfields with less than 60% were experimental psychology and cognitive/psycholinguistics. It is also worth noting that more PhDs were awarded in psychology in 2014 than all the other social sciences combined (anthropology, economics, political science, and sociology) (Doctorate Recipients, 2016).

cognitive psychology
The study of how people perceive, remember, think, speak, and solve problems.

Cognitive psychology is the study of how we perceive information, how we learn and remember, how we acquire and use language, and how we solve problems. For example, a researcher who is concerned with how people visualize objects in their minds is studying cognitive psychology. Those who do research on cognition and learning are often referred to as *experimental psychologists*, because they conduct laboratory experiments to address their research questions.

developmental psychology
The study of how thought and behavior change and remain stable across the life span.

Developmental psychology explores how thought and behavior change and show stability across the life span. This developmental perspective allows us to appreciate that organisms—human or otherwise—change and grow. Developmental psychologists ask such questions as these: How do our reasoning skills or emotional skills change as we age? How does parent-infant bonding affect adult relationships? Does old age bring wisdom?

behavioral neuroscience
The study of the links among brain, mind, and behavior.

biological psychology
The study of the relationship between bodily systems and chemicals and how they influence behavior and thought.

Behavioral neuroscience studies the links among brain, mind, and behavior. Neuroscience cuts across various disciplines and subdisciplines of psychology. One can study the brain functions involved in learning, emotion, social behavior, and mental illness, to name just a few areas. The more general subdiscipline of **biological psychology** includes research on all areas of connection between bodily systems and chemicals and their relationship to behavior and thought. An example of research in biological psychology appears in the chapter "Stress and Health", where we discuss the effects of stress on hormones and behavior. Neuroscience and biological psychology overlap substantially. Biological psychology is an older term that is being replaced by *behavioral neuroscience* in contemporary psychology. Using noninvasive advanced imaging techniques and electrical recordings, behavioral neuroscientists study the structure and functions of the living brain.

Personality psychology considers what makes people unique, as well as the consistencies in people's behavior across time and situations. Personality research addresses questions such as whether our personal traits and dispositions change or stay the same from infancy to childhood to adulthood. A question from this area, for example, might be whether the tendency to be friendly, anxious, or hostile affects one's health, career choice, or interpersonal relationships or whether a friendly or anxious child will necessarily have the same characteristics as an adult.

Social psychology considers how the real or imagined presence of others influences thought, feeling, and behavior. Research on prejudice and racism, for example, looks at how a person of one group perceives and treats people in other groups. Social psychologists ask such questions as these: How does the presence of other people change an individual's thoughts, feelings, or perceptions? Why is someone less likely to help a person in need when there are many people around than when there is no one else around? Why are we attracted to particular kinds of people?

Clinical psychology focuses on the diagnosis and treatment of mental, emotional, and behavioral disorders and ways to promote psychological health. Some clinical psychologists also conduct research and teach. Clinical psychologists work in universities, medical settings, or private practice. As you can see from Figure 1, clinical psychology is the single largest subdiscipline in psychology. In the United States, since the late 1940s, the main approach to training in psychology has been the scientist-practitioner model, in which people with PhDs in clinical psychology should be both therapists and researchers—or at least be trained to be both (Benjamin, 2007). Psychology is a practice as well as a science.

A related field is *counseling psychology*. Counseling psychologists tend to work with less severe psychological disorders than clinical psychologists. They treat and assess relatively healthy people and assist them with career and vocational interests. Training for

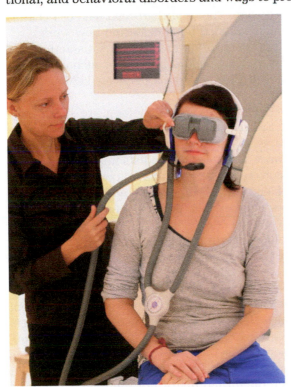
©Matthias Rietschel/AP Images

The woman wearing goggles and headgear is being prepared for a neuroimaging exam in a neuroscience lab.

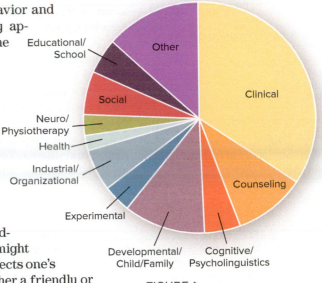

FIGURE 1
PERCENTAGE OF PhDs AWARDED IN THE SUBFIELDS OF PSYCHOLOGY IN 2014. (Adapted from Doctorate Recipients, 2016)

personality psychology
The study of what makes people unique and the consistencies in people's behavior across time and situations.

social psychology
The study of how living among others influences thought, feeling, and behavior.

clinical psychology
The diagnosis and treatment of mental, emotional, and behavioral disorders and the promotion of psychological health.

counseling psychologists is more likely to occur in schools of education than in psychology departments (Norcross et al., 1998).

Other professionals who provide therapy include clinical psychologists who have obtained a PsyD (a professional degree oriented toward nonresearch clinical careers); social workers; marriage and family therapists (who generally have master's degrees); and psychiatrists. Psychiatrists have training in medicine and an MD degree; in addition to offering therapy, they can prescribe drugs.

health psychology
The study of the role psychological factors play in regard to health and illness.

Health psychology examines the role of psychological factors in physical health and illness. Topics in health psychology range from studies of how stress is linked to illness and immune function to studies on the role of social factors in how people interact with health care professionals. Some health psychologists work in disease prevention, treatment, and rehabilitation; thus, this area involves clinical practice as well as research.

educational psychology
The study of how students learn, the effectiveness of particular teaching techniques, the social psychology of schools, and the psychology of teaching.

Educational psychology draws on several other areas of psychology to study how students learn, the effectiveness of particular teaching techniques, the dynamics of school populations, and the psychology of teaching. This field also attempts to understand special populations of students, such as the academically gifted and those with special needs. Educational psychologists are usually academics, theorists, or researchers. *School psychology* is a related field generally practiced by counselors in school settings. Approximately 9% of the doctorates in psychology were awarded in school psychology in 2005–2006.

industrial/organizational (I/O) psychology
The application of psychological concepts and questions to work settings.

Industrial/organizational (I/O) psychology is an applied science, meaning that it involves understanding real-world rather than laboratory behavior (Aamodt, 2010). The industrial and organizational sides focus on two distinct sets of problems. The *industrial* side involves matching employees to their jobs and uses psychological principles and methods to select employees and evaluate job performance. For this reason, the industrial side of I/O psychology is also sometimes referred to as personnel psychology. The *organizational* side of I/O aims to make workers more productive and satisfied by considering how work environments and management styles influence worker motivation, satisfaction, and productivity. I/O is one of the fastest-growing subdisciplines in psychology, with a nearly 50% increase in the number of PhD programs between 1986 and 2004 (Rogelberg & Gill, 2006).

sports psychology
The study of psychological factors in sports and exercise.

forensic psychology
The field that blends psychology, law, and criminal justice.

Two of the smaller and newer disciplines in psychology are sports psychology and forensic psychology. **Sports psychology** examines the psychological factors that affect performance and participation in sports and exercise (Weinberg & Gould, 2007). For instance, sports psychologists might focus on improving athletic performance through techniques such as relaxation and visualization. **Forensic psychology** is a blend of psychology, law, and criminal justice (Adler, 2004). Forensic psychologists make legal evaluations of a person's mental competency to stand trial, the state of mind of a defendant at the time of a crime, the fitness of a parent to have custody of children, and allegations of child abuse. Occasionally, they develop criminal profiles of the type of person who might have committed a particular crime.

As you study the chapters of this text, you may find that one area of psychology especially excites you. Keep in mind, however, that psychology is about how humans think and behave. Thus, all of the topics are useful, many of them are closely intertwined, and there are many reasons for studying psychology, even if you don't become a psychologist. The field of psychology is the outcome of millions of years of humans' interest in their fellow human beings (Feist, 2006). As we will see next, however, the formal history of the field is not quite so old.

1. What subdiscipline of psychology examines how thoughts, feelings, and behaviors change over the life span?
   a. developmental psychology
   b. cognitive psychology
   c. personality psychology
   d. educational psychology

2. A psychologist has conducted a series of studies on which part of the brain is most active during a memory task. She is probably
   a. a developmental psychologist.
   b. a behavioral neuroscientist.

   c. a cognitive psychologist.
   d. an industrial/organizational psychologist.

3. The main difference between a clinical and a counseling psychologist is that counseling psychologists treat
   a. people with more severe psychological disorders.
   b. more children than adults.
   c. people with less severe psychological disorders.
   d. people with learning disabilities only.

Answers can be found at the end of the chapter.

THE ORIGINS OF PSYCHOLOGY

In this section, we look briefly at the origins of the two main forms of psychology: clinical practice and science. The practice of psychology has deeper roots in human history than does the science of psychology. The prehistoric record offers evidence of efforts to heal people's suffering from disturbances of the mind, often in ways we now find alarming. The foundations for psychology as a science date back to the ancient Greeks, and the modern science of psychology originated in the 1870s (Robinson, 1995). First, we consider the practice of psychology, that is, clinical psychology.

shamans
Medicine men or women who treat people with mental problems by driving out their demons with elaborate rituals, such as exorcisms, incantations, and prayers.

A Brief History of the Practice of Clinical Psychology

Disorders of thought and behavior are no doubt as old as humans—indeed, there is evidence that primates (monkeys and apes) are afflicted with psychological disorders such as depression, anxiety, repetitive and functionless behaviors, and self-injuries (Maestripieri et al., 2006; Novak, 2003; Troisi, 2003). Thus, research suggests that these behaviors go back to the ancestors of both species, in this case approximately 6 million years.

Prehistoric Views As far back as the Stone Age (7,000 years ago and maybe even as long as 50,000 years ago), humans tried to cure one another of various mental problems. Most prehistoric cultures had medicine men or women, known as **shamans**, who treated the possessed by driving out demons with elaborate rituals, such as exorcisms, incantations, and prayers. Some of these shamans appeared to have practiced the oldest of all known surgical procedures, trephination.

Trephination involves drilling a small hole in a person's skull, usually less than an inch in diameter (Alt et al., 1997; Weber & Wahl, 2006). Some of these surgeries may have been for medical reasons, such as an attempt to heal a brain injury. Some may also have been performed for psychological reasons, to release the spirits and demons they believed possessed the afflicted person. Anthropological evidence suggests that a surprisingly large percentage of people survived such surgeries—which today's scientists can confirm by identifying bone growth after the procedure—and the surgeons must have had moderately sophisticated knowledge and understanding of the brain (Alt et al., 1997; Weber & Wahl, 2006).

Ancient Views Around 2600 BCE (Before the Common Era), the ancient Chinese moved away from supernatural explanations of psychological disorders toward

©SSPL/The Image Works

The hole in this skull may have been created by trephination, a prehistoric practice believed to release spirits or demons responsible for psychological disturbances.

 What do you think actually happens to those who undergo such a procedure?

natural and physiological explanations (Tseng, 1973). Specifically, they made connections between a person's bodily organs and emotions. The heart housed the mind; the liver, the spiritual soul; the lung, the animal soul; the spleen, ideas and intelligence; and the kidneys, will and vitality. The ancient Egyptians and Greeks also sought natural explanations for psychological disorders. In the second century BCE, the ancient Egyptians apparently used narcotics to treat pain (Finger, 1994). The Greek physician Hippocrates (460–377 BCE) was the first to write about a man suffering from a phobia of heights—now called acrophobia.

Medieval to Early Modern Views   In medieval Europe from approximately 400 to 1400 CE (Common Era), psychological disorders were again attributed to supernatural causes. In the worldview that dominated this era and the Renaissance (from about 1400 to the early 1600s), people were thought to be possessed by demons, spirits, and the devil—not by physical disorders. These views were taken to an extreme during the Inquisition, when the Catholic Church investigated witchcraft and heresy as part of a broad campaign to eliminate dissent from established Church dogma. Some witchcraft practices were viewed as harmless and even beneficial, but others were branded as the work of the devil. In order to distinguish good witchcraft from bad, Church officials held inquisitions and trials, using several techniques to determine whether a person was a witch (D. N. Robinson, 1995). Sometimes the accused was prodded with a metal pole and spears; if she felt no pain, she was protected by the devil and therefore was a witch. In another common method, the *float test*, the woman's hands and feet were tied, and she was thrown into a lake or river. If she floated, she had to be guilty, because only the devil could make someone float; if she sank, she was innocent—but had drowned (Robinson, 1995). The most common punishment for the infrequent survivor of the float test—deemed to be a witch—was being burned at the stake. To be fair, numerous writers during the 14th to 16th centuries argued that witchery was caused not by spirits and supernatural elements but rather by natural ones, such as hallucinations or "melancholia"—what we would now call depression (Robinson, 1995; Veith, 1965).

©Bettmann/Getty Images

In the Middle Ages, people who were judged to be witches could be burned at the stake. Some of them may have had psychological disorders that caused them to behave strangely.

 Although we see these as very outdated reactions to those who may be mentally ill, can you think of modern-day reactions that one day may also seem as outdated?

During the witch hunts of the 16th and 17th centuries, the first facilities for the mentally ill—called **asylums**—were built throughout Europe. The most famous, or infamous, of these was located at St. Mary of Bethlehem in London, England. Although it had served as a hospital for the mentally ill and others since the 1300s, Henry VIII designated it as a hospital for the insane in 1547. It was really no more than a storage house for the mentally ill and other social castaways. For the most part, early efforts to "treat" mental illness focused on removing afflicted people from society rather than helping them adjust to society. The conditions were deplorable and chaotic—patients were put in windowless and filthy rooms and were chained and shackled to the walls. The local population, including William Shakespeare, called the place *Bedlam*, a shortened version of *Bethlehem*, and that is how the term came to be associated with chaotic and noisy conditions.

In response to these inhumane conditions, reform movements in support of **moral treatment** emerged in Europe and the United States. The main idea was to provide a relaxing place where patients would be treated with dignity and care. The first major proponent of humane therapies was the Frenchman Philippe Pinel in 1783. Dorothea Dix pioneered moral treatment in the United States. After visiting a prison in 1841 and witnessing the abhorrent and inhumane treatment of the inmates, some of them suffering from psychological disorders, Dix vowed to change these conditions. Over the next 40 years, she helped open 30 homes throughout North America (Nolen-Hoeksema, 2007). Moral therapies were among the first forms of treatment that regularly helped people get better.

Modern Views   The last decades of the 1800s also saw the emergence of the first truly modern view of psychological disorders—the idea that they are simply one form of illness and should be treated as medical conditions, with appropriate diagnosis and therapy. This view is now known as the "medical model" perspective in clinical psychology. In the 1880s and 1890s, the German psychiatrist Emil Kraepelin collected data on the various kinds of psychological disorders and began systematically classifying and diagnosing them (Shepard, 1995). He popularized the term *dementia praecox* (premature dementia), which he later changed to *schizophrenia*, to refer to the major thought disorder known previously as "split mind." He was also the first to distinguish thought disorders (schizophrenia) from the mood disorders of melancholia (depression) and manic depression (bipolar disorder; Jablensky & Woodbury, 1995). In short, his views were a major influence on diagnostic categories formulated during the 20th century.

Around the turn of the 20th century in Austria, Sigmund Freud developed a form of therapy called psychoanalysis. A clinical approach to understanding and treating psychological disorders, **psychoanalysis** assumes that the unconscious mind is the most powerful force behind thought and behavior and that dreams have meaning and are the most direct route to the unconscious mind (Freud, 1900/1953). It also assumes that our experiences during childhood are a powerful force in the development of our adult personality. Psychoanalysis assumes that people use psychological defenses to protect themselves against threatening impulses, thoughts, feelings, and fantasies. Last, it assumes that the unconscious blocking, or repression, of disturbing thoughts and impulses—especially sexual and aggressive impulses—is at the heart of all maladaptive adult behavior.

By the mid-20th century, three of the major modern developments in clinical psychology had emerged: psychotherapy, drug therapy, and modern criteria for diagnosing mental disorders. For example, one common form of modern therapy—cognitive-behavioral—focuses on changing a person's maladaptive thought and behavior patterns by discussing and rewarding more appropriate ways of thinking and behaving. Although we will consider the modern diagnostic criteria in detail in the chapter "Psychological Disorders" and *psychotherapy* (psychological assessment and treatment by a trained therapist) and drug therapy in detail in the chapter "Treatment of Psychological Disorders", it is appropriate

asylums
Facilities for treating the mentally ill in Europe during the Middle Ages and into the 19th century.

moral treatment
A 19th-century approach to treating the mentally ill with dignity in a caring environment.

Connection

Disturbance, dysfunction, distress, and deviance must be present for the diagnosis of psychological disorders. The *DSM-5* describes specific symptoms of more than 250 different disorders.

See "Defining Psychological Disorders," in the chapter "Psychological Disorders". (p. 569)

psychoanalysis
A clinically based approach to understanding and treating psychological disorders; assumes that the unconscious mind is the most powerful force behind thought and behavior.

Source: Library of Congress, Prints & Photographs Division, Sigmund Freud Collection [LC-USZ62-72266]

Sigmund Freud

to conclude our discussion of the history of psychology as a clinical practice with a brief introduction to the classification system that guides the diagnosis of psychological disorders today.

When diagnosing psychological disorders, psychologists use the *Diagnostic and Statistical Manual*. Currently in its fifth edition, this standardized reference is referred to as the *Diagnostic and Statistical Manual–5*, or *DSM-5* (American Psychiatric Association, 2013). Originally published in 1952, the *DSM* includes diagnoses for more than 250 psychological disorders. The various editions of the *DSM* have incorporated new findings and added new disorders, objectively describing the behaviors and symptoms of each disorder, so that psychologists from all perspectives can agree on a single diagnosis for an individual with a given set of symptoms. You might find it surprising to know, however, that this goal of universal agreement often is not achieved, so different clinicians hold different views about what constitutes a mental disorder. Occasionally, the *DSM* authors have removed behavior patterns (such as homosexuality, which was deleted from the list of disorders recognized by the American Psychiatric Association in 1973) that do not meet updated diagnostic criteria. Further, practitioners from the various subfields do not always agree with each other about the definitions of a given disorder. Cognitive-behavioral practitioners view depression, for example, as the patient's distorted thinking ("I am worthless"), whereas psychodynamic practitioners might consider the same person's depression (and expressed thoughts) to be the result of unconscious disturbing family relationship patterns that need to be made conscious. Clearly, perspective matters when it comes to psychological treatment, and we must continually question what we know from the perspective we are adopting.

A Brief History of Scientific Psychology

As with all sciences, scientific psychology can claim philosophy as one of its parent disciplines. By the middle of the 1800s, however, psychology had grown away from philosophy to become a science. Let's look briefly at this history.

The Philosophy of Empiricism   Perhaps the most important philosophical question for psychology is the nature of knowledge and how human beings create knowledge. Does knowledge come from reflection and thinking or from experience? In the 4th century BCE, the Greek philosopher Plato argued for the former and his student Aristotle for the latter. In 17th-century Europe, however, the English philosopher John Locke established the view that knowledge and thoughts come from experience and observations, a point of view known as **empiricism**. Specifically, Locke argued that the mind begins as a *tabula rasa*, or blank slate, onto which experience writes the contents of the mind (Locke, 1690/1959).

empiricism
The view that all knowledge and thoughts come from experience.

This view that the mind simply receives what our sensory organs—eyes, ears, nose, skin, and tongue—take in from the outside world is very important in philosophy and psychology. In contrast to scientists, however, philosophers do not collect data to test their ideas. Psychology gained its independence from philosophy when researchers started to examine and test human sensations and perception using scientific methods. Psychology as a modern empirical science tests predictions about behavior with systematic observations and gathered data. In the mid- to late 1800s, many German universities were starting scientific laboratories in physics, chemistry, and medicine. In the 1870s, they opened the first laboratories in psychology.

The Psychophysics of Human Perception   The starting point for empiricism is that we know and experience the world through our five senses of seeing, hearing, tasting, smelling, and touching. Because of the profound influence of the empiricists, in the 1870s physicists who wanted to understand how people process and experience the sensations of sound, light, smell, taste, and touch developed the field of **psychophysics**—the psychology of physical sensations. By doing so, these physicists started the scientific discipline of psychology. The reasoning was that if the mind consists only of what we sense, then understanding the senses will lead to a direct understanding of the mind.

One important principle of psychophysics is that the perception of physical properties is not the same as the physical properties themselves. To demonstrate, let's consider the classic question, What weighs more, a pound of feathers or a pound of bricks? You might be thinking, How dumb do they think I am? I've heard that so many times. They weigh the same! A pound is a pound. Maybe, for that answer is true only for the objective, physical property of weight. The *perceived* weight of the two—a psychological property—would be very different. Researchers found that, when people's estimates of the weights of both items are empirically tested, contrary to common sense, people think a pound of bricks weighs two to three times as much as a pound of feathers (Benjamin, 2007). If you don't believe us, try it for yourself.

In essence, the scientists who first developed psychophysics were the first experimental psychologists. Ernst Weber (1795–1878) did some of the first research in perception and laid the groundwork for what later became known as psychophysics. For instance, he investigated the smallest change in weight or length that people could discern. Then, in 1850, building on Weber's work, his mentor, Gustav Fechner (1801–1889), had a sudden realization that one could study the psychological and physical worlds. Fechner coined the term *psychophysics* for this new discipline, and he went on to refine some of Weber's principles of perception (Fancher, 1996).

A physician and physicist, Hermann von Helmholtz (1821–1894), not only made important contributions to the study of memory, physiology, and color vision but also made key contributions to the laws of conservation in physics and to music theory, meteorology, and geometry; he designed a workable telephone years before Alexander Graham Bell (Benjamin, 2007). In addition, he was the first to calculate the speed of a nerve impulse at about 90 feet per second. With the work of these pioneers, psychophysics took the first steps toward establishing psychology as a science.

©Bettmann/Getty Images

Wilhelm Wundt

Psychology blossomed into a full-fledged science with the help of Wilhelm Wundt (1832–1920). In 1879 (remember this date!), Wundt set up a psychology laboratory in Leipzig, Germany, now considered the birthplace of experimental psychology. Although others went before Wundt, he is credited with giving psychology its independence from philosophy and physiology (Benjamin, 2007; Fancher, 1996). He did so by applying the scientific methods of physiology and physics to questions of philosophy (Benjamin, 2007). Before Wundt, people evaluated the question of how the mind worked only by way of argument, not by scientific investigation. By establishing a laboratory, Wundt created a place where the best young minds could learn the science of psychology, and come to learn they did. Wundt single-handedly trained more than 180 students in his laboratory. Of these, more than 100 came from countries other than Germany and then returned to their native countries, taking their knowledge of experimental psychology with them.

An American, G. Stanley Hall (1844–1924), went to Germany to learn from Wundt. At Harvard, Hall also studied with William James, who is considered the founder of American psychology. Hall holds the distinction of earning the first PhD (1878) in psychology in the United States as James's student. He opened the first psychology laboratory in the United States at Johns Hopkins University in Baltimore, officially establishing psychology as a science in this country. He also founded the American Psychological Association (APA) and became its first president in 1892. Hall started the first scientific journal in American psychology,

©Bettmann/Getty Images

William James

the *American Journal of Psychology*. Finally, he was able to persuade both Sigmund Freud and his famous protégé, Carl Jung, to make their only journey to the United States and give lectures at Clark University in Massachusetts in 1909. G. Stanley Hall was also the teacher and mentor of Francis Cecil Sumner (1895–1954), the first African American to earn a PhD in psychology (1920). From 1928 until his death in 1954, Sumner chaired the psychology department at Howard University, where he conducted research on equality and justice.

Another of William James's students, Mary Whiton Calkins (1863–1930), became the first female president of APA in 1905. Harvard was an all-male university until 1920, and the male students did not want to have a woman in class, so she and James had to conduct their coursework in James's home. Calkins went on to complete the requirements for the PhD, although Harvard would not grant her the degree, simply because she was a woman (Benjamin, 2007). Nevertheless, Calkins had an accomplished academic career. She taught at Wellesley College and conducted research on dreaming, gender issues, and self-image (Furumoto, 1981). James acknowledged her to be among the best students he had ever encountered (Benjamin, 2007).

Structuralism and Functionalism   What is the best way to understand the human mind, by examining its parts or its function? In the last decades of the 1800s, psychology weathered its first major scientific debate, with two different perspectives on how to study thought and behavior. The field was divided over whether it was more important to study the *elements* or the *functions* behind human thought and behavior. Focus on the elements of mind led to the school of thought known as structuralism, whereas focus on the functions of mind led to the school of thought known as functionalism. Edward Titchener (1867–1927), a British American psychologist trained by Wilhelm Wundt, coined both terms.

According to **structuralism**, breaking down experience into its elemental parts offered the best way to understand thought and behavior. Structuralists believed that a detailed analysis of experience as it happened provided the most accurate glimpse into the workings of the human mind. Their method was **introspection**, looking into one's own mind for information about the nature of conscious experience. Structuralists divided each experience into its smallest elements. Wundt, the chief proponent of structuralism, wanted to describe human experience in terms of the elements that combined to produce it (Benjamin, 2007). For example, structuralists, like chemists describing elements, would not describe a peach as "a good peach" but rather would describe their experience with the peach as sweet, round, slightly orange, fuzzy, wet, and juicy.

Influenced by Charles Darwin's theory of natural selection, psychologists who supported **functionalism** thought it was better to look at why the mind worked the way it did rather than to describe its parts. The functionalists asked, "Why do people think, feel, or perceive, and how did these abilities come to be?" Functionalists used introspection as well. William James, the most famous functionalist, relied on introspection as a primary method of understanding how the mind worked.

James's and Wundt's methods of introspection were impressive attempts to describe the conscious mind. Eventually, however, introspection failed as a method of science because of difficulties in reaching a consensus as to the nature of certain experiences. Moreover, the rise of psychology as the science of *observable* behavior led to complete rejection of the study of the mind. It also gave way to the rise of behaviorism.

Behaviorism   In 1913, a little-known 34-year-old psychologist, John Watson, directly challenged the use of introspection. He founded **behaviorism**, which asserts that psychology can be a true science only if it examines observable

structuralism
The 19th-century school of psychology that argued that breaking down experience into its elemental parts offers the best way to understand thought and behavior.

introspection
The main method of investigation for structuralists; it involves looking into one's own mind for information about the nature of conscious experience.

functionalism
The 19th-century school of psychology that argued it was better to look at why the mind works the way it does than to describe its parts.

behaviorism
A school of psychology that proposed that psychology can be a true science only if it examines observable behavior, not ideas, thoughts, feelings, or motives.

behavior, not ideas, thoughts, feelings, or motives. In Watson's view, mental experiences are hypothetical concepts, for they cannot be directly measured. As long as psychology focused on such internal states, it would forever be a false science. Behaviorism is an extreme form of environmentalism, the view that all behavior comes from experience interacting with the world. It is the school of psychology that most clearly expresses John Locke's ideas about our minds being a blank slate at birth.

A decade or so after behaviorism emerged, it became the dominant force in experimental psychology. Its most famous figure, B. F. Skinner (1904–1990), was largely responsible for making behaviorism the major approach in experimental psychology, a position it held for nearly 50 years. Skinner modified Watson's ideas and argued that consequences shape behavior.

Humanistic and Positive Psychology During the first half of the 20th century, the two major schools of thought in psychology were split along the divide between practice and science. On the therapeutic side were psychoanalysis and Freud, and on the scientific side were behaviorism and Skinner. In the 1940s and 1950s, Abraham Maslow and Carl Rogers presented an alternative to both of these perspectives. They argued that both psychoanalysis and behaviorism ignored people at their best, and neither approach considered what it meant to be psychologically healthy. Maslow and Rogers proposed an alternative called **humanistic psychology**, which promoted personal growth and meaning as a way of reaching one's highest potential.

The humanistic movement had waned by the late 1970s, mostly because it had moved away from its research and scientific base. It surfaced again in the late 1990s, however, when Martin Seligman and Mihaly Csikszentmihalyi started the positive psychology movement (Seligman & Csikszentmihalyi, 2000). **Positive psychology** shares with humanism a belief that psychology should focus on studying, understanding, and promoting healthy and positive psychological functioning. It does so with a better appreciation than humanistic psychology for the importance of studying well-being from a scientific perspective. As you will see in this text, much of contemporary psychology embraces the positive psychological view.

Cognitivism After Watson banished thoughts, feelings, and motives as the focal point of the modern science of psychology in the 1910s, research into these topics nearly disappeared from the field for almost 50 years. Two events kept them in the minds of psychologists, however. First, in the 1920s and 1930s, a movement in Germany called Gestalt psychology attracted worldwide attention. Led by Max Wertheimer (1880–1943), **Gestalt psychology**—after the German word for "whole form"—proposed that perception occurs in unified wholes, where the whole is more than the sum of its parts. As the Gestaltists suspected, our brains actively shape sensory information into perceptions. For an example of this phenomenon, look at Figure 2. You see a triangle within three circles, but no triangle actually exists. The brain, however, organizes your perception of the markings on the page into the shape of a triangle.

Second, mental processes returned to psychology full force in the 1950s and 1960s—just when the influence of behaviorism was at its peak. The

©U.S. Navy Brien Aho, HO/AP Images

This dolphin is being trained by means of shaping, a behaviorist technique that rewards animals for small changes in behavior as they learn a desired behavior pattern, such as leaping out of the water on cue.

 Can you think of undesirable human behaviors that could be shaped with rewards to lessen them or to make them go away?

humanistic psychology
A theory of psychology that focuses on personal growth and meaning as a way of reaching one's highest potential.

positive psychology
A scientific approach to studying, understanding, and promoting healthy and positive psychological functioning.

Gestalt psychology
A theory of psychology that maintains that we perceive things as wholes rather than as a compilation of parts.

FIGURE 2
A DEMONSTRATION OF GESTALT PSYCHOLOGY.

 Why do you see a triangle even though no triangle actually exists?

new emphasis was really a forgotten focus on the processes that fascinated Fechner, Wundt, and Helmholtz in the 19th century: sensation, perception, and mental processes. The term *mental*, however, had lost its appeal. Instead, a new word for thought and mental processes appeared: *cognition* (Benjamin, 2007; Gardner, 1987).

By the 1960s, the field of cognitive science had been born, with a focus on the scientific study of thought (Gardner, 1987). In addition to freeing itself from the label *mental*, cognitive science made use of a new modern metaphor for the human mind—the computer. A fairly recent innovation at the time, the computer seemed to have a lot in common with the human mind. Computers store, retrieve, and process information, just as the brain stores, retrieves, and processes sensations, memories, and ideas. Sensation was the input; perception was the interpretation and processing of the input; and behavior and thoughts were the output. By the 1980s, cognitive science had combined many disciplines in addition to psychology—namely, linguistics, philosophy, anthropology, artificial intelligence, and neuroscience (Gardner, 1987).

Some of the thinking in this new cognitive movement was based on a book by the British psychologist Frederick Bartlett (1886–1969). Bartlett wrote that memory is not an objective and accurate representation of events but rather a highly personal reconstruction based on one's own beliefs, ideas, and point of view. For example, racial-ethnic stereotypes are frameworks that can alter memory (Graham & Lowery, 2004). If a witness to a crime holds a bias about how likely a crime is to be perpetrated by a person of a certain racial-ethnic background, the witness may misremember the appearance of the accused. This example illustrates that, as Bartlett argued, when people remember, they reconstruct experience in terms of what is most relevant to them rather than providing an unbiased account of events. Bartlett showed that our cognitive frameworks organize how we experience the world. This view is now well accepted in psychology, though Bartlett's insights were unappreciated in the United States for decades (Benjamin, 2007).

Connection

Our genetic code is not set in stone at birth. Genes are turned on or off by experiences we have, foods we eat, and even foods our mothers ate while pregnant with us.

See "The Environment Can Change Gene Expression: Epigenetics," in the chapter "The Biology of Behavior". (p. 79)

Challenge Your Assumptions

True or False? Genetic influence on our thoughts and actions is set at birth and can't be changed.

False: Experience can and does change how and when genes get expressed.

Behavioral Genetics, Behavioral Neuroscience, and Evolutionary Psychology By the 1980s, more and more psychologists had become receptive to the ideas that who we are and what we do and think are very much influenced by genetic factors (behavioral genetics) and brain activity (behavioral neuroscience), with a long evolutionary past (evolutionary psychology). The roots of this approach lie in many related fields. Recent behavioral genetic research has overturned a long-held notion that genetic influence is set at birth and is unchanging. We now know that genes get turned on and off by experience—that is, genetic influence changes how we think and behave over the course of our lives. Similarly, evolutionary psychology was jump-started in 1992 when John Tooby and Leda Cosmides (1992) published "The Psychological Foundations of Culture" in a seminal book on evolutionary psychology. These developments all began to shift psychology toward a more complex view of the origins of human thought and behavior as products of nature and nurture, enhanced by new brain imaging techniques and the sequencing of the human genome.

Our review of the history of psychological science, summarized in Figure 3, has only scratched the surface of how psychologists think about human thought and behavior, about mind, body, and experience. Debates and theories about how and why we think and act the way we do go back thousands of years. Some of the key debates remain unresolved to this day, primarily because in many cases no one perspective explains the whole story of how things work. These systems of thought have profoundly influenced the development of psychology. Let's now consider the major ways of thinking about mind, body, and experience that have shaped modern psychological science.

FIGURE 3
KEY FIGURES AND EVENTS IN THE HISTORY OF PSYCHOLOGY.

460–377 BCE
Hippocrates describes a patient suffering from mental disorder

5,000 BCE
Trephination is used to release the spirits and demons from the mind

1690
John Locke proposes that the mind is a blank slate to be written on by experience

1860
Gustav Fechner publishes *Elemente der Psychophysik*, establishing the discipline of psychophysics

1879
Wilhelm Wundt opens first psychology laboratory in Leipzig, Germany

1890
William James publishes *Principles of Psychology*, a text in 2 volumes

1892
G. Stanley Hall, a founding father of American Psychological Association (APA), becomes its first president

1900
Sigmund Freud introduces his psychoanalytic theory of behavior with the publication of *Interpretation of Dreams*

1905
Mary Whiton Calkins becomes first female president of APA

1912
Max Wertheimer develops the principles of Gestalt psychology

1913
John B. Watson establishes behaviorism to study observable behavior

1920
Francis Cecil Sumner becomes first African American to earn PhD in psychology

1932
Frederick Bartlett lays the foundation for cognitive science with his book *Remembering*

1938
B. F. Skinner publishes *The Behavior of Organisms,* outlining his version of behaviorism

1951
Carl Rogers publishes *Client-Centered Therapy,* advocating a new humanistic approach emphasizing personal growth

1950
Karen Horney published *Neurosis and Human Growth* outlining her psychoanalytic social theory as an alternative to Freud's psychosexual theory

1953
Abraham Maslow's *Motivation and Personality* outlines the stages of growth leading to personal fulfillment

1965
Jean Piaget publishes *The Child's Conception of Number*

1974
Eleanor Maccoby and Carol Jacklin publish a seminal book on gender, *The Psychology of Sex Differences*

1992
John Tooby and Leda Cosmides publish a landmark chapter "The Evolutionary Foundations of Culture" that jump-starts evolutionary psychology

1998
Martin Seligman starts the positive psychology movement with Mihaly Csíkszentmihalyi to study and promote psychological well-being

Timeline markers: 1860, 1870, 1880, 1890, 1900, 1910, 1920, 1930, 1940, 1950, 1960, 1970, 1980, 1990, 2000

1. What perspective in psychology assumes that the unconscious is the most powerful force behind most behavior?
   a. trephination
   b. cognitive psychology
   c. structuralism
   d. psychoanalysis

2. _____ argued that thoughts, feelings, and motives are unimportant in understanding human behavior.
   a. Behaviorists
   b. Psychoanalysts

   c. Functionalists
   d. Gestalt psychologists

3. Positive psychology is a modern version of which school of thought?
   a. structuralism
   b. humanism
   c. functionalism
   d. introspectionism

Answers can be found at the end of the chapter.

PSYCHOLOGICAL PERSPECTIVES: EXPLAINING HUMAN BEHAVIOR

One of the primary functions of science is to describe and explain how the world works. Psychologists attempt to explain how human thought, emotion, motivation, and behavior work. Yet, people are so complex that many different perspectives have developed on how to best explain human thought and behavior. These perspectives make different assumptions and focus on different aspects of behavior. In psychology, there are at least seven major perspectives that explain human behavior. These perspectives are distinct but can be and sometimes are integrated. After all, it's not all black and white.

Psychoanalytic-Psychodynamic

Beginning with Freud, psychoanalytic and then later the psychodynamic approaches focus on the importance of early childhood experience and relationships with parents as guiding forces that shape personality development. Additionally, this view sees the unconscious mind and motives as much more powerful than the conscious awareness. Psychoanalysis traditionally used dream interpretation and uncovering the unconscious thoughts, feelings, and impulses as a main form of treatment of neurosis and mental illness.

Behaviorism-Learning

Behaviorists argue that if you want to understand behavior then focus only on behavior, not hypothetical and unobservable internals states such as thoughts, feelings, drives, or motives. All behaviors are learned through association and/or their consequences (whether it is reinforced or punished). To shape desired behavior, we have to understand and then establish the conditions that bring about those particular behaviors.

Humanistic-Positive

Humanistic and positive psychologists assume that people strive toward meaning, growth, well-being, happiness, and psychological health; positive emotions and happiness foster psychological health and pro-social behavior. Understanding these evolved positive aspects of human behavior provides just as much insight into human nature as does understanding the pathological aspects (Seligman, 2003).

Cognitive

How we think about ourselves, other people, and the world, as well as the assumptions we make and the strategies we use for solving problems and interacting with others are the keys to understanding differences between people. The particular language we learn and use shapes our way of thinking and perceiving. Memory formation is not a passive process but is shaped by our experiences, attitudes, and personalities. In short, what we do is shaped by how we think and perceive the world.

Sociocultural/Cross-Cultural

The immediate (micro; family, friends) and larger (macro; region and nation) environments impact and mold a person's personality from birth on. One can't understand people without understanding the place and context in which they grew up. Cultures differ along particular dimensions—such as collectivism-individualism or masculinity-femininity—and these cultural differences influence the thought and behavior of individuals within each culture. Psychological outcomes can also be compared between cultures and there are both similarities and differences across cultures.

Neuropsychological-Behavioral Genetic

Behavior, thought, feelings, and personality are influenced by differences in basic genetic, epigenetic, and neurological systems between individuals. The reason some people have different traits, dispositions, and ways of thinking stem from differences in their genotype and central nervous system (brain structures and neurochemistry).

Evolutionary

Because they are based on evolved brain systems, human thought, behavior, and personality have been shaped by forces of evolution (natural and sexual selection) over millions of years. The body, brain, and environment coexist and co-evolved and so more than any other psychological perspective the evolutionary perspective emphasizes that what we think, feel, and do is always an interaction between nature (biological) and nurture (environment).

In addition to these seven psychological perspectives, there are two other overarching issues that have colored much of psychology over the previous few decades: the nature-nurture debate and an increased appreciation for the evolution of human behavior.

The Nature-Nurture Debate

For millennia, thinkers have argued over what determines our personality and behavior—innate biology or life experience (Pinker, 2004)—a conflict known as the *nature-nurture debate*. The nature-only view is that who we are comes from inborn tendencies and genetically based traits.

On the one hand, the nature-only position argues that inborn and innate (that is, genetic and biological) qualities are the strongest determinants of thought and behavior. We are born predisposed toward particular personality traits and styles of thinking and behaving. On the other hand, the nurture-only side states that we are all essentially the same at birth and that we are the product of our experiences. As we have already considered, John Locke (1690/1959) popularized

Perspective	Primary Assumptions	Focus	Key Figures
Psychoanalytic-Psychodynamic	• first 5 years of life most shape personality • unconscious forces are most important	unconscious thoughts and motives	Freud Adler Jung Horney
Behavioral-Learning	• only explanation for behavior is the conditions that create behavior • learning occurs through association and consequences of the behavior	behavior, learning, and environmental conditions	Pavlov Watson Skinner Bandura
Cognitive	• thoughts, heuristics, and assumptions are the primary forces behind behavior	thoughts, language, assumptions, memory, decision-making strategies	Chomsky Piaget Kahneman Tversky
Humanistic-Positive	• people strive to live meaningful, happy lives • people are motivated by growth and psychological health	meaningful life, psychological well-being, and growth	Maslow Rogers Seligman
Sociocultural	• thought, behavior, and personality are mostly products of social and cultural conditions • there are both similarities and differences in thought, personality and behavior cross-culturally	cultural and society	Hofstede Triandis
Neuropsychology-Behavioral Genetic	• the foundation for thought and behavior is biological and genetic forces	brain structures, neurochemicals, and genes	Kandel Milner Bouchard Plomin
Evolutionary	• human thought and behavior have been shaped by evolutionary forces (natural and sexual selection)	adaptive mechanisms	Tooby Cosmides Buss

FIGURE 4
SUMMARY OF SEVEN MAJOR PERSPECTIVES IN PSYCHOLOGY.

the idea that the newborn human mind is a blank slate on which the experiences of life are written. This accumulation of experiences makes us who we are. This view means that anything is possible. You can be anything you want to be. This notion is a very Western, very North American idea. It stands as the cornerstone of democracy, free will, and equality (Pinker, 2002).

Pitting nature against nurture, however, gets us nowhere. It creates a false split, or false dichotomy, that hinders our understanding of the mind and behavior. Almost nothing in psychology can be categorized as either nature or nurture—not learning, not memory, not cognition, not emotion, not even social behavior! These forces work together almost all the time; they are interdependent.

Throughout this text, we will point out many cases in which environmental and genetic forces work together to shape who we are (Rutter, 2002). For example, in the processes of learning and remembering, certain genes in the brain are turned on or off by what happens to us (Kandel, 2006). New connections between brain cells result from these changes in the genes. Consequently, the brains of people and animals reared in richly stimulating environments differ from the brains of people reared in understimulating, neglectful, or abusive environments.

What we are born with and what we are exposed to interact to create thought and behavior. For decades, many psychologists have shied away from the idea of an interrelationship, clinging to the nature-nurture debate. Old habits die hard. To fully appreciate human behavior, we must take a broader view. All creatures are born with genetic instructions, but even before birth environmental factors alter the ways in which genes are expressed. Throughout life, genetic factors, such as a familial predisposition toward anxiety, assert themselves. Rather than pitting nature against nurture, we prefer the phrase **nature through nurture**, whereby the environment—be it the womb or the world outside—interacts continuously with biology to shape who we are and what we do (Begley, 2007; Pinker, 2004; Ridley, 2003).

nature through nurture
The position that the environment constantly interacts with biology to shape who we are and what we do.

The Evolution of Human Behavior

One principle that plays an important role in understanding human behavior is evolution. The basics of this theory are more complex than most of us realize. Here we briefly explain the fundamental processes of evolution.

Evolution means "change." With respect to biological species, **evolution** is the change over time in the frequency with which specific genes occur within a breeding species (Buss, 1999). What does the frequency of gene transmission have to do with behavior? Our genes contain instructions for making all the proteins in our bodies. Proteins in turn make up a lot of what we are: cell membranes, hormones, enzymes, and muscle tissue, for instance. These constituents carry out our intentions, in our brains and in our bodies. Thus, behaviors have genetic bases that are affected by many environmental factors. Human interaction with the world influences which genes are passed on to future generations, and these in turn shape human behavior. These changes take place by *natural and sexual selection*.

evolution
The change over time in the frequency with which specific genes occur within a breeding species.

©Natural History Museum, London/Science Source

©NHPA/Photoshot

In industrial England in the 1800s, the peppered moth, which was originally mostly white, blended into the white lichen on trees. Pollution killed the white lichen on trees and put the original white moth in danger of being easy prey. Some started to become darker to blend in with the lichenless trees. Can you see both moths in each image? The white one on the right is so well camouflaged that a red circle had to be drawn to show its location.

 How does this exemplify Darwin's idea of natural selection?

To understand how Darwin's idea of evolution works, consider a population of beetles:

FIGURE 5

HOW NATURAL SELECTION WORKS. Natural selection is one of the basic mechanisms of evolution. This hypothetical example shows how natural selection might change the predominant color of a population of beetles from green to brown.

1 **There is variation in traits.**

Some beetles are green and some are brown.

3 **There is heredity.**

The surviving brown beetles have brown baby beetles because this trait has a genetic basis.

4 **There is the end result.**

The more advantageous trait, brown coloration, allows the beetle to have more offspring and becomes more common in the population. If this process continues, eventually, all individuals in the population will be brown.

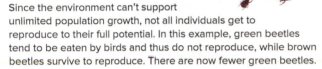

2 **There is differential reproduction.**

Since the environment can't support unlimited population growth, not all individuals get to reproduce to their full potential. In this example, green beetles tend to be eaten by birds and thus do not reproduce, while brown beetles survive to reproduce. There are now fewer green beetles.

(Charles Darwin): Source: Library of Congress Prints & Photographs Division [LC-DIG-ggbain-03485]; (green beetle below Charles Darwin): ©Melinda Fawver/Getty Images; (stages 1 and 2): ©W.E. Garrett/National Geographic/Getty Images; (stage 3): ©Ingram Publishing/Fotosearch RF; (stage 4): ©Denise McCullough

natural selection
A feedback process whereby nature favors one design over another because it has an impact on reproduction.

First described by the 19th-century English naturalist Charles Darwin (1809–1882), **natural selection** is formally defined as a feedback process whereby nature favors one design over another, depending on whether it has an impact on reproduction. This process takes a long time to work, but it ultimately shapes who we are and how species evolve. Charles Darwin's great contribution was not the theory of evolution itself but rather his explanation of *how evolution works*—that is, by natural selection.

Natural selection occurs by chance. Every once in a while, genes change for no apparent reason. Spontaneous changes in genes, called *chance mutations*, can alter the design of a structure or a set of behaviors. Let's suppose that a chance mutation in a population of green beetles results in a brown beetle. If the brown beetle is less visible to predators, it might have more success in surviving and reproducing, as Figure 5 shows. When it reproduces, the brown beetle passes on its "brown" genes to its offspring.

The brown offspring have a better survival rate, which means they are more likely to reproduce. Eventually, this physiological trait becomes common among members of the species. The complete change takes many generations, but eventually the entire beetle species will be brown (Tooby & Cosmides, 1992). The key in natural selection is that the behaviors have to increase reproductive success, because reproduction and gene transmission drive the whole process. The accumulation of chance mutations underlies evolutionary change. Each generation is a product of beneficial modifications from its evolutionary past.

Another form of selection happens not through mutation and chance but rather by being attractive to members of the opposite sex. Darwin in fact proposed a second form of selection, namely **sexual selection**, which operates when members of the opposite sex find certain traits attractive or appealing and therefore over long periods of times these traits become more common in the population (Darwin, 1859; Miller, 2000).

Natural and sexual selection create structures, behaviors, and traits that solve adaptive problems. Among the adaptive problems that our early human

sexual selection
Operates when members of the opposite sex find certain traits attractive or appealing and therefore over long periods of times these traits become more common in the population.

ancestors faced were avoiding predators, choosing nutritious foods, finding a mate, and communicating effectively with others. **Adaptations** are inherited solutions to ancestral problems that have been naturally and sexually selected because they directly contribute in some way to reproductive success (Tooby & Cosmides, 1992). Adaptations evolved to solve problems in past generations, not current ones. In other words, we are living with traits and tendencies that benefited our ancestors. Even though these tendencies might not seem to enhance our fitness in today's world, eons spent in harsher environments have left us predisposed to perform certain social behaviors when a situation calls forth ancient patterns. Consider our preference for fatty foods. In our evolutionary past, eating fat was a good strategy. Early humans, as hunter-gatherers, did not know when they would find food. If they found fat, they ate it, because fat could be stored in the body and used later when food might be scarce. For this reason, humans evolved to like fat. Modern society, however, offers easy access to food. Now eating fat is not the best strategy, because we don't need to store it for future use. More food will be available when we need it. So we eat fat, store it up, and carry it around as extra weight. Human cravings have not changed much, even though our environments have.

Evolutionary psychology is the branch of psychology that aims to uncover the adaptive problems the human mind may have solved in the distant past and the effect of evolution on behavior today. Rather than just describing what the mind does, evolutionary psychologists are interested in the functions of the human mind (Tooby & Cosmides, 1992). Evolutionary changes in organs and bodily structures—or color, as in our beetle example—are not difficult to understand, but how do human behaviors evolve?

Let's consider the emotions as an example of a behavioral adaptation. In the chapter "Motivation and Emotion", we discuss emotions in detail and explore the feelings that move us powerfully. For now, imagine that you are driving on the highway and the car in the lane next to you has just cut you off. You have to slam on your brakes to keep from smashing into it, and you are shaking with fright. The possible car accident is an immediate cause of your fear.

Why do you experience this intense bodily reaction called fear in the first place? The answer, from an evolutionary perspective, is that fear was naturally

Adaptations
Inherited solutions to ancestral problems that have been selected for because they contribute in some way to reproductive success.

evolutionary psychology
The branch of psychology that studies human behavior by asking what adaptive problems it may have solved for our early ancestors.

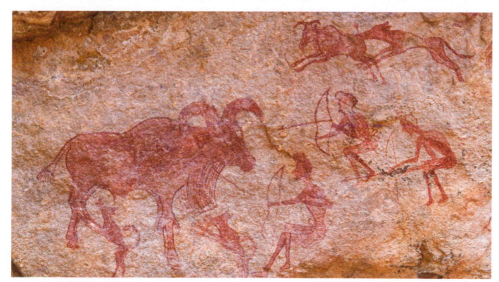

©Frank Lukasseck/Getty Images

Early hunters, like the ones portrayed in this ancient rock painting from the Tadrart Acacus of Libya, ate fat when it was available, and their bodies stored the excess in order to survive when food was scarce. This adaptation has persisted for thousands of years, even though for most people access to food is not a problem.

selected to solve an adaptive problem. What we call fear—including the way it moves our bodies, impels us to act, and makes our hearts race—evolved because it helps us deal quickly and efficiently with danger (Ekman, 2003). Eons ago, a genetic variation occurred in a human that somehow led to a specific way of responding to threatening circumstances—quick action to avoid being killed—and the human was able to avoid harm and reproduce more readily; that is, it had an advantage. Without thinking about it, the ancestor who recognized a beast that could kill her while she was picking berries just wanted to get out of harm's way. Experiencing fear, she was more likely to escape death. This woman survived, reproduced, and passed on a genetic tendency to experience fear to the next generation. Thus, emotions are behavioral adaptations. They are quick and ready response patterns that tell us whether something is good or bad for our well-being (Ekman, 2003; Lazarus, 1991).

Not all products of evolution are adaptations. Sometimes things evolve because they solve one problem and just happen to solve another one too. These structures or features that perform a function that did not arise through natural selection are often called *by-products* or, more technically, *exaptations* (Buss, 1999; Gould & Vrba, 1982). An example of a by-product is feathers. Feathers probably evolved for insulation in flightless dinosaurs, but they turned out to be useful for flight in birds, the dinosaurs' descendants. Because feathers did not evolve for that purpose, they are considered by-products ("Exaptations," 2006). Evolutionary changes in bodies and brains are prime examples of how nature and nurture interact to shape the psychology of human thought and behavior.

Nothing illustrates more vividly than evolution how nature and nurture work together. Depending on how they enable organisms to respond to their environment, certain characteristics of animals predominate or not—such as the brown color of a beetle and the fear response in humans. Nature and nurture work together to create our bodies (including our brains) and behavior. They are interdependent—they depend on and interact with each other.

Quick Quiz 4: Psychological Perspectives: Explaining Human Behavior

1. Charles Darwin's great contribution was the theory of
   a. how evolution works (natural selection).
   b. evolution.
   c. psychoanalysis.
   d. adaptations.

2. Which phrase most accurately reflects a modern perspective in psychology?
   a. nature versus nurture
   b. nature over nurture
   c. nurture over nature
   d. nature through nurture

3. A _____ psychologist would be most interested in understanding what it means to be fully functioning, whereas a _____ psychologist would focus on what people do and not what they think or feel.
   a. cognitive; psychoanalytic
   b. psychoanalytic; social-learning
   c. evolutionary; biological
   d. humanistic; behavioral

4. The perspective that argues that unconscious thoughts and feelings are most important in a person's personality is
   a. Behaviorism-Learning.
   b. Humanism-Positive.
   c. Cognitive.
   d. Psychoanalysis-Psychodynamic.

Answers can be found at the end of the chapter.

NO ONE PERSPECTIVE TELLS THE WHOLE STORY IN PSYCHOLOGY

As we have seen in this chapter, in order to fully appreciate the complexity of human thought and behavior, one must consider a wide variety of perspectives—no one perspective tells the whole story. Throughout this text we highlight diverse explanations of human thought and behavior. This variety of perspectives raises the question, How does one resolve the various views? There are two strategies for answering this question: by using science and critical thinking and by making connections.

Challenging Assumptions and Not Believing Everything You Think—The Art of Critical Thinking

Whether we are evaluating the ideas of a Facebook feed or the merits of a scientific perspective, we need to use our skills as critical thinkers to distinguish fact from fiction. You've probably heard about "critical thinking" quite often. Teachers are always talking about getting their students to think critically.

To apply critical thinking skills, we should ask ourselves, What is the evidence for this conclusion, and is it valid? Suppose you are on a jury in a murder trial. The primary evidence on which the case is based is eyewitness testimony: Two people picked out the defendant from a lineup. The prosecutor offers no other concrete evidence, such as DNA findings, fingerprints, bloodstains, or ballistic (bullet) matching. Your job is to decide whether the defendant committed the murder. You will want to draw on your critical thinking skills, because in this situation ignoring evidence and basing judgments on bias can have costly, even deadly, consequences.

So what exactly is critical thinking? We can answer this question in part by examining the origin of the word *critical*. It comes from the ancient Greek word *kritikos* and means "to question, to make sense of, and to be able to analyze; or to be skilled at judging" (Chaffee, 1999, p. 32). Educator Paul Chance has provided a more complete definition of **critical thinking**: "The ability to analyze facts, generate and organize ideas, defend opinions, make comparisons, draw inferences, evaluate arguments, and solve problems" (Chance, 1986, p. 6). The core traits of critical thinking are sound analysis, evaluation, and the formation of ideas based on the evidence at hand.

In the late 1980s a group of educators, philosophers, psychologists, and biological and physical scientists organized a conference around the topic of critical thinking in education, and there they arrived at a consensus on what it means to be a good critical thinker. They were nearly unanimous in identifying six activities or qualities that define critical thinking (Facione, 1990).

What a Critical Thinker Does

- Analyze
- Evaluate
- Make inferences
- Interpret
- Explain
- Self-regulate

If you become skilled in these activities, or at least in most of them, you will be able to think critically. In particular, you will be able to counter assertions that have little basis in reality, and you will know the difference between sound and faulty reasoning. For instance, the following argument was made by Charles Johnson, a former president of the International Flat Earth Research Society: "Nobody knows anything about the true shape of the world. The known, inhabited world is flat. Just as a guess, I'd say that the dome of heaven is about 4,000 miles away, and the stars are about as far as San Francisco is from Boston."

Instead of simply saying "That's silly," "That's stupid," or "That's just wrong," a critical thinker would examine the claim by analyzing it, evaluating it, and

Challenge Your Assumptions

True or False? Psychologists agree that most of human thought and behavior cannot be explained by one perspective.

True: Human thought and behavior are so complex and determined by so many different factors that no one perspective can fully capture the richness of human psychology.

critical thinking
A process by which one analyzes, evaluates, and forms ideas.

Challenge Your Assumptions

True or False? Critical thinking involves seeing only the weaknesses and flaws in ideas.

False: Critical thinking involves seeing both strengths and weaknesses in claims and evidence.

FIGURE 6
EVIDENCE THAT THE EARTH IS NOT FLAT.
The drawing on the left shows how a ship would appear as it came into view if Earth were flat. On the right we see the ship coming into view on a round Earth.

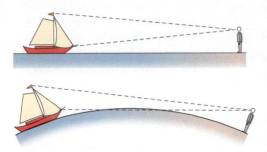

 Which view is correct?

Metacognitive thinking
The process that includes the ability first to think and then to reflect on one's own thinking.

drawing conclusions based on the facts and evidence at hand. A great deal of evidence directly and clearly contradicts the belief that Earth is flat. Just consider these two pieces of evidence: (1) The top of a ship is the last thing we see as it sails out to sea because it is sailing on a sphere rather than on a flat surface (see Figure 6), and (2) images and photographs taken from spaceships and satellites show Earth as a round sphere with half of it shining in the light of the sun.

Critical thinking and its cousin, scientific thinking, both involve being able to think metacognitively. **Metacognitive thinking** requires the ability first to think and then to reflect on one's own thinking (Feist, 2006b; Kuhn & Pearsall, 2000). People who can think metacognitively are able to question their own thinking (see Figure 7). This ability is not universal, however. Without specific training, many people find it difficult to question their own thinking. If one were able to do so as a matter of course, one could more readily dismiss a line of thinking as wrong when it was not supported by evidence.

Science tests our assumptions against observation from the real world. Think about it: People thought the world was flat until explorers began to map out the surface of the Earth. Because it is based on skepticism, the scientific view encourages critical thinking—that is, not believing everything we think. By comparing our assumptions with real-world observation, science helps us choose among competing explanations of behavior. For example, one recent popular theory has been that something in childhood vaccines causes autism. Over the last 10 years, scientists have conducted many studies of the vaccine-autism explanation and have found no support for it. As we discuss in the research ethics section of "Conducting Research in Psychology," the original study on which the argument had been based turned out to be fraudulent, consisting of false data.

Although collecting observations and conducting research help us choose one viewpoint over another, sometimes more than one perspective can be correct. Consider the psychological disorder of schizophrenia. For years people attributed the development of this disorder mostly to upbringing, arguing for a pure "nurture" explanation. Then biological explanations, such as an imbalance of particular neurotransmitters, became fashionable. The most recent research suggests that schizophrenia

FIGURE 7
METACOGNITIVE THINKING. In an era marked by 24/7 information overload, we often leap to overly simplistic or incorrect conclusions based on what we think we "know."

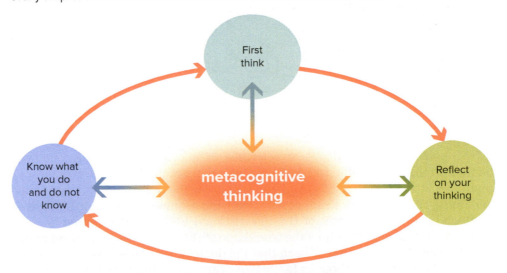

 Can you think of a time when you were surprised by what you didn't know after you felt confident, such as on an exam or some other experience?

emerges from an interaction of biological and environmental influences—in a very real sense, elements of both explanations are correct (Moffitt, Caspi, & Rutter, 2005). The more open we are to diverse perspectives, the better able we will be to explain the whole and often surprising picture of human behavior.

We believe strongly that modern psychological science tells us that we must combine multiple perspectives in order to come to a complete understanding of human thought and behavior. One of the overarching themes of multiple perspectives is the proverbial nature-nurture question. Psychological science shows that almost every fundamental aspect of human behavior—whether it is brain development, learning, intelligence, perception, personality, social behavior, or psychological disorders—develops from a complex interplay of biological and environmental forces, of nature and nurture.

Research can also lead us to surprising findings, sometimes challenging our most basic assumptions. For example, a young neuroscientist named Helen Mayberg parted paths with most of her colleagues and did not focus on drug therapies to treat depression. She focused instead directly on the brain. In so doing she stumbled on a surprising and counterintuitive discovery: A particular part of the brain is overactive in depressed people (Mayberg, 1997, 2003). She went on to pioneer treatment for depression by stimulating the part of the brain that was overactive.

There is a psychology behind the science of psychology, and there are personal stories for every discovery (Feist, 2006b). Seeing the dynamic and often personal side of psychological science leads to a better appreciation of how psychological science came about and may help you challenge assumptions to break new ground.

Connection

Area 25 is a region in the front of the brain; it is overly active in people with depression. A therapy known as "deep brain stimulation" can calm this area down and lead to a sudden decrease in depressed symptoms for some people.

See "Challenging Assumptions in the Treatment of Severe Depression," in the chapter "Treatment of Psychological Disorders". (p. 618)

Connections within and between Chapters

To bring together the various perspectives, we also explicitly connect theories and findings throughout the text. Seeing connections is a creative act, and psychological ideas and research findings are connected sometimes in obvious ways and sometimes in surprising ways. Learning to bring together ideas is an important part of learning to think critically. To facilitate this skill, we connect concepts both within and between chapters, as we just did with deep brain stimulation and depression. We do so by means of a "Connection" note alongside the primary narrative, in which we provide section, chapter, and page number to facilitate easy access to these related ideas. By regularly returning to ideas from the same or different chapters, we can put them in a different context.

As a way of reviewing and connecting all of the important topics in each chapter, but in an applied way, we end each chapter with a section titled "Bringing It All Together". In this section, we explore one topic that brings together most of the main concepts and ideas in the chapter. For example, in this chapter, we consider how psychologists in different subfields of psychology have begun to study the effects of electronic social interactions on human behavior.

Quick Quiz 5: No One Perspective Tells the Whole Story in Psychology

1. Which of the following is a technique we argue for integrating the many perspectives in psychology?
   a. using not believing everything you think
   b. using the scientific method
   c. making connections within and between chapters
   d. all of the above

2. Research on the association between vaccines and autism has shown
   a. no connection between the two.
   b. a weak connection between the two.
   c. a strong connection between the two.
   d. inconclusive results.

Answers can be found at the end of the chapter.

Bringing It All Together

Making Connections in Psychology

Studying Electronic Social Interactions

There are nearly a dozen ways a person can interact with others electronically—via email, blogs, phone calls, chat rooms, texting, instant messaging, audio or video chats, gaming (either solo or multiplayer), videos, photos, bulletin boards, and social network sites (SNSs). Humans have taken to electronic forms of interaction like fish to water. As a form of behavior that is evolving at a rapid pace, electronic social interaction holds great interest for psychologists in all of the subfields you read about in this chapter. Let's consider how psychologists from some of these areas might study electronic communication and its effects on human behavior and thought.

©Alejandro Rivera/Getty Images RF

 How does technology change how we learn, think, feel, and behave with others?

Cognitive Psychology

Cognitive scientists typically are interested in how we learn, speak, remember, think, and reason. They are also interested in attention. The widespread use of mobile devices has sparked a number of research questions. The most obvious one concerns how drivers can pay attention to driving while talking on a mobile device. Researchers who have examined the effect of talking on a hands-free mobile device while driving report that a person's ability to operate a car while doing so is significantly impaired and is even similar to the ability to drive while drunk (Caird et al., 2008; Strayer, Drews, & Couch, 2006). In addition, attitudes and beliefs about how dangerous and how common mobile phone use is while driving predict using phones while driving (Hafetz et al., 2010; Zhou et al., 2009): Those who think most about receiving phone calls and think about their phones while they are off are most likely to have accidents while driving (O'Connor et al., 2013).

Developmental Psychology

Developmental psychologists study how we change over the life span. They might ask questions like these: At what age is a person too young to form electronic social networks? At what age does participation in Internet social networks peak? Will they always be for the younger generation, or will people 60 and older use them? Does gender affect interest and participation in SNSs? How have mobile phones and other electronic methods of communicating changed the way teenagers interact with others?

Researchers have already given us answers to some of these questions. Some suggest that older teenage girls and young women are more likely to participate in social networking sites than are boys and young men (Boyd, 2007; Hargittai, 2008). A recent study found that 13-year-olds check social media up to 100 times a day, with one 13-year-old girl saying "I would rather not eat for a week than get my phone taken away. It's really bad. I literally feel like I'm going to die" (Hadad, 2015, p. 1). Moreover, 50% of teens admit to being "addicted" to their cell phones (Felt & Robb, 2016). College men are more likely to use SNSs to begin new relationships, whereas college women are more likely to use them to maintain existing relationships (Muscanell & Guadagno, 2012). Electronic interactions are popular with adolescents because of psychological factors: identity, autonomy, intimacy, and sexuality (Subrahmanyam & Greenfield, 2008; Walsh, White, & Young, 2009). One reason the popularity of electronic interactions declines with age may be that these issues decline in importance as one moves from early adulthood to middle and late adulthood (Erikson, 1982; Harris Interactive, 2008).

Social Psychology

More than just about any other area of psychology, social psychology lends itself to a rich set of research questions regarding electronic interactions. Texting in particular and mobile device use in general are the primary tools for staying connected to friends and peers (Harris Interactive, 2008; Walsh et al., 2009). One of the first Internet applications for social purposes was online dating services. Such forms of electronic interaction may be a preferred method of contact for people with high social anxiety (Stevens & Morris, 2007). Although most people who use online dating services tend to be over 30, college-age teens and young adults are increasingly using them as well (Stevens & Morris, 2007; Valkenburg & Peter, 2007b). Contrary to what some people originally thought, however, electronic interactions cannot easily be used to hide one's "real personality" and to avoid ever having real face-to-face contact with others. Research on this phenomenon suggests that people use the Internet not simply to interact with others from afar but also to arrange real face-to-face meetings (Couch & Liamputtong, 2008).

Electronic interactions have led to new behaviors and language as the boundaries between public and private have broken down. For instance, being *privately public* means connecting with many other people while being relatively nonpublic about revealing who you are. Being *publicly private* means you disclose a lot of details of your private life and may or may not limit access to your site (Lange, 2008).

Another electronic behavior is "friending," which raises ancient issues of being "popular," socially excluded, rejected, or accepted. In one tragic case of online rejection, a 13-year-old girl was so distraught over being rejected by a boy online that she committed suicide. The even greater tragedy, however, was that the boy did not exist: A neighbor's mother allegedly had made him up to get back at the girl for making disparaging remarks about her daughter.

Personality Psychology

A personality psychologist could ask many questions about electronic interaction and presentation—such as "Are people who interact extensively with other people via Facebook more or less outgoing than those who do not?" Moreover, how much of people's personality is reflected in their Facebook profiles? Scientific literature consistently finds that people who are extraverted are more likely than introverts to use Facebook and have a wider network of social relationships (Amichai-Hamburger & Vinitzky, 2010; Nadkarni & Hofmann, 2012). Yet introverts are more likely than extraverts to spend more time on Facebook and have a more favorable attitude toward it (Orr et al., 2009).

Health Psychology

A very innovative and at least partially successful application of electronic media is using a mobile device to access health information and symptoms of various diseases.

A program in San Francisco, California, has phone numbers for people to call if they suspect they have a particular disease, often a sexual disease. The embarrassment of having to ask questions face-to-face is taken away when one can call or text to obtain a health diagnosis anonymously.

Clinical Psychology

Clinical psychologists can diagnose disorders of technology use but also use the same technologies to help treat people with various kinds of disorders. When do SNSs and other electronic interactions become a problem? Can one become "addicted" to such behavior, and can such interactions become dangerous to those involved? One of the main criteria for a mental illness is that it interferes with everyday life and functioning. If one is online for 10–12 hours a day, is that healthy? What about the danger involved in meeting someone in person whom you know only from online interaction? Sexual predators use these connections to meet victims. They contact potential victims through chat rooms, instant messages, and email. According to one study, one in seven teens (ages 10–17) have been sexually solicited online (Ybarra & Mitchell, 2008).

There is also the psychologically interesting phenomenon of creating an alternative personality, or avatar, in the gaming world. People sometimes take on personalities that are very different from their own in an online world that allows them to say things they would not in direct, face-to-face contact. This ability to be people we are not has allowed psychotherapists to use avatar personality games, such as Second Life®, to help people overcome their social anxieties in real life (Gottschalk, 2010; Lisetti et al., 2009). Similarly, video services such as SKYPE and GoogleChat are increasingly used to connect psychotherapist and patient, who can now be in different states if need be.

We hope this chapter has helped you appreciate the richness and excitement of psychology as a clinical practice and science. More than that, we hope it encourages you to become an active and critical student of human behavior: Don't believe everything you think, and question how conclusions are drawn—even conclusions in this text. We hope that at this point, as a first step toward active learning and investigating, you are asking, How do psychologists know all this? How do they do research? In the next chapter, we discuss the techniques by which psychological scientists study mental processes and behavior. Welcome to the fascinating world of psychology.

Chapter Review

WHAT IS PSYCHOLOGY?

- Psychology is the scientific study of thought and behavior. We can see psychology all around us—in our own thoughts and feelings, in the behavior of our friends and relatives, and in how we interpret others' behaviors. As a field, it prepares us well not only for life in general but also for a wide variety of professions in which social interaction plays a key role.

- As a discipline, psychology is both a practice and a science. Clinical psychologists and counselors treat mental, emotional, and behavioral disorders and promote psychological health. Clinical psychologists also conduct research on psychological disorders and health. They practice psychology. As a science,

©michaeljung/iStock/Getty Images RF

psychology is the field of study in which researchers examine how the mind works and the rules that govern behavior within and between individuals.

SUBDISCIPLINES OF PSYCHOLOGY

- As a broad field, psychology comprises several subdisciplines, or areas of focused study, including cognitive, developmental, social, personality, health, educational, and industrial/organizational psychology.

- Neuroscience explores the links among brain, mind, and behavior and thus cuts across other subdisciplines.

THE ORIGINS OF PSYCHOLOGY

- The practice of psychology goes back to prehistoric times. Thousands of years ago, humans drilled holes in the skull to treat brain injury and perhaps mental anguish.

- In the Middle Ages, the mentally ill were often treated as if possessed by demons. A few hundred years later, asylums served as storage houses for the severely mentally disabled.

- The late 1800s and early 1900s witnessed the beginning of more humane and more sophisticated treatment of people with psychological disorders.

- Around the turn of the 20th century, Sigmund Freud developed psychoanalysis to treat people suffering from disorders. By the middle of the 20th century, modern diagnostic criteria for mental disorders, psychotherapy, and drug therapy had emerged.

- The history of psychology as a science is not nearly as old as that of clinical practice, although its origins in philosophy go back to the ancient Greeks. Psychological science emerged from a tradition of empiricism and observations of the world.

- John Locke's 17th-century view of the mind as a blank slate on which experience writes the contents influences psychology to this day.

- The first psychological scientists did experimental work in perception and laid the groundwork for

psychophysics. Only when laboratories started to empirically examine and test human sensations and perception did psychology gain its independence from philosophy and become a science.

- Wilhelm Wundt opened the first laboratory in experimental psychology in Leipzig, Germany, in 1879. Key figures in the birth of scientific psychology in the United States include William James and G. Stanley Hall.

- The biggest development in psychological research in the United States was the birth of behaviorism in the early 20th century. According to behaviorism, all behavior comes from experience. Founded by John Watson, behaviorism reached its pinnacle with B. F. Skinner.

- Behaviorism proved a very useful model for developing methods of studying learning in humans and animals, but it left the unobservable world of the mind unexplained. This all changed with the cognitive revolution of the 1950s and 1960s. Initially, cognitive science used the computer as a model for the way the human mind processes and stores sensations, memories, and ideas.

- Many fields that have older origins came together in the psychology of the 1980s and 1990s: neuroscience, behavioral genetics, and evolutionary psychology.

PSYCHOLOGICAL PERSPECTIVES: EXPLAINING HUMAN BEHAVIOR

- Psychological science in the 21st century has reintegrated biological and environmental explanations of human thought and behavior.

- The fully modern view squares explanations of behavior with the principles of evolution. It also surpasses old absolutes, such as the nature-nurture debate and mind-body dualism.

NO ONE PERSPECTIVE TELLS THE WHOLE STORY IN PSYCHOLOGY

- Multiple perspectives are often needed to fully explain the complexity of human thought and behavior.

- To integrate these multiple perspectives, it helps to use the methods of science and critical thinking and to integrate and connect related ideas and concepts.

BRINGING IT ALL TOGETHER: MAKING CONNECTIONS IN PSYCHOLOGY

- The world of electronic interaction provides a context for research in many subdisciplines of psychology. For example, personality psychologists have examined which types of people are more likely to use social networking sites (SNSs); social psychologists have studied whether SNSs operate as real-life social networks do; and developmental psychologists have begun to explore how the use of email, SNSs, and texting varies by age and gender.

Key Terms

adaptations
asylums
behavioral neuroscience
behaviorism
biological psychology
clinical psychology
cognitive psychology
critical thinking
developmental psychology
educational psychology
empiricism
evolutionary psychology

evolution
forensic psychology
functionalism
Gestalt psychology
health psychology
humanistic psychology
industrial/organizational (I/O)
    psychology
introspection
metacognitive thinking
moral treatment
nature through nurture

natural selection
personality psychology
positive psychology
psychoanalysis
psychology
psychophysics
sexual selection
shamans
social psychology
sports psychology
structuralism

Quick Quiz Answers

Quick Quiz 1: 1.d; 2.d; 3.c **Quick Quiz 2:** 1.a; 2.b; 3.c **Quick Quiz 3:** 1.d; 2.a; 3.b **Quick Quiz 4:** 1.a; 2.d; 3.d; 4.d
Quick Quiz 5: 1.d; 2.a

2 Conducting Research in Psychology

Chapter Outline

Challenge Your Assumptions

True or False?

- Psychology is not a science. (see page 38)

- Disgust and doubt activate the same part of the brain. (see page 39)

- Scientific research that is published in scientific journals is reliable and valid. (see page 42)

- Knowing what you're looking for in an experiment has no effect on the outcome. (see page 58)

- Eating sugar makes children hyperactive. (see page 64)

©Jane Underwood/My Third Eye Photography/Moment Select/Getty Images

Y ou are at your apartment near campus one summer day when the police knock at your door. After they confirm your identity, they arrest you on suspicion of armed robbery. The cops handcuff your hands, put you in the police car, and take you down to the police station. There you are booked, fingerprinted, and placed in a detention cell. You are then blindfolded and driven to a nearby prison, where you are stripped, sprayed with a delousing agent, and made to stand nude and alone in the cell yard. Finally, you are given a uniform, photographed, and assigned to a prison cell. But you have done nothing, and the people who arrested you knew this.

This scenario may seem far-fetched, but it actually happened to 10 male college students in the summer of 1971 in Palo Alto, California. They had previously agreed to participate in a "psychological study on 'prison life' in return for payment of $15 a day" (Haney, Banks, & Zimbardo, 1973, p. 73). Yet the officers who arrested them said nothing about a connection between their arrest and their agreement to participate. Philip Zimbardo conducted this study—now known as the Stanford Prison Experiment—to examine whether normal people might behave in extreme ways when thrust into situations that place extreme demands on them. In this case, they readily took on roles that made them either powerful or powerless (Haney et al., 1973). Zimbardo chose 21 carefully screened male student volunteers and assigned them to be either "guards" or "prisoners" in a simulated prison environment for 2 weeks. All were briefed beforehand about what the conditions would be like in the mock prison. All the students signed a form, consenting to participate. Six days into the simulation, however, the experiment had taken such an unexpected turn that Zimbardo had to end the study—the students were playing their roles too well. Prisoners went back and forth between plotting riots and having emotional breakdowns—getting sick and crying, for instance. Guards became extremely authoritarian, restricting the prisoners' personal freedom almost completely. They dehumanized the prisoners by referring to each one only by his assigned number, never by name. They put anyone suspected of "disobeying" and being "a bad prisoner" in solitary confinement. The line between fiction and reality, between assigned role and true identity, blurred. In fact, half of the "prisoners" had to be released ahead of schedule, because they were experiencing extreme emotional distress as a result of their "incarceration."

Zimbardo's study served as a springboard for additional research on group behavior, and it provided a strong incentive for prison reform. Interest in this study continues today. In 2015 a Hollywood movie was even made entitled *The Stanford Prison Experiment* (http:// www.prisonexp.org/movie). Still, the Stanford Prison Experiment also provoked great concern about the treatment of human participants in research. What hypothesis was Zimbardo testing? Were the scientific gains worth the trauma caused to these young men? These are questions of research ethics, one of many topics of research methods in psychology covered in this chapter. We will first look, however, at psychology as a science and the methods of scientific inquiry applied in psychological research. We will then turn to the subject of how psychologists collect, analyze, and interpret data—processes that become the building blocks of knowledge in the field.

THE NATURE OF SCIENCE

Science is about testing intuitive assumptions regarding how the world works, observing the world, and being open-minded to unexpected findings. Some of science's most important discoveries happened only because the scientists were open to surprising and unexpected results. Fundamentally, science entails collecting observations, or *data*, from the real world and evaluating whether the data support our ideas or not. The Stanford Prison Experiment fulfilled these criteria, and we will refer to this example several times in our discussion of research methods, measures, and ethics.

Common Sense and Logic

Science involves more than common sense, logic, and pure observation. Although reason and sharp powers of observation can lead to knowledge, they have limitations. Consider common sense, the intuitive ability to understand the world. Often common sense is quite useful: Don't go too close to that cliff. Don't rouse that sleeping bear. Don't eat food that smells rotten. Sometimes, though, common sense leads us astray. In psychology, our intuitive ideas about people's behavior are often contradictory or flat-out wrong. For example, most of us intuitively believe that who we are is influenced by our parents, family, friends, and society. It is equally obvious, especially to parents, that children come into the world as unique people, with their own temperaments, and people who grow up in similar environments do not have identical personalities. To what extent are we the products of our environment, and how much do we owe to heredity? Common sense cannot answer that question, but science can.

Rationalism is the view that using logic and reason is the way to understand how the world works. Logic is also a powerful tool in the scientist's arsenal, but it can tell us only how the world *should* work, not how the world actually works. Sometimes the world is not logical. A classic example of the shortcoming of logic is seen in the work of the ancient Greek philosopher Aristotle. He argued that heavier objects should fall to the ground at a faster rate than lighter objects. Sounds reasonable, right? Unfortunately, it's wrong. For 2,000 years, however, the argument was accepted simply because the great philosopher Aristotle wrote it and it made intuitive sense. It took the genius of Galileo to say, "Wait a minute. Is that really true? Let me do some tests to see whether it is true." He did and discovered that Aristotle was wrong (Crump, 2001); the weight of an object does not affect its rate of speed when falling. Science combines logic with research and experimentation.

The Limits of Observation

Recall from The Origins of Psychology (in chapter "Introduction to Psychology") that empiricism is the view that our observations and experience, not pure reason and logic, are another path to knowledge. Science is empirical in that it is based on observations and experience. Science relies on observation, but even observation can lead us astray. Our knowledge of the world comes through our five senses, but they can be fairly easily fooled, as any good magician or artist can demonstrate—and as we explore in some detail in the chapter "Sensing and Perceiving Our World". Even when we are not being intentionally fooled, the way in which our brains organize and interpret sensory experiences may vary from person to person.

Another problem with observation is that people tend to generalize from their observations and assume that what they witness in one situation applies to all similar situations. Imagine you are visiting another country for the first

Connection

How do psychologists tease apart the question of how much of a trait is due to genetics and how much is due to environment? A common approach is to study twins (both identical and fraternal) who are reared apart or reared together.

See "The Relative Effects of Genes and Environment Can Be Teased Apart," in the chapter "The Biology of Behavior". (p. 79)

rationalism
The view that using logic and reason is the way to understand how the world works.

©SonyaLang/iStockphoto/Getty Images RF

Reality can be different from what we think. Our perceptions are not the same as what is really out there. Camouflaged animals are just one example.

 Can you think of other common examples of perceptions that don't reflect reality?

time. Let's say the first person you have any extended interaction with is rude, and a second, briefer interaction goes along the same lines. Granted, you have lots of language difficulties; nevertheless, you might conclude that all people from that country are rude. After all, that has been your experience. Those, however, were only two interactions, and after a couple of days you might meet other people who are quite nice. The point is that one or two cases are not a solid basis for a generalization. Scientists must collect numerous observations and conduct several studies on a topic before generalizing their conclusions.

What Is Science?

Is physics a science? Few would argue that it is not. What about biology? Psychology? Astrology? How does one decide? Now that we have looked at some of the components of science and explored their limitations, let's consider the larger question: What *is* science? People often think only of the physical sciences as "science," but science comes in at least three distinct flavors (Feist, 2006b):

- physical science,
- biological science, and
- social science.

As we mentioned in the chapter "Introduction to Psychology", psychology is a social science (see Figure 1).

The physical sciences study the world of things—the inanimate world of stars, light, waves, atoms, the Earth, compounds, and molecules. These sciences include physics, astronomy, chemistry, and geology. The biological sciences study plants and animals in the broadest sense. These sciences include biology, zoology, genetics, and botany. Finally, the social sciences study humans, both

FIGURE **1**

SIMPLIFIED MAP OF THE SCIENCES: THE STUDY OF THINGS, PLANTS, ANIMALS, AND PEOPLE.

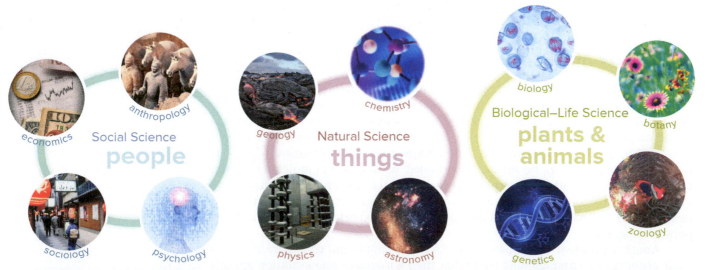

(economics): ©Tetra Images/Getty Images RF; (anthropology): ©Pixtal/agefotostock RF; (sociology): ©Glow Images RF; (psychology): ©Chad Baker/Getty Images RF; (geology): ©Jason Weingart Photography RF; (chemistry): ©Wayne Calabrese/Getty Images; (physics): ©Kim Steele/Getty Images RF; (astronomy): NOAO/AURA/NSF; (biology): ©Steven P. Lynch; (botany): ©Thinkstock Images/Stockbyte/Getty Images RF; (genetics): ©Andrey Prokhorov/Getty Images RF; (zoology): Dr. Dwayne Meadows, NOAA/NMFS/OPR

©Shaun Curry/AFP/Getty Images

Dr. Andrew Wakefield published a scientific paper claiming that autism spectrum disorder was often caused by vaccines for measles, mumps, and rubella. There were many problems with the paper from the outset, not the least of which was its small, unrepresentative sample size (12 children). Many scientists and medical panels could not confirm the results and were highly skeptical of Dr. Wakefield's findings. Unfortunately, the paper created quite a bit of publicity, and many parents ignored standard vaccination schedules, leading to numerous deaths from preventable diseases. After a 7-year investigation, the original paper was deemed fraudulent by the *British Medical Journal* and retracted (withdrawn). The investigation concluded that Dr. Wakefield had altered the results of his study to make vaccines appear to be the cause of autism spectrum disorder.

as individuals and as groups. These sciences include anthropology, sociology, economics, and psychology.

Science is as much a way of thinking or a set of attitudes as it is a set of procedures. **Scientific thinking** involves the reasoning skills required to generate, test, and revise theories (Koslowski, 1996; Kuhn, Amsel, & O'Loughlin, 1988; Zimmerman, 2007). What we believe or theorize about the world and what the world is actually like, in the form of evidence, are two different things. Scientific thinking keeps these two things separate. In other words, scientists remember that belief is not the same as reality.

There are three attitudes central to scientific thinking. The first is to *question authority*—including scientific authority. Be skeptical (see Figure 2). Don't just take the word of an expert; test ideas yourself. The expert might be right, or not. That advice extends to textbooks—including this one. Wonder. Question. Ask for the evidence. Be a critical thinker. Also question your *own* ideas. Make your own observations—be empirical. Our natural inclination is to really like our own ideas, especially if they occur to us in a flash of insight. As one bumper sticker extols, "Don't believe everything you think." Believing something does not make it true.

The second attitude of science is *open skepticism* (Sagan, 1987). Doubt and skepticism are hallmarks of critical and scientific reasoning. The French philosopher Voltaire put scientific skepticism most bluntly: "Doubt is uncomfortable, certainty is ridiculous"; however, skepticism for skepticism's sake is also not scientific, but stubborn. Scientists are ultimately open to accepting whatever the evidence reveals, however bizarre it may be and however much they may not like it or want it to be the case. For example, could placing an electrical stimulator deep in the brain, as if it were a switch, turn off depression? That sounds like a far-fetched treatment, worthy of skepticism, but it does work for some people (Mayberg et al., 2005). Confirming Voltaire's assertion that doubt is uncomfortable, brain imaging evidence suggests that doubt and skepticism are associated with areas of the brain involved in the sensation of taste and disgust (and belief with reward and pleasure), so doubt is a less pleasant state than belief (Harris, Sheth, & Cohen, 2008; Harris et al., 2009; Shermer, 2011).

The third scientific attitude is *intellectual honesty*. When the central tenet of knowing is not what people think and believe, but rather how nature behaves, then we must accept the data and follow them wherever they take us. If a researcher falsifies results or interprets them in a biased way, then other scientists will not arrive at the same results if they repeat the study. Every so often we hear of a scientist who faked data in order to gain fame or funding. For the most part, however, the fact that scientists must submit their work to the scrutiny of other scientists helps ensure the honest and accurate presentation of results.

All sciences—whether physics, chemistry, biology, or psychology—share the general properties of open inquiry that we have discussed. Let's now turn to the specific methods scientists use to acquire new and accurate knowledge of the world.

scientific thinking
A process using the cognitive skills required to generate, test, and revise theories.

FIGURE 2
Science is an attitude that requires us to keep open eyes and questioning minds.

Don't believe
everything
you think

©Westend61/Getty Images RF

 Can you think of some ideas you've had that you no longer believe?

Challenge Your Assumptions

True or False? Disgust and doubt activate the same part of the brain.
True: When we disbelieve a statement, the same region of the brain that is involved in perceptions of taste and disgust is also activated.

The Scientific Method

Science depends on the use of sound methods to produce trustworthy results that can be confirmed independently by other researchers. The **scientific method** by which scientists conduct research consists of five processes: **O**bserve, **P**redict, **T**est, **I**nterpret, and **C**ommunicate (O-P-T-I-C; see the Research Process for this chapter, Figure 3). In the *observation* and *prediction* stages of a study, researchers develop expectations about an observed phenomenon. They express their expectations as a **theory**, defined as a set of related assumptions from which testable predictions can be made. Theories organize and explain what we have observed and guide what we will observe (Popper, 1965). To put it simply, theories are not facts—they explain facts. Our observations of the world are always either unconsciously or consciously theory-driven, if you understand that theory in this broader sense means little more than "having an expectation." In science, however, a theory is more than a guess. Scientific theories must be tied to real evidence, they must organize observations, and they must generate expectations that can be tested systematically.

A **hypothesis** is a specific, informed, and testable prediction of what kind of outcome should occur under a particular condition. For example, consider the real-life study that suggests that caffeine increases sex drive in female rats (Guarraci & Benson, 2005). The hypothesis may have been phrased this way: "Female rats that consume caffeine will have more couplings with male rats than female rats that do not consume caffeine." This hypothesis predicts that a particular form of behavior (coupling with male rats) will occur in a specific group (female rats) under particular conditions (the influence of caffeine). The more specific a hypothesis is, the more easily each component can be changed to determine what effect it has on the outcome.

To *test* their hypotheses (the third stage of the scientific method), scientists select one of a number of established research methods, along with the appropriate measurement techniques. Selecting the methods involves choosing a design for the study, the tools that will create the conditions of the study, and the tools for measuring responses (such as how often each female rat allows a male to mount her). One basic principle of all scientific research is that measures and tools need to be both reliable and valid. **Reliability** means the test or measure gives us a consistent result over time or between different raters. **Validity** means when a scientist claims to measure a particular concept, such as sex drive for example, she really is measuring that concept and not something else. We will examine each of these elements in the next section "Research Designs in Psychology".

In the fourth step of the scientific method, scientists use mathematical techniques to *interpret* the results and determine whether they are significant (not just a matter of chance) and whether they closely fit the prediction. Do psychologists' ideas of how people behave hold up, or must they be revised? Let's say that the caffeine-consuming female rats coupled more frequently with males than did nonconsuming females. Might this enhanced sexual interest hold for all rats or just those few we studied? Statistics, a branch of mathematics we will discuss shortly, helps answer that question.

The fifth stage of the scientific method is to *communicate* the results. Generally, scientists publish their findings in a peer-reviewed professional journal. Following a standardized format, the researchers report their hypotheses, describe their research design and the conditions of the study, summarize the results, and share their conclusions. In their reports, researchers also consider the broader implications of their results. What might the effects of caffeine on sexuality in female rats mean for our understanding of caffeine, arousal, and sex in female humans? Publication also serves an important role in making research findings part of the public domain. Such exposure not only indicates that colleagues who reviewed the study found it to be credible but also allows other researchers to repeat and/or build on the research. It is important to point out, however, that not all published scientific papers are of equal quality (that is, use equally reliable and valid measures and techniques).

---

scientific method
The procedures by which scientists conduct research, consisting of five basic processes: observation, prediction, testing, interpretation, and communication.

theory
A set of related assumptions from which scientists can make testable predictions.

hypothesis
A specific, informed, and testable prediction of the outcome of a particular set of conditions in a research design.

reliability
The consistency of a measurement, such as an intelligence test.

validity
The degree to which a test accurately measures what it purports to measure, such as intelligence, and not something else, and the degree to which it predicts real-world outcomes.

Connection

Are IQ and personality tests reliable and valid?

See "Measuring Intelligence" in the chapter "Intelligence, Problem Solving, and Creativity," p. 373; and "How Is Personality Measured?," in the chapter "Personality: The Uniqueness of the Individual," (p. 515).

Research Process

FIGURE 3

THE SCIENTIFIC METHOD. The scientific method consists of an ongoing cycle of observation, prediction, testing, interpretation, and communication (OPTIC). Research begins with observation, but it doesn't end with communication. Publishing the results of a study allows other researchers to repeat the procedure and confirm the results.

Observe
Researchers working with rats observe their behavior.

1

Communicate
5 Publish findings of "Caffeine and mating behavior in female rats" via peer review process.

Predict
2 Propose a hypothesis based in theory: Caffeine will make female rats seek more couplings with males.

Test
3 Collect data: How often do females on caffeine allow males to mate and how often do females not on caffeine allow males to mate?

Interpret
4 Analyze resulting data to confirm or disconfirm the theory-prediction.

Challenge Your Assumptions

True or False? Scientific research that is published in scientific journals is reliable and valid.

False: Even published scientific studies are of varying degrees of reliability and validity, so it is always important to ask "on what evidence are they drawing their conclusions?"

As when reading any kind of information, one should always ask "how did they come to that conclusion?" and "on what evidence did they draw that conclusion?"

Replication is the repetition of a study to confirm the results. The advancement of science hinges on replication. No matter how interesting and exciting results are, if they cannot be duplicated, the original findings may have been accidental. Whether a result holds or not, new predictions can be generated from the data, leading in turn to new studies. For example, recently, a team of more than 50 social psychologists from around the world replicated 13 classic findings in social psychology and found that although 10 of the 13 findings were replicated, the strength of the findings decreased (Klein et al., 2014). Three did not replicate and the field now knows that they were by chance and cannot be trusted. The other 10 findings are real (if a bit smaller in size) and can be built upon. This finding confirms the cumulative nature of scientific progress.

What Science Is Not: Pseudoscience

Do you believe that the planets and stars determine our destiny, that aliens have visited Earth, or that the human mind is capable of moving or altering physical objects? Astrology, unidentified flying objects (UFOs), and extrasensory perception (ESP) are certainly fascinating topics to ponder. As thinking beings, we try to understand things that science may not explain to our satisfaction. Many of us are willing to believe things that science and skeptics easily dismiss. For example, in 2015 a Chapman University poll of 1,500 representative American adults found the following (Ledbetter, 2015):

- Fifty percent endorsed at least one paranormal belief (e.g., ghosts, ESP, astrology, etc.).
- Forty-one percent believed that spirits inhabit haunted places.
- Twenty-seven percent believe the dead can communicate with the living.
- Twenty-one percent believe aliens have visited Earth.

Similarly, a 2015 survey of of more than 1,000 American adults reported that 72% believed in angels, 42% in demonic possession, and 62% believed the Earth was made 6,000 years ago (creationism), only 45% believed in the theory of evolution, and 56% believed in UFOs (*What People*, 2009).

People often claim there is "scientific evidence" for certain unusual phenomena, but that does not mean the evidence is truly scientific. There is also false science, or *pseudo*science. **Pseudoscience** refers to practices that appear to be and claim to be science but, in fact, do not use the scientific method to come to their conclusions. What makes something pseudoscientific comes more from the way it is studied than from the content area. According to Derry (1999) pseudoscience practitioners

1. make no real advances in knowledge,
2. disregard well-known and established facts that contradict their claims,
3. do not challenge or question their own assumptions,
4. tend to offer vague or incomplete explanations of how they came to their conclusions, and
5. tend to use unsound logic in making their arguments (see Figure 4).

FIGURE 4

THE CHARACTERISTICS OF PSEUDOSCIENCE. It is wise to be skeptical of claims that aren't supported by scientific evidence.

©akud/iStock/Getty Images RF

1 Lacks the cumulative progress seen in science
2 Disregards real-world observations and established facts/results and contradicts what is already known
3 Lacks internal skepticism
4 Only vaguely explains how conclusions are reached
5 Uses loose and distorted logic

 What makes something a false science, or pseudoscience?

Philosophy, art, music, and religion, for instance, are not pseudosciences because they do not claim to be science. Pseudoscientific claims have been made for alchemy, creation science, intelligent design, attempts to create perpetual motion machines, astrology, alien abduction, psychokinesis, and some forms of mental telepathy.

Perhaps the most pervasive pseudoscience is astrology, which uses the positions of the sun, moon, and planets to explain an individual's personality traits and to predict the future. There simply is no credible scientific evidence that the positions of the moon, planets, and stars and one's time and place of birth have any influence on personality or life course (Hartmann, Reuter, & Nyborga, 2006; Shermer, 1997; Zarka, 2011), yet about one in four American adults believe in astrology.

Overall, telekinesis, astrology, alien abduction explanations of UFOs, and creation science, to name a few, meet the criteria for pseudoscience. For instance, astrology or ESP as fields of study are very much the same in their knowledge and ideas as they were 50 years ago, neither doubts and questions their own assumptions, methods, or results, and the conclusions are often vague and non-testable. In all fairness, there have been some peer-reviewed reliable observations of UFOs and some scientifically sound evidence for precognition (anticipating the future) and telepathy (Bem, 2011; Bem & Horonton, 1994; Bem, Palmer, & Broughton, 2001; Rosenthal, 1986). However, other attempts to replicate these findings have not been successful (Galak, LeBeouf, Nelson, & Simmons, 2012; Rouder & Morey, 2011). Had they been replicated, we would be forced to accept them, at least tentatively. Remember, open skepticism is the hallmark of science. If there is scientifically sound evidence for something—even if it is difficult to explain—and it has been replicated, then we have to accept it. The key is to know how to distinguish sound from unsound evidence.

Quick Quiz 1: The Nature of Science

1. The scientific method consists of
   a. observing, predicting, testing.
   b. observing, predicting, trying.
   c. observing, predicting, testing, communicating.
   d. observing, predicting, testing, interpreting, communicating.

2. Which of the following is NOT a characteristic of science?
   a. It is cumulative.
   b. It is a search for truth.
   c. It is an attitude.
   d. It requires intellectual honesty.

3. Scientific theories are
   a. a set of related assumptions that guide and explain observations and allow testable predictions to be made.
   b. educated guesses.
   c. hunches.
   d. hypotheses.

4. What distinguishes science from pseudoscience?
   a. the use of statistics
   b. the content area studied
   c. open skepticism
   d. the search for truth

Answers can be found at the end of the chapter.

RESEARCH DESIGNS IN PSYCHOLOGY

Science involves testing ideas about how the world works, but how do we design studies that test our ideas? This question confronts anyone wanting to answer a psychological question scientifically.

Principles of Research Design

Like other sciences, psychology makes use of several types of **research designs**— plans for how to conduct a study. The design chosen for a given study depends on the question being asked. Some questions can best be answered by randomly placing people in different groups in a laboratory to see whether a treatment causes a

research designs
Plans of action for how to conduct a scientific study.

©Ciaran Griffin/Stockbyte/Getty Images RF

Researchers often work with a small sample of the population they're interested in studying.

 Can a small sample represent the larger population? If so, how is that done?

change in behavior. Other questions have to be studied by questionnaires or surveys. Still other questions can best be answered simply by making initial observations and seeing what people do in the real world. Sometimes researchers analyze the results of many studies on the same topic to look for trends.

In this section, we examine variations in research designs, along with their advantages and disadvantages. We begin by defining a few key terms common to all research designs in psychology.

A general goal of psychological research is to measure change in behavior, thought, or brain activity. A **variable** is anything that changes, or varies, within or between individuals. People differ from one another on age, gender, weight, intelligence, level of anxiety, and extraversion, to name a few psychological variables. Psychologists do research by predicting how and when variables influence each other. For instance, a psychologist who is interested in whether girls develop verbal skills at a different rate than boys focuses on two variables: gender and vocabulary.

All researchers must pay careful attention to how they obtain participants for a study. The first step is for the researchers to decide the makeup of the entire group, or **population**, in which they are interested. In psychology, populations can be composed of, for example, animals, adolescents, boys or girls of any age, college students, or students at a particular school. How many are older than 50 or younger than 20? How many are European American, African American, Asian American, Pacific Islander, or Native American? How many have high school educations, and how many have college educations?

Can you think of a problem that would occur if a researcher tried to collect data directly on an entire population? Because most populations are too large to survey or interview directly, researchers draw on small subsets of each population, called **samples**. A sample of a population of college students, for instance, might consist of students enrolled in one or more universities in a particular geographic area. Research is almost always conducted on samples, not populations. If researchers want to draw valid conclusions or make accurate predictions about a population, it is important that their samples accurately represent the population in terms of age, gender, ethnicity, or any other variables of interest. When a poll is wrong in predicting who will win an election, it is often because the polled sample did not accurately represent the population.

variable
A characteristic that changes, or "varies," such as age, gender, weight, intelligence, anxiety, and extraversion.

population
The entire group a researcher is interested in—for example, all humans, all adolescents, all boys, all girls, all college students.

samples
Subsets of the population studied in a research project.

Descriptive Studies

Ideas for studies often start with specific and personal experiences or events—one person being painfully shy; someone rushing onto train tracks to rescue a person who had fallen in front of an ongoing train; or, having personal experience with trauma. These experiences can be and often are the driving force behind a person's desire to study them more systematically.

The point is that single events and single cases often lead to new ideas and new lines of research. When a researcher is interested in a question or topic that is relatively new to the field, often the wisest approach may be to use a descriptive design. In general, in **descriptive designs** the researcher makes no prediction and does not try to control any variables. She simply defines a problem of interest and describes as carefully as possible the variable of interest. The basic question in a descriptive design is, What is variable X? For example, What is love? What is genius? What is apathy? The psychologist makes careful observations, often in the real world outside the research lab. Descriptive studies usually occur during the exploratory phase of research, in which the researcher is looking for meaningful patterns that might lead to predictions later on; they generally do not involve testing hypotheses. Survey research is an exception since it can involve testing predictions. The researcher then notes possible relationships or patterns that may be used in other designs as the basis for testable predictions (see Figure 5). Four of the most common kinds of descriptive methods in psychology are case studies, naturalistic observations, qualitative research/interviews, and surveys.

Case Study   Psychotherapists have been making use of insights gained from individual cases for more than 100 years. A **case study** involves the observation

descriptive designs
Study designs in which the researcher defines a problem and variable of interest but makes no prediction and does not control or manipulate anything.

case study
A study design in which a psychologist, often a therapist, observes one person over a long period of time.

FIGURE 5

CHARACTERISTICS OF DESCRIPTIVE STUDIES. In descriptive studies, researchers look for patterns that might help them create testable hypotheses.

descriptive studies	What type of questions might be researched?	What is the most suitable method of answering the question?	What is the best use for this kind of study?	What is the main limitation of this kind of study?
	Single variable, such as **How do people flirt?**	Case study, observation, survey, or interviews/qualitative research	To find patterns that might lead to predictions for more complete research project **To start describing observed flirtation behavior**	Hypotheses are not tested **Cannot look at cause and effect**

©Kelly Redinger/Design Pics

©Michael Nichols/National Geographic Creative

Primatologist Jane Goodall is famous for her observational studies of chimpanzees in the wild.

of one person, often over a long period of time. Much wisdom and knowledge of human behavior can come from careful observation of one individual over time. Because case studies are based on one-on-one relationships, often lasting years, they offer deep insights that surveys and questionnaires often miss. Sometimes studying the lives of extraordinary individuals, such as van Gogh, Lincoln, Marie Curie, Einstein, or even Hitler, can tell us much about creativity, greatness, genius, or evil.

An area of psychology called *psychobiography* combines psychology with history to understand human behavior through the study of individual lives in historical context (Elms, 1993; Runyan, 1982; Schultz, 2005). Like other descriptive research, case studies and psychobiographies do not test hypotheses but can be a rich source for them. One has to be careful with case studies, however, because not all cases are generalizable to other people. That is why case studies are often a starting point for the development of testable hypotheses.

naturalistic observation
A study in which the researcher unobtrusively observes and records behavior in the real world.

Naturalistic Observation   A second kind of descriptive method is **naturalistic observation**, in which the researcher observes and records behavior in the real world. The researcher tries to be as unobtrusive as possible so as not to influence the behavior of interest. Naturalistic observation is more often the design of choice in comparative psychology by researchers who study nonhuman behavior (especially primates) to determine what is and is not unique about our species.

Developmental psychologists occasionally also conduct naturalistic observations. For example, the developmental psychologist Edward Tronick of Harvard University has made detailed naturalistic observations of the infants of the Efe people in Zaire. He has tracked these children from 5 months through 3 years to understand how the Efe culture's communal pattern of child rearing influences social development in children (Tronick, Morelli, & Ivey, 1992). Although the traditional Western view is that having a primary caregiver is best for the social and emotional well-being of a child, Tronick's research suggests that the use of multiple, communal caregivers can also foster children's social and emotional well-being.

The advantage of naturalistic observation is that it gives researchers a look at real behavior in the real world rather than in a controlled setting—such as in a laboratory, where people might not behave naturally. Few psychologists use naturalistic observation, however, because conditions cannot be controlled and cause-and-effect relationships between variables cannot be demonstrated.

Qualitative Research   Letting people say what they want in responding to questions is the essence of an interview. **Interviews** occur between two people, one asking the questions and the other answering, usually in open-ended answers. Sometimes interview questions are predetermined or structured and sometimes they are spontaneous or unstructured. Interviews are an example of **qualitative research**, which involves data gathered from open-ended and unstructured answers rather than quantitative or numeric answers. The advantage to qualitative research, namely the open-ended and flexible answers, is also its disadvantage. How does one interpret, summarize, and make sense of a person's interview answers? Just as importantly, how do we compare one person's answers to another's and get a general sense of what the trends are? These are difficulties of qualitative research.

Survey Research   Surveys do not have these difficulties because more often than not, they restrict the possible answers to some kind of numeric rating scale, such as 1 for "completely disagree," 3 for "neither disagree nor agree," and 5 for "completely agree." Research that collects information using any kind of numeric and quantifiable scale and often has limited response options is referred to as **quantitative research**. These are structured and quantitative answers and can be summarized and calculated for trends and averages. Yet, answers are restricted to a few categories and sometimes the response options are too limited and do not capture the person's true ideas or attitudes. A common example of a limited response option is when a respondent has to answer on a 1 to 5 scale from "completely disagree" to "completely agree." Sometimes survey research is descriptive and exploratory and other times it may propose and test hypotheses.

There is another concern with survey research. Think about your own response when you are contacted via phone or email about participating in a scientific survey. Many of us don't want to participate and ignore the request. So how does a researcher know that people who participate are not different from people who don't participate? Maybe those who participate are older or younger, have more education or less education. In other words, we need to know that the information we collect comes from people who represent the group we are interested in, which is known as a **representative sample** (see Figure 6). **Sampling** is the procedure researchers use to obtain participants from a population.

Representative sample

population

Unrepresentative sample

FIGURE 6

SAMPLING. For practical reasons, research is typically conducted with small samples of the population of interest. If a psychologist wanted to study a population of 2,200 people (each face in the figure represents 100 people), he or she would aim for a sample that represented the makeup of the whole group. Thus, if 27% of the population were blue, the researcher would want 27% of the sample population to be blue, as shown in the pie chart on the left. Contrary to what many students think, *representative* does *not* mean that all groups have the same numbers.

©Bettmann/Getty Images

Americans were shocked by Alfred Kinsey's initial reports on male and female sexual behavior. Kinsey was the first researcher to survey people about their sexual behavior. For better or worse, his publications changed attitudes about sex.

The well-known Kinsey surveys of male and female sexual behavior provide good examples of the strengths and weaknesses of survey research (Kinsey, Pomeroy, & Martin, 1948; Kinsey et al., 1953). Make no mistake—just publishing such research caused an uproar in both the scientific community and the general public at the time. Kinsey reported, for instance, that up to 50% of the interviewed men but only about half as many (26%) of the women had had extramarital affairs. Another widely cited finding was that approximately 10% of the population could be considered homosexual. The impact of Kinsey's research has been profound. By itself it began the science of studying human sexuality and permanently changed people's views. For example, Kinsey was the first to consider sexual orientation on a continuum from 0 (completely heterosexual) to 6 (completely homosexual) rather than as an either-or state with only two options. This approach remains a lasting contribution of his studies.

By today's standards, however, Kinsey's techniques for interviewing and collecting data were rather primitive. He didn't use representative sampling and oversampled people in Indiana (his home state) and in prisons—both of which led to biased results. In addition, he interviewed people face-to-face about the most personal and private details of their sex lives, also making it more likely they provided less than honest and biased answers.

Correlational Studies

Once an area of study has developed far enough that predictions can be made, but for various reasons people cannot be randomly assigned to groups or variables cannot be manipulated, a researcher might choose to test hypotheses by means of a correlational study. **Correlational designs** measure two or more variables and their relationship to one another. In this design, the basic question is, Is X related to Y? For instance, "Is sugar consumption related to increased activity levels in children?" If so, how strong is the relationship, and is increased sugar consumption associated (correlated) with increased activity levels, as we would predict, or does activity decrease as sugar consumption increases? Or is there no clear relationship?

Correlational studies are useful when the experimenter cannot manipulate or control the variables. For example, it would be unethical to raise one group of children one way and another group another way in order to study parenting behavior. We could use a good questionnaire to find out whether parents' scores related to their parenting behavior are consistently associated with particular behavioral outcomes in children. In fact, many questions in developmental psychology, personality psychology, and even clinical psychology are examined with correlational techniques.

The major limitation of the correlational approach is that it does not establish whether one variable actually causes the other. Parental neglect in childhood might be associated with antisocial behavior in adolescence, but that does not necessarily mean that neglect causes antisocial behavior. Some other variable (e.g., high levels of testosterone, poverty, antisocial friends) might be the cause of the behavior. We must always be mindful that correlation is necessary for causation but is not sufficient by itself to establish causation (see Figure 7).

correlational designs
Studies that measure two or more variables and their relationship to one another; not designed to show causation.

©Peter Cade/Getty Images

 Do you think sugar makes kids hyperactive? What does the evidence show?

FIGURE **7**

CHARACTERISTICS OF CORRELATIONAL STUDIES. These studies measure two or more variables and their relationship to one another.

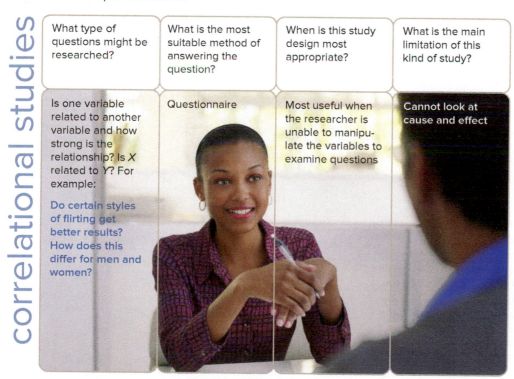

correlational studies

What type of questions might be researched?	What is the most suitable method of answering the question?	When is this study design most appropriate?	What is the main limitation of this kind of study?
Is one variable related to another variable and how strong is the relationship? Is *X* related to *Y*? For example: Do certain styles of flirting get better results? How does this differ for men and women?	Questionnaire	Most useful when the researcher is unable to manipulate the variables to examine questions	Cannot look at cause and effect

©Chris Ryan/agefotostock RF

correlation coefficients

Statistics that range from –1.0 to +1.0 and assess the strength and direction of association between two variables.

Psychologists often use a statistic called the correlation coefficient to draw conclusions from their correlational studies. **Correlation coefficients** tell us whether two variables relate to each other and the direction of the relationship. Correlations range between –1.00 and +1.00, with coefficients near 0.00 indicating that there is no relationship between the two variables. A 0.00 correlation means that knowing about one variable tells us nothing about the other. As a correlation approaches +1.00 or –1.00, the strength of the relationship increases.

Correlation coefficients can be positive or negative. If the relationship is positive, then as a group's score on variable X increases, its score on variable Y also increases. Height and weight are positively correlated—taller people generally weigh more than shorter people. For negative correlations, as one variable increases, the other decreases. Alcohol consumption and motor skills are negatively correlated—the more alcohol people consume, the less physically coordinated they become.

To further demonstrate correlation, let's consider the positive correlation between students' scores on midterm and final exams. By calculating a correlation, we know whether students who do well on the midterm are likely to do well on the final. Based on a sample of 76 students in one of our classes, we found a correlation of +0.57 between midterm and final exam grades. This means that, generally, students who did well on the midterm did well on the final. Likewise, those who did poorly on the midterm tended to do poorly on the final. The correlation, however, was not extremely high, so there was some inconsistency. Some people performed differently on the two exams. When we plot these scores, we see more clearly how individuals did on each exam (see Figure 8). Each dot represents one student's scores on both exams. For example, one student scored an 86 on the midterm but only a 66 on the final.

When interpreting correlations, it is important to remember that a correlation does not mean there is a causal relationship between the two variables. *Correlation is necessary but not sufficient for causation.* When one variable causes another, it must be correlated with it, but just because variable X is correlated with variable Y, it does not mean that X causes Y. The supposed cause may be an

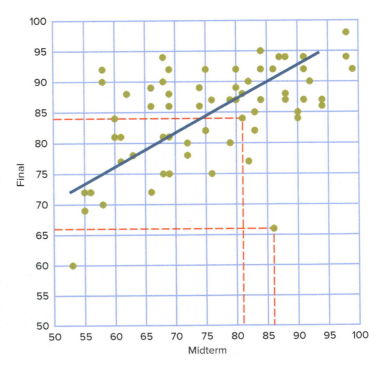

FIGURE 8

EXAMPLE OF A SCATTERPLOT OF POSITIVE CORRELATION: STUDENTS' SCORES ON A MIDTERM AND A FINAL EXAM. The correlation between scores on the midterm and final is +.57, which means that in general the students who do well on the midterm tend to do well on the final. It also means that students who do poorly on the midterm tend to do poorly on the final. Each circle is a particular student's scores on the midterm and final. For example, one student scored an 81 on the midterm (vertical dashed line) and an 84 on the final (horizontal dashed line). Students above the diagonal line did better on the final than expected. Students below the diagonal line performed worse on the final than expected. For example, one student scored an 86 on the midterm but only a 66 on the final.

effect, or a third variable may be the cause. What if hairiness and aggression in men were positively correlated? Would that imply that being hairy makes a man more aggressive? No. In fact, both hairiness and aggressiveness are related to a third variable, the male sex hormone testosterone (Simpson, 2001 see Figure 9).

Experimental Studies

Often people use the word *experiment* to refer to any research study, but in science an experiment is something quite specific. All psychological studies measure behavior, but a true **experiment** has two unique characteristics:

1. Experimental manipulation of a predicted cause, the independent variable
2. Random assignment of participants to control and experimental groups or conditions, meaning that each participant has an equal chance of being placed in each group

   The **independent variable** in an experiment is an attribute the experimenter manipulates under controlled conditions. The independent variable is the condition the researcher predicts will cause a particular outcome. The **dependent variable** is the outcome, or response to the experimental manipulation. You can think of the independent variable as the "cause" and the dependent variable as the "effect," although reality is not always so simple. If there is a causal connection between the two, then the responses *depend* on the treatment, hence the name *dependent variable.*

   Earlier we mentioned the hypothesis that sugar consumption makes kids overly active. In this example, sugar levels consumed would be the independent variable and behavioral activity level the dependent variable. Recall the study of the effect of caffeine on sex drive in rats. Is caffeine the independent or dependent variable? What about sex drive? Figure 10 features other examples of independent and dependent variables.

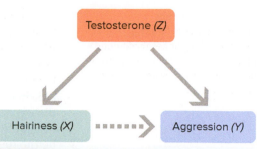

FIGURE 9

CORRELATION IS NOT CAUSATION. Hairiness (*X*) and aggression (*Y*) may be correlated, but that does not mean hairiness causes aggression. In reality, a third variable (testosterone, *Z*) is the cause of both of them (Simpson, 2001). The solid lines imply cause; the dashed line implies correlation.

experiment
A research design that includes independent and dependent variables and random assignment of participants to control and experimental groups or conditions.

independent variable
A property that is manipulated by the experimenter under controlled conditions to determine whether it causes the predicted outcome of an experiment.

dependent variable
In an experiment, the outcome or response to the experimental manipulation.

You want to know the effect of *X* on *Y*

FIGURE 10

INDEPENDENT AND DEPENDENT VARIABLES. Remember: The response, or dependent variable (DV), depends on the treatment. It is the treatment, or independent variable (IV), that the researcher manipulates.

Number of people present *(X)* and likelihood of helping someone in distress *(Y)*

Hours of sleep *(X)* and performance on a test *(Y)*

Relaxation training *(X)* and blood pressure *(Y)*

Independent variable:
Number of people present

Dependent variable:
Likelihood of helping

Independent variable:
Number of hours asleep

Dependent variable:
Test grade

Independent variable:
Relaxation training

Dependent variable:
Blood pressure

random assignment
The method used to assign participants to different research conditions, so that all participants have the same chance of being in any specific group.

experimental group
A group consisting of those participants who will receive the treatment or whatever is predicted to change behavior.

control group
A group of research participants who are treated in exactly the same manner as the experimental group, except that they do not receive the independent variable, or treatment.

placebo
A substance or treatment that appears identical to the actual treatment but lacks the active substance.

confounding variable
The variable whose influence on the dependent variable cannot be separated from the independent variable being examined.

Random assignment is a method used to assign participants to different research conditions to guarantee that each person has the same chance of being in one group as another. Random assignment is achieved with either a random numbers table or some other unbiased technique. Random assignment is critical, because it ensures that *on average* the groups will be similar with respect to all possible variables, such as gender, intelligence, motivation, and memory, when the experiment begins. If the groups are the same on these qualities at the beginning of the study, then any differences between the groups at the end are likely to be the result of the independent variable.

Experimenters randomly assign participants to either an experimental group or the control group. An **experimental group** consists of participants who receive the treatment or whatever is thought to change behavior. In the sugar consumption and activity study, for example, the experimental group would receive a designated amount of sugar.

The **control group** consists of participants who are treated in exactly the same manner as the experimental group but with one crucial difference: They do not receive the independent variable, or treatment. Instead, they often receive no special treatment or, in some cases, they get a **placebo**, a substance or treatment that appears identical to the actual treatment but lacks the active substance. In a study on sugar consumption and activity level, an appropriate placebo could be an artificial sweetener. The experimental group would receive the treatment (sugar), and the control group would be treated exactly the same way but would not receive the actual treatment. Instead, the control group could receive a food flavored with an artificial sweetener.

Experimental and control groups must be equivalent at the outset of an experimental study so as to minimize the possibility that other characteristics could explain any difference found after the administration of the treatment. If two groups of children are similar at the start and if one group differs from the other on activity level after receiving different amounts of sugar, then we can conclude that the treatment caused the observed effect. That is, different levels of sugar consumption caused the differences in activity level.

In our hypothetical study on sugar and activity, for instance, we would want to include equal numbers of boys and girls in the experimental and control groups and match them with respect to age, ethnicity, and other characteristics, so that we could attribute differences in activity level following treatment to differences in sugar consumption only. Suppose we didn't do a good job of randomly assigning participants to our two conditions and the experimental group ended up with 90% boys but the control group had 90% girls. If, after administering the sugar to the experimental group and the placebo (sugar substitute) to the control group, we found a difference in activity, then we would have two possible explanations for the difference: gender and sugar. Either being male or female caused the difference or consuming large amounts of sugar did. In this case, gender would be a **confounding variable**—an additional variable that the researcher failed to control for in the experimental design (too many males), and one that could be responsible for a change in the dependent variable (activity level). Because most of the people in the experimental group were male and consumed sugar, we do not know whether being male or consuming sugar was responsible for the difference in active behavior. These two variables are confounded and cannot be teased apart.

The power of the experimental design is that it allows us to say that the independent variable (treatment) caused changes in the dependent variable, as long as everything other than the independent variable was held constant (see Figure 11). Random assignment guarantees group equivalence on a number of variables and prevents ambiguity over whether effects might be due to other differences between the groups.

FIGURE 11

CHARACTERISTICS OF EXPERIMENTAL STUDIES. Only in true experimental designs, in which researchers manipulate the independent variable and measure its effects on the dependent variable, can researchers determine cause and effect. By itself, correlation is not causation.

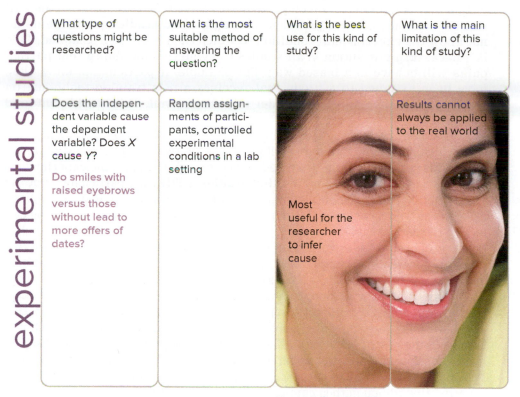

experimental studies

What type of questions might be researched?	What is the most suitable method of answering the question?	What is the best use for this kind of study?	What is the main limitation of this kind of study?
Does the independent variable cause the dependent variable? Does *X* cause *Y*? Do smiles with raised eyebrows versus those without lead to more offers of dates?	Random assignments of participants, controlled experimental conditions in a lab setting	Most useful for the researcher to infer cause	Results cannot always be applied to the real world

©Purestock/SuperStock RF

In addition to random assignment to control and experimental groups, a true experiment requires experimental control of the independent variable. Thus, researchers must make sure that all environmental conditions (such as noise level and room size) are equivalent for the two groups. Again, the goal is to make sure that nothing affects the dependent variable besides the independent variable.

In our experiment on sugar consumption and activity level, we first must randomly assign participants to either the experimental group (in which participants receive some amount of sugar) or the control group (in which participants receive some sugar substitute). The outcome of interest is activity level, so each group might be videotaped for a short period 30 minutes after eating the sugar or sugar substitute. What if the room where the experimental group was given the sugar was several degrees warmer than the room where the control group received the sugar substitute, and our results showed that the participants in the warmer room were more active? Could we feel confident that sugar led to increased activity level? No, because the heat in that room may have caused the increase in activity level. In this case, room temperature would be the confounding variable.

There is a design that has one quality of an experiment (the manipulation of an independent variable), but not the other (random assignment), a design known as a **quasi-experimental design** (Shadish, Cook, & Campbell, 2002). It is called "quasi" because it is partly or almost an experimental design. It is often used with human participants, because we cannot randomly assign them to ethically untenable conditions, such as depression or childhood abuse or

quasi-experimental design
A research method similar to an experimental design except that it makes use of naturally occurring groups rather than randomly assigning subjects to groups.

even personality traits such as extroversion. In these situations, the researchers use preexisting groups but then manipulate a variable to see how the groups respond.

Any knowledge that participants and experimenters have about the experimental conditions to which participants have been assigned can also affect the outcome of an experiment. In **single-blind studies**, participants do not know the experimental condition to which they have been assigned. This is a necessary precaution in all studies to avoid the possibility that participants will behave in a biased way. For example, if participants know they have been assigned to a group that receives a new training technique on memory, then they might try harder to perform well. This would confound the results.

Another possible problem can come from the experimenter knowing who is in which group and unintentionally treating the two groups somewhat differently. This could lead to the predicted outcome simply because the experimenter has biased the results. In **double-blind studies**, neither the participants nor the researchers (at least the ones administering the treatment) know who has been assigned to which condition. Ideally, then, neither the participants nor those collecting the data should know which group is the experimental group and which is the control group. The advantage of double-blind studies is that they prevent two potential problems with experimental designs: experimenter expectancy effects and demand characteristics. **Experimenter expectancy effects** occur when the behavior of the participants is influenced by the experimenter's knowledge of who is in which condition (Rosenthal, 1976, 1994). **Demand characteristics** are subtle cues given by experimenters to the participants as to how they should behave in the role of participant. These cues may be provided unconsciously, or even consciously. The latter apparently happened, for example, in the Stanford Prison Study when before the study began, Zimbardo suggested to the assigned "guards" that although they cannot abuse or torture, they can create fear, boredom, frustration, lack of privacy, and control (Zimbardo, 2007). That is precisely what the guards did.

Longitudinal Studies

People change over time—our brains, thoughts, feelings, personality, motivations. In fact, every aspect of us changes. The only way to study change over time is with longitudinal studies. **Longitudinal designs** make observations of the same people over time, ranging from months to decades. These kinds of studies are not only useful for studying change over time, but also can be used to study how specific causes affect specific outcomes. For example, we cannot randomly assign young children to live in abusive or neglectful home environments. But some children do and some do not. So if we follow these groups over time, we can examine the outcomes of such living conditions on thought and behavior. Longitudinal studies often combine observational, correlational, and quasi-experimental techniques.

Twin-Adoption Studies

One of the most important questions in psychology is how much of our thought, behavior, personality, and mental health stems from built-in biological forces (nurture) and how much is from learning and the environmental (nature). The nature-nurture topic runs throughout the book and our answer is always it is "both/and" not "either/or." How do researchers conduct research to answer these questions? They primarily use two different methods: twin-adoption studies and gene-by-environment studies.

single-blind studies
Studies in which participants do not know the experimental condition (group) to which they have been assigned.

double-blind studies
Studies in which neither the participants nor the researchers administering the treatment know who has been assigned to the experimental or control group.

experimenter expectancy effects
A result that occurs when the behavior of the participants is influenced by the experimenter's knowledge of who is in the control group and who is in the experimental group.

demand characteristics
Subtle, often unconscious, cues given by experimenters to the participants as to how they should behave in the role of participant.

longitudinal designs
Make observations of the same people over time, ranging from months to decades.

Twin-Adoption Studies   The best way to untangle the effects of genetics and environment is to study twins who are adopted or not and compare them to other siblings who are adopted or not, which is what **twin-adoption studies** do. We will be discussing twin-adoption research throughout the rest of the book, so it is important that you understand the logic of how these studies tease apart the extent to which nature and nurture is involved in creating differences or similarities between people.

The easiest way to understand how twin-adoption research teases nature and nurture effects apart is to realize that there are three forms of similarity: genetic (nature), environmental (nurture), and trait.

Genetic similarity varies based on degree of relationship, for example in cases of twins, siblings, and parents and their children. Genetic similarity ranges from 100% with **identical twins** (split from a single egg) to 0% with unrelated people, such as adopted siblings. In between 100% and 0% we have **fraternal twins** (two eggs fertilized by two sperm), siblings, and parents and their children. These all share 50% of their genes.

Environments vary in many ways, the most obvious being raised in the same house (together) or not (apart). Researchers who make use of twin-adoption methods then look for how similar or different these different groups are on a given trait in order to calculate how much of the variation in that trait is due to genetic influence, or its heritability.

Researchers cannot for obvious reasons assign people to different genetic or environmental conditions to see what effect each one has on a trait. So they turn to what exists in nature to tease the two apart. The logic of all of this is laid out in Figure 12. Let's just take two of these hypothetical cases from Figure 12. First, if identical twins (100% genetically alike) are raised apart (different environments) and yet they still are very similar on certain traits such as their height, weight, intelligence, or personality, then we would know that genes play a large role in the variation of those traits. Likewise, if adopted siblings (0% genetically alike) who are raised together (same environment) share strong similarities on these traits, then we have to conclude that environment plays a large role in the variation of those traits.

twin-adoption studies
Research into hereditary influence on twins, both identical and fraternal, who were raised apart (adopted) and who were raised together.

©Monkey Business Images/Shutterstock.com

Twins form a natural population for teasing apart the influences of genetics and environment on development.

identical twins
Twins that develop from a single fertilized egg that splits into two independent cells.

fraternal twins
Twins that develop from two different eggs fertilized by two different sperm.

FIGURE **12**
Logic of Strong versus Weak Genetic and Environmental Influence from Twin-Adoption Research

Four Hypothetical Situations from Twin-Adoptions Studies: Logic of Strong versus Weak Genetic Influence

Genetic Similarity (%)		Environmental Similarity		Trait Similarity		Conclusion
100% (Identical Twins)	+	Raised Apart	+	High (same)	→	Strong Genetic Influence
100% (Identical Twins)	+	Raised Apart	+	Low (different)	→	Strong Environmental Influence (Weak Genetic)
0% (Adopted Siblings)	+	Raised Together	+	High (same)	→	Strong Environmental Influence (Weak Genetic)
0% (Adopted Siblings)	+	Raised Together	+	Low (different)	→	Strong Genetic Influence

 How do researchers know how much of a trait is under genetic or environmental influence?

gene-by-environment interaction research
A method of studying heritability by comparing genetic markers; allows researchers to assess how genetic differences interact with the environment to produce certain behaviors in some people but not in others.

Gene-by-Environment Studies The second technique in the study of heritability, **gene-by-environment interaction research**, allows researchers to assess how genetic differences interact with the environment to produce certain behavior in some people but not in others (Moffitt, Caspi, & Rutter, 2005; Thapar, Langley, & Asherson, 2007). Instead of using twins, family members, and adoptees to vary genetic similarity, gene-by-environment studies directly measure genetic variation in parts of the genome itself and examine how such variation interacts with different kinds of environments to produce different behaviors or traits.

Meta-Analysis

As powerful as results may be from an individual study, the real power of scientific results comes from the cumulative overall findings from all studies on a given topic. If a topic or question has been sufficiently studied, researchers may choose to stand back and analyze all the results of the numerous studies on a given topic. For example, a researcher interested in the effects of media violence on children's aggressive behavior might want to know what all of the research—not just one or two studies—suggests.

meta-analysis
A research technique for combining all research results on one question and drawing a conclusion.

effect size
A measure of the strength of the relationship between two variables or the extent of an experimental effect.

Meta-analysis is a quantitative method for combining the results of all the published and even unpublished results on one question and drawing a conclusion based on the entire set of studies on the topic. To do a meta-analysis, the researcher converts the findings of each study into a standardized statistic known as effect size. **Effect size** is a measure of the strength of the relationship between two variables. The average effect size across all studies reflects what the literature overall says on a topic or question. For example, a meta-analysis of 28 different studies from the United States, Europe, and Asia compared technology-based learning (e.g., tablets, laptops, and smart phones) to traditional non-technology-based instruction and found that students using tablets learned better than those without. The average effect size for these 28 studies was 0.23, meaning that students using tablets scored 0.23 of a standard deviation (the average variation around the mean) higher on learning outcomes compared to students with no tablets (Tamin et al., 2015). (See "Making Sense of Data with Statistics" later in this chapter.) In short, meta-analysis tells us whether all of the research on a topic has or has not led to consistent findings and what the effect size is. It is more reliable than the results of any single study.

Big Data

More than 1 billion of the world's 7 billion people use some form of social media (Facebook, Twitter, Instagram, and others). With the increase in storage and speed of the Internet and the proliferation of mobile apps, a whole new way of collecting data on human behavior has arisen—so-called "big data." **Big Data** consists of the extremely vast amounts of information from websites and apps that is collected and analyzed by unusually large and sophisticated computer programs. Big Data come mostly from social media, smartphones, and wearable devices, but sometimes from the scientific literature itself (Augur, 2016).

big data
Extremely large amount of data captured from online behaviors (especially social media), which are then collected and analyzed for patterns by sophisticated analytic programs.

In psychology, compared to the traditional survey, questionnaire, and even experimental techniques, Big Data afford a much more extensive and reliable means of measuring interests, social relationships, personality, emotion, political attitudes, exercise behaviors, brain activity and structure, and language just to name a few (Schwartz & Ungar, 2015). For example, Tan and colleagues (2016) used Big Data to find and narrow down all brain studies on hippocampus size (a brain structure most notably associated with learning and memory) and gender. By doing so, they narrowed the field down to 76 studies with more than 6,000 participants. Further, using meta-analysis, once they controlled for overall brain size (because men are larger and have larger overall brains), the researchers found there was no size difference in the hippocampi of men and women, further eroding the assumption that men and women have different brains. This study took advantage of both Big Data and meta-analysis.

Quick Quiz 2: Research Methods in Psychology

1. Dr. Lovejoy wanted to do research on real-world conditions that lead to aggression in 10-year-old children, defining aggression as "intent to harm another person." She went to a local elementary school and videotaped a 10-minute recess period. She and her trained coders then coded the behavior of every child and counted the number of times each child acted aggressively. This is an example of what kind of research design?
   a. descriptive   c. case study
   b. correlational   d. experimental

2. If Dr. Lovejoy wanted to examine whether certain personality traits make aggression more likely, she would probably use what kind of research design?
   a. descriptive
   b. correlational
   c. interview
   d. experimental

3. Researchers have consistently found that married men live longer than single men. From this finding, we can conclude that
   a. if a man gets married, he adds years to his life.
   b. marriage causes men to live longer.

   c. being single causes men to die earlier.
   d. marriage correlates with longer life in men.

4. In research on whether sugar causes hyperactivity, researchers randomly assign children to receive no sugar, small amounts of sugar, or large amounts of sugar. They then observe and code activity levels. In this case, the sugar level is the
   a. outcome variable.
   b. dependent variable.
   c. independent variable.
   d. control condition.

5. In contrast to other kinds of research designs, a true experimental design must have two things:
   a. random assignment of participants to conditions and statistical analysis.
   b. random assignment of participants to conditions and manipulation of an independent variable.
   c. manipulation of an independent variable and a dependent variable.
   d. hypothesis testing and observation.

Answers can be found at the end of the chapter.

CHALLENGING ASSUMPTIONS IN THE OBJECTIVITY OF EXPERIMENTAL RESEARCH

You don't have to be a scientist to understand that it would be wrong and unethical for an experimenter to tell participants how to behave and what to do. Even for the participants to know what group they are in or what the hypotheses of the study are is bad science and biases behavior. Can what the experimenter knows change the behavior of the participants?

In a classic case of scientific serendipity, Robert Rosenthal's PhD thesis challenged the assumption that experimenters who randomly assign animals or people to conditions and manipulate an independent variable are being quite objective—that is, these procedures assure objective results. He discovered the assumption of objectivity was wrong when he set out to conduct a study on perceived success and intelligence. Rosenthal hypothesized that people who believed they were successful would be more likely to see success in others. To test this idea, he conducted an experiment in which he told one group of participants they had done well on an intelligence test and another group they had done poorly on an intelligence test. Rosenthal randomly assigned participants to be in one of these conditions (there was also a neutral control condition in which participants received no feedback on the intelligence test). Then he asked all groups to look at photographs of people doing various tasks and rate how successful they thought

Courtesy of the University of California, Riverside

Robert Rosenthal

the people in the photos were. He reasoned that people who are told they did well on an intelligence test should see more success in photographs of people doing various tasks than people who are told they did not do well on the test.

As a good scientist, Rosenthal compared the average test scores of the participants assigned to different conditions before giving them any feedback on their performance—that is, before the experimental treatment. The reason is simple: If the treatment causes a difference in behavior for the different groups, the researcher needs to make sure the groups started out behaving the same way before treatment. To Rosenthal's dismay, the groups did differ before receiving treatment. They were also different in exactly the way that favored his hypothesis!

Given random assignment, the only difference in the groups at the outset was Rosenthal's knowledge of who was in which group. Somehow, by knowing who was in which group, he created behaviors that favored his hypothesis. He was forced to conclude that, even when trying to be "scientific" and "objective," researchers bias results unintentionally in their favor by subtle voice changes or gestures. Instead of having a wonderful "aha moment" of scientific discovery, Rosenthal had more of an "oh no" moment: "What I recall was a panic experience when I realized I'd ruined the results of my doctoral dissertation by unintentionally influencing my research participants to respond in a biased manner because of my expectations" (Rosenthal, personal communication, April 18, 2010).

Rosenthal decided to systematically study what he came to call experimenter expectancy effects. Through several experiments, he confirmed that experimenter expectancies can ruin even the best-designed studies. Also, he discovered that two other surprising factors can change the outcome of the study as well. First, if the study involves direct interaction between an experimenter and participants, the experimenter's age, ethnicity, personality, and gender can influence the participants' behavior (Rosenthal, 1976). Second, Rosenthal stumbled upon a more general phenomenon known as **self-fulfilling prophecy**. A self-fulfilling prophecy occurs when our belief or expectation that something is going to happen unknowingly makes it happen. For example, if research assistants know the study's hypothesis, they may unconsciously affect the behavior of the participants and make the predicted outcome more likely to happen. Or if a teacher does not expect a student to do very well and then ignores that student, the student may well not do well, fulfilling the expectation of the teacher.

Ten years after Rosenthal's first publication on experimenter expectancy effect, more than 300 other studies confirmed his results (Rosenthal & Rubin, 1978). Such expectancies affect animal participants as well as humans (Jussim & Harber, 2005; Rosenthal & Fode, 1963). Rosenthal's demonstration of experimenter expectancy effects and self-fulfilling prophecies also led to the development of double-blind procedures in science. Think about it: If what experimenters know about a study can affect the results, then they'd better be as blind to experimental conditions as the participants are. All of this came to be because Rosenthal "messed up" his dissertation and unintentionally challenged the assumptions of the best way to conduct scientific experiments.

self-fulfilling prophecy
A statement that affects events to cause the prediction to become true.

Challenge Your Assumptions

True or False? Knowing what you're looking for in an experiment has no effect on the outcome.

False: Even when being careful, if the researcher is aware of the hypothesis, he or she may unconsciously act differently and unintentionally affect the behavior of the participants.

Quick Quiz 3: Challenging Assumptions in the Objectivity of Experimental Research

1. One explanation for experimenter expectancy effect is
   a. double-blind studies.
   b. self-fulfilling prophecy.
   c. confounding variables.
   d. experimental manipulation.

2. The best way to lessen the effects of experimenter expectancy is to design a study that uses
   a. single-blind methods.
   b. double-blind methods.
   c. triple-blind methods.
   d. quasi-experimental methods.

Answers can be found at the end of the chapter.

COMMONLY USED MEASURES OF PSYCHOLOGICAL RESEARCH

In addition to different study methods, when psychologists conduct research, they rely on a vast array of tools to measure variables relevant to their research questions. The tools and techniques they use to assess thought and behavior are called **measures**. Measures in psychological science tend to fall into three categories: self-report, behavioral, and physiological. To study complex behaviors, researchers may employ multiple measures (see Figure 13).

measures
The tools and techniques used to assess thought or behavior.

Self-Report Measures

Self-reports are people's written or oral accounts of their thoughts, feelings, or actions. Two kinds of self-report measures are commonly used in psychology:

- Interviews
- Questionnaires

self-reports
Written or oral accounts of a person's thoughts, feelings, or actions.

In an interview, a researcher asks a set of questions, and the respondent usually answers in any way he or she feels is appropriate. The answers are often open-ended and not constrained by the researcher. (See the section "Descriptive Studies", for additional discussion on interviews.)

In a questionnaire, responses are limited to the choices given in the questionnaire. In the Stanford Prison Experiment, for example, the researchers used several questionnaires to keep track of the psychological states of the prisoners and guards. They had participants complete mood questionnaires many times during the study, so that the researchers could track any emotional changes the participants experienced. The participants also completed forms that assessed personality characteristics, such as trustworthiness and orderliness, that might be related to how they acted in a prison environment (Haney et al., 1973).

Self-report questionnaires are easy to use, especially in the context of collecting data from a large number of people at once. They are also relatively inexpensive. If designed carefully, questionnaires can provide important information

FIGURE **13**
COMMONLY USED MEASURES IN PSYCHOLOGY.

	Description	Use	Limitations
self-reports	Participants' written or oral accounts of thoughts, actions, feelings	Interviews and questionnaires	Social desirability bias Lack of clear insight into one's own behavior
behavioral measures	Objective observation of actions in either natural or lab settings	Small-scale studies on behavior	Time required to train coders and conduct coding Participants may modify their behavior
physiological measures	Data collection of bodily responses under certain conditions	Studies to determine the magnitude of physiological change	Specialized training on expensive equipment, on how to collect measurements, and on data interpretation
multiple measures	Several measures combined to acquire data on one aspect of behavior	Offset limitation of any single measurement Complex behaviors to study	Expensive and time-consuming

 Why does the best research strategy involve using as many techniques as possible to study the same question?

social desirability bias
The tendency toward favorable self-presentation that could lead to inaccurate self-reports.

behavioral measures
Measures based on systematic observation of people's actions either in their normal environment or in a laboratory setting.

on key psychological variables. A major problem with self-reports, however, is that people are not always the best sources of information about themselves. Why? Sometimes, as a reflection of the tendency toward social desirability, called **social desirability bias**, people present themselves more favorably than they really are, not wanting to reveal what they are really thinking or feeling to others for fear of looking bad. Presented with questions about social prejudice, for example, respondents might try to avoid giving answers that suggest they are prejudiced against a particular group. Another problem with self-reports is that we have to assume that people are accurate witnesses to their own experiences. Of course, there is no way to know exactly what a person is thinking without asking that person, but people do not always have clear insight into how they might behave (Nisbett & Wilson, 1977).

Behavioral Measures

Behavioral measures involve the systematic observation of people's actions either in their normal environment (that is, naturalistic observation) or in a laboratory setting. A psychologist interested in aggression might bring people into a laboratory, place them in a situation that elicits aggressive behavior, and videotape the responses. Afterward, trained coders observe the videos and, using a prescribed method, code the level of aggressive behavior exhibited by each person. Training is essential for the coders, so that they can evaluate the video and apply the codes in a reliable, consistent manner.

Behavioral measures are less susceptible to social desirability bias than are self-report measures. They also provide more objective measurements, because they come from a trained outside observer, rather than from the participants themselves. This is a concern for researchers on topics for which people are not likely to provide accurate information in self-report instruments. In the study of emotion, for example, measuring facial expressions from video reveals things about how people are feeling that they might not reveal on questionnaires (Rosenberg & Ekman, 2000).

One drawback of behavioral measures is that people may modify their behavior if they know they are being observed and/or measured. The major drawback of

©Spencer Grant/PhotoEdit

 What are some advantages and disadvantages to collecting data via observation?

behavioral measurement, however, is that it can be time-intensive; it takes time to train coders to use the coding schemes, to collect behavioral data, and to prepare the coded data for analysis. As a case in point, one of the most widely used methods for coding facial expressions of emotion requires intensive training, on the order of 100 hours, for people to be able to use it correctly (Ekman, Friesen, & Hager, 2002)! Moreover, researchers can collect data on only a few participants at once, and therefore behavioral measures are often impractical for large-scale studies.

Physiological Measures

Physiological measures provide data on bodily responses. For years, research-ers relied on physiological information to index possible changes in psychological states—for example, to determine the magnitude of a stress reaction. Research on stress and anxiety often measures electrical changes in involuntary bodily responses, such as heart rate, sweating, and respiration, as well as hormonal changes in the blood that are sensitive to changes in psychological states. Some researchers measure brain activity while people perform certain tasks to deter-mine the speed and general location of cognitive processes in the brain.

We will look at specific brain imaging technologies in the chapter "The Biol-ogy of Behavior". Here we note simply that they have enhanced our understanding of the brain's structure and function tremendously. However, these technologies, and even more simple ones, such as the measurement of heart rate, often require specialized training in the use of equipment, collection of measurements, and in-terpretation of data. Further, some of the equipment is expensive to buy and main-tain. Outside the health care delivery system, only major research universities with medical schools tend to have them. In addition, researchers need years of training and experience in order to use these machines and interpret the data they generate.

physiological measures
Measures of bodily responses, such as blood pressure or heart rate, used to determine changes in psychological state.

Quick Quiz 4: Commonly Used Measures of Psychological Research

1. An advantage of self-report questionnaires is that they are easy to administer to large numbers of participants. A disadvantage of questionnaires is that
   a. they cost too much.
   b. people do not always accurately report their true thoughts or feelings.
   c. scoring responses is subjective.
   d. they have low reliability.
2. One advantage of behavioral measures compared with self-reported measures is that they
   a. are less prone to social desirability bias.
   b. are less time-intensive.

   c. are always more valid.
   d. cost less.
3. A psychologist who is interested in how brain activity relates to behavior will most likely use which kind of measure?
   a. interview
   b. questionnaire
   c. behavioral
   d. physiological

Answers can be found at the end of the chapter.

MAKING SENSE OF DATA WITH STATISTICS

Once researchers collect data, they must make sense of them. Raw data are dif-ficult to interpret. They are, after all, just a bunch of numbers. It helps to have some way to organize the information and give it meaning. To make sense of in-formation, scientists use **statistics**, mathematical procedures for collecting, ana-lyzing, interpreting, and presenting numeric data. For example, researchers use

statistics
The collection, analysis, interpreta-tion, and presentation of numerical data.

statistics to describe and simplify data and to understand how variables relate to one another. There are two classes of statistics: descriptive and inferential.

Descriptive Statistics

descriptive statistics
Measures used to describe and summarize research.

mean
The arithmetic average of a series of numbers.

median
The score that separates the lower half of scores from the upper half.

mode
A statistic that represents the most commonly occurring score or value.

standard deviation
A statistical measure of how much scores in a sample vary around the mean.

frequency
The number of times a particular score occurs in a set of data.

normal distribution
A bell curve; a plot of how frequent data are that is perfectly symmetrical, with most scores clustering in the middle and only a few scores at the extremes.

The first step in understanding research results involves calculating **descriptive statistics**, which simply tell researchers the range, average, and variability of the scores. For instance, one useful way to describe data is by calculating the center, or average, of the scores. There are three ways to calculate an average—the mean, median, and mode. The **mean** is the arithmetic average of a series of numbers. It is calculated by adding all the numbers together and dividing by the number of scores in the series. An example of a mean is your GPA, which averages the numeric grade points for all of the courses you have taken. The **median** is the middle score, which separates the lower half of scores from the upper half. The **mode** is the most frequently occurring score.

Sometimes scores vary widely among participants, but the mean, median, and mode do not reveal anything about how spread out—or how varied—scores are. For example, one person's 3.0 GPA could come from getting B's in all his courses, while another person's 3.0 could result from getting A's in half her classes and C's in the other half. The second student has much more variable grades than the first. The most common way to represent variability in data is to calculate the **standard deviation**, a statistical measure of how much scores in a sample vary around the mean. A higher standard deviation indicates more variability (more spread); a lower one indicates less variability (less spread). In the example, the student with all B's would have a lower standard deviation than the student with A's and C's.

Another useful way of describing data is by plotting, or graphing, their frequency. **Frequency** is the number of times a particular score occurs in a set of data. A graph of frequency scores is known as a distribution. To graph a distribution, we place the scores on the horizontal axis, or X-axis, and their frequencies on the vertical axis, or Y-axis. When we do this for many psychological variables, such as intelligence or personality, we end up with a very symmetrical shape to our distribution, which is commonly referred to as either a **normal distribution** or a "bell curve"—because it looks like a bell (see Figure 14).

Let's look at a concrete example of a normal distribution with the well-known intelligence quotient (IQ). If we gave 1,000 children an IQ test and plotted

FIGURE **14**

BELL CURVE. Psychological variables, such as intelligence, show a normal distribution, which is represented by a bell curve.

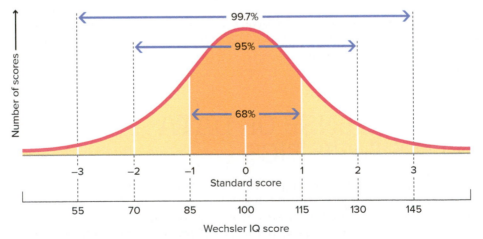

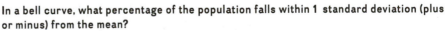
In a bell curve, what percentage of the population falls within 1 standard deviation (plus or minus) from the mean?

all 1,000 scores, we would end up with something very close to a symmetrical, bell-shaped distribution. Very few children would score 70 or below, and very few children would score 130 or above. These are infrequent or rare scores. The majority of children would be right around the average, or mean, of 100. In fact, two-thirds (68%, to be exact) would be within 1 standard deviation (15 points) of the mean. These are frequent or common scores. Moreover, about 95% would be within 2 standard deviations, or between 70 and 130.

How do we know this? We know it because we know the exact shape of a normal distribution in the general population of people being studied. Knowing the shape of the distribution allows us to make inferences from our specific sample to the general population. For example, because a normal distribution has a precise shape, we know exactly what percentage of scores is within 1 standard deviation of the mean (68%) and how many are within 2 standard deviations of the mean (95%). This is why we know that a mean IQ score of 70 or lower or 130 or higher occurs only 5 times in 100—both are very unlikely to occur by chance. This quality of allowing conclusions or inferences to be drawn about populations is the starting point for the second class of statistics, inferential statistics.

Inferential Statistics

We do not draw any conclusions from descriptive results. We just describe the scores with them. **Inferential statistics**, however, allow us to test hypotheses and draw a conclusion (that is, make an inference) as to how likely a sample score is to occur in a population. They also allow us to determine how likely it is that two or more samples came from the same population. In other words, inferential statistics use probability and the normal distribution to rule out chance as an explanation for why group scores are different.

What is an acceptable level of chance before we say that a score is not likely to occur by chance? Five in 100 (5%) is the most frequent choice made by psychological researchers and is referred to as the *probability level*. So if we obtain two means and our statistical analysis tells us there is only a 5% or less chance that these means come from the same population, we conclude that the numbers are not just different but statistically different and therefore not likely to be due to chance.

Researchers use many kinds of statistical analyses to rule out chance, but the most basic ones involve the comparison of two or more means. To compare just two means, we use a statistic known as the **t-test**. The basic logic of t-tests is to determine whether the means for your two groups are so different that they are not likely to come from the same population. If our two groups are part of an experiment and one is the experimental group and the other the control group, then we are determining whether our treatment caused a significant effect, seen in different means. In short, t-tests allow us to test our hypotheses and rule out chance as an explanation.

Let's look at an example, by returning to a question we considered earlier: Does sugar cause hyperactive behavior in children? We will make the common-sense prediction that sugar does cause hyperactive behavior. We randomly assign 100 children to consume sugar (experimental group); another 100 children do not consume sugar (control group). We then wait 30 minutes—to let the sugar effect kick in—and observe their behavior for an additional 30 minutes. We video record each child's behavior and code it on number of "high activity acts." If sugar causes activity levels to increase, then the sugar groups number of high activity acts should be higher than those of the no-sugar group. Our data show that the experimental (sugar) group exhibited an average of 9.23 high activity behaviors in the 30 minutes after eating the sugar; the control (no-sugar) group exhibited an average of 7.61 such behaviors. On the face of it, our hypothesis seems to be supported. After all, 9.23 is higher than 7.61. However, we need to conduct a statistical test to determine whether the difference in the number of hyperactive behaviors between our groups of kids who ate sugar versus those who did not really represents a true difference between these two different populations of kids in the real world.

inferential statistics
Analyses of data that allow us to test hypotheses and make an inference as to how likely a sample score is to occur in a population.

t-test
A statistic that compares two means to see whether they could come from the same population.

Psychology in the Real World

Challenge the Assumptions of Advertisers' Statistics

Learning about research methods plays a crucial role in understanding psychological science, but it offers huge practical advantages as well. You can learn how to look at claims in the news and advertisements with a critical eye to challenge your assumptions about things that matter to you in your own life. Much of what you learn in this class may be forgotten not long after you leave college, but you are bombarded with advertisements dozens of times each day, something that will continue throughout your life. So let's look briefly at three scenarios that will help you be a more critical and intelligent consumer of information.

Scenario 1
A billboard advertising a popular hybrid vehicle: "The car more people would buy again"

That sounds great! Not only is the car good for the environment (which is one reason to get it), but it also gets great mileage (which will save you money) and people like it (they must, if they say they would buy it again). Are you sold yet?

Wait a minute. What does the ad actually say? The car more people would buy again. More than what? The meaning of this claim depends entirely on what this vehicle is being compared to. The implication is that more people would buy this car again than would buy any other car. What did they actually compare it to?

Other hybrids?
All other cars?
A horse and buggy?

These are things you need to know. Otherwise, you can't judge what the statement means. Advertisers regularly leave out such information and hope you will fill in the blank with what helps them most. In this case, they hope and assume you fill in the blank with "all other cars."

Scenario 2
In an ad in the morning paper, Company B reports on a recent lab study showing that just a half ounce of its new drug—let's call it No-Cold—killed 37,202 germs in a test tube in less than 15 seconds! (adapted from Huff, 1954)

The implication is that No-Cold is a great cold medicine—perhaps better than others—on the basis of these hard scientific data. Let's take this claim apart, though. Can you see what is wrong with this statement? Here are a few things to consider:

1. Just because a substance works well in a test tube does not mean it will work in the human throat or respiratory tract. The test tube is a controlled environment, whereas a host of factors interact in the human body. Temperature, moisture, other bacteria, the human immune system, and phlegm are just a few examples of such factors.

2. The ad doesn't say what kind of germs No-Cold killed. Were they the ones that cause colds? (The common cold is caused by a variety of viruses.) Medical researchers still have little idea of the specific viruses

---

The t-test is the test to use in this case, the purpose of which is to determine whether the difference between the two means $(9.23 - 7.61 = 1.62)$ is a chance occurrence or not. If we calculate our t-test and find out that the probability (p-level) that these two means came from the same population is 0.55, then we cannot rule out chance as an explanation. Because there is a 55% chance our two means came from the same population, we conclude the means are not significantly different from each other; children who eat sugar are no more active than those who do not. In this case, our hypothesis is *not* supported, and we are forced to conclude that we have no evidence that sugar increases activity level. These figures are hypothetical but completely consistent with the actual literature on the topic of sugar and activity level (Flora & Polenick, 2013; Krummel, Seligson, & Guthrie, 1996).

Rejecting a hypothesis is never fun. We may have really wanted sugar to be a cause of activity level and, in fact, most parents believe this; however, it is not what the evidence shows, and we have to conclude that sugar does not cause hyperactive behavior, regardless of what we want to believe. This is a perfect example of a very widely held assumption being false. Scientists keep a distance

Challenge Your Assumptions

True or False? Eating sugar makes children hyperactive.

False: There is no evidence supporting the belief that sugar intake directly affects hyperactivity.

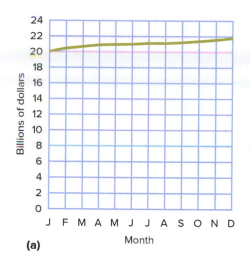

(a)

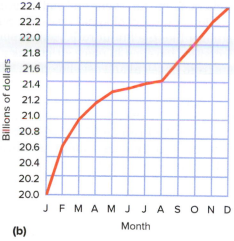

(b)

FIGURE 15
BILLIONS OF DOLLARS SPENT ON EDUCATION.

If you wanted to persuade someone that education spending is out of control, which graph would you use to make your case?

(germs) that cause colds, though some of them have been isolated. Were these germs even relevant to colds? Were they even viruses? Can you identify any other problems with the ad?

Scenario 3
Graphic displays of data can be misleading.

Consider Figures 15a and 15b, both of which depict the billions of dollars spent on education over a 1-year period. Figure 15b seems to show a much bigger increase in spending on education than Figure 15a. If you look closely, however, both depict a $2 billion increase in spending over a 1-year period. The information contained in each picture is exactly the same, but the slopes of the lines differ dramatically. This difference stems from how the illustrations' vertical axes are segmented. If you want to imply that the spending increases in education are insufficient, then you might graph them as shown in Figure 15a, which has $2 billion increments, so it shows a gradual increase across the year. Figure 15b, on the other hand, uses $0.2 billion increments. Businesses, journalists, and politicians can mislead people by graphically distorting data.

from their ideas; they don't believe what they think, at least not until it can be confirmed and replicated.

As useful and helpful as statistics are to help us understand our results, be aware that they also can be and are used to mislead people.

Quick Quiz 5: Making Sense of Data with Statistics

1. If two sets of scores have the same mean, then
   a. they must have the same variability.
   b. they must have similar variabilities.
   c. they must have different variabilities.
   d. their variabilities could be the same or they could be different.

2. Why is GPA a good example of the statistic *mean*?
   a. It is calculated by adding scores and dividing by the number of scores.
   b. It is a good measure of how well a student is doing.
   c. It measures the spread, or variability, of a student's performance.
   d. We can plot it on a graph.

3. Scores that are widely spread apart have a
   a. high standard deviation.
   b. low standard deviation.
   c. high mean.
   d. low reliability.

Answers can be found at the end of the chapter.

ethics
The rules governing the conduct of a person or group in general or in a specific situation—or more simply, standards of right and wrong.

plagiarism
Is when someone presents words or ideas of other people as their own.

falsification
Is the changing, altering, or deleting scientific data.

fabrication
Presenting or publishing scientific results that are made up.

RESEARCH ETHICS

Due to current ethical guidelines, some of the most important and classic studies in psychology could not be performed today. One of them is the Stanford Prison Experiment, which you read about at the beginning of this chapter. This experiment subjected participants to conditions that so altered their behavior the researchers had to intervene and end the study early. In 1971, there were few ethical limitations on psychological research. Since then, and partly as a consequence of studies like the Stanford Prison Experiment, professional organizations and universities have put in place strict ethical guidelines to protect research participants from physical and psychological harm.

Ethics are the rules governing the conduct of a person or group in general or in a specific situation; stated more simply, ethics are standards of right and wrong. What are the ethical boundaries of the treatment of humans and animals in psychological research? In psychology today, nearly every study conducted with humans and animals must pass through a rigorous review of its methods by a panel of experts. If the proposed study does not meet the standards, it cannot be approved. Ethics involve rules against scientific misconduct and rules for treatment of human participants and animals.

Scientific Misconduct

Ethical violations and scientific misconduct in science range from honest errors or mistakes to fraud. Errors can be the result of carelessness, bias, or mistakes, but tend not to be intentional. Scientific misconduct, however, is intentional and therefore the most serious ethical violation. According to both the National Science Foundation and the American Psychological Association, scientific fraud or misconduct comes in three forms: plagiarism, falsification, and fabrication (Code of Federal Regulations-689, 2002; Research Misconduct, n.d.). **Plagiarism** is when someone presents the words or ideas of other people as their own. **Falsification** is changing, altering, or deleting data. The most serious and blatant form of scientific misconduct and fraud is when a researcher commits scientific **fabrication**, that is, presenting or publishing scientific results that are made up.

Fortunately, fraud and misconduct are relatively rare in science—estimates are about 1 in 5,000 to 1 in 23,000 papers need to be taken back or retracted for serious errors or misconduct (Steen, 2010; Steen et al., 2013). One of the worst recent cases of scientific fraud recently involved a social psychologist by the name of Diederik Stapel, who was an up-and-coming psychologist, publishing in the top journals. But one of his studies did not provide the results he predicted. In his words: "I said, you know what, I am going to create the dataset" (Bhattacharrjee, 2013). So he sat down at his kitchen table and literally fabricated an entire dataset. It worked. The paper was published in a top psychological journal. Over the next dozen years or so, a total of 55 scientific articles and 10 PhD theses were based on fabricated data. When it was all over, Stapel was fired, lost his career, and admitted "I have failed as a scientist" (Bhattacharrjee, 2013).

Ethical Treatment of Human Participants

Fraud or errors are one thing but ethical issues also arise in the treatment of participants and animals. For example, the classic series of studies by Stanley Milgram in the early 1960s. Milgram's landmark research on obedience is discussed in more detail in the chapter "Social Behavior", but we mention it here for

Courtesy of Philip Zimbardo

In the Stanford Prison Experiment, college students assigned to the role of either a prison guard or a prisoner acted their parts so well that they blurred the distinction between reality and the world created for this study. The extreme distress experienced by some of the prisoners forced the researchers to end the simulation earlier than planned.

 Do you think the experimenter pushed the participants too far?

its pivotal role in the development of ethical guidelines for human psychological research. Milgram, like many other social psychologists of the mid-20th century, was both fascinated and horrified by the atrocities of the Holocaust and wondered to what extent psychological factors influenced people's willingness to carry out the orders of the Nazi regime. Milgram predicted that most people are not inherently evil and argued that there might be powerful aspects of social situations that make people obey orders from authority figures. He designed an experiment to test systematically the question of whether decent people could be made to inflict harm on others.

Briefly, Milgram's studies of obedience involved a simulation in which participants were misled about the true nature of the experiment. Thinking that they were part of an experiment on learning, they administered what they thought were electrical shocks to punish the "learner," who was in another room, for making errors. In spite of protests from the learner when increasingly intense shocks occurred, the experimenter pressured the "teachers" to continue administering shocks. Some people withdrew from the study, but most of the participants continued to shock the learner. After the study, Milgram fully explained to his participants that the learner had never been shocked or in pain at all (Milgram, 1974).

Milgram's study provided important data on how easily decent people could be persuaded by the sheer force of a situation to do cruel things. What is more, Milgram conducted many replications and variations of his findings, which helped build knowledge about human social behavior. Was it worth the distress it exerted on the participants?

One could ask the same of the Stanford Prison Experiment. Zimbardo appears to have coached the guards by suggesting behaviors they could do and these are the one's they ended up doing. Although the prison experiment led to some reform in U.S. prisons, it is hard to know whether the deception of the participants and the emotional breakdowns some of them experienced was worth it. What do you think?

The Milgram study is one of the most widely discussed studies in the history of psychology. A number of psychologists protested it on ethical grounds (Baumrind, 1964). The uproar led to the creation of explicit guidelines for the ethical treatment of human subjects. Today all psychological and medical researchers must adhere to the following guidelines:

1. *Informed consent:* Tell participants in general terms what the study is about, what they will do and how long it will take, what the known risks and benefits are, and whom to contact with questions. They must also be told that they have the right to withdraw at any time without penalty. This information is provided in written form and the participant signs it, signifying consent. If a participant is under the age of 18, informed consent must be granted by a legal guardian. Informed consent can be omitted only in situations such as completely anonymous surveys.

2. *Respect for persons:* Safeguard the dignity and autonomy of the individual and take extra precautions when dealing with study participants, such as children, who are less likely to understand that their participation is voluntary.

3. *Beneficence:* Inform participants of costs and benefits of participation; minimize costs for participants and maximize benefits. For example, many have argued that the Milgram study was worth the distress (cost) it may have caused participants, for the benefit of the knowledge we have gained about how readily decent people can be led astray by powerful social situations. In fact, many of the participants said that they were grateful for this opportunity to gain knowledge about themselves that they would have not predicted (Milgram, 1974).

4. *Privacy and confidentiality:* Protect the privacy of the participant, generally by keeping all responses confidential. Confidentiality ensures that participants' identities are never directly connected with the data they provide in a study.

5. *Justice:* Benefits and costs must be distributed equally among participants.

In Milgram's study, participants were led to believe they were taking part in a learning study when, in fact, they were participating in a study on obedience to authority. Is this kind of deception ever justified? The answer (according to the American Psychological Association, APA) is that deception is to be avoided whenever possible, but it is permissible if these conditions are met: It can be fully justified by its significant potential scientific, educational, or applied value; it is part of the research design; there is no alternative to deception; and full debriefing occurs afterward. **Debriefing** is the process of informing participants of the exact purposes of the study—including the hypotheses—revealing any and all deceptive practices and explaining why they were necessary to conduct the study and ultimately what the results of the study were.

debriefing
The explanation of the purposes of a study following data collection.

Debriefing is required to minimize any negative effects (e.g., distress) experienced as a result of the deception. Deception comes in different shades and degrees. In the Stanford Prison Experiment, all participants were fully informed about the fact that they would be assigned the roles of a prisoner or a guard. In that sense there was no deception. They were not informed of the details and the extent to which being in this study would be like being in a real prison world. They were not told upfront that, if they were assigned to the "prisoner" role, they would be strip-searched. When they were taken from their homes, the "prisoners" were not told this was part of the study. Not informing participants of the research hypotheses may be deceptive but necessary to prevent biased and invalid responses. Not telling participants that they might experience physical pain or psychological distress is a much more severe form of deception and is not ethically permissible.

institutional review boards (IRBs)
Organizations that evaluate research proposals to make sure research involving humans does not cause undue harm or distress.

Today, to ensure adherence to ethical guidelines, **institutional review boards (IRBs)** evaluate proposed research before it is conducted to make sure research involving humans does not cause undue harm or distress. Should Milgram's study have been permitted? Were his procedures ethical by today's standards? To this day, there are people who make strong cases both for and against the Milgram study on ethical grounds, as we have discussed. It is harder to justify what Zimbardo did in the prison experiment.

Ethical Treatment of Animals

Human participants are generally protected by the ethical guidelines itemized in the previous section. What about animals? They cannot consent, so how do we ethically treat animals in research?

The use of nonhuman species in psychological research is even more controversial than is research with humans. There is a long history in psychology of conducting research on animals. Typically, such studies concern topics that are harder to explore in humans. We cannot, for instance, isolate human children from their parents to see what effect an impoverished environment has on brain development. Researchers have done so with animals. The subfields of biological psychology and learning most often use animals for research. For instance, to determine what exactly a particular brain structure does, one needs to compare individuals who have healthy structures to those who do not. With humans this might be done by studying the behavior of individuals with accidental brain injury or disease and comparing it to the behavior of normal humans. Injury and disease, however, never strike two people in precisely the same way, so it is not possible to reach definite conclusions about the way the brain works by just looking at accidents and illness. Surgically removing the brain structure is another

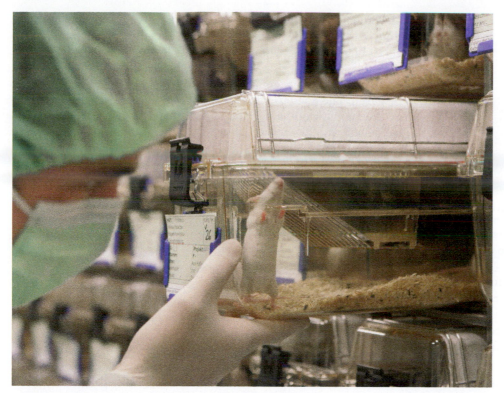

©Wolfgang Flamisch/Getty Images

Strict laws and ethical standards govern the treatment of animals used in research.

 What are the pros and cons of using animals for scientific research?

way to determine function, but this approach is obviously unethical with humans. In contrast, nonhuman animals, usually laboratory rats, offer the possibility of more highly controlled studies of selective brain damage. For example, damage could be inflicted on part of a brain structure in one group of rats while another group is left alone. Then the rats' behaviors and abilities could be observed to see whether there were any differences between the groups.

Animals cannot consent to research, and if they could, they would not likely agree to any of this. Indeed, it is an ongoing debate as to how much animal research should be permissible at all. Because animal research has led to many treatments for disease (e.g., cancer, heart disease), as well as advances in understanding basic neuroscientific processes (such as the effects of environment on brain cell growth), it is widely considered to be acceptable. Animal research is acceptable, that is, as long as the general conditions and treatment of the animals is humane.

If informed consent is the key to ethical treatment of human research participants, then humane treatment is the key to the ethical use of animal subjects. The standards for humane treatment of research animals involve complex legal issues. State and federal laws generally require housing the animals in clean, sanitary, and adequately sized structures. In addition, separate IRBs evaluate proposals for animal research. They require researchers to ensure the animals' comfort, health, and humane treatment, which also means keeping discomfort, infection, illness, and pain to an absolute minimum at all times. If a study requires euthanizing the animal, it must be done as painlessly as possible.

Despite the existence of legal and ethical safeguards and the importance for medical research in humans, some animal rights groups argue that any and all animal research should be discontinued, unless it directly benefits the animals. These groups contend that computer modeling can give us much of the knowledge sought in animal studies and eliminates the need for research with animals. In addition, current brain imaging techniques, which allow researchers to view images of the living human brain, reduce the need to sacrifice animals to examine their brain structures.

As is true of all ethical issues, complex and legitimate opposing needs must be balanced in research. The need to know, understand, and treat illness must be balanced against the needs, well-being, and rights of participants and animals. Consequently, the debate and discussion about ethical treatment of humans and animals must be ongoing and evolving.

Quick Quiz 6: Research Ethics

1. When conducting research with humans, researchers
   a. never have to obtain informed consent if it interferes with the research.
   b. almost always must obtain informed consent.
   c. always must obtain informed consent.
   d. used to be required to obtain informed consent, but this requirement has been discontinued.

2. Current guidelines on research ethics state that, when studying humans, deception
   a. must be avoided whenever possible.
   b. can be used only if it's part of the research design.
   c. must be followed by debriefing.

   d. must be fully justified.
   e. all of the above.

3. Ethical guidelines for research with nonhuman animals state that
   a. informed consent is always required.
   b. ethical and humane conditions must exist throughout the research process.
   c. computer modeling must always be tried before research with animals.
   d. deception can be used if fully justified.

Answers can be found at the end of the chapter.

Bringing It All Together

Making Connections in Psychological Research

How Is Technology Changing How We Think, Feel, and Behave?

Technology in general—wearable devices, laptops, desktops, and tablets—is transforming how we learn, think, remember, interact, and behave. More specifically, social media such as Instagram, Facebook, YouTube, and Twitter keep us constantly connected to family, friends, and others. Together, these technologies are changing how we think, feel, and behave, and therefore make a perfect topic to bring together all the major ideas discussed in the chapter—the nature of science, research methods, and research ethics.

Descriptive Research Designs

Descriptive research aims to simply observe and describe behavior and historically, this research has involved watching people behave in a real world setting. The "real world," however, is becoming increasingly the online world. Park and colleagues (2016) for example analyzed the language use of more than 65,000 Facebook volunteers. Park and colleagues found that when updating their status

on Facebook, women were more likely to use friendlier, warmer, and more socially oriented language compared to men. For example, women more often than men used words such as "wonderful," "happy," "excited," "baby," "daughter," and "thankful." Men, by contrast, were more likely to use words about sex, work, money, politics, video games, or sports, such as "freedom," "government," "win," "lose," "xbox," or "enemy." Men were also more likely to use crude, sexual language than women. In short, women were more likely to discuss social topics and men more likely to discuss activities or things.

Correlational Research Designs

Correlational research makes predictions about whether or not two or more variables are related to each other. Karpinski and colleagues (2012) addressed the question of the relationship between social network site (SNS) use per day and academic performance and whether multitasking disrupts or facilitates studying.

The sample consisted of 590 undergraduate students and 285 graduate students in the United States and Europe. They found a negative relationship between social network site use and multitasking and GPA—meaning the more overall time spent on SNS and the more multitasking spent per day was associated with lower GPAs. Unsurprisingly, they also found that studying more is associated with higher GPAs.

Studies sometimes combine research strategies. For example, Rosen et al. (2012) combined observational and correlational strategies in a study on Facebook use and academic performance. Researchers went to the homes of more than 250 middle school, high school, and college students and observed whether and how much students used social media while studying. Researchers also collected more general data via questionnaire on social media use and academic performance (GPA). On average, students lasted no more than 6 minutes on studying before switching to social media, and those who went to social media most had the lowest GPAs. Like Karpinski and colleagues, the main finding from this study was that staying on task (not multitasking) and not accessing FB while studying was correlated with a higher GPA.

Experimental Research Designs

From a scientific perspective, the study of distraction and cell phone use lends itself easily to the experimental method, because cell phone use can be easily manipulated as the independent variable. Probably the oldest and most established research on the effects of technology on behavior focus on how cell phone use affects driving. In general, the results are clear: Using any kind of device, including hands-free, has costs in terms of attention and reaction times while driving (Delgado, Wanner, & McDonald, 2016; Engelberg, Hill, Rybar, & Styer, 2015; McDonald & Sommers, 2015). Moreover, using a cell phone while driving decreases awareness that one's driving is impaired (Sanbonmatsu, Strayer, Biondi, Behrends, & Moore, 2015).

Using an experimental design, Papadakaki and colleagues (2016) had 50 professional (taxi) drivers go through a driver simulator under four different conditions: control (drive only), talking on cell phone, reading a text, and answering a text. Outcome measures were how much their steering deviated from a center line, how much they changed their speed, and whether they were able to maintain a 3-second distance behind a car. The researchers found that reading and sending a text impaired steering, ability to maintain a constant speed, and following distance. Speaking on the phone diminished the driver's ability to maintain a constant speed and steering. Other similar experimental research has reported that driving while talking on a hands-free phone is as dangerous as driving with a blood alcohol content (BAC) level of 0.08, the legally drunk level in all 50 U.S. states (Strayer, Drews, & Couch, 2006).

©Hero Images/Getty Images RF

Social network site (SNS) use while studying disrupts and interferes with the learning process. Students who do this regularly tend to have lower grades.

 How much time do you spend on social networks while studying?

Ethics in Studying Technology and Behavior

Big Data in particular raises questions about ethics, given that people often do not even know their data are being collated and analyzed by researchers. For instance, in 2014 psychological researchers at a U.S. university collaborated with a Facebook data analyst and tested the hypothesis that positive Facebook feeds about friends' lives actually lowers the recipients' mood—that is, that moods can be contagious (Kramer, Guillory, & Hancock, 2014). On close to 700,000 Facebook users the researchers manipulated their likelihood of receiving positive and negative feeds (based on the kind of words in the post). Different users had positive or negative mood posts decreased or increased. The researchers found that when positive mood posts were increased, people tended to post fewer positive mood posts. Likewise, a decrease in negative mood posts led to an increase in positive mood posts.

The problem is not with the study in itself but the fact that researchers at a university bypassed informed consent and went by Facebook data use policy that did not explicitly stipulate that Facebook data can be used for research purposes. Private companies like Facebook can and do use data without users' knowledge for commercial purposes. But university researchers have a different standard that requires "informed consent" and approval by the university's "Institutional Review Board"—neither of which happened in this study. Although the researchers were technically correct and were collaborating with a data scientist at Facebook, there was a public outcry over the study's borderline ethical violations. Four months after the study was conducted, Facebook changed its data use policy to include the word "research." People now have an opt-out policy for research on their Facebook data use policy.

Chapter Review

THE NATURE OF SCIENCE

- Science is about empirically testing our ideas and learning whether our understanding of the world is correct.

- The key attitudes of science are skepticism, openness to new ideas based on evidence, and intellectual honesty.

- The scientific method by which research is conducted can be summed up by OPTIC: Observing, Predicting, Testing, Interpreting, and Communicating. Scientists start with observations of the world, make predictions once they see a pattern, devise a study to test predictions, interpret results with the aid of statistics and decide whether the prediction was correct, and publish their work to clearly describe findings to others. These new findings lead to new predictions, and the whole process begins anew.

- Pseudoscience lacks cumulative progress, disregards empirical facts, lacks skepticism of its own assumptions,

©Jane Underwood/My.Third.Eye Photography/Moment Select/Getty Images

and vaguely describes how it came to its conclusions, which often stem from loose and distorted logic.

- In experimental designs, researchers randomly assign participants to conditions and carefully manipulate the predicted cause (independent variable), then look for differences in outcome (dependent variables). True experiments address the question "Does X cause Y?"

RESEARCH DESIGNS IN PSYCHOLOGY

- Psychologists use three types of research designs to test their ideas: descriptive designs, correlational designs, and experimental designs.

- In descriptive designs, researchers simply observe and describe what they see. They address the question "What is X?" They don't manipulate anything or have any predictions to test.

- In correlational designs, researchers measure two or more things carefully to see whether or not they are related. They address the question "Is X related to Y?" These designs use correlational statistics to interpret the results and to make and test hypotheses, but they do not allow researchers to draw any conclusions about causality.

- Researchers use correlation coefficients to assess the strength and direction of association between two variables.

- In experimental designs, researchers randomly assign participants to conditions and carefully manipulate the predicted cause (independent variable), then look for differences in outcome (dependent variables). True experiments address the question "Does X cause Y?"

- Meta-analysis is a quantitative method for combining the results of all the published and even unpublished results on one question and drawing a conclusion based on the entire set of studies on the topic.

- Big Data consists of the extremely vast amounts of information from websites and apps that is collected and analyzed by unusually large and sophisticated computer programs.

CHALLENGING ASSUMPTIONS IN THE OBJECTIVITY OF EXPERIMENTAL RESEARCH

- Researchers can unintentionally affect the outcome of results if they are aware of the study's hypotheses.

- In order to lessen these effects, double-blind procedures, in which both the participant and the experimenter are blind to the study's hypotheses, need to be implemented.

COMMONLY USED MEASURES OF PSYCHOLOGICAL RESEARCH

- Psychological researchers draw on several types of tools to measure variables relevant to their research questions. These measures fall into three major categories: self-report, behavioral, and physiological.

- Self-reports are people's written or oral accounts of their thoughts, feelings, or actions.

- Behavioral measurements involve systematic observation of people's actions in either their normal life situations (naturalistic observation) or laboratory situations.

- Physiological measures include various types of measures of bodily responses. Each measure has strengths and weaknesses. By employing multiple measures, researchers offset the limitations of any given measure.

MAKING SENSE OF DATA WITH STATISTICS

- Descriptive statistics organize data for interpretation and help researchers evaluate their hypotheses. The mean is the arithmetic average of a set of data. The median is the score that separates the lower half of scores from the upper half.

- Variability is the spread between the lowest and highest values in a set of data; it is measured in terms of the standard deviation around the mean.

- Inferential statistics go beyond describing data and allow researchers to test hypotheses and rule out chance as an explanation for the findings.

RESEARCH ETHICS

- Ethics are standards of right and wrong that guide people's behavior.

- Professional ethics have been developed to protect the rights of humans and animals that participate in psychological research. Researchers must obtain informed consent from human participants before a study begins. Animals cannot provide informed consent, but strict ethical guidelines ensure humane living conditions and treatment.

BRINGING IT ALL TOGETHER: MAKING CONNECTIONS IN PSYCHOLOGICAL RESEARCH

- Research on how technology affects thought, feelings, and behavior is becoming more and more common in psychology. For example, studies using descriptive, correlational, and experimental methods have examined how multitasking while studying or driving leads to lower academic performance or impairs reaction time and steering ability while driving.

Key Terms

behavioral measures
big data
case study
confounding variable
control group
correlational designs
correlation coefficients
debriefing
demand characteristics
dependent variable
descriptive designs
descriptive statistics
double-blind studies
effect size
ethics
experiment
experimental group
experimenter expectancy
    effects
fabrication
falsification
fraternal twins
frequency

gene-by-environment interaction
    research
hypothesis
identical twins
independent variable
inferential statistics
institutional review boards
    (IRBs)
interviews
longitudinal designs
mean
measures
median
meta-analysis
mode
naturalistic observation
normal distribution
physiological measures
placebo
plagiarism
population
pseudoscience
qualitative research

quantitative research
quasi-experimental design
random assignment
rationalism
reliability
replication
representative sample
research designs
samples
sampling
scientific method
scientific thinking
self-fulfilling prophecy
self-reports
single-blind studies
social desirability bias
standard deviation
statistics
t-test
theory
twin-adoption studies
validity
variable

Quick Quiz Answers

Quick Quiz 1: 1.d; 2.b; 3.a; 4.c   **Quick Quiz 2:** 1.a; 2.b; 3.d; 4.c; 5.b   **Quick Quiz 3:** 1.b.; 2.b   **Quick Quiz 4:** 1.b; 2.a; 3.d
Quick Quiz 5: 1.d; 2.a; 3.a   **Quick Quiz 6:** 1.c; 2.e; 3.b

3 The Biology of Behavior

Chapter Outline

Challenge Your Assumptions

True or False?

- Genetically influenced traits are set and unchanging after conception. (see page 80)

- Neanderthals had larger brains than we (*H. sapiens*) do. (see page 94)

- Only long-term learning increases the number and structure of neurons in your brain. (see page 98)

- In people who are blind, areas of the brain involved in vision do not function. (see page 106)

- Only infants and children are capable of forming new neurons. (see page 108)

©Gage/Getty Images

See the painting in Figure 1. It is pleasing, colorful, and nicely done. It features realistic color, perspective, and shadowing. It seems, perhaps, not extraordinary—except by virtue of its maker. He cannot see at all.

Born blind to an impoverished family in Turkey, Esref Armagan started drawing at a young age; later he began painting with oils and acrylics. Armagan has been actively painting for over 35 years. His work strikes us not only for its beauty but also for how it depicts objects in a way that a sighted person would see them. How can someone who has never seen anything in his life create beautiful paintings that depict realistic images? It seems as if his brain is doing something that his eyes cannot.

You can experience how this is possible at the Tactile Dome, part of the Exploratorium in San Francisco. Once there, you enter a room full of common, recognizable objects, such as a cheese grater, an egg carton, and a sieve. You look at them and feel them.

Then you proceed through a pitch-black tunnel. As you find your way through it by touch, you feel the common objects you saw earlier. When you reach the end, you are prompted to think back and remember your way through the tunnel. Surprisingly, the memory of what you encountered along the path in the dark with your hands is visual! Your brain has taken a tactile experience and unwittingly converted it into a visual memory. How?

The Tactile Dome and the skills of Esref Armagan both suggest that our experience of the world is not a direct representation of what is out there. The brain can change our experiences—give us visual memories for tactile experiences. The brain is both fixed and flexible in how it acts. While most of us use the rear portion of our brains to process visual information, Esref Armagan uses that area when he paints by the feel of his hands.

FIGURE 1

PAINTING BY ESREF ARMAGAN, A BLIND PAINTER. Besides being beautiful to look at, Armagan's vivid, realistic paintings and drawings challenge conventional thinking about the brain and its ability to adapt and overcome limitations imposed on it.

©Images & Stories/Alamy

 Can you think of how Armagan is able to paint with color, shadow, and perspective, even though he has never seen any of these?

In this chapter and the next, we will explore what is known about how the brain works, supports behavior, and is transformed by experience. Our main task in this chapter is to introduce the biological systems that are most relevant to a basic understanding of psychology. We will explore the workings of the nervous system, the relationship between behavior and chemicals called hormones, and the role of heredity and evolution in shaping the brain and behavior. Throughout this chapter we will highlight the ways that biological and environmental forces constantly interact and influence who we are, what we do, and how we feel. We will also see how biological systems involved in thought and behavior—genes, brain structures, brain cells, and so on—are open to ongoing modification from the environment (LaFreniere & MacDonald, 2013; Ottersen, 2010).

GENES AND BEHAVIOR

We seldom have trouble accepting the idea that heredity is responsible for outward family resemblances, such as the shape of the nose and face, height, and the color of hair and skin. But when it comes to behavior, many of us are uncomfortable with the idea that heredity might strongly influence what we think and do. Research has revealed that heredity strongly shapes our behavior and experience, although it does not operate in a simple, deterministic way.

Before we can explore how our hereditary material and behavior are linked, we must first determine the structures and mechanisms involved in heredity. Your genetic material is composed mainly of **DNA (deoxyribonucleic acid)** and is passed down in the form of chromosomes from both your mother and your father. A **chromosome** is a very long thread of DNA wrapped around proteins to hold it all together. You inherit 23 chromosomes from one parent and 23 chromosomes from the other parent such that you end up with 23 *pairs* of chromosomes (46 individual chromosomes) in every cell of your body. Together, the total amount of your unique DNA is referred to as your **genome**. Each person's unique and incomparable genome is called his or her **genotype**.

In our genome we carry our entire ancestral history (Pickrell & Reich, 2014; Tucci & Akey, 2016). Recently companies have developed the technology to commercially analyze anyone's genome and tell them which geographical regions of world their ancestors came from. For instance, a report might show that someone has an ancestry makeup that is 29% Asian Native American, 22% European, and 3% sub-Saharan African, when in fact, all the person ever knew about was her Asian Native American ancestry. Our genetic makeup is more complex than we often believe, and is yet another example of the interaction between nature (genes) and nurture (geography and place).

But our unique genotype that each of us is born with is not the end point but the starting point of gene expression. What form a gene takes and how it gets expressed in observable characteristics is known as the **phenotype**. As we see at the end of this section, there are many ways in which our genes get turned on or off from our experience, many after the genome is established.

Within your genome, some information that codes for the production of proteins. That is what **genes** do—they are the segments of DNA that code for protein synthesis, and are therefore the functional segment of DNA. In fact, the vast majority of DNA (98%) is not genetic because it does not code for proteins (Zimmer, 2015). It's not "junk" as some biologists used to say because it does other things, but it does not code for proteins. The proteins that are coded from genes in turn make up most chemicals and structures in the body (see Figure 2). As a result, genes have a profound control over physical characteristics, such as height or hair color, by directing the synthesis of proteins. In addition, there are genes that code for proteins responsible for making up your brain and the chemicals it needs to make you feel happy or sad. Thus, genes play an important role in shaping how you think and feel.

Most traits, such as height, weight, intelligence, and personality, are the result of many dozens or even hundreds of genes and these are known as **polygenic** traits. Any characteristic that cannot be placed in a small number of categories and ranges from a little to a lot is polygenic (Clark & Grunstein, 2000; Plomin, DeFries, Knopik, & Neiderhiser, 2013). All psychological and almost all physical traits in humans are polygenic (Ebstein, 2006; Plomin et al., 2013). By contrast, traits that have a one-to-one connection to a gene are known as **monogenic** traits. Humans have very few traits that result from a single gene.

Lactose tolerance/intolerance is one of the few examples of a monogenic trait in humans. Everyone can metabolize lactose (digest milk) as an infant,

DNA (deoxyribonucleic acid)
A large molecule that contains genes.

chromosome
A coiled-up thread of DNA.

genome
All the genetic information in DNA.

genotype
The entire genetic makeup of an organism.

phenotype
An organism's observed characteristics.

genes
Small segments of DNA that contain information for producing proteins.

polygenic
The process by which many genes interact to create a single characteristic.

monogenic
The hereditary passing on of traits determined by a single gene.

FIGURE 2

DNA, CHROMOSOMES, AND THE HUMAN CELL. Every cell in the human body contains the same genetic material distributed in 23 pairs of chromosomes.

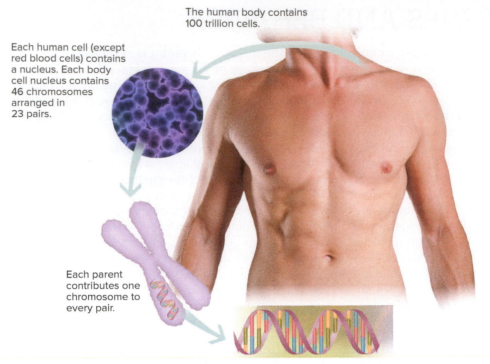

The human body contains 100 trillion cells.

Each human cell (except red blood cells) contains a nucleus. Each body cell nucleus contains 46 chromosomes arranged in 23 pairs.

Each parent contributes one chromosome to every pair.

Each chromosome contains numerous genes, segments of DNA that contain instructions to make proteins—the building blocks of life.

(cells): ©phil morley/Getty Images RF; (torso): ©Juice Images/Alamy RF

mutation
A random change in genetic sequence.

alleles
Different forms of a gene.

dominant alleles
Alleles that show their effect even if there is only one allele for that trait in the pair.

recessive alleles
Alleles that show their effects only when both alleles are the same.

©2005 Kathy Hutchins/Hutchins Ph/Newscom

Actors (and siblings) Maggie and Jake Gyllenhaal inherited their blue eyes from their parents. Blue eyes are a recessive trait, which means that each parent must possess at least one allele for blue eyes.

but most people lose this ability with age, because the activity of lactase (the protein that breaks down lactose) decreases. Some humans, however, have a change, or **mutation**, in their genetic sequence that allows lactase activity to persist into adulthood, so they can eat and drink dairy products without getting an upset stomach. This means that some people have one form of the gene, which allows lactase persistence (they are lactose tolerant), and some people have another form, which results in lactase nonpersistence (they are lactose intolerant). These different forms of a gene are known as **alleles** (Clark & Grunstein, 2000; Starr & Taggart, 2004), one of which you inherit from your mother and the other from your father.

If you receive alleles for lactose tolerance from both your mother and your father, then you will digest dairy products easily into adulthood.

However, what happens if you inherit one lactose tolerant gene and one lactose intolerant gene from your parents? The lactase persistent or tolerant allele is dominant over the intolerant one. **Dominant alleles** show their effect even if there is only one copy of that allele in the pair. So if you have one of each kind of allele (tolerant and intolerant) chances are you will still be able to digest some dairy products. Alternatively, **recessive alleles** show their effects only when both alleles are the same. Consequently, a person will be lactose intolerant only if he or she receives a lactase persistent allele from each parent.

Principles of Behavioral Genetics

To understand how heredity affects behavior, psychologists turn to the science of **behavioral genetics** (Fuller & Thompson, 1960; Plomin et al., 2013). There are three principles of behavioral genetics that are especially relevant to psychology:

1. The relationship between specific genes and behavior is complex, usually with many genes involved in each trait.
2. By studying twins and adoptees, as well as genetic markers, behavioral geneticists may disentangle the contributions of heredity (nature) and environment (nurture) that influence behavior.
3. The environment influences how and when genes affect behavior.

The Connection between Genes and Behavior Is Complex   The connection between genes and behavior is complex. To understand how genes influence behavior, we must abandon the notion of simple causation (Rutter, 2006). Genes seldom make behaviors a certainty. For example, no single gene causes anxiety. Both genetic and environmental factors make anxiety more likely to trouble some people than others.

In a few cases, having a specific gene guarantees an outcome—such as the incurable neuromuscular disease called Huntington's—but these outcomes are primarily physical, not behavioral. Typically, a specific gene plays only a small part in creating a given behavior, which is precisely what happens in polygenic traits. For example, there is wide variation in intelligence because numerous genes contribute to it. Other examples of polygenic traits are skin color, mental disorders, personality traits (such as whether a person is likely to be adventurous), height, and weight (Clark & Grunstein, 2000; Ebstein, 2006; Evans et al., 2007). Environmental events such as smoking during pregnancy, early childhood experiences, stress or trauma, and enriched environments all interact with genes to make specific behaviors more or less likely.

The Relative Effects of Genes and Environment Can Be Teased Apart   The extent to which a characteristic is influenced by genetics is known as **heritability**. The second principle of behavioral genetics is that teasing apart and identifying genetic and environmental influences on behavior can be done but requires special techniques. Recall from the chapter "Conducting Research in Psychology" that researchers use two different research methods to study the relative effects of nature and nurture (heritability), namely twin-adoption studies and gene-by-environment studies.

Twin-adoption studies take advantage of the fact that genetic similarity ranges from 0% (strangers) to 100% (identical twins) and environmental similarity ranges from a little (different families) to a lot (same families). Genetic influence or heritability is strongest when twins—who have high genetic similarity—are still very much alike on traits even when they are raised by different families. Environmental influence is strongest when adopted siblings—who have no genetic similarity—are still very much alike on traits when they are raised by the same family.

Gene-by-environment studies do not use twins but rather examine whether genes that vary in people are correlated with particular trait. An example of this kind of research is seen from the findings that people with certain genetic markers are more likely to be depressed, anxious, or hyperactive than people without those markers (Moffitt, Caspi, & Rutter, 2005; Thapar, Langley, & Asherson, 2007).

The Environment Can Change Gene Expression: Epigenetics   The third—and, in many ways, the most important—principle of behavioral genetics is a relatively new one, epigenetics. **Epigenetics** is the study of changes in the way genes are expressed—that is, are activated (turned "on") or deactivated

---

behavioral genetics
The scientific study of the role of heredity in behavior.

Connection

Genetic influence accounts for about 50% of the differences in performance on intelligence tests, leaving about the same amount to be explained by nongenetic influences.

See "The Nature and Nurture of Human Intelligence," in the chapter "Intelligence, Problem Solving, and Creativity," p. 383

heritability
The extent to which a characteristic is influenced by genetics.

epigenetics
The study of changes in the way genes are turned on or off without a change in the sequence of DNA.

©Sam Edwards/Glow Images RF

The field of study known as epigenetics examines how experience can turn genes on or off.

 What implications does this have for what we eat, drink, and are exposed to?

(turned "off")—without changing the sequence of DNA (Meaney, 2010; Plomin et al., 2013). Some substances that we eat, drink, or get exposed to result in molecules attaching to certain base pairs of genes. By doing so these tags turn off or on the gene expression process. Put differently, epigenetics involves heritable changes to DNA that are independent of the genetic sequence yet influence its expression. This means that experience (nurture) shapes our nature.

The food we eat, the drugs we take, and our exposure to certain chemicals in the environment, among other things, can have epigenetic consequences. Contrary to what many people think, genes are not destiny. They are simply the starting point for biological structures. Many things—including experience—can turn genes on or off. Epigenetic effects have been demonstrated in a host of psychological traits—including attention deficit hyperactivity disorder (ADHD), aggression, dementia, obesity, and anxiety, just to name a few (Curley et al., 2011; Cropley et al., 2016; Mill & Petronis, 2008; Sweatt, 2010).

What is even more amazing is that these environmentally produced tags can be inherited—passed on from parent to offspring. In other words, genetics is not the only way inheritance works. It also works via epigenetics (Meaney, 2010; Zimmer-Gembeck & Collins, 2008). An activated gene in your grandparent that gets turned off environmentally in one of your parents can be inherited by you as a deactivated gene. This secondary form of inheritance via epigenetics is sometimes referred to as *soft inheritance* to contrast it with traditional genetically based inheritance (Graff & Mansury, 2008). The term soft inheritance is another example of how nature and nurture work side-by-side.

Epigenetics offers one explanation for why identical twins—whose genomes are 100% alike—end up being not completely identical on numerous traits. For instance, they do not have identical fingerprints and sometimes not even the same gender identity (see the chapter "Human Development"). Recent longitudinal research shows that differences in epigenetic tags in identical twins already exist in early to middle childhood and that these differences can be related to personality differences in twins (Kaminsky et al., 2008; Wong et al., 2010). In short, although identical twins share 100% of their genotype, their phenotype—or their observed characteristics—may be subtly (even strikingly) different because different epigenetic tags are turning different genes on or off. Genes are not destiny.

Quick Quiz 1: Genes and Behavior

1. Genes occur in pairs, or alternate forms of each other, called
   a. chromosomes.
   b. alleles.
   c. base pairs.
   d. ribosomes.

2. Why are twin-adoption studies powerful ways to untangle the effects of genes and the environment on thought and behavior?
   a. They allow both genetic and environmental similarity to be compared and contrasted.
   b. Twins share genes.

   c. They allow for understanding epigenetic influences.
   d. They allow researchers to experimentally manipulate genetic and environmental similarity.

3. Nurturing behavior in rats can produce calmer, less stressed offspring because genes that are involved in stress reactions are turned off. This is an example of
   a. epigenetics.
   b. genetic engineering.
   c. recessive genes.
   d. dominant genes.

Answers can be found at the end of the chapter.

THE NERVOUS SYSTEM

The human genome contains an estimated up to 30,000 genes (National Human Genome Research Institute, 2010). At least half of these genes code for proteins in the brain, where they play a central role in seeing, hearing, thinking, memory, learning, movement, and all other behavior. The brain mediates all of our experiences and orchestrates our responses to those experiences.

The nervous system controls all the actions and automatic processes of the body. Ultimately, everything we experience and do results from the activity of nerve cells, which are organized in a net of circuits far more complex than any electrical system you could imagine.

Organization of the Nervous System

The human nervous system has two main parts and several components, as depicted in Figure 3. It is divided into the **central nervous system (CNS)**, which includes the brain and spinal cord, and the **peripheral nervous system**, which consists of all the other nerve cells in the body. The peripheral nervous system includes the somatic nervous system and the autonomic nervous system. The **somatic nervous system** serves the skeletal muscles of the body: It sends messages out to the skeletal muscles from the CNS and transmits sensory information back to the CNS from the skeletal muscles. The **autonomic nervous system (ANS)** serves the involuntary systems of the body, such as the internal organs and glands.

Autonomic means "self-governing," and to a large extent the structures served by the autonomic nervous system control bodily processes over which we have little conscious control, such as changes in heart rate and blood pressure. The ANS has two main branches: the **sympathetic nervous system** and the

central nervous system (CNS)
The part of the nervous system that comprises the brain and spinal cord.

peripheral nervous system
The part of the nervous system that comprises all the nerve cells in the body outside the central nervous system.

somatic nervous system
Nerve cells of the peripheral nervous system that serve the skeletal muscles. Somatic nerves transmit from the central nervous system (CNS) to the skeletal muscles and sensory information from the skeletal muscles back to the CNS.

autonomic nervous system (ANS)
All the nerves of the peripheral nervous system that serve involuntary systems of the body, such as the internal organs and glands.

sympathetic nervous system
The branch of the autonomic nervous system that activates bodily systems in times of emergency.

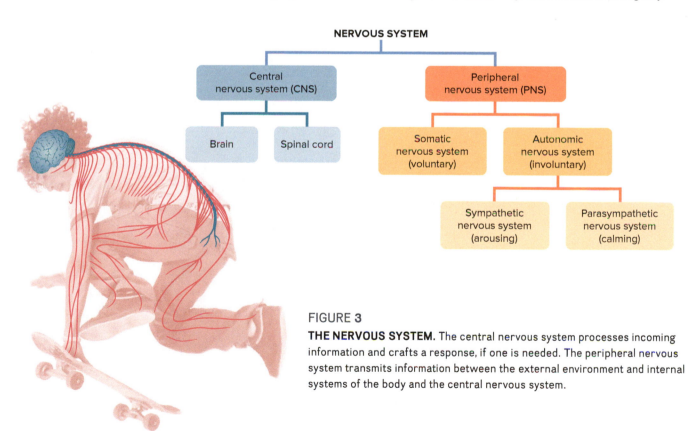

FIGURE **3**

THE NERVOUS SYSTEM. The central nervous system processes incoming information and crafts a response, if one is needed. The peripheral nervous system transmits information between the external environment and internal systems of the body and the central nervous system.

parasympathetic nervous system. The nerves of both of these systems control muscles in organs such as the stomach, small intestine, and bladder and in glands such as the sweat glands. The sympathetic nervous system activates bodily systems in times of emergency by increasing the heart rate, dilating the pupils of the eyes, or inhibiting digestion. It is responsible for what the physiologist Walter Cannon (1939) labeled the *fight-or-flight response*. The function of the parasympathetic nervous system is largely one of relaxation, returning the body to a less active, restful state. All of the systems that are aroused by the sympathetic nervous system are relaxed by the parasympathetic nervous system (see Figure 4).

FIGURE **4**
THE SYMPATHETIC AND PARASYMPATHETIC NERVOUS SYSTEMS. The sympathetic nervous system prepares the body for action, whereas the parasympathetic nervous system returns it to a relaxed and resting state.

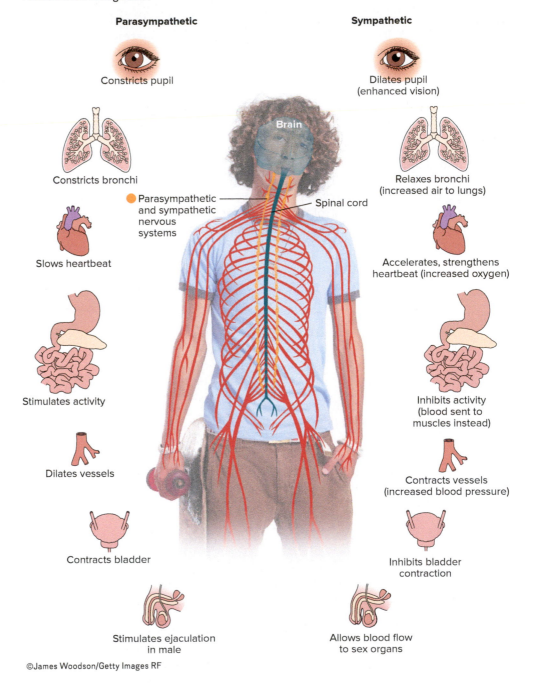

Parasympathetic

Sympathetic

Constricts pupil — Dilates pupil (enhanced vision)

Constricts bronchi — Relaxes bronchi (increased air to lungs)

Parasympathetic and sympathetic nervous systems — Spinal cord

Slows heartbeat — Accelerates, strengthens heartbeat (increased oxygen)

Stimulates activity — Inhibits activity (blood sent to muscles instead)

Dilates vessels — Contracts vessels (increased blood pressure)

Contracts bladder — Inhibits bladder contraction

Stimulates ejaculation in male — Allows blood flow to sex organs

Brain

©James Woodson/Getty Images RF

Because of its effects on these various bodily systems, the ANS produces many of the physical sensations we experience during emotional arousal, such as a racing heart or sweaty palms.

The Cells of the Nervous System: Glial Cells and Neurons

Without a nervous system, we would have no sensory experiences—no seeing, hearing, touching, tasting, smelling, or feeling. We would also have no thoughts, memories, or emotions. Everything we sense or do is accomplished by means of nerve cells.

The central nervous system is made up of two types of cells: glial cells and neurons. *Glia* is the Greek word for "glue." Indeed **glial cells** serve the primary function of holding the CNS together. For years their primary functions were thought to be structural support for the CNS and the removal of cellular debris (Kandel, 2000b). We now know that glial cells also play an important role in communication between neurons, produce the material that insulates neurons (myelin), aid cell metabolism, help form the blood–brain barrier, play a key role in the control of breathing, regulate neuronal transmission, and may play an important role in neural regeneration repair after brain injury (Ballanyi, Panaitescu, & Ruangkittisakul, 2010; Benner et al., 2013; Charsar, Urban, & Lepore, 2016; Eroglu & Barres, 2010; Li & Chen, 2016; Verkhratsky, Rodríguez, & Parpura, 2012). Glial cell abnormalities may also play a role in the development of schizophrenia (Bernstein et al., 2015).

Neurons are the cells that process and transmit information throughout the nervous system. Within the brain, neurons receive, integrate, and generate messages. By most estimates, there are more than 10 billion neurons in the human brain. Each neuron has approximately 10,000 connections to other neurons, making for trillions of neural connections in the human brain (Hyman, 2005; Nauta & Feirtag, 1979). Thus, it is understandable why some scientists consider the human brain to be one of the most complex structures in the known universe. Over the last 125 years, three major principles of neuroscience have emerged concerning the neuron and how it communicates with other neurons (Kandel, 2006):

1. Neurons are the building blocks of the nervous system. All the major structures of the brain are composed of neurons.

2. Information travels within a neuron in the form of an electrical signal by action potentials.

3. Information is transmitted between neurons by means of chemicals called **neurotransmitters**.

Let's explore each of these principles to better understand the mechanisms of brain function and behavior.

The Structure and Types of Neurons   Whereas most cells in the body have a round shape, neurons are spidery, with long branches and projections. Neurons are so small that they cannot be seen with the naked eye; only a strong microscope can magnify them enough to be viewed and described. In the late 1800s, the Spanish anatomist Santiago Ramón y Cajal deciphered the precise nature and structure of nerve cells, which he named neurons. It was Ramón y Cajal who identified the three major parts of the neuron: cell body, dendrites, and axon.

As in other cells, the cell body, or **soma**, of the neuron contains a *nucleus* and other components needed for cell maintenance and function (see Figure 5). The genes that direct neural change and growth lie within the nucleus itself. Extending from one side of the soma is a long projection called an **axon**, which transmits electrical impulses toward the adjacent neuron. On the other side of the soma are **dendrites**, fingerlike projections that receive incoming messages from other neurons.

glial cells
Central nervous system cells that provide structural support, promote efficient communication between neurons, and serve as scavengers, removing cellular debris.

neurons
The cells that process and transmit information in the nervous system.

neurotransmitters
Chemicals that transmit information between neurons.

soma
The cell body of the neuron.

axon
A long projection that extends from a neuron's soma; it transmits electrical impulses toward the adjacent neuron and stimulates the release of neurotransmitters.

dendrites
Fingerlike projections from a neuron's soma that receive incoming messages from other neurons.

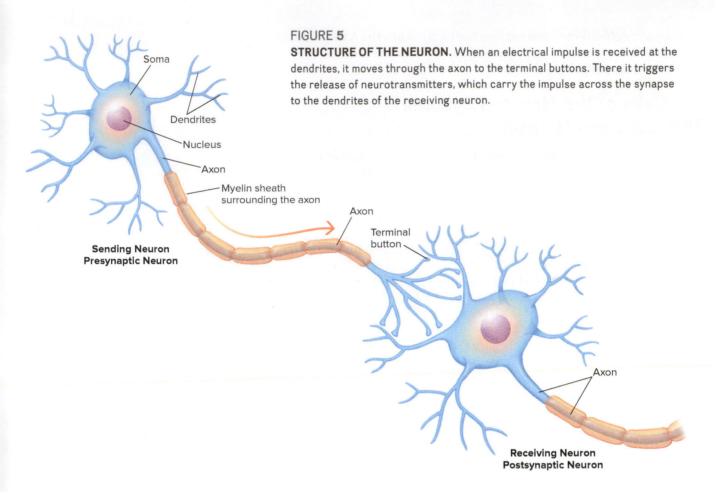

FIGURE 5

STRUCTURE OF THE NEURON. When an electrical impulse is received at the dendrites, it moves through the axon to the terminal buttons. There it triggers the release of neurotransmitters, which carry the impulse across the synapse to the dendrites of the receiving neuron.

Soma

Dendrites

Nucleus

Axon

Myelin sheath surrounding the axon

Sending Neuron Presynaptic Neuron

Axon

Terminal button

Axon

Receiving Neuron Postsynaptic Neuron

myelin sheath
The fatty substance wrapped around some axons, which insulates the axon, making the nerve impulse travel more efficiently.

synapse
The junction between an axon and the adjacent neuron, where information is transmitted from one neuron to another.

terminal button
A little knob at the end of the axon that contains tiny sacs of neurotransmitters.

sensory neurons
Nerve cells that receive incoming sensory information from the sense organs (eye, ear, skin, tongue, nose).

motor neurons
Nerve cells that carry commands for movement from the brain to the muscles of the body.

mirror neurons
Nerve cells that are active when we observe others performing an action as well as when we are performing the same action.

The axons of some neurons are wrapped in a fatty **myelin sheath**. Just like rubber around an electrical wire, the myelin sheath insulates the axon, so that the impulse travels more efficiently, strengthening the connection to adjacent neurons. The process of *myelination* is a gradual one that starts before birth, is facilitated in breast-fed babies, and continues into early adulthood (Deoni et al., 2013; Fields, 2008). The glial cells are responsible for creating the myelin that insulates axons throughout the nervous system (Simons & Nave, 2016). The junction between the axon and the adjacent neuron is known as the **synapse**. At the end of the axon, at each synapse, is a **terminal button** containing tiny sacs of neurotransmitters. When an electrical impulse reaches the terminal button, it triggers the release of neurotransmitter molecules into the gap between neurons, known as the *synaptic cleft*. The neurotransmitter carries the signal across the synaptic cleft to the next neuron.

There are three kinds of neurons: sensory neurons, motor neurons, and interneurons. **Sensory neurons** receive incoming sensory information from the sense organs (eyes, ears, skin, tongue, and nose). Any sensation you receive—anything you see, hear, touch, taste, or smell—activates sensory neurons, which take the message to the brain for processing.

Motor neurons take commands from the brain and carry them to the muscles of the body. Each time you move any muscle in your body, intentionally or not, motor neurons are at work. Researchers have identified motor neurons that are active when monkeys observe others performing an action, as well as when the monkeys undertake the same action (Rizzolatti et al., 1996). Neurons that behave this way, called **mirror neurons**, appear to play an important role in learning by observation (Lametti & Watkins, 2016).

The most definitive work on mirror neurons has been conducted on monkeys because it has been possible to record directly from single neurons deep in their brains. So far, this has not been done with humans, but there is indirect evidence

©John Lund/Blend Images LLC RF

Sensory and motor neurons working in concert with the brain make this sprinter's elegant strides possible.

of systems of neurons acting as mirrors in humans (Debes, 2010). One piece of evidence is from studies that measure brain activity while people engage in various tasks that involve imitation or observation. Such evidence suggests that human mirror neuron systems are activated when we process social cues from others (Coudé et al., 2016; Mainieri et al., 2013). Certain patterns of electrical activity measured from the cerebral cortex may be a sign of human mirror neuron system, though this remains a matter of debate in neuroscience (Hobson & Bishop, 2016). The discovery of mirror neurons has changed the way we make sense of a wide range of human experiences, including how we interpret the emotions of and feel empathy toward others.

Interneurons communicate only with other neurons. Most interneurons connect neurons in one part of the brain with neurons in another part. Others receive information from sensory neurons and transmit it to motor neurons for action. If you touched a sharp object, interneurons in your spinal cord would receive pain information from sensory neurons in your fingers and communicate it to motor neurons in the muscles of your arm, so that you could pull away. Interneurons are the most common kind of neuron in the brain, outnumbering sensory and motor neurons by at least 10 to 1 (Nauta & Feirtag, 1979). They play a crucial role in the inhibition of impulses between one brain region and another (Crandall & Connors, 2016). Dysfunction in these important inhibitory circuits has been implicated in disorders associated with overexcitation in the brain, such as epilepsy and schizophrenia (Marin, 2012) and may play a role in the memory deficits of Alzheimer's disease (Schmid et al., 2016).

Neural Communication   Neural communication is a two-step process: action potential and neurotransmission.

The Action Potential   The **action potential**, an electrical and chemical process, is the positively charged impulse that moves one way down an axon.

Connection

Mirror neurons support learning by imitation as well as empathy.

See "The Developing Infant and Child," in the chapter "Human Development," p. 171; "Imitation, Mirror Neurons, and Learning," in the chapter "Learning," p. 324; and "Prosocial Behavior," in the chapter "Social Behavior," p. 552.

interneurons
Neurons that communicate only with other neurons.

action potential
The impulse of positive charge that runs down an axon.

This happens by virtue of changes in the neuron itself. The neuron, like all cells in the body, is surrounded by a membrane that is somewhat permeable, letting only certain particles move through it. The fluid inside and outside the cell contains electrically charged particles called **ions**. Positively charged sodium and potassium ions and negatively charged chloride ions are the most common. Channels in the membrane of the neuron allow ions to flow between the inside and outside of the cell. Some of these channels are always open. Others, called *voltage-dependent channels*, open only when certain electrical conditions are met.

Due to the flow of ions into and out of the neuron, there is a difference in charge inside the cell compared to outside at all times. In the resting state, there is an excess of negatively charged particles inside the axon, whereas the fluid outside the axon has a positive charge. When a neuron is at rest, the charge difference, known as a *potential*, between the inside and the outside of the axon is −70 millivolts (mV). This value is the **resting potential** of the neuronal membrane (see Figure 6a).

Neurons do not stay at rest, however. An incoming impulse—which may have been stimulated by events as different as pressure to the skin and the thought of a loved one—can temporarily change the potential. Here is how touch can stimulate a neural impulse: A message received from sense receptors in the skin or from other neurons changes the axonal membrane's permeability, especially to positively charged sodium ions. If an incoming impulse increases the positive charge inside the neuron to a certain threshold, the neuron becomes *depolarized* and fires an action potential, a surge in positive charge (see Figure 6b). The sodium channels at the top of the axon fly open, and positively charged sodium ions pour into the cell. The influx of sodium leads to a brief spike in positive charge, raising the membrane potential from −70 mV to +40 mV.

Once initiated, the action potential causes sodium channels to close and potassium voltage-dependent channels to open (see Figure 6c). As positively charged potassium ions flow out of the cell, the membrane potential returns to its resting state of −70 mV. While the neuron is returning to its resting state, it temporarily becomes supernegatively charged. During this brief period, known as the **refractory period**, the neuron cannot generate another action potential.

We can summarize the electrical changes in the neuron from resting to action potential to refractory period and back to the resting state as follows (see Figure 6d):

1. Resting potential is −70 mV.

2. If an incoming impulse causes sufficient depolarization, voltage-dependent sodium channels open and sodium ions flood into the neuron.

3. The influx of positively charged sodium ions quickly raises the membrane potential to +40 mV. This surge in positive charge inside the cell is the action potential.

4. When the membrane potential reaches +40 mV, the sodium channels close and potassium channels open. The outward flow of positively charged potassium ions restores the negative charge inside the cell.

This process repeats all along the axon, as the impulse moves toward the synapse. As the action potential subsides in one area, it immediately depolarizes the next portion of membrane, causing sodium channels to open there, continuing the action potential. This process of how an impulse moves down the axon is known as *propogation*. Like a wave, the action potential travels along the axon, until it reaches the terminal buttons. In myelinated neurons, the action potential travels faster still, as depolarization occurs only at gaps in the myelin sheath and the action potential jumps from gap to gap (see Figure 5). The gaps

FIGURE 6
HOW NEURONS FIRE: MEMBRANES AND VOLTAGE CHANGES IN ACTION POTENTIALS

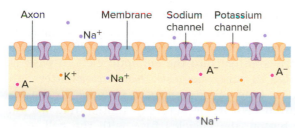

(a) Resting potential: Time 1.
In the resting neuron, the fluid outside the axon contains a higher concentration of positive ions than the inside of the axon, which contains many negatively charged anions (A–).

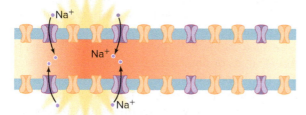

(b) Action potential: Time 2.
An action potential occurs in response to stimulation of the neuron. Sodium channels in the axonal membrane open, and positively charged sodium ions (NA+) pour into the axon, temporarily raising the charge inside the axon up to +40 mV.

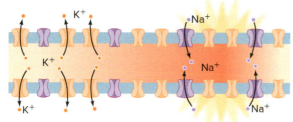

(c) Resting potential restored: Time 3.
As the impulse moves on down the axon, potassium (K+) channels open, allowing more K+ to flood out of the cell, restoring the negative resting potential (–70 mV).

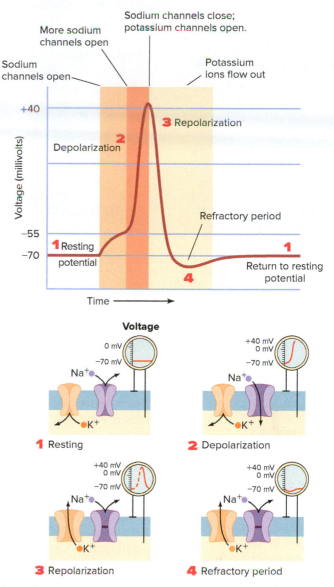

(d) This graph depicts the electrical changes that occur during each stage of an action potential (resting, depolarization, repolarization, refractory period). The top portion shows changes in voltage over time as measured by direct recording from single neurons in animal research. The lower four pictures show the membrane changes that correspond to each stage. The electrical changes of an action potential occur in a few thousandths of a second. During the refractory period, no new action potential can be generated.

 How does a neural firing (action potential) happen?

in the myelin sheath across which the action potential jumps are known as the **nodes of Ranvier**.

How fast are action potentials? In the 1920s, Edgar Douglas Adrian recorded individual action potentials of sensory neurons and confirmed a speed of about 100 feet per second (Kandel, 2006). Adrian's work also confirmed the existence of a threshold—a point of no return. Once the charge inside the neuron exceeds threshold (and *only* if it exceeds threshold), the action potential fires. This is

node of Ranvier
The gap(s) in the myelin sheath across which the action potential jumps.

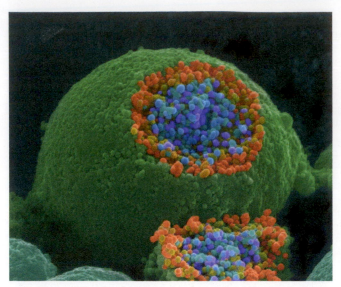

Source: Tina Carvalho/NIH-NIGMS

In this image taken by a scanning electron microscope, we see a terminal button that has been broken to show vesicles (colored balls). Neurotransmitters reside in the vesicles.

all-or-none principle
The idea that, once the threshold has been crossed, either an action potential fires or it does not.

synaptic vesicles
Tiny sacs in the terminal buttons that contain neurotransmitters.

enzymatic degradation
A way of removing excess neurotransmitter from the synapse in which enzymes specific for that neurotransmitter bind with the neurotransmitter and destroy it.

reuptake
A way of removing excess neurotransmitter from the synapse, in which excess neurotransmitter is returned to the sending, or presynaptic, neuron for storage in vesicles and future use.

graded potentials
Small changes in membrane potential that by themselves are insufficient to trigger an action potential.

glutamate
A major excitatory neurotransmitter in the brain that increases the likelihood that a postsynaptic neuron will fire; important in learning, memory, neural processing, and brain development.

known as the **all-or-none principle**; that is, either an action potential fires or it does not.

Neurotransmission The arrival of an action potential at the terminal buttons of a neuron triggers the second phase in neural communication—the release of neurotransmitters into the synaptic cleft to pass on the impulse to other neurons. Neurotransmitters are packaged in sacs called **synaptic vesicles** in the terminal button. When an action potential reaches the terminal button, the vesicles fuse with the cell membrane of the terminal and release neurotransmitter molecules into the synaptic cleft, where they may be taken up by receptors in the dendrites of adjacent neurons (Schwartz, 2000).

In a synapse, the neuron on the receiving end is known as the *postsynaptic* neuron. Neurotransmitters bind with receptors in the postsynaptic neuron in a lock-and-key type of arrangement (see Figure 7). There are many different types of neurotransmitters, each of which binds only with a specific receptor. For example, some receptors bind only with the neurotransmitter acetylcholine. If other neurotransmitters come in contact with acetylcholine receptors, they will not bind and no signal will be transmitted.

Not all of the neurotransmitter molecules that are released into the synaptic cleft bind with receptors. Usually, excess neurotransmitter remains in the synaptic cleft and needs to be removed. There are two removal methods: (1) **enzymatic degradation**, in which enzymes specific to that neurotransmitter bind with the neurotransmitter and destroy it, and (2) **reuptake**, which returns excess neurotransmitter to the sending, or *presynaptic*, neuron for storage in vesicles and future use. Even the neurotransmitter that binds to the dendrites of the receiving or *postsynaptic* neuron does not stay there. Eventually, it disengages from the receptor and floats away.

After a neurotransmitter binds to a receptor on the postsynaptic neuron, a series of changes occurs in that neuron's cell membrane. These small changes in membrane potential are called **graded potentials**. Unlike action potentials, these are not "all-or-none." Rather, they affect the likelihood that an action potential will occur in the receiving neuron. Some neurotransmitters, called *inhibitory* neurotransmitters, create graded potentials that decrease the likelihood of a neuron firing. One such neurotransmitter is GABA (gamma-aminobutyric acid). In contrast, *excitatory* neurotransmitters create graded potentials that increase the likelihood of an action potential. **Glutamate** is the most common excitatory neurotransmitter in the brain.

The excitatory potentials bring the neuron closer to threshold, while the inhibitory potentials bring it further away from threshold. The soma in the postsynaptic neuron *integrates* the various graded potentials. If the integrated message from these graded potentials depolarizes the axon enough to cross the threshold, then an action potential will occur.

Common Neurotransmitters

Within the past century, researchers have discovered at least 100 distinct neurotransmitters and related chemical messengers and have learned what most of them do, though the exact number of neurotransmitters is unknown. Of the known neurotransmitters, those most relevant for the study of human thought and behavior are acetylcholine, dopamine, epinephrine, norepinephrine,

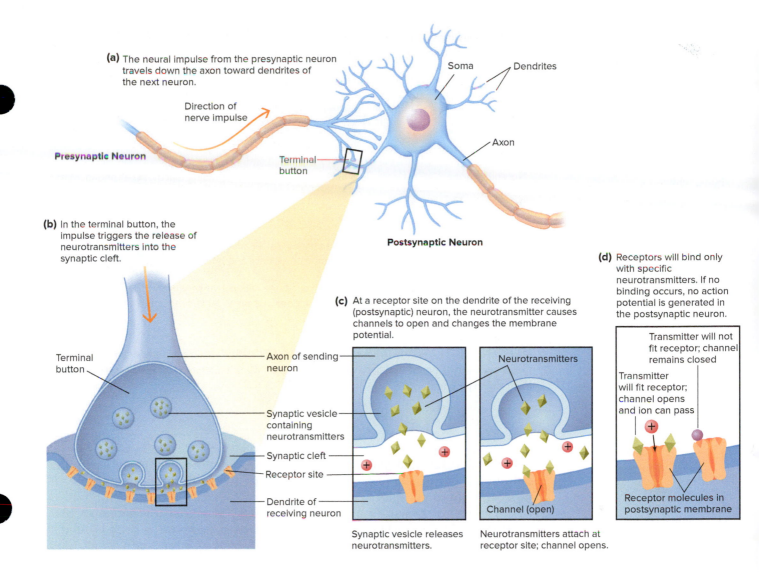

(a) The neural impulse from the presynaptic neuron travels down the axon toward dendrites of the next neuron.

Direction of nerve impulse

Soma　　　Dendrites

Presynaptic Neuron

Axon

Terminal button

Postsynaptic Neuron

(b) In the terminal button, the impulse triggers the release of neurotransmitters into the synaptic cleft.

Terminal button

Axon of sending neuron

Synaptic vesicle containing neurotransmitters

Synaptic cleft

Receptor site

Dendrite of receiving neuron

(c) At a receptor site on the dendrite of the receiving (postsynaptic) neuron, the neurotransmitter causes channels to open and changes the membrane potential.

Neurotransmitters

Channel (open)

Synaptic vesicle releases neurotransmitters.

Neurotransmitters attach at receptor site; channel opens.

(d) Receptors will bind only with specific neurotransmitters. If no binding occurs, no action potential is generated in the postsynaptic neuron.

Transmitter will not fit receptor; channel remains closed

Transmitter will fit receptor; channel opens and ion can pass

Receptor molecules in postsynaptic membrane

FIGURE 7

HOW SYNAPSES AND NEUROTRANSMITTERS WORK. In (a), two neurons connect, a presynaptic neuron and a postsynaptic neuron. They do not touch, but terminal buttons in the presynaptic neuron form a synaptic cleft with the postsynaptic neuron. In (b), the synaptic cleft has been enlarged to show the synaptic vesicles that carry neurotransmitters. They release neurotransmitters into the cleft where they bind to receptor sites on the postsynaptic neuron. In (c), we see a further enlargement of the neurotransmitters being released into the synaptic cleft and binding to receptor sites in the postsynaptic neuron. In (d), each receptor site binds to only one specific kind of neurotransmitter. Below is a three-dimensional artistic interpretation of neurons in the brain.

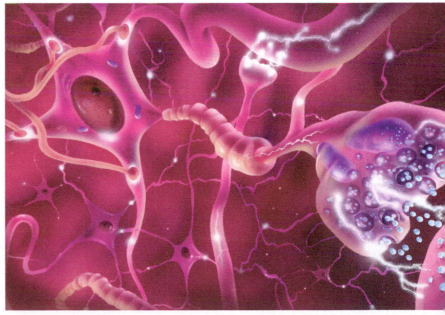

Neurotransmitter	Major Function
Acetylcholine	Slows ANS activity; eating, drinking, neuromuscular junction; involved in learning, memory, sleeping, and dreaming
Dopamine	Plays an important role in arousal, mood (especially positive mood); oversupply correlates with schizophrenia; voluntary muscle control
Epinephrine	Increases ANS activity; fight-or-flight response
Norepinephrine	Affects CNS activity; plays role in increasing alertness, attention
Serotonin	Plays role in mood, sleep, eating, temperature regulation; undersupply correlates with anxiety and depression
GABA	Is the major inhibitory neurotransmitter in the brain; slows CNS function; correlates with anxiety and intoxication
Glutamate	Is the most common excitatory neurotransmitter in the brain; involved in learning and memory; may be involved in schizophrenia

FIGURE 8

MAJOR NEUROTRANSMITTERS AND THEIR FUNCTIONS. Neurotransmitters can be excitatory, increasing the likelihood of an action potential, or inhibitory, decreasing the likelihood of an action potential.

serotonin, GABA, and glutamate (see Figure 8). Neurotransmitters are found only in the brain. They are synthesized inside the neuron for the purpose of neurotransmission.

The neurotransmitter **acetylcholine (ACh)** is released at synapses that control muscle movement (these are known as *neuromuscular junctions*), and it also released at synapses involved in learning, memory, attention, sleeping, and dreaming. Whether ACh excites muscles or slows them down depends on what kind of receptor receives it. Furthermore, researchers have discovered that the degenerative memory disorder called Alzheimer's disease results at least partly from a decrease in ACh activity and that ACh drug enhancers aid memory. ACh enhancers are now used to treat memory disorders, such as Alzheimer's disease, and they seem to slow the progression of memory loss (Czech & Adessi, 2004; Selkoe, 2002).

Dopamine is involved in voluntarily controlling your muscles and is released during feelings of pleasure or reward. Eating a good meal, doing well on an exam, having an orgasm, or drinking a glass of water when really thirsty—each of these behaviors stimulates dopamine activity in the brain (Hamer & Copeland, 1998; Kringelbach & Berridge, 2015). Because dopamine activity makes us feel good, many drug addictions involve increased dopamine activity. For instance, cocaine blocks the reuptake of dopamine into the presynaptic neuron, leaving it in the synaptic cleft for a longer period of time before it binds to receptors in the postsynaptic neuron (Bradberry, 2007). The result is a feeling of euphoria and pleasure.

Epinephrine and **norepinephrine** primarily have energizing and arousing properties. (Epinephrine was formerly called *adrenaline*, a term that is still widely used in everyday speech—"Wow! What an adrenaline rush!") Both are produced in the brain and by the adrenal glands that rest atop the kidneys. Epinephrine tends not to affect mental states, whereas norepinephrine increases mental arousal and alertness. Norepinephrine activity also leads to physical

acetylcholine (ACh)
A neurotransmitter that controls muscle movement and plays a role in mental processes such as learning, memory, attention, sleeping, and dreaming.

dopamine
A neurotransmitter released in response to behaviors that feel good or are rewarding to the person or animal; also involved in voluntary motor control.

epinephrine
Also known as adrenaline, a neurotransmitter that arouses bodily systems (such as increasing heart rate).

norepinephrine
A neurotransmitter that activates the sympathetic response to stress, increasing heart rate, rate of respiration, and blood pressure in support of rapid action.

arousal—increased heart rate and blood pressure. People who suffer from ADHD have unusually low norepinephrine levels, and treatment sometimes includes drugs to increase norepinephrine levels (Barr et al., 2002).

Serotonin plays a role in a wide range of behaviors, including dreaming and controlling emotional states such as anger, anxiety, and depression. People who are generally anxious and/or depressed often have low levels of serotonin (Caspi, Sugden, et al., 2003; Frokjaer et al., 2009; Kendler et al., 2005). Drugs that block the reuptake of serotonin in the synapse are used to treat anxiety and depression. It is well known that depression runs in families (Weissman et al., 2016). Serotonin related genes appear to modulate family risk for depression (Bansal et al., 2016).

People who are consistently angry and/or aggressive (especially males) often have abnormally low levels of serotonin as well. The administration of serotonin reduces aggressive behavior in monkeys (Suomi, 2005). The street drug ecstasy or molly (MDMA), which makes people feel social, affectionate, and euphoric, stimulates extremely high levels of serotonin. Ironically, however, ecstasy ultimately interferes with the brain's ability to produce serotonin, and so depression can be an unpleasant side effect of the drug (de Win et al., 2004). The psychedelic state created by hallucinogenic drugs, such as psilocybin mushrooms, appears to involve the activation of serotonergic systems (Muthukumaraswamy et al., 2013).

Gamma-aminobutyric acid, or GABA, is a major inhibitory neurotransmitter in the brain. Remember that inhibitory neurotransmitters tell the postsynaptic neurons *not* to fire. GABA slows CNS activity and is necessary for the regulation and control of neural activity. Without it, the central nervous system would have no "brakes" and could run out of control. One theory about epilepsy is that GABA does not function properly in people who suffer from the disorder (Laschet et al., 2007). Many drugs classified as depressants, such as alcohol, increase GABA activity in the brain and lead to relaxing yet ultimately uncoordinated states. Because GABA inhibits much of the CNS activity that keeps us conscious, alert, and able to form memories, large amounts of alcohol consumption can lead to memory lapses, blackouts, loss of consciousness, and even death (White, 2003). Stress can increase GABA and thereby increase its inhibitory effects on organs such as the large intestine, which might be one reason why some people experience diarrhea when under extreme stress (Reed et al., 2016).

Glutamate, the brain's major excitatory neurotransmitter, is important in learning, memory, neural processing, and brain development. More specifically, glutamate facilitates growth and change in neurons and the migration of neurons to different sites in the brain, all of which are basic processes of early brain development (Nadarajah & Parnavelas, 2002). It also amplifies some neural transmissions, so that a person can tell the difference between important and less important information. For example, is it more important to notice that a car is skidding out of control in front of you or that your shoes are still the same color they were when you put them on this morning? Glutamate boosts the signals about the car. The physiologically stimulating effects of nicotine in tobacco stem from glutamate synapses (Guillem & Peoples, 2010). The balance between the excitatory effects of glutamate and the inhibitory effects of GABA may be involved in supporting the repetitive motor behaviors seen in autistic spectrum disorder (Dickinson, Jones, & Milne, 2016).

©Rommel Canlas/Shutterstock.com

The street drug known as ecstasy or molly stimulates the release of high levels of the neurotransmitter serotonin, which makes people temporarily feel euphoric and affectionate. By interfering with the body's ability to produce serotonin, however, ecstasy eventually may cause depression in some people.

Summary of the Steps in Neural Transmission

We have considered the complex phenomena of action potentials and neurotransmission and described the neurotransmitters involved in human thought and behavior. Before we discuss the major structures of the brain, let's take time to summarize the process of neural communication.

- The information in neural transmission always travels in one direction in the neuron—from the dendrites to the soma to the axon to the synapses. This process begins with information received from the sense organs or other neurons, which generate a nerve impulse.

- The dendrites receive a message from other neurons. That message, in the form of an electrical and chemical impulse, is then integrated in the soma.

- If the excitatory messages pass the threshold intensity, an action potential will occur, sending the nerve impulse down the axon. If the inhibitory messages win out, the likelihood that the postsynaptic neuron will fire goes down.

- The nerve impulse, known as the action potential, travels down the axon, jumping from one space in the axon's myelin sheath to the next, because channels are opening and closing in the axon's membrane. Ions, mostly sodium and potassium, pass in and out of the membrane.

- This impulse of opening and closing channels travels like a wave down the length of the axon, where the electrical charge stimulates the release of neurotransmitter molecules in the cell's synapses and terminal buttons.

- The neurotransmitters are released into the space between neurons, known as the synaptic cleft. Neurotransmitters released by the presynaptic neuron then bind with receptors in the membrane of the postsynaptic neuron.

- This binding of neurotransmitter to receptor creates electrical changes in the postsynaptic neuron's cell membrane, at its dendrites. Some neurotransmitters tend to be excitatory and increase the likelihood of an action potential. Others tend to be inhibitory and decrease the likelihood of an action potential.

- The transmission process is repeated in postsynaptic neurons, which now become presynaptic neurons.

Quick Quiz 2: The Nervous System

1. Which branch of the nervous system is responsible for the fight-or-flight response?
   a. the parasympathetic nervous system
   b. the somatic nervous system
   c. the sympathetic nervous system
   d. the central nervous system

2. The fingerlike projections on neurons that receive input from other neurons are called
   a. dendrites.
   b. nuclei.
   c. axons.
   d. terminal buttons.

3. What property of the neuron is most directly responsible for the changes that lead up to an action potential?
   a. sodium ions outside the cell
   b. its permeable membrane
   c. chloride ions inside the cell
   d. the flux of potassium ions

4. What is the most common excitatory neurotransmitter in the brain?
   a. GABA
   b. serotonin
   c. glutamate
   d. acetylcholine

Answers can be found at the end of the chapter.

THE BRAIN

The brain is a collection of neurons and glial cells that controls all the major functions of the body; produces thoughts, emotions, and behavior; and makes us human. This jellylike mass at the top of the spine has been mapped and described in astonishing detail. Here we consider the evolution of the brain, look at key brain regions, and explore what is currently known about their specialized functions. At this point, the picture is still far from complete, and neuroscientists continue to piece it together.

Evolution of the Human Brain

Evolution provides a fundamental example of how biology and environment interact. As we discussed in the chapter "Introduction to Psychology," over long periods of time, nature selects traits and behaviors that work well in a given environment. Recall the example of the beetle population becoming more brown than green as brown beetles blended into their surroundings better and were more likely to survive and reproduce. This natural selection process gradually leads to big changes in living forms and structures—from cells to muscles to brains to new species.

The human brain has been shaped, via natural selection, by the world in which humans have lived. It is worth noting that brains do not fossilize to allow a present-day analysis, but the skulls that hold them do. By looking at the size and shape of skulls from all animals and over very long time periods, scientists can glean something about how and when human brains evolved. The evolution of the human brain is a fascinating story. Although the details lie well beyond the scope of this book, we can consider a general outline of brain evolution (Dunbar, 2001; Jerison, 2000; Klein, 1999; Striedter, 2005).

When did the very first brain show up on the planet? Arthropods, which have no backbone and external skeleton, were probably the first organisms with a central nervous system (brain) about 520 million years ago (Ma et al., 2015). Within a few million years, the first primitive vertebrates (animals with backbones) appeared. They were jawless fish, and they had a bigger mass of nerve cells than flatworms (Jerison, 2000). The first land animals came into existence around 450 million years ago and the first mammals around 200 million years ago. Land animals had more than a bundle of neurons above the spinal cord; they had complex brains with numerous structures.

The first primates lived around 55 million years ago—10 million years after the dinosaurs went extinct (Jerison, 2000; Zhang et al., 2008). Compared to other mammals, birds, reptiles, and fish, primates have relatively large amounts of brain cortex, allowing more complex thinking and problem solving. The earliest ancestors of humans appeared in Africa about 6 million years ago. One of our closest evolutionary relatives, the Neanderthals (*Homo neanderthalensis*), lived from about 350,000 to 28,000 years ago, when they were replaced by our species (*Homo sapiens*). Neanderthals had brains slightly larger, on average, than those of modern humans (see Figure 9).

Photo ©Xiaoya Ma http://nhm.academia.edu/XiaoyaMa

The very first brain on earth probably belonged to this 520 million year old arthropod.

©Tom McHugh/Science Source

Neanderthals had larger but less complex brains than modern humans do.

 Can you think of how this is the case—that is, what makes a brain complex?

Challenge Your Assumptions

True or False? Neanderthals had larger brains than we (*H. sapiens*) do.

True: Average Neanderthal brain volume was slightly greater than ours (1,450 cc to 1,300 cc).

Nevertheless, these early humans did not produce highly complex tools, may have possessed very rudimentary language, and never made symbolic pieces of art, at least none that have been found. Their brains were modern in size but not modern in function. It is possible, therefore, that the modern human brain took up to 100,000 years to become fully wired and complex, all the while staying the same overall size.

Australopithecus (4 million years ago)	*Homo erectus* (1.6 million to 100,000 years ago)	Neanderthal (350,000 to 28,000 years ago)	*Homo sapiens* (200,000 years ago to present)
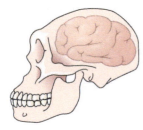	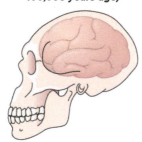	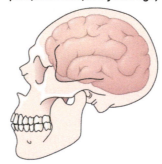	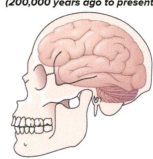
The brain capacity ranges from 450 to 650 cubic centimeters (cc).	Further development of skull and jaw are evident and brain capacity is 900 cc.	The human skull has now taken shape: The skull case has elongated to hold a complex brain of 1,450 cc.	The deeply convoluted brain reflects growth in areas concerned with higher mental processes (1,300 cc).

FIGURE 9

EVOLUTION OF THE HUMAN BRAIN OVER THE LAST 4 MILLION YEARS. An early form of prehuman, *Australopithecus*, had a brain about one-third the size of the modern human (*H. sapiens*) brain. In general, the overall brain size has grown over the course of 4 million years. But note that Neanderthal's brain was slightly larger than ours. Just as important as overall size for modern human thought and behavior is the relative enlargement of the frontal lobe area. This can be seen in the less-sloped forehead of modern humans compared to their earlier ancestors.

FIGURE 10

THREE MAIN BRAIN STRUCTURES: HINDBRAIN, MIDBRAIN, AND FOREBRAIN. The hindbrain regulates breathing, heart rate, arousal, and other basic survival functions. The midbrain controls eye muscles, processes auditory and visual information, and initiates voluntary movement. The forebrain controls cognitive, sensory, and motor function and regulates temperature, reproductive function, eating, sleeping, and emotions.

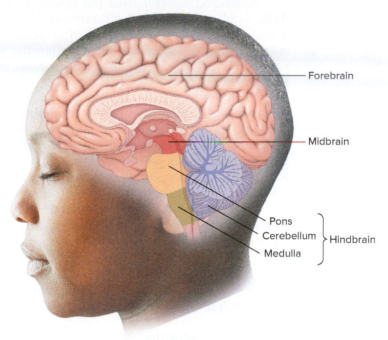

©Peter Griffith/Getty Images RF

Overview of Brain Regions

In evolutionary terms, then, the human brain is the result of a few hundred million years of natural selection. The three major regions of the brain, in order from earliest to develop to newest, are the hindbrain, the midbrain, and the forebrain (see Figure 10). By comparing the relative size of each region in distinct kinds of animals that vary in evolutionary age (see Figure 11), we gain an appreciation of how these regions evolved. When we compare brains from these different groups, we see an increase in size of the forebrain in humans and other primates (Jerison, 2000).

FIGURE 11

THE BRAIN STRUCTURE OF MAMMALS. Mammals have many of the same brain structures, but of different relative sizes. Notice how much larger the cerebral cortex is in humans than in chimpanzees, cats, and rats. Also notice the increase in brain folds in primates.

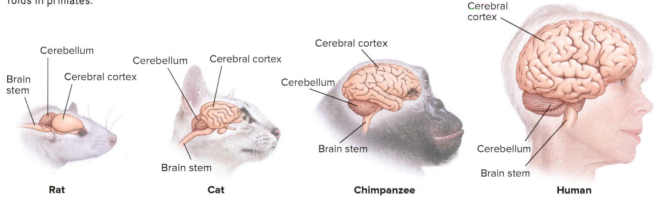

 What are the main differences you notice in these brains?

©Kraig Scarbinsky/Getty Images RF

Swallowing is one of a number of involuntary behaviors controlled by the medulla.

medulla
A hindbrain structure that extends directly from the spinal cord; regulates breathing, heart rate, and blood pressure.

reflexes
Inborn and involuntary behaviors—such as coughing, swallowing, sneezing, or vomiting—that are elicited by very specific stimuli.

pons
A hindbrain structure that serves as a bridge between lower brain regions and higher midbrain and forebrain activity.

cerebellum
A hindbrain structure involved in body movement, balance, coordination, fine-tuning motor skills, and cognitive activities such as learning and language.

reticular formation
A network of nerve fibers that runs up through both the hindbrain and the midbrain; it is crucial to waking up and falling asleep.

thalamus
A forebrain structure that receives information from the senses and relays it to the cerebral cortex for processing.

Hindbrain   The oldest brain region is the hindbrain, the region directly connected to the spinal cord. Hindbrain structures regulate breathing, heart rate, arousal, and other basic functions of survival. There are three main parts of the hindbrain: the medulla, the pons, and the cerebellum.

Extending directly from the spinal cord, the **medulla** regulates breathing, heart rate, and blood pressure. It is also involved in various kinds of involuntary, reflexive responses such as as coughing, swallowing, sneezing, and vomiting. **Reflexes** are inborn, involuntary behaviors that are elicited by very specific stimuli (Anokhin, 2013).

The **pons** serves as a bridge between lower brain regions and higher midbrain and forebrain activity, thereby playing an important role in regulating many of the same automatic functions as the medulla as well as body movement, including facial expressions (Müri, 2016). For instance, information about body movement and various sensations is relayed from the cortex via the pons to the cerebellum.

The **cerebellum**, or "little brain," contains more neurons than any other single part of the brain. It is responsible for body movement, balance, coordination, and fine-motor skills such as typing and piano playing. The cerebellum is also important in cognitive activities such as learning and language, and abnormalities in the cerebellum may be linked to cognitive as well as motor abnormalities (Amaral, 2000; Salman & Tsai, 2016; Stroodley & Schmahmann, 2009).

Midbrain   The next brain region to evolve after the hindbrain was the smallest of the three major areas, the midbrain. Different parts of the midbrain control the eye muscles, process auditory and visual information, and initiate voluntary movement of the body. People with Parkinson's disease have problems with midbrain functioning, due to the loss of neurons that use dopamine there, and so they shake uncontrollably (Vogt Weisenhorn, Giesert, & Wurst, 2016). The midbrain, the medulla, and the pons together are sometimes referred to as the *brain stem*.

A network of nerves called the **reticular formation** runs through both the hindbrain and the midbrain (*reticular* means "netlike"). The reticular formation plays a key role in wakefulness. Among the first neuroscientists to study the reticular formation were Giuseppe Moruzzi and Horace Magoun. In a classic study, Moruzzi and Magoun electrically stimulated the reticular formation of a sleeping cat, and it immediately awoke. When they *lesioned*, or damaged, its connection to higher brain systems, the cat went into a deep coma, from which it never recovered. No kind of pinching or loud noises would arouse the cat (Moruzzi & Magoun, 1949). To this day, the reticular formation is still considered a major player in the maintenance of wakefulness (Koch et al., 2016).

Forebrain   The last major region to evolve was the largest part of the human brain, the forebrain. It consists of the cerebrum and numerous other structures, including the thalamus and the limbic system. Collectively, the structures of the forebrain control cognitive, sensory, and motor function and regulate temperature, reproductive functions, eating, sleeping, and the display of emotions. Most forebrain structures are *bilateral*; that is, there are two of them, one on each side of the brain.

From the bottom up, the first forebrain structure is the **thalamus**, which receives input from the ears, eyes, skin, or taste buds and relays sensory information to the part of the cerebral cortex most responsible for processing that specific kind of sensory information. For this reason, the thalamus is often called a sensory relay station. Olfaction (the sense of smell) is unique in this case. It has a thalamic relay, but unlike the other senses, it has direct connections to the

FIGURE 12

THE LIMBIC SYSTEM. The limbic system controls motivation and emotion. It includes the hypothalamus, hippocampus, amygdala, and cingulate gyrus.

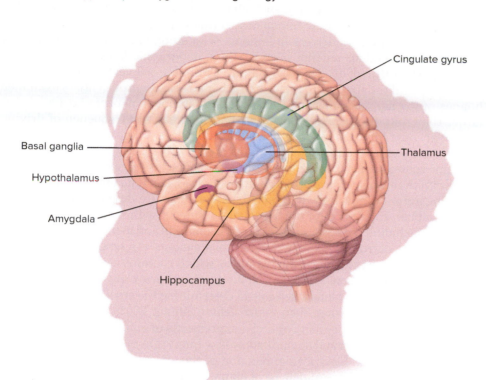

Cingulate gyrus

Basal ganglia

Hypothalamus

Amygdala

Thalamus

Hippocampus

 Can you think of certain kinds of drives and emotions that result from activation of the limbic system?

memory and emotional processing areas of the brain in the limbic system as well (see below), which is one of the reasons why smells can trigger powerful emotional memories very quickly (Courtiol & Wilson, 2016).

The Limbic System   In the middle of the brain, directly around the thalamus, lies a set of structures, traditionally referred to as a group. The **limbic system** (see Figure 12) is a group of forebrain structures that share important functions in emotion, memory, and motivation, including the hypothalamus, amygdala, hippocampus, and the cingulate gyrus. There is some debate as to whether these structures work together as a system. Some neuroscientists suggest either that the term *limbic system* should be abandoned altogether or that we should speak of limbic systems or networks instead (Rolls, 2015).

The structure directly below the thalamus is the hypothalamus (hypo means "below"). The **hypothalamus** regulates almost all of our major drives and motives, including hunger, thirst, temperature, and sexual behavior. It also controls the pituitary gland, which is responsible for producing and controlling the hormones our bodies produce. Researchers in the 1940s discovered the hypothalamus's role in eating: Lesioning one part of it produced overeating and obesity in animals, whereas lesioning another part of the hypothalamus led to undereating (Kupfermann, Kandel, & Iversen, 2000). In particular, pathways from the hindbrain send crucial information to the hypothalamus about energy needs, which helps the hypothalamus regulate food intake (Utoyama et al., 2016). The hypothalamus is also involved in sexual arousal (Brunetti et al., 2008; Karama et al., 2002).

Wrapped around the thalamus is the **hippocampus**, which plays a vital role in learning and memory. Sensory information from the sense organs goes to the

How does this picture make you feel? The structures of the limbic system play a key part in emotion and motivation.

limbic system
A connection group of forebrain structures (hypothalamus, amygdala, hippocampus, and cingulate gyrus) that share important functions in emotion memory and motivation and regulate autonomic and endocrine function.

hypothalamus
A limbic structure; the master regulator of almost all major drives and motives we have, such as hunger, thirst, temperature, and sexual behavior; also controls the pituitary gland.

hippocampus
A limbic structure that wraps itself around the thalamus; plays a vital role in learning and memory.

Connection

The various appetites of the hypothalamus play a big role in motivating behavior.

See the chapter, "Motivation and Emotion." (p. 404)

amygdala
A small, almond-shaped structure located directly in front of the hippocampus; has connections with many important brain regions and is important for processing emotional information, especially that related to fear.

Challenge Your Assumptions

True or False? Only long-term learning increases the number and structure of neurons in your brain.

True: Whenever we learn and retain information long term, neurons in our brains actually grow and change. The same does not happen with short-term learning that is soon forgotten.

©Karen Moskowitz/Getty Images

One of the special functions of the amygdala is to recognize situations for which fear is an appropriate response.

 What would happen if humans were not able to experience fear?

cingulate gyrus
A beltlike structure in the middle of the brain; plays an important role in attention and cognitive control.

basal ganglia
A collection of structures surrounding the thalamus; involved in voluntary motor control.

hippocampus. If these events are important enough, they are processed in the hippocampus and eventually established as lasting memories.

As we will see throughout this text, learning and memory change the brain. The brain structure most open to such change is the hippocampus. To get a feel for the kind of research that demonstrates this capacity, let's look at research conducted with taxicab drivers in London. Why study taxi drivers? Their work requires a tremendous amount of spatial and geographic knowledge, and they have to pass a difficult driving test (Maguire, Woollett, & Spiers, 2006). They must know where all the streets are relative to other streets. Neuroscientists examined images of the hippocampus and found that the hippocampi of taxi drivers were larger than that of other drivers. Moreover, the stress and frequency of driving did not account for these hippocampal size differences. Compared to bus drivers, taxi drivers had larger hippocampi (Maguire et al., 2006). Why? Bus drivers drive the same route every day, so they need to learn much less about the spatial layout of the city than taxi drivers. As this study suggests, learning changes the brain.

The **amygdala** is a small, almond-shaped structure directly in front of the hippocampus. Anatomically, the amygdala connects with many other areas of the brain, including the structures involved in emotion and memory: the hypothalamus, which controls the autonomic nervous system; the hippocampus, which plays a crucial role in memory; the thalamus, which contains neurons that receive information from the sense organs; and the cerebral cortex. By virtue of its prime location, the amygdala plays a key role in determining the emotional significance of stimuli, especially when they evoke fear (Öhman, 2002; Phelps & LeDoux, 2005), as well as the processing of facial expressions of emotion (Wu et al., 2016).

Studies in animals and humans show how important the amygdala is to emotions, especially fear. Electrical stimulation of the amygdala in cats makes them arch their backs in an angry-defensive manner, a response suggesting that anger and aggression involve the amygdala. Moreover, when aggressive monkeys had this region of the brain surgically lesioned, they became tame and nonaggressive. They also became fearless; for instance, rather than fleeing from snakes, they approached them (Klüver & Bucy, 1939; Meunier & Bachevalier, 2002). Similarly, in cases of disease, injury, or surgery to the human amygdala, people often lose their aggressive tendencies. They become mild-mannered yet also fearless. Additionally, our ability to recognize certain emotional expressions on other people's faces—especially fear—involves the amygdala (Adolphs, Gosselin, et al., 2005; Wu et al., 2016). Without the amygdala, we cannot learn appropriate emotional responses, especially to potentially dangerous situations. The amygdala, along with the hypothalamus and other brain structures, is also activated during sexual arousal (Fonteille & Stoléru, 2011; Hamann et al., 2004; Karama et al., 2002).

The **cingulate gyrus** is a beltlike structure in the middle of the brain. Portions of the cingulate gyrus, in particular the front part, play an important role in attention and cognitive control (Botvinick, Cohen, & Carter, 2004). When people are first trying to figure out a difficult problem and preparing to solve it, parts of the cingulate gyrus are activated (Kounios et al., 2006; Qiu et al., 2010). In contrast, this area seems to malfunction in people with schizophrenia, who have major difficulties in focusing their attention (Carter et al., 1997).

The **basal ganglia** are a collection of structures surrounding the thalamus; they are involved in voluntary motor control. Several movement-related neurological disorders, including Parkinson's disease and Huntington's disease, affect the functioning of neurons in this region. Individuals who have these disorders suffer from jerky, often uncontrollable movements. Often considered part of the limbic system, the basal ganglia reside on both sides of the thalamus and above the limbic system. They connect with the cerebral cortex, thalamus, and brain stem (Kopell et al., 2006).

The Cerebrum and Cerebral Cortex

The uppermost portion of the brain, the **cerebrum**, is folded into convolutions and divided into two large hemispheres. When most of us think about the human brain, we typically envision the outer layer, with all of its convolutions. This outer layer is called the **cerebral cortex**. The cortex is only about one-tenth to one-fifth of an inch thick, yet it is in this very thin layer of brain that much of human thought, planning, perception, and consciousness takes place. In short, it is the site of all brain activity that makes us most human.

The cerebrum is composed of four large areas called *lobes*, each of which carries out distinct functions. These lobes are bilateral, which means they are located on both the left and right sides of the brain. The four lobes are the frontal, temporal, parietal, and occipital (see Figure 13). The *frontal lobes*, in the front of the brain, make up one-third of the area of the cerebral cortex. One important region of the frontal lobe, descending from the top of the head toward the center of the brain, is the *primary motor cortex*. One of the earliest discoveries about the brain's frontal lobes involved the motor cortex. In the 1860s, while caring for wounded soldiers, the German physiologist Eduard Hitzig noticed that touching the surface of a specific side of the brain caused a soldier's body to twitch on the opposite side.

Hitzig then discovered that, as he moved the stimulation along this strip of cortex and stimulated one small region at a time, different parts of the soldier's body moved. More importantly, he was the first researcher to discover and study something that few believed: Different parts of the cortex are responsible for different functions—a phenomenon known as *cortical localization* (Finger, 1994).

The frontal lobe carries out many important functions, including attention, holding things in mind while we solve problems, planning, abstract thinking, control of impulses, creativity, and social awareness (Miller & Cummings, 1999; Stuss & Knight, 2002). The frontal lobes are more interconnected with other brain regions than any other part of the brain and therefore are able to integrate much brain activity. This integration allows for insight and creative problem solving (Fuster, 1999). For example, connections between the frontal lobes and the hippocampus and temporal lobe facilitate tasks involving language and memory, respectively. More than any other part of the brain, the frontal lobes are what make humans human. They are also the "youngest" brain systems to evolve and the last to fully develop in individuals. The frontal lobes continue to develop until the early 20s. Children and teenagers act more impulsively than adults partially because their frontal lobes are not fully developed.

FIGURE 13

FOUR LOBES OF THE CEREBRAL CORTEX. Each of the four lobes has a counterpart on the opposite side of the brain. Most important for thinking, planning, and integrating the brain's activity are the frontal lobes. The parietal lobes integrate the sensation and perception of touch. Visual information is processed in the occipital lobes, whereas hearing is processed in the temporal lobes.

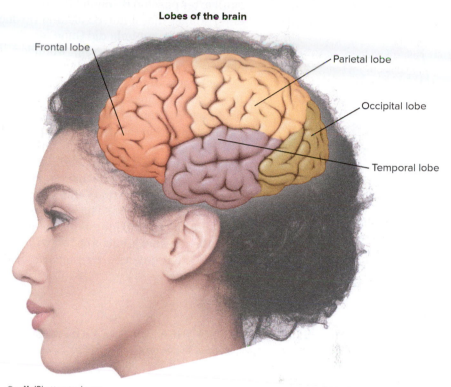

Lobes of the brain

Frontal lobe
Parietal lobe
Occipital lobe
Temporal lobe

©paffy/Shutterstock.com

cerebrum
Each of the large halves of the brain; covered with convolutions, or folds.

cerebral cortex
The thin outer layer of the cerebrum, in which much of human thought, planning, perception, and consciousness takes place.

FIGURE 14
PHINEAS GAGE'S ACCIDENT.
Miraculously, Gage survived, but his personality changed dramatically as a result of the injury to his frontal lobe.

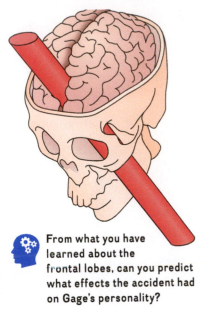

 From what you have learned about the frontal lobes, can you predict what effects the accident had on Gage's personality?

Probably the most famous story in neuroscience comes from the first case study of frontal lobe involvement in impulse control and personality (Macmillan, 2000). In September 1848, a 25-year-old railroad foreman, Phineas Gage, was laying railroad ties. While hammering a tamping iron (an iron bar), Gage accidentally ignited gun powder used to lay the track, and it exploded. The iron bar shot upward, entered Gage's left cheek, and exited through the top of his skull after passing through his frontal lobe (see Figure 14). The iron bar was traveling so fast that it moved cleanly through Gage's head and landed 25 feet away. Miraculously, not only did Gage survive, but he never even lost consciousness!

Although not mortally wounded, Gage suffered immediate and obvious changes to his personality. Before the accident, he had been a mild-mannered but clever businessman. After the accident, he was stubborn, impulsive, and argumentative, and at times he said offensive things. Gage's accident was one of the first documented cases of marked personality change following an injury to the frontal lobes, suggesting that these areas play a key role in regulating social behavior.

The *parietal lobes*, which make up the top and rear sections of the brain, are important in the sensation and perception of touch. The frontmost portion of the parietal lobes is the **somatosensory cortex**. When different parts of the body are touched, different parts of this strip of cortex are activated—whether fingertips, limbs, or the genitalia. The somatosensory cortex lies directly behind the *motor cortex* of the frontal lobe, which controls the voluntary movement of the body. In fact, these two regions are "twins." The areas of the motor and somatosensory cortexes that govern specific parts of the body are parallel to and directly next to each other (see Figure 15). For example, the part of the motor cortex involved

FIGURE 15
MOTOR AND SOMATOSENSORY CORTEXES OF THE BRAIN. Note that the regions of the motor and somatosensory cortexes are "twins." The face, lips, or toes, for example, activate the same areas of both cortexes. The arrows going down into the lower brain region represent motor neurons, and the arrows coming up into the somatosensory cortex correspond to sensory neurons.

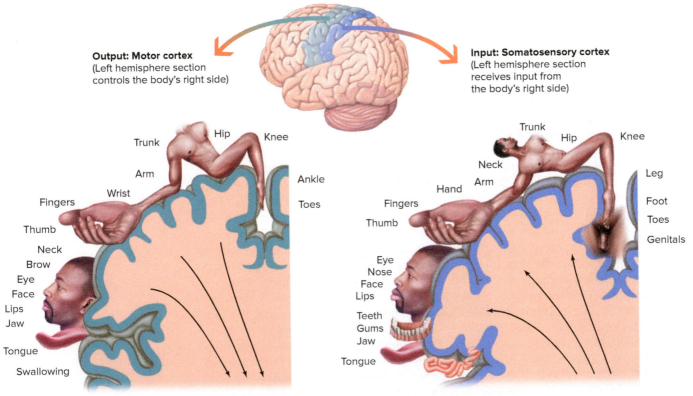

 Can you think of why the distorted size differences are shown in various body parts?

in moving the lips is directly opposite the region of the sensory cortex where we sense that our lips are being touched. Notice from Figure 16—which shows that the more sensitive portions of the body appear bigger—that touch sensation at the fingertips is much more sensitive than that hip, for example. Brain representation of sensation from the sex organs is a bit more complicated, however, as sexual stimulation involves more than just touch. Sensation of the sex organs is represented not just on the somatosensory cortex but also in the insula (Cazala, Vienney, & Stoléru, 2015).

Neural signals from the motor cortex can communicate with computers to control robotic arms or artificial limbs, as explained in "Psychology in the Real World."

The *temporal lobes* lie directly below the frontal and parietal lobes and right behind the ears. The temporal lobes have many different functions, but the main one is hearing. The temporal lobes house the *auditory cortex*, where sound information arrives from the thalamus for processing. Here, we "hear" our mother's voice, a symphony, an approaching car, or any other sound. The temporal lobes also house and connect with the hippocampus and amygdala and, so, are also involved in memory and emotion (Ventura-Bort et al., 2016).

The *occipital lobes* occupy the rear of the brain. The optic nerve travels from the eye to the thalamus and then to the occipital lobes—specifically, to the *primary visual cortex*. Visual information is processed in the visual cortex, where we "see" and "imagine." Neuroscientists have discovered that different neurons in the visual cortex are activated when we see horizontal lines, diagonal lines, and vertical lines. In other words, individual neurons are specialized for the many different aspects of vision, including shape, color, shadow, light, and orientation (Wurtz & Kandel, 2000a).

The **insula** is a small structure deep inside the cerebrum, in the area that separates the temporal lobe from the parietal lobe. The insula is active in the perception of bodily sensations, emotional states, empathy, and addictive behavior (Damasio, 2000; Naqvi et al., 2007). It communicates with structures of the limbic system and higher brain areas involved in decision making. The insula also plays a key role in our awareness of our bodies as our own (Tsakiris et al., 2007). The insula may play a key role impulsive behavior and may be crucial for understanding the compulsions underlying many addictions (Belin-Rauscent et al., 2016).

Cerebral Hemispheres The human cerebrum is divided into two equal *hemispheres*. Although they look similar, the hemispheres differ in shape, size, and function. In general terms, the left hemisphere processes information in a more focused and analytic manner, whereas the right hemisphere integrates information in a more holistic, or broader, manner (Beeman & Bowden, 2000; Beever & Chiarello, 2009). Insights and solutions to problems are more likely to occur in the right hemisphere.

The hemispheres do not operate independently, however. The **corpus callosum**, the thick band of nerve fibers connecting the two hemispheres, provides a channel for extensive communication between the hemispheres in both logical and creative tasks.

Perhaps the best-known and biggest functional difference between the cerebral hemispheres is in language. Speech and language comprehension involve two separate regions in the left hemisphere. The French physician Paul Broca is credited with being the first "neuropsychologist." He deserves this title because his work in the early 1860s demonstrated for the first time that specific parts of the brain control particular behaviors (Kandel, 2006). Broca was the first to test the predictions of a fellow physiologist, Ernest Auburtin, who diagnosed a "softening of the anterior lobes" in a patient who understood but could not produce speech (Kolb & Whishaw, 2003, p. 11). He had a type of **aphasia**, a deficit in the ability to speak or comprehend language. Broca had a similar patient who shortly thereafter died, at which time Broca performed an autopsy and confirmed Auburtin's

somatosensory cortex
A strip of the parietal lobe involved in the processing and perception of sensory information from the body, especially temperature, touch, pressure, and pain.

insula
A small structure inside the cerebrum that plays an important role in the perception of bodily sensations, emotional states, empathy, and addictive behavior.

corpus callosum
Nerve fibers that connect the two hemispheres of the brain.

aphasia
A deficit in the ability to speak or comprehend language.

Psychology in the Real World

Neuroprosthetics: Thought Control of Artificial Limbs

Think about how incredible it is that we can use our thoughts to control voluntary movement. You might think, *I want to scratch my nose*, and then instantaneously lift your arm and move a finger to scratch your nose. When injury or disease destroys connections between the CNS and the skeletal muscles, a person's intention to move a limb—say, to pick up a coffee cup—cannot reach the muscles needed to lift the cup. Thoughts cannot lead to action. Similarly, the limbs cannot send information about felt touch, temperature, or pressure back to the brain.

Attempts to reconnect brain and limb lie at the center of *neuroprosthetics*, a field in which the brain, computing, and robotics come together to help people who no longer have functional limbs (Eapen et al., 2016). People can learn to control movements of an artificial limb (or a *prosthetic*) with only their thoughts. How? Neural activity is recorded from key areas of the brain, and then action potentials are converted into digital signals, which then can be used to control a prosthetic or paralyzed limb (Hargrove et al., 2013). Thoughts are converted to action, whereby a robotic arm can then execute the neural instructions of "lift the arm."

©Chip Somodevilla/Staff/Getty Images

An artificial arm created by the Applied Physics Laboratory at Johns Hopkins University. The wearer or user of this limb can control the action of the arm with his thoughts, as well as feel sensations with the limb, thanks to an interface between electrodes implanted in his brain and sensors in the limb. These developments in prosthetics are a major area of work in Neurotechnology.

What would be needed so that thoughts can control an artificial limb? First, one would need to know which neurons in the motor cortex control intentional movement. Such mapping of individual neurons can be done in a surgical lab setting. Studies on monkeys, in which electrodes were placed on specific areas of the motor cortex, have helped map the motor cortex of the monkey brain, mapping both muscle control and action patterns in the brain (Graziano, 2016) and helped monkeys learn to control artificial limbs with thoughts (Foley, 2016). In laboratory studies, paralyzed patients can use their intentional thoughts toward movement to control a robotic arm, which may prove to be a help for quality of life if these changes can move out into their daily lives (Davis et al., 2016; Hochberg et al., 2012).

In one of the key studies in neuroprosthetics, researchers implanted electrodes deep into the brains of two monkeys to record signals from neurons in the motor cortex. They used nerve-blocking drugs to temporarily paralyze the animals' arms. Then they wanted to see whether they could use a brain-machine interface to have these neural signals stimulate muscles in the monkeys. In spite of almost completely paralyzed wrists, the monkeys were able to use this cortically controlled system to control the contraction of four forearm muscles (Pohlmeyer et al., 2009).

Brain control of a paralyzed or artificial limb is fascinating, but if if one could *feel* what that limb does, then all the better. Researchers at Johns Hopkins University created a system that helped a 28-year-old man who had been paralyzed for over a decade to feel pressure in his fingers, using a robotic arm and brain implants. They implanted electrodes in both motor and sensory areas of the cortex and then tested whether the man could determine which finger they were touching. The man was able to identify with near-perfect accuracy where he was being touched, even when blindfolded (Hotson et al., 2016).

Work in neuroprosthetics has taken off, with an emphasis on perfecting the relationship between brain and limb (Davis et al., 2016). Though the challenge is even greater with weight-bearing limbs like the legs, the connections between the robotic legs and the body's own muscle activity (near amputation site, for example) offer great promise for lower limb amputees as well (Bercich et al., 2016). The future is now.

conjecture. He found that a cyst had damaged a small region in the left frontal lobe. Broca went on to discover similar damage in eight other aphasia patients (Pinker, 1994). These clinical findings have been confirmed by modern brain imaging techniques: People with aphasia often have damage or lesions in the same region of the left frontal lobe. This region, responsible for the ability to produce speech, is commonly referred to as **Broca's area**, (see Figure 16) and this type of aphasia is known as Broca's aphasia.

About 20 years after Broca found the area of the brain now named for him, a German physiologist, Carl Wernicke, discovered that damage to another region of the left hemisphere creates a different language problem. This area of the left temporal lobe, now called **Wernicke's area**, is responsible for speech comprehension. Wernicke's aphasia, in contrast to Broca's aphasia, results in fluent, grammatical streams of speech that lacks meaning. A patient with this disorder who was asked why he was in the hospital responded, "Boy, I'm sweating. I'm awfully nervous, you know, once in awhile I get caught up, I can't mention the tarripoi, a month ago, quite a little, I've done a lot well, I impose a lot, while, on the other hand, you know what I mean, I have to run around, look it over, trebbin and all that sort of stuff" (as quoted in Pinker, 1994, p. 316).

Although it is clear that the Broca's and Wernicke's regions are involved in language production and comprehension, recent evidence using more modern technologies than lesion studies—such as fMRI—has started to challenge the simple one-to-one model of these brain areas and language (Dick, Bernal, & Tremblay, 2013; Poeppel et al., 2012; Tremblay & Dick, 2016). It is becoming more and more clear that speaking and understanding language involves a wider network of brain regions than simply the Broca's and Wernicke's regions, including right hemisphere regions.

Communication between the Hemispheres   As we have seen, the two hemispheres of the brain do not operate independently. All communication between one side of the brain and the other travels across the corpus callosum.

In the early 1960s, a former prisoner of war from World War II developed epileptic seizures as a result of a failed parachute jump. The seizures were so severe that his doctor approached Roger Sperry, a local researcher who had begun to do research on the corpus callosum, for help (Finger, 1994). Previous medical evidence had suggested that cutting the bundle of nerves between the two hemispheres could stop epileptic seizures. Because the war veteran's seizures had become life threatening, Sperry recommended surgery, which was very successful. Not only did the man's seizures stop, but there was also no noticeable change in his personality or intelligence. However, Sperry and his colleagues soon discovered a fascinating problem. The man could not name things that were presented to his left visual field, but he could do so with things presented to his right visual field. Why?

Recall that language—both speech and comprehension—resides in the left hemisphere of the human brain. In addition, information from our right visual field (the right portion of the visual scope of each eye) goes to the left occipital cortex, whereas information from the left visual field (the left portion of the visual scope of each eye) goes to the right occipital cortex (see Figure 17). The information from the left visual field could not get transferred to the language centers in the *left* hemisphere. He could, however, consistently pick up with his left hand the image he saw! Thus, because the right hemisphere (where the image was projected) controls the left side of the body, he could move his hand to the correct object (see Figure 18). This *split-brain research* shows that we can know something even if we cannot name it (Sperry, Gazzaniga, & Bogen, 1969).

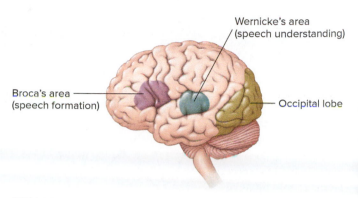

FIGURE 16

WERNICKE'S AND BROCA'S AREAS AND THE OCCIPITAL LOBES. The occipital lobes are home to the visual cortex. As we'll see later, thinking involves both verbal and visual representations.

Broca's area
The area in the left frontal lobe responsible for the ability to produce speech.

Wernicke's area
The area deep in the left temporal lobe responsible for the ability to speak in meaningful sentences and to comprehend the meaning of speech.

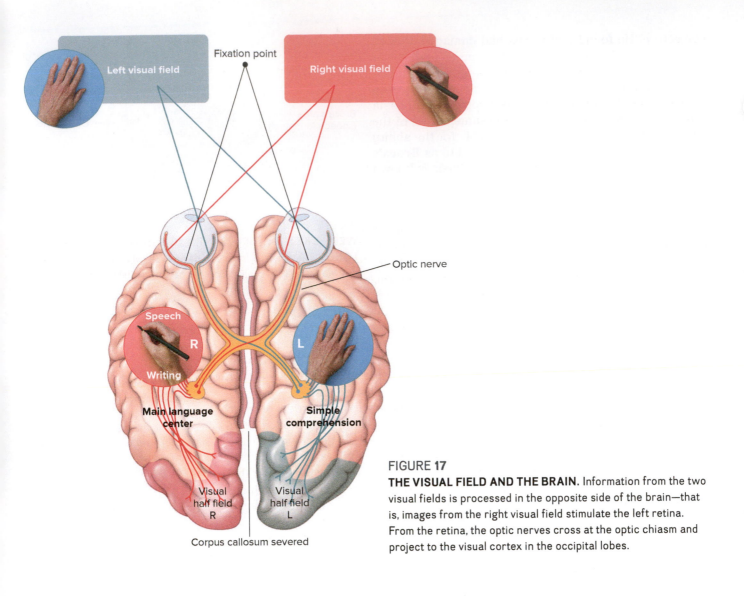

FIGURE 17

THE VISUAL FIELD AND THE BRAIN. Information from the two visual fields is processed in the opposite side of the brain—that is, images from the right visual field stimulate the left retina. From the retina, the optic nerves cross at the optic chiasm and project to the visual cortex in the occipital lobes.

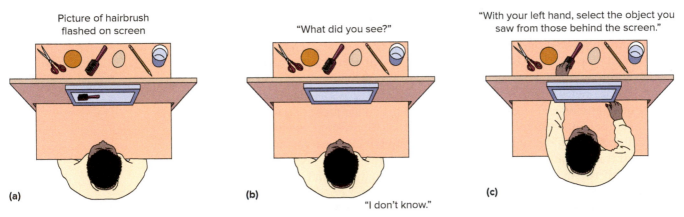

FIGURE 18

PERCEPTION AND LANGUAGE IN A SPLIT-BRAIN PATIENT. In (a), a person who has had an operation to cut the corpus callosum is shown an object (hairbrush) to his left visual field. In (b), when asked what he saw, he cannot say, because his language production center (Broca's area) is in his left hemisphere. Because the image is shown to his left visual field, only his right visual cortex perceives it. With a split corpus callosum, there is no way for that information to cross from the right hemisphere to the left. So he is unable to say what he saw. In (c), however, he is able to pick up the object he saw with his left hand. Why his left hand? Because it is controlled by his right hemisphere, which did, in fact, perceive the brush.

Brain Plasticity and Neurogenesis

When scientists began mapping the brain in the late 19th century, they did so by stimulating various brain regions in animals and observing the behavioral changes that such stimulation caused; they then diagrammed the locations of functions in the cerebral cortex (Kandel, 2006). Such mapping contributed to the notion that brain function was fixed: Certain brain regions had certain functions. But as far back as the early 20th century, researchers had stimulated different places on the motor cortex in several different monkeys and had found that maps generated from such stimulation varied from monkey to monkey. They were as individual as fingerprints.

In the early 20th century, other neuroscientists mapped the motor cortexes of several monkeys many times during a 4-month period. They found that neural areas corresponding to the movement of specific fingers changed to reflect changes in the animal's patterns of movement over that time period (Jenkins et al., 1990). By the 1970s, there was evidence that learning occurs through synaptic change. These findings were only the tip of the iceberg. Since the 1990s, numerous principles of brain plasticity have emerged (Perry, 2002). First and most generally, **neuroplasticity** is the brain's ability to adopt new functions, reorganize itself, or make new neural connections throughout life, as a function of experience. Second, almost every major structure of the neuron is capable of experience-based change.

Third, not all regions of the brain are equally plastic. For example, the part of the brain most involved in learning, the hippocampus, is more plastic than just about any other part of the brain. Finally, brain plasticity varies with age, being strongest in infancy and early childhood and gradually decreasing with age. Contrary to popular belief, at no time in our lives does the brain lose its ability to grow new neurons. Neuroplasticity occurs in all stages of life, though the different parts of the brain are not equally plastic at all times. In fact, a woman's brain is most plastic during reproduction—a flexibility that appears to benefit the baby (Pawluski, Lambert, & Kinsley, 2016).

These four principles of brain plasticity are summarized in Figure 19. Experience-based change in the nervous system occurs in several ways. Most common are the formation of new neurons, the growth of dendrites in existing neurons, and the formation of new synapses. The process of developing new neurons is known as **neurogenesis**. The growth and formation of new dendrites is called **arborization** (from the Latin *arbor*, meaning "tree"), because dendrites are like branches on a tree. Probably the best-known example of neuroplasticity, however, is **synaptogenesis**, the formation of entirely new synapses or connections with other neurons—the basis of learning (Yates, 2016).

Although these principles of neuroplasticity are universal—that is, they apply to everyone—some of the strongest evidence for them comes out of research on people with different kinds of sensory deficits, such as blindness or deafness. It is in deafness and blindness that we see most clearly how flexible the brain really is. Brain function and localization vary considerably on the basis of the experience of the individual brain.

neuroplasticity
The brain's ability to adopt new functions, reorganize itself, or make new neural connections throughout life, as a function of experience.

neurogenesis
The development of new neurons.

arborization
The growth and formation of new dendrites.

synaptogenesis
The formation of entirely new synapses or connections with other neurons.

FIGURE **19**
FOUR PRINCIPLES OF BRAIN PLASTICITY.

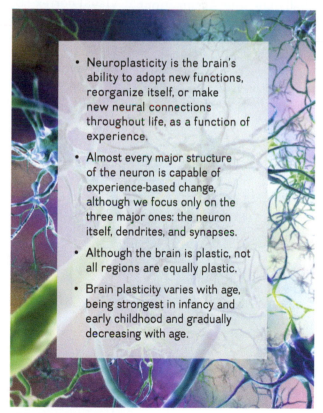

- Neuroplasticity is the brain's ability to adopt new functions, reorganize itself, or make new neural connections throughout life, as a function of experience.

- Almost every major structure of the neuron is capable of experience-based change, although we focus only on the three major ones: the neuron itself, dendrites, and synapses.

- Although the brain is plastic, not all regions are equally plastic.

- Brain plasticity varies with age, being strongest in infancy and early childhood and gradually decreasing with age.

©Hybrid Medical/Science Source

©Kobby Dagan/Shutterstock.com

Stevie Wonder, blind since infancy, is a gifted and successful musician.

In most hearing people, the area called the *auditory cortex* processes sound. Although labeled by its function, anatomically the auditory cortex is actually a section of the temporal lobe. It is called the auditory cortex because the sensory neurons from the inner ear go there. But if those neurons don't pick up any sounds, what does this area of the brain do?

For centuries, scientists and others have observed that deaf people see better than hearing people and that blind people hear better than sighted people. The neuroscientist Helen Neville always thought there must be truth to these observations. In the process of testing these assumptions, she discovered that, overall, blind people are not better at hearing. They are not more sensitive to softer sounds than sighted people. Similarly, deaf people do not excel at all kinds of vision, nor are they able to see fainter images than do hearing people.

What Neville found, however, was that deaf and blind people are more expert in peripheral sensory experiences. Deaf people have better *peripheral* vision than sighted people—they are better at seeing things "out of the corner of their eyes" (Bavelier et al., 2000). They have better motion detection as well, and this seems to be processed by the auditory cortex. Just as deaf people see better at the periphery, those who are blind don't hear better overall, but their *peripheral* hearing—hearing for things around the edges of a sound field (rather than the center)—is better than that of sighted people. These peripheral sounds are processed by the visual cortex (Bavelier et al., 2000). According to Neville, "This was some of the first evidence that brain specializations such as auditory cortex are not anatomically determined" (Neville, as quoted in Begley, 2007, p. 84). In short, by virtue of neural plasticity, the brain compensates for deficits in one sensory modality by reorganizing and rewiring unused regions to take on new functions (Murphy et al., 2016). Once again, we see how forces of nature and nurture interact to shape human thought and behavior and how psychological research leads to startling changes in our assumptions.

Challenge Your Assumptions

True or False? In people who are blind, the areas of the brain involved in vision do not function.
False: The visual cortex takes on new functions, such as processing auditory information, in blind people.

Quick Quiz 3: The Brain

1. This region of the brain was the last to evolve. It is also the biggest part of the brain.
   a. cerebellum
   b. forebrain
   c. hindbrain
   d. pons

2. Which limbic structure plays a crucial role in fear?
   a. hypothalamus
   b. basal ganglia
   c. amygdala
   d. hippocampus

3. Where is the somatosensory cortex?
   a. in the occipital lobes
   b. in the frontal lobes
   c. in the temporal lobes
   d. in the parietal lobes

Answers can be found at the end of the chapter.

CHALLENGING ASSUMPTIONS ABOUT NEURAL GROWTH IN THE ADULT BRAIN

Neurons are unique cells in the body. Unlike many other cells, including hair, blood, and skin cells, nerve cells do not grow and die on an hourly basis. Nor do they divide. Because of these two facts, discovered by the Spanish physician and Nobel Prize–winner Santiago Ramón y Cajal more than 100 years ago, the prevailing wisdom was that neurons were incapable of growth, at least after early childhood.

These observations led Ramón y Cajal to put forth the *neuron doctrine*, which declared that neurons do not regenerate. Until the 1990s, researchers and physicians alike accepted the idea that, once a region of the brain was damaged, its function was lost forever. All neural growth and change were understood to be limited to fetal and childhood development, and the adult brain did not change.

Early Evidence of Neurogenesis in Adults

By the early 1960s, however, an accumulation of evidence began to suggest that adult brains do change. Perhaps the first empirical demonstration of neural growth (neurogenesis) occurred when neuroscientists detected evidence of cell division (evidence of growth) in the brains of adult rats (Bryans, 1959).

In the early 1960s, Joseph Altman published a series of groundbreaking studies with adult rats and cats. Armed with a new cell-labeling technique, Altman found evidence of the growth of new neurons in several brain areas that are crucial for learning and memory (Altman & Das, 1966; Gross, 2000). Even though his reports appeared in prestigious journals, Altman's findings were almost completely ignored or discounted. Why? He was working alone, and he was a little-known researcher who violated the dogma, or strongly accepted view.

As often happens with ideas that radically challenge basic assumptions and long-held beliefs, neuroscientists and others either trivialized or ignored Altman's findings of adult neurogenesis. What does it take for a movement to change a well-entrenched, century-old idea? In this case, three scientific events took place during the 1980s and 1990s that finally turned the tide of disbelief.

First, a series of studies on birds showed exceptional neural growth in many areas of the adult avian brain, including the hippocampus (Nottebohm, 1985). Second, there was increasing evidence for the formation of new synaptic connections in the brains of rats when they were raised in enriched environments, more so than normally occurs with development (Comery et al., 1996). For example, rats that lived in cages with playmates, wheels to run on, and toys showed more dendritic growth than those that lived alone in sparse cages (Rosenzweig & Bennett, 1969). Third, in the 1990s, researchers began to find solid evidence for neurogenesis in one region of the hippocampus in adult rats, monkeys, and humans. Neurogenesis was no longer something seen only in birds and rats. There was no more denying that neural growth occurs in humans.

Key Figures in the Discovery of Neural Growth in Adults

The person most responsible for demonstrating neurogenesis in humans is Fred "Rusty" Gage (ironically, a cousin of the famous Phineas Gage who had

©Sergey Uryadnikov/Shutterstock.com

Animals reared in naturalistic settings have higher rates of neurogenesis than those reared in cages.

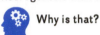 Why is that?

Challenge Your Assumptions

True or False? Only infants and children are capable of forming new neurons.

False: Although neural growths slows in adulthood compared to childhood, it never stops.

Connection

Learning results in new synapses, dendrites, and even neurons in certain regions of the brain. Regular exercise also stimulates neural growth.

See "Synaptic Change during Learning," in the chapter "Learning," p. 326, and "Research on Health-Relevant Behavior," in the chapter "Stress and Health," p. 480

an iron rod blast through his skull; Gage, 2002; Gage, Kemperman, & Song, 2008). How is this research done in humans if researchers cannot train humans and then slice open their brains to see if neural growth has occurred? Current brain imaging techniques cannot detect the growth of new cells. Gage and his researchers, some of whom did medical research, hit upon the solution that allowed them to detect new neural growth in humans. It involves injecting people with a substance called BrdU, which is incorporated into dividing cells so that they can be identified.

However, there is a problem with BrdU: You can't simply inject humans with it, because it is radioactive, but—here was the big breakthrough—some people have to have it injected for medical reasons. Gage and his colleague Peter Erikkson knew that some cancer patients receive this injection as part of their therapy. Because it identifies new cells, it is used to track how aggressively cancerous tumors are growing. After some patients who had been injected with BrdU died, Gage and Erikkson examined their hippocampus tissue. Based on the presence of BrdU, they found new cells in the adult human hippocampus (Begley, 2007; Erikkson et al., 1998). It was the same part of the hippocampus that earlier had shown the greatest neuronal growth in rats and monkeys.

Another of the key figures in demonstrating new neural growth in adult primates has been Elizabeth Gould (Glasper, Leuner, & Gould, 2008). She and her colleagues have compared rates of neurogenesis and synaptic growth in the brains of primates living in naturalistic settings with those living in lab cages. The naturalistic settings simulated a wild environment, with natural vegetation where the animals could search for food, among other activities. The brains of the animals that lived in these environmentally complex settings showed brain growth in areas important for thinking and feeling. They also had higher rates of neurogenesis and more connections between neurons than the animals reared in cages. In other studies, Gould and her colleagues found that stress and impoverished environments resulted in less neurogenesis in mammals (Mirescu & Gould, 2006; Mirescu et al., 2006).

Because of the onslaught of findings demonstrating neurogenesis in adult animals during the 1990s, the dogma of no new neural growth finally died. Now we know that neurons and their dendrites and synapses change, grow, and die in both young and old animals—including humans—depending on the kind of stimulation they receive from the outside world. When we learn anything, and even when we exercise, neurons in the brain are changed.

Quick Quiz 4: Challenging Assumptions about Neural Growth in the Adult Brain

1. The brain's ability to adopt new functions, reorganize itself, and make new neural connections is known as
   a. neuroplasticity.
   b. neurogenesis.
   c. the neuron doctrine.
   d. localization of function.

2. In what region of the human brain is there the most evidence of neurogenesis?
   a. frontal cortex
   b. hypothalamus
   c. amygdala
   d. hippocampus

Answers can be found at the end of the chapter.

MEASURING THE BRAIN

To be able to look into the brain as it is working was a long-time dream of philosophers and scientists. In the last few decades, realizing this wish has become possible. At least three techniques are now commonly used to measure brain activity in psychological research.

Electroencephalography

Researchers use **electroencephalography (EEG)** to record the electrical activity of the brain. The procedure involves placing electrodes, metal disks attached to wires, on a person's scalp. The electrodes are usually mounted in a fabric cap that fits snugly over the head. Typically, the person is performing certain tasks while the electrical activity is recorded. EEG is superior to other brain imaging techniques in showing *when* brain activity occurs. It is not very accurate, however, at indicating precisely *where* activity occurs (see Figure 20).

Event-related potential (ERP) is a special technique that extracts electrical activity from raw EEG data to measure cognitive processes. To examine ERPs, one gathers electrical recordings from an EEG cap on research participants who are performing cognitive or emotional tasks, such as trying to attend to an object on a computer screen, remember a list of words, or view emotionally charged slides. Typically, raw EEG data provide a summary of all the electrical activity in the brain that happens at a particular time. Generally, this level of detail is fine for measuring states of wakefulness, for example, but more temporal precision is needed to see a brain reaction to a particular stimulus, such as a flashing light or a line. To examine ERPs, researchers use an averaging process that allows them to filter out all electrical activity except the activity related to the stimulus the person is processing in a controlled experiment.

Because they are based on EEG, ERPs provide excellent temporal resolution (they show brain activity linked with psychological tasks almost immediately in time) but poor spatial resolution. Spatial resolution involves how tiny an area can be pinpointed as being active at a certain time. Two other techniques provide better spatial resolution than EEG: MRI and PET.

Magnetic Resonance Imaging (MRI) and Functional MRI (fMRI)

MRI stands for **magnetic resonance imaging**. MRI uses magnetic fields to produce very finely detailed images of the structure of the brain and other soft tissues. In MRI, the patient lies on a platform or bed, which slides into a tube surrounded by a circular magnet. The magnet, along with radio waves, is used to produce a signal, which is then processed by computer. The computer then produces an image with an amazing level of detail (see Figure 21). MRI provides static pictures, very useful for looking at structures, such as when someone is injured, but MRI does not tell us anything about *activity*.

A variation on MRI, **functional MRI (fMRI)**, does tell us about brain activity. Using magnets, fMRI produces indirect, high-resolution images of activity based on how the brain uses oxygen, rather than a direct "readout" of nerve impulses. The images show where brain activity is occurring during particular

FIGURE 20
ELECTROENCEPHALOGRAPHY (EEG). One of the authors (Erika) in an EEG cap for a study on brain activity and facial expression of emotion: The dots on her face allow for video motion capture of facial expression changes.

Courtesy of Erika Rosenberg

 Do measurements taken from the scalp determine precisely where in the brain activity is happening for different tasks such as whether the amygdala or hippocampus is activated? Explain.

electroencephalography (EEG)
A method for measuring brain activity in which the electrical activity of the brain is recorded from electrodes placed on a person's scalp.

event-related potential (ERP)
A technique that extracts electrical activity from raw EEG data to measure cognitive processes.

magnetic resonance imaging (MRI)
A brain imaging technique that uses magnetic fields to produce detailed images of the structure of the brain and other soft tissues.

functional MRI (fMRI)
A brain imaging technique that uses magnetic fields to produce detailed images of activity in areas of the brain and other soft tissues.

FIGURE 21

BRAIN IMAGING TECHNOLOGY. MRI equipment takes very clear, detailed images of soft tissue, including the brain, but it doesn't record brain activity. Both PET scans and fMRI, in contrast, highlight brain activity.

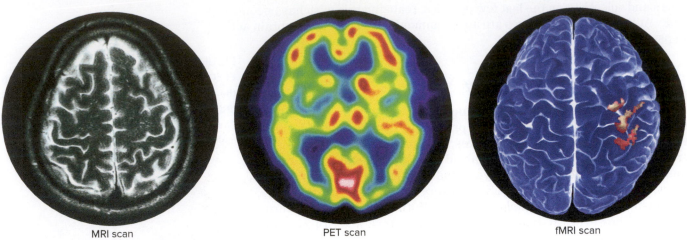

MRI scan   PET scan   fMRI scan

(MRI): ©Photopix/Getty Images; (PET): ©Department of Nuclear Medicine, Charing Cross Hospital/Science Source; (fMRI): ©ISM/Phototake

 Which of these techniques gives the most precise location of brain activity?

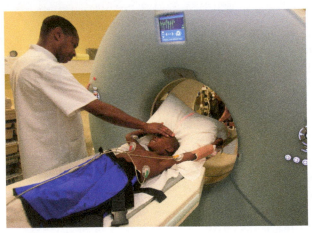

©Philippe Lissac/Getty Images

A young boy being prepped for a brain imaging procedure in an fMRI machine.

tasks by tracking blood oxygen use in brain tissue, as shown in Figure 21. In this way, researchers can see which areas of the brain are using the most oxygen (and presumably are most active) during certain tasks (Casey, Davidson, & Rosen, 2002; Lagopoulos, 2007), which indicates which areas are active during each task.

Although fMRI provides a much better measure of *where* activity occurs than EEG does, it still has drawbacks. For one thing, it is very expensive. Also, it does not provide very precise measures of *when* activation occurs in response to a particular stimulus or task. It is not entirely clear exactly how directly fMRI images reflect underlying neural activity (Lagopoulos, 2007), even though people assume that the signal changes reflect brain activity in directly underlying areas. A number of factors involved in how the measurements are taken can impact how closely the fMRI data reflect directly underlying areas of brain activity (Rath et al., 2016).

Regardless of any limitations, fMRI has become the favored measure of brain activity in psychology and neuroscience—so much so that many nonexperts think we have the ability to infer psychological processes or feeling states from fMRI data (Rose, 2016). The Research Process for this chapter illustrates one such example—the use of fMRI to study how people perceive faces (see Figure 22).

Positron Emission Tomography (PET)

positron emission tomography (PET)
A brain imaging technique that measures blood flow to active areas in the brain.

Positron emission tomography (PET) measures blood flow to brain areas in the active brain (see Figure 21). From these measurements, researchers and doctors can determine which brain areas are active during certain situations.

PET involves injecting the participant or patient with a radioactive form of oxygen (or glucose). The brain then takes up the oxygen during cell metabolism. Thanks to the radioactive label on the oxygen, scanners and computers can be used to create images of the brain regions using that oxygen during a certain task. Although the results are very informative, the use of radioactive substances means PET is not completely risk-free. fMRI is a much safer way to image metabolism in the brain.

Diffusion Tensor Imaging (DTI)

The imaging techniques we have discussed so far focus on measuring the structure or activity of clusters of somas of neurons. What is known as the **gray matter** is the brain tissue composed of grayish neuron cell bodies, because the soma or cell body is where cell metabolism takes place and thus oxygen is used by the cell. Information, however, is communicated among different areas of the brain via long fibers of myelinated axons, which are not typically well imaged by MRI or PET. Because these axons are covered with whitish myelin, they are called **white matter**.

Several methods have been developed for better imaging white matter, or neural fibers. The most widely used method for white matter measurement is **diffusion tensor imaging (DTI)**, which is a type of MRI adapted for better imaging of myelinated fibers and *tracts* (collections of myelinated fibers) and their microstructure. DTI helps neurosurgeons locate important tracts to avoid during surgeries, and this type of imaging shows promise in studying the connections among brain areas (Emsell, Van Hecke, & Tournier, 2016; Durante & Dunson, 2016; Jones, Knösche, & Turner, 2012). For instance, one study looked at the connections between the amygdala and both the orbitofrontal cortex and the anterior temporal lobe. Both of these areas have been shown to play a role in social behavior. The researchers also measured real-life social networks by means of a questionnaire. The more connected these regions were by fibers as per the DTI measure, the bigger the social network (Hampton et al., 2016). Some neuroscientists argue that more research should focus on connectivity among brain areas rather than the areas themselves. We expect DTI and other white matter imaging techniques to become increasingly popular rather than less so.

Near Infrared Spectrometry (NIRS)

Another method for producing images of brain tissue that is much less expensive than MRI and fMRI is **near infrared spectrometry** (NIRS; Jöbsis, 1977). Most simply, NIRS uses light rather than magnets to produces images of brain tissue. When light passes through any substance—whether it is fabric or a leaf or your skin—some of the light is absorbed by the substance through which it passes and some light escapes. NIRS is portable, so it can be used in many places and situations and with populations that fMRI cannot, such as with infants (Watanabe et al., 2016). fNIRS has been used in basic research in mapping which areas of the brain are associated with various cognitive skills. One of the ways NIRS has been used in clinical work is to examine brain structure and function in people with brain injury from accident or stroke (Sen, Gopinath, & Robertson, 2016). In short, it performs almost as well as fMRI at much lower cost.

gray matter
Is the brain tissue composed of neuron cell bodies.

white matter
Brain tissue made up of white myelinated axons.

diffusion tensor imaging
A method of brain measurement similar to MRI that provides a measure of white matter rather than grey matter; ideal for examining connections between brain regions, rather than those regions themselves.

near infrared spectrometry (NIRS)
Uses light rather than magnets to produces images of brain tissue.

Research Process

1 Research Question

Is any part of the brain dedicated to seeing faces and no other object? Likewise, is there a part of the brain dedicated exclusively to perceiving places (such as buildings)? If so, are these brain regions equally active when you imagine a face or place and when you actually see one?

2 Method

Previous research had found one distinct part of the brain activated when we see a face (the fusiform face area, FFA) and a different area of the brain (the parahippocampal place area, PPA) activated when we see a place or a building. O'Craven and Kanwisher (2000) wanted to confirm this result and extend it by seeing whether the activity was as strong when just imagining faces or places as it was when seeing these images.

Eight participants were placed inside an fMRI machine and then viewed images of either famous faces or familiar buildings on their university campus. For the imagining condition, participants were read the names of famous people and places and asked to close their eyes and form a "vivid mental image" of each one.

3 Results

Results confirmed the FFA showed high activity (% signal change) for faces but low activity for places, whereas the PPA showed the opposite (see graph). Moreover, the results for imagining faces and places showed the same pattern of results, only less strongly.

4 Conclusion

Different regions of the brain are dedicated to very specific kinds of visual stimuli. We know this only because fMRI technology allows us to see specific areas of brain activity when we are shown different kinds of objects and given different kinds of tasks.

FIGURE 22

DISTINCT BRAIN REGIONS INVOLVED IN IMAGINING AND PERCEIVING FACES AND PLACES. ("Mental Imagery of Faces and Places Activates Corresponding Stimulus-Specific Brain Regions," by K. M. O'Craven and N. N. Kanwisher, 2000, *Journal of Cognitive Neuroscience, 12,* 1013–1023. doi:10.1162/08989290051137549.)

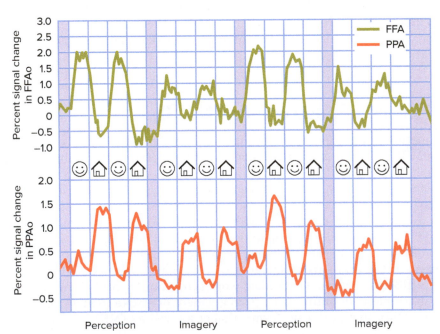

Source: "Mental Imagery of Faces and Places Activates Corresponding Stimulus-Specific Brain Regions," by K. M. O'Craven and N. N. Kanwisher, 2000, *Journal of Cognitive Neuroscience, 12,* 1013–1023. doi:10.1162/08989290051137549

1. Which brain measurement technique best shows when neural activity has occurred?
   a. PET
   b. MRI
   c. EEG
   d. fMRI

2. Betty has an injury to a particular part of her brain and suddenly has trouble imagining, recognizing, and interpreting faces. What region of the brain was likely affected and which technology told us this?
   a. parahippocampal place area (PPA); MRI
   b. parahippocampal place area (PPA); fMRI
   c. fusiform face area (FFA); EEG
   d. fusiform face area (FFA); fMRI

Answers can be found at the end of the chapter.

THE ENDOCRINE SYSTEM

In the nervous system, neurons communicate information electrochemically by means of membrane changes and neurotransmitters released into the synaptic cleft. In the **endocrine system**, glands secrete chemicals called **hormones**, which travel through the bloodstream to tissues and organs all over the body and regulate body functions. Hormones also play a crucial role in regulating metabolism, growth, reproduction, mood, and other processes.

Figure 23 depicts some of the major endocrine glands of the body. The hypothalamus is a brain structure that controls the **pituitary gland**, known as the master gland of the body because it secretes hormones that control the release of hormones from glands elsewhere in the body. The *thyroid* gland sits in the neck region and releases hormones that control the rate of metabolism, the process by which the body converts nutritional substances into energy. The *pancreas* releases hormones, including insulin, that play a vital role in regulating blood sugar levels. The sex glands (ovaries and testes) release sex hormones, which lead to the development of sex characteristics (such as body hair and breast development), sex drive, and other aspects of sexual maturation.

The **adrenal glands**, which sit atop the kidneys, release hormones in response to stress and emotions. They also help regulate heart rate, blood pressure, and blood sugar. In addition, the adrenal glands produce **catecholamines**, a class of chemicals that includes the neurotransmitters dopamine, norepinephrine, and epinephrine, which control ANS activation. Norepinephrine activates the sympathetic nervous system, increasing the heart rate, rate of respiration, and blood pressure in order to support rapid action of the body. The adrenal glands also release stress hormones, such as **cortisol**, which is responsible for maintaining the activation of bodily systems during prolonged stress.

The endocrine system works in conjunction with the nervous system and in a dynamic relationship with the brain. An example is its control of the female menstrual cycle. Each month, the hypothalamus sends signals to the pituitary gland to release hormones that stimulate a woman's ovaries to develop (mature) an egg. As part of the process, the ovary itself releases hormones that prepare the womb to receive a fertilized egg. If the egg is fertilized, the ovaries send hormonal feedback to the hypothalamus, so that it will not stimulate further egg development.

endocrine system
The system of glands that secrete and regulate hormones in the body.

hormones
Chemicals, secreted by glands, that travel in the bloodstream and carry messages to tissues and organs all over the body.

pituitary gland
The master endocrine gland of the body; controls the release of hormones from glands throughout the body.

adrenal glands
Endocrine structures that release hormones important in regulating the stress response and emotions.

catecholamines
Chemicals released from the adrenal glands that function as hormones and as neurotransmitters to control ANS activation.

cortisol
A stress hormone produced by the body to ensure that the body gets enough fuel during emotional arousal and stress.

FIGURE 23

THE ENDOCRINE SYSTEM. The endocrine system consists of numerous glands throughout the body. The pancreas, for example, releases insulin, which is important in transporting sugars (glucose) from the bloodstream into the cells. Cells then use the glucose as their energy source. The thyroid gland regulates metabolism.

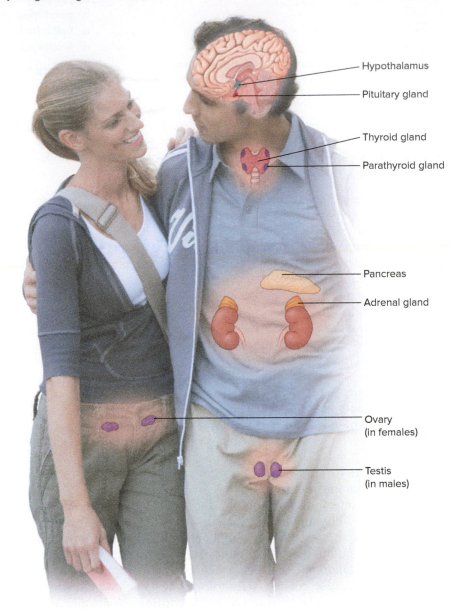

©Laurence Mouton/Getty Images RF

Quick Quiz 6: The Endocrine System

1. How do hormones differ from neurotransmitters?
   a. Hormones are proteins; neurotransmitters are fats.
   b. Hormones carry messages in the bloodstream; neurotransmitters carry messages across synapses.
   c. Hormones have no effect on mood; neurotransmitters do.
   d. All of the above are correct.

2. What is the name of the stress hormone released by the adrenal glands?
   a. catecholamine
   b. insulin
   c. thyroxin
   d. cortisol

Answers can be found at the end of the chapter.

Bringing It All Together

Making Connections in the Biology of Behavior

What Esref Armagan's Story Reveals about the Brain

This chapter opened with a profile of the blind artist Esref Armagan. Besides being a fine example of someone creatively overcoming a disability, Armagan's story offers us a way to connect much of the material in this chapter.

When Armagan paints, he uses a Braille stylus (writing instrument) to sketch out his drawing by laying down bumps on paper. With his other hand, he follows the raised bumps to "see" what he has put down (Motluk, 2005). He then transfers this sketch to canvas and applies acrylic paint with his fingers, one color at a time. Armagan waits for each color to dry before applying another, so that they will not blend or smear too much. No one helps him when he paints, and his paintings are entirely his own creations.

Armagan has learned much from talking with other people, such as what the typical colors of certain objects are. He always keeps his paints lined up in the same order, so that he can find the right color. His sense of perspective is harder to explain. He portrays perspective with uncanny realism, far beyond what any other blind painter has ever achieved (Kennedy & Juricevic, 2006). He says he learned this from talking with others, as well as from feeling his way in the world (*Biography*, n.d.).

Armagan's skill appears to have at least some inborn basis, given how early he started without receiving any instruction. Before age 6, he drew in the dirt and scratched drawings on the furniture in his home. His parents, wanting to save their furniture, finally gave him drawing materials (Kennedy & Juricevic, 2006; Motluk, 2005)—something not usually offered to blind children. This early, automatic, and almost compulsive behavior suggests that something about how his brain is wired drove young Esref to draw, and genetics likely played a role.

What senses does Armagan use while painting? Like many blind people, Armagan relies mostly on his sense of touch. Interestingly, he needs total silence while working. In many blind people, the so-called visual centers of the brain are used to process hearing (Röder, 2006).

How can we explain Armagan's act of painting in the context of the nervous system? As Armagan moves the stylus to create bumps on paper and moves his fingers over those bumps, the sensations from his fingertips stimulate his sensory neurons. These neurons in turn stimulate interneurons in different regions of the brain, which eventually stimulate motor neurons to move his hands and fingers in precise ways to execute his painting.

Throughout this process, millions of neurons are firing. As Armagan moves his hands and fingers and begins to paint, the neurons send impulses to other neurons. Some of the messages are excitatory; some are inhibitory. If a neuron receives a preponderance of excitatory impulses

Esref Armagan with some of his paintings.

and the membrane potential changes sufficiently, it will fire in an all-or-none fashion. At this point, the cell membrane opens channels, letting potassium out and sodium in. The wave of opening and closing channels moves the impulse down the axon and stimulates the release of neurotransmitters in vesicles in the terminal buttons. The neurotransmitters are released into the synaptic cleft, where they bind with receptor sites in postsynaptic neurons, get taken back up into the presynaptic neuron, or degrade. The message is then relayed to the next (postsynaptic) neurons.

What neurotransmitters are most likely to be involved in painting? As Armagan sketches and paints, he voluntarily moves his arms, hands, and fingers. Voluntary motor movements of muscles use synapses involving dopamine and acetylcholine. His attention and focus while painting, and his blocking out of auditory stimulation, increase his levels of norepinephrine as well. Additionally, the learning and memory needed for his artistry involve the effects of acetylcholine and glutamate in various parts of the brain.

There is activity throughout his brain, in brain stem structures as well as in the forebrain. As Armagan paints, as is true for anything he does, his breathing, heart rate, body temperature, and even consciousness are regulated by his medulla (see Figure 24). Armagan's thalamus transfers and relays most of the sensory information coming into various parts of his brain for different kinds of processing. As he develops new ideas for what he wants to paint, his hippocampus is active in sending those ideas to the frontal lobes for memory or to various cortexes for more permanent storage.

In order to paint, Armagan needs to plan and execute the actions of painting. The frontal lobes play a key role in planning and keeping in mind the tasks needed to paint. His motor cortex controls the movement of his legs, arms,

hands, and fingers. His basal ganglia help carry out the commands to move the various parts of his body. Perhaps Armagan decides to put his fingers in the paint container to his left. The parietal lobes get involved in orienting his body in space, and the frontal lobes plan the action to reach for the paint pot to his left. When he is ready to move his hand, the signal from these cortical areas travels to the cerebellum to control fine movement, then to the pons, the medulla, and finally the spinal cord to the nerves that control the muscles in his hand and arm. All this occurs in an instant. His brain gets feedback on the position of his hand and makes needed adjustments: a complex interplay among the somatosensory cortex (which receives sensory input from his fingers and arms as he paints), the insula, and the cerebellum.

Armagan is one of the few blind people with the ability to accurately portray depth and perspective in his drawings and paintings. When asked to draw a cube and then rotate it once and then once again, he draws it in perfect perspective, with horizontal and vertical lines converging at imaginary points in the distance (Kennedy & Juricevic, 2006). This ability to render perspective accurately in three dimensions is processed in the parietal lobes near the top and back of his brain. The visual images that Armagan forms from his sense of touch activate the occipital lobe.

When sighted people imagine something, their visual cortex (in the occipital lobe) is active, but in a much weaker way than when they actually look at something. When Armagan imagines an object, his visual cortex is even less active than that. But when he paints, his occipital cortex becomes so active that it cannot easily be distinguished from a sighted person's visual cortex as the person actually sees something (Begley, 2007; Motluk, 2005). Armagan's brain appears to be seeing.

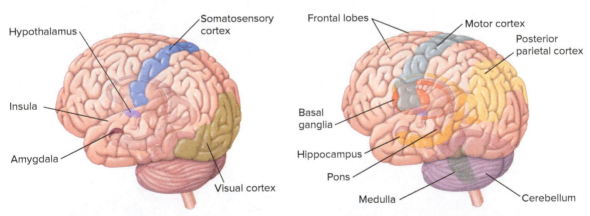

FIGURE 24
SOME OF THE BRAIN REGIONS INVOLVED WHEN ESREF ARMAGAN PAINTS. When he is drawing or painting, Armagan uses many different regions of the brain. Most interestingly, Armagan's visual cortex is active in forming images of what he paints. These images do not stem from his visual system (eyes) but rather from his sense of touch (fingers). When Armagan touches something, his occipital lobes are as active as a sighted person's occipital lobes are when seeing something. In other words, he forms visual images, but they come from touching rather than seeing.

Because Armagan has been blind since birth, his visual cortex has never received any visual input (light), but that part of his brain didn't merely die or stop functioning. In many blind people, the visual cortex takes on hearing functions, enabling them to hear certain types of sounds better than sighted people can (Röder, 2006), and they use the visual cortex to imagine soundscapes and visual landscapes (Murphy et al., 2016). Armagan's occipital cortex indeed is very active when he paints, but he is receiving tactile (touch) and not visual input.

Furthermore, in most blind people who read Braille, the visual cortex is active in processing tactile and verbal memory function, but Armagan can't read Braille and his visual cortex is not recruited for any aspect of language. His memory for language is rather poor. He is a very "visual" person, but his visual images are built from tactile information. There is evidence from neuroscientists that this plasticity of the occipital lobes is the norm—it usually processes tactile information, verbal information, or both for blind people (Amedi et al., 2005). Armagan's life, abilities, and brain illustrate that the brain is both highly plastic *and* specialized (Begley, 2007). The so-called visual part of his brain found something to do. Increasingly, we are seeing such examples, such as deaf people using the auditory cortex to improve their vision (Shiell, Champoux, & Zatorre, 2016).

Chapter Review

©Gage/Getty Images

GENES AND BEHAVIOR

- At least four principles of behavioral genetics are important for psychology: (1) The relationship between specific genes and behavior is complex. (2) Most specific behaviors derive from many genes. (3) Behavioral genetics employs studies of twins and adoptees to disentangle the contributions of heredity and environment to behavior. (4) The environment influences how and when genes affect behavior.

- The extent to which a characteristic is influenced by genetics is known as heritability. Researchers use twin-adoption studies and gene-by-environment designs to study heritability.

THE NERVOUS SYSTEM

- There are two kinds of cells in the central nervous system: glial cells and neurons.

- Glial cells provide structural support, among other important functions.

- Neurons transmit information throughout the nervous system by means of action potentials. Messages are received by the branchlike dendrites and cell bodies of neighboring neurons; these messages create changes in the membrane of the receiving neuron. If the right conditions are met, then neurons fire in an all-or-none fashion.

- Action potentials move down the length of the axon as channels in the membrane open and close, allowing ions to move into and out of the axon. The action potential stimulates the release of neurotransmitters from the terminal buttons into the synaptic cleft.

- Neurotransmitters bind to receptor sites on the dendrites of postsynaptic neurons, allowing an action potential to be generated if the charge threshold is surpassed. Excess neurotransmitter is either taken back into the original neuron or broken down in the synaptic cleft.

THE BRAIN

- The brain is divided into three major regions: the hindbrain, midbrain, and forebrain.

- The topmost brain structures are the cerebrum and cerebral cortex, which are the seat of abstract reasoning, planning, and higher-order thought.

- The cerebrum comprises four lobes: The frontal lobes are involved in abstract reasoning, self-control, and motor control; the temporal lobes house the auditory cortex; the parietal lobes process tactile and spatial information; and the occipital lobes house the visual cortex.

- The left and right hemispheres of the brain carry out somewhat different functions. The biggest difference between the hemispheres is language, which is usually controlled by the left hemisphere.

- One major shift in our understanding of the brain over the last 15–20 years is how much neurons and brain structures are shaped by experience. New neurons form, new dendrites grow, and new synapses are created across the life span, especially in infancy and early childhood.

CHALLENGING ASSUMPTIONS ABOUT NEURAL GROWTH IN THE ADULT BRAIN

- Although first uncovered in the 1960s, evidence for neural growth in adult brains was not fully appreciated and accepted until the 1990s and 2000s.

MEASURING THE BRAIN

- Various methods offer glimpses into the brain and its functions.

- Electroencephalography (EEG) measures electrical activity from scalp readings.

- Magnetic resonance imaging (MRI) measures blood flow changes in the brain without the added risk of the radioactive dyes used in PET scans. The adaptation of MRI to functional MRIs (fMRI) allows researchers to determine which brain areas are active during specific tasks.

THE ENDOCRINE SYSTEM

- In the endocrine system, glands secrete chemicals called hormones, which travel in the bloodstream to tissues and organs all over the body.

- The pituitary gland, called the master gland of the body, controls the release of hormones from other glands in the body.

- The adrenal glands secrete hormones involved in sympathetic nervous system responses and stress.

BRINGING IT ALL TOGETHER: MAKING CONNECTIONS IN THE BIOLOGY OF BEHAVIOR

- The story of Esref Armagan offers a glimpse of the brain in action.

- As Armagan moves his hands and fingers and begins to paint, the neurons send impulses to other neurons. Activation occurs in many regions of the brain. The cerebellum fine-tunes his movements by attending to whether his body is moving appropriately with the right amount of effort.

- The visual images that Armagan forms from his sense of touch activate the same region of the brain that is active when seeing people see something: the occipital lobe.

Key Terms

acetylcholine (ACh)
action potential
adrenal glands
alleles
all-or-none principle
amygdala
aphasia
arborization
autonomic nervous system (ANS)
axon
basal ganglia
behavioral genetics
Broca's area
catecholamines
central nervous system (CNS)

cerebellum
cerebral cortex
cerebrum
chromosome
cingulate gyrus
corpus callosum
cortisol
dendrites
diffusion tensor imaging (DTI)
DNA (deoxyribonucleic acid)
dominant alleles
dopamine
electroencephalography (EEG)
endocrine system
enzymatic degradation

epigenetics
epinephrine
event-related potential (ERP)
fraternal twins
functional MRI (fMRI)
GABA (gamma-aminobutyric acid)
gene-by-environment interaction research
genes
genome
genotype
glial cells
glutamate
graded potentials
gray matter

heritability
hippocampus
hormones
hypothalamus
identical twins
insula
interneurons
ions
magnetic resonance imaging (MRI)
medulla
mirror neurons
monogenic
motor neurons
mutation
myelin sheath
near infrared spectrometry (NIRS)

neurogenesis
neurons
neuroplasticity
neurotransmitters
norepinephrine
parasympathetic nervous system
peripheral nervous system
phenotype
pituitary gland
polygenic
pons
positron emission tomography (PET)
recessive alleles
reflexes
refractory period
resting potential

reticular formation
reuptake
sensory neurons
serotonin
soma
somatic nervous system
sympathetic nervous system
synapse
synaptic vesicles
synaptogenesis
terminal button
thalamus
twin-adoption studies
Wernicke's area
white matter

Quick Quiz Answers

Quiz Quiz 1: 1. b; **2.** a; **3.** a   **Quick Quiz 2: 1.** c; **2.** a; **3.** b; **4.** c   **Quick Quiz 3: 1.** b; **2.** c; **3.** d   **Quick Quiz 4: 1.** a; **2.** d   **Quick Quiz 5: 1.** c; **2.** d   **Quick Quiz 6: 1.** b; **2.** d

4 Sensing and Perceiving Our World

Chapter Outline

Challenge Your Assumptions

True or False?

- Only one organ is involved in vision: the eyes. (see page 132)

- Some visual neurons fire only when presented with images of the actress Halle Berry. (see page 132)

- Color is a property of objects in the world. (see page 134)

- Different regions of the tongue contain taste buds for specific types of taste, such as sweet or bitter. (see page 154)

- The experience of "seeing sounds" or "hearing colors" occurs only under the influence of drugs. (see page 155)

When Ben Underwood was 3 years old, he had both eyes removed. He had a rare and malignant eye cancer, and removing the eyes altogether was his best shot at survival. When he woke up from the surgery, he said, "Mom, I can't see you anymore, Mom." But his mother said, "Yes you can see me. You can see me with your hands. You can see me with your ears. You can see me with your nose. I said baby, you can still see" (*Extraordinary People*, 2007). Ben's mother wanted him to think of himself as normal, and he did. He learned to ride a bike, played basketball, and walked everywhere. He did all of these things without any aid whatsoever, other than a clicking tongue and his ability to "echolocate" (use differences in pitch when sounds bounce off objects of different sizes and distances), which he taught himself. When he was 4, he was in the car with the window rolled down, listening to the passing sounds. He astonished his mother by saying, "Mom, do you see that big building out there?" She said, "Yeah, I can see that big building but how can you see it?"(*Extraordinary People*, 2007). He was "seeing" the buildings by the different sounds the building made compared to open spaces or other kinds of buildings.

Tragically, when Ben was 16 the cancer returned, and he died in 2009, yet Ben's legacy lives on. Inspired by Ben, and with the aid of echolocation proponent Daniel Kish, schools for the blind in Scotland and Israel are teaching their students to use echolocation to help them maneuver and get around (Kloosterman, 2009; Macaskill, 2008).

Ben's ability to "see" with sound is but one fascinating example of the flexibility in how humans sense and perceive their world. Every moment of every day we are bombarded with stimulation—sights, sounds, tastes, smells, and textures. In this chapter we examine the interface between the outer world and our inner experience by looking at how we sense and perceive external stimuli. Sometimes there is a one-to-one correspondence between the kind of stimulation our sense organs receive (such as light) and our perceptual experience (sight). Other times, one sense can replace another (as in Ben's case). For each of the major sensory systems, we will examine how physical information is transformed into neural signals, how the brain processes that information, and how our knowledge and expectations can shape our sensory experiences.

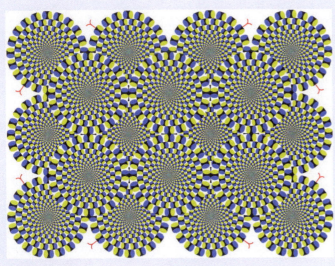

©Yonghui Shi/Alamy

 Stare at the center of the circles. Do they move? We perceive with our brains and sometimes our brain can be fooled by what it senses.

THE LONG, STRANGE TRIP FROM SENSATION TO PERCEPTION

How does the outer world become the inner world that we perceive, understand, and make sense out of? The better that animals can sense what is happening in the world around them, the better they can survive and reproduce. Yet the apparently

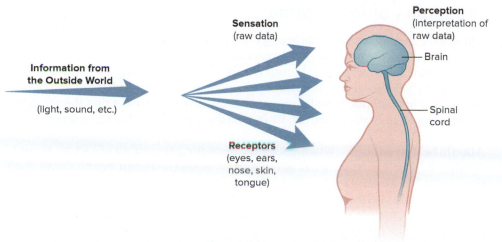

Sensation
(raw data)

Perception
(interpretation of raw data)

Information from the Outside World

(light, sound, etc.)

Receptors
(eyes, ears, nose, skin, tongue)

Brain

Spinal cord

FIGURE 1

THE PATH FROM OUTSIDE WORLD TO SENSING TO PERCEPTION

The outside world can never be directly sensed, but rather is filtered first through our particular sense organs (sensation) and then interpreted and given meaning in our brain (perception).

simple act of interpreting the sound vibrations hitting your ear as someone's calling your name, for example, is a complex process involving both the sense organs and the brain. The sense organs transform information from its physical form (light or sound waves or chemicals) into a nerve impulse and transmit it to the brain, which organizes that information, interprets it, and then initiates a response. It all happens in an instant and without effort on our part. Think about that for a second: Vibrations in your ear become your friend's voice; light waves that hit your retina become images of your home. How does sensation become perception?

This interplay between taking in information from the outside world and interpreting it is what sensation and perception are all about (see Figure 1). **Sensation** is the stimulation of our sense organs by the outer world. Eyes are sensitive to light waves, ears to sounds, skin to touch and pressure, tongues to tastes, and noses to odors.

Perception is the act of organizing and interpreting sensory experience. It is how our psychological world represents our physical world. If you had not been taught to read, the symbols on this page would not be words but rather meaningless marks. You read and make sense of the marks on the page because you spent years learning to speak and read English, and your brain transforms the raw sensory experience into meaningful concepts. We can have different experiences of the real world because individuals can experience the same physical object in different ways.

As we mentioned in the chapter "The Biology of Behavior," the brain organizes and interprets sensory experience to give it meaning. Before the brain can create meaning from sensory information, our sense organs transform physical stimuli from the outer world to a form that the brain can use—action potentials.

Basic Sensory Processes

Imagine if you were constantly aware of the sensations that bombard your sense organs, such as the sound of the air conditioner and traffic; the sight of the chair you're sitting on and the rug on the floor; the smells in the air; and the feel of your clothing against your skin. If you were constantly sensing all this, you would suffer from sensory overload. Our sensitivity diminishes when we have constant stimulation, a process known as **sensory adaptation**. Sensory adaptation ensures that we notice changes in stimulation more than stimulation itself.

The sense organs convert physical stimuli into neural impulses. This conversion of physical into neural information is called **transduction**, such as when cells in the retina change light waves to neural energy, when hair cells in the inner ear change sound waves to neural energy, when chemicals in the air bind to receptors in the nose, when food chemicals stimulate taste buds on the tongue, and when pressure and temperature stimulate nerve cells in the skin. In short, transduction is when the outer world becomes the inner world.

Sensation
A physical process: the stimulation of our sense organs by features of the outer world.

Perception
A psychological process: the act of organizing and interpreting sensory experience.

sensory adaptation
The process by which our sensitivity diminishes when an object constantly stimulates our senses.

transduction
The conversion of physical into neural information.

Principles of Perception

Some of the earliest experiments in psychology were in the field of *psychophysics*, the study of how people psychologically perceive (*psycho-*) physical stimuli ("physics") such as light, sound waves, and touch (Read, 2015; see the chapter "Introduction to Psychology"). Some basic principles of perception have emerged from over a century of research in this area, including absolute threshold, signal detection theory, difference threshold, and perceptual set. We outline these principles briefly in this section.

Absolute Threshold When do we go from not sensing an object or event to sensing it? For example, what is the softest sound you can hear? These questions concern **absolute threshold**, the lowest intensity level of a stimulus we can detect half of the time. A common way to assess absolute thresholds is for a researcher to present stimuli, such as light, of different intensities to a research participant. The intensity level that a participant can see 50% of the time is that person's absolute threshold for light. Imagine that six light intensities, whose values are 150, 160, 170, 180, 190, and 200, are presented 10 times each. Of these values, a participant detects the 180 value 50% of the time. Then 180 is this person's absolute threshold for this light stimulus (**Goldstein, 2007**). It is important to point out, however, that people differ in their absolute thresholds with some people being more sensitive than others. For instance, introverts compared to extraverts are more sensitive to most sensory stimulation, including sound, smells, light, and pain (**Aron & Aron, 1997; Aron et al., 2012; Jagiellowicz, 2011; Koelega, 1992; Stelmack & Geen, 1992**). Similarly, depression is related to less sensitivity to pain and cold perception (**Boettger, Grossman, & Bär, 2013**).

Psychologists have made some general conclusions about thresholds of perception (see Figure 2). Classic research from the 1960s reported that, under ideal laboratory conditions, an average person on a very clear night can detect a single candle from 30 miles away or can distinguish 2 gallons of water with only 1 teaspoon of sugar as being different from 2 gallons of pure water (Galanter, 1962).

Absolute thresholds, however, are not constant; they change depending on the cost of making an error, motivation, and even personality. There are a few

absolute threshold
The lowest intensity level of a stimulus a person can detect half of the time.

FIGURE 2

ABSOLUTE SENSORY THRESHOLDS. How much of a stimulus must be present for us to notice it? These are the smallest amounts of a stimulus that most humans can perceive (Smith, 1998).

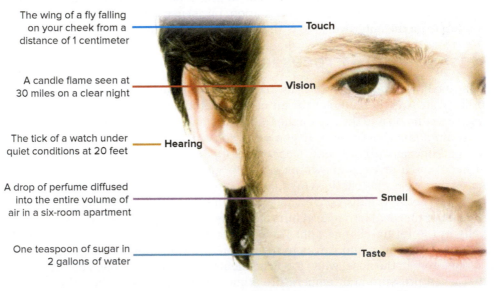

The wing of a fly falling on your cheek from a distance of 1 centimeter — Touch

A candle flame seen at 30 miles on a clear night — Vision

The tick of a watch under quiet conditions at 20 feet — Hearing

A drop of perfume diffused into the entire volume of air in a six-room apartment — Smell

One teaspoon of sugar in 2 gallons of water — Taste

©PhotoAlto/Alix Minde/Getty Images RF

©John Luke/Stockbyte/Getty Images RF

 Why is it important for certain jobs to have people with more awareness of low-intensity signals, and what does it say about how we measure absolute thresholds?

problems with measuring general absolute thresholds. Detecting sensations is a matter not only of the intensity of the stimulus but also of the person's decision-making process in a particular context. **Signal detection theory** attempts to separate "signal" from "noise" and takes into account both stimulus intensity and the decision-making processes people use in detecting a stimulus.

In signal detection research, a low-intensity stimulus is presented on some occasions but not presented on other occasions (Green & Swets, 1974; Swets, 1964; Wickens, 2002). Instead of having a 50% detection line, which is at threshold, signal detection experiments present only a single, low-intensity stimulus. Let's use the air traffic controller example where incorrectly detecting an airplane can cost people their lives. In signal detection research, a controller has 100 chances to detect a faint signal on the radar. During the 100 chances, the signal is present only about half the time. There are two kinds of correct responses the controller can make: A *hit* occurs when she accurately believes a signal (plane) is present; a *correct rejection* occurs when she accurately believes a signal is not present. Likewise, there are also two kinds of errors the controller wants to avoid: A *false alarm* ("false positive") is the believing that something (plane) is there when it is not; a *miss* ("false negative") is not detecting something when it is present. In this example, a miss is often a more serious mistake than a false alarm—that is, not believing a plane is there when it is, compared to believing a plane is present when it is not, That is why controllers tend to have sensitive absolute thresholds. Figure 3 summarizes the possible outcomes in signal detection theory.

In a signal detection study, the participant's responses create a profile of hits, misses, false alarms, and correct rejections. Using the classic method of absolute threshold, a person's threshold is assumed to be constant (for example, light intensity of 180). But in signal detection, it is assumed that a person's absolute threshold fluctuates, sometimes being more sensitive and other times being less sensitive, depending on the cost of failing to detect the stimulus.

Difference Threshold   Absolute thresholds involve perceiving or not perceiving a stimulus. But what about perceiving when a stimulus changes? Once we already perceive a stimulus, how much does it have to change

signal detection theory
The viewpoint that both stimulus intensity and decision-making processes are involved in the detection of a stimulus.

	Participant's Response	
	"Yes"	*"No"*
Stimulus Present	Hit	Miss
Stimulus Absent	False alarm	Correct rejection

FIGURE 3

POSSIBLE OUTCOMES IN SIGNAL DETECTION RESEARCH.
In signal detection theory, the participant's responses create a profile of hits, misses, false alarms, and correct rejections.

difference threshold
The smallest amount of change between two stimuli that a person can detect half of the time.

just noticeable difference
Is a difference threshold that is the smallest change in a stimulus that can be perceived most of the time.

Weber's law
The finding that the size of a just noticeable difference is a constant fraction of the intensity of the stimulus.

perceptual set
The effect of frame of mind on perception; a tendency to perceive stimuli in a certain manner.

before we notice that change? This threshold is known as a **difference threshold**. Difference thresholds are relative thresholds and are also referred to as **just noticeable differences (JND)** because they involve the smallest difference that is noticeable. For example, being able to perceive slight differences is essential to a piano tuner, who has to be able to distinguish the slightest change in pitch to tune the instrument. Importantly, people differ in their JND sensitivity. For instance, the piano tuner will no doubt recognize differences in pitch that most people will not.

The laws of just noticeable differences in sensory perception go back to Ernst Weber, who in 1834 discovered that the size of the JND is a constant fraction of the intensity of the stimulus, a finding that came to be known as **Weber's law**. To explain Weber's law more concretely, if you are given two weights, one at 100 grams and the other at 103 grams, you would probably be able to say, "Yes, these two objects are different in weight." But you might not be able to detect the difference between a 100-gram object and a 102-gram object. In this case, 3 grams, or 3%, is the JND. In fact, classic research demonstrated that 3% is the JND for weight perception (Canter & Hirsch, 1955). Even if you had much heavier objects—say, of 100 and 102 *kilo*grams—you would not perceive a difference in their weight.

Perceptual Set   We have already made clear that perception happens in the brain, after transduction of the stimulus at the sense organ. So our experience of seeing, hearing, or tasting is primarily a result of brain processing.

Other things going on in the brain at the time of sensory processing can influence perceptual experience. In particular, our frame of mind, which is ultimately coded in the brain, can impact how we perceive things. The effect of frame of mind on perception is known as **perceptual set**. Perceptual set makes us more likely to perceive one thing than another and explains the adage "we see what we want to see and hear what we want to hear." Figure 4 reproduces an image from a classic study of perceptual set. Bruner and Minturn (1955) showed two groups of research participants this image. However, each of the groups saw a different set of items before viewing the image. One group saw a series of numbers; the other saw a series of letters. Of those who saw the numbers first, the vast majority said that this image was the number "13." For those who saw letters first, the vast majority saw the figure as a "B." Thus, what people had seen prior to the test image created an expectation, or perceptual set, for how they perceived what came next. Beliefs, motives, culture, and emotions all act as perceptual sets when we perceive events in the world.

People who hold particular political beliefs will perceive any one event in a way that is consistent with those beliefs (Blais et al., 2010; Munro, Lasane, & Leary, 2010; Richardson, Huddy, & Morgan, 2008). Political jokes, airport security, presidential debates, and news releases are among the many situations that are perceived one way by liberals and another way by conservatives. In one study, people differed in their perceptions of a biracial candidate's skin color depending on whether they were likely to vote for that candidate or not (Caruso, Mead, & Balcetis, 2009). As we will discuss in the chapter "Social Behavior," many of the attitudes and opinions we hold can influence how we perceive and interpret information that we bring in from the world around us.

FIGURE 4
A DEMONSTRATION OF PERCEPTUAL SET. On a quick look, what do you see here?

 What conditions might lead to people having different perceptions of this image?

Quick Quiz 1: The Long, Strange Trip from Sensation to Perception

1. The conversion of physical into neural information is called
   a. conduction.
   b. transduction.
   c. perception.
   d. adaptation.

2. Which of the following may act as a perceptual set in constructing our visual experience?
   a. mood
   b. expectation
   c. knowledge of how the world works
   d. all of the above

Answers can be found at the end of the chapter.

VISION

Most mammals rely on smell over all other senses, but humans are predominantly visual creatures. We rely so much on our sense of sight that we often ignore other types of information. Why is vision so important? In terms of evolution, being able to see helps us know where we are, what other people might want from us, and whether there is danger nearby. As hunter-gathers, our vision is critical for locating prey and avoiding danger, as well as for finding the foods we can eat. We also rely on hearing, the second most important sense, and smelling. But vision is king, and it starts with the eye.

Sensing Visual Stimuli

What does the eye do? It bends light, converts light energy to neural energy, and sends that information to the brain for further processing. The eye is the gateway to vision, but very little of what we experience as vision actually happens in the eye. Visual perception happens in the brain, with input from the eye. Before we explore the more complicated matter of how the brain sees, let's look briefly at how light travels through the eye and how it converts light energy to neural energy.

Vision and the Eye   Light enters the eye at the **cornea**, a clear, hard covering that protects the lens. It then passes through liquid until it reaches a hole called the **pupil**. Light enters the interior of the eye through the pupil. The colored part of the eye, the **iris**, adjusts the pupil to control the amount of light entering. The light then passes through the **lens**, which bends the light rays. Through a process known as **accommodation**, muscles around the lens alter its shape to adjust to viewing objects at different distances and to allow the lens to focus light on the retina.

Finally, the **retina** is a thin layer of nerve tissue that lines the back of the eye, whose main function to to convert light energy into neural energy. As indicated in Figure 5, the light that hits the retina travels through several cell layers before processing begins. Note how the image hits the retina upside down. The brain reorients the inverted image, so that our world is right side up. The deepest layer of cells, where processing of light energy begins, is made up of **photoreceptors**. The two types of photoreceptors in the retina—rods and cones—convert light energy into neural impulses.

Rods play a key role in night vision, as they are most responsive to dark-and-light contrast. They work well at low illumination. We have all experienced rods in action. Consider what happens when someone turns out the lights. At first, everything is completely dark. Then, with a bit of time, we begin to see shapes and forms, although we cannot really see colors. The process of adjustment to seeing in the dark, known as **dark adaptation**, can take up to 30 minutes and reflects the rods at work (Rushton, 1961). Rods are very sensitive, however, and sudden exposure to light can quickly cancel out their effectiveness.

Cones, on the other hand, are responsible for color vision and are most functional in conditions of bright light. They act much more quickly than rods. On exposure to light, cones reach maximum effectiveness in about 5 minutes, because the chemicals involved in their function replenish quickly (Rushton, 1961). The **fovea**, a spot on the back of the retina, contains the highest concentration of cones in the retina. We see images with the greatest clarity when they are focused on the fovea. So **visual acuity**, or our ability to see clearly, depends on our cones. Animals that have the most cones have the best acuity.

Vision and the Brain   After transduction at the photoreceptor layer, visual information is processed by different layers of cells in the retina. One of these layers is made up of *ganglion cells*, the axons of which make up the optic nerve. The **optic nerve** transmits signals from the eye to the brain. The point at which

---

cornea
The clear, hard covering that protects the lens of the eye.

pupil
The opening in the iris through which light enters the eye.

iris
The muscle that forms the colored part of the eye; it adjusts the pupil to regulate the amount of light that enters the eye.

lens
The structure that sits behind the pupil; it bends the light rays that enter the eye to focus images on the retina.

accommodation
The process by which the muscles control the shape of the lens to adjust to viewing objects at different distances.

retina
The thin layer of nerve tissue that lines the back of the eye.

photoreceptors
Cells in the retina (called rods and cones) that convert light energy into nerve energy.

rods
Photoreceptors that function in low illumination and play a key role in night vision; responsive to dark and light contrast.

dark adaptation
The process of adjustment to seeing in the dark.

cones
Photoreceptors that are responsible for color vision and are most functional in conditions of bright light.

fovea
A spot on the back of the retina that contains the highest concentration of cones in the retina; place of clearest vision.

visual acuity
The ability to see clearly.

optic nerve
The structure composed of the axons of ganglion cells from the retina that carry visual information from the eye to the brain.

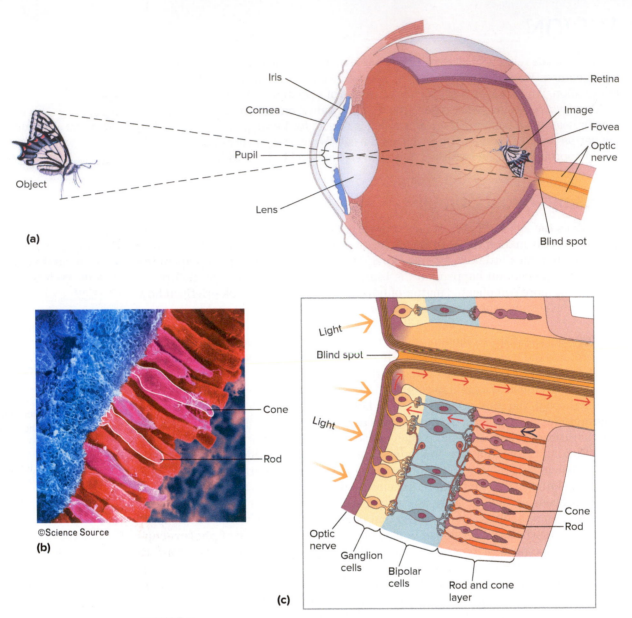

FIGURE 5

THE EYE AND ITS RECEPTOR CELLS. In (a), we see all the main structures of the eye. Notice that the image of the butterfly is projected upside down on the retina in the back of the eye. In (b), we see the layers of cells in the retina, including the photoreceptors (rods and cones). In (c), an enlarged view of the retina shows the layers of the cells involved in processing light. Light hits the retina and is processed first by the photoreceptors (deepest layers), then by the *bipolar cells*, which send the light to the ganglion cells.

the optic nerve exits the eye is called the *blind spot* of the retina because this location has no receptor cells and therefore nothing is seen.

Another interesting detail about the focusing of the visual image on the retina concerns how well we see. In people with normal vision, the lens projects the image to hit just on the retina. In people who are nearsighted (myopic), the image focuses slightly in front of the retina (see Figure 6). Nearsighted people can see close objects clearly, but distant objects are fuzzy. In people who are farsighted (hyperopic), the image focuses behind the retina. They can see distant objects

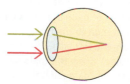

Uncorrected

In **nearsightedness,** the lens focuses
the image in front of the retina.

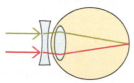

Corrected

In **nearsightedness** with a minus lens
for correction, the image focuses directly
on the retina.

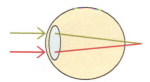

Uncorrected

In **farsightedness,** the lens focuses
the image past the retina.

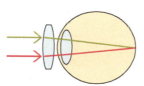

Corrected

In **farsightedness** with a plus lens
for correction, the image focuses directly
on the retina.

FIGURE 6

NEARSIGHTEDNESS AND FARSIGHTEDNESS. In nearsightedness, the uncorrected lens of the
eye focuses the image short of the retina. In farsightedness, the uncorrected lens focuses the
image past the retina. With corrective lenses, the image is accurately projected on the retina.

clearly, but close objects are fuzzy. As people age, the lens becomes less flexible,
and it is more likely that the visual image will focus behind the retina. This is an
age-related form of farsightedness (presbyopia).

Exactly what happens when visual information arrives in the brain? The
optic nerve carries impulses to the thalamus and, ultimately, to the visual cortex of the occipital lobes. This journey is *not* straightforward: As you can see in
Figure 7, the information from the left visual field is processed in the brain's right
hemisphere, and the information from the right visual field is processed in the
brain's left hemisphere. How the visual information gets to these hemispheres is
a bit complicated. Let's look at this process more closely.

In Figure 7, notice that, in each eye, each half of the retina (the area at the
back) sends out its own axons. Thus, each optic nerve has two strands. One strand
contains axons that travel from the retina to the thalamus and on to the visual cortex of the *same* side of the brain as the eye from which the axons come. The other
strand crosses to the *opposite* side of the brain in an area called the **optic chiasm.**

The first stop in the brain for most of the optic nerve fibers is the thalamus.
If the pathways to the thalamus are cut, visual perception is not possible, beyond
some crude ability to detect the presence of a stimulus (Wurtz & Kandel, 2000a).
As we discussed in the chapter "The Biology of Behavior," the thalamus serves as
a relay station for most of the major sense inputs to the brain, taking information
from the sense organs and sending it to the relevant area of the cerebral cortex
for processing. The thalamus does more than just relay information, though. Real
visual processing occurs there. A cluster of the neuron cell bodies in the thalamus forms the *lateral geniculate nucleus (LGN)*. Visual information creates a
point-by-point representation on the tissue of the LGN. Patterns of neural firing
that correspond to the shape projected on a specific region of the retina affect
a similar layout of cells in the LGN. So the retina and the LGN represent visual
information in similar ways (Wurtz & Kandel, 2000a).

optic chiasm
The point at which strands of the
optic nerve from half of each eye
cross over to the opposite side
of the brain.

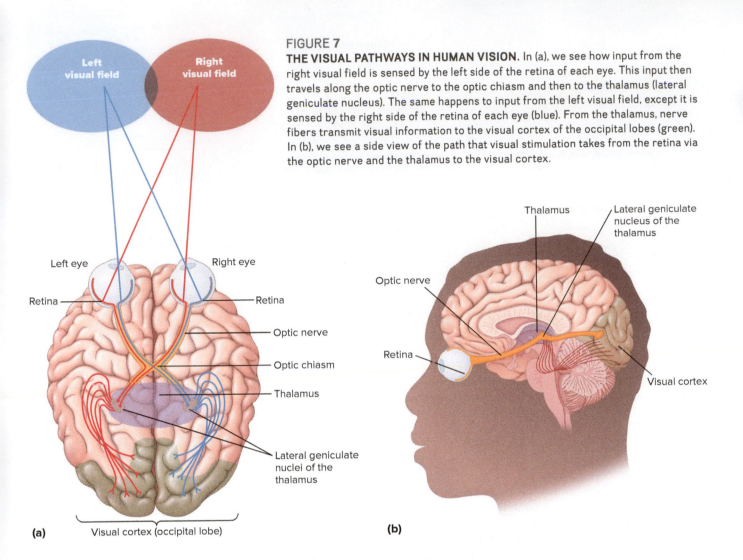

FIGURE 7

THE VISUAL PATHWAYS IN HUMAN VISION. In (a), we see how input from the right visual field is sensed by the left side of the retina of each eye. This input then travels along the optic nerve to the optic chiasm and then to the thalamus (lateral geniculate nucleus). The same happens to input from the left visual field, except it is sensed by the right side of the retina of each eye (blue). From the thalamus, nerve fibers transmit visual information to the visual cortex of the occipital lobes (green). In (b), we see a side view of the path that visual stimulation takes from the retina via the optic nerve and the thalamus to the visual cortex.

Fibers from the LGN in the thalamus then travel to the visual cortex in the occipital lobes. Neurons in the visual cortex analyze the retinal image in terms of its various patterns, contrasts, lines, and edges. Different cortical cells handle different aspects of this analysis, as a breakthrough discovery by Hubel and Wiesel demonstrated.

Vision and Specific Neurons   Researchers had known for decades that, after leaving the retina, optic fibers go to the visual portion of the thalamus (the LGN) and then travel to the visual cortex in the occipital lobes. The work, however, of Hubel and Wiesel—for which they won the Nobel Prize in 1981—showed something astounding and challenged all the science of the day: Individual neurons fire only because of very specific visual information. Some neurons fire only to angled lines; some only to movement; and some only to edges. Hubel and Wiesel were able to record specialized activity of individual cells in the brain's vision area by implanting electrodes into the visual cortex of cats. As a result, in the visual cortex they discovered neurons called **feature detectors**, which analyze the retinal image and respond to specific aspects of shapes, such as angles and movements (Hubel & Wiesel, 1962, 1979).

More specifically, Hubel and Wiesel discovered three types of neurons in the visual cortex that act as feature detectors:

- Simple cells
- Complex cells
- Hypercomplex cells

feature detectors
Neurons in the visual cortex that analyze the retinal image and respond to specific aspects of shapes, such as angles and movements.

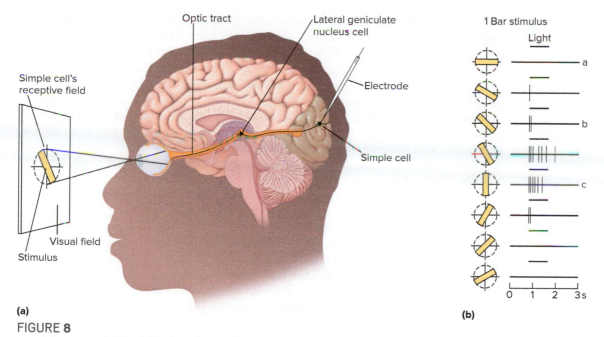

(a)

(b)

FIGURE 8

NEURAL ACTIVITY OF A SIMPLE CELL THAT IS RECEPTIVE TO ONE PARTICULAR DIAGONAL ORIENTATION. In (a), we see the stimulus on a visual field and how this simple cell is receptive to lines tilted from about 11 o'clock to 5 o'clock as if it were a clock face. In (b), each vertical line to the right of the stimulus represents a neural impulse. The cell begins to fire more often as the stimulus (line) approaches the angle to which the cell is the most responsive. As the stimulus passes that orientation on its way back to horizontal, the cell fires less and less frequently. Otherwise, this cell does not fire.

Simple cells respond to very specific information, such as a bar of light oriented at a particular angle. Some simple cells respond to only one angle or orientation, while others respond to other angles of orientation or to edges, shapes, and sizes of lines. As seen in Figure 8a, a particular simple cell might be receptive only to a diagonal line of a particular orientation. As seen in Figure 8b, recordings from this one simple cell show activity only to lines that match its receptive field, which in this case is a diagonal line from about 11 o'clock to 5 o'clock (\). The cell begins to fire more often as the stimulus (line) approaches the angle to which the cell is most responsive. As the stimulus passes that orientation on its way back to horizontal, the cell fires less and less often. This is the activity of just one simple cell, which responds only to visual stimuli that stay still or are in the middle of its receptive field.

Other cells, called *complex cells*, receive input from many different simple cells and are receptive to particular stimuli in different parts of the receptive field. Unlike simple cells, complex cells are also sensitive to the movement of an image and respond if the image appears anywhere in the visual field.

Finally, *hypercomplex cells* receive inputs from many complex cells, so they fire in response to patterns of lines. If some simple cells are responsive to / and others to \, then the hypercomplex cells are sensitive to the entire configuration of \/\/. Hypercomplex cells, therefore, are partially involved in integrating pieces of visual information into whole parts. Much of the integration into whole parts occurs when the visual cortex sends the images to other parts of the brain, such as the frontal or parietal lobes (Perry & Zeki, 2000; Wurtz & Kandel, 2000b). The cortex does not passively accept the nerve impulses from the retina and thalamus; it actively transforms the signals by first breaking them down and then putting them back together.

Challenge Your Assumptions

True or False? Only one organ is involved in vision: the eyes.

False: Our eyes take in visual information but it does not mean anything to us until our brains organize and interpret it. Our brains are just as important for seeing as our eyes.

Hubel and Wiesel made an even more monumental early discovery of neuroplasticity when they closed one eye of a newborn cat. In the first weeks in a cat's life, when its brain is growing most rapidly, visual experience is critical for brain structures to develop all the neural connections needed to see well. If a cat is blinded or has its eyes closed for a week or more during this important stage of development, its visual cortex does not develop properly and the animal's vision is forever stunted. If one eye is closed early in life for an extended period of time, the part of the brain receiving messages from the closed eye soon begins to receive and process visual messages from the one good eye. Moreover, it is not merely light that the developing brain needs if vision is to properly develop but also lines, shapes, and colors—the full visual experience. Eyes alone are not enough to see. We need neural growth in our brains to really see; we have to learn to see.

A dramatic demonstration in humans of the principle neuroplasticity of the brain and how it needs to develop in order to see comes from the case of Mike May and others like him. May lost his vision at age 3. Four decades later, he had surgery to repair his eyes, in which doctors replaced the corneas (the clear outer layer of the eye) and other tissues. The surgery gave May working eyes, but he could not miraculously "see" right after his surgery. He could barely make out vague shapes, colors, and light. It took him months to learn how to see again. Finally, 3 years after the surgery, Mike's vision started to approach normal. Many formerly blind people never fully recover their vision; if they have been blind since birth, they never quite obtain normal vision (Kurson, 2007). Seeing requires the right environmental stimulation (in this case, light) and neurons specialized for vision. It requires both sensation and perception, which involve a complex dance of environmental input and biology, of nature and nurture. In short, visual perception is softwired and requires input from the environment in order to develop.

Challenging Assumptions in How Neurons "Recognize" Human Faces

After Hubel and Wiesel's groundbreaking work, other researchers continued to find different cortical cells that fire in response to certain visual stimuli. Some neurons, for example, respond only to faces. What happens when cells are stimulated with a specific face? The answer may surprise you.

Some of the first evidence for a specific region of the brain being dedicated to face recognition came from O'Craven and Kanwisher (2000). Simply imagining a face compared to a physical place activates different regions of the brain. Imaging a face activates neurons in the fusiform face area, whereas imaging a place activates neurons in the parahippocampal place area. In 2005 Rodrigo Quian Quiroga and his colleagues decided to test how selective individual neurons really are (Quiroga et al., 2005). They took advantage of surgical procedures already being conducted on people with epileptic seizures to test the activity of individual neurons. The brains of these patients were being probed with electrodes that measured the activity of single neurons, so Quiroga and colleagues piggybacked onto that procedure to examine whether single neurons fire to specific images of famous and nonfamous people, animals, and buildings. The famous people included former U.S. president Bill Clinton, and actresses Jennifer Aniston and Halle Berry. The results of the study were stunning and surprising. As Quiroga put it, "The first time we saw a neuron firing to seven different pictures of Jennifer Aniston—and nothing else—we literally jumped out of our chairs" (Martindale, 2005, p. 22). This finding has been dubbed the "Halle Berry neuron," even though it applies to more than just Halle Berry. Recent research has extended this finding and has demonstrated that just thinking about Halle Berry (not actually seeing a picture of her) is enough to stimulate the "Halle Berry neuron" (Sanders, 2009).

Does that mean we are born with Halle Berry neurons? No. What it does mean is that, based on our exposure and interest in certain things or people,

Challenge Your Assumptions

True or False? Some visual neurons fire only when presented with images of the actress Halle Berry.

False: Believe it or not, single neurons learn specific faces and fire only when those particular faces are perceived.

©Michael Tran/FilmMagic/Getty Images

Do you have a Halle Berry neuron?

single cells can come to represent a category of things, such as all things Halle Berry-ish. It also means that neurons are not passive switches but rather are more like computers or even "thinking" cellular organisms.

Perceiving Visual Stimuli

The eye is where we sense visual information and the brain is where we make sense of it (perceive visual information). But making sense of (perceiving) the neural information from the eye involves many different acts of perception: color, motion, depth, size, and patterns, among others. Each of these perceptual processes works together to help us recognize objects in the world. Let us look at how these perceptual processes function to allow us to see the world as we do.

Perceiving Color

We tend to think of color as a property of the objects we see: "That rose is red" or "the sky is blue." You may be surprised to learn that color is not a property of objects—it is a property of us. Our perception of color depends on our photoreceptors, our brains, and the physical characteristics of the stimulus we look at. Let's start with the physical stimulus. Color perception is partly determined by wavelength, measured in billionths of a meter, or nanometers (nm). The spectrum of color visible to humans ranges from 350 nm, which most of us perceive to be the color violet, to 750 nm, which most of us perceive as red. Light that we perceive as green is at 550 nm. Figure 9 shows the spectrum of light visible to humans.

Humans and other primates are unique when it comes to vision in mammals. Primates—humans included—have three kinds of cones: those that are sensitive to red, to green, or to blue wavelengths of light (Jacobs & Nathans, 2009). Humans therefore are *trichromatic* (sensitive to three colors; see Figure 10). The million colors we see are simply combinations of different intensities of these three wavelengths. All mammals other than primates are sensitive to only two pigments—that is, they are *dichromatic*, sensitive only to blue (short) and green (medium) wavelengths (see Figure 10).

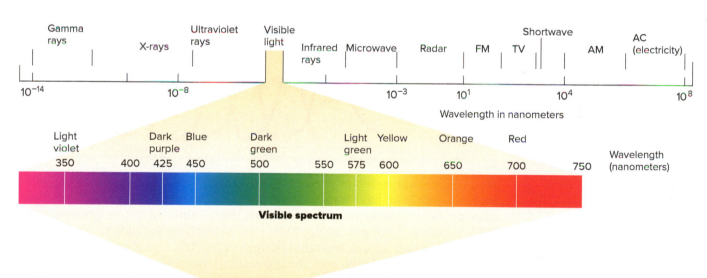

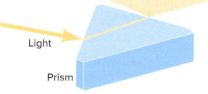

FIGURE 9

LIGHT WAVES AND THE ELECTROMAGNETIC SPECTRUM. The entire electromagnetic spectrum ranges from gamma waves at the shortest end to AC current at the longest end. Between these two extremes is a very narrow band of wavelengths visible to the human eye. Visible light ranges from about 350 nanometers (violet) to about 750 nanometers (red).

FIGURE 10

DIFFERENT TYPES OF COLOR VISION IN DIFFERENT ANIMALS.

Humans with normal color vision have three different cones (*triachromatic*), sensitive to different wavelengths of light: blue (short), green (medium), and yellow-red (long). Most mammals are *dichromatic* and see only the short and medium wavelengths. The most common form of human color blindness is dichromatic and is a deficiency in the middle (green) wavelengths. A few human and many birds and fish are *tetrachromatic*, seeing in the very short wavelength (ultraviolet) as well as short, medium, and long.

 Why do some people have color blindness, and why do most mammals view colors differently than we do?

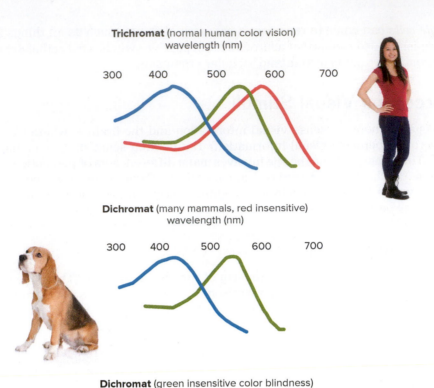

Trichromat (normal human color vision)
wavelength (nm)

Dichromat (many mammals, red insensitive)
wavelength (nm)

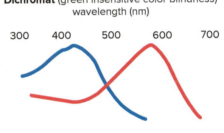

Dichromat (green insensitive color blindness)
wavelength (nm)

Tetrachromat (many birds, 2–3% of humans)
wavelength (nm)

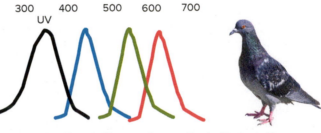

girl: ©shipfactory/Shutterstock; dog: ©Ermolaev Alexander/Shutterstock; pigeon: ©s_oleg/Shutterstock

Many nocturnal animals are sensitive to only one wavelength. Many birds and fish, however, have cones sensitive to four different wavelengths of light, making them *tetrachromatic* (Goldsmith, 2006; Jameson, 2009; Jameson et al., 2016; Osorio & Vorobyev, 2005). Their cone sensitivity extends to wavelengths shorter than blue and violet—that is, ultraviolet light (see Figure 10). A few humans (approximately 2% and always women) are tetrachromatic. Tetrachromatic people see 100 million colors compared to the 1 million colors that most people see, and because they have more cones, their vision is also sharper than most (Jameson, 2009).

Two Theories of Color Vision Psychological science has offered two main theories of color perception that explain different aspects of how most humans see color. Let's consider the aspects of each perception.

FIGURE 11

COLOR AFTERIMAGE. Stare at the white spot in the middle of the green and black flag for about 10 seconds, and then stare at the black dot in the white rectangle on the right. You will see, very briefly, a regular red, white, and blue American flag. Trichromatic color theory cannot account for this afterimage, but opponent-process theory can.

Young and Helmholtz developed their theory of color vision around the idea that people have three kinds of cones: red, green, and blue. We now know this is anatomically correct, but Young and Helmholtz did not. They inferred it from their experiments on color perception (Read, 2015). Their **trichromatic color theory** reasoned that all the color we experience must result from a mixing of these three colors of light, but mixing light is not like mixing paints. Mix red, green, and blue light together in equal amounts and you get white; with paints, you get a brownish muck. Light color mixing actually occurs inside the eye, in terms of how different kinds of cones respond to different wavelengths of light. How much each cone is stimulated determines the color we see. For most people, the perception of yellow occurs with equal stimulation of red and green cones, plus a smidgen of blue cone stimulation. So trichromatic color theory went a long way toward explaining how humans see color, but it has limitations.

Even though trichromatic color explains how photoreceptors process colored light, it cannot explain some aspects of color vision, such as **afterimages**, visual images that remain after removal of the stimulus. Figure 11 demonstrates a popular color afterimage.

Ewald Hering (1878) proposed **opponent-process theory** to explain color vision. He said that cones are linked together in three opposing color pairs: blue/yellow, red/green, and black/white. The members of the color pairs oppose one another, whereby activation of one member of the pair inhibits activity in the other. Opponent-process theory can account for the color afterimage of the American flag, and it helps explain some types of color blindness, as well as why we never experience some colors, such as reddish-green or yellowish-blue.

Current research indicates that both theories account for how human color vision works. The trichromatic theory better explains color processing at the red, blue, and green cones in the retina. Opponent-process theory better explains how cells in the lateral geniculate nucleus (LGN) of the thalamus and visual cortex process color information. In these brain areas, some cells are excited by red and inhibited by green stimuli (Lennie, 2000). Also, opponent-process theory can explain color afterimages, whereas trichromatic theory cannot.

Deficiencies in Color Vision   There are many types of color blindness. Only about 10 people in a million actually fail to see color at all (Goldstein, 2007). More commonly, *color blindness* refers to a weakness or deficiency in the perception of certain colors, usually resulting from an inherited pigment deficiency in the photoreceptors. To be clear, color blindness almost never means that a person sees the world in black and white, but rather sees fewer colors. The most common

trichromatic color theory
The theory that all color that we experience results from a mixing of three colors of light (red, green, and blue).

afterimages
Visual images that remain after removal of or looking away from the stimulus.

opponent-process theory
The theory that color vision results from cones linked together in three pairs of opposing colors, so that activation of one member of the pair inhibits activity in the other.

FIGURE 12

RED-GREEN COLOR BLINDNESS. Normal color vision on the left; red-green (green insensitive) color blindness on the right (deuteranopia). If these two images look the same, then you may be red-green color blind.

©Leontura/Getty Images RF

form, often seen in men and boys due to the pattern of inheritance, occurs from a deficiency in cones sensitive to green (medium-wavelength) light (see Figure 12). People with this disorder have trouble distinguishing some shades of green from red, may see green and brown as similar, or might have difficulty distinguishing blue and purple (purple has more red in it, so when a person cannot pick up on the red, purple and blue look alike). Yellow-blue deficiencies are less common.

Color blindness may be an evolutionary vestige of mammals most commonly being sensitive to only short and medium wavelengths rather than long (Jacobs & Nathans, 2009). When mice had a gene introduced to them that made them trichromatic (sensitive to long wavelengths as well as short and medium wavelengths), they could suddenly distinguish colors the way trichromatic humans do (Smallwood et al., 2003).

Perceiving Motion

Feature detectors play a role in how we perceive movement and form. We perceive movement when an image moves across the retina. Simple and complex cells respond to either the orientation or the direction of moving images. Sometimes these moving images truly reflect movement in the world around us.

As we view any scene, at least two factors contribute to how we perceive movement: (1) the background against which an object moves and (2) the size of the object. When an object moves across a complex background, it appears to move faster than when it moves across a simple background. For example, a deer running across a field, with mountains and trees in the background, will seem to move faster than one running across a wide open plain, simply because the background objects provide references that help us note the change of position in the deer. The human visual system is quite sensitive to changes in the position of objects, a sensitivity that appears to decline a bit with age (Bennett, Sekuler, & Sekuler, 2007).

Size matters too. Smaller objects appear to move faster than larger objects, when all else is equal. If we see a domestic rabbit and a mule deer run across a wide open plain, the rabbit will appear to be running faster because of its size, even though these two animals run at about the same speed.

We can also be fooled into thinking something is moving when it is not. We refer to this illusion as *apparent motion* because our brains interpret images that move across our retinas as movement. The "moving" lights on a movie theater marquee are a rapid succession of bulbs lighting up in a row. Even though we know the lights are not moving, we still interpret this illusion as movement.

Perceiving Depth

We take for granted that we see things in three dimensions and can discriminate what is near from what is far; this is called **depth perception**, a remarkable skill, given that the image projected on the retina is two-dimensional. How does this work? Two major aspects of human visual anatomy and processing allow for depth perception: binocular and monocular depth cues.

Binocular Depth Cues **Binocular depth cues** rely on input from both eyes. One key binocular cue to depth comes from the fact that the eyes are separated by a few inches, so the images from each eye provide slightly different viewpoints. The difference in these retinal images, or **binocular disparity**, plays a key role in our ability to perceive depth (Read, 2015). To see how this works, hold a finger out in front of you. Close one eye, open it, and then close the other eye: You will see how the image shifts slightly to one side, depending on which eye is closed and which eye is opened. The brain integrates these two slightly different two-dimensional images into a single three-dimensional image. Many animals are capable of depth perception, but this quality depends on the location of the eyes in the head.

Three-dimensional TV and movies make use of binocular depth cues for their effect. Just as humans have two eyes slightly apart, 3-D movies are filmed with two cameras slightly apart. Traditionally, one camera films with a red filter and the other camera with a blue filter. On the screen both images are projected, but when the moviegoer puts on red and blue glasses, each eye sees only one of the two separate images (see Figure 13). The brain then integrates these two images into one, and the effect is perceived as three-dimensional. Rather than using color to filter the images, modern 3-D technology in movie theaters uses polarizing filters to do the same. The effect is the same: Each eye sees only one perspective, which is merged in the brain as three-dimensional.

Monocular Depth Cues We derive a great deal of information about depth from the numerous **monocular depth cues** (*monocular* means "one eye") that do not require two eyes to be effective. These cues allow people who are blind in one eye to perceive some depth. Our knowledge of many of these cues derives from the seminal work of James Gibson (1950, 1966). Let's discuss some of the most common ones. *Linear perspective* involves parallel lines that converge, or come together, the farther away they are from the viewer. The more they converge, the greater distance we perceive. See Figure 14a for this classic effect

depth perception
The ability to see things in three dimensions and to discriminate what is near from what is far.

binocular depth cues
Aids to depth perception that rely on input from both eyes.

binocular disparity
The difference in retinal images due to the fact that our two eyes are separated by a few inches and is an important cue in depth perception.

monocular depth cues
Aids to depth perception that do not require two eyes.

FIGURE 13

MODERN TECHNOLOGY FOR THREE-DIMENSIONAL TELEVISION AND MOVIES. Two cameras are needed for modern 3-D technology. Each camera records with a differently angled polarizing filter—either horizontal or vertical. Once a movie is made and projected, the moviegoer wears polarizing glasses. One lens filters out the vertical image and leaves only the horizontal one; the other eyeglass lens filters out the horizontal image and leaves only the vertical one. Each eye, therefore, sees only one image. The brain then integrates these two slightly different images, so that we see them as being three-dimensional.

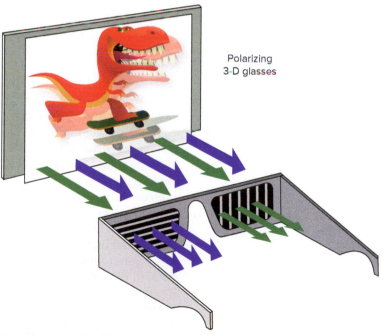

Polarizing 3-D glasses

(Adapted from: id work/iStock Exclusive/Getty Images.)

FIGURE 14
MONOCULAR CUES TO DEPTH

(a) linear perspective

(b) texture gradient

(c) atmospheric perspective

(d) interposition

a: ©Spike Mafford/Photodisc/Getty Images RF; b: ©Barbara Chase/Stockbyte/Getty Images RF; c: ©Terry Moore/Stocktrek Images/Getty Images RF; d: ©Humberto Olarte Cupas/Alamy RF

 What characteristics of these images allow for depth perception, even in people who do not have binocular vision?

in railroad tracks. *Texture gradient* is a monocular depth cue that causes the texture of a surface to appear more tightly packed together as the surface moves to the background. These changes in textural information help us judge depth.

Notice in Figure 14b that the red poppies are more tightly packed at the top of the picture, which makes us think that those flowers are farther away. Another cue, *atmospheric perspective*, comes from looking across a vast space into the distance in the outdoors. Anyone who has stood at the edge of the Grand Canyon has seen atmospheric perspective at work. We look through air and particles in the air (more so when the air is polluted). Objects farther away appear more blurred and bluish as a result (see Figure 14c). Another monocular depth cue is *interposition*, the partial blocking of objects farther away from the viewer by objects closer to the viewer, which overlap those farther away. This is a reliable cue to depth. Look at the image in Figure 14d. The closer lemons hide part of the one behind them, which is farther away.

Visual illusions sometimes make use of the way the brain interprets depth cues. In Figure 15, which line is longer, the one on the right or the one on the left? If you take a ruler to the page, you find that both line segments are identical in length, but many people report that the one on the right looks longer. Why do we see it that way? This illusion, known as the Müller-Lyer illusion, results from our tendency to see the right line as the inside corner of a room and the left one as the

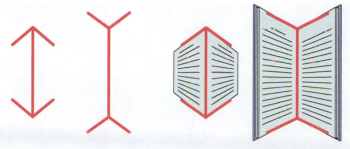

FIGURE 15

THE MÜLLER-LYER ILLUSION. Which line is longer?

outside corner of a room or building, making use of the monocular depth cue of linear perspective.

Another commonly experienced illusion results from monocular depth cues. Take a look at Figure 16. Distance cues (horizon) make objects look bigger than they are. More famously, the *moon illusion* occurs when the moon is closer to the horizon (see Figure 17). At that time, it appears to be much larger than when it is farther from the horizon. Of course, the moon is not any larger, so why does this happen? Scientists offer several explanations for the moon illusion, and although no answer provides one true cause for the illusion, nearly all explanations involve cues to depth perception (Goldstein, 2007).

One explanation is that, when the moon is near the horizon, we see it against other cues that indicate we are looking off into the distance (such as buildings interposed on the moon, possibly roads that offer cues to linear perspective, and

FIGURE 16

ANOTHER ILLUSION OF SIZE AND DEPTH PERCEPTION

 Is the figure in the front smaller than the one in the back? No. Both are exactly the same size. Measure them and see for yourself. Why don't you believe they are all the same size? Like the moon illusion in **Figure 18**, this illusion comes about by our brain believing objects nearer the horizon are larger than those closer to us.

FIGURE **17**

MOON ILLUSION. Distance cues make the moon look bigger on the horizon.

so on). Another way to look at it is this: When the moon is in the middle of the night sky, there are no cues to distance, no objects with which to compare it, and a huge sky surrounds it. Relative to the sky, the moon does not look so big. When the moon is on the horizon, however, we view it against objects whose size we know. Relative to those earthly objects, the moon looks enormous, as it is (Baird, Wagner, & Fuld, 1990).

Perceiving Size and Shape

We know what familiar objects look like. We also know that, when they change position or distance in relation to us, they remain the same. Nevertheless, the images on our retinas change shape and size as objects move through space. The brain's ability to preserve perception of such objects in spite of the changes in retinal image is known as **perceptual constancy**. We will look at two types: constancy of size and of shape.

Size Constancy We see things as the same size regardless of the changing size of the image on the retina, because we know what the size of the object is. If you see your friend Jayson, who is about 6 feet tall, walking away from you, the size of his image on your retina shrinks, yet you do not suddenly think, Oh no, Jayson is shrinking! Your knowledge of Jayson's height and your knowledge that people maintain their height even when they move away from you prevent you from interpreting the smaller retinal image as a smaller person. Also, distance cues, such as linear perspective, indicate that the road Jayson is walking on is in the distance, and your brain makes use of this information *plus* your knowledge of Jayson's size to keep his size constant in your mind.

A stunning demonstration of distortions in the perception of size is the Ames room. In the photograph in Figure 18a, the child on the right looks enormous compared to the one on the left. It turns out, however, that the room is not rectangular (as we expect it to be) but rather trapezoidal, and the girl on the right is standing much closer to the peephole through which the viewer looks (Figure 18b). So the distance cues we tend to rely on are not available, and we perceive the two people as equally far away, which makes the child on the right appear enormous.

Shape Constancy People know the shapes of common things, just as they know their sizes. The brain uses this knowledge to override changing retinal

perceptual constancy
The ability of the brain to preserve perception of objects in spite of changes in retinal image when an object changes in position or distance from the viewer.

FIGURE 18
THE AMES ROOM

(a)

©Mauro Fermariello/Science Source

 These two children are about the same size, so why does the child on the right appear enormous compared to the child on the left? What does the Ames room demonstration show about perceptual constancy?

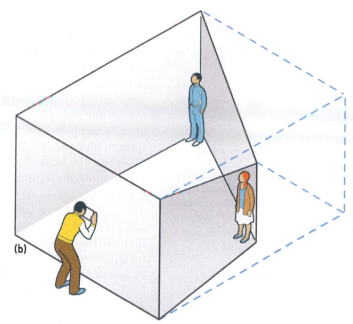

(b)

images that might make the world very confusing. Take a look at Figure 19. When we see a door that is closed, it looks like a rectangle (and this is what the 2-D image on our retina looks like). A door that is partially open looks like a trapezoid. Still, we would not think that the door has suddenly changed shape. The brain corrects our perception based on our previous knowledge that doors retain their shape when they change position.

Perceiving Patterns and Wholes

How is it that we recognize a set of marks on a page as a letter or a shape rather than just a bunch of markings? We know that the letter *E* is more than just one long, vertical line segment plus three shorter, horizontal line segments. The Gestalt psychologists recognized that often we perceive wholes as more than merely the sum of their parts. *Gestalt* is a German word that means "form," "pattern," or "shape." German researchers Max Wertheimer, Kurt Koffka, and Wolfgang Köhler studied visual perception in the early 20th century and described a set of principles or laws by which people organize elements of figures or scenes into whole objects. The major Gestalt laws of visual organization are similarity, continuity, proximity, closure, and figure-ground.

What do you see when you look at Figure 20? Most people with normal color vision would report seeing two lines of blue dots alternating with two lines of red dots. You would not say, "Oh, 20 dots; some are red and some are blue." Instead, you group the elements that are like one another together into a perceptual unit—the red dots go together and the blue dots go together. This Gestalt tendency to group like objects together is known as **similarity**.

similarity
A Gestalt law that says we tend to group like objects together in visual perception.

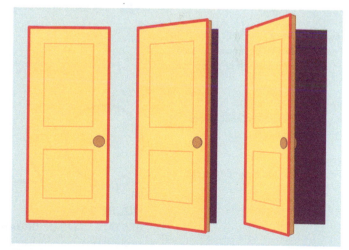

FIGURE 19

SHAPE CONSTANCY. Even though the two-dimensional retinal image of the door changes in shape from rectangular to trapezoidal when the door is opened, we know the door's shape hasn't changed.

FIGURE 20

GESTALT LAWS OF ORGANIZATION: SIMILARITY

 Do you see this figure as two rows of blue and two rows of red dots or as 20 dots, some red and some blue? Why do people have different perceptions about the whole?

FIGURE 21

GESTALT LAWS OF ORGANIZATION: CONTINUITY

continuity
The Gestalt law that says we see points or lines in such a way that they follow a continuous path.

proximity
A Gestalt law that says we tend to group objects together that are near one another.

law of closure
The tendency to perceive a whole object in the absence of complete information.

figure
A specific object in front of an unformed background.

ground
The background behind objects or figures.

According to the Gestalt law of **continuity**, we see points or lines in such a way that they follow a continuous path. For example, consider the first drawing in Figure 21. We see a straight line running through a curved line. We do *not* see the first drawing as a result of combining the two pieces from the second drawing.

The Gestalt law of **proximity** says that we tend to group together objects that are near one another. Figure 22 shows a series of blue boxes. Most people say they see four pairs of boxes, rather than eight boxes, because of the spacing. The first two are closer together than the second and third, and the third and fourth are closer together than the fourth and fifth, and so on.

Take a look at Figure 23a. Most observers see these figures as distinct shapes (a circle and two triangles) rather than lines, curves, and spheres, even though they are incomplete. The **law of closure** occurs when we perceive a whole object in the absence of complete information. The drawing in Figure 23b provides another example of how our perceiving brain completes the drawing to see a duck.

Another key Gestalt notion concerns how we separate things into **figure** and **ground**, where the figure is the thing that stands in front of a somewhat unformed background. Gestalt psychologists pointed out that we readily separate a figure from its background in order to perceive it. Perhaps the most famous example of figure-ground effects is the face-vase figure, a version of which is shown in Figure 24a. Notice that you can view the figure either as a blue vase against a light background or as two facial profiles (with blue space between them). It is impossible to see both the vase and the faces at the same moment. Dutch painter M. C. Escher regularly used figure-ground effects in his paintings (Figure 24b).

Numerous visual illusions stem from Gestalt figure-ground principles, many of which have hidden figures, as in Figure 25. Once you know what to look for in the picture, the hidden object becomes figural and you cannot help but see it. Try it for yourself.

FIGURE 22

GESTALT LAWS OF ORGANIZATION: PROXIMITY

 How would you describe what you see here? Four pairs or eight single boxes? Which do you think most people see, and why?

(a)   (b)

FIGURE 23

GESTALT LAWS OF ORGANIZATION: CLOSURE. Challenge your perceptions: There really is no circle, triangle, or duck in the images—the "whole" appears only in your mind.

 How and why do you view these images as whole?

FIGURE 24
FIGURE-GROUND EFFECTS

(a)

(b)

©Zsschreiner/Shutterstock.com

 In (a), is it a vase or two faces? In (b), in the center of the image do you see butterflies or spiders?

FIGURE 25

FIGURE-GROUND EFFECTS IN SCENE PERCEPTION. Do you see the owl in the picture above? If not, see end of chapter to find out what you may have missed. See p. 161

Artist: Julian Jusim

1. Neurons called _____ in the visual cortex analyze the retinal image and respond to aspects of shapes, such as angles and movements.
   a. subjective contours
   b. shape-responsive cells
   c. feature detectors
   d. horizontal cells

2. How did Hubel and Wiesel discover that some cortical neurons respond to seeing lines of a specific orientation?
   a. by using fMRI to study cat brain function during visual tasks
   b. by inserting electrodes into single cells in the visual cortex
   c. through surgical removal of cortical tissue
   d. with EEG

3. After leaving the retina, what is the first stop in the brain for processing of visual information?

   a. the occipital cortex
   b. the parietal lobe
   c. the hypothalamus
   d. the thalamus

4. Which of the following is NOT a monocular depth cue?
   a. linear perspective
   b. 3-D movies
   c. texture gradient
   d. interposition

5. The brain's ability to preserve perception of objects in spite of the changes in retinal image is known as
   a. interrelative consistency.
   b. proximity.
   c. visual stability.
   d. perceptual constancy.

Answers can be found at the end of the chapter.

HEARING

We could clearly make the case that sight is the most important sense for humans. So much of our lives revolves around what we see. The science of vision is much more developed than the science of any other sense, but people who are both blind and deaf beg to differ, as the American author Helen Keller put it eloquently when she wrote

> I am just as deaf as I am blind. The problems of deafness are deep and more complex, if not more important, than those of blindness. Deafness is a much worse misfortune. For it means the loss of the most vital stimulus—the sound of the voice that brings language, sets thoughts astir and keeps us in the intellectual company of man. (Helen Keller, as quoted in Ackerman, 1990, p. 191)

Just as vision starts when we sense light waves, hearing begins when we sense sound waves. Sound waves must travel through a medium, or we cannot hear them. Sound waves can move through fluid or air, but most of the time we hear sound waves that travel through air. Sound waves travel much more slowly than light waves, which is why you hear thunder after you have seen lightning.

The Physics of Sound and the Psychophysics of Hearing

We perceive different shapes and sizes of sound waves as different sounds. Hearing is affected by three physical properties of the sound wave: its amplitude, frequency, and purity. The height, or *amplitude*, of the sound wave determines what we perceive as loudness. The taller the wave is, the louder the sound. The scale for a sound's loudness is decibels (dB), starting with 0, which is the threshold for normal human hearing. The scale has no upper limit, but sounds above 150–170 dB are seldom registered anywhere.

A whisper is about 30 dB, a regular human conversation is about 55–60 dB, a jackhammer is about 90 dB, a very loud bar or nightclub is around 100–110 dB, a very loud rock concert is about 110–120 dB, and a jet airplane is about 130–140 dB. If you ever were to hear a sound at 160 dB, your eardrum would burst.

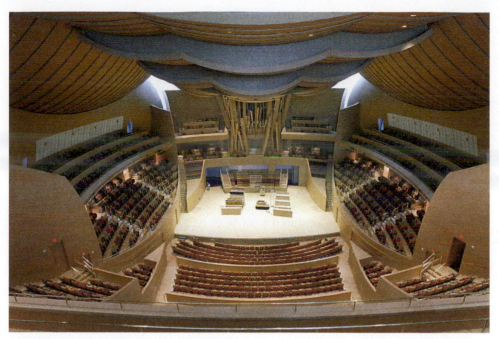

©Hector Mata/AFP/Getty Images

Theaters and concert halls are designed to reflect and absorb sound, so that wherever you sit you can hear the performance. For musicians, however, constant exposure to loud music can cause hearing loss.

Believe it or not, car sound system competitions, such as "dB Drag Racing," regularly achieve sound in the 150–160 dB range. The record stands at 171 dB, about as loud as the Space Shuttle at launch! Needless to say, these levels are strictly for competition, and no one is in the car during the competition. Blue whales produce the loudest sound of any living animal ever recorded, reaching up to 188 dB (Cummings & Thompson, 1971).

The *frequency* of a sound wave, or how many waves occur in a given period of time, is what we perceive as the sound's pitch. Frequency is measured in units called *hertz (Hz)*, which is how many times the wave cycles per second. The higher the frequency, the higher the pitch. For example, the higher keys on a piano—those farther to the right—are of higher pitch than the lower keys. The range for human pitch perception is from about 20 Hz to about 20,000 Hz, but most people cannot hear sounds at either extreme. Sounds below 20 Hz are called *subsonic* and above 20,000 are called *ultrasonic*. Most sounds we hear are in the range of 400 to 4,000 Hz. The human voice generally produces sounds ranging from 200 to 800 Hz, and a piano plays notes ranging from 30 to 4,000 Hz.

The third property of sound waves, *purity*, is the complexity of the wave. Some sound waves are pretty simple, made of only one frequency (see Figure 26). Most waves are *complex*; that is, they contain a mixture of frequencies. A sound's purity or unique tonal quality, which we perceive as **timbre** (pronounced "tamber"), is determined by how many frequencies are present in the wave. Musicians often refer to timbre as the "color" or "quality" of sound. Timbre, for example, allows us to distinguish a middle C (256 Hz) as being from either a piano or a violin or even one middle C on one piano from that of another piano. They are all 256 Hz and may even be of equal loudness, but we have no trouble telling them apart because they produce waves of different purities. So when musicians fall in love with the "sound" of one guitar or piano over another, it is the timbre they are falling in love with.

timbre
Is the quality or "color" of a particular sound and is a result of the sound's complexity or number of sound frequencies.

Pure wave

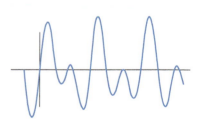

Complex wave

FIGURE 26
PURE AND COMPLEX SOUND WAVES. A pure sound wave consists of only one wave, whereas a complex wave is a mixture of more than one wave.

The Ear

As the structures on the sides of our head, our ears have very little to do with hearing itself. These external structures, called *pinnae*, collect and funnel sounds into the passage called the *auditory canal*. Once inside this canal, sound vibrations travel to the eardrum, or **tympanic membrane**. The auditory canal and tympanic membrane make up the *outer ear*. The sound waves on the tympanic membrane set into motion the bones of the *middle ear*: the hammer, anvil, and stirrup (see Figure 27). These bones do more than just vibrate, however: They amplify the waves, so that they have more than 20 times the energy they had entering the ear. The hammer hits the anvil, and the anvil moves the stirrup. The vibration of the stirrup in turn sets into motion a series of important changes in the *inner ear*.

The inner ear includes the cochlea and semicircular canals. The **semicircular canals** play a key role in maintaining a sense of balance. As the stirrup vibrates, it moves a membrane that covers the inner ear, called the *oval window*. The vibrations on the oval window send movement through the fluid-filled cavity of the **cochlea**, a bony tube, curled like a snail's shell and filled with fluid. The **basilar membrane** runs through the cochlea. Within the basilar membrane of the cochlea are **hair cells**, which are the sensory receptors for sound, just as the photoreceptors are for vision. As the vibrations move through the cochlear fluid, the basilar membrane vibrates,

tympanic membrane
The eardrum.

semicircular canals
A structure of the inner ear involved in maintaining balance.

cochlea
A bony tube of the inner ear, which is curled like a snail's shell and filled with fluid.

basilar membrane
A membrane that runs through the cochlea; contains the hair cells.

hair cells
Inner ear sensory receptors for sound that transduce sound vibrations into neural impulses.

FIGURE **27**

ANATOMY OF THE HUMAN EAR. Sound waves hit the outer ear and travel down the auditory canal, where they hit the eardrum and cause vibrations, setting in motion the bones of the middle ear (hammer, anvil, and stirrup). The bones vibrate and amplify the waves, where they vibrate the oval window. The vibrations cause fluid in the cochlea to bend the hair cells. Stimulation of the hair cells transduces sound vibrations into electrical impulses, which can generate an action potential in the auditory nerve. An electrical impulse is then sent to the brain's auditory cortex for processing and interpretation.

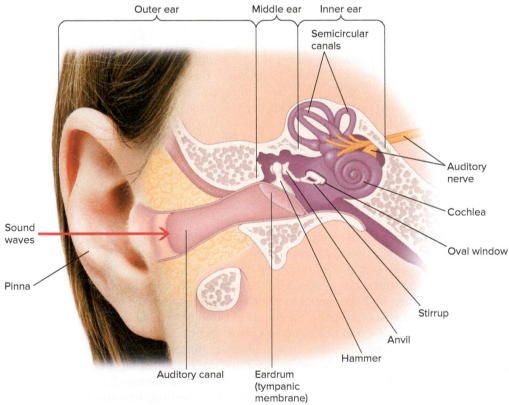

©PhotoAlto/Alix Minde/Getty Images RF

Psychology in the Real World

Hearing Loss Can Happen in Young People Too

Most people take their hearing for granted, but there is a good chance that at some point in your lifetime you will suffer some degree of hearing loss. Studies often divide the causes of hearing loss into the categories of age-related and noise exposure, but these two are related. Being exposed to loud noise levels over long periods of time leads to a loss of hearing after 10–15 years.

Noise often leads to age-related hearing loss, especially in the high-frequency range of 5,000–15,000 Hz (Lutman & Spencer, 1991). In a large-scale study of exposure to noise at work, it was found that middle-aged to older men (ages 45 to 70) have their threshold for hearing high-frequency sounds (4,000 Hz and higher) raised by 10 dB compared to men not exposed to such noise at work (Tambs et al., 2006). A 10 dB increase translates to sound that is 10 times as intense, which we perceive as twice as loud. Factory or machine workers exposed to noise at the 90 dB level for 8 hours a day, 5 days a week suffer permanent hearing loss after 10 years on the job (Bauer et al., 1991; Lutman & Spencer, 1991). Similarly, rock musicians exposed to noise levels 95–107 dB, when tested before and after concerts, showed both temporary and permanent hearing loss (Gunderson, Moline, & Catalano, 1997). Musician hearing loss primarily depends upon number of hours per week one plays, rather than number of years spent as a musician (Halevi-Katz et al., 2015). Finally, 7.5% of military personnel who were deployed to combat report hearing loss, which is higher than the rate young adults in general (5.5%) (Wells et al., 2015; Zelaya, Lucas, & Hoffman, 2015).

Many people believe it's mostly the elderly who suffer from hearing loss. Due to the ubiquity of personal listening devices, however, younger people are now suffering some degree of hearing loss as well. Personal listening devices have maximum decibel levels of around 115–125 dB, about the loudness of a rock concert. In a meta-analysis of 26 separate studies, Jiang and colleagues (2016) reported that more than 58% of teens and young adults listened to more than the daily recommended noise dose. This recommended dose is a ratio of decibel level and time, but two examples are if you listen at 85 dB, you can listen for 8 hours/day, but at 105 dB, you cannot exceed 5 minutes/day (NIOSH, 1998). It is not surprising therefore that since the first iPod was released in late 2001 hearing loss of any kind in teens has increased from 15% in 1988–1994 to 19.5% by 2005–2006 (Shargorodsky et al., 2010). By 2013 the rate was up to 21.5% (Sulaiman et al., 2013). As with older adults, hearing loss in teens is also most likely in the high-frequency range (National Institute on Deafness, 2008). Earbud-style headphones are the most problematic, as they let in the most ambient noise (Hodgetts, Szarko, & Rieger, 2009). Ambient noise comes from your surrounding environment and when that is louder, you have to turn the volume up to hear the music. Most young people claim to understand the risks of hearing loss due to frequent personal listening device use, and some research shows that certain messages to teens about the dangers of loud music can reduce their exposure to high volume music in those who are motivated to reduce hearing loss (De Bruijn et al., 2016). The following are some guidelines for listening to a personal listening device without causing long-term damage to your ears (Knox, 2007):

- Limit earphone listening to an hour a day, at a setting no greater than 6 on a 10-notch scale.
- If someone can hear earphone "leakage" from several feet away, it is too loud.
- If someone has ringing in the ears or a feeling of fullness in the ear, or if speech sounds are muffled after a listening session, the music was too loud.
- Try over-the-ear headphones rather than earbuds.

making the hair cells bend. As they bend, they transduce the sound vibrations into electrical impulses, which may generate an action potential in the **auditory nerve**.

Hair cells vary in size depending on their location in the cochlea. The smallest hair cells are nearest the oval window, and the largest hair cells are in the coiled-up center part of the cochlea. There is a one-to-one connection between the size of a hair cell and its sensitivity to different frequencies of sound. The smallest cells are sensitive to the highest frequencies (up to 20,000 Hz), and the largest hair cells are sensitive to the lowest frequencies (down to 20 Hz; see Figure 28). The louder the sound, the bigger the vibration in the cochlear fluid, the more stimulation of the hair cells, the faster the rate of action potentials in the auditory nerve, and the louder the sound we perceive. If the hair cells in the inner ear become damaged, as can happen when a person is exposed to very loud

auditory nerve
The nerve that receives action potentials from the hair cells and transmits auditory information to the brain.

FIGURE 28

DIFFERENT PARTS OF THE COCHLEA PROCESS DIFFERENT FREQUENCIES OF SOUND. The highest frequencies of sound stimulate the narrowest region of the cochlea. The small hair cells here are sensitive to high-frequency (higher-pitch) sounds in the range of 15,000 to 20,000 cycles per second (Hertz). The largest hair cells are in the wide center portion of the cochlea. These hair cells respond to low-frequency (low-pitch) sounds in the range of 20 to 100 cycles per second.

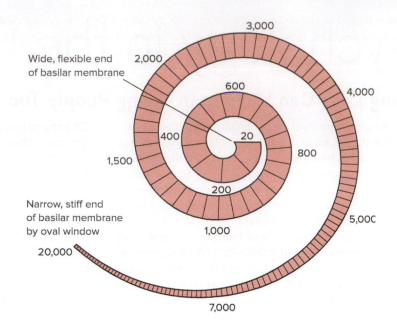

noises once or moderately loud noises (such as machines) over long periods of time, the person can suffer irreparable hearing loss. For more information about hearing loss, see "Psychology in the Real World."

Hearing in the Brain

After sound energy is changed to neural energy in the cochlea, the hair cells synapse with the auditory neurons that transmit the sound impulses to the thalamus in the brain. From there, the neural impulses are relayed to various parts of the brain, including the brain stem and the temporal lobes, home of the auditory cortex. Recall that the visual pathways go through the LGN. The auditory pathways go from the cochlea to the *inferior colliculus* in the brain stem and from there to the *medial (middle) geniculate nucleus (MGN)* of the thalamus. Lastly, due to the brain's neuroplasticity, it is true that people who are born deaf partly make up for lack of hearing with heightened sensitivity of other senses, especially touch but even sight (Karns et al., 2012). The brain is plastic and does not waste the auditory cortex. Instead, it simply takes on new sensory functions.

Quick Quiz 3: Hearing

1. The _____ of a sound wave determines what we perceive as loudness.
   a. frequency
   b. shape
   c. amplitude
   d. width

2. Which structure is responsible for the transduction of sound vibrations into action potentials?
   a. tympanic membrane
   b. cochlea
   c. stapes
   d. hair cells

Answers can be found at the end of the chapter.

THE BODILY SENSES

We feel things on our skin and in our organs. The largest contact surface area any sensory input has with our bodies is the skin, and it is carefully mapped in the somatosensory cortex in the parietal lobe of the brain (Blakeslee & Blakeslee, 2007).

The senses based in the skin, body, or any membrane surfaces are known as the **bodily senses**, which include knowing where our body parts are. We also sense things inside our bodies—organ pain, levels of heart rate, depth of breathing, to name a few. There are at least six distinct bodily or somatic senses: touch, temperature, pain, position/motion, balance, and interoception (perception of bodily sensations). Of these six senses, we will discuss touch and pain.

Touch

Imagine that your eyes are closed and someone puts an object in your left hand. For a minute, you feel its weight, shape, hardness, and temperature. Then the person puts something in your right hand. You conclude, with eyes still shut, that the first is a screwdriver and the second is a pen. How are you able to do this?

The top layers of skin have receptor cells that are sensitive to different tactile qualities—some to shape, some to grooves, some to vibrations and movements. These receptor cells are known as **mechanoreceptors**, and they are like the photoreceptors in the eye and the hair cells in the ear. There are four kinds of mechanoreceptors; each kind has a unique profile of sensitivity. Some of the mechanoreceptors are slow to change, and others are fast with variations in tactile stimulation. Some are sensitive to fine details, whereas others are not. For example, slowly drag your fingertip over a quarter. You can feel the bumps and grooves, thanks to fine-detail receptors in your skin. Some mechanoreceptors also sense movement and vibration, such as when someone runs fingers over your forearm. You have far fewer mechanoreceptors on the soles of your feet than on your fingertips, probably a good thing—it would be overwhelmingly uncomfortable to have extremely sensitive soles.

Women have finer tactile sensitivity in their fingertips than men, but this appears to be due to smaller fingertip size in women (Peters, Hackeman, & Goldreich, 2009). The cells for tactile sensation are more densely packed in smaller fingers. When men and women with equal-sized fingertips are compared, their tactile sensitivity is the same.

Like photoreceptors in the eye, mechanoreceptors mark only the beginning of the journey from sensation to perception. The sensory qualities (shape, size, hardness, and temperature) of the screwdriver and pen stimulate different kinds of mechanoreceptors in the skin, but the resulting sensory impulses must travel to the brain to be processed and interpreted. When something touches our fingertips, forearm, or shoulder, a dedicated region of cortex becomes active, and we perceive the sensation of being touched. Tactile sensations from our skin travel via sensory neurons to the spinal cord and up to the brain. The first major structure involved in processing bodily sensations is the thalamus, which relays the impulses to the somatosensory cortex in the parietal lobes.

Again, due to neuroplasticity, repeated sensory and motor tactile experience changes the amount of cortex involved in processing a particular sensation or movement. The general location in the somatosensory cortex stays the same, but the areas of the cortex devoted to that experience or function grow (Jenkins et al., 1990; Ostry et al., 2010). The more one body region is touched or stimulated, the more sensory or motor cortex is used to process information from the mechanoreceptors. Musicians who play stringed instruments, such as a violin, use the right hand to bow and the left hand to play the notes. Researchers have found that experienced violinists have larger representations, or *brain maps*, of the hand and finger regions of the somatosensory cortex than do non-musicians (Pantev et al., 2001).

Pain

We need pain to survive. People born with an extremely rare genetic insensitivity to pain can be severely injured or killed, because they don't know they have been harmed (Watkins & Maier, 2003). **Pain** is a complex emotional and sensory

bodily senses
The senses based in the skin, the body, or any membrane surfaces.

Connection

The part of the brain involved in the sense of touch is the somatosensory cortex.

See Figure 15 in the chapter "The Biology of Behavior". (p. 100)

mechanoreceptors
Receptor cells in the skin that are sensitive to different tactile qualities, such as shape, grooves, vibrations, and movements.

pain
A complex emotional and sensory experience associated with actual or potential tissue damage.

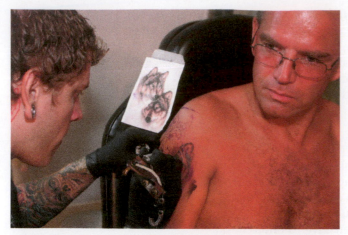
©Jeff Greenberg 2 of 6/Alamy

©The Tennessean, John Partipilo/AP Photo

Pain is subjective, and the perception of pain varies from one person to another. Some people may perceive the experience of getting a tattoo as moderately uncomfortable. Others might find it to be quite painful.

phantom limb pain
Occurs when a person who has lost an arm or leg continues to feel pain in the lost limb.

nociceptive pain
Pain from skin and/or tissue damage or injury.

experience associated with actual or potential tissue damage (Merskey & Bogduk, 1994). It is usually very unpleasant, but people vary widely in their experiences of pain, what they think is painful, and whether they might even enjoy pain (Schwerdtfeger, 2007). Some people feel no pain during great injury (such as soldiers in battle situations), and others feel pain when no tissue damage is present. The latter situation occurs with **phantom limb pain**, when people who have lost a limb feel pain in the missing arm or leg. Such cases dramatically show how pain is not just a direct result of tissue damage, but an experience in the brain as well. Pain also is enhanced by one's reaction to the injury. Often the emotional reaction to pain creates as much suffering as the actual tissue damage.

Pain Perception How do we sense and perceive pain? It's not merely touch gone too far. Damage to the skin is only one kind of pain. Other forms include organ tissue and nerve damage, as well as joint inflammation. Pain from skin and/or tissue damage or injury is called **nociceptive pain**. The skin has pain receptors that are sensitive to heat, cold, chemical irritation, and pressure; all these pain receptors are kinds of *nociceptors* (Basbaum & Jessell, 2000). Getting frostbite, suffering from chemical burns, and hitting your thumb with a hammer all hurt because these events stimulate nociceptors in the skin. The nociceptors send signals to the spinal cord and then to the brain, signaling that damage has occurred. The brain can then initiate an appropriate response, such as pulling your hand away from a hot burner. You can now see why not experiencing pain would be so dangerous!

Many brain structures are involved in the perception of skin damage alone. A partial list of brain structures activated by skin-based pain includes the thalamus, hypothalamus, limbic system, insula, and anterior cingulate cortex (see Figure 29; Goldstein, 2007). A somewhat surprising finding is that some of the same brain regions and neurochemicals activated when we experience physical pain are also activated during emotional pain—especially when we are rejected by others or see others receive shocks (Eisenberger, 2013; Singer et al., 2004). For example, the class of drugs known as opiates relieves both physical and emotional pain, which is one reason they can be so easily abused (Crain, Crain, & Crain, 2013; Panksepp, 1998). Moreover, the brain regions active in both physical and emotional pain are the anterior cingulate cortex (ACC) and the insula (see Figure 29). Even more fascinating, the same brain regions (ACC and insula) are activated whether we experience pain directly or observe someone else get hurt (Singer et al., 2004; Zaki et al., 2016). Interestingly, those who are born without the ability to experience pain also do not experience pain when others get hurt (Danziger et al., 2006). In short, the brain reacts much the same way to pain whether it is physical (in self or other) or emotional.

Emotion and pain systems interact considerably, as indicated by the well-established observation that emotional states can influence pain perception. Certain negative emotions—such as sadness—worsen the pain experience, whereas positive emotions can lessen it (Berna et al., 2010; Villemure & Schweinhardt, 2010). Scientists are just beginning to understand the brain mechanisms involved in emotional modulation of pain. Apparently, in the transmission of pain signals

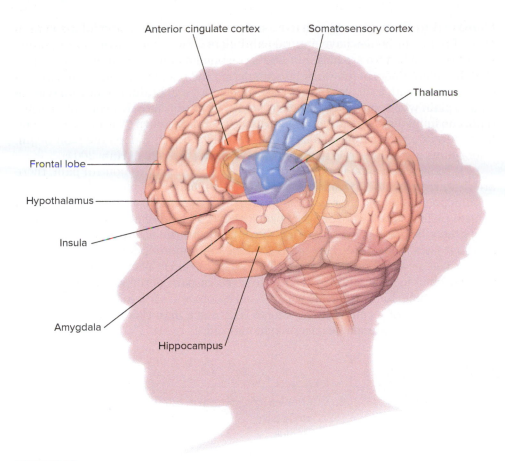

Anterior cingulate cortex

Somatosensory cortex

Thalamus

Frontal lobe

Hypothalamus

Insula

Amygdala

Hippocampus

FIGURE 29

THE BRAIN AND PAIN. What structures are activated during the perception of physical pain? Which of these are involved in emotional pain?

between the spinal cord and brain, there are many opportunities for communication with the brain systems involved in emotion (Roy et al., 2009).

Explaining Pain   One of the more influential explanations for pain comes from Ronald Melzack and Patrick Wall (1965, 1988). Their **gate control theory of pain** proposes that the spinal cord regulates the experience of pain by "gating" the transmission of pain information at the level of the spinal cord. The *gate* is not literally a gate but rather a competition between signals coming from different-sized axons or nerve fibers. More specifically, pain signals are sent via smaller nerve fibers than non-pain signals. Experienced pain is all about the balance and imbalance between signals from the pain fibers (small) relative to the non-pain fibers (large). When injury to skin or tissue occurs, for instance, there is more signaling from small pain fibers than the larger non-pain ones. The "gate" has opened. On the other hand, when there are more signals from the larger non-pain fibers pain is not experienced. The "gate" has closed. This is why small levels of pain can be blocked by rubbing one's skin or even acupuncture: The non-pain signals dominate and override or close the gate of the pain signals being sent to the brain (White, 2006).

What is most interesting about the gate control theory of pain is the idea that inhibitory channels can come from the brain as well as the body. Messages sent by the brain itself can close off the fibers in the spinal cord that are involved in pain sensations. Thoughts, feelings, and beliefs can affect pain sensations, which is one reason people vary so much in their perception of pain. Different people experiencing the same level of pain may have completely different experiences of their pain.

gate control theory of pain
The idea that the spinal cord regulates the experience of pain by the balancing of signals to the brain from small pain nerve fibers and larger non-pain fibers. The pain "gate" opens when more pain signals are sent to the brain than non-pain signals. Pain is blocked when the reverse happens.

Controlling Pain   In addition to thoughts and feelings that control the experience of pain, our bodies have natural painkillers called *endorphins* (*endogenous morphines*). When we are hurt, our bodies respond by releasing these substances (Fields, 2009). Endorphins work by stimulating the release of neurotransmitters that interfere with pain messages in the spinal cord and brain. Endorphin release may explain why some people, such as soldiers and automobile accident victims, report no immediate sensations of pain after a horrible injury (Warga, 1987). Only hours afterward or maybe the next day while in a hospital does the pain begin. Endorphins also play a role in acupuncture-based pain relief (Han, 2004).

If thoughts, feelings, and endorphins are not enough to control pain, there are drug treatments. For small aches and pains, many people take aspirin, acetaminophen, ibuprofen, or other similar drugs. Generally, these drugs work to control inflammation (Loeser & Melzack, 1999). For more severe pain, doctors may prescribe opioids, which are a class of drugs known as *analgesics*, meaning "without pain." Morphine, heroin, oxycodone, and hydrocodone are all opioids. All but heroin are commonly prescribed for pain relief. They deaden or lessen pain by blocking the neural activity involved in pain perception (Crain et al., 2013). Morphine, for example, is widely used before and after medical procedures and in the care of terminally ill patients. There is a high risk of dependency on opioids, so their use must be carefully monitored.

Quick Quiz 4: The Bodily Senses

1. The receptor cells for touch that reside in the skin are called
   a. tactile cilia.
   b. mechanoreceptors.
   c. interoceptors.
   d. receptive fields.

2. Our bodies have natural painkillers called
   a. analgesics.
   b. opioids.
   c. endorphins.
   d. acetaminophens.

Answers can be found at the end of the chapter.

THE CHEMICAL SENSES: SMELL AND TASTE

Smell and taste are chemical senses, because they respond to contact with molecules from objects we encounter in the world. Smell and taste are very important survival-related senses, for they govern our choices about what we take into our bodies. As such, these senses are very sensitive, are heightened during pregnancy, and can trigger emotional reactions (Profet, 1992; Rolls, 2004).

Unlike receptors for other senses, receptors for chemical molecules are regularly replaced, because they are constantly exposed not only to the chemicals in food but also to dirt and bacteria that can impair function (Goldstein, 2007). Smell and taste receptors are replaced every few weeks.

Smell (Olfaction)

olfactory sensory neurons
The sensory receptors for smell that reside high up inside the nose.

olfactory bulb
A forebrain structure that sends information either directly to the smell-processing areas in the cortex or indirectly to the cortex by way of the thalamus.

A small area high in the lining of the nasal cavity contains the **olfactory sensory neurons**, which are the receptors for smell (see Figure 30). These neurons contain hairlike projections called *cilia*, which are similar to the hair cells in the inner ear. The cilia convert the chemical information in odor molecules into neural impulses.

When chemicals come in contact with the cilia, transduction occurs, and the olfactory message travels to the **olfactory bulb** in the forebrain. The olfactory bulb sends information either directly to the smell-processing areas in the cortex or indirectly to the cortex by way of the thalamus (Buck, 2000). The *primary olfactory* *cortex* resides in the temporal lobe; the *secondary olfactory cortex* is in the frontal lobe near the eyes (see Figure 31).

Some fibers from the olfactory bulb go directly to the amygdala, which sends smell information to the hypothalamus, thalamus, and frontal cortex. You may recall that the amygdala plays a key role in emotional responses and connects to memory areas such as the hippocampus. These connections may explain why smells can instantly evoke an emotional memory (Herz, 2004). The smell of cedar wood, for example, immediately transports one of the authors (Greg) to his grandmother's attic in Kansas.

Just as there are specific photoreceptors for different primary colors, different odors stimulate different olfactory neurons. Most mammals have hundreds of different types of olfactory sensory neurons; these account for their highly discriminating sense of smell (Fleischer, Breer, & Strotmann, 2009). Greater concentrations of odors stimulate a greater number of sensory neurons; as a result, we perceive the same odor presented at different concentrations as entirely different smells. People differ considerably in their ability to sense odors. Some people lose the ability to sense smell with infection or injury, but usually this is short-term.

Animals have a heightened sense of smell compared to humans: We rely on dogs to sniff out suspects and bombs. Grizzly bears can locate dead animals from miles away and will readily feed on them (Bauer & Bauer, 1996). Sharks can detect one drop of blood in 25 gallons of water (Marks, 2006).

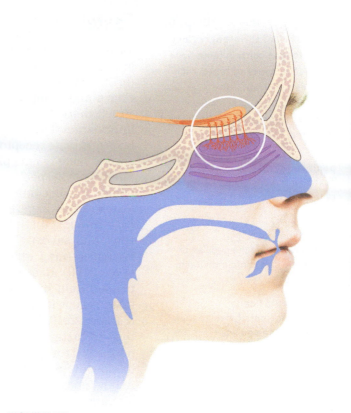

FIGURE **30**

OLFACTORY RECEPTORS IN THE NASAL CAVITY. The receptors in the nasal cavity, called cilia, are like the hair cells in the ear. They change chemical stimulation received from smells to nerve signals that are sent to the brain for processing and interpreting.

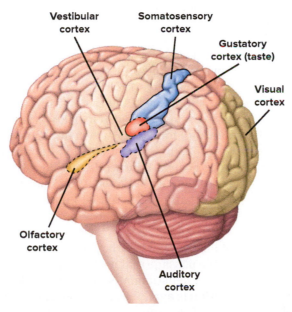

FIGURE **31**

FIVE SENSORY CORTICES IN THE BRAIN: OLFACTORY (SMELL), GUSTATORY (TASTE), VISUAL (VISION), AUDITORY (HEARING), AND SOMATOSENORY (TOUCH)

 Where are the major brain regions involves with each of the five senses?

Taste

True or False? Different regions of the tongue contain taste buds for specific types of taste, such as sweet or bitter.

False: Recent evidence shows taste receptor cells are distributed throughout the tongue.

papillae
Textured structures on the surface of the tongue; contain thousands of taste buds.

taste buds
Structures inside the papillae of the tongue that contain the taste receptor cells.

taste receptor cells
Sensory receptors for taste that reside in the taste buds.

gustatory cortex
The cortical region of the brain located in the insula area of the frontal lobe where taste sensations are processed and interpreted.

Taste evolved as a way of telling animals whether something was edible or not and in particular whether it was likely to be energy-rich (sweet) or noxious (bitter) (Peng et al., 2015). A close look at the human tongue reveals all kinds of ridges and bumps. These textured structures, called **papillae**, contain about 10,000 **taste buds**. Dozens of **taste receptor cells** on each bud process taste information. The papillae in the central part of the tongue contain very few taste buds and taste receptor cells, so we do not taste from that region. Human experience of taste results primarily from the stimulation of taste buds throughout the tongue, not in specific regions as was once thought. When chemicals from food or liquid come in contact with the tips of these taste buds, a chain of events unfolds, leading to the experience of taste.

Humans distinguish among five basic taste qualities: bitter, sweet, salty, sour, and savory. There is increasing evidence that a sixth taste quality—fattiness—may exist as well, but further research is needed (Garcia-Bailo et al., 2009). Researchers once thought that receptors for the different tastes resided only in certain regions of the tongue, but we now know that these taste receptor cells are distributed in many regions (Buck, 2000; Chaudhari & Roper, 2010; Huang et al., 2006). Although specific receptors exist for each type of taste, the savory experience—also known as *umami* from the Japanese word for "good flavor"—comes from the combined sensory experience of monosodium glutamate (MSG; a flavor enhancer, traditionally used in many Asian foods) and the perception of savory odors (Kawamura & Kare, 1987; McCabe & Rolls, 2007). The combined factors that produce the savory flavor point to the important roles both taste and smell play in our experiences of flavor in general.

Just as there are cortical regions for seeing, hearing, touching, and smelling, there is one for tasting. It is known as the **gustatory cortex** and is located in the insula region of the frontal lobe right where the temporal and parietal lobes intersect (see Figure 32). Interestingly, the five different tastes (sweet, sour, bitter, salty, savory/umami) activate slightly different areas of the gustatory cortex for different people, but the regions stay consistent within the same person (Schoenfeld et al., 2004).

Both smell and taste are involved in the experience of flavor (Goldstein, 2007). Have you ever noticed how dull food tastes when you have a cold? This is because your sense of smell is impaired. Try squeezing your nostrils shut while tasting an apple or any other food. Notice the flavor. Then release your nostrils and take another bite. You will notice more intense "appleness" with your nostrils open, because food aromas contribute greatly to the experience of flavor (Lawless et al., 2004). When the nose is shut, olfactory receptors in the passage that connects the oral and nasal cavities do not get stimulated. As a result, less olfactory information is available, and taste is impaired.

The experience of flavor showcases the brain's ability to combine sensory information to produce a unique sensory experience. In some people, sensory experiences sometimes combine in even more unusual ways. The next section, on synesthesia, focuses on these cases.

©Ahn Young-joon/AP Photo

Because dogs have a keen sense of smell, humans often employ them to locate illegal drugs, explosives, criminals, and missing people.

1. The primary olfactory cortex resides in which lobe of the brain?
   a. temporal
   b. frontal
   c. parietal
   d. occipital

2. Humans have taste receptor cells for what flavors?
   a. sweet, sour, salty, sharp, savory
   b. sweet, sour, bitter, salty, sharp
   c. sweet, sour, bitter, salty, savory
   d. sweet, sour, salty, sharp

Answers can be found at the end of the chapter.

SYNESTHESIA

Many of us use expressions such as "he was green with envy" or "her anger was red hot." We use these colors metaphorically, knowing full well he is not really green and her anger is not really red, but what if we literally experienced numbers as colors or touch as tastes? A surprisingly large segment of the population—about 4%–5%—can do just that (Simner et al., 2006). They experience what is known as **synesthesia**, which occurs when a person experiences sensations in one sense when a different sense is stimulated (Cytowic, 1989; Ramachandran & Hubbard, 2003; Spector & Maurer, 2009; Ward, 2013). In short, synesthesia occurs when the senses get mixed up and don't stay separate. Some people with this condition experience yellow when they hear a tone such as middle C. Others taste shapes.

As it turns out, however, synesthesia can be manipulated such that most anyone can experience it. For example, in research reported by **Rosenblum (2010)**, sounds while eating can change perception of how food tastes. Participants were asked to eat chips and at the same time sounds were played, with some sounds being loud and some being bright. Not knowing any connection between the sounds and eating, participants were simply asked to rate how fresh, crisp, soft, or stale the chips tasted. The chips were all exactly the same but people rated them differently depending on the sounds that played while eating. Bright and loud sounds, for instance, made the chip taste fresher and crispier. This study demonstrates how different senses—in this case sound and taste—can easily become interconnected or synesthetic.

The most common form of synesthesia is the one in which people experience numbers or sometimes letters as colors (Ramachandran & Hubbard, 2003; Spector & Maurer, 2009). One way that scientists were able to discover that synesthesia is a real perceptual phenomenon and not just a learned association or merely an overly active sense of metaphor was to administer perceptual tests such as the one in Figure 32 (5s and 2s). In the figure on the left, there are a few 5s within the 2s. For most of us, they are hard to pinpoint, and it takes us a while to determine how many there are, but a person who sees 5s as blue and 2s as red, as shown on the right, has no trouble seeing that there are six 5s, forming a triangle.

How does synesthesia happen? The most well-established explanation is that synesthesia results from a cross-wiring or cross-activation of sensory neurons in various parts of the brain (Hubbard & Ramachandran, 2005; Spector & Maurer, 2009; Tomson et al., 2013; van Leeuwen et al., 2011). Cross-activation occurs when two areas of the brain, normally kept separate, become activated at the same time by the same stimulus. In synesthesia, the brain regions involved in color perception cross-activate with sensations of numbers. As it turns out, one region of the temporal lobe is active in processing both color sensations and numbers and is therefore the most likely area of cross-activation in this form of synesthesia (Hubbard & Ramachandran, 2005;

synesthesia
An unusual sensory experience in which a person experiences sensations in one sense when a different sense is stimulated.

Challenge Your Assumptions

True or False? The experience of "seeing sounds" or "hearing colors" occurs only under the influence of drugs.

False: About 4% of the population regularly has a crossover of sensory experience where they "see sounds" or "hear colors." This is known as synesthesia.

FIGURE **32**

SYNESTHESIA. People who perceive numbers as colors would have no trouble distinguishing the numbers 5 and 2 in the square on the left. They would see the numbers in color, as shown in the example on the right.

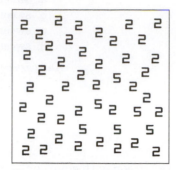

The way a person without synesthesia sees it

The way a person with synesthesia sees it

(Source: From Ramachandran, V. S., & Hubbard, E. M. (2003, May). Hearing colors, tasting shapes. *Scientific American*, 228, 52–59.)

Ramachandran & Hubbard, 2003). Some evidence suggests that this sensory cross-wiring is a result of unusual neural development, including a failure to prune synaptic connections that are temporary in early stages of development (Spector & Maurer, 2009; Ward, 2013). Many infants have these cross-wired neurons connecting different sensory systems, but with age and experience they get pruned or eliminated. They do not appear to be pruned in people with synesthesia. Finally, certain hallucinogenic drugs can temporarily create synesthetic experiences, such as when people see musical sounds as colors. The brain mechanisms responsible for this kind of synesthesia are not well described (Weil & Rosen, 1998).

Bringing It All Together

Making Connections in Sensation and Perception

Differences across Cultures

Throughout this chapter we have touched on ways in which people differ in sensory perception. For example, some people are more sensitive to bitter tastes than others. Individual differences in perception may result from differences in perceptual set, or frame of mind. Thus, it stands to reason that growing up in a certain environment, with particular beliefs, ways of viewing things, and physical settings, might impact how one perceives the world. Culture and place can serve as perceptual sets. Most research on the cultural influences on perception has focused on three sense systems: vision, olfaction, and pain.

Cultural Variation in Visual Perception
Differences exist across cultures in response to certain visual images that use monocular cues to depth. Look again at the Müller-Lyer line illusion in Figure 15. Recall that linear perspective explains why people see the line on the right as longer than the one on the left when the lines are, in fact, equal. Do people who grow up in a world with no corners view these drawings the same way we do? Researchers have studied the effects of living in a *carpentered world*—an environment with constructed buildings with many right angles—on various people's perceptions of depth. Navajos who have lived at least 10 years in round huts are much less likely to see the lines of Figure 15 as differing in length, for they are not accustomed to rooms with edges (Pedersen & Wheeler, 1983). A similar effect has been reported in studies of children living in Zambia, in a rural setting with few modern buildings (Stewart, 1973), but Navajos and Zambians who have lived in the presence

FIGURE 33

A PICTURE FOR DEPTH PERCEPTION TASKS TESTED ON BANTU

 Is the hunter after the elephant or the gazelle? How might your explanation of this scene depend on your cultural perspective? (Based on Hudson, 1960.)

of corners do experience the Müller-Lyer illusion (Matsumoto & Juang, 2004). Experience modifies perception.

Moreover, Hudson (1960) studied the perception of depth cues in the Bantu people of the Niger-Congo region of Africa. He showed people the picture depicted in Figure 33 and others similar to it. He then asked them to explain what was going on in the scene. When people from the United States, Europe, and India viewed such a picture, they said the hunter was going after the gazelle, as the elephant was clearly in the distance. Bantu people, however, said the hunter was attacking the elephant. So the Bantu do not appear to use relative size differences as cues to depth because they don't see the elephant as being in the background. Why? The Bantu people's response may result from not having much experience with two-dimensional drawings like the figure. Interestingly, Bantu who had been educated in European schools said the hunter was going for the gazelle (Matsumoto & Juang, 2004).

As we have just seen, different cultural backgrounds can impact not only illusions and depth perception but also foreground and background. People from Eastern cultures tend to perceive the world more as a whole, with people, objects, and the context being connected and belonging together. Westerners, however, tend to focus most on foreground objects and less on the background and periphery (Nisbett et al., 2001). The Research Process for this chapter (see Figure 34) focuses on cultural influences on how people perceive and recall figural versus background information in visual scenes (Masuda & Nisbett, 2001). The findings are consistent with the more established observation that Eastern people view themselves as embedded in the larger world rather than as independent entities (Markus & Kitayama, 1991). In another example of top-down processing, one's orientation toward life and the world can shape visual perception and memory.

Cultural Variation in Olfactory Experience

Smell is an interesting sense to compare across cultures, in part because it is a highly emotional sense. Because smells elicit emotions so readily, cultures often develop strong rules or norms about which smells are okay and which ones aren't and differ widely on the acceptability of odors based on experience, climate, and cuisine. Also, different places vary in their standards for cleanliness and for what is acceptable body odor (Hannigan, 1995). Do people who are raised so differently with respect to what is typical to smell or what it is okay to smell like show differences in scent detection in controlled experiments?

The ability to describe and name smells seems to vary across different cultures and languages (Classen, 2012; Doty et al., 1985; Majid & Levinson, 2011). For instance, Korean Americans performed better than African Americans and European Americans on odor detection tasks, and both of these groups performed better than native Japanese. In other research on smell and culture, English-speaking people consistently reported great difficulty in describing and identifying common smells like coffee, peanut butter, and chocolate. Typically, participants could only correctly identify approximately one-half of the smells and they would fumble in trying to describe it. When researchers went to the Jahai rain-forest culture in Malay, however, they found not only greater accuracy but also that the Jahai had little trouble putting into words what they smelled.

Other aspects of smell may be less susceptible to cultural effects. Consider gender differences in smell perception. Women tend to be more sensitive to smells than men (Brand & Millot, 2001; Kobayashi et al., 2006). When researchers tested how well native Japanese and Americans of African, European, and Korean descent could identify odors in a controlled laboratory setting (Doty et al., 1985), although they found cultural differences and gender differences. In each culture women outperformed men.

Cultural Variation in Pain

Given the large role that subjective factors play in pain perception, many researchers have looked at cultural, gender, and ethnic differences in pain (Al-Atiyyat, 2009; Wickelgren, 2009). There are big differences among people in pain tolerance, and we can even experience pain in the absence of any real tissue damage—remember phantom limb pain? One general finding is that women tend to have a lower pain threshold than men; that is, they more quickly say a stimulus is painful as it becomes more intense (Wickelgren, 2009). Moreover, there are clear cultural differences in tolerance for pain. In one of the most painful of human experiences, childbirth, we see widely differing perceptions of how painful it is.

For example, the Yap who live in the South Pacific consider childbirth to be simply a part of everyday life. Yap women routinely work in the fields right up until childbirth

©Tengku Bahar/AFP/Getty Images

Cultural differences in pain perception are evident in this photo, taken during the Hindu festival of Thaipusam in Malaysia.

and are often back at work the next day. What is even more interesting is that Yap fathers experience the pain of childbirth, and they are the ones who stay in bed to recover after the birth of the child (Kroeber, 1948). In the Huichol tribe of Mexico, so that fathers-to-be would go through their own painful birth process along with the mothers in labor, a string would be tied around the man's testicles. The woman in labor would hold the other end of the string, and with each contraction she experienced, she would pull on the string (Cassidy, 2006)!

Research Process

1 Research Question

Do people from an Eastern culture (Japan) focus more on and have better recall for objects in the background and periphery of a scene than people from a Western culture (United States)?

2 Method

For this quasi-experimental study by Masuda and Nisbett (2001), participants came into the laboratory individually and sat down at a computer. They watched a 20-second video of the scene depicted here. The large fish are considered foreground. Plants, small fish, and the other nonmoving animals (rocks and snail) are considered background. Arrows indicate the direction in which the fish and other objects moved during the scene. After viewing the video, participants orally described what they had seen. Trained coders rated the number of statements they made about various aspects of the scene, such as foreground and background fish, the small stationary animals, and the plants.

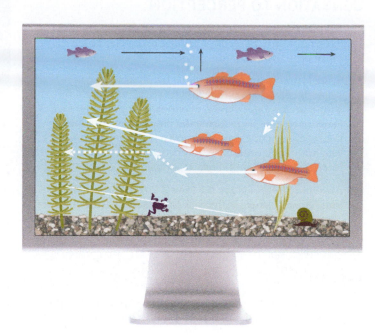

FIGURE 34

FOREGROUND-BACKGROUND. How does culture influence the way we perceive visual information?

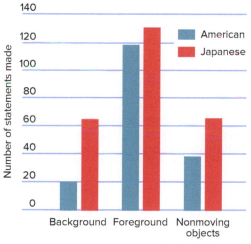

3 Results

As predicted, and consistent with cultural values and attitudes, the Japanese commented much more on the background and nonmoving animals (snail and frog) than the Americans did. There was no significant difference in how much people from each culture commented on the large fish in the foreground.

4 Conclusion

How we perceive everyday scenes is influenced by our culture. Our brains have been shaped by the assumptions and values of our society. In this case, people in Eastern cultures, such as Japan, tend to focus on background, foreground, and nonmoving objects, whereas those in Western cultures, such as the United States, tend to focus more on the foreground and moving objects only. This research is consistent with the more established observation that Eastern people view themselves as rooted in the larger world rather than as independent individuals.

(Source: "Attending Holistically versus Analytically: Comparing the Context Sensitivity of Japanese and Americans," by T. Masuda and R. E. Nisbett, 2001, *Journal of Personality and Social Psychology*, 81, 922–934.)

Chapter Review

THE LONG, STRANGE TRIP FROM SENSATION TO PERCEPTION

- Sensation is the stimulation of our sense organs by the external world. Perception is the process by which the brain organizes and interprets sensory experience.

- Stimulation of the sense organs involves taking in sensory energy from the outside world, whether it be sound waves, light waves, chemicals, or pressure. Our sensory system transforms the physical energy into neural energy in a process known as transduction. The brain then organizes the transformed information, interprets it, and initiates a response.

- Absolute thresholds are the lowest levels of a stimulus that humans sense. Difference thresholds are the smallest amounts of change in stimulus that a person detects.

©Güldenhaupt/Moment/Getty Images RF

- According to Weber's law, the smallest detectable change is a constant proportion of the intensity of the original stimulus.

- Our frame of mind affects our perception of objects and is known as our perceptual set.

VISION

- The eye bends light, converts light energy into electrical energy, and sends that information to the brain for further processing.

- Vision happens in the brain, in the lateral geniculate nucleus (LGN) of the thalamus and in the visual cortex in the occipital lobes.

- Hubel and Wiesel demonstrated that single cells in the visual cortex act as feature detectors, and there are three kinds for vision: simple cells, complex cells, and hypercomplex cells. Integration of this feature information occurs in the parietal and temporal cortexes.

- Depth perception is the ability to figure out how far or near objects are. One cue for depth perception is binocular disparity, the fact that our two eyes provide slightly different viewpoints, which our brains integrate into a single 3-D image. Monocular depth cues include linear perspective, texture gradient, atmospheric perspective, and interposition.

- The brain organizes visual sensations with Gestalt laws of similarity, continuity, proximity, and closure.

- Separating figures from backgrounds helps us organize visual sensations, but it also makes us vulnerable to illusions.

HEARING

- Humans respond to three different properties of sound waves: We perceive amplitude as loudness, frequency as pitch, and purity as timbre.

- The receptor hair cells in the cochlea are sensitive to different frequencies of sound waves and convert the mechanical energy of sound into neural energy for processing in the auditory cortex.

THE BODILY SENSES

- The bodily senses include sensations of touch, temperature, pain, balance, position/motion, and interoception.

- The brain regions most involved in touch are the thalamus and the somatosensory cortex in the parietal lobes. Pain sensations are processed mainly by the insula and the anterior cingulate cortex in the frontal lobes.

THE CHEMICAL SENSES: SMELL AND TASTE

- The retina contains two types of photoreceptor cells, called rods and cones. Cones are sensitive to red, green, and blue light waves, whereas rods are sensitive to light and are responsible for dark adaptation.

- The trichromatic theory of color vision states that we perceive the full range of colors as different combinations of three colors. The opponent-process theory says that cones are linked together in three opposing color pairs: blue/yellow, red/green, and black/white.

- Smell receptors in the nose contain olfactory sensory neurons, which convert chemical information into neural information. The olfactory message goes to the olfactory bulb and then to the primary olfactory cortex in the temporal lobe.

- Information about taste is processed in the taste buds of the tongue. Humans distinguish among five basic taste qualities: bitter, sweet, salty, sour, and savory.

SYNESTHESIA

- Synesthesia occurs when one sensory system is activated by the stimulation of a different sensory system, and the neurons are cross-activated in the brain.

- In the most common form of synesthesia, people experience letters or numbers as colors.

BRINGING IT ALL TOGETHER: MAKING CONNECTIONS IN SENSATION AND PERCEPTION

- Variations in experience across cultures influence the way people see, smell, and feel pain.

- Ethnic and cultural differences aside, women are more sensitive to smells than are men.

Key Terms

absolute threshold
accommodation
afterimages
auditory nerve
basilar membrane
binocular depth cues
binocular disparity
bodily senses
bottom-up processing
cochlea
cones
continuity
cornea
dark adaptation
depth perception
difference threshold
feature detectors
figure
fovea
gate control theory of pain

ground
gustatory cortex
hair cells
iris
just noticeable difference (JND)
law of closure
lens
mechanoreceptors
monocular depth cues
nociceptive pain
olfactory bulb
olfactory sensory neurons
opponent-process theory
optic chiasm
optic nerve
pain
papillae
perception
perceptual constancy
perceptual set

phantom limb pain
photoreceptors
proximity
pupil
retina
rods
semicircular canals
sensation
sensory adaptation
signal detection theory
similarity
synesthesia
taste buds
taste receptor cells
timbre
transduction
trichromatic color theory
tympanic membrane
visual acuity
Weber's law

Quick Quiz Answers

Quick Quiz 1: 1.b; 2.d   **Quick Quiz 2:** 1.c; 2.b; 3.d; 4.b; 5.d   **Quick Quiz 3:** 1.c; 2.d
Quick Quiz 4: 1.b; 2.c   **Quick Quiz 5:** 1.a; 2.c   Solution to Figure 26 on p. 143:

Artist: Julian Jusim

5 Human Development

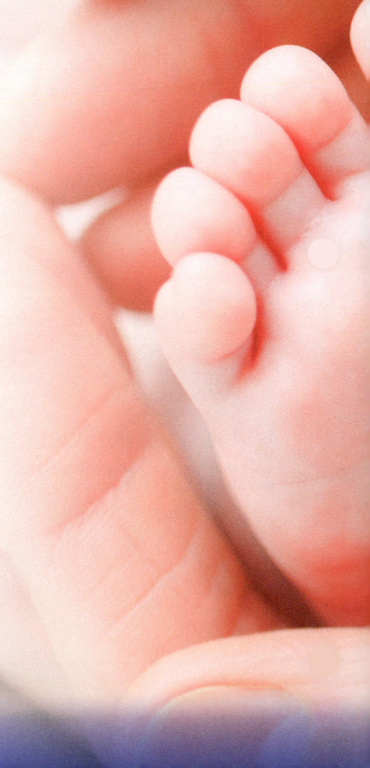

Chapter Outline

Challenge Your Assumptions

True or False?

- The heart develops before the brain. (see page 165)

- Schizophrenia in an offspring is more likely if the mother is exposed to a virus while pregnant. (see page 169)

- Differences in human temperament already exist before birth. (see page 171)

- Babies are born able to see and hear as well as adults. (see page 172)

- Being regularly touched as a newborn increases both physical and mental health later in life. (see page 187)

- Parents are the main social influence on development up through late adolescence. (see page 195)

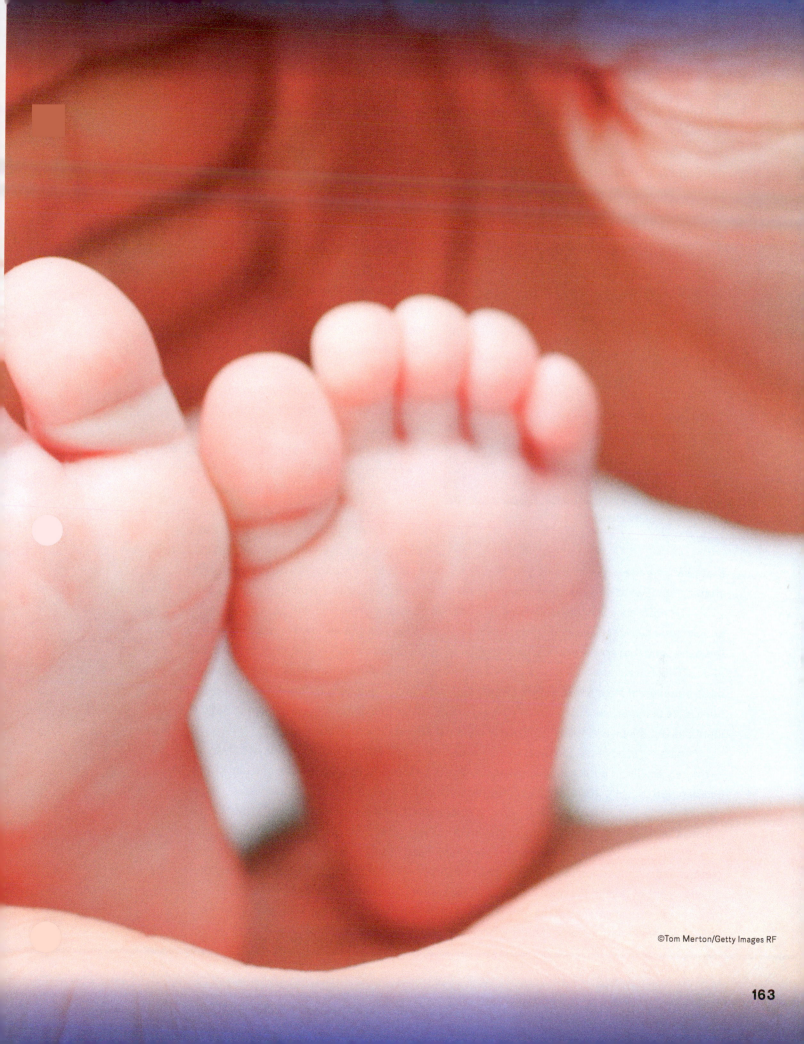

©Tom Merton/Getty Images RF

S eldom have two identical twins been more different than Wyatt and Jonas. Both born male, but by age 2, Wyatt was clearly identifying as a girl. He asked his mother things like "when do I get to be a girl?" and "when does my penis fall off?" (Nutt, 2015). Wyatt was quite persistent, being clear that he was a "girl in a boy's body." Wyatt's mother and twin brother accepted this as just who Wyatt was, but his father and most other people had a difficult time understanding how a young "boy" could really be a girl. From childhood on, Wyatt dressed like a girl and by age 9 identified socially as a girl. By 15 Wyatt transitioned and officially changed his name to Nicole.

©Bill O'Leary/The Washington Post/Getty Images

Nicole and Jonas

Identical twins are "identical" because they start from one fertilized egg (monozygotic), which for reasons unknown splits into two developing fetuses with identical genetic information. Why might one "identical" twin look slightly different from the other, or why might one develop schizophrenia as a young adult whereas the other does not? Genotype is not phenotype. Many events can occur between the time genotype is established at conception and the time traits get expressed as phenotypes over the course of a lifetime. Genetic mutations and different placenta (saclike organ in which the fetus lives) can be two reasons for differences in identical twins (Bruder et al., 2008; Segal, 1999). Epigenetics—environmental events that change gene expression—is another (Fraga et al., 2005). These events define development, shaping somewhat different paths even for identical twins before and after birth.

The difference between genotype and phenotype is very clear from the case of Nicole and Jonas. Their case also highlights the fact that anatomy and gender identity are not one and the same, and that processes before and after birth continue to mold gender identity (Pasterski et al., 2015; Sasaki et al., 2016). As we will see in more detail at the end of this chapter, sexual differentiation of male and female is affected by many things, including different levels of sex-hormones being present during brain development. Nicole and Jonas may have been genetically identical, but they were not epigenetically identical. Genes are not destiny.

To be sure, however, identical twins—even when separated at birth—are almost always extremely similar in personality, intelligence, illness histories, and even careers and marriages (Holden, 1980; Lynn, 2006; Schein & Bernstein, 2007; Segal, 1999). But not always.

human development
The study of change and continuity in the individual across the life span.

The science of human development helps explain why. **Human development** is the process of how genotype becomes phenotype and therefore how we change and remain the same over the course of a lifetime, from conception to death. Forces of nature and nurture are involved in shaping the development of human thought, behavior, and personality, and even gender identity. Developmental psychology examines any and all influences of change over the life span—genetic, epigenetic, neurological, cognitive, social, moral, emotional, and personality.

THE DEVELOPING FETUS

From conception until birth, we grow from a single cell to a fully formed, but still developing, human. The brain is the first major organ to form. The heart develops about a week later. (It is strange to think we have a brain before we have a heart!) A little more than 8 months later, when we are born, the brain has more than 100 billion cells.

We pass more biological milestones before birth than we will during the rest of our lives. Development in the womb is incredibly fast and complex and includes not only physical growth but psychological development as well. Personality and cognitive traits are already being shaped before we are born.

Challenge Your Assumptions

True or False? The heart develops before the brain.

False: A rudimentary brain develops before the heart.

Stages of Prenatal Development

Life before birth is commonly divided into three distinct stages: germinal, embryonic, and fetal. The **germinal stage** begins at conception and lasts for 2 weeks. At conception, the fertilized egg is a single-celled **zygote** which starts dividing rapidly around 36 hours after conception. By day 7, the multicelled organism—now called a blastocyst—travels down the mother's fallopian tube and attaches to the uterine wall (see Figure 1). This process is far from risk-free: Between 30% and 50% of blastocysts do not implant properly, and the pregnancy ends without the woman's having known she was pregnant (Gupta et al., 2007).

germinal stage
The first prenatal stage of development, which begins at conception and lasts 2 weeks.

zygote
The single cell that results when a sperm fertilizes an egg.

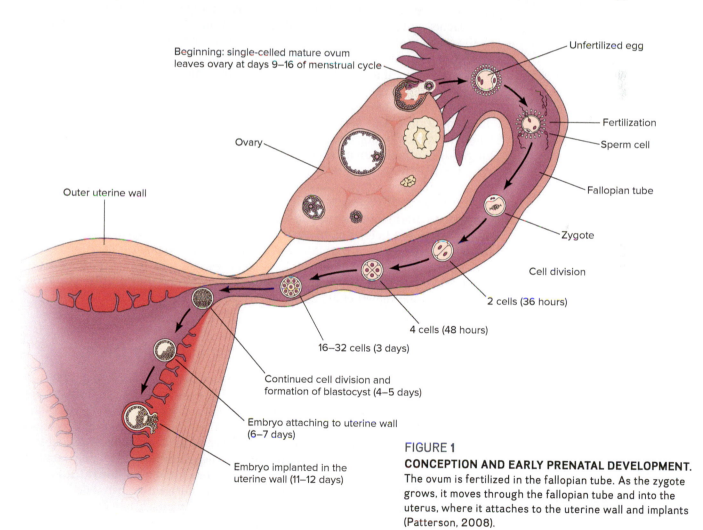

Beginning: single-celled mature ovum leaves ovary at days 9–16 of menstrual cycle

Unfertilized egg

Ovary

Fertilization

Sperm cell

Fallopian tube

Outer uterine wall

Zygote

Cell division

2 cells (36 hours)

4 cells (48 hours)

16–32 cells (3 days)

Continued cell division and formation of blastocyst (4–5 days)

Embryo attaching to uterine wall (6–7 days)

Embryo implanted in the uterine wall (11–12 days)

FIGURE 1

CONCEPTION AND EARLY PRENATAL DEVELOPMENT. The ovum is fertilized in the fallopian tube. As the zygote grows, it moves through the fallopian tube and into the uterus, where it attaches to the uterine wall and implants (Patterson, 2008).

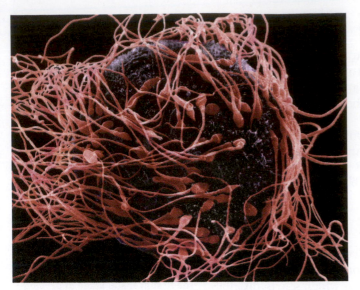
©David M. Phillips/Science Source

In this highly magnified image, an egg is being fertilized, with many sperm surrounding a single egg. Only one sperm will succeed in penetrating the egg.

embryo
A developing organism from 2 weeks until about 8 weeks after conception.

embryonic stage
The second prenatal stage, from 2 weeks to 8 weeks after conception, when all of the major organs form.

fetal stage
The third prenatal stage, which begins with the formation of bone cells 8 weeks after conception and ends at birth.

neural migration
The movement of neurons from one part of the fetal brain to their more permanent destination; occurs during months 3–5 of the fetal stage.

If implantation is successful, the second stage of prenatal development begins, at about 2 weeks after conception. At this point, the growing bundle of cells is officially an **embryo**. The **embryonic stage** is marked by the formation of the major organs: the nervous system, heart, eyes, ears, arms, legs, teeth, palate, and external genitalia. Embryonic development continues until about 8 weeks after conception.

In Figure 2, we see the timetable for prenatal development. Each bar in Figure 2 shows when major structures develop and how long it takes. Notice that the central nervous system (brain and spinal cord) takes the longest amount of time to develop. Most major abnormalities occur only in the early stages of development, when exposure to environmental hazards, such as drugs or illness, can cause serious defects.

The key event that distinguishes the embryonic stage from the third stage, the **fetal stage**, is the formation of bone cells at 8 weeks after conception. By this time, all the major organs have already begun to form. Between 8 and 12 weeks into development, the heartbeat can be detected with a stethoscope. Organs continue to grow and mature while the fetus rapidly increases in size.

Genetically, sex is determined at conception; girls have two X chromosomes (XX) and boys an X and a Y (XY). Until about seven weeks after conception there are no physical traits distinguishing male and female. Then, at around seven weeks gestation, if a Y chromosome is present, male organs start to form. If no Y chromosome is present, then female organs start to form.

Genetic influences may be the first but are not the final influence on sexual differentiation. There seems to be a sensitivity period during fetal development when the effects of hormones on sexual differentiation have a much stronger and longer-term effect than after birth and beyond (Berenbaum & Beltz, 2011).

Epigenetic processes in utero and after birth are also involved because exposure of the brain to sex-hormones changes which genes get turned on or off during sex differentiation (McCarthy & Nugent, 2015). In utero, exposure to sex-specific hormones like estrogen and testosterone produce long-term changes in the brain and behavior. In particular, a region of the hypothalamus (preoptic area) is involved in regulating sexual behavior. Exposure of this and other areas of the brain to relatively high levels of testosterone masculinizes the brain and behavior in both males and females (Berenbaum & Beltz, 2011; Clarkson & Herbison, 2016; Nugent et al., 2015).

Brain and Sensory Development before Birth

As mentioned earlier, the brain is the first major organ to develop, and it is still growing rapidly at birth (see Figure 3). By the time an infant is born, its head has grown to 25% of its adult weight, whereas its body is only 5% of its adult weight (see Figure 4). During the fetal stage, the rate of new neural growth can be approximately 3 million neurons per minute at its peak (Purves & Lichtman, 1985). From months 3 through 5 of pregnancy, neurons move from one part of the brain to their more permanent home in a process known as **neural migration** (Nadarajah & Parnavelas, 2002). Factors that interfere with normal neural migration, such as prenatal exposure to certain toxins or viruses, can increase the risk of psychological disorders (Kandel, 2006).

FIGURE 2

PRENATAL DEVELOPMENT TIMELINE. Does the brain develop before or after the heart completes its development? Review the graph to find out. Each bar shows when major structures develop and how long it takes for development to be completed. Note that the central nervous system begins developing in the third week after conception and continues to develop nearly the entire time we are in the womb. The blue section of each bar indicates when major abnormalities can occur if growth goes awry. After that crucial period, minor abnormalities can still occur.

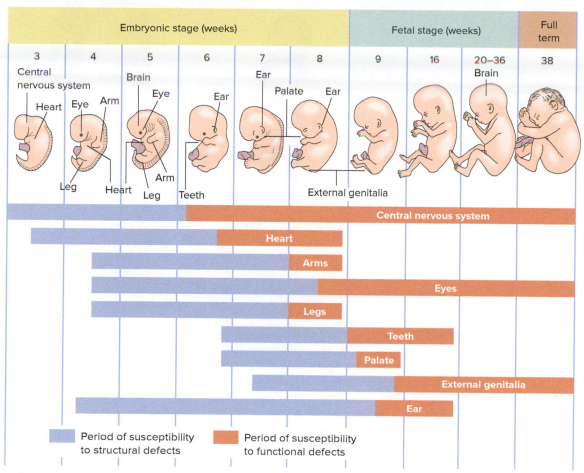

(Hetheringon, E. M. (2006). *Child Psychology: A Contemporary Viewpoint*, 6th edition, Figure 3.2, p. 89.)

FIGURE 3

PRENATAL BRAIN DEVELOPMENT. The size and complexity of the brain increase dramatically in the weeks and months following conception.

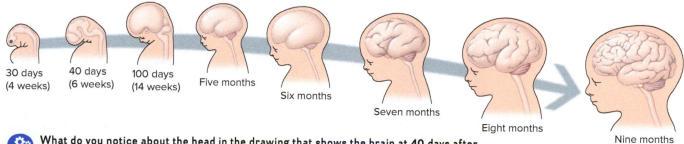

What do you notice about the head in the drawing that shows the brain at 40 days after conception?

Soon after the formation of the nervous system, the embryo begins to move its limbs. By 4 to 6 months after conception, the fetus's movements are noticeable (DiPietro et al., 1996). Mothers can feel the fetus moving as early as 16 weeks into pregnancy, although it may feel a little like abdominal gas or "butterflies."

FIGURE 4

NEWBORN AND CHILD BRAIN AND BODY AS A PERCENTAGE OF ADULT WEIGHT. The size and complexity of the brain increase dramatically in the weeks and months following conception.

	Newborn	2 years	4 years
Percentage of total weight			
Brain	25%	75%	90%
Body	5%	20%	20%

©Francisco Cruz/Purestock/SuperStock RF; middle: ©Purestock/SuperStock RF; ©RubberBall Productions/Getty Images RF

Generally, male fetuses are more active than females, suggesting their greater activity levels after birth may be inborn (DiPietro et al., 1996).

The major sensory systems develop at different times and at different rates. After conception, the neurons connecting the ear to the brain are complete around 18 weeks, and the fetus begins to respond to sound around 26 weeks (6 months; Kisilevsky, Muir, & Low, 1992). A few weeks later, fetuses find their mother's voice soothing, and they prefer the sound of their mother's voice to others (DeCasper &

 Kanye West or Mozart—can a fetus hear the difference? How so, and what would be its reactions to the different music styles?

©Artiga Photo/Masterfile

Fifer, 1980; DeCasper & Spence, 1986). How can researchers possibly know what a fetus prefers? They monitor the fetus's heart rate. Slowed heart rate indicates attention, interest, or orienting response, whereas an increased heart rate indicates fear or distress (Groome et al., 2000). Moreover, particular sounds and music to which fetuses are exposed change their neural networks and these sounds and music are retained in memory for at least 4 months after birth (Partanen et al., 2013; Partanen, Kujala, Näätänen, et al., 2013). In other words, learning already occurs prior to birth!

Taste- and odor-related chemicals from the mother's diet are present in amniotic fluid (Mennella, Johnson, & Beauchamp, 1995). In turn, fetuses are sensitive to odors in the amniotic fluid before birth, and they remember these smells. When pregnant women consumed anise-flavored foods during the last stages of pregnancy, their newborns liked the smell of anise more than babies whose moms did not consume the flavor (Schaal, Marlier, & Soussignan, 2000).

Such studies suggest that our taste preferences may start in the womb (Beauchamp & Mennella, 2009; Hopson, 1998). By 13 to 15 weeks after conception, the taste buds of a fetus look very much like those of an adult (Bradley, 1972). Researchers do not know whether the fetus uses the taste buds, but babies born prematurely—who would otherwise still be developing in the womb—prefer sweet flavors, suggesting that this taste preference exists in the womb (Beauchamp & Mennella, 2009; Mennella & Beauchamp, 1996).

The sense that is least well developed in the fetus is vision (Hopson, 1998). Fetuses do not open their eyes. Also, as discussed in chapters "The Biology of Behavior" and "Sensing and Perceiving Our World", vision perception occurs in the brain, which needs visual stimulation to develop the sense of sight (Ptito & Desgent, 2006). Because it is not receiving visual stimulation, the fetus's brain is not developing the appropriate neural connections in the visual cortex to respond to visual imagery. Thus, at birth, infants cannot see things clearly unless the objects are close to the face. Infants cannot see as well as adults until they are at least 6 months old, whereas their hearing is almost adultlike soon after birth.

Nature and Nurture Influences on Fetal Development

To a fetus, the mother's womb is its only "environment." Thus, what a pregnant mother eats, drinks, smokes, feels, and experiences play an important role in fetal development, such as both subtle and profound effects on biological systems in the developing fetus. Nature and nurture work together to shape who we are and who we become. Specifically, **prenatal programming** is the process by which events in the womb alter the development of physical and psychological health (Coe & Lubach, 2008). Of particular concern in this context are **teratogens** or substances that can cause permanent damage to the developing embryo or fetus.

Maternal Nutrition and Teratogens   Doctors know that what a pregnant woman eats and drinks affects the health of the fetus and even of the infant and child for years after birth. Both schizophrenia and antisocial personality disorder are more likely to occur if the mother is malnourished during pregnancy (Neugebauer, Hoek, & Susser, 1999; Wahlbeck et al., 2001). Similarly, if pregnant women smoke, the risk of the child developing bipolar disorder later in life doubles (Talati et al., 2013).

As it turns out, the body may have a built-in toxin detector called pregnancy sickness, commonly referred to as "morning sickness." Pregnant women often develop aversions to certain foods, and some get nauseated and even vomit regularly (Profet, 1992). Pregnancy sickness is worst during the first 3 months, when the fetus's major organs develop and the embryo is most vulnerable to teratogens, and it occurs most commonly with exposure to foods susceptible to molds (such as aged cheeses) and to bitter substances (such as coffee), possibly because these foods can cause birth defects (Keeler, 1983).

prenatal programming
The process by which events in the womb alter the development of physical and psychological health.

teratogens
Substances that can disrupt normal prenatal development and cause lifelong deficits.

Challenge Your Assumptions

True or False? Schizophrenia in an offspring is more likely if the mother is exposed to a virus while pregnant.

True: The odds increase fourfold (from 1% to 4%) of developing schizophrenia if the mother is afflicted with a viral illness, such as the flu, while pregnant.

Compared with the brain of a typical child (bottom), what does the brain of a child with FASD (top) look like? What would cause such underdevelopment?

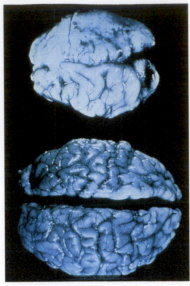

Photo by Sterling K. Clarren, M.D.

Maternal nutrition—a key part of the developing baby's environment—provides one of the most important examples of epigenetics, the study of how the environment affects gene expression (see the chapter "The Biology of Behavior"). Certain kinds of maternal diet during pregnancy can lead to obesity in offspring—whether or not the mother is obese. In one study, researchers randomly assigned two genetically identical strands of female laboratory mice to receive two kinds of diet while pregnant (Dolinoy & Jirtle, 2008). Group A received a diet rich in substances that activate a gene that causes weight gain, while Group B received a diet rich in nutritional supplements (folic acid and B_{12}) that protect against such weight gain. The results showed that the *offspring* of the Group A mice became obese. The diet of the pregnant mother led to obesity in the offspring, and not the child's diet after birth. Equally noteworthy is that the diet of the Group B mice appeared to protect against obesity in their off spring (Dolinoy & Jirtle, 2008; Waterland & Jirtle, 2003).

Teratogens   Substances from the external environment impact fetal and infant development. Because all major body parts are forming and growing during the embryonic and fetal stages, the fetus is quite susceptible to birth defects. Known teratogens include viruses, such as those that cause rubella (measles) and the flu; alcohol; nicotine; prescription drugs, such as the antidepressants Prozac and Zoloft; and radiation. Viruses may have a major impact early in pregnancy and relatively little effect toward the end of pregnancy. If a pregnant woman develops an infection, such as the flu, especially during months 4–6 of pregnancy, the risk of schizophrenia increases for the child later in life (Brown, 2006; Khandaker, Dibben, & Jones, 2012; Koenig, 2006).

Maternal substance use can also cause serious prenatal and postnatal problems. Pregnant women who drink alcohol take chances with their developing baby, as there is no known safe level of alcohol consumption during pregnancy (Centers for Disease Control and Prevention [CDC], 2017). The most serious effect of prenatal alcohol exposure is **fetal alcohol spectrum disorder (FASD)**, which causes damage to the brain and central nervous system; intellectual disability; low birth weight; physical abnormalities in the face, head, heart, and joints; and behavioral problems (Burd et al., 2007; May & Gossage, 2001; Medina & Krahe, 2008; Moore et al., 2007; Sen & Swaminathan, 2007; Uylings, 2006).

Another teratogen is nicotine; exposure from maternal smoking interferes with the oxygen supply to the fetus. Such exposure can lead to premature and low-birth-weight babies as well as increased risk for stillbirth, the delivery of a dead fetus (CDC, 2017; Zigler, Finn-Stevenson, & Hall, 2002).

Prescription drugs pose other potential risks for the developing fetus. Many women take prescription drugs during pregnancy, especially if they were taking them before they learned they were pregnant. Research on animals and humans generally indicates that the antidepressants Zoloft and Prozac can cause respiratory problems, increased risk of preterm birth, and short-lasting effects on motor development (Huang et al., 2013; Maschi et al., 2008; Moses-Kolko et al., 2005). The safest course of action is to avoid these drugs prior to pregnancy, if at all possible.

Prenatal Personality Development

Before the 1990s, most people, including psychologists, thought that personality was something that starts to develop only after birth, maybe not until one is a toddler. A finding that challenged these assumptions revealed that temperament begins before birth. **Temperament** is the biologically based tendency to behave in particular ways

fetal alcohol spectrum disorder (FASD)
A consequence of prenatal alcohol exposure that causes multiple problems, notably brain damage.

Connection

How does having the flu while pregnant influence the way neurons grow in the developing fetus and increase its vulnerability to schizophrenia later in life?

See "Schizophrenia," in the chapter "Psychological Disorders." (p. 576)

temperament
The biologically based tendency to behave in particular ways from very early in life.

from very early in life. To be clear, temperament involves mostly unique behaviors, whereas personality also involves unique traits, feelings, beliefs, attitudes, goals, and motivations. So personality develops out of temperament differences.

In one study on prenatal temperament, Janet DiPietro and her colleagues (1996) showed that fetal activity and fetal heart rate predict temperament differences over the first year of life. In particular, a high heart rate in a 36-week-old fetus foreshadowed less predictable eating and sleeping habits at 3 and 6 months after birth. A high heart rate also predicted a less emotional infant at 6 months after birth.

What happens to the mother while pregnant may affect not only the temperament of the fetus but the temperament and personality later of the infant as well. As we discuss in more detail in the chapter "Personality: The Uniqueness of the Individual," **personality** stems from temperament and is the consistently unique way in which an individual behaves, thinks, feels, and is motivated over time and in many different situations. Mothers who are depressed or anxious or who experience a lot of stress during pregnancy are more likely to have infants who are temperamentally "difficult" and "fussy"(Austin et al., 2004; Gutteling et al., 2005). Thus, temperament and sensitivity to stress are set not only by our genes (nature) but also by our mothers' experiences (nurture).

personality
The unique and relatively enduring set of behaviors, feelings, thoughts, and motives that characterize an individual.

Quick Quiz 1: The Developing Fetus

1. Life before birth is commonly divided into three distinct stages: the _____, embryonic, and fetal stages.
   a. gestational
   b. seminal
   c. germinal
   d. cellular

2. How can researchers tell which sounds a fetus prefers to hear?
   a. by measuring the position of the fetus in the womb
   b. by measuring changes in fetal heart rate in response to sounds
   c. by taking a reading of fetal respiration
   d. It is not possible to measure fetal preferences.

3. Teratogens are
   a. substances that can cause birth defects.
   b. genes that turn on or off with exposure to viruses.
   c. inborn fetal taste preferences.
   d. factors that influence the generation of fetal brain tissue.

Answers can be found at the end of the chapter.

THE DEVELOPING INFANT AND CHILD

Because it's still developing, the newborn human brain is more responsive than that of other animals to its surroundings. This distinction allows nurture to shape human nature more than is the case for most animals.

Physical Development in Infancy and Childhood

Adults take for granted the ability to act at will, yet when first born, humans are completely incapable of acting intentionally. Motor and sensory systems develop substantially in newborns. In this section, we explore how physical growth, motor skills, and sensory capacities develop in infancy and early childhood. We examine how experience and the brain interact to shape early human experience.

Early Motor Development   When we speak of motor development, we are referring to changes in physical movement and body control. Figure 5 outlines the major milestones of motor development during the first 15 months. Although the sequence is predictable, the exact age at which children reach each milestone varies. For example, our son Jerry did not crawl until he was 9 months old, but he walked at 10 months. Our son Evan, on the other hand, crawled at 7½ months and then started walking at about 12 months.

FIGURE 5

MAJOR MOTOR DEVELOPMENT MILESTONES IN INFANCY AND TODDLERHOOD. Some children reach these milestones earlier than others, but most achieve them within the range indicated by the purple bars.

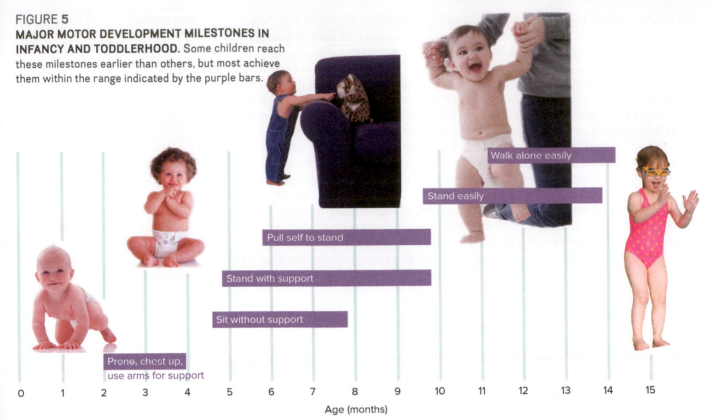

Walk alone easily

Stand easily

Pull self to stand

Stand with support

Sit without support

Prone, chest up, use arms for support

Age (months)

0 1 2 3 4 5 6 7 8 9 10 11 12 13 14 15

happy baby: ©Image Source RF; baby girl wearing a diaper: ©Image Source RF; Baby and tiger: ©Image Source RF; mother helping daughter: ©JGI/Jamie Grill/Blend Images LLC RF; 3 year old girl swimming: ©Pixtal/agefotostock RF

Early in infancy, babies start to show intentional movements. First, they look at their mother with an unfocused gaze, and then they turn their head to look at her. By about 2 months of age, babies lying on their stomach can lift their head. A 3-month-old who is fascinated by a stuffed ring dangling in front of him will suddenly, though not very smoothly, grab for it. At 4 months, babies can hold objects. By 6 months, many can sit by themselves, without any help. By 7 months, babies can pull themselves up and hold on to furniture, and at about 8 to 9 months, they walk from sofa to coffee table by holding on to the furniture. Many babies take their first steps around their first birthday, though it may be some time—at about 17 months of age—before they settle into walking on their own (Patterson, 2008).

Other motor responses are more specific. If you give a newborn baby your finger, she will grasp it tightly. If you stroke her cheek, she will turn her head, open-mouthed in expectation of a breast, a reflex called *rooting*. Grasping and rooting are among several reflexes—involuntary responses to very specific stimuli—present at birth.

It takes a while before young children can turn knobs and pick up tiny objects. These *fine motor skills* involve the coordination of many smaller muscles, along with information from the eyes, in the service of some task. Fine motor development shows up, for example, in children's drawing skills. Two-year-olds typically show very crude crayon scribbles, but by age 3 or 4 children can make crude drawings of people, and by age 5 most kids can print letters, dress alone, and use silverware (Gardner, 1980; Patterson, 2008). Training in fine motor skills actually aids kindergartners' attention, especially in girls, showing just how joined cognition and action can be (Stewart, Rule, & Giordano, 2007).

Early Sensory Development   As noted earlier, the five major senses develop at different rates. Hearing is almost fully developed at birth, but a newborn's vision is only about 20-600, meaning that infants see an object that is 20 feet away as indistinctly as an adult with normal vision would see an object 600 feet away (see Figure 6).

Challenge Your Assumptions

True or False? Babies are born able to see and hear as well as adults.

False: Newborn vision is only 20-600 and becomes adultlike (20-20) only around age 3; hearing becomes adultlike by about age 6 months.

Visual sharpness, or acuity, continues to improve during infancy, and by 6 months of age, vision is 20-100. By age 3 or 4, a child's vision is similar to an adult's (Banks & Salapatek, 1983). You may be surprised to learn that newborns do not see colors very well and are best able to see black-and-white edges and patterns (Fantz, 1963). Color vision approximates that of adults by 4 months of age (Kellman & Arterberry, 2006).

Experience is crucial in the development of vision, as it is in all aspects of human development. The occipital cortex of the brain has to be stimulated by visual input, so that it can develop the proper synaptic connections needed to process visual information. It is for this reason that young infants respond chiefly to visual stimuli within 8 to 12 inches of their faces.

Can all babies who have normal vision in both eyes and can crawl see the world in three dimensions? In a study that has become a classic, Gibson and Walk (1960) tested this question by creating a *visual cliff* to test depth perception in babies who have learned to crawl (see Figure 7). They placed clear Plexiglas (hard plastic) over one end of a crawl area to make it look as though there was a steep drop in the middle. They put a baby on one end of the crawl area and asked the mother to stand at the end with the drop. The mother's role was to encourage the baby to crawl across the clear plastic surface to her. In this study, babies stopped crawling when they reached the visual cliff, indicating that, at least by the time they learn to crawl, babies can perceive depth.

Early Brain Development Experiences such as eating, exercising, and learning mold our brains throughout life, but especially in infancy and childhood. With learning and experience, certain synaptic connections strengthen, whereas those that don't receive stimulation from the environment die off—a process known as **pruning** nature's way of making the brain more efficient (Baltes, Reuter-Lorenz, & Rösler, 2006; Greenough, Volkmar, & Juraska, 1973; Perry, 2002). Pruning is not only about creating a more efficient brain but is also required for normal brain development. Research shows that problems with neural pruning may result in neurological disorders, such as autism or schizophrenia (Cusack et al., 2013; Rapoport et al., 2009).

After birth, the brain continues to grow new neurons (see Figure 8). Contrary to scientific thought as recently as 15 years ago, brain growth continues throughout the life span. The rate of change slows down considerably after the age of 6, increases in early adolescence, and then settles again after adolescence (Chechik, Meilijson, & Ruppin, 1999; Sakai, 2005).

In some 9-year-old children showing early signs of puberty, gray matter in the prefrontal and parietal regions of the brain surprisingly *decreases* somewhat in volume (Giedd et al., 1999; Peper et al., 2009). Such decreases in gray matter volume suggest that pruning—in which unused neurons die—is still occurring late in childhood. Recall that gray matter consists of the cell

FIGURE 6
VISUAL ACUITY IN INFANTS. These are computer simulations of what a picture of a human face looks like to a 1-month-old, 2-month-old, 3-month-old, and 1-year-old (top to bottom).

pruning
The degradation of synapses and dying off of neurons that are not strengthened by experience.

©Kevin Peterson/Getty Images RF

What do you notice about the change in visual acuity, color, and depth over the first year of life?

FIGURE 7
THE VISUAL CLIFF

Connection

Experience is crucial in the formation of synaptic connections and the growth of neurons in the brain throughout the life span. Unused synapses are left to die. Pruning is nature's way of making the brain function more efficiently.

See "Brain Plasticity and Neurogenesis," in the chapter "The Biology of Behavior." (p. 105)

©Enrico Ferorelli   ©Enrico Ferorelli

 In what appears to be a cliff by using a clear sheet of plastic, do you think babies will stop at the edge? Explain.

FIGURE 8

NEURAL GROWTH DURING THE FIRST 15 MONTHS OF LIFE

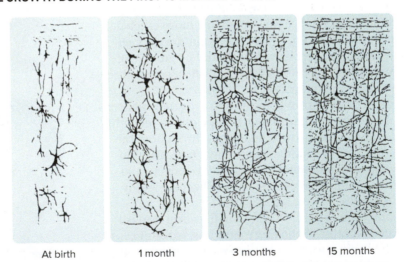

At birth   1 month   3 months   15 months

(Adapted from *The postnatal development of the human cerebral cortex, Vols. I–VIII*, by Jesse LeRoy Conel. Harvard University Press, 1939).

 Describe what happens during neural growth and what happens to neurons and synapses not reinforced by learning.

bodies and is a measure of the number of neurons; white matter is made up of the axons and myelin (see Figure 9). The number of neurons (gray matter) starts to decline in adolescence, but white matter (axons and connectivity) continues to grow into one's 40s (Westlye et al., 2010).

Because pruning is based on input from the environment, the quality of the environments in which we are raised influences how our brains develop. Normal and enriched environments create more complex neural connections, whereas abusive, neglectful, and impoverished environments create less-developed neural connections and fewer of them (Mirescu & Gould, 2006). An example of how experience can positively shape the brain is seen in the findings that physically fit children are also more cognitively fit; that is, they do better in reasoning tasks and school in general (Castelli et al., 2007; Hillman et al., 2009). "Psychology in the Real World" looks at another type of experience—musical training—that influences brain growth and cognitive development.

Neglect exists when caregivers fail to provide basic sensory experience and stimulation to a child during key periods of development (Perry, 2002). Timing is critical. A dramatic instance of the effect of neglect and abuse on the development of the human brain comes from research on children who spent their early years in Romanian orphanages, where they were confined much of the time to cribs and had very limited stimulation. Figure 10 shows a PET scan from one of the orphans alongside one from a typically developing child. The red to yellow areas in Figure 10a represent the active regions in the brain of a normal child. Figure 10b shows the brain activity of a Romanian orphan who was neglected from birth. As you can see, brain activity is greatly diminished in the orphan (Cicchetti, 2001). Similarly, research shows decreases in brain size in children raised in severely neglectful homes. These deficits can be overcome if the children are removed from the neglectful environment—sooner rather than later, however. The longer they stay in the deprived environment, the less likely it is that they will recover (Perry, 2002).

Findings in neuroscience suggest that children's brains are more plastic and more sensitive to stimulation from the outside world than are the brains of older people. Part of the reason is that young brains are more flexible because they have less myelin, which makes neural transmission more efficient but at a cost to neuroplasticity. In the chapter "The Biology of Behavior," we noted that many axons are covered with a myelin sheath, the fatty insulation that allows nerve impulses to travel faster. Few neurons are myelinated at birth; with age, myelination increases (Fields, 2008; Peper et al., 2009). Figure 11 shows the relative increases in myelin over time from age 4 to age 20.

Early Cognitive Development

With brain growth come advances in the ability to think, pay attention, reason, remember, learn, and solve problems. How do cognitive skills grow, and how can we study them in babies who cannot speak yet? The answer is that infants look at things longer when they are interested in them, and such looking can indicate preference. Researchers who study infants have come to rely on visual preference as their primary means of studying infant thought and attention (Richards, Reynolds, & Courage, 2010).

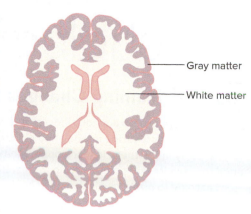

FIGURE 9

WHITE AND GRAY MATTER IN THE HUMAN BRAIN

FIGURE 10

BRAIN DEVELOPMENT IN A NORMAL CHILD COMPARED TO A DEPRIVED AND NEGLECTED CHILD

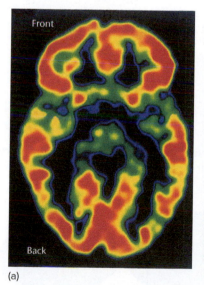
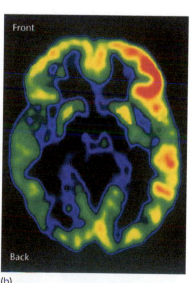

(a)   (b)

Courtesy of Dr. Harry T. Chugani, Children's Hospital of Michigan

If red represents high levels of brain activity and blue relatively less brain activity, what do these two images tell you about the brain of (a) a typically developing child and (b) a child who experienced deprivation and neglect in an orphanage? (Cicchetti, 2001)

Psychology in the Real World

Musical Training Changes the Brain

The brain develops throughout life, yet it is most responsive to stimulation during infancy and childhood. In other words, early in life there is more opportunity for experience to leave its mark on the brain (Stiles, 2008).

Learning to play a musical instrument is a fascinating example of how experience changes the brain, or of how nature and nurture work together to create who we are. If you want to learn guitar, you must learn how to finger on the neck, how to hold your fingers and press the strings firmly enough to get a clear sound, and how the fingering movements relate to the notes on different musical scales. In the chapter "The Biology of Behavior," we discussed how monkeys trained in a finger-tapping task showed substantial increases in the amount of somatosensory cortex devoted to the fingertips compared to both the amount they had before training and the amount in untrained monkeys (Jenkins et al., 1990). Can we see similar effects in the brains of string instrument players?

Researchers who were curious about this question applied a slight pressure to each finger on each hand of right-handed musicians and nonmusicians of various ages. Using fMRI, they mapped the brain's responses to this pressure. For musicians, the area on the somatosensory cortex devoted to those fingers on the side of the brain that controls the fingering left hand was bigger than the area that controls the nonfingering right hand, and musicians who started playing before the age of 12 showed the most pronounced differences. The somatosensory maps did not differ between sides in the brains of nonmusicians (Elbert et al., 1995; Vaquero

et al., 2016). So musical training may change brain organization, especially for people who start training as children.

Musical training appears to shape the structure of the brain as well. People who have had intensive musical training have a thicker corpus callosum and more brain growth in regions associated with music-related skills than do nonmusicians, and the difference is even greater if they started their training before age 7 (Schlaug et al., 1995; Vaquero et al., 2016). A thicker corpus callosum makes for greater communication between the two sides of the brain. Also, musicians have larger cerebellums (an area involved in motor coordination) than do nonmusicians (Hutchinson et al., 2003). Other research shows that, the earlier musical training begins, the greater the degree of activation of the music-processing areas of the brain (left auditory cortex) when listening to music (Ohnishi et al., 2001; Vaquero et al., 2016), and evidence indicates significant growth in brain regions of 6-year-old children after just 15 months of musical training compared to those without training (Hyde et al., 2009).

Moreover, as the brain regions involved in moving muscles and processing sound grew, the better the children's musical performance became. Recent evidence points to musical training enhancing neural activity in the hippocampus, which is the brain region most involved in learning and memory (Herdener et al., 2010). Most impressive, perhaps, is the finding that these neuroplastic effects of musical training last well into adulthood (Skoe & Kraus, 2012).

The findings discussed so far are correlational. Recall a lesson from the chapter "Conducting Research in

FIGURE 11

MYELINATION IN THE DEVELOPING BRAIN. In the figure, unmyelinated neurons appear yellow and orange. Myelinated neurons appear purple.

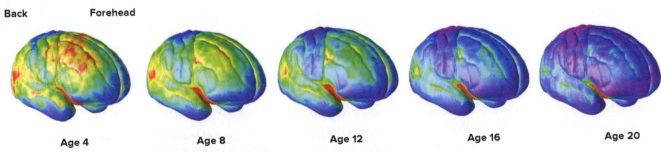

Back   Forehead

Age 4   Age 8   Age 12   Age 16   Age 20

Courtesy of Paul Thompson, Laboratory of Neuro Imaging, UCLA

 What does myelin do for developing brains? (Fields, 2008)

Psychology": Correlation is necessary but not sufficient for causation. Correlational findings suggest that musical training can shape the brain, but they do not lead to the conclusion that musical training necessarily *causes* brain growth. One way to address the problem of correlation is to do an experiment, which is what Alvaro Pascual-Leone, professor of neurology at Harvard University, did. He taught people who had never before played piano a one-hand, five-finger exercise. They repeated the exercise in 2-hour practice sessions for 5 days, and then they were given a test involving 20 repetitions of the exercise (responses measured by computer for speed, etc.). As skill improved, cortical representation for the finger muscles involved in the task increased (Pascual-Leone, 2001). Next, participants were randomly assigned either to continue daily practice of the exercise for 4 more weeks or to stop practicing. For those who stopped practicing, within 1 week, brain maps returned to the way they were before training. For those who continued practicing, brain map changes continued. In short, if you don't use it, you lose it!

Your parents may have wanted you to take music lessons "because it would be good for you." Well, there is evidence, as difficult as it may be for you to believe, that your parents were correct about this. Musical training enhances cognitive skills beyond those directly related to music, such as verbal memory, verbal reasoning, nonverbal reasoning, and mathematical reasoning, as well as IQ in general (Forgeard et al., 2008; Ho, Cheung, & Chan, 2003; Rodrigues, Loureiro, & Caramelli, 2010; Schellenberg, 2004, 2006, 2011, 2016; Spelke, 2008). For example, music

©Fuse/Corbis/Getty Images RF

training is positively correlated with intelligence test scores in children and college students, and this relationship is strongest for people who have trained longer (Schellenberg, 2006, 2016). Recent evidence, however, suggests that high intelligence is more of a cause than an effect of musical training, with high cognitive ability children more likely to take music lessons than average or low cognitive ability children (Schellenberg, 2011). High intelligence extends neuroplasticity and the sensitivity periods for learning, meaning that musical training can shape the brain even more and for a longer period of time in those with high intelligence (Brant et al., 2013).

When infants from 4 to 7 months of age pay attention to something for more than a few seconds, brain activity narrows from many brain regions to more specific brain regions (Richards et al., 2010). This finding suggests that the brain is becoming more organized and efficient during the first 6 months of life, and this increased brain organization leads to increased ability to pay attention and focus on one thing during the first year of life (Richards et al., 2010).

If there is one important thing developmental psychologists have learned about infants over the last 20 years, it is that infants are smarter than we ever thought. Alison Gopnik summarized these findings in her book *The Philosophical Baby* (2009). Infant perception, knowledge of the world, and even problem-solving skills are much more sophisticated than previously thought. For example, 8-month-old infants understand the basics of statistics and probability. To arrive at this finding, a researcher put mostly white but a few red Ping-Pong balls into a box, then reached into the box and pulled out a few white but many red balls (Xu & Garcia, 2008). The babies registered that this was very unlikely; they looked a lot longer at this situation than when the researcher pulled out many white and only a few red balls (Xu & Garcia, 2008). Psychologists therefore call babies "intuitive statisticians"—without any training, they know some events are very unlikely.

©Bettmann/Getty Images

Jean Piaget

Stage	Approximate Age (years)	Core Cognitive Capacities
Sensorimotor	0–2	Knowledge is through senses (tasting, seeing, smelling, touching, hearing) Object permanence develops between 4 and 9 months
Preoperational	2–5	Verbal and egocentric thinking develop Can do mentally what once could only do physically Conservation of shape, number, liquid not yet possible
Concrete Operational	6–11	Conservation of shape, number, liquid are now possible Logic and reasoning develop, but are limited to appearance and what is concretely observed
Formal Operational	12 and up	Abstract reasoning—principles and ideals develop Systematic problem solving is now possible (no longer just trial and error) Ability to think about and reflect upon one's thinking (metacognition) Scientific reasoning

FIGURE 12

PIAGET'S STAGES OF COGNITIVE DEVELOPMENT

sensorimotor stage
Piaget's first stage of cognitive development (ages 0–2), when infants learn about the world by using their senses and by moving their bodies.

object permanence
The ability to realize that objects still exist when they are not being sensed.

So we have learned from developmental science that infants and young children have many specific perceptual and cognitive skills that develop rapidly over time. Is there a model of general cognitive development from infancy to adulthood? Yes, it was proposed by Jean Piaget. Jean Piaget's (1954) principles of cognitive development from birth throughout childhood outline stages at which certain cognitive capacities appear. Relying primarily on observations of his own three children, Piaget outlined four phases of cognitive development from birth through adolescence, which he called the sensorimotor, preoperational, concrete operational, and formal operational stages. Figure 12 summarizes Piaget's theory of cognitive development.

Piaget called the first stage of cognitive development the **sensorimotor stage** because it characterizes the way infants learn about the world through their senses and their own movements. Young children sense more than they "think" and come to understand the world by manipulating and moving through it. Piaget also observed that, during the first 8 or 9 months, a child has no concept of **object permanence**, which is the ability to realize that objects still exist when they are not being sensed (Piaget, 1954). In other words, it is "out of sight, out of mind" for young infants. When an object is hidden from them, they will not look for it, even if they see someone hide it. Around 9 months of age, however, infants will move a cloth or look under something to find the hidden object, because they have begun to remember that objects continue to exist even when they are not directly sensed. Mastering object permanence is a hallmark of the sensorimotor stage.

Renée Baillargeon and colleagues conducted intriguing research using a different technique that challenged Piaget's argument that infants develop object permanence at about 9 months (Baillargeon & DeVos, 1991). They measured infants' responses to both expected and impossible events (see Figure 13). First, infants were shown an inclined track and a screen that was lowered or raised in front of the track. They learned that, when a car rolls down the track, the car keeps rolling behind the lowered screen and appears on the other side of it. They were not surprised to see the car, even though it was hidden for a short time by the lowered screen. They were shown this event many times, until they got used to it—that is, until it became expected. In the next sequence, everything was the same except that the researchers placed a toy mouse *behind* the track while the

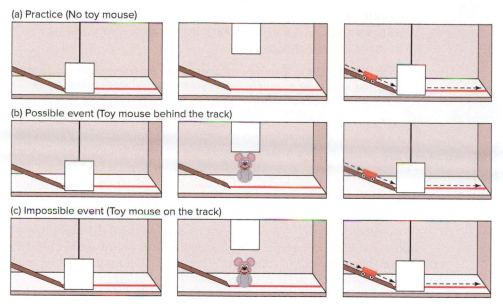

(a) Practice (No toy mouse)

(b) Possible event (Toy mouse behind the track)

(c) Impossible event (Toy mouse on the track)

FIGURE 13

THE DEVELOPMENT OF OBJECT PERMANENCE. In the practice sessions (a), children learn that cars can still roll all the way to the wall, because the screen is in front of the track, not blocking the car's path. In the possible session (b), they are not surprised to again see the car roll all the way to the wall, because the mouse was behind, not on, the track. But in the impossible session (c), the infants were surprised to see the car roll all the way to the wall, because the mouse should have blocked it (unbeknownst to the children, the mouse had been removed while the screen was down).

 How do the researchers know whether the young child was surprised or not? (Baillargeon and DeVos, 1991)

babies watched. Again, they were not surprised to see the car roll behind the lowered screen and appear on the other side of it.

Then something impossible happened. The researchers placed the mouse *on* the track while the infants watched. When the screen was down, hiding the mouse from the infants' view, the experimenters removed the mouse. The researchers found that, when the car rolled down the track and kept rolling (impossible if the mouse were still on the track), the infants were quite surprised, which Baillargeon and DeVos were able to tell by studying the infants' eyes. When things go as expected, infants get bored and stop looking at the event, but when they witness an impossible event, their eyes widen and they keep looking. Infants as young as 4 months of age, not 9 months, realize objects still exist even when they do not see them. Piaget was right about object permanence but wrong about the age at which it first happens.

At around age 2, with the emergence of symbolic thought, children move into Piaget's second stage of cognitive development—the **preoperational stage**, a period that lasts until about age 5 or 6. Symbolic thinking involves using symbols, such as words or letters, to represent ideas or objects. The cognitive limitations of the preoperational stage include animistic thinking, egocentrism, and lack of conservation.

Animistic thinking refers to the idea that inanimate objects are alive. For example, Piaget reported on a child in this stage who was asked whether the sun moved. The child answered, "Yes, when one walks, it follows." When the child was asked why it moves, he responded, "Because when one walks, it goes too." Finally, when the child was asked whether the sun was alive, he responded, "Of course, otherwise it wouldn't follow us; it couldn't shine" (Piaget, 1972b, p. 215).

Egocentrism is the tendency to view the world only from one's own perspective. Piaget and Inhelder (1967) designed the *three mountains task* to

preoperational stage
The second major stage of cognitive development (ages 2–5), which begins with the emergence of symbolic thought.

animistic thinking
A belief that inanimate objects are alive.

egocentrism
Viewing the world from one's own perspective and not being capable of seeing things from another person's perspective.

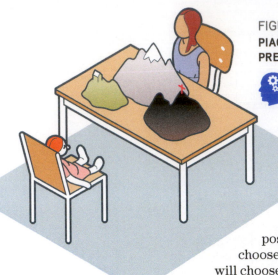

FIGURE 14

PIAGET'S THREE MOUNTAINS TASK: EGOCENTRIC PERCEPTION OF PREOPERATIONAL CHILDREN

When asked to describe what the doll can see from the other side of the table, how do children in the preoperational stage respond, and why? (Patterson, 2008)

measure young children's egocentrism (see Figure 14). For this demonstration, three mountains are placed on a small table. The child sits on one side of the table, and a doll is placed in a chair on the other side of the table. The experimenter asks the child to describe how the doll sees the three mountains. Typically, the three possible perspectives are drawn on a board and the child has to choose the correct perspective. Egocentric, preoperational children will choose the perspective from which *they* see the mountains; they cannot visualize them from the doll's point of view.

Conservation is the ability to recognize that, when some properties (such as shape) of an object change, other properties (such as volume) remain constant. During preoperational thinking, the child cannot yet recognize that amounts stay the same when shapes change. Psychologists say that they are unable to conserve. Piaget used many objects and situations to examine conservation. Figure 15 shows a number of them.

conservation
Recognition that when some properties (such as shape) of an object change, other properties (such as volume) remain constant.

	Original setup	Alter as shown	Ask child	Usual answer
conservation of liquid			Which has more liquid?	
conservation of mass			Do they both weigh the same, or does one weigh more than the other?	
conservation of number			Are there still as many pennies as nickels, or more of one than the other?	
conservation of length			Are they the same length, or is one longer?	
conservation of length			Is one pencil as long as the other, or is one longer?	

FIGURE 15

DIFFERENT KINDS OF CONSERVATION TASKS. Children in the preoperational stage don't realize that the quantity of something doesn't change if it is rearranged. (Seifert, Hoffnung, & Hoffnung, 2000)

Let's look at conservation of liquid as an example. This task involves filling two glasses of the same shape and size with equal amounts of water. The child confirms that the two glasses contain the same amount of water. Then the child pours one of the glasses of water into a third container, which is wider but shorter than the first two. The child does nothing to the second. When asked whether the two glasses contain the same amount of water, the child will say no if he or she lacks the ability to conserve. Usually, the child will say that the tall, thin container has more water than the short, wide one.

During Piaget's third stage, called the **concrete operational stage** (ages 6–11), children can perform mental operations on real, or concrete, objects and events—but they still have trouble with abstract ideas and reasoning. The ability to reverse events is one type of operation a child masters in this stage. One of the yardsticks that measures whether a child has moved from preoperational to concrete operational thinking is the ability to conserve, such as when the child realizes that an amount of liquid doesn't change when pouring it from one container into another of

©Tony Freeman/PhotoEdit

 After a 4- or 5-year-old child (preoperational) sees liquid poured from a short, fat container to a tall, thin one, does the child think the amount of liquid is more than or is the same as when it was in the short container? What did Piaget's research tell us?

different shape. In this stage, logic remains concrete and limited to objects that a child directly observes. The child can reason that the amount of liquid she or he sees go from one glass into the other must remain the same but would have trouble solving a problem of this type: "If Susan is half as old as Robert, and Robert is twice as old as Samantha, then how old is Samantha compared to Susan?"

With the onset of adolescence, children gain the ability to reason about abstract concepts and problems. Piaget called this phase of cognitive development the **formal operational stage** (Inhelder & Piaget, 1958; Piaget, 1972b). During this stage, formal logic becomes possible. Here is an example: "If Maria is a woman, and all women are mortal, then Maria is mortal." In addition, adolescents develop scientific reasoning and hypothesis-testing skills. We'll go into more detail about this stage of cognitive development in the section on adolescence.

One limitation to Piaget's theory is it omitted the social component to cognitive development. The Russian psychologist Lev Vygotsky developed a more social view of cognitive development than Piaget. Vygotsky (1978), for instance, argued that cognitive development does not happen in a vacuum but rather must be understood in its social context. Other people can and do affect what we learn. Vygotsky coined the phrase **zone of proximal development** and defined it as the distance between what a child can learn alone and what that child can learn assisted by someone else, usually an adult. The idea of a zone of proximal development is that, when a child is near his or her potential (in the zone), a more experienced person can aid the child in learning more and learning faster than the child would alone. Learning, therefore, is best understood as a social process.

Theory of Mind Knowing and understanding what other people are thinking, wanting, or feeling is a critical skill in human society. The term **theory of mind** refers to our knowledge and ideas of how other people's minds work. The important questions from a development perspective are when and how does such a skill emerge and how does it change with age?

concrete operational stage
Piaget's third stage of cognitive development, which spans ages 6–11, during which the child can perform mental operations—such as reversing—on real objects or events.

formal operational stage
Piaget's final stage of cognitive development, from age 11 or 12 on through adulthood, when formal logic is possible.

zone of proximal development
The distance between what a child can learn alone and what that child can learn assisted by someone else, usually an adult.

theory of mind
Ideas and knowledge about how other people's minds work.

Most adults—especially those who learn to think critically—know that people believe things that sometimes are not true. They may even come to realize that their own beliefs may not always be true. Children under the age of 4 are cognitively incapable of understanding that people may believe things that are not true. Psychologists created the *false-belief* task to explore children's theory of mind and the stage at which they come to know that others may hold false beliefs (Wimmer & Perner, 1983). For the false-belief task, a child between the ages of 3 and 5 sits with an experimenter at a table. The experimenter has cardboard cutouts of a story. In the first cutout, Sally puts her marble in a basket. In the next picture, Sally goes away. In the next scene, Ann takes the marble from the basket and puts it in a box. In the final scene, Sally returns. The researcher asks this critical false-belief question: Where will Sally look for her marble, in the box or the basket? A 3-year-old will say that Sally will look in the box, because a 3-year-old cannot distinguish what she or he knows from what Sally knows. Around age 4, however, children can disentangle their own beliefs from other people's beliefs and say, "Sally will look in the basket," because they understand that Sally doesn't know that Ann moved the marble (Gopnik, Meltzoff, & Kuhl, 1999; Sullivan, Zaitchik, & Tager-Flusberg, 1994; Wimmer & Perner, 1983).

Development of Moral Reasoning

As children develop cognitive skills, social skills, and theory of mind, they also develop a sense of right and wrong. Most likely, social and cognitive skills work together to help the child make sense of the workings of the world.

The most well-known account of the development of moral reasoning comes from Lawrence Kohlberg (1981), who studied the development of moral reasoning in children and adults by giving them a moral dilemma and recording the reasons they provided for their responses. Their responses were less important to him than was the reasoning behind them.

The dilemma Kohlberg commonly presented to his participants was the "Heinz Dilemma," as follows:

> A woman was near death from a special kind of cancer. There was one drug that the doctors thought might save her. It was a form of radium that a druggist in the same town had recently discovered. The drug was expensive to make, but the druggist was charging ten times what the drug cost him to produce. He paid $200 for the radium and charged $2,000 for a small dose of the drug. The sick woman's husband, Heinz, went to everyone he knew to borrow the money, but he could only get together about $1,000, which is half of what it cost. He told the druggist that his wife was dying and asked him to sell it cheaper or let him pay later. But the druggist said: "No, I discovered the drug and I'm going to make money from it." So Heinz got desperate and broke into the man's store to steal the drug for his wife. Should Heinz have broken into the laboratory to steal the drug for his wife? Why or why not? (Kohlberg, 1981)

After analyzing the reasoning that people of different ages gave in response to these questions, Kohlberg proposed a three-stage theory of moral reasoning. In Kohlberg's view, moral reasoning moves from being focused on the self to being increasingly focused on others, with a basis in clear personal principles of morality and ethics (see Figure 16).

In the first, and least developed, level of moral reasoning, the **preconventional level** the responses tend to be something like this: "Heinz should not steal the drug because he will get in trouble and go to jail." The reasoning behind the answer has

preconventional level
The first level in Kohlberg's theory of moral reasoning, focusing on avoiding punishment or maximizing rewards.

	Motive–reasoning
pre-conventional	To avoid punishment Judgments are based on personal needs
conventional	Rules are rules and they are not to be broken Judgments are based on needs of society; individual needs serve group needs
post-conventional	Willing to break law—and suffer the consequences—if it is perceived as unjust or immoral Judgments balance needs of society with personal convictions

FIGURE 16

SUMMARY OF KOHLBERG'S STAGES OF MORAL REASONING. Kohlberg saw a possible progression through three stages of moral reasoning, but not everyone reaches the postconventional stage.

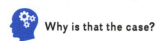 **Why is that the case?**

to do with avoiding punishment or maximizing reward. Children obey rules because their parents tell them to comply.

In the second level, the **conventional level** the person might respond with "Heinz should not steal the drug because stealing is wrong. Society cannot function if people steal all the time." At this level, the person values caring, trust, and relationships, as well as social order and lawfulness.

In the third level of moral reasoning—the **postconventional level**—a person might respond, "Although it is legally wrong, Heinz should steal the drug to save his wife's life. But he also has to be willing to suffer the consequences and go to jail if need be." In this case, the person acknowledges both the norm and the law but argues that there are universal moral rules that may trump unjust or immoral local rules. Therefore, disobeying the more local rule or law may be necessary. This is the principle of civil disobedience embraced by great moral leaders from Henry David Thoreau to Mahatma Gandhi to Martin Luther King, Jr., to Rosa Parks, who exhibited well-developed moral codes for which they were willing to sacrifice their lives, if need be, to set right unjust and immoral laws and societies. When Rosa Parks refused to take a seat in the back of the bus and thus violated local law, she exhibited postconventional moral reasoning.

Research supports Kohlberg's argument that children tend to reason preconventionally and adults conventionally (Carroll & Rest, 1981; Lapsley, 2006). Moreover, research on moral reasoning in different cultures all over the world offers support for the first two stages of Kohlberg's model but challenges his argument for a third. Snarey (1985) reviewed 45 studies on the development of moral reasoning in 27 countries and found universal support for the preconventional and conventional levels of moral reasoning. The postconventional level, however, appears to be limited to Western cultures, which place a strong emphasis on individual values, and postconventional moral reasoning is heavily based in a personal moral code. In contrast, many non-Western cultures emphasize the importance of the group and community, so the highest level of moral reasoning would be likely to involve compassion and caring for others, altruism, and family honor, values that Kohlberg did not measure (Matsumoto & Juang, 2004).

conventional level
The second level in Kohlberg's theory of moral reasoning, during which the person values caring, trust, and relationships as well as the social order and lawfulness.

postconventional level
The third level in Kohlberg's theory of moral reasoning, in which the person recognizes universal moral rules that may trump unjust or immoral local rules.

©Lee Lockwood/Time & Life Pictures/Getty Images

Lawrence Kohlberg

Personality Development during Infancy

After birth, some infants soon settle into a predictable routine. Others do not. Some are generally happy, and others are fussy. Some infants also have lower thresholds for stimulation than others. Based on their classic study of such differences, Alexander Thomas and Stella Chess (1977, 1996) developed an influential model of temperament, with three general categories, that is still widely accepted: the easy child, the difficult child, and the slow-to-warm-up child. The *easy child* is predictable in daily functions, is happy most of the time, and is adaptable. About 40% of children fell into this category. The *difficult child* is unpredictable in daily functions, is unhappy most of the time, and is slow to adapt to new situations. About 10% fell into this category. The *slow-to-warm-up child* is mildly intense in his or her reactions to new situations and mildly irregular in the daily patterns of eating, sleeping, and eliminating. Although his or her first response to new situations might be negative, after repeated exposures, he or she develops an approaching style. About 15% of the children fell into this category. About 35% of the children were not classified by these three dimensions.

Early Socioemotional Development

All mammals need warmth and contact to survive and flourish. Human babies need constant care in order to survive to early childhood. They seem programmed from birth to form close relationships with their primary caregivers. Thanks to some pioneering research that began in the mid-20th century, we know that the quality of those relationships can have lifelong implications.

imprinting
The rapid and innate learning of the characteristics of a caregiver very soon after birth.

Attachment   Some animals, especially birds, follow and imitate the first large creature they see immediately after birth, a behavior called **imprinting.** The newborn sees this creature as a protector. Usually, this creature also happens to *be* the protector (mom or dad), so it is a good strategy (Lorenz, 1935, 1937). Newborn humans cannot follow around the first large creature they see, so they do not imprint. They *attach* (Kirkpatrick, 2005).

attachment
The strong emotional connection that develops early in life between infants and their caregivers.

In everyday usage, *attachment* means "connectedness." In human development, **attachment** refers to the strong emotional connection that develops early in life to keep infants close to their caregivers. This relationship shapes the child's social and emotional development and forms the foundation for social relationships later in life.

Psychologist John Bowlby (1969) described the process of emotional attachment between infants and their caregivers and the emotional distress that develops when they are separated. He proposed that the major function of this affection-based bonding system is to protect infants from predation and other threats to survival. In his observations of human infants and primates, Bowlby noted that they both went through a clear sequence of reactions—from protest, to despair, to detachment. Bowlby defined **separation anxiety** as the distress reaction shown by babies (typically at around 9 months of age) when they are separated from their primary caregiver.

separation anxiety
The distress reaction shown by babies when they are separated from their primary caregiver (typically shown at around 9 months of age).

On the basis of such observations, Bowlby (1969, 1973, 1980) developed his *attachment theory*, which rests on two fundamental assumptions. First, a responsive and accessible caregiver creates a secure base for the child, who needs to know that the caregiver is accessible and dependable. With a dependable caregiver, the child can develop confidence and security in exploring the world. The bonding relationship serves the critical function of attaching the caregiver to the infant, thereby making the survival of the infant, and ultimately the species, more likely.

The second assumption of attachment theory is that infants internalize the bonding relationship, which provides a mental model on which they build future friendships and love relationships. Therefore, attachment to a caregiver is the most critical of all relationships. In order for bonding to take place, infants must be more than merely a passive receptor to the caregiver's behavior. It is a bidirectional relationship—the infant and the caregiver respond to each other and influence each other's behavior.

Influenced by Bowlby's work, Mary Ainsworth and her associates (1978) developed a technique for testing Bowlby's assumptions about attachment of infant and caregiver. This procedure, known as the *strange situation*, consists of a 20-minute laboratory session that creates a mildly stressful situation for the baby. The strange situation is designed to see how much the caregiver is a safe haven when the infant is distressed and a "secure base" from which to explore.

Here is how the strange situation works: After a 1-minute introduction, the caregiver and her 12-month-old infant are left alone in a playroom. Then a stranger comes into the room, and after a few minutes the stranger begins a brief interaction with the infant. The caregiver then leaves for two separate 3-minute periods. During the first period, the infant is left alone with the stranger. During the second period, the infant is left completely alone. Then caregiver and child are reunited. The critical behavior that Ainsworth and colleagues rated was how the distressed infant reacted when the caregiver returned.

From the behavior in this context, Ainsworth et al. (1978) and others described one secure attachment style and three types of insecure attachment. Based on temperamental and contextual factors, babies who are **securely attached** to parents may or may not be distressed on separation. The key issue is that they initiate contact with the parent on return and then can return to play. Securely attached infants are confident in the accessibility and responsiveness of their caregiver, and this security and dependability provide the child with the foundation for play and exploration when the caregiver is absent. About 65% of infants are securely attached.

In all three kinds of insecure attachment, infants lack the ability to engage in effective play and exploration. These three types are insecure-avoidant, insecure-resistant, and insecure-disorganized/disoriented.

Insecure-Avoidant An insecure-avoidant infant often shows little to no distress in separation episodes, although physiological measures suggest that the infant is indeed under stress. When the caregiver returns, the infant tends to ignore and avoid her, focusing instead on something else in the room. The infant's avoidance on reunion may reflect the expectation that a bid for more contact would be followed by the parent's rejection. The avoidant classification is most common in Western cultures (15%–20% in the United States and Europe). In cultures such as Africa and Japan, where infant care practices involve almost constant physical contact between mother and infant, the classification is rare (True, Pisani, & Oumar, 2001).

Insecure-Resistant An insecure-resistant infant cannot be comforted by the caregiver on reunion and shows difficulty in returning to play. Some babies actively resist contact with the parents at this stage, and others act more passive. The infant's resistance and distress during the reunion may reflect the infant's lack of confidence in being comforted. On average, only about 10%–15% of infants are classified as insecure-resistant (van IJzendoorn & Sagi, 1999).

Insecure-Disorganized/Disoriented These infants show odd, conflicted behaviors in the strange situation. They might approach the caregiver on reunion, but they do so with their heads averted. Or they might freeze in place for 50 seconds in the caregiver's presence (Main & Solomon, 1990). Theory and research suggest that these infants are frightened (Main & Hesse, 1990). Kids who have been maltreated are more likely to be insecure-disorganized, and home observations suggest they are afraid of their parents. Not all parents of infants classified as insecure-disorganized/disoriented maltreat their infants (Hesse & Main, 2006). This classification is considered the most insecure, because infants' fear of their attachment figures inhibits the development of a strategy for effective regulation of stress.

securely attached
An attachment style characterized by infants who will gradually explore new situations when the caregiver leaves and initiate contact when the caregiver returns after separation.

FIGURE 17

THE CLOTH AND WIRE MOTHERS
FROM HARLOW'S RESEARCH

©Nina Leen/Getty Images

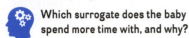

Which surrogate does the baby spend more time with, and why?

The infant-caregiver relationship provides the first context for the development of love in the baby's life. Some research suggests that this initial relationship helps shape adult romantic love relationships because the attachment style from infancy brings something to bear on the ways one connects—or doesn't connect—with a romantic partner (Hazan & Shaver, 1987).

Challenging Assumptions in the Importance of Physical Contact for Well-Being   Up until the 1950s, most people—and most psychologists, for that matter—assumed that if children were well fed and well sheltered they would grow and develop normally. Physical touch and contact were considered nice but not necessary for normal, healthy development. As it turns out, this assumption was wrong.

Harry Harlow thought there might be more to infants' desire for contact than a need for nourishment. To test his hunch that the need for something soft to hold is as fundamental as the need for nutrition, Harlow and his colleagues carried out a series of studies with newborn monkeys, which they separated from their mothers (Arling & Harlow, 1967; Harlow, 1958). They housed them with two types of surrogate mothers constructed of wire and wood (see Figure 17). One was composed of just a wire frame with a crude head. The other was a wire frame covered with soft terry cloth. Both "mothers" were heated, and either could be hooked up to a bottle of milk.

In the first study, Harlow removed eight monkeys from their mothers shortly after birth. Cloth and wire mothers were housed in cubicles attached to the infants' cages. By random assignment, half the monkeys received milk from the wire mother; the other half got their milk from the cloth mother. Harlow used the amount of time spent with a surrogate mother as a measure of the affection bond. He found that contact comfort was much more important than the source of food in determining which surrogate mother the monkeys preferred (Harlow, 1958).

Regardless of whether a baby monkey nursed from the cloth mother or the wire mother, it spent most of its time with the cloth one (see Figure 18). Monkeys fed by wire surrogates quickly got milk from the wire mom and then ran over to the cloth mom to cuddle. Harlow's findings thus challenged the belief that feeding was the basis for the bond between babies and mothers. He went so far as to say that contact is as essential a function of nursing in humans as is nutrition.

However, having a cloth surrogate mother was clearly not as good as having a real mother. In follow-up research, Harlow found that monkeys raised without mothers (including some raised with cloth surrogates) were negligent and abusive mothers when they had their own babies. They failed to give their babies proper contact or even to feed them correctly (Arling & Harlow, 1967).

Because of Harlow's work, physical contact came to be considered central to optimal human development, but not all babies get enough of it. As researcher Tiffany Field noted, preterm human babies who spend weeks or months in special hospital beds, where they are kept warm, protected from infection, and monitored by the latest technology, are rarely touched.

What might be the effects of this deprivation among the neediest babies? To explore this question, Field and her colleagues (1986) tested the impact of touch on tiny premature infants. She randomly assigned 40 preterm infants from a hospital's newborn intensive care unit to either receive touch therapy (experimental group) or not (control group). All of the premature infants lived in isolettes, plastic-covered bassinets designed to prevent infection. The touch therapy involved gently stroking the baby with warmed hands (no gloves)

FIGURE **18**

TIME MONKEYS SPENT ON CLOTH VERSUS WIRE SURROGATE "MOTHERS." Whether the baby monkeys were fed by the wire mother or the cloth mother, all of them preferred the comfort of the cloth mother. (Harlow, 1958)

Graph:
Legend: Fed on cloth mother; Fed on wire mother
Y-axis: Mean hours per day (0, 6, 12, 18, 24)
X-axis: Days of age (1–5, 6–10, 11–15, 16–20, 21–25)
Hours per day spent with cloth mother
Hours per day spent with wire mother

through portholes in the isolette for 15 minutes, three times a day for 10 days. What Field and colleagues found was truly surprising: The regularly touched babies, who had the same diets as those who were not regularly touched, gained significantly more weight and were released from the hospital sooner (see Figure 19). Later research showed the same effect in weight gain when mothers touched their preterm infants (Field et al., 2004).

Developing Relationships and Emotions   It is no doubt frustrating at times to be a baby. Think about it: There are things you need and want, and you are not yet able to ask for them, other than by crying. Yet babies learn other ways to communicate their needs to their caregivers, even before they can talk. One way is by facial expression. At just 7 hours old, newborns can imitate, or *mimic*, simple adult facial expressions (Meltzoff & Moore, 1977, 1983). By imitating others, infants learn to make facial expressions that help them communicate their needs (Iacoboni & Mazziota, 2007). Such infant imitation may be a result of mirror neuron systems in the brain, although the brain mechanisms involved in imitation may extend beyond mirroring (Grossberg & Vladusich, 2010; Lepage & Théoret, 2007).

Babies also seem to know at a very young age what the facial expressions of others mean. Four-month-olds show different patterns of visual attention to angry, fearful, and sad facial expressions in a peek-a-boo game (Montague & Walker-Andrews, 2001). Moreover, older babies know how to look to their primary caregivers, whom they know they can trust, for information about emotion and situations.

The visual cliff discussed earlier as a way of testing babies' depth perception has also been used to study whether babies look to their caregivers for information about safety (Sorce et al., 1985). If the mother showed fear or anger on her face, the baby did not move over the cliff, but most babies went willingly over the cliff when the mom smiled. What this means is that, by the age of 1, children can make sense of their mothers' emotional facial expressions and use them to know what to do. This ability to make use of social and emotional information from another person, especially a caregiver, is known as **social referencing** (Campos & Stenberg, 1981).

The research on social referencing shows that babies understand the meaning of some facial expressions much earlier than age 1. On the basis of studies measuring visual preference and brain activity, we know that by 7 months babies can discriminate between fearful and happy faces. Babies of this age also understand the emotional meaning of the voice (intonation changes) that tends to go with certain emotional states, such as happy, angry, or sad (Grossman, Striano, & Friederici, 2006). Well before 1 year of age, then, babies possess a basic ability to interpret other people's emotions.

Development of Emotions and Impulse Control   Babies show emotions very early in life—though not with the subtle variations that adults do. They start with pleasure and pain after birth, and somewhat later they respond to mom's voice or face with a smile. This transition occurs between 2 and 3 months of age (Lavelli & Fogel, 2005). A month later, they laugh in response to playful social interaction.

Signs of anger in facial expression occur as early as 4 months. How do you make young babies angry? One way is to restrain their movement, simply by holding their arms firmly. Between the ages of 4 and 7 months, infants begin to show facial expressions similar to adult expressions of anger when restrained, and the more frustrated they get, the more they show it (Stenberg, Campos, & Emde, 1983).

Other studies tell us that babies may not be able to differentiate their emotions the way adults can (Bridges, 1932). There is evidence that babies use "anger faces" in situations where they might feel fear, such as when they see a noisy toy gorilla head. So it is not clear whether the anger faces at this age are specific to

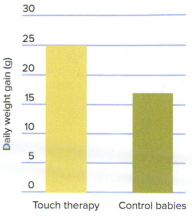

FIGURE 19

WEIGHT GAIN IN PREMATURE INFANTS WHO DID OR DID NOT RECEIVE TOUCH THERAPY. The graph shows the amount of weight gained per day, in grams. Over time, the difference in the weights of the two groups could be expected to increase. Along with the added weight, the massaged babies gained better overall health (Field et al., 1986).

Challenge Your Assumptions

True or False? Being regularly touched as a newborn increases both physical and mental health later in life.

True: The simple act of regularly stroking and touching a newborn facilitates physical and mental growth and well-being.

social referencing
The ability to make use of social and emotional information from another person—especially a caregiver—in an uncertain situation.

Connection

One way we learn is by imitating someone else's behavior. This type of learning, seen also in infant mimicry, may be based on mirror neuron systems in the brain.

To learn about these systems, see "The Cells of the Nervous System: Glial Cells and Neurons," in the chapter "The Biology of Behavior," p. 83; and "Imitation, Mirror Neurons, and Learning," in the chapter "Learning," p. 324.

situations that generally provoke anger (Camras et al., 2007; Oster, 2005). With further development and experience, babies refine their emotional expressions.

Learning to regulate and control emotion is not easy for most children. **emotional competence** is the ability to control emotions and know when it is appropriate to express them (Saarni, 1999; Trentacosta & Izard, 2007). The development of emotional competence starts as early as preschool and continues throughout childhood (Feng et al., 2008; Grolnick, McMenamy, & Kurowski, 2006; Saarni, 1984). Moreover, the better children do in school and the fewer stressful and dysfunctional situations they have at home, the more emotionally skilled and competent they become (Feng et al., 2008; Spinrad et al., 2006).

Related to emotional competence is the ability to control one's impulses. In many ways, maturing and growing up involves the increasing ability to not act on every impulse. One of the best-known and now classic studies on the development of impulse control was conducted by Walter Mischel beginning in the 1960s (2015; Mischel & Ebbesen, 1970; Mischel, Ebbesen, & Zeiss, 1972; Mischel, Shoda, & Rodriguez, 1989). Mischel and colleagues simply had 3- to 5-year-old children come in to his laboratory where the child was given a choice between a few treats, such as a pretzel or a marshmallow. But with a catch. The child could have his or her one preferred treat right now, or if the child could wait 15 minutes while the experimenter left the room, he or she would be given two of treats. As it turns out, some children could wait longer than others—that is, they had greater impulse control or willpower. Children who waited were better able to distract themselves with thoughts of other things than children who could not wait. See the Research Process (Figure 20) for more details and findings.

One aspect of emotional competence is learning to regulate one's emotional behavior. By the age of 9, children realize the impact of their reactions on other people's feelings. Carolyn Saarni (1984) conducted a classic series of studies to uncover how children learn to modify their emotional expressions in the presence of others. She gave first-grade (age 7), third-grade (age 9), and fifth-grade (age 11) children a task to complete and told them that afterward they would get a very desirable toy. The children, however, received a less-than-desirable toy either alone or in the presence of the experimenter. When alone, kids readily showed their disappointment. In the presence of the experimenter, the young children (age 7) readily showed their disappointment, but those ages 9 and 11 tried to inhibit facial expressions of negative emotion when receiving an undesirable gift so as not to hurt the experimenter's feelings. Such social smiling comes only with age and maturity (Simonds et al., 2007).

Peer Interaction   As children get older, their social world expands from the intimate environment of the home to include play with other children. Although attachment to the primary caregiver is important for the baby and young child, relations with other children have a big impact after early childhood (Harris, 1998). Indeed, in early childhood, children do not even interact much with other children, even if other children are playing nearby. Children begin to interact socially during play at about age 3 (Howes & Matheson, 1992).

Most people assume that parents are the biggest influence in a child's life, so they are surprised to learn that, by mid- to late childhood, peers are probably an even bigger influence than parents on a child's development. Why? Peers share equal standing or status in terms of age, gender, skill, or power, so they are important role models. How early does peer influence begin? A study of over 100 British children shows that even 5-year-olds are sensitive to peer criticism. Kids who are more attuned to social and emotional information are more likely to display this sensitivity. Researchers have evaluated children's skills with social and emotional information by giving them tasks such as identifying facial expressions of emotion and determining what a puppet in an acted-out scene or a character in a story might do or feel (Cutting & Dunn, 2002).

emotional competence
The ability to control emotions and know when it is appropriate to express certain emotions.

Research Process

1 Research Questions

Can 3- to 5-year children delay gratification and resist the urge for one immediate treat (marshmallow) if they can wait and have two treats later (Mischel et al., 1972)? Further, do distraction strategies help resist the urge for the treat?

2 Method

©Image Source Plus/Alamy RF

Children came to the lab one at a time and an experimenter showed the child toys he or she could play with after a game. The game involved the experimenter leaving the room but could be brought back immediately if the child summoned him with a small bell. Further, the game's rule was that the child could have two treats (marshmallows, for example) if he or she could wait the full amount of time (usually 15 minutes). If the child could not wait, then he or she was instructed to ring the bell and the experimenter will return and the child could have one rather than two of the treats.

Researchers manipulated the child's thoughts or actions by asking the child to think or do different things while the experimenter went out of the room. In one condition, children were asked to think anything fun (FUN GROUP) such as singing a song or playing with toys. In a second condition, other children were told they can play with a toy slinky (TOY GROUP). And in a third condition, other children were not told anything specific (NO DISTRACTION GROUP) about what they could think or do while the experimenter is gone.

3 Results

Mischel and colleagues found that the children who were provided distraction options did a much better job resisting their urge to eat the treat compared to those who were provided no distraction options (see Figure 20). Cognitive distraction (FUN) works slightly better than behavioral distraction (TOY).

In other versions of the study, children were provided with no distraction suggestions and had to develop, or not, their own strategies of distraction. The most important findings occurred when Mischel and colleagues followed up various samples from early childhood into their teens, 20s, and 30s. Those children who decades earlier had controlled their impulse to did better in school, scored higher on the SAT, and were able to cope with frustration and stress better than those children who could not control their impulse (Mischel, 2015; Mischel et al., 1989; Mischel et al., 2011).

FIGURE 20
WAITING TIME (MIN) FOR THREE GROUPS

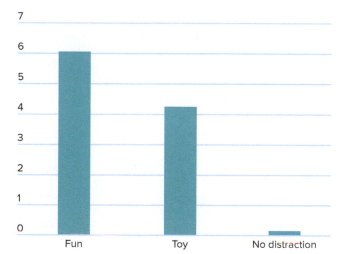

(Mischel, W., Ebbesen, E. B., & Zeiss, A. R. (1972). Cognitive and attentional mechanisms in delay of gratification. *Journal of Personality and Social Psychology*, 21(2), 204–218. Available at https://doi.org/10.1037/h00321982), 204–218. Available at https://doi.org/10.1037/h0032198)

4 Conclusion

Distraction is an important self-control mechanism and the ability to control impulses beginning in early childhood predicts adolescent and adult academic achievement and intellectual ability.

In peer interactions, children tend to sort themselves out by gender. First, even when not pressured by adults to do so, children flock to same-sex playmates (Maccoby & Jacklin, 1987). Second, these gender differences in play occur all over the world—in Europe, the United States, Asia, and Africa (Omark, Omark, & Edelman, 1973; Whiting & Edwards, 1988). Eleanor Maccoby (2000) has attributed this same-sex interaction preference to shared preferences for certain types of play. Boys prefer rough-and-tumble play, whereas girls opt for cooperative play (Green & Cillessen, 2008; Maccoby, 2000). Only in adolescence do boys and girls begin to move toward opposite-sex interactions.

Childhood Temperament and Personality Development   What does early childhood temperament predict about adult personality and behavior? One longitudinal study evaluated 1,000 New Zealand children over an 18-year period. The children were assessed on many temperamental, cognitive, medical, and motor dimensions at age 3 and then again about every 2 to 2.5 years until they were 21 years old (Caspi, 2000). Ratings by parents of their children at age 3 revealed three basic types of temperament: well-adjusted, undercontrolled, and inhibited.

Eighteen years after the initial assessment, the individuals whose parents had classified them as undercontrolled (impulsive and prone to temper tantrums) at age 3 were impulsive and likely to engage in thrill-seeking behaviors. Compared to well-adjusted kids, this group was also much more likely to be aggressive and hostile, to have more relationship conflict, and to abuse alcohol.

At age 21, the inhibited children were less likely to have social support and were more likely to avoid risk and harm, to be nonassertive and overcontrolled, and to suffer from prolonged depression. They also were somewhat more likely than well-adjusted individuals to attempt suicide or have problems with alcohol. Further, they were about as likely as well-adjusted types (and less likely than the undercontrolled individuals) to have committed a criminal offense. Finally, as adults, inhibited children reported the least amount of social, emotional, and financial support from others. In sum, our temperament at age 3 seems to continue shaping our personalities into adulthood (Kagan, 2003).

A separate study assessed 3- and 4-year-old children for openness to new experiences; that is, they were tested on how curious, exploratory, creative, and imaginative they were. These individuals were assessed again at ages 18 and 23 (Gjerde & Cardilla, 2009). Interestingly, the open and imaginative young boys tended to become self-assured, flexible, and resilient young adults. The results

©Steve Wisbauer/Getty Images RF   ©IML Image Group Ltd/Alamy

 Are children born with different temperaments and personality, or do they only learn to be different from experience?

were rather different for the open and imaginative young girls. They tended to become relatively anxious and self-doubting young women. This finding may be explained by socialization differences whereby boys are more encouraged than girls to realize their cognitive potential (Gjerde & Cardilla, 2009). Who we are as young children does foreshadow, sometimes in predictable and other times in unpredictable ways, whom we become as adults.

Quick Quiz 2: The Developing Infant and Child

1. In the newborn infant, the sense of _____ is almost fully developed, but the sense of _____ continues to change and improve over the first few years of life.
   a. taste; hearing
   b. vision; taste
   c. vision; hearing
   d. hearing; vision

2. With learning and experience, certain synaptic connections grow stronger, while those that are not strengthened by experience degrade and die off. This process is known as
   a. neural efficiency.
   b. honing.
   c. pruning.
   d. reductionism.

3. People who have had intensive musical training have _____ than nonmusicians.
   a. thicker finger pads
   b. a thicker corpus callosum
   c. a thicker cerebellum
   d. a thicker caudate nucleus

4. Piaget's _____ stage of cognitive development begins when the child can conserve; that is, knows that the amount of a liquid or substance stays the same even when it changes shape.
   a. sensorimotor
   b. abstract-ideational
   c. logical operations
   d. concrete operations

Answers can be found at the end of the chapter.

THE DEVELOPING ADOLESCENT

Adolescence is the transition period between childhood and early adulthood, beginning at about age 11 or 12 and lasting until around age 18. Adolescence is a tumultuous time, made both exciting and difficult by all the changes that have to take place in a relatively short period to turn a girl into a woman and a boy into a man.

adolescence
The transition period between childhood and adulthood.

Physical Development in Adolescence

Puberty, the period when sexual maturation begins, marks the beginning of adolescence. During puberty, major hormonal changes prepare the body for reproduction and stimulate changes in body size and proportions. On average, girls reach puberty at about age 11 and boys at about age 13. The changes that mark the beginning of puberty stem from the release of sex hormones. First, the pituitary gland sends hormonal signals to the sex glands, telling them to mature. The sex glands, or *gonads*, then release sex hormones (see Figure 21). The male gonads are called *testes*; the female gonads are the *ovaries*. The testes release the male sex hormone *testosterone*, which initiates the physical changes we associate with male maturation, such as facial and pubic hair, deepening of the voice, widening of the shoulders, and growth of the penis. The release of the female sex hormone *estradiol* from the ovaries transforms girls into women, with the growth of breasts, the widening of hips, and an increase in body fat.

puberty
The period when sexual maturation begins; it marks the beginning of adolescence.

In girls, breast development can start as early as age 10. The next major change is the onset of menstruation, known as **menarche**. You may be surprised to learn that menstruation is not solely a biological event; indeed, it is also affected

menarche
The first menstrual period.

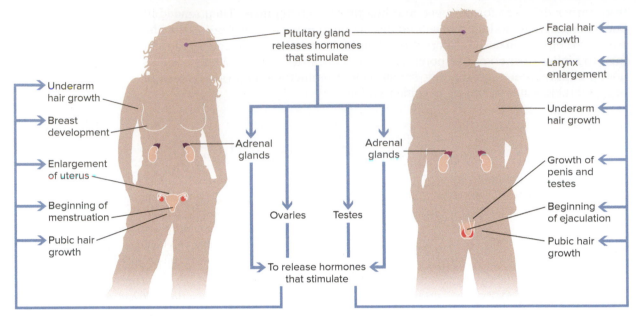

FIGURE 21
PHYSICAL DEVELOPMENT OF MALES AND FEMALES DURING PUBERTY

©Thinkstock/Getty Images RF

In the United States, girls start puberty about 2 years earlier than boys. African American girls begin maturing somewhat earlier than European American girls.

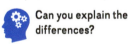 **Can you explain the differences?**

spermarche
The first ejaculation.

by cultural and environmental events. The age of menarche is highly variable, but it often occurs by age 12. In most Western cultures, the age of menarche has dropped from about age 16 during the 1800s to 12 or 13 today. The beginning of menstruation marks the beginning of fertility for a young woman, so this is an important developmental milestone.

In boys, the event that signals readiness to reproduce is **spermarche**, or the first ejaculation. Usually, the first ejaculation is unexpected, and it occurs as a nocturnal emission, or "wet dream." Once a male has ejaculated, technically he can father a child. This presents a primary problem of adolescence: In boys and girls, the body is ready for parenthood far earlier than the mind is.

Cognitive and Brain Development in Adolescence

As the body undergoes dramatic transformation, changes continue to unfold in the brain. During adolescence, children gain the ability to reason about abstract concepts and problems. Recall that Piaget called this stage formal operational, when teens begin to think abstractly and may show the ability to engage in scientific reasoning and hypothesis testing.

Adolescents and even adults do not all develop this reasoning ability to the same degree (Klahr, 2000; Kuhn, Amsel, & O'Loughlin, 1988; Kuhn & Pearsall, 2000; Wilkening & Sodian, 2005). The extent to which they do is related to their ability to think and solve problems systematically, rather than relying on the trial-and-error method that children use. It is also related to the ability to distinguish one's thoughts about how the world works from the evidence for how it really works (Kuhn & Pearsall, 2000). For example, believing that the position of the planets affects human personality does not make it so. Good scientific thinkers realize the world may or may not operate the way they think it does, so they devise step-by-step ways of testing their ideas. This requires the ability to think about alternatives and to question their own thinking.

With adolescence and formal operations, young people begin to ask abstract philosophical, religious, and political questions and form their own beliefs.

Moreover, with abstract thinking comes the ability to consider alternatives—not just how things are but how they could be. For instance, science fiction and Internet gaming appeal to adolescents because they involve abstract, imaginative, and alternative forms of thinking.

The cognitive developments of adolescence, such as abstract reasoning and logical thinking, are linked with the dramatic brain development occurring during this period. The frontal lobes are the last areas of the brain to fully develop, and they continue to mature until late adolescence or early adulthood (Fuster, 2002; Miller & Cummings, 1999; Sowell et al., 2001). They are involved in planning, attention, working memory, abstract thought, and impulse control. The onset of formal operational and scientific thinking occurs after the frontal lobes have developed more fully (Kwon & Lawson, 2000).

It is not so much that the frontal lobes and other brain regions are growing in size but rather that they are growing in neural complexity. Complexity is seen in more myelin and white matter, greater neural coordination or synchrony, and neural pruning. In general, there is a direct relationship between cognitive development and brain development.

A multitude of changes occur in brain development throughout adolescence:

- The brain develops more myelin around the axons, as well as more neural connections (Fields, 2008; Perrin et al., 2009; Sabbagh, 2006; Sakai, 2005; Shaw et al., 2006). As seen in Figure 11, myelination proceeds from the back of the brain to the frontal lobes during the period from childhood to adolescence. The rate and locations of myelination differ between boys and girls (Fields, 2008; Perrin et al., 2009; Schmithorst, Holland, & Dardzinski, 2008). In girls, this increased white matter organization is in the right hemisphere; in boys, it is in the left hemisphere (Schmithorst et al., 2008). This is one of numerous examples of developmental differences in the brains of boys and girls as they move into the teen years.

- *Neural synchrony*, or the ability of certain types of brain waves to work together to allow for coordinated activity in the brain, also increases throughout adolescence and possibly into early adulthood (Uhlhaas et al., 2009). Abnormal neural synchrony appears to play a role in such disorders as autism and schizophrenia (Uhlhaas & Singer, 2010).

- *Synaptic pruning* reaches its final stages, whereby rarely used synapses are allowed to die off to make the brain more efficient (de Graaf-Peters & Hadders-Algra, 2006; Paus, Keshavan, & Giedd, 2008).

How the brain develops and, in particular, how the cortex develops affect intelligence. Philip Shaw and colleagues (2006) periodically scanned the brains of more than 300 participants during childhood and adolescence and discovered something surprising. At age 7 the highly intelligent children had thinner frontal cortexes, but by mid-adolescence their cortexes had become thicker than those of the children with average intelligence. Moreover, by age 19 the thickness of the cortex in the two groups was the same (see Figure 22). So the cortex grows thicker into adolescence, and the brains of highly intelligent people are more elastic and trace a different developmental path.

If so much brain growth is occurring, why do teens often seem absent-minded and/or prone to risky and impulsive behavior? Research on other mammals offers some clues to this question. "Teen" mice taught how to learn a maze perform much more slowly than both prepubescent and adult mice. They also have an increased abundance of GABAnergic receptors in the hippocampus at that time, which impairs learning (Shen et al., 2010). Impaired hippocampus functioning, therefore, may be responsible for questionable and risky behavior seen in teen mice and, by extension, teen humans.

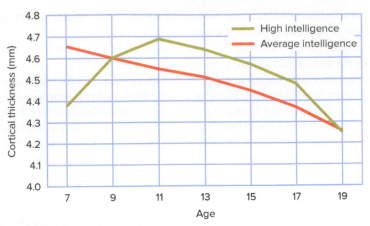

FIGURE 22

THE DEVELOPING BRAIN: CORTICAL THICKNESS AND INTELLIGENCE

 Can you think of any reasons highly intelligent children at age 7 have a thinner cortex but between the ages of 11 and 17 they have a thicker cortex than average intelligent children? (Shaw, et al., **2006**)

In teens, the frontal lobes become overloaded during complex and demanding tasks, whereas the workload is distributed more evenly throughout the brain in adults (Sabbagh, 2006). Moreover, although teenagers have the same basic reasoning skills as adults, the more sophisticated cognitive skills, such as the ability to plan ahead or evaluate the possible consequences of a decision, do not develop until late adolescence or young adulthood (Steinberg, 2010). The tendency of teenagers to engage in impulsive and risky behavior, such as driving at excessive speeds and fighting, can be partly explained by these findings of brain development.

The active development of the teen brain—the growing brain structures, increased myelination, neural synchrony, and synaptic pruning—also helps explain why people are more vulnerable to brain-related dysfunctions and disorders during adolescence (Paus et al., 2008). When so many changes are happening in the brain, it is more vulnerable to toxins and diseases that affect the nervous system.

Social Development in Adolescence

The changes to the brain during adolescence influence social as well as cognitive behavior. Areas of the brain involved in how we interpret other people's faces, our understanding of emotion, and "theory of mind" are still developing into the teen years. These areas include the amygdala, portions of the temporal lobe, and the medial prefrontal cortex (mPFC; Sebastian et al., 2010). For instance, teens use slightly different brain regions to process certain emotions than do adults, indicating that further change occurs during the teen years (Burnett et al., 2008).

Teens are also more sensitive than adults to rejection. In a laboratory task in which a teen is left out of simulated group play (a computer game with unseen partners) and then ostracized for it, the omitted teens showed a much stronger response to rejection than did adults in the same situation. It may be that the sensitivity to rejection in teen years is related to the extended period of development in the prefrontal cortex that occurs over the course of adolescence, but more research is needed to confirm this hypothesis (Sebastian et al., 2010).

With the onset of puberty and adolescence, children begin to focus on the questions of who they are. Just as we try on clothes to see what fits, adolescents try on identities to see what looks good and feels comfortable. One way teens experiment with identity is in how they relate to groups, which groups they identify with, and how they present themselves to others more generally. Group identifications can be very important, long-lasting, and quite distressing to teens if they are challenged (Lemay & Ashmore, 2004). For instance, one of your authors (Erika) ran track and cross-country in high school. Being a runner—an athlete—became an important part of her identity, as did relating to the community of runners at school. This identification lasted well through adulthood. Although identity development occurs across the life span, teens are more self-conscious about the changes associated with them and experience changes more intensely than do children or adults (Steinberg, 2005, 2010).

Puberty brings profound changes not only in the body but also in relationships. Family becomes less central, and peer relationships become the focus of life. Having close, intimate friends during adolescence is associated with many positive social and emotional outcomes, such as self-confidence, better relationships with parents and authority figures, better performance in school, and even better overall adjustment and feelings of self-worth in adulthood (Bagwell, Newcomb, & Bukowski, 1998). In contrast, feeling isolated and lacking close peer relationships during adolescence are associated with poorer performance in school, more conflict with parents and authority figures, and lower self-esteem.

In the teen years, peers start to replace parents as a source of identification (Bukowski & Sippola, 2001; Pugh & Hart, 1999). In the search for who they are, adolescents look to their friends for answers. The values and social rules operating within different peer groups give teens "identity templates," which they use to define themselves (Pugh & Hart, 1999). Moreover, perceived pressure and criticism from others (mother and friends, for instance) foretell whether or not disordered eating might emerge in both male and female teens (Shomaker & Furman, 2009). Reactions from parents and peers also play a role in whether teens end up using alcohol and cigarettes (Kristjansson et al., 2010).

Compared to childhood, however, the most obvious change in adolescent social development is the emergence of sexual interest and sexual relationships. Not only do teens become interested in sexual relationships, but sexual thoughts and feelings also occupy much of their attention and time. The average age for first sexual intercourse for men and women is around 17 years old, although there is quite a bit of variability (Chandra et al., 2005). A sexually mature body combined with a brain that is not fully developed can result in bad judgment, as shown in the high rates of unplanned pregnancy and sexually transmitted diseases in teens (CDC, 2005). Sexuality and sexual activity influence how teens think of themselves. Being sexually active increases self-esteem and enhances self-concept in both boys and girls, but it also can lead to an increase in risky behavior (Houlihan et al., 2008).

Sexual orientation and gender identity are important components to the development of identity during adolescence. To be clear, sexual orientation and gender identity are not related. **Gender identity** is who a person identifies as, whereas **sexual orientation** is who a person is attracted to. As the doctor who worked with the twin Nicole (with whose case we opened the chapter) put it: "sexual orientation is who you go to bed with; gender identity is who you go to bed as" (Spack, 2014). In 2015, 93% of teenagers between the ages of 13 and 17 described themselves as predominantly *heterosexual* (interested only in the opposite sex), about 1% as either predominantly *homosexual* (interested only in the same sex), 2% as *bisexual* (interested in both sexes), and about 3% as unsure about their orientation (Lenhart, Anderson, & Smith, 2015). Another survey showed that about 6% of teens are heterosexual with same-sex attraction/fantasy or behavior (Zhao et al., 2010).

Transgender identity occurs when one identifies with the opposite gender one was assigned at birth. It is true that most people identify with the gender

gender identity
Is the gender one feels oneself to be internally.

sexual orientation
The disposition to be attracted to someone of the opposite sex (heterosexual), the same sex (homosexual) or both sexes (bisexual)

transgender identity
Occurs when one identifies with the opposite gender one was assigned at birth.

FIGURE 23

ERIKSON'S EIGHT STAGES OF PERSONALITY DEVELOPMENT. EACH STAGE HAS A CORE STRENGTH (SHOWN IN BOLD TYPE) AND A CRISIS TO RESOLVE

8 Old age
Wisdom
Integrity vs. despair, disgust

7 Adulthood
Care
Generativity vs. stagnation

6 Young adulthood
Love
Intimacy vs. isolation

5 Adolescence
Fidelity
Identity vs. identity confusion

4 School age
Competence
Industry vs. inferiority

3 Play age
Purpose
Initiative vs. guilt

2 Early childhood
Will
Autonomy vs. shame and doubt

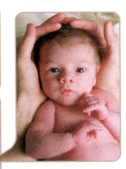

1 Infancy
Hope
Basic trust vs. basic mistrust

text: From *The Life Cycle Completed: A Review* by Erik H. Erikson. Copyright 1982 by Rikan Enterprises, Ltd.; photos: 1: ©FrareDavis PhotographyStockbyte/Getty Images RF; 2: ©Ariel Skelley/Blend Images; 3: ©Laurence Moulton/PhotoAlto/PictureQuest RF; 4: ©Terry Vine/Blend Images LLC RF; 5: ©Blend Images LLC RF; 6: ©Stockbyte/Getty Images RF; 7: ©Monkey Business Images/Shutterstock.com; 8: ©ESB Professional/Shutterstock.com

cis-gendered
Is when a person's gender identity is the same (cis) as their sex assigned at birth.

they are born—that is, they are **cis-gendered** (where "cis" means "same"). But not everyone does. A 2015 Pew Research Center survey reported that 3% of U.S. teens ages 13 to 17 identify as transgender (Lenhart et al., 2015).

For some people, especially those who are intense, consistent, and persistent in their atypical identity, transgender identity is not something that is easy to change (Steensma et al., 2013). For others, however, who are less consistent and persistent, their atypical gender identity may not continue during or after puberty (Steensma et al., 2013). In fact, some studies report between two-thirds and three-fourths of those who identify atypically in childhood no longer do in adolescence (Steensma et al., 2013; Wallien & Cohen-Kettenis, 2008). For them, gender identity is more fluid and changeable.

Finally, some adolescents explore their identity through experimenting with drugs and alcohol (Duncan, Duncan, & Strycker, 2006; Tang & Orwin, 2009). Both parental and peer behavior influence whether someone will start drinking and how his or her drinking behavior develops.

Personality Development in Adolescence

Although many aspects of temperament and personality are stable over time, our personalities also grow and change as we age. Adolescence is a time of more rapid personality change than adulthood (Syed & Seiffge-Krenke, 2013). Erik Erikson (1968) proposed a model of personality development with eight stages, each defined by an identity crisis or conflict (see Figure 23). According to Erikson, an identity crisis is an opportunity for adaptive or maladaptive adjustment. Each stage consists of a conflict from which a person may emerge either more adjusted or less adjusted.

Erikson (1968) saw *identity versus identity confusion* as the major conflict during adolescent personality development. Testing, experimenting, and trying on identities are the norm during adolescence. This searching for and trying on various identities has been labeled *identity exploration* (Marcia, 1966). Experimenting and exploring allow a person to find out which identities work and which ones don't. The three primary areas of identity formation during adolescence are in the domains of sexual identity, ideological identity (religion and politics), and occupational identity (career decisions). The basic strength that develops in adolescence is fidelity, a sense of faith and commitment to an identity. Moreover, Erikson argued that having some solid sense of identity during adolescence was crucial for forming mature and healthy relationships in early adulthood. Otherwise, the person loses their identity in the relationship.

©Prisma by Dukas Presseagentur GmbH/Alamy

Experimenting with different styles of dress appeals to adolescents in the midst of identity formation.

Quick Quiz 3: The Developing Adolescent

1. What event marks the beginning of adolescence?
   a. puberty
   b. formal operations
   c. growth of body hair
   d. all of the above
2. In which area of the brain does significant development occur during adolescence?
   a. occipital lobes
   b. hippocampus
   c. frontal lobes
   d. cerebellum

Answers can be found at the end of the chapter.

THE DEVELOPING ADULT

As adolescence draws to a close and people enter their 20s, the transition from high school to college or work increases independence. Many changes to behavior occur with the transition from the teens to the 20s, and even across the life span.

Early Adulthood

Major changes in thinking, feeling, and behavior occur during childhood and adolescence, but what happens when you turn 18? Are you suddenly grown-up and "all done"? Not by a long shot. By the time most young people have reached sexual maturity, their lives are still in great flux. Further changes associated with assuming responsibilities for one's own finances, housing, clothing, and career shape the time between adolescence and young adulthood. Although some reliance on parents persists throughout college, when a person reaches adulthood, some threshold has been crossed. This threshold, however, is not defined by landmarks in physical and psychological development, as is the case for childhood and adolescence. Rather, the movement into adulthood entails successful passage through certain life transitions, which end in nearly complete independence from one's parents.

Emerging Adulthood   Arnett (2004) uses the term **emerging adulthood** for the phase between adolescence and young adulthood, which spans ages 18–25. Emerging adulthood is a phase of transition between the teen years and adulthood. Teens rely

emerging adulthood
The transitional phase between adolescence and young adulthood; includes ages 18–25 years.

1 **identity exploration**	Who am I *really*?
2 **instability**	Job Relationships Education
3 **self-focused**	More so than childhood and adolescence, because most people during this phase go through some stage of living alone
4 **feeling in-between**	Between both adolescence and adulthood
5 **age of possibilities**	Anything is possible for the future

FIGURE 24
STATE OF EMERGING ADULTHOOD

 What factors figure into identity formation of emerging adulthood? (Arnett, 2004)

on their parents for food, clothing, and housing. At about age 18, things change. Young people in their late teens know that soon they will have to assume greater responsibility for keeping themselves alive, and this has broad-reaching implications for behavior and thought.

As young people enter college or the workforce, financial responsibility starts to shift to their shoulders. They continue to try on many behaviors and self-concepts (just as teens do), but this experimentation is tinged by the realization that soon they will have to stabilize a bit and assume more responsibility for their own livelihoods. Whether or not someone goes to college affects the timing of certain developmental milestones. Women who do not go to college marry and have their first child substantially earlier than those who do (Klein, 2004).

The key changes during emerging adulthood center on coping with increased responsibility and recognizing the need to make decisions about some of the things one has been exploring (Arnett, 2006). Figure 24 shows the key features of emerging adulthood. Although much brain development has happened by the time of emerging adulthood, the brain continues to change and grow. The prefrontal cortex continues to develop and fibers there are increasingly myelinated, which facilitates neural communication. Brain structure changes as well (de Graaf-Peters & Hadders-Algra, 2006). For example, brain areas that organize incoming sensory information and help generate emotional responses change significantly from the early to late teen years (Bennett & Baird, 2006). Similarly, researchers are learning to extend neural plasticity into adulthood with the use of various drugs. For instance, in a study by Gervain and colleagues young adult males (ages 18–27) were able to develop superior pitch perception if they were randomly assigned to receive a mood stabilizer (valproic acid, otherwise known as Depakote) compared to those assigned to receive a placebo (Gervain et al., 2013). Even more impressive, when the two groups switched (placebo group got the mood stabilizer and vice versa) the effect still held. In sum, mood stabilizing drugs can extend into adulthood the critical period for certain kinds of learning.

An emerging adult necessarily has an emerging identity. Numerous issues figure into identity formation, but we will discuss four: career identity, sexual and sexual-orientation identity, gender identity, and ethnic identity.

Career Identity By the time young people are finishing high school, they need to start looking for a job or go to college to train for a career. These choices involve a great deal of soul searching about such questions as how to spend their time, what are their life goals, and what, exactly, might they offer the world (Park, 2015; Porfeli & Skorikov, 2010).

Sexual Identity and Sexual-Orientation The age of first sexual experience varies by culture, ethnicity, and education, among other factors (Jordahl & Lohman, 2009). In this country, most people become sexually active during adolescence, on average by about age 17 for both men and women (Chandra et al., 2005). Although sexual behavior begins in the teens, issues surrounding psychological sexual maturation and experience occur also in the late teens and extend well into the early 20s. Although young men and women tend to begin sexual activity around the same time, men accumulate sexual encounters more rapidly between the ages of 16 and 26 than do women (Zimmer-Gembeck & Collins, 2008). Adolescents experiment with relationships and partners. Fifty years ago, young people were expected to settle down with a single partner by their early 20s. Today, if you make a commitment to someone you have dated for a while in high school, it is considered a mistake (Arnett, 2004).

Sexual orientation concerns the gender to which we are sexually attracted and comes in three forms: opposite sex (heterosexual), same-sex (homosexual), and both sexes (bisexual). Those who readily know they are heterosexual may have a hard enough time developing a sense of sexual identity during adolescence and emerging adulthood, but for those who are either confused about their orientation or identify as lesbian, gay, bisexual, or transgender (LGBT), it is even harder. The additional pressure from and challenge of dealing with other people's negative attitudes toward their orientation and attempts to fit into a heterosexual identity that is not theirs are linked with depressed mood and even higher incidences of suicide than in heterosexual students (Smith et al., 2016; Spencer & Patrick, 2009). These young adults often experience a unique kind of "minority stress" that is different from the pressures experienced by other minorities: There's no guaranteed familial support. Hence, the support from friends becomes even more important.

©James Drake /*Sports Illustrated*/Getty Images

Bruce Jenner, 1976

Gender Identity In the adolescent development section we reported that 3% of U.S. teens identify as transgender. For adults, the figure is between 0.3% and 0.5% who identify themselves as "non-binary" and a similar percentage (0.4%) do so in the United Kingdom (Conron, Scott, Stowell, & Landers, 2012; Gates, 2011; Titman, 2014). That is about 1 in every 200 to 330 people.

In recent times, the highest-profile case of someone identifying with the gender they were not born with is Caitlyn Jenner. Bruce Jenner grew up as the all-American boy and man and went on to win the "world's greatest (male) athlete award" by winning the 1976 decathlon at the summer Olympics. As many people now know, however, Bruce is now Caitlyn (and parent of the Kardashian girls). In 2015, at age 65, Jenner went public with her male to female transition and became Caitlyn.

Forces of nature and nurture help explain the development of gender identity. Gender identity is influenced by differences in genes, hormones, and brain structures. First, variants of particular genes have been associated with transgender identity (Klink & Den Heijer, 2014; Saraswat, Weinand, & Safer, 2015). Second, twin-adoption research shows that identical twins are more likely to share the same gender identity than fraternal twins (Bailey, Dunne, & Martin, 2000; Heylens et al., 2012). Third, research has uncovered various brain activity and brain structure differences in transgender individuals compared to cis-gendered individuals (Kreukels & Guillamon, 2016; Russo, 2016; Saraswat et al., 2015; Zhou et al., 1995).

Social and cognitive theories explain gender and gender identity development as a product of environmental, personal, and behavioral forces (Bussey & Bandura, 1999; Martin et al., 2012). Environmental forces include social and cultures norms of appropriate male and female behavior. Some cultures make very strong distinctions of what is male and female and even have laws enforcing them. And yet it may be a surprise to many but some cultures believe, such as the Bugis of Indonesia, that five genders exist (male, female, male to female, female to male, and both male and female). Similarly, cultures within India, Pakistan, and Nepal acknowledge three genders: male, female, and transgender (Nutt, 2015).

©Kevin Winter/Getty Images

Caitlyn Jenner, 2015

Ethnic Identity For people of mixed racial heritage, who constitute roughly 2% of the adult U.S. population, and a higher percentage of younger people (U.S. Census Bureau, 2009b), the awareness of one's ethnic identity increases from adolescence to emerging adulthood (French et al., 2006; Syed & Azmitia, 2010). Each parent or grandparent may push for his or her identity to be adopted as the prominent one, and the young person

Gay couples struggle with more identity and acceptance issues than heterosexual couples.

young adulthood
The development stage that usually happens by the mid-20s, when people complete the key developmental tasks of emerging adulthood.

has to decide for him- or herself which one feels right. For example, Rosa is of Chinese and Mexican heritage. She says she feels more Chinese than Mexican, due to her mother's influence (Arnett, 2004).

Biracial people of all ages resist having to identify with one racial group over the other. Doing so can be stressful (Townsend, Markus, & Bergsieker, 2009). Even such mundane tasks as completing simple surveys may force them to choose. Recent versions of the SAT, for example, require students to complete a brief demographic questionnaire on their age, sex, ethnicity, and so on. According to Heidi Durrow (whose mother is Dutch and father is African American), when asked to identify her race, "The satisfactory answer usually isn't: I'm black *and* white. Other people want mixed-race kids to choose who they are" (*Reimagining*, 2010). The same debate followed President Obama—whose father was African and whose mother was European American—throughout the 2008 election and even onto his 2010 census form, where he selected African American as his racial identity. Indeed, biracial children often feel rejected by both groups (Crawford & Alaggia, 2008). Some feel unsupported by parents who do not understand their dilemma.

Young Adulthood How do you know when you are an adult? At a certain point, some threshold has been crossed, but the criteria for adulthood vary from culture to culture (Cheah & Nelson, 2004). Though some cultures still have rituals of transformation, most modern technological societies rely on the assumption that certain responsibilities occur when the person reaches a certain age. Usually, the transition to **Young Adulthood** occurs in the 20s, though certain life transitions represent more significant markers than does age (Arnett, 2004; see Figure 25). In young adulthood, financial and living arrangements have settled down, and many people marry or form other long-term partnerships (though this, too, is changing). These tasks all push the person to become increasingly engaged with the outside world (Burt & Masten, 2010).

Aberg and colleagues (2009) studied over a million Swedish men who had enlisted for military service at age 18, and they examined data on intelligence, cardiovascular fitness, and muscular strength outcome measures. They found a positive correlation between cardiovascular fitness (but not muscular strength) and better cognitive scores. Further, people whose cardiovascular fitness had improved from 15 to 18 years of age

FIGURE 25
ARE YOU AN ADULT?

1 Do you accept responsibility for yourself?

2 Do you make independent decisions about major life events?

3 Are you financially independent?

had higher intelligence scores at age 18 years than those whose cardiovascular fitness had declined over that time. What this means is that physical fitness and cognitive functioning are linked in young adulthood. Not only the middle-aged and elderly can benefit cognitively from being physically fit. Young adults can too.

Marriage Over the past 50 years, the average age at which people marry has increased from the early 20s to the mid- to late 20s for both men and women, though women tend to marry a bit earlier overall (see Figure 26; Liu, Elliott, & Umberson, 2009; U.S. Census Bureau, 2009a). Why is marriage being delayed? More people are pursuing higher education, a trend that accounts for the lengthening of young adulthood generally (Arnett, 2004). In addition, more people are living together prior to marriage, though according to survey research, living together before engagement does not predict better marital satisfaction down the line (Rhoades, Stanley, & Markman, 2009).

Parenthood One clear marker of reaching adulthood is having a child, although about 15% of adults never have children, and many people consider themselves to be adults before they become parents (Goodwin, McGill, & Chandra, 2009). The age at which people have their first child has increased steadily over the years, primarily because time spent in college and training means that it takes longer to settle down in industrialized nations (Kokko, Pulkkinen, & Mesiäinen, 2009). As shown in Figure 27, there is a direct relationship between education and age of having a first child. Just under 90% of women who drop out of high school have a first child before age 25, whereas less than 25% of women who finish college have a child before age 25 (Martinez, Daniels, & Chandra, 2012).

Personality may also play a role in whether and when people become parents. For instance, shy men become fathers later than men who are not shy. By contrast, shy girls are more conventional and thus even more likely to parent early—less likely to be moving into the world of careers (Caspi, Elder, & Bem, 1988). Both men and women who tend to avoid harm and risk are less likely to have children at all (Jokela et al., 2010).

Early Adult Personality Development
Having a solid sense of self and identity is important for early adulthood—the period during one's 20s. In this stage, Erikson believed the primary conflict is between *intimacy and isolation*. Erikson defined **intimacy** as the ability to fuse one's identity with another's without the fear of losing it (Erikson, 1968). If an individual does not develop a relatively secure sense of identity as an adolescent, forming intimate relationships may not be possible during young adulthood. Before they have completely figured out who they are, people may develop very close love relationships and then let the relationship define who they are. Their identity gets lost in the relationship. Then, years later, the relationship may end—because as each person develops his or her own identity, differences surface. The core strength to emerge in young adulthood is *love*, which involves commitment, passion, cooperation, competition, and friendship (Erikson, 1982).

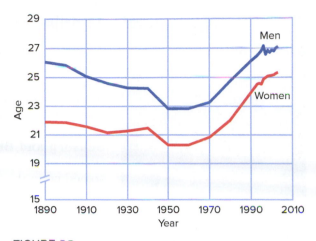

FIGURE 26

U.S. MEDIAN AGE AT FIRST MARRIAGE, 1890–2010. The median age of first marriage has always been above 23 for men and above 21 for women, except in the 1950s, when they were both lower.

 What are some of the reasons the median age is now higher than it has been in more than 100 years?

intimacy
As defined by Erikson, the ability to fuse one's identity with another's without the fear of losing it.

FIGURE 27

AGE AT FIRST BIRTH FOR WOMEN AGES 22–44 YEARS, BY EDUCATION: UNITED STATES, 2006–2010

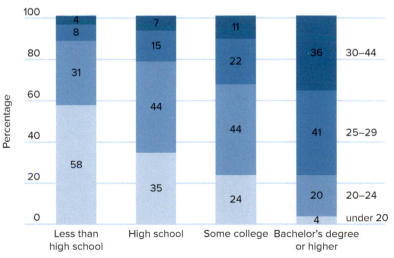

(Martinez et al., 2012).

Middle Adulthood

©Ted Streshinsky Photographic Archive/Getty Images

Erik Erikson

After establishing a career and settling down in long-term relationships and, often, having children, one moves into middle adulthood—generally acknowledged to be the ages between 40 and 60 or 65 (Santrock, 2010). Like all developmental stages, middle adulthood has its own unique challenges, two of which involve sensory and physical development.

Sensory and Brain Development Many people experience some loss of vision, hearing, or both by middle adulthood. Most people need reading glasses sometime in their 40s, as the lens of the eye loses flexibility (Goldstein, 2007). For those who already wear glasses or contacts as adults, bifocals may become necessary as they enter their late 40s.

On average, about 10% of adults suffer from normal hearing loss, defined as difficulty in hearing normal conversation, but age, gender, and profession are the three biggest predictors of hearing loss (see Figure 28). A recent large-scale study found that as many as 50% of older adults (mean age of 67) experience some degree of hearing loss (Chia et al., 2007). Certain professions are much more prone to suffering hearing loss than others, with farming/agriculture, mining, construction, manufacturing, and certain forms of music being highest on the list (*Work-related hearing loss*, 2001). By age 50, 49% of miners have significant hearing loss, and by age 60 the figure is 70% (*Work-related hearing loss*, 2001). Exposure to loud sounds throughout life, such as rock concerts, heavy machinery, and overuse of headphones, accounts for many hearing problems in people over 40 (Liu et al., 2015; Wallhagen et al., 1997). Age-related hearing deficits can stem from problems with the ears, the auditory nerve, or various brain areas and are more common in men than women (Pearson et al., 1995; Tremblay & Ross, 2007). High-pitched, high-frequency sounds become harder to hear as people get older. Some people report that, as they age, they can hear conversations but cannot always understand them.

Some people also experience a loss of sensitivity to taste and smell, though these changes vary considerably among individuals. Taste buds lose sensitivity, although the ones affected—sweet, salty, bitter, or savory—vary from person to person. These changes do not seem to adversely affect appetite, however (Kremer et al., 2007). As many as half of people over 65 demonstrate significant loss of smell (Toussaint et al., 2015).

In spite of the potential for sensory losses, the brain remains quite plastic and generative throughout adulthood (Leuner & Gould, 2010). Although the rate of neurogenesis tapers off in middle adulthood compared to young adulthood, in the hippocampus in particular, new neurons still form. The amount of neurogenesis depends on a number of factors. Opportunities for continued learning throughout life appear to aid neurogenesis, while stress and anxiety hinder it (Leuner & Gould, 2010; Morgenstern, Lombardi, & Schinder, 2008).

Personality Development during Middle Adulthood Carl Jung (1931/1960) argued that in midlife people are confronting the unfulfilled parts of their personality and ideally are developing them as a counterbalance to the other, more fully developed parts of themselves. The process through which someone's personality becomes whole and balanced is what Jung called **individuation**. During middle adulthood a formerly very extroverted and masculine man might become more solitary and less focused on being "macho," but some middle-aged adults cling to their youth, deny their undeveloped selves, and spiral into a crisis of midlife. Jung believed that this midlife crisis is seen in higher divorce rates and more mental breakdowns during midlife than earlier in life.

individuation
The process of a person's personality becoming whole and full.

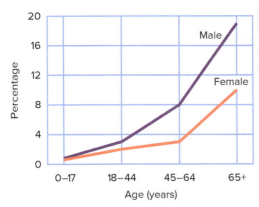

FIGURE 28

PREVALENCE OF HEARING LOSS BY AGE GROUP AND GENDER. From childhood to middle age, men and women are equally likely to suffer hearing loss. After middle age, men far outnumber women in suffering from hearing loss.

Erik Erikson proposed that in midlife the crisis we confront is *generativity versus stagnation*. He defined **generativity** as the creation of new ideas, products, or people (Erikson, 1982). Parenting, starting a business, and creating a work of art are different ways of being generative. **Stagnation** occurs when the adult becomes more self-focused than oriented toward others and does not contribute in a productive way to society or family. The core strength of adulthood is *care*, being committed to and caring for the people, ideas, and products one has generated.

A very popular notion of midlife imagines that nearly everyone goes through some kind of "midlife crisis"—quitting their jobs, getting divorced, buying a sports car, contemplating the meaning of life, and becoming painfully aware of the passage of time and impending death. These ideas are, in fact, based on psychological theory, most notably the work of Jung and Erikson. Indeed, a minority of people do experience crises and major life changes during middle adulthood, but the scientific evidence for a crisis being universal or widespread is lacking (Freund & Ritter, 2009; Wethington, 2000). Overall satisfaction with life, however, does reach a low point for most adults in midlife (ages 40 to 55), rises into one's 60s and 70s, and then falls again in one's 80s (Baird et al., 2010).

Late Adulthood

The last stage of life begins around age 65 and is labeled "late adulthood." Of the many significant developmental changes occurring during late adulthood, we will focus only on cognition, personality development, and death.

Normal changes in the brain occur with age. Just as body mass gradually decreases with age, so does brain mass (Enzinger et al., 2005). Most normal cognitive decline with aging results in brain changes to the frontal lobes, the part of the brain most involved in working memory, planning, and abstract reasoning (Braver & Barch, 2002; Raz, 2000).

The older brain does not change as rapidly as the younger brain, but it remains dynamic (Baltes et al., 2006; Gervain et al., 2013). New experiences and mastery of new skills continue to give rise to neural branching and growth throughout life (Kemperman, 2006). Learning new skills, such as a new language, a new game, or a new computer activity, can lead to new neural growth (Cotman et al., 2007). Taking up a musical instrument can also stimulate brain growth (Pascual-Leone, 2001; see "Psychology in the Real World" earlier in this chapter).

People often complain about memory problems as they get older, yet cognitive decline in adulthood is a complex topic. Some abilities, such as expertise in a given area, take time to develop and reach a peak in middle adulthood (Kim & Hasher, 2005). Verbal memory actually peaks after age 50 (Schaie, 1996). Declines do occur in other kinds of memory, however, especially the kind involved in processing information and maintaining information while making decisions. The rate of decline does not become noticeable until people reach their 60s or 70s. Even then, healthy older people in their 70s who receive training in memory skills show improvements not only in cognitive performance but also in their ability to manage the tasks of daily living, such as shopping, food preparation, financial management, and household tasks (Willis et al., 2006).

In terms of intelligence, we must first distinguish between two distinct kinds—fluid and crystallized. **Fluid intelligence** involves raw mental ability, pattern recognition, and abstract reasoning and is applied to a problem that a person has never confronted before. Problems that require finding relationships, understanding implications, and drawing conclusions all require fluid intelligence. Neither culture nor vocabulary influence fluid intelligence. Knowledge that we have gained from experience and learning, education, and practice, however, is called **crystallized intelligence**, which is influenced by how large your vocabulary is, as well as your knowledge of your culture. Being asked whether

generativity
A term Erik Erikson used to describe the process in adulthood of creating new ideas, products, or people.

stagnation
A situation in which an adult becomes more self-focused than oriented toward others and does not contribute in a productive way to society or family.

fluid intelligence
Raw mental ability, pattern recognition, and abstract reasoning that can be applied to a problem one has never confronted before.

crystallized intelligence
The kind of knowledge that one gains from experience and learning, education, and practice.

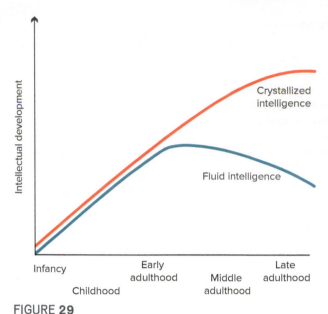

FIGURE 29

COGNITIVE DEVELOPMENT OVER THE LIFE SPAN

 What is crystallized intelligence, and what is fluid intelligence? Why does crystallized intelligence level off at a much later stage than fluid intelligence?

dementia

A loss of mental function, in which many cognitive processes are impaired, such as the ability to remember, reason, solve problems, make decisions, and use language.

Alzheimer's disease

A degenerative disease marked by progressive cognitive decline and characterized by a collection of symptoms, including confusion, memory loss, mood swings, and eventual loss of physical function.

Dalmatian is to dog as oriole is to bird is an example of a problem that requires crystallized intelligence.

One of the clearest developmental changes in adult intelligence is the gradual decline in fluid intelligence beginning in middle adulthood, but the strengthening of crystallized intelligence (Schaie, 1996; see Figure 29). Only in very late adulthood do we see a leveling off in acquired knowledge and crystallized intelligence. How quickly one processes information, keeping things in mind while solving problems (working memory), and how well one recalls events are key components of fluid intelligence. These skills reach a peak in one's 20s and 30s and then begin to decline (Basak et al., 2008; Hedden & Gabrieli, 2004; Nilsson, 2003; Schaie, 1996).

One way to stave off, or at least reduce, cognitive decline with aging is to exercise (Bherer, Erickson, & Liu Ambrose, 2013). Older people who had been inactive improved significantly in a wide range of cognitive tasks after aerobic exercise training compared to a control group that did not exercise (Colcombe & Kramer, 2003). Similarly, engaging in meaningful, challenging work can make a huge difference for thinking and the brain.

One cognitive benefit of aging is wisdom, the ability to know what matters, to live well, and to show good judgment (Baltes & Smith, 2008). Wisdom comes with learning from the situations in which we find ourselves. The more we experience, the more we learn about what is important and how to manage our time (Carstensen, 2006). Wisdom also comes from learning not to take things too seriously.

Sometimes more than just normal forgetting occurs with aging. **Dementia** is an unusual degree of loss in cognitive functions and includes memory problems and difficulty in reasoning, solving problems, making decisions, and using language. Age is a risk factor for dementia, but in and of itself, aging does not cause dementia (Fratiglioni, Winblad, & von Strauss, 2007).

Several neurological conditions, including stroke and **Alzheimer's disease**, can lead to dementia in the elderly. It may be impossible to determine which condition is responsible for dementia, because they share symptoms. A *stroke* occurs when a blood vessel that serves the brain is blocked. As a result, the brain tissue served by that vessel does not receive the oxygen and nutrients it needs, and it dies. Multiple strokes are a common source of dementia in the elderly (Schneider et al., 2007). Dead brain tissue after a stroke makes for many little (or sometimes big) cognitive impairments, such as memory loss and confusion.

Alzheimer's disease is a degenerative disease marked by progressive cognitive decline, with symptoms including confusion, memory loss, mood swings, brain pathology, and eventual loss of physical and bodily function (Figure 30). Usually affecting older people, Alzheimer's accounts for 60%–70% of the cases of dementia among the elderly (Fratiglioni et al., 2007). *Early-onset Alzheimer's* affects people younger than 65 (Alzheimer's Association, 2008).

Currently, the only way Alzheimer's can be diagnosed definitively is by examining brain tissue after death, although recent progress in brain imaging (such as MRI) may help identify early risk factors (Schmand, Eikelenboom, & van Gool, 2011; Wermke et al., 2008). For the most part, physicians diagnose Alzheimer's by noting a collection of symptoms and structural brain changes (from brain imaging) that they cannot attribute to anything else.

The defining anatomical feature of Alzheimer's is the presence of patches of dead tissue in the brain, especially in the hippocampus and areas of the cortex (Kalat, 2007). As a result, the affected person experiences lapses in memory, confusion, and other cognitive impairments. In addition, low levels of the neurotransmitter acetylcholine inhibit memory formation in people with Alzheimer's (Akaike, 2006). Alzheimer's is progressive, which means that it worsens over time and eventually is fatal. Currently, there is no cure for Alzheimer's, although some drugs do seem to slow the progression of the disease (Hansen et al., 2007). There have been recent advances in developing drugs carried on extremely small fat droplets that may one day protect people against the disease (Gregori et al., 2016).

Some evidence suggests that neurogenesis, the growth of new neurons, in the adult brain might offset or even prevent the kind of neural degeneration seen in Alzheimer's and other age-related brain disorders, such as Parkinson's disease (Kaliman et al., 2011; Petzinger et al., 2013). One of the benefits of aerobic exercise—brisk physical activity that causes the heart and lungs to work harder to meet the body's increased need for oxygen—is that it appears to protect against a decline in higher mental processing and may actually make the brain grow (Bherer et al., 2013; Colcombe et al., 2006; Kaliman et al., 2011; Petzinger et al., 2013). Recent evidence suggests that changes in gene expression (epigenetic influences) may be responsible for the effect that exercise has on neural growth (Kaliman et al., 2011). Environmental enrichment is known to improve memory and learning, improve brain plasticity, and interact with genetic factors to reduce progressive degenerative diseases of the nervous system in rodents (Nithianantharajah & Hannan, 2006). It can also stimulate neurogenesis in humans and help counteract the cognitive effects of neural degeneration (Kempermann, 2006; Steiner, Wolf, & Kempermann, 2006).

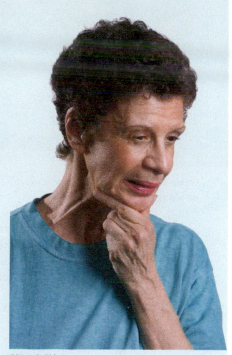

FIGURE 30

TYPICAL SIGNS AND SYMPTOMS OF ALZHEIMER'S DISEASE. According to the Alzheimer's Association (2016), as many as 5.4 million people in the United States may be living with this fatal disease, most of them over 65.

- General confusion, disorientation to date, time, or place

- Apathy, irritability, depression, anxiety

- Problems with language, math, abstract thinking, and judgment

- Personality changes with strange quirks or inappropriate behaviors

- Wandering, hiding objects, problems with eating and sleeping

- Late in the disease, paranoia and delusions possible

- Toward the end, total loss of self and inability to control bodily functions

©Lars A. Niki

Helpguide.org, copyright 2001–2011. Helpguide's articles on Alzheimer's, visit www.Helpguide.org

©George Shelley/Corbis/Getty Images

For these aging baseball players, an active lifestyle has cognitive and social benefits, as well as physical benefits.

©Sarto/Lund/Getty Images

 What are the benefits of aerobic exercise in preventing mental decline in old age?

Personality Development in Late Adulthood The final stage of Erikson's theory of personality development is old age, starting around age 60 or 65. The conflict of old age is between *integrity* and *despair*. Integrity is the feeling of being whole and integrated. It is the sense that all of one's life decisions are coming together. The core strength of old age is *wisdom*. Erikson defined wisdom as being informed and knowledgeable about life and yet having a detachment from it that comes only with old age, when one is no longer in the throes of establishing a family and career.

Death and Dying

Death can be defined in medical terms, though the criteria have changed. Physicians used to pronounce people dead when vital signs, such as heart rate and breathing, ceased. Today medical technology can keep a body alive when the brain is no longer functioning. Brain death occurs when no measurable electrical activity in the brain is evident, but life support equipment may maintain vital signs long after the brain has stopped functioning.

In psychological terms, death is a complex event that marks the end of life. In Western culture, we don't emphasize talking about death. Some Eastern cultures take a different view. In Buddhism, for example, acceptance of death and of the fact that life is not a permanent condition is a touchstone against which life is evaluated. Knowing one has limited time on Earth helps give meaning to daily life (Rinpoche, 1992). Some people with terminal illnesses report that knowing their time is limited helps them find meaning in their lives. Accessing such meaning seems to lessen their despair about dying (Carlozzi et al., 2016).

People may move through a series of stages in dealing with the end of life. Based on her extensive talks with dying patients, Elizabeth Kübler-Ross (1969) detailed the stages people may move through after learning they are going to die. Initially, they experience denial, a sense of utter disbelief that they are going to die. Next comes anger, in which the dying person feels the injustice of it all. At this stage, the dying person asks, "Why me?" In the bargaining stage, people start negotiating with God or whatever forces of nature they feel may control their fate to try to buy more time. Once the certainty of death sets in, depression may ensue. Finally, there is acceptance of death and the end of life. During this final stage, people often come to terms with their own passing.

Increasingly, people in the United States and other Western countries prepare for death by resolving differences with family and friends and accomplishing their life goals. Some people prepare special rituals or events to mark the final stage of life or to say good-bye to friends and family (Bourgeois & Johnson, 2004). We have only so much control over when we die, but by preparing psychologically for it, not just for ourselves but also for the loved ones who will be left behind, we can bring comfort to many people. Palliative care and hospice are growing branches of medicine that are devoted to end-of-life care (Morrison et al., 2005). The main goal of palliative care is to ease suffering and to make the dying person as comfortable as possible rather than to cure or treat the patient. Similarly, hospice focuses on the overall needs of the patient and family members, such as physical comfort, emotional care, and a dignified death.

Quick Quiz 4: The Developing Adult

1. Which of the following enhances neural growth in adulthood?
   a. ginkgo biloba
   b. diet
   c. caffeine
   d. aerobic exercise

2. What is necessary for a definitive diagnosis of Alzheimer's disease?
   a. an fMRI
   b. an autopsy
   c. an EEG
   d. psychological testing

3. As people age and become more aware of their limited time on Earth, they become more _____ about how they expend their resources in personal and emotional relationships.
   a. selective
   b. anxious
   c. regretful
   d. concerned

Answers can be found at the end of the chapter.

Bringing It All Together

Making Connections in Human Development

Influence of Technology on Lifespan Development

One topic that cuts across all stages of human development is how technology affects our thought, behavior, personality, and social interactions. Because there is so much research on technology use across the lifespan, we review it here to bring together all stages of human development.

Technology and Infant and Child Development

There is some evidence that infants who learn to use the computer and do tasks other than play games are more likely to be able to read a few years earlier than children who use the computer just to play games (Calvert et al., 2005; Castles et al., 2013). Other findings, however, suggest that early media use is associated with having attention deficits later in childhood (Nikkelen et al., 2015).

It will not come as a surprise that media use in general consumes much time in the day of an average child. The latest figures from a Common Sense Survey of children and teens in the United States in 2015 found that children (ages 8–12) spend about 2.5 hours a day watching TV or DVD/videos and about 1.3 hours/day playing video/computer/mobile games (Rideout, 2016) (see Figure 31). Altogether, the average 8- to 12-year-old spends almost as much time each day on media as in classroom (about 6 hours/day).

Children who watch the most TV tend to do slightly worse at school than children who watch little TV (Pellicer-Chenoll et al., 2015; Schmidt & Vandewater, 2008), but that is not the full picture. One of the central findings on early TV viewing and learning is that what children watch matters more than how much they watch. If they watch educational programs, they tend to do better in school, and if they watch noneducational programs, they tend to do worse (Huston et al., 1999; Schmidt & Vandewater, 2008).

Certain kinds of video training may have positive effects on the brains of young children as well. With a simple attention-training computer program, children's brains show more efficient processing in the frontal lobes, where executive planning and attention and focus are most active (Posner & Rothbart, 2007). Moreover, researchers report that video games can enhance cognitive skills such as mental rotation, visual tracking, and even certain kinds of problem solving (De Lisi & Wolford, 2002; Dye & Bavelier, 2004; Holmes, Gathercole, & Dunning, 2009; Schmidt & Vandewater, 2008). One study reported that, in low-income families, children who frequently use the Internet at home had higher scores on standardized tests than did children who used it very infrequently (Jackson et al., 2006). Similarly, fourth- and fifth-grade urban children who were given laptops at school and who used email frequently had high self-efficacy (confidence in being able to do well) in math and science courses (Shank & Cotten, 2014).

The news on technology and cognitive development, however, is not all positive. Cyberbullying, of course, is a serious problem all over the world (Baek & Bullock, 2014; Festl & Quandt, 2016). Researchers report that kids who heavily use TV, DVD, social networking, and computers tend to have problems with paying attention and keeping their focus (Nikkelen, Vossen, & Valkenberg, 2015; Schmidt & Vandewater, 2008; Shank & Cotten, 2014). More than 10 hours a week of electronic media use correlates with a lack of physical exercise and poor school performance (Pellicer-Chenoll et al., 2015; Schmidt & Vandewater, 2008; Vik et al., 2013).

FIGURE 31
MEDIA ACTIVITY AMONG U.S. YOUTH IN 2015

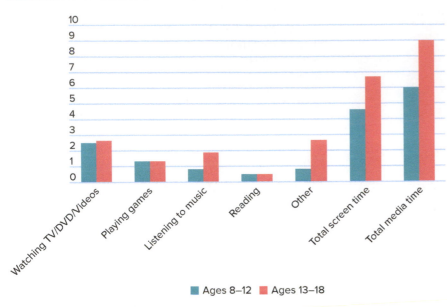

■ Ages 8–12 ■ Ages 13–18

(Source: Adapted from Rideout, V. (2016). Measuring time spent with media: The Common Sense census of media use by US 8- to 18-year-olds. *Journal of Children and Media*, 10(1), 138–144. http://doi.org/10.1080 /17482798.2016.1129808)

Heavy amounts of video gaming—but not TV viewing—were associated with being overweight in children (Atkin, Sharp, Corder, & Van Sluijs, 2014; Vik et al., 2013).

Technology and Adolescent Development

If there is an age group that has been most influenced by technology, it is adolescents. They are even referred to as Digital Natives. Ninety-two percent of 13- to 17-year-olds in the United States go online every day and 24% go online "almost constantly" (Lenhart, 2015). Eighty-seven percent of teens aged 13 to 17 either own or have access to desktop or laptop computers, 73% to a smartphone, 58% to a tablet, and 30% to a basic cell phone. African American teens have the highest smartphone ownership at 85% (Lenhart, 2015).

Family income seems to impact the type of social media teens use. At all incomes brackets Facebook is most popular compared to Instagram, Snapchat, and Twitter. But as we see in Figure 32, Facebook is more popular among lower income teens (Lenhart, 2015).

The latest figures from a Common Sense Survey of teens in the United States in 2015 found that teens (ages 13–18) spend about 2.6 hours a day watching TV or DVD/videos and about 1.3 hours/day playing video/computer/mobile games (Rideout, 2016) (see Figure 31). Altogether, the average teenager spends more time each day on media than in classroom (9 hours/day). Teens who are at risk for compulsive problematic Internet use (PIU) are those who lack social activity, are anxious, and use alcohol (Chérif, Ayadi, Khemekhem, Moalla, & Ghribi, 2014).

How does the widespread "multitasking" in teens affect their attention, learning, or problem solving? Contrary to what many people believe, multitasking comes at a cost.

Especially when problems are relatively difficult, multitasking lowers overall performance on that task (Adler & Benbunan-Fich, 2015). Moreover, perpetually heavy multitaskers are less able to filter out irrelevant information and are more likely to get distracted while working on problem-solving tasks than are light multitaskers (Ophir, Nass, & Wagner, 2009). Teens who are heavy multitaskers compared to those who are light multitaskers do not do as well on standardized achievement tests in math and English, have poorer working memory, and are more impulsive (Cain, Leonard, Gabrieli, & Finn, 2016). Similarly, driving while using a hands-free cell phone distracts drivers enough that their reaction time and coordination are on par with someone who is legally drunk (Strayer, Drews, & Couch, 2006). Texting, which requires hand and thumb coordination as well as attention, appears to be even more dangerous while driving (LaPrecious et al., 2009; Yannis et al., 2016). With the advent of self-driving cars, the question of cell phone use and texting while driving may well become moot: The car will be driving itself!

Technology and Adult Development

Technology is becoming more crucial for young adults who are in the midst of two major life transitions: forming long-term romantic relationships and deciding on and entering a career. Traditional ways of meeting potential life partners have begun to change over the last generation or two. Work, school, family, and friends still are the most common ways in which people meet life partners, with about 86% of adults having never used online dating (Pew Research Center, 2016).

FIGURE 32
MOST OFTEN USED SOCIAL MEDIA BY INCOME.

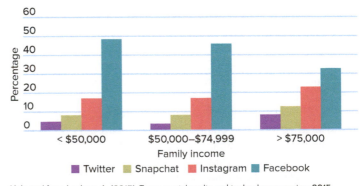

■ Twitter ■ Snapchat ■ Instagram ■ Facebook

(Adapted from Lenhart, A. (2015). Teens, social media and technology overview 2015: Smartphones facilitate shifts in communication landscape for teens. Pew Research Center, (April), 1–47. Available at http://doi.org/10.1016/j.chb.2015.08.026)

Yet, online dating is gaining in popularity with each passing year both among young adults and older adults (Pew Research Center, 2016) (see Figure 33). The sharpest increase was among young adults aged 18 to 24—their online dating nearly tripled between 2013 and 2015 (from 10% to 27%). There are both perceived pros and cons to online dating. For example, 80% of adults who use online dating say it is good way to meet people and 61% say it is an easier and faster way to meet people. Forty-five-percent of users, however, believe it is more dangerous than other methods of dating and 31% believe it leads too easily to short-term dating because there are always other people to date (Pew Research Center, 2016). Online relationship seekers have many things in common with traditional date seekers, but they also have a few differences. Online daters place higher value on communication and physical attractiveness than do offline daters (Rosen et al., 2007).

Researchers have also uncovered differences in how younger and older adults present themselves and talk on online dating sites. Dating profiles of younger adults (ages 18–49) are more likely to use first person singular (I, me, my) words and describe work and achievement compared to profiles of older adults (ages 50 and up). By contrast, profiles of older adults were more likely to contain first-person plural (we, our) and words that describe positive emotions and health (Davis & Fingerman, 2015). How much emotion and self-disclosure an online ad reveals increases the chance of receiving a response (at least in women). For example, ads that used words such as "wonderful" or "excited" had more positive responses than ads that used milder words, such as "fine" or "happy" (Rosen et al., 2007).

As any of us who uses social media knows, we tend to present our best selves or what some call our "Facebook selves" on social media. We post our best meals, best vacations, our achievements, our joys—not our failures, conflicts, and mundane experiences. And research backs up this overly positive self-presentation on social media (Dorethy, Fiebert, & Warren, 2014).

FIGURE 33

USE OF ONLINE DATING SITES OR APPS BY YOUNG ADULTS. Percent in each age group who have ever used an online dating site and/or mobile dating app.

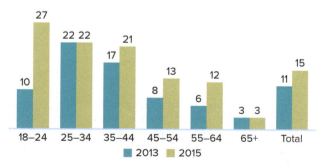

(Pew Research Center. (2016). 15% of American adults have used online dating sites or mobile dating apps. Pew Research. Retrieved October 23, 2016 from http://www.pewinternet.org/2016/02/11/15-percent-of-american-adults-have-used-online-dating-sites-or-mobile-dating-apps/)

As it also turns out, people in general and especially those who compare themselves to others feel worse about themselves after comparing themselves to their "friends" on Facebook (de Vries & Kühne, 2015). College students high in social comparison (sensitive to and awareness of others, less certain self-concept) use Facebook more frequently than those low in social comparison. More importantly when presented with other people's Facebook profiles, those high in social comparison see larger drops in their self-esteem and self-perception. That is, ironically, it makes them feel worse about themselves (Vogel, Rose, Okdie, Eckles, & Franz, 2015). As Vogel and colleagues put it, they "compare and despair." In addition, after young (ages 17–25) women looked at their Facebook accounts for 10 minutes compared to a magazine website they reported being in a worse mood and having lower body image evaluations (Fardouly, Diedrichs, Vartanian, & Halliwell, 2015). Facebook use in college women was associated with disordered eating, but only if the women also did a lot of comparisons of their bodies to those of others (Walker et al., 2015). In fact, if they did not engage in physical comparisons online, heavy Facebook users actually were less likely to suffer eating disorders than those who made lots of online comparisons of bodies. In young adults, heavy social media use is associated with increased odds of suffering from depression (Lin et al., 2016). Of course, this does not tell use cause or causal direction; do depressed people use more social media or does using social media lead to depression?

But social media use is clearly not all bad. If students use social media for social functions and communication, heavy social media use is associated with higher overall well-being (Wang, Jackson, Gaskin, & Wang, 2014). Moreover, the negative effects on body image decline with age, with the effect on adults and older adults being significantly less than on young adults (Hayes, Van Stolk-Cooke, & Muench, 2015).

By age 65, many people notice some degree of cognitive decline, especially in memory and selective attention, planning, and cognitive control. Most of these processes are working memory and executive functioning processes and involve frontal lobe activity (Basak et al., 2008; Raz, 2000).

It is very tempting to believe that if we just stay cognitively active and even play "brain games" that we can ward off our inevitable cognitive decline with age. Numerous companies have formed over the last 10 years in an attempt to cash in on the hope of aging adults to maintain mental sharpness. Indeed, there has been much publicity and nearly an equal amount of controversy concerning the effectiveness of "brain games" to enhance cognitive functioning in the elderly (Simons et al., 2016). There are a few questions to ask about "brain training" and cognitive function in the elderly. First, are these activities effective, and second if they are do their benefits generalize outside of the training they provide? There have been numerous studies showing these games can lead to slowing of decline in cognitive functioning (Basak et al., 2008; Litwin, Schwartz, & Damri, 2016; McArdle & Prindle, 2008; Willis et al., 2006). But it is also clear that the claims by the companies of the effectiveness of these games are overblown and overstated and some companies have been legally forced to pull back on their claims (Simons et al., 2016).

The assumption and sometimes the claim of these companies is that such cognitive enhancement will transfer over into everyday life. The research, however, tends to show that the cognitive improvements can extend beyond the type of training they received (Basak et al., 2008;

McArdle & Prindle, 2008; Simons et al., 2016). There is some promising new research, however, that combines brain training with mild electrical (transcranial direct current) stimulation or tDCS and results showed that learning was more likely to transfer to everyday life when combined with electrical stimulation (Looi et al., 2016).

It is clear to see that technology is used by every age group and have a tremendous impact on all aspects of development. It will no doubt continue to influence even more of human thought, behavior, personality, and social interaction in the years to come.

Chapter Review

THE DEVELOPING FETUS

- Life before birth is divided into the germinal, embryonic, and fetal stages.

- Prenatal programming refers to a change in developmental trajectory for certain health outcomes that are established in the womb.

- Two common sources of prenatal programming are maternal nutrition and substances known as teratogens, which can harm the developing infant. Mild to profound

©Tom Merton/Getty Images RF

changes in the brain and body of the fetus can result from diet and chemicals the pregnant mother takes into her body.

THE DEVELOPING INFANT AND CHILD

- The five major senses develop at different rates. Hearing is almost fully developed at birth, but vision is not.

- Learning and experience strengthen certain synaptic connections. Through pruning, synaptic connections that are not reinforced and strengthened by experience degrade and ultimately die off.

- Piaget proposed four major stages of cognitive development: (1) the sensorimotor stage, with object permanence being the major accomplishment; (2) the preoperational stage, when young children begin to think systematically; (3) the concrete operational stage, when school-age children master conservation, the knowledge that the total amount of something stays

the same even when its shape or arrangement changes; and (4) the formal operational stage, during which adolescents begin to think logically and abstractly.

- The ability to know and understand what other people are thinking, wanting, or feeling is called theory of mind, typically developed around age 4, when children recognize that other people's beliefs may be different from their own.

- In human development, attachment refers to the strong emotional connection that develops early in life to keep infants close to their caregivers. Comfort and touch in infancy are crucial to healthy development.

THE DEVELOPING ADOLESCENT

- For girls, a major change during adolescence is the first menstrual period, known as menarche. For boys, the equivalent change is spermarche, the first ejaculation.

- Brain development continues in adolescence, with the frontal lobes being the last part of the brain to mature.

- Social relationships become paramount in adolescence. Girls tend to have one or two deep friendships and more intimate relationships than boys. Sexual maturity brings sexual behavior, with most adolescents being sexually active by age 18.

THE DEVELOPING ADULT

- Most sensory systems (for example, vision and hearing) gradually decline after middle age.

- Cognitive decline is complex but not inevitable in adults; it mostly begins in the late 60s or early 70s.

- Age is a risk factor for dementia, a loss of mental function in which many cognitive processes, such as the ability to remember, reason, solve problems, make decisions, and use language, are impaired.

- Alzheimer's disease is a degenerative condition marked by progressive cognitive decline, confusion, memory loss, mood swings, as well as eventual loss of physical function.

- Healthy aging is possible through physical exercise and cognitive training.

- One cognitive benefit of aging is wisdom, or the ability to know what matters; to live well; and to show good judgment.

BRINGING IT ALL TOGETHER: MAKING CONNECTIONS IN HUMAN DEVELOPMENT

- Male-female is a fundamental dimension on which people differ and are categorized by others.

- Some cultures, however, assume there are three to five genders.

- *Transgender identity* exists when a person identifies with the gender opposite their birth (natal) sex. For about 0.3% of the population natal sex is not the gender they identify with.

- Sex differentiation begins but doesn't end with genes. Hormones also continue to mold brains and behavior during development.

- Brains of transgender individuals are not really like those of natal males or females. They have certain

brain structures and neural activity profiles that are in between males and females.

- For many people, their gender identity is not easily changed. For others, it can fluctuate and change.

- Transgender individuals compared to non-transgender (cis-gender) individuals tend to suffer higher levels of discrimination, anxiety, depression, and even suicide starting in adolescence and continuing through late adulthood.

- Transgender people are most likely to reveal their identity to the partners and friends compared to parents, siblings, and coworkers. The younger cohort of transgender people tend to be more open about their identity than the older cohort.

Key Terms

adolescence
Alzheimer's disease
animistic thinking
attachment
cis-gendered
concrete operational stage
conservation
conventional level
crystallized intelligence
dementia
egocentrism
embryo
embryonic stage
emerging adulthood
emotional competence
fetal alcohol spectrum disorder (FASD)
fetal stage

fluid intelligence
formal operational stage
gender identity
generativity
germinal stage
human development
imprinting
individuation
intimacy
menarche
neural migration
object permanence
personality
postconventional level
preconventional level
prenatal programming
preoperational stage

pruning
puberty
securely attached
sensorimotor stage
separation anxiety
sexual orientation
social referencing
spermarche
stagnation
temperament
teratogens
theory of mind
transgender identity
young adulthood
zone of proximal development
zygote

Quick Quiz Answers

Quick Quiz 1: 1.c; **2.** b;**3.**a   **Quick Quiz 2: 1.**d; **2.**c; **3.**b; **4.**d
Quick Quiz 3: 1.d; **2.**c   **Quick Quiz 4: 1.**d; **2.**b; **3.**a

6 Consciousness

Chapter Outline

Challenge Your Assumptions

True or False?

- Texting while driving is as dangerous as driving drunk. (see page 223)

- With practice, most people can multitask effectively. (see page 225)

- Meditation practice can improve your SAT score. (see page 229)

- You can make up for lost sleep. (see page 236)

- Marijuana is ineffective as medicine. (see page 252)

©Chris Tobin/Getty Images RF

On Super Bowl Sunday, January 30, 1994, David, the brother of author Greg Feist, was hit by a car while riding his bicycle home from work. He crashed onto the windshield and then landed on the street. He was not wearing his helmet. Fortunately for David, within just a few minutes, emergency workers whisked him off to one of the top trauma centers in the country. David had suffered a severe traumatic brain injury.

When we arrived at the hospital, David was in a coma. We asked the trauma nurse to explain just how comatose he was. They use a scale, ranging from 3 to 15, to rate the degree of coma and nonresponsiveness. David was a 4. We asked what a 4 meant in practical terms. The nurse picked up the small bottle of saline solution from David's bedside table. "You see this?" she asked. "This is a 3." David was barely alive.

Two weeks after the accident, David opened his eyes, but he was nonresponsive. Five months later, he emerged from what the doctors called a vegetative state and began responding to input from the outside world. Witnessing David's nearly miraculous recovery over the next year not only pushed the limits of our concepts of life and death but also illustrated just how delicate states of consciousness can be.

For a long time, the topic of consciousness—something that occupies the center of our psychological experience—was a neglected area in psychology. Thanks to the cognitive revolution, evolutionary psychology, and neuroscience, which all returned mental phenomena to the forefront of psychological research, the scientific study of consciousness is back. In this chapter, we review what the science of psychology reveals about consciousness.

In particular, we'll explore what consciousness is, examine how we know the contents of our own minds, look at how psychologists have studied the conscious mind, and consider how meditation, sleep, drugs, hypnosis, and mental exercises can modify consciousness. Finally, we'll return to the consciousness-altering effects of brain injury.

WHAT IS CONSCIOUSNESS?

Consider what happens if you walk out of a dark house onto a sunny porch. Many signals assault the brain: The bright light from the sky hits your eyes, which send information to visual processing areas in the thalamus and occipital cortex. The heat from the sun bathes your skin, and temperature sensors there send impulses to the thalamus, somatosensory cortex, and brain stem areas that regulate body temperature. The scent of the jasmine flowers in the garden wafts through your nostrils, quickly moving to the olfactory bulb and emotional centers in the brain, perhaps triggering pleasant memories of the jasmine that grew along the fence of your grandmother's house so many years ago. The brain processes these signals instantaneously and simultaneously, and they come together into the experience of being on the front porch in the sun. They come together in your consciousness.

consciousness
An awareness of one's surroundings and of what's in one's mind at a given moment; includes aspects of being awake and aware.

In spite of its central role in our experience, consciousness is not easily defined. Most simply, **consciousness** is the awareness of one's surroundings and of what is in one's mind at a given moment. It is our experience of a moment as we move through it, as well as the capacity to take in and process information briefly before sending it to specialized areas for further use or storage. Consciousness can change very quickly and dramatically whenever new information arrives.

Imagine the change in your experience if you stepped off the porch from your jasmine-laced memory into a pile of dog droppings!

Consider again the example of standing on the front porch with your brain receiving and processing sensory information from all around you. When the connections among the various processing areas of the brain areas become strong enough, a conscious experience occurs (Engel, Debener, & Kranczioch, 2006). These various sensory elements are brought together in consciousness.

Still, much of what we do does not require deliberate, conscious thought. Without thinking about it, we can lift our fingers, choose whom we prefer to talk with, and know how to tie our shoes (Bargh, 1997; Baumeister, Masicampo, & Vohs, 2011). If this is so, why do we need consciousness? Baumeister and his colleagues (2010, 2011), who reviewed volumes of research in psychology on this question, argue that consciousness is required for any mental processes that involve imagining situations, such as planning future behavior. Also, consciousness is crucial for mental tasks that require working with sequences of information, such as counting, speaking and understanding languages, logical reasoning, and helping people share experiences (Baumeister & Masicampo, 2010; Baumeister et al., 2011).

Many studies have examined the processes of consciousness, including sleeping, dreaming, wakefulness, perception, sensation, responsiveness, and awareness, but the subjective aspect of being a conscious human—*what it feels like* to be in love, see red, or have an idea—has eluded science. The focus of this chapter is on psychology's contribution to understanding conscious processes and to developing methods that may bring the subjective aspect of consciousness into clearer view.

Theories of Consciousness

Few questions have perplexed the world's thinkers longer than how does consciousness comes about—is it a product of the brain or some greater mystery? What exactly is consciousness anyway? We know what it feels like to be happy, to eat a peach, to have a cold. Is there a scientific explanation for this feeling or quality? We describe briefly three different cognitive perspectives on consciousness. Each of these views see consciousness as a quality that emerges from the brain's integration of the various types of information processing that it does all the time, in networks spread all over the brain.

1. **Consciousness is a global workspace** (Baars, 1997). According to *global workspace theory*, consciousness is a place where we temporarily attend to information at hand or deemed important. It is the place where the spotlight of attention lands on the contents of our minds—that illuminated place is where for the moment you can know what you are working with, feeling, and thinking. The global workspace idea offers a good explanation for what consciousness is, but it does not explain how it arises.

2. **Conscious awareness occurs when neurons from many distinct brain regions work together—a process referred to as *synchronization*.** Imaging techniques, such as fMRI, reveal synchronization in brain regions that are equally active. When synchronization occurs, we might have a conscious experience (Kranczioch et al., 2005). Imagine that you see an apple: Before you experience "apple," several areas of your brain are active, such as those responding to the object's shape (round) and color (red) and where the object is in your visual field. The synchrony of cell assemblies may be what binds together these separate experiences (of round and red) into the experience of an apple. By identifying this process, neuroscience is beginning to address how a moment of conscious experience actually occurs in the global workspace (Engel et al., 2006).

3. **Consciousness is a learned process**. Cleeremans's (2011) *radical plasticity theory* explains consciousness as a skill the brain acquires, not as a inherent property of the brain or a skill controlled by particular brain region.

Cleeremans (2011) offers this analogy for consciousness: A thermostat can be considered "sensitive" to temperature, but there is no way a thermostat actually knows that it is sensitive to temperature, nor does it care. Also, a thermostat does not know that it regulates temperature, it just *does* (Chalmers, 2007). The brain, however, learns to perform new skills all the time, and we develop a sense that *we* do them—there is an agent behind them (I see, I hear, and so on). Or put another way, there is a subject having the experiences.

How does the brain come to inform us that we have experiences? Our brain is processing all kinds of information all the time, and we are unaware of most of it. One idea is that consciousness emerges as the information from seeing, hearing, problem solving, remembering (to just name a few things our brain can do) is linked with our internal states, including emotions (Cleeremans, 2011). From these linkages our brains learn our preferences—we like certain experiences more than others. Those events or objects we like form who we are and tag what is worth recalling again. This is similar to the way "liking" songs in Pandora makes those songs or certain elements of those songs (time signature, key, genre) more likely to appear again in a given station. Consciousness is something that the brain learns to do by a process of regularly interpreting it's own actions and attempting to predict what will happen in the future.

Global workspace theory says that if we pay attention to something, then it should be conscious. Awareness is all-or-none, depending on whether the spotlight of attention shines on the information in question. But the radical plasticity theory says the brain learns to be aware, so one should be able to capture the process of awareness emerging gradually, in an incremental fashion. Simply put, partial awareness should occur. One study compared participants' self-reported degree of awareness of visual stimuli in a color categorization (which is considered to be low-level processing) with a word categorization task (higher-level visual processing) (Windy & Cleeremans, 2015). For the lower-level tasks, participants' ratings indicated partial awareness of the stimuli, but in the word categorization task—which is cognitively more demanding—awareness was all-or-none. That is, they either saw the word or they did not. Evidence of partial awareness in the low-level task suggests that consciousness is not always an all-or-none phenomenon.

TWO DIMENSIONS OF CONSCIOUSNESS: WAKEFULNESS AND AWARENESS

We defined consciousness as the extent to which we are aware of our surroundings and of what's in our minds at a given moment. But consciousness really has two aspects: the degree to which we are awake and the degree to which we are aware. **Wakefulness** refers to alertness, or the extent to which a person is awake or asleep. **Awareness** refers to the monitoring of information from the environment and from one's own thoughts (Brown & Ryan, 2003). Often, wakefulness and awareness go hand in hand, but they do not always work together. A person can be awake but not very aware, as is true in vegetative states or severe drunkenness.

Variations in consciousness can be explained in terms of degrees of wakefulness and awareness (Laureys, 2007). Figure 1 shows how the two dimensions of wakefulness and awareness can explain a variety of states of consciousness. Coma, for example, is characterized by very low wakefulness and awareness. The other extreme of consciousness is characterized by high wakefulness and

wakefulness
The degree of alertness reflecting whether a person is awake or asleep.

awareness
Monitoring of information from the environment and from one's own thoughts.

FIGURE 1

TWO DIMENSIONS OF CONSCIOUSNESS. Consciousness exists on a continuum from low to high wakefulness and from little to high awareness.

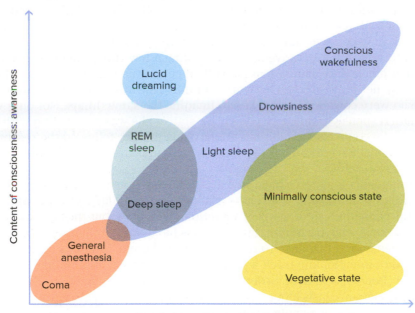

(From Laureys, S. (2007). Eyes open, brain shut. *Scientific American*, 296, 84–89. Art by Melissa Thomas, p. 87. Used with permission by Melissa Thomas.)

 Looking at Figure 1, what is the difference between a coma and a vegetative state? Between deep sleep and lucid dreaming? Between light sleep and full wakefulness? (Laureys, 2007)

awareness. In contrast, the vegetative state is wakeful but not very aware, as was the case when David opened his eyes but did not respond to the outside world. Let's look at variations in consciousness in more detail, starting with minimal consciousness and moving to moderate and full consciousness.

Minimal Consciousness

If you have ever fainted, you have experienced a loss of consciousness. **Coma**, in which the eyes are closed and the person is unresponsive, is a much more severe and enduring loss of consciousness than fainting. People cannot be roused from a coma as they can be roused from sleep. Coma generally results from illness or brain injury that damages areas of the brain that control wakefulness—in particular, the reticular activating system of the brain stem (Bernat, 2006). The **reticular activating system** is involved in alertness and the transition between wakefulness and sleep. In fact, comatose people whose brains show normal sleep patterns are more likely to regain consciousness than are those who do not exhibit these patterns (Fischer, 2004). In an exciting new study, researchers uncovered three crucial brain regions involved in consciousness (Fischer et al., 2016). One is a small part of the brainstem (pontine tegmentum) that when damaged often results in coma. This brainstem region is also connected to two regions of the cortex associated with consciousness, the anterior insula and the cingulate cortex. In coma, the pathway between these two cortical regions becomes disconnected.

In the **vegetative state**, the eyes might be open, but the person is otherwise unresponsive (Kondziella et al., 2016). In fact, the vegetative state has been defined as "wakefulness without awareness" (Bernat, 2006, p. 1181). Physicians used to think that anyone who was vegetative could neither perceive or respond

coma
A state of consciousness in which the eyes are closed and the person is unresponsive and unarousable.

reticular activating system
A bundle of nerves in the brainstem that are involved in wakefulness and the transition between wakefulness and sleep.

vegetative state
A state of minimal consciousness in which the eyes might be open, but the person is otherwise unresponsive.

to stimuli from the environment, because such folks seemed to be completely unresponsive. We now know this is not always the case.

Clever studies utilizing measures of brain activity have led to major changes in how people with reduced conscious awareness are treated and diagnosed. One highly publicized case study ignited a deeper understanding of the responsiveness of the brain in vegetative states (Owen et al., 2006). Researchers asked a young woman who was in a vegetative state to imagine a few things, such as walking through her house and playing tennis, while they scanned her brain using fMRI. Surprisingly, her brain showed activation in the same areas as did the brains of people who were conscious and asked to imagine the same things. Not only was this woman responsive while in a vegetative state—she was responding with her brain—but she could also exhibit intentional thought: She followed the researchers' instructions. Several other case studies have appeared with similar results (Kondziella et al., 2016).

Such patients may have been in transition from a vegetative state to what is now called a minimally conscious state (Laureys, 2007). People who are **minimally conscious** show signs of intentional behavior, but they cannot communicate. People who are minimally conscious have opened their eyes but show very little behavioral response to the world around them. Whereas a vegetative person cannot intentionally track a person with the eyes, a minimally conscious person can (Bender, Jox, Grill, Straube, & Lulé, 2015; Kondziella et al., 2016).

A large meta-analysis looked at several fMRI studies of brain activity shown by minimally conscious people when they performed guided mental tasks. The results suggest that minimally conscious people often have more mental activity than their observable behavior suggests. Even among people who would have been previously designated vegetative (in their degree of nonresponsiveness), at least 15% can follow verbal commands with their minds as indicated by changes in brain activity, and up to 40% still classified as "vegetative" show signs of minimal consciousness (Kondziella et al., 2016).

There is a new diagnostic category called **disorders of consciousness** (or DoCs) to encompass the variety of ways in which wakefulness and awareness might vary when compromised. DoCs can range from persistent vegetative state to minimally conscious. Up to 40% of the people with DoCs may have been mistakenly categorized as "vegetative," and almost 90% of unresponsive individuals previously considered "unclassifiable" might well be minimally conscious (Schnakers et al., 2009).

Determining a person's degree of awareness remains a complicated medical and ethical issue. When there is no observable behavioral response to stimulation from the environment, neuroimaging techniques, such as fMRI, are the best way of assessing whether someone who is behaviorally nonresponsive is conscious at all (Kondziella et al., 2016; Owen, 2013).

Moderate Consciousness

Between the extremes of a complete lack of consciousness and full consciousness lies a realm that accounts for much of what our minds do—manage business and process information just below the threshold of conscious awareness. Freud used the term *preconscious* to describe material that is potentially accessible but not currently available to awareness (Freud, 1933/1964). An example is the so-called *tip-of-the-tongue phenomenon* (Galin, 1994). We know a person's name, and we know we know it, but we can't come up with it. The experience of knowing that we know a name is conscious, even if we cannot bring the name into awareness. This state can be thought of as *moderate consciousness*.

When we sleep and dream, we are moderately conscious. We may be roused by sounds that are important to us, while ignoring others. But during sleep there is a perceptual wall in our consciousness that prevents us from perceiving most sensations of the outer world. Psychologists study many other processes that operate at the boundaries of awareness, several of which we discuss in the chapter "Memory."

Full Consciousness

Even when fully awake we experience fluctuations in consciousness—alertness ebbs and flows. There are periods when we are more alert and present than normal. We may be stimulated and even excited. Or we may become so involved in what we are doing that we lose a sense of time and forget where we are. Some psychologists have called this state *flow* (Csikszentmihalyi, 1990). Flow exists when we thrive in our ability to rise to the occasion of challenging tasks. Think of a sport or craft you really love to do and do well. Think of the times when you were involved in such an activity and everything "clicked" all at once—everything you did was just right. This is the flow state. Our attention is so focused and everything goes so smoothly that an hour may feel like a minute or a minute like an hour. We are so engaged with the experience that time does not matter at all.

Another state of full consciousness is **mindfulness**, a heightened awareness of the present moment, of events in one's environment and events in one's own mind. When you are talking with a friend, you can be aware of what your friend is saying, how he looks, how his words and tone of voice affect how you feel, and what you are feeling in your own body and mind in response to him (Brown & Ryan, 2003; Kabat-Zinn, 1990). A more mindful person attends to all of these things; a less mindful person might notice only the friend's words. People vary considerably in how mindful they are, just as they differ in their personalities Kristeller, et al., 2006; Brown & Ryan, 2003). People can develop their mindfulness skills using mental training techniques, such as meditation.

mindfulness
A heightened awareness of the present moment, whether of events in one's environment or in one's own mind.

Quick Quiz 1: Two Dimensions of Consciousness: Wakefulness and Awareness

1. Which brain region plays a key role in maintaining wakefulness?
   a. prefrontal cortex
   b. cerebellum
   c. amygdala
   d. reticular formation

2. _____ is a heightened awareness of the present moment, which can be applied to events in one's environment and events in one's own mind.
   a. Wakefulness
   b. Attention
   c. Mindfulness
   d. Optimism

Answers can be found at the end of the chapter.

ATTENTION: FOCUSING CONSCIOUSNESS

Being conscious—being awake and aware—involves attending to particular parts of our world, so attention is a key aspect of consciousness. It is how we direct the spotlight of awareness.

We can be aware of only a finite amount of material at a time. **Attention** is the limited capacity to process information that is under conscious control (Styles, 2006). When you are in class, it is not possible to text your friend, or look at a social media site, as well as pay attention to the lecture. If you are texting your thoughts to a friend, you cannot also listen carefully to what the professor is saying. There are several types of attention. We will examine three attentional processes that help determine the contents of consciousness at any given moment: selective attention, sustained attention, and the shifting of attention through multitasking.

attention
The limited capacity to process information that is under conscious control.

Selective Attention

Imagine being in a crowded room where several people are talking, although you want to listen to just one person. You filter out unwanted noise to focus on what you want to hear. If attention is a general process, then focusing conscious attention even more narrowly is **selective attention**, the ability to focus awareness on specific features in the environment while ignoring others. When your professor asks for your "undivided attention," then, she is really interested in getting your selective attention.

The classic scientific evidence for selective attention came from research on a "dichotic listening task" (Broadbent, 1954). In these studies, a participant received one message in one ear and another message in the other ear. Typically, researchers presented several messages to both ears and then told the participant to pay attention to just one ear (the attended ear). They then measured recall for items presented to both ears. Recall was much better for the attended ear. If people were instructed to attend to the left ear message, they showed little to no memory of the message presented to the right (unattended) ear (Broadbent, 1954; Styles, 2006).

If the material presented to the unattended ear is meaningful in some way, it may make its way into consciousness (Treisman, 1964). If you were at a large party, trying to follow a conversation in spite of a lot of background noise, and someone in another part of the room mentioned your name, you would immediately become aware of the other conversation. Previously, you tuned out the background noise, so that you could follow the first conversation. Now that you have heard your name in that background conversation, however, it occupies the foreground of consciousness and you must attend to it. This particular ability to filter out auditory stimuli and then to refocus attention when you hear your name is called the *cocktail party effect* (Moray, 1959; see Figure 2). One simulated cocktail party study used event-related potentials (ERPs) to assess brain activity during focused and simple divided attention tasks in participants of various ages (Getzmann et al., 2016). Older participants performed far worse in divided attention tasks compare to focused attention tasks—a difference

FIGURE **2**

THE COCKTAIL PARTY EFFECT. The cocktail party effect is the ability to filter out auditory stimuli and then to refocus attention when you hear your name.

©Skynesher/iStock/Getty Images RF

 Explain when this effect is most likely to occur.

not seen in the younger participants, though one must be clear that this was a speech-related task. Such differences might not hold for attention for different stimuli.

When we selectively attend, we focus so much on certain things that we are blind to other things. Focusing attention can create gaps in attention and perception. Many magic tricks take advantage of the fact that, with our attention diverted, we can easily be fooled. In one study that clearly demonstrates gaps in attention. Try the video attention task at this link, which showcases the research of Simons and Chabris (1999) (https://www.youtube.com/watch?v=IGQmdoK_ZfY). If you watched the video, did you notice the gorilla? For those of you who cannot watch the video, here is what it featured. First, viewers were instructed to watch the basketball players onscreen and simply count the number of times the players on the team wearing white T-shirts passed the ball. About half the participants were dumbfounded to learn afterward that they completely missed seeing a person dressed in a gorilla suit walk into the game, pause for a second to beat his chest, and then walk off screen. They were so focused on counting passes made by people wearing white shirts that they ignored everything else. Attending closely to one thing can blind us to other events, even gorillas walking into a basketball game. This phenomenon by which we fail to notice unexpected objects in our surroundings is referred to as *inattentional blindness*.

If we can be inattentive in spite of efforts to attend, does that mean we can prevent the intrusion of unwanted information during concentration? If you are reading an engrossing novel, is it possible to tune out the sounds of your roommate's TV? The *perceptual load model* states that we do not notice potential distracters when a primary task consumes all of our attentional capacity (Lavie et al., 2004). When a primary task is minimally demanding, however, distracters can capture our awareness. Perceptual load theory might explain, for example, why it is easier to ignore the TV when you are lost in an engrossing novel than when you are reading a boring chapter in your textbook (ahem). It might also explain deadly errors, such as not seeing a pedestrian while driving and simultaneously writing or reading a text message.

Research by Murphy and Greene (2015) applies perceptual load theory to the study of distracted driving. They did a series of studies using a driving simulator that required to the driver to complete tasks that varied in how cognitively demanding they were. In one study, for instance, drivers had to fit their car through passageways that were either clearly too big or too small for the car (low perceptual load) or those that were barely big enough for the car to pass through (high perceptual load). In another study, they had to find a red Mercedes among a group of silver (low perceptual load) or red (high perceptual load) cars. The key dependent variables involved how well they noticed distracters presented during those conditions. All distracters were relevant to road driving, such as a pedestrian on the side of the road or a loud horn.

In the high perceptual load conditions, the drivers failed to notice the distracters. That is, if the task was demanding (such as fitting into a tight space), then the distracter was not noticed. So, the more demanding driving tasks created inattentional blindness and deafness to other stimuli. The drivers didn't notice the pedestrians on the side of road or the horn when they were busy with the work of driving. What about when the load is even higher—say, when you are busy with any driving task and engrossed in a text? Murphy and Greene's findings suggest that you might miss driving hazards completely, with potentially catastrophic consequences. For more information on the effect of mobile phone use on attention while driving, see "Psychology in the Real World."

Psychology in the Real World

The Hazards of Distracted Driving

Most people know that it is dangerous (and illegal in most states) to text while driving, but many continue to do it anyway. A recent survey indicates that 83% of teen drivers texted or sent emails at least once while driving in the past month, and more than half said they did so more than 20% of the time (Ehsani, Li, & Simons-Morton, 2015). Given that self-reports of behaviors considered unhealthy or dangerous are often underreported, we can assume actual frequencies of texting while driving is greater than this number. Texting is a deadly problem. It's the number one cause of driver death in teens (Fitch et al., 2013) and accounted for 10% of driving fatalities across all ages in 2014 (NHTSA, 2014). It also plays a causal role in about 60% of all crashes (AAA Newsroom, 2015). The first increase in traffic deaths in over 6 years occurred in 2015 after years of a steady decline—a change presumed linked to distracted driving (National Center for Health Statistics, 2016).

How does operating a phone or other mobile device impair driving? Think of all a person has to manage while driving: scanning the road, operating the pedals and gears, watching for other cars and pedestrians, monitoring driving speed, and remembering directions. These tasks demand a lot from our awareness. Texts and calls place additional demands on our already limited resources of attention. At the most basic level, texting takes one's eyes off the road. Onboard video monitoring of real-life driving behavior tells us that, on average, the eyes are diverted from the road for roughly 5 sec per text message. That might not sound like much, but for a car traveling 55 mph, this translates to driving the length of a football field without looking (Virginia Tech Transportation Institute, July 29, 2009). More than a decade's worth of research now shows that texting, speaking on a hands-free/Bluetooth or handheld device, and even operating a built-in touchscreen in your vehicle interferes with the attentional resources and perceptual skills needed for safe driving by diverting attention from the demanding tasks of safely operating and navigating a car, thereby creating more driving errors, crashes, and fatalities (Caird et al., 2014; NHTSA, 2015, Simmons, Hicks, & Caird, 2016). Mobile activities that require drivers to take their eyes of the road are linked with the greatest risks to safety (Simmons et al., 2016).

Perceptual load theory (Murphy & Greene, 2015) offers one explanation for why, when faced with too much information to manage, drivers make mistakes in resource allocation (diverting attention to a conversation in lieu of the road), some of which are fatal. Indeed, fMRI research reveals decreases in activity in areas of the brain needed for driving—such as those involved in processing spatial information and increases in activity in those involved in language processing when driving simulator study participants listened to sentences while driving. This finding suggests that conversations divert attentional resources from the task of driving (Just, Keller, & Cynkar, 2008).

Drivers drink coffee, eat, and have conversations. Aren't these activities at least as distracting as texting or talking? Yes, but only for new drivers. A real-life driving study examined onboard videos of driving behavior in new teen versus experienced drivers (Klauer et al., 2014). Behavioral analysis revealed that several possible distractions led to accidents involving novice drivers, including conversations with other passengers, looking at something in the vehicle, eating, singing and/or dancing to music, as well as texting and talking on the phone. In experienced drivers, however, the only potential distraction that predicted accidents was mobile phone use (Klauer et al., 2014). Indeed, inexperience with driving is one factor that plays a big role in how much people text and in how much texting affects driving performance. In a driving simulator task, new drivers made substantially more errors (such as drifting out of their own lanes and not noticing traffic signs and spent 400% more time with their eyes off the road) while texting (Hosking, Young, & Regan, 2006). One large meta-analysis combined the results of hundreds of simulator and real-life studies of effects of texting-while-driving and offers a glimpse of the range of behaviors and how they impact specific

Sustained Attention

Staying focused on a task is difficult, especially if the task both requires a high degree of concentration and can have life-or-death consequences. As we discussed in the chapter "Sensing and Perceiving Our World," air traffic controllers must focus on an airplane on a visual display. To do so, they must coordinate with other airplanes, controllers, and pilots to make sure that each plane lands where it should without crossing the paths of other planes that are landing or taking off. This ability to maintain focused awareness on a target is known as **sustained attention**.

sustained attention
The ability to maintain focused awareness on a target or an idea.

Source: back street view; Jalal-e-Ale Ahamad;Tiran,Iran,mapio.net/Evan Feist

driving outcomes (Caird et al., 2014). The analysis provided strong evidence that both typing and reading texts while driving affected eye movements, impaired stimulus detection and reaction times, led to more collisions, and influenced maintenance of speed and headway (distance between vehicles). Typing texts led to more problems than reading text alone, but reading alone still influenced many of the outcomes (as reading still requires looking away from the road).

Not everyone texts behind the wheel—some are more likely than others. Teens who text or talk on the phone while driving are more likely to be risk takers generally, have friends who text and drive, and tend to underestimate the risks of their texting behavior (Beck & Watters, 2016). Also, one study suggests that thinking compulsively about messages and phones even when the devices are turned off is linked with having more accidents automobile accidents (O'Conner et al., 2013). Additionally, feeling attached to the phone increases the odds of using it while driving, over and above perceptions of risk (Weller et al., 2013). Not surprisingly, insufficient sleep worsens the effects of distracted driving on unintended lane shifts and other risks to driver safety (Anderson & Horne, 2013), as does alcohol consumption (Ammar et al., 2016). People who already have

attentional deficits are even more prone to driving performance deficit while texting (Kingery et al., 2015).

Phone-related distraction is not the only safety problem we face when texting on roadways—what about when people cross the street texting? One virtual-reality study looked at the effects of texting-related distraction out of the vehicle and into the hands of the pedestrian (see inserted photo) (Banducci et al., 2016). After being trained on the system, participants were measured on their pedestrian behavior (how well they crossed the street, etc.) and were either texted by an experimenter, called, or not disturbed at all. Texts and calls were sent and received on the tablet next to the participant (see inserted photo). Both phone conversations and texting led to fewer safe crossings and longer crossing times than the no distraction control condition. Why do people continue to engage in such dangerous behavior? This question applies to all unhealthful habits (e.g., why do people eat too much sugar or smoke cigarettes, or drink?) and it seems that social pressure, observing parents who text and drive, education level, and social norms to reply to texts quickly all play a role (Delgado, Wanner, & McDonald, 2016). The main strategy to curb this habit is education and laws (many states prohibit texting and handheld talking), as well as apps that prevent mobile phone use while a vehicle is in motion by detecting whether the vehicle is moving. Time will tell whether these measures make a difference, but it is clear that drivers are challenged with more opportunities for distraction each year. Can we scale back, or must we move instead toward cars that drive themselves? Tesla is promoting the latter approach, but we are not there yet.

Challenge Your Assumptions

True or False? Texting while driving is as dangerous as driving drunk.

True: Texting while driving creates distraction-related driving risks comparable to those of people driving under the influence of alcohol. driving drunk.

What are the limits of people's abilities to sustain their focused attention on one task? The airline industry needs to know this, as do many other industries that require careful attention on the part of their employees. Researchers study sustained attention using tasks such as the Continuous Performance Test (CPT). Imagine having to detect the letter *Y* among other, similar letters (such as *X*s) shown very rapidly, one by one, on a computer screen. The CPT requires that the participant maintain attentional focus for an extended period of time. Most people cannot perform well on CPT tasks for more than about 15 minutes, and their accuracy in detecting targets declines considerably after 5 to 7 minutes (Nuechterlein & Parasuraman, 1983; Parasuraman, 1998).

©Oliver Multhaup/AP Photo

For air traffic controllers, the ability to sustain attention for long stretches of time is fundamental to the safety of air travelers. Yet research suggests that most people have difficulty focusing attention on a continuous performance task for more than 15 minutes.

 What does this suggest about highly focused occupations, such as air traffic controller?

Multitasking: The Implications of Shifting Attention

Sustained attention is compromised during multitasking (Moisala et al., 2016). We think about multitasking as a modern problem that emerged from our increasingly digital lifestyles, but research on multitasking began in the mid-20th century, on industrial psychological research questions on jobs that involved competing demands on one's attention (e.g., pilots, air traffic controllers). Early on, the data indicated that people cannot typically do two things in parallel; rather, they switch between tasks, or leave and return, repeatedly, while trying to keep in mind the previous task before moving to others (Meyer & Kieras, 1997).

The evidence suggests that truly concurrent, or parallel, task performance rarely occurs, or to put it another way, people really cannot multitask effectively (Borst, Taatgen, & van Rijn, 2010; Courage, Bakhtiar, Fitzpatrick, Kenny, & Brandeau, 2015). Instead, what we consider to be multitasking really involves fast switching of one's attention from task to task. Switching from task to task necessarily interrupts sustained attention. Also, the person loses time when he or she makes the switch, especially on more complex tasks. That is, if a person switches from simple task to simple task (such as from watching a video to checking a social networking site [SNS]), the amount of lost time is low, but if he or she moves away from a more substantial task (such as writing a paper or reading an article) to an SNS and back, then more time is lost. Switching also compromises memory for the tasks at hand. A study of office workers showed that, once people switched away from their work to another activity, they forgot what they were doing prior to the distraction (Gonzalez & Mark, 2004). In order to compensate for interrupted work, people tend to work faster. The cost of this sped-up, interrupted work, however, is more stress (Mark, Gudith, & Klocke, 2008).

Multitasking compromises learning. Foerde and colleagues (2006) asked students to perform a weather prediction task. Half were randomly assigned to do the task with distraction (listening to beeps on headphones), half without the distraction. While both groups recalled what they learned with similar accuracy, the distraction group members were less able to extrapolate what they had learned from the task to another weather prediction simulation.

Salvucci and Taatgen (2008) proposed the *threaded cognition* theory of multitasking behavior to explain limitations on concurrent multitasking. According to threaded cognition theory, although we can be involved in more than one task at a time, a particular resource (e.g., a perceptual system, a cognitive system, a motor system) can only be used by one task at a time. For instance, if two tasks require the involvement of your vision (such as monitoring the road while driving and reading a text message), only one of them can progress, and involvement with one task will necessarily interfere with the other. If a resource is needed by more than one task, a bottleneck, or backup, can develop in the attempt to access consciousness (Borst et al., 2010). There is also a central control mechanism that may have to decide when to allocate resources, which we might think of as the cook in the kitchen who decides what to do and when to do it (Salvucci & Taatgen, 2008). For instance, if you have to engage in a new task (such as driving to a new location you do not have memorized), you cannot also speak on a cell phone.

Thus, there is a bottleneck with multitasking, a place where tasks compete for access to the workspace of consciousness or where attention is focused at a given point in time. This is a key reason multitasking is much more likely an exercise in rapid switching between tasks rather than actual performance of two at the same time.

There is increasing evidence that SNSs, such as Instagram, are the source of most of college students' multitasking behavior while working (Judd, 2014). Indeed, increases in use of SNS sites in class are associated with decrements in GPA, more so than other technological distractions, such as texting (Junco, 2012). If such distractions are a problem for you, apps are available that will allow you to set a given amount of time in which access to Instagram, Snapchat, Reddit, or other SNSs is blocked. The "Psychology in the Real World" feature showcases an extremely dangerous kind of multitasking: using a cell phone while driving.

Due to the overwhelming popularity of portable devices, people are multitasking more than ever. Quite apart from the problems of multitasking, just having a mobile device with you and allowing it to compete for your attention means that it is siphoning off a portion of your already limited conscious resources all the time. Consider these statistics about usage: 67% of cell owners say they check their phones (for messages, etc.) even in the absence of ringing or vibrating; 44% of mobile users have kept their phones near the bed, so that they don't miss any messages (Brenner, 2013).

Some people swear they can do more than one thing at a time, without compromising their performance on either task. Watson and Strayer (2010) conducted a study to see if there really are any "supertaskers" who show no performance decrements in an auditory attentional task in the presence of distractors. All participants were tested in a single-task versus a dual-task condition. A vast majority of people showed significant decrements in attention in the dual task condition, but 2.5% showed no decrement. The authors concluded that there are a few "supertaskers" out there who have excellent mechanisms of cognitive control, but the vast majority of us cannot do it.

One of your authors, Erika, went without her phone for a couple of days when it was water-damaged and noticed just how often she had the impulse simply to reach for and check it. Taking one mobile-free day a week is a useful practice to help remind you of how much your experience is tethered to your mobile device.

1. What term best describes not perceiving a person in a gorilla suit when asked to count the number of people playing basketball?
   a. inattentional blindness
   b. not paying attention
   c. absent-mindedness
   d. minimally conscious state

2. You are at a loud gathering, talking to a friend. The noise of the chatter is nearly deafening, but all of a sudden you hear your name spoken above the noise. This is known as the
   a. self-recognition effect.
   b. cocktail party effect.
   c. attentional effect.
   d. divided attention effect.

Answers can be found at the end of the chapter.

TRAINING CONSCIOUSNESS: MEDITATION

Anytime you read, reason, solve problems, or learn something new, you are sharpening your mental skills. Some age-old techniques, however, are designed specifically to train the conscious mind. **Meditation** refers to a wide variety of practices that people use to calm the mind, stabilize concentration, focus attention, and enhance awareness of the present moment. There are many types of meditation techniques, with different goals. To improve concentration, meditators might spend minutes or even hours sitting still, relaxed yet alert, focusing their attention on the sensations of breathing, noticing how the breath moves into and out of their mouths and noses. In this case, meditators attempt to keep their attention on the breath. If their minds wander, they bring their attention back to the breath. This simple, ancient practice calms the mind and stabilizes attention (Wallace, 2006).

Psychologists and neuroscientists study the effects of such meditative practices on mental processes, emotion, and brain function. This research illustrates the dynamic relationship between mental life and neural structure.

Meditation and Conscious Experience

Many forms of meditation develop mindfulness, a fully conscious state of heightened awareness of the present moment. Unlike concentration techniques, mindfulness meditation encourages attention to the details of momentary experience, such as all the thoughts, feelings, and sensations available at present (Baer et al., 2006). People with high scores on mindfulness questionnaires also score high on measures of well-being and optimism, are more in tune with their emotional states, and are less self-conscious and anxious. In addition, people who practice meditation consistently have higher mindfulness scores than those who do not (Brown & Ryan, 2003), but the findings of such correlational studies do not tell us definitively that mindfulness causes these changes. Numerous studies have examine the effectiveness of mindfulness-based meditation training programs, as they appear to have beneficial effects to enhance well-being, reduce stress, decrease depression, improve physical health, and reduce pain (Rowe, Hirsch, & Anderson, 2007; R. E. Jung et al., 2010; Kabat-Zinn et al., 1998; Sahdra et al., 2011; Teasdale et al., 2000; Zeidan et al., 2011). Mindfulness training also shows promise in helped prevent distraction and improved reading performance in people with attentional deficits and dyslexia (Tarrasch, Berman, & Friedmann, 2016).

Many meditation techniques (such as focusing on the sensations of breathing) aim to improve attentional skills. Whether meditation can improve performance on attentional tasks is a question that psychological science really first started addressing in the past decade. In the first true experiment on this question, 64 experienced meditators were randomly assigned to a control group or to receive intensive

meditation
Practices that people use to calm the mind, stabilize concentration, focus attention, and enhance awareness of the present moment.

Connection

Every time you make a memory or learn something new, you change your brain by strengthening synaptic connections or growing new neurons.

See "Synaptic Change during Learning," in the chapter "Learning." (p. 326)

training in concentration meditation (similar to the breathing technique described at the beginning of this section), which they practiced for several hours a day for 3 months. All participants were assessed before, during, and after the 3-month training (MacLean et al., 2010). Specifically, concentration meditation makes people perceive visual objects—lines, at least—with greater sensitivity and helps them attend to such objects longer (which is an increase in sustained attention). These effects are akin to having sharper vision for a longer period of time. The same type of training also improves response inhibition, which is the ability to resist impulsive responding (Sahdra et al., 2011). Shorter-term training in meditation, such as completion of an 8-week training course, also increases vigilance (Lutz et al., 2009) and enhances working memory, or the capacity to keep multiple things in mind while solving problems or making decisions, in adolescents as well as adults (Quach, Mano, & Alexander, 2016; van Vugt & Jha, 2011). Recent studies show that an 8-week training course in mindfulness meditation can reduce the likelihood of attention shifts among multiple tasks, reduce job stress, and improve memory, potentially counteracting multitasking in stressful work environments (Levy et al., 2012). Across three studies, Brown and his colleagues (2016) showed the overall degree of mindfulness (as measured by self-report inventory) people reported was correlated positively with memory performance and,

© Copyright Dan Piraro. Used by permission

further, that brief training in mindful attention improved performance on a memory task. This finding makes sense given that mindfulness training is essentially attentional training and attention plays a key role in marking things as "worth remembering" in our minds.

Meditation Training and the Brain

Meditation changes brain function and structure. After 8 weeks of mindfulness meditation training, people with no previous meditation experience showed significant increases in EEG activity in the left frontal cortex (an area associated with positive mood) and decreases in negative mood (Davidson et al., 2003). These EEG changes persisted for at least 4 months after training. Another study has linked meditation-related changes in brain activity with quicker performance in an attentional task. Such findings help tell us whether measurable differences in brain activity really mean anything in terms of actual behavior (Lutz et al., 2009).

In another study, MRI scans revealed thicker brain tissue in the areas of the cortex associated with attention, sensitivity to bodily sensations, and the processing of external sensory information in very experienced meditators compared to a group of nonmeditators (Lazar et al., 2005). Those who had meditated the longest showed the greatest cortical thickness in certain areas. The finding has since been replicated in a study of Zen meditators (Grant et al., 2010). Such correlational findings suggest that meditation can grow the brain, but an experimental design is required to uncover a causal link between meditation training and brain changes. Experimental studies that train people new to meditation can better address whether meditation caused such brain changes. Compared to a control group, novices assigned to an 8-week meditation training program showed a greater density in brain tissue in the areas relevant to attention and emotion processing, which appeared to be linked with changes in emotional well-being over the 8-week period (Hölzel et al., 2010). This density of tissue indicates more neuron cell bodies—or more neurons! A meta-analysis that addressed the question of whether meditation changed brain structure carefully selected only those of hundreds of studies with the best experimental methods. The researchers analyzed the

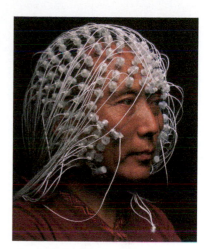

©Cary Wolinsky/Aurora Photos/Getty Images

Meditation, an integral part of the Buddhist spiritual practice for thousands of years, develops concentration and mindfulness. Here a Buddhist monk is being outfitted with EEG electrodes for monitoring his brain during meditation.

Connection

Attention is the first step in getting an experience into short-term memory and potentially to long-term memory.

See "Short-Term and Working Memory," in the chapter "Memory." (p. 269)

results of 36 studies on the topic in both long-term meditators and those who took an 8-week standardized, mindfulness meditation class. Similar brain changes were found in the novices after the 8-week class as seen in experienced meditators in previous work: specifically in the prefrontal cortex, cingulate cortex, insula, and hippocampus. Also the new meditators showed changes in areas of the brain key to emotional processing: namely, the amygdala (Gotink, Meijboom, Vernooij, Smits, & Hunink, 2016).

For more on whether meditation training can improve memory, see "Research Process" (Figure 5).

Quick Quiz 3: Training Consciousness: Meditation

1. Which of the following does meditation appear to improve?
   a. mindfulness
   b. attention
   c. well-being
   d. all of the above

2. A study of brain images of experienced meditators and a comparison group of nonmeditators found that the experienced meditators' brains showed evidence of

   a. thicker cortex in brain areas associated with attention and sensitivity to sensory information.
   b. more diverse synaptic connections throughout the cerebellum.
   c. cortical thinning throughout motor areas but thickening in frontal areas.
   d. less synaptic death than in nonmeditators.

Answers can be found at the end of the chapter.

SLEEPING AND DREAMING

Meditation offers specific practices for working with consciousness. Yet consciousness varies constantly on a daily basis without much intervention, by virtue of our degree of wakefulness or our moods. In this section, we discuss two major sources of variation of consciousness: sleeping and dreaming.

Sleeping

A 5-year-old boy once described sleep to one of your authors as "when I go to my bed and I think about nothing." Typically, we think of sleep as a time of rest and relaxation, when we put the day's events out of our minds. Though a time of rest, sleep is, in fact, a very active process. We behave while we sleep—moving, dreaming, sometimes even talking and walking. The sleeping brain is very active, but it is only partially processing information from the outside world.

Sleep has two essential characteristics: It creates a perceptual wall between the conscious mind and the outside world, and the sleeping state can be reversed in an instant by waking (Dement, 1999). In sleep, awareness of the outside world is greatly diminished, but not completely. The mind is still able to filter relevant from irrelevant stimuli: A baby's cry may awaken a parent, but much louder sounds (such as a TV blaring in the room) may not. Moreover, because sleep is reversible, it is different from coma.

circadian rhythms

The variations in physiological processes that cycle within approximately a 24-hour period, including the sleep–wake cycle.

Sleep and Circadian Rhythms Sleep occurs in the context of a daily cycle, which follows a pattern known as a circadian rhythm. **Circadian rhythms** are the variations in physiological processes that cycle within approximately a 24-hour period. Many physiological systems, including the sleep–wake cycle, feeding, hormone production, and cellular regeneration, vary on a circadian basis (Refinetti, 2006), as do psychological processes, such as memory (Reichert, Maire, Schmidt, & Cajochen, 2016) and mood (McClung, 2015). The mood disorder of depression may well result, in part, from a circadian pattern of arousal that differs from what most people experience (McClung, 2015).

In Figure 4 we see how three bodily processes—body temperature, the hormone melatonin, and alertness—fluctuate on a circadian cycle. Body temperature, for instance, peaks a few hours before bed and soon after waking up, then

Research Process

1 Research Question

Can just 2 weeks of mindfulness meditation training improve working memory and Graduate Record Exam (GRE) performance and reduce mind wandering?

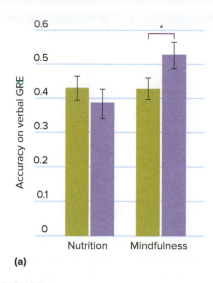
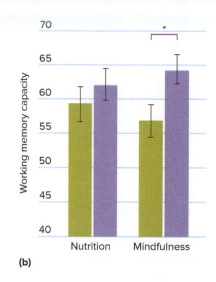
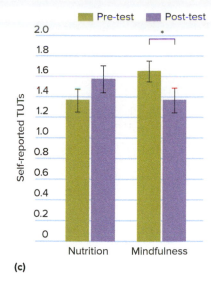

(a)   (b)   (c)

FIGURE 3

CAN MINDFULNESS MEDITATION TRAINING IMPROVE WORKING MEMORY AND GRE PERFORMANCE? Pre- and post-training scores on working GRE (a), working memory (b), and mind wandering (c) for those in nutrition class (control group) and those in mindfulness training class (experimental group). TUT = task-unrelated thought; mind wandering. Asterisks (*) indicate statistically significant differences between the two groups ($p > .05$). (Mrazek et al., 2013).

2 Method

Forty-eight undergraduate students (34 females) were randomly assigned to either the experimental (mindfulness training) or the control (nutrition class) condition. One week before and then again 1 week after these courses participants took cognitive tests (working memory and GRE verbal subtest).

The mindfulness training met four times a week for 45 minutes a session and lasted 2 weeks. The mindfulness class focused on posture and breath, allowing the mind to rest instead of suppressing thoughts, lessening distracting thoughts and reframing them as mental projections. A *nutrition class* also met four times a week for 2 weeks and students had to log their daily food intakes (but did not have to make any changes to their diets). *Working memory* was assessed with an operation span task, where participants saw three letters presented one at a time and had to recall those letters in correct order immediately afterwards. Finally, *mind wandering* was assessed by asking participants at unpredictable times during the GRE and working memory tasks how much their attention was focused on the task at hand.

3 Results

GRE, working memory, and mind wandering scores prior to training and the class were the same between the two groups. But after the 2 weeks of training, those in mindfulness meditation course had improved their working memory and the GRE scores and lowered their mind wandering compared to the nutrition class students. Because the groups were the same before but different after the training sessions, the likely cause of the change was the training.

4 Conclusion

Mindfulness training in as little as 2 weeks can have significant impact on improving memory and verbal problem solving while also reducing the mind's tendency to wander between tasks.

Challenge Your Assumptions

True or False? Meditation practice can improve your SAT score.

True: Research has linked meditation-related changes in brain activity with quicker and better performance in tasks that measure attentional skills.

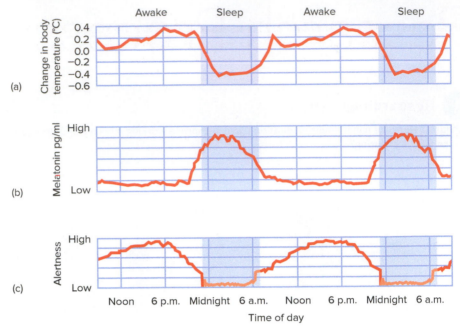

FIGURE **4**

HUMAN CIRCADIAN CYCLES. Our body temperature (a), melatonin levels (b), and alertness (c) fluctuate regularly on 24-hour circadian cycles. (Monk, Folkarc, & Wedderburn, 1996)

drops during sleep. That our bodies go through 24-hour cycles is the reason we are sharper at some times of the day than others and why we experience jet lag. Shortening or lengthening our days by traveling across time zones throws the circadian cycles off, and it takes time for the body to readjust to the new daily cycle.

The body has an internal timekeeper located in the hypothalamus, called the suprachiasmatic nucleus (SCN), which regulates physiological activity on daily cycles (Moore & Eichler, 1972; Weaver, 1998). When the retina in the eye senses light in the morning, it stimulates the SCN, which in turn signals the nearby *pineal gland* to decrease the amount of melatonin it releases (Itri et al., 2004). *Melatonin* is a hormone that plays a role in relaxation and drowsiness. In the evening, decreased activity in the SCN prompts the secretion of melatonin, which increases relaxation. Because of melatonin's role in regulating sleep, melatonin supplements are often taken to combat the effects of jet lag. The daylight shifts of travel affect the body's secretion of melatonin (Wieczorek, Blazejczyk, & Morita, 2016). Although research suggests that, for some people, taking melatonin can be effective in reducing the disruptive effects of jet travel (more so when we travel ahead in time than backward in time) (Waterhouse, Atkinson, & Reilly, 2007), the mechanisms are not well understood.

The Sleeping Brain   People used to assume that the brain was relatively inactive during sleep, except for dreaming. In the 1950s, Nathaniel Kleitman and Eugene Aserinsky were studying attention in children and noticed that, when children lost attention and fell asleep, their eyes moved rapidly underneath their eyelids (Bulkeley, 1997). Not only were these movements important in sleep, but they occurred in everyone throughout the night. Kleitman and Aserinsky coined the term **rapid eye movements (REM)** to describe their discovery (Dement, 1999). The discovery of REM revolutionized the study of sleep and dreaming.

The brain, as it turns out, is very active during sleep. With EEG technology, scientists have learned that sleep changes throughout the night, and distinct patterns of brain activity characterize these changes (Bulkeley, 1997; Dement, 1999). Each state of wakefulness and sleep has its own pattern of brain electrical activity. **Beta waves** are rapid, low-energy waves that occur when we are awake and alert. **Alpha waves** occur when we are awake but relaxed and drowsy.

rapid eye movements (REM)
Quick movements of the eye that occur during sleep, thought to mark phases of dreaming.

beta waves
The pattern of brain activity when one is awake; rapid, low-energy waves.

alpha waves
The pattern of brain activity when one is relaxed and drowsy; slower, higher-energy waves than beta waves.

FIGURE 5

TYPES OF BRAIN WAVES AND DIFFERENT STAGES OF CONSCIOUSNESS AND SLEEP.

Each stage of wakefulness and sleep is marked by a unique pattern of brain wave. For the typical 7-hour night of sleep for an adult, there are about five cycles of sleep

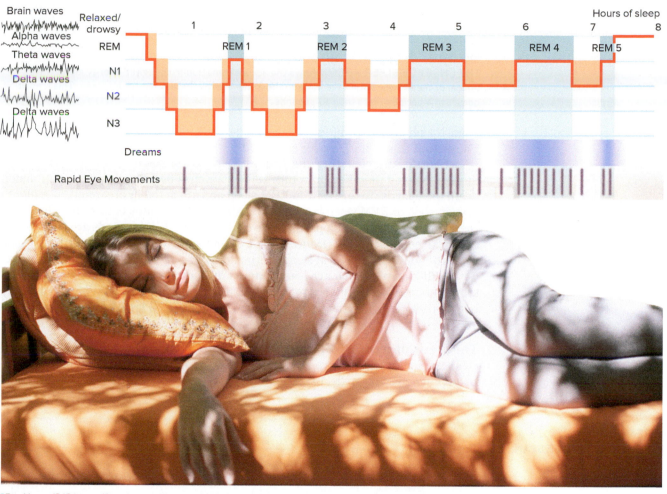

©Tom Merton/OJO Images/Getty Images RF

 What happens to the amount of dreaming as the night progresses?

Non-REM sleep (NREM or just "N") has relatively few eye movements; those that occur are slow. There are three stages of non-REM sleep, each marked by unique brain wave patterns (see Figure 5). **Theta waves**, slower and lower energy waves than alpha, occur as we enter N1 sleep—when the sensory curtain drops and we are no longer responsive to the outside world. The precise moment when we fall asleep is readily apparent on an EEG display—we move from alpha to slower and lower energy theta wave activity (see Figure 6). N1 sleep, however, is a light sleep, and not much stimulation is needed to awaken us from it.

After about 5–7 minutes in N1, we move to N2 sleep, when the theta waves now show short periods of extremely fast and somewhat higher-energy *sleep spindles*. The other unique markers of Stage 2 sleep are sudden, high-energy *K-complexes*. After a short period of time, we move from N2 to N3 sleep, which initially consists of theta waves with some higher-energy **delta waves**. As we progress through N3, however, more and more delta waves appear, and we have fewer and fewer sleep spindles and K-complexes. When the latter disappear completely, we have entered our deepest sleep. This deepest stage is still N3, though it used to be referred to as Stage 4. EEG research shows that it actually is indistinguishable

non-REM
The form of sleep with few eye movements, which are slow rather than fast.

theta waves
A pattern of brain activity during N1 sleep; slower, lower-energy waves than alpha waves.

delta waves
Type of brain activity that dominates N3 sleep; higher energy than theta waves.

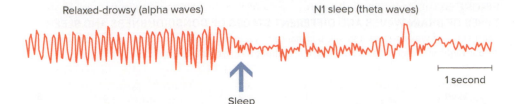

Relaxed-drowsy (alpha waves)   N1 sleep (theta waves)

1 second

Sleep

FIGURE 6

THE ONSET OF SLEEP. An EEG shows the abrupt transition from higher-energy alpha waves typical of the drowsy but awake state to the lower-energy theta waves of N1 sleep. This transition occurs in a period of less than 10 seconds.

from N3 physiologically, so we no longer talk of Stage 4 (Iber, Ancoli-Israel, Chesson, & Quan, 2007; Moser et al., 2009).

Shortly after entering the deepest part of N3 sleep, we start going back through N2 and then N1. On return to N1, our eyes begin to move rapidly underneath the eyelids. We are now in REM sleep and are actively dreaming. The night's first episode of REM sleep lasts for only about 8–10 minutes before the whole process starts over. With each progressive cycle, the non-REM periods are shorter and the REM periods longer (Dement, 1999). Adults move through about four to six cycles of non-REM and REM sleep every night. Each cycle lasts roughly 90 minutes.

Full-blown dreams are less common during non-REM than REM sleep, but they do occur regularly. Up to 70% of non-REM periods may involve dreaming, but the dreams differ from REM dreams: They tend to be less detailed, less active, and more like regular thinking (Bulkeley, 1997; Foulkes, 1996; Kahan, 2001).

The Development of Sleep over the Life Span Newborns of many species, especially humans, spend more time in REM sleep than in non-REM sleep. In humans, REM sleep declines rapidly over the life span (see Figure 7). Although

FIGURE 7
SLEEP ACROSS THE LIFE SPAN

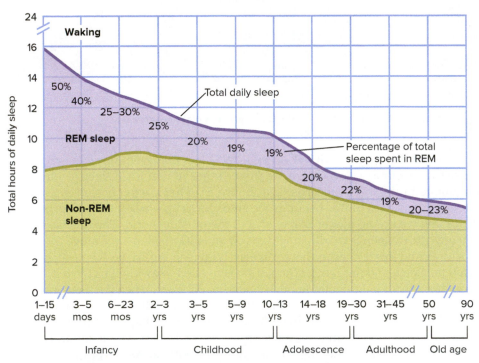

(Source: Adapted from Roffwarg, H. P., Muzio, J. N., & Dement, W. C. (1966). Ontogenetic development of human dream-sleep cycle. *Science, 152*, 604, Figure 1.)

 Which groups require more hours of sleep and more time in **REM sleep**? From what you have learned about brain development, why do you think that is the case?

newborns typically sleep for only a few hours at a time—much to the chagrin of their sleep-deprived parents—they might spend a total of 8 hours in REM sleep and another 8 hours in non-REM sleep *per day*. The percentage of total sleep that is REM stays close to 50% for the first 3 months of life. By 8 months, it has fallen to 33%, and by age 1 it has dropped to about 28%. During adolescence and adulthood, the amount of sleep that involves REM steadily decreases.

The fact that newborns and infants spend so much more time in REM sleep than adults has led some researchers to hypothesize that the main function of REM sleep is to assist in brain growth and development. The amount of REM sleep over the life span does correspond to the degree of brain plasticity and neural growth (Dement, 1999). Our brains are most plastic in infancy and childhood and less so in adulthood—precisely the pattern seen in REM sleep. REM sleep, just like new neural growth, continues throughout our lives—it just decreases with age.

Getting enough sleep is important for health, as we have seen. Large-scale studies of the population suggest, however, that too much sleep is harmful as well. The optimal length night's sleep for long life is about 7 hours, on average. Getting too much less or too much more than 7 hours on a regular basis is associated with a shorter lifespan (Liu et al., 2016). What seems optimal for health is the right amount of sleep—more is not necessarily better. A meta-analysis of 16 prospective studies on sleep and mortality looked at the relationship between the amount of sleep people averaged nightly over their lifetimes and death (from any cause). People who slept between 6 and 8 hours a day lived longer than those who slept much less or more than that amount (Cappuccio et al., 2010).

The Function of Sleep Sleep supports several restorative processes in the CNS: neural growth, metabolic cleanup in the brain, memory consolidation, and protection against cellular damage (Bellesi et al., 2013; Xie et al., 2013; see Figure 8).

FIGURE **8**
THE FUNCTIONS OF SLEEP. A good night's sleep before an exam may do more for your performance than an all-night cram session.

to help with metabolic cleanup in the brain
to restore neural growth
to consolidate memory
to produce enzymes that protect
against cellular damage

©Chris Ryan/age fotostock RF

Sleep also seems to help in the cleanup of cerebral toxins that build up throughout the day. In mice, there are substantial increases in the exchange of cerebrospinal fluid with intracellular fluid during sleep compared to waking states (Xie et al., 2013). Each of these effects appears to be important for optimal function and well-being.

Sleep deprivation inhibits the growth of new neurons and impairs production of the chemicals that make up the myelin sheath, which is crucial for the smooth and rapid conduction of neural impulses (Bellesi, 2015). (This is something to think about the next time you consider staying up all night to cram for a test.) Children who experience chronic sleep disturbances show decreased connectivity and neuron loss in key memory areas of the brain, which has long-term implications for cognitive development (Jan et al., 2010).

Studies in mice show that the proliferation of a cell that plays an important role in myelin production (oligodendrocyte precursor cells, or OPCs) doubles during sleep, and it increases with the amount of time spent in REM sleep. OPC production actually decreases during wakefulness, so adequate sleep appears to be very important for adequate myelin production. These findings may have implications for multiple sclerosis, the symptoms of which worsen during periods of sleep loss (Bellesi et al., 2013).

Sleep appears to be crucial for several types of learning, primarily because it affects memory (Mantua, Baran, & Spencer, 2016; Reichert et al., 2016; Schreiner & Rasch, 2016). For instance, both young and elderly adults who learn a mirror-tracing task (see Figure 9, below) perform better if they learn the task shortly before sleep than if they learn it in the morning (Mantua et al., 2016). Sleep also helps learning in infants. Researchers played sounds of an artificial language (e.g., *dapu*, *dobi*, *diti*, and *bugo*) to babies at various times of day. They then measured the babies' recognition of the sounds by means of an approach often used in infants who cannot yet speak—head turning. Infants tend to orient their heads to noises, sights, or smells they have experienced before. Babies oriented more often to previously heard sounds that were learned before sleeping than to sounds learned at different times of day (Simon et al., 2016).

Not only does sleep affect learning, but learning affects the structure of sleep. In the elderly, learning-related sleep changes have a beneficial effect on sleep structure (Conte, Carobbi, Errico, & Ficca, 2012). In a home-based sleep and learning study in older adults (mean age of 72.5 years), participants recorded their normal sleep patterns (e.g., waking times, napping times, and going to sleep times) for

FIGURE 9
LEARNING AND SLEEP. (a) Mirror-tracing task. (b) Two figures used during the learning phase.

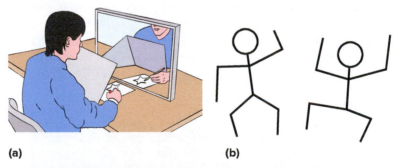

(a)　　　　　　　　　　　　　　　(b)

(Source: Mantua, J., Baran, B., & Spencer, R. M. (2016). *Experimental Brain Research, 234(2)*, 587–595. doi: 10.1007/s00221-015-4490-7)

 A mirror tracing task from Mantua, Baran, and Spencer (2016, p. 589). Both older and younger adult perform better on this task if they learn right before sleeping rather than earlier in the day.

several days. An experimenter visited the home to train each participant on a task involving learning word pairs, which was administered right before sleep. To measure sleep patterns, participants wore a portable device that collected EEG and other physiological information while they slept in their own beds. Compared to nights when they did not learn a new task before sleeping, sleep after learning lasted longer, showed more complete sleep cycles, and contained fewer awakenings in the night. These improvements in stability and continuity of sleep suggest that learning before bed has a beneficial reorganizing effect on sleep (Conte et al., 2012).

The relationship between sleep and memory is not always straightforward. Apparently, it is not just a matter of total sleep hours but also *when* you sleep that matters. What appears to be really important for learning and memory is getting sleep at the appropriate (or your normal) place in the circadian cycle (Buxton et al., 2012).

Neuroimaging studies of people learning to navigate a virtual maze show increases in activation in the hippocampus, the brain structure that is central to memory formation and learning (see the chapters "The Biology of Behavior," "Memory," and "Learning"). If people sleep after this training, the same kind of hippocampal activity resurfaces during slow-wave sleep. The more hippocampal activation shown during slow-wave sleep, the better the person performs on the task the next day (Peigneux et al., 2004; Stickgold & Walker, 2007). In short, task learning is replayed in the brain during sleep, and this brain practice helps performance the next day. Napping after learning a task may improve performance as well (Wamsley, Tucker, Payne & Stickgold, 2010). In fact, napping improves memory for language even in infants (Horvath, Myers, Foster, & Plunkett, 2015). It is interesting that a group with language learning challenges—children with dyslexia—often have disturbed sleep patterns (Carotenuto, Esposito, Cortese, Laino, & Verrotti, 2016).

Sleep not only helps make memories more solid—as in the maze learning example—but also makes them more accessible later (Dumay, 2016). How this happens is unclear, but perhaps by getting rid of material we do not need so that the material we need is easier to access. So we have to forget some things that we learn, so that we better remember the key points. Recent findings that sleep leads to synaptic pruning (see Chapter 3) occurs during sleep (de Vivo et al., 2017), which is associated with forgetting.

Another important function of sleep is fighting cell damage. When our bodies use energy through the process of metabolism, some cells are damaged. Specifically, when we metabolize oxygen, by-products of this process known as *free radicals* damage cells, including brain cells (Harmon, 2006). Sleep aids cell function by triggering the production of enzymes that fight cell damage (Ramanathan et al., 2002). Similarly, sleep slows metabolism itself, thereby slowing the rate of cell damage (Wouters-Adriaens & Westerterp, 2006). Chronic sleep deprivation can lead to DNA damage, and it accelerates cellular aging (Carroll et al., 2016). Cancer, which results from aberrations in the cellular growth process, may be affected by sleep (Blask, 2009). One large-scale study indicates that too little sleep correlates with an increased risk of certain types of breast cancer in both black and white women (Xiao et al., 2016). Chronic restrictions on the duration of sleep and the timing of sleep may increase the risk of other illnesses, such as diabetes (Anothaisintawee, Reutrakul, Van Cauter, & Thakkinstian, 2016).

Sleep Deprivation and Sleep Debt   Given the health benefits of sleep, what are the consequences of not getting enough sleep? In the United States, 40% of adults suffer from sleep deprivation (Dement, 1999). Are you one of them? You are probably sleep deprived if you need an alarm clock to wake up, if you sleep longer on the weekends than on weekdays, or if you fall asleep during lectures (Maas, 1998).

Recent surveys show that the typical adult gets about 6 hours and 40 minutes of sleep on weekdays and 7 hours and 25 minutes on weekends (National Sleep Foundation, 2008). Sleep expert William Dement (1999) developed the concept of *sleep debt* to represent the amount of sleep our brains owe our bodies. It is like a monetary debt that must be "paid back." Simply put, if you get 2 hours less sleep one night, then you owe your body 2 hours additional sleep the next night (or within a few days). Sleeping longer on weekends is a way to pay back a little bit of the sleep debt accumulated during the week.

Most people don't pay back their sleep debt, so they pay in other ways: day-time drowsiness, the use of stimulants (such as caffeine or nicotine), a lack of focused attention, and impaired learning and memory. The most dangerous pay-back comes in the form of accidents. A high percentage of automobile, airplane, boating, and job-related accidents are caused by drowsiness related to sleep debt and/or night shift work, although people drastically underestimate the risks of drowsy driving (Lee et al., 2016; Watling et al., 2016).

Smartphones, tablets, laptops, and televisions activate arousal and make it difficult to sleep. Screens on these devices (LED) emit enough light to trick the brain into thinking it is daytime, which interferes with the sleep–wake cycle (https://sleepfoundation.org/ask-the-expert/electronics-the-bedroom). Texting and other types of screen use in bed is a major cause of sleeplessness and daytime drowsi-ness in teens (Fossum et al., 2014; Johansson, Petrisko, & Chasens, 2016).

(See Figure 10 for tips on how to get a good night's sleep.)

Not surprisingly, sleep deprivation affects mental health as well. Scores on measures of anxiety, depression, and paranoia increase with sleep loss (Kahn-Greene et al., 2007; McClung, 2015). In terms of daily sleep variations, the effects might not be immediate, and wear and tear might take a few days to show up. Bar-ber and colleagues (2010) asked students to complete a daily sleep log as well as online diaries of psychological symptoms and perceived stress in life over a 5-day period (Monday through Friday). They found that a few days of sleep deficiency early in the week, even when people try to offset this debt with subsequent sleep, can contribute to psychological strain later in the week (Barber et al., 2010). Not all sleep loss can be replenished, and inconsistent sleep patterns can wear us down.

---

tips for better sleep

- Go to bed and get up at the same time each day.
- Avoid caffeine, nicotine, beer, wine, and liquor in the 4 to 6 hours before bedtime.
- Don't exercise within 2 hours of bedtime.
- Don't eat large meals within 2 hours of bedtime.
- Don't nap later than 3 p.m.
- Sleep in a dark, quiet room that isn't too hot or cold for you.
- If you can't fall asleep within 20 minutes, get up and do something quiet.
- Wind down in the 30 minutes before bedtime by doing something relaxing.
- Avoid electronic screens, such as those of your phone, tablet, laptop, or TV, for at least 20 minutes before bedtime, and do not allow them to disturb you during sleep.

©Ferlistockphoto/iStock/Getty Images RF

FIGURE 10

SLEEP BETTER. Everyone has trouble falling asleep occasionally. Following these simple suggestions can help you avoid persistent problems with sleeplessness. (National Sleep Foundation, 2008)

Disorders of Sleep For most people, sleeping 6 to 8 hours a day is a welcome experience, notwithstanding the occasional nightmare or restless night. For an estimated 20% of the U.S. population, however, nighttime is often fraught with problems (Dement, 1999). Let's consider four disorders of sleep: insomnia, sleepwalking, narcolepsy, and hypersomnia.

Insomnia is defined as taking more than 20 minutes to fall asleep, having trouble staying asleep, and/or not feeling rested after a night's sleep for 2 or more consecutive weeks (Krystal, 2005). About 19% U.S. adults suffer from insomnia (Ford et al., 2015). Some sleep experts consider insomnia more a symptom of other maladies than a disorder in its own right, although there is some debate on this matter (Stepanski, 2006). There are many possible causes of insomnia, for instance, restless leg syndrome, erratic hours, medical conditions, psychological disorders (such as depression), and excessive use of alcohol (Dement, 1999; Roehrs, Zorick, & Roth, 2000). Iron deficiency may also cause insomnia. This fact might explain why women, who are more likely to be iron deficient, show higher rates of insomnia than men (Lee, 2006; Mizuno et al., 2005).

Drug treatments for insomnia, such as the popular sleep aid Ambien, work by increasing the effects of gamma-aminobutyric acid (GABA), the neurotransmitter that decreases central nervous system activity. In this way, sleep aids produce a general feeling of relaxation. Several non-drug therapies, such as meditation and cognitive-behavioral therapy, help relieve symptoms of insomnia as well (Babson, Feldner, & Badour, 2010; Ong, Shapiro, & Manber, 2008). *Imagery rehearsal*, in which one rewrites a nightmare and mentally rehearses images from the newly re-scripted scenario while awake, is effective in treating nightmare-related insomnia (Wellisch & Cohen, 2011). Another non-drug treatment for insomnia is mindfulness meditation (Garland, Zhou, Gonzalez, & Rodriguez, 2016), which may improve sleep quality even in people who do not experience insomnia (Kaul et al., 2010).

Sleepwalking occurs when a person gets out of bed during sleep, usually during the first third of the sleep cycle, and engages in activities that normally occur during wakefulness, such as walking, eating, dressing, or bathing. People who sleepwalk are difficult to rouse and do not remember having been up after waking in the morning. Because sleepwalking occurs during non-REM sleep, the sleepwalker is not likely to be acting out a dream. Sleepwalking occurs in about 4%–15% of children and about 1.5%–2.5% of adults (Guilleminault et al., 2005).

Narcolepsy, another sleep disorder, is defined by excessive daytime sleepiness. People with this condition may fall asleep at inopportune times throughout the day, often with little to no warning. They may also experience *cataplexy*, a weakness of facial muscles and the muscles in limbs (Nishino et al., 2015). The origin of narcolepsy may lie in disrupted nighttime sleep patterns. Narcolepsy is often a function of insomnia; EEG studies reveal that people who suffer from narcolepsy show some abnormality in sleep spindles and disruption of REM sleeping patterns. Narcolepsy appears to have a genetic basis. It is most often treated with amphetamines (stimulants), which help prevent daytime sleepiness, and antidepressants, which can help with cataplexy. Neither treatment addresses the nighttime sleep disruptions (Broderick & Guilleminault, 2016).

Sleep apnea is a sleeping disorder characterized by brief pauses in breathing during sleep (NHLBI, 2012). Apnea can cause disruption in the sleep cycle, which leads to daytime fatigue. Apnea may be *obstructive* or *central*. Obstructive apnea is caused by airflow blockage and can cause snoring. This type of apnea is more common in people who are overweight, and weight loss is a first course of treatment. Less common is *central* apnea, which is a result of abnormalities in brain structures that control breathing.

Hypersomnia exists when a person sleeps more than 10 hours a day for 2 weeks or more. Hypersomnia involves strong urges to nap throughout the day, often at inappropriate times, such as during meals or in the middle of conversations. It can be caused by other sleep disorders, such as apnea, brain injury, or depression.

insomnia
A sleep difficulty characterized by difficulty falling and staying asleep, as well as not feeling rested.

sleepwalking
A sleep difficulty characterized by activities occurring during non-REM sleep that usually occur when one is awake, such as walking and eating.

narcolepsy
A sleep disorder characterized by excessive daytime sleepiness and weakness in facial and limb muscles.

sleep apnea
A sleeping disorder characterized by brief pauses in breathing during sleep.

hypersomnia
A sleep difficulty characterized by sleeping more than 10 hours a day for 2 weeks or more; includes an urge to nap during inappropriate times.

©Universal History Archive/Getty Images

Sleepwalking is more common in children than in adults, possibly because it occurs during non-REM sleep, and adults spend less time in non-REM sleep than children do.

night terrors
A state that occurs when a person walks around, speaks incoherently, and ultimately awakens, terrified, from sleep.

Adolescents who commit suicide are more likely to have suffered from hypersomnia than are those who do not commit suicide (Goldstein, Bridge, & Brent, 2008).

Night terrors occur when a person, often a child, speaks incoherently and ultimately awakens suddenly in a terrified state from sleep; night terrors may also involve walking around in one's sleep (Smith, Comella, & Högl, 2008). The individual may scream, bolt upright from bed, and appear very confused and frightened. He or she may wake up sweating and breathing very fast, with dilated pupils. The episodes generally last 10–20 minutes, and then the person returns to a normal sleep. The next morning the individual usually has no recollection of the event. Although night terrors are rare in adults, the adults who do suffer from them tend to exhibit higher levels of depression, anxiety, and obsessive-compulsive traits (Kales et al., 1980). To be clear, night terrors are *not* nightmares, which are typical dreams with a frightening plot. Night terrors do not occur during REM sleep and are not associated with dreams.

Nightmares are frightening or distressing dreams. We all have nightmares from time to time, but some people experience nightmares of such intensity and/or frequency that it can cause insomnia, make their sleep very irregular, or form the basis of serious stress. Nightmares are a huge problem for veterans with posttraumatic stress disorder (PTSD), as well as for people dealing with ongoing severe stress or trauma presented by adverse life experiences, such as cancer patients (Berlin, Means, & Edinger, 2010; Wellisch & Cohen, 2011).

Dreaming

dreams
Images, thoughts, and feelings experienced during sleep.

Dreaming is one of the most fascinating features of consciousness, but what are dreams exactly? **Dreams** are the succession of images, thoughts, and feelings we experience while asleep. The images are loosely connected by unusual associations and not well recalled afterward. Most of us dream numerous times each night, yet we rarely recall our dreams on waking. When people in sleep labs are awakened, they report dreaming almost always if they were in REM sleep and somewhat regularly if they were in non-REM sleep (Bulkeley, 1997; Dement, 1999).

Do dreams have real meaning, or do they simply reflect the random activity of a complex brain? Psychologists from different perspectives disagree on what dreams are and what they mean.

Psychoanalytic Theory   In *The Interpretation of Dreams*, Sigmund Freud wrote that dreams are "the royal road to the unconscious" (1900/1953, p. 608). He argued that conflicting impulses, thoughts, feelings, and drives that threaten the waking mind are released as a visual compromise in distorted and disguised form by the sleeping mind. In this view, each dream is an attempt to fulfill unacceptable desires or satisfy unconscious wishes.

According to Freud's theory, dreams operate on two distinct levels of consciousness. The dream that we consciously recall after waking up is only the surface level, which Freud called the **manifest level**. The deeper, unconscious level, where the true meaning of a dream lies, he labeled the **latent level**. In his clinical practice, Freud used psychoanalysis to uncover the latent meaning of his clients' dreams in order to help them resolve the hidden conflicts from which their problems arose.

Biological Theory   One influential biological theory of dreams has been AIM theory, which argues that dreams are devoid of meaning and are a result of random brain activity (Hobson, 2001, 2002). **AIM** stands for three biologically based dimensions of consciousness: **a**ctivation, **i**nput, and **m**ode. *Activation* refers to the amount of neural activation and ranges from low to high activation. *Input* refers to whether stimulation is internal or external. Finally, *mode* refers to the mental state—from logical (wakeful) to loose-illogical (dreaming). These three dimensions (A-I-M) make up a cube, and all states of consciousness occupy a different space in this cube (see Figure 11). For example, waking is a highly active, external, and logical mode of consciousness residing in the upper-back-right portion of the cube. Non-REM sleep is moderately active, external, and logical and resides in the middle of the cube. By contrast, REM sleep is highly active, internal, and loose and therefore occupies the lower-front-right portion of the cube.

Cognitive Theory   According to cognitive psychologists, dreams are not that different from everyday thinking. Research shows that some of the standard processes that we use during our waking life, such as imagery, memory, speech, and problem solving, operate in a similar manner during dreaming (Cavallero & Foulkes,

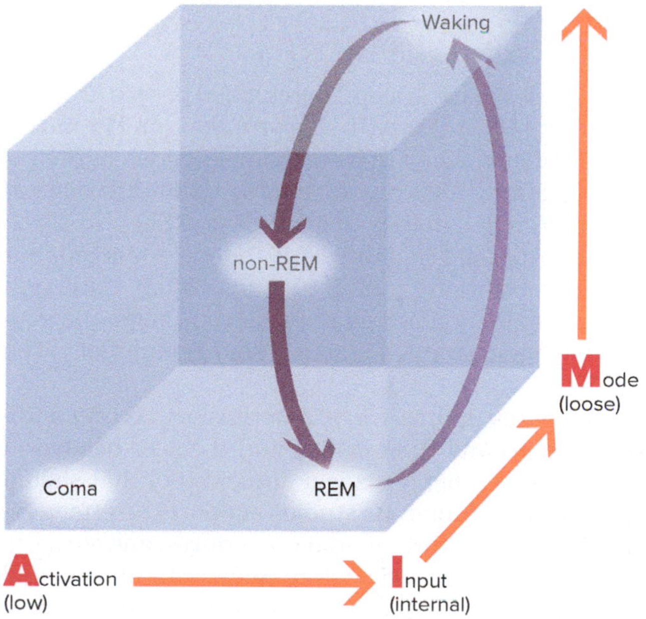

manifest level
Freud's surface level of dreams, recalled upon waking.

latent level
Freud's deeper, unconscious level of dreams; their meaning is found at this level.

AIM
Three biologically based dimensions of consciousness—activation, input, and mode.

FIGURE 11
HOBSON'S AIM MODEL OF CONSCIOUSNESS. What are the three dimensions of consciousness and their ranges? Each state of consciousness occupies a unique place in this three-dimensional space. Our days normally cycle between waking, non-REM, and REM sleep states of consciousness. (Hobson, 2001)

1993; Kahan, 2001). Some people develop an ability to know when they are dreaming (lucid dreaming) and can therefore control the events and outcomes of the dreams (LaBerge, 1985). Others are able to reflect on and evaluate their experiences while dreaming (Kahan, 2001; Kahan & LaBerge, 1994). Also, recall that dreaming occurs during both REM and non-REM periods. Dreaming that occurs during non-REM sleep is closer to waking thought than is REM sleep dreaming—it is less visual, more verbal, and not as loose and unusual in its associations (Dement, 1999; Kahan, 2001).

Combined Theories   Some recent theories promote an integration of cognitive and biological perspectives on dreaming. One such cognitive-biological view suggests that dreams consolidate long-term memories first by strengthening the neural traces of recent events and then by integrating these traces with already stored memories. Dreams also keep existing memories stable, even when new experiences attempt to interfere with older memories (Payne & Nadel, 2004). Particular hormones, such as cortisol, are involved in strengthening these neural connections to consolidate memory. Cortisol levels change throughout sleep stages, with peaks of cortisol matching REM stages of sleep (Payne & Kensinger, 2010; Payne & Nadel, 2004; Weitzman et al., 1971).

Quick Quiz 4: Sleeping and Dreaming

1. When a perceptual wall between the conscious mind and the outside world emerges and we are in a state that is immediately reversible, we are
   a. sleep.
   b. unconscious.
   c. vegetative.
   d. minimally conscious.

2. Research shows that sleep functions to
   a. give our cells some energy.
   b. facilitate learning and memory.
   c. facilitate neural growth.
   d. both b and c

3. Dreaming is most active during what kind of sleep?
   a. non-REM
   b. REM
   c. Stage 3
   d. N1

4. In lucid dreaming, people become aware that they are dreaming and can sometimes even control their dreams. Lucid dreaming is most consistent with which theory of dreams?
   a. psychoanalytic
   b. biological
   c. cognitive
   d. none of the above

Answers can be found at the end of the chapter.

HYPNOSIS

hypnosis
A state characterized by focused attention, suggestibility, absorption, lack of voluntary control over behavior, and suspension of critical faculties; occurs when instructed by someone trained in hypnosis; may be therapeutic.

Although the Greek word root *hypnos* means "sleep," hypnotized people are very much awake but have little voluntary control over their own behavior. **Hypnosis** is a state of mind that occurs in compliance with instructions and is characterized by focused attention, suggestibility, absorption, lack of voluntary control over behavior, and suspension of critical faculties of mind (Raz & Shapiro, 2002; Stewart, 2005). People may be more easily hypnotized if they are relaxed, but they can be hypnotized without relaxation (Raz & Shapiro, 2002). Although about 65% of the population is mildly to moderately responsive to hypnotic suggestion, only about 15% are highly hypnotizable (Hilgard, 1965; Song, 2006). The rest are resistant to hypnosis.

The mention of hypnosis conjures up images of a performer putting audience volunteers into sleeplike trances and then instructing them to behave in ways that are out of character; however, hypnosis is a clinical tool that should not be confused with stage techniques. Numerous studies support the effectiveness of hypnosis for pain relief during childbirth, dental procedures, and surgery. Further, hypnosis may be effective in treating nicotine addiction, nausea and vomiting related to chemotherapy, and anxiety associated with certain medical

©William Thomas Cain/Getty Images

Hypnosis therapy has helped people quit smoking. This group of smokers is being hypnotized to believe that cigarettes taste like vomit.

procedures (Lang et al., 2006; Montgomery, DuHamel, & Redd, 2000; Patterson, 2004; Stewart, 2005). The therapeutic benefits of hypnosis are not fully understood, but the availability of brain imaging techniques has motivated efforts to document its effectiveness and to learn how it works to reduce pain (Flammer & Bongartz, 2003; Stewart, 2005). We now know that, during hypnosis, cortical areas activated during normal pain situations (during wakefulness) are not activated at all (Vanhaudenhuyse et al., 2009).

It is not easy to offer a general explanation for how hypnosis works, and theorists offer a range of different perspectives. First, some theorists consider hypnosis to be a state in which one part of the brain operates independently. Ernest Hilgard (1977) showed that under hypnosis one aspect of a person's mind can remain aware and open to stimulation from the outside (such as the hypnotist's voice) while other parts are cut off from external input.

A second theory maintains that hypnosis does not alter consciousness, nor do hypnotized individuals give up control of their behavior. Instead, they behave the way they think a hypnotized person would behave. In short, they are role-playing (Orne, 1959). For decades, this was the prevailing scientific view on hypnosis.

Neuroscientific research suggests a different, third, explanation—that hypnosis is not imitation but rather real brain activity. Neuroscientist Amir Raz and his colleagues have studied whether hypnosis might help eliminate the **Stroop effect**, which is a delayed reaction when there is a mismatch between font color and the meaning of the color word (Raz, Fan, & Posner, 2005). The Stroop task tests visual selective attention; it measures how people deal with conflicting verbal and color information. In a typical Stroop test, participants view the names of colors, such as green, red, and blue, printed in different colors and must name the color in which the word is printed. People are slower to identify the color of words that are printed in a different color from the meaning of the word (such as when the word *blue* is printed in yellow ink) than words that are printed in the same color (*blue* printed in blue). The delay in reaction time caused by mismatching color words and the color in which the words are printed is known as the Stroop effect (Stroop, 1935; see Figure 12).

Raz and his colleagues (2005) hypnotized 16 people—8 of whom were highly hypnotizable and 8 less hypnotizable. While hypnotized, the participants received instruction on a Stroop test that they would perform a few days later in an fMRI scanner. After the hypnosis session, all the participants received a posthypnotic suggestion, which is a suggestive statement that a particular behavior will occur sometime in the future. Participants were told that during the test they would see

Stroop effect
A delay in reaction time when the colors of words on a test and their meaning differ.

FIGURE 12

THE STROOP EFFECT. Study participants will name the color of the letters more rapidly when their color matches the meaning of the word compared to when there is a mismatch.

 Why do you think this is?

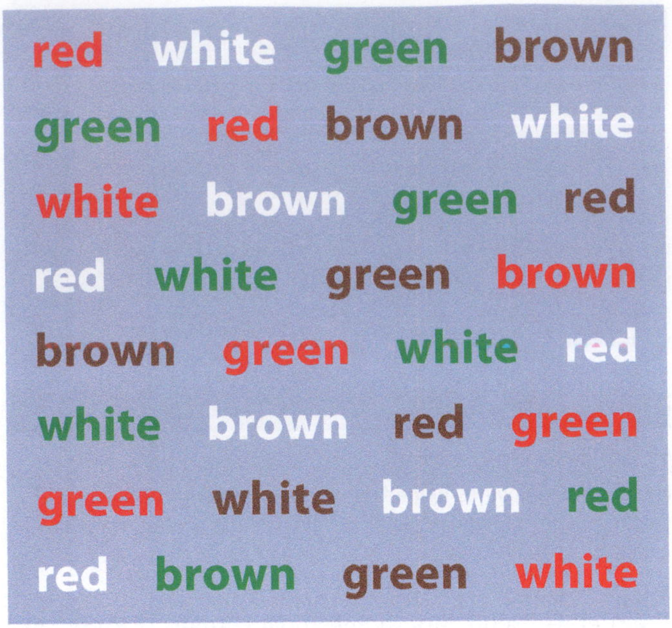

gibberish words in different colors and have to push a button corresponding to the actual color of the letters. The words they saw during the test were names of colors.

Highly hypnotizable people who received the "gibberish" suggestion identified the colors faster than the less hypnotizable people who received the same suggestion. Brain scans taken during the Stroop test showed that the highly hypnotizable people had less activity in the areas of the brain that normally process word meaning, so these areas did not interfere with color recognition. The less hypnotizable people were not able to suppress the Stroop effect. In response to the posthypnotic suggestion, the highly hypnotizable people saw real words as gibberish, so they attended only to identifying the color of the letters. These findings support the idea that hypnosis is a real effect in the brain, not just imitation.

Another set of studies addressed the question of whether hypnosis involves role-playing (Derbyshire et al., 2004; Raij et al., 2005). Some participants were administered mild pain, others imagined pain, and a third group experienced hypnotized pain. Hypnotically induced pain activated the same brain circuit as did the real pain. Also, participants reported actually feeling pain for both real and hypnotically induced pain, but not for imagined pain. So both hypnotic pain and real pain activate the same brain regions and produce the same subjective feelings. Imagining pain does not have the same effects. Hypnotic pain, then, is not just an imitation of the real thing. As far as the brain is concerned, it is the same thing.

Quick Quiz 5: Hypnosis

1. Scientific research has demonstrated that hypnosis
   a. is a real phenomenon.
   b. is not real but learned.
   c. is only an imagined state of mind.
   d. is something everyone experiences.

2. A groundbreaking area of research has demonstrated that, under hypnosis,

   a. hypnotically induced pain creates a subjective experience similar to real pain.
   b. people turn off the areas of the brain that normally process the meaning of words.
   c. hypnotically induced pain activates the same brain circuit as real pain does.
   d. all of the above are correct.

Answers can be found at the end of the chapter.

ALTERING CONSCIOUSNESS WITH DRUGS

Hypnosis creates profound alterations in consciousness for some people. Drugs can change consciousness too. In this section, we will focus on the type of drug known as **psychoactive drugs**, naturally occurring or synthesized substances that, when ingested or otherwise taken into the body, reliably produce qualitative changes in conscious experience.

Psychoactive drug use is universal among humans. Every culture in every recorded age has used mind-altering substances. People use psychoactive drugs for many reasons: to aid in spiritual practice, to improve their health, to explore the self, to regulate mood, to escape boredom and despair, to enhance sensory experience, to stimulate artistic creativity and performance, and to promote social interaction (Weil & Rosen, 1998). Whatever the reason, habitual use of psychoactive drugs can lead to abuse.

Problems arise when people become dependent on a drug to maintain normal function and to cope with the challenges of daily life. For some drugs, repeated use causes **tolerance**, meaning people require increasing amounts of the drug to get the desired effect. **Withdrawal symptoms** are the adverse effects people with physical dependence experience if they stop using a drug. The drugs that lead to physical dependence create the most severe withdrawal symptoms. Alcohol withdrawal for an alcoholic creates many unpleasant side effects, such as delirium tremens (often referred to as the DTs), the symptoms of which may include tremors, insomnia, irritability, seizures, confusion, **hallucinations** (convincing sensory experiences that occur in the absence of an external stimulus), nausea and vomiting, and agitation. In some cases the DTs lead to death.

Sometimes people compulsively use a substance to alleviate boredom, regulate mood, or cope with the challenges of everyday life. People who regularly take sleeping aids to help them fall asleep at night may be unable to sleep without them, even if they are not physically dependent on them. The essence of a compulsive behavior is the inability to control or regulate it. **Addiction** results from habitual use or physical and psychological dependence on a substance. People who are addicted continue to use a substance in spite of knowing that it is harmful and often in spite of attempts to quit.

In this section we survey the behavioral, psychological, and neurological effects of the major classes of psychoactive drugs: depressants, stimulants, and hallucinogens (see Figure 13). We will consider illegal substances as well as the most commonly used and abused legal ones.

Depressants

Depressants slow down central nervous system activity. Alcohol, sedatives, and opioids (narcotics) are all depressants. In low doses, these drugs generally calm the body and mind. In high doses, they can slow down heart rate and brain activity to dangerously low levels. Alcohol and sedatives increase the activity of GABA, the main inhibitory neurotransmitter in the brain, and decrease the activity of glutamate, the main excitatory neurotransmitter in the brain. If taken during pregnancy, alcohol and sedatives can destroy developing neurons in the fetus's brain, leading to learning disabilities, poor judgment, or intellectual disability (Farber & Olney, 2003). Additionally, combining alcohol with sedatives can be lethal. The opioids work differently, as we will see, but they can be equally dangerous. Let's look in more detail at each type of depressant.

psychoactive drugs
Naturally occurring or synthesized substances that, when ingested or otherwise taken into the body, reliably produce qualitative changes in conscious experience.

tolerance
The need to consume increasing amounts of a drug to get the desired effect.

withdrawal symptoms
The adverse effects people with physical dependence experience if they stop using a drug.

hallucinations
Convincing sensory experiences that occur in the absence of an external stimulus.

addiction
A condition that results from habitual use or physical and psychological dependence on a substance.

depressants
Substances that decrease or slow down central nervous system activity.

Drug classification	Short-term effects	Risks
Depressants Alcohol	Relaxation, depressed brain activity, slowed behavior, reduced inhibitions	Accidents, brain damage, liver damage, blackouts, birth defects
Sedatives	Relaxation, sleep	Accidents, slowed heart rate, possible death
Opioids	Euphoria, pain relief, bodily relaxation	Slowed heart rate and breathing, death
Stimulants Caffeine	Alertness, nervousness, increased heart rate	Anxiety, insomnia
Nicotine	Arousal, stimulation, increased heart rate	Cardiovascular disease, lung cancer risk with smoking
Cocaine	Exhilaration, euphoria, irritability	Insomnia, heart attack, paranoia
Amphetamines	Increased alertness, excitability, difficulty concentrating	Insomnia, paranoia, accelerated heart rate
Ecstasy (MDMA)	Mild amphetamine and hallucinogenic effects, high body temperature and dehydration; sense of well-being and social connectedness	Depression, mental deficits, cardiovascular problems
Hallucinogens Marijuana	Euphoric feelings, relaxation, mild hallucinations, time distortion, attention and memory impairment, fatigue	Memory problems, respiratory illness, immune system impairment
LSD	Strong hallucinations, distorted time perception, synesthesia	Accidents, insomnia
Psilocybin	Hallucinations, change in mood, possible spiritual experience	Anxiety, impaired thinking, nausea

FIGURE 13
COMMON PSYCHOACTIVE DRUGS, THEIR PRIMARY EFFECTS ON CONSCIOUSNESS, AND THEIR RISKS. Only caffeine, nicotine, marijuana, and LSD do not carry a risk of overdose, resulting in death.

Alcohol   Alcohol is the most widely used depressant. How quickly alcohol is absorbed into the bloodstream depends on a variety of factors, including the amount of food in the stomach and the person's body mass. The amount of alcohol in the bloodstream is the common measure of inebriation known as blood alcohol concentration (BAC). BAC is measured in milligrams of alcohol per 100 milliliters of blood (milligrams %), so a BAC of 0.10 means that one-tenth of 1%, or 1/1,000th, of one's blood content is alcohol. Figure 14 shows the amount of alcohol one must consume to reach 0.08 BAC, which is currently the legal limit for driving in all states in the United States, for various body weights. The figure includes various effects for different BACs.

The more alcohol a person consumes, the more obvious the depressant effects become, sometimes leading to blackouts. These effects are counterintuitive to the loose feeling that many people get in the early stages of drinking alcohol. This apparently stimulating effect occurs because alcohol suppresses the higher social regulatory functions of the cerebral cortex, thereby lowering inhibitions.

Alcohol consumption creates numerous health hazards: accidents resulting in injury or death, usually caused by drunk driving; sudden death from binge drinking; blackouts; and increased risk of liver and throat cancers. Liver damage is one of the better-known health effects of drinking alcohol. Over time, heavy drinking, which is defined as more than five drinks per day, leads to fat

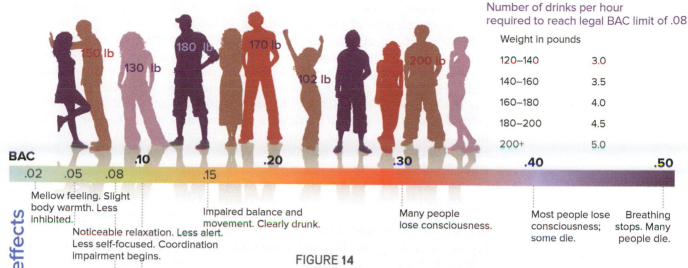

Number of drinks per hour
required to reach legal BAC limit of .08

Weight in pounds	
120–140	3.0
140–160	3.5
160–180	4.0
180–200	4.5
200+	5.0

BAC .02 .05 .08 .10 .15 .20 .30 .40 .50

effects

Mellow feeling. Slight body warmth. Less inhibited.

Noticeable relaxation. Less alert. Less self-focused. Coordination impairment begins.

Drunk driving limit. Definite impairment in coordination and judgment.

Noisy. Possible embarrassing behavior. Mood swings. Reduction in reaction time.

Impaired balance and movement. Clearly drunk.

Many people lose consciousness.

Most people lose consciousness; some die.

Breathing stops. Many people die.

FIGURE 14

BLOOD ALCOHOL CONCENTRATION (BAC) AND ITS EFFECTS ON THE CENTRAL NERVOUS SYSTEM. The legal maximum BAC for driving is 0.08, but even at lower levels our reflexes and judgment may be impaired. The number of drinks it takes to reach 0.08 BAC varies with weight.

 What other factors besides weight affect how quickly someone passes over the 0.08 BAC level?

accumulation and blocks blood flow in the liver. Without an adequate blood supply, liver tissue cannot function properly and dies. Chronic alcoholism causes *cirrhosis*, the accumulation of nonfunctional scar tissue in the liver, an irreversible and eventually fatal condition.

Another powerful example of the interaction between biology and environment is that heavy drinking over a prolonged period actually shrinks the brain. Brain tissue is lost, creating widespread deficits in cognition and behavior (Mechtcheriakov et al., 2007; Oscar-Berman & Marinkovic, 2003; see Figure 15). For example, frontal lobe damage leads to deficits in planning, working memory, and abstract reasoning, whereas damage to the hippocampus leads to deficits in learning and memory. When a person is drinking heavily, reductions in both white and gray matter can occur (Sullivan, Harris, & Pfefferbaum, 2010). Chronic alcohol use has been associated with permanent damage and shrinkage to the thalamus, which affects circuits underlying various memory processes (Pitel, Segobin, Ritz, Eustache, & Beaunieux, 2015). With abstinence from alcohol, the brain can recover much of its lost volume, especially in the first month of abstinence (Gazdzinski, Durazzo, & Meyerhoff, 2005; Kubota et al., 2001).

Binge drinking is usually defined as at least five drinks for men and four for women over a 2-hr period (Jackson, 2008; Wechsler, Lee, & Kuo, 2002). Some researchers argue, however, that not all binge drinkers are alike and that these figures do not predict various

Connection

The brain continues to develop throughout adolescence, which makes it quite vulnerable to the effects of drugs and alcohol.

See "The Developing Adolescent," in the chapter "Human Development." (p. 191–197)

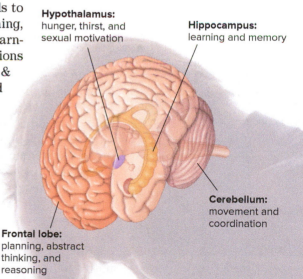

Hypothalamus: hunger, thirst, and sexual motivation

Hippocampus: learning and memory

Cerebellum: movement and coordination

Frontal lobe: planning, abstract thinking, and reasoning

FIGURE 15

BRAIN REGIONS MOST AFFECTED BY EXCESSIVE DRINKING. The main regions of the brain most affected by long-term and excessive drinking include the frontal lobes (planning and abstract thinking and reasoning); the hippocampus (learning and memory); the hypothalamus (hunger, thirst, and sexual motivation); and the cerebellum (movement and coordination).

health consequences very well (Harvard, 2016). However defined, engaging in frequent episodes of consuming many drinks in a short period of time is an unhealthy pattern of behavior that is becoming increasingly common among both high school and college students. Among teens, although the frequency of "modest" binge drinking (around 5 drinks in one sitting) has decreased among 12th graders, the number who engage in extreme binge drinking (10–15) has not changed (Veliz, McCabe, & Boyd, 2016). The group at greatest risk for binge drinking is boys who participate in more than one sport (Veliz, McCabe, & Boyd, 2016). About 40% of college students binge drink, and the numbers are rising (National Institute on Alcohol Abuse and Alcoholism, 2005; Wechsler et al., 2002).

As dangerous and deadly as alcohol can be, mild to moderate alcohol intake, generally defined as no more than two drinks a day, appears to provide protective effects for cardiovascular health. With moderate alcohol use, blood levels rise for the beneficial form of cholesterol (HDL), which has protective effects on the cardiovascular system (King, Mainous, & Geesey, 2008). Although these cardiovascular benefits were initially linked to red wine only, research now shows that many forms of alcohol convey the same advantages (Hines & Rimm, 2001; Sacco et al., 1999). The health benefits of alcohol are hotly debated, though, largely due to the health risks of alcoholism. The lack of controlled, prospective studies on the development of cardiovascular disease make it difficult to resolve the debate (Mukamal & Ding, 2016).

Sedatives Sedatives create a feeling of stupor similar to that of alcohol intoxication. Prescription sedatives, such as barbiturates and benzodiazepines, slow the heart rate, relax skeletal muscles, and tranquilize the mind. Medically, barbiturates are used in anesthesia to calm people down during certain medical procedures and as a temporary sleeping aid. Examples of barbiturates are secobarbital (Seconal) and pentobarbital (Nembutal). Benzodiazepines are often used to induce relaxation or calm one who is agitated, examples include diazepam (Valium) and chlordiazepoxide (Librium). All of these sedatives have the potential for both physical and psychological dependence, can be lethal at high doses, and should be used only under strict medical supervision. Sedative use most often begins with a medical prescription (for anxiety or before painful medical procedures), and abuse can develop quickly (Shin et al., 2016; Kendler et al., 2015).

©Theo Wargo/Staff/WireImage/Getty Images

The rock and pop megastar, Prince, died on April 21, 2016 of an accidental overdose of the opioid fentanyl.

Opioids Another class of depressants is the opioids (also called narcotics), a term that applies to all drugs derived from opium or chemicals similar to opium. Such drugs may be derived from natural sources (such as morphine), may be partially synthetic (such as heroin), or may be entirely synthetic (such as fentanyl). Modern synthetic opioids include oxycodone (Percocet or Percodan), which is prescribed for moderate to severe pain, and hydrocodone (Vicodin), which is prescribed for milder pain.

The effects of specific opioids vary, depending on the form and strength of the substance. Opioids depress central nervous system activity, slowing heart rate, respiration, and digestion and suppressing the cough center. In fact, pharmaceutical companies marketed heroin as a cough suppressant in the early 20th century. Prescription cough medicines today often include codeine, a safer alternative to heroin.

Opioids have been used for centuries as pain relievers. These drugs make use of the body's own naturally occurring opioid systems. Our own bodies produce *endorphins*, opioid-like proteins that bind to opioid receptors in the brain and act as natural painkillers. The more potent opioids—opium, morphine, and heroin—produce feelings of overwhelming bliss, euphoria, and bodily relaxation. The feeling is so good that nothing else matters. As one intravenous heroin user said, "It's so good. Don't even try it once" (Weil & Rosen, 1998).

Generally, opioids (including the newer, widely prescribed synthetic opioids) have a high potential for abuse (Paulozzi, 2006). Contrary to the popular image, not all users of opioids are junkies on the street. Some people develop a tolerance for opioids while being treated for chronic pain (Gallagher & Rosenthal, 2008).

Opioids slow the heart and breathing; high doses can kill by stopping the heart and breathing (Hayes, Klein-Schwartz, & Doyon, 2008). For many of these drugs, the amount required to feel an effect may not be that much less than the amount that can be deadly, especially in people who have developed tolerance. Some newer therapeutic opioids, such as buprenorphine, can be taken at higher doses with less risk of overdose (Johnson, Fudala, & Payne, 2005).

Stimulants

Stimulants activate the nervous system. Although many stimulants are illegal, two of the most widely used psychoactive drugs are the legal stimulants caffeine and nicotine.

stimulants
Substances that activate the nervous system.

Caffeine   If you drink coffee, tea, cocoa, or certain soft drinks (including energy drinks) regularly, you are a stimulant user (see Figure 16). Caffeine is the world's most commonly consumed psychoactive drug, ingested by 90% of North American adults on a daily basis (Lovett, 2005). The effects of mild to moderate caffeine intake are increased alertness, increased heart rate, loss of motor coordination, insomnia, and nervousness. Too much caffeine can make people jittery and anxious. Caffeine is also a diuretic, which means it increases urine output.

FIGURE 16
CAFFEINE CONTENT, IN MILLIGRAMS (MG), OF SEVERAL POPULAR BEVERAGES. Is your favorite pick-me-up listed here?

photos: (coffee): ©John A. Rizzo/Stockbyte/Getty Images RF; (espresso): ©Foodcollection RF; (cola): ©Foodcollection RF; (tea): ©Pixtal/SuperStock RF

 How does it affect your performance and awareness?

Caffeine in 8 oz of beverage (mg)

	mg	Beverage
	115–175	Drip coffee
	100	Espresso coffee*
	60	Brewed black tea
	53	Red Bull
	36.7	Mountain Dew
	25	Pepsi Cola
	22.7	Coca-Cola
	15	Green tea
	3	Decaf coffee, brewed

A single espresso is about 2 ounces rather than 8 ounces

If regular caffeine users stop consuming caffeine, they can experience withdrawal symptoms, the most common of which is headache. Giving up caffeine can also lead to fatigue and decreased energy, depressed mood, and difficulty concentrating (Juliano & Griffiths, 2004). These withdrawal effects show that caffeine creates physical dependence. To eliminate these negative withdrawal effects, people who want to stop using caffeine should gradually reduce their consumption over time.

Nicotine The active drug in tobacco, nicotine, is a powerful stimulant. Tobacco is used throughout the world. As of 2015, approximately 15% of American adults smoked cigarettes regularly (over 36.5 million people), which is lower than the figure from 5 years prior (CDC, 2016).

Smoking tobacco puts nicotine into the bloodstream almost immediately; within 8 seconds of inhalation, it reaches the brain. As a stimulant, nicotine increases heart rate and rate of respiration, and it creates a feeling of arousal. Over time, the cardiovascular arousal associated with nicotine use increases the risk of high blood pressure and heart disease. Ironically, many nicotine users report that cigarettes calm them down. This perception may stem from the fact that nicotine relaxes the skeletal muscles even as it arouses the autonomic nervous system.

Nicotine is extremely addictive. It creates high tolerance, physical dependence, and unpleasant withdrawal symptoms, such as headaches, fatigue, irritability, anxiety, and insomnia (Przulj, McRobbie, & Hajek, 2016). The high that heroin creates is more intense than the feeling of arousal from cigarettes, and the disruption to daily life of the heroin addict is more extreme than that of the smoker, but in terms of how difficult it is to quit, nicotine ranks higher than heroin (Keenan et al., 1994).

There are many known health risks in smoking. Cigarette smoking reduces life expectancy on average by 10 years, increases the risk for lung cancer more than 10-fold, and triples the risk of death from heart disease in both men and women (CDC, 2001; Doll et al., 2004). The U.S. surgeon general has reported that smoking is also conclusively linked to leukemia, cataracts, pneumonia, and cancers of the cervix, kidney, pancreas, and stomach.

Tobacco smoke contains many cancer-causing agents that trigger severe damage to DNA and can inhibit DNA repair in lung cells. Tobacco smoke also contains carbon monoxide, a toxic substance that displaces oxygen in the bloodstream, depriving tissues of needed oxygen. This is one reason smokers often feel out of breath (CDC, 2001; Doll et al., 2004; Feng et al., 2006; Health and Human Services, 2004). Carbon monoxide from smoking also makes people look older than they are, because it reduces the blood supply to skin tissue. Tobacco smoking increases skin wrinkles even in young smokers (Koh et al., 2002).

Cocaine For centuries, South American Indians have chewed the coca leaf for its stimulant and digestion-aiding properties (Weil & Rosen, 1998). The most notable component in the coca plant is cocaine, a psychoactive substance that when isolated from the coca leaf is a much stronger stimulant than chewed coca. When snorted, cocaine increases heart rate and produces a short-lived but intense rush of euphoria. It can also lead to a sense of invulnerability and power. Physiologically, cocaine induces a sense of exhilaration by increasing the availability of the neurotransmitters dopamine and serotonin in synapses (Mateo et al., 2004).

The brevity of the cocaine high helps explain why people abuse it—they keep chasing after a short-lived euphoria with even more cocaine. Some people inject (free-base) cocaine or smoke crack cocaine, a form of cocaine that is sold on the streets in pellets. Along with being extremely addictive, cocaine

Connection

Principles of conditioning interact with the drug effects of nicotine to support the habit of smoking.

See "Why Do People Smoke" in the chapter "Learning." (p. 327)

can cause other health problems, including increased heart rate and irregular heartbeat, increased risk of heart attack, and, occasionally, death (Weil & Rosen, 1998).

Amphetamines Amphetamines are synthetically produced compounds that produce long-lasting excitation of the sympathetic nervous system, the part of the nervous system that keeps us ready for action. There are three main forms, all of which are pills: methamphetamin, dextroamphetamine (Dexedrine), and amphetamine sulfate (Benzedrine, or "speed"). Methamphetamine is highly addictive. The street drug called crystal meth is a crystallized form of methamphetamine that is smoked, though people who abuse amphetamines get them from health care providers. Adderall (which is a combination of methamphetamine and dextroampthetamine) is widely prescribe for attention deficit hyperactivity disorder (ADHD). This ready availability may play a role in the widespread abuse of Adderall on college campuses in the United States (Taylor, 2015; Watson, Arcona, & Antonuccio, 2015).

Amphetamines raise heart rate, increase motivation, and elevate mood. The effects vary with the dosage and manner of use, but other short-term effects may include insomnia, stomach distress, headaches, decreased libido, and difficulty concentrating. Long-term use can lead to severe depression, paranoia, loss of control over one's behavior, and in some cases amphetamine psychosis, a condition marked by hallucinations. Withdrawal from chronic amphetamine use creates unpleasant symptoms, such as fatigue, anxiety and depression, hunger, overeating, and disordered thought and behavior.

MDMA The psychoactive drug MDMA (3,4-methylenedioxymethamphetamine), also known as Molly or Ecstasy (the name varies depending on the supposed purity of the drug), acts as both a stimulant and a mild hallucinogen. MDMA produces mild sensory hallucinations as well as physiological arousal. It is sometimes called "the love drug," because it produces feelings of euphoria, warmth, and connectedness with others. Among friends, it dissolves interpersonal barriers and produces feelings of affection and a desire to touch and hug. MDMA improves the recognition of emotion expressions in others, enhances empathic connection, and increases the willingness to help others (Hysek et al., 2013). The drug promotes affiliation in nonhuman primates as well. For example, macaques injected with MDMA show more grooming and object play than controls and these effects increase with higher doses of the drug (Ballesta, Reymond, Pozzobon, & Duhame, 2016).

The social and emotional effects of MDMA may be why this drug has become popular in dance clubs and at live music concerts, but the greater accessibility of emotions is also a reason why MDMA has received attention for its therapeutic applications. MDMA can be helpful in the treatment of post-traumatic stress disorder (PTSD), in the context of psychotherapy, largely because it makes emotions more accessible (Oehen et al., 2013; Sessa, 2016). PTSD (as we will discuss in the chapter "Psychological Disorders") is triggered by a horrifying life event (e.g., experiencing war, witnessing the murder of a loved one, surviving a horrific natural disaster), and those who suffer from it experience anxiety and flashbacks, and they have lost access to their original experience around the trauma, which impedes the treatment of the condition.

The dangers of MDMA include increased risk of depression with repeated use, slower processing times on cognitive tasks, and greater impulsivity (Halpern et al., 2004). Long-term effects include persistent mental deficits, low mood, and serotonin deficiencies in certain areas of the brain (Parrott, 2013). Probably the biggest risk associated with MDMA use is the risk of it being mixed with other

Connection

Our moods are tightly linked to transmitter systems in the brain. Dopamine is released when we feel good, and serotonin affects how sociable and affectionate we feel.

See "Common Neurotransmitters," in the chapter "The Biology of Behavior." (p. 90)

substances that are even more dangerous. Often suppliers cut it with additives, such as amphetamines, cough medicines, and bath salts (synthetic substances called *cathinones*, which can mimic the effects of stimulants), all of which can be very harmful or even fatal in combination or in amounts that the user is unaware of ingesting.

Hallucinogens

hallucinogens
Substances that create distorted perceptions of reality ranging from mild to extreme.

The third major class of psychoactive drugs is the hallucinogens. As the name implies, **hallucinogens** create distorted perceptions of reality, ranging from mild to extreme. Sometimes they also alter thought and mood. There are numerous hallucinogens, but we will discuss only marijuana, LSD, and psilocybin.

Marijuana   Marijuana comes from the blossoms and leaves of the *Cannabis sativa* plant. For centuries, people have used the hemp fibers for clothing and other practical goods. They use the blossoms to alter consciousness and for medicinal properties. The active ingredient in cannabis is tetrahydrocannibinol (THC), a plant cannabinoid, which affects the brain and body when people eat or smoke it. Marijuana alters mood to create euphoria and changes perception, especially one's perception of time and food. It makes time appear to slow down and makes food more desirable (Crystal, Maxwell, & Hohmann, 2003; Nicoll & Alger, 2004). In fact, medical marijuana appears to be helpful in treating a variety of gastrointestinal disorders (Isfort & Gerich, 2016).

Marijuana is classified as a hallucinogen, although people rarely experience hallucinations when using low or moderate doses. Such experiences occur more readily when people eat it. It takes longer for the effects to be felt when ingested (whereas the drug reaches the brain in seconds when smoked), so people are more likely to consume larger amounts unintentionally.

Marijuana does not lead to withdrawal symptoms the way nicotine and heroin do. In the course of long-term habitual use, however, people develop cravings for marijuana when they are without it, and these cravings have a

©Rod Rolle/Getty Images

In light of marijuana's known effectiveness in treating certain medical conditions, 25 U.S. states, plus the District of Columbia (as of late 2016) have legalized marijuana use for medical purposes. Seven states and the District of Columbia have legalized recreational use of marijuana: Alaska, California, Colorado, Massachusetts, Nevada, Oregon, and Washington.

physiological basis (Wölfling, Flor, & Grüsser, 2008). People can become dependent on marijuana or use it compulsively. In a word, marijuana use can become a habit.

Many researchers have argued that regular marijuana smoking increases the risk for lung cancer, as marijuana smoke contains many of the same cancer-causing agents as cigarette smoke (Tashkin et al., 2002). One large-scale study, however, found no increased risk for lung cancer among heavy marijuana smokers compared to nonsmokers (Tashkin, 2006). A study in New Zealand, for example, showed a moderate increase in lung cancer in heavy pot smokers under the age of 55 (Aldington et al., 2008). The results for marijuana smoking causing lung cancer and other types of cancers is inconsistent across studies, in spite of the evidence that marijuana smoke contains carcinogens (Huang et al., 2015). Heavy marijuana smoking increases the likelihood of a variety of respiratory illnesses, can cause immune system impairment, and appears to lead to memory problems (Kanayama et al., 2004; Tashkin et al., 2002).

Regular marijuana use is common in adolescents who later develop schizophrenia, which has led some people to suggest a link between marijuana use and schizophrenia in people who might be genetically predisposed to this disorder (Arseneault et al., 2004). There is evidence of rapid increases in pot use in the few years before the schizophrenia onset in teens with the disorder (Kelley et al., 2016). Daily marijuana use, however, has little to no effect on brain structure or volume in either teens or adults, despite claims to the contrary (Weiland et al., 2015). And yet, heavy marijuana use (that is, daily) in teens is associated with deficiencies in attention, learning, memory, motivation, processing speed, and even overall IQ (although the last effect can be reversed with abstinence) (Jacobous et al., 2010; Squeglia & Gray, 2016; Trezza et al., 2008; Winward et al., 2014).

Contrary to U.S. government reports that marijuana has no medical value, marijuana and the **endocannabinoids**, a class of marijuana-like chemicals produced by our own bodies, offer promise for the medical treatment of various physical and even some psychological disorders ("Marijuana Research," 2004; Nicoll & Alger, 2004). Marijuana is known for its effective prevention and treatment of nausea: It has been recommended and prescribed for people who suffer chemotherapy-related nausea or the involuntary weight loss due to cancer and other chronic conditions (Birdsall, Birdsall, & Tims, 2016). Research shows that marijuana may help people eat not by increasing appetite but by making food appear more appealing (Nicoll & Alger, 2004). Additionally, marijuana and its derivatives may be helpful for the treatment of pain. Marijuana-activated receptors in brain areas modulate pain and may work more safely and more effectively than opioids (Hohmann et al., 2005). Cannabinoids such as marijuana and medical cannabis preparations reduce the symptoms of neuropathic pain, one of the most common types of chronic pain, and they show promise in the treatment of migraine headaches (Rahn & Hohmann, 2009). There is also evidence that THC and other cannabinoids may be helpful in the treatment of Alzheimer's disease (Currais et al., 2016) and cancer (Ware, 2016).

As of 2016, 25 U.S. states, plus the District of Columbia, had legalized marijuana for medical use. Recreational marijuana use is fully legal in four states (Alaska, Colorado, Oregon, Washington) and the District of Columbia. Nationally the tide is turning toward more widespread accessibility of this popular drug, which will allow for more research into the pros and cons of using it. A recent survey in an eminent medical journal show that about 10% of marijuana users nationally use it for medical reasons, up to 21% of whom currently reside in states where it was not legal for medical use at the time of the survey (Compton et al., 2016). This second figure suggests that doctors are prescribing marijuana outside states where it is legal.

endocannabinoids
Natural, marijuana-like substances produced by the body.

LSD   LSD (lysergic acid diethylamide-25), or "acid," is a synthesized form of lysergic acid, which is derived from the grain fungus ergot. People notice dramatic changes in conscious experience when they ingest LSD. These experiences include altered visual perceptions (such as seeing the tracks that your hand makes when you move it through the air or seeing the lines dance about on a page), enhanced color perception, hallucinations, and synesthesia, which is when we "see" sounds or "hear" visual images (see the chapter "Sensing and Perceiving Our World"). Neurochemically, LSD appears to work by increasing the levels of the neurotransmitters dopamine and serotonin. Serotonin activity in turn increases the excitatory neurotransmitter glutamate, which may play a role in creating hallucinations (Marek & Aghajanian, 1996; Scruggs, Schmidt, & Deutch, 2003). Still, we do not know exactly how drugs like LSD create hallucinations. Neuroimaging research suggests that when in the psychedelic state, the brain's background intrinsic activity levels have a more profound influence on the processing of visual information than when one is in the resting, drug-free state, creating unusual visual images (Carhart-Harris et al., 2016).

The known side effects of LSD include increased body temperature, increased blood pressure, insomnia, and psychosis-like symptoms in some people. Because it can temporarily separate a person from reality, for some people LSD use can lead to panic and negative experiences, known as bad trips. For other people, it can have the opposite effect and lead to very profound, life-altering experiences (Strassman, 1984; Weil & Rosen, 1998).

Psilocybin   Psilocybin is the active ingredient of hallucinogenic mushrooms. Experimental studies on the use of psilocybin show that the "trips" can lead to profound spiritual experiences, even in studies where people were "blind" to what they were taking (Griffiths et al., 2006). What is more, the spiritual insights they experienced seemed to be fairly stable, as they endured 14 months following the drug exposure (Griffiths et al., 2008), and mood improvements endured for a similar amount of time (Griffiths et al., 2011). Mood changes from psilocybin seem to be dependent on synapses using serotonin, a neurotransmitter associated with positive moods (Kometer et al., 2012). Psilocybin-related spiritual changes seem to be consistent with changes in personality occasioned by psilocybin experience. Controlled studies of the effects of a single, controlled dose of psilocybin in people who have had no experience with the drug show that the psychedelic experience is so profound that it can change personality, making people score significantly higher on the basic personality dimension of "openness to experience" from before taking high doses of the drug in just one session (MacLean, Johnson, & Griffiths, 2011). Marijuana, psilocybin, and LSD all appear to help relieve headache pain—in particular, cluster headaches, a type of migraine (McGenney, 2012; Schindler et al., 2015).

Quick Quiz 6: Altering Consciousness with Drugs

1. Even though it can make people feel more aroused in social settings, this popular drug is a depressant.
   a. alcohol
   b. heroin
   c. cocaine
   d. marijuana

2. This stimulant can be as addictive as heroin.
   a. caffeine
   b. ecstasy
   c. nicotine
   d. morphine

Answers can be found at the end of the chapter.

Bringing It All Together

Making Connections in Consciousness

Brain Injury Revisited

Remember David? Today, nearly two decades after his brain injury, David functions pretty well. His most profound deficits are problems with consciousness that affect attention, memory, and learning. By revisiting David's situation and the effects of brain injury on consciousness in general, we can integrate many of the topics addressed in this chapter.

David moved through various stages of conscious awareness in his first year of recovery. He went from comatose to vegetative to responsive in 5 months, but even when he was responding to the outside world, he was minimally conscious. In some cases of brain injury, this is a transitional state to full consciousness; sometimes it is a permanent state. Fortunately, in David's case, minimal consciousness eventually led to full consciousness. His brain gradually became more and more responsive. How does this happen? We do not know for sure. What we do know is that people with damage to lower brain regions that control basic functions, such as sleep–wake cycles, are less likely to regain consciousness than are people with damage to the cerebral cortex (Laureys, 2007). David had cortical damage.

David's consciousness bears permanent scars from his injury. When he is working on a task, David can suddenly become distracted and forget what he is doing. We all experience this kind of distraction from time to time, but for David it can be disabling. He might be emptying the dishwasher and overhear someone saying something about baseball. Hearing the word *baseball*, David might look up and—as a fanatic about baseball statistics—suddenly have some thought about the sport. He will then ask Greg if he knew, say, that Joe DiMaggio had a lifetime fielding percentage of 0.978. Then he'll head to his room to send an email to his other brother about the same topic. By the time he's finished sending the email, David has forgotten all about emptying the dishwasher.

Such distractibility may be due to problems with selective attention. Indeed, David has a hard time staying on task and filtering out or setting aside information to deal with at a later time. As soon as he heard *baseball,* David thought of Joe DiMaggio and simply had to talk about him. He couldn't set the topic aside briefly. As a result, he lost the ability to continue unloading the dishwasher. People with brain damage, especially to the frontal lobes, have trouble blocking out extraneous information and using selective attention to stay on task (Ries & Marks, 2005). Some studies show that such individuals perform poorly on the Stroop test, possibly because it takes them longer to process information overall (Mathias & Wheaton, 2007). For David, a related problem is an inability to concentrate on one thing for any extended period of time; he shows deficits in sustained attention. Research confirms that, in general, people with traumatic brain injury have deficits in sustained attention (Malkinson & Bartolomeo, 2016; Mathias & Wheaton, 2007).

Sleeping and dreaming may also change with brain injury. How people sleep while comatose or vegetative may be an important predictor of recovery. People in coma who show more organized EEG patterns during sleep have less disability later and a greater likelihood of survival than those whose brain patterns are less organized while sleeping (Valente et al., 2002). After they have regained consciousness, sleep and wakefulness may be disrupted. David's sleep is not normal. He suffers from hypersomnia, or excessive sleeping. Sometimes he sleeps 14 hours a day; other times he has trouble sleeping at night and naps frequently throughout the day. Insomnia and chronic fatigue are also common in people with traumatic brain injury (Ouellet, Beaulieu-Bonneau, & Morin, 2006; Ouellet & Morin, 2006).

Brain injury can also lead to disruptions in dreaming, probably as a consequence of disordered sleep, though this doesn't seem to be a problem for David. It may depend on the location of the brain injury. Some people who sleep normally following traumatic brain injury nevertheless have problems with dreaming, indicating that different areas of the brain may be responsible for sleeping and dreaming. People with damage to the areas of cortex involved in the integration of sensory information and the limbic system and areas around it or the links between these areas show the greatest dreaming deficits and, in some cases, a total absence of dreaming (Domhoff, 2001; Solms, 2000). Although not dreaming might seem insignificant, many people who experience a total lack of dreaming due to brain injury also lack "initiative, curiosity, and fantasy" in waking life (Domhoff, 2001, p. 16).

Finally, drug use and abuse can occur in people who are coping with the challenges of a brain injury. It is most common among those who experience depression and anxiety (Anson & Ponsford, 2006).

Chapter Review

WHAT IS CONSCIOUSNESS?

- Consciousness is an awareness of one's surroundings and of what's in one's mind at a given moment. It is also the limited portion of the mind of which we are aware at any given moment, sometimes called a global workspace.

©Chris Tobin/Getty Images RF

TWO DIMENSIONS OF CONSCIOUSNESS: WAKEFULNESS AND AWARENESS

- Consciousness has two aspects: the degree to which we are awake and the degree to which we are aware.

- Three levels of consciousness stem from these two dimensions. First, *minimal consciousness* refers to states when people are barely awake or aware, such as coma and vegetative states. Second, moderate consciousness includes phenomena such as being preconscious, having words on the tip of the tongue, and sleeping and dreaming. Third, full consciousness is a high degree of wakefulness and awareness and ranges from normal waking states to states of flow and mindfulness.

ATTENTION: FOCUSING CONSCIOUSNESS

- Attention is focused awareness.

- Selective attention is the process by which we filter out unwanted stimuli while focusing on other stimuli. It can result in inattentional blindness, the failure to notice the unexpected. Sustained attention is the ability to stay focused on one thing.

TRAINING CONSCIOUSNESS: MEDITATION

- Meditation is a form of mental training that can be used to calm the mind, stabilize concentration, or enhance awareness of the present moment.

- Evidence from brain imaging studies suggests that meditation has lasting effects on mood, concentration, and learning.

SLEEPING AND DREAMING

- Four stages of sleep are characterized by different EEG patterns. We move through Stages 1–3 roughly once every 90 minutes during the night. Rapid eye movement (REM) sleep occurs only during Stage 1 sleep, when most dreaming occurs. Most sleep consists of non-REM sleep.

- Sleep is important for three major restorative processes: neural growth, memory consolidation, and the formation of enzymes that protect against cellular damage.

- Sleep disorders affect nearly 20% of the U.S. population. Insomnia, sleepwalking, narcolepsy, and hypersomnia are the most common sleep disorders.

- Dreams consist of images, thoughts, and feelings that we experience while we sleep. Freud maintained that dreams are attempts to fulfill unconscious wishes. A biological theory of dreams, AIM, argues that dreaming is the result of moderate levels of brain activation and internal focus, coupled with looseness of thought. The cognitive view argues that dreams do not differ greatly from normal waking forms of thinking, as seen most clearly in lucid dreaming.

HYPNOSIS

- Hypnosis is a state of mind that occurs naturally and is established by compliance with instructions. It is characterized by focused attention, suggestibility, absorption, lack of voluntary control over behavior, and suspension of critical faculties of mind.

- Research not only shows that hypnosis has a real physiological and neurological basis but also points to ways that hypnosis may serve as a model for understanding attention.

ALTERING CONSCIOUSNESS WITH DRUGS

- A psychoactive drug is a naturally occurring or synthesized substance that produces qualitative changes in conscious experience. The three major categories of psychoactive drugs are depressants, stimulants, and hallucinogens.

- Depressants decrease central nervous system activity. Alcohol, sedatives, and opioids are all depressants. Typically, people develop tolerance for these drugs quickly, withdrawal is unpleasant, and the risk of overdose is high.

- Stimulants increase central nervous system activity.

- The most commonly used stimulants are caffeine and nicotine. Cocaine, amphetamines, and ecstasy all have stronger stimulant properties than caffeine and nicotine and carry a high risk of abuse and physical and psychological problems.

- Hallucinogens create altered sensations and perceptions. The two most widely known examples are marijuana and LSD. Heavy marijuana smoking increases the risk of respiratory ailments, impairs immune system functioning, and can lead to memory problems. Marijuana mimics the effects of endocannabinoids, pain-relieving substances produced in the body.

BRINGING IT ALL TOGETHER: MAKING CONNECTIONS IN CONSCIOUSNESS

- Brain injury can affect many different aspects of consciousness, depending on the location and extent of the damage.

- As happened to David, brain damage interferes with selective attention, creating difficulties with staying on task, as well as with sleep and dreaming.

Key Terms

addiction
AIM
alpha waves
attention
awareness
beta waves
circadian rhythms
coma
consciousness
delta waves
depressants
disorders of consciousness
dreams
endocannabinoids

hallucinations
hallucinogens
hypersomnia
hypnosis
insomnia
latent level
manifest level
meditation
mindfulness
narcolepsy
night terrors
non-REM
psychoactive drugs
rapid eye movements (REM)

reticular activating system
selective attention
sleep apnea
sleepwalking
stimulants
Stroop effect
sustained attention
theta waves
tolerance
vegetative state
wakefulness
withdrawal symptoms

Quick Quiz Answers

Quiz 1: 1. d; **2.** c   **Quick Quiz 2: 1.** a; **2.** b   **Quick Quiz 3: 1.** d; **2.** a   **Quick Quiz 4: 1.** a; **2.** d; **3.** b; **4.** c
Quick Quiz 5: 1. a; **2.** d   **Quick Quiz 6: 1.** a; **2.** c

7 Memory

Chapter Outline

Challenge Your Assumptions

True or False?

- Memory of traumatic events cannot be inherited from a previous generation. (see page 264)

- We can know things we don't remember. (see page 274)

- No one can remember every single day of his or her adult life. (see page 275)

- Higher doses of stimulants are better at enhancing memories than lower doses. (see page 279)

- Mild electrical stimulation to the brain can improve your memory. (see page 282)

- When victims of a crime get a good look at perpetrators of crimes, odds are quite good they could accurately pick them out of a photo lineup. (see page 286)

©Robert Daly/Getty Images

257

When he was 7 years old, Henry Molaison—better known to scientists as H. M.—was hit by a bicyclist (Corkin, 1984). He suffered a brain injury, which resulted in severe epileptic seizures. To stop these seizures, doctors removed the hippocampus on both sides of H. M.'s brain, as well as the adjoining brain structures. The seizures stopped, but at quite a cost: H. M. lost the ability to form new memories. He lived forever in the present.

©Dan Tuffs/Getty Images

Jill Price

Evan was switching back and forth between Instagram, Facebook, and his Spanish homework for which he had an quiz the next day. He was "studying" for 4 or 5 hours, more than enough time, he thought, to master the Spanish material and do well on the quiz. To no one's surprise except his own, he got a C– on the quiz.

Kim Peek had a tested IQ of 65 and yet everything he read he could remember years later. He could tell you every zip code and area code in the country, any birthdate of any president. He had nearly perfect recall of any facts he had ever learned. Yet, he could not dress himself as an adult.

As a college student in the 1980s, Jennifer Thompson was sexually assaulted in the middle of the night at her apartment (Thompson-Cannino, Cotton, & Torneo, 2009). She was determined, if she survived, to identify the rapist and was very careful to study his face, height, mannerisms, etc. Eleven days later she helped police make a composite sketch and a few days after that Ronald Cotton was arrested for the rape. Mostly based on this eye-witness account, Cotton was convicted and spent 11 years in prison before DNA evidence exonerated him and confirmed what he claimed all along. He was not the rapist.

Jill Price can remember something about every single day of her life extending back to at least childhood (Price, 2008). Her ability to remember extends back to 18 months of age, when she remembers being in her crib (Parker, Cahill, & McGaugh, 2006). So if you name any day since 1980, she will have a memory for that day, but the truly remarkable thing is that her memories are instantaneous—she doesn't have to work to recall them. "*November 14, 1981,* a Saturday: My dad's forty-fifth birthday. That night a school group I was joining, the Rasonians, was initiating new members and taking us out in Westwood. *July 18, 1984,* a Wednesday: A quiet summer day. I picked up the book *Helter Skelter* and read it for the second time" (Price, 2008, p. 10). What is equally fascinating about Jill is that her IQ is only average and she is somewhat below average in memorizing lists of words or numbers.

In each of these vignettes, we see an important principle of memory at work. With Henry it is how certain parts of our brain, in particular, the hippocampus are vitally important for forming new long-term memories. With Evan it is how not properly attending to and taking in information interferes with our ability to recall and learn it. With Jennifer it is how absolute certainty in our memory is no guarantee that the memory is accurate. Finally, with Jill it is how remarkable and unlearned some memory ability can be and also that different types of memory exist.

These cases and the countless more systematic studies on memory have a powerful story to tell psychological scientists about the nature of memory. There are at least five "chapters" to the story of memory:

1. There are multiple stages in how memories are formed and many different psychological processes aid or impede memory formation.

2. There are different types of memory that last for different amounts of time, some of which are conscious and others unconscious.

3. Different memory systems involve different areas of the brain and long-term but not short-term memory involves the growth of new neural structures.

4. Memory is a reconstructive act that changes over time and is inherently filled with distortion and bias.

5. Forgetting and memory loss is a part of the memory process and comes about for different reasons.

FORMING MEMORIES

Without memories our entire sense of self, our personalities, and relationships would not be possible. Memories are essential to every aspect of our life. The questions therefore become: what is memory, how do memories form, and are there different kinds of memory? This chapter answers each of these questions.

First, **memory,** in its most general form, is our ability to take in, solidify, store, and then use information. In this section we delve into the process by which memories form. To be clear, memory does not need to be, and often is not, conscious and something we can put into words, which we discuss in more detail in the next section on "Types of Memory". To foreshadow the main message of these two sections: Memory is not one process nor is it only one kind.

memory
The ability to take in, solidify, store and use information; also the store of what has been learned and remembered.

Four Steps in Forming Memories

We define memory as taking in (encoding), solidifying (consolidating), keeping (storing), and then using (retrieving) information. In other words, there are four steps in how we form memories. Let us look at each step a bit more closely.

Encoding: Taking In Information   The first step in forming memories involves taking in, or encoding, our sensory experiences. **Encoding** is the means by which we attend to, take in, and process new information. We take in information from our five senses—what we see, hear, taste, feel, and smell. This phase is absolutely crucial for memory formation because much of our "faulty memory" happens because we don't take it in well. Our mind pays attention to some sensory experiences and ignores others. Attention drives the encoding process. If we fail to pay attention or try to multitask, an experience is not going to be processed deeply enough to be stored for a long period.

encoding
The process by which the brain attends to, takes in, and integrates new information; the first stage of long-term memory formation.

automatic processing
Encoding of information that occurs with little effort or conscious attention to the task.

Psychologists describe two kinds of encoding processes: one that happens with little effort and one that takes significant effort (Hasher & Zacks, 1979). **Automatic processing** happens with little effort or conscious attention to the task. Because these experiences are automatic, our recall of them does not improve much with practice. Furthermore, they are often not processed as deeply and are less likely to be recalled later. For instance, you most likely encoded what you ate for breakfast this morning without trying, but by this evening you may have trouble recalling what you ate hours earlier. Episodic memory involves this kind of automatic processing.

Now think about what you learn in college. You read the text, attend lectures, take notes, and study those notes, usually multiple times. Before an exam, you then go over these materials again and again. Needless to say, this kind of learning takes work. **Effortful processing** occurs when we carefully attend to and put conscious effort into remembering information. Effortful processing is the basis of semantic memory, and it usually involves rehearsal of the information, so that it goes from short-term to long-term memory. Interestingly, advancing age tends to lessen recall for events and experiences that require effortful processing, but not for those that involve automatic processing (Hasher & Zacks, 1979).

effortful processing
Encoding of information that occurs with careful attention and conscious effort.

A common way to encode information deeply is to use mnemonic (pronounced neh'-mon-ik) devices. A **mnemonic device** is a scheme that helps people remember information. Rhyming, chunking, and rehearsal are types of mnemonic devices. Others include imagery and acronyms. Imagery can be used to remember a set of words or a list of objects in a set order. Simply form a mental image of each word or object in a specific place along a route you know very well, such as from your home to your school. Rehearse this a few times. Then when you need to recall the word or object list, take a mental stroll along the familiar path and the visual images of the list should be relatively easy to recall (Thompson & Madigan, 2005).

mnemonic device
A method devised to help us remember information, such as a rhyme or an acronym.

Acronyms are a type of mnemonic device. We usually create acronyms by combining the first letters of each word or object we need to remember. Acronyms work best when they form a word we can pronounce or some other meaningful unit. For example, the acronym RADAR is easier to remember than "**R**adio **D**etection **a**nd **R**anging" and "ROY G. BIV" is easier to remember the colors of the rainbow than "red, orange, yellow, green, blue, indigo, and violet."

You might have your own favorite mnemonic devices to help you encode material that you need to know for an exam. If you have never tried this approach to studying, you might be surprised at how much it improves memory.

Consolidation: Solidifying Information The second stage of memory formation is **consolidation,** the process of establishing, stabilizing, or solidifying a memory (Kandel, 2006; McGaugh, 2000; Moscovitch, 2010). A consolidated memory is resistant to distraction, interference, and decay (Dubai, 2004). As we'll discuss in some detail shortly, new proteins are manufactured in the brain during long-term memory formation, and consolidation provides time for these proteins to develop. Once the proteins needed for consolidation have formed, a memory is beyond the effects of interference and decay.

consolidation
The process of establishing, stabilizing, or solidifying a memory; the second stage of long-term memory formation.

Sleep plays an important role in memory consolidation. Psychologists have long known that we recall information better after we "sleep on it" than after the same amount of time if we stay awake. Recent findings indicate that not only does sleep stabilize the memory but it also enhances memory and makes it stronger (Walker & Stickgold, 2006; Wamsley, Tucker, Payne, Benavides, & Stickgold, 2010). Moreover, sleep deprivation has been shown to have a detrimental effect on memory (Stickgold, 2005). We can conclude, then, that cramming all night before an exam is not the best study strategy. (We'll consider better alternatives in the "Bringing It All Together" section at the end of this chapter.) Research shows that learning over long periods of time and evenly spaced sessions leads to better recall (Kornell & Bjork, 2007; Kornell et al., 2010).

Storage: Keeping Information The third step in memory formation happens once memories have been encoded and consolidated, and they are ready to be stored. Storing a memory is akin to putting something—say, a birthday gift purchased months ahead of time—away in a special place where you can find it later. **Storage,** the retention of memory over time, is the third stage of memory formation. We organize and store memories in at least three ways: in hierarchies, schemas, and networks.

We use **hierarchies** to organize related information from the most specific feature they have in common to the most general. An example is the hierarchy human (specific), hominid (less specific), primate, mammal, and animal (general). Each step moves to a more general category in the hierarchy.

Schemas are mental frameworks that develop from our experiences with particular objects or events. They act as a filter through which we encode and organize information about our world. Once formed, schemas tell us how people, objects, and events are most likely to look or act. Because schemas help us organize and understand experiences, they can also aid memory and recall. For instance, if your favorite childhood pet was a Chihuahua, your schema of Chihuahuas would be a very positive one that predisposes you to expect other Chihuahuas to act as friendly and fun-loving as yours did. Because you had so many happy experiences with your Chihuahua as a child, when you see one now you are able to most easily remember the enjoyable experiences you had with your own pet. Likewise, you are less likely to remember the negative and aggressive experiences you may have had with your dog, because they do not fit your schema of the happy Chihuahua. For better and for worse, schemas bias our memory and perception.

Hierarchies and concepts bring order and organization to our perceptions and experiences. The psychological process that binds concepts together is *association*. Associations are linked together in networks by their degree of closeness or relatedness (Hopfield, 1982). An **associative network** is a chain of associations between related concepts. Each concept or association in a network is referred to as a *node*. The links between the nodes are associations. When people think of a concept, and its node is activated, they are primed and more likely to make an association to a nearby concept or node (Collins & Loftus, 1975). Figure 1 illustrates an associative network for the concept of fire engine. "Fire engine" activates both vehicle and color networks of association, and it may well activate others not shown here (such as emergency).

Neural networks also use associations to explain how memory works. Unlike associative networks, *neural networks* are computer models that imitate the way neurons talk to each other (Chappell & Humphreys, 1994). Neural networks have nodes, too, but their nodes are not single concepts, such as colors or vehicles. Rather, these nodes are information-processing units. Neural networks are analogous to the nervous system, where the nodes in a network are single cells (neurons) that can process information. The more the nodes in a neural network communicate with each other, the stronger the link between

storage
The retention of memory over time; the third stage of long-term memory formation.

hierarchies
Ways of organizing related pieces of information from the most specific feature they have in common to the most general.

schemas
Mental frameworks that develop from our experiences with particular people, objects, or events.

associative network
A chain of associations between related concepts.

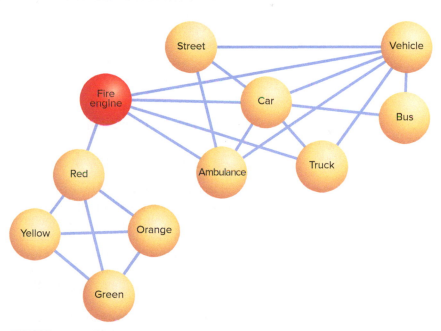

FIGURE 1

AN ASSOCIATIVE NETWORK. Associative networks are chains of association between related concepts or nodes that get activated. The closer concepts are to each other, the more directly related they are and the more likely they are to activate the other node. The network for "fire engine" is a rich associative network of related concepts (Collins & Loftus, 1975).

nodes. As we will discuss later in this chapter and in the next, repeated connection between neurons leads to stronger connections, as well as stronger memories and learning (Hebb, 1949).

Well-known models of memory storage that integrate associative and neural networks are parallel distributed processing. *Parallel distributed processing (PDP)* models propose that associations involve the simultaneous activity of many nodes (McClelland, 1988; McClelland & Rogers, 2003; McClelland & Rumelhart, 1985). Many nodes can fire at the same time, spreading or distributing activation to other nodes in the network. This spread of activation can serve a priming function, making certain memories more likely than others to be stored. Recent work in neuroscience reveals that such PDP models may do a good job of explaining how neurons and genes work together to store new long-term memories (Mendelsohn, Furman, & Dudai, 2010; Miyashita et al., 2008).

Retrieval: Getting and Using Information   After memories are encoded, consolidated, and stored, they ultimately need to be used and retrieved. **Retrieval** is the recovery and use of information stored in memory. It's remembering where you put that birthday gift you bought early—or that you even bought one—when it comes time to present it to your friend. The ease of retrieval and the time frame over which we can recall a particular event or piece of knowledge is determined by the previous stages of memory. How did we encode it? Did we consolidate it? Did we store it where we can access it? Additionally, whenever we retrieve a memory, we need to focus our attention on remembering, which requires working memory. Retrieval, attention, and working memory are related activities.

Some memories require conscious effort for retrieval. An example is the date of a friend's birthday—factual information that is encoded and stored for later recall. But factual information is not always properly encoded and stored, and we cannot always retrieve it at will. A common retrieval problem is the inability to remember the name of a person only minutes after meeting her, even if we repeated her name immediately after hearing it. What most likely happens in this situation is that we fail to pay enough attention to the person's name when we first hear it and focus instead on the whole social interaction. Consequently, we do not encode, consolidate, and store the name very deeply. When we try to retrieve it, we cannot. We'll explore retrieval problems in more detail when we talk about forgetting, and later the "Bringing It All Together" section outlines some strategies for improving retrieval.

Aids to Memory Formation

Many things help us to take in or encode our sensory experience. Among the more important ones are paying attention, processing the information deeply, sleeping on it, and feeling strong emotion around the experience.

Attention is absolutely essential in the first step in forming memories. Not attending to, paying partial attention, or being distracted while we are experiencing something means it stands little chance of being taken in and encoded (see "Impediments to Memory Formation," next section).

Attention   As we saw in the opening part of the chapter with Evan, not paying attention to information when first exposed to it almost guarantees that it will not get encoded and processed well and therefore stands almost no chance of being remembered well. As we elaborate in the next section of this chapter, attention is the first step in moving from the earliest and most temporary sensory experiences (hearing, smelling, seeing, tasting, or touching something) and getting it in our minds to be processed, stored, and then recalled (Bollinger et al., 2010; Griffin & Nobre, 2003; Ravizza, Uitvlugt, & Hazeltine, 2016; Santangelo & Macaluso, 2013). Recall from the section on "Encoding" that many strategies can be used to attend to information such as effortful processing, using mnemonic devices and acronyms that aid memory formation.

Depth of Processing   Processing information deeply rather than superficially is one of the best ways to recall it. This means encoding it deeply. The connection between encoding and remembering is at the core of the levels-of-processing approach to memory (Craik & Lockhart, 1972). The idea behind **levels of processing** is that, the more deeply people encode information, the better they will recall it. Thomas Hyde and James Jenkins (1973) created a standard procedure for manipulating depth of processing in which they typically presented a list of about 28 words with a 5-second interval between words.

Participants heard beforehand that they would be given a list of words and should focus on a specific aspect of the words. Participants were not told that they would be asked to recall as many words as possible, so they were somewhat surprised when they were asked to recall them.

Based on word-recall studies, researchers have identified three levels of processing: structural, phonemic, and semantic (Craik & Tulving, 1975; Hyde & Jenkins, 1973; see Figure 2). *Structural processing* is the shallowest level.

When studying structural processing, researchers might have directed participants to focus on the structure of a word by asking questions such as "Is the word in capital letters?" To study *phonemic processing*, or midlevel processing, they asked questions to focus participants' attention on the sound of the word, such as "Does the word rhyme with _____ ?" *Semantic processing* is the deepest level of processing. Participants in studies of semantic processing were asked to think about the meaning of the words and answer questions such as "Would the word fit the sentence: 'He met a _____ in the street?'"

Results across many studies find the best recall when words are encoded more deeply and worse recall for words that are processed less deeply (Craik & Tulving, 1975; Hyde & Jenkins, 1973; Lockhart & Craik, 1990). Craik and Tulving (1975) conducted 10 experiments in which they manipulated the participants' level of processing with target words (between 48 and 60 words) and found that, the deeper the level of processing became, the better the recall was (see Figure 3).

Recent research suggests that information that is encoded more deeply activates the left prefrontal cortex and left temporal lobe more than information that is processed shallowly (Rose, Craik, & Buchsbaum, 2015). The take-away message is that, the more deeply you process material, the better you will remember it. We will come back to this point in our discussion of the role of memory in studying at the end of this chapter.

Sleep   More and more evidence is suggesting that a major benefit of getting a good night's sleep is not just to rest your body but to aid in learning and memory and cognitive functioning in general (Mazza et al., 2016; Wixted & Cai, 2014). Emotional events also benefit from being recalled after sleep (Baran et al., 2012; Payne & Kensinger, 2010). In addition, recent evidence suggests that sleep not only protects memories from being forgotten, but it also makes memories

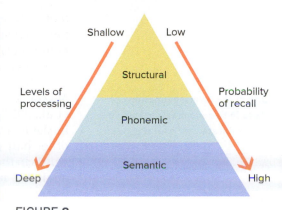

FIGURE 2

LEVELS-OF-PROCESSING MODEL OF MEMORY AND RECALL. The level at which we process information affects the probability of recall. The deeper we process information, the more likely we are to recall it. Structural processing is the shallowest level of processing and the least likely to be recalled. Semantic processing is both the deepest and the most likely to be recalled (Craik & Lockhart, 1972).

levels of processing
The concept that the more deeply people encode information, the better they will recall it.

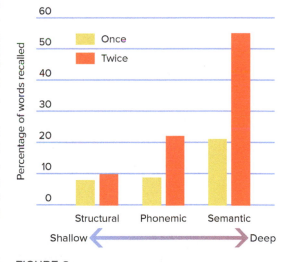

FIGURE 3

RESULTS OF LEVELS OF PROCESSING AND RECALL. These results show that, the more deeply people process information, the better they recall it. If people are presented a word list twice, the effect of depth of processing on recall is even stronger (Craik & Lockhart, 1972).

more accessible to recall (Dumay, 2016). Finally, retention is best the sooner a person falls asleep after taking in the information (Payne et al., 2012). Recall is better when a person falls asleep one hour after learning material compared to 12 hours after learning the material. There is less interference.

To give just one example of the research on how sleep benefits memory: Mazza and colleagues taught students 16 foreign vocabulary words (Mazza et al., 2016). Half of the students were randomly assigned to learn all 16 words in the morning and relearn all of them again that very day (wake group). The other half (the sleep group) were randomly assigned to learn all of the same words in the evening of one day, sleep all night, and then relearn all of the words again the next morning. The memories of both groups were tested 1 week and 6 months later. At both time periods, the sleep group outperformed the wake group. After one week, the sleep group recalled 15 of the words and the wake group 11. After 6 months the sleep group still recalled 9 of the words whereas the wake group only recalled 3. The authors concluded that not only is sleeping a good memory strategy, but that sleeping between two learning sessions is better still.

Emotion   Why is it that you can remember in great detail the events of your first date but cannot recall what you ate for breakfast 3 days ago? Generally speaking, emotional memories are easier to recall than are factual ones. Emotions help us encode and retrieve memories. When emotions occur—especially negative ones—attention is focused and details are noted, because emotions usually are connected with events that have important implications for the individual. As such, these events may be important to recall.

How does emotion help memory? One way, as we'll see in more detail in the "Memory and the Brain" section later in this chapter, is through biochemical and genetic processes. Emotional events switch on genes that build proteins to strengthen the synaptic connections between neurons. These proteins also stimulate the formation of new synapses and even new neurons (Kandel, 2006). All of these structures make the memory "stick" for a long period of time.

Additionally, emotion helps memory by way of anatomy. Important structures for memory—the amygdala and the hippocampus—are linked to key structures for emotion. These two structures lie next to each other in the brain and are connected by many nerve fibers. Indeed, these two structures become activated simultaneously during emotional experiences (Strange & Dolan, 2006). The amygdala is involved in assigning emotional significance to events and is crucial in encoding information relevant to emotional experiences, especially fear (Dolcos, LeBar, & Cabeza, 2005; Phelps & LeDoux, 2005; Sigurdsson et al., 2007). People remember the visual details of an object better if negative emotions were aroused while viewing it (Kensinger, Garoff-Eaton, & Schacter, 2007). One mechanism through which emotional arousal affects memory formation is the release of norepinephrine (Tully & Bolshakov, 2010). This neurotransmitter makes synaptic connections between neurons more plastic—that is, it changes the structure of the synaptic connections. Neural plasticity in turn is necessary for making the connection between synapses stronger; hence, an event becomes more memorable. Moreover, as unbelievable as it may seem, olfactory memories paired with fear experiences through conditioning—at least in mice—seem to be passed down to the next generations via epigenetic processes (Dias & Ressler, 2013). Second- and third-generation mice have the same fear response to a conditioned smell that their parents and grandparents had. In short, traumatic memories may well be inherited.

No doubt there are certain powerful events you remember vividly. For instance, most people remember exactly what they were doing when two jets flew into the World Trade Center towers on September 11, 2001. Your authors

Connection

One of the primary functions of sleep is to consolidate memories and facilitate new neural growth.

See "Sleeping," in the chapter "Consciousness." (p. 228)

Challenge Your Assumptions

True or False? Memory of traumatic events cannot be inherited from a previous generation.

False: Conditioned fears are experienced in mice one and two generations removed from the original conditioned fear.

©Andrew Lichtenstein/Corbis Historical/Getty Images

Powerful, rare, and emotional events can produce lifelong memories, but they are still subject to many of the same distortions as memories of normal, everyday events.

 What events in your life have produced "flashbulb memories"?

also know exactly what they were doing when they heard John Lennon was killed (Erika was doing her American history homework, in her red chenille bathrobe, when her brother told her of the announcement on *Monday Night Football*).

A special kind of emotional memory occurs when a detailed snapshot memory forms for what we were doing when we first heard of a major, often public, and emotionally charged event. This kind of memory is known as a **flashbulb memory** (Brown & Kulik, 1977). These recollections tend to be highly charged with emotion, which marks them for recall in some way. Flashbulb memories are remarkable for two reasons: They are very long-lasting (often lasting a lifetime) and people remain very confident in the accuracy of what they were doing when they learned of the event, even though their accuracy/consistency is not very high (Conway, Skitka, Hemmerich, & Kershaw, 2009; Hirst et al., 2015; Lanciano, Curci, & Semin, 2010). For example, Hirst and colleagues (2015) conducted four separate surveys with the same people immediately following September 11, 2001 and then one year later, 3 years later, and finally 10 years later. What they found was the flashbulb memory became inconsistent 1 year later and then often became consistent and leveled off. For example, here are the four accounts of one participant's flashbulb memory of 9/11: "Kitchen, making breakfast" (immediate); "In dorm room, folding laundry" (1 year later); "Ironing in dorm room" (3 years later); and "In dorm room, ironing" (10 years later) (Hirst et al., 2015, p. 617). Note the change during the first year, and then the consistency over the next 9 years, which was a fairly common finding. Interestingly, Hirst and colleagues also found that even though the inaccuracies in the flashbulb memory ("where was I") tend to get repeated over the years, the inaccuracies in the event memory ("what happened") tend to get corrected over the years.

flashbulb memory
Is a detailed snapshot memory for what we were doing when we first heard of a major, public, and emotionally charged event.

Impediments to Memory Formation

Some experiences enhance but others impede or interfere with encoding and recall of memories, such as distraction (for example, multitasking) and emotion. Notice that emotion can both aid and and impede encoding and memory. It is not surprising that just as paying attention is the key to memory formation, that being distracted is the key to poor memory formation.

Distraction (Multitasking)   There are fewer more common devices of distraction these days than our cell phones. Talking on a cell phone while writing an email can only lead to poor encoding of the phone conversation, the email, or both. We are much less likely to remember things when we try to multitask. Divided attention and multitasking are enemies of memory because they interfere with the first necessary steps of memory formation (Clapp et al., 2011; Dindar & Akbulut, 2016; van der Schuur, Baumgartner, Sumter, & Valkenburg, 2015). A classic example of this is the common finding that using a laptop to take notes in lecture interferes with learning and grades (Bellur, Nowak, & Hull, 2015; Levine, Waite, & Bowman, 2012; Sana, Weston, & Cepeda, 2013; van der Schuur et al., 2015). It is not the laptop in itself, but rather the distractions of the web, email, YouTube, Facebook, etc., that lead to poor encoding of material and inferior recall and learning. It is nearly impossible to take in and later recall information when being distracted by other forms of information.

Emotion   The relationship between emotion and memory is far from perfect. Emotion can help us remember events but the recall will not always be accurate. Sometimes emotions distort our memories. The details of emotional memories tend to be less accurate than those of non-emotional memories (Phelps & Sharot, 2008). Emotional memories are often held with great confidence, but with blindness to their inaccuracy. In addition, in terms of autobiographical memories, when people look back over their lives, they recall the pleasant times rather than the negative ones. So there is a positive bias in autobiographical memory recall. The "good ol' days" are good partly because we remember the good more readily than we remember the bad (Walker, Skowronski, & Thompson, 2003). Research suggests that the emotional goals we have prior to an event, like what we hope for or are afraid of, narrow our attention and make us vulnerable to misinformation and distortion of our memories (Kaplan et al., 2016).

Connection

Besides the ability to consciously recall a memory, what other forms of consciousness affect our behavior without our knowing it?

See "Two Dimensions of Consciousness: Wakefulness and Awareness," in the chapter "Consciousness." (p. 216)

Quick Quiz 1: Forming Memories

1. David was thinking about baseball statistics when his mother told him to make sure to call his Uncle Jim for his birthday. Two hours later, David's mom asked him if he had called his uncle yet and he said he did not even remember her asking him to. Which memory process is probably where David's memory failure occurred?
   a. Encoding
   b. Consolidation
   c. Storage
   d. Retrieval

2. Jennifer studied for a week for her psychology exam. She took careful notes, made note cards, reviewed them many times, and even had her roommate test her. She even developed visual images and mnemonics for help her learn the four steps in forming memories. But when she read a question on the exam about this material, she got confused and got it wrong. Which memory process is probably where Jennifer's memory failure occurred?

   a. Encoding
   b. Consolidation
   c. Storage
   d. Retrieval

3. Roberto and Stephen both studied a total of about 10 hours for a Chem exam. They both used many of the same study strategies such as making in-depth notes, reading the chapter multiple times, and rehearsing the material many times. Roberto, however, spread his 10 hours of studying over 1 week with 8 hours of sleep each night. Stephen crammed his 10 hours in from 7 p.m. to 5 a.m. the night and morning of the exam and then got 3 hours of sleep for his 9 a.m. exam. Who is most likely to do best on the exam and why?
   a. Roberto; Consolidation
   b. Stephen; Consolidation
   c. Roberto; Retrieval
   d. Stephen; Retrieval

Answers can be found at the end of the chapter.

TYPES OF MEMORY

Until the 1950s, psychologists thought of memory as one thing. Either people remembered things or they didn't. As we've seen so often throughout the history of psychology, a single case in science changed our understanding and made it clear that there are different kinds of memory. The case involved Henry Molaison. When he was 7 years old, Molaison—better known to scientists as H. M.—was hit by a bicyclist (Corkin, 1984; Squire, 2009). He suffered a brain injury, which soon thereafter resulted in severe epileptic seizures. To stop these seizures, doctors removed the hippocampus on both sides of H. M.'s brain, as well as the adjoining brain structures (see Figure 4). The seizures stopped, but at quite a cost: H. M. lost the ability to form new memories. He lived forever in the present.

Brenda Milner, the neuropsychologist who examined H. M. regularly for more than 30 years, had to introduce herself each time they met. What makes H. M.'s story even more remarkable is that most of the memories he had formed prior to the surgery, at age 27, remained intact.

Milner's (1962) work with Molaison provided the first documented evidence of distinct kinds of memory in operation. For example, she gave him a standard learning task, in which he had to trace inside the outline of a star while looking at the star in a mirror (see Figure 5a). This task is particularly difficult because the mirror image of every movement is reversed. True to Milner's expectations, H. M. had no recollection of doing this task, even though he had been trained on it for days and had even done it up to 10 times in 1 day.

Each time he did it, H. M. said that it was a completely new task. Yet contrary to what you might expect, some part of his brain knew and remembered the task, because the drawings improved the more often he worked on them (see Figure 5). Although Molaison may have lost the ability to form new memories of his experiences, some type of memory formation must have occurred, or he would not have improved on the task.

©Owen Egan

Brenda Milner

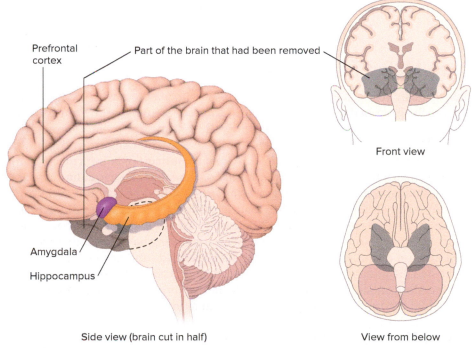

Prefrontal cortex

Part of the brain that had been removed

Amygdala

Hippocampus

Side view (brain cut in half)

Front view

View from below

FIGURE 4

PORTIONS OF H. M.'S BRAIN REMOVED DURING SURGERY. Patient H. M. had most of his hippocampus and the adjacent tissues in the temporal lobe removed from both hemispheres of his brain (Carey, 2008).

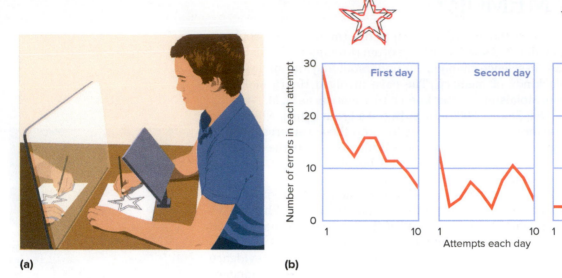

(a)　　　　　　　**(b)**

FIGURE 5

A CASE STUDY OF MEMORY WITHOUT RECOLLECTION. Although H. M.'s memory problems prevented him from recalling ever having completed this star tracing task, some part of his brain clearly did "recall" the task. He got better and better at it over time (Kandel, 2006; Kandel, Kupferman, & Iversen, 2000).

How might one explain this contradictory finding? As H. M.'s case illustrates, being unable to consciously recall experiences doesn't mean there is no memory of an event. We are incapable of intentionally bringing into awareness much of what we remember, such as memories that have been put away for some time or memories for how to do things, such as tie one's shoes or ride a bike. Many things we know are outside of conscious awareness. Milner's research with H. M. ushered in a new understanding of memory and how memory comes in distinct types.

Three Major Types of Memory

three-stage model of memory
The classification of memories based on duration as sensory, short-term, and long-term.

sensory memory
The part of memory that holds information in its original sensory form for a very brief period of time, usually about half a second or less.

short-term memory
The part of memory that temporarily (for 2 to 30 seconds) stores a limited amount of information before it is either transferred to long-term storage or forgotten.

long-term memory
The part of memory that has the capacity to store a vast amount of information for as little as 30 seconds and as long as a lifetime.

Memories can last less a second or a lifetime. Psychologists who study memory distinguish three major types of memory that occur in stages (Figure 6). The **three-stage model of memory** classifies three types of memories based on how long the memories last: sensory memory, short-term memory, and long-term memory (Atkinson & Shiffrin, 1971). **Sensory memory** holds information in its original sensory form for a very brief period of time, usually about half a second or less. **Short-term memory** temporarily stores a limited amount of information before it is either transferred to long-term storage or forgotten. Information stays in short-term memory for 2 to 30 seconds—about long enough to remember a phone number before you dial it. **Long-term memory** has the capacity to store a vast amount of information for as little as 30 seconds and as long as a lifetime. Here reside the memories of your first pet and your knowledge of how to read. As the three-stage model suggests, memory formation is an active, dynamic process. Let's look at the types and stages of memory in more depth.

Sensory Memory　As we interact with the world, our sensory systems are stimulated—we may smell, taste, feel, see, or hear an experience. In fact, two or more sensory systems may contribute information about a single experience, as when we dig into a bag of buttery popcorn while watching a scary movie. In the chapter "Sensing and Perceiving Our World," we saw that

FIGURE 6

THREE TYPES OF MEMORY. When our sense organs are stimulated, the nervous system forms a very brief image, or trace, of what we saw, heard, tasted, felt, or smelled (sensory memory). If we don't attend to it, we forget it immediately. If we do pay attention, the information is passed on to short-term memory. Here, if we attend to it only briefly, it will remain in short-term memory as long as we need it, but then it will be forgotten. If we rehearse it over and over, the information is processed more deeply and passed on to long-term memory. If we encode the information deeply, it becomes a long-term memory. Some long-term memories fade or are forgotten over time (Atkinson & Shiffrin, 1971).

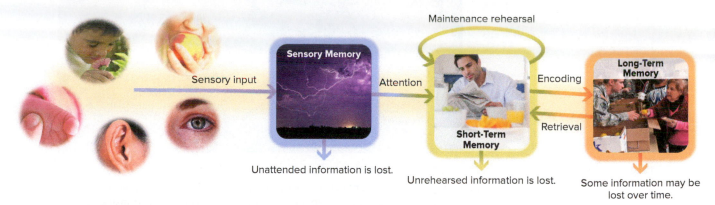

sensory neurons respond to sensory stimuli by sending signals to the brain for processing. Sensory memory is made up of the brief traces of a sensation left by the firing of neurons in the brain. These traces last from less than half a second up to 2 or 3 seconds. Sensation is the first step toward the creation of a long-term memory.

Because seeing and hearing are key sources of information for humans, the two kinds of sensory memory that have received the most attention from memory researchers are iconic and echoic memory (Craik, 1979). *Iconic memory* is a brief visual record left on the retina of the eye, whereas *echoic memory* is the short-term retention of sounds. In a simple laboratory demonstration of iconic memory, four digits, such as "5 4 7 1," are flashed on a computer screen for 30 milliseconds. (A millisecond is a thousandth of a second.) Then the screen goes blank. At 30 milliseconds, the information is barely perceived at all. Yet when a blank screen follows the numbers, most people have no trouble recalling them. However, if the same four digits are followed on the screen by "# # # #," people have a lot of trouble recalling any digits and often report that they did not see any digits at all (Thompson & Madigan, 2005). The presentation of the symbols interferes with the ability to recall the digits. This demonstration suggests that all sensory memory traces are preserved for very short periods of time and are very fragile.

Short-Term and Working Memory   After we sense information, we either ignore it or start to process it more deeply. If we process it more, the first step involves holding a limited amount of information for a short period of time, otherwise known as short-term memory (Cowan, 2008). If we do this in the service of working on a problem or carrying out an action, we make use of our **working memory.** Working memory is used, for example, when we are following a recipe or solving a math problem.

Although short-term memory and working memory are very similar, and some psychologists use them interchangeably, they are not identical. Working memory makes use of information in short-term memory. It is for this reason,

working memory
The part of memory required to attend to and solve a problem at hand.

©Brand X Pictures/Getty Images RF

How good are you at remembering names of people after meeting them for the first time? Unless you rehearse them, names often don't make the transition to long-term memory.

that working memory but not short-term memory is associated with intellectual ability and intelligence (Cowan, 2008).

Short-Term Memory Capacity   Most of us hear someone's phone number, repeat it a few times, and then place the call. The number of items that can be held in short-term memory is called short-term memory capacity, and it is limited to about seven items (Feldman-Barrett, Tugade, & Engle, 2004; Miller, 1956). It is not a coincidence that local phone numbers in this country contain seven digits. The short-term memory capacity of most people is between five and nine units of letters, digits, or chunks of information, but there are substantial individual differences in this capacity. Some people struggle with three or four bits of information, whereas others easily handle 11 or 12 (Baddeley, 2003).

One of the best ways to increase short-term memory capacity is to transform what you want to remember into a smaller set of meaningful units, or chunks, a process known as **chunking** (Thompson & Madigan, 2005). For example, 4155557982 is much more difficult to remember than the chunks of (415) 555-7982. Social Security numbers follow the same idea: 555-66-8888 is easier to remember than 555668888.

How Working Memory Works   Similar to how memory in general forms (encoding, consolidating, storing, and retrieving), one researcher, Alan Baddeley (2003, 2007), has suggested that working memory consists of three distinct processes: *attending to a stimulus, storing* information about the stimulus, and *rehearsing* the stored process to help solve a problem. In Baddeley's model, the first process, focusing and switching attention, is carried out by a master attentional control system. This attention system is supported by three temporary storage systems, one for sounds and language (phonological loop), one for images and spatial relations (visuospatial sketchpad), and one that provides temporary storage for specific events (an episodic buffer; see Figure 7).

The *central executive* decides where to focus attention and selectively hones in on specific aspects of a stimulus. Attention allows us to focus on the task at hand and develop a plan for solving a problem. We are bombarded by dozens of sensations every second. How do we know which are important and deserve our

chunking
Breaking down a list of items to be remembered into a smaller set of meaningful units.

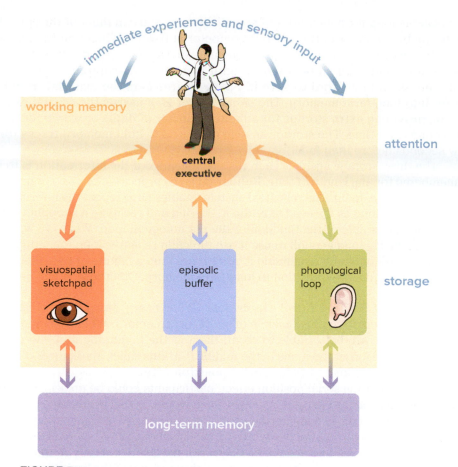

immediate experiences and sensory input

working memory

central executive

attention

visuospatial sketchpad

episodic buffer

phonological loop

storage

long-term memory

FIGURE 7

BADDELEY'S MODEL OF WORKING MEMORY. The four components of working memory are the central executive, which focuses attention, and three storage systems (visuospatial sketchpad, episodic buffer, and phonological loop). Once our attention is focused on something, we need short-term places to store the relevant information. Images and spatial relations are stored in one storage center; events and experiences in another; and language and sounds in another (Baddeley, 2003).

attention and which we can ignore? According to Baddeley's model, children and people with brain injuries (at least those with frontal lobe damage) have a difficult time screening out irrelevant information, because they lack well-developed or fully functioning central executives.

Once information is taken in and attended to, it is sent to a temporary store: the *visuospatial sketchpad* if it is visual or spatial information, the episodic buffer if it is a specific event or experience, or the *phonological loop* if it is sound or linguistic information.

The *visuospatial sketchpad,* as the name implies, briefly provides storage for visual and spatial sensations, such as images, photos, scenes, and three-dimensional objects. Like verbal information stored in the phonological loop, a visual image created on the visuospatial sketchpad lasts only seconds before it fades—unless we attend to it and process it more deeply. Normally, we can hold a small number of images (three or four) in short-term storage. An example is a cognitive map that you visualize while someone is giving you directions to an unfamiliar location. If you are going to find your way there, however, you have to move this map from sensory memory to short-term memory by verbalizing and rehearsing the directions ("left at the stop sign, right at the Quicki-Mart … "). Depending on how complex the directions are, you might even move them to long-term memory. The *episodic buffer* is a temporary store for information that will become long-term memories of specific events. You can think of the episodic buffer as being like a buffer in your computer software. When you type something in a word processing program, such as Microsoft Word, the typed letters reside in a temporary store, a buffer, until you save the material to your hard disk, unless you tell Word to save it. Saving it transfers the material from the buffer into long-term memory. The *phonological loop* assists the central executive by providing extra storage for a limited number of digits or words for up to 30 seconds at a time. The storage system allows us to hold memory traces for a few seconds before they fade.

The three storage systems each require rehearsal if the information is to be remembered for any length of time. **Rehearsal** is the process of reciting or practicing material repeatedly. The rehearsal system enables us to repeat the information to ourselves as long as we need to retain it. Storing and recalling a shopping list is an everyday example of the function of the phonological loop. When we want to remember the list long enough to use it, we typically rehearse it by repeating it to ourselves. If we continue rehearsing it, after more than a minute or two, the information might make the transition to long-term memory. Otherwise, it will be lost.

The Serial Position Effect In the late 19th century, Mary Whiton Calkins observed an interesting phenomenon of short-term memory. When learning a list of items, people are better able to recall them at the beginning and end of the list; they tend to forget the items in the middle (Calkins, 1898; Madigan & O'Hara, 1992). This effect is known as the **serial position effect.**

In studies of the serial position effect, participants could be presented with a list of 15 words read at 1-second intervals. They would be told in advance that they will be asked to recall as many as they could, in any order. Typically, about 50% of the participants recall the first two words on the list, about 50%–75% recall the words near the end of the list, and about 90%–95% recall the last two words on the list. Recall for the beginning and end of the list is pretty good, but only about 25% of the participants recall words in the middle of the list. The tendency to preferentially recall items at the beginning of a list is known as the *primacy effect*, whereas recall for items at the end of a list is known as the *recency effect* (see Figure 8).

The main explanation offered for the primacy effect is that the items in the beginning of the list are quickly rehearsed and transferred to long-term memory storage, so they are remembered. The items in the middle of the list haven't made that trip to long-term memory yet. The recency effect results from those items at the end still being held in short-term memory. They are therefore accessible. The items in the middle cannot be rehearsed as more and more items are being added to the list. Neuroimaging data support the idea that the serial position effect results from both short-term and long-term memory processes and greater brain activation during early (primary) and late (recency) stages of perceiving stimuli (Azizian & Polich, 2007; Talmi et al., 2005). Because of the serial position effect, we are more likely to remember the first and last parts of a book, TV program, movie, or commercial than to recall the middle. Writers, directors, and politicians know about this tendency, either consciously or not, and try to place the most important information near the beginning and end of their works.

rehearsal
The process of repeatedly practicing material, so that it enters long-term memory.

serial position effect
The tendency to have better recall for items in a list according to their position in the list.

FIGURE 8

SERIAL POSITION EFFECTS AND RECALL. People have the best recall of items that are in the beginning of a series (primacy) or at the end of a series (recency). The recency effects go away if people are given a distracting task, such as having to recall digits before recalling the words in a list.

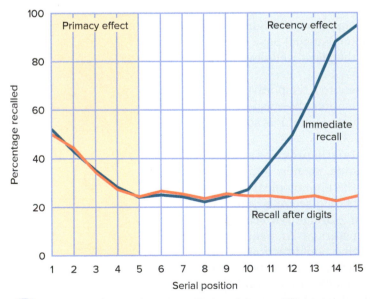

 How might the serial position effect explain our ability to remember some parts of books or movies better than other parts? (Thompson & Madigan, 2005)

Long-Term Memory   In April 2006, during the centennial of the 1906 San Francisco earthquake, a 109-year-old survivor reported these two memories from that disaster: "I remember the smell of the smoke [from the fires afterward] … and the cow running down California Street with its tail in the air" (Nolte & Yollin, 2006). Memories that are 100 years old definitely qualify as long-term memories! Yet according to our definition of long-term memory as "any information that is stored for at least 30 to 40 seconds and up to a lifetime," things that you remember from earlier today—the topic of a psychology lecture, for example—are also in long-term storage. So is information you remember for only a few weeks, such as material for your next midterm exam. Will you remember the material you learned in this course 20 years from now? That depends on a number of factors, but primarily it depends on how often you use or rehearse the information.

Long-term memory is what most people think of when they think of memory. Long-term memory is also the most complex form of memory: There are two distinct types and four distinct stages of processing. Long-term memory can be divided into whether it is conscious or not (implicit/explicit). Then, if conscious, does it involve memories of events or facts. If unconscious, does it involve memory of skills or procedures for carrying out an action (Figure 9).

Types of Long-Term Memory   People often forget specific things, but they typically do not forget how to tie their shoes, ride a bike, or even add 6 to 12. How is it possible that a person can forget names but almost never forget skills such as simple arithmetic? The short answer is that there is more than one type of long-term memory, and the types operate differently. At the broadest level, there are two types: implicit and explicit memory. How to ride a bike or add is implicit; where you left your car keys is explicit. H. M.'s case, described at the beginning of the chapter, is important partly because it helped psychologists change their long-held perspective on memory by distinguishing between implicit and explicit memory.

Implicit Memory   When we know or remember something but don't consciously know we remember it, we are tapping into **implicit memory**, also known as *nondeclarative memory*, because we cannot directly recall this type of memory. Instead, implicit memory is based on prior experience, and it is the place where we store knowledge of previous experience, such as skills we perform automatically once we have mastered them—how to ride a bicycle, for instance. If asked to describe how we perform these skills, we can't do so very well. Although we can perform many skills automatically, we don't have ready access to the memory of the many steps they require (Kandel, Kupfermann, & Iversen, 2000).

Implicit memory comes in two forms, procedural memory and priming. **Procedural memory** is knowledge we hold for almost any behavior or physical skill we learn, whether it is how to play golf, ride a bike, drive a car, or tie a shoe. The star-tracing task that H. M. worked on (Figure 5) is another example of procedural memory. Part of his brain remembered the mirror task because his performance improved each time he did it. The part of his brain responsible for conscious recall did not remember the task, however.

Priming is a kind of implicit memory that occurs when recall is improved by prior exposure to the same or similar stimuli. In one laboratory demonstration of priming, people with memory problems (an amnesia group) were compared to individuals without such problems (a comparison group) on a word-learning task.

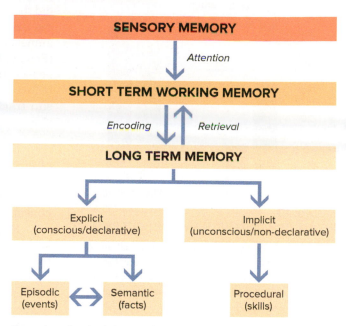

FIGURE 9
MAJOR TYPES OF MEMORY

(Source: https://missshanks2014.wordpress.com/types-of-long-term-memory/)

What kind of memory is remembering your first kiss?

implicit memory
A kind of memory made up of knowledge based on previous experience, such as skills that we perform automatically once we have mastered them; resides outside conscious awareness.

procedural memory
A kind of memory made up of implicit knowledge for almost any behavior or physical skill we have learned.

Challenge Your Assumptions

True or False? We can know things we don't remember.

True: Many things we know we have no conscious verbal recollection of.

priming
A kind of implicit memory that arises when recall is improved by earlier exposure to the same or similar stimuli.

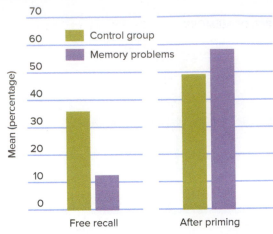

FIGURE 10
RECALL OF WORDS WITH AND WITHOUT PRIMING

 What effect does priming have on recall, and does priming affect people with memory problems differently than those with no memory problems? Looking at the figure, what would you conclude? (Squire, 1987)

explicit memory
Knowledge that consists of the conscious recall of facts and events; also known as declarative memory.

semantic memory
A form of memory that recalls facts and general knowledge, such as what we learn in school.

episodic memory
The form of memory that recalls the experiences we have had.

highly superior autobiographical memory (HSAM)
Occurs when people can recall in considerable detail personal events from almost any day of their adolescent and adult life.

Challenge Your Assumptions

True or False? No one can remember every single day of his or her adult life.
False: Although quite rare, a few dozen people do have the ability to recall some specific event from every single day of their adult and some even younger lives.

When asked to recall a list of words they were exposed to, the people in the amnesia group demonstrated much less recall than did the comparison group (see Figure 10), but when they were given the first three letters of the words as a prime, or memory aid, the amnesia group performed at least as well as the comparison group (Squire, 1987). What is intriguing about this outcome is that the amnesia group had no conscious recollection of having seen the words before. Like H. M., who was primed by his previous learning of the star-tracing task, people with severe long-term memory problems show a remarkable ability to recall words if they have been primed.

Explicit Memory **Explicit memory** is the conscious recall of facts and events. Explicit memory is sometimes called *declarative memory*, because it refers to memories that can be deliberately accessed or *declared*. There are two distinct kinds of explicit-conscious memory: semantic and episodic (Tulving, 1972, 1985).

Semantic memory is our memory for facts and knowledge, such as what we learn in school. **Episodic memory** is our memory for the events (episodes) we have lived through. Remembering that Baton Rouge is the capital of Louisiana is an example of semantic memory, whereas remembering your high school graduation is an episodic memory. Kim Peek, whom we met at the opening of this chapter, could remember most every detail of any book he has ever read and all the streets and area codes in the country. He, therefore, had incredible semantic memory.

Episodic memories are more personal and autobiographical than semantic memories. Jill Price, whom we met at the opening of the chapter, and a few dozen other people in the world, have what is known as **highly superior autobiographical memory (HSAM)** whereby they can recall in considerable detail personal events (episodes) from almost any day of their adolescent and adult life (LePort et al., 2016; Parker et al., 2006). Recent research with people with highly superior autobiographical memory reveals that they are not better than most people at recall after short periods of time, such as 1 week. But from 1 month out, they far surpass most people in detail and accuracy of recall (LePort et al., 2016). What is truly remarkable is how these detailed memories persist at the 1-year and 10-year

©Digital Vision RF

Images associated with events such as high school graduation are stored temporarily by the visuospatial sketchpad in short-term memory before making the trip to long-term episodic memory. The emotions that accompany such occasions increase the likelihood that our memories of them will last a lifetime.

follow-ups. In a sense, they are unable to forget. Interestingly, this same research uncovered a high incidence of obsessive-compulsive behavior in people with HSAM, which suggests this memory ability might be a form of obsessive-compulsive thinking.

In addition to Kim Peek and Jill Price, someone else with an incredible explicit memory is Daniel Tammet, whose abilities have to do with numbers. Tammet memorized 22,514 digits of pi in just 3 weeks. Most people can recall perhaps 7–10 digits of pi without too much trouble (3.14159265…), but Daniel carried out this feat to more than 22,500 digits! What makes his accomplishment all the more amazing is that there is no pattern in pi, and he recalled the digits without a single mistake.

It took him more than 5 hours to recite the numbers. His "trick" is an uncanny ability to see numbers as shapes and colors. As he described in his memoir, he does not remember numerals but rather a landscape of shapes and colors (Tammet, 2006). In fact, his rendition of how he sees the first 20 digits of pi is presented in Figure 11 .

FIGURE 11

EXTRAORDINARY NUMERIC MEMORY. This is Daniel Tammet's description of how he sees the first 20 digits of pi; he memorized 22,514 digits in just 3 weeks.

©Jérôme Tabet

Quick Quiz 2: Types of Memory

1. Suppose you met a person who could remember things that happened well before she had surgery but who was now incapable of forming new long-term memories. What part of her brain was most likely affected by the surgery?
   a. hypothalamus
   b. hippocampus
   c. insula
   d. amygdala

2. The brief traces of a touch or a smell left by the firing of neurons in the brain are examples of
   a. perceptual memory.
   b. long-term potentiation.
   c. implicit memory.
   d. sensory memory.

3. What kind of memory do we use to keep someone's phone number in mind long enough to put it in our contacts?
   a. working memory
   b. iconic memory
   c. long-term memory
   d. sensory memory

4. What type of memory allows us to perform skills, such as tying our shoes, automatically once we have mastered them?
   a. explicit memory
   b. declarative memory
   c. procedural memory
   d. echoic memory

Answers can be found at the end of the chapter.

MEMORY AND THE BRAIN

It boggles the mind to realize that memories are really just changes in and connections among clusters of neurons. Indeed, the brain is where memory happens. There are two major neurological systems involved in every aspect of memory: neurons and brain regions. Neurons grow and change with the birth and death of memories. That is, neuroplasticity is the key to memory formation. Furthermore, distinct regions of the brain are most involved in the birth and death of memories.

Neuroplasticity and Memory

In the first half of the 20th century, much of psychology ignored the biological basis of memory and learning, but not all psychologists did. Based on his studies of brain anatomy and behavior, Donald Hebb (1949) developed a theory of how neural connections form and how synaptic connections change with learning and memory.

Hebb proposed that, when the synapse of one neuron repeatedly fires and excites another neuron, there is a permanent change in the receiving neuron, the excitatory neuron, or both, which strengthens the synaptic connection. This strengthening process is called **long-term potentiation** (LTP; Whitlock et al., 2006). When synapses fire more readily, learning becomes easier and more efficient.

Hebb further suggested that repeated stimulation of a group of neurons leads to the formation of *cell assemblies*, networks of nerve cells that persist even after stimulation has stopped. The more times synapses in these assemblies fire together, Hebb asserted, the stronger the network becomes, increasing the likelihood that they will fire together again. Simply put, *neurons that fire together, wire together* (see Figure 12). Initially, neurons are not connected, but with stimulation, clusters of neurons fire together. If repeated and continued, these clusters form long-term bonds and are consolidated into a memory. What is now referred to as Hebb's law led to another important conclusion from his theory: *Use it or lose it*. If the cell assemblies are not stimulated repeatedly, eventually the synaptic connections weaken and we forget.

As we discussed in the previous section, no one suspected a link between the hippocampus and memory formation, however, until a student of Hebb's, Brenda Milner, reported clinical observations of Henry Molaison (H. M.). Her observations supported Hebb's theories (Corkin, 1984; Milner, 1962; Milner, Corkin, & Teuber, 1968; Penfield & Milner, 1958). Moving beyond the case study approach of Milner, Eric Kandel and his colleagues were able to conduct systematic research into the biological basis of learning and memory.

Kandel (2001) wanted to study memory and learning in the neurologically simplest animal he knew, the sea slug (*Aplysia*). Sea slugs have far fewer neurons than humans, and their neurons can also be seen with the naked eye. When Kandel's group administered a shock to the tail of the sea slug, it responded with a defensive posture. If the researchers administered the shock only once, the sea slug's defensive response persisted for only about 10 minutes. If the shock was administered four or five times in close succession, the sea slug exhibited the same defensive response to the shock days later. The sea slug had created a long-term memory of how to react to a shock (Pinsker et al., 1973). Kandel's conclusion: "Conversion from short-term to long-term memory storage requires spaced repetition—practice makes perfect, even in snails" (Kandel, 2001, p. 294).

Following up on these findings, Kandel set out to learn just how repeated experience changes the brain. What he found provides an intriguing example of the interaction of nurture and nature. Kandel and his colleagues discovered that repeated stimulation of a neuron actually sends signals to the nucleus of the cell, where its DNA is stored. These signals trigger the production of *CREB*, a potein that switches

FIGURE 12
NEURAL FORMATION OF NEW MEMORY—LONG-TERM POTENTIATION

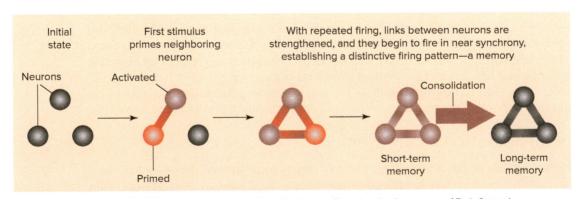

(Adapted from Adler, J. [2012, May]. Erasing painful memories. *Scientific American*. Reproduced with permission of Emily Cooper.)

on the genes responsible for the development of new synapses. Repetition brings about the growth of new synapses, which stabilize a new memory (see Figure 13). Both the timing and the frequency of neural firing are crucial in making a memory permanent. By repeatedly pulling away from a shock, the sea slug rehearsed and remembered a defensive behavior. Thus, experience from the outside world (repeated stimulation) changes genes and the way in which they are expressed (Kandel, 2006).

People, too, need to rehearse an idea or a thought many times in order to create a long-term memory. Strong emotions also make memories stick. In the process, our brains literally grow more synapses, thereby strengthening the neural connections—they become different brains. Experience changes the brain, and these changes then change how we respond to our environment. Kandel found the link between behavior and long-term memory that Hebb had speculated about in his model. These findings laid the foundation for developing drugs that help memory and/or delay memory declines in dementia (see "Psychology in the Real World").

©Tim Laman/Getty Images RF

In Kandel's study, the sea slug (Aplysia) created a long-term memory of how to react to shock.

 Why did Kandel want to use a sea slug to study human memory?

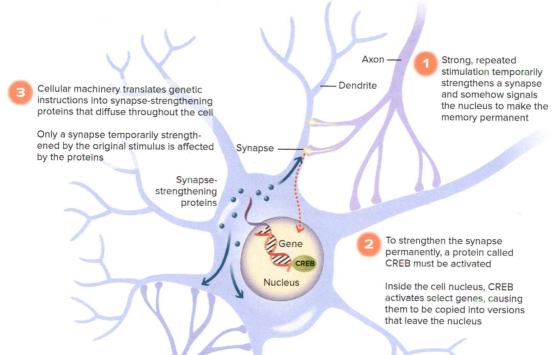

3 Cellular machinery translates genetic instructions into synapse-strengthening proteins that diffuse throughout the cell

Only a synapse temporarily strengthened by the original stimulus is affected by the proteins

Synapse-strengthening proteins

Axon

Dendrite

Synapse

1 Strong, repeated stimulation temporarily strengthens a synapse and somehow signals the nucleus to make the memory permanent

Gene

CREB

Nucleus

2 To strengthen the synapse permanently, a protein called CREB must be activated

Inside the cell nucleus, CREB activates select genes, causing them to be copied into versions that leave the nucleus

FIGURE 13

HOW MEMORIES STICK. When we experience something emotionally important or an experience is repeated over and over, synapses fire repeated neural impulses, as if to say, "This is important; remember this event" (1). These repeated neural firings in turn strengthen the synapse by activating a protein called CREB (2). CREB then turns on certain genes, which set into motion a process that builds other proteins that strengthen the synaptic connection (3). This process makes memories last in our minds, in effect "tattooing" the event in our brains. Thus, the timing and frequency of neural firings are crucial in making a memory permanent—an idea or a thought needs to be rehearsed many times if it is to pass from short-term to long-term memory (Fields, 2005).

Connection

Kandel's findings explain how and why the brains of mice reared in enriched environments are heavier and have more dendrites than the brains of mice reared in impoverished environments.

See "Brain Plasticity and Neurogenesis," in the chapter "The Biology of Behavior." (p. 105)

Psychology in the Real World

Manipulating Memory with Drugs and Drinks

We have learned in this chapter how memories are formed from neural connections being strengthened and even from new dendrite and neural growth. The regular and consistent firing of neurons consolidates their connectivity, and memories form from these connections. Cells that fire together, wire together.

As it turns out, there is now both basic and applied research on how and why particular drugs do or do not enhance memory. Memory researchers, including Kandel and his colleagues, have joined the quest for new drugs to enhance not just memory decline but also memory in general. This research has demonstrated the power of the gene-regulating protein CREB to help form memories (Alberini & Chen, 2012; Stern & Alberini, 2013; Xia et al., 2009; Yin et al., 1995). Indeed, flies bred to have an excess of CREB demonstrated super powers of memory: Instead of needing 10 trials to learn to avoid a scented room, they needed only one trial (Yin et al., 1995). Based on this basic science, others are researching drugs that stimulate the production of CREB and other memory-enhancing proteins in the brain (Xia et al., 2009). Recent research suggests that because it contains a metabolite of CREB, the spice cinnamon may help improve memory (Modi et al., 2016). Clinical trials with all of these findings, however, with humans are still at least a few years away.

A number of memory-oriented biotech companies, however, have started developing memory-enhancing drugs (Mangialasche et al., 2010). These drugs have focused on enhancing memory in general as well as slowing the onset of age-related cognitive decline. The Food and Drug Administration (FDA) has approved two drugs for the treatment of Alzheimer's disease: Aricept and Reminyl. Both of these drugs boost levels of *acetylcholine*, a memory-enhancing neurotransmitter that is deficient in Alzheimer's patients (Birks, 2009; Hansen et al., 2008).

Laboratory research has found drugs that block or dampen the process of memory formation. More specifically these drugs block protein synthesis required for forming new long-term memories (Cai et al., 2012; Soeter & Kindt, 2015). Why would they want to do that? The most obvious application of this kind of drug is to prevent traumatic experiences—such as abuse, car accidents, or war experiences—from developing into posttraumatic stress disorder (PTSD), a condition in which a person who has experienced an extremely traumatic event, such as being a crime victim or a soldier in battle, relives the event over and over. The way these drugs work is by blocking the protein synthesis that Kandel's lab demonstrated is needed in the formation of long-term memories (Adler, 2012; Lauzon et al., 2013; Pittman et al., 2002; Soeter & Kindt, 2010, 2015; Yao et al., 2008). Commercial drugs to dampen traumatic memories, however, are still in the developmental stage and are years away from being on the market.

Can prescription and nonprescription stimulants and herbal medications enhance memory? There are no doubt bogus and unscientific claims about how pills, herbs, and drinks can enhance memory, such as a headline from an ad in the *San Francisco Chronicle* (January 13, 2013): "Memory Pill Helps the Brain Like Prescription Glasses Help the Eyes." The ad went on to claim that the pill "helps users match the memory power of others 15 years younger in as little as 30 days!"

Contrary to what many college students believe, there is mixed evidence that the nonmedicinal use of stimulants, such as Adderall or Ritalin, improves

Brain Regions Most Involved in Memory

At the beginning of this chapter we introduced H. M., who lost the ability to make new long-term memories after having his hippocampus and nearby brain sections removed. Why was he still able to retrieve memories stored before the surgery? And how was he able to learn the star-tracing task more and more rapidly each time it was presented, even though he didn't remember learning it before? Each of the types of memory (sensory, working, short-term, and long-term) involves slight different regions of the brain.

The overview of sensory, short-term, working, and long-term memory systems and the brain is this: Sensory memories are processed (encoded) in the various sensory cortexes; short-term memory is processed in the hippocampus and frontal lobes; and long-term memories are stored in different parts of the cortex and subcortex and retrieved with the help of areas associated with the **prefrontal cortex.**

prefrontal cortex
The frontmost region of the frontal lobes; plays an important role in attention, appropriate social behavior, impulse control, and working memory.

memory (Ilieva, Boland, & Farah, 2013; Ilieva, Hook, & Farah, 2015). In a meta-analysis of 48 studies on more than 1,400 participants, the positive effects on cognitive functioning of these drugs happen is more likely in low doses (< 20mg) (Ilevia, Hook, & Farah, 2015; see also Mehta, Sahakian, & Robbins, 2001). Higher doses of prescription stimulants can actually interfere with and block memory formation (Devilbiss & Berridge, 2008). Similarly, caffeine in general and over-the-counter energy drinks (with caffeine and other chemicals, such as taurine) in particular have mixed effects in their capacity to enhance memory (Giles et al., 2012; Howard & Marczinski, 2010). There is nonclinical trial evidence that long-term, regular consumption of foods and drinks rich in a chemical compound known as *flavonoids* can enhance memory and preserve cognitive function in elderly people by protecting neurons, stimulating blood flow, and inducing neurogenesis (Spencer, 2010). Grapes, blueberries, green tea, and cacao beans (made into chocolate) are rich in flavonoids. The more definitive clinical trial research has yet to be carried out.

Research on herbal medication and memory enhancement is also mixed. Numerous claims of herbal effects on memory are unsupported, but the most solid evidence suggests that the ground-up leaves of the ginkgo biloba tree can be moderately effective in delaying symptoms of mild to moderate Alzheimer's disease (Le Bars et al., 1997).

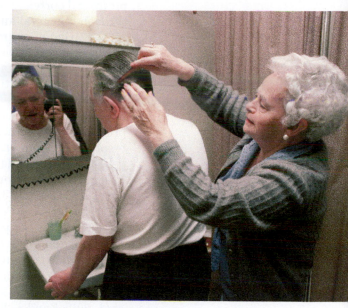

©Stephanie Maze/Corbis Documentary/Getty Images

The science of memory has led to some promising treatments for problems with memory, yet not all "memory pills" are equally effective. Be leery of pills that claim to "increase your mental power." One day, however, Alzheimer's disease and other memory problems may be a thing of the past.

 Which drugs or drinks are more effective at enhancing memory than others?

More recent and clinical trial evidence, however, has failed to support these earlier findings (Hirsch, 2013; Vellas et al., 2012). In short, don't believe everything you read or everything you remember!

The prefrontal cortex is the frontmost region of the frontal lobes. It plays an important part in attention, appropriate social behavior, impulse control, and working memory (Baier et al., 2010). Now that we know something about the three types of memory, we can explore the brain regions involved in memory.

Sensory Memory and the Brain Our sensory memory system is fairly straightforward. Recall that sensory neurons carry information about external stimuli from our sense organs to different parts of the brain. First, the sensation travels to the thalamus, which then relays the sensory information to the cerebral cortex for further processing. Three of the five sensory systems have a dedicated sensory cortex for processing sensory stimuli. The visual cortex is located in the occipital lobes, the auditory cortex is in the temporal lobes, and the somatosensory (touch) cortex is in the parietal lobes. Taste and smell do not have their own processing regions, although a particular smell can elicit a very strong and immediate memory, even if it's been decades since you were exposed to that scent.

Connection

Why do smells evoke particularly strong and specific memories?

See "Smell (Olfaction)," in the chapter "Sensing and Perceiving Our World". (p. 152)

optogenetics
A treatment that uses a combination of light stimulation and genetics to manipulate the activity of individual neurons.

Short-Term and Working Memory and the Brain The prefrontal cortex determines what information in the environment is worthy of our attention. Only then does a sensory memory make its way from the prefrontal cortex to the hippocampus. In other words, the encoding stage of memory formation activates the prefrontal cortex as well as the hippocampus, where the memory is consolidated through rehearsal and repetition (R. D. Fields, 2005; Kandel et al., 2000). The repeated firing of neural impulses necessary to convert a short-term memory into a long-term one occurs mostly in the hippocampus. Memory consolidation in the hippocampus may take hours, days, or sometimes weeks before the memory is transferred back to the cortex for permanent storage. As mentioned earlier, think of the hippocampus as being like a librarian—with aid from the frontal lobes, it processes, organizes, and directs memories and then returns them to the appropriate location in the cortex for long-term storage. New techniques such as high resolution imaging and **optogenetics** (a combined technique of light (opto) and genetics to manipulate and stimulate precise clusters of neurons) have recently uncovered much more precise regions of the hippocampus, such as the dentate gyrus and C1 and C3, involved in memory formation (Denny et al., 2014; Goshen, 2014; Nabavi, Fox, Proulx, Lin, Tsien, & Malinow, 2014; Yushkevich et al., 2015).

The hippocampus does not do all of the work in working memory, however. Attention and focus also require the prefrontal cortex. Remember that key functions of working memory are to focus attention and to plan action. When we speak, read, solve problems, or make some other use of working memory, we rely on the prefrontal cortex to keep the crucial information accessible (Baddeley, 1998; Baier et al., 2010; Kandel, 2006; B. L. Miller & Cummings, 1999; Miyake et al., 2000).

The other main function of working memory is rehearsal. Auditory input is processed and rehearsed via the phonological loop from the prefrontal cortex to the language comprehension center (Wernicke's region) in the rear of the left parietal lobes (Paulesu, Frith, & Frackowiak, 1993; Schacter, 2001). The processing pathway for visual information and the visuospatial sketchpad goes from the prefrontal cortex to the temporal lobes (for spatial information) and then to the occipital lobes (for visual information; Baddeley, 2003). Figure 14 highlights the regions of the brain that play a role in short-term (working) memory.

Connection

Optogenetic techniques are now being used to treat various mental disorders, from depression and anxiety to obsessive-compulsive disorder (OCD) and alcoholism.

See "Emerging Therapies" in chapter "Treatment of Psychological Disorders". (p. 636)

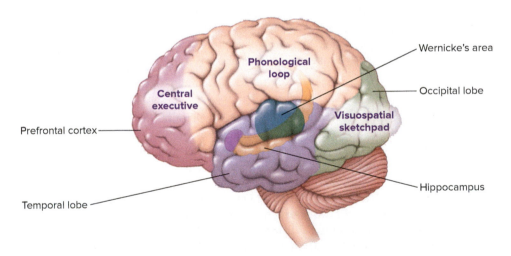

FIGURE 14

BRAIN REGIONS INVOLVED IN WORKING MEMORY. The prefrontal cortex focuses attention on sensory stimuli and holds information long enough for us to solve a problem; then it transfers the information to the hippocampus for memory consolidation. The temporal and occipital lobes, as well as Wernicke's area, are active in the rehearsal of the auditory and visuospatial information needed by working memory.

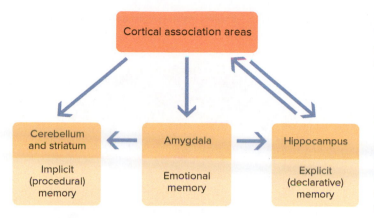

FIGURE 15

THREE LONG-TERM MEMORY SYSTEMS. Memories begin with parallel output from cortical sensory association areas, such as the auditory or visual association areas. Depending on the kind of memory system involved, the output goes to different brain regions. For instance, when we learn to do things (often implicit procedures), output goes mostly to the cerebellum and striatum. When we experience an emotional event, output goes to the amygdala. And when we remember explicit personal events (episodes), facts, and information, output goes mostly to the hippocampus. Those rehearsed and attended-to memories are then returned and stored in the cortical areas from which they came. Think of the hippocampus as being more like a librarian than a library. It processes, organizes, and directs memories and then returns them to the appropriate location in the cortex for long-term storage (Eichenbaum, 2010).

Long-Term Memory and the Brain As noted in the previous section, there are multiple long-term memory systems, and each system involves its own distinct brain regions (Eichenbaum, 2010). One anatomically based model of memory systems proposes three long-term memory systems: procedural-implicit, emotional, and declarative-explicit (see Figure 15).

Long-term memories begin with sensations being processed into output from cortical sensory association areas, such as the auditory or visual association areas. Depending on the kind of memory system involved, the output goes to different brain regions. For instance, when we are learning to do things (implicit procedures), output goes mostly to the cerebellum and striatum. When we experience an emotional event, output goes to the amygdala. And when we consciously and explicitly remember personal events (episodes), facts, and information, output goes mostly to the hippocampus. After being processed by the hippocampus, however, the memory is stored back in the cortical association area from where it came.

H. M. had a very difficult time making new long-term explicit memories because of the damage to his hippocampus and surrounding areas. He could learn tasks such as the star-tracing task, however, because his cerebellum and striatum, which are involved in implicitly learning to carry out procedures, were intact.

We store the different types of long-term memory in different places in the brain. Explicit long-term memories are stored in the cortex, specifically in the area where the original sensation was processed (Ji & Wilson, 2007). Implicit memories are stored in structures in the subcortex, specifically in the striatum (part of the basal ganglia), amygdala, and cerebellum (Kandel, 2006; see Figure 16).

When we actively try to recall information, especially words, from long-term memory, we use the prefrontal cortex (Gershberg & Shimamura, 1995; Mangels et al., 1996; Thompson & Madigan, 2005). Retrieving information requires attention and focus, and hence it involves working memory, which is predominantly an activity of the prefrontal cortex.

Implicit memories of learned skills are also processed and stored in different parts of the brain. Priming, for example, occurs mostly in the cortex. Procedural memories for skills and habits involve the striatum. The amygdala is crucial for associating particular events with emotional responses, such as happiness or fear. So when we learn to associate a neighbor's house with a mean dog and we become afraid of going there, the amygdala is the part of our brain that is most involved.

As we have mentioned, memories for behaviors and skills are implicit, and we process them mostly in the subcortex. We process and store explicit memories for events and facts mostly in the cortex. This can occur only if the hippocampus is intact and can pass them on for long-term cortical storage. Even if part of the hippocampus is removed, we cannot easily form new long-term memories. Damage to the areas of

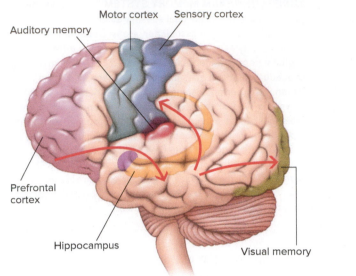

Explicit Memory Storage

Auditory memory

Motor cortex   Sensory cortex

Prefrontal cortex

Hippocampus

Visual memory

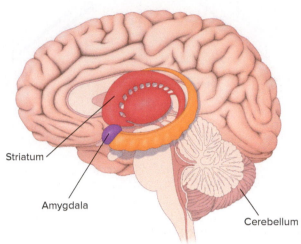

Implicit Memory Storage

Striatum

Amygdala

Cerebellum

FIGURE **16**

BRAIN REGIONS INVOLVED IN LONG-TERM MEMORY. Many different brain areas are involved in memory. The hippocampus is involved in laying down and retrieving memories, particularly personal ones and those related to finding your way about. After being processed in the hippocampus, explicit long-term memories are returned to the cortex for storage in the area where the sensory information was processed originally. Implicit memories are processed and stored in the cortex, the striatum, and the amygdala (Kandel, 2006).

the cortex involved in processing particular kinds of information can lead to deficits in that knowledge system. For instance, damage to the temporal lobe often results in problems with one's sense of direction—that is, spatial problems. In the chapter "Consciousness," we introduced David, who suffered a major brain injury when hit by a car. David's injury involved portions of the left temporal lobe of his brain. Since his accident, David can get lost easily in almost any location except his immediate neighborhood, which he sees daily. Even there, he knows that, if he wanders more than a few blocks down the street, he may become disoriented and lose his way.

The importance of the amygdala in making emotional events memorable is seen in people with damaged amygdalas. They do not recall emotional events better than non-emotional events (Adolphs et al., 1997). In fact, there is evidence that amygdala damage can impair memories for the overall feeling of an event, but not for details. The details are still there, but the emotional accent is gone (Adolphs, Tranel, & Buchanan, 2005). Moreover, damage to the left amygdala results in deficits in verbal recall of emotional events (Buchanan et al., 2001).

Challenging Assumptions in Brain Stimulation and Memory

It is perhaps obvious—at least in retrospect—that drugs that alter neural functioning and change gene expression in the brain can enhance or dampen memory formation, but what about electrical charges applied on the outside of the skull? Could they possibly accomplish the same thing? It almost seems like voodoo, magic, or pseudoscience to make such a claim.

There is a growing body of scientific evidence, however, that stimulating the brain with very weak electrical charges can indeed enhance memory and learning. The modern form of this research was so hard to believe to established scientists that it took more than 5 years before a scientific journal accepted the basic finding. The scientist who challenged the field's assumptions, Alberto Priori, put it this way: "People kept telling me it can't be true, it's too easy and simple" (Hurley, 2013, p. 51). Other criticisms were that the charge was too weak to pass through the skull (less than 10 milliamps) or that it was too dangerous. As it turns out, none of the criticisms were true (Hurley, 2013).

Electrical stimulation of the brain in one form or another has been around for more than 250 years. Indeed, Ben Franklin suffered amnesia after accidentally administering an electric shock to his head (Kadosh & Elliot, 2013). Its medical use goes back to the 1740s, and it was used successfully to treat people with depression as early as 1804 (Utz et al., 2010). In the mid-1960s, Albert (1966) was the first to report its positive effect on memory consolidation. It wasn't until the mid- to late 1990s, however, with Priori's work that the modern period of brain stimulation research really took off as a field of research (Priori et al., 1998).

Electrical stimulation of the brain is technically called **transcranial direct current stimulation,** or tDCS. The basic idea is straightforward: A very weak voltage (less than 10 one-thousands of an amp or 10 milliamps) is administered via at least two electrodes (at least one positive and at least one negative) placed on the scalp (see Figure 17). The technique is both painless and safe (Utz et al., 2010). The research on cognitive enhancement and tDCS has reported that positively charged (anodal) stimulation increases memory in general and that negatively charged (cathodal) stimulation interferes with memory (Brasil-Neto, 2012; Dedoncker et al., 2016; Fregni et al., 2005; Utz et al., 2010). More specifically, implicit memory and working memory are enhanced when part of the left prefrontal cortex (PFC) is stimulated (Dedoncker et al., 2016; Fregni et al., 2005; Kincses et al., 2004; Utz et al., 2010; see Research Process, Figure 18, for more details of the Fregni et al., 2005 study). Research has also shown that transcranial electrical stimulation during sleep improves recall of word pairs and of pictures in young and older adults (Ladenbauer et al., 2016; Marshall et al., 2004); and of the temporoparietal lobes improves word recognition memory in Alzheimer's patients (Ferrucci et al., 2008).

transcranial direct current stimulation (tDCS)
Electrical stimulation of the brain.

FIGURE **17**

TRANSCRANIAL DIRECT CURRENT STIMULATION. A typical transcranial direct current stimulation (tDCS) setup.

©Neuroscience Research Australia

 Can very low voltage (less than 10 milliamps) enhance memory formation? How?
Growing evidence suggests that it can.

Research Process

1 Research Question

Does very weak electrical stimulation of the prefrontal cortex (PFC) enhance working memory?

2 Method

To assess working memory, participants were presented with a letter (A–J) for 30 milliseconds on a computer screen. A new letter was displayed every 2 seconds. The working memory task was to recall whether a letter was the same as one presented three letters previously and hence is dubbed the "three back task."

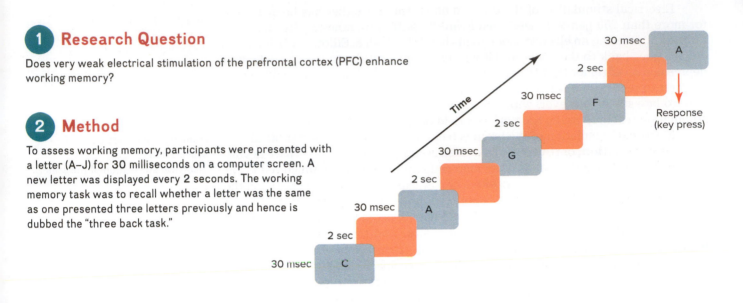

Starting 5 min prior to and continuing during the 5 min duration of the working memory task participants received very weak (< 10 milliamp) electrical brain stimulation (tDCS; total time was 10 min). For baseline comparison, participants also underwent the same procedure except with a "sham" stimulation (that is, no stimulation was actually administered). Half of the participants received the active stimulation first and half the sham first and there was a 1-hour "wash out" session in between sessions to erase any effects of the previous session.

3 Results

When the PFC was stimulated total number of letters recalled out of 30 was significantly higher than when during sham stimulation.

4 Conclusion

A brief (10-min) transcranial direct current stimulation (tDCS) of the prefrontal cortex (PFC) does enhance working memory.

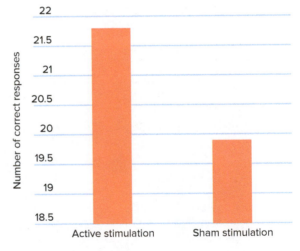

FIGURE **18**

ELECTRICAL STIMULATION AND WORKING MEMORY. In the 2005 study by Fregni and his colleagues, letters are presented for 30 milliseconds (ms), followed by a 2 second orange screen, followed by another 30 ms presentation of a different letter (Fregni et al., 2005).

1. When we actively try to recall information, especially words, from long-term memory, we use the
   a. occipital cortex.
   b. prefrontal cortex.
   c. parietal cortex.
   d. parahippocampal gyrus.

2. Rehearsal makes memories stick. So does
   a. drunkenness.
   b. storage.
   c. emotion.
   d. fatigue.

3. Neurons that _____ together, _____ together.
   a. grow; sow
   b. lie; die
   c. synapse; degrade
   d. fire; wire

4. One sea slug had frequent and closely-spaced-in-time puffs of air administered to it. Another had frequent puffs but they were not closely spaced. Yet another slug had one puff administered to it. Which one is most likely to remember this aversive event?
   a. the one with frequent and closely spaced air puffs
   b. the one with frequent but not closely spaced air puffs
   c. the one with one air puff
   d. They all are equally likely to remember the event.

5. CREB is a(n) _____ that switches on genes responsible for the development of new synapses.
   a. amino acid
   b. protein
   c. neurotransmitter
   d. enzyme

6. For which of the following is there at least some scientific evidence that it can enhance memory?
   a. caffeine
   b. ginkgo biloba
   c. drugs that enhance the protein CREB
   d. all of the above

Answers can be found at the end of the chapter.

MALLEABILITY OF MEMORY

One of the major discoveries over the last 25 years in the science of memory is how changing, malleable, and fallible memories and memory formation are. Memory is more an act of continuous reconstruction than objective construction of events. We would like to think that memories are accurate and objective depictions of reality, as if our minds were simply recording events like a video camera. We know that is not true. There are numerous ways in which memory is dynamic and fallible, including reconsolidation, selective and divided attention, eyewitness testimony, false memories, recovered memories, and suggestibility and misinformation. The message is clear: Challenge your assumptions about memory and don't believe everything you remember.

Reconsolidation

The very act of recalling an event changes it (Cai et al., 2012; Levy, Kuhl, & Wagner, 2010; Nader, Schafe, & Le Doux, 2000). Soon after forming, memories are vulnerable to disappearing unless they get strengthened and consolidated. But what is really fascinating is that already formed and consolidated memories become vulnerable again each time they are recalled and must be consolidated all over again. This process is known formally as **reconsolidation** and happens when the reactivation of a memory temporarily weakens the original memory and a new consolidation happens, but this time resulting a slightly different memory (Cai et al., 2012; Kroes et al., 2014; Nader et al., 2000; Soeter & Kindt, 2015). In short, with reconsolidation, the process of remembering changes our original memory. The original research on reconsolidation by Nader and colleagues (2000) was the inspiration behind the romantic science-fiction movie *Eternal Sunshine of the Spotless Mind.*

reconsolidation
Occurs when a reactivation of a memory weakens the original memory and a new consolidation happens, but this time resulting a slightly different memory.

Selective and Divided Attention

As we have seen throughout this chapter, attention is the first step in getting an experience into short-term memory and potentially to long-term memory. But attention by its very nature is selective. If it weren't we would be completely overwhelmed by the chaos of sensory experience. But because we have different minds with different values, attitudes, beliefs, and experiences we select different things to pay attention to, even in the same event. As we saw in the chapter "Consciousness," this is known as selective attention. Therefore, our memories of events are always somewhat uniquely our own. Different people remember the same events differently because they pay attention to different parts of the experience and it means different things to them (James et al., 2016; Mifflin, Chorney, & Dick, 2016). This is normal, natural, and unavoidable. But it does lead to memory distortion.

Divided attention is similar to yet different from selective attention. Divided attention exists when we are trying to focus on more than one activity at once. When we try to focus on multiple activities at once, and are distracted during the encoding process, our memory for either activity suffers (Craik et al., 1996; Fernandes & Moscovitch, 2000; Fernandes et al., 2016; Weeks & Hasher, 2016).

Challenge Your Assumptions

True or False? When victims of a crime get a good look at the perpetrators of crimes, odds are quite good they could accurately pick them out of a photo lineup.

False: Eyewitness memories, even if they are reported soon after the crime, range from mildly inaccurate to severely inaccurate.

Eyewitness Testimony

Elizabeth Loftus has conducted the most systematic research on two major types of memory distortion: eyewitness testimony and false and recovered memories. Her findings changed our understanding of how memory works. Eyewitness testimony can sometimes be the deciding evidence presented at a trial, so the reliability of eyewitnesses' recall is a central concern for judges, lawyers, and jurors. Historically, lawyers and jurors have been prone to believe the testimony of eyewitnesses unless it was contradicted by firm, hard evidence. As it turns out, there are lots of problems with the eyewitness memories of crimes (Schacter & Loftus, 2013).

A case in point is the rape case of Jennifer Thompson. It is worth telling in a bit more detail as a example of faulty eyewitness memory. Recall the case at the beginning of this chapter of Jennifer Thompson and Ronald Cotton (Thompson-Cannino, Cotton, & Torneo, 2009). Although Jennifer studied the face of her rapist as carefully and as meticulously as she could under the circumstances, the actual rapist, Bobby Poole, was never in the photo lineup or in the live lineup. But someone who looked incredibly similar to Poole was, namely, Ronald Cotton. In Thompson's mind then Cotton became the rapist because memory is not perfect. Ironically, Cotton and Poole ended up in the same prison—Poole had been arrested and convicted on another rape charge—and people in the prison would confuse the two. Because of this evidence, Cotton was granted a second trial. But at the second trial, when Jennifer saw both Poole and Cotton together in the same courtroom, she still identified Cotton as her rapist. So Cotton was convicted yet again. It wasn't until years later that DNA testing, which did not exist yet for the first two trials, exonerated Cotton and convicted Poole. Cotton, however, spent 11 years in prison for a crime he did not commit. The only evidence against him was someone's memory. Amazingly, Cotton not only understood and forgave Thompson, the two became close friends and wrote a book together about their case called *Picking Cotton* (Thompson-Cannino et al., 2009). They still tour the country together speaking on behalf of judicial reform.

False Memories

The most fascinating, if not the most disturbing, example of suggestibility comes from research on false memories and recovered memories. **False memories** are memories for events that never happened but were suggested by someone or something (Kaplan et al., 2015; Loftus, 1997; Loftus & Pickrell, 1995). With a false memory, an individual develops an actual memory, sometimes very elaborate and detailed, based on false information. Loftus pioneered the technique of suggesting falsely that subjects in her studies experienced some event and then later asking them about their memories of that event. To be sure, a majority of the subjects never recalled anything, but across eight studies, on average 31% of the participants did create false memories (Lindsay et al., 2004). In case you are wondering, people with highly superior autobiographical memory—such as Jill Price, whom we discussed in the opening of the chapter—are not immune to false memories (Patihis et al., 2013).

Recovered Memories

A **recovered memory** is supposedly from a real event—a memory that was encoded and stored but is not retrieved for a long period of time; the memory is retrieved after a later event brings it suddenly to consciousness. Recovered memories have been blocked or repressed for years. Recent research shows that people who suffered childhood sexual abuse do, in fact, have less specific autobiographical memories than people who did not suffer childhood sexual abuse (Raymaekers et al., 2010). They are not likely to remember specific events on specific days from their childhood. Their memories tend to be general—for example, "when I was about 9, one summer our family took a trip to New York. But I can't recall any specific details of the trip." Interestingly, however, compared to people with recovered memories, those who were abused and had continuous recall of the event (that is, did not have to recover the memory later) have equally poor specific autobiographical memories (Raymaekers et al., 2010). Traumatic events may alter how people store memories and, as a defense, make them less likely to be specific in their recall.

The topic of recovered memories, however, is controversial (Lynn et al., 2015). Sometimes they are triggered while a person is under the care of a psychotherapist. Controversy arises when it is not clear whether the psychotherapist has helped a patient recover a memory of an actual event or has unwittingly suggested an event that the client "remembers." If the event involves traumatic experiences, such as physical or sexual abuse, and people's lives are at stake, recovered memory becomes an explosive topic, as it did when the phenomenon first came to light in the early 1990s.

Suggestibility and Misinformation

Another form of memory distortion and malleability is **suggestibility,** which occurs when memories are implanted in our minds based on leading questions, comments, or suggestions from someone else or some other source. We are most prone to suggestions that are present in the interval between our original experience and the time we are asked to recall it.

Loftus and her colleagues were among the first memory researchers to demonstrate that people's memories of events, even under the best of circumstances, are not very accurate and are susceptible to suggestion (Loftus, 1974, 1996, 2003). In one classic study, Loftus (1974) showed participants

©Steve Cole/Getty Images

Leading questions might influence how an eyewitness recalls a car accident. Did these cars "hit" each other or "smash" each other?

an event on videotape and then asked them to answer questions, some of which contained misleading evidence or suggestions about the event they had just witnessed. A misleading suggestion, for instance, could be about what a person on the tape was wearing. After answering these questions, participants were asked to recall specific details about the event they had seen on videotape. The results showed that participants are likely to incorporate suggestions about the wrong clothing into their memory and even elaborate on them.

Another classic study from Loftus's lab indicates how changing the wording of a question impacts people's recall for events. People will estimate higher speeds of travel when asked "How fast were the cars going when they *smashed* into each other?" rather than "How fast were the cars going when they hit each other?" (Loftus, 2003). With the first question, people also are more likely to report seeing broken glass than with the second question, simply because one word in the question is different. This effect is unconscious: People have no idea and will even deny that they have responded differently to the different wording in the questions.

Related to suggestibility distortion of memory is the misinformation effect. The **misinformation effect** occurs when information learned after the original event (crime) is wrong or misleading but gets incorporated into the memory as true (Loftus, 2005). Even brief exposure to misinformation can lead to long-term false memories (Zhu et al., 2012). The good news is that the misinformation effect can be greatly reduced (cut in half) by simply warning people in advance that not all information may be accurate (Blank & Launay, 2014). Moreover, not everyone is equally susceptible to the misinformation effect. People with strong memories, high intelligence, good face recognition, and with personalities that are open to experience and depressed are less vulnerable to the misinformation effect (Zhu et al., 2010a, 2010b).

misinformation effect
Occurs when information learned after an original event (e.g., crime) is wrong or misleading but gets incorporated into the memory as true.

1. Which technology metaphor is best for how memories work?
   a. camera
   b. video camera
   c. text editor
   d. typewriter

2. The fact that changing the wording of a question impacts people's recall for events illustrates which kind of forgetting?
   a. retroactive interference
   b. traceability
   c. rephrasing
   d. suggestibility

3. Gwendolyn is 29 years old and is now convinced that she was abused as a child. From the time she was 9 until she was 28, however, she had no recollection of the abuse. Gwendolyn has
   a. a false memory.
   b. long-term memory loss.
   c. amnesia.
   d. a recovered memory.

Answers can be found at the end of the chapter.

FORGETTING AND MEMORY LOSS

We all forget things. In fact, forgetting can be quite necessary. Once information is no longer useful or need or used, it degrades in our brains. **Forgetting** occurs when memories degrade, decline, or die. Just as there are different kinds of memory, there are also different kinds of forgetting.

Forms of Forgetting

One reason we forget is **interference,** which occurs when other information competes with the information we are trying to recall. Interference can happen in one of two ways (Jacoby, Hessels, & Bopp, 2001). First, **retroactive interference** occurs when new experiences or information cause people to forget previously learned experiences or information. Memory's vulnerability to interference from information that follows immediately after an event has profound applications. For example, the recall of a crime by an eyewitness, even if only minutes after the crime (which it usually is not), will be distorted by the events that occur in those few minutes (or hours or days or weeks) after the crime. A second type of interference, **proactive interference,** occurs when previously learned information interferes with the learning of new information. Perhaps the serial position effect occurs because the process of remembering the first words interferes proactively with recall of the middle words.

Research on forgetting began in the 1880s with Herman Ebbinghaus, who found that recall shows a steady decline over time (Erdelyi, 2010). This decline is what is now called Ebbinghaus's **forgetting curve.** A classic demonstration of the forgetting curve comes from the work of Norman Slamecka and Brian McElree (1983). Participants in their research were given a long list of words to learn. Some saw the list once; others saw it three times. Moreover, some were asked to recall the list either immediately or 1, 2, 3, or 4 days later. When Slamecka and McElree plotted the results, they produced the classic forgetting curve. Recall was between 70% and 80% immediately, but it declined steadily for each additional day between learning and recalling the word list (see Figure 19). It is noteworthy that seeing the list three times, compared to once, increased recall only a little bit.

forgetting
The weakening or loss of memories over time.

interference
Disruption of memory because other information competes with the information we are trying to recall.

retroactive interference
Disruption of memory because new experiences or information causes people to forget previously learned experiences or information.

proactive interference
Disruption of memory because previously learned information interferes with the learning of new information.

forgetting curve
A graphic depiction of how recall steadily declines over time.

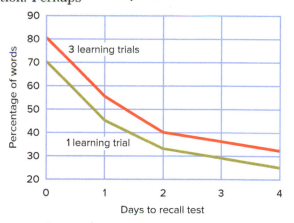

FIGURE 19

THE FORGETTING CURVE. Forgetting happens in a predictable way over time. The forgetting curve shows that, with each passing day, we remember less, though the rate of decline slows (Slamecka & McElree, 1983).

absent-mindedness
A form of forgetfulness that results
from inattention.

Most normal forgetting occurs because we don't pay close attention when we first learn or experience something, so we never encode or consolidate the memory very well. In contrast, **absent-mindedness** is a form of forgetfulness that involves attention as well as memory (Cheyne, Carriere, & Smilek, 2006; Robertson, 2003). For example, Sandra is distraught over not being able to find her keys. After spending 10 minutes looking all over the house in all of the obvious places, she finally goes out the front door to the car, only to discover that the keys are still in the lock to the house. Such experiences happen when we do not pay close attention or we divide our attention among different tasks.

Absent-mindedness increases with age, but it typically is not a problem until people reach their 70s (Schacter, 2001). Due to the slowing of processing speed and less ability to filter out irrelevant information with age, some degree of dementia or age-related memory decline is common in people in their 60s and 70s (Salthouse, 2000; Van Gerven et al., 2007). As is true with all cognitive capacities, there are vast differences among individuals in memory decline with age. Some people show little decline into their 90s, while others begin to experience it in their 40s.

Connection

Most people think they can multi-task well. Research shows otherwise—especially when it comes to talking on the phone while driving.

See "Sustained Attention," in the chapter "Consciousness." (p. 222)

Regular aerobic exercise, higher education level, and certain personality traits act as a buffer against age-related memory decline (Caselli et al., 2016; Nouchi et al., 2014; Schmand et al., 1997; ten Brinke et al., 2015). For example, Caselli and colleagues (2016) in a longitudinal study of healthy elderly adults found that those high in the personality trait of conscientiousness (being detail oriented, careful, and orderly) had less cognitive and memory decline as they aged compared to those low in the trait. Moreover, those high in neuroticism (anxiety and depression prone) showed greater cognitive decline. One of the few cross-cultural studies to compare age-related memory decline found no cultural differences in the effect (Crook et al., 1992). Age-related memory decline, in other words, appears to be universal (Matsumoto & Juang, 2004).

blocking
The inability to retrieve some information that once was stored.

repression
The unconscious act of keeping threatening thoughts, feelings, or impulses out of consciousness.

amnesia
Memory loss due to brain injury or disease.

anterograde amnesia
The inability to remember events and experiences that occur after an injury or the onset of a disease.

Another form of forgetting is **blocking,** or the inability to retrieve some information that once was stored—say, a person's name or an old phone number (Schacter, 2001). It simply won't resurface, despite our efforts. One example of blocking is the frustrating *tip-of-the-tongue* phenomenon in which we can almost recall something but the memory eludes us. We might even know that the word begins with a particular letter. We say to ourselves, I know it! It's right there. I can even see her face. Her name begins with an M. More often than not, it does begin with that letter. **Repression,** in which the retrieval of memories that have been encoded and stored is actively inhibited, is another example of blocking. Memories of a traumatic experience are more likely to be repressed than are other memories. The implication is that, under the right circumstances—during psychotherapy, for instance—the person may suddenly remember the repressed event. We come back to this topic in the next section when we discuss "recovered memories."

Memory Loss Caused by Brain Injury and Disease

When people forget due to injury or disease to the brain, the condition is known as **amnesia.** Two types of amnesia associated with organic injury or disease are anterograde amnesia and retrograde amnesia (Collinson, Meyyappan, & Rosenfeld, 2009). **Anterograde amnesia** is the inability to remember events and experiences that occur *after* an injury or the onset of a disease. People with anterograde amnesia fail to make new long-term memories. They recall experiences for only a short period of time, perhaps 10 minutes or less. H. M., whose case we recounted earlier in the chapter, had anterograde amnesia after his hippocampus had been removed. **Retrograde amnesia** is an inability to recall events or experiences that happened *before* the onset of the disease or injury. The memory loss in this type of amnesia might involve only the incident that preceded it or might include years of memories. Accidents almost always result in retrograde amnesia of the event itself. Car accident victims, for instance, will usually say that they do not remember the accident.

retrograde amnesia
An inability to recall events or experiences that happened before the onset of a disease or injury.

One of your author's brother, David, suffered a brain injury (from the chapter "Consciousness") that resulted in problems with both anterograde and retrograde amnesia. A typical example of David's anterograde amnesia is that, on meeting friends who visit infrequently, David will forget having met them at all and say, "Have I told you about my memory problem?"

An example of the retrograde amnesia that David experiences is that he cannot remember anything that happened in the months before his accident, which includes completing a very difficult bicycle ride, which he would have considered "the memory of a lifetime." His accident erased this event from his long-term memory, likely because the region of his cortex that stored those memories was permanently damaged or destroyed.

As we discussed in the chapter "Human Development," a severe form of age-related memory loss occurs in the organic brain disease known dementia, the most common form of which is Alzheimer's disease. Although it can affect people in their 40s or 50s, Alzheimer's disease usually strikes people in their 60s, 70s, and 80s (Toyota et al., 2007). It results in progressive memory loss, ending with complete memory loss. For instance, forgetting the death of a spouse is common among people who suffer from moderate to severe forms of Alzheimer's. They may go through the whole grieving process over and over, as if each time someone reminds them that their loved ones are gone they are hearing the news for the first time. In Alzheimer's disease, experiences are lost due to anterograde amnesia, which can be caused by retroactive interference and absent-mindedness.

Quick Quiz 5: Forgetting and Memory Loss

1. Sofia is fluent in Spanish and is now trying to learn French. Much of it comes easy to her, yet she keeps forgetting some French words that are similar to yet different from their Spanish equivalent. The kind of forgetting that Sofia is suffering from is
   a. amnesia.
   b. retroactive interference.
   c. proactive interference.
   d. blocking.

2. Jon was in an automobile accident. It has now been a month since his accident, and he has no recollection of the 2 days after the accident. He suffers from
   a. anterograde amnesia.
   b. retrograde amnesia.

   c. posttraumatic amnesia.
   d. selective amnesia.

3. The predictable pattern of forgetting that shows that we forget more and more over time but that the rate of forgetting declines with time is known as _____.
   a. absent-mindedness
   b. forgetting curve
   c. repression
   d. anterograde amnesia

Answers can be found at the end of the chapter.

Bringing It All Together

Making Connections in Memory

How to Study

One of the most common questions students have while learning about memory in introductory psychology is "How can I use this material to study more efficiently?" This question may come up after the first exam, especially from students who expected an A but got a C. "What did I do wrong? I reread my notes, highlighted the book; how come I didn't do better?" It turns out that the things that worked for you in high school might not work anymore. To master a lot of complex new material, you may have to adopt new study strategies. You can make psychological science work for you by using the years of research about memory to optimize how to learn new material and prepare for exams (Bjork, 2001; Kornell & Bjork, 2007; Kornell et al., 2010; Soderstrom et al., 2016).

Consider that anything you hear in lecture or read in the book—after a brief stint in sensory memory—is in that vulnerable place called short-term memory. Your job is to move this information into long-term memory and then to retrieve it for an exam. In particular, the material you learn in any class—new facts, terms, processes, and so on—is semantic memory. Like all long-term memories, how well you remember this material begins with encoding.

1. *Go to class and pay attention.* Attending and paying attention in lecture is the first very important step. If there is something you don't understand when the instructor first mentions it, ask a question about it right away. If you are too shy to do so in class or you can't get a word in edgewise with your instructor, note it in the margin of your notes, so that you can go back to it later. Consider that, if you don't attend to it now, you'll forget it by the end of class. Why?

   The interference of new material presented afterward, the fact that your stomach is growling, and thoughts of getting to your next class in time will make it difficult for you to remember what you wanted to ask. If you don't rehearse or work with the material in some way, it will be gone. By being in class and hearing in more detail what was posted on the lecture outline and what you read in the text, you give yourself another context in which to work with the material: engaging your attention. Avoid creating sources of interference, such as talking with a friend, text messaging, or emailing during lecture. If you start optimizing how you encode material in class, you will be ahead of the game. If you can do this, you are much more likely to store the information in long-term memory and be able to retrieve it easily during the exam. Who knows, some of the information might even stay with you longer than that.

2. *Read the text before class.* To increase the odds of learning and remembering the material for a long period of time, it is important to read the material in the text, because it helps you establish a network of associations in which to fit the new material, so that when you hear your instructor talk about it, you have a place to put the information—you can make the associations. A related encoding tool is connecting the new material you learn to things you have already experienced, so you begin to build more associations.

   What else can help at the encoding stage? Many professors post lecture outlines electronically before class, which, like reading the text in advance, gives you the opportunity to begin encoding and storing material from the upcoming lecture before you get there. Reading through both lecture material and text assignments before going to class *primes* you to process the lecture material in a deep and meaningful way.

3. *Study deeply, not shallowly.* In addition to the lecture and book information, you can improve the way you study the material outside of class. What you have learned from levels of processing theory can help you in your approach to studying. According to depth of processing theory and research, the more deeply you process material, the better you will be able to recall it. Rereading notes and highlighting the text are both examples of shallow processing; they involve rote rehearsal. You want to process the material semantically, to work with the meaning of the material, which enhances your depth of processing and memory. Simply reading a definition of a term such as storage over and over again is not all that different from repeating a list of nonsense words, but if you attempt to work with the meaning of the material,

you will remember it better. Think about it. *Storage* is a word we use a lot, and you only recently saw it related to memory. In everyday speech, it means "to put something away and keep it there," such as storing your memorabilia from high school in the attic of your parents' house. You put your yearbooks, varsity jacket, and track trophies into a box and take them to the attic. You label the box and make a mental note—maybe even a cognitive map—of where you put the box, so that you will be able to retrieve it later. Memory storage is just like this. It is the process of putting something away and leaving it there for future use. If you can elaborate your understanding of concepts such as storage in this way, you don't have to remember their word-for-word definitions, because you understand what they mean. That's good semantic processing. Add a few salient visual images to the mix—maybe an old bicycle and Darth Vader costume in the attic—and your depth of processing increases.

Also, the more different ways you work with material, the better you learn it. Connecting the concept of storage with your own experience— storing your high school things in a box—places *storage* into a semantic network of associations, with meaningful nodes in other networks: high school (friends, sports, classes, graduation), your parents' attic (and all the attic junk you know is up there), and boxes and other forms of storage (file cabinets, closets). By making the material personally relevant, you are adding the element of emotional significance, which strengthens the associations. Moreover, every time you succeed at storing information deeply and permanently in long-term memory, you change your brain. Proteins in your neurons are activating genes that promote the growth of new dendrites and synapses.

Research on student study habits shows that spacing out study activities is also important. Students tend to cram right before an exam, thinking that this is the most effective approach to learning. However, spacing things out and covering topics or chapters in separate study sessions, using both studying and self-testing of that material, is much more effective

for long-term memory (Kornell & Bjork, 2007; Kornell et al., 2010).

4. *Form a study group.* Another way to increase depth of processing is to form a study group. Getting together with a few other students to review and discuss the material before an exam can be enormously helpful, as long as you prepare beforehand. Meeting with your peers to discuss course material adds new information, fills in gaps, and helps build up new semantic networks, but most importantly it offers a context in which to talk about the material. You might also have a peer who can explain a concept in a way that your instructor did not. Study groups foster discourse, social interaction, and the need to make another person understand you. This requires semantic processing, preparation, and some emotional charge. It is also important to have time between meeting with the study group and taking the test, so that you can go over any lingering questions that may have arisen during study group and consolidate your learning. To be sure that the material you are studying becomes consolidated, or firmly established, make a point of sleeping well after studying.

5. *Devise meaningful mnemonics.* Will you be able to access the information you learned when you need it? What can you do while studying to facilitate retrieval? Reviewing material with a study group is like a practice test, which is a nice evaluation of retrieval ability. Also, using an easy-to-remember mnemonic device during encoding may make it easier to retrieve the information later. If you make a concept personally relevant and integrate it into a semantic network, you can provide yourself with labels or tags as memory prompts. So, for example, to remember the meaning of memory storage, you can just think *attic* and you will activate that whole network of associations.

6. *Get good sleep.* As we have seen in both the chapter "Consciousness" and this chapter, getting a good night's sleep is one of the best and most effective ways to consolidate what we learn during the day. While "pulling an all-nighter" is a college tradition, just understand that it actually cost you cognitively—your memory and retention suffers.

Chapter Review

FORMING MEMORIES

- There are four main steps involved in forming a memory: encoding, consolidating, storing, and retrieving information.

- Encoding involves attending to and taking in the information.

- Consolidation is the process of establishing and solidifying the memory, aided by rehearsal and sleep.

- Storage involves keeping the memory and retaining it over time.

- Retrieval is the process of recalling and making use of the information when it is needed.

- Aids to memory formation include attention, depth of processing, sleep, and emotion.

©Robert Daly/Getty Images

- Impediments to memory formation including distraction and emotion.

TYPES OF MEMORY

- Memory systems are classified as sensory, short-term/working, and long-term.

- Sensory memory is the brief trace of a sensory experience that lasts from less than half a second to 2 or 3 seconds. Iconic memory is the trace memory of a visual sensation. Echoic memory is the short-term retention of sounds.

- Short-term memory holds a limited amount of information for about 2 to 30 seconds, or as long as we continue to rehearse it, before we either transfer it to long-term memory or forget it. Baddeley's model

of working memory describes how we are able to hold information in working memory while solving a problem.

- The serial position effect is a phenomenon of short-term memory whereby we most likely remember information that comes first and last in a series.

- Long-term memory is the repository of any material that we retain for between 30 seconds and a lifetime. It includes implicit memory, in which skills, behaviors, and procedures we don't consciously retrieve are stored, and explicit memories of events (episodes) and facts (semantic) stored for conscious recall.

MEMORY AND THE BRAIN

- Clusters of neurons that fire together are the biological foundation of memory (long-term potentiation).

- Different memories are processed in different areas of the brain. Sensory memories are processed primarily by their respective sensory cortexes. Short-term memories are processed mostly by the hippocampus and frontal lobes. Long-term memories are stored for the most part in the areas of the cortex where they were processed as sensory memories.

- Repetition and sometimes strong emotion initiate neural activity that converts short-term memories into long-term memories. In long-term memory formation, proteins activate genes, which turn on the production of new dendrites and synapses.

- In short-term memory, existing synapses grow stronger with rehearsal, but no new ones form.

- Certain drugs, drinks, and transcranial direct current stimulation can enhance (or block) memory formation.

MALLEABILITY OF MEMORY

- Memory is a reconstructive and changing process more than an objective recording of events.

- Examples of memory's dynamic and changing nature include selective attention, eyewitness testimony, false memories, and recovered memories.

FORGETTING AND MEMORY LOSS

- One form of forgetting is interference, which can happen in one of two ways. Retroactive interference occurs

when new experiences or information cause people to forget previously learned experiences or information.

Proactive interference occurs when previously learned information interferes with the learning of new information.

- Injury or disease to the brain can cause memory loss or amnesia.

- Anterograde amnesia is forgetting events *after* to the injury or disease, whereas retrograde amnesia is forgetting events *before* the injury or disease.

BRINGING IT ALL TOGETHER: MAKING CONNECTIONS IN MEMORY

- Going to class and paying attention to lectures help you encode lecture material deeply.

- Reading the book before a lecture will help you build a richer network of associations of the lecture material.

- You can process material deeply by rehearsing and spacing out your studying.

- Forming a study group facilitates deeper processing of material, because you have to learn by generating information, not simply reading or hearing it.

Key Terms

absent-mindedness
amnesia
anterograde amnesia
associative network
automatic processing
blocking
chunking
consolidation
effortful processing
encoding
episodic memory
explicit memory
false memories
flashbulb memories
forgetting
forgetting curve
hierarchies

highly superior autobiographical memory (HSAM)
implicit memory
interference
levels of processing
long-term memory
long-term potentiation (LTP)
memory
misinformation effect
mnemonic device
optogenetics
prefrontal cortex
priming
proactive interference
procedural memory
reconsolidation
recovered memory

rehearsal
repression
retrieval
retroactive interference
retrograde amnesia
schemas
semantic memory
sensory memory
serial position effect
short-term memory
storage
suggestibility
three-stage model of memory
transcranial direct current stimulation (tDCS)
working memory

Quick Quiz Answers

Quick Quiz 1: 1. a; **2.** d; **3.** a   **Quick Quiz 2: 1.** b; **2.** d; **3.** a; **4.** c   **Quick Quiz 3: 1.** b; **2.** c; **3.** d; **4.** a; **5.** b; **6.** d
Quick Quiz 4: 1. c; **2.** d; **3.** d   **Quick Quiz 5: 1.** c; **2.** a; **3.** b

8 Learning

Chapter Outline

Challenge Your Assumptions

True or False?

- Negative reinforcement is the same as punishment. (see page 307)

- Humans and rats basically learn in the same way. (see page 314)

- Kids are not affected by watching violence in movies or killing in video games. (see page 320)

- Bees learn by watching other bees perform a new task. (see page 321)

©Andrea Golden/Getty Images RF

We are constantly responding to events in the world. Some situations produce lasting changes in us, whereas others do not. Consider these ways in which situations might change a person:

- You are in a well-lit room and someone suddenly turns off the lights. At first you cannot see, but gradually, as your pupils dilate to let in more light in the dim surroundings, your eyes adapt to the dark and you can discern some objects you could not see previously.

- When Rashida enters her grandmother's home, there is always a distinct scent of eucalyptus and black pepper. After staying a little while inside the house, however, she no longer notices the smells at all.

- When he was a child, Ahn was regularly bullied by a boy named Ryan. As an adult, whenever he meets a person named Ryan, Ahn's palms start to sweat and his heart races.

- A young girl sees her mother putting on makeup in a mirror and pursing her lips while applying lipstick. The girl copies her mother's lip movements. Later that afternoon the girl looks in the mirror again, and she purses her lips.

- A father teaches his 5-year-old son how to make a peanut butter sandwich. The next day, the boy successfully makes himself a peanut butter sandwich.

- You visit a new restaurant. The food is delicious and the service is good, so you plan to go again.

Which of these cases do you consider to be examples of learning? *Dark adaptation* is a sensory process, in which the muscles of the iris contract in response to low illumination levels. Eyes can do this automatically, and they will do it in any situation of low illumination without *any* prior experience.

The fact that Rashida could no longer notice the scent of her grandmother's house is an example of *habituation*, the sensory process by which organisms adapt to constant stimulation. The result is a change in response—from smelling odors to not smelling them—that stems from experience. The change is a fairly short-lived one, however. An argument can be made that habituation is not learning, because it can disappear immediately with a slight change in the stimulus. For example, if Rashida just stepped outside for a minute and then went back inside, she would notice the scent again. Still, habituation is often regarded as learning in its simplest form (Carew & Kandel, 1973).

Ahn's fear and anxiety when he meets any Ryan is a form of *learning by association*. Ahn associates *Ryan* with intimidation and violence, and that learned association is long lasting, thereby affecting his immediate response to all Ryans for several years to come.

The girl copying her mother's behavior is *mimicry*. The fact that the girl repeated the lip-pursing gesture later that afternoon suggests that she learned to do it by watching and copying her mother. Learning by observation also played a role in the way the boy learned how to make a sandwich from watching his father.

In the restaurant example, our choice of restaurant was rewarded by good service and food, both of which are consequences that increase the likelihood that we will return to the same restaurant in the future.

In this chapter we will explore what learning is. In so doing, we will examine three major theories of learning—classical conditioning, operant conditioning, and social learning theory. We will also explore the role of evolution in learning and how learning both emerges from and changes the brain.

BASIC PROCESSES OF LEARNING

Psychologists define **learning** as an enduring change in behavior that occurs with experience. This definition sounds simple, but there are many forms of learning—from a child developing a preference for certain foods to a student learning a foreign language. As we try things out in the world, changes in sensation, perception, behavior, and brain functions alter who we are, what we know, what we feel, and what we can do. The essence of learning involves acquiring new knowledge, skills, values, or behaviors.

Learning and memory work together. Without them, we could not process, retain, or make use of new information. Learning occurs when information moves from short-term to long-term memory. During this process, new knowledge is stored in networks in the brain. For this reason, we don't have to learn to ride a bicycle every time we want to go for a spin. Once we have mastered the skill, we can retrieve that knowledge from memory and pedal away without thinking about it.

learning
Enduring changes in behavior that occur with experience.

Association

Association occurs when you experience one object or situation that is linked with another. Think of it as learning by connection. Learning by association can be powerful, and we all experience it. We learn to link bells with class starting and certain smells with powerful memories. Consider the case of how one of your authors, Erika, learned to associate a beloved food with nausea. Erika gets severe motion sickness on boats, in cars, and sometimes on planes. Several years ago, she joined friends on a deep-sea fishing trip. Having taken prescription anti-nausea medication in preparation for the trip, she was confident she would have a good day. Before leaving the yacht harbor that morning, the folks in the boating party ate some doughnuts. Erika chose her favorite flavor, old-fashioned chocolate. Twenty minutes later, the boat left the harbor. Within 5 minutes, Erika was vomiting, and she was violently ill for the next several hours before the boat turned around. Unfortunately, due to no fault of the doughnut, Erika had made a strong association between chocolate doughnuts and seasickness. For 10 years thereafter, the mere sight or smell of a chocolate doughnut nauseated her.

Associations form simply as a result of two events occurring together, whether or not the relationship between them makes any sense. In our example, the taste and smell of the doughnut was linked with nausea in Erika's mind, even though motion (not the doughnut) had caused her sickness. Association is at the core of this kind of learning, known as condition taste aversion. By virtue of their connection, one event may come to suggest that the other will occur.

association
A process by which two pieces of information from the environment are repeatedly linked, so that we begin to connect them in our minds.

CONDITIONING MODELS OF LEARNING

Conditioning is the process by which a behavior becomes more likely due to association with events that occur in the organism's environment. Erika, for example, was *conditioned* to feel nausea to chocolate doughnuts, because she associated that food with the growing motion sickness she felt as the boat left the yacht harbor.

At the most basic level, one can distinguish between two types of conditioning: classical and operant. Both are forms of associative learning. In classical conditioning, organisms learn from connections or associations between stimuli. In operant conditioning, organisms learn from the consequences of their behavior. Let's look at these two forms of conditioning in more detail.

conditioning
A form of associative learning in which behaviors are triggered by associations with events in the environment.

Classical Conditioning

In **classical conditioning**, learning occurs when a neutral stimulus becomes associated with a stimulus to which the learner has an automatic, inborn response. Exactly how this works will become clearer if we consider the pioneering example of Ivan Pavlov and his dogs.

Pavlov's Dogs   Ivan Pavlov received the Nobel Prize in Medicine in 1904 for his research on saliva and digestion. While he was studying digestion in dogs, Pavlov (1906, 1928) discovered classical conditioning quite accidentally—a famous example of how scientists looking at one thing inadvertently discover another.

In order to examine digestive enzymes in the dogs' saliva, Pavlov and his technicians placed tubes in the dogs' mouths to collect their saliva. Then they placed meat powder in their mouths, which naturally produces salivation. After doing this for a while, Pavlov noticed that the dogs began to salivate even before the meat powder was presented. It was as if the sounds of the technician preparing the apparatus signaled to the dogs that meat powder was about to come (Fancher, 1996). Pavlov reasoned that the dogs had formed an association between a stimulus that had no inherent food value (the sound of the apparatus) and one that did (the meat powder). This made him wonder: Could he teach a dog to salivate to something else?

(top): ©Time & Life Pictures/Getty Images;
(bottom): ©Pictorial Press Ltd/Alamy

Pavlov and his dogs

Pavlov designed a laboratory experiment that mimicked the conditions in which the dogs salivated to sounds made by the technician. Working with various dogs, Pavlov rang a bell just before showing them the meat powder. The bell can be considered a **neutral stimulus**, because by itself it has no effect on salivation or appetite. The dogs had no previous experience with the bell. They salivated to the meat powder, because dogs always salivate to meat powder, from the first time they smell it. Salivation is a reflex, an automatic response to a particular stimulus (food) that requires no learning.

Pavlov presented the bell along with the meat powder to the dogs over and over again. The dogs salivated. Then he tried presenting the bell alone to see if the dogs might now link the bell with the meat powder in the way the first dogs linked the noise of the apparatus with the meat powder. The dogs salivated to the bell alone. By virtue of the association made during repeated pairings with meat powder, the bell had come to signal "meat powder" to the dogs. The dogs had learned that they would get meat powder after the bell sounded.

How Classical Conditioning Works   Pavlov called the kind of learning he'd observed the *conditioning of reflexes*; psychologists now call it *classical conditioning*. He coined the term **unconditioned response (UCR)** to describe an automatic, involuntary response to a stimulus. *Unconditioned* simply means "unlearned." In Pavlov's research, salivation was the UCR. Pavlov used the term **unconditioned stimulus (UCS)** to refer to the environmental input (meat powder) that always produced the same unlearned, involuntary response (salivation). Without learning, the UCS always produces the UCR; in Pavlov's experiment, meat powder—the UCS—always led to salivation—the UCR.

Food makes you salivate, pressure on your eye makes you blink, and a tap just below your kneecap causes your leg to jerk forward. These reflexes are unlearned, fixed responses to specific types of environmental stimuli. Pavlov defined reflexes, such as salivation in response to food, as fixed stimulus-response patterns. Classical conditioning is the modification of these stimulus-response (S-R) relationships with experience. Pavlov presented the neutral stimulus (bell) right before the UCS (meat powder); salivation in the presence of meat powder was the UCR.

After repeated pairings of the bell with meat powder and the bell alone led to salivation, the bell became a *conditioned stimulus*. A **conditioned stimulus (CS)** is a previously neutral stimulus that an organism learns to associate with

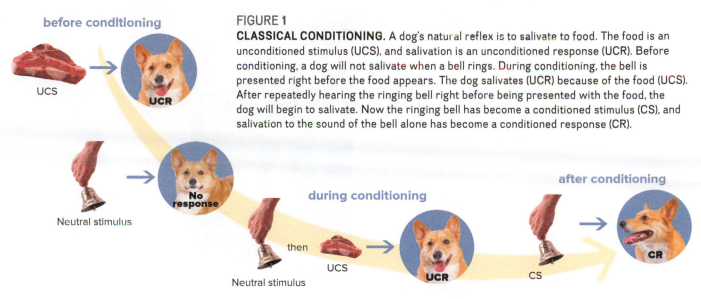

UCS

UCR

No response

Neutral stimulus

Neutral stimulus

then

UCS

during conditioning

UCR

CS

after conditioning

CR

FIGURE 1

CLASSICAL CONDITIONING. A dog's natural reflex is to salivate to food. The food is an unconditioned stimulus (UCS), and salivation is an unconditioned response (UCR). Before conditioning, a dog will not salivate when a bell rings. During conditioning, the bell is presented right before the food appears. The dog salivates (UCR) because of the food (UCS). After repeatedly hearing the ringing bell right before being presented with the food, the dog will begin to salivate. Now the ringing bell has become a conditioned stimulus (CS), and salivation to the sound of the bell alone has become a conditioned response (CR).

(steak): ©Stewart Waller/fStop/Getty Images RF; (bell): ©Pixtal/SuperStock RF

the UCS. If salivation occurred in response to the CS (as it did in Pavlov's experiment), it would then be called a conditioned response. A **conditioned response (CR)** is a behavior that an organism learns to perform when presented with the CS alone. Figure 1 shows how classical conditioning works.

Notice that Figure 1 shows the neutral stimulus being presented just before the UCS. This process is known as *forward conditioning*. One can also present the neutral stimulus and UCS simultaneously. When the neutral stimulus follows the UCS, a process called *backward conditioning*, conditioning is less successful. An example of backward conditioning would be sounding the bell after presenting the food to Pavlov's dogs.

Based on repeated, painstakingly careful experimentation, Pavlov laid out certain criteria for stimulus-response conditioning to succeed (Pavlov, 1906, 1928). Two of the most fundamental criteria are as follows:

1. Multiple pairings of UCS and neutral stimulus (CS) are usually necessary for an association to occur and for the CS to produce the conditioned response (occasionally conditioning can occur after a single pairing).

2. The UCS and CS must be paired or presented very close together in time in order for an association to form.

Good examples of classical conditioning can be found in our everyday experiences with seemingly mundane objects or places. Miguel, for instance, once got bullied at the shopping mall. Now every time he enters the mall, Miguel feels his heart race and gets anxious, because the mall setting (an otherwise neutral or even pleasant place for him) was unfortunately linked with a frightening, painful experience he had with an aggressive classmate. That bullying episode was the unconditioned stimulus, his fear of bullying the unconditioned response, which became a conditioned response to the shopping mall, which happened to be the place where the bullying occurred.

When a behavior has been conditioned to occur in the presence of a given stimulus, it may also increase in the presence of similar stimuli. **Stimulus generalization**, the term for this phenomenon, is defined as the extension of the association between UCS and CS to a broad array of similar stimuli. For instance, for several years, Erika felt nauseated not only to chocolate doughnuts but also to glazed doughnuts. The opposite of stimulus generalization is stimulus discrimination. **Stimulus discrimination** occurs when a CR (such as salivation) occurs only to exactly the stimulus to which it was conditioned. If Pavlov's dogs did not salivate to a buzzer but only to a bell, they would discriminate the conditioned stimulus (bell) from other stimuli (buzzers, clicks, and so on).

conditioned response (CR)
A behavior that an organism learns to perform when presented with the CS.

stimulus generalization
Extension of the association between UCS and CS to include a broad array of similar stimuli.

stimulus discrimination
The restriction of a CR (such as salivation) to only the exact CS to which it was conditioned.

Unconditioned stimulus: bullied at the mall ①

Unconditioned response: fear and heart racing ②

③ **Conditioned response: fear when approaching the mall**

④ **Extinction: repeated exposure to the mall without being bullied**

©SpeedKingz/Shutterstock

FIGURE 2

CLASSICAL CONDITIONING IN THE REAL WORLD. Miguel was bullied (unconditioned stimulus) at the mall and it frightened him a lot (fear and heart racing is unconditioned response to aggression). He now reacts with fear every time he approaches the mall, even though the bully usually is not there (conditioned response). After enough exposure to the mall without being bullied, however, Miguel can learn to not react with fear. At this point, the conditioned response (fear) is extinguished.

extinction
The weakening and disappearance of a conditioned response in the absence of reinforcement.

Can a conditioned response be unlearned? Would you expect Pavlov's dogs to continue salivating indefinitely in response to the bell alone? It turns out that the dogs gradually stopped salivating to the bell (CS) once they learned that the bell was no longer being accompanied by meat powder (UCS). This weakening and disappearance of a conditioned response is called **extinction**, and it occurs when the UCS is no longer paired with the CS. It can be difficult to extinguish behaviors. Sometimes it takes 100 or more presentations of a CS without the UCS to achieve extinction, and still the behavior might return.

Consider the case of Miguel again, who had had a bad experience with bullying at the mall and learned to fear the shopping mall. Repeated exposure to the shopping mall when no bullying occurs will reduce and eventually eliminate his conditioned fear, which is an example of extinction (see Figure 2). A graph depicting the process of extinction appears in Figure 3.

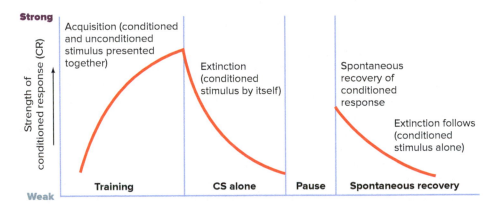

FIGURE 3

ACQUISITION, EXTINCTION, AND SPONTANEOUS RECOVERY IN CLASSICAL CONDITIONING. The graph shows how a conditioned response (CR) gradually becomes stronger during conditioning, weakens when the conditioned stimulus (CS) is no longer paired with the UCS, and disappears (extinction). Following a pause during which the CS is not presented, spontaneous recovery of the CR may occur briefly before it is extinguished again.

The sudden reappearance of an extinguished response is known as **spontaneous recovery** (see Figure 3). One example of spontaneous recovery comes from a man one of your authors recently met (let's call him Gino) who was involved in a car accident. Gino's car was sideswiped as he was making a blind turn from a parking lot. After the accident, Gino would have a panic attack whenever he passed that lot, so he couldn't park there. Several months later the attacks stopped, and he started parking there again. Then, one day as he approached the parking lot, Gino had an unexpected panic attack. A learned response he thought had been extinguished suddenly came back. Research on spontaneous recovery suggests that extinction never completely eliminates the response, only suppresses it (Moody, Sunsay, & Bouton, 2006). After a response has been extinguished, it is quite common for it to reappear spontaneously if a person returns to the setting where the conditioning originally took place.

spontaneous recovery
The sudden reappearance of an extinguished response.

Why does classical conditioning—the ability to associate innate stimulus-response patterns with novel stimuli—work? It may be adaptive in an evolutionary sense. We need to be able to associate certain types of stimuli with potential harm and to respond quickly to new stimuli that present threats. For instance, we might not be hardwired to see long, sharp metal objects as dangerous, but once we see that pressing one of them against the skin causes bleeding, then we know it is dangerous. Most animals can learn such things readily, and it helps them survive and reproduce. It is by virtue of experience and association that many objects acquire their meaning for us. That knives are dangerous is something we learn. The fact that classical conditioning is a powerful learning device for nearly all creatures suggests that it has advantages for survival.

The Conditioning of Little Albert   Pavlov's work caught the attention of young psychologists in the United States in the early 20th century. They saw in Pavlov's research the first systematic account of a scientific procedure for studying behavior. One American psychologist, John Watson, felt strongly that classical conditioning could be used to shape human behavior:

> Give me a dozen healthy infants, well-formed, and my own specified world to bring them up in and I'll guarantee to take any one at random and train him to become any type of specialist I might select—doctor, lawyer, artist, merchant-chief, and yes, even beggar-man and thief, regardless of his talents, penchants, tendencies, abilities, vocations, and race of his ancestors. (Watson, 1925, p. 82)

Watson's complete faith in the ability to mold human behavior seems naive today, and some would even call it dangerous. Yet Watson and his view of infants as blank slates helped push psychology—which Watson defined as "the study of behavior"—forward as a science. To Watson, classical conditioning offered a model for transforming the field.

In a classic study of the power of conditioning techniques, Watson conditioned a baby, known as Little Albert, to fear white rats and other white, fluffy objects. When Watson and his colleague Rosalie Rayner first met Albert, they brought out a white rat and showed it to him. He was curious but not afraid of it. Then Watson and Rayner (1920) paired the presentation of the rat with a very loud noise (the sound of a hammer striking a steel bar right behind Albert's head). Naturally, the loud sound (a UCS) startled Albert (the UCR), and he got very upset.

After repeated pairings of the loud sound with the rat, seeing the rat alone (the CS) upset Albert. On further testing, Albert's fear grew to include an intense emotional response not only to white rats but also to many other white, fluffy items, including John Watson's fake white beard. This is an example of stimulus generalization.

Regrettably, Little Albert did not undergo deconditioning (Watson & Rayner, 1920). Controversy surrounded this case for years, and it is still not clear what happened to Little Albert. We see in this case that psychology in its infancy lacked clear ethical guidelines for research. Watson's "experiment" raised many ethical issues, particularly about the need to safeguard the rights of individuals who cannot

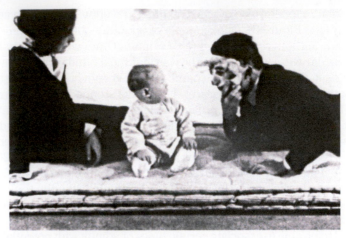

Courtesy of Prof. Benjamin Harris, University of New Hampshire

Little Albert with Rosalie Rayner and John B. Watson. Due to stimulus generalization, Little Albert came to have an intense emotional response not only to white rats, but also to other white, fluffy items, like John Watson's fake white beard.

Connection

The ethics of human research today would not allow Watson to do his research on Little Albert.

See "Ethical Treatment of Human Participants," in the chapter "Conducting Research in Psychology." (p. 66)

law of effect
The consequences of a behavior increase (or decrease) the likelihood that the behavior will be repeated.

operant conditioning
The process of changing behavior by manipulating the consequences of that behavior.

give informed consent to participate in research. Still, Watson is remembered as the father of behaviorism for his role in establishing psychology as the study of behavior. Recently, evidence shared from one man thought to be Little Albert suggests he may have had some brain abnormalities at birth, which would suggest he was not the "normal" infant Watson proclaimed him to be (Fridlund et al., 2012), though there is some controversy, however, as to whether that man was Little Albert or not. The leading theory is that he was Albert Barger, who was quite normal as a child but did have a fear of dogs as an adult (Powell et al., 2014).

Operant Conditioning

Unlike Little Albert's fear of white rats and other reactions that people can elicit from other people, some behaviors occur spontaneously. In the late 19th century, Edward L. Thorndike (1905) noted that rewarding consequences can make a spontaneous behavior more likely to occur again. He found that a cat would escape from a specially designed cage if left to its own devices for a while, not necessarily because it figured out how to get out but because certain motions were rewarded by the door opening (see Figure 4). This reward made it more likely that the specific behavior that led to the door opening would happen again if the cat were again confined in the same cage. In addition, the time it took the cat to escape decreased over time. The plot of the rate at which learning occurs over time is known as a *learning curve* (see Figure 4). In the same way, you might go back to a café you had casually walked into if you found out that it had free wireless Internet service and gave out tasty samples of its pastries. Thorndike labeled this principle the **law of effect**, which states that the consequences of a behavior increase (or decrease) the likelihood that the behavior will be repeated.

Like Thorndike, B. F. Skinner viewed the consequences of an individual's actions as the most important determinants of behavior (Skinner, 1938, 1953). Skinner set out to explain the environmental factors that led Thorndike's cat to learn to open the cage (or you to return to the café). Skinner wanted to know how disorganized, spontaneous behavior becomes organized, and exactly what role the consequences of an action play in the organization of the response. Figure 5 shows how consequences may increase behavior.

Skinner (1938) coined the term *operant* to refer to behavior that acts—or operates—on the environment to produce specific consequences. **Operant conditioning** is the process of modifying behavior by manipulating the consequences

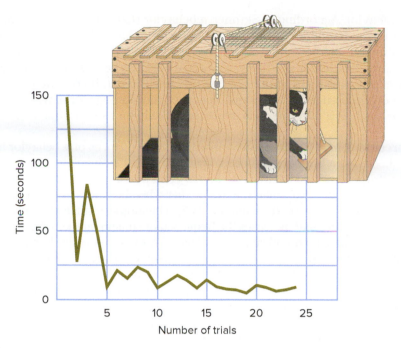

FIGURE 4

THE LEARNING CURVE. Depicted here is the box from which Thorndike's cats learned to escape. Thorndike found that a cat would escape from a specially designed cage if left to its own devices for a while, not necessarily because it figured out how to get out but because certain motions eventually were rewarded by the door's opening. This reward of the opening door made it more likely that the specific behavior that had led to the opening door would happen again if the cat were again confined in the same cage. The graph shows the amount of time it took the cat to escape. Initially, it took more than 2 minutes, but after just a few trials, the cat could consistently escape in about 10 seconds.

FIGURE 5

THREE EXAMPLES OF HOW CONSEQUENCES CAN INCREASE OR REINFORCE BEHAVIOR

(texting): ©Hero/Corbis/Glow Images RF; (checking social media): ©Digital Vision/Getty Images RF; (drinking coffee): ©Thinkstock/agefotostock RF

of that behavior. According to Skinner, a behavior that is rewarded is more likely to occur again. If a hungry animal does something that is followed by the presentation of food, then the animal is more likely to repeat the behavior that preceded the food presentation. If a café gives you free wireless access, you might go back. In contrast to classical conditioning, which modifies an involuntary or even reflexive behavior (such as salivation), operant conditioning works when voluntary behavior (such as a movement) is made more likely by its consequences.

Reinforcement and Punishment   When the consequences of a behavior increase the likelihood that a behavior will occur again, the behavior is reinforced, or strengthened. A **reinforcer** is any internal or external event that increases a behavior. When a baby sees he can get a big smile from his mother when he smiles at her, he is likely to smile more often (Adamson & Bakeman, 1985). The mother's smile in response to the infant's is a reinforcer that increases the frequency of smiling by the baby, because parental smiles are inherently rewarding to babies. This is a key point. Reinforcers have to be things that the learner wants in order for them to influence the likelihood that a behavior will occur again. For example, you will continue getting paid on a regular basis if you do your job. You want the money, so you keep working hard, but if your employer gave you paper clips for your hard work, you'd probably quit. Similarly, if your credit card company offered iTunes credits for using your card, you might use it more often. This last case shows how corporations apply principles of operant conditioning to make a profit. All of these examples differ from classical conditioning, in which two things become linked because they occur together, whether or not they are inherently rewarding.

With operant conditioning, Skinner developed a programmatic approach to using schedules of reinforcement for modifying behavior. This basic system has been applied widely with much success in education, animal training, and numerous behavioral treatments for everything from weight loss and smoking cessation to the treatment of autism in children (Cannon et al., 2016; Wood et al., 2015).

There are two kinds of reinforcers: primary and secondary. **Primary reinforcers** are not learned. They are innate and often satisfy biological needs. Food, water, sex, and even artificial sweeteners are primary reinforcers (Vaughan, 2009). Many drugs, such as caffeine and nicotine, are primary reinforcers by virtue of their stimulating effects on the central nervous system (Bernardi & Spanagel, 2013). **Secondary (conditioned) reinforcers**, such as money, grades, and peer approval, are learned by association. That is, a neutral object or situation acquires reinforcing properties by virtue of its association with inherently rewarding objects or situations (such as food or sex). Advertisers regularly take advantage of this fact. Consider ads for sports cars. If a sports car is always shown in commercials with sexy, attractive individuals, then it becomes linked in memory with something that is inherently desirable. The car itself becomes a secondary reinforcer due to its association with sex.

Reinforcement can be positive or negative. The terms "positive" and "negative" do not refer to being good or bad, but rather to whether a stimulus is added to a situation (positive) or taken away (negative). **Positive reinforcement** occurs when the presentation or addition of a stimulus to a situation increases the likelihood of a behavior. Giving extra credit points for turning in homework on time would be positive reinforcement if it led to students submitting their assignments on time. The term **negative reinforcement** refers to the removal of a stimulus

reinforcer
An internal or external event that increases the frequency of a behavior.

©Bachrach/Getty Images

B. F. Skinner

primary reinforcers
Innate, unlearned reinforcers that satisfy biological needs (such as food, water, or sex).

secondary (conditioned) reinforcers
Reinforcers that are learned by association, usually via classical conditioning (such as money, grades, and peer approval).

positive reinforcement
The presentation or addition of a stimulus after a behavior occurs that increases how often that behavior will occur.

negative reinforcement
The removal of a stimulus after a behavior to increase the frequency of that behavior.

A smile is inherently rewarding for babies.

How might the principles of operant conditioning explain why the baby would smile at Mommy even more?

©Marc Debnam/Digital Vision/Getty Images RF

to *increase* behavior. Frequently, the stimulus removed is something unpleasant. As an example, consider the beeper that sounds in your car until you fasten your seat belt. The *removal* of the annoying beeping is negative reinforcement for fastening the seat belt.

Is the distinction between positive and negative reinforcement important? Some behavioral psychologists have argued that it is unnecessary and, at times, difficult to make (Baron & Galizio, 2006; Michael, 1975). Here is an illustration of how this distinction can be confusing. Let's say you drink coffee to wake up. From one perspective, the wakefulness induced by the caffeine is positive reinforcement for drinking coffee, but are you really increasing wakefulness or decreasing fatigue (which would be negative reinforcement for drinking coffee)? Either way, the consequence for behavior is the same—you drink more coffee.

Negative reinforcement is often confused with **punishment**, which is any stimulus that *decreases* the frequency of a behavior. Like reinforcement, punishment can be positive or negative. Remember, however, that punishers *decrease* the frequency of behavior. By definition, negative reinforcers *increase* desired behaviors, so they cannot be punishers.

Typically, when most people think of punishment, they think of **positive punishment**, the addition of a stimulus that decreases behavior. A classic example of a positive punisher is spanking. Spanking a child (adding a stimulus) is positive punishment if it decreases the undesirable behavior. Similarly, if you are fined for parking in the faculty lot and stop parking there, you have received positive punishment. **Negative punishment** decreases behavior by removing a stimulus, usually a desirable stimulus. Revoking a child's TV-watching privileges for repeatedly hitting a sibling is a form of negative punishment if it stops the hitting. Figure 6 summarizes positive and negative forms of punishment and reinforcement.

Skinner emphasized that reinforcement is a much more effective way of modifying behavior than is punishment (Skinner, 1953). Specifically, using reinforcement to increase desirable behaviors works better than using punishment in an attempt to decrease undesirable behaviors. Let's say a girl hit her brother

punishment
A stimulus that decreases the frequency of a behavior.

positive punishment
The addition of a stimulus that decreases behavior.

negative punishment
The removal of a stimulus to decrease behavior.

result:	(+) add a stimulus	(−) take away a stimulus
increase in behavior using reinforcement	**Positive reinforcement** You exercise a few times and feel better. **Result:** You exercise more often.	**Negative reinforcement** You buckle your seat belt and the annoying buzzer sound is removed. **Result:** You continue using your seat belt.
decrease in behavior using punishment	**Positive punishment** You park in the faculty parking lot. You then receive a fine. **Result:** You stop parking in the faculty lot.	**Negative punishment** You talk back to your mom. She takes away TV and videos for a week. **Result:** You stop talking back to your mom.

FIGURE 6
POSITIVE AND NEGATIVE REINFORCEMENT AND PUNISHMENT IN OPERANT CONDITIONING. It is the actual result, not the intended result, that matters. For example, if an intended punisher does not decrease the behavior, it is not a punishment.

because he took away her toy. Instead of punishing the girl for hitting her brother, the parents could reinforce more desirable behaviors for dealing with the stolen toy—the girl could tell her brother that it upset her that he took the toy and suggest that, if he would please give it back, they could share it for a while. When the little girl acted in this preferable way, the parents could commend her, perhaps by giving her special privileges (such as more playtime). This in turn would increase the likelihood that the girl would use something more appropriate than physical retaliation. Punishment, as it focuses on decreasing or eliminating behaviors, doesn't tell kids what they should be doing, only what they shouldn't be doing. Reinforcement offers them an alternative.

How Operant Conditioning Works   In classical conditioning, organisms learn about the relationships between stimuli; in operant conditioning, organisms learn from the consequences of their behavior. The basic idea behind operant conditioning is that any behavior that is reinforced becomes strengthened and is more likely to occur in the future. Behaviors are reinforced because they are instrumental in obtaining particular results.

Substance use and abuse can be learned through operant conditioning. When people try a substance such as alcohol or nicotine for the first time and it makes them feel elated (a positive reinforcer) or removes their fears (a negative reinforcer), they will be more likely to use that drug again in the future. The problem with many drugs (especially alcohol and nicotine) is that the body adjusts to their presence, and more and more of the drug is required to get the desired effect. When increasing amounts of the drug are required to obtain reinforcement—to get "high," then the behavior of taking the drug increases even more. This is one reason drug addictions are so powerful and hard to overcome.

Skinner box
A simple chamber in which a small animal can move around, with a food dispenser and a response lever to trigger food delivery.

To test his conditioning principles, Skinner created the **Skinner box**, a simple chamber in which a small animal can move around, with a food dispenser and a response lever to trigger food delivery (see Figure 7). The Skinner box has been modified in recent years to allow for computer collection of responses, but many laboratories still use chambers very similar to Skinner's original device.

How exactly does someone do operant conditioning? How can you get a rat to press a lever? Rats have no inherent interest in lever pressing. You might give the rat a food pellet for pressing the lever, but how do you get the animal to press the lever in the first place?

Skinner trained a rat to perform a desired behavior (such as lever pressing) by reinforcing behaviors that occurred when the rat came closer and closer to pressing the lever. If you put a rat in a Skinner box, sooner or later—as a function of its random movements—it will come closer to the lever. When it does, you reinforce that behavior by giving it some food.

Eventually, the rat makes an association between getting closer to a particular region of the chamber and food appearing. More specifically, the rat learns that the appearance of food seems to be contingent on getting over to that region of the chamber. The researcher then increases the requirements for food presentation. Now brushing up against the lever will be reinforced with a food pellet. Finally, the rat has to press the lever to get the food.

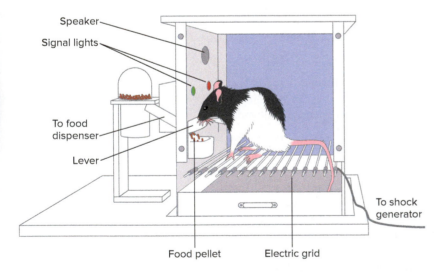

Speaker
Signal lights
To food dispenser
Lever
Food pellet
Electric grid
To shock generator

FIGURE 7
THE SKINNER BOX. This modern Skinner box provides a small space in which the rat can move and a lever to press that delivers food as a reinforcer. A small region of the floor can be set up to deliver a shock as a punisher. The rat learns through punishment to avoid that region of the floor. (Source: Weiten, W., School Sample Box for Weiten's *Psychology: Themes and Variations (with Concept Charts)*, 7th edition © 2007, Cengage.)

©Bettmann/Getty Images

Through shaping and reinforcement, pigeons can learn to discriminate colors.

Gradually reinforcing behaviors that come closer and closer to the target behavior will eventually produce the target behavior. The reinforcement of successive approximations of a desired behavior is called **shaping**. Shaping behavior is a bit like shaping clay, for the idea really is that an organism can be molded to do things that it typically wouldn't do. Professional trainers rely on shaping to get animals to perform tricks or to be guide dogs to assist people with disabilities.

Does shaping work with humans? Let's say you're trying to teach your friend how to drive a car with a stick shift. The first time he tries, even if he makes a few mistakes and stalls a few times, you might give him lots of encouragement and praise. Later, when you're trying to get him to master changing gears smoothly, you give praise only when each movement is done correctly. You are reinforcing successive approximations of the desired behavior, and as your student gets closer and closer to the desired behavior, the criteria for reinforcement become more stringent. By the 15th attempt, bucking forward a few feet before stalling gets no praise. In fact, there are numerous applications of shaping in humans. Parents use it all the time to help teach their children new tasks (e.g., how to ride a bicycle).

In operant conditioning, extinction occurs when a behavior stops being reinforced. So if a rat presses the lever and repeatedly gets no food, the lever-pressing behavior will decrease and eventually disappear. If you keep leaving phone or text messages for someone you want to ask on a date, but he or she never returns your calls or texts, eventually you will stop trying to contact this person. The calling or texting behavior has been extinguished. Figure 8 compares classical and operant conditioning.

Applications of Operant Conditioning Operant conditioning also offers a powerful method for modifying behavior in the treatment of several disorders in humans, such as phobias (severe, specific fears), nicotine addiction, and learning disabilities (Anthonisen et al., 2005; Lamb et al., 2004; Lovaas, 1987). Treatment programs based on operant methods effectively reduce self-harming behaviors in adults with intellectual deficiencies (Chowdhury & Benson, 2011) and in suicidal teens with borderline personality disorder (Klein & Miller, 2011). Shaping is used to help improve the attention span in people with schizophrenia (Silverstein, Menditto, & Stuve, 2001).

One important application of operant conditioning is for the treatment of autism (Bradshaw, Steiner, Gengoux, & Koegel, 2015; Lovaas, 1987; Soorya, Carpenter, & Romanczyk, 2011). Applied behavioral analysis (ABA), developed by

shaping
The reinforcement of successive approximations of a desired behavior.

FIGURE 8
THE DIFFERENCES BETWEEN CLASSICAL AND OPERANT CONDITIONING

	Classical conditioning	Operant conditioning
basic principle	Forming a new association between previously neutral stimulus and a response that used to occur automatically to a biologically important stimulus.	Reinforcement increases the frequency of a behavior. Punishment decreases the frequency of a behavior.
nature of behavior	The behavior is based on an organism's involuntary behavior: its reflexes. The behavior is elicited by the unconditioned stimulus (UCS) or conditioned stimulus (CS).	The behavior is based on an organism's voluntary action. The consequence of the behavior creates the likelihood of its increasing or decreasing the behavior.
order of events	Before conditioning occurs, a UCS leads to a UCR. After conditioning, a CS leads to a CR.	Reinforcement leads to an increase in behavior. Punishment leads to a decrease in behavior.
example	 Manuel is bullied at the mall (UCS). He experiences fear and heart racing (UCR). He then experiences fear (CR) whenever he approaches the mall (CS).	**Negative reinforcement** Buckling a seat belt removes the annoying buzzer, so you're more likely to buckle the seat belt again. **Negative punishment** A child who misbehaves and loses TV and video for a week is less likely to repeat that behavior again.

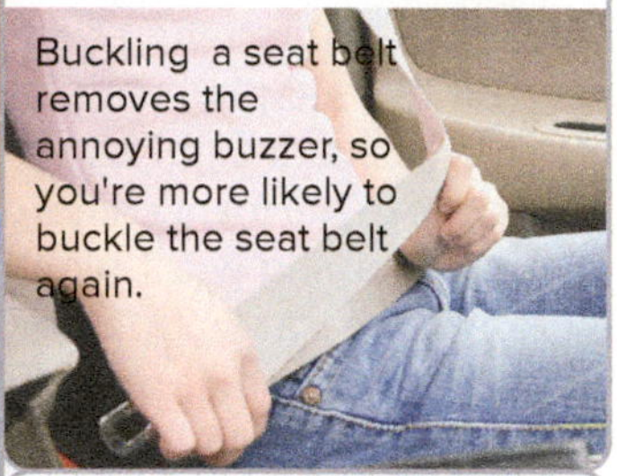

(teenage boy): ©SpeedKingz/Shutterstock; (seatbelt): ©Ned Frisk/Blend Images RF; (sad girl): ©Digital Vision/PunchStock RF

Ivar Lovaas at UCLA, uses reinforcement to increase the frequency of adaptive behaviors in autistic children and, in some cases, punishment to decrease the likelihood of maladaptive behaviors. The intensive program involves ignoring harmful or undesirable behaviors, such as hand flapping, twirling, or licking of objects, as well as aggressive behaviors. It also involves reinforcing desirable behaviors, such as contact with others and appropriate toy play. Although ABA appears to be quite effective in reducing many harmful and aggressive behaviors in young autistic children and in improving cognitive functions across many age groups, it appears to be a bit less effective in improving the social and emotional challenges of autism (Beadle-Brown, Murphy, & Wing, 2006; Matson et al., 2012; Virués-Ortega, 2010). Operant conditioning has also been applied to the treatment of attentional disorders, as discussed in "Psychology in the Real World."

Psychology in the Real World

Behavior Modification for the Treatment of Attentional Disorders

Have you ever tried to break a habit—like nail biting, hair twisting, or binge eating? If so, then you know how difficult it is to change human behavior. Operant and classical conditioning techniques have been among the most effective psychological tools for behavior change. Behavior modification is the application of methods of conditioning for behavior change. Just as one can "shape" a pigeon to peck at a lever (which they are not naturally inclined to do), you can train yourself to stick to an exercise program or eat fewer sugary snacks.

Behavior modification techniques are part of effective treatment programs for many psychological disorders, from anorexia to autism to depression (Martin & Pear, 2015). They are a go-to method for their ability to produce lasting, observable effects on behavior by use of reinforcement, extinction, and sometimes mild punishment. Attentional disorders are widespread and behavior modification shows promise as part of long-term effective treatment in many cases (Page et al., 2016; Pelham et al., 2016).

Attentional disorders usually appear early in life, although they may not be diagnosed until adulthood. There are many types of attentional deficit disorders and many degrees of severity that share symptoms of distraction, difficulty in focusing attention, behavioral unrest, and impulsive behavior (*DSM-5*, 2013) [see the chapter "Psychological Disorders"]. Medications are used frequently as a first line of treatment because stimulants increase attention and focus. However, these have undesirable side-effects, so psychological treatments are more desirable because they are not setting up unhealthful behavior patterns.

Behavioral treatments for attentional deficits are designed to reduce certain behaviors that tend to create problems for the child or the environment he or she is in, such as fidgeting, rule breaking, speaking without permission, leaving one's seat during instruction, and instigating conflict in and out of the classroom. The desirable behaviors include staying on task and improvements in school performance (Pelham et al., 2016). You might notice that there is more emphasis on removing rather than on promoting behaviors. For the task of reducing undesirable behaviors, simple reinforcement—which increases behaviors—is not used. Instead, these programs make use of extinction techniques. If you recall, to extinguish or stop a behavior, reinforcement for a behavior is eliminated. The idea is that once it no longer is reinforced, it will stop occurring (which is the definition of extinction). For instance, learning to ignore a child's temper tantrum, rather than attending to it, can decrease the likelihood of it occurring in the future.

Many behavioral programs for the treatment of attentional disorders are parent training programs, by which the parents are taught how to reward certain desirable behaviors and withhold reinforcement for others. For example, some programs teach reward systems, such as giving points to children when they perform well in their work, are cooperative group members, or ask for a toy politely rather than grabbing it. To reduce behaviors such as class disruption, leaving without permission, or getting off-task, teachers or parents might remove reinforcement by ignoring the child or even apply slight punishment, such as harsh words in front of others or white noise (Cook, Johnson, & Bradley-Johnson, 2015). Other programs try to focus more on increasing healthful behavior patterns and improving relationships between parent and child (Tarver, Daley, & Sayal, 2014).

Research comparing behavior treatment and medications in a large number of trial and across a large number of people shows that the most effective treatments combine behavior modification and drugs. Beginning with behavior modification and gradually working in medication in targeted ways seems most beneficial in terms of changing behavior (Pelham et al., 2016). This kind of combined therapy also is more cost effective for the family and health care systems (Page et al., 2016).

Critical commentary: There is some controversy as to whether eliminating undesirable behaviors and making kids fit a "well-behaved" norm is best for development and honors the unique qualities of each child. What do you think about using operant conditioning to make people fit a societal standard of what "normal" should be?

Schedules of Reinforcement   Reinforcers can be arranged (scheduled) to follow behavior under a variety of conditions or rules, called **schedules of reinforcement**. Although a powerful tool in the laboratory, it is sometimes difficult to describe complex human behavior in terms of simple reinforcement schedules. Nonetheless, there are some parallels.

schedules of reinforcement
Patterns of intermittent reinforcement distinguished by whether reinforcement occurs after a set number of responses or after a certain amount of time has passed since the last reinforcement.

continuous reinforcement
Reinforcement of a behavior every time it occurs.

intermittent reinforcement
Reinforcement of a behavior—but not after every response.

fixed-ratio (FR) schedule
A pattern of intermittent reinforcement in which reinforcement follows a set number of responses.

variable-ratio (VR) schedule
A pattern of intermittent reinforcement in which the number of responses needed for reinforcement changes.

Reinforcers may be presented every time a behavior occurs or only occasionally. **Continuous reinforcement** means rewarding a behavior every time it occurs. Giving a dog a biscuit every time it jumps is continuous reinforcement.

Intermittent reinforcement does not occur after every response. Intermittent reinforcement produces a stronger behavioral response than continuous reinforcement does. Why? The explanation has to do with memory and expectation. If an animal gets a food pellet every time it hits a lever, it will remember and expect that food will appear each time it presses the lever, but if it sometimes receives food after one lever press and other times it takes five or 10 presses, the animal will not learn a predictable pattern. It will keep responding as fast as possible in hope that eventually it will receive food, because it is not sure when food will come.

It is well documented that intermittent reinforcement produces stronger responses—in terms of both rate of responding and resistance to extinction—than does continuous reinforcement (Ferster & Skinner, 1957). Think about your own behavior: How often do you check email each day? Maybe you check it several times a day. Some people are essentially "addicted" to email or social network sites, checking them dozens of times a day. This behavior is very easy to explain in terms of operant conditioning. Occasionally, a very important or interesting (reinforcing) email or post arrives, but we don't know when the next one will come (intermittent), so we check and we check, each time hoping for that important message, a behavior shaped by intermittent reinforcement.

Skinner identified four schedules of reinforcement (see Figure 9). These schedules can be distinguished on the basis of whether reinforcement occurs after a set number of responses or after a certain amount of time has passed since the last reinforcement.

In a **fixed-ratio (FR) schedule**, reinforcement follows a set number of responses. The pattern becomes predictable, so the response rate is not steady. Typically, there is a pause in response immediately after reinforcement occurs, and then the response rate increases. An FR schedule produces a steep, stepwise pattern of response, as shown in Figure 10. One example is a worker being paid by the number of units he or she produces, whether the units are pajama sets or pizzas delivered. A worker whose wages or tips depend on the number he or she produces will work faster, possibly risking injury, to make more money.

A **variable-ratio (VR) schedule**, in which the number of responses needed for reinforcement varies, produces a very steady rate of response, because the individual is not quite sure how many responses are

FIGURE **9**

SCHEDULES OF REINFORCEMENT. Workers who are paid for the number of units they produce are reinforced on a fixed-ratio schedule. Winnings from playing slot machines vary in amount and in the interval between payoffs, which reinforce behavior on a variable-ratio schedule. An example of a fixed-interval schedule is not attending lecture after taking an exam. A variable-interval schedule occurs when you continue to text a friend, who doesn't respond, until you get an answer; the number of times you have to text varies over time.

(factory workers): ©PeerPoint/Alamy; (slots): ©Brand X Pictures RF; (lecture): ©dpa picture alliance/Alamy; (cellphone): ©Morakot Kawinchan/Shutterstock.com

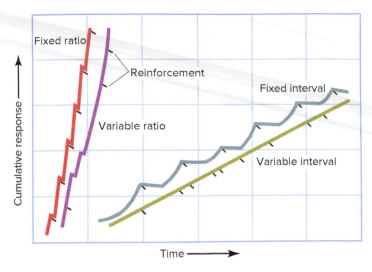

FIGURE 10

EFFECTS OF DIFFERENT SCHEDULES OF REINFORCEMENT ON LEARNING. Different schedules of reinforcement lead to different rates of response. Each hash mark indicates when a reinforcer is administered. Ratio schedules of reinforcement result in more of the reinforced behavior being performed over a given amount of time (the two steep slopes) than interval schedules of reinforcement (the two flatter slopes). Also, the fixed-interval schedule leads to the classic "scallop" effect, which indicates that responses decrease immediately after the reinforcer is administered and then increase again as the next reinforcer draws near.

necessary to obtain reinforcement (see Figure 10). VR schedules produce reinforcement around a mean number of responses, but the exact ratio differs for each trial. Thus, the mean may be set at 10 responses, but some trials may require 10 responses for reinforcement, some 20, some five, some seven, and so on. A slot machine is an example of a device that delivers reinforcement on a VR schedule. The player cannot know how many pulls of the slot machine arm it will take to win. On one occasion it might take just one pull to win a small jackpot. Other times dozens of quarters might be spent before winning. Casinos make a lot of money capitalizing on the steady rate of response produced by a variable-ratio schedule—gamblers do not.

In a **fixed-interval (FI) schedule**, reinforcement always follows the first response after a set amount of time—say, every 4 seconds. This produces a pattern in which the rate of response immediately following reinforcement is low. The response rate accelerates as the time of reinforcement approaches. A graph of the FI schedule produces a scalloped pattern, as in Figure 10. An example of the effects of a fixed-interval schedule is one's studying behavior before and after a test. If tests are given every 4 weeks, students learn that immediately after the test their performance will not be evaluated, so we would expect to see a drop in the rate of studying at that time. The same is true of class attendance before and after exams.

In a **variable-interval (VI) schedule**, the first response is reinforced after time periods of different durations have passed. The researcher sets a mean interval length around which the intervals will vary. For example, the mean interval may be 5 seconds, but sometimes reinforcement occurs after 10 seconds, sometimes after 1 second, sometimes after 5 seconds, and so on. The variable nature of the interval makes it difficult for the subject to predict when reinforcement will occur. Variable-interval schedules therefore produce a steady, moderate rate of response (see Figure 10). Suppose you are trying to reach a good friend on the phone, but every time you call you get her voice mail. You can tell she is on the line already, so you keep calling back every few minutes to see if she is off.

fixed-interval (FI) schedule
A pattern of intermittent reinforcement in which responses are always reinforced after a set period of time has passed.

variable-interval (VI) schedule
A pattern of intermittent reinforcement in which responses are reinforced after time periods of different duration have passed.

conversation can last only so long. Eventually, she will pick up the phone
(... reward), but the wait time is unpredictable. In other words, reinforcement
...ows a variable-interval schedule.

Challenging Assumptions about Conditioning Models of Learning

Assumptions

Humans and rats ba-
in the same way.
animals learn from
..on (classical condition-
.d reinforcement (operant
.itioning).

Traditional learning theory assumes that the principles of conditioning are universal—classical conditioning and operant conditioning each work pretty much the same way in different species of animals. In fact, Skinner maintained that, given the proper reinforcement, almost any animal could be taught to do almost anything. Supporting this view, there is recent evidence that bumble bees can learn through reward and reinforcement to drag a small round disk by pulling a string attached to it (Alem et al., 2016).

Skinner's faith in universal principles of learning was so strong that he was convinced that what he learned about a rat or pigeon in a conditioning chamber was representative of most species' learning in any context. In one sense Skinner was correct. The biochemical processes involved in learning and memory are the same in slugs as in humans (Kandel, 2006). Skinner was also suggesting that we could understand learning by training behavior, not because it is inherently interesting to us or to the animal but rather because trained behavior is easily observed. The specific species or the behavior does not make a difference; however, some of the basic assumptions of conditioning models of learning did not go unchallenged. Three domains of research challenged traditional learning theory:

- Conditioned taste aversion
- Instinctive drift
- Latent learning

conditioned taste aversion
The learned avoidance of a particular taste or food.

Conditioned Taste Aversion As we discussed, Erika's chocolate doughnut and deep-sea fishing experience led to a case of **conditioned taste aversion**, the learned avoidance of a particular taste when nausea occurs at about the same time as the food (Garcia, Kimeldorf, & Koelling, 1955). Whether or not the food actually causes the sickness, it is experienced that way in future encounters.

Traditional learning theory would explain conditioned taste aversion as a special case of classical conditioning, in which a neutral or even pleasant taste is linked with the unconditioned causes of nausea. This learned association (say, between a doughnut and nausea) is not much different from the one made by Pavlov's dogs (see Figure 11). The catch is that classical conditioning requires repeated pairings of the CS and the UCS to create and maintain a conditioned response, but in the case of the chocolate doughnut, the doughnut (the CS) acquired the ability to induce nausea (CR) after a brief pairing with the motion of the boat (UCS), more than 30 minutes after the doughnut was eaten.

The person responsible for discovering and describing this kind of learning was John Garcia. In the 1950s Garcia and his colleagues wondered whether rats in their laboratory had developed a taste aversion for the food and water they had consumed while they received radiation for one of the lab's experiments. He and his colleagues (1955) at the U.S. Naval Laboratory decided to look more closely at this phenomenon by conditioning rats to develop an aversion to a taste they liked—saccharin water. They began with the following questions:

1. Could taste aversion to saccharin water occur by pairing the taste with radiation (a UCS for nausea)?

2. How long would the taste aversion last without repeated exposure to radiation (the UCS)?

©UCLA Psychology

John Garcia

FIGURE 11
A CLASSICAL CONDITIONING MODEL OF TASTE AVERSION

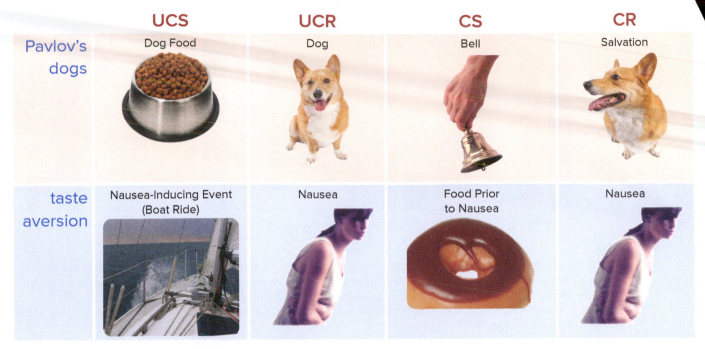

	UCS	UCR	CS	CR
Pavlov's dogs	Dog Food	Dog	Bell	Salvation
taste aversion	Nausea-Inducing Event (Boat Ride)	Nausea	Food Prior to Nausea	Nausea

(dog food): ©Lew Robertson/Corbis RF; (bell): ©Pixtal/SuperStock RF; (boat ride): ©Ingram Publishing/SuperStock RF; (nausea): ©Colin Anderson/Stockbyte/Getty Images RF; (donut): ©Dynamic Graphics/PunchStock RF

Garcia's team varied the type of fluid presented during a radiation period (plain water or saccharin water) and the radiation exposure level (none, low, or moderate dose). One control group had access to plain water during a 6-hour period of exposure to radiation (irradiation). Another control group received saccharin water and no radiation. In the experimental conditions, rats received saccharin water during periods of low or moderate irradiation. According to traditional classical conditioning, the UCS and CS must be paired very closely in time—typically, no more than a few seconds apart. However, in some cases, several minutes passed between the time the rats were irradiated (UCS) and the time they drank the fluid (CS).

Following the conditioning period in which the rats were irradiated or not, all the rats were housed in cages with two drinking bottles, one containing plain water and one with saccharin water. At this time, taste aversion was measured, and the dependent variable was how much saccharin water the rats consumed.

There were no changes in the control groups' water preferences, but in the two experimental groups, aversion occurred (see Figure 12). Regardless of radiation level, rats that had been drinking saccharin water during irradiation consumed significantly less saccharin water after conditioning. This result answered the first question the researchers had posed: Rats could be conditioned to avoid a taste they previously liked. Also, the drop in intake of saccharin water lasted for at least 30 days. This finding answered the second question about how long such conditioning might last.

Percentage of fluid intake after radiation

Legend:
- No radiation
- Low radiation
- Moderate radiation

y-axis: 0, 20, 40, 60, 80, 100
x-axis: Water, Saccharin
Fluid during irradiation

FIGURE 12

CONDITIONED TASTE AVERSION. Compared to rats that received no nausea-producing radiation, rats exposed to radiation (UCS) while drinking saccharin water (CS) developed a long-lasting aversion to saccharin water (CR).

Which item in this story is analogous to the chocolate doughnut in Erika's story of conditioned taste aversion? (Garcia et al., 1955)

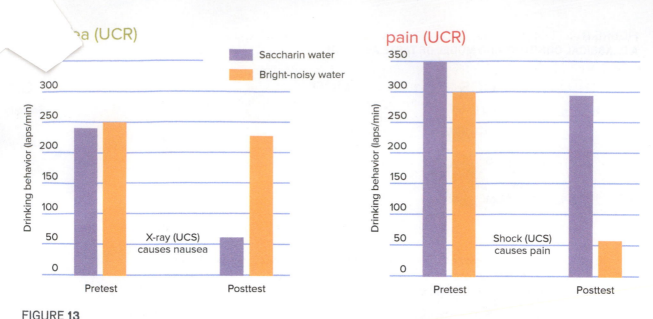

FIGURE 13

LIMITS ON CONDITIONED TASTE AVERSION. Contrary to predictions from traditional learning theory, taste aversion conditioning depends on the stimulus. Conditioned taste aversion occurs only to the kind of stimulus that makes biological sense. For example, nausea produces aversion to taste, but not to noise and light, as shown in the graph on the left. Pain produces aversion to frightening stimuli, such as noise and bright lights, but not to saccharin water, as shown in the graph on the right. (Garcia & Koelling, 1966)

Garcia's subsequent research derailed another assumption of traditional learning theory: that reflexive responses (such as nausea) could be conditioned to any kind of stimulus. Garcia and Koelling (1966) varied the type of aversive stimulus (UCS) to which rats were exposed and the type of neutral stimulus (CS). Nausea (the UCR) was induced by exposure to x-rays, whereas pain (the other UCR) was induced by electrical shocks sent through the floor of the cage. When the rat licked the drinking tube, it received the CS of either saccharin water or "bright-noisy water" (plain water accompanied by a light and a buzzer that went on when the rat touched the drinking tube). The UCS for half the rats was irradiation-induced nausea. The other half received a shock. The irradiated rats avoided the sweet water but not the bright-noisy water (see Figure 13), whereas the rats that had received a mildly painful shock avoided the bright-noisy water but not the sweet water. The researchers described the first response as "conditioned nausea" and the second as "conditioned fear."

The key finding here is that, contrary to the predictions of traditional learning theory, an organism cannot be conditioned to respond to just any "neutral" stimulus paired with an unconditioned stimulus. We can learn certain things only under certain conditions. In other words, nausea can be conditioned to a taste but not to a light, because taste is relevant to eating, but light is not.

As another example of how research can radically change what we think we know, Garcia's research on taste aversion undermined two key assumptions of classical conditioning: (1) that conditioning could happen only if an organism were exposed repeatedly within a brief time span to the UCS and CS together, and (2) that organisms could learn to associate any two stimuli. With respect to the first assumption, Garcia showed in other research that the CS and UCS can be separated by as much as 75 minutes and still lead to conditioned taste aversion (Garcia, Ervin, & Koelling, 1966). With respect to the second assumption, the "bright-noisy water" findings showed that only certain stimuli can be conditioned to produce nausea (Garcia & Koelling, 1966). More specifically, you cannot make someone be nauseated by a sound or a sight as easily as by a taste.

Instinctive Drift Many studies of conditioning used different species in learning experiments. Results from rats were readily assumed to be relevant for humans, but are species really interchangeable? Also, is learning to press a bar equivalent to learning to play the piano? Over many years, it has become clear that the notion of the equivalence of species and tasks is problematic. As it turns out, there are limits to what different species will learn and how they will learn it.

Ironically, this conclusion stemmed from the research of two of Skinner's students, Keller Breland and Marian Breland. Initially, the Brelands (1961) successfully applied traditional operant conditioning principles to shaping all kinds of behaviors in many kinds of animals. In fact, they successfully conditioned 38 different species and more than 6,000 animals.

When they turned their attention to species whose learning behavior had not been studied, however, they began to experience failures. When they tried to condition different animal species to insert poker chips into a vending machine, raccoons rubbed them instead of putting them in the slot machine, pigs rooted them with their snouts, and chickens pecked at them. When describing the raccoons' "problematic behavior," Breland and Breland wrote,

> The rubbing behavior became worse and worse as time went on, in spite of non-reinforcement.... These egregious failures came as a rather considerable shock to us, for there was nothing in our background in behaviorism to prepare us for such gross inabilities to predict and control the behavior of animals with which we had been working for years. (Breland & Breland, 1961, p. 683)

Initially, the Brelands considered such behavior misguided and even titled their article "The Misbehavior of Organisms." Once again, new science toppled old assumptions to offer new perspectives. With research, it became clear to the Brelands that these behaviors were not "misbehaviors" but normal expressions of innate instincts. It seems that raccoons naturally wash, pigs root, and chickens peck. Breland and Breland (1961) called this effect **instinctive drift**, which they defined as learned behavior that shifts toward instinctive, unlearned behavior tendencies.

Instinctive drift challenges the behaviorist conviction that learning always results either from associating an event with an unconditioned stimulus or from shaping by reinforcement or punishment. The Brelands' findings imply that there are biological limitations, or constraints, on learning. According to the **biological constraint model** of learning, some behaviors are naturally more likely to be learned than others (Garcia, McGowan, & Green, 1972; Seligman & Hager, 1972). Biology constrains options so that the adaptive ones are more likely to occur than the maladaptive ones.

Constraints on learning have positive evolutionary implications: They guide organisms in a direction that speeds up learning and aids survival or reproductive success. This model explains instinctive drift. Humans are geared toward learning language—one could say we "instinctively drift" toward speaking. It is very easy for us to learn to speak, assuming we are simply exposed to language early in infancy and childhood. Reading, writing, and arithmetic, however, are not so easily learned, which is one reason we need to go to school to learn these skills. We do not need to go to school to learn to speak. School might help with teaching us formal grammar and syntax, but we all use a grammar and kind of syntax.

Instinctive drift and biological constraints provide excellent examples of the limits nature places on nurture. Biology makes it possible for humans, but not chimpanzees, to talk. Experience interacting with the capacity for speech determines not only whether an individual learns to talk but also the language he or she learns. As we have seen, Garcia's groundbreaking research revised traditional thinking about classical conditioning within the limits of biology.

instinctive drift
Learned behavior that shifts toward instinctive, unlearned behavior tendencies.

biological constraint model
A view on learning which proposes that some behaviors are inherently more likely to be learned than others.

Latent Learning Even before the Brelands studied biological constraints and learning, other psychologists challenged some of the basic assumptions of learning theory. One was Edward Tolman. Like many other learning researchers, Tolman ran rats through mazes. In one key study, hungry rats were randomly assigned to three groups (Tolman & Honzik, 1930). Rats in Group 1 were rewarded with food if they reached the end of a maze. Rats in this group became better and better at maze running, thanks to the reliable reinforcement of a food reward. Rats in Group 2 received no food for their work, and not surprisingly, they never ran the maze very well. They had no reinforcement. These results are what standard behaviorism would predict.

The rats in Group 3, however, received no reinforcement for running the maze—at least not at first. Like Group 2, they did not run the maze very well. But after a set of nonreinforced trials, they started being reinforced with food for their maze running. Suddenly, these rats started running the maze really well. It was as if they had been learning all along. In fact, the Group 3 rats even started performing better than the rats in Group 1.

How might we explain this outcome? Tolman argued that the rats in Group 3 had been learning all along—they just didn't show it before they started being reinforced. **Latent learning** is a type of learning that occurs in the absence of reinforcement and is not demonstrated until later, when reinforcement occurs. Tolman reasoned that these rats had formed internal *cognitive maps*—like pictures in their minds—of the maze from all the practice they had received. When they finally had rewards waiting for them, the rats could use these maps to run the maze more efficiently. It is difficult to know whether the rats really had maps of the maze in their minds. What is clear from these findings is that some learning can occur in the absence of reinforcement. Running the maze, even without rewards, helped the rats in Group 3 run much better when reinforcement was available.

Tolman's important research set the stage for future work on the role of thought in learning, something that Skinner (1990) and other behaviorists deemed irrelevant. Tolman's work also showed that prior experience—whether reinforced or not—aids future learning. Further, it suggested that motivation plays a part in learning. The idea of latent learning implies that learning sometimes stays hidden until the learner is motivated to perform.

latent learning
Learning that occurs in the absence of reinforcement and is not demonstrated until later, when reinforcement occurs.

Connection

People who cannot form new memories nevertheless learn. The body can learn things of which the conscious mind is not aware.

See "Long-Term Memory," in the chapter "Memory". (p. 273)

Quick Quiz 1: Basic Processes and Conditioning Models of Learning

1. Using the definition provided in the text, which is the best example of learning?
   a. A plant moves toward the sun in order to get the best example of sunlight.
   b. A newborn baby automatically grabs a finger placed in its palm.
   c. A cat perks up its ears and looks toward a sound.
   d. Ten-year-old Jerry can snowboard down the mountain after practicing for a week.

2. Because Sela always opens a drawer to get the can opener whenever she feeds her cat, Socks, use a can opener when getting her Socks runs into the kitchen each time he hears someone open a drawer. Socks has
   a. remembered what cat food is.
   b. made an association between the drawer opening and being fed.
   c. habituated to noises in the kitchen.
   d. done none of the above.

3. A rat presses a lever, resulting in food delivery. The rat then presses the lever more frequently. This is an example of
   a. punishment.
   b. higher-order conditioning.
   c. reinforcement.
   d. extinction.

4. In a typical classical conditioning experiment, a neutral stimulus is
   a. repeatedly paired with the unconditioned response.
   b. not paired with any other stimulus.
   c. repeatedly paired with the conditioned stimulus.
   d. repeatedly paired with the unconditioned stimulus.

5. A reinforcer is anything that _____ ; a punisher is anything that _____ .
   a. makes a behavior less likely; makes a behavior more likely

b. makes a behavior more likely; makes a behavior less likely
c. is positive; is negative
d. is shaped; is extinguished

6. A slot machine player cannot know how many pulls of the slot machine arm it will take to win. On one occasion it might take just one pull to win a small jackpot. Other times dozens of quarters might be spent before winning. This payout schedule is what kind of schedule of reinforcement?
a. fixed-interval
b. fixed-ratio
c. variable-interval
d. variable-ratio

Answers can be found at the end of the chapter.

SOCIAL LEARNING THEORY

We all look to others for clues on how to behave. Think about how you first learned to tie your shoes or even to swim. Did someone just explain the way to do it? Or did you try random motions and then get praise from your teacher every time you did something right? There may have been some random successes in your attempts to swim, but chances are you learned the right movements by imitating the actions of your swim teacher or parent. There is more to learning than associating one thing with another (classical conditioning) or doing something and then being reinforced for it (operant conditioning). Classical and operant conditioning explain many aspects of learning, but they neglect the powerful role of modeling in the learning process.

Obviously, people learn from their own experience, from their own successes and failures, and from trial and error, but if we had to learn everything that way, not only would the process take much, much longer but it also would require reinventing what others have already learned, over and over again. Learning by observing others is much more efficient. Albert Bandura proposed that we learn both by doing and by observing.

Bandura's **social learning theory** (1986) goes beyond traditional conditioning approaches to include observation and modeling as major components of learning. Bandura (1986) called learning influenced by the behavior of others **observational learning**. **Modeling** is Bandura's term for observational learning that involves imitating behaviors performed by others. Modeling is everywhere. Younger children mimic the behavior of their older siblings. We pick up figures of speech and mannerisms from our closest friends. Modeling is more likely to occur in some people than in others, more likely after some behaviors than others, and more likely after some consequences than others.

Modeling is only one aspect of social learning theory. According to Bandura (1986), social learning also works through reinforcement. Remember from operant conditioning that the consequences of our behavior influence whether we repeat those behaviors. People learn best those things they are rewarded for doing, whether the rewards are external (such as praise, money, candy) or internal (such as joy and satisfaction). Bandura noted that reinforcement matters not only for the person carrying out the behavior but also for those who watch. Advertisers make use of this phenomenon all the time. When teenagers see young adults getting a lot of attention and having fun while they are drinking beer, they might be more likely to want to drink beer themselves. People will do things they see others doing, especially if the model's behavior is rewarded.

Bandura and his colleagues demonstrated the power of observational learning in a series of classic studies—the Bobo doll studies. Their experiments showed how two key elements of social learning—modeling and reinforcement—affect behavior. The first study focused on the power of observational learning on aggressive behavior (Bandura, Ross, & Ross, 1961). Children observed an adult either being aggressive or not being aggressive with an inflatable doll, called a Bobo doll. Half saw the adult play politely with the Bobo doll. The others saw the adult sock the Bobo doll hard, hit it with a rubber mallet, and kick it around. Afterward, one at a time, the kids entered a room filled with toys (including the ones the model played with) and were allowed free play. Children who had seen the adults act aggressively with the

©Jon Brenneis/Life Magazine/Time & Life Pictures/Getty Images

Albert Bandura

social learning theory
The kind of learning that occurs when we model the behavior of others.

observational learning
Learning influenced by watching the behavior of others.

modeling
The imitation of behaviors performed by others. A kind of observational learning.

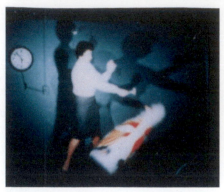
Courtesy of Albert Bandura

Courtesy of Albert Bandura

Children who observed an adult model being aggressive with a Bobo doll (left) in a study by Bandura tended to behave aggressively when given the opportunity to play with the doll (right).

 What kind of learning is this? What conditions might increase the likelihood of children modeling this adult behavior?

doll were much more likely to be aggressive when they had the chance to play with the Bobo than were those who had seen the adults play pleasantly with the doll. In fact, they adopted many of the same actions the adults had used. Thus, these initial studies demonstrated the power of observational learning in aggression.

Another important classic study showed how reinforcement works with modeling to lead to observational learning (Bandura, Ross, & Ross, 1963). Again using an experimental design, this time the researchers introduced another variable: What happened to the models after they had behaved aggressively? The children saw one of four films: one with no models, one with two adult men who interacted in a nonaggressive manner, and two films with adult men who played aggressively with each other, but in one the aggressive man was punished, whereas in the other he was rewarded. The first two films (no model and nonaggressive models) were control conditions, whereas the last two (aggression) were experimental conditions. In the films shown to the experimental groups, one man was aggressive toward the other man. The aggressive man hit the nonaggressive man with a rubber mallet and shot darts at him. He also roughed up the inflatable Bobo doll. A key element of this study is that the films also showed what happened to the aggressive adult after the interaction. There were two possibilities. The aggressive adult was either punished (he lost the conflict and ended up cowering in the corner) or rewarded (he won the conflict and got to play with all the toys) for his aggression. The research design is summarized in Figure 14.

After seeing the film, the children had an opportunity to play with the Bobo doll and other toys they had seen in the film. Just as in the previous set of studies, how the kids acted with the doll and other toys was the main dependent variable. The primary finding from the previous study was replicated: Those who had viewed aggression were more aggressive with the doll than were those who had not seen aggression (see Figure 15), but the consequences for the model also mattered. The children who had seen the aggressive adult rewarded for his aggression were more violent with the toys and Bobo doll than were those who had seen the aggressive adult get punished. Those who had not seen an aggressive model did not show much aggression with the toys, nor did those who had seen the adult punished. These studies show how modeling and reinforcement can work together to influence behavior. Kids are more likely to copy behavior that they see others being rewarded for.

The Bobo doll studies were pivotal in showing how children learn aggression and other violent behaviors from viewing aggression in others. The results, of course, have implications for the effect of violence on television, in movies, and in video games on children and teens. Numerous studies have demonstrated

Challenge Your Assumptions

True or False? Kids are not affected by watching violence in movies or killing in video games.

False: Various studies support the idea that children imitate violence they see, especially if it is reinforced or rewarded.

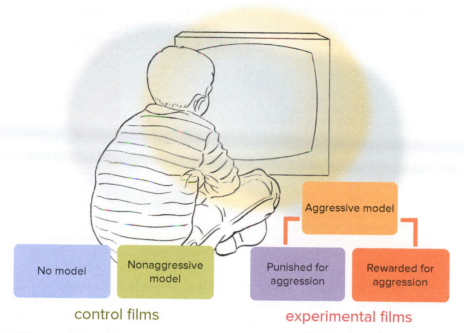

control films   experimental films

FIGURE **14**

EXPERIMENTAL DESIGN FOR BANDURA'S STUDY OF OBSERVATIONAL LEARNING AND AGGRESSION. Children viewed one of four films: one with no model, one with nonaggressive adult models, or one of two with an aggressive adult model, in which the model is either punished for being aggressive or rewarded for it. (Bandura, Ross, & Ross, 1963)

©BananaStock/Getty Images RF

 Do you think there is too much violence in movies and video games? Explain.

that kids behave more violently after exposure to violence in the media (Bushman & Anderson, 2001). Furthermore, children who play violent video games are at increased risk for delinquent behavior (Exelmans, Custers, & Van den Bulck, 2015).

Observational learning is not a uniquely human capacity. The great apes—profoundly social animals—learn from watching what others do. Schuppli and her colleagues (2016) studied the peering behavior of wild orangutans in the wild. Peering is looking at something in an attentive, focused way. And it's not just mammals that learn through observing: believe it or not, even insects—bees at least—have this capacity (Alem et al., 2016).

Challenge Your Assumptions

True or False? Bees learn by watching other bees perform a new task.
True: Many bees, but not all, learned how to pull an object with a string after observing another bee perform this novel task.

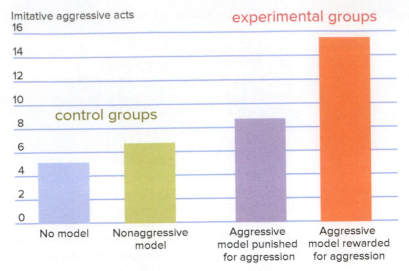

FIGURE **15**

THE EFFECT OF MODELING AND REWARD ON LEARNED AGGRESSIVE BEHAVIOR. This graph depicts the number of imitative aggressive acts by children who had viewed one of four film conditions. The children who had seen the aggressive adults get rewarded for their aggression showed more aggressive acts, such as hitting the Bobo doll with a hammer or punching it, than did the children in the other three categories. (Bandura, Ross, & Ross, 1963)

Quick Quiz 2: Social Learning Theory

1. Barbara just started a new job, and she watches how her colleagues dress and act. The type of learning Barbara is doing is
   a. observational learning.
   b. enactive learning.
   c. operant conditioning.
   d. reinforcement.

2. The major finding(s) from Bandura's Bobo doll experiments were that
   a. children learn to be aggressive by watching other people be aggressive.
   b. children learn to be aggressive by observing reinforced aggression in others.

   c. children learn to be aggressive only if they see someone of the same sex be aggressive.
   d. Both a and b are correct.

3. Research generally shows that children
   a. are not at all likely to be aggressive after watching aggression on TV or in movies.
   b. are likely to be aggressive after watching aggression on TV or in movies.
   c. are more aggressive after watching aggression in movies only if they are from impoverished backgrounds.
   d. know the difference between movies and real life and are not influenced by movie or TV violence.

Answers can be found at the end of the chapter.

HOW NATURE AND NURTURE WORK TOGETHER IN LEARNING

One goal of this book to highlight how environment and biology interact in psychology. Thus far we have emphasized primarily the role of environmental conditions—such as the presence of reinforcers—in learning. Indeed, the early behaviorists refused to study anything that could not be directly observed, including mental processes and any potentially relevant biological structures. Although Skinner acknowledged the role of genetics in behavior, he and Watson ignored the role of cognitive and brain processes in learning, because these could not be observed (Skinner, 1938, 1990).

We now know that learning results from the constant interaction of the brain and the environment. Several very specific brain structures and circuits have been identified for their role in learning. The hippocampus in particular, given its important role in memory, is a major player in learning (Wenger &

Lövden, 2016). One brain imaging study examined the medial temporal lobe and its key connections with other brain structures in children ages 7 to 12 with learning disabilities undergoing math tutoring (Ashkenazi et al., 2013). All the students in the study benefited some from tutoring, but not all equally. Those who improved the most had larger hippocampi than those who did not benefit as much. Further, those students who had strong connections between the hippocampus and PFC and basal ganglia benefited the most from tutoring. In fact, the hippocampus as well as the brain area in which it is located (the medial temporal role) may be the most plastic or modifiable area of the brain, and thereby more susceptible to experience-induced changes than other brain areas (Walhovd et al., 2016).

Biology makes learning possible, and learning changes biology. Extreme forms of behaviorism paint a picture of learning resulting primarily from one's experiences. It is an extreme environmental, or nature-only, view. Few modern behaviorists agree with such a one-sided view. In this section, we look at four learning processes that illustrate the dynamic interplay between nature and nurture in learning: imprinting, imitation, synaptic change, and brain growth with enrichment.

Imprinting

Not all forms of learning depend on reward and reinforcement. A good example is **imprinting**, the rapid and innate learning of the characteristics of a caregiver within a very short period of time after birth (Lorenz, 1935, 1937). Mammals and birds, which are born helpless, need to form a strong bond to a caregiver almost immediately after birth to avoid getting lost or being killed by a predator. We know this from **ethology**, the scientific study of animal behavior, and especially from the work of Austrian ethologist and winner of the 1973 Nobel Prize in Medicine, Konrad Lorenz, who studied imprinting extensively in birds. He observed that, soon after they hatched, ducklings and goslings (baby geese) learned to follow whatever they saw most, be it a mother duck or goose or, surprisingly, a human. This parent figure tends to be the first moving object the young animal sees within the first few days of life. Usually, this figure is the animal's mother, but it need not be, as Lorenz found out when he became an imprinted parent to a flock of goslings.

Imprinting provides clear evidence of a *sensitivity period* in learning: a period when a particular type of learning occurs very readily if an animal is exposed to a particular stimulus or situation. The brain seems to be primed at a particular time for a particular kind of learning. Once the animal has moved beyond that sensitivity period, it becomes much harder, if not impossible, to learn certain skills or make use of certain kinds of information. Once a "parent" has been imprinted on young ducks or geese, that learning is permanent and cannot be unlearned. Imprinting, in other words, can be learned soon after birth—or not at all. After a certain age, imprinting cannot be learned, unlearned, or relearned—it cannot be modified at all.

Although imprinting does not occur in humans, young babies do develop an important bond

imprinting
The rapid and innate learning of the characteristics of a caregiver very soon after birth.

ethology
The scientific study of animal behavior.

Why are these goslings following Konrad Lorenz?

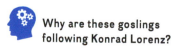

with their primary caregivers that serves much the same function (see the chapter "Human Development"). Imprinting and sensitivity periods in learning remind us that the mind is not a blank slate, able to learn anything at any time, given the right reinforcers and stimuli. The brain is structured in such a way that certain kinds of experiences are more or less easily learned at different periods in life; language learning by humans is one example, as discussed in the chapter "Language and Thought."

Imitation, Mirror Neurons, and Learning

Connection

Mirror neurons help explain why even infants imitate adult behavior so easily.

See "Early Socioemotional Development," in the chapter "Human Development". (p. 184)

embodied cognition
The thought processes involved in representing parts of the body and/or reenacting bodily actions in thoughts.

Humans imitate one another. Imitation is fundamental to the way in which human and nonhuman primates learn. As we discussed in the section on social learning theory, classical and operant conditioning do not take into account the powerful role of imitation in the learning process. Infants begin copying the behavior of adults and other children almost immediately. Babies as young as 7 hours old imitate simple adult facial expressions (Meltzoff & Moore, 1977, 1983).

Imitation by infants may be a result of mirror neuron systems (MNS) in the brain (Lepage & Théoret, 2007), although evidence suggests that MNS only becomes functional sometime between 3 and 6 months of life (Turati et al., 2013). As discussed in Chapter 3, humans and other primates have mirror neurons, which respond in much the same way while watching an action as they do while performing an action (Iacoboni & Mazziotta, 2007; Rizzolatti et al., 1996); see the "Research Process" for this chapter (Figure 16). Simply put, for some neurons in the frontal lobe of the cerebral cortex, the experience of watching someone else do something is like doing it yourself. Mirror neuron systems appear to play a key role what is called **embodied cognition**, which is a term for the thought processes involved in representing parts of the body and/or reenacting bodily actions in thought. When a monkey observes another monkey or a human grab a peanut, the same neurons fire in the frontal lobe as fire when the observing monkey actually grabs a peanut (Fogassi & Ferrari, 2006). It is likely that mirror neuron systems are involved in imitation and social learning (Filimon et al., 2007; Ganepy et al., 2015; Lyons, 2009). It has been suggested that autistic children, who often have trouble imitating others' gestures, may have deficits in mirror neurons (Bernier & Dawson, 2009;

©UpperCut Images/Alamy RF

Like father, like son. We learn by observing and imitating others.

Research Process

1 Research Question

Rizzolatti and colleagues (1996) were studying neurons involved in hand movements in monkeys, when they made an accidental discovery: The same motor neurons fired when the monkey observed an experimenter grabbing an object as when the monkey made a similar action itself. It made the researchers wonder: Does the brain contain neurons that rehearse motor actions during observational learning?

FIGURE 16

THE DISCOVERY OF MIRROR NEURONS. Mirror neurons in the brain respond in much the same way while watching an action as they do when performing an action.

Source: (Rizzolatti, G., Fadiga, L., Gallese, V., & Fogassi, L. [1996]. Premotor cortex and the recognition of motor actions. *Cognitive Brain Research*, 3, 131–41.)

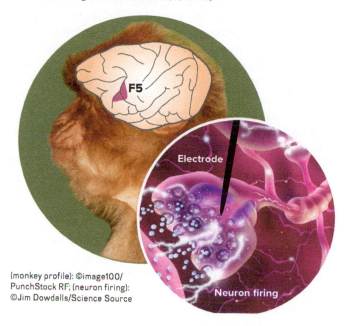

(monkey profile): ©image100/PunchStock RF; (neuron firing): ©Jim Dowdalls/Science Source

2 Method

In a descriptive study of two monkeys, the researchers monitored activity of individual neurons in the motor cortex. They implanted a wire electrode in the motor cortex (area F5) and measured the firing rate of a single neuron while the monkey either grasped a piece of food itself or saw the experimenter pick it up.

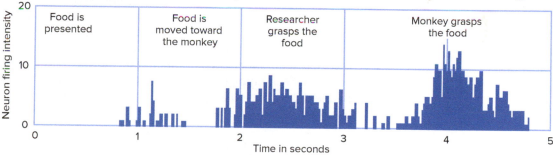

3 Results

The graph shows the results of firing patterns in area F5 when food is presented, when it is moved toward the monkey, when the researcher grasps food, and when the monkey grasps food. The peaks of the graph are taller when the firing rate in area F5 is faster. They are shorter when the firing rate is slower. Notice that there is minimal firing when the monkey simply looks at the food. The firing rates increase during observation of grasping and during grasping itself. More importantly, the pattern of firing is similar when action is observed and when action is made by the monkey itself. Neurons that fire during action and observation of similar actions are called mirror neurons.

4 Conclusion

Mirror neurons support the function of rehearsal during learning. By watching others' actions, we "exercise" the motor regions of the brain involved in making those actions. This, in turn, allows us to perform the same behavior more readily.

©Brand X Pictures/Alamy RF

What effect does regular practice have on synaptic connections?

Oberman & Ramachandran, 2007). Recent research shows, however, that the mirror neuron systems involved in mimicking hand movements (Ruysschaert, Warreyn, Wiersema, Oostra, & Roeyers, 2014) and facial expressions are functional in autistic children, though these motor skills might not get associated with the cognitive skills necessary for understanding another's emotions (Schulte-Rüther et al., 2016).

Synaptic Change during Learning

If you've ever tried to learn a second language, you know that if you don't use it for a while you forget what you've learned. Similarly, you will probably forget much of the material you learn in this class soon after the exam, even if you learn it well to begin with. Why is that?

In the chapter "Memory," we saw what Hebb's work on learning and memory revealed about the plasticity of the brain: "Neurons that fire together, wire together" and "use it or lose it." We also discussed Kandel's studies on the sea slug *Aplysia*. Both areas of research provided experimental evidence of the neural basis of learning and memory (Kandel, 2006; Pinsker et al., 1973). Specifically, certain proteins become activated in short- and long-term memory formation and learning. These proteins change preexisting synaptic connections and cause the growth of new synapses (H. L. Fields, 2005; Kandel, 2001). What this means is that learning *is* the growth of new synapses. Synaptic connections between neurons become stronger and even grow during long-term associative learning. The brain literally grows and changes as we learn. The development and frequent use of new synaptic connections in response to stimulation from the environment strengthen the associated memories and make learning easier. So having experiences repeated over a short period of time is often essential for moving an experience from short-term to long-term memory—that is, for learning to take place. The saying "practice makes perfect" is quite relevant here. To learn and become proficient at something requires repeating the behavior over and over. Synapses need to grow and strengthen.

However, the same synaptic connections will weaken if they aren't used regularly, resulting in forgetting and the loss of learning. Thus, when we stop using learned information, the synapses that support our knowledge weaken and ultimately degrade—and we forget what we once knew. Practice, use, and rehearsal are important in retaining what we have learned.

If you play a musical instrument, you have experienced this phenomenon directly. The more you practice the scales on your piano or guitar, for example, the more synaptic connections you build and the stronger they become. The scales become easier and easier to play. The sensations and movements associated with the increased experience of playing occupy a greater area of your motor cortex and, in effect, change the mapping of touch information in your brain (Pascual-Leone, 2001). If you stop practicing, those connections weaken, the brain map changes, and the scales are harder to recall the next time you try to play.

Experience, Enrichment, and Brain Growth

As we have seen again and again, experience changes the brain. Recall the discussion in the chapter "Conducting Research in Psychology" of the classic work demonstrating that rats reared in enriched or normal environments grow more neural connections and learn to run mazes faster than genetically identical rats raised in impoverished environments (Bennett et al., 1964; Rosenzweig et al., 1962).

Building on this research, later experiments showed that animals do not have to be raised from birth in an enriched environment to benefit. Laboratory mice, for example, can have identical "childhoods" (the first 21 days of their lives) and then be randomly assigned to three different environments: no enrichment, short enrichment (68 days), and long enrichment (6 months). The longer they live in an enriched environment, the more neural growth there is in the hippocampus (Kempermann & Gage, 1999). More importantly, however, simply being in an enriched environment is not even the best way to stimulate the growth of new neurons: Being in an enriched environment that continues to have new and novel forms of stimulation is even better (Kempermann & Gage, 1999). What is more, enrichment can reverse age-related reductions in neural growth (neurogenesis) in rats (Speisman et al., 2013).

In an effort to better understand what aspects of an enriched environment facilitate the growth of new neurons, researchers compared the effects of social interaction, swimming, running, and maze learning on neurogenesis (Pereira et al., 2007; van Praag, Kempermann, & Gage, 1999). Only the running condition led to hippocampal neurogenesis, which is consistent with several studies that show that physical exercise benefits neural growth (Li et al., 2013). Similar enrichment effects on neuron growth occur in other species besides rats, including birds, primates, and humans (Doetsch & Scharff, 2001; Eriksson et al., 1998; Gould et al., 2001; Hillman, Erickson, & Kramer, 2008). In a review of more than 200 studies of both humans and animals, Hötting and Röder (2013) reported that, due to neuroplasticity, physically active people and animals have an increased capacity for learning and other cognitive tasks. In fact, longitudinal research shows that people who are less active and have poorer cardiovascular fitness have smaller brain volume 20 years later (Spartano et al., 2016).

Connection

Can experience and learning generate new neurons in an elderly person?

See "The Developing Adult," in the chapter "Human Development." (p. 197)

Quick Quiz 3: How Nature and Nurture Work Together in Learning

1. Because Konrad Lorenz was the first and only animal baby geese knew for the first few weeks of their lives, they thought Lorenz was their "mother." This kind of association is known as
   a. reinforcement.
   b. imprinting.
   c. learning.
   d. conditioning.

2. What biological structure(s) or system(s) might best explain why we cry along with characters in a sad movie?
   a. mirror neurons
   b. sensory neurons
   c. frontal lobes
   d. hypothalamus

3. Research on learning and the brain has shown that rats raised in impoverished environments
   a. learn just as quickly as rats raised in enriched environments.
   b. have the same number of neurons in the hippocampus as rats raised in enriched environments.
   c. learn more slowly but have the same number of neurons and synaptic connections as rats raised in enriched environments.
   d. learn more slowly and have fewer neurons and synaptic connections than rats raised in enriched environments.

Answers can be found at the end of the chapter.

Bringing It All Together

Making Connections in Learning

Why Do People Smoke?

As you have probably figured out by now, human behavior is complex, so it should be no surprise that any given behavior may be acquired and maintained by means of several types of learning (classical, operant, and/or social), all operating in the context of a human being who has a personality and history. Consider, for example, cigarette smoking (see Figure 17). The acquisition of smoking behavior—how people become smokers in the

		Model or stimulus	Reinforcement	Behavior
starting to smoke . . .	**Social learning theory**	Hang out with friends who smoke	Friends look cool	Begin smoking
continuing to smoke . . .	**Operant conditioning**		**Positive reinforcement** Increased feelings of peer acceptance of smoking **Negative reinforcement** Reduced stress levels	Continue smoking
discouraging smoking . . .	**Operant conditioning**		**Positive punishment** Health consequences **Negative punishment** Smoking restricted in public places	Less smoking
	Classical conditioning	Pairing cigarette smoking with: **UCS** Image of a smoker's lungs **UCR** Feeling of revulsion in response to image of smoker's lungs		Less likely to smoke once an association is made between smoking and lung damage

FIGURE 17

HOW LEARNING THEORIES EXPLAIN SMOKING BEHAVIOR

 How do different theories of learning explain why people start smoking and continue smoking?

first place—is perhaps best explained by social learning theory (Bandura, 1969, 1986). The sensory qualities of cigarette smoking on first experience are anything but pleasant—coughing, dizziness, and nausea—but most smokers start smoking as teenagers, and most teens start smoking because they seek some of the rewards that appear to come with smoking: coolness, peer acceptance, looking like an adult. (All of these rewards are secondary reinforcers, which acquire their reinforcing characteristics by means of classical and operant conditioning.) Kids see that others who smoke get some of these rewards for smoking. Thus, they might model smoking behavior in order to obtain these rewards themselves (Jaber et al., 2016). They might view "being seen as cool"—a form of peer acceptance—as desirable, so being seen as cool becomes a reinforcer for the smoking behaviors of others. "Whenever Mom gets stressed, she smokes a cigarette

to relax—maybe that will work for me too" is another example of social learning.

Once someone has become an established smoker, operant conditioning helps maintain smoking behavior. Smoking is bolstered by a number of positive reinforcers: arousal of the sympathetic nervous system (the "rush" of smoking), mild relaxation of the muscles, and, in some cases, increased peer acceptance. Smoking also has a number of negative reinforcers, such as the removal of stress, the removal of social isolation for some smokers, and a reduced appetite. The power of these reinforcers, combined with the physiologically addictive properties of nicotine, makes it very difficult to quit smoking. Moreover, the potential punishers of smoking—a substantially increased risk of lung cancer and heart disease—are threats that are so far off in the future for teens that they tend to ignore them. It is for this reason that some psychologists who are concerned with preventing teen smoking have tried to link smoking with unpleasant images and effects (such as ugliness and social rejection). The hope is that, by using both classical and operant conditioning, they can make smoking appear less rewarding. In order to discourage smoking, some public health campaigns show pictures of diseased lungs or smokers who look older than they are. It is an effort to teach people to have an unpleasant association with a cigarette and therefore stop smoking.

Like many complex human behaviors, smoking derives from numerous other influences besides conditioning. Gender, personality, and sociocultural characteristics are some of the factors that may interact with conditioning and biology to influence people to start smoking and affect whether they successfully quit.

Although numerous studies have found no evidence for gender differences in the factors related to smoking, one large-scale study found that gender influences susceptibility to smoking, the way people work with their urges to smoke, and the ability to successfully quit (Ellickson, Tucker, & Klein, 2001). Whether friends smoke plays a stronger role in whether adolescent girls attempt and succeed at quitting smoking than it does in boys. In a study of the effects of smoking abstinence (and therefore nicotine withdrawal) on craving and cognitive performance in male and female adolescent smokers, girls reported greater tobacco cravings and symptoms of nicotine withdrawal than boys, but boys performed worse on two cognitive tasks during nicotine withdrawal (Jacobsen et al., 2005). Taken together, these studies suggest that gender may interact with social and cognitive factors to maintain smoking by influencing whether teens decide to attempt to quit (girls have more social pressures to try to quit) and the extent to which the effects of nicotine withdrawal are debilitating (the adverse effects on performance are worse for boys). These are just some of the factors that may explain why more boys smoke than girls, although the gap is narrowing (Robinson & Klesges, 1997). This may be an unfortunate by-product of an increasing social and economic status of women worldwide. Large-sample surveys indicate that as gender empowerment increases, so does the proportion of women smoking relevant to men (Hitchman & Fong, 2011).

Other research shows that personality style predicts whether people start smoking and whether they try to stop, introducing yet another variable into this complex behavior. A study of personality and smoking found that people who are more sociable, impulsive, rebellious, hostile, and sensation seeking are more likely to start smoking and less likely to quit successfully than those who do not have these personal characteristics (Lipkus et al., 1994). This finding fits with established theory that extraverts are more likely to be smokers than introverts, because extraverts have a physiological need for stimulation and therefore seek experiences that are physiologically arousing, such as smoking, drinking, and thrill-seeking feats (Eysenck, 1980; O'Conner, 2016). Furthermore, a lack of certain cognitive skills, including long-term thinking and planning abilities, in some adolescents may predispose them to smoke. Not having a long-term perspective, they fail to understand the negative effects of smoking on health (Dinn, Aycicegi, & Harris, 2004). This explanation makes sense if we consider the prevalence of health promotion efforts designed to discourage people from smoking. The urges or need for stimulation may combine with cognitive factors and social learning (modeling peer behavior) to make it very difficult for some people to resist smoking.

The presence of models for smoking (such as parents and friends) figures among the environmental factors that influence smoking behavior. A recent study of more than 10,000 European teenagers revealed that teens modeled both parents' smoking behavior, but especially their same-sex parent (Alves et al., 2016). For example, teen boys were 1.90 times more likely to smoke if their father smoked than if he didn't and 1.77 times more likely if their mother smoked. Even more pronounced, teen girls were 1.42 times more likely to smoke if their fathers smoked and a whopping 3.36 times more likely to smoke if their mothers smoked than if she didn't. The modeling of parental smoking, therefore seems to have an even stronger effect on girls than boys.

These findings indicate that cultural variables (ethnic group), social factors (the availability of role models), and basic principles of learning (observational learning) can all interact to influence whether young people start smoking (Amin & Lhila, 2016; Ellickson et al., 2004).

Given the role that reinforcement plays in the acquisition of smoking behavior, it is not surprising that operant conditioning has been used to help people kick the smoking habit. **Behavior modification** techniques, which apply the principles of operant conditioning to changing behavior, have been particularly effective in helping people quit smoking, especially when combined with nicotine replacement therapies (such as gum or the patch), which ease the symptoms of withdrawal. Smokers who participate in such programs are likely to live longer than those who don't (Anthonisen et al., 2005).

behavior modification
The principles of operant conditioning used to change behavior.

Chapter Review

BASIC PROCESSES OF LEARNING

- Learning is an enduring change in behavior that results from experience. It involves changes in sensation, perception, behavior, and brain function.

- Learning by association is a simple form of learning that links two pieces of information from the environment with one another because, in our experience, they repeatedly occur together.

CONDITIONING MODELS OF LEARNING

- Classical conditioning centers on stimulus-response (SR) relationships. It involves the modification of reflexes with experience. A conditioned response occurs when a neutral stimulus (such as a bell) elicits what was previously an unconditioned response (such as salivation) to an unconditioned stimulus (such as food) when it is presented alone. After conditioning, the neutral stimulus is called a conditioned stimulus.

- In operant conditioning, the consequences of spontaneous behavior are manipulated in order to elicit the desired behavior. According to Skinner, certain consequences make a behavior more likely to occur again. When the consequences of a behavior increase the likelihood that a behavior will occur again, the behavior has been reinforced. Reinforcement can be positive (something added) or negative (something subtracted).

- In contrast, punishment decreases the likelihood that a behavior will occur again. The stimuli used for reinforcement and punishment are unrelated to the target behavior. Shaping is the reinforcement of successive approximations of a desired behavior.

- Reinforcement may be presented every time a behavior occurs or only occasionally. Intermittent reinforcement, reinforcement that does not occur after every response, produces a stronger behavioral response

©Andrea Golden/Getty Images RF

than does continuous reinforcement. Four schedules of reinforcement dictate how an intermittent reinforcement might be implemented: fixed-ratio, variable-ratio, fixed-interval, and variable-interval.

- Conditioned taste aversion, the learned avoidance of a particular taste or food if sickness occurs at the same time as or shortly after exposure to it, can develop after only one exposure. The time lapse between exposure and sickness may be an hour or more.

- Biological constraints limit the development of a conditioned response to a neutral stimulus that is relevant to the situation. For example, it is easier to make someone nauseated by a taste than by a sound or a sight.

- Biology limits behavioral options in order to make the adaptive ones more likely. The biological constraint model of learning suggests that some behaviors are inherently more likely to be learned than others. Instinctive drift, in which an organism fails to learn the target behavior because it conflicts with a stronger instinctive behavior, is a type of biological constraint.

- Latent learning occurs in the absence of reinforcement and is not demonstrated until later, when reinforcement occurs.

SOCIAL LEARNING THEORY

- Social learning theory takes into account the role of social influence in learning. Imitation, or modeling, plays a key role in how we learn, and it can work with reinforcement to shape behavior. Bandura proposed that

reinforcement makes learning more likely not only for the person doing the behavior but also for observers.

- Modeling is the process of observing and imitating behaviors performed by others, particularly behaviors that are rewarded in others.

HOW NATURE AND NURTURE WORK TOGETHER IN LEARNING

- Examples of the bidirectional relationship between learning and the brain include imprinting, the rapid and innate learning of the characteristics of a caregiver within a very short period of time after birth; sensitivity

periods, when the brain is most receptive to learning certain skills; imitation; the growth and strengthening of synaptic connections in response to environmental stimuli; and environmental enrichment.

BRINGING IT ALL TOGETHER: MAKING CONNECTIONS IN LEARNING

- All of the major learning perspectives, as well as other factors, are needed to fully explain behaviors such as smoking.

- Applications derived from models of learning, such as behavior modification, may help people unlearn unwanted or undesirable behaviors, such as smoking.

Key Terms

association
behavior modification
biological constraint model
classical conditioning
conditioned response (CR)
conditioned stimulus (CS)
conditioned taste aversion
conditioning
continuous reinforcement
embodied cognition
ethology
extinction
fixed-interval (FI) schedule
fixed-ratio (FR) schedule

instinctive drift
intermittent reinforcement
latent learning
law of effect
learning
modeling
negative punishment
neutral stimulus
negative reinforcement
observational learning
operant conditioning
positive punishment
positive reinforcement
primary reinforcers

punishment
reinforcer
schedules of reinforcement
secondary (conditioned) reinforcers
shaping
Skinner box
social learning theory
spontaneous recovery
stimulus discrimination
stimulus generalization
unconditioned response (UCR)
unconditioned stimulus (UCS)
variable-interval (VI) schedule
variable-ratio (VR) schedule

Quick Quiz Answers

Quick Quiz 1: 1. d; **2.** b; **3.** c; **4.** d; **5.** b; **6.** d   **Quick Quiz 2: 1.** a; **2.** d; **3.** b   **Quick Quiz 3: 1.** b; **2.** a; **3.** d

9 Language and Thought

Chapter Outline

Language
Thinking, Reasoning, and Decision Making
Chapter Review

Challenge Your Assumptions

True or False?

- Humans have to be taught grammar. (see page 341)

- People who speak different languages think about time differently. (see page 347)

- Most educated adults can tell when they are reading "fake" news stories versus fact-based news stories. (see page 355)

- Humans are generally rational in their decision making. (see page 358)

- Adults can learn to speak a second language more easily than children. (see page 361)

- Children raised from infancy with two languages (bilingually) do not confuse the two languages. (see page 363)

W hen one of the authors of this text (GJF) was 17 years old, he spent a year in Germany as an exchange student, living with a German family and attending a German *Gymnasium* (High School). Before then he spoke essentially no German, but after lots of hard work he became relatively fluent in about 6 months. But the hardest thing about learning German for him was not simply the new vocabulary and that there are 16 forms of "the" and 16 forms of "a" but also the fact that the German language has a more complex sentence structure (more subordinate clauses), verbs are often placed at the end not beginning of clauses, and there are concepts that exist in German but not English. For instance, *Gemütlichkeit* roughly can be translated as "cozy" or "comfortable," but because it stems from the German word for "heart, mind, or feeling" it also means something more: It has a social meaning of the feeling one gets by being welcome and comfortable in a social context, especially when celebrating. The German "Beer Garden" is the classic venue for experiencing *Gemütlichkeit*. As he became more and more fluent in German, what began to dawn on Greg, as it certainly has for anyone who has learned a second language, especially as an adult, is that language is not just a way of speaking and communicating. Rather, it is also a way of thinking.

Indeed, a recent study of English and German monolinguals and bilinguals showed that those who speak only English or only German think differently about the world. English speakers tend to describe action only ("A woman is walking"), whereas German speakers also include goals in the action ("A woman walks toward her car."). German speakers are more holisitic and English speakers more focused on action (Athanasopoulas et al., 2015). In short, language and thought are separate and yet intimately tied together.

This chapter introduces the psychology of language and thought, both separately and together. First we look at language by exploring its nature, evolution, and development in humans. Then we turn to current psychological research and theory concerning how we represent our thoughts visually and verbally. We look at how people reason, form judgments, and make decisions. Finally, we bring all these topics together by examining how and when learning a second language changes our brains and affects our ability to reason, solve problems, and think flexibly. We will continue the discussion of thought in the chapter "Intelligence, Problem Solving, and Creativity," where we discuss intelligence, problem solving, and creativity.

LANGUAGE

If you lived 300,000 years ago, before language was fully developed, how would you think and communicate if everyone you met could only grunt and groan? Much like the other primates on the planet, you would communicate with other humans only about immediate, concrete states. Everything you knew would be experienced directly through smell, taste, hearing, sight, or touch. Your memory would be limited chiefly to events in the recent past; you would have no language with which to process events and store them in long-term memory. Without language, culture and civilization as we now know it could not exist, and your ways of thinking, understanding, and transmitting knowledge would be limited to the here and now.

The Nature of Language

Linguists define **human language** as an open and symbolic communication system that has rules of grammar and allows its users to express abstract and distant ideas (Bickerton, 1995). To be *open* is to have a dynamic system free to change, and to be *symbolic* is to have no real connection between a sound and the meaning or idea associated with it. For example, words are open in that they change meaning over time (compare modern English to Shakespearean English). Sounds are parts of words that symbolize meaning and ideas. Symbolic refers to the idea that words and letters are symbols and not to be taken literally. The concept "book" in English uses other symbols in other languages to be expressed ("libro" in Spanish, for instance) but the concept is essentially the same.

Words in turn are put together in ways that follow the rules of syntax and grammar. **Syntax** refers to the rules for arranging words and symbols in sentences (or parts of sentences), whereas **grammar** comprises the entire set of rules for combining symbols and sounds to speak and write a particular language and includes such things in English as subject-verb agreement, plurals, and the use of possessives.

The easiest way to demonstrate the arbitrary nature of the connection between sound and meaning is to point out that we can say exactly the same sentence in almost every language in the world, of which there are nearly 7,000. For example, "I am reading the book" can also be "Ich lese das Buch" in German, "Estoy leyendo el libro" in Spanish, "Je lis le livre" in French, and "Я читаю книгу" in Russian. Each language has its own distinct sounds for saying the same thing. The specific word and sound of the word is therefore arbitrary (book versus libro, for example), but the meaning of the word is not. The concept "book" is very much the same regardless of language. Because this is true, ideas can often be directly translated—more or less—from one language to another, a topic we return to in "Bringing It All Together" at the end of the chapter.

Human language is unique because it is the only system capable of transmitting abstract ideas. Although most animals communicate, for the most part they are able to signal to other members of their species only their immediate and concrete states, such as being angry, threatened, hungry, hurt, or eager to reproduce (Deacon, 1997). Humans can discuss not only immediate feelings and needs but also abstract and remote ideas or states of being, such as infinity, God, the afterlife, the universe—or whether Macs are better than PCs.

©Patrick Rolands/Shutterstock.com

Bonobos do communicate with one another—not with words but by leaving trail markers on the floor of the tropical forests where they live.

 If bonobos (pygmy chimps) could speak, what would these two be talking about?

human language
A communication system specific to *Homo sapiens*; it is open and symbolic, has rules of grammar, and allows its users to express abstract and distant ideas.

syntax
The rules for arranging words and symbols to form sentences or parts of sentences in a particular language.

grammar
The entire set of rules for combining symbols and sounds to speak and write a particular language.

The Evolution of Language in Humans

As far as we know, earlier species of humans, such as *Homo erectus* and *Homo neanderthalensis*, had, at most, very rudimentary language, called **protolanguage**, or pre-language (Arbib, Liebal, & Pika, 2008; Givón & Malle, 2002; Johansson, 2013). No one knows for sure when fully grammatical language first appeared, but archaeologists and linguists suggest that probably only our species (*Homo sapiens*) has used grammatical and syntactical language. If so, language is less than 150,000 years old.

protolanguage
Very rudimentary language; also known as pre-language; used by earlier species of *Homo*.

Because the development of fully grammatical language is such a big and unusual step, scientists think that the evolution of language and evolution of the brain were intertwined. Anthropologists and psychologists suggest that the complexity of the human brain and the human ability to use language co-evolved. As our ancestors moved from protolanguage to grammatical language, they required brains with greater working memory and the ability for abstract thought (Arbib et al., 2008; Deacon, 1997; Dunbar, 2001).

As the human brain, and especially the frontal lobes, grew larger and larger, people became capable of thinking and communicating more and more complex and abstract thoughts. Increases in the size of human social groups may have triggered an increase in brain size as well. The more complex a group is, the greater is its members' need to communicate and cooperate (Dunbar, 2001). The needs for reciprocating and cooperating also played a role in the evolution of human language (Nowak & Sigmund, 2005).

Language Development in Individuals

If you have ever traveled to a country where you don't speak the language, you know that a foreign language can seem like a single, continuous string of sounds. It is hard to know where one word ends and the next one begins, unless you have been hearing and speaking that language since early childhood. As young children develop their understanding of language, they learn that the sounds coming from the mouths of the people around them are meaningful units that form words.

Recent research shows that language learning is already occurring in the womb, with babies who have been exposed to certain verbal sequences responding to these sequences after birth, whereas babies not exposed to them in utero do not respond to them after birth (Partanen et al., 2013). Moreover, 3-month-old infants' ability to categorize objects is helped by being exposed to either human or primate vocalizations—yet another connection between language and thought (Perszyk & Waxman, 2016).

One principle of language development is the ability to understand words develops before the ability to produce words (Fenson et al., 1994). We can easily observe that comprehension comes first, because babies can do many things that are asked of them, such as pointing to their nose, long before they can say the words associated with those actions. Language comprehension, as we saw in the chapter "The Biology of Behavior," occurs in the left hemisphere of the brain, in the region called Wernicke's area, whereas language production is associated with the left-hemisphere region called Broca's area (see Figure 1). The fact that infants understand language before they start speaking suggests that the Wernicke's area develops before the Broca's area.

Another principle of language development happens when younger infants (for example, 6-month-olds) can discriminate phonetic sounds outside of their native language, whereas a few months later (for example, by 10 or 12 months of age) they can't (Kuhl et al., 2006). After about 12 months they only discriminate sounds in their native language. This principle is known as *neural commitment* because it suggests the neural networks in the brain's language centers are wiring themselves—committing to—one language (or two if bilingual). This is why babies hear more phonetic sounds than children or adults.

Stages of Language Development The first speech sounds humans make consist almost exclusively of vowels, such as "aah, ee, ooh." Most infants begin uttering repeated vowel sounds, called **cooing**, during the first 6 months. Cooing sounds are universal: They vary little from hearing to deaf babies or among babies from all over the world.

Babbling, the infant's experimentation with a complex range of sounds or phonemes, overlaps with cooing, and it starts at around 5 or 6 months of age.

cooing
The first sounds humans make other than crying, consisting almost exclusively of vowels; occurs during the first 6 months of life.

babbling
Sounds made as a result of the infant's experimentation with a complex range of phonemes, which include consonants as well as vowels; starts around 5–6 months of age.

Although babbling includes consonants as wells as vowels, the sounds are not yet recognizable as words. At first, babies babble single syllables, such as "buh" and "duh"; later they utter "gibberish," simply a string of single syllables, such as "da, buh, ma, wee."

At first, babbling babies make many more sounds than they hear in their native language, because babies' brains have not yet been fully shaped by their native language. They can also hear more sounds than their parents can (Jusczyk, 1997; Plunkett, 1997). Adults who speak certain Asian languages—which do not distinguish between "r" and "l," for example—do not perceive a difference between these two sounds, but their toddlers do. As children progress through the babbling stage, and with repeated exposure to the subset of sounds in their native language, they "prune" away sounds that are not used in that language and lose the ability to say or perceive nonnative sounds (Goto, 1971; Kuhl, Stevens, & Hayashi, 2006). Research, however, has demonstrated that adult Japanese speakers can partially relearn how to hear the difference between "r" and "l" with a little training (Ingvalson et al., 2011; McClelland et al., 2002).

At the end of the babbling stage, usually at around 12 months, **one-word utterances** emerge. Now children first speak such classic words as "mama," "dada," "more," and the all-important "no!" One-word utterances are likely descended from protolanguage. Like toddlers, our ancestors probably made up sounds for objects (nouns) and actions (verbs) before they developed more complex sentences (Goldfield, 2000).

Whether a word is at the beginning, middle, or end of a sentence seems to be related to how likely young children are to learn that word. Children tend to acquire words that are spoken at the ends of sentences first. In languages that are structured in the order of subject-verb-object, such as English, children acquire nouns earlier than verbs, because objects are nouns. In languages that are structured subject-object-verb, such as Japanese, children acquire verbs earlier than nouns (Chan, Brandone, & Tardif, 2009; Clancy, 1985; Tardif, Gelman, & Xu, 1999). In English, we say, "Maria read the book," whereas in Japanese people say, "Maria the book read." English-speaking children learn *book* before *read*, whereas Japanese-speaking children learn the Japanese version of *read* before *book*.

This tendency to learn the last word in a sentence first may reflect the memory phenomenon called the *recency effect*, discussed in the chapter "Memory". Starting around 18 months, children make **two-word utterances**, such as "my ball," "mo wawa" (more water), or "go way" (go away). During this phase of language development, parents often find themselves serving as translators for other people, because their children create unique ways of saying things. For instance, our youngest son, Evan, would say "ba" for any kind of water, because he had learned to say "ba" to mean "bottle of water." He extended "ba" to other types of water, such as a lake, pool, or bathtub, which we easily understood. Our babysitters did not, however, so we had to translate "Evanese" for them.

By age 2½ or 3, most children have entered the third phase of language development—the **sentence phase**—in which they begin speaking in fully grammatical sentences. This transition happens so quickly that linguists usually have a tough time studying it. Linguist Steven Pinker uses a boy named Adam as an example. At age 2, Adam would say, "Play checkers. Big drum. I got horn." Less than a year later, at age 3, he would say, "I going come in fourteen minutes. You dress me up like a baby elephant. You know how to put it back together" (Pinker, 1994, pp. 273–274). These sentences may not always be what adults consider grammatically correct, but they are grammatical sentences.

one-word utterances
Single words (such as "mama," "dada," "more," or "no!") occur around 12 months of age.

two-word utterances
Phrases children put together, starting around 18 months, such as "my ball," "mo wawa," or "go way."

sentence phase
The stage when children begin speaking in fully grammatical sentences; usually age 2½ to 3.

©Datacraft/Getty Images RF

By age 3, children have begun to speak in fully grammatical sentences. Also, their brains are nearly adult size.

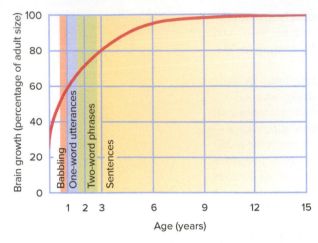

FIGURE 1

THE ASSOCIATION BETWEEN BRAIN GROWTH AND LANGUAGE DEVELOPMENT. As a child's brain approaches its final adult size, the onset and rapid development of language match the rapid growth of the brain. At age 1, when the child's brain is less than 50% of its adult size, the infant is babbling and perhaps saying a few words. By age 3, when the brain is 75%–80% of its adult size, the child has progressed to two-word phrases and short sentences (Sakai, 2005).

In sum, children go through a very predictable sequence in acquiring language: from cooing to babbling, one-word utterances, two-word utterances, and finally adultlike sentence structure, a stage that is reached around age 3. These stages in speech development map remarkably well onto the growth in the child's overall brain size (see Figure 1). There is a steep rise in both brain growth and language between the ages of 1 and 3. The brain of a 3-year-old child has reached about 80% of adult size. At about this age, children can form adultlike sentences.

The Sensitivity Period An important principle of language development is that, if children are not exposed to any human language before a certain age, their language abilities never fully develop (Lenneberg, 1967; Newport, 2003; Uylings, 2006). This sensitivity period, and optimal learning time for language acquisition, begins in the first years of life and ends at about age 12. Severe neglect and lack of exposure to language during this period cause permanent problems in language development. As Uylings (2006) points out, sensitivity periods end after neural pruning and neural wiring have reached their peak, at which point the plasticity of neural connections becomes less flexible.

One of the most dramatic examples of the importance of the sensitivity period in language development is the case of an abused and severely neglected girl, known as "Genie." When she was 2 years old, a family doctor diagnosed Genie as being mildly retarded (Rymer, 1993). Her father, who was mentally unstable, interpreted this to mean that she was severely retarded and needed "protection." He tied her to a chair all day long and caged her in a crib at night. Moreover, he beat her every time she tried to speak and barked at her like a dog. This abuse lasted until Genie was 13½, when her mother finally ran away, taking Genie with her. The local social worker whose help they sought thought Genie was 6 or 7 years old, because she was only 4 feet 6 inches tall and weighed 59 pounds. The social worker arranged for the State of California to take temporary custody of the child. At that time, Genie could speak only a few words, such as "stopit" or "nomore."

At age 17, after 4 years of language training, Genie's language skills were still extremely delayed. She could communicate simple ideas, but her speech was limited mainly to ungrammatical sentences. She said things such as "Spot chew glove" or "Applesauce buy store" (*Transcripts*, 1997). In this sense, her language ability was at the level of a young child's. Her language comprehension, however, was much better than her language production. She understood much of what was said to her. Brain imaging revealed something very unusual about Genie's brain activity while speaking or listening: The activity was located mostly in her right hemisphere (Curtiss, 1977). Recall that language ability is located in the left hemisphere. The case of Genie suggests that left-hemisphere speech development requires stimulation from the environment during a certain sensitivity period if it is to develop properly.

As tragic as Genie's story is, it reveals something very important about language: We need verbal stimulation from others, and we need it while we are young if we are to develop fully and completely the ability to speak. Now in her 50s, Genie lives in supportive foster care. The movie *Mockingbird Don't Sing*, released in 2001, is based on her life.

Because Genie had other cognitive deficits at birth, her case is not a clear test of the sensitivity period hypothesis. Clearer evidence comes from cases of people born deaf who were not spoken to in sign language and did not learn it until later in life. Consistent with the idea of a sensitivity period, deaf people who learn sign language after early childhood never become as proficient as those who learn sign language early in life (DeKeyser & Larson-Hall, 2005).

Theories of Language Acquisition

Unless they suffer from some sort of disease or deficit, all humans learn to speak, including those who were born deaf. Many children who can't hear learn spoken language in order to communicate with hearing individuals, but many rely heavily on sign language as well. Sign language is every bit as complex and communicative as spoken language. This suggests that we have innate, genetically based structures in the brain that enable us to learn language, but the vast differences in how well each of us learns to speak illustrate the importance of environmental stimulation. Different theories of language acquisition emphasize the contributions of nature and nurture to language differently, but they all agree that both are involved.

Sociocultural Theories   We learn language from the people around us. We acquire vocabulary by hearing others speak, and we figure out what they mean by the context (Hoff, 2006; Zhang et al., 2008). Children who hear more total and unique words, and more complex sentences, develop their language faster and more richly than those who do not (Gathercole & Hoff, 2007; Hart & Risley, 1992, 1995; Huttenlocher et al., 2002; Pan et al., 2005). In a review of the evidence for how environment shapes and molds language acquisition, Erika Hoff (2006) provides a partial list of the environmental influences on language. They include culture, socioeconomic status, birth order, school, peers, television, and parents. Each of these influences has a rich research history demonstrating how sociocultural forces shape language development, particularly the timing of vocabulary development.

The richness of a child's vocabulary is very much a function of how many words are spoken in the family. Hart and Risely (1992, 1995) examined language development in 42 families with young children from three different economic and educational groups: professional, middle and working class, and unemployed (welfare). Each month for over 2 years (from when the children were 10 months to 3 years of age), the researchers tape-recorded and analyzed in-home verbal interactions.

One major finding was that the children all started to speak around the same time and they developed good structure and use of language. Children, however, from professional families heard an average of 2,153 words per hour, those from middle- and working-class families heard an average of 1,251 words per hour, and those from unemployed (welfare) families heard an average of 616 words per hour. Extending these numbers to total words heard in a year, by age 4 the children from the unemployed families would have heard about 32 million fewer words than the children from professional families.

These differences in amount of words spoken to translated into differences in the child's own vocabulary (see Figure 2). By age 3, the average vocabulary of the children from unemployed (welfare) families was around 500 words, whereas for professional families it was around 1,100 words. The children from the professional families also heard more encouragement words than discouragement words than did the children from either the working-/middle-class or welfare-recipient families.

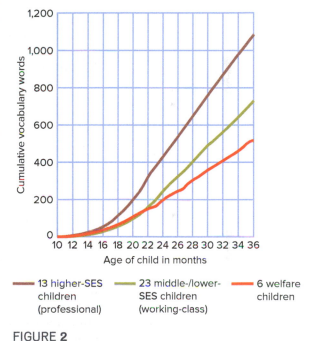

FIGURE 2

DEVELOPMENT OF VOCABULARY AS A FUNCTION OF SOCIOECONOMIC STATUS OF THE FAMILY.
Given the differences between families in the numbers of words spoken to children, it is not surprising that these differences would translate into differences in the children's vocabulary. In this graph we see the development of total vocabulary size over the 2.5-year period in children in three socioeconomic status (SES) groups: professional, middle-/working-class, and unemployed (welfare). By age 3, children from professional families are using more than twice as many different words as children from welfare families (Hart & Risley, 1995).

Much of what we learn comes from imitating family members. Recall that imitation is doing exactly what you see someone else do, and with certain behaviors imitation is evident immediately after birth. Newborns as young as 50 minutes old will stick out their tongues or open their mouths when they see an adult do so (Meltzoff & Moore, 1983). At a slightly older age, babies try to imitate the speech sounds they hear (Kuhl & Meltzoff, 1997). Adults in turn do many things to encourage imitation, such as speaking in a higher pitch, raising and lowering the volume of their voice, using simpler sentence structures, emphasizing the here and now, and using emotion to communicate their messages (Fernald & Morikawa, 1993; Rice, 1989). These changes in adult speech patterns—which appear to be universal—are referred to as **child-directed speech**.

The richness of verbal stimulation from family members affects the timing of a child's vocabulary development (Hoff, 2006). For instance, the children of very verbally responsive mothers reach the 50-word vocabulary milestone a full 5 months earlier than do children of less verbally responsive mothers. More generally, much of the differences in the timing of the child's vocabulary development can be explained by three characteristics of the mother: her socioeconomic status, her vocabulary use, and her personality characteristics.

Although these are mostly social processes we have been discussing, they also demonstrate profound interdependence with brain processes, which is yet another example of the interplay between nature and nurture. Mirror neurons, the clusters of brain cells that fire not only when an individual performs a task (such as sticking out one's tongue) but also when an individual observes another person do the same task, facilitate social learning and imitation (Rizzolatti & Arbib, 1998; Rizzolatti & Craighero, 2004). Many human social skills, including speech, develop because our brains allow and foster such social learning.

Conditioning and Learning Theory Another classic nurture or environmental-behavioral perspective of how we learn language is B. F. Skinner's (1957) conditioning and learning theory. Skinner argued that language exists because it is reinforced and shaped. He proposed that we speak not because we want to convey an idea or a feeling but rather because we have been reinforced for doing so. What are the conditions that bring about or reinforce verbal behavior? According to Skinner, children learn to speak a particular language because, when they say anything that even comes close to a word, the parents smile and say things like "Wow! She said 'mama'!" The parents' reaction has a reinforcing effect, making the child more likely to say that word.

As we just discussed, young children begin language development by cooing, then babbling, then uttering one and two words until they begin to say short phrases and sentences. Skinner explained this progression in terms of shaping, successive approximations, and reinforcement: The first approximation of a complex behavior will be reinforced. When a toddler utters "mama," she gets more of her mother's attention and smiles than she does when she utters "baba." The child learns first that the word *mama* matters and soon thereafter learns what it means. In a short while the child is saying "mama go bye-bye." Each step is subsequently reinforced until the child reaches the final behavior—in this case, speaking in fully grammatical sentences, such as "Mommy is going away."

Nativist Theory There is little doubt that language development, such as the acquisition of certain words, is shaped partly by parental responses. When a child correctly names an object for the first time, the parents lavish much praise and encouragement: "Yes, that's right! Spot is a doggy!" However, such reinforcement does not occur as consistently for other aspects of language development, such as syntax and grammar rules. Still, children seem to learn these aspects with little difficulty, and they tend to *overgeneralize* language rules; they may add *ed* to *run* to form the past tense because adding *ed* is the typical way of forming

child-directed speech
Changes in adult speech patterns—apparently universal—when speaking to young children or infants; characterized by higher pitch, changes in voice volume, use of simpler sentences, emphasis on the here and now, and use of emotion to communicate messages.

Connection

One reason newborn infants are capable of imitating behavior immediately after birth is that humans and other animals have mirror neurons.

See "The Cells of the Nervous System: Glial Cells and Neurons," in the chapter "The Biology of Behavior," p. 83, and "Imitation, Mirror Neurons, and Learning," in the chapter "Learning," p. 334.

the past tense in English. Instead of saying "Spot ran," then, the child says "Spot runned." Reinforcement cannot explain this formation, because children most likely have never heard "runned" from their parents and, so, have not been reinforced for using it. In other words, it is impossible to learn novel utterances through imitation and reinforcement. One cannot use shaping to teach someone to say something no one has ever said. So Skinner's explanation of language acquisition cannot fully explain how we learn language.

Some linguists contend that we discover language rather than learn it, that language development is "native," or inborn, the main assumption of the **nativist view of language**. In this view, the brain is structured, or "wired," for language learning; as you have learned, Broca's and Wernicke's areas are dedicated to speech production and comprehension, respectively. The linguist Noam Chomsky (1972, 1986) has argued that humans are born with a **language acquisition device (LAD)**—an innate, biologically based capacity to acquire language. Just as birds are biologically built to fly, humans are biologically built to speak. We are not born with a capacity to learn a particular language, such as Chinese or English, but rather we are simply born with a capacity to learn "language." Further, Chomsky (1972, 2000) has suggested that there is essentially a single universal grammar underlying all human languages; each language is simply a specific expression of this universal grammar.

Chomsky argues for a built-in language acquisition device (LAD) partly because of how easily and automatically humans learn to do this very complex and difficult thing: speak in complete and grammatical sentences. It is universal, and it develops intuitively in children in about the same way and at the same time all over the world, regardless of which language they learn. Any child can learn equally easily any language as his or her native language. If you grew up in certain regions of Africa, you would be speaking Swahili; certain parts of Asia, Mandarin; certain parts of Europe, German.

Although there are universal principles for language, each language sets limits, or parameters, for what is correct in terms of word orders and other aspects. Parameters are often binary, like an "on-off" switch. For example, one parameter question is "do verbs go before or after subjects?" There are only two answers to this parameter for each language—yes or no. To take English and Japanese as an example: verbs go before objects in English but after them in Japanese. Parameters make clear why it is relatively easy for a child to learn a particular language. Once children learn the parameters or rules of their language, forming grammatically correct sentences becomes relatively easy because of a built-in language acquisition device (Dunbar, 2001; Pinker, 1994).

Nature, Nurture, and Language Learning   As we have seen, different theoretical perspectives emphasize different contributions of nature and nurture. Social and learning theorists argue for the importance of social input and stimulation, whereas nativist theorists argue for the importance of brain structures and genetic factors. One difference between the two perspectives is environmental theories tend to focus more on vocabulary and nativist theories more on grammar. Vocabulary of a particular language obviously has to be learned, but our brains are more hardwired for intuitively acquiring grammatical rules of language.

Both perspectives are needed to fully explain language. In general, most scholars of language agree that acquiring language involves natural abilities, which are modified by the language learner's environment (Hoff, 2006; Lidz & Gleitman, 2004; MacWhinney, 1999). The term *innately guided learning* captures the interaction between nature and nurture very well (Elman et al., 1996). We learn to speak, but in doing so we are guided by our innate capacity for language learning. The importance of both nature and nurture is starkly illustrated by the case of Genie: She could speak, and even learned a few words as a child, but her environment was so barren that her language development was severely stunted.

nativist view of language
The idea that we discover language rather than learn it, that language development is inborn.

language acquisition device (LAD)
An innate, biologically based capacity to acquire language, proposed by Noam Chomsky as part of his nativist view of language.

©ChinaFotoPress/Getty Images

Noam Chomsky

Challenge Your Assumptions

True or False? Humans have to be taught grammar.

False: The human brain evolved and is wired for language (grammar). Vocabulary must be learned but grammatical rules are acquired intuitively and easily, with no formal teaching.

©Gwyn Photography/Getty Images

Do you agree with Chomsky that native languages are acquired automatically and with little to no effort?

Still, genetic factors and innate structures have a stronger influence on some aspects of language development, whereas environmental conditions have a greater influence on other aspects. For instance, grammar is more innate and genetically influenced than is vocabulary, which is more strongly shaped by input from the environment (Dale et al., 2000; Hoff, 2006). Recall that one common way to determine how much of a trait is due to genetic influence is to compare identical twin pairs to fraternal twin pairs (see the chapter "Conducting Research in Psychology"). If a trait is strongly genetically influenced, it will show much stronger correlations in identical twins than in fraternal twins, because identical twins are more genetically alike. Dale and colleagues 2000) compared vocabulary and grammar skills in 1,008 identical twin pairs to the same skills in 1,890 fraternal twin pairs; all were about 2 years old. The children's parents assessed their vocabulary and grammar skills by completing questionnaires dealing with the kinds of words and sentences their children could say. Identical twin pairs were more similar in vocabulary and grammar. Figures from the study show that genetics influences about 25% of vocabulary development and about 40% of learning about grammar (Dale et al., 2000).

Moreover, brain systems not only are involved with language development but also change together over time (Szaflarski et al., 2006). Not surprisingly, between the ages of 5 and 11 years, the brain regions associated with language (Broca's area and Wernicke's area; see Figure 3) increase in activity during language processing.

Animals of all kinds communicate with members of their own species. Birds sing songs to tell other birds where they are, that they want to mate, or that a predator is nearby; sometimes they sing just for the fun of it (Rothenberg, 2005). Whales sing long, melancholic (to human ears) tones that other whales hear from miles away. Bees dance to tell other bees where nectar can be found and even learning socially (via observation) how to perform novel behaviors, like pulling a string (Alem et al., 2016). Chimps communicate through

©golf9c9333/Getty Images RF

Studies of twins, like these fraternal twins, suggest that grammar is influenced more by genetics than by the environment, whereas vocabulary is influenced more by the environment than by genetics.

DEVELOPMENT OF LANGUAGE REGIONS IN THE BRAIN. Brain regions that decrease in activity from ages 5 to 11 are shown in A, whereas brain regions that gain in activity during language processing are shown in B. The regions that decrease are in the left insula, cingulate gyrus, and thalamus, whereas the regions that increase in activity are the well-known Broca's and Wernicke's regions of the left hemisphere (Szaflarski et al., 2006).

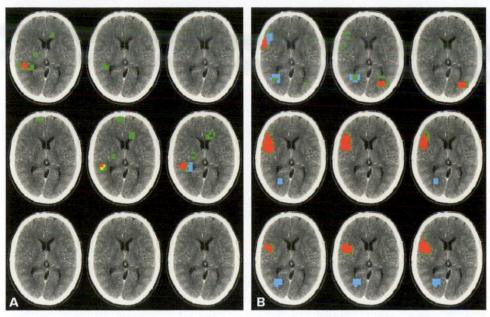

©Bob Masters/Alamy

dozens of specific gestures such as "let's groom," "flirt with me," or "climb onto my back" (Hobaiter & Byrne, 2014). Chimps use observational/social learning to teach other chimps how to use tools (Hobaiter et al., 2014). Bonobo chimps use vocalizations in flexible and meaningful ways to communicate with each other (Clay et al., 2015). However, apes in the wild tend to communicate only what they want other apes to do—not their internal states, feelings, or desires, as humans often do (Tomasello & Hermann, 2010). But do these forms of animal communication represent the ability to use language as humans do?

Can Other Species Learn Human Language?

For centuries it was argued that the capacity for language is what separates humans from other animals. Yet if humans share almost all of their genes with chimps, and humans and apes share a common ancestor from roughly 6 million years ago, an obvious question is, Is it possible for apes to learn human language?

Bonobos in the wild make the same vocalization in different contexts, such as when traveling, feeding, or grooming, which suggests the same signal means different things in different contexts (Clay et al., 2015). Such flexible communication has long been thought to be unique to humans. Bonobos and chimps, however, do not have a vocal apparatus that allows them to speak, so they are physically incapable of making the same range of sounds that humans can (see Figure 4). The only way humans can teach apes to communicate is to use a nonvocal sign language, most often American Sign Language (ASL). A number of captive apes have learned ASL to different degrees and have been able to communicate with humans. Allen and Beatrix Gardner, for instance, have compiled more than 400 ASL signs that three chimps named Dar, Tatu, and Moja acquired in the course of extensive training (Gardner, Gardner, & Van Cantfort, 1989). Their first chimp, Washoe, learned to sign almost 200 distinct words. Another chimp, Sarah,

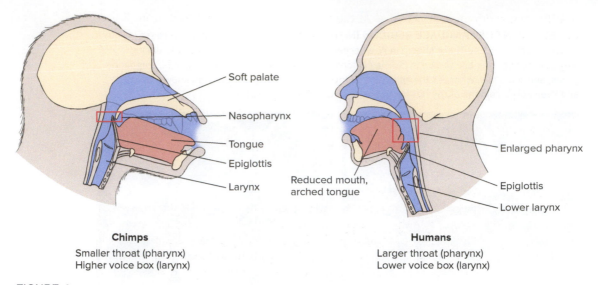

Soft palate

Nasopharynx

Tongue

Epiglottis

Larynx

Reduced mouth, arched tongue

Enlarged pharynx

Epiglottis

Lower larynx

Chimps
Smaller throat (pharynx)
Higher voice box (larynx)

Humans
Larger throat (pharynx)
Lower voice box (larynx)

FIGURE **4**

VOCAL ANATOMY OF CHIMPS AND HUMANS. Vocal structures (throat, voice box, tongue) determine the kinds of sounds chimps and humans are capable of making (Deacon, 1997).

developed a vocabulary of about 100 words (Premack, 1971). Perhaps the most linguistically gifted ape to date is Kanzi, a bonobo chimp (Cohen, 2010; Rumbaugh, Beran, & Savage-Rumbaugh, 2003).

Kanzi was the son of Matata, which had been caught wild in Zaire. When Matata was an adult, linguist Sue Savage-Rumbaugh attempted to teach her sign language, with limited success. Kanzi was present during these training sessions but was not formally taught any signs. Savage-Rumbaugh soon discovered, however, that Kanzi had been paying attention to the signs being taught to his mother. Moreover, he learned more quickly and developed a larger vocabulary than his mother. The research team decided to compare Kanzi's language comprehension to that

©Frans Lanting/www.lanting.com

Kanzi, a bonobo that understands at least 3,000 English words, uses symbols to communicate with his teacher, linguist Sue Savage-Rumbaugh.

of a 2½-year-old human child, Alia. At the time, Kanzi was 7 years old. Both Kanzi and Alia were given 660 spoken requests to see whether they understood them well enough to carry them out. The requests were things such as "Take the shoe to the bathroom," "Give Karen an apple," and "Put the pine needles in the refrigerator" and reversals such as "Make the doggie bite the snake," then "Make the snake bite the doggie" (Rumbaugh et al., 2003, p. 411). Alia and Kanzi performed these commands at very similar levels of success—about 70%. Since then, Kanzi, now 27 years old, has learned to comprehend as many as 3,000 English words (Raffaele, 2006).

If apes can learn sign language, do they use it to talk with each other? The answer seems to be sometimes, in some circumstances, and in some species of ape. So what do apes sign to one another about? Fouts and colleagues (1984) analyzed the types of conversations five signing chimpanzees had among themselves. They found that 88% of the conversations were about social interaction, play, and reassurance, whereas the other 12% were about feeding, grooming, cleaning, discipline, and chimps signing, or "talking," to themselves (just as we humans talk to ourselves; Fouts et al., 1984). More incredibly, one chimp, also named Washoe, spontaneously began teaching her adopted son, Loulis, how to sign (Fouts, 1997). Human trainers were careful not to sign around Loulis to ensure that he would learn only from Washoe. After just 8 weeks with Washoe, Loulis regularly signed with humans, and after 18 months he had learned about 20 signs.

However, even the most linguistically talented apes compared to humans are limited in their language ability on speed, sentence length, and sentence structure. First, the developmental sequence in which they acquire signs is slower than the sequence in which humans do so. A gorilla named Koko acquired signs at about half the speed of very young human children (Parker & McKinney, 1999), and Loulis learned only about one sign a month during his first 18 months of learning. Second, apes seldom progress beyond two- or three-word combinations, which means that their highest level of language learning is equivalent to the level achieved by a toddler in terms of vocabulary and sentence structure. Adult apes may have vocabularies of 100 to 300 words, whereas an average high school student knows 60,000 words (Hauser, Chomsky, & Fitch, 2002; Parker & McKinney, 1999). Third, nonhuman primates seldom either understand or consistently use correct word order (syntax). For example, one chimp, named Nim Chimsky, after linguist Noam Chomsky, would alternate among "Banana give Nim," "Give Nim banana," and "Banana Nim give" (Terrace, 1987).

Given the successes and limits of language acquisition by apes, the scientific community is split on the question of whether apes really can use language to communicate with humans (Cohen, 2010; Pepperberg, 2016). On the one hand, some researchers emphasize the linguistic abilities of apes. Often they have raised these apes as children of their own and taught them language. Such close relationships can also bias their perceptions, causing them to see things that may or may not be there. On the other hand, others, often linguists with little direct experience with apes, emphasize the linguistic limitations of apes. The main conclusion to draw from these opposing views is that the capacity for learning language in rudimentary form evolved from our early ancestors—ancestors common to both humans and apes (Deacon, 1997).

Language, Culture, and Thought

Does the language we speak cause us to see the world in a particular way? Can people who speak vastly different languages communicate effectively, even in translation? After we learn our native language, can we still learn about concepts that do not exist in our language but only in other languages?

According to the *Whorf-Sapir hypothesis*, language creates thought as much as thought creates language (Whorf, 1956). Anthropologists Benjamin Whorf and Edward Sapir, the authors of the Whorf-Sapir hypothesis, suggested that language shapes our thoughts and perceptions to such an extent that people

Courtesy of Daniel L. Everett

Support for the linguistic determinism hypothesis comes from studies of the Pirahã tribe in Brazil.

 Think what it would be like to try to understand an idea or a concept for which you had no word.

linguistic determinism hypothesis
The proposition that our language determines our way of thinking and our perceptions of the world; the view taken by Sapir and Whorf.

who speak languages that lack a common foundation, such as English and Chinese, have difficulty directly communicating and translating their ideas from one language to the other. Taken to its logical conclusion, the Whorf-Sapir view leads to the **linguistic determinism hypothesis**, which states that our language determines our way of thinking and our perceptions of the world. In this view, if there are no words for certain objects or concepts in one's language, it is not possible to think about those objects or concepts.

An example offers support for the linguistic determinism hypothesis. The Pirahã, a very small tribe of only about 200 people living in the Amazon area of Brazil, are challenging some of science's most basic notions of language, numbers, memory, perception, and thought (Everett, 2005). The Pirahã have no words for the numbers higher than 2. As a result, it is nearly impossible for them to learn concepts such as 10. Because of their language, and not because of intelligence, they have difficulty learning simple arithmetic relationships, such as 3 + 1 (Gordon, 2004).

Linguists studying the Pirahã claim that the Pirahã have no way to include one clause within another and do not construct sentences that start with words such as *when, before,* and *after.* They can construct only independent clauses. For example, they cannot say something like "When I finish eating, I want to speak to you." Instead, they must say two things: "I finish eating. I speak to you" (Bower, 2005). This claim is radical, because it directly challenges the concept of a universal grammar. According to Chomsky, a cornerstone of universal grammar is that all languages embed clauses within clauses. The Pirahã, however, do not construct sentences that start with words such as *when, before,* and *after,* and as a result they are limited to talking about the here and now and only about what is directly observable. Not surprisingly, they lack stories about the ancient past—they have no stories, for instance, of how the world began, and they refer only to known, living relatives.

Nonetheless, the view that language determines our thinking is almost certainly overstated. Most research on the topic shows how language influences rather than determines our thinking (Anthasopoulos et al., 2015; Boroditsky, 2011a; Newcombe & Uttal, 2006; Regier & Kay, 2009; Regier et al., 2010). Speakers of different languages also have different mental models about time and use different gestures to point to past and future (Boroditsky, 2001, 2011b; Fuhrman et al., 2011). For instance, although both English and Mandarin speakers use metaphors of forward and backward to talk about time, only Mandarin speakers use up (earlier) and down (later) also. Written language also matters since languages written left to right are more likely to conceptualize the future to the right and languages (such as Mandarin, Arabic, and Hebrew) that write from right to left are more likely to conceptualize the future to the left (Fuhrman et al., 2011).

The influence of language on thought is known as *linguistic relativism*. For instance, when infants are exposed to vocalizations (compared to music), they get better at learning categories (Perszky & Waxman, 2016). Another example of linguistic relativism was reported in a study on how language affects color perception (Winawer et al., 2007). Russian has distinct words for lighter blues (*goluboy*) and darker blues (*siniy*). English has only *blue*. When researchers presented 20 different shades of blue to both Russian and English speakers, they discovered that Russian speakers were faster—by milliseconds—at discriminating between these two shades of blue that came from within the same category (either within *goluboy* or within *siniy*) than when they came from different categories of blue; see the Research Process for this chapter (Figure 5). For English speakers, however, who have no words for the different categories of blue, the category of blue made no difference. This is a typical finding on how language influences but does not determine thinking and perception.

As these examples illustrate, thought, memory, number, and perception are all tied to language. In fact, language is a close cousin to thought—humans rely on language for organizing, storing, and communicating ideas. Our ability to think, reason, and make decisions often takes verbal form. Let's therefore turn our attention to human thought, reasoning, and decision making.

Quick Quiz 1: Language

1. A language's rules for arranging words and symbols in a sentence or parts of a sentence is called
   a. grammar.
   b. lexicon.
   c. syntax.
   d. representation.

2. During which stage of language development do babies make many more sounds than they hear in their native languages?
   a. babbling
   b. cooing
   c. one-word utterances
   d. telegraphic speech

3. According to Skinner, children learn to speak a particular language because

   a. they possess an inherent ability to speak.
   b. they engage in imitation of what they hear.
   c. they have a language acquisition device.
   d. they get reinforcement from their parents for various utterances.

4. Which theory of language argues that, if there are no words for certain objects or concepts in one's language, one is unable to think about those objects or concepts?
   a. nativist theory
   b. theory of innately guided learning
   c. linguistic determinism hypothesis
   d. Skinnerian theory of language

Answers can be found at the end of the chapter.

THINKING, REASONING, AND DECISION MAKING

What does it mean to know something? If our bodies do something automatically, such as breathing or digesting food, can we say that we know how to breathe and digest or that we just do it?

These questions suggest that knowledge is distinct from instinct, and certainly it is. In this section we explore some questions about mental processes, such as how we come to know anything, as well as how we know that we know anything. Psychologists use the word **cognition**, which means "to know," to refer to the mental processes involved in acquiring, processing, and storing knowledge. Recall that cognitive psychology is the science of how people think, learn,

cognition
Mental processes involved in acquiring, processing, and storing knowledge.

Research Process

① Research Question

Is people's ability to discriminate colors altered by language? Unlike English, Russian has two distinct words for lighter blues (*goluboy*) and darker blues (*siniy*); English does not. Does knowledge of these different color categories affect how quickly a person can discriminate between different shades of blue?

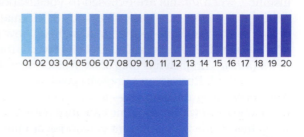

② Method

Winawer and colleagues (**2007**) designed a quasi-experiment to measure color discrimination performance in native English and Russian speakers in a simple perceptual task. Twenty color stimuli spanning the Russian *siniy/goluboy* range were used. The participants viewed colors arranged in a triad (*right*). Their task was to indicate as quickly and accurately as possible which of the two bottom color squares was identical to the top square.

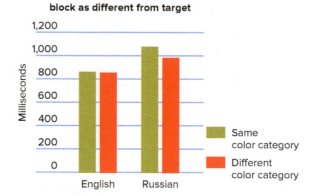

③ Results

Russian speakers were faster at discriminating blues that came from different color categories than at discriminating blues that came from within the same category. For English speakers, response time did not differ for same versus different category of blue, because there is only one category of blue in English.

Mean reaction time to identify color block as different from target

④ Conclusion

Knowledge of words for different categories of blue does affect how quickly people can discriminate between examples of blue. Notice, however, that the English speakers performed very well overall—in fact, they were faster than Russian speakers—but their performance was not affected by the different language categories. Language knowledge can influence thought.

FIGURE **5**

LANGUAGE AND COLOR DISCRIMINATION. Words for colors influence our perception of thinking about those colors. (Winawer, J., Witthoft, N., Frank, M. C., Wu, L., Wade, A. R., & Boroditsky, L. [2007]). Russian blues reveal effect of language on color discrimination. *Proceedings of the National Academy of Sciences*, 104, 7780–7785.

remember, and perceive (Sternberg, 2006a). Humans are unique in their ability to represent ideas and think abstract and symbolic thoughts.

We will consider three fundamental questions about cognition and reasoning:

- How do we represent thoughts in our minds?
- How do we reason about evidence?
- How do we make judgments and decisions?

How Do We Represent Thoughts in Our Minds?

Have you ever wondered, Where exactly in my brain is a thought? Cognitive psychologists and neuroscientists have and have even conducted research to find an answer. Cognitive psychologists, however, frame the question this way: How do we store or represent thoughts in our minds?

Even with the most up-to-date brain imaging technology, we cannot actually see inside the brain as it conjures up an image or comes up with a solution to a problem. Imaging techniques can only measure changes in blood flow, which suggest brain activity. We cannot and probably never will be able to *see* thoughts and ideas, but it is clear that we all have thoughts, memories, and ideas, so the question arises: How do we use our brains to store and maintain these mental processes?

Cognitive psychologists approach this question by proposing that we store and process ideas, knowledge, and memories as *mental representations*. A **mental representation** is a structure in the mind—such as an idea or image—that stands for something else, such as an external object or thing (Thagard, 2005). In general, mental representations are frequently not about things we are currently sensing (seeing, touching, or smelling, for instance) but rather about things we sensed in the past. Mental representations, therefore, allow us to think about and remember things in the past and to imagine things in the future. They also allow us to think about abstract ideas that have no physical existence, such as love, truth, beauty, and justice. For the most part, we represent ideas and thoughts in our minds with images (visually) and with words (verbally).

Visual Representation   We think in both images and words. The visual system, located mostly in the occipital lobes (see the chapter "Sensing and Perceiving Our World", Figure 7), is older in evolutionary terms than the verbal system. It also develops before verbal ability (Givón, 2002). Consider how babies respond to picture books before they learn to talk.

Every animal with eyes perceives visual images, but only those animals with significant cortex are better able to keep and store visual sensations in mind after the sensory stimulation stops. Indeed, visual perception occurs while the stimulus is still present, as we learned in the chapter "Sensing and Perceiving Our World". **Visual imagery**, however, consists of visual representations created by the brain after the original stimulus is no longer present (Kosslyn, 2005). The brain is active much the same way during visual imagery as it is during visual perception. Thus, you would have a hard time distinguishing between a brain image of someone actually perceiving something and a brain image of someone imagining seeing the same thing (Thompson & Kosslyn, 2000).

Being able to imagine things that are not currently being perceived is a very useful and complex skill, although about 2% of the population cannot do it at all (Kosslyn, 2002). People clearly differ in their ability to imagine an event or object in their "mind's eye" (Ganis, Thompson, & Kosslyn, 2009; Kosslyn, Van Kleeck, & Kirby, 1990). If you have the ability to imagine outcomes, you can make them more likely to happen. For instance, if you first form a mental image of an ideal performance, such as hitting a home run or playing a piece of music without errors, you are more likely to perform that activity better (Hale, Seiser, & McGuire, 2005).

©Stockbyte/PunchStock RF

 How does the brain store and maintain mental processes?

mental representation
A structure in the mind—such as an idea or image—that stands for something else, such as an external object or thing sensed in the past or future, not the present.

visual imagery
Visual representations created by the brain after the original stimulus is no longer present.

©Dave and Les Jacobs/Blend Images LLC RF

Many successful athletes use visual imaging to improve their performance. Visualizing success can help make it happen.

Neuroscientists have shown that the brain is activated in much the same way while imagining a task as it is while performing that task (Bonnet et al., 1997). So next time you are getting ready to play a game of tennis or perform a Mozart sonata, imagine doing your best. It can help you succeed.

Visual imagery and visual imagination can also be critical to many creative accomplishments, in both art and science (Miller, 1996). Albert Einstein made it quite clear that words were not involved or came after the fact when he was developing his most creative ideas. When describing how he came up with his ideas for the theory of relativity, Einstein said, "These thoughts did not come in any verbal formulation. I rarely think in words at all. A thought comes and I may try to express it in words later" (quoted in Wertheimer, 1959, p. 228). He often visually imagined certain thought experiments, such as riding on a light beam or traveling at the speed of light in an elevator. Other physicists have argued that Einstein's great creativity dried up when he could no longer produce such visual images (Feist, 2006b).

mental rotation
The process of imagining an object turning in three-dimensional space.

The process of imagining an object rotating in three-dimensional space is known as **mental rotation**. Look at the shapes in Figure 6. The pairs are either the same or different, and your task is to decide which is which. If you are like most people, it will take you about 2.5 seconds for each pair to determine whether the two shapes are the same (a and b) or different (c).

Researchers examining gender differences in the performance of mental rotation tasks have reported moderate to large gender effects, with boys and men

  (a) 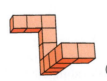 (b) 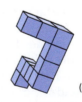 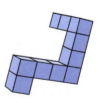 (c)

FIGURE 6

MENTAL ROTATION. In this example, the figures on the right are always rotated 80 degrees compared to the figures on the left. It takes most people about 2.5 seconds to mentally rotate the figures. The pairs in (a) and (b) are the same, whereas the pair in (c) is different (Shepard & Metzler, 1971).

generally doing better than girls and women (Geary & DeSoto, 2001; Halpern, 2004; Hyde, 1990). Cross-cultural research has shown that these effects also appear in China, Ecuador, Ireland, and Japan (Flaherty, 2005; Geary & DeSoto, 2001; Silverman, Choi, & Peters, 2007). It may not only be gender directly that leads to differences in spatial ability but also one's gender role identification. That is, in a meta-analysis of 12 studies, girls and women and boys and men who self-identify as "masculine" have higher spatial ability scores than those who identify as "feminine" (Reilly & Neumann, 2013).

One possible cause of this gender difference in spatial ability appears to be levels of the male sex hormone testosterone (Kimura, 2007). Female rats injected with testosterone during development perform better than noninjected female rats on spatial tasks like maze running (Berenbaum, Korman, & Leveroni, 1995). The relationship in humans, however, among testosterone, gender, and spatial ability is complex and not linear (Ceci &Williams, 2010). In humans, it is females with relatively high levels and males with relatively low levels of testosterone who perform best on spatial tasks. So it is too simple to say that high levels of testosterone alone result in better spatial skills. In humans, this is true only for women. For men, having low levels of testosterone leads to better spatial skills (Ceci & Williams, 2010; Hines et al., 2003).

Verbal Representation   A major function of the human brain is to organize and classify our perceptions into categories. We call this "thinking." One way in which humans organize their environment is by naming things and giving them labels. We organize our sensory experience by putting like with like and then distinguishing that group of things from other groups of things. We do this by first finding similar features (categories) and then forming mental concepts based on those similarities (concepts).

Perceiving similar features in objects, ideas, or events and treating them as if they are the same is what we mean by **category**. "Animals," "plants," or "trees" are examples of categories. For instance, all things that move and eat belong to the category "animal," whereas all living things that grow out of the earth and do not eat are in the category "plants." Categories can be either *well defined* (e.g., triangles, cars) or *fuzzy* (e.g., good, consciousness). In addition, some examples of a category fit that category better than others. "Robin" for example, fits and represents the category "bird" better than does "ostrich," because ostriches cannot fly, are big, and have long legs. The best-fitting examples of a category are known as **prototypes** (Rosch, 1973). Thus, a robin is a better prototype for the category "bird" than an ostrich is.

The abstract knowledge and understanding we have of a category is known as a **concept**. Concepts are mental representations of categories. As an example, "animals" is a category, but "animal" is a concept. The category of animals consists of many specific examples, such as dogs, birds, fish, etc., whereas "animal" is the general and abstract understanding that some things are living, eat organic matter, breathe, and move from place to place. Concepts help us organize our perceptions of the world. We can store and process these concepts in at least two ways: in a hierarchy and by parallel distributed processing, which we discussed in the chapter "Memory". A **concept hierarchy** lets us know that certain concepts are related in a particular way, with some being general and others specific. In so doing, it helps us order and understand our world.

In Figure 7, we present a hierarchical model of living things (McClelland & Rogers, 2003; Quillian, 1968; Rumelhart, 1990). For instance, animals such as birds and fish are closer to each other and farther away from plants, such as trees and flowers. The location of a concept is based on its relation to other concepts. "Living thing" is the most general conceptual category, of which there are two particular examples, "plants" and "animals." The propositional relationship between nodes takes the form of "CAN," "HAS," or "IS." An animal CAN move, HAS skin, and IS a bird or fish, whereas a plant HAS roots and IS a flower or tree.

category
Consist of perceiving similar features in objects, ideas, or events and treating them as if they are the same.

prototypes
The best-fitting examples of a category.

concept
A mental grouping of objects, events, or people.

concept hierarchy
An arrangement of related concepts in a particular way, with some being general and others specific.

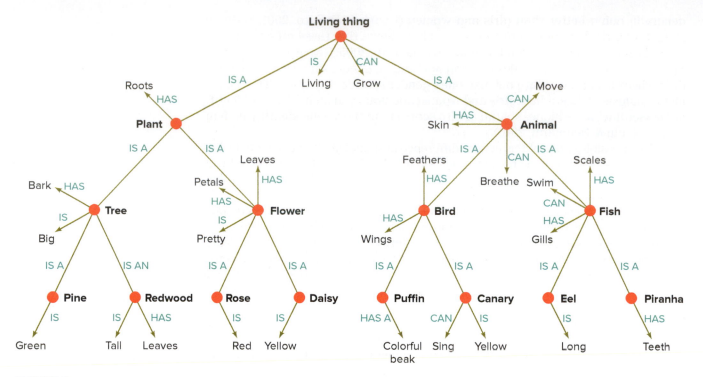

FIGURE 7

A HIERARCHICAL MODEL OF THE VERBAL CONCEPT "LIVING THING." Concepts, printed in bold type, are represented by circles, or nodes, and are interconnected. The properties of concepts are depicted by arrows, which represent statements. Relationships are shown in CAPS. The concept Flower, for instance, HAS petals and leaves, IS pretty, IS a plant, and IS a rose or a daisy. The concept Plant is more general than Rose and Daisy (McClelland & Rogers, 2003).

A fish in turn HAS scales and gills, IS a salmon, and CAN swim. We can use these relationships and networks to reason about things: If a bird can fly and a robin is a bird, then a robin can fly.

Now that we have developed concepts and categories to help organize the mind's representations, how do we use them to make sense of our world and to reason about them? In the next section we'll consider an answer to this question as we talk about humans' reasoning ability.

How Do We Reason about Evidence?

reasoning
The process of drawing inferences or conclusions from principles and evidence.

Almost anytime we use the word *because*, we are reasoning (for example, "She is smiling at me because she likes me"). **Reasoning** is the process of drawing inferences or conclusions from principles and evidence (Sternberg, 2006a). Sometimes reasoning allows us to draw sound or correct conclusions, yet this is not always the case. Consider the statement "The FBI and CIA are both out to get me because I always see people looking at me." The conclusion is not a sound one, for it is based only on the evidence that people are looking at the individual. It's probably not correct, either.

Two Forms of Reasoning

deductive reasoning
Reasoning from general statements of what is known to specific conclusions.

Cognitive psychologists distinguish between two kinds of reasoning drawn from formal logic: deductive and inductive. **Deductive reasoning** occurs when we reason from general statements of what is known to specific conclusions. It goes from the general to the specific. The specific conclusion is always correct if the general statement is true—for instance,

All humans are mortal (premise A).
Socrates is human (premise B).
Therefore, Socrates must be mortal (conclusion).

That Socrates is mortal is a logical conclusion that has to be true if the two premises are true. Consider the following:

All humans are green (premise A).
Socrates is a human (premise B).
Therefore, Socrates must be green (false conclusion).

This reasoning obviously leads to a false conclusion, because it is based on false premise A. Even though the structure of the two arguments is exactly the same, one leads to a correct conclusion, but the other does not. When scientists make specific predictions from their general theories, they are engaging in deductive reasoning.

Inductive reasoning draws general conclusions from specific evidence. Inductive reasoning, therefore, goes from the specific to the general. Such conclusions are less certain than those drawn from deductive reasoning, because many different conclusions might be consistent with a specific fact. With induction, the best we can hope for are highly likely conclusions. An example is "All the peaches I have eaten have been sweet; therefore, all peaches are sweet." All it takes is one unsweet peach to undermine that conclusion. A better inductive conclusion would be that *most* peaches are sweet. When scientists develop theories, they use inductive reasoning, because they offer general statements that explain many specific facts or observations. When we use inductive reasoning, we often use **causal inferences**, judgments about whether one thing causes another thing (Koslowski, 1996): "Every time I get chilled, I catch a cold. So getting chilled must cause colds."

Inductive reasoning and causal inferences are related to a phenomenon seen in most people, including scientists: **confirmation bias**, or the tendency to selectively attend to information that supports one's general beliefs while ignoring information or evidence that contradicts one's beliefs. In the 1960s, Peter Wason conducted classic research to demonstrate the pervasiveness of confirmation bias. Wason (1960) decided to find out whether people propose and test hypotheses systematically and, more to the point, whether they would be more likely to falsify or to confirm their own theories.

Wason gave students the task of determining the hidden rule behind a sequence of three numbers, known as a *triplet*. The students were asked to guess at the rule by writing down triplets that they thought conformed to it and the reason they selected them. They could make as many guesses and explanatory statements as they wished, until they thought they knew the rule. The experimenter, who knew the hidden rule, could answer only "yes" or "no" to the students' guesses and was not allowed to say whether their reasons were correct or incorrect. For instance, if the experimenter gave the students the triplet "2–4–6," the students might guess a triplet of "6–8–10" and state that the hidden rule is "continuous series of even numbers." In this case, the guess is right but the rule is incorrect, so the experimenter would say "yes" to the guess but "no" to the rule. The students would then have to keep proposing triplets to test other reasons until they came up with the specific rule.

Out of frustration, students could throw out a triplet with seemingly no pattern to it, such as "1–10–21." Imagine their surprise when the experimenter said "yes" to that seemingly nonsensical triplet! Yet the triplet "1–10–21" conformed to the rule the experimenter had in mind, because that rule was simply "three numbers that must ascend in order of magnitude." As this experiment shows, people are so inclined to test only ideas that confirm their beliefs that they forget that one of the best ways to

inductive reasoning
Reasoning to general conclusions from specific evidence.

causal inferences
Judgments about causation of one thing by another.

confirmation bias
The tendency to selectively attend to information that supports one's general beliefs while ignoring information or evidence that contradicts one's beliefs.

Psychology in the Real World

Critical Thinking and Detecting Fake News

The year 2016, especially during the presidential election in the United States, was the year that "fake news" became big news. The Internet is full of "click bait" sites that make sensational and sometimes fabricated claims—often with just enough reality to make them plausible. Money and profit is often the motive: the more views, the more money. Knowing how to do this can even be a matter of life and death. For example, upon reading many web stories that Hillary Clinton was behind a child sex-ring operation at a pizzeria, a man drove a few hundred miles to stop it. Upon getting to the restaurant he ended up firing his rifle. Fortunately, no one was injured. Of course, none of these allegations were true. They were fake conspiracy theories. After being arrested, the man was quoted as saying, "The intel on this wasn't 100 percent" ("*Pizzagate" shooting suspect*, 2016). But he was gullible enough to believe them without questioning them.

So how are we to suss out real from fake information and prevent from being duped? This is where critical thinking comes in. To apply critical thinking skills, we should ask ourselves, What is the evidence for this conclusion, and is it valid? Suppose you are on a jury in a murder trial. The primary evidence on which the case is based is eyewitness testimony: Two people picked out the defendant from a lineup. The prosecutor offers no other concrete evidence, such as DNA findings, fingerprints, bloodstains, or ballistic (bullet) matching. Your job is to decide whether the defendant committed the murder. You will want to draw on your critical thinking skills, because in this situation ignoring evidence and basing judgments on bias can have costly, even deadly, consequences.

Unfortunately, many people, including adults, sometimes lack critical and scientific thinking skills (Ransdell, 2010). Recall that scientific thinking is metacognitive thinking that is used to generate, test, reflect upon, and revise theories. Deanna Kuhn studied the connection between scientific and informal (everyday) reasoning in adults (Kuhn, 1993). She asked 160 people (teenagers and people in their 20s, 40s, and 60s) their theories on three topics: What causes prisoners to return to a life of crime, what causes children to fail in school, and what causes unemployment? After stating their theories, participants were asked for evidence on which they based their ideas. Only 40% of the participants could give actual evidence—information based on actual observations that bear on the theory's correctness. For instance, a man in his 20s who theorized that poor nutrition causes children to fail in school answered the question "What would show that?" with "[They get poor grades because] they are lacking something in their body." He fails to understand what evidence is and how it is different from his beliefs. He simply restates his belief in a different way. When asked to come up with reasons their thinking may be wrong, many actively resisted. As one participant said, "If I knew from the evidence that I'm wrong, I wouldn't say what I am saying." Others were even more stubborn, saying things such as "They'll never prove me wrong." Scientific and critical thinking both require that we be open to evidence that bears on whether our ideas are correct or not, even if we are not happy with the evidence.

Fake news and claims, especially when it comes to politics, are so common that just a little bit of questioning and detective work is all it takes to determine whether something that sounds too good to be true, or that confirms my political values too easily, may be bogus. For example, Snopes.com

test an idea is to try to tear it down or disconfirm it, the foundation of the scientific method. Most people, though, look only for information that confirms what they already believe and seldom look for information that disconfirms what they think.

Critical and Scientific Thinking

As we first discussed in the chapter "Introduction to Psychology", critical thinking is a particular form of reasoning that involves our ability to question, evaluate, and analyze information and to then form sound opinions based on evidence. At its core, it is making sound evidence-based judgments. In these days of massive amounts of information and beliefs of all kinds being thrown our way on the Internet, we have to be able to know the difference between ideas and arguments that have evidence behind them versus those that don't. For this we need to be able to think critically. See "Psychology in the Real World" to learn how to develop critical thinking outside the classroom.

©Sathi Soma/AP Photo

This man believed the conspiracy theory that Hillary Clinton was behind an underground child sex ring at a pizza parlor near Washington, DC. Believing the story and that he had to stop it, he drove a few hundred miles and ended up shooting his rifle at the scene. Here he is surrendering to authorities. He later acknowledged "The intel on this wasn't 100 percent."

Challenge Your Assumptions

True or False? Most educated adults can tell when they are reading "fake" news stories versus fact-based news stories.
False: Many adults, even well-educated ones, can be duped or fooled by fake news sites.

or Urbanmyths.com are two widely available sources on the web that suss out the fake from the real claims.

Unfortunately, a critical eye toward these fake news sites is not very common. A recent survey found that 75% of American adults believed a fake news headline. Believing fake news is especially likely for those whose main source of news is Facebook (McCarthy, 2016).

Developing critical thinking has consequences beyond the classroom and even beyond studies in psychology, as the story of the pizzeria–child sex ring conspiracy story suggests. To summarize, the critical and scientific thinker is:

- habitually inquisitive and skeptical
- aware of the difference between belief and evidence
- willing to put one's beliefs to the test
- trustful of reason and evidence
- open-minded
- flexible and fair-minded in evaluation
- honest in facing personal biases
- prudent in making judgments
- willing to reconsider
- willing to go beyond the headline and check the source of the information (for fake news sites)
- likely to check web-based claims against fact-checking sites such as Snopes.com or Urbanmyths.com

With a few basic critical thinking skills developed, we can avoid living in a "post-fact" era. Facts and evidence matter and with critical thinking we will be able to know the difference between fake and real news and information.

As we showed in the chapter "Conducting Research in Psychology," scientific thinking is closely connected to critical thinking and involves the ability to know and understand that our thoughts and beliefs are separate from evidence. Just because we believe something doesn't make it true. The essence of science and scientific thinking is forming beliefs (hypotheses) that then are empirically tested to determine whether they are valid or not. The starting point of scientific thinking is questioning and being skeptical about the validity of an idea, and only when it withstands the rigors of empirical testing do we decide there is enough evidence for us to believe it.

How Do We Make Judgments and Decisions?

Should you go to class or not? Should you wear a green or brown shirt? Paper or plastic? Can you make it across the street without getting hit by that car? Should you have a glass of water or a soda? We make hundreds of decisions every day, and each of those decisions is based on many different assumptions, judgments, and estimates. We also make judgments countless times each day. Every time we say things such as "I decided . . .," "Chances are . . .," "It is unlikely . . .," or "She probably did that because . . .," we are judging how likely something is to happen.

As it turns out, most often we use mental shortcuts to make decisions. These shortcuts, known as **heuristics**, are methods for making complex and uncertain decisions and judgments (Kahneman & Tversky, 1972). Consider the thought processes involved in deciding how to avoid being hit by a car when crossing a busy street. Instead of reasoning out each step systematically, we check oncoming traffic in both directions and quickly judge how fast the cars are moving and how fast we can get across. We base the decision to step off the curb or not on our quick judgment of the pace of the oncoming cars. We usually don't debate with ourselves for very long before making that decision. Heuristics allow us to come to quick and efficient decisions. We use many types of heuristics. Here we look briefly at the two most common types: the representativeness heuristic and the availability heuristic.

The Representativeness Heuristic   We use the **representativeness heuristic** when we estimate the probability of one event based on how typical or representative it is of another event (Tversky & Kahneman, 1974). For example, consider this information about Joe: He is not overweight, wears glasses, and reads poetry. Now we ask you to answer this question: Is Joe more likely to be a truck driver or a professor of English at an Ivy League university? It's simply an *either-or* decision that most people get wrong: Joe is more likely to be a truck driver!

To understand why this is so, we need to be aware of **base-rates**, or how common something is in the population as a whole. The concept of a base rate can be applied to people, events, or things. For example, 6 out of 100,000 people contract brain cancer in a given year; that is, the base rate for brain cancer. Taking the four descriptors *truck driver*, *not overweight*, *wears glasses*, and *reads poetry*, let's consider the base rates for those segments of the U.S. population. First (assuming that by *truck driver* we mean a semi driver), there are about 3 million truck drivers in the United States (*Trucking Stats and FAQ's*, n.d.). Second, because about two-thirds of the adults in the U.S. population are overweight (see the chapter "Motivation and Emotion"), we can use the figure 67% to determine how many truck drivers are overweight—about 2 million. This leaves 1 million truck drivers who are not overweight. Third, about 50% of adults wear corrective lenses (National Eye Institute, 2002). Fifty percent of 1 million leaves us with 500,000 not-overweight, glasses-wearing truck drivers. Last, it is difficult to estimate how many people read poetry, but even a very conservative figure of 1% of the population leaves us with 5,000 truck drivers who wear glasses, are not overweight, and read poetry. Once we have established that figure, we can simply ask ourselves whether there are more than 5,000 professors of English at the eight Ivy League universities. There are approximately 50 professors of English at each of the eight schools, meaning there are about 400 Ivy League English professors. So, in fact, even though it goes against our prejudices, Joe is more likely to be a truck driver than a professor of English at an Ivy League university. The information (not overweight, glasses, poetry) is so *representative* of an English professor and not a truck driver that we ignored the base-rate differences when we made our initial decision. There are simply many more truck drivers than English professors.

The Availability Heuristic   The second major type of heuristic is the **availability heuristic,** which is a strategy we use when we make decisions

---

heuristics
Mental shortcuts; methods for making complex and uncertain decisions and judgments.

representativeness heuristic
A strategy we use to estimate the probability of one event based on how typical it is of another event.

base-rate
Is how common is an event or trait in the general population.

availability heuristic
A device we use to make decisions based on the ease with which estimates come to mind or how available they are to our awareness.

©McGraw-Hill Education/Gary He, photographer

Finding one item in a large supermarket is made easier by heuristics. If you're looking for cold juice, you can narrow your search to a few places where cold beverages are stored and ignore all the other aisles. Deciding on a specific juice drink might be harder.

based on the ease with which estimates come to mind or how available they are to our awareness (Tversky & Kahneman, 1974). One example of the availability heuristic occurs when people are asked whether they are more likely to be killed while flying in an airplane or while driving in a car. Some might answer that they are more likely to be killed in plane crashes, even though statistics show that far more fatalities are caused by auto accidents than by plane crashes. According to the National Safety Council (*The odds of dying from ...* , 2010), in 2006 the odds of dying in one's lifetime in an automobile accident was 1 in 85, whereas the odds of dying in a plane crash during one's lifetime was 1 in 5,682—a ratio of about 66 to 1. We may want to believe we are safer in cars than airplanes, but remember, "don't believe everything you think."

We may think we have a greater chance of dying in a plane crash because the thought of such a death conjures up dramatic images, referred to as *vividness*. Thoughts of large numbers of people dying violent deaths in plane crashes, therefore, are readily available because they are vivid. Vividness and availability lead us to overestimate how likely certain events are.

Additional research by Kahneman and Tversky (1972) revealed other areas in which people are less than rational in their decision making and judgments. For example, if people were rational they would realize that the odds of two events occurring together can never exceed the odds of either A or B occurring separately. Let's consider a specific example: The odds of your both (A) winning the lottery and (B) getting a promotion on the same day can never be greater than the odds of either one of these events happening alone. Sometimes, though, we get information that can be so representative of a stereotype that it biases us, and we are likely to

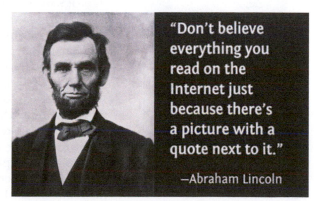

"Don't believe everything you read on the Internet just because there's a picture with a quote next to it."

—Abraham Lincoln

Library of Congress Prints & Photographs Divison [LC-USZ62-13016]

forget this simple rule of logic and make an error in judgment. Take the classic example of Linda offered by Tversky and Kahneman (1983, p. 297):

> Linda is 31 years old, single, outspoken, and very bright. She majored in philosophy. As a student, she was deeply concerned with issues of discrimination and social justice, and participated in anti-nuclear demonstrations.

Now you are asked the odds of each of the following: (A) that Linda is active in the feminist movement, (B) that Linda is a bank teller, and (C) that Linda is a bank teller and is active in the feminist movement. It is clear that A is more likely than B, but what about B compared to C? Remember that the combination of two events cannot be more likely than either event separately. Yet because what we are told about Linda is representative of feminists (A) and not of bank tellers (B), we are likely to say what 85% of the participants said—namely, that (C) is more likely than (B). In this case, the representativeness heuristic led to an error known as the **conjunction fallacy**, which occurs when people say that the combination of two events is more likely than either event alone.

These findings and others like them point to the conclusion that people sometimes ignore base rates, sometimes are biased by stereotypes, and sometimes use shortcuts to arrive quickly, but not completely rationally, at their decisions and conclusions. In short, Kahneman and Tversky demonstrated that people bypass fully rational decision making and make use of automatic shortcuts in their reasoning and judgments.

Heuristics and their importance in decision making and judgments are relatively new concepts in psychology. These notions developed from research in the early 1970s by Kahneman and Tversky. How they came up with the idea for carrying out this research provides an interesting glimpse into how psychologists make discoveries by challenging assumptions held by other scientists.

Challenging Assumptions in Human Rationality Are the mental processes you use to make decisions based on reasonable, rational thought? Are you sure? Most of us like to think we are always reasonable and rational, yet a Nobel Prize was awarded in 2002 for findings showing that people often make decisions, especially economic decisions, that are not rational and reasonable.

For much of the 20th century, cognitive scientists and economists who studied human decision making believed that people generally make rational decisions. Specifically, it was thought that, when given a choice between two or more options, humans will choose the one that is most likely to help them achieve their particular goals—that is, the rational choice. Economists called this *rational choice theory* (Scott, 2000).

As we saw in the case of confirmation bias, not all reasoning is rational. In the 1970s, Tversky and Kahneman began to challenge rational choice theory with their research on human judgment and decision making. Their collaboration began when both were at the Hebrew University in Israel, where Kahneman was teaching a graduate seminar in applied psychology. "In what turned out to be a life-changing event," Kahneman writes, "I asked my younger colleague Amos Tversky to tell the class about what was going on in his field of judgment and decision-making" (Kahneman, 2002). In the seminar, Tversky demonstrated how people make judgments about the probability of events. He combined red and white poker chips in two different bags and in two different ratios as an example. He explained that people are generally rational in their judgments; they take into account differences in base rates. Using his bags of poker chips, he demonstrated that the odds are higher that a red chip will come from a bag

conjunction fallacy
An error in logic that occurs when people say the combination of two events is more likely than either event alone.

©Sean Gallup/Getty Images for Burda Media

Daniel Kahneman

with a base rate of 70/30 red to white chips than from a bag with a base rate of 30/70 red to white chips.

Tversky's conclusion that people are rational and make use of base-rate information, however, started a lively debate in the seminar, as Kahneman later described:

> The idea . . . did not seem to fit with the everyday observation of people commonly jumping to conclusions. [Tversky] went in to the seminar believing in his findings that people are relatively rational judges but left with that belief shaken. . . . I do remember that Amos and I decided to meet for lunch to discuss our hunches about the manner in which probabilities are "really" judged. There we exchanged personal accounts of our own recurrent errors of judgment in this domain, and decided to study the statistical intuitions of experts. (Kahneman, 2002)

As Kahneman recently recounted, it was this back and forth in that seminar that led him to realize that he and Tversky were an "exceptional team" (personal communication, October 1, 2010). From there, they went on to do research which demonstrated that people are often less than rational in their decision making. These conclusions changed psychology, economics, and philosophy (e.g., Tversky & Kahneman, 1974).

To some economists and philosophers, Kahneman and Tversky's findings were nothing short of revolutionary, although not everyone appreciated them. A well-known American philosopher told Kahneman, who had started to describe some of his findings at a dinner party, "I am not really interested in the psychology of stupidity," and walked away (Kahneman, 2002).

By the late 1970s Kahneman and Tversky had begun to apply their ideas of decision making to economics (Kahneman & Tversky, 1979). They were particularly intrigued by situations that pitted people's intuitions against their rational choices. They discovered that people often make economic decisions based on intuition rather than rational choice. For example, which of the following would you pick?

a. A coin toss (50-50) chance for $1,000
b. $460 for sure

Most people choose the certain option (certainty effect). But what about the following choices? Which would you choose?

a. A 100% chance of losing $3,000
b. An 80% chance of losing $4,000 and a 20% chance of losing nothing

Now which of the following would you choose?

c. A 100% chance of winning $3,000
d. An 80% chance of winning $4,000 and a 20% chance of winning nothing

Only 20% of the people chose d, whereas 92% of the people chose b (Kahneman & Tversky, 1979). People treat wins and losses differently. People are risk-averse when faced with the prospect of winning and risk-loving when faced with the prospect of losing. Put differently, people are more averse to losing money than they are attracted to winning it. Most people will not choose an option in which they might lose $20 unless they have a chance of gaining at least $40. Notice the asymmetry in this. A $20 loss has to be balanced by a $40 gain, not $20. These results are not what standard (rational) economic theory would predict, but they are what Kahneman and Tversky's "prospect theory" predicted.

Amos Tversky

Many of us are not rational consumers. The fact that we cannot afford to buy three pairs of shoes at a time does not mean that we do not buy them.

©Eileen Bach/Getty Images

Quick Quiz 2: Thinking, Reasoning, and Decision Making

1. Structures in the mind—such as an idea or image—that stand for something else, such as an external object or thing, are known as
   a. memories.
   b. mental representations.
   c. mental rotation.
   d. visions.

2. Which of the following would be considered a prototype for fruit?
   a. kiwi
   b. tomato
   c. avocado
   d. apple

3. When we reason from general statements of what is known to specific conclusions, we are engaging in
   a. hypothesis testing.
   b. inductive reasoning.
   c. deductive reasoning.
   d. logic.

4. What distinguishes scientific thinking from nonscientific thinking?
   a. the ability to separate belief from evidence
   b. the ability to reason
   c. concept formation
   d. the use of heuristics

5. _____ are mental shortcuts for making complex and uncertain decisions and judgments.
   a. Categories
   b. Schemas
   c. Calculations
   d. Heuristics

6. Which of the following makes people believe they are more likely to die in a plane crash than a car crash?
   a. the fear schema
   b. the availability heuristic
   c. concept formation
   d. the representativeness heuristic

Answers can be found at the end of the chapter.

Bringing It All Together

Making Connections in Language and Thought

Learning a Second Language

As we saw with Greg at the beginning of the chapter, learning second languages can be difficult and challenging. But it also offers cognitive advantages and insight into the connection between thought and language that speaking only one language does not. Vocabulary tests often reveal higher vocabulary in monolingual children than bilingual children, but the latter have better executive functioning skills than the former (Bialystok et al., 2010; Hoff et al., 2012). Bilingualism offers a perfect topic to bring together research findings on how language and thought are closely connected, because we can address these questions:

1. When are our brains most sensitive to learning a second language, and why can some people speak a second language with no accent from their first language?

2. Is a second language processed differently in the brain than a first language?

3. Do we think and reason differently in different languages?

4. Does learning a second language make us more creative and more able to think about our thinking (metacognitive)?

Sensitivity Periods and Second-Language Acquisition

There is a sensitive period for second-language acquisition: Children learn second languages more quickly than adults do and speak them more fluently (Birdsong, 2006; DeKeyser & Larson-Hall, 2005; Kim et al., 1997; Sakai, 2005; Uylings, 2006). A strong negative correlation exists between the age of learning the second language and the proficiency of speaking that language (DeKeyser & Larson-Hall, 2005). The younger a person is when he or she acquires the second language, the more proficiently the person speaks that language. Starting around age 7, learning a second language starts to become a little more difficult, and proficiency

is reduced; and by around early adolescence (ages 13 to 15) the sensitive period for learning to speak a second language without an accent appears to end (Birdsong, 2005; Flege, Munro, & MacKay, 1995a, 1995b; Long, 1990; Jiang et al., 2009; Oyama, 1976; Sakai, 2005). For example, native English speakers evaluated the strength of the accent in English spoken by Italian immigrants to the United States (Oyama, 1976). The length of time the immigrants had been in the United States did not affect the strength or thickness of their accent, but the age at which they had moved to the United States did. If they were 6 when they immigrated and had been in the country for only 2 years, they had much less of an accent than if they were 30 years old when they learned the language but had been in the United States for 10 years. A systematic review of the literature by Long (1990) confirmed this finding from dozens of studies. Thus, as a time for learning to speak a second language without an accent, childhood is better than adolescence and adolescence is better than adulthood. Although the finding is robust that age of second-language acquisition affects the accent level of nonnative speakers, numerous social factors lessen this effect, such as continued education, the amount of second language that is used, and gender (Flege, 1999; Flege et al., 1995a, 1995b; Hakuta, Bialystok, & Wiley, 2003).

Second-Language Learning and the Brain

People who are fluent in two languages apparently are capable of more efficient cognitive processing than

Challenge Your Assumptions

True or False? Adults can learn to speak a second language more easily than children.

False: The window for learning to speak a second language easily and with little effort seems to be early to mid-adolescence.

©Andrew Rich/Getty Images RF

those who speak only one. Psychologists examined the ability of speakers of one and two languages to perform cognitive tasks (Bialystok et al., 2006). They found that those who spoke two languages performed better on the cognitive tasks and continued to do so later in life.

Learning another language may also have a long-term beneficial effect on the brain. When matched for age, gender, and other qualities, elderly speakers of two languages develop dementia more than 4 years later than do elderly speakers of only one language (Bialystok & Craik, 2010). What is most interesting about these results is that they once again support the view that stimulation from the environment—in this case, learning another language—can enrich our brains and enable them to process information more efficiently.

Neuroscientists have begun to demonstrate even more directly the long-lasting effects of learning two languages. First, compared to single-language 6- to 9-month-old infants, bilingual infants of the same age do not discriminate similar sounds; by 10 to 11 months, however, there are no differences between the two groups in their ability to discriminate sounds (Garcia-Sierra et al., 2011). This suggests that the brains of bilingual babies are more responsive to a wide range of sounds, which in turn may explain their greater cognitive flexibility later in life.

Second, compared to single-language speakers, bilingual speakers have brain regions that are more plastic (changeble) and more highly connected (Li, Legault, & Litcofsky, 2014), and also have a greater density of neurons in the language centers of the brain (Mechelli et al., 2004). Additionally, neural density is proportional to the age at which the person learned the second language. The earlier the second language is learned, the greater the neural density (Mechelli et al., 2004). Bilingual people compared to monolingual people also have more neural volume (gray matter) in the frontal lobe regions involved with executive function (abstract reasoning, working memory, and planning) (Olulade et al., 2016; Pliatsikas & Luk, 2016). In addition, the part of the brain most involved in memory formation—the hippocampus—grows in as little of 10 weeks after starting to learn a foreign language (Bellander et al., 2016). All of these findings demonstrate yet again the neuroplasticity of how the brain is shaped by experience—in this case, language exposure.

Third, bilingual people exhibit differences in brain activation, depending on when they learned their second language (Bloch et al., 2009; Kim et al., 1997). What is most fascinating is that the brains of people who learn a second or third language early in life are more efficient at language processing and more similar when speaking in both languages than are the brains of people who learn a second language late in life (Bloch et al., 2009). If someone learns a second language early in life, essentially at the same time they learn their first language, the brain regions that are active during speech (production) overlap almost completely. On the other hand, if a person learns a second language years after learning the first language, the brain regions that are active during speech (production) are next to each other but hardly overlap (see Figure 8).

What is equally fascinating is that the same pattern does not hold for comprehension or listening. The brains of both early and late second-language learners show the same areas of activation when the learners are listening to their first and second languages (Kim et al., 1997). Thus, the age at which a person learns a second language is reflected in differences in the brain, but only in areas involved in producing rather than understanding speech.

These studies support the idea of *sensitivity period* in the brain for language acquisition: With age it becomes more and more difficult to pronounce words in a second language as a native speaker. Moreover, learning multiple languages early in life seems to extend the timeframe the brain is plastic and open to language development (Garcia-Sierra et al., 2011; Kuhl et al., 2008).

Reasoning in a Second Language

It is difficult enough to get through a college entrance exam, such as the Scholastic Aptitude Test (SAT), in one's native language. Imagine doing it in a second language in which you are not perfectly fluent. Each year thousands of foreign students seeking admission to American universities undertake this challenge. The SAT includes questions that require deductive reasoning, such as text comprehension. In research that compared students' deductive reasoning in their native language and their deductive reasoning in a second language, not surprisingly the students performed better in their native language (D'Anglejan, 1979). In addition, being bilingual has an adverse effect on reading but not math performance on the SAT (DeDonno, Rivera-Torres, Monis, & Fagan, 2014). Therefore, it is quite possible that the validity of these tests for nonnative speakers is somewhat questionable and that the scores do not accurately portray the aptitude of the test-takers.

Cognitive Advantages of Second-Language Acquisition

Research and first person experience shows that children exposed to two languages do not confuse the two languages and intuitively understand which language to use when speaking to different people. One explanation for why children do not confuse which language

FIGURE 8

ACTIVATION IN BROCA'S AREA FOR LATE LEARNERS AND EARLY LEARNERS OF A SECOND LANGUAGE. People who learn a second language later in life (after the age of 16) use different areas of the brain to produce speech in two languages, as shown by the images on the left. People who learn a second language in childhood show activation in overlapping areas of the brain when producing speech in two languages, as shown on the right. In other words, the brain of the early learner responds almost identically when the person is speaking either language. Perhaps the reason that late learners are less fluent is that the brain treats the two languages differently (Kim et al., 1997).

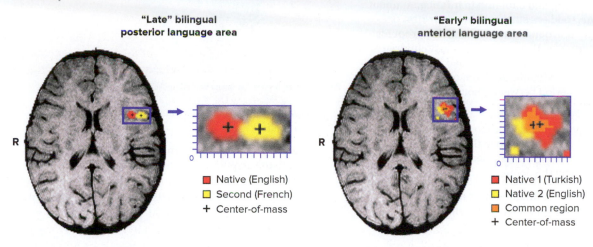

"Late" bilingual
posterior language area

"Early" bilingual
anterior language area

■ Native (English)
■ Second (French)
+ Center-of-mass

■ Native 1 (Turkish)
■ Native 2 (English)
■ Common region
+ Center-of-mass

©Du Cane Medical Imaging Ltd./Science Source

to speak to which group of people is "theory of mind," a topic we first introduced in the chapter "Human Development." By about age 4, children understand that other people's thoughts and ideas are different from their own. Research shows that bilingual children and adults are more skilled in theory of mind tasks than are monolingual children and adults, suggesting that they are aware of what the person they are speaking to knows and does not know (Cox et al., 2016; Kovács, 2009; Tare & Gelman, 2010).

Accurately knowing what you do and do not know and being able to monitor your thinking as you work on a problem are two hallmarks of metacognition. Because learning a second language requires one to think about one's thinking, some linguists and psychologists have proposed that bilingual children should be better than monolingual children at knowing what they know and monitoring their thinking (Barac & Bialystok, 2012; Jimenez, Garcia, & Pearson, 1994; Ruan, 2004; Tobias & Everson, 2002; Wenden, 1998). The findings of research on this question are mixed. It may be, however, that metacognitive thinking is more pronounced when one is first learning a second language than later, when one is rather fluent (Tobias & Everson, 2002).

Challenge Your Assumptions

True or False? Children raised from infancy with two languages (bilingually) do not confuse the two languages.
True: Probably because they are sensitive to what other people know and don't know, bilingual children seldom mix up languages or speak the wrong language to someone.

Other studies have also reported at least partial support for the idea that speaking two languages facilitates creative, flexible, and original problem solving (Kovács & Mehler, 2009; Landry, 1973; Lasagabaster, 2000; Ricciardelli, 1992; Zhang, 2010). In a quantitative review (meta-analysis) of a large body of research, Ricciardelli reported that 20 out of 24 published studies had found that bilingual students scored higher on creativity tasks than did monolingual students. Flexible and creative thinking thus is closely aligned with metacognitive thinking (Sternberg, 2004).

Finally, research shows that learning second languages helps with various cognitive abilities, such as reading, memory, and intelligence, as well as delays onset of dementia and facilitates recovery from stroke (Alladi et al., 2016; Bak et al., 2014; Ljungberg et al., 2013).

Chapter Review

©Eternity in an Instant/The Image Bank/Getty Images

LANGUAGE

- Human language is an open, symbolic communication system that follows rules of syntax and grammar.

- Individuals develop language in a four-stage sequence, beginning with cooing and babbling in infancy. At about 12 months of age, toddlers start making their first one-word utterances. At around 18 months, babies progress to two-word utterances. By age 2½ to 3, most children enter the short-sentence phase. Continued language development requires stimulation from other people during a sensitive period between about the first 6 years of life and age 12.

- There are three major theories of language.
  - Social-cultural theories propose that we learn vocabulary by hearing others speak and figure out what they mean by the context.

  - Conditioning and learning theories argue that language is like any other learned behavior, something that occurs because it is reinforced and shaped.

  - Nativist theories argue that humans possess a language acquisition device (LAD), an innate, biologically based capacity to acquire language that comes with a general and universal grammar.

THINKING, REASONING, AND DECISION MAKING

- Cognitive psychology is the scientific study of how people think, learn, remember, and perceive.

- We use visual and verbal representations in our minds as mental structures or processes for an image or idea. Concepts and categories are mental representations we use to organize our world. Prototypes are the best-fitting examples of a category.

- We use reasoning to draw inferences, or conclusions, from principles and evidence. In deductive reasoning, we start with a general statement of what is known and draw specific conclusions from it. We use inductive reasoning to draw general conclusions from specific evidence. These conclusions are less certain, because many different conclusions might be consistent with a specific fact.

- Confirmation bias is the tendency to selectively attend to information that confirms one's general beliefs while ignoring information or evidence that contradicts one's beliefs.

- Critical thinking uses sound reasoning when analyzing facts, generating and organizing ideas, defending opinions, making comparisons, drawing inferences, evaluating arguments, and solving problems.

- Scientific thinking is metacognitive thinking used to generate, test, reflect upon, and revise theories.

- Heuristics are shortcuts we use in making judgments. We use the representativeness heuristic when we estimate the probability of one event based on how typical it is of another event. We use the availability heuristic to make estimates based on the ease with which we can bring an event or object to mind.

BRINGING IT ALL TOGETHER: MAKING CONNECTIONS IN LANGUAGE AND THOUGHT

- Children who learn a second language early, during a sensitive period that ends around age 15, speak it more easily, fluently, without an accent, and with greater proficiency than do older children or adults.

- Bilingualism appears to enhance cognitive processing and is associated with a lower rate of dementia in the elderly.

- People who learn a second language in childhood process both languages in roughly the same area of the brain, whereas in later learners, processing of the two languages occurs in two scarcely overlapping areas.

- At least initially, learning a second language may enhance metacognition, the knowledge of what we know and don't know, and foster flexible thinking and creative problem solving.

Key Terms

availability heuristic

babbling

base-rate

category

causal inferences

child-directed speech

cognition

concept

concept hierarchy

confirmation bias

conjunction fallacy

cooing

deductive reasoning

grammar

heuristics

human language

inductive reasoning

language acquisition device (LAD)

linguistic determinism hypothesis

mental representation

mental rotation

nativist view of language

one-word utterances

protolanguage

prototypes

reasoning

representativeness heuristic

sentence phase

syntax

two-word utterances

visual imagery

Quick Quiz Answers

Quick Quiz 1: 1. c; **2.** a; **3.** d; **4.** c

Quick Quiz 2: 1. b; **2.** d; **3.** c; **4.** a; **5.** d; **6.** b

10 Intelligence, Problem Solving, and Creativity

Chapter Outline

Challenge Your Assumptions

True or False?

- Intelligence is a single, general capacity. (see page 369)

- Some people can know things without ever having learned them. (see page 383)

- People with high IQs have larger brains. (see page 384)

- As people get older, genetics plays a stronger and stronger role in how intelligent they are. (see page 385)

- Creative thought and behavior happen when a person has original and novel ideas. (see page 394)

- Creative people are more "right-brained" than less creative people. (see page 397)

- People with very high IQs are geniuses. (see page 401)

B ob, a sixth-grader, was petrified by the woman who was about to administer an IQ test. "As she distributed the test booklets, I could feel my insides chill" (Sternberg, 1988, p. ix). Sure enough, as Bob attempted to solve the problems, his fears and anxieties got the best of him. He could hardly concentrate and couldn't finish. "I knew I had bombed. . . . There are those who think they fail but really succeed, and there are those who really fail. Unfortunately, I was among the latter" (p. ix). Then to add to the humiliation, Bob was sent to retake the test with fifth-graders; however, his fears of taking the test with his peers went away completely, and this time he did very well on the IQ test.

As a child, Scott had an auditory processing disability that made processing words in real time difficult. This made school and learning a challenge. "When I performed poorly on an IQ test, I had to repeat third grade. I remember thinking to myself: *Gosh, I must be really behind if they don't think I'm ready to handle fourth grade*" (Kaufman, 2013, p. ii, emphasis in the original). Scott was placed in special education classes, where the expectations for learning and success were very low. He felt quite ungifted growing up.

Finally, what do Tom Cruise, Thomas Edison, Bob Weir, Alexander Graham Bell, Albert Einstein, Robin Williams, Cher, Leonardo da Vinci, Henry Ford, John Lennon, Stephen Spielberg, and Whoopi Goldberg all have in common? They are (were) all dyslexic; they had a reading/learning disability (*Famous people*, 2013).

Bob (Robert Sternberg) went on to attend Yale as an undergraduate; he earned a PhD from Stanford and became a world famous professor of psychology, with expertise in intelligence and creativity. As we see later in the chapter, Sternberg has been one of the main voices challenging traditional conceptualizations of intelligence. Scott (S. B. Kaufman) earned a PhD from Yale (and was a student of Sternberg's). Using his personal experiences and his research on the topic, he authored a best-selling book entitled *Ungifted: Intelligence Redefined*. To be sure, the list of incredibly talented and creative people with learning disabilities is vast.

As these cases show, conventional intelligence may be inadequate to explain greatness, and they raise questions about what intelligence is and how it relates to genius and creativity. Are we born smart, or does this capacity grow with training? Is intelligence a single, general skill or many different skills? Psychologists agree that there are capacities that shape how smart people are, and these constitute the three central topics of this chapter: intelligence, problem solving, and creativity. In this chapter, we will discuss what intelligence is and how it is measured, we will look at a practical ability called *problem solving*, and then we will examine the process of solving problems in unique ways known as *creativity*. Throughout, we aim to show how these topics overlap considerably yet also reveal distinct capabilities of the human mind.

INTELLIGENCE

Many people consider intelligence the primary trait that sets humans apart from other animals, but what is intelligence? Is it the same as being generally smart, or is it more complex? Is it a single ability or many different abilities? Intelligence can be defined in a number of ways, and even the experts cannot agree on a definition. Over the years, groups of intelligence experts have convened for the purpose of defining intelligence (Neisser et al., 1996; Snyderman & Rothman, 1987; Sternberg & Detterman, 1986).

Question	Theory	Summary
How intelligent are you?	Spearman's general intelligence (g)	Intelligence is a single, general capacity.
How are you intelligent?	Thurstone's multiple factors	Intelligence consists of 7 primary mental abilities, including spatial ability, memory, perceptual speed, and word fluency.
How are you intelligent?	Cattell–Horn–Carroll (CHC) hierarchical intelligence	Intelligence can be broken down into 3 levels of ability: general, broad, and narrow.
How are you intelligent?	Sternberg's triarchic theory	Intelligence is made up of 3 abilities (analytical, creative, and practical) necessary for success.
How are you intelligent?	Gardner's multiple intelligences	Intelligence includes at least 8 distinct capacities, including musical intelligence, interpersonal intelligence, and bodily kinesthetic intelligence.

FIGURE 1

THEORETICAL PERSPECTIVES ON INTELLIGENCE. There are two principal views of intelligence. One considers intelligence as a single, measurable ability. The other looks at intelligence as comprising several distinct abilities.

Defining Intelligence

Intelligence may be our inherent potential for learning, how fast we are able to learn, or the body of knowledge we possess. It may also include the ability to do things in ways that other people have never tried. The definition of intelligence that we will use encompasses all these qualities. According to the experts, **intelligence** is a set of cognitive skills that includes abstract thinking, reasoning, problem solving, and the ability to acquire knowledge. Other, less-agreed-on qualities of intelligence include mathematical ability, general knowledge, and creativity (see Figure 1).

Theories of Intelligence

Theories of intelligence started sprouting up in the early 1900s, soon after the first modern intelligence tests appeared. Two distinct views dominate our understanding of intelligence. One view says that intelligence is a single, general ability; the other says that intelligence consists of multiple abilities. Theories of intelligence that argue intelligence is a single, general ability asks the question: *How intelligent are you?* Theories of intelligence that argue intelligence consists of multiple intelligences ask the question: *How are you intelligent?*

Traditional Models of Intelligence: Intelligence as a Single, General Ability Charles Spearman (1904, 1923) developed the first theory of intelligence and proposed that it is best thought of as a single, general capacity, or ability. Spearman came to this conclusion after research consistently showed that specific dimensions, or factors, of intelligence—are correlated strongly with one another, suggesting that they were all measuring pretty much the same thing. The three dimensions that are correlated are verbal, spatial, and quantitative intelligence. **Verbal intelligence** is the ability to solve problems and analyze information using language-based reasoning. It includes knowledge of vocabulary and producing and comprehending written or spoken language. **Spatial intelligence** is defined as the ability or mental skill to solve spatial problems such as navigating and visualizing objects from different angles. Finally, **quantitative intelligence** is the ability to reason and solve problems by carrying out mathematical operations and by using logic. Spearman discovered that people who achieve high scores on the verbal section of an intelligence test, for example, are also likely to have high scores on the spatial and quantitative sections.

intelligence
A set of cognitive skills that includes abstract thinking, reasoning, problem solving, and the ability to acquire knowledge.

Challenge Your Assumptions

True or False? Intelligence is a single, general capacity.

Neither True nor False: Some psychologists and educators argue that intelligence is one general, intercorrelated skill, whereas others argue it is many distinct, relatively uncorrelated abilities.

verbal intelligence
Is the ability to solve problems and analyze information using language-based reasoning.

spatial intelligence
Is defined as ability or mental skill to solve spatial problems such as navigating, and visualizing objects from different angles.

quantitative intelligence
Is the ability to reason and solve problems by carrying out mathematical operations and using logic.

g-factor theory
Spearman's theory that intelligence is a single general (g) factor made up of specific components.

Spearman's theory is now known as a **g-factor theory** of intelligence, because it describes intelligence as a single, *general* factor made up of specific components. This theory influenced intelligence test construction for most of the 20th century. Most intelligence tests determine a person's overall intelligence score by his or her scores on specific subtests. G-factor theory implies that this single number accurately reflects a person's intelligence—the higher, the better. A person who scores 115 on an intelligence test is generally more intelligent than a person who scores 100, a perspective illustrated by the question, How intelligent are you? (see Figure 1). The theory of general intelligence allows us to assign a single number (an overall IQ score) to represent how intelligent a person is.

Challenging Assumptions of Traditional Views of Intelligence: Intelligence as Multiple Abilities Critics of the g-factor theory insisted that test scores by themselves ignore important aspects of intelligence that the traditional tests don't measure. This view, the **multiple-factor theory of intelligence**, holds that the different aspects of intelligence are distinct enough that multiple abilities must be considered, not just one. This perspective is illustrated by the question, How are you intelligent? (see Figure 1).

multiple-factor theory of intelligence
The idea that intelligence consists of distinct dimensions and is not just a single factor.

One of the first people to "break intelligence in two" was Raymond Cattell, with his notion of fluid and crystallized intelligence (Horn & Cattell, 1966), terms introduced in the chapter "Human Development." Recall that **fluid intelligence** involves raw mental ability, pattern recognition, and abstract reasoning and is applied to a problem that you have never confronted before. It is called "fluid" because it involves new problems and requires flexible solutions. Fluid intelligence is not a result of what you have already learned and nor is it influenced by culture or the size of your vocabulary. Instead, it simply involves how fast you learn new things. So some people just learn new things more quickly and easily than others. One commonly used measure of fluid intelligence is *Raven's Progressive Matrices Test* (see Figure 2). Matrix reasoning is fluid intelligence, because it does not depend on acquired knowledge and involves the ability to find patterns.

fluid intelligence
Raw mental ability, pattern recognition, and abstract reasoning that can be applied to a problem one has never confronted before.

By contrast, **crystallized intelligence** involves using already learned skills, experience, and knowledge to solve problems. Because it involves what we have already learned (acquired) knowledge, crystallized intelligence becomes more and more stable with time—much like a crystal. Crystallized intelligence is more influenced by culture, experience, and environment than fluid intelligence. This form of intelligence stems from the size of your vocabulary, as well as your knowledge of your culture.

crystallized intelligence
The kind of knowledge that one gains from experience and learning, education, and practice.

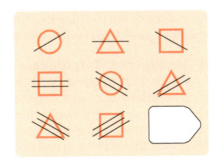

FIGURE **2**

AN EXAMPLE FROM RAVEN'S PROGRESSIVE MATRICES TEST. This sample problem requires fluid intelligence. It is nonverbal and requires pattern recognition, not prior acquired knowledge. For this reason, this test is often considered a "culture-free" test of intelligence.

 Can you figure out which of the numbered bottom figures would be next in the series of nine? (Simulated items similar to those in the Raven's Progressive Matrices.)

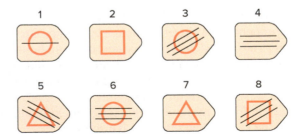

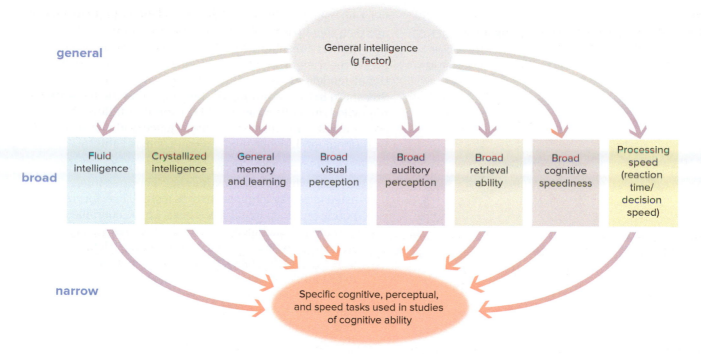

FIGURE 3

THE CATTELL-HORN-CARROLL (CHC) MODEL OF INTELLIGENCE. This hierarchical model integrates the concept of a general intelligence with several, broadly defined abilities, including fluid and crystallized intelligence. The broad categories consist of more specific abilities, such as speed of reasoning (fluid intelligence) and language comprehension (crystallized intelligence) (Carroll, 1993).

For example, understanding the meaning of a written paragraph requires crystallized intelligence, because it requires you to use your experience and knowledge to solve the problem. Vocabulary tests are also measures of crystallized intelligence.

John Carroll (1993) further subdivided intelligence when he reviewed and integrated more than 450 sets of intelligence data published from the 1930s to the mid-1980s and concluded that the Cattell-Horn model of fluid and crystallized intelligence best fit the existing evidence. Carroll extended the model, however, arguing that intelligence actually consists of three levels, arranged in a hierarchy. At the top is **general intelligence**, at the middle is **broad intelligence**, and at the bottom is **narrow intelligence**. General intelligence is very similar to Spearman's concept of "g." Broad intelligence is between general and narrow levels of intelligence and consists of abilities such as crystallized and fluid intelligence, as well as memory, learning, and processing speed. Narrow intelligence consists of nearly 70 distinct abilities, such as speed of reasoning and general sequential reasoning for fluid intelligence and reading, spelling, and language comprehension for crystallized intelligence (see Figure 3). Because this model includes Cattell and Horn's crystallized and fluid intelligence, it has become known as the Cattell-Horn-Carroll (CHC) model of intelligence.

As we discussed in the chapter "Human Development," different aspects of intelligence develop and peak at different ages. Not only does knowledge-based crystallized intelligence improve until middle age, more specifically vocabulary, short-term working memory (digit span and visual problems) remain rather constant and only dip after age 65 (Hartshorne & Germine, 2015). For example, in Figure 4 are the results from more than 10,000 people on four aspects of intelligence (digit symbol coding, visual working memory, digit span working memory, and vocabulary) and we see a continuous increase in vocabulary ability all throughout life, declines in

general intelligence
One of Carroll's three levels of intelligence; very similar to Spearman's concept of "g."

broad intelligence
One of Carroll's three levels of intelligence; includes abilities such as crystallized and fluid intelligence, memory, learning, and processing speed.

narrow intelligence
One of Carroll's three levels of intelligence; includes many distinct abilities.

Connection

As we go from young adulthood to middle adulthood, our acquired knowledge and experience-based (crystallized) intelligence continues to improve. Abstract, flexible, and culture-free (fluid) intelligence, however, peaks during our 20s.

See "The Developing Adult," in the chapter "Human Development." (p. 197)

FIGURE 4

AGE AND DIFFERENT COMPONENTS OF INTELLIGENCE

z-scores are IQ scores that have been converted to have a mean of zero. Any score above zero is better than average; any score below zero is below average.

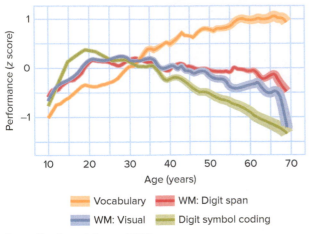

 What aspect of intelligence continues to rise until our late 60s? Which one peaks at age 20 and then shows a steady decline?

successful intelligence
According to Sternberg, an integrated set of abilities needed to attain success in life.

triarchic theory of intelligence
Sternberg's three-part model of intelligence, including analytic, creative, and practical intelligence.

©Michelle McLoughlin/AP Photo

Robert Sternberg

©Madridismo.Org/Shutterstock.com

 How do athletes use practical intelligence to solve problems on the court or field?

working memory only after age 65, and an early peak (age 20) and then steady decline only in digit span coding.

Robert Sternberg and Howard Gardner, however, proposed theories of intelligence that further challenged traditional models of general intelligence. We first encountered Sternberg in the beginning of the chapter as the test-anxious boy who "flunked" an IQ test. He took this failure, however, as a spark for his interest in intelligence and challenged the traditional intelligence model as one general ability:

> Almost all my ideas for research have emerged from areas in which I have weaknesses. I became interested in psychology because, as a child, I performed poorly on group intelligence tests. I have continued my study of intelligence even until the present day, still trying to figure out what went wrong when I took those tests. (I like to attribute my poor scores to test anxiety, although that may be a rationalization.) . . . So I recommend to you that, if you are bad at something, you use that as a basis to get new ideas about what you can study in psychology! (Personal communication, May 30, 2010)

In fact, Sternberg has spent a career focusing not simply on intelligence but on **successful intelligence**, which he defines as an integrated set of information-processing and cognitive abilities needed for life success (Sternberg, 2005, p. 104). Three interrelated but distinct abilities make up successful intelligence: analytic, creative, and practical intelligence (Sternberg, 1985, 2006b). Sternberg's three-part theory is known as the **triarchic theory of intelligence**.

The first type of intelligence, *analytic intelligence*, involves judging, evaluating, or comparing and contrasting information (Sternberg, 1988). Analytic intelligence resembles the kind of academic intelligence that leads to high scores on tests of intelligence. For example, an analytic problem might require a person to decipher the meaning of an uncommon word from its context in a sentence, or it might ask the person to determine the next number in a series of numbers (Sternberg, 2003).

The second form of intelligence is *creative intelligence*, which involves coming up with fresh and useful ideas for solving problems. For example, a person might be given a number of cartoon images and then be asked to come up with a caption for each one (Sternberg, 2006b). Traditional measures of intelligence do not measure creative intelligence well.

The third processing skill, *practical intelligence*, is the ability to solve problems of everyday life efficiently. Practical intelligence plays a role in knowing how to do one's job well and requires knowledge and skills that one learns "on the street" rather than in the classroom. A practical intelligence problem might ask people to come up with three solutions to an everyday problem they are currently experiencing in their lives, such as how to live on a fixed income (Sternberg, 2003).

The person who has developed the most elaborate theory of multiple intelligences is Howard Gardner (1983, 1993). He argues that intelligence consists of at least eight distinct capacities: linguistic, mathematical-logical, musical, bodily-kinesthetic, spatial, intrapersonal, interpersonal, and naturalistic. *Naturalistic intelligence*, for instance, is the ability to recognize, classify, and understand the plants and animals in one's environment. In cultures that have formal science, highly skilled people in this domain of intelligence are likely to become biologists, botanists, and animal scientists or veterinarians.

In cultures without formal science, they are the most talented hunters, gatherers, and farmers. *Interpersonal intelligence* is the ability to perceive and understand

Intelligence	Definition	Representative Professions
linguistic	Ability to learn, understand, and use both spoken and written language	Poets, writers, lawyers, politicians
logical-mathematical	Ability to analyze information and problems logically and to perform mathematical operations	Scientists, engineers, accountants
musical	Ability in performing, composing, or appreciating musical patterns	Musicians, dancers, song-writers
bodily-kinesthetic	Ability to use one's body or parts of it to solve problems or create products	Athletes, dancers, mechanics, craftspeople
spatial	Ability to think about and solve problems in three-dimensional space	Navigators, pilots, architects, sculptors
interpersonal	Ability to understand and be aware of other people's intentions, motivations, thoughts, and desires; also the ability to work well with and get along with others	Psychologists, social workers, teachers, politicians
intrapersonal	Ability to be aware of, understand, and regulate one's own behavior, thoughts, feelings, and motivations	Psychologists, monks, priests
naturalistic	Ability to recognize, classify, and understand the plants and animals in one's environment	Naturalists, biologists, botanists, veterinarians, hunters, farmers

FIGURE 5

GARDNER'S MULTIPLE INTELLIGENCES. The far-right column lists professions that are well served by each ability.

other people's intentions, emotions, motives, and behaviors and is very closely related to what other psychologists refer to as "emotional intelligence." Interpersonally intelligent people therefore work well and know how to get along with others. See Figure 5 for a complete listing, with definitions, of Gardner's eight intelligences. Gardner's theory has had an impact on educators and numerous schools around the world have developed their entire curriculum around teaching to and developing the broad range of multiple intelligences (see "Psychology in the Real World").

Scholars are strongly divided, however, over Gardner's theory. On the one side, those who have the most problems with it tend to be psychologists, because they see little value in calling skills such as music, movement, and social skills "intelligence" and argue that Gardner has not provided tests of these intelligences. Yet, in the last few years, there is growing evidence that the eight intelligences can be reliably and validly measured (Aleksic & Ivanovic, 2016; Bas, 2016; Hanafin, 2014). On the other side, for some psychologists and many educators Gardner's ideas address two important facts overlooked by traditional models of intelligence: (1) Different students learn in different ways, and (2) some students who have demonstrated ability in some areas fail academic subjects and do poorly on traditional intelligence tests (Kornhaber, Fierros, & Veenema, 2004). They may even drop out of school.

Measuring Intelligence

Like various theories of intelligence, tests of intelligence (commonly called IQ tests) are controversial. They raise questions such as these: How does someone interpret a person's score on an intelligence test? Where does a person stand compared to everyone else? How do we know that a given test is any good at all? The numerous attempts to answer these questions over the years have been based on the way intelligence was understood at the time the tests were devised.

©Kris Connor/Getty Images

Howard Gardner

Psychology in the Real World

Bringing Multiple Intelligences to School

The chief motivation behind bringing multiple intelligences (MI) to the school setting is to avoid some of the limitations of traditional testing and teaching that discourage students who do not do well. Gardner (1999) realized that testing in the usual sense would have to be abandoned and classrooms would have to be arranged and equipped with materials that stimulate and foster each of the forms of intelligence. Under this model, classrooms may be arranged with areas meant for dance, exercise, and construction. The materials may include board games, art and music materials, nature specimens (e.g., a fish tank), and natural objects.

An educational principle based on MI theory is that children should have some freedom to choose activities on their own. If they ignore certain kinds of activities, their teachers provide encouragement and "bridges" for them to try the neglected activities. If students are reluctant to tell stories, a teacher might encourage them to build a diorama (a three-dimensional model). The teacher might then ask the students to tell a story about what is happening to the people and animals in the diorama.

More than 40 schools in the United States and even more abroad have been designed to put into practice the development of all Gardner's forms of intelligence (Armstrong, 2009; Hanafin, 2014; Kornhaber et al., 2004; Kunkel, 2009). Examples include the New City School in St. Louis, Missouri and the Key Learning Community in Indianapolis, Indiana. The Key Learning Community opened in 1987 as a public elementary and middle school. Assessment takes place at the end of the school year, when each student presents a project based on any or all of the intelligences on which he or she has focused during the year. Students often present their project as a performance, such as a play, a poetry reading, or an artistic interpretation. They may also write papers on what they have learned. Each presentation is videotaped and put into the student's portfolio, which serves as a record of the student's cognitive and emotional development. Students in these schools still must take the local school district's standardized tests, and when they do, they perform at least as well as students from other schools (*Key Learning Community*, n.d.; Kornhaber et al., 2004). Moreover, most of the schools adopting this model have reported that the MI approach helped decrease disciplinary problems and increase parent participation. Finally, the performance of students with learning disabilities improved markedly when they attended MI schools.

In short, the MI schools teach to different learning styles and to their students' different intellectual talents. For some students, at least, this alternative fosters academic achievement that might not occur in a traditional setting.

Evaluating the effectiveness of programs like the Key Learning Community is difficult in a culture dominated by test scores as the main criterion of success (Kunkel, 2009). This is especially true because MI-based programs emphasize community service, the completion of projects, and apprenticeships. In a recent survey of Key students (among a community with a 73% poverty rate, which works against successfully completing school in traditional school settings), the results showed that 88% of Key students graduate and 91% go on to further education or training after high school (Kunkel, 2009).

©C.W. McKeen/Syracuse Newspapers/The Image Works

 Should naturalistic intelligence be nurtured in the same way as mathematical skills, verbal ability, and at least five other kinds of intelligence?

Traditional Measures of Intelligence   Intelligence tests were among the first psychological tests. The French scholar Alfred Binet deserves the most credit for developing the first true test of intelligence. In the early 1900s, the government hired Binet to identify students who would benefit most from special instruction techniques. For this purpose, Binet and a colleague, Theodore Simon, developed a test containing 30 problems of increasing difficulty. Their idea that the ability to solve increasingly difficult problems depends on age became widely influential and has since become known as **mental age**, the age a child has reached, regardless of chronological age, based on his or her performance on an intelligence test relative to other children. If, for example, a child solves problems that the average 12-year-old solves, regardless of how old the child actually is, then that child has a mental age of 12. Mental age is a norm, or average, because it is based on what most children at a particular age level can do.

A few years after Binet developed the concept of mental age, a German psychologist, William Stern, introduced the *intelligence ratio*, in which mental age (MA) is divided by chronological age (CA) and multiplied by 100 to determine an intelligence score. The ratio of mental age over chronological age is commonly known as a person's *intelligence quotient*, or *IQ*. If a child had a mental age of 10 and was 10 years old, she had an IQ of 100 (10/10 × 100). But if she had a mental age of 12 and was only 10 years old, she had an IQ of 120; if she had a mental age of 8 and was 10 years old, her IQ was 80. This ratio was very useful in the early years of IQ testing with children, but it is no longer used. Today IQ scores are based on how well a child does on tests relative to norms or standards established by testing children of the same age.

About 10 years after Binet published his first test, Lewis Terman, an American psychologist, translated the test for American students. Because Terman taught at Stanford University, he named the test the *Stanford-Binet test*. The most significant changes Terman made were to establish national norms and to adopt and apply the ratio score of MA/CA to a widely used IQ test.

In the 1930s, David Wechsler created new intelligence tests to measure adult intelligence. Wechsler's test became known as the *Wechsler Adult Intelligence Scale*, or *WAIS* (Wechsler, 1944, 1958). Later he developed a test for children, the *Wechsler Intelligence Scale for Children* (*WISC*). At present, these two tests are the ones most frequently administered in the United States (Wasserman & Tulsky, 2005). To sample the kinds of problems included on one of these IQ tests, see Figure 6. The current versions of both the Stanford-Binet and the WAIS are based on modern theories about intelligence.

Courtesy of Nadeen & Alan Kaufman

Alan Kaufman

Modern Measures of Intelligence   For 50 years, IQ tests were based on the assumption that intelligence is a single quality. The developers of both the Stanford-Binet and the Wechsler tests failed to take into account Jean Piaget's work on cognitive development and newer findings from neuroscience. As discussed in the chapter "Human Development," Piaget found that the cognitive abilities of young children are fundamentally different from those of adolescents and that cognitive development occurs in stages rather than gradually over time. Adolescents can reason abstractly, for example, but young children cannot; however, IQ tests continued to give very similar problems to young children, teenagers, and adults, changing only the level of difficulty. Moreover, until the 1980s, IQ test developers ignored advances in neuroscience (Kaufman, 1979). In the late 20th century, a new approach to intelligence testing incorporated Piaget's ideas, findings from neuroscience, and learning style differences.

As advances in neuroscience led to greater understanding of how the brain solves problems, psychologists became increasingly aware of the limits of existing IQ tests. By the late 1970s, alternatives to the two dominant IQ tests

Courtesy of Nadeen & Alan Kaufman

Nadeen Kaufman

Similarities

An individual must think logically and abstractly to answer a number of questions about how things might be similar.

Example: "In what ways are boats and trains the same?"

Comprehension

This subscale is designed to measure an individual's judgment and common sense.

Example: "Why do individuals buy automobile insurance?"

Picture Arrangement

A series of pictures out of sequence is shown to an individual, who is asked to place them in their proper order to tell an appropriate story. This subscale evaluates how individuals integrate information to make it logical and meaningful.

Example: "The pictures below need to be placed in an appropriate order to tell a story."

Block Design

An individual must assemble a set of multicolored blocks to match designs that the examiner shows. Visual-motor coordination, perceptual organization, and the ability to visualize spatially are assessed.

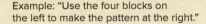

Example: "Use the four blocks on the left to make the pattern at the right."

FIGURE 6

IQ TEST PROBLEMS SIMILAR TO THOSE ON THE WECHSLER ADULT INTELLIGENCE SCALE (WAIS). The WAIS and the Wechsler Intelligence Scale for Children are the most widely administered intelligence tests in the United States.

(Stanford-Binet and Wechsler) began to be published. One of the best known of these alternatives, developed by Nadeen and Alan Kaufman, is the *Kaufman-Assessment Battery for Children*, or *K-ABC* (Kaufman & Kaufman, 1983). The K-ABC differed from the Stanford-Binet and Wechsler tests in four ways. First, it was the first IQ test to be guided by theories of intelligence, in particular Cattell and Horn's concepts of fluid and crystallized intelligence and Piaget's theory of cognitive development. Second, influenced by Piaget, the Kaufmans included fundamentally different kinds of problems for children of different ages, as well as problems at varied levels of difficulty. Third, unlike older tests, the K-ABC measured several distinct aspects of intelligence. Finally, influenced by neuroscience and information processing theory, the K-ABC assessed different types of learning styles. In this sense, the K-ABC was the first of many intelligence

that results from a condition known as trisomy-21, in which a person has three rather than two number 21 chromosomes, is an example of a chromosomal cause. The genetic cause of Down syndrome is not fully known, but it is related to maternal age. Children born to older women are more likely to develop trisomy-21 and Down syndrome (*What causes Down syndrome?* 2011). Fragile X syndrome is a disorder on the X chromosome, resulting in the abnormal development of a gene involved in neural development. People with Fragile X syndrome often have stunted cognitive development and social interactions.

As we first discussed in the chapter "Consciousness," fetal alcohol syndrome is a prenatal cause of intellectual disability, and it occurs when the mother drinks while pregnant (Streissguth et al., 1989). If the pregnant mother is also exposed to other chemicals—for example, lead, manganese, or mercury—that affect brain development or is physically abused, the risk of intellectual disability also increases (Dietrich et al., 1991; Jacobson & Jacobson, 2000; Mash & Wolf, 2010; Solan & Lindow, 2014).

Finally, environmental deprivation, such as neglect and poor nutrition, is to blame for some cases of milder intellectual disability. Sometimes called **familial-cultural intellectual disability**, this type is more prevalent among people of low socioeconomic status, tends to occur in more than one family member, and tends to be mild (Kerig & Wenar, 2006; Mash & Wolf, 2010). Genetics play no role in this form of intellectual disability.

Giftedness   Giftedness lies at the high end of the intelligence spectrum. Starting in about the third grade in the United States, students who do very well in school and well on standardized tests of intelligence are sometimes placed in "gifted" programs. In most schools, children are admitted to such a program if they score 130–140 or above on a standardized IQ test, such as the WISC or Stanford-Binet.

Prodigies   A **prodigy** is a young person who is extremely gifted and precocious in one area, such as math, music, art, or chess, and is at least average in intelligence (Feldman, 2004). Most often, prodigies are under the age of 20. Sometimes they possess extreme talent in more than one domain, such as math and language. Probably the world's most famous child prodigy was Wolfgang Amadeus Mozart, who was playing keyboard by age 3 and composing symphonies by age 8. Although they are relatively rare, some people display extreme early talent in visual arts. Akiane Kramarik is an example. She was sketching incredibly lifelike drawings by age 4 and producing world-class paintings by age 9. She loves drawing and painting so much that she wakes each morning at 4 a.m. to express herself on canvas (Kramarik, 2006). What makes Kramarik even more unusual is that she is also an accomplished and published poet. In short, she is both visually and verbally gifted.

In addition to documenting individual cases of intellectual prodigies, researchers have conducted large-scale studies of mathematical prodigies. The best known of these is the Study for Mathematically Precocious Youth (SMPY; Stanley, 1996). Begun in 1971, the SMPY is a 50-year longitudinal study of extremely talented people, especially in math. To qualify for the SMPY, students had to score 700 on the SAT-Quantitative and 630 or higher on the SAT-Verbal *before*

©Mikael Vaisanen/Corbis/Getty Images

Like this happy couple, many people with Down syndrome have full, productive lives in spite of their intellectual limitations.

familial-cultural intellectual disability
Occurs when environmental deprivation, such as neglect and poor nutrition, is to blame for some cases of milder intellectual disability. Genetics play no role in this form of disability.

prodigy
A young person who is extremely gifted and precocious in one area and at least average in intelligence.

©Art Akiane LLC

Akiane Kramarik is a gifted young artist who has been painting and drawing since she was a small child. With her parents' encouragement, she has developed her natural creative abilities to an extraordinary level. She also writes poetry.

their 13th birthday. Only about 1 in 10,000 test-takers achieves a score of 700 or above (Lubinski & Benbow, 2006). Students in the latter group go on to have very successful careers. Follow-up research 30–40 years later showed that many of them attended top universities at both the undergraduate and graduate levels and then went on to become successful scientists, mathematicians, engineers, and doctors (Kell, Lubinski, & Benbow, 2013; Lubinski, Benbow, & Kell, 2014; Wai, Lubinski, & Benbow, 2009).

savant syndrome
A very rare condition in which people with serious mental handicaps also show isolated areas of ability or brilliance.

Savants Since at least the 1700s, there have been reports of people with **savant syndrome,** a very rare condition characterized by serious mental handicaps and isolated areas of ability or remarkable giftedness (Treffert, 2006). Savants (the word savant comes from the French word for "knowing") have low overall intelligence, typically with an IQ below 70, and an incredible ability for calculating numbers, recalling events, playing music, or drawing. Many of these individuals cannot speak at all or speak poorly.

Although it is difficult to know for sure, by some estimates, there are only about 100 savants in the world today, about 50% of whom suffer from autistic spectrum disorder and the other 50% from some other kind of psychological disorder, such as brain injury, epilepsy, or intellectual disability (Treffert, 2006). Savant syndrome occurs most often in five major areas of talent: music (usually piano), art, math, calendar calculations, and spatial/mechanical skills (Treffert, 2006). A relatively common form is seen in individuals who can immediately calculate the day of the week on which a particular date in history fell. For example, if asked to name the day of the week for June 15, 1899, they would correctly answer "Thursday." Others with savant syndrome can take apart clocks, toys, bicycles, and other machines and rebuild them with expert precision. Psychologists do not fully understand savant syndrome, but what is clear is that it involves skills and abilities that cannot be learned or taught. Moreover, it almost always exists in someone with some sort of brain abnormality, which suggests that the non-learned ability might be associated with unusual brain structure or function (Treffort, 2006).

In the chapter "Memory," we met Daniel Tammet, whose uncanny memory skills enable him to recall pi to 22,514 digits and calculate complex mathematical problems almost instantaneously. Tammet has savant syndrome as well as high-functioning autism and synesthesia, which, as you might recall from the chapter "Sensing and Perceiving Our World," occurs when a person experiences sensations in one sense when a different sense is stimulated. In Tammet's case, he sees each number as a distinct color and shape, and this is the secret behind his uncanny memory for numbers and calculations. For example, he finds the 762nd to 769th digits (a series of six 9s) of pi to be a beautiful "deep, thick rim of dark blue light" (Tammet, 2006, p. 179). Recent research points to superior math ability among children with high-functioning autism compared to typically developing children (Iuculano et al., 2014).

Another person with savant syndrome was Kim Peek. Although Peek was most famous as the inspiration for the movie *Rain Man*, his abilities went much further than the movie suggests. He was one of the world's only true speed-readers—he could read a page in about 3 seconds and retain essentially every word. Incredibly, Peek memorized about 9,000 books after reading them only *once*. He immediately provided biographical information about any of the U.S. presidents; could tell you the zip code of any city or borough in the United States; and could identify who composed almost any piece of classical music, stating where it was composed and when it was first performed. Like some other savants, he also could tell you more or less instantly the day of the week on which any date in history fell.

Given his phenomenal abilities, it is easy to forget that Peek was unable to do many basic things—such as dress himself. Indeed, his tested IQ was 73, which is in the range for people with severe autism. Socially, he was very awkward, and he liked to repeat certain phrases, saying over and over again how great was the person he had just met. He also did not understand metaphors such as "get a hold of yourself." Instead, he interpreted everything literally. His adaptive functioning skills were poor, and his father had to take care of him on a daily basis. A scan of his brain revealed that Peek, like some other savants, had no corpus callosum and very little cerebellum (Treffert & Christensen, 2005). The absence of a corpus callosum means that information processed in one of the brain's hemispheres cannot be communicated to the other hemisphere.

The Nature and Nurture of Human Intelligence

If you want to start an argument, all you need to do is take a strong stance on one of the following positions: (1) A person's intelligence is determined almost completely by genetics, or (2) a person's intelligence is determined almost completely by the environment in which he or she is raised. Most people realize that intelligence results from a combination of "being born that way" and "being brought up that way" by our family and teachers. What is most remarkable is the complexity of the interaction between these two forces.

Obviously, the brain is the source of intelligence. The idea that brain size and intelligence are related is an old idea, going back to at least the 1830s (Pietschnig et al., 2015). It has also been controversial (Gould, 1981). Part of the problem came from poor measures of brain volume. With the advent of more sophisticated and accurate technology, however, such as magnetic resonance imaging (MRI), researchers have in fact uncovered a modest positive relationship—a correlation between 0.25 and 0.40, on average—between brain volume and intelligence (McDaniel, 2005; Miller & Penke, 2007; Pietschnig et al., 2015; Woodley of Menie et al., 2016; Ziegler et al., 2013). These findings suggest that highly intelligent people on average have more brain volume than less intelligent people. This relationship seems to be strongest with greater parietal-frontal lobe integration—regions associated with working memory, executive functioning, and attention (Basten, Hilger, & Fiebach, 2015; Jung & Haier, 2007). Indeed, some researchers currently suggest that more important than overall brain volume in intelligence is activity in specific brain

Challenge Your Assumptions

True or False? Some people can know things without ever having learned them.

True: Savants who have abilities such as knowing calendar dates, musical pieces, calculations, and machines without studying them are examples of how some people can know things without having learned them.

Connection

Daniel Tammet uses mnemonic devices, a memory tool, to help him remember the value of pi. He retraces the shapes, colors, and textures in his head and then just reads the number. How do mnemonic devices aid memory?

See "Long-Term Memory," in the chapter "Memory." (p. 273)

FIGURE 9
The image of the connectome, or mapping of all neural connections in the brain.

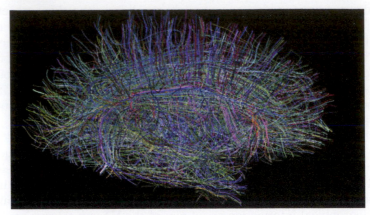

©Photo Researchers, Inc/Alamy

 Does higher neural connectivity lead to higher intelligence or higher intelligence lead to higher neural connectivity?

Challenge Your Assumptions

True or False? People with high IQs have larger brains.

True: Brain volume, especially in the regions of the brain that control working memory and executive function, is increased in people with high IQ compared to those with average IQ.

connectome
The map of all neural networks in the human brain; the wiring diagram of the brain.

regions, such as the frontal lobes, neocortex, and the hippocampus (Pietschnig et al., 2015; Woodley of Menie et al., 2016).

Another example of the interaction between nature and nurture (brain plasticity) on intelligence is the research on intelligence and the **connectome** or the entire map of neural connections in the human brain (see Figure 9). Recent research reveals that people with higher levels of brain connectivity tend to have higher overall IQ (especially fluid intelligence) than people with lower connectivity (Smith et al., 2015). Although causal direction cannot be definitely determined from this research, it is likely that connectivity and intelligence mutually interact to boost each other—connectivity leading to higher intelligence and higher intelligence leading to greater connectivity.

Another way we see the interaction between environment and biological forces is in how the brain responds differently to different kinds of problems, intelligence problems among them. The region most often involved in various IQ tasks is the prefrontal cortex (Colom et al., 2009; DeYoung et al., 2009; Duncan et al., 2000; Haier et al., 2004; Jung & Haier, 2007). When a person is working on verbal tasks, only the left prefrontal region of the brain is activated. When an individual is working on spatial tasks, however, the prefrontal cortexes of both the left and the right hemispheres, as well as the occipital cortex, are activated (Duncan et al., 2000; Haier et al., 2004; Jung & Haier, 2007). Moreover, the frontal lobe is more involved when an individual is performing fluid intelligence tasks, such as pattern recognition, than when the person is performing tasks that involve crystallized intelligence and learned experiences (Gray & Thompson, 2004).

Furthermore, twin-adoption and family studies demonstrate the interconnectedness of nature and nurture in intelligence. As we saw in the chapter "The Biology of Behavior," these kinds of studies allow researchers to hold one factor constant while varying the other one. The more genetically related people are, the more similar they are in IQ, even if reared apart (see Figure 10). Identical twins reared apart are more similar in their levels of intelligence than are fraternal twins reared together. Similarly, dozens of studies have shown that adopted children's overall intelligence is more similar to that of their biological parents than to that of their adoptive parents (Munsinger, 1975). Yet adoption—hence, the environment—can also enhance a child's IQ (van IJzendoorn & Juffer, 2005). Compared to orphans not adopted, adopted children tend to have higher IQs. In sum, genetic factors ("nature," or heritability) account for about 50% of the variability in intelligence among individuals; environment ("nurture") accounts for about 40%; the remaining 10% is, as yet, unexplained (Grigorenko, 2000; Lynn, 2006; Plomin & Petrill, 1997).

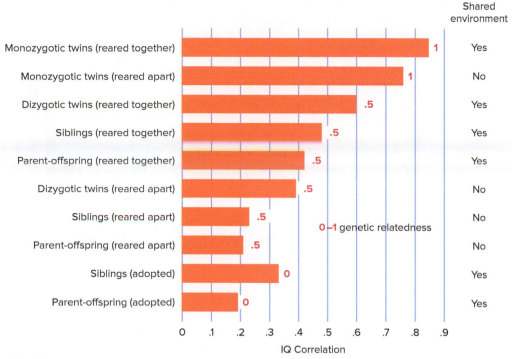

FIGURE 10

GENETIC AND ENVIRONMENTAL EFFECTS ON IQ. The numbers in orange represent genetic relatedness. Genetic relatedness of 1 means 100% genetic similarity; 0.5 means 50% genetic similarity; and 0 means no genetic similarity. Monozygotic twins are identical twins. Dizygotic twins are fraternal twins. (Adapted from Grigorenko, 2000; Plomin & Petrill, 1997).

One fascinating set of findings concerns the fact that from infancy to adolescence the environment has progressively less of an influence on intelligence (Bartels et al., 2002; Bouchard & McGue, 1981; Brant et al., 2009; Tucker-Drob et al., 2011). Children above the median (50th percentile) on IQ, however, have a longer period of being influenced by the environment (sensitivity period) than those below the median (Brant et al., 2013). That is, high-IQ children show a pattern of neuroplasticity that is more childlike (i.e., more "plastic"), because they have neural networks that are shaped longer by the environment.

The concept of reaction range provides further evidence for the interaction of biology and environment in determining a person's intelligence. A **reaction range** is a genetically determined range within which a given trait, such as intelligence, may fall; that trait's exact value, however, depends on the quality of the individual's environment (Gottlieb, 1991; Scarr, 1981; Turkheimer & Gottesman, 1991; Weinberg, 1989). For most people in most environments, the reaction range for IQ is about 25 points—meaning that a given person may end up scoring anywhere in a 25-point range on an IQ test, depending on the kind of environment in which he or she was raised (Weinberg, 1989). Being raised in an enriched environment means someone is likely to obtain an IQ score near the upper limit of his or her reaction range; being raised in an impoverished environment means one is likely to obtain a score near the lower limit; and being raised in a normal environment means one is likely to obtain a score in the middle of his or her reaction range (see Figure 11). The important point here is that genes do not determine behavior but rather establish the range of possible behaviors.

Environment, however, is a complex thing. Only part of the environmental influence on intelligence comes from being in the same household and sharing experiences. The other part comes from experiences that family members do not share—each person's unique environmental experiences. One such experience is

Challenge Your Assumptions

True or False? As people get older, genetics plays a stronger and stronger role in how intelligent they are.

True: Heritability, or genetic influence, increases its influence with age from infancy to adolescence.

reaction range

For a given trait, such as IQ, the genetically determined range of responses by an individual to his or her environment.

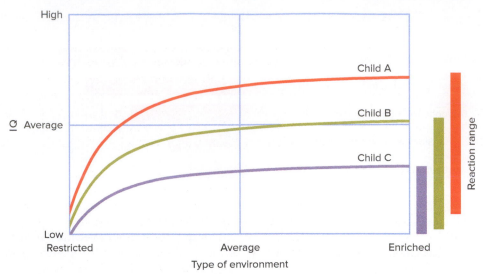

FIGURE 11

REACTION RANGE AND INTELLIGENCE. The concept of reaction range suggests that heredity places upper and lower limits on an individual's potential, but environment determines whether the individual reaches the upper limit or a point somewhere between the upper limit and lower limit. This graph shows hypothetical reaction ranges for three children (A, B, and C) and how their surroundings can shape their IQs. With enriched environments, all three can reach their individual upper limits, as shown on the right side of the graph.

 What does this graph tell you about the effect of a restricted environment on intelligence? (Seifert, Hoffnung, & Hoffnung, 2000)

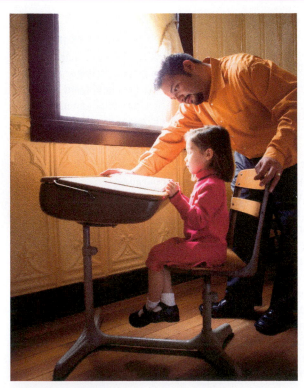

©Somos Photography/Veer RF

Reading to children regularly from the time they are very young as part of an enriched environment may enhance their IQ.

the prenatal environment and what happens to the fetus during pregnancy. Toxins ingested by the mother, either intentionally or unintentionally, may influence the child's intelligence. Alcohol, drugs, and viral infections in a pregnant woman can seriously lower her child's overall intelligence (Dietrich et al., 1991; Jacobson & Jacobson, 2000; Ruff, 1999; Steinhausen & Spohr, 1998; Streissguth et al., 1989).

Other aspects of intelligence stem from the joint influence of nature and nurture factors. One such example is birth weight. For many years, researchers and physicians have known that insufficient birth weight—a sign of severe prenatal malnutrition—creates a high risk for cognitive impairment (and thus impaired intelligence) later in life. Only recently, however, has anyone examined whether birth weight matters for children born at a normal weight. Broekman and colleagues (2009) obtained birth weight, head measurement, and length information on over 1,500 children born in Singapore. All infants were born in the normal healthy weight/size range. After the children had reached age 7, the researchers conducted yearly intelligence testing on them. Longer birth length, higher birth weight, and larger head circumference within the normal birth size range (neither undernourished nor obese) are associated with higher IQ scores later in childhood; the bigger children had higher IQs. Why might this be? Certain prenatal factors affecting fetal growth, such as maternal stress, also influence cognitive development. When a pregnant woman is under severe stress, her stress hormones might affect the growth of new neurons in the baby's brain (Oitzl et al., 2010).

Group Differences in Intelligence Scores

Given the importance of intelligence to success in life, the question of whether there are group differences in intelligence is bound to stir up controversy (Fancher, 1985). Research on this topic has political and social implications, and from time to time scientists who have studied group differences in intelligence have been harassed or threatened. If there are differences in intelligence between racial-ethnic groups or genders, what should we do as a society to compensate for those differences to level the playing field? Can that even be done?

Race-Ethnicity and Intelligence   In the 1960s and 1970s, Arthur Jensen received death threats for publishing research that not only reported differences in IQ among racial-ethnic groups but also argued that, because IQ is under genetic influence, racial-ethnic differences in IQ must be at least partly genetic in origin (Jensen, 1969). It was another highly controversial book, published in the mid-1990s, that most recently ignited an academic, political, and cultural firestorm over intelligence. The book was called simply *The Bell Curve*, but its subtitle hinted at the more controversial contents: *Intelligence and Class Structure in American Life*. The authors, Richard Herrnstein and Charles Murray (1994), summarized the results of a study on racial-ethnic group differences, social class, and intelligence among 12,000 individuals. They concluded what many others had before and since: First, racial-ethnic groups vary on IQ scores; second, differences in IQ contribute, to a large extent, to differences in education and income (Gottfredson, 1997). Their conclusion suggested that group differences in IQ, and hence in education and income, can be explained in part by genetics.

After *The Bell Curve*, when all of the smoke cleared and tempers settled down, there was still no widely accepted and agreed-on explanation for racial-ethnic differences on IQ scores. There are a few schools of thought on the causes (in addition to the one that attributes the difference in part to genetics). Some experts maintain that racial-ethnic differences in IQ result from biases in IQ tests that favor people from certain cultural backgrounds over others (Ford, 2008; Reynolds, 2000). Others have argued that differences in IQ scores based on race-ethnicity are meaningless, because race is mostly a social construct with little scientific support or biological foundation (Sternberg, Grigorenko, & Kidd, 2005). These psychologists also point out that heritability findings apply only within the group of people studied, not between groups. So it is a misinterpretation of heritability to argue that group differences are due to genetics, even if IQ is heritable (Sternberg et al., 2005).

The conclusion that genetics influences intelligence is often interpreted—or misinterpreted—as implying that IQ levels are determined at birth or conception. If this were so, then trying to change IQ levels with intervention programs such as Head Start would likely be unsuccessful (Herrnstein & Murray, 1994). Such a conclusion is faulty for two reasons. First, genes interact with environmental forces, and therefore environment can shape gene expression. We saw this in the chapter "The Biology of Behavior" with the concept of epigenesis. Similarly, the concept of a reaction range makes clear the connection between genes and the environment. Second, interventions have succeeded in changing IQ levels. Children raised under conditions of severe neglect and abuse who were adopted within the first few years of life showed tremendous growth in brain size and gains in IQ scores. Those adopted later in life or not adopted at all did not show increases in IQ scores (Perry, 2002). Moreover, one longitudinal study randomly assigned infants either to an early educational intervention program or to a control group. All children were from socially disadvantaged households. The intervention program lasted until age 5 and focused on language, social, emotional, and cognitive stimulation. The children from both groups were studied again at ages 12, 15, and 21. The findings were clear: During adolescence and early adulthood, those

©Purestock/SuperStock RF

Men and women may have their differences, but intelligence isn't one of them.

who had been in the intervention program had higher IQ scores, performed better in school, and obtained higher-paying jobs than those in the control condition (Campbell & Ramey, 1995; Campbell et al., 2002). In short, both genetic and environmental forces play important roles in determining IQ scores.

Gender and Intelligence Larry Hedges and Amy Nowell (1995) reviewed six nationally representative sets of IQ scores. Each set ranged from 12,000 to 73,000 participants altogether. They concluded that there are relatively few differences between the sexes in cognitive ability; men and women are equally intelligent. Indeed, most research on overall intelligence and gender has reported no difference between men and women on average.

There is one area of variability in intelligence among men and women, illustrated in Figure 12. Men are more likely than women to score at either end of the range, especially in some areas, and more frequently score at the high or low end of the scale on tests of science, math, spatial reasoning, and social studies (Ceci & Williams, 2007; Gallagher & Kaufman, 2005). Some recent evidence suggests that self-identifying as masculine—for both men and women—is associated with increased spatial skills (Reilly & Neumann, 2013). Women, however, consistently tend to do better than men in writing, reading comprehension, perceptual speed, and associative memory (Deary et al., 2003; Hedges & Nowell, 1995; Maccoby & Jacklin, 1974).

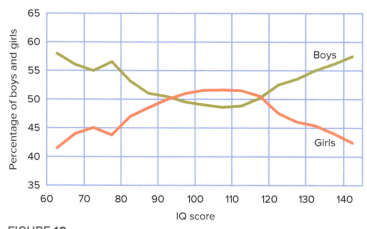

FIGURE **12**
GENDER VARIABILITY IN INTELLIGENCE. Results from more than 80,000 Scottish children found that mean IQ scores were nearly identical. Mean IQ was 100.5 for boys and 100.6 for girls. Boys were much more likely to be at the two extreme ends of intelligence, however. They made up 58% of the scores at 60 and 140, whereas girls made up only about 42% of those scores (Deary et al., 2003).

Non-Western Views of Intelligence

Ask people in the United States or Europe what it means to be intelligent. Then ask people in Kenya, China, Malaysia, and Bolivia. No doubt you will get very different answers. Western cultures emphasize verbal and cognitive skills first, whereas many African cultures see social skills, such as being socially responsible, cooperative, and active in family and social life, to be crucial aspects of intelligence (Ruzgis & Grigorenko, 1994; Serpell, 1982). Asian cultures have traditionally emphasized humility, awareness, doing the right thing, and mindfulness as important qualities of intelligence (Sternberg, 2000). Doing well in school and being quick to learn are not universally acknowledged to be essential qualities of intelligence. Sternberg and his colleagues have examined practical intelligence in cultures where academic intelligence is not valued as highly as it is in Western cultures. They have found that children in Kenya and Tanzania may not do well at solving "bookish" analytic problems but do very well at solving everyday, practical problems (Sternberg, 1998).

Problems that require intelligence are just one kind of problem we face. Problem solving—our next topic—pervades almost everything we do, from our choice of a major in college to our choice of friends, where we live, how we vote, and so on.

Quick Quiz 10.1: Intelligence

1. Which of the following skills is NOT part of the definition of intelligence?
   a. abstract reasoning
   b. problem solving
   c. knowledge acquisition
   d. remote associations

2. Historically, a child's IQ was calculated by dividing _____ by chronological age and multiplying by _____.
   a. perceptual skill; 100
   b. mental age; 50
   c. perceptual skill; 50
   d. mental age; 100

3. The Kaufmans changed the field of intelligence testing by developing an IQ test that
   a. could be universally applied.
   b. was grounded in psychological theory and knowledge of the brain.

c. was reliable and valid.
d. was culture-free and fair.

4. _____ involves raw mental ability, pattern recognition, and abstract reasoning and is applied to a problem that a person has never confronted before.
   a. Crystallized intelligence
   b. Narrow intelligence
   c. Fluid intelligence
   d. General intelligence

5. Someone who is good at detecting whether a person is lying has high
   a. interpersonal intelligence.
   b. naturalistic intelligence.
   c. practical intelligence.
   d. creative intelligence.

Answers can be found at the end of the chapter.

PROBLEM SOLVING

None of us go through a day without having to solve a problem, because every time we face a task that we do not know how to carry out, we are confronted with a problem (Simon, 1978). On any given day, you may have to budget your time so that you can study for your test and go to a party with friends or figure out the most efficient route to drive to a place you have never visited.

Psychologists have examined how people go about solving problems, often by presenting research participants with problems and studying how they solve them. Take a few minutes to work on each of the following problems. Some are easy but others not so easy, but give them a try. We will return to each problem later in the section.

- How would you solve the problem of rising world temperatures?
- Pretend you have three jars (A, B, and C), each containing a set amount of water. Add or subtract the given amounts in each jar to come up with a set final amount. For instance, Jar A holds 21 units of water, Jar B 127 units, and Jar C 3 units. Using any of the jars, discard or add water as needed to end up with 100 units of water. Figure 13 shows some variations you can try.

Problem	Jar A	Jar B	Jar C	Obtained the amount
1	21	127	3	100
2	14	163	25	99
3	18	43	10	5
4	9	42	6	21
5	20	59	4	31
6	23	49	3	20
7	15	39	3	18

FIGURE **13**

WATER JAR PROBLEMS AND MENTAL SET. The task is to use any combination of Jars A, B, and C, subtracting or adding jars of "water" to obtain the desired amount (Luchins & Luchins, 1970).

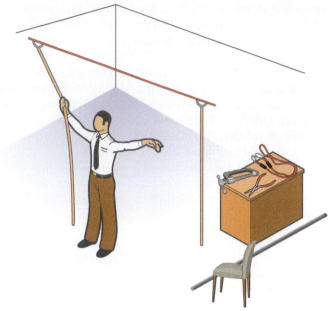

FIGURE **14**

TWO-STRING PROBLEM. How do you connect two strings if you can't reach the second one without dropping the first one? (*The answer appears at the end of the chapter.*)

- Figure 14 is a picture of a person in a room with two strings hanging from the ceiling. Also in the room are a pole, clamp, extension cord, table, chair, and a pair of pliers. The task is to tie the two pieces of string together. The strings, however, are too short for the person to hold onto one and grab the other. How would you go about tying the strings together?

- In Figure 15a, how would you mount the candle on the wall without having it drip wax on the floor?

- Look at the nine dots in Figure 15b. Connect all the dots using only four straight lines without lifting up your pen or pencil from the paper once you've started.

- In Figure 15c, arrange six matchsticks of equal length to make four equilateral triangles, the sides of which are one matchstick long.

Types of Problems

convergent thinking problems
Problems that have known solutions and require analytic thinking and the use of learned strategies and knowledge to come up with the correct answer.

divergent thinking problems
Problems that have no known solutions and require novel solutions.

Convergent thinking problems have known solutions, which can be reached by narrowing down a set of possible answers. Intelligence tests and college entrance exams include convergent problems. Figuring out how to operate a new coffeemaker is a convergent problem. There is one right way to brew coffee with a given machine. Convergent problems require analytic thinking and crystallized intelligence—the problem solver has to analyze the problem and then apply learned strategies and knowledge to come up with the answer.

Some problems, however, may not have a known solution. Consider the question posed earlier: How would you solve the problem of rising world temperatures? There are many possible solutions to such problems, some of which work better than others. These kinds of problems are known as **divergent thinking problems**. To solve them, we must break away from our normal problem-solving

The Candle Problem

How would you mount a candle on a wall so that it won't drip wax on a table or a floor while it is burning?

(a)

The Nine-Dot Problem

Take out a piece of paper and copy the arrangement of dots shown below. Without lifting your pencil, connect the dots using only four straight lines.

(b)

The Six-Matchstick Problem

Arrange six matchsticks of equal length to make four equilateral triangles, the sides of which are one matchstick long.

(c)

FIGURE 15

PROBLEM SOLVING. (a) How would you mount the candle on the wall without having it drip wax on the floor while it is burning? (b) Connect all nine dots with four straight lines—without lifting your pencil. (c) Arrange six matchsticks of equal length to make four equilateral triangles, the sides of which are one matchstick long. *(The answers to [b] and [c] appear at the end of the chapter)*.

strategies and make unusual associations to arrive at novel ways of thinking about a problem. Imagine that your new dormmate snores so loudly you can't sleep. How would you solve this problem? Divergence may lead to redefining the problem in a way that makes finding a solution more likely. These kinds of problems require fluid and creative intelligence.

Solution Strategies

Psychologists describe three kinds of strategies people use to solve different kinds of problems: algorithms, insight, and thinking outside the box. When you were solving the water jug problems in Figure 13, did you realize that the last two could be solved much more easily than the first five? If you are like about 75% of the population, you continued to use the solution pattern you may have discovered in solving the first few problems. **Algorithms** are step-by-step formulas or procedures for solving problems. In this case, the algorithm is "Jar B – Jar A – Jar C (twice)."

Not all solutions involve algorithms. Some occur with a flash of insight. One of the best-known examples of insight occurred in ancient Greece, when the philosopher-scientist Archimedes solved the problem of how to determine whether a crown contained anything besides gold. The solution came to him in a flash when he saw the water level rise as he entered the public baths. Because gold is heavier than other metals, it will displace more water, so by seeing how much water it displaced, Archimedes would be able to determine whether the crown was pure gold without melting it down. The insight excited him so much that, without pausing to dress, he ran out of the baths, yelling, *"Eureka!"* (Greek for "I have found it!"). In honor of Archimedes, these kinds of sudden solutions are referred to as either **Eureka insights** or **insight solutions**.

A modern version of a "Eureka solution" happened to George de Mestral, a Swiss engineer (Stephens, 2007). de Mestral often went on hikes in the Alps with his dog. When they returned home, he noticed that his clothes and his dog's fur had caught thistle burrs, which he found on close inspection to have hooks on the ends. The dog's fur and his clothes contained loops that snagged the plants. In a flash, de Mestral realized that a fastener could be made to connect to loops. The best part about the hook-and-loop system was that it

algorithm
A step-by-step procedure or formula for solving a problem.

Eureka insight (insight solution)
A sudden solution that comes to mind in a flash.

was easily reversible and could be fastened over and over again. de Mestral invented Velcro, now a common fastener of such things as shoe straps, backpacks, and clothing.

One solution to the two-string problem in Figure 14 often comes as a Eureka insight (Maier, 1931). With or without a hint of the string swaying, you might have suddenly realized that the pliers or any other heavy object could be used as a weight (after you had cut the string a bit so it could swing). You could tie it to the shorter string, then swing into motion. As you stood holding the other string, the weighted string would swing over; you could grab it and tie the two together.

The third problem-solving strategy is turning a problem around and thinking about it from a different perspective. If you have ever heard the phrase "thinking outside the box," you now know where it comes from—the nine-dot problem (Figure 15b). **Thinking outside the box** requires you to break free of self-imposed conceptual constraints and think about a problem differently in order to solve it. If you came up with a solution, it required that you go outside the self-imposed "box" that the nine dots create in your mind. There is no such box in reality, but you perceive one. Once you think outside the box, a couple of solutions may come to you rather easily (see the end of the chapter for the solution). Creative thinkers regularly think flexibly and differently about problems by challenging their own assumptions (Feist, 1999).

Obstacles to Solutions

The difficulties people encounter in solving the nine-dot problem also point to some of the common obstacles we face in solving all kinds of problems. One of the biggest blocks to solving a problem is cognitive **fixation**, or the inability to break out of a particular mind-set in order to think about a problem from a fresh perspective. Fixation prevents many people from seeing possible solutions to the match problem (Figure 15c). It is difficult, for example, to see that you must think in three dimensions in order to solve the match-triangle problem (see end of chapter for solution in three dimensions). This solution may not be obvious because people become fixated on a self-imposed mental set in which "I have to solve this problem in two dimensions." Note that the instructions do not require this—people unconsciously impose such rules themselves.

Solutions themselves can sometimes be an obstacle: For the jar problem, the algorithm used to solve it also creates a **mental set**, which is a tendency to continue to use problem-solving strategies that have worked in the past, even if better solutions are available (Luchins & Luchins, 1970). This mental set probably made you miss the easier solutions to Problems 6 and 7 in Figure 13: Jar A – Jar C and Jar A + Jar C, respectively. Luchins and Luchins (1970) found that, if Problems 1 to 5 were not given first, 100% of adults saw the direct solution. In contrast, if they first received Problems 1 to 5 and had to develop an algorithm, only 24% found the more direct solutions to Problems 6 and 7. Education and training also create mental sets. When we learn solution strategies in school and in the workplace, we learn how to solve problems. Sometimes these solutions are algorithms and sometimes insights, but strategies can blind us to more novel, efficient, and even creative solutions. It becomes hard to step back and see problems from a fresh perspective.

Another obstacle to successful problem solving is our tendency to be blind to unusual uses of common, everyday things or procedures: This is known as **functional fixedness** (Duncker, 1945). A good example of functional fixedness occurs when people try to solve the two-string problem. People are used to thinking of pliers as tools for holding or gripping something so that it can be turned,

---

thinking outside the box
An approach to problem solving that requires breaking free of self-imposed conceptual constraints and thinking about a problem differently in order to solve it.

fixation
The inability to break out of a particular mind-set in order to think about a problem from a fresh perspective.

mental set
A tendency to continue to use problem-solving strategies that have worked in the past, even if better solutions are available.

functional fixedness
A mind-set in which one is blind to unusual uses of common, everyday things or procedures.

twisted, or cut, but a pair of pliers can also be used as a weight at the end of a string to cause it to swing like a pendulum. Figuring out a new way to use pliers is an example of thinking outside the box to find a creative solution to a problem. As mentioned earlier, creative thinkers often think differently about how to solve a problem.

Quick Quiz 10.2: Problem Solving

1. What kind of problems require you to narrow down the range of possible solutions to arrive at the correct answer?
   a. simple problems
   b. convergent thinking problems
   c. algorithms
   d. divergent thinking problems

2. A child discovers that 2×2 is the same as $2 + 2$. He therefore wrongly concludes that 3×3 is the same as $3 + 3$. What tendency is affecting this child's problem-solving strategies?
   a. mental set
   b. divergent thinking

   c. test bias
   d. response bias

3. An inability to break out of a particular frame of mind in order to think about a problem from a fresh perspective is known as
   a. perpetuation.
   b. mental set.
   c. fixation.
   d. functional fixedness.

Answers can be found at the end of the chapter.

CREATIVITY

What was it about Leonardo da Vinci that made him so versatile as an artist and inventor? What was going on in the mind of Isaac Newton when he realized the significance of an apple falling from a tree? Why are some people able to paint magnificent landscapes, while others can hardly draw a straight line? The answer is that these individuals are more creative than the average person.

The ability to think or act creatively is highly prized in our society (Feist, 1999, 2016; Sawyer, 2006; Simonton, 1999). All of society's advances—artistic, musical, industrial, governmental, legal, and scientific—happen because a person or group of people come up with a creative idea. Creative thinking is related to, yet distinct from, both intelligence and problem solving.

What Is Creativity?

Read the following two paragraphs, written by different people, and think about what each one means and whether they are equally "creative":

> They're all so different Boylan talking about the shape of my foot he noticed at once even before he was introduced when I was in the DBC with Poldy laughing and trying to listen I was waggling my foot we both ordered 2 teas and plain bread and butter I saw him looking with his two old maids of sisters when I stood up and asked the girl where it was what do I care with it dropping out of me and that black closed breeches he made me buy takes you half an hour to let down wetting all myself always with some brand new fad every other week. . . .

This creation in which we live began with the Dominant Nature as an Identification Body of a completed evolutionary Strong Material creation in a Major Body Resistance Force. And is fulfilling the Nature Identification in a like Weaker Material Identification creation in which Two Major Bodies have already fulfilled radio body balances, and embodying a Third Material Identification Embodiment of both.

Challenge Your Assumptions

True or False? Creative thought and behavior happen when a person has original and novel ideas.

False: Originality and novelty by themselves are not enough to determine that a person's thought and behavior is creative; the thoughts or behavior must also be meaningful and useful (to someone).

creativity
Thinking and/or behavior that is both novel—original and useful—and adaptive.

The first paragraph is an excerpt from James Joyce's great novel *Ulysses*. The second paragraph was written by a person who has schizophrenia and is an example of what is called *word salad*, a collection of words that are mixed up in sentences with no real meaning (White, 1964). These two paragraphs demonstrate an essential point about what creativity is and what it is not. It is not simply original thinking, for the paragraphs are equally original. They are both unusual, and both give voice to sentences that probably had not been uttered or written before these writers penned them. For something to be deemed creative, however, it not only has to be original but also must be useful or adaptive and solve a problem. Joyce's paragraph does that because it's part of solving the problem of telling a story. The second paragraph is not creative, because it is not useful or meaningful to someone and it does not solve a problem.

Creativity, then, is thought or behavior that is both novel (original) and meaningful (Amabile, 1996; Beghetto & Kaufman, 2007; Feist, 1999, 2016; MacKinnon, 1970; Plucker, Beghetto, & Dow, 2004). The meaningful criterion requires that someone at some time sees value and usefulness in the creative accomplishment. Truly creative works are often appreciated in the creator's lifetime, but not always. For instance, Vincent van Gogh sold very few of his paintings while alive, but his creative genius is now fully appreciated by novices and experts alike, and his paintings are worth millions.

Stages of Creative Problem Solving

Creative problem solving is a process with distinct stages. Long ago, Graham Wallas (1926) identified four stages of creative problem solving: preparation, incubation, insight, and elaboration-verification. The first stage, *preparation*, involves discovering and defining the problem and then attempting to solve it. This leads to the second stage, *incubation*, or putting the problem aside for a while and working on something else. The third stage, *insight*, is a Eureka moment when the solution comes immediately to mind. The fourth, and final, stage of creative problem solving is *elaboration-verification*. The solution, even if it has the feel of certainty, still needs to be confirmed. How it is confirmed depends on what kind of task is involved. The verification process is different for everyday problems and for problems in art, literature, music, science, technology, invention, or philosophy.

Creativity and the Brain

Imagine what was going on in Newton's brain when he "discovered" gravity or in Einstein's when he came up with the theory of relativity. Of course, we'll never know what was going on in the minds of these geniuses from the past, but neuroscientists are beginning to uncover what happens in the brain when a typical person has a Eureka insight or when creative people solve problems compared to less creative people (Jung et al., 2010, 2013). The research has revealed three consistent findings:

- Creative ideas activate frontal and parietal lobe regions of the brain.
- Insights occur in the right hemisphere rather than the left.
- Creative people solving creative problems show more integrated and balanced activity between their right and left frontal lobes.

Marie Curie

Leonardo da Vinci

Virginia Woolf

Vincent van Gogh

Albert Einstein

a: ©Time & Life Pictures/Getty Images; b: ©Pixtal/agefotostock RF; c: ©Popperfoto/Getty Images; d: ©Francis G. Mayer/Corbis/VCG/Getty Images; e: Source: Library of Congress Prints & Photographs Division [LC-USZC4-4940]

 Can you think of other creative geniuses who changed society in some important way?

Creative Insight Results in Increased Frontal and Parietal Lobe Activity The frontal lobes are active in abstract reasoning, planning, focused working memory, and the integration of sensory input. Creativity involves integrating ideas in novel and valuable ways. It is not surprising, therefore, that modern neuroscience supports the conclusion that creative problem solving and insights involve frontal lobe activity (Carlsson, Wendt, & Risberg, 2000; Chow & Cummings, 1999; Feist, 2004; Folley & Park, 2005; Mell, Howard, & Miller, 2003; Takeuchi et al., 2010). Recent research using diffusion tensor imaging (DTI) examined whether greater neural connection in the frontal lobe is associated with greater levels of creativity (Durante & Dunson, 2016). Greater connectivity suggests more myelinated neurons and hence more efficient communication between the neurons. Recall from the chapter "The Biology of Behavior" that DTI measures white matter connections which are covered with (white) myelin, which facilitates neural transmission. It may be that more creative people have both more connections between neurons and more myelin. Further research, however, is needed to confirm this idea.

Additionally, creative thought engages not only frontal lobes, but also the parietal lobes. In fact, a newly named brain network consisting of and connecting parts of the frontal and parietal lobes is most clearly involved in creative thought (Jung et al., 2010, 2013). Dubbed the **default mode network,** it is a region of the frontal and parietal lobes that is active when a person is not really engaged in any particular behavior or focused attention—that is, their brain is on "default mode" (Raichle & Snyder, 2007; Raichle et al., 2001). It is essentially active when we are daydreaming and "mind wandering." These findings may explain why taking a shower, daydreaming, walking, and just being bored can be ideal conditions for creative ideas (Mann & Cadman, 2014; Oppezzo & Schwartz, 2014).

Creative Insight and the Right Hemisphere One kind of problem that has been used in creativity/brain research is a *remote association* word problem (Mednick & Mednick, 1967). Remote association problems display three words at one time to the participant, who must then come up with a single word that could be used with all three of the words. The single word could be added to each of the words to create a compound word, or it could modify one of

default mode network
A brain network that consists of regions of the frontal and parietal lobes that are active when a person is not focused on anything in particular from the outside and becomes less active when a person is focused on a particular stimulus.

FIGURE 16
Default brain network (from Graner et al. 2013).

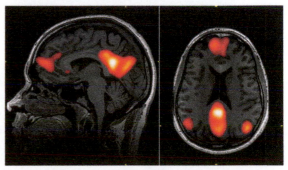

John Graner, Neuroimaging Department, National Intrepid Center of Excellence, Walter Reed National Military Medical Center, 8901 Wisconsin Avenue, Bethesda, MD 20889, USA. /http://www.frontiersin.org/Neurotrauma/10.3389/fneur.2013.00016/full

Research Process

 Research Question

Do creative people use more of their right-hemisphere than less creative people—that is, are they more "right-brained"?

 Method

First, Jung and colleagues (2010) assessed creativity and brain activity using diffusion tensor imaging (DTI), which measures connections involving white matter in the brain. They assessed creativity by giving participants the "Unusual Uses" test in which participants are asked to think of as many unusual uses as they can in 3 minutes for an everyday object such as a brick or paper clip. They also reported on their areas of creative achievement in music, arts, creative writing, cooking, and science.

Two other statistical researchers, Durante and Dunson (2016), then re-analyzed Jung and colleagues' data using sophisticated statistics involving probability analyses. This procedure involved training computers to sort through the original data and identify any brain structure differences in the white matter.

 Results

When splitting the groups into the top and bottom 15% on creativity, Durante and Dunson found significantly greater white matter connectivity between the right and left hemispheres in creative people compared to less creative people (see Figure 1). Green lines mean that connection was greater in creative compared to less creative people. These differences were mostly isolated to the frontal lobes of the brain.

 Conclusion

The "creative right brain" idea is more fiction than fact. Creative people make more balanced use of the parts of the brain involved in focused attention, abstract reasoning, and planning while solving problems than do less creative people. This finding may appear to contradict what we just said about the importance of the right hemisphere in creative problem solving, but it does not. The right hemisphere findings are from noncreative participants who are coming up with insight solutions. The balanced and integrated hemisphere result comes from comparing creative to less creative people.

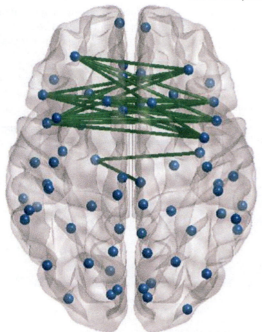

FIGURE **17**

BALANCED AND INTEGRATED BRAIN ACTIVITY IN CREATIVE PEOPLE.
Green lines represent more connectivity in creative compared to less creative people

Source: "Bayesian Inference and Testing of Group Differences in Brain Networks" by D. Durante & D. B. Dunson, 2016, Bayesian Analysis, doi: 10.1214/16-BA1030-160; Photo: ©D. Durante & D.B. Dunson, 2016

the displayed words in some way. This requires the participant to form a nonobvious, or "remote," association in order to solve the problem. If the three words were *French*, *shoe*, and *car*, what one word could you think of that could be used with the other three? What if the three words were *pine*, *crab*, and *sauce*? (*The answers appear at the end of the chapter.*) Interestingly, people often solve these kinds of problems with Eureka insights.

In one set of studies, researchers presented remote association tests to either the right or left visual fields of participants. These participants were not selected for high or low levels of creativity. The researchers presented the information to the individual visual fields because they wanted to control which hemisphere of the brain processed the information. Recall from the chapter "The Biology of Behavior" that information presented to the left visual field is processed in the brain's right hemisphere and information presented to the right visual field is processed in the brain's left hemisphere. When the problem was presented in the left visual field and processed in the right hemisphere, insight into the problems occurred much more frequently than when the problem was presented to the right visual field and processed in the left hemisphere (Beeman & Bowden, 2000; Bowden & Jung-Beeman, 2003; Kounios & Beeman, 2015). Moreover, when researchers took brain images using fMRI and EEG while people were solving insight problems, they found that sudden insights consistently activated the right hemisphere more than the left (Bowden et al., 2005). Similarly, patients with damage to the frontal region of their right hemisphere are less able to solve problems requiring insight than people without damage to their right hemisphere (Miller & Tippett, 1996).

Creativity and Integrated Activity between the Hemispheres The third consistent finding from the neuroscience of creativity is that, when solving problems, creative people have more balanced brain activity between the hemispheres than less creative people (Durante & Dunson, 2016; Takeuchi et al., 2010). In particular, while solving problems, they show equally active areas in their right and left frontal lobes, which translates into a widening rather than a narrowing of attention and a greater flexibility in moving from one way of thinking to another (Carlsson et al., 2000; Goel & Vartanian, 2005); see the Research Process for this chapter (Figure 17). Widening one's attention and being able to shift ways of thinking easily and flexibly are hallmarks of creative thinking (Feist, 2004; Martindale, 1999).

Cognitive Processes in Creative Thinking

Creative thinking entails unique cognitive processes (Lee & Therriault, 2011). Psychologists who study the cognitive aspects of creative thought have focused on visual thinking, fluency, flexibility, and originality. Visual imagery occurs when we see a solution in our "mind's eye." Many scientists, artists, and writers solve problems by using creative mental images (Miller & Tippett, 1996). Einstein, for example, often visualized a situation, such as riding in an elevator traveling at the speed of light. Imagining such a scenario and then thinking about what would happen to a light beam he emitted led to his discovery of the theory of relativity.

Cognitive psychologists have developed clever experiments to test people's ability to come up with creative mental images. They display images of letters or geometric shapes and ask participants to combine some of them in a creative way (Finke, Ward, & Smith, 1992). Figure 18a contains a set of such objects. Three of these images are chosen at random during each trial, and the participant's task is to assemble them in such a way as to create a recognizable shape or pattern. Various solutions are presented in Figure 18b.

The ability to produce many ideas is central to creative thought. Having many ideas, or being fluent in producing ideas, is called **ideational fluency**

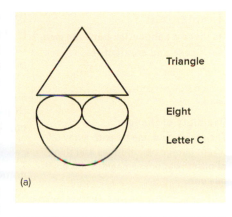

Triangle

Eight

Letter C

(a)

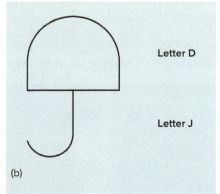

Letter D

Letter J

(b)

FIGURE 18
CREATIVE PROBLEM SOLVING USING MENTAL IMAGERY. (a) Three stimulus shapes at a time are presented to a person, whose task it is to combine them in any way to produce a single image or object. (b) These are some of the solutions created using the shapes in (a) (Finke et al., 1992).

Challenge Your Assumptions

True or False? Creative people are more "right-brained" than less creative people.

False: Although insight does activate more right than hemisphere, creative people actually have more integrated and connected brain hemispheres than less creative people.

ideational fluency
The ability to produce many ideas.

Connection

Is there a connection between mental illness and creativity?

See "Bringing It All Together," in the chapter "Psychological Disorders." (p. 602)

flexibility of thought
The ability to come up with many different categories of ideas and think of other responses besides the obvious one.

originality
The ability to come up with unusual and novel ideas.

FIGURE 19
PERSONALITY TRAITS SHARED BY CREATIVE ARTISTS AND SCIENTISTS.

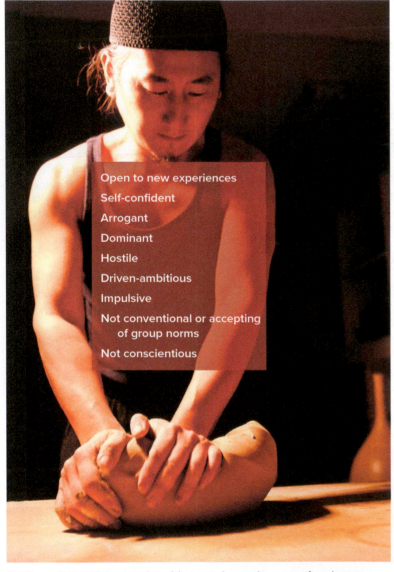

Open to new experiences
Self-confident
Arrogant
Dominant
Hostile
Driven-ambitious
Impulsive
Not conventional or accepting of group norms
Not conscientious

Text: Source: Feist, 1998; A meta-analysis of the impact of personality on scientific and artistic creativity. *Personality and Social Psychological Review, 2*, 290–309; photo; ©Imagemore Co., Ltd./ Getty Images RF

(Guilford, 1967). Highly creative people usually come up with more ideas for a given problem than less creative people do. Not all the ideas will be equally useful, but having a large number of ideas increases the chance that any one of them will be a useful or adaptive solution to the problem at hand. J. P. Guilford developed the *Alternate Uses* test to measure creativity. In this test, participants are given a common object, such as a brick or a pencil, and are asked to write down all the possible uses they can think of for the object within a limited amount of time. An ideationally fluent person can list many alternate uses for the object within a short period.

The ability to produce many ideas does not by itself guarantee that one can break out of one's mental set and think of unusual uses. A creative person can also come up with many different categories of ideas and think of other responses besides the obvious one. This ability is called **flexibility of thought** (Guilford, 1967). In the Alternate Uses test, flexibility of thought is gauged by the number of categories of response a person offers. If all the answers for the uses of a brick involve building something, the person is not displaying flexible thinking but remaining within one, rather obvious category. In contrast, coming up with uses that involve building, painting, writing, weights, step stools, and ballasts means a person is a flexible thinker, because those uses cut across many different categories.

The third cognitive process involved in creative thought is **originality**, which means thinking of unusual and novel ideas. In the Alternate Uses test, the test-taker's originality is scored by comparing his or her responses to a set of norms developed from the answers given by thousands of respondents who have already taken the test. A person's answer is scored as original if it is rare or uncommon compared to the norms. Again using the brick as an example, a higher originality score is given to "step stool" than to "paperweight," because there are fewer instances of "step stool" in the norms. In this sense, an original response is the same as an infrequent response, but originality in itself is not enough to explain creative thought. Creative thinking occurs when a person combines all three cognitive processes at once—fluency, flexibility, and originality.

The Creative Personality

We have seen how creative people differ from others by their brain activity and cognitive style. What about their personalities? Do creative people tend to have unique personalities? If so, what personality characteristics tend to be found in highly creative people? The best way to answer these questions is by looking at what all the published studies on the topic say—that is, by conducting a meta-analysis.

Feist (1998) conducted such a meta-analysis by locating all the published studies that reported the personality qualities of artists and scientists (see also Batey & Furnham, 2008).

Twenty-six studies on almost 5,000 participants had reported the personality traits of scientists compared to norms; 29 studies on almost 4,400 participants had reported the personality traits of artists compared to norms. Creative artists and scientists do share some common personality traits (see Figure 19). One of the most pronounced personality traits of creative artists and scientists, is openness to experience, which is the tendency to enjoy and seek out new experiences, new foods, new places, and new ideas. Highly creative people have this quality, which is not surprising, given that creativity involves novel thoughts and behavior (Batey, Furnham, & Safiullina, 2010; Furnham & Bachtiar, 2008; Greengross, Martin, & Miller, 2012; Hughes, Furnham, & Batey, 2013; Prabhu, Sutton, & Sauser, 2008). Also, they are unconventional and tend to have a firm belief that they possess a better way of doing things. In some, this comes off as self-confidence and in others as arrogance (Feist, 1993). Despite the similarities, artists are more emotionally sensitive and unstable than scientists (Feist, 1998; Ludwig, 1995).

Quick Quiz 10.3: Creativity

1. Creative thinking or behavior is both novel and
   a. interesting.
   b. artistic.
   c. meaningful.
   d. unusual.

2. The four stages of creative problem solving are preparation, incubation, insight, and
   a. elaboration-verification.
   b. validation.
   c. discrimination.
   d. resolution.

3. When compared to less creative people, creative people show what pattern of brain activity while solving problems?
   a. asymmetry between the hemispheres
   b. balance between the hemispheres
   c. parietal lobe activation
   d. occipital lobe activation

4. What is measured by the task in which participants are asked to think of as many different uses for a brick as they can?
   a. originality
   b. flexibility of thought
   c. functional fixedness
   d. both a and b

Answers can be found at the end of the chapter.

Bringing It All Together

Making Connections in Intelligence, Problem Solving, and Creativity

Genius, Intelligence, and Creativity

For many people, finding out that someone has an extremely high IQ (140 and above) is enough to call him or her a "genius," but are all very smart people necessarily geniuses? Moreover, does having an extremely high IQ mean the person will be creative? These are fascinating and important questions and they beg two other questions:

1. What is genius?
2. Is intelligence necessary and sufficient for creativity?

What Is Genius?

What makes someone a genius? Is superior intelligence enough? Consider Marilyn vos Savant. Most people have not heard of her, although she writes a weekly nationally syndicated column for *Parade* magazine. She has the world's highest recorded IQ ever—an off-the-chart 228—yet she has not created master works of note. Genius is not, as some have claimed, simply being smart or having a very high IQ (Simonton, 1999). Having an IQ of 130 or 140, which puts someone in the top 1% or higher of the population, does not guarantee producing creative works of lasting influence.

Something other than intelligence must go into the making of a genius. **Genius** is high intelligence combined with

genius
High intelligence combined with creative accomplishments that have a tremendous impact on a given field.

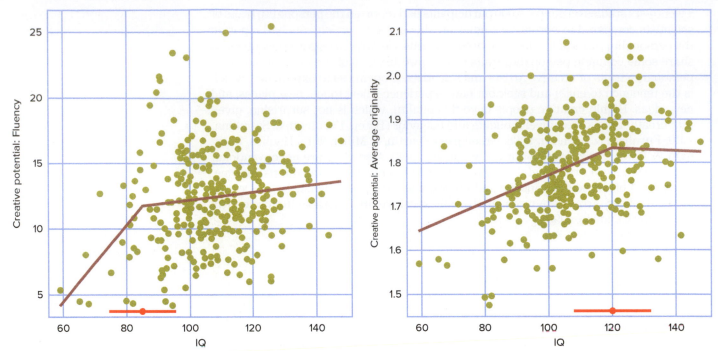

(a) An IQ of 85 is the breakpoint, or threshold, for the relationship between IQ and fluency/number of ideas (creative potential).

(b) An IQ of 120 is the breakpoint for the relationship between IQ and originality of ideas (creative potential).

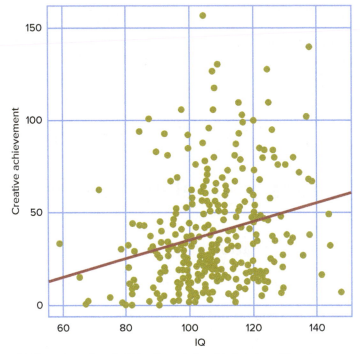

(c) There is no threshold for the relationship between IQ and creative achievement.

FIGURE 20

IQ THRESHOLDS FOR CREATIVE POTENTIAL (FLUENCY AND ORIGINALITY) AND CREATIVE ACHIEVEMENT. In these scatterplots, each dot represents a person's IQ score and his or her score on a different measure of creativity. The line through the dots represents the slope of the relationship. A diagonal line is a significant relationship, but a flat line is no relationship. The sharp change in direction of the line is the threshold, or breakpoint (Jauk et al., 2013).

 What does the threshold, or breakpoint, tell you about whether IQ is a necessary and sufficient condition for different forms of creative potential and creative achievement?

creative accomplishments that have a tremendous impact on a given field (Simonton, 1999). The paintings, plays, buildings, novels, and scientific discoveries of geniuses change their respective fields. Literature was never the same after Shakespeare or Virginia Woolf. Physics has not been the same since Newton, Einstein, and Marie Curie. Art has not been the same since van Gogh and Picasso. Music has not been the same since Bach and Beethoven. If people's accomplishments change their field, other people appreciate their importance sooner or later. Having a major impact on a field and being appreciated for the accomplishments is what distinguishes genius from genius-like IQ. For every Shakespeare, Beethoven, Leonardo, and Einstein, there are many more people with equally high intelligence who make no significant contributions to society. Moreover, there have been people of truly monumental creative accomplishment whose intelligence was only somewhat above average. Charles Darwin, was—by his own admission—of only modestly high intelligence (Simonton, 1999), but his accomplishments have had as much impact on science and culture as those of just about any other person. By this standard, he was a genius.

Is Intelligence Necessary and Sufficient for Creativity?

Genius, by definition, and creativity are closely related, but what about intelligence and creativity? Does being really smart make a person more creative? The relationship between intelligence and creativity is not a simple one. Starting in the 1950s and 1960s, creativity researchers concluded there was a threshold on intelligence, below which the relationship with creativity was positive, above which there was no relationship (Guilford, 1967). A threshold is the point at which the relationship goes from being significant to not significant, which was argued to be an IQ of 120. Creativity and intelligence were positively related below an IQ of 120 but unrelated above this threshold. This would imply that intelligence is a necessary condition, but not a sufficient one, for creativity.

More recent investigations, however, have shown a more complex relationship between intelligence and creativity (Jauk et al., 2013; Joy, 2012; Jung et al., 2009; Karwowski & Gralewski, 2013; Kaufman & Plucker, 2011; Kim, 2005; Nusbaum & Silvia, 2011; Preckel, Holling, & Wiese, 2006). For example, Jauk and colleagues (2013) report different thresholds for different aspects of creative potential (doing well on tests of creativity). If number of ideas (fluency) is the measure of creative potential, the threshold is only an IQ of 85; however, if originality of ideas is the measure of potential, then support for the threshold of 120 is reported (see Figures 20a and 20b). In other words, high intelligence predicts original ideas more than just quantity or number of ideas. Moreover, when the measure of creativity is achievement (actually producing creative works in art, music, or science), there is no threshold (see Figure 20c). Intelligence is positively related to creativity—meaning that, the more intelligent people are, the more likely they are to produce creative works.

Challenge Your Assumptions

True or False? People with very high IQs are geniuses.

False: IQ alone does not determine genius; genius requires creative accomplishments that change some aspect of society.

Chapter Review

INTELLIGENCE

- Intelligence is a set of cognitive skills that includes abstract thinking, reasoning, problem solving, and the ability to acquire knowledge.

- There are two major theories of the nature of intelligence. The single-factor, or general-factor, theory argues that intelligence at its core is one, overall ability. The other theory, the multifactor theory, says that intelligence consists of multiple abilities.

- Some of the factors of intelligence in the multifactor theory are crystallized and fluid intelligence, as well as analytic, practical, musical, and bodily-kinesthetic intelligence.

- Measures of intelligence, including the Stanford-Binet test and the Wechsler Adult Scale of

©Dave Fimbres Photography/Getty Images RF

Intelligence (WAIS), tend to be reliable and predictive of certain outcomes (school achievement), but not others (happiness or satisfaction with one's job).

- Intelligence ranges widely on a continuum from very low to very high. On the extremely low end is intellectual disability and on the extremely high end is giftedness.

- Group differences in IQ exist for race and gender, yet there is much debate concerning the possible explanations for these differences.

PROBLEM SOLVING

- Two distinct kinds of problem exist. Convergent thinking problems have known solutions, which can be reached by narrowing down a set of possible answers. Divergent thinking problems have no known solution; they require us to break away from our normal problem-solving strategies and make unusual associations to arrive at novel ways of thinking about a problem.

- People use different kinds of strategies to solve problems. Algorithms are formulas that guarantee correct solutions to particular problems. Thinking outside the box requires one to break free of self-imposed conceptual constraints and think about a problem differently in order to solve it. Eureka insights involve a sudden understanding of a solution.

- Obstacles to solutions include fixation, or an inability to break out of a particular mind-set in order to think about a problem from a fresh perspective; mental set, the tendency to continue to use problem-solving strategies that have worked in the past; and functional fixedness, the tendency to be blind to unusual uses of common, everyday things or procedures.

CREATIVITY

- Creativity is thought or behavior that is both novel and meaningful or adaptive.

- Genius is closely related to creativity in that it combines high intelligence with achievements that change entire fields (art, music, science, technology, business).

- Researchers have uncovered three principles of creative thinking and the brain: Creative insight increases frontal lobe activity; insights occur in the right hemisphere rather than the left; and creative people solving creative problems show more balanced activity between their right and left frontal lobes. Cognitive processes commonly associated with creative thinking are visual imagery, flexibility (coming up with many different categories of ideas), ideational fluency (the ability to produce many ideas), and originality (thinking of novel solutions).

- Creative people tend to have open, self-confident, arrogant, and unconventional personalities.

BRINGING IT ALL TOGETHER: MAKING CONNECTIONS IN INTELLIGENCE, PROBLEM SOLVING, AND CREATIVITY

- Intelligence, genius, and creativity are related but distinct concepts. Intelligence appears to be necessary but not sufficient for both genius and creativity.

Key Terms

adaptive behavior
algorithm
broad intelligence
Connectome
construct validity
convergent thinking problems
creativity
crystallized intelligence
cultural test bias
default mode network
divergent thinking problems
Down syndrome
Eureka insight (insight solution)
familial-cultural intellectual disability
fixation

flexibility of thought
fluid intelligence
functional fixedness
general intelligence
g-factor theory
genius
ideational fluency
internal reliability
intellectual disability
intelligence
mental age
mental set
multiple-factor theory of intelligence
narrow intelligence
originality

predictive validity
quantitative intelligence
prodigy
reaction range
reliability
savant syndrome
spatial intelligence
successful intelligence
test bias
test fairness
test-retest reliability
thinking outside the box
triarchic theory of intelligence
validity
verbal intelligence

Quick Quiz Answers

Quiz 1: 1. d; **2.** d; **3.** b; **4.** c; **5.** a   **Quick Quiz 2: 1.** b; **2.** a; **3.** c   **Quick Quiz 3: 1.** c; **2.** a; **3.** b; **4.** d

The solution to the first remote association is "horn" and the second is "apple" on p. 397

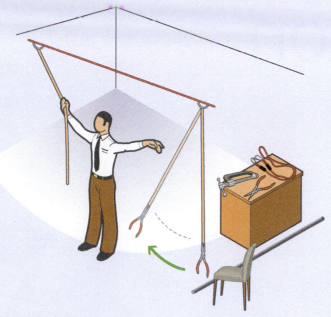

SOLUTION TO FIGURE 14.

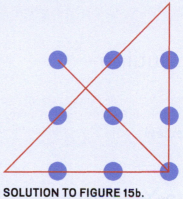

SOLUTION TO FIGURE 15b.
Can you think of any others?

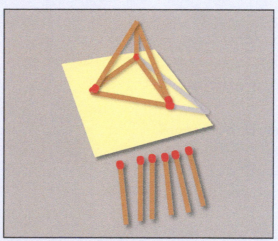

SOLUTION TO FIGURE 15c.

11 Motivation and Emotion

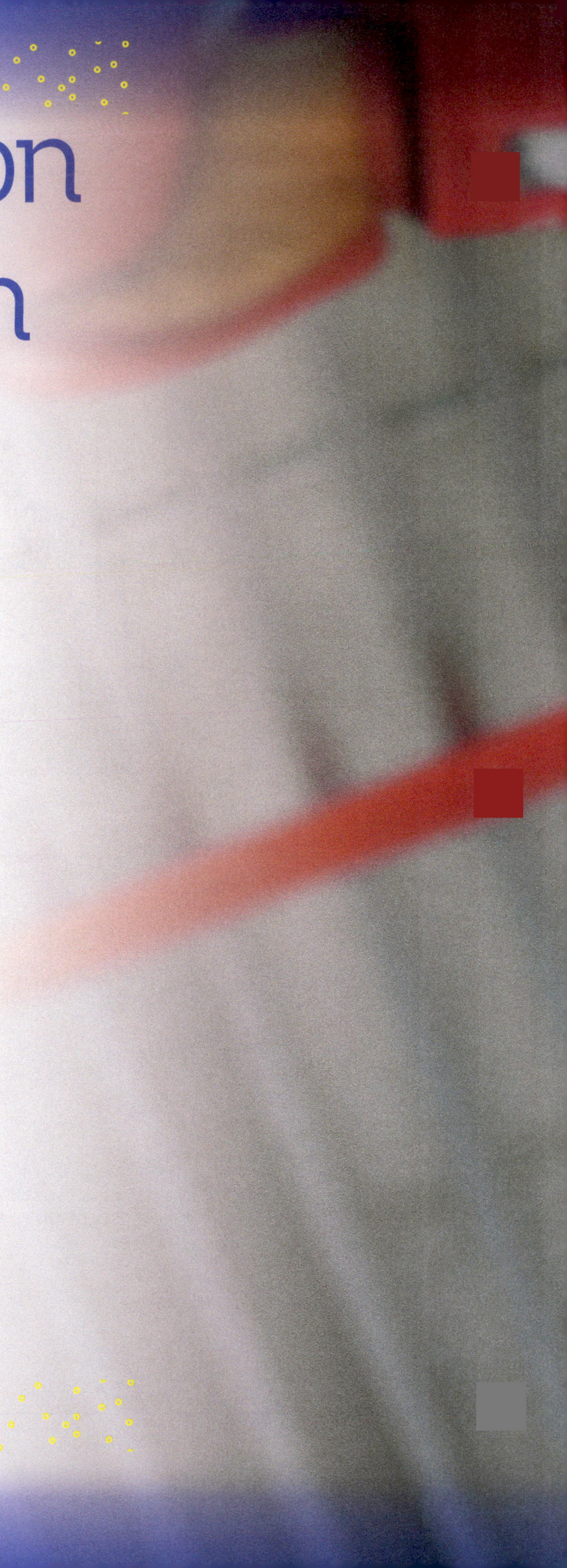

Chapter Outline

Motivation
Emotion
Chapter Review

Challenge Your Assumptions

True or False?

- Craving sweet, fatty, and salty foods is a socially and culturally determined preference. (see page 412)

- Eating smaller and more frequent meals can help you lose weight. (see page 415)

- Women are just as likely as men to engage in casual sex. (see page 421)

- Many species of animals engage in homosexual behavior. (see page 421)

- Facial expressions of emotion are very different from culture to culture. (see page 438)

- More money leads to greater happiness. (see page 451)

©Jade/Getty Images RF

Beck Weathers was finally doing what he long dreamed of doing: climbing Mt. Everest. Being a pathologist, Weathers had already accomplished a lot in his 49 years, but he also struggled with bouts of depression and found challenging exercises to be effective ways of coping with his depression (Weathers, 2000).

All went well for the 2 months Weathers and his team spent on Mt. Everest to adjust to the altitude and conditions until they finally decided conditions were right to attempt to summit the 29,029-foot (8,848-meter) peak: Weathers had to stop slightly below the 28,000-foot mark. Completely exhausted, depleted of oxygen, and literally blinded by the conditions, Weathers could not continue and promised his guide, Rob Hall, he would wait for his return from summiting with another client.

Not knowing that his guide and the other client would wind up in trouble, Weathers waited hours. He refused offers by two groups to help him back down because of his promise to Hall. After hours of waiting alone, Beck finally joined a few others going down the mountain, but it was too late. They got caught in a fierce storm that came out of nowhere and had to spend the night in nearly 100 mph winds and temperatures of 30 below zero Fahrenheit.

The next morning Anatoli Boukreev, a Russian guide, came upon Beck's five-person group. The storm was still blasting at full force, so Boukreev could not guide more than one or two at a time down to the 26,000-foot Camp Four. Even though he believed that the remaining two people, one of whom was Weathers, were dead or better left for dead, he did send another rescue team up. When the rescuers got to the duo lying in the snow, they both were still breathing but close to death. It would be dangerous to try to take them down the mountain, so they were left for dead—again. Word got back to camp, and a phone call was made to his wife in Dallas, informing her of Beck's death.

Weathers remained in the subzero temperatures and snow for more than 12 hours, and "[t]hen . . . for some unknowable reason a light went on in the reptilian core of Beck's inanimate brain and he floated back to consciousness" (Krakauer, 1996, p. 264). When he first woke up in the snow, Weathers thought he was in a dream. He was no longer cold, and he was motivated to survive: "I was overwhelmed by an enormous, encompassing sense of melancholy. That I would not say good-bye to my family, that I would never again say 'I love you' to my wife, that I would never again hold my children, was just not acceptable. 'Keep moving' I said to myself again and again" (Weathers, 2000, Chapter 6, para. 28).

He fell many times on his way down to camp. After finding his way back to Camp Four, using wind direction as his only guide, and getting into a sleeping bag, the people there were still convinced that he would be dead by morning and was left alone to die—yet again! Only Jon Krakauer, best-selling author of *Into Thin Air*, decided to check on Weathers as others prepared to leave the camp the next day and "was shocked to discover that Beck was still alive" (Krakauer, 1996, p. 267).

After another day of horrifically difficult climbing, being guided footstep by footstep, Weathers finally made it to a lower camp at around 20,000 feet, but how was he going to make it off the mountain? The answer was one last beyond-belief act of heroism: the highest helicopter rescue ever performed by Madan Khatri Chhetri. At that elevation, helicopters can't get enough lift. The pilot risked his own life, but he succeeded, and Beck Weathers survived beyond all expectation and reason.

Weathers's survival is not only one of miraculous drive and motivation but also one of how emotion can often fuel motivation. The thought of never seeing his wife and children again gave Weathers the strength and perseverance to make it back down to camp. Although he was left for dead three times and ended up losing both hands and his nose to frostbite, Weathers survived and became a better husband and father (Weathers, 2000). Motivation and emotion are important forces of survival, and in this chapter we explore how these two forces shape human thought and behavior.

MOTIVATION

Consider what the following situations have in common:

A baby seeking a nipple
A girl studying for a math exam
A homeless person searching for food in a garbage can
A scientist conducting research
A couple having sex
A man climbing Mt. Everest

These are all examples of motivated behaviors. Babies seek the nipple because they need contact and nutrition; a girl might study for a test because she finds the material fascinating. There might be various reasons for a behavior, but each involves **motivation**, the urge to move toward one's goals, an energetic push toward accomplishing tasks, such as getting dinner, getting rich, and getting lucky.

Needs, drives, and incentives all contribute to motivation. **Needs** are states of cellular or bodily deficiency that compel drives. These are what your body seeks. Examples are your needs for water, food, and oxygen. **Drives** occur when our bodies are deficient in some internal need. If we are extremely thirsty, we are driven to drink. All our physiological needs have drive components. Figure 1 shows the drive components associated with various physiological and psychological needs. Motivated behaviors, therefore, result from needs and drives.

If drives push us into action, then incentives pull us into action. An **incentive** is any external object or event that motivates behavior. In general, drives come from the body, whereas incentives come from the environment. Financial independence, a gold medal at the Olympics, and academic success are all possible incentives behind training or studying.

Models of Motivation

Psychologists propose many models, or explanations, for motivation. Some focus more on internal drives, some more on external incentives, and others on both.

The Drive Reduction Model   When our physiological systems are out of balance or depleted, we are driven to reduce this depleted state (Hull, 1943; McKinley et al., 2004; Strombach, Strang, Park, & Kenning, 2016; Weisinger et al., 1993). Recall that a drive is the perceived internal state of tension that arises when our bodies are lacking in some basic physiological capacity, such as food or water. Central to drive reduction is the idea of maintaining physiological balance, or

motivation
The urge to move toward one's goals; to accomplish tasks.

needs
Inherently biological states of deficiency (cellular or bodily) that compel drives.

drives
The perceived states of tension that occur when our bodies are deficient in some need, creating an urge to relieve the tension.

incentive
Any external object or event that motivates behavior.

FIGURE 1

a: ©didi/amanaimages/Corbis RF; b: ©Ryan McVay/Getty Images RF; c: ©Corbis/VCG/Getty Images

Which needs and drives motivate studying behavior?

homeostasis
The process by which all organisms work to maintain physiological equilibrium, or balance around an optimal set point.

set point
The ideal fixed setting of a particular physiological system, such as internal body temperature.

homeostasis (Cannon, 1929). Whether they know it or not, all bodies aim to maintain physiological equilibrium around an optimal **set point**, the ideal, fixed setting of a particular physiological system. Set points are important mechanisms that allow homeostasis to work. We have set points for hunger, thirst, respiration, and many other drives. For example, if we get too cold, we shiver to warm up as the body tries to warm itself with physical activity. The "normal" human body temperature of 98.6°F is like setting your thermostat to 68°F to warm your home (see Figure 2). When the temperature in the room has fallen more than a degree or two lower than the set point, the thermostat switches on the heater. Once the temperature has been brought back within the ideal set-point range, the thermostat turns off. In short, set points guide us to a "happy medium" in our needs. Our bodies automatically work to achieve states that are "just right."

For homeostasis to work, our bodies must have sensors that detect their current states and any changes that cause them to deviate from the set point. Most of these sensory detectors are mechanisms in the brain. If our bodily states move too far from the set point, these mechanisms motivate us to take action—to raid the refrigerator, for example—to reduce our state of discomfort. Certain brain mechanisms evaluate the options and decide what to do to meet a biological need based on the information the brain is getting from our organs and tissues.

FIGURE 2

MODELS OF HOMEOSTASIS. Detectors in the brain stabilize the body's physiological state by comparing the current state (for example, blood sugar level, body fluids, body temperature) to a set point. If the body is far from the set point, the organism is motivated to correct the imbalance (for example, by seeking food or putting on a sweater). Sensory feedback to the brain tells it when the set point has been achieved, and the brain then tells the body to stop correcting. This feedback system keeps the body's physiological systems at their ideal set point (Berridge, 2004).

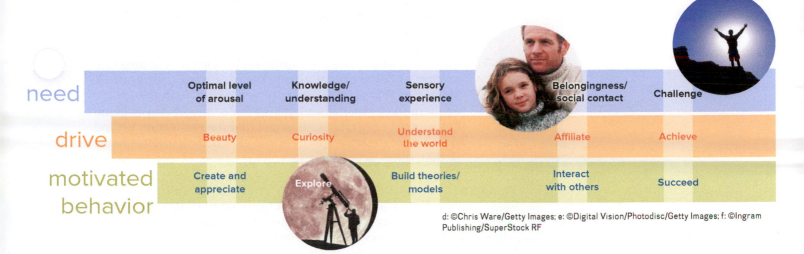

need	Optimal level of arousal	Knowledge/ understanding	Sensory experience	Belongingness/ social contact	Challenge
drive	Beauty	Curiosity	Understand the world	Affiliate	Achieve
motivated behavior	Create and appreciate	Explore	Build theories/ models	Interact with others	Succeed

d: ©Chris Ware/Getty Images; e: ©Digital Vision/Photodisc/Getty Images; f: ©Ingram Publishing/SuperStock RF

The Optimal Arousal Model When do we operate at our best? Can we be too wound up to perform well? The "optimal level of arousal" is another model that focuses on internal drive states; it is based on research by Yerkes and Dodson (1908). According to the optimal arousal model, we function best when we are moderately aroused, or energized. Both low and high arousal/ energy levels lead to poor performance (Yerkes & Dodson, 1908). The finding is so common that it is now referred to as the **Yerkes-Dodson law** (see Figure 3). Consider the case of making a public speech, especially if you are not accustomed to such tasks. If you are too relaxed, you might not have the motivation to prepare. If you are too nervous, your voice might quiver and you might forget what you were supposed to say. If you are just mildly excited and/or challenged by the task, however, you are energized and motivated but not incapacitated by too much arousal.

The optimal arousal model of motivation argues that humans are motivated to be in situations that are neither too stimulating nor not stimulating enough. Support for the optimal arousal model comes from sensory deprivation research. It involves having a person lie down on a bed or in a sensory deprivation (saltwater) tank. Classic research from the 1950s demonstrated that people could not remain in sensory deprivation for more than 2 to 3 days, even if they were paid double their daily wage for each day they remained in the tank (Bexton, Heron, & Scott, 1954). After long periods of sensory deprivation, people begin to hallucinate, their cognitive ability and concentration suffer, and they develop childish emotional responses. Sensory deprivation in rodents shrinks the brain regions most involved in the senses that have been deprived, another example of the plasticity of the brain (Cheetham et al., 2007; Denizet, Cotter, Lledo, & Lazarini, 2016).

In the 1990s, Mihaly Csikszentmihalyi introduced the concept of *flow* to describe how people perform best and are most creative when they are optimally challenged relative to their abilities (Csikszentmihalyi, 1990, 1996). According to this school of thought, needs such as curiosity, learning, interest, beauty-aesthetics, competence, challenge, flow states, and optimal experiences are motivated by the desire

Yerkes-Dodson law
The principle that moderate levels of arousal lead to optimal performance.

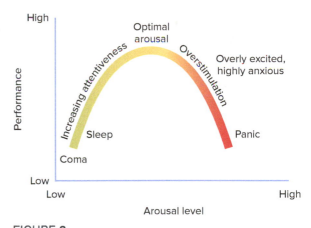

FIGURE 3

YERKES-DODSON LAW. The Yerkes-Dodson law states that performance is best when we are optimally aroused; to be optimally aroused is to be moderately aroused. Performance is worst when we are either not very aroused (asleep or not paying attention) or overly aroused (highly excited or anxious) (Smith, 1998).

FIGURE 4
MASLOW'S HIERARCHY OF NEEDS.

Self-
actualization

Esteem needs

Love and belongingness needs

Safety and security needs

Physiological needs

Adapted from: A. Maslow, "Hierarchy of Needs," from *Motivation and Personality* (1970). New York: Harper Row.

 Is it possible to satisfy needs of personal development, such as self-actualization, when physiological needs, such as hunger, are not met? Why or why not?

to be optimally aroused and engaged with the task or activity with which one if engaged (Berlyne, 1960; Csikszentmihalyi, 1990; Deci & Ryan, 1985; Silvia, 2006). When in flow states, people are not aware of time passing and are very absorbed in the task in which they are engaged—so much so that they lose a sense of being separate from the task itself (Sadlo, 2016). Many find this experience quite rewarding, both due to the exhilaration it can induce but also due to the feeling of being in the groove or flow. Some argue that the motivation behind training for extreme sports or the elite artistic performance is that these activities can engage states of optimal flow (Brymer & Mackenzie, 2017).

The Evolutionary Model A third model of motivation that focuses on internal drive states is evolutionary theory. The biological purpose of any living organism is to survive and reproduce (perpetuate the species). The processes of natural and sexual selection have shaped motivation over time to make all animals, including humans, *want* those things that help them survive and reproduce (Buss, 2003). As a result, the major motives involve basic survival and reproduction needs and drives: hunger, thirst, body-temperature regulation, oxygen, and sex. Our bodies "know" they want food, water, oxygen, and—after adolescence—sex. We don't have to learn these behaviors. They are automatic and instinctive. Desires, wants, and needs have been shaped over the course of human evolution to guide behavior either toward adaptive or away from maladaptive actions (Buss, 2003; Miller, 2000).

The Hierarchical Model Another model of motivation, which combines drives and incentives, is Abraham Maslow's hierarchy of needs (Maslow, 1970). The essence of Maslow's hierarchy is simple: Needs range from the most basic physiological necessities to the highest, most psychological needs for growth and fulfillment (see Figure 4). At the lowest level of the hierarchy are *physiological needs*, such as the needs for food, water, oxygen, and adequate body temperature. At the next level are *safety needs*, which include physical security, stability, dependency, protection, and freedom from threats, such as war, assault, and terrorism. We need to be fed and out of danger's way before we can pay attention to higher-level needs.

The third level in the hierarchy consists of the *love and belongingness needs*, including the desire for friendship, sex, a mate, and children, as well as the desire to belong to a family or social group. The fourth level in Maslow's hierarchy of needs is the *need for esteem*—that is, the need to be liked, appreciated, and respected by other people as well as oneself. The need for esteem is behind the desire to achieve and succeed. The top level in the hierarchy is the need for **self-actualization**, the full realization of one's potentials and abilities in life. Only when lower-level needs have been satisfied can people focus on higher-level needs. For example, hunger and safety needs must be met before self-actualization needs can be fulfilled.

Maslow's hierarchy, as well known as it is, has had relatively little scientific support or updating. In 2010, however, Doug Kenrick and colleagues bridged the evolutionary and hierarchical models of motivation by modifying Maslow's hierarchy from an evolutionary perspective (Kenrick et al., 2010; see Figure 5). The new model builds on the basic needs—physiological, safety (protection), love and belongingness (affiliation), and esteem—and replaces self-actualization with three types of reproductive goals: acquiring a mate, retaining

self-actualization
The inherent drive to realize one's full potential.

a mate, and parenting. In addition, in the new model, the levels overlap rather than replace earlier needs, clarifying that they do not go away but can be activated whenever needed.

Although we have numerous drive states, the two most basic ones are hunger and sex. Hunger is the drive behind survival, and sex is the drive behind reproduction.

Hunger: Survival of the Individual

All animals need to replenish the energy continuously being used by their bodies. The rate at which we consume energy is known as *metabolism*. When our energy has been depleted, hunger drives us to replenish it by eating. Hunger is not just an internal biological process, however. It is the product of biological processes interacting with external, environmental ones.

The Biology of When We Eat   Internal signals control the desire to eat or stop eating. From a drive-reduction perspective, being hungry depends not only on how much food we have consumed recently but also on how much energy is available for organ function. Hunger has four biological components: the stomach, the blood, the brain, and hormones and neurochemicals.

When we get hungry, our stomach starts to growl from gastric secretions the brain activates when we think of, see, or smell food. Hunger can also cause the stomach to contract when the stomach and small intestine have been relatively empty for about 2 hours. Although stomach contractions correspond with hunger pangs, they do not cause hunger. You might be surprised to learn that people who have their stomachs removed for medical reasons still feel hunger, as do rats whose nerves between the stomach and the brain have been cut (Brown & Wallace, 1980; Cannon & Washburn, 1912). Thus, the stomach does not act by itself to produce feelings of hunger; other biological systems are also involved.

One of these other signals comes from blood sugar. **Glucose**, a simple sugar in the blood that provides energy for cells throughout the body, including the brain, is the most important source of energy for the body. Although fat and protein provide their own forms of energy, some organs, including the brain, can use only glucose. Our blood sugar level drops when we don't eat for long periods, and the hypothalamus, which monitors glucose levels, will trigger the drive to obtain food.

As with almost all behavior, many regions of the brain are involved in eating. The hypothalamus regulates all basic physiological needs and acts as hunger's sensory detector. The body signals the hypothalamus about the nutritional needs of the cells. Various parts of the hypothalamus in turn send signals to different brain regions to either start or stop eating (Berthoud, 2002; Stellar, 1954).

Hormones and neurochemicals also play a role in hunger. Some of these substances stimulate appetite; others suppress it (Rowland, Li, & Morien, 1996; Simpson & Bloom, 2010; Williams et al., 2004). Two of the numerous hormones that stimulate appetite are neuropeptide Y (NPY) and ghrelin (Williams et al., 2004). When an animal is hungry or underfed, NPY is released in the hypothalamus to stimulate appetite. Ghrelin stimulates the release of dopamine (the feel-good neurotransmitter) and sends hunger signals to the brain, thereby stimulating hunger (Simpson & Bloom, 2010). Ghrelin levels rise when we are hungry and fall drastically after we eat.

FIGURE 5

EVOLUTIONARY UPDATE TO MASLOW'S HIERARCHY OF NEEDS. An evolutionary revision of Maslow's hierarchy of needs replaces self-actualization at the highest level with three levels of reproductive needs, in the order of their developmental appearance (acquiring a mate, retaining a mate, and parenting). Another change is that the new model conceptualizes the stages as overlapping, rather than replacing, previous stages.

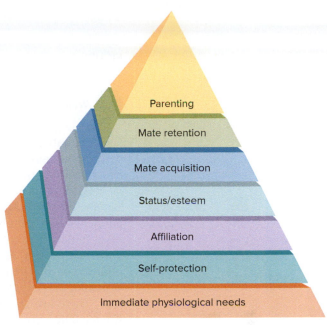

Source: Kenrick, D.T., Griskevicius, V., Neuberg, S.L., & Schaller, M. (2010). Renovating the pyramid of needs: Contemporary extensions built upon ancient foundations. *Perspective on Psychological Science*, 5, 292–314. Doi: 10.1177/1745691610369469

glucose
A simple sugar that provides energy for cells throughout the body, including the brain.

Hormones and Neurochemicals Involved in Hunger

Hormone/Neurochemical	Increase Appetite	Decrease Appetite
Neuropeptide Y (NPY)	✓	
Ghrelin	✓	
Endocannabinoids	✓	
Insulin		✓
Leptin		✓

FIGURE 6

HORMONES AND NEUROCHEMICALS INVOLVED IN HUNGER.

 Which hormones and neurochemicals are involved in making us feel hunger or full?

Endocannabinoids are marijuana-related naturally occurring neurochemicals that can also increase appetite. Blocking receptor sites for endocannabinoids leads to a decrease in eating and to weight loss (Kirkham, 2005; Morello et al., 2016).

Among the hormones that suppress appetite are insulin and leptin (Simpson & Bloom, 2010; Williams et al., 2004). One of the most important hormonal effects on hunger comes from insulin, which is produced by the pancreas. Rising glucose levels stimulate insulin production; insulin in turn transports glucose out of the blood and into the cells. As a result, hunger decreases. Leptin is produced by fat cells and inhibits neurons in the hypothalamus that contain NPY (appetite stimulant), thereby signaling the body that it has had enough to eat (Friedman & Halaas, 1998).

There are specific cells in the hypothalamus that regulate appetite (Chen & Knight, 2016). Some of these cells make us hungry and promote eating, while others stop our hunger and stop eating. The "stop eating" neurons are regulated by leptin (which reduces hunger) and another neurohormone, ghrelin (which increases hunger). Sensory information about food—such as odors or sights of food—can activate and regulate the neurons responsible for hunger (Chen, Lin, Kuo, & Knight, 2015).

The Psychology of What We Eat   What we eat is shaped by both nature and nurture. We crave foods that are essential to our bodies but that were scarce during early periods of human evolution, but we also learn to like and crave particular foods common in our culture.

Food preferences are very much shaped by evolutionary forces. Without realizing it, most humans crave the basic nutrients that our bodies require and that were scarce during ancestral times: sugar, salt, and fat. The fast-food industry capitalizes on this fact by creating foods that are rich in these substances (Moss, 2013). Companies conduct research to determine precisely the optimal levels of flavors that people crave—the so-called bliss point. Sweets and fats are no longer scarce in industrialized society, and their easy access and overconsumption contribute to increasing problems of obesity.

Our choice of what we eat is also driven by culture. That some people eat cows and others worms is, for the most part, culturally determined. Different cultures expose children to different flavors. Different cultures expose children to unique flavor combinations or shape food preferences while people are young. For instance, people in very cold climates commonly eat raw animal fat: Icelanders eat raw whale blubber pickled in whey; the Inuit eat raw seal fat. In contrast, cow brains and tongue are commonly eaten in Mexico. Exposure does not immediately lead to preference, however (Pliner, 1982; Rozin, 1996), and genetic factors also pay a role in food preference (Smith et al., 2016). It often takes multiple exposures before children will come to like a food that they initially disliked (Birch & Fisher, 1996; Birch & Marlin, 1982). Breastfed babies can develop preferences or aversions

Connection

Endocannabinoids and their relative, marijuana, are used medically to treat cancer patients who are on chemotherapy, because they stimulate appetite.

See "Hallucinogens," in the chapter "Consciousness." (p. 250)

Challenge Your Assumptions

True or False? Craving sweet, fatty, and salty foods is a socially and culturally determined preference.

False: The fact that we crave basic foodstuffs is very much a product of evolution.

to foods from their mothers, as flavors pass through breastmilk—this is a form of early exposure (Nicklaus, 2016). The more often people eat certain foods, the more they like them. Once people develop a preference for a kind of food, they are motivated and even driven to eat that kind of food. If you develop a strong liking for Mexican food, but then spend a year studying in Europe or Asia, where there is little Mexican food, you will probably be driven to seek out any kind of burrito.

The Motive to Be Thin and the Tendency toward Obesity Fat provides a way of storing energy for future use. In our evolutionary past, this was important in case food became scarce, but in modern, industrialized societies with abundant food, fat is a liability.

Because our lifestyle generally is sedentary compared with earlier times, we need less food to be healthy. Our ideas about beauty have also been transformed as a result of having more food available than we need. Thinness has come to define attractiveness, and being thin has become a cultural obsession. For example, 61% of high school girls in the United States are trying to lose weight (Daee et al., 2002). Among U.S. adults, 73% of women and 55% of men wish to weigh less (Yaemsiri, Slining, & Agarwal, 2011). The obsession with thinness sometimes leads to the development of eating disorders. At the same time, obesity rates have increased dramatically over the last 50 years.

How do we define obesity? Any definition of being overweight must consider both height and weight. Therefore, in evaluating an individual's weight, the U.S. government and medical doctors use body mass index (BMI), which is determined by dividing weight by height squared to yield a weight-to-height ratio (see Figure 7). The ideal BMI is between 19 and 24, with 25 to 29 considered overweight and 30 or above considered obese. According to the Centers for Disease Control and Prevention (CDC), in 2008, more than one-third of adult Americans were obese, one-third were overweight, and less than one-third were of ideal weight (Flegal et al., 2010). Moreover, rates of obesity have climbed rapidly over the last 25 years—from 12% in 1991, to 18% in 1998, to 36% in 2010 (Ogden, Lamb, Carroll, & Flegal, 2010). To be sure, BMI alone is not a complete measure of fitness, because it does not take muscle mass into account. For 18% of people, BMI is misleading (National Health & Nutrition Examination Survey, 2005–2006). For instance, 12% of adults are "healthy overweight"; that is, they are above 25 on BMI (overweight) but have less than 25% body fat. A better all-around index, therefore, takes waist circumference into account as well as BMI. To address these problems, a new measure known as "Body Volume Indicator" (BVI) was introduced in 2017 that not only considers height and weight but more importantly mass distribution around the waist, known as "belly fat." As you may imagine, there is an app for this that uses two photos of the person (from the front and side) and then calculates BVI. This is a more valid index of healthy and unhealthy weight than BMI since belly fat is the most direct predictor of health outcomes.

People who are overweight tend to misperceive their body image as lighter than it really is. In a study of more than 3,500 young Mexican adults (ages 18–20), most of the normal-weight people (79%) accurately perceived their weight as normal by BMI standards. The obese people (BMI ≥ 30), however, greatly underestimated their weight: Only 9.5% accurately classified themselves as obese (Andrade et al., 2012). Similar misperceptions of body image in overweight Canadian children and adolescents have been reported (Maximova et al., 2008).

Weight gain is subject to environmental influence, but biological factors also play a role. Genes appear to be responsible for about 70% of adult weight (Allison et al., 1994; Hamer & Copeland, 1998). One study found that adults who had been adopted as children were much closer in weight to their biological parents than to their adoptive parents (Maes, Neale, & Eaves, 1997). In addition, in some obese people the gene that produces the hormone leptin, which normally suppresses appetite, has suffered a mutation and therefore does not function properly (Hamer &

©Vittorio Zunino Celotto/Getty Images

Actress Jennifer Lawrence is clear about liking her body and not wanting to be hungry to make other people happy: "You look how you look, you have to be comfortable. What are you going to do? Be hungry every single day to make other people happy? That's just dumb."

	Normal						Overweight					Obese									
BMI	**19**	**20**	**21**	**22**	**23**	**24**	**25**	**26**	**27**	**28**	**29**	**30**	**31**	**32**	**33**	**34**	**35**	**36**	**37**	**38**	**39**
Height (inches)																					
58	91	96	100	105	110	115	119	124	129	134	138	143	148	153	158	162	167	172	177	181	186
59	94	99	104	109	114	119	124	128	133	138	143	148	153	158	163	168	173	178	183	188	193
60	97	102	107	112	118	123	128	133	138	143	148	153	158	163	168	174	179	184	189	194	199
61	100	106	111	116	122	127	132	137	143	148	153	158	164	169	174	180	185	190	195	201	206
62	104	109	115	120	126	131	136	142	147	153	158	164	169	175	180	186	191	196	202	207	213
63	107	113	118	124	130	135	141	146	152	158	163	169	175	180	186	191	197	203	208	214	220
64	110	116	122	128	134	140	145	151	157	163	169	174	180	186	192	197	204	209	215	221	227
65	114	120	126	132	138	144	150	156	162	168	174	180	186	192	198	204	210	216	222	228	234
66	118	124	130	136	142	148	155	161	167	173	179	186	192	198	204	210	216	223	229	235	241
67	121	127	134	140	146	153	159	166	172	178	185	191	198	204	211	217	223	230	236	242	249
68	125	131	138	144	151	158	164	171	177	184	190	197	203	210	216	223	230	236	243	249	256
69	128	135	142	149	155	162	169	176	182	189	196	203	209	216	223	230	236	243	250	257	263
70	132	139	146	153	160	167	174	181	188	195	202	209	216	222	229	235	243	250	257	264	271
71	136	143	150	157	165	172	179	186	193	200	208	215	222	229	236	243	250	257	265	272	279
72	140	147	154	162	169	177	184	191	199	206	213	221	228	235	242	250	258	265	272	279	287
73	144	151	159	166	174	182	189	197	204	212	219	227	235	242	250	257	265	272	280	288	295
74	148	155	163	171	179	186	194	202	210	218	225	233	241	249	256	264	272	280	287	295	303
75	152	160	168	176	184	192	200	208	216	224	232	240	248	256	264	272	279	287	295	303	311
76	156	154	172	180	189	197	205	213	221	230	238	246	254	263	271	279	287	295	304	312	320

FIGURE 7

BODY MASS INDEX (BMI).

 Do you consider yourself to be normal, overweight, or obese? BMI provides a good, initial indicator of whether your estimate is on target. To determine your body mass index, find your height in the left column and go across to your body weight. Then, at the top of the chart, locate the BMI for your height and weight. Because BMI does not take muscle mass into account, it is best to also include waist circumference and mass in determining the health risk of one's weight, as is done by a newer measure, Body Volume Indicator.

Copeland, 1998). African Americans are at high risk for obesity, and a number of genes have been identified that play a role in this predisposition (Liu et al., 2016).

Genes also control the number of fat cells a person has, which has been set by childhood and adolescence and does not change much after that (Spalding et al., 2008). Each year about 10% of our fat cells die, but they are replaced by roughly the same number of new ones (Spalding et al., 2008). Dieting does not change this. When people diet, they are not decreasing the number of fats cells they have but rather how much fat each cell stores. Because the number fat cells stays the same regardless of diet, it it hard hard to keep off weight that has been lost.

Common Myths about Dieting: Challenging Assumptions about Diet
There are some widely held beliefs about weight loss that have little or no empirical or scientific support. We review two here. First, the most pervasive and misleading myths involve fats and carbohydrates. The thinking is that low-fat and low-carb diets are good and high-fat and high-carb diets are bad, but it's not that simple (Ebbeling et al., 2007; Howard et al., 2006). There are different kinds of fats and carbohydrates; some are good and healthy, while others are not. Saturated fats, found in red meats, are less healthy and lead to greater weight gain than unsaturated fats, such as those found in avocado or olive oil. Likewise, carbohydrates can be simple or complex, with high-fiber foods being high in complex carbs and sugars being high in simple carbs. A more sound approach to losing weight and having a healthful diet is to aim for a low-glycemic (blood sugar level) diet, defined as approximately 40% carbohydrate, 40% fat, and 20% protein (Ebbeling et al., 2007). A low-fat diet by comparison consists of approximately 20% fat.

In general, it is healthier and easier to lose weight when diets are relatively low glycemic (e.g., fruits, vegetables, grains, and beans), which means avoiding high-glycemic foods, such as white bread, pasta, rice, baked goods, and low-fiber cereals.[1] Low-glycemic foods are digested more slowly than high-glycemic foods and hence a person feels full longer and eats less. Research is clear that high-glycemic diets are risk factors for coronary heart disease and adult-onset diabetes (Dong et al., 2012; Salmerón et al., 1997).

The second idea worth challenging about eating is that having smaller but more frequent meals (say, five or six) a day is one way to lose weight. The scientific evidence for this is mixed at best and seems contradictory (Cameron, Cyr, & Doucet, 2010; Parks & McCrory, 2005). Eating smaller, more frequent meals does not lead to weight loss, but controlling portions while not adding more frequent meals *does* (Rock et al., 2016).

Challenge Your Assumptions

True or False? Eating smaller and more frequent meals can help you lose weight.

False: The evidence suggests that small, frequent meals do not lead to weight loss.

Why Dieting Does Not Work—and What Does   For everyone who has tried to lose weight by dieting, we have bad news for you: Dieting generally does not work—not in the long-term, at least. Traci Mann and colleagues (2007) conducted a meta-analysis of 31 high-quality published studies on long-term weight loss from dieting and reported that diets work only for a minority of the population. People typically lose about 5 to 10 pounds within the first 6 months they start dieting (Mann et al., 2007). Within 2 to 5 years, however, the vast majority has not only gained all of the weight back but also weigh more than when they started dieting.

Even worse, the dieters in the studies would have been better off if they had never dieted at all. Their weight would have been the same, but their bodies would not have gone through the stressful yo-yoing in weight. Losing and regaining weight is associated with heart disease, stroke, diabetes, and altered immune function. The reason for the nearly inevitable regaining of the original weight is due to the fact that metabolism slows down after weight loss. That has been known for a long time. But a more recent study of participants on the hit TV show "The Biggest Loser" pointed to surprising reason why it's often better to not lose lots of weight: years after the weight loss and the person has often regained the weight, the metabolism never speeds back up (Fothergill et al., 2016). This is why it would be better in the long run to never lose the weight—metabolism would be higher and the person's weight would not yo-yo up and down.

Courtesy of Traci Mann

Traci Mann

Health and social scientists have accumulated a fairly clear body of evidence for the kinds of lifestyle changes that are needed for losing weight and keeping it off for more than a year (Centers for Disease Control and Prevention, 2015; Chaput & Tremblay, 2012; Christakis & Fowler, 2009; Culvers, 2010; Murray, 2009):

- Eat slowly—it takes 20 minutes after eating before your brain knows you are full.
- Write down what you eat for at least 1 month.
- Monitor your weight regularly (at least a few times a month).
- Choose low-fat and/or whole-grain foods (a low-glycemic diet) as snacks.
- Eat breakfast every day.
- Follow a healthy and realistic eating pattern—don't set ridiculous goals for yourself.
- Eat what you want but in moderation.
- Stop eating when you feel full.

[1]The glycemic index places foods on a scale from 0 to 100, with 100 being highest in glycemia. Foods in the 70 to 100 range are considered high glycemic; 56 to 69 are considered moderate; and 55 or below are considered low glycemic. If you are interested in seeing the glycemic index score for 100 common foods, go to http://www.health.harvard.edu/newsweek/Glycemic_index_and_glycemic_load_for_100_foods.htm

- Drink lots of water, which, among other things, fills your stomach and decreases a tendency to overeat.
- Ensure at least moderate physical activity each day totaling approximately 30 minutes (could be as short as three 10-minute sessions).
- Get support from your friends and family.
- Get good sleep.

The last two points deserve elaboration. Research confirms the remarkable power of our social groups to affect our overall health and lifestyle habits, including weight loss and weight gain (Christakis & Fowler, 2009). For example, one study reported that only 23% of those who enrolled alone in a weight-loss program kept the weight off 10 months after treatment compared to 66% of those who enrolled with friends and received social support training (Wing & Jeffery, 1999). On average, those who were recruited with friends lost 33% more weight than those who were recruited alone.

Sometimes a support network helps with weight loss—other times it doesn't. A large-scale survey study in Greece showed that the *type* of social support friends offer really matters more than the amount of social support—especially when it comes to keeping weight off (Karfopoulou et al., 2016). Over 400 participants completed questionnaires online about their weight, eating habits, medical history, and the comments of the support network (family, friends, colleagues). They conducted telephone interviews to obtain information about recent eating patterns. The social support questionnaire contained several statements about the kinds of supportive comments people might offer. People who regained right after loss were more likely to receive instructions on how to behave from their supportive friends/family (e.g., "Reminded me to eat healthy or low-fat foods" or "Encouraged me to be more physically active"); whereas people who maintained their weight loss received more compliments (e.g., "Complimented me on my eating habits") or active involvement from friends with their goals ("Offered to participate in physical activity with me") (Karfopoulou et al., 2016).

We create our real-world social networks as a function of what we are hoping to get and who we like being around. A study of over 7,000 people in a national poll reveals the complex showed that when motivated to lose weight, people tend to prefer to be around other people who are heavier and motivated to lose. In terms of what predicts actual weight loss, however, the more the person trying to lose is connected with thinner people, the more likely they were to lose weight (Andersson & Christakis, 2016).

Most people understand that physical exercise is not only important for weight loss, but for maintenance of weight loss as well. According to a survey study of over 1,000 African American women—a group at high risk for obesity—whether they exercised a lot or not, being *sedentary* (just generally not active, sitting much of the day) was negatively correlated with maintaining weight and positively correlated with BMI (Taylor et al., 2015).

Another surprising finding on weight loss concerns its connection with adequate sleep. People who do not get enough sleep have more trouble losing weight than those who get adequate sleep (Chaput & Tremblay, 2012; Chaput, Després, & Tremblay, 2007). There are two reasons for this. First, sleep deprivation seems to change brain signals, making food more appealing (and hence the person eats more). Second, sleep deprivation decreases the activity of the appetite-suppressing hormone leptin, leading to a sense of never being full. This is yet another reason to get a good night's sleep!

Eating Disorders   Some people develop such concern about their bodies and how much they weigh that they develop an eating disorder. Although we discuss psychological disorders more fully in the chapter "Psychological Disorders," we briefly introduce the concept here. For any behavior to be disordered, it must be dysfunctional, disturbing, distressing, and deviant (American Psychiatric Association, 2013). Dysfunction is interference with everyday functioning, as well as disruption of one's personal and professional life. *Disturbing* and *distressing* imply that the behavior is not wanted and causes stress for either the person suffering from it or the individual's family, friends, and social contacts. *Deviant* implies that these are not common, everyday behaviors but relatively rare in the population.

Eating disorders meet the criteria for a psychological disorder. The two primary types of eating disorders are anorexia nervosa and bulimia nervosa. **Anorexia nervosa** involves an extreme fear about being overweight that leads to a severe restriction of food intake (American Psychiatric Association, 2013). This caloric restriction typically does not allow a person to maintain at least 85% of the low end of his or her ideal weight—that is, a BMI about 16 or less. At its core, anorexia involves an extremely distorted body image, with the person believing he or she is too heavy regardless of how thin he or she really is. BMIs in the range of 15 or less can lead to death, and about 4% of those who suffer from anorexia will die from the disorder (Crow et al., 2009).

The second well-known eating disorder is bulimia nervosa. A person suffering from **bulimia nervosa** is prone to binge eating and feeling a lack of control during the eating session. Binge eating involves eating much more food at one time than the average person would, such as having a half gallon of ice cream as a late-night snack. A person with bulimia regularly engages in self-induced vomiting, the use of laxatives or diuretics, strict dieting or fasting, or vigorous exercise in order to prevent weight gain.

The causes of anorexia and bulimia are unknown, although a number of factors appear to put people at risk for this disorder, such as reactivity to stress, genetics, epigenetics, social pressure, and personality. In short, they result from both nature and nurture. Women are much more likely than men to develop

anorexia nervosa
An eating disorder in which people cannot maintain 85% of their ideal body weight for their height, have an intense fear of eating, and have a distorted body image.

bulimia nervosa
An eating disorder characterized by binge eating and a perceived lack of control during the eating session.

©Martin Grimes/Newsom (first): ©Dfree/Shutterstock.com; (second): ©Joe Seer/Shutterstock.com (third)

The ups and downs of anorexia nervosa: celebrity Nicole Richie has struggled with anorexia for years. These three panels illustrate the yoyo effect of living with anorexia.

anorexia or bulimia (Nolen-Hoeksema, 2007). Women with eating disorders show higher physiological reactivity to stress.

A growing body of literature has examined the genetic and epigenetic basis of eating disorders (Bulik et al., 2016; Thornton et al., 2016). For example, according to a review of many twin and twin-adoption studies, genes explain about 60% of the variance in eating disorders. Moreover, people who had demonstrated a proneness to anxiety, depression, and low self-esteem (as measured by the trait of neuroticism) later were more likely to develop anorexia. In fact, as a group people (Taylor et al., 2016). Anorexics are also more conscientious, more introverted, and less open to new situations than are non-anorexics (Bollen & Wojciechowski, 2004). Questionnaire studies suggest that both men and women with eating disorders seek approval from others and are more likely to have insecure attachments to their caregivers (Abbate-Daga et al., 2010). They are also more likely to have attentional deficits and hyperactivity (Brewerton & Duncan, 2016).

A number of factors play a role in whether one develops an eating disorders. The social setting and behavior of peers plays a key role. Binge eating spread in social groups—especially sororities (Crandall, 1988; Cruwys et al., 2016). Girls and women are more likely to develop eating disorders (American Psychiatric Association, 2013), especially European American middle to upper class girls, though this is changing. More and more young men are at risk than ever before (Vo, Lau, & Rubinstein, 2016), and it is becoming more common in African American, Asian American, and Latina girls. Hispanic women are much less likely than White women to develop anorexia, but they are about equally likely to be bulimic (Perez, Ohrt, & Hoek, 2016). Girls who attend schools with a high percentage of female students and who have college-educated parents are also more susceptible (Bould et al., 2016). It has been shown numerous times, often in very large-scale studies, that young women who are high achievers in school are at high risk for disordered eating (Sunquist et al., 2016). Perhaps the risk factor of having a college-educated parent may help explain why high-achieving young women have a higher risk for disordered eating.

Sex: Survival of the Species

Without food, we would starve to death. Without sex, individuals would not die, but, if everyone went without sex, our species would die. At the species level, we have sex to propagate the species. As individuals, we have sex because it is enjoyable.

Human Sexual Response   Like many basic questions, "What is sex?" is more complex than it would appear. We define **sexual behavior** as actions that produce arousal and increase the likelihood of orgasm.

Masters and Johnson (1966) were the first scientists to study the human sexual response systematically and directly. One of their major findings was that men and women go through four phases of sexual arousal—excitement, plateau, orgasm, and resolution—but they do so somewhat differently (see Figure 8). The major signs of the initial excitement phase are vaginal lubrication in females and erection in males. In the plateau phase, the excitement level remains high but is pre-orgasmic. In men, the plateau phase might be rather short, but orgasm almost always follows. In women, the plateau phase often lasts longer than in men but is not necessarily followed by orgasm. Some women stay in the plateau phase for a while, then pass to the resolution phase without achieving orgasm. These women also have a gradual resolution phase. An even more striking gender difference is the ability of women to have multiple orgasms. Men always have a refractory period immediately following orgasm in which erection is lost and orgasm is not possible.

Updated models of female sexual arousal suggest that the initial sexual response in women involves more psychological processes than simply desire and arousal (Basson, 2000). Desire and arousal do not happen spontaneously in many women, who often require the right balance of thoughts and feelings dealing with

sexual behavior
Actions that produce arousal and increase the likelihood of orgasm.

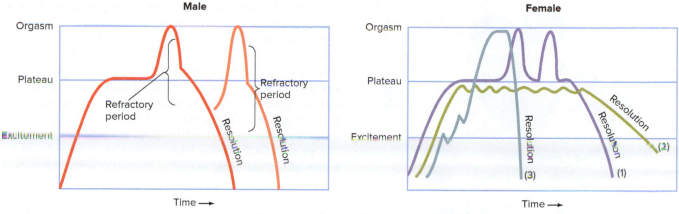

FIGURE 8

THE SEXUAL RESPONSE CYCLE IN MEN AND WOMEN. The four phases are excitement, plateau, orgasm, and resolution. Women are more varied in their sexual response than men. There are at least three distinct types of response in women. In (1), we see a response pattern much like men's, except that there is a possibility of multiple orgasm. In (2), we see a woman who gets aroused and stays at the plateau level, never reaching orgasm. In (3), we see a pattern in which the woman gets aroused and excited, skips the plateau phase, and has a quick resolution phase. In men, there is only one pattern, though a second orgasm can occur after a refractory period (Passer & Smith, 1998).

intimacy, closeness, trust, and lack of fear and anxiety. These thoughts and feelings play off and feed arousal, which in turn leads to deeper feelings of intimacy and closeness. Arousal continues to increase and may or may not lead to orgasm, but arousal and excitement are important and meaningful even without orgasm (Basson, 2000).

The Biology of Sexual Behavior This newer model of sexual response matches well with brain imaging research on sexual arousal and orgasm. Many of the brain regions involved in emotion, which we will discuss shortly, are also involved in the stages of sexual arousal prior to orgasm. As is true of many physiological drives, such as hunger, the hypothalamus plays a crucial role in sexual behavior (Dominguez & Hull, 2005; Hines, 2010). In humans, lesions in the back portion of the hypothalamus lead to a decrease in sexual behavior, whereas electrical stimulation of the same region leads to an increase in sexual behavior, especially in males (Dominguez & Hull, 2005). In addition, the part of the hypothalamus involved in sexual behavior is larger in men than in women (Allen & Gorski, 2007).

When experiencing an orgasm many brain regions are involved, such as the somatosensory cortex, nucleus accumbens, limbic system, cerebellum, hypothalamus, and prefrontal cortex (Komisaruk & Whipple, 2005). Although women's orgasms last a little longer than men's (20 versus 10 seconds), brain activation is very similar in women and men during orgasm (Poeppl, Langguth, Rupprecht, Safton et al., 2016; Stoléru et al., 2012). Paradoxically, orgasm actually requires certain brain regions—those involved with fear—to shut down. Gert Holstege and colleagues from the Netherlands took brain images of women while they were having an orgasm (being manually stimulated by their partners) and while they were faking it (Georgiadis et al., 2006). Achieving a real orgasm always involved deactivation of the brain regions associated with fear and anxiety in the amygdala and hippocampus, as well as parts of the cortex involved in consciousness. During faked orgasms, however, these brain regions remained activated. For men, brain deactivation occurred only in the left amygdala during orgasm (Holstege et al., 2003). One brain difference between men and women may help explain why women but not men can experience multiple orgasms. Immediately after orgasm certain brain regions in men become unresponsive to further stimulation but not so in women (Komisaruk & Whipple, 2005; Mallick et al., 2007; Stoléru et al., 2012).

©wavebreakmedia/Shutterstock.com

Testosterone, the primary male sex hormone, also controls women's sex drive.

Testosterone, the major male sex hormone, controls sex drive in both men and women (Morris et al., 1987; Persky et al., 1978; Regan, 2016). The role of testosterone in the female sex drive was discovered accidentally when women whose adrenal glands had been removed lost their sex drive (Waxenberg, Drellich, & Sutherland, 1959). The adrenal glands produce testosterone. Moreover, younger women have both higher levels of male sex hormones and more frequent sexual activity than do older women (Persky et al., 1982). Males and females with high baseline levels of testosterone are more sexually active at earlier ages and engage in sex more frequently than those with low baseline levels of testosterone. It's not surprising that testosterone treatments increase sex drive in both men and women (Bolour & Braunstein, 2005).

In most species, females are not continually receptive to males. In women, there also is some regular cyclical activity and sexual desire in the course of their 28-day menstrual cycle. Sex drive in women is strongest around ovulation and again before and after menstruation (Bullivant et al., 2004; Elaut et al., 2016; Udry, Morris, & Waller, 1973). The strongest cyclical effect for women, however, occurs in relation to their fantasies involving men other than their regular sex partner (Buss, 2003), which increases in frequency and intensity as women approach ovulation (Bullivant et al., 2004). Such an increase in sex drive makes sense from an evolutionary and biological perspective, because a woman is most likely to become pregnant during ovulation. This is a case in which biological motives drive behavior.

Culture and Sexual Behavior   What is acceptable and normal sexual behavior varies from culture to culture. Perspectives on this basic human experience are many and varied. In a classic study of sexual behavior and culture, Clellan Ford and Frank Beach (1951) studied attitudes toward sex before and after marriage in 190 cultures. They identified three kinds of societies in terms of sexual attitudes. First, restrictive societies restrict sex before and outside of marriage. Second, semirestrictive societies place formal prohibitions on pre- and extramarital sex that are not strictly enforce. Third, permissive societies place few restrictions on sex. Thirty years later, Broude and Greene (1980) conducted a similar study of 141 non-Western cultures and found that, for women, premarital sex was mildly to moderately disapproved of in 30% of the societies and strongly disapproved of in 26%. Extramarital sex was common among men in 69% of the cultures and among women in 57% of the cultures.

Gender and the Drive for Casual Sex   The belief that men are more promiscuous than women is widespread, but is it true? In a word, yes. Research consistently shows that men are more willing to engage in and are more interested in casual sex (see, for example, Bailey et al., 2000; Buss, 2003; Clark & Hatfield, 1989; Maticka-Tyndale, Harold, & Opperman, 2003; Schmitt, 2003; Townsend et al., 2015). For instance, in a meta-analysis of 177 studies of gender and sexual attitudes and behavior published between 1966 and 1990, Oliver and Hyde (1993) reported that men, on average, have much more positive attitudes toward casual sex and are slightly more likely to approve of premarital or extramarital sex. A follow-up meta-analysis of research published between 1993 and 2007 found similar but somewhat smaller gender differences in casual sex (Petersen & Hyde, 2010). Similarly, Schmitt (2003) collected data from more than 16,000 men and women in 52 nations and 6 continents and found universal support for men preferring more variety and greater number of sexual partners than women in both the short-term and long-term. The result of men compared to women having more variety of sexual partners seems to hold in the elderly as well (Waite et al., 2009).

Russell Clark III and Elaine Hatfield (1989, 2003) conducted a classic study on the question of gender differences and casual sex. Research assistants approached strangers of the opposite sex and asked them whether they would be willing to go on a date, come over to their place, or go to bed with them. As you can see in the "Research Process" for this chapter (Figure 9), the results were striking. Three-quarters of the men said they were willing to have sex with a stranger of the opposite sex, but not one woman was willing to do so!

Parental investment theory offers an explanation for the gender difference in attitude toward casual sex. If pregnancy results, the cost of having sex is quite different for men and women (Trivers, 1972). Biologically, the only assured contribution from men to parenthood is the act of sex itself. If a woman becomes pregnant, however, her contribution includes 9 months of carrying the fetus, a good portion of which might involve pregnancy sickness; the painful labor and delivery; and approximately 18 years of caring for the child. Therefore, women would be less motivated to have sex with little emotional commitment—a single sexual encounter could have consequences that endure a lifetime.

Sexual Orientation   Historically, sexual orientation was thought of as an either-or proposition: A person was either heterosexual or homosexual. In the 1940s, however, Alfred Kinsey proposed a radically new view of sexual orientation: It exists on a continuum from exclusively heterosexual to exclusively homosexual (Kinsey, Pomeroy, & Martin, 1948). After interviewing thousands of individuals, Kinsey and his colleagues realized that sexual orientation was not either-or. So they devised a 7-point scale from 0 to 6, with 0 being exclusively heterosexual. Current research generally supports this continuum of sexual orientation (Bailey et al., 2016; Chandra et al., 2011; Savin-Williams & Vrangalova, 2013). For example, there is growing evidence for people who identify as "mostly heterosexual," or who have a strong but not exclusive leaning toward opposite sex partners (Chandra et al., 2011; Savin-Williams & Vrangalova, 2013).

Approximately 90% of U.S. men and women identify as exclusively heterosexual (Chandra et al., 2011). Between 1% and 5% of the adult male population and 1% and 3.5% of the adult female population classify themselves as predominantly homosexual (Bailey et al., 2016; Chandra et al., 2011; Tarmann, 2002). For men, sexual orientation tends to be either-or, producing a dip between 2 and 4 on Kinsey's 7-point scale (the bisexual range). For women, however, there is a more gradual decrease from exclusively heterosexual to exclusively homosexual, with more women identifying themselves as mostly heterosexual or bisexual (Chandra et al., 2009; Diamond, 2008; Hamer & Copeland, 1998; Rahman, 2005; Savin-Williams & Vrangalova, 2013).

Recall from our discussion in "Human Development" that sexual orientation and gender identity are unrelated. Sexual orientation involves who we are attracted to, whereas gender identity involves who we identify as. Most people identify with the sex they have at birth (cis-gendered), but some identify with the opposite sex (transgendered), and there are variations in between these ends of the spectrum (Bailey et al., 2016). We discuss gender identity in more detail in the chapter "Human Development".

What causes a person to be sexually attracted to someone of the opposite sex or the same sex? The age-old nature-nurture question inevitably arises: Is sexual orientation more a result of biology or of upbringing and environment? As usual, forces of nature and nurture are involved in sexual orientation, and in complex ways (Bailey, Dunne, & Martin, 2000).

The biological foundation of sexual orientation can be seen from four sources: animal observations, hormonal influences in the womb, neuroscience, and genetics. First, naturalistic observations of animals suggest that same-sex pairings may be much more common than previously thought. Same-sex sexual

Challenge Your Assumptions

True or False? Women are just as likely as men to engage in casual sex. False: Women are, in fact, less willing to engage in casual sex with a stranger than are men. Can you think of reasons that might be?

sexual orientation
Sexual orientation refers to a person's inherent romantic, emotional and sexual attraction to other people—whether same sex, opposite sex, or both.

Challenge Your Assumptions

True or False? Many species of animals engage in homosexual behavior. True: Homosexual behavior in animals is more common than previously believed.

Research Process

① Research Question

Are there differences between men and women in their interest in casual sex? The researchers hypothesized that men are more eager for casual sex than are women.

② Method

Clark and Hatfield (1989) developed a brief survey to address the research question. Research assistants who were college students approached students of the opposite sex. After a brief introduction, the research assistant would ask each student one of these questions: "Would you go out with me tonight?" "Would you come over to my apartment tonight?" or "Would you go to bed with me tonight?"

FIGURE 9
GENDER AND CASUAL SEX. A simple survey revealed gender differences in the interest in casual sex.

©Roberto Westbrook/Getty Images RF

③ Results

This table gives responses to the various questions, by gender.

④ Conclusion

Men and women were equally likely to agree to go on a date with someone they didn't really know. As the proposal became increasingly intimate, however, women backed off. Consistent with the hypothesis, men were much more likely than women to agree to have sex. This finding would be predicted by parental investment theory, which states that the cost of having sex is quite different for men and women.

Percentage saying "yes"

Question	Men	Women
"Would you go out with me tonight?"	56%	50%
"Would you come over to my apartment tonight?"	69%	6%
"Would you go to bed with me tonight?"	75%	0%

©C Squared Studios/Getty Images RF

Source: "Gender Differences in Willingness to Engage in Casual Sex," by R. D. Clark III and E. Hatfield, 1989, *Journal of Psychology and Human Sexuality, 2,* 39–55.

 Do more men or women agree to casual sex with an opposite-sex stranger? Why do you think that is the case?

behavior is seen in numerous species, including beetles, penguins, and snakes (Bailey & Zuk, 2009). In the Laysan albatross, for example, more than 30% of parental couples are all female, which care for eggs and raise young together (Young, Zaun, & VanderWerf, 2008).

Second, research has uncovered brain structure and brain activation differences associated with sexual preference and sexual orientation (Witelson et al., 2008; Poeppl, Langguth, Rupprech, Laird, & Eickhoff, 2016). The hypothalamus also seems to be involved in sexual orientation, which is not surprising, given its key role in sexual behavior (Hines, 2010). Because he knew from previous research that men had larger hypothalami than women, Simon LeVay (1991) decided see whether this structure was also different in gay and straight men. He found that the hypothalamus was substantially smaller in gay men than in straight men—about the size of women's. Because this was a correlational study, however, we cannot know whether the small size of this brain region causes homosexuality or whether homosexual behavior shapes this region of the brain.

Finally, genetic research suggests that sexual orientation is partly under genetic influence, at least in men. Studies of twins indicate that genetics plays a bigger role in determining sexual orientation in men than in women. For women, environmental factors seem to have a strong influence on sexual orientation. Female twins raised in the same household are much more likely to have the same sexual orientation than are female twins raised in different households, regardless of whether they are identical or fraternal twins. For males, the degree of genetic relationship seems to matter most in twin sexual orientation (Bailey et al., 2000; Demir & Dickson, 2005; Hamer & Copeland, 1998; Hyde, 2005; Rahman, 2005). Recently, some biologists have argued that epigenetic influences during fetal development, more than genetic influences, play a role in the development of sexual orientation (Rice, Friberg, & Gavrilets, 2012). Genes being turned off by epigenetic markers may be affecting the development of sexual orientation.

At the interface between biological and environmental explanations involved in sexual orientation are epigenetic influences. There is evidence that our first biological environment—the womb—exerts a long-term effect on our sexual orientation. Recall that epigenetic effects are from events that occur after conception and that change gene expression. One of these epigenetic effects can be exposure to sex hormones in utero, such as high levels of testosterone exposure to female fetuses or low levels of testosterone to male fetuses. Research suggests that females exposed to high levels of testosterone in utero and who therefore have congenital adrenal hyperplasia (CAH) are more likely to develop non-heterosexual orientation compared to female fetuses exposed to lower levels of testosterone (Hines, 2010; Meyer-Bahlburg et al., 2008; Ngun & Vilain, 2014). Another example of prenatal hormone exposure comes from the finding that the odds of homosexual orientation in males increase with each male pregnancy of the mother (Blanchard, 2004; Ngun & Vilain, 2014). This is known as the fraternal birth order effect. The explanation seems to be that with each male birth, there is less androgen (testosterone) exposure to the male fetus and this affects development of sexual orientation (Cohen, 2002; Ellis & Ames, 1987; Hines, 2010; Rahman, 2005).

Social-environmental theories of sexual orientation in general tend point to the importance of social experiences in shaping sexual orientation. Some of the social influences on the development of sexual orientation include early peer

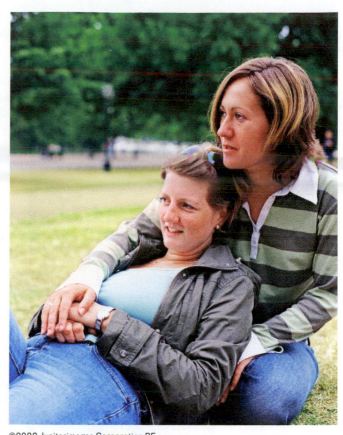

©2009 Jupiterimages Corporation RF

Sexual orientation is influenced by both nature and nurture.

©blue jean images/Getty Images RF

relations, gender atypical play, and differences in how parents treat boys and girls (Bailey et al., 2016).

Many studies report that engaging in play more typical of the opposite sex early in childhood predicts a homosexual orientation later in life, in both men and women (Bailey & Zucker, 1995; Bailey et al., 2016; Cohen, 2002; Rieger et al., 2008; Steensma et al., 2013). It is important to point out, however, that these are just correlations and not causal relationships, meaning being gender atypical in childhood does not make homosexual orientation in adulthood inevitable—it just increases the odds.

Another suggestion that social factors can affect sexual orientation is its changeability or fluidity over time. A general finding here is that women's sexual orientation is more likely to change than men's (Bailey et al., 2016; Diamond, 2003, 2008; Kinnish, Strassberg, & Turner, 2005; Manley et al., 2015). Sexual fluidity is also seen in heterosexual men in prison who engage in homosexual behavior (Gibson & Hensley, 2013). Given this changeability, some researchers argue that sexual orientation is a construction of society (Asthana & Oostvogels, 2001; Chaline, 2010; Dube & Kamath, 2013).

Culture also plays a big role in the attitudes and acceptance of homosexual behavior. Ten years ago it was almost unimaginable that gay marriage would be the law of the land in the United States and in many other countries. Especially since the Supreme Court ruling in 2015 that same-sex marriage was legal, attitudes toward same-sex marriage have changed drastically. As recently as 2010, the majority of Americans were opposed to same-sex marriage (McCarthy, 2016). According to a Gallop poll in May of 2016, 61% of American adults believed same-sex marriage should be recognized by law (37% were opposed). For 18- to 29-year-olds, by 2016, 83% said same-sex marriage is okay, up 42% since 1996. Interestingly, older Americans' attitudes are also changing with a 39% increase in acceptance by people 65 years old and older (up from 14% to 53% from 1996 to 2016) (McCarthy, 2016). Recent evidence suggest that social media such as Facebook may be playing a role in increasing empathy for and positive attitudes toward same-sex marriage and transgender identity (Manjoo, 2016). Yet the world over, homosexual behavior is not universally accepted—in fact, is still punishable by death in some countries (Bailey et al., 2016).

In sum, biology could start the development of sexual orientation, which in turn would be strengthened or discouraged by environmental factors. The two sets of explanations work best in cooperation.

The Needs to Belong (Affiliation) and to Excel

As we saw in Maslow's hierarchy of needs, human needs extend beyond the physiological needs of hunger and sex. The need for social contact and belonging—what psychologists call affiliation—and the need to excel and compete with others—what psychologists call achievement—are universal.

The Need to Belong: Affiliation   As we discuss in more detail in the chapter "Social Behavior," humans are inherently social and affiliative creatures. Just think about how important it has been throughout your life—elementary school, middle school, high school, and now college—to have friends and to be accepted, even before there were Facebook friends and Instagram and Twitter followers. We depend on other people our entire lives, especially at life's beginning and end. It is

©David Malan/Getty Images RF

What does your social network look like?

not surprising, therefore, that our need to belong and to be accepted by others is one of the strongest of all human needs (Adler, 1956; Baumeister & Leary, 1995; Murray, 1938/1962). Particular parts of our brains are dedicated to and are activated uniquely by affiliation needs (DeWall et al., 2012; Eisenberger et al., 2003; Quirin et al., 2013). Further, some psychologists argue that one's self-esteem, or sense of worth, is directly a function of being accepted or rejected by other people (Leary, 2007). Being accepted by others increases our self-esteem, whereas being rejected lowers it.

No doubt one reason that social networks sites became instantly popular the world over was they tapped in to our need to connect and to belong (Lee & Chiou, 2013). If social networks are forms of belonging and connection, and belonging increases self-esteem, then it stands to reason that the use of social network sites (SNSs), such as Facebook, can increase self-esteem and well-being—and it does (Kim & Lee, 2011; Nadkarni & Hofmann, 2012; Yu et al., 2010). Research also reveals that SNS use is associated with number of friends (both in person and online), a need to be liked by many people (popularity), extraversion, and a lack of social loneliness (Nadkarni & Hofmann, 2012; Ryan & Xenos, 2011; Utz, Tanis, & Vermeulen, 2012).

The opposite of being accepted is being rejected, which can be one of the more painful experiences in life. A lack of belongingness leads to both physical and psychological problems, ranging from having more health problems to being more likely to commit suicide (Baumeister & Leary, 1995; Nadkarni & Hofmann, 2012). Moreover, being rejected or being bullied makes people more prone to anger and aggression toward others (Leary, Twenge, & Quinlivan, 2006). Many explosive, violent episodes are preceded by a person's being fired from work or being rejected by peers, a lover, or a spouse (Williams & Zudro, 2001). For example, many of the high-profile school shootings over the last 12 years, such as Columbine, Virginia Tech, and Sandy Hook, were carried out by boys and men who were teased, bullied, or rejected by their peers (Leary et al., 2003).

The Need to Excel: Achievement   Some people, such as successful athletes, businesspeople, and politicians, have a tremendous need to excel and to be the best at what they do, but in truth, almost everyone strives to overcome shortcomings and imperfections (Adler, 1956). In the process, some people compete fiercely with other people, whereas others compete more with themselves.

Courtesy of Jerry Feist

One of your authors (Greg)—inspired by his 15-year-old son Jerry's desire to climb a mountain—at the 14,179-foot peak of Mt. Shasta in July 2013. After waking up at 12:45 a.m. and leaving base camp at 9,900 feet at 2:15 a.m., Greg and Jerry reached the peak by 9:45 a.m. Drive, motivation, and perseverance, in addition to training and preparation (and good luck with weather), are a must in order to pull off such a physical and mental challenge.

achievement motivation
A desire to do things well and overcome obstacles.

The motivation to succeed raises the question of how to define achievement. David McClelland and his colleague John Atkinson emphasized that **achievement motivation** is a desire to do things well and overcome difficulties and obstacles (McClelland, 1985). However, those obstacles can be measured only in terms of one's goals. When David Feist (whom you met in the chapter "Consciousness") was coming out of his vegetative state following his bicycle accident, lifting a finger was a tremendous achievement, yet for a highly driven, accomplished, and motivated athlete, a silver medal at the Olympics might be a crushing defeat.

Atkinson (1964) argued that the tendency to achieve success is a function of three things: motivation to succeed, the expectation of success, and the incentive value of the success (see also McClelland, 1985). Let's apply Atkinson's model to your motivation to obtain a good grade in this introductory psychology course. Your *motivation to succeed* is the extent to which you want to be successful, which differs for everyone. For some students, an *A—* might be disappointing, whereas for others, a *B+* might be a great accomplishment.

Expectation of success is an individual's evaluation of the likelihood of succeeding at a task. Your evaluation of your performance in this course consists of two beliefs: whether you have the ability to do well and what the actual outcome is likely to be. These two beliefs may not match. For instance, some students may see themselves as quite capable of doing well, but because of some missed classes, they may not obtain a high grade for the course.

Incentive value stems from two factors. First, success at the task has to be important to you. Second, the more difficult the task and the lower the odds of succeeding at it, the more meaningful and satisfying it'll be if you do succeed. The incentive value for doing well in introductory psychology differs, depending on what a good grade in the course means to you. If you are a psychology major and if your GPA plays an important role in your class standing or your scholarship, then your introductory psychology grade might have a higher incentive value than it would if you were a physics major taking the course to satisfy a general education requirement. Succeeding at something that is considered very difficult means more to most people than succeeding at something they consider easy, but the degree of difficulty may not provide much useful feedback about abilities.

Motivation in the Workplace

What keeps someone motivated to do well in a job? Industrial/organizational (I/O) psychologists study motivation and behavior in work contexts (Aamodt, 2010). Consider an I/O question very important to businesses: What motivates employees to work at their best?

Three Models of Employee Motivation   What would you prefer most in your job—money or interesting, enjoyable work? The most sensible answer is probably "both." In fact, "interesting work," "good wages," and "job security" have been the top priorities among employees in surveys from the 1940s onward (Wiley, 1997).

From a behavioral perspective, the bottom line for business is productivity. Historically, many businesses and companies have operated using principles of operant conditioning to motivate workers to perform well—that is, good behavior is rewarded by pay increases, promotions, and incentives. More recently, however, some companies have questioned whether money and reward are really the best motivators and instead have emphasized supportive and pleasant work environments, autonomy, enjoyment, and challenge in their workers. There are at least three competing models of how to best motivate workers and make them more productive:

- Extrinsic motivation
- Intrinsic motivation
- Organizational support for the well-being of employees

Extrinsic Motivation   Some models, influenced by Skinner's discoveries of the power of reinforcement to shape behavior, argue that reward, money, and feedback are all important as powerful shapers of workplace behavior (Aamodt, 2010; Eisenberger & Cameron, 1996). Known as **extrinsic motivation**, this motivation comes from outside the person and usually involves rewards and praise. Extrinsic motivators are used to get people to do things they themselves wouldn't normally do or perhaps don't like doing, as when children get an allowance for cleaning their rooms and doing the dishes.

Psychological research offers much support for the power of reward and extrinsic motivation on behavior (Bandura, 1997; Eisenberger, Rhoades, & Cameron, 1999; Gneezy, Meier, & Rey-Biel, 2011; Harackiewicz & Sansone, 1991; Skinner, 1971). Reward not only can increase a particular behavior but also can increase performance and feelings of competency. When rewards are connected directly to performance, workers will be more motivated to do a job well than when they simply receive positive feedback without a reward (Harackiewicz & Sansone, 1991).

However, extrinsic motivation has its drawbacks (D'Ausilio, 2008; Gneezy et al., 2011); it requires the reward to be constant. If the reward goes away, the motivation to continue goes away and the worker stops doing the rewarded behavior. Similarly, if the reward stays the same and doesn't increase, motivation will drop. The bar must constantly be raised, and pay must continue increasing. In addition, reward has a way of narrowing focus, so it works for simple tasks, but narrow focus hinders creative thinking and the expanded focus required to solve difficult problems. Finally, reward can sometimes remove a person's own desire to perform a task out of pure enjoyment. If people perceive that they are being controlled by others, then their own intrinsic interest in doing the task dwindles, because reward and evaluation by other people undercut one's own pleasure in doing a task. For example, if you enjoyed reading in middle school and then your parents started paying you for every 25 pages you read, you might start reading for money rather than for pleasure. In this case, your intrinsic enjoyment of reading would have been destroyed by external reward.

Intrinsic Motivation   The rock musician Tom Petty recently summed up the second model of work motivation very well: "I think any time you're making a living at what you love to do, you're blessed. That's what I try to instill in my kids. Go after what you really love and find a way to make that work for you, and then you'll be a happy person" (Fong-Torres, 2010). **Intrinsic motivation** happens when you want to do something simply because you enjoy doing it. This type of motivation has four components (Amabile & Khaire, 2008; Amabile et al., 1994; Deci & Ryan, 1985; Miao, Lund, & Evan et al., 2009):

- *Challenge*: How much do you enjoy the thrill and excitement of new challenges?
- *Enjoyment*: How much pleasure do you receive from the process of doing the task?
- *Mastery*: Do you gain a sense of accomplishment and pride in doing a difficult task?

extrinsic motivation
Motivation that comes from outside the person and usually involves rewards and praises.

intrinsic motivation
Motivation that comes from within a person and includes the elements of challenge, enjoyment, mastery, and autonomy.

Extrinsic
motivation

Intrinsic
motivation

Perceived support by supervisors
and organizations

a: ©Brand X Pictures/PunchStock RF; b: ©Image
Source c: ©Jacobs Stock Photography/Jupiterimages RF

 **What kind of motivation do you think
is most effective in the workplace:
extrinsic or intrinsic? Explain.**

perceived organizational support
Employees' beliefs about how much
the organization appreciates and
supports their contributions and
well-being.

- *Autonomy and self-determination*: Do you believe that you are free to determine much of what you do and how you do it?

Teresa Amabile and her colleagues argue that intrinsic motivators help employees work creatively and productively (Amabile & Khaire, 2008; Amabile & Kramer, 2007). They present evidence that the companies that most successfully motivate their employees and inspire their creativity are those that

- don't have executives who think they are the only source of good ideas but rather elicit and champion ideas from anyone in the company, as long as they are good, creative ideas;

- open the organization to a diverse number of perspectives, based on ethnicity, gender, age, and experience;

- have managers or executives who know when to put controls on the creative process (commercialization phase) and when not to (idea generation phase); and

- create positive emotions in workers, such as satisfaction, pride, and elation, because positive emotion is likely to make workers more creative, productive, and committed to the company.

Intrinsic motivation changes as life circumstances change. We see this with the various components of intrinsic motivation (Miao et al., 2009). For example, the need for challenge rises for employees in their 20s to 30s but then drops as they move toward late middle age and the end of their careers. However, enjoyment, which is the emotional component of intrinsic motivation, drops only a little over the course of one's career. Environmental factors such as career stage interact with biological causes to shape motivation, however. A large area of research is devoted to understanding the neural mechanisms of reward and the role they play in motivating behavior (Hidi, 2016).

Perceived Support by Supervisors and Organizations How much employees believe that the organization appreciates and supports their contributions and well-being, known as **perceived organizational support**, plays a big role in keeping them motivated and committed to working at that company (Allen, Shore, & Griffeth, 2003; Eisenberger et al., 2002; Kottke & Sharafinski, 1988; Shore & Wayne, 1993; Yoon & Thye, 2000). Few things can be more deflating than working hard at something and then having it taken for granted or not appreciated by the people whose opinions matter most to you. Eder and R. Eisenberger (2008) reported research that supports the idea that, when employees work at companies that care about their well-being, they are happier at their jobs, experience less stress, and are more motivated to stay at their jobs. In addition, they are less likely to miss workdays, be late for work, or take long lunch breaks.

In another study, Allen, Shore, and Griffeth (2003) predicted that perceived organizational support would be positively related to both how committed employees were to their company and how satisfied with their jobs they would be. Two samples were studied: first, 264 salespeople at a large department store in

FIGURE 10
MODEL LINKING ORGANIZATIONAL SUPPORT TO COMMITMENT TO STAY WITH A COMPANY.

Source: Adapted from D. G. Allen et al., 2003

the southeastern United States and, second, 442 insurance agents at a large national insurance company. Allen and colleagues found that perceptions of fairness and opportunity affect perceptions of organizational support, which affect the likelihood of commitment to a company (see Figure 10).

Quick Quiz 1: Motivation

1. Which model of motivation can be compared to the thermostat in your house?
   a. evolutionary
   b. drive-reduction
   c. optimal arousal
   d. hierarchical

2. In addition to blood sugar (glucose) and the hypothalamus, and as discussed in this chapter, what is another important biological system involved in regulating hunger?
   a. adrenaline
   b. the liver
   c. hormones
   d. protein

3. Most research on weight loss has reported that
   a. losing weight is very difficult for most people.
   b. losing weight is relatively easy initially, but keeping it off is very difficult.
   c. keeping weight off is relatively easy for most people.
   d. losing weight is relatively easy and so is keeping it off.

4. Which of the following statements is FALSE?
   a. Testosterone is both a cause and an effect of sexual behavior.
   b. Testosterone is associated with sex drive in both men and women.
   c. Testosterone is associated with sex drive in men only.
   d. Men and women have different sexual response cycles.

Answers can be found at the end of the chapter.

EMOTION

Emotions are also powerful motivators of human behavior, though they differ from basic drives, such as hunger, thirst, and sex, in several ways. First, drives are linked to very specific needs or triggers, whereas emotions are not (Tomkins, 1962, 1981). Hunger comes from a need for food, thirst from a need for water, physical desire from a need for sex. Happiness, in contrast, occurs in response to an infinite variety of triggers, such as smelling a rose, visiting a friend, reading a good story, or watching a sunset. Second, emotions can override biological drives (Tomkins, 1962). Sexual desire is a powerful motivator, but it can be derailed by emotion. Recall that sexual orgasm cannot occur unless the areas of the brain involved in fear and anxiety are shut down (Georgiadis et al., 2006). The emotion of disgust can easily override the fundamental drive of hunger. How can an emotion turn off a basic biological need? Disgust is important for survival. It arises when we come across something that is potentially toxic or harmful and capitalizes on our inborn aversion to contamination (Oaten, Stevenson, & Case, 2009; Rozin & Fallon, 1987). It is preferable for spoiled food to elicit such a response, because it decreases our chances of eating food containing harmful bacteria, molds, or parasites. Simply put, emotions can shut down the drives of hunger, thirst, and sex (Chohra & Madani, 2016; Neuberg, Kenrick, & Schaller, 2011; Oaten et al., 2009).

Some emotions, like disgust and fear, are very primitive, survival-oriented responses to certain kinds of situations that are present in many species in the animal kingdom (Ekman, 1992). Others, like embarrassment and shame, require a sense of right and wrong and may be present only in humans and animals, such as chimps, that live in groups in which social rules operate (Hall & Brosnan, 2016).

What Are Emotions?

Emotions are brief, acute changes in conscious experience and physiology that occur in response to a meaningful situation in a person's environment. They emerge from our interactions with the world and are triggered by situations that are relevant to our personal goals, physical safety, or well-being. Because emotions stem from situations that are important to us, they reveal much about what makes us tick.

Types of Affect Psychologists use the term *affect* to refer to a variety of emotional phenomena, including emotions, moods, and affective traits. Emotions make us pay attention, forcing us to set priorities and deal with life-relevant situations, connect with others, and attain our goals (Armenta, Fritz, & Lyubomirsky, 2016; Ekman, 1992; Lazarus, 1991). They occupy the foreground of our consciousness, often dominating our awareness. In fact, emotions can impact memory, perception, attention, and decision making (Cohen, 2005; Phelps, 2006).

Moods are changes in affect that fluctuate throughout the day or over several days. We experience moods both physiologically and psychologically, and they tend to last longer than most emotions (Davidson, 1994; Ekman, 1984; Forgas, 2016). Moods make certain emotions more likely to occur than others. An irritable mood, for instance, makes people more easily angered than usual. If you are irritated, a slight inconvenience that normally would not bother you, such as having to wait in a slow line at the supermarket, might cause you to speak rudely to the clerk.

Some emotional qualities are longer lasting, however. **Affective traits** are enduring aspects of our personalities that set the threshold for the occurrence of particular emotional states, such as hostility (which potentiates anger) or anxiety (which potentiates fear; Blalock, Kashdan, & Farmer, 2016; Ekman, 1984; Rosenberg, 1998). People who have the affective trait of hostility aren't always angry, but they have hair triggers. If they get cut off in traffic, they are more likely to shout an obscenity at the other driver. For several minutes or likely even longer, hostile people will continue focusing on the event—how they were wronged—making for repeated and/or prolonged experiences of anger (Ekman, 2003).

Basic Emotions Although humans experience an infinite variety of emotional states, a small set of emotions appears to be common to all humans and, thus, may be a product of our evolutionary past (Ekman, 1992). These **basic emotions**—anger, disgust, fear, happiness, sadness, and surprise (see Figure 11)—are fundamental states that play a role in essential life tasks, such as protecting oneself and loved ones from harm (fear), progressing toward the realization of a goal (happiness), or experiencing irrevocable loss (sadness) (Ekman, 1992; Lang & Bradley, 2010; Oatley & Johnson-Laird, 2011). The basic emotions are not single states; rather, they are categories or groups of related emotions, what Ekman (1992) describes as emotion families. For instance, the fear family, which includes anxiety, trepidation, and nervousness, may arise in response to a threat to physical safety. The happiness family includes joy, contentment, elation, amusement, and exhilaration, among others.

emotions
Brief, acute changes in conscious experience and physiology that occur in response to a personally meaningful situation.

Connection

Emotional events are remembered better than nonemotional events, almost as if they were seared into our brains.

See "Memory and the Brain," in the chapter "Memory." (p. 275)

moods
Affective states that operate in the background of consciousness and tend to last longer than most emotions.

affective traits
Stable predispositions toward certain types of emotional responses.

basic emotions
The set of emotions that are common to all humans; includes anger, disgust, fear, happiness, sadness, and surprise.

©Monkey Business Images/Shutterstock.com

 Judging from his facial expression, what do you think this man is feeling?

Emotions as Evolutionary Adaptations   Why do we have emotions? From an evolutionary perspective, emotions are adaptations to particular problems in our ancestral past and so contributed to survival and reproductive success (Tooby & Cosmides, 1990). According to one evolutionary view, emotions bring our physiological systems together to help us deal efficiently with critical situations (Levenson, 1988; Mauss et al., 2005; Rosenberg & Ekman, 1994). When danger approaches, the heart pumps blood to the skeletal muscles to enable quick movement in case escape is necessary, the respiratory system works harder to bring in more oxygen, and the brain prioritizes attention, so that we can figure out what we need to do to protect ourselves. This view of emotions as organized responses best illustrates the adaptive value of negative emotions, such as anger and fear, which enable people to respond efficiently to a significant challenge or obstacle. There is evidence from studies of both ANS physiology and brain that each basic emotion has a unique physiological signature, which is consistent with the view that they organize the systems of the body for particular responses (Ekman, Levenson, & Friesen, 1983; Saarimäki et al., 2016).

What about happiness or other emotions that are not responses to obstacles or threats? Positive emotions, such as contentment, happiness, love, and amusement, solve different kinds of adaptive problems. According to the **broaden-and-build model**, positive emotions widen our cognitive perspective, making our thinking more expansive and enabling the acquisition of new skills and enhance well-being (Fredrickson, 1998, 2001, 2016). Negative emotions promote a narrow, vigilant way of looking at the world (Derryberry & Tucker, 1994). Play, for example, especially the rough-and-tumble play of animals and young children, is a kind of fun that helps develop physical and strategic skills, which may be useful for hunting, escaping, or defensive fighting.

What evidence do we have that positive emotions broaden and build? Several studies suggest that positive emotions broaden one's attentional focus (Fredrickson & Branigan, 2005; Stanko-Kaczmarek & Kaczmarek, 2016). When in positive moods, people perform poorly on tasks of selective attention that require a narrow focus but better on tasks that require a broader attentional focus (Rowe, Hirsch, & Anderson,

Basic emotions	Self-conscious emotions
Anger	Embarrassment
Disgust	Guilt
Fear	Humiliation
Happiness	Pride
Sadness	Shame
Surprise	

FIGURE 11
BASIC AND SELF-CONSCIOUS EMOTIONS. (Ekman, 1992; Tracy & Robins, 2007)

broaden-and-build model
Fredrickson's model for positive emotions, which posits that they widen our cognitive perspective and help us acquire useful life skills.

2007). Also, when people show authentic smiles of enjoyment, attention is broadened (Johnson, Waugh, & Fredrickson, 2010). A broadening of thinking induced by positive emotional states may also underlie the effects of positive emotion on creative thinking (Fredrickson, 1998). In a standard creative thinking task in which people were instructed to think of as many uses as they could for a brick, people in a positive mood thought of more uses (and more novel uses) than those experiencing negative emotions (Isen, Daubman, & Nowicki, 1987; Rowe et al., 2007). In a perceptual task, positive emotions also enhance attention to visual information in the outer edges of a visual display, compared to the center (Wadlinger & Isaacowitz, 2006).

The ability of positive emotions to alter the scope of attention may be beneficial to people who get caught in certain negative patterns of thinking. People who suffer from depression tend to get stuck in ruts of negative thinking, when thoughts of being worthless and unlikeable can interfere with reaching out to others when they need help or comfort. One set of studies experimented with the idea of giving depressed people brief "infusions" of positive emotional experiences of gratitude and feelings of elevation by having them read or write about experiences of these emotions. The intention here was to get the depressed person in a better mood to shift the focus of thinking from a negative orientation to one with more possibilities. Brief "infusions" of elevation did increase the likelihood of depressed people to seek help. Infusions of gratitude did not increase the likelihood of depressed people to seek help—the authors think that reminding people who are depressed to be grateful might have led to feelings of guilt (Siegel & Thomson, 2016).

Self-Conscious Emotions The pride a child feels at learning how to ride a bike and the shame of being caught in a lie are examples of **self-conscious emotions**, which occur as a function of how well we live up to our expectations, the expectations of others, or the rules set by society (Tracy & Robins, 2007; Tangney et al., 2007; see Figure 11). These emotions, which include shame, guilt, humiliation, embarrassment, and pride, require a sense of self and the ability to reflect on one's own actions. Let's look at pride and embarrassment in detail.

Pride has a recognizable expression, which involves body movements, a smile, the head tilted upward, and a slightly expanded chest (see Figure 12). This

self-conscious emotions
Types of emotion that require a sense of self and the ability to reflect on actions; they occur as a function of meeting expectations (or not) and abiding (or not) by society's rules.

FIGURE **12**

THE EXPRESSION OF PRIDE. Jamaican sprinter Usain Bolt shows the typical pride display after winning the gold medal in the 100-meter sprint. This display is innate; even blind people who have never seen it make the same pose after a victory.

©Tom Jenkins/Getty Images

behavior is recognized as pride by children and adults in America and by people in a preliterate, socially isolated tribe in West Africa (Tracy & Robins, 2008). These cross-cultural recognition data from very diverse groups suggest that this pride expression may be common across the globe, but more data are needed. People show elements of this behavior when in situations that produce pride, such as winning medals at the Olympics (Tracy & Matsumoto, 2008). Pride is an emotion that is associated with superiority over others and higher social status—even in cultures that do not value social status differences (Tracy et al., 2013). Just as there are gender differences in the expression of positive emotions generally, with young girls and teens showing more than boys (Chaplin & Aldao, 2013), there seem to be differences in pride expression as well (Webb et al., 2016).

We all know what it feels like to be embarrassed. You are admiring yourself in the mirror when you realize your roommate has walked in and caught you preening. Embarrassment involves an unintentional revelation about yourself to someone else. Being embarrassed makes you feel self-conscious, as if you have violated some social rule. People often get giggly when embarrassed and act as if they want to make amends for some sort of social transgression (Keltner, 1995; Tangney et al., 2007). Keltner (1995) describes the facial expression of embarrassment, which he argues appeases and placates those who have seen one's mistake. The embarrassment expression involves a sequence of facial and gestural actions, each of which may correspond to some sort of social function (see Figure 13).

In another study, Feinberg, Willer, and Keltner (2012) asked people to imagine themselves in various embarrassing situations (such as asking a woman with a protruding stomach if she is pregnant and finding out she is not!) and to recall an embarrassing experience by spending 4 minutes telling this story aloud to a video camera. Analyses of the videotaped behavior, questionnaire data, and performance on game tasks revealed that the people who expressed more embarrassment were more concerned about others in social situations and more generous in their offerings of money to others (Feinberg et al., 2012). These findings

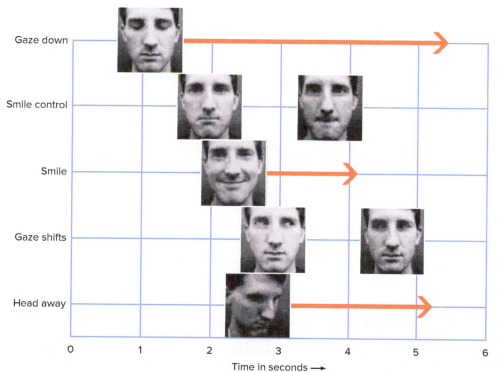

FIGURE 13

THE FACIAL EXPRESSION OF EMBARRASSMENT. The display of embarrassment involves a sequence of actions, each of which might serve a social function. First there is a smile, which may reflect amusement at one's own transgression. Then the eyes gaze away, as if to indicate a desire to escape the awkward situation. Smile control is an attempt to dampen the amusement, as well as looking downward and turning the head away (Keltner, 1995).

Source: Keltner, Dacher, "Signs of Appeasement: Evidence for the Distinct Displays of Embarrassment, Amusement, and Shame," *Journal of Personality and Social Psychology,* 1995, Vol. 68, No. 3, 441–454, Fig. 1. American Psychological Association

FIGURE 14

Most people would be likely to recognize this facial expression as fear.

Courtesy of the authors

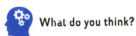 **What do you think?**

suggest that embarrassing experiences, though often uncomfortable, may provide an important prosocial function.

Emotion as a Process

Imagine you are hiking in the mountains and a cougar crosses your path. Your heart starts racing, your breathing speeds up, and you start sweating. You want to get away as fast as possible, but you are not sure if you should run or freeze. Very likely, your face looks like the one shown in Figure 14. You are frightened. Fear provides one example of how emotions quickly change our experience, physiology, and behavior. For decades psychologists debated which of these three aspects best defined what an emotion is. Most researchers today agree that emotions are characterized by all of these components, which unfold in time. The *emotion process* (see Figure 15) shows us how the components of emotion emerge (Gross, 2002; Lazarus, 1991; Levenson et al., 1994).

Emotions emerge in response to situations we encounter in the world or in our thoughts, called *antecedent events*. Not everyone responds to the same situation in the same way. An individual evaluates the antecedent event to determine whether it is potentially harmful or beneficial as per such criteria as safety or personal goals (Lazarus, 1991). Depending on the results of that appraisal, he or she may experience an emotional response.

The emotional response in turn produces changes in physiology, behavior, expression, and felt experience. The direction of the arrows moving from left to right in Figure 15 is only part of the story. As the reverse-curved arrow suggests, the process can move in the other direction as well. That is, the activation of facial and physiological responses might enhance the emotion, becoming yet another kind of input for a new emotional experience. Levenson (2003) points out that, in addition to the antecedent events that are external to us, there may be internal inputs into the emotion process, inputs provided by facial and physiological changes. Once we generate emotions, we sometimes attempt to modify them, regulate them, or make them go away, which in turn involves new appraisals and new responses. To some extent, then, the emotion process moves in a loop rather than in a single direction.

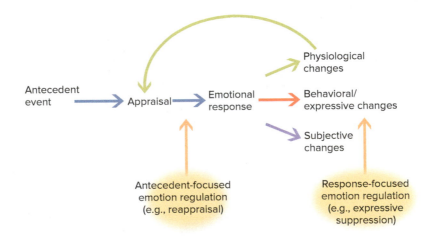

FIGURE 15

THE EMOTION PROCESS. Emotions start with an event that is appraised as relevant to one's goals. If the event is deemed relevant, an emotional response begins, which consists of physiological changes, behavioral and expressive changes, and subjective changes in feelings. Changes in the body's physiology, behavior, and subjective feelings then feed back to the appraisal process and become inputs for experiencing new emotions. Attempts to regulate (modify, change, or suppress) emotion can occur early or late in the emotion process.

Appraisal in the Emotion Process   Whether an event or a situation leads to an emotion depends on how the person appraises it. **Appraisal** is the evaluation of a situation with respect to how relevant it is to one's own welfare (Lazarus, 1991). Appraisal need not be a conscious, deliberate thought process. Most of the time it probably occurs automatically, outside of awareness, and it may occur in an instant (Barrett, Ochsner, & Gross, 2007).

Appraisal drives the process by which emotions are elicited (Roseman, 1984; Scherer, Dan, & Flykt, 2006). It explains why the level of happiness expressed by Olympic athletes can be greater for winners of bronze medals (third place) than for winners of silver medal (second place; Medvec, Madey, & Gilovich, 1995). Bronze medalists can easily imagine an alternative outcome: They may not have even placed. Compared to that outcome, third is great. Silver medalists, on the other hand, can easily imagine having won first place! Compared to that outcome, second might be felt as disappointing.

Examples of appraisal dimensions include control (how much control you feel you have in a situation), agency (whether you or someone else made something happen), pleasantness, and fairness (Ellsworth & Scherer, 2003). The type of appraisal that occurs determines the type of the emotion generated. Fear, for instance, arises in situations of uncertainty and over which we feel we have little control (Arnold, 1960; Ellsworth & Scherer, 2003; Lazarus, 1991).

Although it may be impossible to study the quick or automatic type of appraisals as they happen, research on people's understanding of situations and their responses to them can indirectly inform us as to what appraisals they might be making in various situations (Smith & Ellsworth, 1987). To illustrate, Tong and colleagues (2009) conducted a set of studies on the relationship between situations and emotions, and how those relationships were linked to certain dimensions of appraisal. Students read brief stories describing common situations that can occur in other students' lives (for example, managing the demands of an important class) and answered questions about how they would have responded to the situations. They also completed ratings of appraisal dimensions for each story. For instance, to assess the degree to which someone felt control over a situation, participants rated how much they agreed with comments such as "I feel that I can control what happens." Results showed that, as predicted, emotions resulted from specific appraisals of the situation. Sadness was likely in stories in which the participants perceived that they had little control and were not responsible for the situation (that is, they had no agency). Another study looked at the real-life emotion in a high-stakes situation to see if people's ratings on appraisal components predicted their emotions in an important situation. Professional fencers provided ratings on a questionnaire measuring appraisal components—such as how much threat or challenge they felt before an important fencing match (Doron & Martinet, 2016). People who perceived challenge in the match were more

appraisal
The evaluation of a situation with respect to how relevant it is to one's own welfare; drives the process by which emotions are elicited.

What frightens you? Many people are afraid of potentially threatening situations over which they have little control.

©Martin Barraud/Getty Images

likely to feel positive emotions and perform well; perceiving the match as threatening was linked to negative emotions and poorer performance (Doron & Martinet, 2016).

Regulation of Emotion   People can intentionally or unintentionally change their emotions or the extent to which they experience certain emotions. The term **emotion regulation** refers to the cognitive and behavioral efforts people use to modify their emotions. Figure 15 shows how attempts to regulate emotions may occur at the beginning or end of the emotion process (Gross, 1998; Gross, Richards, & John, 2006). An example of emotion regulation that can occur early in the emotion process is **reappraisal**, in which people reevaluate their views of an event so that a different emotion results. Rather than seeing your next midterm as an opportunity for failure, an outlook that might create fear or anxiety, you might reappraise the exam as a challenging opportunity to prove how much you have learned, an outlook that can lead to eager anticipation.

Another kind of emotion regulation operates when people want to make an unpleasant feeling go away. An example of this kind of strategy is **expressive suppression**, the deliberate attempt to inhibit the outward display of an emotion (Gross et al., 2006). In order to avoid a confrontation, you might literally bite your lip rather than tell your roommates that they are slobs for letting the dishes pile up. Instructing people to suppress their negative emotions can decrease the experience of negative emotion, but it increases activation of the sympathetic nervous system and sustains the emotional response (Gross & Levenson, 1997). When it becomes a habitual way of responding to negative emotion, a lifetime of emotional suppression can have harmful health consequences, such as increasing the likelihood of overeating, obesity, and heart disease (Bahremand et al., 2016; Görlach et al., 2016).

The Emotional Response   Whether processed consciously or automatically, emotional responses emerge from events appraised as relevant to one's safety or personal goals. As shown in Figure 15, the **emotional response** includes physiological, behavioral/expressive, and subjective changes.

Physiological Changes in Emotion   Emotions produce physiological changes, such as increases in heart rate and respiration rate. The physiological system responsible for changes during an emotional response is the autonomic nervous system (ANS), which governs structures and processes over which we have little conscious control, such as changes in heart rate and blood pressure and the release of hormones. The ANS plays a crucial role in emotional response because it activates other systems that are needed for action, including the circulatory and respiratory systems.

Once elicited, emotions engage the ANS almost immediately. For emotions that are concerned with survival and protection from harm, such as fear, the sympathetic branch of the ANS is activated. Sympathetic activity mobilizes body resources into an organized response to a real or imagined environmental threat. The heart pumps blood rapidly to the muscles; oxygen intake in the lungs increases; and processes that are not immediately necessary for action, such as digestion, shut down, so that energy is conserved for more urgent body functions.

The patterns of ANS activity can vary, depending on the emotion elicited. Anger increases heart rate more than fear does; disgust slows the heart (Ekman, Levenson, & Friesen, 1983; Levenson, Ekman, & Friesen, 1990). Such autonomic nervous system changes appear to be common to people all over the world (Levenson et al., 1992; Tsai, Levenson, & Carstensen, 2000; Tsai et al., 2002). Cross-cultural data on the physiology of emotion support the view of emotions as evolutionarily old, as does evidence of emotion in nonhuman

emotion regulation
The cognitive and behavioral efforts people make to modify their emotions.

reappraisal
An emotion regulation strategy in which one reevaluates an event, so that a different emotion results.

expressive suppression
A response-focused strategy for regulating emotion that involves the deliberate attempt to inhibit the outward manifestation of an emotion.

emotional response
The physiological, behavioral/expressive, and subjective changes that occur when emotions are generated.

primates, other mammals, birds, and even fish (Paul, Harding, & Mendl, 2005). Emotion-like responses have even been documented in bees (Perry, Baciadonna, & Chittka, 2016).

Positive emotions engage the parasympathetic branch of the ANS, purportedly returning the body to a more relaxed, responsive state (Levenson, 2003). For example, Fredrickson and Levenson (1998) showed participants a fear-eliciting film and followed it with clips known to elicit sadness, amusement, contentment, or no emotions at all. They measured cardiovascular activity while the participants viewed the films and again afterward. Cardiovascular activation elicited by the negative film returned to baseline levels more quickly in people who saw a pleasant film following the fear film than for those people who saw sad or neutral films after the fear film. This finding suggests that positive emotions may help "undo" the effects of negative emotional arousal by activating the parasympathetic nervous system, which helps return the body to a state of relaxation after arousal.

Behavioral-Expressive Changes in Emotion   Emotions create expressive changes in the face and voice, as well as behavioral tendencies toward particular types of action (Frijda, 1986). People show their emotions—knowingly or not—through both verbal and nonverbal means, such as changes in facial behavior and vocal intonation. Although researchers have studied both facial and vocal expressions of emotion, the most extensive body of research has focused on facial expressions.

Facial Expression of Emotion   Humans are predisposed to respond to faces. Newborn babies mimic the facial expressions of adults. At 5 months they can discriminate between different types of facial expressions of emotion; and by 1 year of age they rely on the faces of their caregivers to convey important information about how they might act (Meltzoff & Moore, 1977; Schwartz, Izard, & Ansul, 1985; Sorce et al., 1985). There are specialized neurons in the brain for responding to faces, and certain brain areas are specialized for particular facial expressions, such as fear (Adolphs et al., 1994, 2005; Kanwisher, 2000).

Much of what we know about facial expression of emotion was originally based on studies of people's ability to recognize emotion in the human face. Charles Darwin was the first modern thinker to formally propose that facial expressions reveal different emotions and offer a theory for the evolution of emotional expression in *The Expression of the Emotions in Man and Animals* (Darwin, 1872/1998). Darwin described in detail how people and animals display emotions through their faces and bodies.

It was not until the 1960s, however, that psychologists began conducting the research that directly addressed Darwin's claims. In his early studies of people's judgments of emotion in the human face, Silvan Tomkins showed participants numerous photographs of European Americans posing different emotions and asked them to decide which emotion may have been felt. Researchers obtained pretty strong evidence of agreement on the emotional meaning of those facial expressions, with roughly 70% or more of the respondents providing the same answer for each photo. Most people recognize facial expression similar to that in Figure 14 as fear. Similarly, when Ekman and Friesen showed Tomkins's pictures to people in the United States, Japan, Argentina, and Chile, there was a high degree of consensus on the emotional meanings of a core set of facial expressions (Ekman & Friesen, 1969). At about the same time, Carroll Izard's (1969) study and results also supported the high level of consensus on the meaning of facial expressions of emotion across numerous cultural groups. These studies and others backed Darwin's (1872/1998) assertion that the facial expressions of certain "basic" emotions, such as anger, disgust, fear, happiness, sadness, and surprise, are **universal**, or common to all human beings.

universal
Common to all human beings and seen in cultures all over the world.

©Fine Art Images/Getty Images

©Ken Graham/Getty Images

 Is Leonardo da Vinci's Mona Lisa smiling out of pleasure or merely posing a smile in her portrait?

 Do facial expressions of emotion have the same meaning in different cultural groups? What do you think this child is feeling?

One problem with these early studies on emotion recognition, however, is that all the participants lived in literate, industrialized cultures. Maybe the findings of cross-cultural consistency in facial expression recognition reflected the spread of the popular media rather than the existence of a universal human skill. People in Japan and the United States might have agreed on the emotional meaning of certain expressions because they had seen portrayals of actors in movies. The only way to resolve this question was to collect data from preliterate people who were isolated from industrialized society, which is what Ekman did by studying an isolated, preliterate group: the Fore tribe from Papua New Guinea.

Ekman and his colleagues showed pictures of facial expressions of emotion—similar to those that had been used in other studies—to find out which emotions, if any, the Fore tribe members saw (Ekman, Sorenson, & Friesen, 1969). But how could he gather such data from a culture without a written language? After experimenting fairly unsuccessfully with a few different approaches, he settled on a technique that had been used with children, who also do not have a written language. The method involved presenting stories about emotional situations to New Guineans and showing them a set of three photographed faces per story. Examples of the stories are "He [she] is angry and about to fight" (which should lead participants to pick an "angry" face) or "She [he] is looking at something that smells bad" (for disgust). Then the experimenter asked the listeners which of the three faces matched the story. With this method, the degree of consensus was much higher.

Both children and adult New Guineans consistently discriminated the "correct" face from other faces; that is, they consistently matched a given story with the face that would have been predicted, and the results matched the data from studies of people in literate cultures (Ekman & Friesen, 1971). Results showed that the range of agreement was relatively high for five of the six basic emotions

Challenge Your Assumptions

True or False? Facial expressions of emotion are very different from culture to culture.

False: There is widespread agreement across cultures on the meaning of basic facial expression of emotion.

FIGURE 16

CONSISTENCY IN EXPRESSIONS OF BASIC EMOTION ACROSS LITERATE AND PRELITERATE CULTURES.

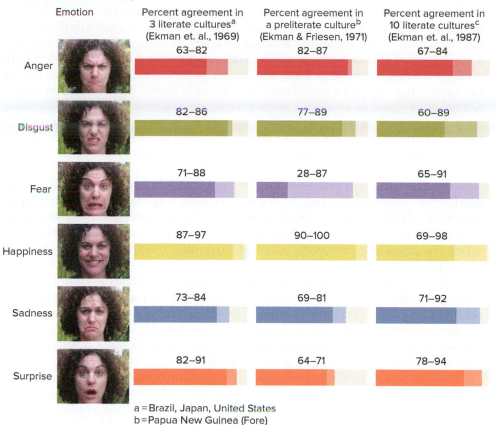

Emotion	Percent agreement in 3 literate cultures[a] (Ekman et. al., 1969)	Percent agreement in a preliterate culture[b] (Ekman & Friesen, 1971)	Percent agreement in 10 literate cultures[c] (Ekman et. al., 1987)
Anger	63–82	82–87	67–84
Disgust	82–86	77–89	60–89
Fear	71–88	28–87	65–91
Happiness	87–97	90–100	69–98
Sadness	73–84	69–81	71–92
Surprise	82–91	64–71	78–94

a = Brazil, Japan, United States
b = Papua New Guinea (Fore)
c = Estonia, Germany (West), Greece, Hong Kong, Italy, Japan, Scotland, Sumatra, Turkey, United States

Courtesy of Erika Rosenberg

(Ekman & Friesen, 1971; Ekman & Friesen, 1969). Follow-up research conducted 20 years later showed similar high-level agreement across 10 literate cultures (Ekman et al., 1987). For summaries of facial recognition data across several cross-cultural studies, see Figure 16.

Universality does not require 100% consistency in people's recognition of emotion. Culture, gender, personality, and other contextual factors can influence how we interpret other people's facial expressions (Haidt & Keltner, 1999). In spite of the factors that pull for differences, there is a remarkable consistency in the human understanding of a core set of basic emotions. One modern application of the universality of recognizing a small set of basic emotion expressions is in the use of emojis. Most text programs add social media sites have a small set of emojis that reflect the basic emotions (in addition to others, like winking, that communicate other information). Basic emotion emojis are used cross-culturally, and change the meaning of text by coloring it with emotional tone 😄😡😞 (Kaye, Malone, & Wall, 2016).

Numerous studies that measure facial behavior from video show that many of the same expressions (and variations) recognized cross-culturally also occur in spontaneous behavior (Ekman & Rosenberg, 2005). The **Facial Action Coding System (FACS)** is a widely used method by which coders describe the observable muscular movements that are possible in the human face (Ekman & Friesen, 1978). Using FACS, researchers have found that many different facial expressions recognized across cultures—such as those for anger, disgust, fear, happiness,

Facial Action Coding System (FACS)
A widely used method for measuring all observable muscular movements that are possible in the human face.

FIGURE 17
A DUCHENNE SMILE VERSUS A NON-DUCHENNE SMILE. Both photos depict a smile of the same intensity, but they differ in the involvement of the muscles around the eyes.

Photos: Courtesy of Erika Rosenberg

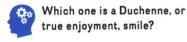

Which one is a Duchenne, or true enjoyment, smile?

sadness, and surprise—are also shown when people spontaneously experience emotions in both laboratory experiments and real-life contexts (Ekman & Rosenberg, 2005; Lupis, Lerman, & Wolf, 2014).

The most recognizable facial expression of emotion is the smile of happiness. However, research using FACS shows that only certain smiles indicate truly felt enjoyment. Other smiles are used for a variety of interpersonal reasons, such as to be polite in conversation or to mask negative emotions. A smile that both pulls up the lip corners diagonally and contracts the band of muscles that circles the eye to create crow's feet and raise the cheeks is known as a **Duchenne smile**. A Duchenne smile is a genuine smile that expresses true enjoyment. When we smile for social reasons and are not genuinely happy, we use only the lips and not the band of muscles around the eye, which is called a non-Duchenne smile (Davidson et al., 1990; Ekman, Davidson, & Friesen, 1990). Figure 17 compares the two.

Vocal Expression of Emotion Have you ever noticed how your voice can betray you? Consider the first time you ever gave a speech. You may have had your hair and clothes in fine order; perhaps your facial expressions showed great composure; and you knew your speech well, having practiced it over and over. When the time came, however, your voice quivered or even squeaked! Why did this happen?

The voice is very sensitive to emotional arousal, because the autonomic nervous system has projections to the vocal chords. Thus, nervousness leaks through the voice (Bachorowski, 1999; Scherer et al., 1991). In studies of actors' portrayals of emotions through spoken nonsense sentences, certain emotions (anger, fear, joy) were associated with higher pitch and volume, while sadness was associated with lower pitch and volume (Scherer et al., 1991).

We have discussed how people can recognize emotion from the face, but can you tell what someone is feeling simply by hearing changes in their voice? Even though there is cultural variability, vocal emotion recognition appears to be a basic human social skill (Scherer, Banse, & Wallbott, 2001). Research suggests that people do a fairly good job of recognizing emotion from the voice alone. For example, when asked to provide what they think are vocalizations for each of 22 different recorded emotional states, people can guess which emotion the speaker is trying to convey (Simon-Thomas et al., 2009).

There may be differences among positive emotion vocalizations (Simon-Thomas et al., 2009). For instance, laughter is a well-known vocal expression of emotion. Studies of people watching funny films show that there are several different types of laughs (Bachorowski, Smoski, & Owren, 2001). Some people grunt or snort, while others open their mouths with a big guffaw. Voiced laughs—those that involve vibration of the vocal fold and typically involve expelling air out of the mouth—generate more positive ratings when evaluated on such features as likability, sexiness, and friendliness (Bachorowski & Owren, 2001). Simply put, voiced laughs make people happy.

Vocal and facial response systems can work together in emotion expression. The same vocalization can sound different depending on the speaker's facial expression. This happens because lip movements affect vocal characteristics. In fact, people can hear smiles and frowns—when presented with recordings of statements made when people are smiling and frowning, people can accurately perceive the difference (Bachorowski, 1999; Tartter, 1980).

Subjective Experience of Emotion The third component of the emotional response is referred to as the **subjective experience of emotion**, which refers to the quality of our conscious experience during an emotional response. When people talk about how an emotion *feels*, they are referring to subjective experience. Each emotion creates a unique feeling: Anger feels different from sadness, which feels different from happiness. The subjective aspect of emotion draws on

FIGURE 18
WHAT BODY SENSATIONS DO YOU ASSOCIATE WITH VARIOUS EMOTIONS?

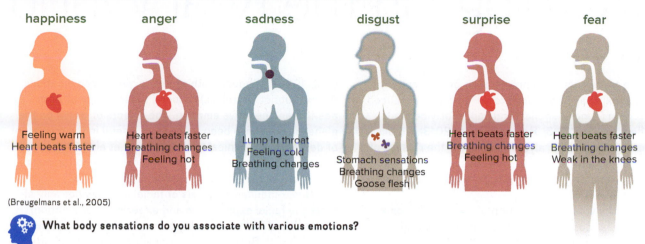

| happiness | anger | sadness | disgust | surprise | fear |

Feeling warm
Heart beats faster

Heart beats faster
Breathing changes
Feeling hot

Lump in throat
Feeling cold
Breathing changes

Stomach sensations
Breathing changes
Goose flesh

Heart beats faster
Breathing changes
Feeling hot

Heart beats faster
Breathing changes
Weak in the knees

(Breugelmans et al., 2005)

What body sensations do you associate with various emotions?

bodily changes, as well as effects on cognition, for emotions can activate associations with images and memories of significant events.

What produces subjective feelings of emotion? For centuries theorists have argued over this question. Perhaps the most influential theory was proposed by William James (1884) and Carl Lange (1885/1992). The **James-Lange theory of emotion** says that our perception of the physiological changes that accompany emotions creates the subjective emotional experience. Without the perception of bodily changes, they argued, there is no emotional experience. Moreover, the changes that accompany different emotional states are unique. We experience fear as feeling different from sadness because we perceive different body changes for each emotion—in short, "I am trembling, and therefore I am afraid; or I feel a lump in my throat, and therefore I am sad."

The James-Lange theory is not without its critics, most notable among them Walter Cannon (1927), who argued that feedback from bodily organs is not specific enough to account for the varieties of emotional experience. Still, several lines of evidence support the James-Lange view that sensory feedback from physiologically activated body systems plays a role in emotional experience. When people in many cultures are asked to identify the body sensations associated with emotions, they differentiate among several emotional states. For instance, "stomach sensations" are associated most strongly with disgust, and sadness with a lump in the throat (Breugelmans et al., 2005; see Figure 18).

Research on facial feedback also supports the idea that feedback from body sensations creates emotional experience. The **facial feedback hypothesis** posits that sensory feedback from the facial musculature during expression affects emotional experience (Tomkins, 1962). Sensory neurons from the face do innervate key emotion areas of the brain, especially the amygdala (Hennenlotter et al., 2009). In fact, research suggests that our facial expressions enhance our emotional feelings. People report feeling a particular emotion when they pose on their faces the muscular movements of that emotion expression (Strack, Martin, & Stepper, 1988). Ratings of pleasantness increase when certain key emotion-relevant facial muscles are contracted (Dimberg & Söderkvist, 2011). Additionally, the better that people pose facial expressions of emotion, the more intensely they feel those emotions (Ekman et al., 1983; Levenson et al., 1990). Recently, the popularity of the cosmetic use of Botox, which reduces wrinkling by paralyzing facial muscles, has led to a flurry of studies on the effects of reduced facial feedback on emotional experience, well-being, and psychological health (see the "Psychology in the Real World" box).

James-Lange theory of emotion
The idea that it is the perception of the physiological changes that accompany emotions that produces the subjective emotional experience.

facial feedback hypothesis
Sensory feedback from the facial musculature during expression affects emotional experience.

Psychology in the Real World

Botox and Emotion

Botox is the trade name of a preparation of a potentially lethal neurotoxin called *botulism toxin*, a protein produced by a bacterium found in spoiled and improperly canned foods (Allergan, Inc., 2013; Rossetto et al., 2013). Botulism toxin causes muscular paralysis by blocking the release of acetylcholine at neuromuscular synapses, which can be fatal if the involuntary muscles of breathing are affected (Rossetto et al., 2013).

How did the voluntary injection of a poison become the most popular cosmetic procedure in the general population (Lorenc et al., 2013)? In 1989, **Clark and Berris (2005)** documented the usefulness of micro-doses of botulism toxin as a treatment for people who had developed facial asymmetries due to partial paralysis from stroke or other health problems. They also noticed a diminution of wrinkles in the paralyzed areas, and the cosmetic applications became obvious. Botox reduces wrinkles by paralyzing facial muscles by relaxing muscular contractions underlying facial creases. As a result, the area looks smoother and younger. The effects wear off after about 6 months or so, at which time many people get new injections. Botox is commonly injected into the area between the eyebrows where short, vertical wrinkles, often referred to as "glabellar frown lines," appear. Under normal conditions, the muscles (most notably, the *corrugator* muscles) underlying these wrinkles pull the eyebrows together and down. These actions occur in the expression of many negative emotions, including anger, sadness, and fear.

What are the consequences of these muscles not working for months at a time? As we know from research on the facial feedback hypothesis, sensory feedback from the facial muscles enhances emotional experience (Dimberg & Söderkvist, 2011). Paralyzing facial muscles would impair facial feedback and possibly diminish emotional experience. Initial studies found that Botox does reduce negative emotional experience (Alam et al., 2008). For example, Davis and colleagues (2010) showed emotionally evocative films to people who had received either Botox injections or injections with Restalyne, a cosmetic wrinkle filler that does not paralyze muscles (the filler was the control condition) in the glabellar region and around the crow's feet of the eyes (an area that can be involved in smiles of enjoyment (Ekman et al., 1990). Although both groups experienced emotions, Botox (but not Restalyne) reduced the intensity of *both* positive and negative emotion. The effects of Botox on the glabellar area have been found to be useful in the treatment of depression in clinical trials (Wollmer et al., 2012), but the effects of crow's feet injections on positive emotion suggest we should be careful about where Botox is used.

Botox-induced paralysis of facial muscles not only affects the facial expressions and experience of emotion, it can also affect one's ability to read emotions in others. Injection with Botox impairs people's ability to read others' facial expressions of emotions, most likely by impairing facial mimicry (Neal & Chartrand, 2011). Mimicry occurs when people imitate the behavior of others without realizing it. Facial mimicry, probably by means of facial feedback, contributes to our ability to recognize emotional expressions in others and plays an important role in the development of empathy (Chartrand & Dalton, 2009; Wood et al., 2016). By extension, we can see how long-term Botox use might impair socioemotional capacities.

The absence of facial movement in the processing of emotional information seems to extend beyond our ability to recognize other people's facial expressions—it may play an important role in how we process emotional information of all types. Havas and colleagues (2010) asked women before and after they received Botox injections to read happy, sad, and angry sentences. After each sentence, the participant was asked to respond to a simple yes/no comprehension question, which could be answered with a single keystroke. The researchers were interested in how long it took the participants to make the keystroke. Reaction times were significantly longer after Botox injections, which suggests that the inhibition of facial feedback from Botox impairs the processing of emotional information. More recent work indicates Botox impairs recognition of facial expression—women who had Botox performed worse on identifying low intensity, subtle expression of both positive and negative emotion (Baumeister, Papa, & Foroni, 2016).

What would happen if injections were very close to the muscles involved in smiling? Not only would that have implications for personal experience, but it would also have profound effects on social interaction.

Emotion and the Brain

So far we have examined the emotion process in detail, from the eliciting event to the appraisal mechanisms that bring forth the emotional response to the resulting changes in physiology, expression, and experience. Missing from this picture is the brain, which participates in every aspect of the emotion process.

Affective neuroscience, the field devoted to studying the brain's role in emotion, is rapidly growing. Most current evidence tells us that emotional information is processed in brain circuits that involve several brain structures, and emotion processing is highly interlinked with cognitive processing (Pessoa, 2008). There is no single structure that could be called an "emotion center" in the brain. Rather, several structures that communicate with one another and other brain areas are involved. We can identify some key areas for emotion processing, including the amygdala, the prefrontal cortex, the anterior cingulate cortex, the hypothalamus, and the insula (see Figure 19).

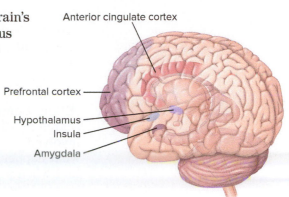

Anterior cingulate cortex
Prefrontal cortex
Hypothalamus
Insula
Amygdala

FIGURE 19
FIVE MAJOR PLAYERS IN THE EMOTIONAL BRAIN. No single area of the brain is responsible for emotion, but the amygdala, prefrontal cortex, anterior cingulate cortex, hypothalamus, and the insula play key roles in the way we experience emotion and remember emotional experiences.

The Amygdala Anatomically, the amygdala has connections with many important brain regions, including structures that appear to be involved in emotion and memory: the hypothalamus, which controls the ANS; the hippocampus, which plays a crucial role in memory; the thalamus, which receives information from the sense organs; and the cerebral cortex. The amygdala appears to contribute to appraisal of the emotional significance of stimuli, with a specialized function for noticing fear-relevant information (Johansen et al., 2011; Öhman, 2002; Phelps & LeDoux, 2005).

Much of the research on the amygdala has centered on its pivotal role in quick appraisals during threatening or fear-inducing situations (LeDoux, 1996, 2000). Along these lines, Joseph LeDoux and his colleagues have used classical conditioning of fear in rats as a model for studying emotion in the human brain (Johansen et al., 2011; Wilensky et al., 2006). In their experiment, a rat is exposed to a tone, which is emotionally neutral at first. Then the tone is repeatedly paired with an aversive stimulus, an electric shock (the unconditioned stimulus, or UCS). After repeated pairings with the shock, the tone itself becomes a fear-eliciting stimulus (the conditioned stimulus, or CS). When the researchers examined the circuitry of fear conditioning in the rat brain, they found that the side and middle of the amygdala are most active in learning to be afraid of the tone (Johansen et al., 2011; Wilensky et al., 2006).

The amygdala's role in fear is well documented in humans and other species (Johansen et al., 2011; Mühlberger et al., 2011). People with damaged amygdalae do not show normal physiological reactions under fear conditioning. They tend to trust faces that most people find to be untrustworthy and have trouble recognizing facial expressions of fear, especially in the eyes (Adolphs et al., 1994, 2005; Adolphs, Tranel, & Damasio, 1998; Phelps & LeDoux, 2005). Brain imaging studies of people with intact brains reveal increased amygdala activation when they are exposed to fear faces, and an inactive amygdala when they view other facial expressions of emotion (Breiter et al., 1996). Whereas certain regions of the amygdala are more involved in fear, other regions are more involved in anger and rage (Panksepp, 2000). Tumors of the amygdala have been found in violent criminals, such as in Charles Whitman, who climbed the tower at the University of Texas in 1966 and in 90 minutes killed 19 people and wounded 38 with a semi-automatic weapon (Austin Police Dept., 1966).

The Prefrontal Cortex The case of Phineas Gage, the 19th-century railroad worker who survived a severe injury to his prefrontal cortex (see the chapter "The Biology of Behavior"), provided early evidence of the importance of the prefrontal cortex in emotion and personality. Gage's prefrontal cortex injury transformed him from a relatively mild-mannered man into an impatient, easily enraged individual. More recently, studies show that the prefrontal cortex is one of the more active regions of the brain in the experience of emotions. Damage to the left prefrontal cortex results in depression

(Morris et al., 1996; Sackeim et al., 1982). According to EEG studies that measure cortical activity, clinically depressed people show less activity in the left prefrontal cortex than do nondepressed people (Davidson, 2001; Herrington et al., 2010).

The prefrontal cortex plays a key role in emotional appraisal—probably due to its involvement in planning, impulse control, and working memory (Etkin, Egner, & Kalish, 2011; Miyake et al., 2000; Morawetz et al., 2016). Research in affective neuroscience shows that the prefrontal cortex is crucially involved in evaluating the relevance of events in the world to oneself, which is what happens when one is appraising a situation. Brain imaging studies show that when people are asked to think of their own name the medial prefrontal cortex is activated more than when they are asked to think of names of fictitious characters (Abraham, 2013; Perrin et al., 2005). A similar pattern is seen for tasks where people make judgments about others who share similar political views versus those who do not (Falk, Spunt, & Lieberman, 2012). Such findings have been taken to imply that the prefrontal cortex is important for self-relevant thinking.

Several studies suggest that the left prefrontal cortex is more involved in the experience of positive emotions than the right (Davidson, 2004; Davidson et al., 1990; Mühlberger et al., 2011). These regions are primarily involved in emotions that have *approach* components, which means they make the organism move toward something or someone. Positive emotions involve a lot of approach—we move toward the things that make us happy. But there are some negative emotions that involve approach as well; namely anger, which often makes us feel like lashing out at someone (Harmon-Jones, 2003).

The Anterior Cingulate Cortex   The anterior cingulate cortex is involved in emotion-related thought and, most likely, appraisal. A meta-analysis of more than 55 brain imaging studies concluded that the anterior cingulate cortex is active when people either recall or imagine emotional experiences (Phan et al., 2002; also see Figure 19). Other evidence points to the anterior cingulate cortex being closely linked to the appraisal and expression of emotion (Etkin et al., 2011). The anterior cingulate cortex is also the brain region that is active in both physical pain and the pain of rejection or exclusion (Eisenberger et al., 2003; Etkin et al., 2011; Zaki et al., 2016). Anatomical studies of primate brains indicate that pathways between the anterior cingulate cortex and amygdala and portions of the prefrontal cortex are important to emotion regulation (García-Cabezas & Barbas, 2016).

The Hypothalamus   The hypothalamus is well known as a pleasure or reward center, as such it is involved in the feeling of emotions. Animals will forgo food and drink to receive stimulation there (Olds & Milner, 1954), and humans report feeling pleasure when this region is stimulated (Heath, 1975). Also, the hypothalamus plays a key role in directing various other areas of the brain involved in emotional responses, such as the ANS, hormone systems, and muscular action (McGaugh, 2016).

The Insula   Finally, we are beginning to appreciate the important role of the insula in emotion as well. The insula is the brain structure most involved in interoception, or the perception of sensations arising within the body. In fMRI studies, the insula is active during the experience of pain and empathy for another's pain (Singer et al., 2004). This brain structure also appears to play an important role in disgust, which is an emotion associated with a high degree of internal bodily sensations. Visualizing disgusting scenes leads to activation of the insula as well as the ACC (Schienle, Shäfer, & Vaitl, 2008). Insular activity is reduced when women attempt to regulate their disgust with reappraisal (Giuliani, Drabant, & Gross, 2010; Goldin et al., 2008). Certain areas of the insula are so specific to disgust that they show activation to facial expressions of disgust but not to those of distaste (von dem Hagen et al., 2009). A recent study in which the insula was stimulated in people who had deep brain implants showed that electrical stimulation of the insula actually impaired recognition of disgust expression but not other facial expressions (Papagno et al., 2016)! Clearly more research is needed to understand exactly how this brain center is linked with emotion and disgust, in particular.

The neuropeptide oxytocin is well known for its role in lactation and bonding in mammals, especially females (Campbell, 2008). We now know that it plays a broad role in positive emotional states, especially those involving affiliation or connection with others (Lee et al., 2009). When adults are given doses of oxytocin, both males and females are more likely to want to be around other people (Campbell, 2008), to help others (Ebstein et al., 2010), to cooperate with others (Declerck, Boone, & Kiyonari, 2010), and to show greater generosity toward others (Zak, Stanton, & Ahmadi, 2007). Also, oxytocin makes people better at recognizing facial expressions of happiness, especially subtle ones (which are harder to read), but not the other emotions. It's as if oxytocin enhances responsiveness to positive emotional states, especially when the information is subtle (Marsh, Yu, Pine, & Blair, 2010). These effects of oxytocin on connection and responsiveness to the emotions of others has led some to wonder whether oxytocin might be beneficial to the treatment of social deficits in autism, a disorder marked by great difficulties with perception of others' emotions (Guastella & Hickie, 2016).

©LWA/Getty Images

 What happens when we experience positive emotions?

How Culture Impacts Emotion Expression

The research on facial expression recognition from New Guinea led to an integration of the two competing perspectives, culture differences and universality. Soon after returning from New Guinea, Ekman (1972) proposed the **neurocultural theory of emotion** to account for the fact that certain aspects of emotion, such as the facial expressions and physiological changes of basic emotions, are similar in all humans, whereas other aspects, such as how people appraise situations and regulate their emotion expressions in front of others, vary from one culture to another.

Anthropologists have offered numerous examples of cultural variability in emotion expression—such as the case of Samurai women who smiled broadly after learning that their husbands or sons had died in battle (Ekman, 1973). Such examples suggest that facial expressions of happiness and sadness are not universal. How can the findings on the universality of facial expressions jibe with the fact that there are cultural differences in emotions? Ekman and Friesen (Ekman, 1972; Friesen, 1972) proposed the concept of display rules to address this dilemma. **Display rules** are learned norms or rules, often taught very early, about when it is appropriate to show certain expressions of emotion and to whom one should show them (Ekman, 1972). As it turns out, Samurai women were expected to be proud of a son or husband who had been killed in battle, and the society required them to display joy at the news. In the United States we expect

Connection

The prefrontal cortex plays a key role in working memory by evaluating sensory information and designating it for storage or disposal.

See "Short-Term and Working Memory and the Brain," in the chapter "Memory." (p. 280)

neurocultural theory of emotion
Ekman's explanation that some aspects of emotion, such as facial expressions and physiological changes associated with emotion, are universal and others, such as emotion regulation, are culturally derived.

display rules
Learned norms or rules, often taught very early, about when it is appropriate to express certain emotions and to whom one should show them.

©Ronald Grant/Mary Evans/The Image Works

Culture affects emotion expression in many ways. *Schadenfreude* is a German expression that combines the words for "harm or injury" (*schaden*) and "joy" (*freude*) and is used to describe the times when people gain pleasure or joy from other people's misfortune or injury, such as when a rival gets hurt or when someone we don't like is humiliated. It is even seen in slapstick comedy.

winners not to boast, losers not to mope, and men not to cry in public (although this last norm is changing).

The first empirical support for display rules came from a study comparing disgust expressions in American and Japanese students (Ekman, 1972; Friesen, 1972). Both groups viewed a film showing a very graphic medical procedure, but in two different conditions: in the presence of an authority figure and alone. When alone, both groups felt perfectly comfortable expressing the obvious response—disgust. When in the presence of an authority figure, the Japanese students did not show disgust, and they masked their responses with non-Duchenne (fake) smiles. American students, however, showed about the same level of disgust in both conditions. The expressive differences between groups emerged in a situation in which the cultures had very different norms about expression, but not in the solo viewing condition. More recent research on display rules and expression supports and extends these original findings (Matsumoto, Yoo & Fontaine, 2008). There are notable variations in the intensity of facial expressions of emotion across cultures, even across smaller groups, such as European Americans (Tsai & Chentsova-Dutton, 2003). Overwhelmingly, people across many cultures show remarkably similar emotion displays in highly emotional situations—in the Olympics, for example (Matsumoto & Willingham, 2006).

The findings on display rules illustrate how many of the differences observed between cultures may be a function of differences in the regulation of emotion. You may recall that earlier we mentioned that once emotions are generated, people make attempts to manage them (this is known as emotion regulation). For instance, countries that value interconnectedness and sharing more than individualism (Asian countries versus Europe, the United States, Canada) report higher levels of emotional suppression of negative emotion—which is motivated by a fear of spreading the negative emotion in the larger social group (Ford & Mauss, 2015).

Darwin (1872/1998) asserted that facial expressions evolved due to their functional role in survival, which if true would speak to why some expressions may be universal. For instance, the expression of fear, with its raised brows and widely opened eyes, increased the scope of vision for someone looking for options for escape. Recent research shows that people posing fear faces actually see better in tests of peripheral vision and quickness of eye movements. These appearance changes may actually reveal the function of the fear face hypothesized by Darwin—to enable people to respond more quickly to danger (Susskind et al., 2008).

There seem to be some universals in vocalizations of emotion as well. Motherese, the singsongy manner with which mothers speak to their babies, shows remarkable consistency worldwide and may be a unique adaptation particularly suited to infant perception (Fernald, 1992). Nonverbal vocalizations of emotion, such as grunts, retching noises, and laughs, also seem to be recognized cross-culturally (Sauter et al., 2010). In a study using methods very similar to those Ekman used with a preliterate New Guinea culture to classify facial expressions, Sauter and colleagues (2010) asked Namibians to match voices with the emotion stories that may have elicited them. Namibians and native English speakers made remarkably similar judgments, despite being from widely separate cultures.

In sum, when and how we express emotion on our face is determined both by innate, biologically determined factors and by culturally learned influences, such as display rules, that may vary from one culture to another. The evidence strongly suggests that all humans share a core set of basic facial expressions of emotion, though there remains some debate as to the exact forms of some of these expressions (Yoder, Widen, & Russell, 2016).

Gender and Emotion

If cultural factors can influence emotion expression, what about gender, which is both culturally and biologically driven? People all around the world think women are more emotional than men (Fischer & Manstead, 2000), but what do the data say? An overwhelming amount of data speak to no sex differences in emotion, but a few areas stand out as potential areas of difference: the verbal description of emotion, facial expression, and brain physiology.

Women talk more about emotions than men do. In a study of older married couples discussing an area of conflict in their marriage, the women were more likely to use words expressing distress and anger, whereas the men were more likely to withdraw from conflict (Levenson, Carstensen, & Gottman, 1994). Women are more likely to describe their reactions to a particular experience with more refinement than men, using phrases such as "I felt angry and upset" rather than the more general phrase "I felt bad" (Barrett et al., 2000).

Women outperform men in accurately recognizing facial expressions of emotion, especially more subtle emotion expressions (Hall & Matsumoto, 2004; Hoffmann et al., 2010; Merten, 2005). This benefit may extend beyond face recognition. Collignon and colleagues (2010) compared men's and women's processing of emotional information about fear and disgust from several channels: the face alone, the voice alone, and both together. Women outperformed men in the recognition of emotion across all three modes of presentation.

What about actual emotional expressions when one is experiencing emotions? In general, women are more expressive and smile more often than men (LaFrance, Hecht, & Paluk, 2003), and even young girls and teens show more positive emotion expression compared to boys overall (Chaplin & Aldao, 2013). Otherwise, there

©Andersen Ross/Blend Images/Corbis RF

Women tend to talk about emotions more than men do, but there is little difference in the facial expressions of men and women during emotional experiences.

is very little evidence of consistent sex differences in the facial expression of emotion, though there is evidence that when research extends across a more varied social and economic situations these gender differences look different. For instance, a recent study looked at the emotions of low-income teen girls and boys when in a stressful situation; namely, when giving a speech in front of a panel of adult judges (Panjwani et al., 2016). They coded the facial expressions the kids showed during the speech (average age of 15 years) from video. As consistent with previous work and cultural stereotypes, girls showed more facial expression of happiness and shame than boys. But contrary to stereotypes, girls also showed more expressions of contempt (Panjwani et al., 2016). These findings suggest that a long held belief about sex differences may be clouded by having studied mainly middle to upper-class kids in nonthreatening situations, and there is a need for more diversity of sample and situation in emotion research.

A few studies have noted sex differences in how the brain processes emotions. Exposure to pictures of animal or human attacks provokes greater amygdala activation in men than in women, which suggests a greater tendency toward aggressive action in men (Schienle et al., 2008). Also, during efforts to regulate emotion by cognitive reappraisal, men and women show different patterns of brain activation, which suggests that men and women may use different brain areas to modulate their emotional responses (Domes et al., 2010). A recent meta-analysis of many different studies reported that women in general show greater left amygdala activation to fear and negative affect, whereas men show greater left amygdala activity to positive emotion (Stevens & Hamann, 2012). Further research is needed, however, to fully appreciate the meaning of these differences. Generally, the similarities between the sexes in terms of emotion and the brain outweigh the differences (Wagner & Ochsner, 2005).

Emotional Intelligence

Culture and gender can shape emotional behavior, but there are individual differences in the way people use and regulate their emotions. Varying emotional skills suggest the existence of an underlying emotional intelligence that varies among people, as with IQ.

In the mid-1990s Daniel Goleman published the book *Emotional Intelligence*, which popularized the idea that emotional skills are crucial in determining how well one does in life—both professionally and personally. Goleman (1995) drew heavily on research by Peter Salovey and John Mayer, who had introduced the concept of emotional intelligence in 1990 (Salovey & Mayer, 1990). **Emotional intelligence** is the ability to recognize emotions in oneself and others, empathic understanding, and the skills for regulating emotions in oneself and others, which may be at least as important to one's success in life as academic achievement.

emotional intelligence
The ability to recognize emotions in oneself and others, empathic understanding, and skills for regulating emotions in oneself and others.

A natural application of this work is in the field of education. Researchers have taught schoolchildren strategies for regulating emotion in order to reduce maladaptive behavior and improve academic performance; these strategies are referred to as *socioemotional learning*, or SEL (Conduct Problems Prevention Research Group, 1999a, 1999b; Kam, Greenberg, & Kusché, 2004). Typically, IQ is seen as the best predictor of school performance. We now know that training in emotional skills not only improves emotional behavior and functioning but also enhances cognitive performance as well as school performance (Hogan et al., 2010).

One groundbreaking SEL program is PATHS (Providing Alternative Thinking Strategies), developed by Mark Greenberg and Carol Kusché (Greenberg & Kusché, 1998; Kusché & Greenberg, 1994). The PATHS program gives teachers a detailed curriculum for improving children's emotional awareness and regulation skills and for enhancing their social competence. Research in which classrooms were randomly assigned to receive the PATHS curriculum or not (thereby continuing as usual) shows that PATHS leads to improvements in social and emotional skills in high-risk children, a reduction of aggressive behaviors in both normal and special-needs children, fewer depressive symptoms in special-needs kids, and improvements in classroom functioning (Conduct Problems Prevention Research Group, 1999a, 1999b; Kam et al., 2004). Other prevention programs, such as Head Start, have also applied the theory and methods of emotion research to decrease behavior problems in schools, and initial results are promising (Izard et al., 2004).

More than a decade after the implementation of major SEL programs, it is possible to see how the development of socioemotional learning might be linked to academic success. A large-scale meta-analysis of more than 500 studies shows that SEL programs significantly improve children's academic performance (Durlak et al., 2007). Specifically, children who participate in these programs have better attendance and exhibit less disruptive classroom behavior; they like school more and have higher GPAs. These effects seem to hold at different ages and in vastly different cultures. For example, emotional intelligence has been linked to improved performance in graduate students in India (Srivastava & Naveen, 2016), business students in Pakistan (Malik & Shahid, 2016), and nursing students in Spain (Roso-Bas, Jiménez, & García-Buades, 2016).

Emotional intelligence may be an enduring characteristic or skill—like other forms of intelligence. Several questionnaires are designed to measure emotional intelligence, much as intelligence tests have traditionally been used to measure IQ. Two such instruments are the EQ-I (Bar-On, 2004) and the Mayer-Salovey-Caruso Emotional Intelligence Test, or MSCEIT (Mayer et al., 2003). With such tools, researchers can look at the relationship between emotional intelligence scores and other academic and nonacademic variables. Such trait measures of emotional intelligence correlate with higher GPA in adolescent boys and girls (Hogan et al., 2010), less job burnout in teachers (Platsidou, 2010), better coping with stress (Mikolajczak & Luminet, 2008), and improvements in mental and physical health (Schutte et al., 2007).

Quick Quiz 2: Emotion

1. The fact that sexual orgasm cannot occur unless the areas of the brain involved in fear and anxiety are shut down illustrates what basic feature of emotions versus drives?
   a. Drives have supremacy over emotions.
   b. Emotions can override biological drives.
   c. Emotions and drives serve similar masters.
   d. Drives must be resolved before emotions can motivate behavior.

2. Which of the following is NOT a self-conscious emotion?
   a. pride
   b. embarrassment
   c. hostility
   d. shame

3. According to the view of emotions as a process, _____ initiate(s) the process by which emotions are elicited.
   a. emotional responses
   b. expressive changes
   c. physiological changes
   d. appraisal

4. Which of the following is NOT a basic emotion?
   a. fear
   b. happiness
   c. disgust
   d. shame

5. The social norm set forth by our culture, which says that winners should not gloat, is an example of a(n)
   a. display rule.
   b. human universal.
   c. affective trail.
   d. antecedent event.

6. The _____ appears to play a very important role in noticing fear-relevant information.
   a. amygdala
   b. hypothalamus
   c. prefrontal cortex
   d. insula

7. Which kind of emotion phrases are women more apt to use than men?
   a. more general comments, such as "I feel bad"
   b. more specific comments, such as "I am upset and angry"
   c. more affective imagery, such as "my fear is blue and cold"
   d. phrases such as "I will blow my top!"

Answers can be found at the end of the chapter.

Bringing It All Together

Making Connections in Motivation and Emotion

Living a Satisfied and Well-Lived Life

Emotion and motivation go together. Both are activated when issues of well-being, survival, and appetite are involved (Lang & Bradley, 2010). We are motivated and driven to keep doing things that are beneficial to our well-being. When we achieve important goals that we were driven to work on, we feel happy and/or proud. Likewise, if we fail, we experience sadness, anger, anxiety, or depression.

What do we want out of life? For many of us the answer is happiness and a good life. Two topics that integrate much of what we have discussed on motivation and emotion are living a satisfied life and living a flourishing life (eudemonia).

Motivation, Emotion, and a Satisfied Life

The word *happiness* often refers to a brief emotion, but it can also refer to **life satisfaction**, our overall evaluation of our own lives and how we are doing (Diener et al., 1999). Psychologists consider life satisfaction to be a subset of **subjective well-being**, which also includes satisfaction in domains such as career, family, finances, and social networks. Maslow's hierarchical model of motivation offers a useful framework for a discussion of motivation and happiness, since both basic and higher-level needs contribute to life satisfaction.

life satisfaction
The overall evaluation we make of our lives and an aspect of subjective well-being.

subjective well-being
The state that consists of life satisfaction, domain satisfactions, and positive and negative affect.

Basic Needs and Happiness

It is a well-known adage that money cannot buy happiness, but basic needs must be met for a person to be relatively satisfied with life. Accordingly, industrialized countries have higher levels of well-being than nonindustrialized countries, because those in industrialized nations are more likely to have food and shelter (see Figure 20). In modern society, we require money to buy food, clothes, and shelter.

At a national level, in the early stages of a country's development, increased income makes people happier with their lives. After a relatively modest level of increased income, however, money makes little difference and may even be a hindrance to happiness. In general, the higher a country's gross national product (GNP), the higher its well-being, but there are many exceptions, especially in Latin America. Countries such as Mexico and Colombia are just as happy as countries such as Denmark, Iceland, and Switzerland, in spite of having only half their per-person GNP. Moreover, when absolute income rose in the United States from the late 1940s to the late 1990s, well-being and life satisfaction stayed constant (Diener & Seligman, 2004).

Income gap worldwide—the difference between highest and lowest incomes in nation—is another way to measure

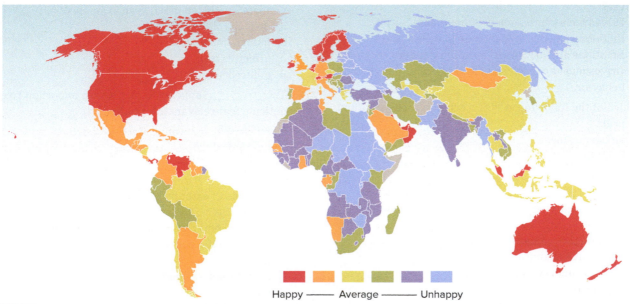

Happy —— Average —— Unhappy

FIGURE 20
WORLD HAPPINESS MAP. This map of subjective well-being closely matches projections based on poverty and national income, indicating that fulfilling basic needs is a prerequisite for happiness.

True or False? More money leads to greater happiness.

Somewhat True, Somewhat False: Modest gains in income lead to higher levels of happiness; after that, there is no increase.

economic status. Higher income gaps mean there is a greater disparity in incomes, which may have an impact on well-being, if we assume that more equality would lead to happiness. Studies are surprisingly mixed on this topic (Schneider, 2016).

At the individual level, there is a modest and complex relationship between income and overall life satisfaction as well. Having more money does make people slightly happier, but this is true only for those driven by money (Diener et al., 1999; Nickerson et al., 2003). The relationship between spending money and being happy depends on whom you are spending it. In an experiment, people assigned randomly to spend money on others were happier than those who spent it on themselves (Dunn, Aknin, & Norton, 2008).

Diet and weight also relate to overall happiness in various ways. First, having a healthy diet is associated with high life satisfaction (Due et al., 1991; Valois et al., 2003). On the other hand, being overweight—having a body mass index higher than 25—is associated with low life satisfaction (Ball, Crawford, & Kenardy, 2004; Nieman et al., 2000; Sarlio-Lähteenkorva, 2001; Zullig, Pun, & Huebner, 2007). Second, long-term weight loss, which less than 10% of dieters are able to maintain, is related to increases in life satisfaction (Korkeila et al., 1998; Valois et al., 2003). Obese people who have had gastric bypass surgery experience enhanced well-being after their procedure (Bocchieri Riccardi, 2007).

Having a satisfying sex life can be a source of overall happiness and well-being. A worldwide survey of more than 27,000 men and women from 29 countries found a positive relationship between how happy people were in their lives in general and how happy they were in their sexual lives (Laumann et al., 2006). Subjective well-being and sexual satisfaction were highest in European and Western cultures (e.g., Germany, Austria, Spain, Canada, and the United States).

Higher Needs and Happiness

Once a person or a country crosses the $12,000 per-person-per-year GNP, close relationships matter most for overall levels of happiness (Headey, 2008). This would explain why people from Denmark are consistently the happiest people on the planet. The Danish are more interested in fostering healthy relationships than in increasing their personal wealth or climbing the career ladder (Christensen, Herskind, & Vaupel, 2006).

Bruce Headey (2008) reported in a 20-year longitudinal study that people who value noncompetitive goals, such as spending time with a spouse, children, and friends, tend to become happier and more satisfied with life over time. However, people who most value competitive achievement goals, such as career advancement and material gains, actually decrease in happiness over time. When the main goal is monetary or career-advancing, all

that people have to look forward to after they achieve their goals is more competition—not a recipe for happiness and well-being.

Another higher-level need is the cognitive need to explore and understand the world. People who are curious and challenge themselves tend to be happier than people who would rather stick with what they know (Diener et al., 1999; Gallagher & Lopez, 2007; Headey, 2008). This finding is consistent with the broaden-and-build model of positive emotion we discussed earlier, which assumes that positive emotional states lead to expansive thoughts and behavior. The connection between openness to novel experiences and life satisfaction is also consistent with the optimal arousal theories of motivation, which assert that people seek out challenging and moderately arousing situations for optimal performance.

Motivation, Emotion, and the Well-Lived Life

Being happy and satisfied with one's life is obviously important, but so is a well-lived, meaningful, and fully functioning life. What role do motivation and emotion play in living the well-lived life?

The Well-Lived Life and Intrinsic Motivation

Recall the distinction between intrinsic and extrinsic motivation: Intrinsic motivation involves doing activities because we enjoy the process of doing them and they are ends in themselves, whereas extrinsic motivation involves doing activities because they bring us external reward and recognition and are a means to an end.

Living the well-lived life is most often driven by intrinsic goals and motives of doing activities that we find inherently enjoyable (Ryan, Huta, & Deci, 2008). For instance, if someone has a career that enables them to spend each day doing things they inherently enjoy, they are happier. It is not the pay nor other people's viewpoints, but rather that one is satisfied with they spend their time. People who flourish are those who exhibit high levels of well-being while showing few signs of mental illness (Keyes & Lopez, 2002). Although flourishing in life certainly involves positive emotions, reaching a certain states of lasting well-being depends as much on how we lead our lives as what we do to simply feel good.

People who live a well-lived life are also characterized by finding meaning in life. There is a purpose to their actions, and well-being stems from a balance between positive emotions and sense of motivation (Barrett-Cheetham et al., 2016). As is true of Maslow's self-actualizing people, they often are driven by a sense of purpose beyond their own personal lives. They find meaning in their lives in general and even in negative and tragic experiences, which tend to be associated with life satisfaction and happiness (King & Hicks, 2012). Historically, the search for meaning has been associated with spirituality, which also appears to play a role in people's search for a lasting sense of well-being (Argyle, 2001; Holder, Coleman, & Wallace, 2010; Van Cappellen et al., 2016).

The Well-Lived Life, Affiliation, and Positive Emotions

The need for human contact and relationship is deep-seated in human evolution. As we saw with the concept of attachment (see the chapter on "Human Development"), all mammals—especially humans—require others during early stages of life for their very survival. The social needs for relatedness and affiliation are general conditions of being human, but people who flourish and have a well-lived life experience these even more strongly than most (Ryan et al., 2008). As a result of this greater sense of connection to others, these individuals often experience a deep sense of empathy with and compassion for others (Ryan et al., 2008).

Flourishers—as people who live life well are called—are also more likely to experience more positive emotional states, and they report more frequency of feeling satisfied, having a life with direction, and contributing to society

(Catalino & Fredrickson, 2011; Fredrickson & Losada, 2005; Keyes, 2002). Catalino and Fredrickson (2011) found that when flourishers experience pleasant everyday events they get a bigger "boost" from positive emotions than nonflourishers do; that is, they feel better about these experiences. Similarly, Fredrickson and Losada (2005) reported that those who are flourishing have more than a 3 to 1 ratio of positive to negative emotional experiences. Moreover, there is preliminary evidence that a sense of well-being marked by flourishing (as opposed to just a sustained sense of feeling good) is related to a form of gene expression that appears to be related to physical health and longevity (Fredrickson, 2016). Living a satisfied life may well be a key to long life.

Chapter Review

©Jade/Getty Images RF

MOTIVATION

- The psychology of motivation addresses the question of why people do what they do.

- Motivation encompasses needs, drives, and motivated behavior. A motive is anything that energizes or directs behavior.

- Needs are states of cellular or bodily deficiency that compel drives, such as the need for water, food, and oxygen. Drives are the perceived states of tension that occur when our bodies are deficient in some need—such as thirst, hunger, or breathing.

- Maslow organized the forces that drive human behavior into a hierarchy, in which lower-level biological needs are subordinate to higher-level needs.

- Hunger is a basic drive that ensures that we take in sufficient nutrition to survive.

- Internal signals of hunger include sensations of the stomach and blood glucose levels, both of which are coordinated by sensors in the brain; external signals for hunger include the sight and smell of food, as well as culturally influenced preferences.

- Eating disorders are complex and dangerous outcomes of a culture obsessed with thinness. At the same time,

rates of obesity have increased dramatically over the last 50 years in the United States.

- Like all human motives, sexual desire results from a complex interplay of both biological and social forces.

- The hypothalamus plays an important role in sexual arousal.

- Hormones, especially testosterone, regulate sexual drive.

- Research on gender differences and casual sex tends to find that males are more likely than females to engage in casual sex.

- Sexual orientation is a motive that involves both biological and social influences.

- The need to belong and to connect with others is one of the strongest and most basic of human needs and is behind the popularity of social networking.

- One's tendency to achieve success is a function of three things: motivation to succeed, expectation of success, and the incentive value of the success.

- Motivation to work comes in three kinds: extrinsic motivators (rewards, money, and positive feedback), intrinsic motivators (pleasure, joy, challenge, and autonomy), and organizational support (belief that the company cares about you and your well-being).

EMOTION

- Unlike the longer-lasting moods and affective traits, emotions are acute, multifaceted responses to important events in our environment.

- Emotion can best be understood as a process that unfolds over time, beginning with exposure to an antecedent event, then appraisal.

- Appraisal determines whether an emotion occurs.

- Emotional responses include changes in behavior/expression, physiology, and subjective experience.

- Emotion regulation is an umbrella term for anything we do to try to change or otherwise manipulate the emotions we experience.

- From an evolutionary perspective, emotions organize bodily systems for a quick and efficient response to an important environmental event. This model applies best to negative emotions. Positive emotions, according to the broaden-and-build model, expand our thinking and help us develop knowledge and skills.

- The facial expressions of a set of basic emotions—anger, disgust, fear, happiness, sadness, and surprise—are recognized universally and appear to have evolutionary significance.

- Self-conscious emotions are a function of how well we live up to our expectations, the expectations of others, or the rules set by society. They require a sense of self and the ability to reflect on one's own actions. Shame, guilt, humiliation, embarrassment, and pride are examples of self-conscious emotions.

- Display rules show how cultural factors can lead to differences in the expression of emotion. Cultural variability is less apparent in the physiological changes associated with emotions.

- Physiological changes of negative emotions tend to be associated with higher arousal and activation of the sympathetic branch of the autonomic nervous system. Many physiological changes of positive emotions engage the parasympathetic nervous system to relax the body.

- Scientists are not sure what produces the subjective experience of emotion. The James-Lange theory holds that the perception of bodily changes plays an important role in an emotional experience.

- The brain is involved in every aspect of the emotion process, from appraisal to regulation. Although many brain structures appear to be crucial to emotions, the amygdala and the prefrontal cortex are major players.

- Men and women differ in how they talk about their emotional experiences, and women tend to smile more than men. The sexes, however, are much more similar than different in their emotionality.

- Emotional intelligence is the ability to recognize emotions in oneself and others, the development of empathic understanding, and the skills for regulating emotions in oneself and others; it may be at least as important to one's success in life as academic achievement.

BRINGING IT ALL TOGETHER: MAKING CONNECTIONS IN MOTIVATION AND EMOTION

- Happiness, life satisfaction, and subjective well-being are not directly related to income.

- People who flourish and live the well-lived life are driven more by intrinsic pleasure, find more meaning in both positive and negative events, and are more likely to experience positive emotion than are those who are not flourishing.

Key Terms

achievement motivation
affective traits
anorexia nervosa
appraisal
basic emotions
broaden-and-build model
bulimia nervosa
display rules
drives
Duchenne smile
emotion regulation
emotional intelligence
emotional response
emotions

expressive suppression
extrinsic motivation
Facial Action Coding System (FACS)
facial feedback hypothesis
glucose
homeostasis
incentive
intrinsic motivation
James-Lange theory of emotion
life satisfaction
moods
motivation
needs
neurocultural theory of emotion

perceived organizational support
reappraisal
self-actualization
self-conscious emotions
set point
sexual behavior
sexual orientation
subjective experience of emotion
subjective well-being
universal
Yerkes-Dodson law

Quick Quiz Answers

Quick Quiz 1: 1. b; **2.** c; **3.** b; **4.** c   **Quick Quiz 2: 1.** b; **2.** c; **3.** d; **4.** d; **5.** a; **6.** a; **7.** b

12 Stress and Health

Chapter Outline

Challenge Your Assumptions

True or False?

- There is a gene for stress. (see page 464)

- Stress can shorten your lifespan. (see page 471)

- People who are Type A are really anxious and high-strung. (see page 478)

- Daily showering and shampooing is good for you. (see page 480)

- Exercise can turn fat into muscle after one workout. (see page 483)

- Stress is always bad for your health. (see page 486)

©Westend61/Getty Images RF

Actress Carrie Fisher, *Princess Leia* in the Star Wars films, died suddenly of a heart attack in December of 2016. Millions mourned the loss of their beloved princess, who by all accounts died young. At age 60, Carrie Fisher died younger than the average American woman, who lives 81.2 years (National Center for Health Statistics, 2015). Carrie Fisher was far from the average woman, however. She once illustrated her own uniqueness by pointing out that she had been both a Pez dispenser *and* featured in abnormal psychology textbooks. Carrie had bipolar disorder, which is characterized by extreme mood variation ranging from deep depression to manic energy. She used her wit, compassion, and fame to bring attention to the disease and gave voice to people who live with it. She also had a challenging life—took daily medications to regulate the bipolar disorder, was prone to substance abuse, smoked cigarettes, and struggled with her weight her entire life. Some of these factors—especially smoking, diet, and stress—can elevate one's risk for heart disease, which Carrie had been developing for years (most likely unbeknownst to her).

Carrie Fisher's mother was the Hollywood legend, actress Debbie Reynolds. Despite periods of conflict in their lives, over the past several years Carrie and Debbie had become extremely close, living in individual houses on a shared plot of land, walking freely between their abodes. Neither was married any more. Their daily lives were intertwined.

The day after Carrie died, while planning Carrie's funeral, Debbie died of a stroke. According to her son, Carrie's younger brother, Todd Fisher, Carrie's death was too much stress for his already frail 84-year-old mother to handle: "She said, 'I want to be with Carrie.' And then she was gone."

Did Debbie Reynolds die of a broken heart? Did the stress of dealing with the horrifying news of the death of her only daughter push her body—already weakened with age and a number of lingering health issues—to stop functioning? As we will see in this chapter, stress and other psychological pressures can impact health in a number of ways. One route is by elevating physiological arousal and taxing blood vessels and organ systems. This is what may have killed Debbie Reynolds. Another impact of stress is through health-related behaviors (such as diet, smoking, substance abuse), all of which appear to have played a role in Carrie Fisher's death.

In this chapter we examine the psychological and physiological nature of stress and the related topic of coping. We then survey some major topics in the field of health psychology, a discipline that emerged from an

©Sunset Boulevard/Corbis Historical/Getty Images

 Carrie Fisher as Princess Leia of *Star Wars*.

interest in the effects of stress on physical health. We will highlight how stress both emerges from and modifies mental and physical processes, and explore how differences in people's ability to deal with life's challenges influence the functioning of their bodies as well as how these bodily responses can affect how people think and feel. We will also explore the evidence that some stress can be beneficial to health and well-being as well as harmful.

Source: http://www.bollywoodlife.com/news-gossip/star-wars-princess-leia-carrie-fisher-dies-after-a-massive-heart-attack/

STRESS

The term *stress* can refer to a wide variety of phenomena. We speak of having a stressful life when the pressures of daily life interfere with our ability to maintain a sense of well-being. Sometimes people talk about "feeling stressed," as if stress were an emotional state, one that involved anxiety and exhaustion. Some people are "stressed" by minor events such as a parking ticket or a missed train, whereas others seem to sail through life amid a great number of demands—work, family, school—all the while maintaining a sense of well-being and balance.

Stress occurs when a situation overwhelms a person's perceived ability to meet the demands of that situation. As with emotions, we evaluate our experiences of stressful situations and attempt to cope with the challenges they pose. Suppose you are doing poorly in a class, and you have the final exam in one week. At first, you may feel stressed, but then you realize that, with more review of the material, study group meetings, and more sleep, you could do better. You resolve to make these changes to improve your chances for a good final exam grade. As a result, the feeling of stress may decrease.

stress
A response elicited when a situation overwhelms a person's perceived ability to meet the demands of the situation.

©AlexanderNovikov/iStock/Getty Images RF

Driving, particularly in high-traffic urban areas, can elicit a stress response.

 What physiological changes might we expect to see in this woman right now?

Stress as Stimulus or Response

Stress has different meanings in different contexts. We often think of stress as something that happens *to* us, as situations that push us to the limit or threaten our safety or well-being. Or stress can be the relentless onslaught of difficulties, such as being late on a term paper, the car breaking down, realizing there is no money in the bank, and then getting into an argument with a roommate all in one week. We call these events that push us to the limit or exceed our ability to manage the situation at hand **stressors**. The focus on the situations that cause stress is known as the *stimulus view of stress*.

In contrast, stress can be internal to us; we can think of it as the feeling we experience when events are too much to handle. The *response view of stress* focuses on the physiological changes that occur when someone encounters an excessively challenging situation. Later in the chapter, we explore Hans Selye's view of stress as a physiological response.

Clearly, stress is much more than being in certain challenging situations, and it is much more than physiological responses. Stress emerges from people's interpretations of the relevance of certain stressors to their lives and their ability to deal with them. This *relational view of stress* defines stress as a particular relationship between people and the situations in which they find themselves. That is, how stressful a situation is for you depends on what the situation means to you. For instance, for someone who has not studied or attended class regularly, a final exam might create severe stress. For someone who prepared carefully and attended most classes, the exam might be a challenge, but not unduly stressful.

We will look briefly at the view of stress as a stimulus, which has dominated psychological research for many years. Then we will explore the relational view, before turning to the research on stress as a physiological response, which sets a foundation for our understanding of how stress can affect health.

stressors
Events that trigger a stress response.

FIGURE 1

SOCIAL READJUSTMENT RATING SCALE.
Developed by Holmes and Rahe (1967), this scale quantifies stress in terms of major life changes. The higher the value, the greater the stress associated with the event.

Life Event	Value
Death of spouse	100
Divorce	73
Marital separation	65
Jail term	63
Death of close family member	63
Change in financial state	38
Death of a close friend	37
Change to a different line of work	36
Foreclosure of mortgage	30
Change in responsibilities at work	29
Change in sleeping habits	16
Change in eating habits	15
Vacation	13
Christmas	12
Minor legal violations	11

Source: Holmes, T. H., & Rahe, R. H. (1967). The social readjustment rating scale. *Journal of Psychosomatic Research, 11*, 211–218.

Stress as a Stimulus Some events demand an overwhelming amount of our energy and time. Any number of things can be stressors: obviously unpleasant situations, such as divorce, financial troubles, or illness, but also pleasant situations, such as a wedding or the birth of a child. Psychologists measure stress as a stimulus by quantifying the number of stressors a person experiences during a given period. Two major categories of stressors are major life events and daily hassles.

Any situation that creates a major upheaval in a person's life might lead to stress. Indeed, one approach to measuring stress as a stimulus focuses on major life events. In the late 1960s, Thomas Holmes and Richard Rahe developed the Social Readjustment Rating Scale (SRRS), an instrument to quantify stress in terms of major life changes. This scale, shown in Figure 1, consists of a list of events that might be considered life changing; each is assigned a corresponding life change value. After a person has responded to the questions on the scale, a researcher can calculate the total amount of stress the respondent is experiencing by adding up relative stress values, which were derived from previous research, known as Life Change Units (Holmes & Rahe, 1967).

The SRRS is easy to administer and score, but it has some drawbacks. First, it ignores the fact that people view similar events differently. While some people might find marriage more stressful than a major work change, for others it may be vice versa (Scully, Tosi, & Banning, 2000). Second, by measuring stress in terms of life events, the SRRS fails to consider differences in people's emotional responses to stressors. Nevertheless, the SRRS is still widely used in research on stress and health, and it relates to measures of mental and physical health (Gottlieb & Green, 1984).

Sometimes little things really bother us. The accumulation of minor irritations—traffic, too much homework, relationship troubles—might wear us down, both mentally and physically. The Hassles and Uplifts Scale measures the frequency and intensity of minor irritations (hassles) and the positive events of daily life that may counteract their damaging effects (Kanner et al., 1981). A number of studies report positive correlations between the frequency of daily hassles and self-reported health symptoms (DeLongis, Folkman, & Lazarus, 1988; Feist et al., 1995; Kohn, Lafreniere, & Gurevich, 1991). Some data indicate that hassles are more strongly related to health outcomes than are major life events (Kohn et al., 1991; Weinberger, Hiner, & Tierney, 1987).

Most studies have looked at whether hassles are related to health outcomes in roughly the same time period, but one longitudinal study of U.S. military veterans collected questionnaire data hassles and uplifts over a 16-year period in over 1,300 men (Jeong et al., 2016). In this study, it was not the number of hassles that mattered, but rather the intensity of the hassles—how severe they felt—that predicted mortality. The authors interpreted this to mean that it was the long-term consequences of almost daily stressors that were perceived as intense that led to death (Jeong et al., 2016).

A major limitation to measuring both major life events and hassles is that not all people view situations in the same way. A poorly prepared student might dread an exam, but a student who has studied thoroughly might welcome it as a challenge. This example points to the ways in which people differ in their responses to situations. Using this logic, Lazarus and Folkman (1984) argued that, because people do not view similar situations in the same way, it is misleading to examine stress solely in terms of the situations that may call it forth. We have to look at the person in relation to the situation.

Relationship between Person and Situation   As we saw with emotion, when we first encounter a situation in our environment, we quickly appraise what it means for us. Lazarus and Folkman (1984) talk about two kinds of appraisal. **Primary appraisal** is an assessment of what a situation means to us. The outcome of this appraisal determines whether an emotional response might occur. If we view the event as personally irrelevant, we feel no emotion. If we view it as personally relevant, the event may be either contrary to or consistent with our goals or welfare. If we appraise it as contrary to our well-being, we feel a negative emotion, which might cause stress. If we appraise it as consistent with our well-being, we feel a positive emotion. Figure 2 depicts the process by which different appraisals lead to different emotional outcomes. Even though both pleasant and unpleasant *events* might lead to stress, stress emerges from negative emotional responses to events that we cannot get under control. Any kind of event—pleasant or unpleasant—might lead to such emotional reactions. For example, a wedding is a pleasant event that can be stressful.

Emotional events may escalate into stress when we cannot deal with the demands that the event entails. According to Lazarus and Folkman, we assess the resources available to cope with stress in a process called **secondary appraisal**. When we find ourselves in a stressful situation, we try to figure out what to do about that situation, how to resolve it, or how to make the unpleasant feeling it creates go away.

The Physiology of Stress

When we experience situations as stressful, physiological changes occur in our bodies. Most notably, the autonomic nervous system (ANS), the endocrine system, and the brain interact to create a range of changes in bodily systems.

The ANS, as discussed in the chapter "The Biology of Behavior," consists of all the neurons that serve the organs and the glands. Because it is linked to the body systems that support action, the ANS plays a crucial role in the stress response. These systems include the circulatory system, to pump blood to large muscle groups during times of emergency, and the respiratory system, to provide the oxygen required so that those muscles can function.

primary appraisal
A quick assessment of the meaning of a given environmental event for the individual.

secondary appraisal
Self-assessment of the resources available to cope with stress.

Connection

Like stress, emotions are generated by our appraisals of events in our lives. How we evaluate the meaning of certain situations—whether a smile from a stranger or an upcoming exam—determines whether we feel threatened or joyful in response to that situation.

See "Emotion as a Process," in the chapter "Motivation and Emotion." (p. 434)

FIGURE 2

THE EMOTION/STRESS PROCESS. When events are appraised as threatening, negative emotions occur.

©arek_malang/Shutterstock, ©Jose Luis Pelaez Inc/Blend Images LLC RF, ©Image Source/Getty Images RF, ©John A. Karachewski RF

 According to this model, under what conditions does stress occur?

neuroendocrine system
The hormonal systems involved in emotions and stress.

The second major system involved in stress is the endocrine system, which consists of the major hormone-releasing glands. The term **neuroendocrine system** refers to the hormonal systems involved in emotions and stress. The interactions among various organs, glands, and nervous system chemicals lay the groundwork for the dynamic interplay between psychological experience and physiological functioning.

The hypothalamus, the pituitary gland, and the adrenal glands are key structures in the neuroendocrine regulation of stress responses. The hypothalamus links the nervous system to parts of the endocrine system relevant to emotions and stress: Hypothalamic neurons release chemicals that stimulate the release of hormones from the pituitary gland, which sits just beneath it and is connected to

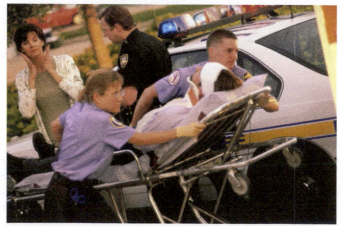

©Ingram Publishing

Physiological changes that enable us to respond quickly during an emergency can take a toll on our bodies if stress persists.

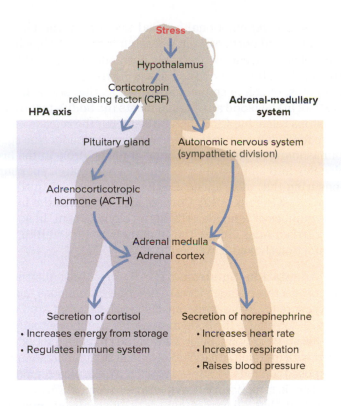

FIGURE 3

THE HPA AXIS AND THE ADRENAL-MEDULLARY SYSTEM. During emotional arousal and stress, the hypothalamus activates the neuroendocrine system to prepare the body's response. The hypothalamus releases CRF, which stimulates the pituitary to release ACTH. ACTH then stimulates the cortex of the adrenal gland to release the "stress hormone" cortisol.

brain stem structures that control the ANS. The pituitary releases hormones that play a key role in the stress response. The adrenal glands, which sit atop the kidneys, release several stress-related hormones: the catecholamines, which control ANS activation, and the **glucocorticoids**, which maintain the activation of physiological systems during emergencies.

Once activated, the hypothalamus initiates a series of endocrine events that profoundly affect the body. Two major neuroendocrine pathways are activated: the adrenal-medullary system and the hypothalamus-pituitary-adrenal axis (see Figure 3). First in line is the **adrenal-medullary system**, in which the hypothalamus sends instructions to the brain stem to activate sympathetic neurons. Then sympathetic neurons tell the adrenal gland to release the important catecholamine norepinephrine. Norepinephrine activates the sympathetic response, increasing heart rate, rate of respiration, and blood pressure to make the body ready for action.

The sympathetic response evolved because rapid mobilization of the body's resources in emergency situations had clear survival and reproductive benefits. In cases of stress, however, this activation is prolonged. Moreover, if we live with prolonged stress-inducing situations, our bodies remain in "emergency mode" for long periods of time. Thus, a response that is adaptive in the short term can take a toll on the body in the long term, leading, for example, to sustained increases in blood pressure and heart rate. Think about how you feel when something startles you: Your heart races; you start breathing heavily; you're in a state of high alert. Now imagine what it would be like to remain in that condition for several days.

The other major neuroendocrine pathway in stress responses is the **hypothalamic-pituitary-adrenal (HPA) axis**. Recall that the hypothalamus releases substances, called releasing factors, that tell the pituitary when to release

glucocorticoids
Hormones responsible for maintaining the activation of physiological systems during emergencies.

adrenal-medullary system
A major neuroendocrine pathway stimulated during stress, in which the hypothalamus activates the sympathetic nervous system.

hypothalamic-pituitary-adrenal (HPA) axis
A major neuroendocrine pathway relevant to the stress response involving the hypothalamus, pituitary gland, and adrenal cortex.

Connection

The sympathetic branch of the ANS activates the body; the parasympathetic branch calms the body. Both play a role in how the body responds to and recovers from stress.

See "The Nervous System," in the chapter "The Biology of Behavior" (p. 81) and "Emotion as a Process," in the chapter "Motivation and Emotion." (p. 434)

general adaptation syndrome (GAS)

As defined by Hans Selye, a generalized, nonspecific set of changes in the body that occur during extreme stress.

alarm stage

The phase of the general adaptation syndrome in which all of the body's resources respond to a perceived threat.

various hormones. During emotional arousal and stress, the hypothalamus releases a substance called corticotropin-releasing factor (CRF), which stimulates the pituitary to release adrenocorticotropic hormone (ACTH). ACTH then stimulates the cortex of the adrenal gland to release cortisol, the major glucocorticoid produced in humans, which is commonly known as the "stress hormone." When the level of cortisol in the blood adequately meets the body's metabolic needs, the hypothalamus stops releasing CRF, thereby reducing the release of cortisol. This kind of negative feedback occurs throughout the neuroendocrine system.

Cortisol has many important functions. It plays a role in the breakdown of complex molecules into simpler ones to release energy and, so, plays an important role in ensuring that more glucose is available for fuel in the bloodstream (Rose, Vegiopoulos, & Herzig, 2010). Cortisol also regulates the immune system, by reducing the number of immune cells in the bloodstream. In so doing, chronically elevated cortisol may impact the immune system's ability to protect the body against infection (Lovell & Wetherell, 2011).

The General Adaptation Syndrome (GAS) In 1946, Austrian physiologist Hans Selye proposed a three-stage model to describe the changes in physiology that occur during exposure to severe stressors. Selye believed that attempts to adapt to overwhelming stressors cause the body to wear down and eventually get sick. With homeostasis as his starting point, Selye viewed the changes the body goes through when confronted with extreme situational demands as manifestations of adaptation to stress. He exposed animals to stressors, such as extreme temperature change, severe electrical shock, radiation, or heavy exercise (Selye, 1976).

Selye proposed that all stress causes a generalized, nonspecific set of changes in the body—no matter what the type of elicitor. He measured hormones, metabolism, organ function, and other variables and observed a consistent pattern of responses regardless of the stressor. Selye (1946) coined the term **general adaptation syndrome (GAS)** to describe this general pattern of responses to prolonged exposure to stress.

The GAS consists of three stages: alarm, resistance, and exhaustion (see Figure 4). Upon exposure to a stressor, an animal enters a state of physiological shock, called the **alarm stage**, which is the body's emergency response to a threat. The alarm stage mobilizes the body's resources to act via the effects of adrenal-medullary activation of the sympathetic nervous system. During this

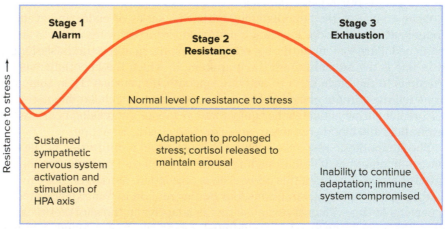

FIGURE 4

SELYE'S GENERAL ADAPTATION SYNDROME (GAS). In the alarm stage, the body's resources are mobilized in response to a stressor. Resistance occurs when the body can no longer sustain the emergency response and the organism must find other ways to ward off the threat. If the threat persists, eventually the body's resources become depleted, physical exhaustion occurs, and illness becomes much more likely.

stage the HPA axis is active as well, and the sustained release of cortisol from the adrenal glands may move from being helpful (by making more fuel available) to being harmful in the long run (by suppressing certain aspects of immune function).

Animals, however, cannot persist in the alarm stage for long. With continued exposure to the stressor, they will either die or find other ways of coping with the enduring threat. When they develop other ways to cope, they enter the second stage of adaptation, the **resistance stage**. Resistance implies that the organism tries to manage the threat. This extended effort, however, takes its toll physically and psychologically by diverting resources from the maintenance of normal bodily functions. With repeated exposure to a stressor, animals enter the **exhaustion stage**. At this stage, their resources for fighting off threats have been depleted, and illness becomes much more likely. Have you ever come down with a cold or other illness a week or so after final exams? You get the idea.

Selye's model laid the groundwork for research on the physiology of stress, but soon it became clear that his GAS model did not fit all stress responses. First, Selye studied extreme physical stressors, such as nearly freezing an animal to death or repeatedly exposing it to severe electrical shock, and subjected animals to these stressors for prolonged periods. Questions arose as to whether the bodily changes that occurred in response to such severe demands in animals provided a good model for enduring the stress of, say, divorce or financial troubles in humans. Second, some researchers questioned the idea that a syndrome of body responses to stress occurred regardless of the type of stressor.

In the 1970s, research challenged Selye's assumption that the stress response is a general one. Mason (1971, 1975) showed that an animal's response to a stressor differed depending on its psychological state. If the animal could anticipate a stressor, it showed a less severe physiological response than an animal that could not anticipate a stressor (Mason, 1971). Further, research conducted during the 1980s showed that different emotions produce different patterns of ANS activation, casting further doubt on Selye's idea of a generalized physiological response to any environmental demand (Ekman, Levenson, & Friesen, 1983).

How We Adapt to Stress   Most accounts of the physiology of stress (such as Selye's) think of stress as a deviation from balance. Recovery from stress occurs when all systems return to normal. This view stems from the notion of homeostasis—the idea that, unless we are being provoked by something, we are humming along at an even-keeled *baseline* state, and we return to the same state after the stress. Moreover, homeostasis implies that just one system in the body struggles to return to baseline at a time (*homeo-* means "same"). Suppose you were walking in a desert: The homeostasis view says that you would sweat to cool your body to return to an ideal temperature. If you think about it for a minute, you'll realize that this is not ideal. If your body did this, you would become dehydrated (Sapolsky, 1998). Thus, a new concept was needed to explain the more complex and dynamic changes that occur when the body is stressed.

Some researchers offer an alternative explanation to how we adapt to stress. Rather than a state of balance, they say, our normal state is one of actively responding to the world around us. This more dynamic, responsive "resting" state is known as **allostasis**, which means that the body achieves stability through change (Karatsoreos & McEwen, 2011; Schulkin, 2005; Sterling & Eyer, 1988). *Allo* means "different" or "changing." Thinking of the baseline state as one of dynamic responsiveness makes it easier to understand the effects of stress on the body (Juster, McEwen, & Lupien, 2010). Back to the example of walking in the desert: The concept of allostasis emphasizes that your body would respond in many ways, not simply by sweating. Your kidneys would start producing less urine; mucous membranes in your eyes and skin would dry out; even your veins and arteries would constrict to maintain blood pressure with a smaller volume of blood.

resistance stage
In the general adaptation syndrome, extended effort by the body to deal with a threat.

exhaustion stage
The phase of the general adaptation syndrome when all resources for fighting the threat have been depleted and illness is more likely.

allostasis
The process by which the body achieves stability through physiological change.

Connection

Do you think an ethics review board would allow Selye to conduct his research on extreme stressors in animals today? Why or why not?

See "Ethical Research with Animals," in the chapter "Conducting Research in Psychology." (p. 68)

The concept of allostasis makes clear that our bodies can respond adaptively to challenge for only a short period of time. If we are pushed too long, the body's active attempts to adapt are sustained, and we are taxed. The body starts to wear down, as the *allostatic load*—the amount of wear and tear on the system to which the body must adapt—becomes too much to bear. This is how stress causes illness. Indeed, scientists are just beginning to get a handle on the complex relationships among nervous, endocrine, and immune systems that can sometimes lead to susceptibility to disease (Verburg-van Kemenade, Cohen, & Chadzinska, 2016).

Stress and the Brain   So far we have emphasized how stress affects a wide array of physiological responses, most of which involve systems outside the central nervous system. What about the brain? We tend to think of stress as being caused by processes within the brain, for it is our interpretations of the events in the world that trigger emotions, but the physiological activation triggered by stress also affects the brain. Cortisol has a profound effect on the hippocampus, a brain structure that plays a pivotal role in memory; the hippocampus contains one of the greatest concentrations of cortisol receptors in the brain (McEwen, De Kloet, & Rostene, 1986). Unfortunately, stress-related cortisol release causes hippocampal dendrites to shrink, which can interfere with several types of memory. Chronic stress reduces neurogenesis (the growth of new neurons) in the hippocampus, and it may inhibit the synaptic plasticity in the hippocampus and neocortex, impacting learning and memory formation (Anacker et al., 2013; Artola, 2008; Wang et al., 2008). Animal research shows that excessive stress in a pregnant mother can affect the development of several brain areas—including the amygdala, hippocampus, hypothalamus, and corpus callosum—in her offspring (Charil et al., 2010). Stress-related brain changes appear to increase the risk of depression and other psychological disorders (Cattaneo & Riva, 2016; de Celis et al., 2016).

Severely adverse experiences early in life—what we would consider serious stressors—can affect the amount of cortisol receptors in the hippocampus (McGowan, 2012). They also show increased susceptibility to chronic diseases of aging (Miller, Chen, & Parker, 2011) and such early life stress can have lasting neurological effects (Vaccarino & Bremner, 2016). The data are inconclusive, however, as to whether minor daily stressors or hassles are linked to cortisol. One recent large-scale study of children measured cortisol from hair samples of over 300 elementary school–aged kids. The researchers also gathered information from the parents about eating habits, activity level, illness symptoms, as well as recent daily hassles. Although cortisol was related to BMI in girls and bodily symptoms in boys, cortisol was unrelated to hassles and other indicators of stress (Gerber et al., 2017).

Coping plays a big role in the duration of stress responses and whether they develop sufficiently to become harmful to the brain and body. In monkeys, more effective coping with stress increases neurogenesis in the hippocampus, which offers the hopeful suggestion that the adverse effects of stress on the brain may be reversible (Lyons et al., 2010). In a fascinating study of rats, researchers found that increased experience with sex—even chronic exposure to sex—also increases neurogenesis in the hippocampus (Leuner, Glasper, & Gould, 2010)!

Stress and Genes   No single "stress gene" dictates how the body responds to stress in the way a cancer gene might turn cancer cells on and off. Instead, several complex processes involving stress, genes, and endocrines regulate the relationship between stress and disease (Cole, 2009, 2010). From this complex area of research, we can distill out a few key points. First, the effects of chronic social isolation on illness appear to be regulated by genetic factors (Cole, 2010; Cole et al., 2007). Also, those genes associated with the human stress response seem critical to certain chronic diseases (Capri et al., 2006). Finally, genes appear to play a role in the relationship between the stress of social isolation and diseases that involve inflammatory processes, such as heart disease and cancer (Cole et al., 2010; Khatami, 2009; Miller, Chen, & Parker, 2011).

Challenge Your Assumptions

True or False? There is a gene for stress.

False: There is no single gene for stress (or any psychological trait).

Connection

The hippocampus, located deep inside the brain, is critical for memory formation.

See "Overview of Brain Regions," in the chapter "The Biology of Behavior," (p. 95) and "Short-Term and Working Memory and the Brain," in the chapter "Memory." (p. 280)

Quick Quiz.1: Stress

1. According to the definition provided in the text, which of the following is the best example of stress?
   a. Maria is studying for one exam.
   b. Maria is studying for three exams on the same day, but she has a handle on all three.
   c. Maria is studying for two exams on the same day and feels unprepared for both of them.
   d. Maria is angry with her boyfriend.

2. This view of stress focuses on the physiological changes that occur when someone encounters an excessively challenging situation.
   a. stimulus
   b. response
   c. relational
   d. situational

3. The model of adaptation to stress that says there is stability through change is the
   a. functional view.
   b. physiological view.
   c. homeostatic view.
   d. allostatic view.

4. Which part of the nervous system becomes most involved when we are feeling stressed?
   a. hypothalamic-pituitary-adrenal (HPA) axis
   b. temporal lobes
   c. hippocampus
   d. frontal lobes

Answers can be found at the end of the chapter.

COPING: THE MANAGEMENT OF STRESS

Generally, **coping** refers to anything people do to deal with or manage stress or emotions. When we walk away from someone who is making us angry or complain about our boss to a friend, we are coping with stresses in our lives. In this section we explore various ways people cope with stress.

coping
The act of dealing with stress or emotions.

Coping Strategies

People don't like feeling bad, so they try to get out of situations that create unpleasantness or look for ways to change their negative feelings. Psychologists Richard Lazarus and Susan Folkman (1984) differentiated between these two types of coping strategies, labeling them *problem-focused* and *emotion-focused* coping. The strategy of social support combines problem-focused and emotion-focused coping strategies. Figure 5 provides an overview of these three coping strategies.

Problem-Focused Coping   **Problem-focused coping** strategies aim to change the situation that is creating stress. If your roommate plays a stereo loudly while you are sleeping, you might choose to discuss it with her, buy earplugs, or cut the speaker wires. Each of these choices is a form of problem-focused coping; each is geared toward changing the situation that created the stress. Examples of problem-focused coping strategies include devising a plan to solve the problem, seeking social support as a way to gather information, and taking assertive action. Problem-focused coping focuses attention on the stress-provoking situation, and we are most likely to use it when we think we can change the situation.

problem-focused coping
A way of dealing with stress that aims to change the situation that is creating stress.

Emotion-Focused Coping   In contrast, **emotion-focused coping** aims to regulate the experience of distress. Lazarus and Folkman describe several forms of emotion-focused coping, including *reappraisal*, the reevaluation of a situation in light of new information or additional thought; *distancing*, or attempting to separate oneself from an emotional experience; *escape-avoidance*, wishful thinking or doing something to get one's mind off the situation (such as going to the movies); *seeking social support* by talking with friends for purposes of emotional support; *self-control*, or trying to regulate one's feelings or actions regarding the problem; and *accepting responsibility*, acknowledging one's role in the stress-eliciting situation (Lazarus & Folkman, 1984).

emotion-focused coping
A way of dealing with stress that aims to regulate the experience of distress.

Strategy	Example

problem-focused strategy

| Solve the problem
Seek social support
Take assertive action | Roommate's stereo too loud:
Focus on how to make it quiet.

An assertive act might be to cut the stereo speaker wires.  |

emotion-focused strategy

| Reappraise
Distancing
Use escape-avoidance
Seek social support
Exercise self-control
Emotional disclosure
Accept responsibility | Break up with a partner:
Focus on how to feel better.

An escape-avoidance act may be to take a vacation to get away from the former partner. Write about it to unburden emotions.  |

social support strategy

| Combines problem-focused and emotion-focused strategies
Develop social connectedness
Seek advice from or talk with friends and loved ones | Support groups:
Giving and showing support to other people may increase longevity.  |

FIGURE 5

COPING STRATEGIES. We tend to apply problem-focused coping strategies to change a stressful situation and emotion-focused coping strategies in situations we feel we cannot control.

(top): ©Floresco Productions/agefotostock RF; (center): ©A. Minde/PhotoAlto RF; (bottom): ©Dave and Les Jacobs/Blend Images LLC RF

When a situation is beyond one's control, certain types of emotion-focused coping—especially reappraisal—can be helpful in regulating the emotional aspects of stress, but other kinds of emotion-focused coping can be problematic. A study of people coping with the loss of a partner to AIDS found that engaging in reappraisal correlated with increases in positive mood (Moskowitz et al., 1996). What exactly is reappraisal? It occurs when one reevaluated a situation, or reinterprets it from the original understanding they had of the situation. For instance, if you see a friend walking down the sidewalk on the other side of the street and you wave, but the person does not look at you or wave back, you might feel hurt. But, if after examining the context, such as the lighting, how far away you were, and how crowded the sidewalk was, you might *reappraise* the situation as one in which the friend could not even see you. They did not wave or smile because they had no idea you were there. One appraisal is more likely to upset you than the other.

Cognitive coping strategies such as reappraisal seem more effective in reducing depression and anxiety in men with HIV than do social support and substance use (Kraaj et al., 2008). The tendency to use of cognitive reappraisal as a strategy to cope with stress has been linked with a protective effect against stress in a number of studies and a number of populations, including people with Type II diabetes (Sagui & Levens, 2016). The ability to reframe one's perceptions to consider a different story for a set of events can be reinforced by mindfulness training, which uses skills from meditation to help people learn how to recognize their thoughts and behavior more keenly. With mindfulness training, even people who deal with chronically stressful situations can learn to use positive reappraisal in the face of adversity (Rayan & Ahmad, 2016).

Willful suppression of upsetting emotions, which is a form of self-control, can lead to chronic physiological arousal and is associated with poor psychological adjustment (Gross & Levenson, 1993; Gross, Richards, & John, 2006). Moreover, some strategies that we use to reduce the experience of distress, such as drinking, smoking, and other forms of drug use, may be maladaptive (Hien & Miele, 2003).

It is widely believed that a good way to cope with stress is to "let it all out." James Pennebaker developed a technique, known as **emotional disclosure**, that enables people to unburden themselves (Pennebaker, 1995). In a typical emotional disclosure task, people are instructed to write for about 15 minutes about a recent emotional experience—in particular, one that they have found troubling, that still bothers them from time to time, and that they haven't discussed much with other people. Participants in the control condition write for a similar amount of time about non-emotional events, such as what they did the day before. Emotional disclosure improves well-being and quality of life (Craft, Davis, & Paulson, 2012), as well as a number of physical health outcomes, including health variables related to HIV/AIDS, immune function, and cancer (O'Cleirigh et al., 2008; Smyth, 1998; Stanton et al., 2002). A few studies, such as a large-scale study of women seeking fertility treatment, show that disclosure did not benefit health outcomes, however (Panagopoulou, Montgomery, & Tarlatzis, 2010). There is evidence that the effectiveness of this intervention may vary for men and women. A brief emotional disclosure intervention dramatically reduced symptoms of PTSD, depression, and HIV in women but not men (Ironson et al., 2013). Also, a recent meta-analysis on the effects of a written emotional disclosure task on psychological and physical health in caregivers (a group of people that often have to endure a great deal of stress) found that while writing about difficult emotions reduced psychological health problems, overall there were few benefits to this group of writing about trauma (Riddle, Smith, & Jones, 2016).

How might writing about one's emotional experiences, especially traumatic ones, benefit health? There are several possible explanations. People in both Western and non-Western cultures believe that confession is beneficial. For the Ndembu of West Africa, for instance, public confession allows for the transformation of negative feelings into positive ones in the community, thereby promoting social harmony (Georges, 1995). It is also thought that *not* working through difficult emotions taxes the body, as research on the association between emotional suppression and ANS arousal suggests (Gross & Levenson, 1993). When confession or disclosure occurs, then, one should observe a decrease in sympathetic nervous system activation or a return to a more relaxed state. In fact, numerous laboratory studies have found that just talking about a traumatic event creates noticeable reductions in autonomic measures such as blood pressure and sweating (Pennebaker, 1995). Writing about positive experiences also benefits mental and physical health, presumably by other mechanisms, such as helping the person maintain a broader focus on life (Burton & King, 2009).

Overall, the research suggests that there is no inherently "good" or "bad" way to cope with stress or regulate emotions. What technique for managing stress is best for your well-being really depends on the context in which it is used (Brockman, Ciarrochia, Parker, & Kashdan, 2016). For instance, when dealing with a terminal illness, some degree of intermittent denial can be helpful to letting one lighten up in the face of death. By contrast, denying you are in debt and have overdue bills is a maladaptive way of coping with the stress of not having enough money (Lazarus, 1983).

Social Support   Social support is a coping strategy that combines problem- and emotion-focused coping. Our friends and loved ones provide advice, give hugs, or simply listen when we are under stress. Social support not only is one

emotional disclosure
A way of coping with stress through writing or talking about the situation.

Connection

Emotion regulation is another term for the strategies we use to alter our emotional state and is similar to *emotion-focused coping*. Both terms refer to efforts to change the way we feel.

See "Emotion as a Process," in the chapter "Motivation and Emotion." (p. 434)

of the most frequently used ways of coping but also can benefit physical health. The *direct effects hypothesis* states that social support is beneficial to mental and physical health whether or not the person is under stress. Sheldon Cohen (2004) has pointed out that being part of a social network guarantees the availability of certain resources. Our social networks may offer guidelines for health-related behaviors, help us regulate our emotions, and give us a sense of identity. We may learn from friends that running or jogging can help us feel better when we're stressed. Examples of social connectedness include being married, belonging to social groups such as churches or clubs, and having many friends. Friends provide an outlet for sharing emotional distress, offering comfort as well as advice.

Alternatively, social support may serve to protect us from the effects of stress under certain conditions. This is known as the *buffering hypothesis*. One influential study found that regular participation in a support group in which members discussed their emotional difficulties improved well-being and extended survival in women with advanced breast cancer (Spiegel et al., 1989), though this finding has not replicated consistently (Edelman et al., 1999; Edmonds, Lockwood, & Cunningham, 1999; Goodwin, 2004; Goodwin et al., 2001).

How well a person is integrated into a *social network* influences health. A social network is simply a cluster of related people, such as family members, spouses, friends, coworkers, or neighbors. This web of friends and acquaintances is related to but not the same as an electronic social network, such as the kind you might have on Facebook or Instagram. When people are well integrated into a social network, social support can buffer the effects of stress by providing interpersonal resources for emotional support and problem solving (Cohen & Wills, 1985). The health benefits of social connectedness include longer life and reduced susceptibility to colds, and a greater likelihood of following doctor's treatment recommendations in health care (Berkman & Glass, 2000; Cohen et al., 2003; Reese et al., 2016). A landmark study that followed more than 12,000 people over 32 years examined the role of social networks in quitting smoking (Christakis & Fowler, 2008). Social networks influenced the likelihood that a person would stop smoking, but not all social connections had the same effect. If a spouse stopped smoking, the chance the other spouse would also stop went up by 67%; if a friend stopped smoking, the chance another friend stopped went up by 36%; and if a coworker stopped smoking, the chance another worker stopped went up by 34%. So the effect of the other person's behavior on any given person depended to some extent on how close they were to each other.

Social networks may be harmful to health as well. In the same study of 12,000 people, researchers looked at the influence of obesity in the same social network. The risk of obesity spread among people who were socially connected. If a person became obese (with a body mass index, or BMI, greater than 30), his or her friends, family members, spouse, or neighbors were more likely to become obese. As was true with smoking, however, not all social connections had the same effect. For instance, if a person's friend became obese over a given period of time, that person's chance of becoming obese increased 57%; if a sibling became obese, the chance increased 40%; and if a spouse became obese, the chance increased 37% (Christakis & Fowler, 2007). Moreover, gender mattered. Individuals of the same gender in a social network influenced same-sexed individuals more than opposite-sexed individuals. In another study, infectious diseases (such as the flu) spread more rapidly among connected individuals than they did among randomly studied groups of people (Christakis & Fowler, 2010). This undesirable aspect of social networks, however, might help in the detection and prevention of further outbreaks. A recent, large-scaled study in Sweden showed that smoking behavior in young women, especially, is supported and shaped by their social interactions

(Miething, Rostila, Edling & Rydgren, 2016). We share healthful habits as well as unhealthful habits with our friends.

The Positive Psychology of Coping

Traditionally, research on stress and coping has focused on how people respond to threatening situations and manage the distress associated with them. For years, however, some psychologists have argued that it is an over-simplification to assume that stress involves only negative emotions and their management (Folkman & Moskowitz, 2000; Lazarus, Kanner, & Folkman, 1980; Seligman & Csikszentmihalyi, 2000). This section discusses various ways in which positive psychological states have been studied in relation to stress and coping.

Positive Traits, Positive Emotions Some people approach the world in a positive way, and as a result, their experience of distress is reduced compared to that of others. *Optimists* tend to emphasize the positive, see the glass as "half full" rather than as "half empty," and believe that things will turn out well (Carver, Scheier, & Segerstrom, 2010). *Pessimists*, by contrast, emphasize the negative; for them, the glass is always half empty and the future uncertain. Optimists are less likely to feel helpless or depressed, adjust better to negative life events, and show better general mental health than do pessimists (Chang, 1998; Smith, Young, & Lee, 2004). Optimism may also benefit physical health (Kubzansky et al., 2001). By seeing the world positively, optimists may appraise events in such a way that negative emotions are less likely and positive emotions more likely. They may be more likely to see potentially stressful situations as challenges rather than threats. Research shows that, the more optimistic a person is, the less likely it is that he or she will die from cardiovascular disease (Giltay et al., 2004). Furthermore, changes in optimism are related to changes in positive emotion that predict immune function (Segerstrom & Sephton, 2010). Surprisingly, believing that you have some control over situations in life, especially traumatic situations, can improve your psychological health (Taylor, 1989). Health psychologist Shelley Taylor has studied various groups of people suffering from chronic, debilitating, and often fatal diseases such as breast cancer, heart disease, and HIV/AIDS. She has found that people who believe they have some control over their illness—in spite of medical evidence to the contrary—are actually happier and less stressed than less optimistic people with the same diseases (Hegelson & Taylor, 1993; Reed et al., 1994; Taylor, 1989). In people recovering from coronary disease, both optimism and gratitude improved how well they maintained healthful behaviors, such as diet and exercise regimens (Millstein et al., 2016).

Positive emotions may facilitate recovery from the physiological effects of negative emotions. One study of men infected with HIV found slower disease progression than in those who were happier (Moskowitz, 2003). Fredrickson and Levenson (1998) showed participants a fear-eliciting film; followed it with a sad, pleasant, or neutral film; and measured cardiovascular activity throughout the film-viewing and post-film-viewing period. Cardiovascular activation elicited by the fear film returned to baseline levels more quickly in people who saw the pleasant film after the fear film, but not in people experiencing the sad or neutral condition. Thus, positive emotions may help the body return to a state of calmness. In fact, research is pointing to a number of potentially beneficial effects of positive emotion on the body—such as lowering blood pressure and regulating cortisol—that we are just beginning to understand (Dockray & Steptoe, 2010).

Tugade and Fredrickson (2004) looked at how resilience affected people's ability to recover from stress. *Resilience* is a personality trait that means being

Connection

The prefrontal cortex plays a key role in the appraisals that generate emotions as well as stress.

See "Motivation and Emotion," in the chapter "Motivation and Emotion". (p. 443)

more flexible and able to bounce back from difficult situations. Resilient people experience quicker recovery from stress-induced cardiovascular arousal, in part because they are more likely to find some positive meaning in a difficult situation (Folkman, 1997; Tugade & Fredrickson, 2004).

Recently, the concept of *grit* has received attention in psychology and the popular press. Grit is related to resilience, but is not identical with it (Duckworth et al., 2007). The two major components of grit are having a resilient response to adverse situations and a stick-to-it-ness or perservering in one's passions and interests over long periods of time (Duckworth & Quinn, 2009). Grit is not only whether one can bounce back from failure but also how much one sticks to tasks over long periods of time. Having the same interest for years and being a hard worker are examples of being gritty. Research has demonstrated that being "gritty" predicts who does well in school, who stays with rigorous military training, and who does well in spelling bees over and above intelligence, personality, or talent (Duckworth et al., 2007; Maddi et al., 2012). Research attempting to understand the brain areas involved in grit and improved performance suggest a key role for structures in the prefrontal cortex (Wang et al., 2016).

Finding Meaning Perhaps the key to psychological health is to be open enough to notice the other things going on in life, even in the midst of tragedy. Positive psychological traits and states do play a big role in whether people are able to find meaning in stressful and tragic events (Folkman, 1997; Folkman & Moskowitz, 2000; Park & Folkman, 1997; Tugade & Fredrickson, 2004). People with terminal illnesses who notice beauty amidst their pain and find opportunities for positive experiences are happier than those who don't, and they may even live longer (Folkman, 1997; Moskowitz, 2003). Resilient people who managed to experience positive moods amidst their despair in the wake of the September 11, 2001 terrorist attacks were more likely to thrive and less likely to fall into depression than those who were less resilient (Fredrickson et al., 2003).

A fascinating line of work, initiated by Elissa Epel and her colleagues (2004) reveals some of the connections between biology and environment that play a role in people's responses to stress and their effects on health. In "Psychology in the Real World," we describe research that stress affects aging at the cellular level.

Quick Quiz 2: Coping

1. You buy earplugs, so that you can sleep when your roommate plays loud music at 1:00 a.m. You have used what kind of coping?
   a. problem-focused
   b. emotion-focused
   c. stimulus-focused
   d. meaning-focused

2. Research has found that having a well-connected social network of friends, family, neighbors, and coworkers is _____ for health outcomes.
   a. never beneficial
   b. sometimes beneficial
   c. sometimes beneficial and sometimes harmful
   d. always beneficial

3. "Seeing the glass as half full," or being optimistic, is likely to have what kind of effect on a person's response to stress and illness?
   a. no real effect
   b. a detrimental effect
   c. a beneficial effect
   d. the same effect as being pessimistic would

4. Who would be most likely to bounce back quickly from a very stressful experience?
   a. a pessimist
   b. a young person
   c. someone who holds in his or her feelings and pretends the event did not happen
   d. a resilient person

Answers can be found at the end of the chapter.

Psychology in the Real World

Does Stress Cause Aging?

Stress often makes people look worn out. As mentioned earlier, this is one of Selye's main ideas: Physiologically, long-term stress wears down the body, making a person more vulnerable to illness ("the exhaustion stage"). People often refer to the stresses of life as wearing them out or causing gray hairs. Is there any evidence, however, that this everyday logic has any basis in the physiology of aging? Can stress actually make you age more quickly?

Contrary to common wisdom, there is little evidence that stress or trauma can suddenly turn a person's hair gray overnight. Most scientific and medical evidence points to purely genetic explanations for hair graying (Nishimura, Granter, & Fisher, 2005; Tobin, 2004). A certain kind of stress does seem to cause gray hair: cellular stress that occurs with aging and toxins from the environment (Nishimura et al., 2005).

Over the last decade or so, however, mounting evidence has accumulated that stress is related to and even causes aging at the cellular level (Lin, Epel, & Blackburn, 2012; Tomiyama et al., 2012). In an innovative study of the physiological effects of stress, psychologist Elissa Epel and her colleagues (2004) examined indicators of cellular aging in healthy women who were biological mothers of either normal or chronically ill children. The mothers reported on the amount of stress they perceived in their daily lives, using a standard questionnaire.

The researchers derived indicators of cellular aging from tests on blood samples collected from each woman. In particular, they examined the telomeres of chromosomes in the DNA of certain white blood cells. *Telomeres* are part of the chromosome involved in replication during the process of cell division. With age, telomeres shorten; moreover, the activity of

telomerase
An enzyme that adds DNA sequences to telomeres.

telomerase, an enzyme that adds DNA sequences to telomeres, decreases with age. Longer telomeres and higher telomerase levels are associated with a longer life in both men and women (Cawthon et al., 2003; Marioni et al., 2016). Telomere length and telomerase levels is also correlated with mortality in people already fighting a disease, such as heart disease (Goglin et al., 2016), though there is some evidence that some these connections might vary by race (Carty et al., 2015).

In a breakthrough study, Epel and her colleagues measured stress not in terms of life conditions per se but in terms of the duration of stress a woman *perceived* in her life; the results showed that, the more stress a woman perceived, the

©Dirk Anschutz/Getty Images

Ask any mother of young children how she feels. Chances are, she'll tell you she's exhausted. Long-term stress that is perceived as severe can speed up the process of cellular aging.

shorter the telomeres and the lower the level of telomerase activity in her blood, conditions that imply older cells. In practical terms, these women's cells were "the equivalent of 9–17 additional years" older than those of women who perceived less stress (Epel et al., 2004, p. 17314).

Since this seminal work, several studies have shown that a number of different stressors have been associated with telomere length, including having major depressive disorder (Garcia-Rizo et al., 2013; Wolkowitz, Epel, Reus, & Mellon, 2010), trauma in war veterans (Bersani et al., 2016), prenatal stress in newborns (Marchetto et al., 2016), and chronic social stress, such as poverty or living with violence (Oliveira et al., 2016). The relationship between telomere length and stress has been replicated several times, though a recent meta-analysis of over 7,000 studies suggests that the relationship might not be particularly strong (Mathur et al., 2016).

If stress can accelerate cellular aging, can engaging in practices that reduce stress or promote well-being enhance cellular health? A study of the psychological and physiological effects of intensive meditation training addressed this question. Positive psychological changes that occur during meditation training are associated with higher activity of telomerase (Jacobs et al., 2010). Specifically, increases in self-reported purpose in life and perceived control predicted greater telomerase activity.

Challenge Your Assumptions

True or False? Stress can shorten your life.
True: Stress accelerates aging at the cellular level.

HOW STRESS AND COPING AFFECT HEALTH

Our discussion so far has implied that stress increases a person's susceptibility to disease. This idea is one of the oldest expressions of the interplay between nature and nurture, and it forms the central tenet of **psychosomatic theory**. Even though people tend to use the term *psychosomatic* to refer to an illness that is "all in the head" or, by implication, "made up," this is a misconception of the theory. Rather, *psychosomatics* deal with how emotional factors can increase the likelihood of certain disorders occurring or worsening. Even the well-known link between stress and ulcers is not a matter of simple causality. Stress increases the likelihood of ulcers by changing the chemical balance in the gut, but certain preconditions must be met for that internal environment to produce ulcers (Yoemans, 2011).

The field of health psychology grew out of psychosomatic medicine. **Health psychology** is the study of psychological factors related to health and illness. It includes disease onset, prevention, treatment, and rehabilitation and involves clinical practice as well as research. Two major approaches can explain the relationship between stress and illness; both illustrate the dynamic interplay among environmental situations, people's interpretations of them, and changes in body functioning. The **physiological reactivity approach** examines how stress cre-

ates sustained physiological activation associated with the stress response can affect body systems in such a way as to increase the likelihood that illness or disease will occur. As such, this model is rooted in psychosomatic medicine. By contrast, the **health behavior approach** focuses on the behaviors in which people engage, such as diet, exercise, or substance abuse, which may make them more

susceptible to illness or may enhance health. These explanations are not mutually exclusive. For example, a person might experience sustained blood pressure elevation due to stress and drink heavily during a time of intense stress, both of which would affect the person's health.

Figure 6 depicts the physiological reactivity model. (We discuss the health behavior approach later in the chapter.) You will notice similarities between this and the emotion/stress process diagram in Figure 2: Each begins with the elicitation of negative emotion and stress. In the physiological reactivity model, however, the activation of the sympathetic nervous system persists and creates

©Steve Prezant/Corbis/Getty Images

Eating in response to stress may make us feel good temporarily, but it may also make us more susceptible to certain diseases.

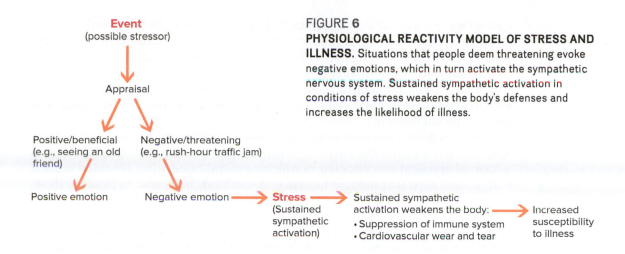

Event
(possible stressor)

Appraisal

Positive/beneficial
(e.g., seeing an old
friend)

Negative/threatening
(e.g., rush-hour traffic jam)

Positive emotion

Negative emotion

Stress
(Sustained
sympathetic
activation)

Sustained sympathetic
activation weakens the body:
• Suppression of immune system
• Cardiovascular wear and tear

Increased
susceptibility
to illness

FIGURE 6

PHYSIOLOGICAL REACTIVITY MODEL OF STRESS AND ILLNESS. Situations that people deem threatening evoke negative emotions, which in turn activate the sympathetic nervous system. Sustained sympathetic activation in conditions of stress weakens the body's defenses and increases the likelihood of illness.

sustained physiological arousal (recall Selye's exhaustion stage). A wide array of body systems may be affected by sustained stress, but a few key systems have been the focus of much research.

The physiological reactivity model starts with sustained physiological arousal. Earlier we said that the sympathetic branch of the autonomic nervous system activates organ systems to enable an animal to respond to emergency situations. The effects of sympathetic arousal on the heart and lungs (increasing pumping and oxygen intake) help the animal act quickly and thus survive. From an evolutionary perspective, these effects were advantageous because of their ability to enable a quick and efficient response; however, the same type of emotional response occurs in daily life, in most cases without an outlet for action, as when you are stuck in traffic or annoyed with a coworker. Thus, the activation persists for hours or days, or it is elicited repeatedly in similar situations over many years. Under such conditions, you can become ill as a result of the recurring arousal produced by stress-related body changes (Sapolsky, 1998).

The **cardiovascular system**, which consists of the heart and all the blood vessels of the body, is especially susceptible to the effects of sustained arousal. During activation of the sympathetic nervous system, heart rate and blood pressure increase. In sustained physiological activation, heart rate and blood pressure remain elevated or are activated repeatedly over extended periods. Frequent blood pressure elevations can damage arteries by reducing their elasticity and increasing the likelihood of fatty buildup. These processes set the stage for heart disease.

The immune system suffers from the effects of sustained arousal as well, and impaired immune function increases susceptibility to disease. How does this work? Sustained activation of the HPA axis leads to sustained release of cortisol, which inhibits the production of certain immune cells. In the short term, the suppression of immune cell production makes sense, because in an emergency immune cells might not be immediately necessary. Over the long term, however, immune suppression makes a person more susceptible to certain diseases.

cardiovascular system
The heart, the blood, and all the blood vessels.

Challenging Assumptions in How the Nervous and Immune Systems Are Linked With the general adaptation syndrome, Hans Selye provided a framework for thinking about how stress might make the body vulnerable to disease. He implied that this vulnerability might be due to the effects of stress on the immune system. No one knew whether psychological factors could affect the immune system at Selye's time, but some groundbreaking research of the 1970s changed all that.

The job of the immune system is to defend the body against foreign substances. Before the 1970s, the prevailing view was that the immune system operated independently of the central nervous system, which implied that the immune system was invulnerable to thoughts, feelings, and stress. As far as anyone knew at the time, there were no anatomical or chemical connections between immune system structures and any aspect of the nervous system that would allow them to communicate. Even though most physicians believed that stress made people sick, or at least sicker, they did not consider it physiologically possible for psychological conditions to have any effect on the immune system; however, that was about to be challenged.

Robert Ader was replicating some classic experiments on conditioned taste aversion. Recall from the chapter "Learning" that conditioned taste aversion is a form of classical conditioning in which a neutral taste, after repeated pairing with a substance that induces nausea and vomiting, will come to produce those characteristics when it is presented alone. In the early research, saccharin water was paired with radiation, which causes nausea (Garcia, Kimeldorf, & Koelling, 1955). In his work, Ader paired a chemical that induces nausea with saccharin water to create taste aversion to the saccharin water. Some rats were exposed to a lot of saccharin water even after they had learned to associate it with nausea, and something else unusual was happening to those rats—they were dying! Why?

Ader remembered that the toxin he was using to induce nausea in the rats also happened to be an *immunosuppressant*; that is, something that inhibits immune system function. Perhaps, he reasoned, in addition to learning to avoid saccharin water, the rats were acquiring conditioned immunosuppression from the repeated pairing of the saccharin solution with the immunosuppressant. But could rats really *learn* to suppress their immune responses?

Ader and his colleague, Nicholas Cohen, designed a series of experiments to determine whether immunosuppression could be classically conditioned in rats (Ader & Cohen, 1975). They conditioned nausea in an experimental group of rats by pairing saccharin water with injections of the immunosuppressant. They also created two control groups: a group that was injected with a placebo around the time they drank saccharin water (which served as a control for the stress-inducing effects of injection in the absence of conditioning) and a group that received the immunosuppressant and plain water (a non-conditioning control group).

Ader and Cohen then tested whether the immune system was, in fact, suppressed in rats with immunosuppressant-induced conditioned taste aversion. They reintroduced the conditioned stimulus, in this case saccharin, and then introduced an **antigen** (a substance foreign to the body). The blood of rats that had been conditioned to avoid saccharin via the immunosuppressant showed much weaker antibody responses to the antigen than did rats injected with the placebo. By demonstrating that one could classically condition the suppression of an antibody response to an antigen, Ader and Cohen had shown that there must be connections between the CNS and the immune system.

The Birth of Psychoneuroimmunology

Not long after Ader and Cohen published their results on conditioned immunosuppression, new findings in biomedical science increased the credibility of their results. In the late 1970s and early 1980s, scientists discovered that the ANS is linked to immune system structures such as the thymus gland and that immune cells have receptors for and can produce certain stress hormones (Smith & Blalock, 1988). There was now solid behavioral and biological evidence for what Selye and others had believed all along—that psychological processes and immune processes interact. The field of **psychoneuroimmunology (PNI)**, the science of how psychological factors relate to immune changes, was born.

Today, the field of PNI examines the relationships among the brain, thought, feeling, endocrine changes, and immune system functioning (Ashley & Demas, 2017). As a discipline, PNI is concerned with any kind of connection between

antigen
Any foreign substance that triggers an immune response.

Connection

Conditioned taste aversion is a type of learning similar to what happened when Pavlov's dogs learned to salivate to the sound of a bell (classical conditioning).

See "Classical Conditioning," in the chapter "Learning." (p. 300)

psychoneuroimmunology (PNI)
The science of how psychological factors relate to changes in the immune system.

psychological processes and the immune system. For instance, there are chemical linkages between psychological processes and immune system changes. Chemicals involved in the stress response, such as cortisol and norepinephrine, influence the number of immune cells produced in the body. This is a means by which stress can affect the immune system.

Furthermore, connections between the central nervous system and immune system are bidirectional. Just as stress can change immune function, certain immune changes (such as the release of chemicals called *cytokines*, which regulate immune response) can feed back and influence brain areas involved in mood regulation (Miller, Capuron, & Raison, 2005; Nishida et al., 2002). The relationship between cytokines and mood may play a role in the development of depression and other mood-related psychological disorders (Bhattacharya et al., 2016).

Overview of the Immune System   The human immune system defends the body against invasion by disease, inspects the body for cells that may take on dangerous mutations, and performs basic housekeeping functions, such as cleaning up cellular debris after an injury. There are two basic lines of defense: natural immunity and acquired immunity. **Natural immunity** consists of a number of inborn processes that help remove foreign substances from the body. These responses typically are very quick, and they provide the first line of defense upon exposure to antigens. Forms of natural immunity include phagocytosis and inflammation. *Phagocytosis* is a process by which a white blood cell engulfs a substance (usually an antigen or another cell) and digests it or moves it to a place where it will be destroyed. *Inflammation* is a process by which tissues are restored following injury. After you cut your finger, for example, blood vessels at the injured area contract and dilate to increase blood flow to the area, creating warmth and redness. The damaged cells release enzymes to destroy invading microorganisms.

The immune system comprises several kinds of white blood cells, including those responsible for phagocytosis. Other white blood cells, called *lymphocytes*, control acquired immunity. **Acquired immunity** involves a number of endocrine and cellular processes that recognize specific antigens and then reproduce specialized cells or circulating proteins to fight those antigens. Acquired immunity is so called because it involves experience—an effective immune response occurs only after prior exposure to a particular antigen. Every cold we get leads to an acquired immune response. As a result, we are less likely to get sick if we encounter that particular virus again. Acquired immune responses take longer to initiate than natural immune responses, because the former involve recognition processes and the duplication of cells. On subsequent exposure to a specific antigen, however, acquired immune responses can be rapid and efficient. Vaccines, for example, provide a safe initial exposure and an acquired immune response that protects us against disease.

Acquired immunity involves two classes of lymphocytes, called B and T lymphocytes. In response to specific antigens, *B lymphocytes* release antibodies into the bloodstream. Antibodies destroy antigens directly. The *T lymphocytes*, or "T cells," fight antigens not by releasing antibodies but by means of cellular processes, collectively known as **cellular immunity**.

Research on Stress, Immune Function, and Health   The physiological reactivity model predicts that the physiological effects of stress, when sustained over time, will eventually weaken the immune system. Theorists have extended the model a step further, reasoning that *immunosuppression* increases susceptibility to disease by reducing the body's ability to fight invading bacteria or viruses or its ability to fight off potentially cancerous cells, or both. This is why psychologists, in collaboration with medical researchers, began conducting studies of stress and immune function (e.g., Cohen et al., 2012). The basic idea is simple: If researchers can show that stress affects immune variables, it should follow that such immune system changes would leave the organism more susceptible to disease. In reality,

natural immunity
The form of immunity that is the first response to antigens.

acquired immunity
Immunity provided by antibodies produced in the body in response to specific antigens.

cellular immunity
The immune response that occurs when T lymphocytes (T cells) fight antigens.

many studies link stress with changes in immune system measures, but very few have shown that these changes affect susceptibility to disease.

Results from animal research show that a variety of chronic stressors can weaken immune responses (Glaser & Kiecolt-Glaser, 2005). Some such stressors tested in animal studies are maternal separation, inescapable shock, abrupt temperature change, and loud noise. Researchers have induced stress in humans by asking them to participate in a stressful task, such as public speaking, or an emotion-evoking task, such as writing about a traumatic event (Pennebaker, Kiecolt-Glaser, & Glaser, 1988). A more common approach to studying stress in human research, however, is to rely on naturally occurring stressors such as: final exams, sleep deprivation, loud noise, abuse, poverty, bereavement, divorce, and caring for an Alzheimer's patient. These studies use various measures of immunity as dependent variables: numbers of certain lymphocytes, tests of how effectively certain lymphocytes function either in a test tube or in a living person, the toxicity of tumor-fighting cells called *natural killer cells*, and the quantities of chemicals that regulate lymphocytes.

The major finding in studies of humans is that stressors are associated with changes in various kinds of immune function, but it is often difficult to know whether the observed immune changes have meaningful effects on health. A few studies address this concern by including measures of illness that are controlled by immune mechanisms. In a study of people caring for Alzheimer's patients, the caregivers and a matched comparison group (all volunteers for the study) received small puncture wounds. They then returned to the laboratory for wound-healing assessments and blood tests to measure immune variables. Compared to the comparison group, the caregivers exhibited substantially slower healing of puncture wounds and reductions in the chemicals involved in healing (Kiecolt-Glaser et al., 1995).

Long-term, chronic abuse, neglect, and poverty in childhood are associated with profound emotional and psychological effects including an increased risk for disease and suicide later in life (Campbell, Walker, & Egede, 2016; Labonte et al., 2012). Labonte and colleagues (2012) studied the brains of people who had committed suicide, some of whom were abused as children (they also studied the brains of controls who had died by means other than suicide). Relative to controls and nonabused suicides, abused suicides had epigenetic changes in gene expression involved in HPA activity consistent with abnormally elevated stress response. As we discussed earlier, the HPA axis is crucial to immune function and a balanced release of hormones in response to stress. Childhood poverty, too, can be a chronic stressor, programming the body to have a long-term elevated stress response (for example, increased cortisol response), leaving people more vulnerable to chronic illness and disease in their 40s and 50s (Miller & Chen, 2013; Miller et al., 2011).

It seems, however, that it is not just the stressful context that matters for long-term outcomes, but the resources one has to deal with them. One longitudinal study of children whose parents underwent divorce during their childhood reported that if the kids perceived their mothers to be warm toward them in adolescence it was related to *lower* cortisol responses to a challenging situation in adulthood (Luecken et al., 2016).

What about stress and the common cold, an infectious illness mediated by the immune system? Sheldon Cohen and his colleagues (Cohen, Tyrrell, & Smith, 1993; Cohen et al., 2003; Cohen et al., 2012) have studied the interplay of stress and social connectedness in people's susceptibility to the common cold. Susceptibility is the key issue here, as exposure to the cold virus does not guarantee that a person will get sick. You and your roommate might both spend time with a friend who is sick, but only one of you might catch the cold. In these studies, Cohen and his colleagues exposed people to a virus; measured perceived stress in some participants as well as external stressors and social networks; and clinically verified whether or not people got sick. They used a clever means by which to measure how sick people were, such as weighing tissues to approximate how much mucus they produced! As it turns out, the perception of stress—rather than the number of stressors to which people had been exposed—predicted whether people developed a cold (Cohen et al., 1993). Further, having more meaningful social interactions in one's daily life reduces susceptibility to colds (Cohen et al., 2003). Perceiving oneself as lower in socioeconomic status also predicts susceptibility to the common cold in people exposed to the virus, independent of one's actual socioeconomic status (Cohen et al., 2008).

The relationship between stress and illness, then, is not driven by the situation as much as by how the individual evaluates that situation. In terms of susceptibility to the common cold, *perceived* stress matters more than actual exposure to stressors; *perceived* low socioeconomic status matters more than actual socioeconomic status. These results remind us of the importance of examining stress not just as a stimulus (number of stressors) but also in terms of how people respond to the stressors and cope with possible stress (transactional view). As discussed earlier, social support and connectedness might buffer the effects of stress by providing interpersonal resources for emotional support and problem solving (Cohen & Wills, 1985).

Psychological Risk Factors for Heart Disease

Heart disease is the number one killer of both men and women in the United States (American Heart Association, 2005; Lethbridge-Cejku & Vickerie, 2005). We saw earlier that the physiological changes associated with negative emotions and stress affect the cardiovascular system. Research has identified a number of psychological risk factors for heart disease, including hostility, anger, and depression.

Type A and Anger For centuries scientists have argued that personality and emotion play a role in the development of heart disease, but research on this topic did not begin until the middle of the 20th century. It began in the waiting room of cardiologist Meyer Friedman's office in San Francisco. A janitor pointed out to Friedman that the upholstery on the chairs in his waiting room was wearing out much more quickly than that on chairs in other waiting rooms. He wondered whether Friedman's patients fidgeted a lot. Friedman said that he had noticed that many of his patients were tense and impatient. Friedman and his colleague Ray Rosenman decided to study the effects of such an emotional style on a person's risk of developing heart disease. They described a set of psychological characteristics they believed put people at risk for heart disease: impatience, competitiveness, hostility, and time urgency. They named it the **Type A Behavior Pattern** (TABP) and explained that this pattern emerges when under conditions of challenge or stress. That is, Type A people are not always impatient and hostile, but when they find themselves in high-pressure situations they exhibit this pattern of behavior.

Type A Behavior Pattern (TABP) A way of responding to challenge or stress, characterized by hostility, impatience, competitiveness, and time urgency.

Friedman and Rosenman hypothesized that people who exhibit the TABP *under provocation* are at greater risk for heart disease than those who do not. After developing an interview to measure Type A behavior, they tracked 3,000 healthy white men for 8 years. They found that Type A behavior predicted the incidence of coronary heart disease, over and above such traditional risk factors as blood pressure, cholesterol, and age (Rosenman et al., 1964). This finding shocked the medical world—no one had anticipated that something psychological could affect heart disease! Other major studies replicated the finding that the presence of Type A behavior predicted the incidence of heart disease and extended it to women (French-Belgian Collaborative Group, 1982; Haynes et al., 1978).

Twenty-two years later, Rosenman and Friedman conducted a follow-up study on their original participants (Rosenman et al., 1975). Surprisingly, Type A behavior did

©Keith Brofsky/Getty Images RF

Is time urgency the component of the Type A Behavior Pattern that predicts heart disease?

not predict death from heart disease in this group. Then another major study of men and women produced null findings as well (Shekelle et al., 1985). Could it really be that Type A behavior did not affect the incidence of heart disease after all?

Remembering that Type A is a collection of various characteristics, Matthews and her colleagues (1977) decided to take a closer look at the follow-up interviews from Friedman and Rosenman's original sample. She reasoned that maybe certain aspects of Type A were still relevant to coronary health, even if the overall pattern did not predict death. Matthews studied how each component of the Type A pattern (hostility, time urgency, competitiveness, and impatience) related to coronary outcomes. As it turned out, *hostility* was the only component that predicted death from heart disease at a 22-year follow-up. As a result of Matthews's findings, the measurement of global Type A has been abandoned, for the most part, in favor of more specific measures of hostility.

Suddenly, the focus changed to the study of hostility and cardiovascular health. In subsequent research, specific measures of hostility again positively correlated with the degree of arterial blockage and other cardiovascular conditions much more so than general Type A behavior did (Suarez, Bates, & Harralson, 1998; Suarez et al., 1993; Suarez & Williams, 1989; Williams et al., 1980).

How might having a hostile personality put someone at greater risk for heart disease? Hostility is an affective trait, which some emotion theorists say sets a threshold for the likelihood of particular emotional responses (Ekman, 1984; Rosenberg, 1998). By this logic, hostile people would have a lower threshold for the elicitation of anger. To link hostility and anger to heart disease, we need to look at a special version of the physiological reactivity model known as the cardiovascular reactivity model (see Figure 7). In the **cardiovascular reactivity (CVR) model**, hostility can increase the likelihood of heart disease through at least two causal routes. On one route, hostility makes the elicitation of anger more likely and more frequent (this route starts with the red arrow in Figure 7). Frequent episodes of anger lead to frequent cardiovascular reactivity. Over time, repeated cardiovascular reactivity sets the stage for the development of coronary artery disease. As coronary artery disease develops, the narrowed arteries deprive the heart of the blood it needs to function properly; thus, progressive coronary artery disease can lead to coronary heart disease. The yellow arrows in the diagram designate the transition between repeated cardiovascular reactivity and coronary artery disease and the later development of coronary heart disease. The second route, indicated by the blue arrow in Figure 7, is a direct path from hostility to how much cardiovascular reactivity certain people experience, without the need for anger.

In support of the first route, research shows that anger does affect cardiovascular outcomes. For instance, anger can lead to heightened and prolonged blood pressure reactivity (Schuler & O'Brien, 1997; Siegman et al., 1992). In coronary patients, the risk of heart attack increases significantly during the hour following an outburst of anger (Moller et al., 1999). A study of coronary patients

cardiovascular reactivity (CVR) model
The hypothesis that hostility can increase the likelihood of heart disease through at least two different causal routes.

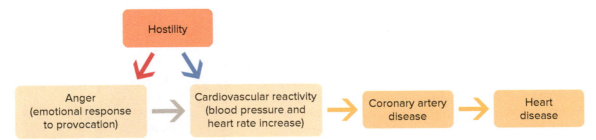

FIGURE 7
CARDIOVASCULAR REACTIVITY MODEL OF STRESS AND ILLNESS. This version of the physiological reactivity model links hostility and anger to heart disease. Repeated cardiovascular reactivity leads to coronary artery disease and heart disease.

undergoing the Type A Structured Interview found that episodes of insufficient blood supply to the muscle of the heart were more likely to occur when those patients displayed facial expressions of anger (Rosenberg et al., 2001).

Depression   A hostile disposition is not the only trait relevant to cardiac health. Depression, a mood disorder involving sadness and lethargy, is also associated with increased severity of symptoms and increased risk of death from coronary heart disease (Geerlings et al., 2002; Glassman & Shapiro, 1998). Large-scale studies show that, for people with coronary heart disease, being clinically depressed significantly increases the risk of death from the disease, in both men and women (Momersteeg et al., 2016; Tully & Cosh, 2013). Also, the chemicals involved in inflammation that present a risk for coronary heart disease are present at higher levels in people who are depressed than in others (Barth et al., 2004; Empana et al., 2005; Mommersteeg et al., 2016). Studies such as these make it hard to know which comes first—the heart disease or the depression. A recent large-scale prospective study, however, showed that depression scores predicted death from cardiovascular disease and overall mortality (Nabi et al., 2010).

The Gut-Brain Axis: How the Critters in Our Intestines Affect Health, Mood, and Behavior

Living in and on most of our body—our gut (intestines), mouth, skin, feet, gums—are trillions of living organisms, for example, bacteria, protozoans, fungi, and even some parasites. Altogether these microbes make up our **microbiome**, the world of tiny organisms that live inside us (Whipps, Lewis, & Cooke, 1988). Historically, bacteria and other microorganisms were considered to be harmful carriers of disease. We now know, however, that these organisms play a very important role in our physical and mental health. Not all or even most bacteria are harmful; in fact, most are beneficial organisms or *probiotics*. A well-balanced and healthy microbiome is absolutely essential to our physical and, as it turns out, mental health.

Although the microbiome resides throughout the body, the most important part of the body hosting these microorganisms is our gut or intestine. There is a bidirectional pathway between the gut and the brain, known as the **gut-brain axis**. This pathway connects the nerves that serve the intestines, the immune system, the HPA axis, neurotransmitters, and hormones. The microbiome of the intestine has a profound effect on the gut-brain axis in many ways, one of which is stress (Carabotti et al., 2015). By means of the HPA axis—the primary stress hormone system—stress can alter the balance of gut bacteria (Dinan & Cryan, 2012; Moloney et al., 2014).

Disruption of the microbiome, known as *dysbiosis*, plays role in the development of obesity, allergies, cardiovascular disease, asthma, diabetes, colitis, and many other conditions (Komaroff, 2017; Montiel-Castro et al., 2013; Pevsner-Fischer et al., 2017; van den Elsen et al., 2017). In a recent study of mice, long-term psychological stress created dysbiosis in the large intestine, which led to inflammation and the bowel disease colitis (Watanabe et al., 2016). Baby rhesus monkeys who have been separated from their mothers experience severe stress, show disturbances in the microbiome, and become more vulnerable to disease (Bailey & Coe, 1999). Stress-related inflammation also plays a role in the development of obesity, heart disease, and the set of disease risk factors known as **metabolic syndrome**. Figure 8 lists some of the diseases affected by changes in the microbiome.

One important lesson, however, from the research on the gut-brain axis is that avoiding dirt and "germs" is not always a good thing for our immune system. Some bacteria may in fact be probiotic and beneficial to

microbiome
The environment of trillions of various microorganisms living with our bodies, which perform important metabolic and physiological functions.

gut-brain axis
The bi-directional pathway between the intestines and the central nervous system, by which changes in the intestinal environment affect the brain and vice versa.

metabolic syndrome
A group of factors related to body composition, weight, and diet that increase risk of stroke, diabetes, and heart disease.

Connection

The gut-brain axis also plays a role in mental health. Several psychological disorders, including anxiety, depression, and autism, are affected by the microbiome.

See "Psychological Disorders," in the chapter "Psychological Disorders." (p. 584)

FIGURE 8
THE GUT-BRAIN AXIS, AND VARIOUS DISEASE OUTCOMES RELATED TO CHANGES IN THE MICROBIOME.

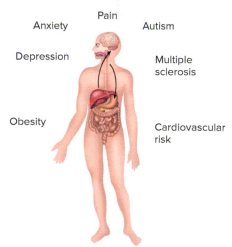

Source: Adapted from Montiel-Castro et al. (2013), p. 3.

©Diane McDonald/Stockbyte/Getty Images RF

A newborn's immune system is still developing. Antibodies present in the mother's breast milk protect the baby from infection until the infant's own immune system has matured.

our physical and mental health. Some researchers argue for a "hygiene hypothesis" that the increase in autoimmune diseases over the last 20–30 years is partly due to the advent of antibacterial soaps and more sterile living conditions (Pollan, 2013; Strachan, 1989). Of course, some bacteria are harmful and many diseases are spread via bacteria and it is misleading and even dangerous to argue against basic hygiene (Bloomfield et al., 2016). For instance, soaps are not a problem, but antibacterial soaps are. It is the balance and overall health of microbiotic system that we should be trying to maintain.

There are many health behaviors that affect and change our microbiome, some of which are listed below.

Birth and breastfeeding. Natural birth and breastfeeding are better than C-section and formula for the infant's microbiome (Mueller et al., 2015).

Diet and Drink. There is now a multimillion dollar industry for probiotic foods that are aimed at improving your gut microbiome. Most scientists, however, who do research on the microbiome say it is too early to know of much of the probiotic craze is just that—a craze—or whether it really is a path to intestinal health and ultimately physical and mental health.

Lifestyle. Over the last 100 years or so much of the West has moved from being predominantly farm-agricultural living to urban living. There has also been a shift to more and more "hygienic" living—daily showers, increase in soaps, especially antibacterial soaps, less exposure to dirt and farm animals. Overall, this has been beneficial and many diseases have been eradicated because of it.

Our current "hygienic" lifestyle comes at a cost to our immune system and the increase in autoimmune diseases, especially allergies. The rates of allergic diseases have risen dramatically in so-called "hygienic" cultures (where clean water, indoor plumbing, and city living prevail) starting in the 1960s and becoming epidemics since the 1980s (Braback, Hjern, & Rasmussen, 2004; Platts-Mills, 2015). In fact, even in Western (currently "hygienic" cultures, allergies were extremely rare before 1870 when farm and outdoor living were more predominant (Platts-Mills, 2015). In less hygienic cultures in Africa, autoimmune diseases are nearly unheard of. In fact, mice that are raised completely germ-free have abnormally high and dysfunctional stress responses (cortisol levels) (Sudo et al., 2004). From this and other research, we know that living germ-free actually increases the stress response.

Kissing. Kissing is one of the more direct exchanges of microorganisms between people. Even though kissing can transfer harmful germs, it also transmits beneficial probiotics between people (Montiel-Castro et al., 2013).

Research on Health-Relevant Behavior

People engage in behaviors that either increase risk for disease or help prevent disease. Some health behaviors are conscious lifestyle choices, such as how and what to eat or whether or not to exercise. Others may begin as conscious choices but over time become habits with serious health implications, such as smoking, drinking alcohol, and taking other drugs. Sometimes, when stressed, people may turn to tobacco, alcohol, or food to calm themselves down or cheer themselves up. This is emotion-focused coping. Long-term use of some of these substances can create health problems and may increase the likelihood of major, sometimes fatal, illnesses.

Smoking   Many smokers say they have a cigarette when they are stressed because it calms them down. However, nicotine, the drug component of cigarette smoke, is a stimulant. Nicotine activates the sympathetic nervous system, increasing heart rate and blood pressure, but relaxes the skeletal muscles, which is probably why some people find it calming. They use nicotine for emotion regulation, but cigarette smoking is harmful to health in many ways. According to the U.S. Department of Health and Human Services (USDHHS, 2006), it is the single most preventable cause of death in the United States. Cigarette smoking reduces life expectancy by an average of 10 years, increases one's risk for lung cancer more than 10-fold, and triples the risk of death from heart disease in both men and women (Centers for Disease Control and Prevention [CDC], 2001; Doll et al., 2004). Smoking also increases the risk of many other cancers, stroke, lung disease, emphysema, and male impotence (USDHHS, 2006). The increased risk of mortality associated with smoking is found in several cultures (Jacobs et al., 1999). Although the rates of smoking in the United States have dropped considerably in recent years, still about 20% of the U.S. population smokes cigarettes. With over 1,000 people a day under the age of 18 in the United States taking up smoking, this is a major health problem (USDHHS, 2006).

We are exposed to *secondhand smoke* by being near someone who is smoking. Analyses of the composition of the smoke burned from the end of a cigarette indicate that it is high in carcinogens (sometimes higher than the smoke inhaled by the smoker) and is a health threat to those who inhale it passively. In fact, a person who breathes secondhand smoke regularly is at increased risk of all the same health problems that the smoker is (USDHHS, 2006).

Drinking Alcohol   Some people drink alcohol to calm down or loosen up. Alcohol is a depressant, which means it slows down central nervous system functions. Alcohol can cause liver damage, and severe alcoholism can lead to a serious liver condition known as cirrhosis (Askgaard et al., 2015; Baan et al., 2007). Heavy alcohol consumption also increases the likelihood of liver cancer and cancers of the digestive tract, not to mention an increased risk for accidents due to alcohol's effect on motor and cognitive performance. Not all the news regarding alcohol is bad, however. Considerable data indicate that regular but moderate alcohol consumption (one to two drinks), especially with food, may reduce the risk of coronary heart disease, the number one killer in the developed world (Guiraud et al., 2008; Renaud & de Lorgeril, 1992). Recent large-scale studies, however, do not suggest that moderate alcohol consumption leads to a longer life (Stockwell et al., 2016).

Diet and Eating   Eating well promotes health. Eating saturated fats, such as those found in meats and dairy products, increases risk for heart disease, while eating other essential fats, such as those found in certain kinds of fish and nuts, may have protective effects (Schaefer, Gleason, & Dansinger, 2005). The consumption of high-fiber, less-fatty foods, such as whole grains and plenty of leafy green vegetables, may help protect against cancers of the colon and rectum, although the data are somewhat inconclusive (Cummings et al., 1992). It is well known that excessive weight gain is risky. Obesity increases a person's risk for heart disease, high blood pressure, adult-onset diabetes, and certain cancers (McTiernan, 2005). Increasingly, we can see how diet, exercise, and lifestyle interact in ways that can profoundly impact health (Powell et al., 2010).

Eating and Stress   Some people eat to cope with stress. In fact, sugary foods in particular help some people feel better and calm down, which makes it likely they will continue to do such eating. Research now supports the connection between eating and stress reduction: Stress increases eating and in turn eating

©BananaStock/Alamy RF

A healthy diet rich in fruits, vegetables, and whole grains and low in fat may protect against heart disease and certain cancers and prevent conditions associated with obesity, such as adult-onset diabetes.

reduces stress reactivity in the HPA axis (Dallman, Pecoraro, & la Fleur, 2005). When a person eats in response to stress, stress-related physiological activity decreases and reward pathways in the brain are stimulated. These areas release endorphins, which make people feel better. Thus, people eat under stress because they get a "good feeling" reward—like a drug high—from the brain (Adam & Epel, 2007). The relationship between stress and eating might vary across individuals, however. Sproesser and colleagues (2014) found that people who eat more under stress eat less when relieved of that stress, while people who eat less under stress might be more likely to eat more when the stress subsides.

Stress-induced eating, however, is risky, as it increases fat in the abdominal area (compared to other places), which is a predictor of heart disease in men and women (Epel et al., 2000; Rexrode, Buring, & Manson, 2001; Rexrode et al., 1998). This is especially true if the stress-induced eating includes sugary junk foods (Kuo et al., 2007).

Exercise   Besides not smoking, one of the best things you can do for your health is to exercise regularly, which reduces the risk of heart disease, stroke, and certain types of cancer (Noda et al., 2005; Thune & Furberg, 2001). Exercise helps keep diabetes under control and slows the rate of bone loss in older women (Cussler et al., 2005). Data show that moderate exercise, even as little as walking 20–25 minutes a day three or four times per week, can extend life by 3 to 4 years (Franco et al., 2005). In addition, exercise offers a healthy way to regulate mood, as it reduces anxiety and depression (Barbour, Edenfield, & Blumenthal, 2007; Binder et al., 2004).

One of the best ways to affect your metabolism, and as a result change your weight, is by exercising regularly. Did you know that introducing just a brief (10 minutes or so) exercise regimen can make a difference in your metabolism? Such metabolic changes can change your genes (Lewis et al., 2010). This lends credibility to the idea that you can change your set point with exercise and thereby eat less.

It's obvious that exercise improves fitness. Regular exercise helps prevent heart disease, reduces the risk of Type II diabetes, offsets certain cancers, and improves mood (Alex et al., 2013; Crouch, Wilson, & Newbury, 2011; Teo et al., 2013). In addition to the cardiovascular benefits, exercise can reduce fat cells and support the cellular processes that grow muscle (Barrés et al., 2012; Ronn et al., 2013). In a study by Ronn and colleagues (2013), researchers took a variety of fitness and health measures from 23 healthy but inactive men, who later underwent a 6-month exercise intervention program, after which they were measured again. The men were more fit and lost weight after the training, but what was most interesting was how epigenetic differences in genes that played a role in fat storage lowered the risk for Type II diabetes and obesity.

Researchers looked at whether a single exercise session could change the genetics of muscle cells of otherwise sedentary people (Barrés et al., 2012). They obtained small tissue samples from participants both before and after a single 400-calorie-burning exercise cycle session. Some were instructed to exercise vigorously, while others were instructed to pedal more gently. They found changes in the DNA methylation of muscle cells after only one workout and these changes were most pronounced among the participants who rode most vigorously.

Exercise also helps your brain. One correlational study found that the most physically fit third- and fifth-grade children also performed the highest on standardized math and reading tests (Hillman, Erickson, & Kramer, 2008). Also, exercise promotes the growth of new neurons (neurogenesis) in the hippocampus, the area of the brain most involved in learning and memory (Pereira et al., 2007). Compared to mice that did not exercise, mice that exercised showed increased activity in their hippocampi after exercising for 2 weeks. They also developed new neurons in the same region of the hippocampus. Increased activity was directly related to neural growth. In fact, similar treadmill studies in rats show that exercise can offset age-related memory loss due to a reduction in neurogenesis in the hippocampus (Kim et al., 2010) and may decrease depressive-like behavior in chronically stressed rats (Marais, Stein, & Daniels, 2009). Similar effects have been found with humans as well; see the "Research Process" for this chapter (Figure 12.8). Being physically fit appears to make the brain fit, and it may offset age-related cognitive decline in the elderly (Bherer, Erickson, & Liu-Ambrose, 2013; Kirk-Sanchez & McGough, 2013; Valenzuela et al., 2012).

Nakajima and colleagues (2010) reported that chronic moderate exercise counteracts the typical age-related decline in methylation (a form of epigenetic change in gene expression, mentioned in the chapter "The Biology of Behavior") in the *ASC* gene, a gene involved in immune function. Such exercise in 65-year-olds returns their *ASC* function to the age of typical 35-year-olds. This is one mechanism to explain some of the health benefits of exercise.

The most recent data suggest that exercise helps the aging brain by preventing inflammation and the related increases in *microglia* cells (Niraula, Sheridan, & Godbout, 2017). Microglia are very small glial cells that play a role in the immune system. They tend to increase with aging and are associated with both depression and cognitive decline (Norden & Godbout, 2013; Santos, Beckman, & Ferreira, 2016).

Although most people realize that exercise has numerous health benefits, many of which receive a great deal of popular press, people are still slow to change their behavior. Human behavior is notoriously difficult to change. Still, it can be done, often by offering reward or incentive for making changes. Jackson and colleagues (Jackson, Gao, & Chen, 2014) studied 26 lean and overweight Chinese women, who viewed images of active (running, dancing, playing tennis, and so on) versus sedentary people (lounging, sitting at a desk), interspersed with images of nature landscapes (as controls), all while in the fMRI scanner. The women were asked to imagine themselves doing these various behaviors. Compared to the leaner women, the overweight women showed brain activation patterns suggesting negative emotional associations with the idea of exercising. Specifically, overweight women showed less activation in brain reward centers and more activation in areas associated with

Challenge Your Assumptions

True or False? Exercise can turn fat into muscle after one workout.

True: Just one session of exercise can turn on genetic processes that convert fat cells to muscle cells.

Research Process

©Zefa RF/Alamy

1 Research Question

Will exercise increase brain activity and stimulate neural growth in humans?

2 Method

Having found that exercise was correlated with neural growth in the hippocampus of mice, Pereira and colleagues (2007) conducted a study to look for the same effects in humans. They recruited 11 adults (ages 21–45) with below average cardiovascular fitness to take part in an exercise program four times a week for 12 weeks. Each session lasted about 1 hour and consisted of a combination of stretching, aerobic training, and cooling down. Brain images were made before and after the training with MRI to measure changes in blood volume, an indirect measure of neural growth.

The hippocampus is the brain region most involved in learning and memory, so participants' memories were tested before and after the program with a list of 20 words read by the experimenter, to find out whether there was any change in memory capacity. Participants were distracted with another word list and were then asked to recall as many words from the original list as they could.

3 Results

MRIs performed before and after the exercise program revealed that cerebral blood flow increased after the program. In addition, participants improved their performance on a cognitive test after 12 weeks of exercise.

4 Conclusion

After exercising regularly, people who had been out of shape showed improvement in memory. This improvement is correlated with—and perhaps a consequence of—new neural growth in the region of the brain most involved in learning and memory, the hippocampus. Although we cannot conclude from the correlations revealed by this study that physical exercise causes improvements in memory, these findings suggest that exercise not only makes the body more fit, but it also makes the brain more fit.

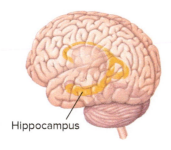
Hippocampus

FIGURE 9
EFFECTS OF EXERCISE ON THE BRAIN.
Physical exercise is as good for the brain as it is for the body.

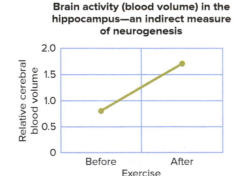

Source: "An In Vivo Correlate of Exercise-Induced Neurogenesis in the Adult Dentate Gyrus," by A. C. Pereira, D. E. Huddleston, A. M. Brickman, A. A. Sosunov, R. Hen, G. M. McKhann, ... S. A. Small, 2007, *Proceedings of the National Academy of Sciences, 104,* 5638–5643.

negative emotional processing. Taken together with other findings that overweight people show evidence of brain-related *positive* activation in response to images of food and eating, this finding builds our understanding of the brain processes involved in struggles with weight.

Meditation for Stress Reduction and Health We have already discussed how positive emotions can reduce the physiological activation caused by negative emotions and how higher positive affect may help people with diseases like AIDS live longer (Moskowitz, 2003). Given the harmful effects of stress, strategies designed to reduce stress can benefit both mental and physical health. One such strategy is meditation.

©Moxie Productions/Blend Images/Getty Images RF

 How might meditation improve health?

Mindfulness meditation involves both paying attention to the present moment and being aware that everything that may arise in one's mind, be it a thought, an emotion, or a sensation, will eventually fade away. The meditator is trained to note experiences as they occur, without clinging to or ascribing value to them. These skills allow one to keep thoughts and emotions in perspective and help an unhealthy obsession with negative emotions (Kabat-Zinn, 1990).

Researchers have applied mindfulness meditation training for stress reduction, pain relief, and the treatment of physical disorders. Kabat-Zinn and his colleagues have developed and studied the effectiveness of a program called Mindfulness-Based Stress Reduction (MBSR) for treating a variety of physical and psychological conditions. MBSR training reduces self-reported pain and pain-related behaviors in people suffering from chronic pain (Kabat-Zinn, Lipworth, & Burney, 1985). Also, MBSR training leads to significant and substantial reductions in anxiety, depression, and fear in people who have various types of anxiety disorder (Kabat-Zinn et al., 1992).

Mindfulness training helps other health conditions as well, especially those that may worsen with stress. Consider psoriasis, an annoying and often painful rash that can be exacerbated by stress (Chapman & Moynihan, 2009). Mindfulness training improves the rate of skin healing in people with psoriasis (Kabat-Zinn et al., 1998). Mindfulness meditation techniques appear to be effective in reducing the stress-related immune changes underlying skin outbreaks. Such meditation training appears to help in treating eating disorders, recovering from substance abuse, and enhancing the quality of life in people with multiple sclerosis (Grossman et al., 2010; Liehr et al., 2010; Masuda & Wendell, 2010).

Connection

Mindfulness meditation can improve well-being, cognition, and brain function.

See "Training Consciousness: Meditation," in the chapter "Consciousness."

Quick Quiz 3: How Stress and Coping Affect Health

1. If a psychologist studies how diet and sleep affect overall health, which view would best match her research?
   a. physiological reactivity
   b. general adaptation syndrome
   c. health behavior approach
   d. homeostasis view

2. Martin is very prone to anger, impatient, and competitive; he is always in a hurry and feeling rushed. Martin probably suffers from
   a. Type A Behavior Pattern.
   b. Type B Behavior Pattern.
   c. hostility.
   d. high drive disorder.

3. Which personality trait is most strongly related to the development of heart disease?
   a. anxiety
   b. hostility
   c. depression
   d. introversion

4. Exercise helps
   a. decrease stress.
   b. improve cardiovascular health.
   c. stimulate neural growth.
   d. all of the above.

Answers can be found at the end of the chapter.

Bringing It All Together

Making Connections in Stress and Health

Good Stress, Bad Stress, and the Power of Belief

Throughout this chapter we have advocated the view that stress is generally bad for your health. We have discussed evidence that stress increases susceptibility to infection, cardiovascular disease, certain cancers, chronic inflammation, and cellular aging. As we have seen, however, the connection between stress and illness in the published literature is far from perfect.

Two recent areas of research challenge the assumption that stress is always bad for you. One area suggests that certain short-term (acute) stress responses might actually be good for our health. The other area shows how our ways of thinking can modify whether we are vulnerable to stress and, subsequently, whether we get sick. Both areas suggest that our notions of the stress and illness relationship have been oversimplified, the discussion of which allows for the integration of many of the important concepts in this chapter.

Challenge Your Assumptions

True or False? Stress is always bad for your health.

False: Not all stress is the same. Acute (short-lived) stress is, in fact, good for your health.

Acute versus Chronic Stress

Short-term (acute) stress is good for your health, but what precisely constitutes *acute* stress and how do we distinguish it from chronic stress? How brief is brief? A leading researcher in this area, Firdhaus Dhabhar (2009) suggests that acute stress is stress that lasts minutes to hours (such as anxiety in the preparation for a final exam), whereas chronic stress lasts months to years (such as having to stay in an abusive relationship).

An increasingly large body of research shows that acute stress may not be harmful to health at all; it might actually be beneficial. Recall Hans Selye's work on the GAS, which argued that, in the short term, stress is an adaptive response by our bodies to deal with emergency. In this new area of work, we are seeing that responding to some challenges with stress may confer benefits to health—more so than not responding at all! How could that be?

Research shows that acute stress may actually promote healing (Dhabhar, 2013). The GAS predicts that in the alarm stage the body mobilizes to deal with

a challenge or threat. Heart rate and respiration increase as an initial response to an emergency (fight or flight) to enable the person to respond quickly (run away from danger, for example). So, too, might an initial immune response mobilize cells to fight antigens (foreign substances) that might enter the body when there is a cut. Most of the research on the benefits of acute stress looked at nonspecific immunity, such as initial skin response to infection, something that has important implications for wound healing (Dhabhar, 2013). What is becoming clear, however, is that acute or short-term stress is more likely to lead to immune system enhancement than long-term stress, which almost always has negative effects on immune measures and healing (Mummert, 2016).

In one key study, mice were randomly assigned to a stress or nonstress condition (being constrained in a plastic tube), then received repeated UV radiation, which can initiate squamous cell carcinoma, a type of skin cancer (Dhabhar, 2009). Researchers repeated this stressor several times during the middle of a 10-week irradiation period and measured whether tumors occurred, what their sizes were, the cell composition of the tumors, and many blood measures. Compared to no-stress controls, the short-term stress group showed fewer tumors, more immune cells, and better immune cell function.

We see these nonstress benefits on a practical level, as well. One groundbreaking study of people undergoing knee surgery showed that the patients who exhibited stress-related immune cell activation had better knee mobility than those who did not (Rosenberger et al., 2009). In other words, mild stress helped them heal faster.

Perceptions of Stress

The second way in which we might question whether stress is always bad for health involves the way thoughts and beliefs can change the effects of stress on health. We have discussed concepts in this chapter that point to how the "goodness" or "badness" of stress depends on whether you perceive or believe that something (a stressor) is overwhelming or not. The question, therefore, is, If you change your mind about stress, can you change how your body responds to it?

Stress in many ways is more subjective than objective—the same experiences will be considered stressful or not by different people. Earlier in the chapter, we questioned the value of viewing "stress" simply in terms of the stimulus that we encounter (e.g., work, marriage, illness, exams) or the response (physiological activation, immune changes). You might also recall the role of appraisal in determining whether a given situation is stressful or not, and the key role of appraisal in that process. Once we have appraised something as threatening and too much to handle and the stress response ensues, how we cope with the stress matters. Coping strategies, such as reappraisal of the situation, can turn something from a stressor into a nonstressor. In this way, not all stress is equal, and certainly not all stress is illness producing.

Reframing situations is not the only way that one might use thoughts to offset the harmful effects of stress. What we believe might do this as well. The belief that stress makes you sick has become almost accepted as a truism in our society, even though—as we have already discussed—the data show that the relationship is not particularly strong and not really clear. Keller and colleagues (2012) examined *beliefs* about whether stress makes you sick might actually make you sick. The study made use of a household survey conducted by the National Center for Health (NCHS, 2000) on almost 30,000 people in the United States who were asked numerous questions about stress: how much stress they experienced over the past year; how much distress they had in their lives; whether they had done anything to reduce the amount of stress in life; what their health behaviors were; and most importantly how much has stress affected their health (a lot, some, hardly, or none). The major dependent variable, or outcome, of interest was whether the respondent had died from *any* cause in the 8-year period following the survey. Death information was obtained from the National Death Index (NDI).

As predicted, those with the highest stress were most likely to die 8 years later. What is most surprising, however, was that it was *not* how much "stress" they had in life but whether they believed stress could make them sick (Keller et al., 2012). Specifically, those who reported the most stress *and* believed stress could make them sick were the most likely to be dead after 8 years! This is alarming but also hopeful, as it shows that we *can* change our beliefs, and therefore our longevity.

We have long known that changing beliefs is a huge aspect of trying to change behavior. Interventions aimed at changing people's beliefs about health have shown mixed effectiveness in changing behavior, mainly because it is very difficult to change beliefs. Consider the number of programs designed to educate people about safe sex and not using drugs—many never have an impact on behavior, because beliefs are so strongly held (Mantler, 2013). Still, some programs aimed at changing one's belief

about health-related behaviors have an impact on health outcomes, such as prenatal smoke exposure in pregnant women (Kazemi, Ehsanpour, & Nekoei-Zahraei, 2012) and colon cancer screening (Rawl et al., 2012). Beliefs and perceptions can be powerful tools in coping with stress and turning bad stress into good stress.

The topics we have discussed herein—especially how variation in perceptions of stress and how people cope with challenges that are manageable versus situations that are unmanageable suggests that a singular concept of "stress" is perhaps an oversimplification. Having some challenge is beneficial to growth (*no pain, no gain*), but too much can push us over the edge. The defining feature to "stress" as per our definition is whether the demands exceed our ability to cope with them. So stress can vary according to how much we can handle it.

Some have proposed distinguishing among three different types of stress: good stress, tolerable stress, and toxic stress (McEwen, 2016). Good stress, sometimes referred to as *eustress*, refers to situations in which we are challenged by difficulty and meet the challenge, often with positive results. A corollary is this: Only when we are stretching our abilities can we acquire new ones. Situations in which we face huge challenge—often with some psychological and physical discomfort—and then successful surmount those challenges is often deemed "worth it." You can look at the simple example of training for excellence in a sport or musical instrument. The practice can be grueling and even stressful, but the rewards make it worth it. This is *eustress* or *good stress*. *Tolerable stress* refers to situations in which we are pressed by life circumstances and may even face disappointing or difficult consequences, but we have adequate coping skills—including ample social support—which helps us get through it relatively unscathed. Examples include: failing an important exam, losing a job, or enduring a break-up. *Toxic stress* is stress so extreme that it wreaks havoc on the body; stress along the lines of what Selye studied—when we are pushed into overwhelming conditions, such as putting a rat in a cage with inescapable shock. For a human, what is "too much" depends to a great extent on what the specific person involved appraises to be too much (some of us can handle more than others), but enduring divorce, a move, financial loss or chronic poverty, and the death of a loved one in a very short period of time might very well qualify. Any kind of trauma would be considered to be toxic stress, such as witnessing someone getting killed in war or a street crime, enduring physical or emotional abuse, or suddenly losing everything in a natural disaster. In fact, trauma has been linked with numerous negative physical and mental health outcomes and harmful health behaviors, especially when it occurs in childhood (Cecil et al., 2017; Nugent, Goldberg, & Uddin, 2016).

Chapter Review

STRESS

- Stress results when we appraise the demands of a situation as exceeding our ability to cope with or manage those demands. Researchers often define stress in terms of events or our physiological responses to certain events.

- Primary appraisal is the initial evaluation of how threatening a situation is. Secondary appraisal involves evaluation of resources to manage the stressful situation or the feelings it generates.

- Most stress-related physiological changes are observed in the autonomic nervous system (ANS), especially the sympathetic branch.

- The adrenal-medullary system controls the release of catecholamines, chemicals that activate heart rate, respiration, and other responses that prepare the organism to deal with emergency situations.

- The hypothalamic-pituitary-adrenal (HPA) axis releases the hormone cortisol, which frees up glucose as a source of energy.

- The stress response is beneficial in short-term, emergency situations but not over the long term. When

©Westend61/Getty Images RF

sustained over time, the stress response can weaken the body.

- Hans Selye proposed a three-stage model, the general adaptation syndrome (GAS), to describe how the body reacts and adapts to chronic, extreme stress. In the alarm stage, the body is in emergency mode and all body systems are activated for quick response. In the resistance stage, the body gradually adjusts to the high level of stress created by the demands of its environment. In the exhaustion stage, the body is unable to sustain the response and becomes more susceptible to illness.

- Mason and others argued that Selye had overlooked the fact that people respond to different situations with different emotions and made a case for greater specificity in the stress response. Research shows that different emotions are indeed associated with different patterns of ANS response.

COPING: THE MANAGEMENT OF STRESS

- Some strategies for coping are problem focused, in that they address how to remedy or change the situation that called forth the stress response. Others are emotion focused, aimed at reducing the emotional distress or unpleasant experience created by a stressful situation.

- Social support can profoundly improve mental and physical health. Social networks influence health behavior, both positively and negatively.

- Some people are more likely than others to believe that they have control over situations, and this belief may make them healthier.

- Some people experience positive affect even in dramatically stressful situations. Positive affect, in turn, may facilitate recovery from the negative emotional arousal of stress.

HOW STRESS AND COPING AFFECT HEALTH

- There are two major approaches to studying how stress leads to illness: the physiological reactivity model and the health behavior model.

- The physiological reactivity model examines how the psychological effects of sustained stress make illness more likely.

- Psychoneuroimmunology (PNI) encompasses research on any type of connection between the CNS and the immune system.

- The work of Ader and Cohen on classically conditioned immunosuppression showed a relationship between psychological processes and changes in immune function.

- The immune system defends the body against disease. Immunity consists of natural and acquired aspects. When antigens are present, lymphocytes either release antibodies into the blood or bind directly with the antigen to disable it.

- Numerous studies have demonstrated the effects of stress on regulation of the immune system. The most convincing argument for a meaningful stress-immune connection comes from studies that measure the experience of stress, immune measures, and related illness outcomes.

- The Type A Behavior Pattern, a way of responding to demanding situations with hostility, time urgency, and competitiveness, can predict the later development of heart disease. The hostility component of the Type A pattern best predicts coronary heart disease.

- The cardiovascular reactivity model offers a perspective for understanding how hostility might increase risk for heart disease. Hostility increases the likelihood and frequency of the physiological effects of anger, which over time increases the likelihood of hardened arteries and, eventually, coronary heart disease.

- The bidirectional pathway between the gut and the brain, known as the gut-brain axis connects the nerves that serve the intestines, the immune system, the HPA axis, neurotransmitters, and hormones. By means of the HPA axis—the primary stress hormone system—stress can alter the balance of gut bacteria, which has many implications for physical health.

- People engage in behaviors that enhance health as well as those that make them more susceptible to illness. Behaviors such as smoking and drinking alcohol increase risk for major illness such as heart disease, cancer, and liver disease. Eating in response to stress also imposes risks.

- Healthy diet and exercise can extend life and enhance brain function.

BRINGING IT ALL TOGETHER: MAKING CONNECTIONS IN STRESS AND HEALTH

- Stress is not inherently good or bad. Different kinds of stress and different perceptions of stress have different effects on our bodies and minds. Acute stress can be beneficial, whereas chronic stress can be harmful.

- Perceiving stress as harmful to us increases its harmful effects on us.

Key Terms

acquired immunity
adrenal-medullary system
alarm stage
allostasis
antigen
cardiovascular reactivity (CVR) model
cardiovascular system
cellular immunity
coping
emotional disclosure
emotion-focused coping

exhaustion stage
general adaptation syndrome (GAS)
glucocorticoids
health behavior approach
health psychology
hypothalamic-pituitary-adrenal (HPA) axis
microbiome
natural immunity
neuroendocrine system
physiological reactivity model

primary appraisal
problem-focused coping
psychoneuroimmunology (PNI)
psychosomatic theory
resistance stage
secondary appraisal
stress
stressors
telomerase
Type A Behavior Pattern (TABP)

Quick Quiz Answers

Quick Quiz 1: 1. c; **2.** b; **3.** d; **4.** a   **Quick Quiz 2: 1.** a; **2.** c; **3.** c; **4.** d   **Quick Quiz 3: 1.** c; **2.** a; **3.** b; **4.** d

13 Personality: The Uniqueness of the Individual

Chapter Outline

Challenge Your Assumptions

True or False?

- Freud's ideas are interesting historically, but have no scientific support. (see page 498)

- Your personality is determined mostly by your family environment. (see page 509)

- Many different kinds of animals have personality in the sense that humans do. (see page 513)

- Facebook "likes" do a better job of predicting your personality than your friends do. (see page 519)

- Your personality predicts future success in your career better than letters of recommendation, educational credentials, or interviews. (see page 518)

- People can usually change their personalities if they try. (see page 521)

Joshua was always a bit of a worrywart and anxious. Ever since he was a small boy, he had more fears and anxieties than most of his friends. For example, he was more afraid of being hit by the baseball in Little League than most others; and as a young child had nighttime fears of monsters and boogymen.

Jackie is very shy and uncomfortable around people she doesn't know well. Around her friends she is talkative and comfortable, but she withdraws and feels uncomfortable in groups of strangers or even acquaintances. She loves reading, prefers being alone to being with lots of people, and cannot stand roller-coasters or other thrill-seeking activities.

Jody has always loved ideas, learning, and exploring new places. She spent a year abroad her senior year of high school, learning Japanese and living with a Japanese family. She is curious about everything and cannot stand routine or being in one place too long. Jody never orders the same thing twice from her favorite restaurant, and her interest in art and music are vast—for example, her musical tastes include anything from Beethoven and Bach to the Beatles and Rolling Stones to Drake and Bruno Mars.

Javale is always warm and friendly and wears a big smile as if its glued to his face. He makes friends with most anybody and is the peace-maker in his own family. Javale is also very helpful and altruistic, willing to help those in need whenever possible.

Jacob is never on time for most appointments or activity, including his college classes. He has no real system for organizing his assignments and notes and often has a bit of trouble locating a specific assignment for a specific class. Jacob also tends to act on impulse, and is often tempted by hanging out with his buddies over attending class. When he was in high school and lived at home and had to do a chore, finishing it half way was good enough for him. Finishing it half way was not good enough, however, for his parents.

The above five hypothetical, but realistic, case studies exemplify each of the five major dimensions of personality, known as the "Big Five." The Big Five—as we see in the "Perspectives on Personality" section of this chapter—are five universal dimensions of personality that we all possess from a little to a lot:

- Neuroticism (Joshua)
- Extraversion (Jackie is low on this dimension.)
- Openness to Experience (Jody)
- Agreeableness (Javale)
- Conscientiousness (Jacob is low on this dimension.)

Yet traits are only one component of personality. The current chapter will discuss not only traits like the Big Five, but also other aspects of the nature of personality—its definition, different theoretical perspectives explaining it, how much of it originates from nature and nurture, and how it is measured scientifically.

DEFINING PERSONALITY

When psychologists use the term *personality*, they are referring to the unique and relatively enduring set of behaviors, feelings, thoughts, and motives that characterize an individual (Feist, Feist, & Roberts, 2013; Roberts & Mroczek, 2008).

The definition of *personality* includes two key components. First, personality is what distinguishes us from one another and makes us unique. Second, personality is relatively enduring, or consistent. Let's consider these key components in more detail.

The first major component of personality involves the uniqueness of an individual's thoughts, feelings, and behavior. Different people will respond to almost every situation in different ways. Consider what happens when one driver cuts in front of another. Some people react to such an incident with "road rage," while others take it in stride. A characteristic of personality—hostility—may determine whether someone responds with road rage or not. Personality, therefore, is about uniqueness, or *individual differences*. The concept of personality would not exist if everyone acted and thought alike. Personality psychology is concerned with the different ways people act in the same situation.

©Robert Glenn/Getty Images

A second component of personality is its relatively enduring consistency: both over time and across different situations. *Consistency over time* is the extent to which a person behaves the same way throughout his or her life span. *Consistency across situations*, in contrast, refers to the consistently unique way a person behaves in different situations.

For example, if a person has a "friendly" personality, she will behave in a friendlier manner than most (uniqueness) at a party, while having coffee with friends, or when meeting someone for the first time (across different situations). Also, from an early age she will be friendlier than most people and probably will be friendlier than most people years from now (over time). This is what we mean by saying that personality is our unique and consistently unique way of behaving.

Friendliness is a personality **trait**, or a disposition to behave consistently in a particular way. Although traits make up a large part of an individual's personality, they are not quite synonymous with it. Personality is the broader term, because it comprises traits but also motives, thoughts, self-concept, and feelings.

trait
A disposition to behave consistently in a particular way.

One important principle of personality traits is that they, like intelligence, are normally distributed in the population. Recall from chapter "Intelligence, Problem Solving, and Creativity" (Figure 8) that a normal distribution exists when a graph of all the scores is symmetrical and bell-shaped. A few people exist at both the extreme low and extreme high ends of the distribution, but most people are average. Consider the Big Five trait of "neuroticism." Neuroticism is the extent to which a person is prone to anxiety, guilt, and sadness on the one hand or is calm, steady, and emotionally stable on the other hand. Most people are in the middle of these two extremes, but a few of us are on the extreme, just like intelligence (see Figure 1). The same is true for extraversion, warmth, and any other personality trait.

Another important principle of traits is that they are directly connected to behavior. They lower **behavioral thresholds**, or the points at which you move from not having a particular response to having one (Allport, 1937; Feist & Barron, 2003; Rosenberg, 1998). A low threshold means you are very likely to behave in a particular way, whereas a high threshold means you are not. For instance, Carlos is shy, which means he has a low threshold for feeling awkward. If he were introduced to a group of strangers, he would likely feel uncomfortable. In the same

behavioral thresholds
The points at which a person moves from not having a particular response to having one.

FIGURE 1

DISTRIBUTION OF NEUROTICISM IN THE POPULATION. When we measure personality traits, such as how prone to anxiety and negative emotion people are, and then plot the number of people at all scores from low to high, we end up with a normal—or bell-shaped—distribution. Most people score in the middle, with a few on the extremes.

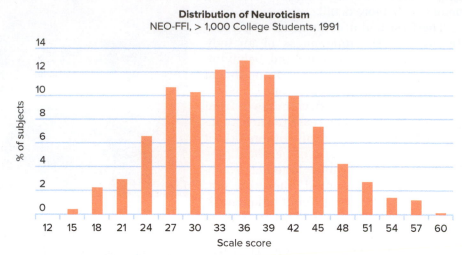

Distribution of Neuroticism
NEO-FFI, > 1,000 College Students, 1991

(Source: https://bspace.berkeley.edu/access/content/group/0f4d90d8-c107-467d-000e-28cb28b3815b/Lecture%20 Supplements/stats_meths/images/neuroticism.gif)

 Where might you be on the distribution?

situation, however, Karen, who is outgoing, would probably feel comfortable, because she has a much higher threshold for social awkwardness. Their optimal levels of arousal—or thresholds—are different. In short, traits lower behavioral thresholds and are directly connected to behavior.

Quick Quiz 1: Defining Personality

1. Two characteristics of personality are
   a. uniqueness and instability in behavior.
   b. uniqueness and consistency in behavior.
   c. consistency in behavior and identity formation.
   d. uniqueness and change in behavior.

2. A statistical property of most personality traits is that they are
   a. unreliably measured.
   b. randomly distributed.
   c. normally distributed.
   d. skewed distributions.

Answers can be found at the end of the chapter.

PERSPECTIVES ON PERSONALITY

Some people are calm and relaxed, but others are regularly nervous and anxious; some are warm and friendly, whereas others are hostile and aggressive. How do we explain such differences in personality style? Let's take a look at the various perspectives that different theorists have provided. The major explanations can be grouped into five distinct theoretical perspectives: psychoanalysis, humanism, social–cognitive learning, trait theory, and evolutionary–biological theory. As you will see, each offers a different perspective on the phenomenon of personality. The primary assumptions and key ideas of each of the five perspectives are presented in Figure 2.

	Assumptions	Theorist	Key ideas
Psychoanalytic	Our personality resides in the unconscious and early childhood experiences lay the foundation for adult personality.	Freud	Unconscious, Preconscious, Conscious, Id, Ego, Superego
		Adler	Striving for superiority Compensation. Inferiority complex, Birth order
		Jung	Personal unconscious, Collective unconscious Archetypes: shadow, anima, animus
		Horney	Basic hostility, basic anxiety, defenses against anxiety
Humanistic–Positive	We have a natural interest in becoming the best person possible.	Maslow	Strive to become the best possible person Self-actualization
		Rogers	Strive toward growth and fulfillment through unconditional positive regard Real self, Ideal self
Social–Cognitive	A person's behavior changes in different situations.	Mischel	Behavior results from the interaction of the cognitive and emotional qualities of the person and the particular situation he or she is in.
Traits	Traits are the major force behind personality.	McCrae/Costa	**O**penness to experience **C**onscientiousness **E**xtraversion **A**greeableness **N**euroticism Five-Factor Model includes: Basic tendencies—biologically based Characteristic adaptations—culturally based
		Allport	Personality is a product of both heredity and environment.
Evolutionary–Biological	We have a biological foundation for our personality traits.	Buss Eysenck	**P**sychoticism **E**xtraversion **N**euroticism Differences in genetics, neurochemistry, and CNS cause personality differences.

FIGURE 2
SUMMARY OF FIVE PERSPECTIVES ON PERSONALITY.

Psychoanalytic Theories

Psychoanalytic theories are all based on or are variations of Freud's seminal ideas.

Sigmund Freud   Undoubtedly the most famous of all psychologists is Sigmund Freud (1856–1939). Freud not only proposed an overarching theory of personality and psychotherapy but also founded the movement known as psychoanalysis and, in the process of doing so, essentially invented the field of psychotherapy.

As mentioned in the chapter "Introduction to Psychology", the starting point for Freud's theory of psychoanalysis is the idea that the unconscious is the most powerful force in personality. More generally, Freud described three layers of

©i love images/Alamy RF

Theories of personality, like all scientific theories, are based on theorists' observations and are used to generate research hypotheses.

What observations about personality does this photograph bring to mind?

Connection

Cognitive psychologists refer to mental processes that occur outside awareness as "implicit" or "automatic." Much of what we learn and remember is implicit.

See "Long-Term Memory and the Brain," in the chapter "Memory" (p. 281) and "Basic Processes of Learning," in the chapter "Learning." (p. 299)

unconscious
One of Freud's three levels of consciousness; it contains all the drives, urges, or instincts that are outside awareness but nonetheless motivate most of our speech, thoughts, feelings, or actions.

id
One of Freud's provinces of the mind; the seat of impulse and desire; the part of our personality that we do not yet own; it owns or controls us.

ego
One of Freud's provinces of the mind; a sense of self; the only part of the mind that is in direct contact with the outside world; operates on the "reality principle."

superego
One of Freud's provinces of the mind; the part of the self that monitors and controls behavior; "stands over us" and evaluates actions in terms of right and wrong; our conscience.

consciousness: unconscious, preconscious, and conscious. The conscious layer is what we are aware of at any given moment in time, whereas the preconscious is just below the surface of awareness. It is not currently conscious but can become so relatively easily. Because the conscious and preconscious layers are less important in Freud's theory, we will focus instead on the unconscious.

According to Freud, the **unconscious** contains all the drives, urges, or instincts that are outside awareness but nonetheless motivate most of our speech, thoughts, feelings, or actions. Before Freud, most people assumed that what we consciously think, feel, and believe is a relatively accurate and important source of information for explaining our behavior and personality.

Freud believed that much of what we do and the reasons we do it are hidden from our awareness and revealed to us only in distorted forms, such as slips of the tongue and dreams (Freud, 1900/1953, 1901/1960). The technique of free association, whereby people are encouraged to speak about anything on their minds without censoring their thoughts, also provides access to the unconscious (see the chapter "Treatment of Psychological Disorders" for a discussion of free association). He developed an elaborate system for interpreting the meaning of dreams, because they were the best way to understand a person's unconscious.

Freud also developed the notion that the human mind has three distinct "provinces," or regions, involved in the control and regulation of impulses. These regions are where the internal conflict between having an impulse and controlling it gets played out. The first province—developed in infancy—is the **id**, the seat of impulse and desire. The id is the part of our personality that owns or controls us. Its sole function is to seek pleasure; it is therefore founded in the "pleasure principle" and operates on the "do it" principle. By the end of the first year of life, a sense of self, or **ego**, has begun to emerge. It is the only part of the mind that is in direct contact with the outside world, and it operates on the "reality principle." If the id wants pleasure, the ego makes a realistic attempt to obtain it. The last part of the mind to develop, around age 2 or 3, is the **superego**, the part of the self that monitors and controls behavior. The superego "stands over us" and evaluates our actions in terms of right and wrong; hence, it is our conscience. It operates on the "moralistic principle," is the control center of the personality, and frequently applies the brakes to the impulses of the id.

In a healthy person, the ego mediates this conflict between impulse and control. Freud believed that some people are mostly id-driven, whereas others are mostly superego-driven. People who are overly impulsive and pleasure seeking have an uncontrolled id. People who are overly controlling and repress their impulses have an exaggerated superego. The healthiest person is one in whom the ego is most developed and can control, in a realistic and healthy way, the conflict between impulse and control (see Figure 3).

Another of Freud's major contributions to psychology is the concept of psychological **defense mechanisms** (S. Freud, 1926/1959). Although Freud first described these mechanisms, his daughter, Anna, developed them further (A. Freud, 1946). Just as the physical body has the immune system to protect us from foreign substances, the purpose of defense mechanisms is to protect us from harmful, threatening, and anxiety-provoking thoughts, feelings, or impulses. All defense mechanisms share two qualities:

- They operate unconsciously.
- They deny and distort reality in some way.

The most basic of all defense mechanisms is repression; it underlies all the other defense mechanisms. **Repression** is the unconscious act of keeping threatening or disturbing thoughts, feelings, or impulses out of consciousness. The impulses that are most likely to be repressed are sexual and aggressive impulses, because these are inherently the most threatening. Although repression may keep these impulses and thoughts out of awareness, they may be expressed in disguised or distorted form. In fact, they often reveal themselves through dreams, slips of the tongue, or neurotic behavior.

Reaction formation occurs when an unpleasant idea, feeling, or impulse is turned into its opposite. This often results in exaggerated or compulsive feelings and behavior (S. Freud, 1926/1959). A woman may resent and even hate her mother, but because these feelings are not acceptable to her or to society, she turns them into showy, exaggerated love. Homophobia is another example: Hatred and aggression toward homosexuals might well be a reaction against fear of one's own latent homosexual impulses.

In **projection**, people deny and repress their own particular ideas, feelings, or impulses and project them onto others. For example, a man may desire a married woman, but instead of recognizing his feelings, he projects his desire onto the woman and believes that she is seducing him.

Another defense is **sublimation**, which involves expressing a socially unacceptable impulse in a socially acceptable and even desirable way. Thus, for example, someone plays football or boxes as a socially acceptable outlet for violent and aggressive impulses. Freud believed that most creative achievements are motivated by sublimated impulses, usually sexual or aggressive. That is, unfulfilled sexual desire or aggressive impulses drive much creative output, which is why sex and violence are such common themes in movies, music, and art.

FIGURE 3

The Conflict Between the Id ("Do It" of the Devil) and the Superego ("Don't Do It" of the Angel)

defense mechanisms
Unconscious strategies the mind uses to protect itself from anxiety by denying and distorting reality in some way.

repression
The unconscious act of keeping threatening thoughts, feelings, or impulses out of consciousness.

reaction formation
A defense mechanism that occurs when an unpleasant idea, feeling, or impulse is turned into its opposite.

FIGURE 4

THE RELATIVE INFLUENCES OF ID, EGO, AND SUPEREGO IN THREE TYPES OF PEOPLE. Freud argued that the relative sizes and strengths of the id, ego, and superego (as symbolized by the size of the circles) contributed to whether a person is overly impulsive, neurotically repressed and overcontrolled, or psychologically balanced and healthy.

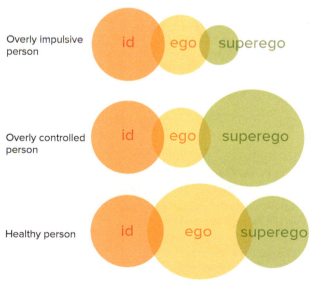

(Feist, Feist, & Roberts, 2013).

©Prisma/Prisma/Superstock

To honor Freud's contributions to psychology, his last home, in London, has been preserved as a museum. His patients would lie on this couch during treatment sessions.

projection
A defense mechanism in which people deny particular ideas, feelings, or impulses and project them onto others.

sublimation
A defense mechanism that involves expressing a socially unacceptable impulse in a socially acceptable way.

striving for superiority
According to Adler, the major drive behind all behavior, whereby humans naturally strive to overcome their inherent inferiorities or deficiencies, both physical and psychological.

compensation
Adler's description of an unconscious reaction people have to cover up their weaknesses and sense of inferiority by striving for superiority.

inferiority complex
An unhealthy need to dominate or upstage others as a way of compensating for feelings of deficiency.

Challenge Your Assumptions

True or False? Freud's ideas are interesting historically, but have no scientific support.

True and False: Some parts of Freud's ideas are supported by modern science (the power of the unconscious and the lasting impact of childhood experiences), but others are not (sexual stages).

Sigmund Freud is one of the most complex figures in the history of psychology. His theories have had a significant and lasting influence on Western thought. Large segments of 20th-century art and literature were directly or indirectly influenced by Freud's views of human nature, from James Joyce's use of stream of consciousness to Salvador Dalí's surrealistic paintings (Adams & Szaluta, 1996; Brivic, 1980; Kimball, 2003). Over the last generation, however, many research-oriented psychologists have dismissed Freud as a pseudoscientist, because he did not support his ideas with research that could be replicated. His status as a scientist is questionable, but his insights as a clinician still have scientific merit. In the late 1990s, a group of neuroscientists began to argue that the latest evidence from neuroscience confirms some parts of Freud's ideas. According to Antonio Damasio, a well-known contemporary neuroscientist, "we can say that Freud's insights on the nature of consciousness are consonant with the most advanced contemporary neuroscience views" (quoted in Solms & Turnbull, 2002, p. 93). Others argue that Freud's ideas about the power of the unconscious, the conflicting nature of motives, and the importance of early childhood experience on adult personality have had a lasting impact and have survived empirical testing (Weston, 1998).

For all of Freud's genius, however, he became dogmatic about his ideas after he had published them. Any followers who seriously challenged them might have been ejected from Freud's inner circle or official society. Some of these followers went on to develop their own theories of psychoanalysis. Among them were Alfred Adler, Carl Jung, and Karen Horney.

Alfred Adler   The first to break away from Freud, Alfred Adler (1870–1937) saw himself as Freud's colleague rather than follower. When he disagreed with Freud on the major motives underlying behavior, he had to resign from the presidency of Freud's Vienna Psychoanalytic Society. Adler's first major assumption was that humans naturally strive to overcome their inherent inferiorities or deficiencies, both physical and psychological. This **striving for superiority**, not sex or aggression, is the major drive behind all behavior (Adler, 1956). Adler introduced the term *compensation* to explain how this process unfolds. **Compensation** is an unconscious reaction people have to cover up their weaknesses and sense of inferiority by striving for superiority. All people, he pointed out, begin life as young, immature, and helpless. As they grow, they strive toward growth and completion. In the process, they attempt to compensate for their feelings of weakness or inferiority. Although all people do this to some extent, some develop an unhealthy need to dominate or upstage others as a way of compensating for feelings of inferiority—that is, they develop an **inferiority complex**.

Another key idea in Adler's theory of individual psychology is the importance of *birth order* in influencing personality (Adler, 1931). Adler was one of the very first psychologists to notice consistent psychological differences in the personalities of first-born, middle-born, and last-born individuals. First-born children tend to have strong feelings of superiority and power. After all, by definition, first-born children are older and more mature than their siblings. First-borns can be nurturing of others, but they are sometimes highly critical and have a strong need to be right. Second children tend to be motivated and cooperative, but they can become overly competitive. Youngest children can be realistically ambitious but also pampered and dependent on others. Finally, only children can be socially mature, but they sometimes lack social interest and have exaggerated feelings of superiority.

Carl Jung　Though younger than Adler, Carl Jung (1875–1961) became more widely known. Jung's signature idea was that the unconscious has two distinct forms: personal and collective (Jung, 1964). The **personal unconscious** consists of all our personally experienced repressed and hidden thoughts, feelings, and motives. This is similar to Freud's notion of the unconscious. Jung also believed, however, that there is a second kind of unconscious, one that belongs not to the individual but to the species. He called it the **collective unconscious**, and it consists of the shared universal experiences of our ancestors—God, mother, life, death, water, earth, aggression, survival—that have been transmitted from generation to generation. Jung decided that there must be some kind of collective unconsciousness that would explain the many instances in which dreams, religions, legends, and myths share the same content, even though the people who created them have never directly or even indirectly communicated with one another. The idea of a collective unconscious came naturally to Jung, because he was extraordinarily well versed in world mythology, world religion, and archaeology.

The collective unconscious is made up of **archetypes**: ancient or archaic images that result from common ancestral experiences. Their content is made manifest most often in our dreams but also in fantasies, hallucinations, myths, and religious themes. Jung postulated many archetypes, including the shadow, anima, and animus. The **shadow** is the dark and morally objectionable part of ourselves. We all have impulses that are dark and disturbing; in fact, most often we project

personal unconscious
According to Jung, the form of consciousness that consists of all our repressed and hidden thoughts, feelings, and motives.

collective unconscious
According to Jung, the form of consciousness that consists of the shared universal experiences of our ancestors—God, mother, life, death, water, earth, aggression, survival—that have been passed down from generation to generation.

archetypes
Ancient or archaic images that result from common ancestral experiences.

shadow
According to Jung, the dark and morally objectionable part of ourselves.

Darth Vader, the villain from the movie *Star Wars*, epitomizes Jung's shadow archetype of the dark, morally repugnant side of human nature.

evil and darkness onto our enemies and deny that we ourselves are evil or capable of it. Shadow figures are found everywhere in politics, literature, and art, not to mention movies: Darth Vader of *Star Wars* clearly personifies the shadow figure.

The **anima** is the female part of the male personality, and the **animus** is the male part of the female personality. All people possess characteristics and traits—not to mention hormones—that are typical of both genders. Yet most people downplay or even repress in themselves the qualities and traits of the opposite sex—men tend to deny and repress their feminine side, or anima, and women tend to deny or repress their masculine side, or animus. As we saw in the chapter "Human Development," however, gender identity has become a topic of exploration for more and more people. Jung argues that full personality development requires acknowledging and being receptive to these unconscious or less well-developed sides of one's personality.

Karen Horney   One of the first major female voices in the psychoanalytic movement was that of Karen Horney (pronounced "horn-eye"; 1885–1952). Compared to Freud, Horney focused more on the social and cultural forces behind neurosis and the neurotic personality, and indeed her approach is labeled "psychoanalytic social theory." The essence of Horney's theory is that neurosis stems from basic hostility and basic anxiety. *Basic hostility* is anger or rage that originates in childhood and stems from fear of being neglected or rejected by one's parents. Because hostility toward one's parents is so threatening, it is often turned inward and converted into *basic anxiety*, which Horney defined as "a feeling of being isolated and helpless in a world conceived as potentially hostile" (1950, p. 18).

Although basic anxiety in itself is not neurotic—it can give rise to normal behaviors—in some people it can result in neurotic behaviors. Horney argued that all people defend themselves against basic anxiety (isolation and helplessness) by developing either normal/spontaneous or neurotic/compulsive defenses that take the shape of particular needs or trends (see Figure 5). If these needs become

FIGURE 5
INTERACTION AMONG HOSTILITY, ANXIETY, AND DEFENSES IN HORNEY'S THEORY. Hostility and anxiety mutually influence one another, and the person then defends him- or herself by developing either normal or neurotic defenses. Horney maintained that we all may develop defenses, but in neurotic individuals, these needs become compulsive.

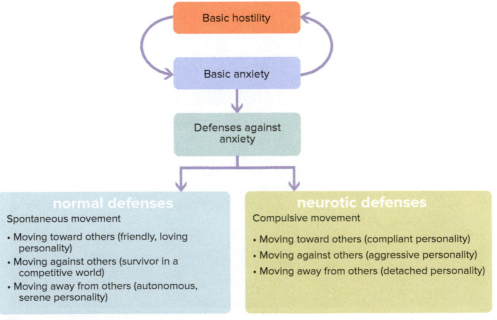

 Can you think of someone you know who uses these defenses normally and someone else who uses them neurotically?

compulsive and the person is unable to switch from one need to another as the situation demands, that person is neurotic. The three neurotic trends or needs are

1. *Moving toward others* (the compliant personality)
2. *Moving against others* (the aggressive personality)
3. *Moving away from others* (the detached personality)

Neurotically moving toward others involves consistently needing or clinging to other people, belittling oneself, getting people to feel sorry for "poor little me," and almost completely repressing feelings of anger and hostility. Neurotically moving against others involves puffing oneself up in an obvious and public manner, "chest-beating," competing against others at almost everything, and being prone to hostility and anger. Finally, neurotically moving away from others involves developing a detached and "cool" demeanor—not responding emotionally, not caring, and being "above it all." One way to avoid feeling isolated and helpless is not to feel anything and avoid committed long-term relationships. Whenever someone tries to get close to a detached person and open up to him or her, the detached person withdraws and closes up (Horney, 1945).

Neuropsychoanalysis One of the major criticisms of Freudian theory has been its lack of empirical or scientific foundation. Critics claimed that it was more "armchair speculation" than scientifically testable hypotheses (Crews, 1998). Although there is some validity to some of these criticisms, it is also true that certain Freudian assumptions—that unconscious motives affect our thinking and reasoning, and that dreams are mostly about repressed ideas—have received recent scientific support (Westen et al., 2006).

In fact, **neuropsychoanalysis**, a scientific movement that combines Freudian ideas with neuroscientific methods (Wright & Panksepp, 2012). By combining the subjective insights into the mind made by Freud with the objective insights of the mind gained by neuroscience, neuropsychoanalysts are closing the divide that existed between Freud's ideas and science. Neuropsychoanalysts argue that at least seven core assumptions made by Freud have received recent scientific support (Solms, 2004; Westen, Gabbard, & Ortigo, 2008; Westen et al., 2006):

neuropsychoanalysis
The scientific movement, started in the late 1990s, that combined Freudian ideas with neuroscientific methods.

- The importance of early childhood experience on later personality development
- Unconscious motivation
- Repression and defense mechanisms
- The pleasure principle
- Primitive drives
- Dreams as wish fulfillment
- Thinking and perception being guided by unconscious motives and emotions

A recent study from a Freudian perspective examined the ways unconscious feelings and motives affect how people judge presidential candidates (Westen et al., 2006). The researchers found that people tended to gloss over contradictions made by their preferred candidate; they didn't see them as real contradictions. They did, however, latch on to the contradictions of their nonpreferred candidate. Such a result is quite consistent with the Freudian notion of repression, where people ignore or deny threatening ideas. In addition, neuroimaging results of the study showed that motivated reasoning involves different brain regions than nonmotivated reasoning. Motivated reasoning is reasoning that is influenced by our wishes and desires.

Humanistic–Positive Psychological Theories

A second major perspective explaining personality comes from a *humanistic approach*, which is optimistic about human nature, believing that humans are naturally interested in realizing their full potential. Humanists argue that psychology needs to study humans at their best as well as at their worst. As Abraham Maslow wrote (1968, p. 5), "Freud supplied us with the sick half of psychology, and we must now fill it with the healthy half." The term *humanism* is not commonly used today, mostly because many adherents of this approach did not conduct empirical research, yet the movement has been rekindled since the late 1990s under a new label: *positive psychology.* Positive psychology embraces and generates empirical research, but its fundamental ideas come from two major thinkers in the humanistic tradition: Abraham Maslow and Carl Rogers (Seligman & Csikszentmihalyi, 2000).

Abraham Maslow   We discussed one of Abraham Maslow's (1908–1970) major ideas in the chapter "Motivation and Emotion": his hierarchy of needs. An important concept that followed from his theory of needs was that of self-actualization, which stood at the top of the hierarchy. This term refers to people's inherent drive to realize their full potential (an idea that was influenced by Adler's notion of striving for superiority; Maslow, 1970). Very few people attain this highest level of the hierarchy of needs, because very few are "fully human," or living life at its fullest and achieving their full potential.

Based on an examination of historical figures whom he considered self-actualizing, Maslow identified a set of characteristics that he believed to be more common in self-actualizing individuals than in other people (Maslow, 1970). He listed 15 characteristics, five of which we summarize here:

Connection

A truly starving person is not concerned with art and beauty. Maslow's hierarchy of needs describes how the basic needs (such as hunger, thirst) must be satisfied before one can pursue the higher needs, such as self-actualization.

See "Models of Motivation," in the chapter "Motivation and Emotion." (p. 407)

1. *Spontaneity, simplicity, naturalness:* Self-actualizing people sometimes can appear quite childlike in their ability to be spontaneous and straightforward; they do not pretend to be what they are not.

2. *Problem-centered (have a "calling"):* Self-actualizing people often experience moments of profound personal importance or personal meaning (what Maslow called "peak experiences"), and these experiences shape the rest of their lives. A sense of what they were meant to do with their lives is suddenly revealed to them, and they devote the rest of their lives to it. These individuals are focused and secure in who they are and what matters most to them—and often their concerns have great philosophical, spiritual, political, artistic, or scientific meaning.

3. *Creativity (self-actualizing rather than specialized):* Problems confront us dozens, if not hundreds, of times each day. Self-actualizing people are able to readily solve problems with originality and novelty. By *creativity,* Maslow does not mean creativity as expressed in art or science (specialized creativity) but rather the kind of creativity that can be found in everyday life (self-actualizing creativity). Practical, everyday creativity is more important than professional achievement, although self-actualized people may be creative in their work as well.

4. *Deep interpersonal relations:* Self-actualizing individuals are likely to have few but profound relationships. They do not call 10 or 15 people their "best friends" or even "friends" but instead may have close relationships with only one or two people. These relationships, however, are intensely intimate; they share deep thoughts and feelings about themselves, each other, and the world.

5. *Resistance to enculturation:* Self-actualizing people are less likely than most people to be influenced by the ideas and attitudes of others. Their ideas are solidly their own; because they have a clear sense of direction in life, they don't look to others for guidance on what to think or how to behave.

Carl Rogers   Another key figure in the humanistic–positive psychology tradition was the psychotherapist Carl Rogers (1902–1987). Rogers developed a unique form of psychotherapy based on the assumption that people naturally strive

©Michael Rougier/Time & Life Pictures/Getty Images

Carl Rogers (second from right) leads a group therapy session. His client-centered therapy approach is discussed in the chapter "Treatment of Psychological Disorders."

toward growth and fulfillment and need unconditional positive regard for that to happen (Rogers, 1980). **Unconditional positive regard** is the ability to respect and appreciate another person unconditionally—that is, regardless of the person's behavior. This may sound easy, but, in fact, it is very difficult. Even if someone violates our basic assumptions of what it means to be a good, decent, and moral person, we still appreciate, respect, and even love him or her as a person. It requires that we separate person from behavior, which can be difficult even for parents and their children. To love people only when they do things that we want and like is to love them conditionally.

In contrast to Maslow, Rogers had a specific, measurable way of defining the self-actualizing tendency and psychological adjustment. To Rogers, all of us have two distinct ways of seeing and evaluating ourselves: as we really are and as we ideally would like to be. The first he called the real self and the second the ideal self (Rogers, 1959). Rogers then defined psychological adjustment as congruence between the real and ideal selves.

In the late 1990s a modern offshoot to humanism began under the name *positive psychology* (Seligman & Csikszentmihalyi, 2000). The core idea behind positive psychology is a focus on positive states and experiences, such as hope, optimism, wisdom, creativity, spirituality, and positive emotions (for example, happiness). In contrast to the humanistic psychologists, however, positive psychologists are more likely to base their ideas in research than in speculation, clinical practice, and observation.

> **unconditional positive regard**
> The acceptance of another person regardless of his or her behavior.

Social–Cognitive Learning Theories

A third major category of personality theory is based on the social–cognitive learning perspective, exemplified by the research and writings of Walter Mischel. As we have seen, personality traits produce consistent behavior over time and across situations. Mischel agreed with the idea that personality involves stable and consistent behavior over time, but he did not completely agree with it involving stable and consistent behavior across situations. A hostile person may be less hostile in one situation (for example, being run into by a child) than in another (for example, being cut off in traffic). Compared to a nonhostile person, he or she is likely to be more hostile in many—but not all—situations. Mischel says that people are not always consistent across all situations (Mischel, 2009; Mischel & Shoda, 1995, 1999), because it would be pathological not to change

FIGURE 6
HYPOTHETICAL PERSON–SITUATION BEHAVIOR INTERACTION.

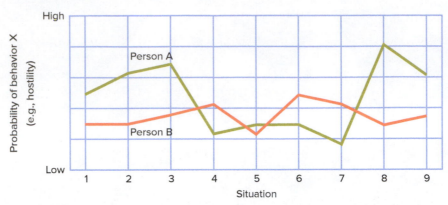

(Mischel & Shoda, 1995)

 Looking at the graph, what conclusion would you draw about which person is more hostile overall, Person A or Person B? People respond to different situations differently, producing unique personality–situation profiles. Here, Person A is more hostile than Person B in the first three situations. They are roughly the same in the middle four situations. So saying that Person A is more hostile than Person B would be misleading and simplistic. It depends on the situation.

one's behavior when the situation changes. The qualities a person brings to each situation interact with the situation to make the behavior change when the situation changes. Figure 6 illustrates how people and situations interact according to Mischel's theory. The figure presents the probabilities of two individuals (A and B) acting in a hostile manner across nine different situations. As you can see, Person A is more likely to be hostile in six of the nine situations, so we would label this person "hostile." Notice two things: (1) There are a few situations in which Person B is more hostile, and (2) Person B is more stable and consistent across all nine situations, whereas Person A is sometimes very hostile but at other times not hostile at all. This hypothetical situation demonstrates how the person, situation, and behavior interact.

Trait Theories

A fourth general perspective that explains personality is the trait approach, which assumes that traits, or dispositions, are the major force behind personality, but which traits are most important? Between the 1930s and the 1980s, dozens of different measures of personality were developed, but almost none of them measured the same personality traits. Some psychologists argued for the central importance of hostility, authoritarianism, introversion, intelligence, repression, and impulsivity, while others cited psychopathic deviance, tolerance, or psychological insight. Until personality psychologists could reach a consensus on a set of traits that make up personality across cultures, no progress could be made in the study of personality, for it would mean different things to different people.

As far back as the 1930s, Gordon Allport (1897–1967) tried to figure out how many personality traits existed (Allport & Odbert, 1936). He began with the idea that language would be a good place to start looking. He argued quite simply that, if a word exists for a trait, it must be important. He approached the problem by taking an English dictionary and combing through it page by page and counting each time a term described a person. After going through and counting all the personally descriptive words, he came away with nearly 18,000 words in English. A few problems arose, however. First, some of these terms—such as *sad*, *angry*, *bored*, or *annoyed*—described temporary states. Others were personal evaluations (*wonderful*, *unhelpful*) or descriptions of

Dimension	Description
Openness (O)	How interested in new experiences or new ideas is someone? How imaginative, original, and curious is he or she?
Conscientiousness (C)	How planned, organized, orderly, hard-working, controlled, persevering, punctual, and ambitious is someone?
Extraversion (E)	How sociable, talkative, active, outgoing, confident, and fun-loving is someone?
Agreeableness (A)	How friendly, warm, trusting, generous, and good-natured is someone?
Neuroticism (N)	How anxious, worrying, tense, emotional, and high-strung is someone?

FIGURE 7

BIG FIVE DIMENSIONS OF PERSONALITY. The acronym OCEAN (or CANOE) will help you remember the five dimensions.

physical traits (*tall, heavy*). Finally, others were essentially synonyms, such as *friendly* and *nice*. When he fixed these problems, he still ended up with more than 4,000 English words that were personally descriptive. He went on to argue, however, that most individuals could typically be described with only about 10 or so central traits.

By the 1980s, personality researchers had amassed evidence for the existence of five universal and widely agreed-upon dimensions of personality (Costa & McCrae, 1992; Digman, 1990; John & Srivastava, 1999). This perspective is known as the **Big Five** or **five-factor model**; the five dimensions are openness to experience, conscientiousness, extraversion, agreeableness, and neuroticism (see Figure 7). An easy way to remember these is to use the acronym O-C-E-A-N or C-A-N-O-E.

The Big Five dimensions are more of a taxonomy, or categorization scheme, than a theory. They describe but do not explain personality. In the 1990s, Robert McCrae (1949) and Paul Costa (1942) proposed a theory around the Big Five personality dimensions. The two primary components of their theory are basic tendencies and characteristic adaptations (McCrae & Costa, 1996, 1999, 2008). The Big Five personality dimensions, along with our talents, aptitudes, and cognitive abilities, are referred to as **basic tendencies**, and they have their origin in biological forces. McCrae and Costa take a clear but somewhat controversial stance in arguing that these basic tendencies are due solely to internal or biological factors such as genes, hormones, and brain structures.

Big Five (five-factor model)
A theory of personality that includes the following five dimensions: openness to experience, conscientiousness, extraversion, agreeableness, and neuroticism (OCEAN).

basic tendencies
The essence of personality: the Big Five personality dimensions, as well as talents, aptitudes, and cognitive abilities.

Evolutionary–Biological Theories

The fifth perspective on personality is the evolutionary–biological approach. Evolution and biology are connected, but for our purposes we treat the two separately.

Evolutionary Explanations of Personality

Two basic problems of all living things are survival and reproduction. These problems must be solved if any species is to survive. Biologists and evolutionary psychologists dub the adaptive solutions to these problems **mechanisms**. *Physical mechanisms* are the bodily organs and systems that solve survival and reproductive problems, whereas *psychological mechanisms* are the internal and specific cognitive, motivational, or personality systems that solve specific problems of survival and reproduction (Buss, 1991, 2011; MacDonald, 1995). Figure 8 lists examples of both physical and psychological mechanisms.

In many animals, but especially humans, personality traits are one form of psychological mechanism that evolved to solve problems of adaptation (Buss,

mechanisms
Adaptive solutions to problems of survival and reproduction.

FIGURE 8
EXAMPLES OF EVOLUTIONARY PROBLEMS (SURVIVAL & REPRODUCTION) AND THEIR SOLUTIONS (MECHANISMS).

Problem	Solution (mechanism)
Survival	*Physical Solution (Mechanism)*
• Taking in information from the outside world	• Eyes, Ears, Tongue, Skin, Nose
• Disease/parasites	• Immune System
• Fending off attacks of predators/enemies	• Strength, Speed
Reproduction	
• Creating offspring	• Sex organs
Survival	*Psychological Solution (Mechanism)*
• Trust/cooperation	• Conscientiousness, Agreeableness
• Alliances	• Dominance, Agreeableness
Reproduction	
• Mate attraction	• Dominance, Intelligence, Creativity
• Intimacy	• Love, Attachment, Agreeableness

2011; Buss & Greiling, 1999; Buss & Hawley, 2011; Duckworth, 2010; MacDonald, 1995; McCrae & Costa, 1999). In this view, personality traits are strategies for solving reproductive and survival problems (Buss, 1991, 2011). MacDonald (1995) refers to personality differences as "viable alternative strategies for maximizing fitness" (sexual and survival). For example, the tendency to be sensitive to threats may well have been adaptive in dangerous environments like those in which our ancestors lived. Heightened anxiety would provide a signal of danger and threat; its absence would quickly lead to extinction of the species. Consider a hunter on the savanna. He hears the growl of a large animal and becomes fearful. If he does not feel anxious, he might not hide, and that would have dire consequences for his safety and his likelihood of catching dinner. By the same token, the other extreme—hypersensitivity to threats—would be debilitating and disruptive to everyday functioning. If the same man who became fearful at hearing the growl of a large animal also became fearful with every rustling of leaves or every sound of the wind, he would have a hard time functioning in everyday life. Having some degree of fearfulness is adaptive, and people with that quality were more likely to survive, reproduce, and pass on that disposition. In addition, for humans to survive we need the trust and cooperation of other people, and group alliances are stronger than individuals. So the trait of conscientiousness, which consists of being dependable and reliable, is a useful trait in this context. So too is being friendly and warm (agreeable) as well as being competitive, strong, and a leader (dominance).

Both natural and sexual selection operate in the evolution of human personality traits. Naturally selected traits are favored if they increase one's chances of survival and reproductive success, whereas sexually selected traits make one more attractive to the opposite sex. For example, intelligence and creativity are sexually selected traits because people are attracted to intelligent and creative people (Buss, 1989; Kaufman et al., 2016; Miller, 2000; Nettle & Clegg, 2005).

To be sure, there are psychologically both costs and benefits to each personality dimension (Nettle, 2006, 2011). Benefits to anxiety are being sensitive to danger or threats, but at a cost of increased difficulty in relationships. Similarly, benefits to extraversion, for example, are an increase in status and sexual relationships, but the costs include an increase of having accidents, disease, or social conflict. The idea is that maladaptive traits, such as anxiety disorders, depression, and obsessive-compulsive disorder, for example, are by-products of more normal and adaptive personality traits, such as anxiety, sadness, and attention to detail and cleanliness. An evolutionary perspective on these traits suggests that if we are going to have these adaptive traits, then the price and risk is that a few people will develop maladaptive, extreme forms of them. Indeed, just as organs break down and fail, so do psychological mechanisms (Baron-Cohen, 1997).

Biological Explanations of Personality

The biological theories of personality assume that differences in personality are partly based in differences in structures and systems in the central nervous system, such as genetics, hormones, and neurotransmitters (Eysenck, 1990; Gray, 1970, 1987). Among the most important of these theories for personality is the one proposed by Hans Eysenck (1916–1997), who argued for the fundamental importance of biology in shaping personality. Eysenck (1947, 1982, 1990) proposed three, rather than five, fundamental dimensions of personality. Two are included in the Big Five, neuroticism and extraversion. The third, *psychoticism*, is a combination of the three other traits from the Big Five of openness, conscientiousness, and agreeableness. Psychoticism consists of traits such as "aggressive," "cold," "antisocial," "impulsive," "egocentric," "non-conforming," and "creative."

Eysenck developed a model in which differences in personality are caused by the combined influences of genes, neurochemistry, and certain characteristics of the central nervous system (Eysenck, 1997). The main idea behind Eysenck's model is that differences in individuals' genomes (DNA) create a different level of arousal and sensitivity to stimulation. These differences in genetics and levels of arousal and sensitivity lead to differences in the three primary dimensions of personality: psychoticism, extraversion, and neuroticism (P-E-N).

Evidence supports the connection between central nervous system arousal and personality traits, especially extraversion-introversion. Specifically, differences in two biological systems lead to differences in introversion and extraversion, namely cortical arousal and sensory thresholds. **Cortical arousal** refers to how active the brain is at a resting state as well as how sensitive it is to stimulation (Eysenck, 1997; Gale, 1983). **Sensory threshold** refers to how much of a stimulus is required for it to be perceived. Because they have higher baseline levels of cortical arousal, introverts require a lower stimulus level to arouse them and reach their "comfort zone" than do extraverts (see Figure 9). Eysenck argued that lower thresholds to arousal imply greater sensitivity to stimuli. Stimulation,

cortical arousal
The brain's level of activity at a resting state and its sensitivity to stimulation.

sensory threshold
Refers to how much of a stimulus is required for it to be perceived.

Introversion	Extroversion
Biology	Biology
☐ Low sensory threshold	☐ High sensory threshold
☐ High cortical arousal at rest	☐ Low cortical arousal at rest
Behavior	Behavior
☐ Withdraw from stimulation	☐ Seek out stimulation
☐ Prefer solitary activities	☐ Prefer group-oriented and arousing experiences
Outcome	Outcome
☐ Maintain stimulation comfort zone	☐ Maintain stimulation comfort zone

FIGURE 9
EYNSENK'S BIOLOGICAL THEORY OF INTROVERSION AND EXTRAVERSION.

whether it is a new place or new people, can easily become overwhelming for an introvert. Therefore, introverts consistently shy away from or withdraw from stimulating environments. By the same token, extraverts, with low cortical arousal and high thresholds of arousal, seek out and enjoy highly stimulating experiences (Eysenck, 1990, 1997). Introversion or inhibition can thus be seen as a way of coping with an inherently aroused and sensitive central nervous system.

Quick Quiz 2: Perspectives on Personality

1. Hatred and aggression toward homosexuals as a reaction to fear of one's own homosexual impulses is an example of which Freudian defense mechanism?
   a. reaction formation
   b. psychosexual stages
   c. repression
   d. projection

2. According to Jung, the collective unconscious is made up of ancient or archaic images that result from common ancestral experiences called
   a. core-relational themes.
   b. the animus.
   c. the inferiority complex.
   d. archetypes.

3. The key assumption of humanistic theorists, such as Maslow and Rogers, is that people
   a. are driven by unconscious motives.
   b. strive toward growth and fulfillment.
   c. learn from observing others.
   d. none of the above.

4. The Big Five dimensions of personality are openness to experience, conscientiousness, extraversion, _____, and _____.
   a. depression; neuroticism
   b. agreeableness; neuroticism
   c. agreeableness; introversion
   d. anxiousness; introversion

Answers can be found at the end of the chapter.

THE ORIGINS OF PERSONALITY

The forces of both nature and nurture shape personality. The interaction between the two can be seen in at least three perspectives and research into personality: genetics, temperament and fetal development, and cross-cultural universality.

Genetics and Personality

Recall from the chapter "The Biology of Behavior" that complex traits are almost never the result of a single gene and that our genome is the starting point, not the end point, for how our genes are expressed (our phenotype). There is no "smart" gene, "shy" gene, or "aggressive" gene. We discuss these two themes in detail later in this section, but first let's look at how *behavioral geneticists* study the relationship between genes and personality.

When studying behavioral genetics, researchers use two major methods to examine the relationship among genetics, behavior, and personality, namely quantitative trait loci studies and twin-adoption studies. In the **quantitative trait loci (QTL) approach**, researchers look for the location of specific bits of DNA on genes that might be associated with particular behaviors. In this sense, it is a search for "genetic markers" of behavior. The traits are quantitative, because they are markers for behaviors that are expressed on a broad continuum, from very little to very much (hence are quantitative). Anxiety is a quantitative trait, because some people are not at all anxious, most people are average, and a few are very anxious. The QTL method uncovers the location on particular genes that is associated with high or low levels of a trait. QTL research points to genetic markers for several basic personality traits, such as novelty or thrill seeking, impulsivity, and neuroticism/anxiety (Benjamin et al., 1996; Hamer & Copeland, 1998; Lesch et al., 1996; Plomin & Caspi, 1999; Retz et al., 2010; Rutter, 2006).

As an example, consider the case of thrill seeking, a trait that entails risk taking. People with this trait may seek out highly exciting activities, such as

quantitative trait loci (QTL) approach
A technique in behavioral genetics that looks for the location on genes that might be associated with particular behaviors.

bungee jumping, mountain climbing, or scuba diving. Thrill-seeking activities create a "rush" of excitement—a positive feeling that may be related to the release of dopamine, a neurotransmitter associated with physiological arousal. Given the possible connection between dopamine and thrill seeking, one theory suggests that people who are deficient in dopamine tend to seek out exciting situations as a way of increasing their dopamine release and making up for deficient levels of dopamine. In the mid-1990s, researchers presented the first genetic evidence to support this theory. The gene *DRD4* is involved in dopamine production in the limbic system, and the longer the gene sequence, the less efficient dopamine production is. In other words, long versions of the *DRD4* gene are associated with less efficient dopamine production. If the theory is correct, people who seek out thrills should have the longer form of this gene, and that is exactly what the research has shown (Ebstein et al., 1996; Hamer & Copeland, 1998).

Another form of quantitative trait loci study, genome-wide association studies, have found very specific gene locations for openness to experience and for conscientiousness (de Moor et al., 2012). Additionally, a meta-analysis of 12 samples revealed a genome-wide association between the serotonin transporter gene and aggressive and antisocial behavior (Tielbeek et al., 2016). In short, people with this particular genetic marker are most likely to be aggressive and antisocial.

As discussed more fully in the chapter "The Biology of Behavior," the second method for examining the effect that genetics plays in behavior and personality is the study of twins, both identical and fraternal, who have been raised together or apart. The amount of similarity between identical versus fraternal twins on a given trait provides a measure of its heritability. In general, twin-adoption studies suggest that between 40% and 60% of the differences in personality traits are genetic/heritable (Bouchard & Loehlin, 2001; Caspi, Roberts, & Shiner, 2003; Krueger & Johnson, 2008; Loehlin et al., 1998; Plomin & Caspi, 1999; Polderman et al., 2015; Tellegen et al., 1988). In other words, an individual's genetic makeup goes about halfway toward explaining his or her basic traits. For instance, the trait of extraversion often correlates around 0.50 for identical twins and around 0.24 for fraternal twins, which leads to a heritability estimate of 48% (see Figure 10). Likewise, between 50% and 55% of the differences in neuroticism and conscientiousness are due to genetics, and about 40% of differences in openness and agreeableness are due to genetics.

FIGURE 10

PERCENTAGE OF GENETIC AND ENVIRONMENTAL INFLUENCE ON PERSONALITY TRAITS. Twin studies indicate that heredity (genetics) accounts for 50%–60% of most traits, slightly less for agreeableness and openness. What's surprising is that the influence of the shared environment (same home and family) on these traits is small, compared with the influence of the non-shared (different home and family) environment.

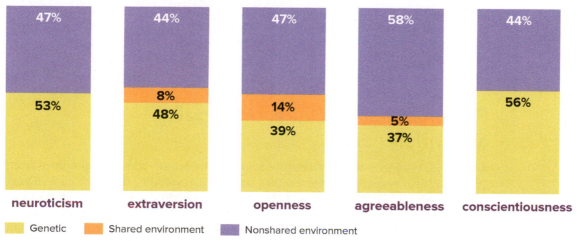

(Plomin & Caspi, 1999)

Connection

Many people think a single gene affects behavior—that we have a gene for "aggression," for example. Any given behavior or personality trait, however, is never the result of a single gene but rather of many genes.

See "Genes and Behavior," in the chapter "The Biology of Behavior." (p. 77)

Connection

Are some babies and toddlers temperamentally fussy and more difficult to care for than others? As we explain in the chapter "Human Development", with very little influence from the environment, some newborns are fussy and unpredictable, and they get upset in new situations, whereas others are generally happy, predictable, and curious in new situations.

See "The Developing Infant and Child," in the chapter "Human Development." (p. 171)

Such a figure leaves roughly 50% of the differences in personality to be explained by three nongenetic sources: shared environment, non-shared environment, and error. Even the environment is not just one thing but needs to be broken into multiple parts. **Shared environment** consists of living conditions that people have in common, such as the same parents, same schools or same peers, whereas **non-shared environment** consists of things like birth order, different parents, different friends, different teachers, and different social groups. Surprisingly, research indicates that the "unshared" environment—differences in birth order or peer groups or even changes in parenting style and attitudes over time—seems to matter most (see Figure 10; Arseneault et al., 2003; Bouchard & Loehlin, 2001; Krueger & Johnson, 2008; Plomin & Caspi, 1999; Rutter, 2006). Personality is influenced by our environment, but surprisingly more by the experiences we do *not* share with our family members, such as peer group influences.

Temperament and the Fetal Environment

Recall from the chapter "Human Development," that temperament is the biologically based disposition to behave in certain ways, which lays the foundation for later personality traits. Evidence suggests that temperament and personality differences are manifest even before birth. Apparently, fetal activity and heart rate can reveal something about temperament differences over the first year of life. In particular, a high heart rate at 36 weeks' gestation (nearly full term) foreshadowed less predictable eating and sleeping habits 3 and 6 months after birth and less emotionality at 6 months after birth. Having high activity levels at 36 weeks' gestation predicted being slow to adapt to new people or situations and having more irregular eating and sleeping habits at 3 and 6 months, as well as being more difficult or fussy at 6 months (DiPietro, 2012; DiPietro et al., 1996).

The prenatal environment may play an important role in shaping personality. One outcome of the prenatal environment is birth weight, with low birth weight being associated with a poor prenatal environment. Recent evidence reports that birth weight is positively correlated with many important outcomes, such as brain volume (Walhovd et al., 2012), and negatively correlated with cautiousness, shyness, and risk aversion later in life—meaning low birth weight babies are more cautious, shy, and risk averse (Waxman et al., 2013).

Another outcome of prenatal environment is differences in serotonin production. These differences play a critical role in brain and neural development, which in turn affect personality development (Oberlander, 2012). Abnormal serotonin function is also involved in the stress response, which is linked with the development of anxiety and depression later in life (McEwen, 2005; Oberlander, 2012). In fact, the amount of stress the mother experiences during pregnancy may alter the infant's own stress response. Infants born to mothers who experienced an unusual amount of stress during pregnancy tend to have impaired stress function; higher baseline levels of stress hormones; and a faster, stronger, and more pronounced physiological response to stress, all of which persist into childhood (Barbazanges et al., 1996; Clark & Schneider, 1997; Rice, Jones, & Thapar, 2007).

Personality and Culture: Universality and Differences

Additional evidence that both nature and nurture shape personality comes from cross-cultural research on personality traits. If personality dispositions are part of our biology, we would expect the same personality dimensions or traits to appear in cultures all over the world. Environment and culture, however, might modify temperament and make certain traits more likely in some societies than in others. There is evidence for both of these perspectives.

Certain personality traits appear to be universal insofar as people all over the world have them, for instance, extraversion, neuroticism, agreeableness, openness to experience, conscientiousness, and psychoticism (Carlo et al., 2014). Research confirms the existence of these personality traits not only in Western cultures (the United States, the United Kingdom, Germany, Australia, Iceland, Spain, Portugal) but also in Asian (China, Japan, South Korea), African (Zimbabwe), Middle Eastern (Iran, Israel), and Pacific Rim (Malaysia and the Philippines) cultures (Benet-Martinez & Oishi, 2008; McCrae, 2002; McCrae & Allik, 2002; McCrae & Costa, 1997). Similarly, one measure of five major dimensions of personality, the NEO-Personality Inventory (PI), has been translated into more than 40 languages, and the same five personality dimensions have emerged in every one (Rolland, 2002).

In general, over the lifespan personality changes in similar ways the world over. One study of more than 880,000 people from 62 countries on every continent reported universal changes in personality (Bleidorn et al., 2013). From early to mid-adulthood, people become less anxious and extraverted and more open, agreeable, and conscientious. People from vastly different cultural backgrounds exhibit these traits—evidence of their universal and biological basis.

However, people in different cultures differ on certain dimensions of personality (Güngör et al., 2013; McCrae et al., 2010). Once again, it is useful to appreciate behavior and personality from multiple perspectives (Bleidorn et al., 2013). For example, personality change over the lifespan is not the same all over the world (Bleidorn et al., 2013). In addition, people in Asian cultures exhibit qualities that fit a dimension of "interpersonal relatedness" that is rarely seen in Western cultures. Interpersonal relatedness includes such behaviors and attitudes as a respectful, obedient demeanor toward others, a belief in saving "face" (allowing a "losing" party to suffer a loss and yet maintain esteem and reputation), and an emphasis on harmonious relationships. This dimension of personality reflects how people in Asian cultures tend to be more concerned about the impact of their behavior on their family, friends, and social groups (known as **collectivism**), whereas people in Western cultures are more concerned with how their behavior will affect their personal goals (known as **individualism**; Cross & Markus, 1999; Hofstede, 2001; Triandis, 1996). Thus, an Asian employee who is offered a promotion that would require relocating to another city may be concerned primarily with how

collectivism
Cultures that tend to be more concerned about the impact of their behavior on their family, friends, and social groups.

individualism
Cultures that are more concerned with how their behavior will affect their own personal goals.

©Blend Images - Noel Hendrickson/Brand X Pictures/Getty Images RF

In Japan and other Asian cultures, respect for others and an emphasis on harmonious interpersonal relationships take precedence over individual concerns. Interpersonal relatedness as a dimension of personality is rare in the West.

the move would affect his family. On the other hand, the primary consideration of a Western employee might be how the move would increase her chances of someday becoming an executive in a major corporation. Research suggests that compared to people in individualist cultures, those in collectivist cultures tend to score higher on the Big Five dimensions of agreeableness and conscientiousness and lower on openness to experience (Realo, Allik, & Vadi, 1997). Cultural differences in personality make clear that environment also affects personality and its development.

Challenging Assumptions in Animal Personality

Courtesy of the Authors

Belle and Scooter—the authors' cats

Years ago, your authors adopted two 7-month-old kittens: "Scooter" (a male) and his sister, "Belle." Now 7 years old, these two cats could hardly be more different in terms of their behavior. Scooter is curious and sociable. He explored every inch of his new home on the first day and forces himself into every one of our activities—eating, watching TV, working at the computer, and sleeping. Not once has he been afraid of any situation. He approaches everything with glee and wonder. Belle, however, has been anxious and shy from the beginning. It took her about 3 days to come out of hiding and become comfortable with her new home. She plays, but not so much with strangers, which we were for the first few days.

To pet owners, the question of animal personality seems to have an obvious answer: Of course, animals have distinct personalities. Just look at Scooter and Belle. To psychologists, the question might seem to be stretching the definition of personality too far. If we claim that animals have personality, might we simply be projecting human qualities onto them, what scientists term *anthropomorphizing*? Most people who have owned more than one cat or dog can identify differences in the personalities of their pets. Some pets are calm, while others are excitable; some are friendly and readily approach strangers, whereas others are more reserved and wary. Even if we can see evidence of personality in animals such as dogs and cats, can we see it in other animals? Do mice have personality? Birds? Reptiles? Fish? Worms?

Until the 1990s, most psychologists would have argued that the term *personality* made sense only as applied to humans. From the 1990s on, however, a solid body of evidence began to challenge the assumption that personality differences are mostly limited to humans (Asher et al., 2016; Cote et al., 2014; Dingemanse et al., 2002; Gosling & John, 1999; Morton et al., 2013; Uher, 2008; Zimmer, 2005). Gosling and Oliver John (1999) conducted a meta-analysis of 19 studies across 12 nonhuman species. They found evidence for at least 14 nonhuman species with personality traits that can be categorized along the same dimensions as human personality. The summary of these findings is presented in Figure 11. Keep in mind that the labels from the Big Five are general labels, and the specific ones used in these studies vary somewhat. For instance, neuroticism is sometimes called emotional stability, excitability, fearfulness, emotional reactivity, fear-avoidance, or emotionality. Agreeableness is sometimes labeled aggression, hostility, understanding, opportunistic, sociability, affection, or fighting-timidity. In addition, dominance-submission is a trait that is often seen and measured in nonhuman animals, but it does not fit into any of the Big Five categories. These ratings of animal personality were made by one of two behavioral observation techniques: either by animal trainers who had extensive knowledge of the individual animals or by trained observers with no history with the animals but who were trained until they could reliably evaluate the dimensions in question.

It may not surprise you that primates and other mammals tend to share the largest number of personality traits with humans (Morton et al., 2013; Weinstein,

FIGURE 11

PERSONALITY DIMENSIONS ACROSS SPECIES. Ratings by trainers who know the animals or by trained observers produced these results, which suggest that animals do have personalities and that they share some traits with humans. Note that domestic dogs and cats have a "competence" or "learning" dimension that is a mixture of openness and conscientiousness. Where no check mark appears, there is no evidence for that trait in that species (Gosling & John, 1999).

	Neuroticism	Extraversion	Agreeableness	Openness	Conscientiousness
chimpanzee	✓	✓	✓		✓
horse[a]	✓	✓	✓		✓
rhesus monkey	✓	✓	✓		
gorilla	✓	✓	✓		
dog	✓	✓	✓		✓[b]
cat	✓	✓	✓		✓[b]
hyena	✓		✓		
pig		✓	✓		
vervet monkey		✓	✓		
donkey		✓	✓		
rat	✓		✓		
guppy	✓	✓			
octopus	✓	✓			
chickadee[c]					

[a]Based on Morris, Gale, and Duffy (2002).
[b]Competence/learning is a mixture of openness and conscientiousness.
[c]Based on Dingemanse et al. (2002).

Capitanio, & Gosling, 2008). Chimpanzees, our closest relative, however, share with humans a distinct "conscientiousness" dimension. Such a finding suggests that conscientiousness—which involves impulse control and therefore requires highly developed brain regions capable of controlling impulses—is the most recently evolved personality trait. Thus, with the exception of chimps and horses, animals other than humans do not possess the required brain structures to control impulse and to organize and plan their activities in advance. Even with chimps, the conscientiousness dimension was somewhat narrowly defined as being methodical, lacking attention, and being goal directed (Freeman et al., 2013). Two very interesting recent findings are that horses high in neuroticism and low in extraversion are most susceptible to pain (Ijichi, Collins, & Elwood, 2013) and that chimps high in openness, dominance, and being methodical spent the longest time working on foraging puzzles that involved finding food (Hopper et al., 2013).

What challenged people's assumptions the most, however, was research reporting that wild birds, fish, and even octopuses possess humanlike personality traits. For instance, in a study of a European bird resembling a chickadee, when researchers placed a foreign object, such as a battery or a Pink Panther doll, into the cage, some birds were consistently curious and explored the novel object, while others consistently withdrew and avoided the object (Dingemanse et al., 2002; Zimmer, 2005). The researchers called these differences in birds "bold" and "shy." These differences are much like those psychologists observe when they place an infant in a room with a stranger. Approach-boldness and shyness-avoidance are also dimensions of human temperament.

Challenge Your Assumptions

True or False? Many different kinds of animals have personality in the sense that humans do.

True: Primates, in particular, but most mammals and even nonmammals share personality traits with humans.

Research Process

1 Research Question

Can the personality and living conditions of pigs affect their levels of optimism?

Pig personalities can be classified as either "proactive" or "reactive." Proactive pigs are quick to explore, curious, aggressive, and behave consistently in different situations. Reactive pigs are inhibited, passive, and behave differently in different situations. Asher and colleagues (2016) predicted that proactive pigs would be more optimistic than reactive pigs and that better living conditions would lead to more optimistic pigs.

©photomaster/Shutterstock.com

2 Method

There were a total of 36 pigs in the study, randomly assigned at four weeks of age to either an enriched or non-enriched living environment. The enriched environment had more space and more straw than the non-enriched environment.

The second variable was personality (proactive-reactive). This was measured at 6 to 8 weeks of age by the speed to which the pig went to a novel and potentially scary object, an orange traffic cone. Pigs that approached this novel, scary object quickly were classified as "proactive" and those who did not approach it quickly were classified as "reactive."

The outcome variable was "optimism," but how does one measure optimism in a pig? Not by a survey of course but by a behavioral test. To set up the optimism test, the researchers first had to train the pigs where "positive" food (chocolate M&Ms) was in their pen and where the "negative" food (coffee beans) was. The positive food was always in one corner and the negative food always in a different corner. Once pigs learned this, the optimism test was how quickly does the pig approach a new unknown food bowl if it is placed near the known negative food? If they go fast, they are "optimistic" because they must think there probably is something good in that bowl. More specifically, "optimism" was scored as 1 if the animal went the same speed to the new unknown bowl as to the known positive food bowl. They received a 0 if they went as fast to the new unknown bowl as to the known negative food bowl ("pessimism").

3 Results

As predicted, the proactive pigs overall were most optimistic. They got to the unknown food bowl almost as fast as they got to the known positive food bowl regardless of whether they were raised in an enriched environment or not. Only for the reactive pigs, however, did their environment matter. If they were raised in an impoverished environment, they were quite pessimistic—that is, only slightly faster than they were getting to their known negative food. But if they were raised in an enriched environment, reactive pigs were actually *faster* to the unknown food bowl than they were to the known positive one (that is why their score was slightly greater than 1.0) (see Figure 12).

4 Conclusion

Proactive pigs are generally more optimistic than reactive pigs, but not always. If the reactive pigs are raised in an enriched environment, then they are the most optimistic pigs of all. This was the first study to demonstrate that personality differences and living environment can combine to affect the levels of "optimism" in pigs.

FIGURE 12

Interaction between pig personality and raised environment on degree of optimism.

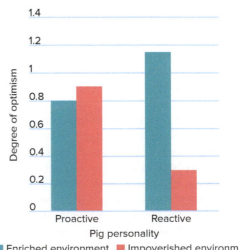

Source: Adapted from Asher et al., 2016.

Quick Quiz 3: The Origins of Personality

1. The genetic marker for thrill seeking involves genetic differences in which neurotransmitter?
   a. dopamine
   b. acetylcholine
   c. serotonin
   d. norepinephrine

2. Which research technique attempts to find specific genetic markers for personality traits?
   a. meta-analysis
   b. analyzing DNA in rats reared together
   c. twin adoption studies
   d. quantitative trait loci studies

3. People in Asian cultures exhibit qualities that suggest a personality dimension of _____ that is rarely seen in Western cultures.
   a. anxiety
   b. interpersonal relatedness
   c. separation distress
   d. agreeableness

4. Which of the human Big Five personality characteristics appears only in humans, chimpanzees, and horses?
   a. openness
   b. extraversion
   c. conscientiousness
   d. agreeableness

Answers can be found at the end of the chapter.

HOW IS PERSONALITY MEASURED?

Defining and explaining personality are of prime importance, but you can define and explain only what you can measure. So how do psychologists measure and study personality? Four distinct methods are most common: behavioral observation, interviewing, projective tests, and questionnaires.

Behavioral Observation

The most direct and objective method for gathering personality data is to observe behavior and simply count specific behaviors that are associated with particular traits, such as aggression, hostility, friendliness, anxiety, or conscientiousness. However, collecting valid data is more difficult than it might seem. For instance, choosing to rate the fairly straightforward example of "aggression" raises many questions. What specific behaviors will count as aggression? Hitting? Insulting? Sarcasm? How does a researcher quantify each behavior—on a continuum from none to a great deal, or simply on the basis of whether it is present or not? Over what time period will the behavior be observed? Where will the behavior take place: in a real-world setting or in a laboratory? Who will rate the behavior? How do we know that different observers will view a given behavior in the same way?

These questions address the issue of measurement in general and reliability in particular. If two or more raters are to accurately rate and agree upon their ratings, there must be **inter-rater reliability**. The researchers must first establish an exact definition of the trait they wish to measure, identify the behaviors that make up that trait, and practice rating it against experienced, expert, and reliable raters. The new raters are deemed "reliable" if their ratings compare well with established norms or expert ratings, usually with a correlation of 0.80 or higher.

When children or others, such as animals, who cannot evaluate or report on their own personalities are being assessed, behavioral observations are required. The advantages of behavioral observations are that they do not depend on people's view of themselves, as self-report measurements do, and they are direct and relatively objective.

Despite these strengths, behavioral observations are costly and time-consuming. Moreover, not all personality traits can be observed by other people. Anxiety and depression, for instance, although they can be expressed through behavior, are often experienced internally and subjectively—external observations can't tell the whole story. For these kinds of personality traits, a person's

inter-rater reliability
A measure of how much agreement there is in ratings when using two or more raters or coders to rate personality or other behaviors.

own reporting—a self-report—is more reliable. Self-reports can be obtained in three ways: interviewing, projective tests, and questionnaires.

Interviewing

Sitting down with another person face-to-face is probably the most natural and comfortable of all personality assessment techniques. Interviewing is an ideal way to gather important information about a person's life. From the participant's perspective, interviewing is usually more engaging and pleasant than completing a questionnaire. The clear advantage for participants is the open-ended nature of the interview, in which they can say anything they wish in response to a question. Of course, there also are disadvantages of interviewing and they mostly involve what to do with the information and how to make sense of it: What does a response mean? How are responses scored and by whom? What criteria are used? These issues are similar to those associated with behavioral ratings, but with interviews the "behavior" is a verbal response to a question that must be coded reliably and accurately. Thus, the ease of interviews from the participant's perspective is offset by the difficulty of scoring responses reliably.

Projective Tests

Projective tests present an ambiguous stimulus or situation to participants and ask them to give their interpretation of or tell a story about what they see. These techniques are based on Freud's notion of "projection" as a defense mechanism, that is, that unconscious wishes, thoughts, and motives will be "projected" onto the other people or situations. By interpreting an entire series of such answers, a psychologist can identify consistent unconscious themes. One of the most widely used projective tests is the Rorschach Inkblot Test.

In the **Rorschach Inkblot Test**, a series of ambiguous inkblots are presented one at a time, and the participant is asked to say what he or she sees in each one (see Figure 13). The responses are recorded and then coded by a trained coder (most often a psychologist or psychotherapist) as to how much human and nonhuman "movement," color, form, and shading the participant sees in each card (Exner, 1974; Masling & Borenstein, 2005). Not only is the test used to measure unconscious motives, but its supporters also claim that responses can help them diagnose various psychological disorders, such as depression, suicidal thoughts, pedophilia, posttraumatic stress disorder, or anxiety disorders (Guarnaccia et al., 2001; Nash et al., 1993; Ryan, Baerwald, & McGlone, 2008; Sloan, Arsenault, & Hilsenroth, 2002; Xiang, Shen, & Li, 2009).

Personality Questionnaires

Because of the expense and time that behavioral ratings and interviews require, along with the relative unreliability of projective tests, the most common way of measuring personality is asking participants to summarize their own behavioral tendencies by means of questionnaires. **Personality questionnaires** consist of individual statements, or items; respondents indicate the extent to which they agree or disagree with each statement as it applies to their personalities. Responses

projective tests
Personality assessments in which the participant is presented with a vague stimulus or situation and asked to interpret it or tell a story about what he or she sees.

Rorschach Inkblot Test
A projective test in which the participant is asked to respond to a series of ambiguous inkblots.

personality questionnaires
Self-report instruments on which respondents indicate the extent to which they agree or disagree with a series of statements as they apply to their personality.

FIGURE **13**
AN INKBLOT SIMILAR TO THOSE FOUND ON A RORSCHACH INKBLOT CARD. In the Rorschach Inkblot Test, a person is asked to interpret the inkblot however he or she wishes. After the participant has interpreted a dozen or more cards, psychologists can form ideas about what kinds of thoughts, feelings, and motives are consistently being "projected."

©Spencer Sutton/Science Source

are usually arranged on a *Likert scale*, which attaches numbers to descriptive responses, such as 1, "completely disagree"; 3, "neither agree nor disagree"; and 5, "completely agree."

Questionnaires are developed with years of validation. But how does a researcher create a new psychological questionnaire? There are two approaches for creating questionnaires, namely the rational method and the empirical method.

The **rational,** or **face valid, method** involves using reason or theory to come up with a question. If we wanted to develop a new measure of anxiety, we could include an item like "I feel anxious much of the time." This is a "face valid" item, because what it measures (anxiety) is clear and can be taken at face value. A frequently used personality questionnaire that uses the face valid method is the NEO-PI (Costa & McCrae, 1992). The problem with such questionnaires, however, is that because the questions are transparent and face valid, participants might give socially desirable or false answers rather than honest ones. For example, for the item "I am anxious much of the time," someone might not want to admit to frequently feeling anxious and hence might not answer honestly.

The **empirical method** focuses on whether responses to various items scientifically or empirically differentiate between the groups it should (Gough & Bradley, 1996). The essence of creating a questionnaire using the empirical method is seen in this example: If preliminary research shows that the statement "I prefer baths to showers" is answered a certain way by anxious people and a different way by nonanxious people (thereby discriminating between these two groups), it is used in a questionnaire for anxiety. This method requires an outside criterion of who is anxious or not, such as a therapist's evaluation of the anxiety levels, to relate to such items. If the empirical evidence shows that it does distinguish the two groups, then it is used in the questionnaire.

Two of the most widely used personality questionnaires were developed using the empirical method: the Minnesota Multiphasic Personality Inventory (MMPI) and the California Personality Inventory (CPI). The MMPI is used by psychotherapists to assess the degree and kind of a person's psychiatric personality traits, such as depression, paranoia, or psychopathic deviance (antisocial personality; Tellegen et al., 2003). The CPI, however, is a measure of nonpathological, or normal, personality traits such as sociability, responsibility, dominance, or self-control (Gough & Bradley, 1996). Both the MMPI and the CPI consist of questions that target groups who answer differently from the general population. In "Psychology in the Real World," we describe how personality predicts college major, career interest, and job performance.

rational (face valid) method
A method for developing questionnaire items that involves using reason or theory to come up with a question.

empirical method
A method for developing questionnaire items that focuses on including questions that characterize the group the questionnaire is intended to distinguish.

Social Network Measurement of Personality

As we have been discussing throughout the text, social networks sites (SNS) such as Facebook, Twitter, and Instagram have changed how we communicate and interact, but did you know that how you use them reflects on who you are and what kind of personality you have?

Believe it or not, recent research suggests that Facebook likes may do a better job at assessing our personality and predicting our behavior than our friends' assessment of our personality (Youyou et al., 2015). In a sample of more than 10,000 people, Youyou and colleagues assessed the accuracy of personality ratings via the correlation between people's Big Five ratings of their own personality and those ratings made by work colleagues, friends, family members, and spouses. Computer ratings were simply the "like" footprint left from Facebook activity. Work colleagues had the lowest agreement with the self-ratings on all of the Big Five personality dimensions ($r = 0.27$), then friends

Psychology in the Real World

Personality and Career Interest and Job Performance

Would you want a surgeon operating on you who is known for being anxious and nervous? How about having a police officer in your hometown who is violent and aggressive? Would you want to buy something from a shy and socially awkward salesperson? Personality is important when it comes to jobs. Would you believe that personality tests do a better job of predicting your future success in your career than interviews, school credentials, or letters of recommendation? They do (Charmorro-Premuzic & Steinmetz, 2013). Conscientiousness is generally the best personality predictor of how well you will perform in your job.

Challenge Your Assumptions

True or False? Your personality predicts future success in your career better than letters of recommendation, educational credentials, or interviews.

True: Although they are not as widely used, personality tests do a better job of predicting future success at jobs than traditional application materials such as educational credentials or interviews.

If you go to your university or college career guidance counselor, he or she will very likely use personality tests in advising you in your career choices (Costa, 1996; Mount et al., 2005). Governments and organizations also rely on them to select the right people for particular jobs (Carless, 1999; De Fruyt & Murvielde, 1999). Indeed, Hammer and Macdaid (1992) provide a list of occupations most and least similar to one's personality. Among other things, personality traits predict the majors and careers we select, what kinds of employers select us, how people perform at jobs, and how likely they are to leave them once they get them.

Personality and Career and College Major Interest

The first stage of job selection—for college students, at least—is picking a major. You may not be surprised to learn that different personality types are attracted to and interested in different kinds of majors. College majors are generally classified using three career codes, with the first one being primary (Emery, 2006). For example, psychology is SIE (Social-Investigative-Enterprising), economics is IAS (Investigative-Artistic-Social), and biology is IRE (Investigative-Realistic-Enterprising).

Personality research consistently shows that different personalities prefer different kinds of careers and college majors. Pulver and Kelly (2008) examined the association between personality and college major using a measure of personality based on Carl Jung's theory, the Myers-Briggs Type Indicator (MBTI; Myers, 1962). The MBTI consists of opposing types: Extraversion-Introversion, Thinking-Feeling, Intuition-Sensing, and Judging-Perceiving. People are classified either as an extravert or an introvert, as a thinker or a feeler, and so on. For example, Intuition-Sensing describes how people prefer to take in information—focused on what is real and actual (sensing) or on patterns and meanings in data (intuiting), whereas Thinking-Feeling describes how people prefer to make decisions—based on logical analysis (thinking) or guided by concern for their impact on others (feeling).

Pulver and Kelly (2008) found that extraverts preferred social and enterprising majors (such as psychology, social work, and elementary education), whereas thinking types preferred realistic and investigative majors (such as mechanical engineering or archaeology). Feeling types preferred artistic and social majors (such as art, music, and theater).

Similarly, Larson and colleagues (2010) examined whether personality scores reliably differentiated majors in 368 undergraduate students, but they used a different measure of personality. In this study, students completed the Multidimensional Personality Questionnaire (MPQ; Tellegen, 2000), a self-reported measure of personality that is scored on 11 primary personality traits, including social closeness, aggression (low agreeableness), harm-avoidance, and absorption.

Results showed that education majors scored higher than engineering majors on social closeness, whereas business majors scored significantly lower on agreeableness than humanities and architecture/design majors. In addition, architecture/design majors were more absorbed than business majors. Elementary education majors scored highest on harm-avoidance (avoiding situations where one can get hurt) and social closeness out of the nine majors. Similar research reported that harm-avoidance is negatively related to realistic interests and specifically interests in mechanical activities (Staggs, Larson, & Borgen, 2007). In other words, mechanical and athletic majors are not as likely as other majors to be afraid or driven to avoid harmful situations.

Personality-Environment Fit and Job Performance

Because so much research shows certain personalities matching certain majors and jobs, researchers have proposed a theory of fit between personality and job. Holland calls this idea "congruence," stating that "people find environments reinforcing and satisfying when environmental patterns resemble their personality patterns" (Holland, 1985, p. 53). I/O psychologists also refer to this notion of congruence as "person-organization fit," or how well matched the person is to his or her work environment (Kristof-Brown, Zimmerman, & Johnson, 2005). Numerous large-scale meta-analyses of over a thousand studies show that fit between personality and job does matter (Assouline & Meier, 1987; Kristof-Brown et al., 2005; Verquer, Beehr, & Wagner, 2003). The better the fit, the more satisfied people are with their jobs, the less likely they are to leave their jobs, and the more successful they will be.

Measures of fit and congruence allow employers not only to use personality measures to recruit/hire workers who best fit the job but also to weed out people who might behave counterproductively. A *counterproductive work behavior* can be defined as anything done by the employee that is intentionally negative for the organization (MacLane & Walmsley, 2010). Such behavior might include such major infractions as betraying company secrets or employee theft, but it may also involve minor transgressions, such as working nonproductively (spending too much time on Facebook or other Internet sites, for example).

What sort of personal characteristics have been linked with counterproductive workplace behavior? Of the traditional Big Five traits, people who are more conscientious, agreeable, and emotionally stable are less likely to engage in behaviors that harm their companies (Berry, Ones, & Sackett, 2007). In another study, a cluster of personality scales from the widely

©Mario Tama/Getty Images

Government and business organizations sometimes use measures of personality in screening job applicants.

 What kind of person do you think would make an effective police officer?

used California Psychological Inventory was able to reliably predict police officers who consistently used excessive force and provided drugs to inmates (Hargrave & Hiatt, 1989). More specifically, the problematic officers scored unusually low on the CPI's Self-control, Socialization, and Responsibility scales.

Personality and Switching Jobs
Personality traits also predict how long people stay in or switch their jobs. Two of the Big Five dimensions—openness to experience and agreeableness—appear to be most predictive of leaving jobs early in one's career. Recall that people with high openness to experience prefer new experiences over routine ones and that people high in agreeableness are warm, caring, and friendly. Researchers have reported that people high in openness and low in agreeableness are most likely to switch jobs and/or companies (Vinson, Connelly, & Ones, 2007; Wille, De Fruyt, & Feys, 2010).

In sum, people who are matched to their jobs make better, happier, more productive employees. Personality has wide-ranging influence over the kinds of careers we are interested in, how well various careers fit who we are, how long we stay, and how well we do in particular careers.

($r = 0.45$), followed by family members ($r = 0.50$) and spouses ($r = 0.58$). The average computer (Facebook like) correlation with self-rated personality was 0.56, outperforming all but the spouses. However, the more "likes" the computer had, the better it became at predicting personality, exceeding even spouses ($r = 0.60$) once 300 likes were added (Youyou et al., 2015). In general, the Facebook likes also outperformed all but self-rated personality on predicting real-world outcomes such as substance use, physical health, depression, impulsivity, and life-satisfaction.

Evidence is mounting that the content of our personal website, posted photos, musical preferences, online profiles, and the number and density of social network site (SNS) friends all predict our personality traits (Ivcevic & Ambady,

Challenge Your Assumptions
True or False? Facebook "likes" do a better job of predicting your personality than your friends do.
True: Research suggests that Facebook "likes" do a better job of predicting our levels of depression, life-satisfaction, impulsivity, and college major better than our friends' personality ratings of us.

2012; Kosinski, Stillwell, & Graepel, 2013; Marcus, Machilek, & Schütz, 2006; Ortigosa, Carro, & Quiroga, 2014; Özgüven & Mucan, 2013; Rentfrow & Gosling, 2003; Whitty et al., 2017). Moreover, specific Facebook "likes" predict specific personality traits. Analyzing the Facebook "likes" of 58,000 people, Kosinski and colleagues (2013) for example found that liking "Nicki Minaj" puts a person in the 92nd percentile on extraversion but only the 37th percentile on openness to experience (see Figure 14). People who like camping tend to be not anxious (high in emotional stability) and conscientious. In short, "likes" can be used to develop specific personality profiles.

Finally, people with different kinds of personalities use Facebook differently. For example, extraverts are more active on SNS, upload more photos, update their status more frequently, and have more posted friends than introverts (Eftekhar, Fullwood, & Morris, 2014; Lee, Ahn, & Kim, 2014; Ong et al., 2011; Michikyan et al., 2014). More agreeable people receive more "likes" and "comments" on their profile pictures (Eftekhar et al., 2014). Given how much of ourselves we put into our social network behavior, it is not surprising that social networks are becoming an important and novel way of assessing who we are, how we present ourselves to others, and our personality.

FIGURE 14
SELECTIVE FACEBOOK "LIKES" AND ONE'S SCORES (PERCENTILES) ON THE BIG FIVE DIMENSIONS OF PERSONALITY. People who "like" *The Colbert Report* are in the 87th percentile on openness to experience but only in the 23rd percentile on extraversion.

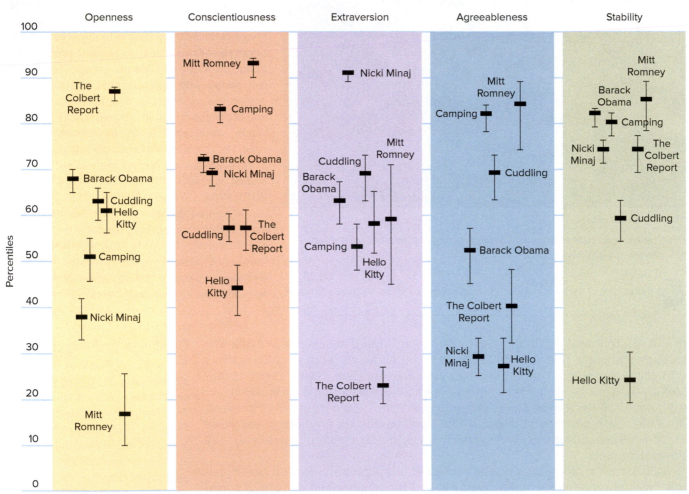

(Source: Kosinski, Stillwell, & Graepel [2013].)

Bringing It All Together

Making Connections in Personality

Does Personality Change over Time?

Personality is at the center of who we are. Recall our definition of personality as the unique and enduring manner in which a person thinks, feels, and behaves. Although it shows considerable stability over our lifetime, it also changes and develops between our infant and adult years. Personality consistency and change illustrate many of the principles discussed in this chapter. All definitions, theories, and measures of personality confront the question of consistency and change of personality.

Personality Consistency

In many ways, it is more difficult to change our personalities than we think. Much of who we are remains rather stable and consistent over our lifetimes. When we talk about personality consistency, however, we mean relative consistency. In fact, that is one of the lessons learned from Walter Mischel's work on how qualities and traits interact with specific situations to bring about different behavior across different situations (Kammrath, Mendoza-Denton, & Mischel, 2005; Mischel, 2009; Mischel & Shoda, 1999). No one is consistent all of the time or in all situations. Consistency is a matter of degree.

Longitudinal studies, those that examine the same people over a period of time, reveal high levels of stability of personality traits. Early in their collaboration, Costa and McCrae (1976) conducted a longitudinal study of personality, expecting to find that personality traits change over time. To their surprise, they found a high degree of stability over a 10-year period. Another set of longitudinal studies revealed very small changes in neuroticism, extraversion, and openness over a period of 6 to 9 years (Costa et al., 2000; McCrae & Costa, 2003).

Challenge Your Assumptions

True or False? People can usually change their personalities if they try.

False: Personality traits are quite stable in adulthood, although there is also some change in early adulthood.

Most parents or observers of infants and toddlers are quick to project subtle signs of their children's interest or talent into the future, but do our personalities and traits at age 3 portend future outcomes such as employment, mental illness, criminal behavior, and quality of interpersonal relationships? Jack and Jeanne Block conducted some of the first long-term studies of human temperament and personality. They conducted interviews, behavioral observations, and personality questionnaires

and found that children who were impulsive, aggressive, and tended to cry at age 3 were most likely to use drugs during adolescence (Block, Block, & Keyes, 1988). Similarly, temperament ratings were made on nearly one thousand 3-year-olds, who were then followed up through their teens, 20s, and 30s. Being undercontrolled and impulsive at age 3 predicted adult alcoholism, drug abuse, and gambling problems (Caspi, 2000; Slutske et al., 2012).

Research from behavior genetics has demonstrated that personality stability between adolescence and adulthood is largely due to genetic factors (Blonigen et al., 2006; Gillespie et al., 2003; Krueger & Johnson, 2008; Takahashi et al., 2007). More specifically, genetics contributes to the personality consistency we see from adolescence to adulthood, whereas environmental factors contribute to both stability and change in personality traits (Takahashi et al., 2007).

Personality Change

We all like to think we can change—that we have the power to change our destructive habits and become a better person. Can we? Research does support some degree of personality change as we move from adolescence through adulthood and as we adapt to changes in life circumstances.

Typical Personality Change across the Life Span

Recent research confirms that some degree of change in personality occurs normally from adolescence to adulthood and into old age (Allemand, Zimprich, & Hendriks, 2008; Josefsson et al., 2013; Letzring, Edmonds, & Hampson, 2014; Lodi-Smith et al., 2009; Roberts & Mroczek, 2008). The most impressive evidence comes from a meta-analysis of 92 studies that assessed personality change in over 50,000 individuals on the Big Five dimensions of personality (Roberts, Walton, & Viechtbauer, 2006). In general, people become steadily more agreeable and conscientious from adolescence to late adulthood (see Figure 15) and tend to become more assertive or dominant and emotionally stable from adolescence to middle adulthood and then level off on these personality dimensions. Finally, people generally become more sociable (social vitality) and open to new experiences from adolescence to early adulthood. These traits level off in adulthood and then decline in older adulthood. The same pattern of change is seen in cross-sectional research that examines personality differences in different age groups at the same time (Allemand et al., 2008). Together, these results make clear that personality is not set in plaster once we reach adulthood.

FIGURE 15

PERSONALITY CHANGE FROM ADOLESCENCE TO LATE ADULTHOOD. This graph shows the results of a meta-analysis of personality change on the Big Five dimensions across 92 studies and involving more than 50,000 individuals. The scale of change is measured in standardized units. 0 units means no change. Emotional stability is the opposite end of neuroticism.

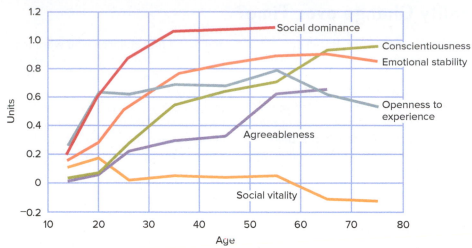

(Roberts, Walton, & Viechtbauer, 2006).

Connection

Children who are rated by their parents as being undercontrolled at age 3 are more likely than other children to have drinking problems, to get in trouble with the law, and even to attempt suicide by age 21.

See "The Developing Infant and Child," in the chapter "Human Development." (p. 171)

Personality Change after Changes in Life Circumstances

Not only does personality show some degree of change during normal life-span development but it also is open to change when we experience big changes in our lives, such as living abroad, becoming a parent, suffering a brain injury, or developing Alzheimer's disease.

Living Abroad and Personality Change

Living in a foreign country for a short or long period of time is becoming more common, especially with the popularity of study abroad programs. This raises two questions related to personality: Are those who decide to study abroad different in personality than those who don't, and what effect does living abroad have on one's personality? Sojourners (those who travel and live abroad) compared to nonsojourners have baseline personalities (before the travel) that are mostly more open and extraverted (Camperio Ciana et al., 2007; Jokela, 2009; Zimmerman & Neyer, 2013). Being open to experience and being

outgoing, sociable, and thrill seeking are qualities that predict who will select the traveling experience.

The answer to the question of whether living abroad changes personality is "yes it does." The personality traits that most consistently change after life abroad are an increase in agreeableness and a decrease in neuroticism; that is, an increase in emotional stability (Zimmerman & Neyer, 2013). Living abroad seems to make people more agreeable and friendly in their interaction with others and less anxious, sad, and depressed. Although more cognitive than personality traits, critical and creative thinking also seem to increase in those who live abroad (Lee, Therriault, & Linderholm, 2012; Savicki et al., 2004). Moreover, personality change seems to happen mostly by people acculturating to the new culture and taking on traits of the new culture (Güngör et al., 2013).

Parenting and Personality Change

Few events change a person as much as becoming the primary caregiver for a totally helpless infant. How does such a major transition affect one's personality? The answer seems to be that it depends on many factors. Paris and Helson (2002) conducted a longitudinal study of female college seniors in their early 20s and followed them until they reached their 50s and 60s. They found that becoming a mother affected personality differently, depending on the woman's evaluation of motherhood. If a woman liked being a full-time mother, then having children led to an increase in her flexibility, self-esteem, adjustment, resourcefulness, and control and a decrease in her dependence and fearfulness. If, however, she did not especially enjoy being a full-time mother, the opposite personality changes were observed.

Other researchers report that parenthood affects the personalities of mothers and fathers differently. Although self-concept in general seems to stay the same for both mothers and fathers, self-esteem goes down and irritability goes up in mothers but not in fathers (Onodera, 2003). Similarly, the gender of the parent interacts with the temperament of the child. Compared to having a child with an "easy temperament," having one with a "difficult temperament" is more likely to increase the father's but not the mother's anxiety (Sirignono & Lachman, 1985). The biggest personality change seems to come from increases in a personal sense of control and mastery if parents have an "easy" child and decreases on these dimensions if they have a "difficult" child (Sirignono & Lachman, 1985). Having a child who is difficult undermines the belief that parents can truly control the life and behavior of their children.

Although not quite parenting, mentoring children by college students can also lead to change in personality. In a study of more than 100 college students who mentored aggressive, at-risk children for three semesters, researchers reported decreases in the mentors' levels of openness, conscientiousness, extraversion, and agreeableness (Faith et al., 2011).

Brain Injury and Personality Change

Do you remember Phineas Gage from the chapter "The Biology of Behavior"? He was the railroad foreman who had a tamping iron shoot through his cheek and out the top of his skull, forever changing his personality (Macmillan, 2000).

Current research on damage to the same part of the frontal lobes where Gage's injury occurred shows similar kinds of personality change. Based on ratings of personality (behavioral observations, Rorschach Inkblots, and semistructured interviews), children and adults who suffer brain injury often lose the ability to control impulses, are socially inappropriate, have a temper, and are more prone to anger (Mathiesen, Förster, & Svendsen, 2004; Max, Robertson, & Lansing, 2001; Max et al., 2006; Rao et al., 2008; Romain, 2008).

Alzheimer's Disease and Personality Change

Alzheimer's disease is a major degenerative brain disease whose hallmarks are severe dementia and memory loss. It eventually affects personality and ultimately leads to death (Azadfar et al., 2014). Using the NEO-PI as a measure of the Big Five personality dimensions, various studies have shown that every Big Five dimension of personality changes after the onset of Alzheimer's (Chatterjee et al., 1992; Clark et al., 2000; Henriques-Calado et al., 2016; Strauss, Pasupathi, & Chatterjee, 1993; Williams, Briggs, & Coleman, 1995):

- Neuroticism increases
- Extraversion increases in some and decreases in others
- Openness decreases
- Agreeableness sometimes decreases
- Conscientiousness decreases

In short, those suffering from Alzheimer's tend to become more anxious, outgoing, and hostile/argumentative, and usually less willing to try new things and less detail-oriented. Some research has reported that personality change can even precede the onset of the disease (Balsis, Carpenter, & Storandt, 2005). In other words, there is a biological basis for our personalities. Changes in the brain are often accompanied by personality changes.

Quick Quiz 4: How Is Personality Measured?

1. The most objective method for gathering information about personality traits is to
   a. observe behavior.
   b. conduct interviews.
   c. administer questionnaires.
   d. do genetic testing.

2. The Rorschach Inkblot Test is an example of which type of personality measurement?
   a. structure interview
   b. questionnaire

   c. projective test
   d. standardized test

3. Scales that use response categories ranging from 1 to 5 (with labels ranging from 1 for "completely agree" to 5 for "completely disagree") are called
   a. ratio scales.
   b. Likert scales.
   c. face valid.
   d. dichotomous.

Answers can be found at the end of the chapter.

Chapter Review

DEFINING PERSONALITY

- Personality is the essence of who we are—both our uniqueness and our consistency. Personality traits function to change behavioral thresholds and make certain behaviors more likely and others less likely.

PERSPECTIVES ON PERSONALITY

- Personality is an expression of both nature and nurture. Personality traits have evolved through natural and sexual selection, in which genetic and environmental forces work in tandem in shaping an individual's personality.

- Studies of infant temperament offer further support for a biological basis for adult personality. Infants make their way into the world with different and unique ways

©Image Source/DigitalVision/Getty Images RF

of behaving. Children may be temperamentally easy, difficult, or slow to warm up.

THE ORIGINS OF PERSONALITY

- Theories of personality organize and explain observations, as well as stimulate testable hypotheses. Five perspectives explain personality differences and development.

- The first perspective, Freud's psychoanalytic theory, assumes distinct levels of consciousness. The most important of these is the unconscious, the level at which most thoughts, feelings, motives, and images reside.

- Freud developed the idea of psychological defense mechanisms, which defend us against psychological threats by unconsciously denying or distorting reality. Repression, for example, is the unconscious process of keeping disturbing thoughts, feelings, or impulses out of consciousness.

- Three followers of Freud broke their ties with him to establish their own views. Alfred Adler argued that striving for superiority is the primary motive underlying almost all behavior. Carl Jung introduced the idea of the personal unconscious and the collective unconscious. Karen Horney developed a psychoanalytic social theory centered on three neurotic trends: moving toward others, moving against others, and moving away from others.

- Contemporary research in neuroscience is beginning to provide empirical support for some of Freud's theories.

- The second perspective, humanistic theory, emphasizes psychological growth and health. Abraham Maslow developed a detailed concept of self-actualization; that is, the inherent tendency to strive to realize one's

full potential. Carl Rogers developed the concept of unconditional positive regard to help people achieve self-fulfillment.

- The third perspective, the social–cognitive learning theory of Walter Mischel, is based on the belief that consistent personality characteristics interact with the environment to produce a person's unique behaviors.

- Trait theory, the fourth perspective, argues for a universal and stable personality structure that consists of five dimensions of personality: openness, conscientiousness, extraversion, agreeableness, and neuroticism (O-C-E-A-N). These traits are normally distributed in the population, with most people falling somewhere between the two extremes on each trait.

- The fifth perspective includes biological theories such as those of Hans Eysenck. Eysenck argued for three fundamental dimensions of personality: psychoticism, extraversion, and neuroticism (P-E-N). Eysenck's theory holds that differences in individuals' cortical arousal and sensitivity threshold lead to differences in introversion and extraversion.

- Confirming the importance of the biological basis of personality, personality psychologists and animal behaviorists have begun to explore the nature of animal personality. They have found not only that other primates and mammals exhibit many consistent and unique personality qualities but also that birds, fish, octopuses, and even insects have personality traits that distinguish one individual from another.

HOW IS PERSONALITY MEASURED?

- Personality is measured in four major ways: observing and coding behavior; interviewing; administering projective tests; and administering structured personality questionnaires.

- Social network use and behavior is a new and upcoming method for measuring personality.

BRINGING IT ALL TOGETHER: MAKING CONNECTIONS IN PERSONALITY

- Most of the major topics in this chapter can be connected by highlighting research demonstrating the stability and change in personality over time. Genetic forces contribute to personality stability, whereas environmental factors contribute to both stability and change.

Key Terms

anima
animus
archetypes
basic tendencies
behavioral thresholds
Big Five (five-factor model)
collective unconscious
collectivism
compensation
cortical arousal
defense mechanisms
ego
empirical method

id
inferiority complex
inter-rater reliability
individualism
mechanisms
neuropsychoanalysis
non-shared environment
personal unconscious
personality questionnaires
projection
projective tests
quantitative trait loci (QTL) approach
rational (face valid) method

reaction formation
repression
Rorschach Inkblot Test
sensory threshold
shadow
shared environment
striving for superiority
sublimation
superego
trait
unconditional positive regard
unconscious

Quick Quiz Answers

Quick Quiz 1: **1.** d; **2.** c   **Quick Quiz 2**: **1.** a; **2.** d; **3.** b; **4.** b
Quick Quiz 3: **1.** a; **2.** d; **3.** b; **4.** c   **Quick Quiz 4**: **1.** a; **2.** c; **3.** b

14 Social Behavior

Chapter Outline

Challenge Your Assumptions

True or False?

©StockFinland/E+/Getty Images

T halia and her closest friend from high school, Deidre, chose to go to the same university. They roomed with other people, but they still saw each other frequently. Although their friendship felt a bit different, Thalia understood that they had different classes and some new friends. For years, Deidre had invited her to the family cabin to go skiing each winter, and Thalia took it for granted that she'd be going again this year, even though she had always been formally asked. When winter rolled around that freshman year, Thalia asked Deidre when they'd be heading to the snow. Deidre said softly, "I invited my new roommate this year." Thalia—stunned—felt like she'd been kicked in the stomach.

Being rejected hurts. In fact, social exclusion creates physical pain. In one study on the neural basis for social pain, participants were taken into a lab with an fMRI scanner and were told they would be involved in an electronic ball tossing game called "Cyberball" (Eisenberger, Shanock, & Williams, 2003; Masten et al., 2009). Once inside the scanner, they could see onscreen a Cyberball game that was apparently in progress between two other participants in scanners in different rooms. Unknown to the original participants, there were no other people playing the game. After watching the "others" play for a few throws, the participants joined in. For a while, the three players continued playing Cyberball together. After seven throws, the other players stopped throwing the ball to the participants and resumed their game. In effect, the participants were left out, as Thalia had been. Participants reported being upset about their exclusion. What's more, the fMRI scans showed activation of brain circuitry involved in physical pain, especially those areas that are involved with how unpleasant pain feels. This kind of *social pain* can be relieved by painkillers like Tylenol (DeWall et al., 2010) and may affect endocrine systems that support social connection (Maner et al., 2010). People who are more sensitive to physical pain are more sensitive to the pain of rejection, and these differences may have a genetic basis (Eisenberger et al., 2006; Way, Taylor, & Eisenberger, 2009).

Challenge Your Assumptions

True or False? Being left out really hurts.

True: When we are excluded, it causes the experience of pain and activates similar brain circuitry as does physical pain.

Drugs that block the effects of endorphins (the body's natural pain killers) actually reduce feelings of social connection (Inagaki et al., 2016). Further, people who trust their interaction partners and have higher self-esteem are less likely to experience social pain when excluded (Yanagisawa, et al., 2011). Finally, people even prefer to administer themselves a mild electrical shock over spending just 10–15 minutes alone with nothing else to do (Wilson et al., 2014).

The plus side of the research on how social exclusion hurts are the findings that social connection feels good. For example, dancing in synchrony with others increases one's threshold to pain and activated feelings of social connection probably by activating endorphins (Tau, Launay, & Dunbar, 2016).

Why does it hurt to be excluded? Like other social animals, humans form important bonds with other members of our species. We depend on other people to raise us and to cooperate with us in the presence of threats (Neuberg & Cottrell, 2006). As a result, the ways in which we relate to others play a huge role in our lives, and the need to belong is ingrained in our biology (Way et al., 2009).

In this chapter, we will discuss why belonging to a group matters to us, as well as other key aspects of social behavior, such as how the presence of other people influences our behavior, how we perceive our social world, how we form attitudes, and how we make friends. These topics are the focus of social psychology, which studies the effects of the real or imagined presence of others on people's thoughts, feelings, and actions. The research in social psychology repeatedly reflects an important theme of this book, that no one perspective tells us everything there is to know about something. What is particularly interesting in social psychology is just how often our perspective on things is influenced in dramatic or subtle ways by others—often without our even being aware of it.

©Glow Images

Dancing in synchrony elevates pain thresholds and increases feelings of social connection (Tau et al., 2016).

GROUP LIVING AND SOCIAL INFLUENCE

The social nature of human beings stems from the importance of group living in our evolutionary history. We are not solitary animals. Group living offered many advantages in human evolution, such as increased safety in the presence of danger, cooperation with others to complete challenging tasks (such as hunting), and child rearing (Brewer & Caporael, 2006; Melis & Semmann, 2010). This heritage explains why people work to preserve group membership and why they modify their behavior when in the presence of others. In this section we examine how the presence of other people affects performance and one's willingness to go along with the group. As we will see, social factors can push people to do things they might not otherwise do.

You may have noticed that sometimes you perform a task better with others around and sometimes you do worse. Such effects are seen in animals as diverse as humans, chimps, birds, and even cockroaches (Gates & Allee, 1933; Klopfer, 1958). The effect of having others present can depend on the situation or task at hand, how easy or difficult the task is, and how excited you are. **Social facilitation** occurs when the presence of others improves our performance. Over a century ago, Norman Triplett (1898) noticed that he bicycled faster when he rode with others. In a laboratory test of the idea that the presence of others improves performance, Triplett asked children to wind a fishing reel as fast as they could. He tested them alone and among other kids doing the same thing. Sure enough, they wound faster when other kids were present—they showed social facilitation, which usually occurs for tasks we find easy, we know well, or we can perform well (Zajonc, 1965).

Connection

Our level of arousal also affects our performance, according to the Yerkes-Dodson law. People perform better on an exam if they are slightly anxious than they would if they were either totally relaxed or very anxious.

See "Models of Motivation," in the chapter "Motivation and Emotion." (p. 407)

social facilitation
A phenomenon in which the presence of others improves one's performance.

social loafing
A phenomenon in which the presence of others causes one to relax one's standards and slack off.

Social loafing is the opposite; it occurs when the presence of others causes individuals to relax their standards (Harkins, 1987). If you are singing in a choir and there are dozens of other voices supporting yours, you are less likely to sing your heart out. You alone are not responsible for the sound, so the diffusion of responsibility alters your behavior (you loaf). If you are singing a solo, you might belt it out—because all the responsibility rests on your shoulders.

Conformity

Social facilitation is a subtle way in which the presence of others changes our actions. More direct social factors also pressure us to act in certain ways. Society imposes rules about acceptable behavior, called **social norms**. Examples of social norms include "Boys don't cry," "Don't pick your nose in public," and "Don't be a sore loser." Norms vary by culture, too. Burping at the dinner table is considered rude in the United States, but in some parts of East Asia, belching is seen as a compliment to the chef.

social norms
Rules about acceptable behavior imposed by the cultural context in which one lives.

Most of the time we conform to the social norms of our culture. **Conformity** occurs when people adjust their behavior to what others are doing or adhere to cultural norms. The reasons for conformity vary, depending on the situation. **Informational social influence** occurs when people conform to the behavior of others because they view them as a source of knowledge about what they are supposed to do. Consider the incoming freshmen who look to other students for information about where to hang out, how to behave in class, and the like. Informational social influence is most pronounced in ambiguous or novel situations. We rely on it all the time, especially as children.

conformity
The tendency of people to adjust their behavior to what others are doing or to adhere to the norms of their culture.

informational social influence
Conformity to the behavior of others because one views them as a source of knowledge about what one is supposed to do.

normative social influence
Conformity to the behavior of others in order to be accepted by them.

Normative social influence is the type of conformity that occurs when people go along with the behavior of others in order to be accepted by the group. A classic example is peer pressure, in which people engage in certain behaviors, such as drinking or trying drugs, so that they will be accepted by a particular social group. This phenomenon is widespread. Look at yourself and your peers. Do you wear the same kinds of clothes? How many of you have similar hairstyles? Consider a more subtle example of normative social influence. You emerge from

©Anthony Plummer/Getty Images

In nomadic cultures, such as Mongolia, extended family groups have traditionally stayed together, sharing food, shelter, livestock, child rearing, and all other aspects of daily life.

 How might communal living in isolated surroundings affect an individual's behavior?

the theater after going to a movie with friends, not sure whether you liked the movie or not, although everyone else in the group loved the film and is talking about it. By the end of the evening you may also be talking about what a great film it was and may have actually convinced yourself that you loved it. We are not always aware of how other people shape our behavior and beliefs.

One of the classic studies of in social psychology, conducted by Solomon Asch in 1951, demonstrates the power of conformity. Asch devoted his career to understanding situations in which perception is not a direct function of the physical properties of stimuli. For example, he found that our perceptions of the angle of a line can be biased by the frame around it (Witkin & Asch, 1948). Asch wondered whether the social world might also shape our perceptions. If pressured by the opinions of others, would people say they saw something that clearly wasn't there? Asch didn't think they would, but he was wrong.

Asch assembled several groups of six or seven people in the lab and told them he was researching visual acuity. He was really interested in conformity but didn't tell his participants what he was really researching, in case the information influenced their behavior. Asch then showed the participants two cards—one with a standard line, the other displaying three lines of varying length. The participant's job was to pick the one line out of the three that matched the standard line. As you can see in Figure 1, the task was easy. This comparison process was repeated 18 times and, on each occasion, participants gave their answers out loud.

The one real participant didn't know that the other so-called participants were *confederates*, people who actually worked for the experimenter. The one real participant was always seated in the last chair and heard the judgments of all of the other group members before making a choice. On the first six trials everyone gave the obvious and correct answer. Starting on the seventh trial, however, the confederates started giving wrong answers. On the first of the rigged trials, the first confederate would glance at the cards and confidently say, "The answer is line 1," even when it clearly was not correct. The next confederate would nod in agreement and say, "Yes, it is line 1." After five or six people in a row gave the wrong answers—remember, this is a *very* easy task—it was the real participant's turn. Participants faced a choice: Agree with everyone else's clearly erroneous judgments or give the answer that they personally thought was correct.

While none of the participants agreed with the group all of the time, 76% of them went along with the group at least once when a group answer was clearly wrong. On average, participants answered incorrectly 37% of the time. Yet when left alone to do the task, participants made errors less than 1% of the time. To summarize, when in the presence of a majority of other people who answered the simple question incorrectly, most of the participants knowingly gave the wrong answer at least once.

How does the design of this study make it a test of normative rather than informational social influence? Judging the lengths of the lines was really easy—there was no need for participants to look to others for information about the right answer. When participants worked alone, they rarely made errors; however, in the situation just described, after all the confederates had given the same wrong answer, many participants conformed by also giving the clearly wrong answer.

Indeed, sometimes people go to great lengths to do what the group is doing, when it does not make sense, especially when groups are engaged in decision making. This phenomenon, called **groupthink**, occurs when the thinking of the

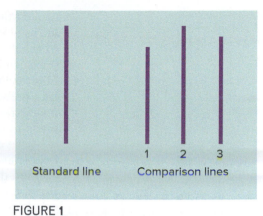

1   2   3

Standard line   Comparison lines

FIGURE 1

STIMULUS LINES PRESENTED TO PARTICIPANTS IN THE ASCH CONFORMITY STUDIES. Each participant was asked to say which of the comparison lines (1, 2, or 3) matched the length of the standard line. The answers were always clear-cut; in this case, the answer is "2." The conformity manipulation involved the confederates in the group giving an obviously wrong answer (such as "1") and then seeing how the participant answered (Passer & Smith, 2008).

groupthink
A situation in which the thinking of the group takes over, so much so that group members forgo logic or critical analysis in the service of reaching a decision.

group takes over, so much so that group members forgo logic or critical analysis in the service of reaching a decision (Janis, 1983). Juries that are hard-pressed to reach a verdict sometimes engage in groupthink, as do governments under pressure. According to the Senate Intelligence Committee's report on intelligence failures leading up to the 2003 invasion of Iraq, the erroneous CIA assertion that Iraq possessed weapons of mass destruction—the primary justification for the invasion—was based on groupthink by an administration invested in finding a reason to attack Iraq (U.S. Senate, 2004).

We can see groupthink operating daily in social media. People post opinions that may or may not be facts, and if enough people agree with it, that opinion gains credibility, even if it is factually wrong. In some online interactions, there is total anonymity; that is, one can operate by an alias so that no one knows who you are. Under such conditions, groupthink can spread more rapidly (Tsikerdekis, 2013). Social networks, in particular, allow for the rapid spread of rumors, bullying, conspiracy theories, or anything someone wants to post. The repetition of such statements gives them credibility, and then they are "liked" or "shared," which makes them increasingly familiar to anyone participating in the network (Webb et al., 2016). Most alarmingly, because people can buy domain names and create any site they like without being reviewed, "fake news" sites have begin to sneak into social media. On many of these sites people post whatever outlandish idea they have, name the site with the word "news" in the title, thus lending the illusion of credibility. False statements are endorsed by people with similar views, eroding individuality and discouraging dissent (Webb et al., 2016).

Culture plays a role in how susceptible people are to social influence. In cultures that value collectivism, groups matter more than the individual. It should not be surprising, then that any group-preserving behavior such as conformity would be valued and encouraged in a collectivist culture. In Japan, a collectivist culture, the company that one works for is elevated to the status of family. An employee is expected to make personal sacrifices for the company to preserve group unity (Miller & Kanazawa, 2000). Psychological scientists have replicated the Asch experiments in Japan and the United States. The results show that people in collectivist cultures like Japan are more likely to conform than are people in individualistic cultures like the United States (Bond & Smith, 1996).

Neuroscience research sheds light on the brain mechanisms involved in conformity. When people are made aware that their beliefs differ from those of most other people in a group, a brain region active when we make an error becomes active (Klucharev et al., 2009; Wu, Luo, & Feng, 2016). In other words, the brain acts as though we've made a mistake when we deviate from the group opinion.

Connection

In an individualistic culture, behavior is determined more by personal goals than by group goals, whereas in a collectivist culture, behavior is determined more by shared goals.

See "Personality and Culture: Universality and Differences," in the chapter "Personality: The Uniqueness of the Individual." (p. 510)

Minority Social Influence

At times a single individual or small number of individuals within a group can influence an entire group. In social psychology, a single person or small group within a larger group is called a *minority*, while the larger group is referred to as the *majority*. Just as the majority pushes for group unity, the minority can push for independence and uniqueness. After all, if people always conformed, how would change occur (Moscovici, 1985)? In order to change the majority view, however, the minority must present a consistent, unwavering message.

Minority social influence refers to what happens when a small number of individuals in a larger group shifts majority opinion by presenting a consistent, unwavering message. Most often, minority opinion shifts majority opinion

minority social influence
When a small number of individuals in a larger group shifts majority opinion by presenting a consistent, unwavering message.

by means of informational social influence. If a group encounters a situation in which the members are unsure of what to do and a minority carefully presents a well-thought-out position to the majority, then the majority might accept it. This is how juries can change course. Juries must provide unanimous decisions, and sometimes only one voice disagrees with the majority. If that minority of one offers a logical argument for the dissenting opinion, the majority view might be changed.

Obedience

Another kind of normative social influence, called **obedience**, occurs when people yield to the social pressure of an authority figure, complying with their demands. Social psychological research on obedience emerged in response to real-life concerns in the aftermath of World War II. The horrific events of the Holocaust raised troubling questions: How could an entire nation endorse the extermination of millions of people? Were *all* Germans evil? Adolf Hitler did not act alone—a supporting cast of thousands was necessary to annihilate so many people. Former Nazi officers who testified in war trials after the war said they were "following orders." The same rationale was offered in 2004 by U.S. soldiers who humiliated and tortured Iraqi prisoners at Abu Ghraib.

Will people do horrible things if an authority figure orders them to do so? One psychologist spurred into action by the Nazi atrocities was Stanley Milgram. A Jew whose family had left Europe before Hitler's rise to power, Milgram spent much of his early academic life trying to make sense of the Holocaust (Blass, 2004). With the support of his graduate advisor, Solomon Asch, Milgram decided to investigate whether people would conform even when their actions could harm others.

Milgram recruited people from the community to participate in an experiment at Yale University. A participant arrived at the lab and sat down next to another supposed participant, who was a confederate. The experimenter, who looked very official in a white lab coat, told both individuals that they would be participating in a study on the effects of mild punishment on memory. He then assigned them to be either a teacher or a learner by asking them to pull a note that said either "teacher" or "learner" from a bowl. The drawing was rigged, however, so that the real participant always landed the "teacher" role and the confederate got the "learner" role. Then the experimenter showed both the teacher and the learner to the room where the learner would sit. The learner's task involved learning and repeating lists of words. The learner was told that every time he made an error he would receive a mild electric shock, delivered by the teacher. With each mistake the shocks would increase in intensity. Both teacher and learner saw the chair where the learner would sit, which had restraints to make sure the electrodes had a good contact when he received the shock. The teacher then received a sample shock of very low voltage to get a sense of what the learner would experience. In actuality, this was the only real shock administered during the entire experiment.

Then they went to the teacher's room. The teacher sat at a table behind a panel of switches. Under each switch was a label indicating voltage level, which ranged, in 15-volt increments, from 15 volts ("mild shock") all the way up to 450 (labeled "XXX"), with 315 volts designated as "Danger: Severe shock" (see Figure 2a). The teacher was reminded that if the learner made mistakes, he or she would have to deliver a shock and with each mistake would have to increase the level.

The experiment began uneventfully. Then the learner made occasional mistakes. At lower levels of shock, the learner gave no real response to the pretend shocks. As the teacher moved up the shock scale and the learner supposedly

obedience
A type of social influence in which a person yields to the will of another person, complying with their demands.

Courtesy of the Graduate Center, CUNY

Stanley Milgram

FIGURE 2

MILGRAM'S STUDY OF OBEDIENCE. (a) This is the control panel seen by the "teacher." (b) Experts consulted by Milgram prior to the study predicted that, at higher voltages, participants would refuse to administer further shocks to the "learner." As the graph shows, the experts were wrong. At the highest voltages, when the experimenter told them the experiment must continue in spite of the "learner's" protests, 60% of the "teachers" continued to administer "shocks." (c) The "learner" is strapped in for Milgram's study (Milgram, 1974).

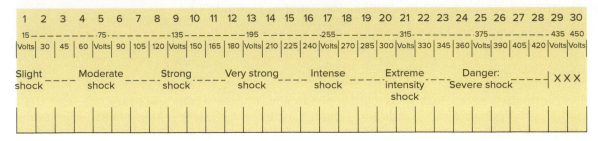

(a) Control panel seen by the "teacher"

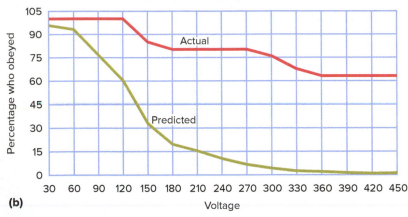

(b)

Voltage

(c)

(c) ©1968 by Stanley Milgram, copyright renewed ©1993 by Alexandra Milgram, and distributed by Penn State Media Sales

made more errors, the teacher and experimenter could hear a yelp of pain come from the learner with each shock. (In fact, the learner played a prerecorded tape of his responses to the shock.) At this point, many teachers asked the experimenter if they should go on, and he would say, "The experiment requires that you go on."

Before beginning the experiments, Milgram polled experts to see how many "teachers" they thought would go along with the experimenter's demands to administer high levels of shock. One group of experts, psychiatrists, predicted that only about 30% would administer shocks as high as 150 volts, less than 4% would go to the 300-volt level, and only 1 person in 1,000 would go all the way to 450 volts. How far do *you* think most people would go in administering shocks?

The results differed drastically from these predictions. As shown in Figure 2b, at 150 volts, the point at which the learner yelled, "Get me out of here! My heart's starting to bother me! I refuse to go on! Let me out!" there was a drop in obedience—from 100% to about 83%. Some participants stopped, but many, although visibly uncomfortable, continued with the experiment. What is alarming is how many people went all the way up to the end of the shock scale, despite the yells and protests (and eventual silence) of the learner. Twenty-six of the 40 participants in the original experiment (65%) went all the way to 450 volts (Milgram, 1963, 1974). Men and women were equally likely to reach the 450-volt level.

Milgram's experiments show that reasonable people may do things that seem cruel and unusual in the presence of powerful social influence. Several

Connection

Do you think participants were treated ethically in the Milgram study? What are the obligations of researchers to ensure the ethical treatment of participants in research?

See "Research Ethics," in the chapter "Conducting Research in Psychology." (p. 66)

FIGURE 3

QUESTIONNAIRE RESPONSES OF PARTICIPANTS IN MILGRAM'S OBEDIENCE STUDY. Despite the distress they experienced during the experiment, the majority of the respondents did not regret their involvement.

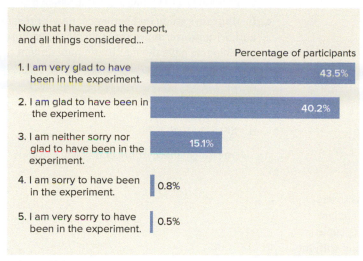

Now that I have read the report, and all things considered...

Percentage of participants

1. I am very glad to have been in the experiment. — 43.5%
2. I am glad to have been in the experiment. — 40.2%
3. I am neither sorry nor glad to have been in the experiment. — 15.1%
4. I am sorry to have been in the experiment. — 0.8%
5. I am very sorry to have been in the experiment. — 0.5%

(Milgram, 1974)

"teachers" did protest and yet went on when the experimenter urged them to continue. When asked, "Who is going to take responsibility if that guy gets hurt?" the experimenter would say, "I have full responsibility, please continue." Somehow, the belief that someone else (the authority figure) was responsible for their actions alleviated feelings of guilt or concern in some of the participants. This is akin to former Nazi officers saying, "I was just following orders," but who really has the final responsibility?

Because participants clearly experienced mental anguish while taking part in the study, it sparked a fierce debate about ethics in research. Milgram contacted his participants later and asked whether they regretted having participated. Less than 2% did (see Figure 3).

You might think that you would never administer those shocks or that people today would know better. Not so.

In the 2000s, Jerry Burger modified Milgram's original study with American college students (Burger, 2009). An important change from the original study was that when the participants began to protest, they were told to continue rather than told that they *had* to continue. Also, once participants passed the 150-volt range, the experiment stopped. By making these changes, the researchers were able to obtain permission from the American Psychological Association to conduct the experiment, which otherwise would not meet current standards for the ethical treatment of human participants. As in Milgram's experiment, Burger reported that two-thirds of the participants obeyed the authority figure and continued to administer shocks after the "learner" began protesting. Milgram's controversial study continues to inspire investigation and reinterpretation, including studies that suggest that people are more likely to follow authority not just for situational reasons but because they think the authority knew the right thing to do (Haslam & Reicher, 2012). There may have been powerful situational issues that made the participant more likely to obey, among them are the fact that the shocks increased in small increments and the fact that the participants experienced time pressures—they did not have much time to mull over whether to continue to administer shocks (Burger, 2014). An even more recent replication of the Milgram study in Poland in 2017, designed to be more ethical, used lower shock levels and yielded nearly identical rates of obedience to Milgram's (Dolinski et al., 2017).

Quick Quiz 1: Group Living and Social Influence

1. Sometimes people perform better—for example, ride a bike faster—when they are in groups than when alone. Social psychologists call this
   a. the Yerkes-Dodson principle.
   b. social loafing.
   c. social facilitation.
   d. conformity.

2. People who are of a minority opinion in a group are most likely to change the opinion of the majority by
   a. getting them to conform to group pressure.
   b. using reason and logic.
   c. trying to shame them.
   d. being consistent and presenting a well-formed persuasive argument.

3. When put in a situation where an individual has to say something about the length of a line that goes against what everyone else in the group has said, most people
   a. eventually conform at least once and go along with the group.
   b. always conform and go along with the group.
   c. never conform and go along with the group.
   d. pretend not to be paying attention.

4. In Milgram's study on obedience, under pressure from an authority figure, approximately what percentage of the participants gave the maximum punishment of 450 volts to the learner's incorrect answers?
   a. 25%
   b. 50%
   c. 65%
   d. 90%

Answers can be found at the end of the chapter.

SOCIAL PERCEPTION

Social processes not only influence our behavior but also guide our perceptions of the behavior of others. For example, we wonder why people do what they do. *Why does Maria wear those clothes?* We wonder whether we can believe what people say. *Is he lying to me?* We form impressions and attitudes about other people. *Ashan is smart.* These are all matters of *social perception*, the way in which we make sense of our social world.

Attribution

attributions
Inferences made about the causes of other people's behavior.

We often wonder why people do the things they do (Kelley & Michela, 1980), and we try to explain their actions. **Attributions** are the inferences we make about the causes of other people's behavior.

Social psychologist Fritz Heider (1958) made an important distinction between two types of attributions. Internal, or *dispositional*, *attributions* ascribe other people's behavior to something within them, such as their personalities, motives, or attitudes. Let's say that Chris flunked a test. A dispositional attribution would be "Chris flunked the test because he is too lazy to study." The person making this attribution assumed that Chris's flunking is a result of something about him, but it is also possible that Chris's failing grade resulted from some external factor. Perhaps the test was too hard. People make external, or *situational*, *attributions* when they think that something outside the person, such as the nature of the situation, is the cause of his or her behavior. If Jake says that Chris failed because the exam was too hard, Jake has made a situational attribution for Chris's grade.

We tend to evaluate our own behavior in different ways depending on whether we have succeeded or failed. For instance, it is likely that Chris would attribute his failure on a test to something about the situation—say, the test was

©sven hagolani/zefa/Corbis/Getty Images

Meeting potential mates in a group of singles might make some people seem shy.

 Would you make the fundamental attribution error in a situation like this and assume that shyness is a personality trait?

too hard or the professor unfair—rather than to his own abilities. If Chris had aced the test, however, it is likely he'd attribute his success to his own skills. Making situational attributions for our failures but dispositional attributions for our successes is known as a **self-serving bias**. For instance, if Martin failed a test and blamed the teacher ("it was a brutally hard test!"), but when he excelled on a test took credit for the success ("I really know this stuff—I aced the test!"), then that is a self-serving bias.

People tend to explain other people's behavior in terms of dispositional attributions rather than situational ones, a bias in judgment known as the **fundamental attribution error** (Ross, 1977). This is not to say that dispositions don't matter but rather that, when making attributions of other people's behavior, we tend to think that dispositional characteristics matter the most. People living in Asian cultures, such as India and Japan, are much less likely to make the fundamental attribution error than are European Americans (Choi, Nisbett, & Norenzayan, 1999). This seems to be due to a cultural tendency for Asians to explain behaviors—even things as extreme as murder—in terms of situations rather than individual characteristics (Morris & Peng, 1994; Norenzayan & Nisbett, 2000). This is due to the fact that most Asian cultures are collectivist—emphasizing the group or "many" over the individual.

Collectivist cultures tend to perceive behavior according to bias that favors the group over the individual, but not always. Many studies have shown that in collectivist cultures, such as China, Korea, and India, people tend to form impressions biased by group or community concerns rather than individual concerns. By contrast, people from individualist cultures, such as United States, France, and

self-serving bias
The tendency to make situational attributions for our failures but dispositional attributions for our successes.

fundamental attribution error
The tendency to explain others' behavior in dispositional rather than situational terms.

England, tend to have social impression shaped by personal concerns (Triandis, 1993). But there are exceptions to this pattern. According to a recent study of over 1,200 teens in China, a collectivist culture, self-serving biases (the very self-centered tendency to view one's achievements as caused by the person but failures as caused by the situation) were just as common in China as in the United States (Hu, Zhang, & Ran, 2016).

Detecting Deception

One way that we try to figure out others is by judging whether or not they are being truthful. Most people think that they know when people lie to them. According to the research, however, most of us are not effective lie detectors. Most people perform no better than the accuracy rate of chance guessing in detecting deception from people's behavior (Ekman & O'Sullivan, 1991).

Why are we unsuccessful at catching liars? Most of us rely on misleading cues. We put too much weight on what people are saying, overinterpret ambiguous nonverbal cues (thinking any sign of nervousness means a person is lying), ignore relevant nonverbal information, and get fooled by signs of warmth and competence (Ekman & O'Sullivan, 1991). If people learn to focus instead on inconsistent behaviors (shaking the head while saying yes) and signs of emotion that don't match what people are saying, then they become better "lie detectors." There are no foolproof ways of detecting deception, however.

The best lie detectors attend to nonverbal information more than verbal information (Frank & Ekman, 1997). In a study of experts who should be good at catching liars, such as U.S. Secret Service agents, FBI agents, CIA agents, police, judges, and psychiatrists, only the Secret Service agents performed significantly better than if they had been guessing (Ekman & O'Sullivan, 1991). Psychologists with a special interest in deception have also been shown to do much better than others in detecting deceit (Ekman, O'Sullivan, & Frank, 1999). The polygraph, the so-called "lie-detector" machine, is unreliable—yielding many false positive results (Faigman, Fienberg, & Stern, 2003). The best objective way of determining whether someone is lying is to look at all the information that is available from a situation—speech, facial expression, vocal tone, situation—to determine if someone is behaving in such a way that suggests they are concealing feelings or information (Ekman & O'Sullivan, 2006). Cognitive processing and response times to tasks and questions tend to slow down when someone is answering questions deceptively (Suchotzki et al., 2017).

Schemas

Whether we are trying to determine if people are lying or simply trying to make sense of simple actions, our own ideas of how the world works influence our perceptions of it. People develop models, or *schemas*, of the social world, which function as lenses through which we filter our perceptions. We first discussed schemas in the chapter "Memory" and defined them broadly as ways of knowing that we develop from our experiences with particular objects or events. In the area of social perception, schemas are ways of knowing that affect how we view our social world.

We rely on schemas when forming impressions of other people, especially when we encounter ambiguous information. Imagine you are invited to dinner and notice that one of the guests has slurred speech and walks shakily across the room. You assume—reasonably—that she is drunk. Later you learn that she has Parkinson's disease, a neurological condition that affects motor coordination. Slurred speech and shaky walking are common symptoms of this disorder.

Connection

Cultural differences in big-picture versus detailed processing are seen in performance on visual perception tasks, too.

See "Perceiving Visual Stimuli," in the chapter "Sensing and Perceiving Our World." (p. 133)

You assumed that the woman was drunk because the schema of drunkenness was much more *accessible* to you than that of Parkinson's disease.

Stereotypes

Schemas of how people are likely to behave based simply on the groups to which they belong are known as **stereotypes**. When we resort to stereotypes, we form conclusions about people before we even interact with them just because they are of a certain race-ethnicity or live in a certain place. As a result, we end up judging people not by their actions but by our notions of how they might act.

Take a look at a few of the common stereotypes that exist in U.S. culture:

Jocks are dumb.
Jews are cheap.
Middle Eastern men with beards might be terrorists.

Each of the examples above reflect unfair generalizations of all people who belong to a particular group simply based on one view of that group. Stereotypes are handy, because they allow for very quick assessments of people based *only* on their membership in certain groups. People resort to stereotypes because they allow for quick—but often inaccurate—impressions, especially if we do not know someone very well.

The human mind has a tendency to categorize and understand all members of a group in terms of characteristics that are typical of the group (Rosch, 1975). So if we meet someone new and learn that he or she belongs to a particular (racial-ethnic, social, political, or religious) group, we rely on what we think we know about that group to anticipate how this new person might behave. fMRI scans show that, when people avoid thinking in this stereotyped way, the prefrontal cortex—an area involved in inhibiting inappropriate responses—is activated (De Neys, Vartanian, & Goel, 2008). This suggests that when you rely on stereotypes you are not thinking carefully.

With stereotypes, we have formed conclusions about people even before we interact with them. Stereotypes may originate in something that is factual but that does not characterize a whole group. The terrorists involved in the September 11, 2001, attacks in the United States, for example, were Middle Eastern men, many of whom had beards—but not all Middle Eastern men with beards are terrorists. Most serial killers in the United States have been young white men. Does that mean all young white men are serial killers (Apsche, 1993)?

During his 2008 run for the presidency, Barack Obama faced numerous stereotypes associated with his name (which has Muslim roots), his mixed-race

stereotypes
Schemas of how people are likely to behave based simply on groups to which they belong; they are oversimplified perspectives of people based solely on their group membership.

Connection

Another name for mental shortcuts we use in decision making is *heuristics*. Heuristics can be adaptive but also can lead to flawed thinking.

See "How Do We Make Judgments and Decisions?" in the chapter "Language and Thought." (p. 355)

©Mareen Fischinger/Getty Images; ©Digital Vision/Photodisc/Getty Images RF; ©Peter Dazeley/Photographer's Choice RF/Getty Images RF

 What stereotypes do these images bring to mind?

ethnicity, and his education. People who did not know much about him were more likely to believe rumors that he was a Muslim (although he is not). The implication that he was a Muslim activated the terrorist stereotype we just discussed. Some rivals stereotyped Obama as an elitist, because he had gone to Harvard Law School. They tried to link him with stereotypical notions that well-educated people are out of touch with average people, even though he had grown up in a low-income household and right out of college had worked with the poor and unemployed in Chicago.

In the 2016 presidential election, the winning candidate established a platform inciting racial tensions, asking for a ban on immigration and, in particular, of people of Muslim descent. Once in office, one of President Trump's first actions was to sign an executive order limiting immigration based on ethnicity. This was fueled by anti-Muslim sentiments in this country (post-911) and motivated further anti-Muslim sentiment.

A recent large-scale survey study in the United States was conducted during the 2016 election, when the Republican candidate—especially Donald Trump—promoted a fear of foreigners, in particular anti-immigrant sentiments toward Mexicans and Muslims. The survey aimed to document the extent to which people in those groups perceived prejudice against them and experienced a sense of dehumanization. **Dehumanization**, a tendency to portray groups of people as devoid of basic qualities or rights attributed to most people, is a common tactic in racial prejudice that aims to make people feel unworthy (Kteily et al., 2015). In the 2016 survey, Mexicans and Muslims in the United States felt increasingly isolated and dehumanized, and this sense of dehumanization increased feelings of aggression toward Americans—the supposed perpetrators of the negative attitudes toward them. In a sense, the anti-Muslim and anti-Mexican negativity bred feelings of not belonging among these groups, which could serve to increase exactly the kind of actions that people who acted prejudice feared—like a self-fulfilling prophecy (Kteily & Bruneau, 2017).

dehumanization
A tendency to portray a group of people as unworthy of human rights and traits—intended to make them feel unworthy.

Exclusion and Inclusion

As a result of having evolved for group living, we tend to judge others and ourselves. These judgments may stem from defending ourselves against other groups and competing with them for limited resources (Neuberg & Cottrell, 2006). That is, the machinery exists for using cognitive and emotional processes to separate "us" from "them." Perceiving others as different from us has several consequences:

1. We sometimes evaluate and treat people differently because of the group they belong to.
2. Our actions are based on in-group/out-group distinctions ("us" versus "them").
3. It hurts to be excluded from our group.

When we show positive feelings toward people in our own group and negative feelings toward those in other groups, we are displaying **in-group/out-group bias**. Think back to the rivalry between your high school and its crosstown rival. Everyone who went to your school was part of your in-group, and you identified with all of them and felt pride belonging to that group. Everyone who went to the other school was part of the out-group, and you felt competitive whenever the two schools interacted. Moreover, you likely made many distinctions between students and groups at your school but categorized

in-group/out-group bias
A tendency to show positive feelings toward people who belong to the same group as we do, and negative feelings toward those in other groups.

FIGURE 4

BRAIN REGIONS ACTIVATED BY SOCIAL PAIN. Exclusion from an electronic ball-tossing game increased blood flow to the same areas of the brain activated by physical pain. The increase in activity in the anterior cingulate cortex (A) and in the right front section of the prefrontal cortex (B) shows up in these fMRI images as patches of orange and yellow (Eisenberger et al., 2003).

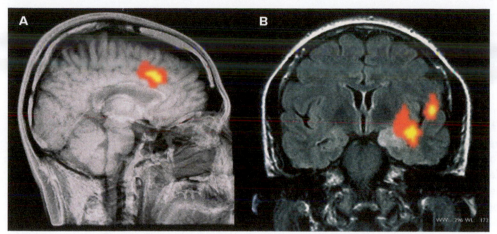

Anterior Cingulate	Right Ventral Prefrontal
x = –8	y = 28

©Chris Gallagher/Science Source; ©BSIP/UIG via Getty Images

everyone who went to the other school into one group: "them." The tendency to see all members of an out-group as the same is known as **out-group homogeneity**.

One result of the human tendency to include and exclude others is that sometimes we get left out. As illustrated by the scenario that opens this chapter, rejection hurts. One possible reason it hurts to be left out is that social connections are as important to us as our physical safety—so important that the brain's physical pain circuits also evolved to signal when we have been excluded from the group (see Figure 4; Eisenberger et al., 2003; MacDonald, Kingsbury, & Shaw, 2005; MacDonald & Leary, 2005; Masten et al., 2009). An interesting corollary of the pain finding is that, when people read friendly messages from those people with whom they feel socially connected, they feel physically warm and show brain activation patterns that correspond to the areas active during actual physical warmth (Inagaki & Eisenberger, 2013). Thus, there appears to be mapping of physical and social pain in our lived experience of others.

In modern life, we separate physical from social needs, but in early human evolution, these two needs were often intertwined. To be included in a social group meant you were fed, you were secure, and you could reproduce. Being excluded threatened not only survival but also the chance to reproduce (MacDonald et al., 2005). The need for connection runs so deep down the phylogenetic tree that you find it in social insects. When raised without social contact, cockroaches show behavioral deficiencies, including poor mating skills, reduced willingness to interact with others, and impaired foraging (Lihoreau, Brepson, & Rivault, 2009).

Humans also form social groups through social networks, which are webs of people who share common interests, professions, or familial relations (Christakis & Fowler, 2009). Both real-life and electronic social networks play an important role in social life. See "Psychology in the Real World."

out-group homogeneity
The tendency to see all members of an out-group as the same.

Psychology in the Real World

The Social Psychology of Social Networks

Real-life social networks form among people who share interests. You might be in one network as a function of your school, another by virtue of familial relationships, and yet another because of your musical taste. Networks are defined by associations among people that branch and spread beyond those people one knows directly (Christakis & Fowler, 2009).

Everything from physical health habits to moods can spread in a social network—often unbeknownst to all involved. By *spread* we mean that these behaviors are more common among members of a network than among people who are not in the same network. Eating behavior, drinking habits, smoking, loneliness, happiness, and cooperative behavior all spread in this way (Cacioppo, Fowler, & Christakis, 2009; Christakis & Fowler, 2007; Fowler & Christakis, 2008, 2010; Rosenquist et al., 2010).

Nicholas Christakis and James Fowler (2009), pioneers in research on real-life (non-electronic) social networks, report that attitudes, behaviors, and habits move through social networks via the *three degrees rule*. For instance, your behavior (say, your food preferences) can affect your friends (one degree) and their friends (two degrees) and their friends' friends (three degrees). So we are influenced by and influence our friends within three degrees of separation, but not much beyond that (Christakis & Fowler, 2009).

How does something like smoking behavior spread in a network? Social psychological processes such as conformity and peer influence play a role; that is, you might be more likely to smoke if the people you know smoke and it is regarded as "OK" to smoke in your social circles. Mimicry, or the process by which we mirror the actions of others, may be one means by which our emotional behavior can impact another person. In such cases, however, the behavior gets distorted as it moves outward toward others, much as a message gets modified when it is passed among many people (Cacioppo, Fowler, & Christakis, 2009).

Real-life social networks have existed for ages, but social networking sites—electronic forums for interaction with friends and acquaintances—are relatively new. Social network sites such Instagram and Snapchat (in the United States) are the major means of social interaction among people ages 15–25; Facebook and Twitter among adults over 30. Even though they are electronic, social network sites influence real-world social connections (Christakis & Fowler, 2009). They are the primary places where people consume news (Boulianne, 2015). Although social networks increase the likelihood of being exposed to differing political views regardless of one's political affiliation, they also increase the likelihood that you will follow news sites that are consistent with your own views and not in opposition to your views (Boulianne, 2015; Kim, 2011). Social networks are also a primary place for promoting political activism, by advertising events such as protests and rallies and encouraging others to sign petitions (Boulianne, 2015).

Still, these two types of networks might work quite differently. Given how Facebook is arranged, ideas and preferences ("likes") instantly spread much more rapidly than they would in a real-world social network. It is possible that the three degrees rule may not apply to social network sites or that the limits of influence may be wider. Also, surveys of Facebook use show that people of all ages share much more private information publicly than they realize (Brandtzæg, Lüders, & Skjetne, 2010). People readily disclose drug and alcohol use more freely on social network sites than they might in real-world public settings (Moran, Snelson, & Elison-Bowers, 2010). Indeed, certain people are more likely to make optimal use of privacy features than others—women more than men and younger people more often than older people (Litt, 2013).

Not everyone is equally interested in using social network sites, and people use them differently. Some users post frequently, while some prefer to read others' postings only. Not surprisingly, a number of personality factors relate to Facebook use, as we discussed in the chapter "Personality: The Uniqueness of the Individual." People who score higher on measures of conscientiousness have more friends; those who score higher on openness to experience are

Prejudice and Discrimination

prejudice
A biased attitude toward a group of people or an individual member of a group based on unfair generalizations about what members of that group are like.

We have discussed many processes that affect group behavior and how we view others. Unfortunately, as people try to make sense of each other and rely on schemas to decide who is similar or who is different, they sometimes use stereotypes to unfairly categorize others, which can fuel prejudice and discrimination.

A **prejudice** is a biased attitude toward a group of people or an individual member of a group based on unfair generalizations about what members of that group are like (Allport, 1954). Prejudicial thinking often stems from stereotypes

©NurPHoto/Getty Images

 How did social networks, such as Facebook and Twitter, play a key role in the revolutions in the Middle East and North Africa in the spring of 2011?

more expressive in their personal profiles; and those who score high on introversion have smaller social networks than extraverts (Amichai-Hamburger & Vinitzky, 2010). People who score either low or high on neuroticism share more information than people with moderate levels of neuroticism. A survey study of college students in the United States found that people who were more impulsive were more likely to exhibit problematic behaviors online, such as swearing and socially inappropriate behavior, and that these behaviors were linked to poor sleep quality and lower GPA (Turel & Bechara, 2017). In China, a recent large-scale study of social network use found that people who score higher on trait measures of narcissism (which reveal how self-focused people are) are more likely to show exhibitionistic behavior and use selfies for profile pictures on Wechat, one of the most popular sites in China (Wang, 2017).

Although Instagram, Snapchat, Facebook, and Twitter are international, Facebook has been banned in China since 2009. Most popular in China and Japan are mobile apps such as QQ and Wechat "Moments." In Japan LINE leads the pack. In Korea, however, Twitter, Facebook, and Snapchat reign supreme.

Payoff for using social media use takes many forms. Many people use social network sites to get reinforcement for their views or images—in Instagram and Facebook terms, one way to measure that is by means of receiving "likes" for one's postings. In fact, the number of "likes" received shapes future posting behavior. People who get reinforced by "likes" for disclosing personal information online (such as posting pictures, relationship status, whereabouts of social activities) are more likely to disclose even more in the future (Trepte & Reinecke, 2013). Also, we tend to "like" the posts of people who "like" our posts. Although many use social network sites primarily for enjoyment, some of the biggest factors that determine usage involve the behavior of our friends. Facebook use is affected by how many of one's peers are using it, as well as perceptions of reciprocity in liking behavior (e.g., if you "like" their stuff, they will "like" yours; Lin & Lu, 2011). Here we see the power of social influence on SNS behavior. Not surprisingly, too much social network use can have ill effects on well-being. People can begin to feel inadequate from seeing the idealistic view of life portrayed by others on social media. A study relating daily diary reports of feelings to social network behavior found that the more people compared themselves to others on Facebook, the more depressive symptoms they reported (Steers, Wickham & Acitelli, 2014).

Both real and virtual social networks spread information to large numbers of people in a short period of time—often to powerful effect. In February 2011, the people of Egypt protested the authoritarian government of Hosni Mubarak. Within a matter of days, early reports and images of police violence against peaceful protestors had spread to millions of young Egyptians via Twitter and Facebook. This, along with other information, incited a successful revolution, which ultimately led to Mubarak's resignation. In 2016, Facebook and Twitter served as major platforms for inciting activism in the protests that followed the presidential election and early months of the Trump administration.

rather than from careful observation of people's behavior. Prejudices are generally negative and often based on insufficient information. Prejudices based on race-ethnicity are called *racism*; those based on sex are called *sexism*. If a business executive does not seriously consider a highly qualified female applicant for a high-level management job because he is convinced that women are not capable of leading a company, his thinking is prejudicial. More precisely, he is sexist. Not offering her an interview—even if she is the best-qualified applicant in the pool— is discrimination. **Discrimination** is the preferential treatment of certain people that is usually driven by prejudicial attitudes. Discrimination can also result from

discrimination
The preferential treatment of certain people, usually driven by prejudicial attitudes.

institutionalized rules, such as the requirement that flight attendants cannot be excessively overweight.

Prejudicial attitudes are learned early in life; and even if they are formally abandoned later in life, these reactions can become quite automatic (Banaji & Greenwald, 1995). Consider the case of Edith, a 21-year-old European American college student who is politically liberal and an activist for progressive causes. However, when Edith walks to her car at night, if an African American man is on the other side of the street, she becomes nervous without knowing why. She is not a racist! Why does this happen? Prejudices can operate outside conscious awareness, and they sometimes stand in stark contrast to one's conscious beliefs (Devine, 1989). Even a person who works hard at being fair may have a hard time overcoming biases that are automatic and deeply learned. There may also be an evolutionary basis for our automatic responses: The mechanism of recognizing group members may have evolved to preserve group harmony, cohesion, and close alliances (Melis & Semmann, 2010; Neuberg & Cottrell, 2006).

Challenging Assumptions in Social Behavior

Prejudice operates both inside and outside a person's awareness. As in Edith's case, much racial-ethnic bias is unconscious and in conflict with consciously held views. Two social psychologists, Mahzarin Banaji and Anthony Greenwald, suspected there was a disconnect between people's conscious and unconscious views of prejudice and developed a way of measuring what they called *implicit bias*.

Social psychologists distinguish between *explicit* and *implicit* prejudice. Explicit ideas are plainly stated. Implicit views are indirect, perhaps unconscious. An explicit reference to a desire to have sex with someone is "I want to go to bed with you." An implicit reference is "Why don't you come by my place and watch a movie with me?" Measuring implicit knowledge and beliefs presents a challenge.

©Harvard University News Office

Mahzarin Banaji

Banaji and Greenwald had become interested in implicit social thought and attitudes but were unhappy about the lack of scientific measures of them (Greenwald & Banaji, 1995). Greenwald and his colleagues had developed a computer program that measured implicit cognitive attitudes toward flowers and insects.

There were four steps to the program. First, participants had to press a computer keyboard letter with their left hand for flowers and a different key with their right hand for insects. Second, they had to do the same for pleasant words (left hand) and unpleasant words (right hand). Third, flowers and pleasant words were combined (left hand), and insects and unpleasant words were combined (right hand). When Greenwald did this, he found these three tasks very easy and did them very quickly. Things changed when he got to the fourth and final condition. Now flowers, which used to be left hand, and insects, which used to be right hand, were switched, but the pleasant and unpleasant words stayed on the same side. In other words, flowers were now paired with unpleasant words and insects with pleasant words. Greenwald was much slower at making these associations. He thought he could get better with practice but, to his surprise, he couldn't. There was no way to change the implicit association. He quickly realized this might be the measure of implicit social attitudes they were seeking (Greenwald, 2009).

When Banaji took the same test, her results looked about the same as Greenwald's. Banaji and Greenwald, though concerned about what their scores might reveal about their own latent attitudes, knew they were on to something. They dubbed the new test the *Implicit Associations Test (IAT)*.

Courtesy of Anthony Greenwald

Anthony Greenwald

Most famously, Greenwald and Banaji applied the IAT to concepts of race and ethnicity. Faster response times on the test indicate that people more readily associate two concepts; slower response times indicate a less automatic association. European Americans tend to respond more slowly to pairings of "black" (words or faces) with positive words than they do to pairings of "black" with negative words (Dasgupta et al., 2000; Greenwald, McGhee, & Schwartz, 1998). This holds even for people whose questionnaire responses indicate that they do not hold racist attitudes. Interestingly, African Americans respond more slowly to pairings of "white American" with positive words than they do to pairings of "white American" with negative words. Banaji and Greenwald (1995) have also reported evidence of implicit gender bias using the IAT; female and male college students more readily associated "fame" with male names than with female names.

In the roughly 30 years since the IAT's publication, hundreds of published research papers, in areas ranging from marketing to neuroscience, have used the IAT technique. IAT scores predict suicidal tendencies, consumer preferences, political preferences, sexual orientation, symptoms of posttraumatic stress disorder, mortality, and drug and alcohol use (Anselmi et al., 2013; Greenwald et al., 2009; Leitner et al., 2016; Lindgren et al., 2013; Nock et al., 2010). Indeed, the IAT is an excellent teaching tool for anyone confronting his or her own implicit prejudice. Results from the test can be used to reduce prejudice and sensitize individuals and groups to the fact that these prejudices operate in subtle yet powerful ways. In 1998, Banaji, Greenwald, and Nosek established a nonprofit organization (Project Implicit) to help people apply the IAT technique. Banaji lives by her own advice. She was so dismayed by her own performance on race- and gender-based IATs—in spite of being a minority woman herself—that she changed her behavior. In addition to the nonprofit work, she does little things to help undo her deeply held biases, such as displaying pictures of prominent black men and women from history in her office.

Recent research links implicit racial bias to in-group death rates (Leitner et al., 2016). Gathering data from the Project Implicit database, which collects IAT responses from a wide variety of respondents around the country, researchers looked at hundreds of thousands of blacks and whites in different areas of the country. They also collected established data on death rates from all causes, and matched those with the areas in which the various respondents lived. The researchers uncovered an interesting relationship between implicit bias toward the opposite racial group and death rates. White implicit bias toward blacks was related to higher white death rates, and black implicit bias toward blacks was related to higher black death rates. Thus, having an implicit bias toward an out-group is associated with death inside one's racial group. Interestingly, there were no such effects for explicit measures of racism. What does this mean? People who are racist and do not acknowledge it openly (which is what implicit racism means) are probably harboring many negative attitudes and conflict about self (Leitner et al., 2016). Racist attitudes toward an out-group can evoke negative emotions and stress, which can have negative health consequences (see the chapter "Stress and Health") and can affect mortality. Internalized racism, whereby one turns the racial bias they feel from others inward toward themselves, is associated with depressive symptoms and other negative psychological consequences in African and Asian Americans (Choi, Israel, & Maeda, 2017).

You can try the IAT yourself at the Project Implicit website: https://implicit.harvard.edu/implicit/

Quick Quiz 2: Social Perception

1. Our tendency to conclude that Alex must have an aggressive personality because we see him hit Bobby once on the playground is an example of
   a. a stereotype.
   b. a prejudice.
   c. deception.
   d. the fundamental attribution error.

2. "College professors are absent-minded" is an example of
   a. an attitude.
   b. an attribution.
   c. a stereotype.
   d. a prejudice.

3. Out-group homogeneity is the tendency to
   a. see people outside our group as looking or acting alike.
   b. see people inside our group as looking or acting alike.
   c. believe people outside our group think the same way we do.
   d. believe people inside our group think the same way we do.
4. Brandon believes women are not very good at math. However, as a computer scientist, he has always been able to treat women the same way he treats men at work. Which of the following statements is true?
   a. Brandon is prejudiced against women.
   b. Brandon's behavior is an example of discrimination.

c. Brandon's beliefs are based on stereotypes.
d. Both a and c are true.

5. Measuring how long it takes a person to pair positive or negative terms with particular ethnic groups is used in social psychology as a measure of
   a. explicit racism.
   b. implicit racism.
   c. stereotypes.
   d. reaction time.

Answers can be found at the end of the chapter.

ATTITUDES AND BEHAVIOR

attitudes
An individual's favorable or unfavorable beliefs, feelings, or actions toward an object, an idea, or a person.

People use the word *attitude* frequently, but what does it mean? Social psychologists define **attitudes** as a person's favorable or unfavorable feelings, beliefs, or actions toward an object, an idea, or a person (Olson & Zanna, 1993). Thus, attitudes have affective, cognitive, and behavioral components. The *affective* component includes the feelings or emotions associated with the belief; the *cognitive* component consists of the rational thoughts and beliefs that make up the attitude; and the *behavioral* component includes the motive to act in a particular way toward the person or object of the attitude. Consider Elizabeth, who is a huge Giants fan. She loves the team (affective), knows all about each starting player (cognitive), and has bought season tickets to their home games (behavioral).

Attitudes differ by how heavily each component is weighted. Some attitudes are more cognitive, such as your beliefs about the best way to slice a mango. Others may be more affective, such as your attitude about the death penalty. Our attitudes and beliefs stem from our history as a species as well as our history as individuals.

The Nature and Nurture of Attitudes

Some of our most basic attitudes may be instinctive, while others are learned. Certain negative attitudes and emotional responses, such as fear of snakes or the nearly universal human revulsion for bodily waste and decaying matter, may be so important for human survival that they are part of our genetic heritage (Buss, 1999). Evolutionary pressures to preserve group membership favor in-group bias (fear of those who are different). Because humans evolved in small social groups in threatening environments, it made sense for people to trust those who were most like them. In addition, the tendency to automatically make quick good-bad and like-dislike assessments is a fundamental cognitive process with clear evolutionary benefits: It helps people make quick decisions in life—threatening situations (Cunningham & Zelazo, 2006; Neuberg & Cottrell, 2006).

On the other hand, many of our attitudes come from experience. In some cases, we learn attitudes through both direct and indirect instruction by others. We may adopt the musical preferences of our friends. Sometimes we like ideas or objects simply because they are familiar. *Mere exposure*, or direct experience with an object, an idea, or a person, increases our overall preference for it (Zajonc, 1968). The things that we come to like from exposure can be trivial, such as abstract symbols, or very meaningful, such as human faces. For example, Zajonc (1968) showed people nonsense words 5, 10, or 25 times; the more often they saw a word, the more they reported liking it. A number of studies now suggest that exposure alone is not enough to set preferences. It is best if the exposures are repeated over and over again (de Zilva et al., 2016).

Mere exposure is a very robust phenomenon, on which advertisers capitalize—by showing you products over and over again they increase the likelihood that you will like them and, hence, buy them (Qin, Koutstaal, & Engel, 2014; Stafford & Grimes, 2012). When people repeat lies over and over again—as in the case of fake news—people are more likely to agree with them and believe they are truths (Garrett, Weeks, & Neo, 2016). Remember groupthink? *This* is groupthink, too.

Attitude Change

Are people willing to switch attitudes based on evidence or a persuasive argument? What role do personality and persuasion play in our willingness to change attitudes? These are just some of the questions asked by social psychologists interested in attitude change. We examine two major reasons for changes in attitude: cognitive dissonance and persuasion.

Cognitive Dissonance   The theory of cognitive dissonance offers one explanation for why and how we change our attitudes. **Cognitive dissonance** is the feeling of discomfort caused by information that is at odds with one's conception of oneself as a reasonable and sensible person (Festinger, 1957). Because we don't like feeling uncomfortable, we are motivated to try to reduce the discomfort. Three options are available for decreasing the discomfort created by dissonance:

1. We can change our behavior to make it consistent with dissonant cognition.
2. We can attempt to justify our behavior by changing one of the cognitions to make it more consistent with our behavior.
3. We can add new cognitions that are consistent with the behavior and that therefore support it.

cognitive dissonance
The feeling of discomfort caused by information that is different from a person's conception of himself or herself as a reasonable and sensible person.

When people experience cognitive dissonance, they go to extreme lengths to reduce it. In this way, they reduce their discomfort and maintain self-esteem. People end up rationalizing or justifying their not-so-adaptive behavior in order to reduce cognitive dissonance.

Smoking offers a classic example of an irrational behavior in which many people engage. Smoking can cause lung cancer, emphysema, and heart disease. Still, many people continue to smoke. True, they are addicted. Cognitively, however, smokers must manage the conflict between their notion of themselves as rational beings and the fact that they engage in a very risky habit. To reduce the unpleasant feeling these dissonant thoughts and behaviors create, people who smoke may behave in one of the three ways just listed, as seen in Figure 5. People will work hard to rationally defend behaviors or strongly held positions in order to reduce the dissonance—the uncomfortable feeling—produced by opposing arguments.

Making use of the tendency toward dissonance around high-risk behaviors, such as smoking, is one approach to treating them. Simmons and colleagues (2013) created a web-based program in which smokers watched a video of health information about the dangers of smoking (or a control video about nutrition). Then they were asked to make a video about themselves for the purpose of "promoting a healthy lifestyle," which would be shown to peers, in which they were asked to mention their smoking as well as other aspects of their lives. This potentially created dissonance, given the antismoking video they had just viewed. Consistent with the idea that people will change behavior or attitudes to reduce dissonance, the smokers with the most dissonant situation (those who viewed the video about the health effects of smoking) had significantly higher scores on a "motivation to quit" questionnaire than those in the control condition (Simmons et al., 2013).

FIGURE 5
COGNITIVE DISSONANCE AND SMOKING. People smoke even though they know it's unhealthy. To reduce their cognitive dissonance, smokers might try one of these approaches, including quitting.

change behavior

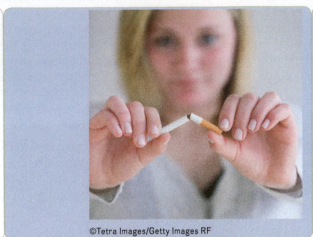

Quit smoking.

©Tetra Images/Getty Images RF

justify smoking by changing cognitions associated with it

"Smoking is not that harmful."
"Results of research on smoking and cancer are not as conclusive as people think they are."

change cognitions so as to justify smoking

"It makes me feel good, so it's worth it, whatever the risk."

©UK Stock Images Ltd/Alamy RF

persuasion
The act of attempting to change the opinions, beliefs, or choices of others by explanation or argument.

Persuasion Persuasion changes attitude as well. **Persuasion** is an attempt by a person or group to change our opinions, beliefs, or choices by explaining or arguing their position. Persuasion is all around us all the time; friends, family, teachers, politicians, salespeople, and advertisers often want to change our minds about something. The success of persuasion depends on three things: who the persuader is (source), the method used to convey the message, and who the receiver (audience) is (Lippa, 1994).

First, how trustworthy, prestigious, and likeable is the source of the message? The more prestigious and trustworthy the persuader, the more likely he or she is to succeed in persuading us. If the persuader is also attractive and familiar, so much the better. This is why people want to buy pain relievers promoted in commercials by famous TV doctors rather than unknown figures. The perceived credibility of the character enhances the credibility of the product.

Second, what methods of persuasion are used? Politicians often rely on fear to convince us to support their policies or candidacy. An example is the so-called Willie Horton ad that was shown during the 1988 U.S. presidential campaign. When Democratic presidential candidate Michael Dukakis was governor of Massachusetts, he supported a weekend release program for prisoners. One of the prisoners, Willie Horton, committed armed robbery and rape during such a weekend. A group supporting the Republican candidate, George H. W. Bush, ran a TV ad showing prisoners walking out of a prison yard with a voice-over about Horton. It ran regularly on stations across the country. It played on people's fears of dangerous criminals, and it linked that fear with Dukakis. That commercial is thought to have played a major role in Dukakis's loss to Bush.

Fear campaigns work only if they actually create fear in the audience (Witte & Allen, 2000). Most ads meant to scare us don't scare us enough to change our behavior. Simply citing statistics about the health risks of smoking is not very effective at getting people to change their behavior. People rarely believe that they will suffer the negative consequences implied by the ads.

Last, who is the targeted audience or receiver of the message? People are not equally malleable in their opinions or behavior. The more people know about a topic and the firmer their prior opinions are, the less likely they are to change their attitudes (Eagly & Chaiken, 1998). Political campaigners know this well. Candidates often focus their efforts—especially near election day—on swing states that either have voted inconsistently in the past or have a mix of party preferences. In regions that have voted Republican for years, say, campaigning by Democratic candidates may be a waste of time.

Quick Quiz 3: Attitudes and Behavior

1. Janice is a college student who is active in politics. She considers voting to be very important for everyone, especially young people. So she volunteers 5 hours a week to staff a table at the student union, encouraging students to register to vote, for any political party. Her stance toward voting is best described as a(n)
   a. belief.
   b. attitude.
   c. attribution.
   d. bias.

2. Levon considers himself to be a healthy person. He eats a healthy diet and exercises 4 days a week, yet he is a smoker. His attitude toward smoking before he became a smoker was very negative. Now that he is a smoker, however, his attitude is not so negative. The change in his attitude is best explained by
   a. attribution.
   b. persuasion.

   c. mere exposure.
   d. cognitive dissonance.

3. Social psychologists have demonstrated that three things matter most in whether an argument will persuade other people or not. The three things are
   a. source, method, and audience.
   b. source, believability, and audience.
   c. logic, believability, and audience.
   d. pressure to conform, source, and authority.

Answers can be found at the end of the chapter.

SOCIAL RELATIONS

We constantly interact with other people. Sometimes these interactions lead to special connections with others that grow into friendship or even love. Other times we clash and find ourselves in conflict with others. In this section we discuss three kinds of social interaction: aggression, helping, and attraction.

Connection

How does hostility differ from anger? Hostility is a personality characteristic that sets the threshold for the emotion of anger.

See "What Are Emotions?" in the chapter "Motivation and Emotion." (p. 430)

The Nature and Nurture of Aggression

aggression
Violent behavior that is intended to cause psychological or physical harm, or both, to another being.

Aggression is part of life. All animals compete with others, both within and outside their species, for survival. Almost every animal can be aggressive, and many animals kill others in order to survive. Humans are unique in that they often engage in aggression and violent behavior even when their survival is not at issue. **Aggression** refers to violent behavior that is intended to cause psychological or physical harm, or both, to another being. By definition, aggression is deliberate. A dentist who performs a root canal may hurt a patient, but we hardly would call that behavior aggressive. Aggression is often provoked by anger, but not always.

When aggression stems from feelings of anger, it is called *hostile aggression*. When aggression is a means to achieve some goal, it is called *instrumental aggression*. The hostile type of aggression is easy to understand. While you are driving, someone cuts you off on the road. You honk and, in response, the other driver makes an obscene hand gesture toward you. The hand gesture is an aggressive action.

An example of instrumental aggression occurs in football when a defensive lineman smashes down a ball carrier to prevent the opponent from scoring. The goal is to prevent scoring by the other team, not to hurt the ball carrier. In this case, the aggressive action is considered to be justified by its instrumental goal.

Where does aggression come from, and why are people aggressive? Some people are more prone to violence than others. An individual's genetic disposition may play a role, but genes by themselves are seldom enough to cause violent behavior (Miczek et al., 2007). Caspi and colleagues (2002) found that, when genetic factors combine with an abusive and neglectful environment, the likelihood of committing violence increases dramatically.

Moreover, research on murderers points to a cluster of traits shared by most of these individuals: being male, growing up in an abusive and neglectful household, having at least one psychological disorder, and having experienced some kind of injury to the head or brain (Pincus, 1999, 2001; Strueber, Lueck, & Roth, 2006–2007; Yang et al., 2010). Having only one of these traits is not enough—all must be present for a person to become antisocial and prone to violence. In other words, the person's disposition interacts with certain environmental influences to make aggressive behavior more likely.

Several brain areas are involved in aggression, including the hypothalamus, the amygdala, and the prefrontal cortex (Pincus, 1999). More specifically, the part of the prefrontal cortex responsible for impulse control often is functionally impaired in aggressive and violent people (Grafman et al., 1996). Amygdala damage is found frequently in murderers (DeLisi, Umphress, & Vaughn, 2009). Similarly, as a result of head injuries, psychopathology, or abuse, murderers may have moderate to severe problems with frontal lobe functioning, which involves impulse control, emotional intelligence, working memory, and attention (Strueber et al., 2006–2007) or reductions in the size of the hippocampus (Yang et al., 2010). Living in a constant state of fear can lead to neural systems being primed for unusually high levels of anxiety, impulsive behavior, and vigilance or a constant state of alertness (Bishop, 2007). These are all conditions that may bring about violent behaviors.

In addition to these brain structures, two hormones are consistently related to high levels of aggression: testosterone and serotonin. A number of lines of evidence point to testosterone's role. As the male sex hormone, it may be responsible for boys being more aggressive than girls at most ages (Maccoby & Jacklin, 1974). In adults, the great majority of people arrested for criminal offenses are men (Strueber et al., 2006–2007). Relatively high levels of testosterone, whether in men or women, correlate positively with a propensity toward violence. Among both male and female prisoners, naturally occurring testosterone levels are higher in criminals convicted of violent crimes than in those convicted of nonviolent crimes (Dabbs, Carr, & Frady, 1995; Dabbs & Hargrove, 1997). In an experimental study, giving testosterone reduced performance on an empathy task in women (University of Cambridge, 2011). Serotonin has a broad range of effects on behavior, one of which is keeping anger and anxiety in check. Research shows that low levels of serotonin make aggression more likely in humans and animals (Moffitt et al., 1998; Raleigh et al., 1991).

Social Influences on Aggression   Situations that prevent us from reaching our goals are likely to make us aggressive. Moreover, the closer we are to our goal when we become frustrated, the more aggressive our response. A classic study by Harris (1974) demonstrated this effect. Confederates of the researchers cut in front of people in lines for movies or crowded restaurants. Sometimes they cut in front of the second person in line; other times they cut in front of someone farther back in line. The response of the person standing behind the intruder was much more aggressive when the confederate cut in front of the person second in line—closest to the goal.

©Shannon Fagan/Getty Images

 Does violence in video games and other visual media increase the likelihood of aggressive behavior?

Similarly, situations that lead to anger stimulate aggression, especially hostile aggression. Threats to our safety or the safety of our families fall into this category. Aggressive responses may be motivated by anger and/or fear. Road rage is a good example of such a situation, and aggressive driving is most likely to happen when people are angry (Nesbit, Conger, & Conger, 2007).

Observing aggressive people and the consequences of their actions can make us more aggressive. This is the fundamental idea behind Albert Bandura's *social learning theory*. Bandura's research demonstrated repeatedly that, if children see adults punching an inflatable Bobo doll, they will do it, too, especially if they see the adult being rewarded for the aggressive behavior.

How does the Bobo doll research apply to real-life aggression? According to longitudinal studies of men and women, the more violence people watch on TV when they are children, the more violent behavior they will exhibit as adults (Huesmann, Moise-Titus, & Podolski, 2003). This correlational result does not prove that TV is the cause of the aggressive behavior; however, more controlled experiments also suggest that watching TV violence leads to aggressive behavior in children. Liebert and Baron (1972) showed a violent TV program to a group of children. The control group saw an exciting but nonviolent sporting event that had the same running time as the violent program. Children were randomly assigned to the two groups. After viewing one of the programs, each child was allowed to play in another room with a group of children. Those who had watched the violent program were far more aggressive in their play than those who saw the nonviolent show.

Until recently, the evidence was overwhelming that exposure to violent programs or video games increased aggression in kids (Bushman & Anderson, 2001; Kirsh, 2006). Results from a recent meta-analysis suggest, however, that the effects of watching violence on aggressive behavior have been exaggerated. It seems many of the studies fail to consider how other factors (such as sex, personality, and family violence) may also play a role in aggressive behavior (Ferguson & Kilburn, 2009). There is clearly a relationship between viewing violence and aggression, but the size of the effects is a matter of great debate (Anderson et al., 2010; Ferguson & Kilburn, 2010).

Whether or not viewing violence increases aggressive behavior, repeatedly seeing or participating in violent action in a virtual world may make young people less sensitive to violence. In one study, researchers randomly assigned more than 250 male and female college students to play either a violent or a nonviolent

Connection

Social learning theory offers an explanation of modeling, the kind of learning in which we imitate the behavior of others.

See "Social Learning Theory," in the chapter "Learning." (p. 319)

prosocial behavior
Action that is beneficial to others.

video game for 20 minutes (Carnagey, Anderson, & Bushman, 2007). Then they measured the participants' physiological responses to films of real-life violence, such as courtroom outbursts, police confrontations, shootings, and prison fights. The students who played the violent video games showed less physiological arousal (as measured by heart rate and sweating) while watching films of real people being stabbed and shot than did the students who had played the nonviolent games. In a similar study, young men with a history of playing video games showed reduced brain activation to real-life violence, and this reduced brain activation correlated with aggression in a behavioral task (Bartholow, Bushman, & Sestir, 2006). Such nonreaction to violence is disturbing.

Prosocial Behavior

Just as people can harm others through aggression, sometimes people can be extraordinarily kind to others. **Prosocial behavior** benefits others. In this section we will explore social processes that benefit others: altruism and empathy.

Sometimes humans do extraordinary things for others at great cost to themselves. Consider the case of Wesley Autrey. One morning in January 2007, Autrey and his two daughters were waiting for the subway in New York City. Suddenly, a teenager standing nearby began convulsing and collapsed on the platform. Among the dozens of people there, only Autrey and a few others stopped to help the young man. They thought they had stabilized him, but the young man got up, tottered, and fell onto the tracks. The headlights of an oncoming train appeared, and in an instant Autrey jumped onto the tracks to help the young man. When Autrey realized that he could not pull the teen off the tracks before the train hit them, he lay on top of him and pressed him down firmly in a bear hug. The train went over both men without touching them.

Autrey heard the screams of onlookers. "We're okay down here," he yelled, "but I've got two daughters up there. Let them know their father's okay." He heard cries of wonder and applause (Buckley, 2007). When interviewed later, Autrey said he had done nothing heroic. He had simply decided to help someone in need. "I didn't want the man's body to get run over," he said. "Plus, I was with my daughters and I didn't want them to see that" (CBS News, 2007).

Would you jump in front of an oncoming train to help a complete stranger? How many people do you think would? What makes people help other people? Most evidence, both from real life and from laboratory studies, indicates that most people would not help a stranger, especially if many others were present but doing nothing. Social psychologists have studied various factors that influence whether people will help others.

The Bystander Effect   Late one night, Kitty Genovese walked from her parked car to her apartment building in New York City after coming home from her job as a bar manager. As she approached the building, Winston Moseley accosted her and stabbed her in the back. She screamed, "Oh my God, he stabbed me! Help me!" Fearing that her cries for help would be heeded, Moseley ran away. Lights went on in the apartment building, at least two people saw the attack, but no one called the police or went to help her. Moseley returned and renewed his attack stabbing her at least 10 more times. Genovese's screams were heard by numerous people, but still no one went to help. One of Kitty's neighbors and friends did make it downstairs and held Kitty as she died. It was only then that one of the witnesses summoned the police.

How could so many people ignore the screams of a young woman being brutally attacked? What kind of attribution—either dispositional or situational—best explains this behavior? The Kitty Genovese case received tons of publicity, it spurred a great deal of research in social psychology, and it was even responsible for establishing the 911 phone call system for emergencies. John Darley and Bibb Latané (1968) used science to understand why no one came to Genovese's rescue. They did an experiment in which research participants heard another participant choking over an intercom (what they actually heard was an audiotape). The researchers led some of the participants to believe that they were the only ones hearing the person choking, while others thought many participants were hearing it. Of the participants who thought they alone were hearing the choking man, 85% tried to help. Of those who thought many other people were also hearing the man choking, only 62% tried to help. Here's the bottom line: The more people who witness an emergency, the less likely any one of them will help. Latané and Darley called this phenomenon the **bystander effect**.

©NY Daily News/Getty Images

In 1964, Kitty Genovese was attacked and killed while residents of her Queens neighborhood, shown in this photo taken after the murder, ignored her screams.

 How does the research on the bystander effect explain why no one came to her aid?

One explanation of the bystander effect involves *diffusion of responsibility*; that is, when there are many people around, an individual's responsibility to act seems decreased. It makes sense when you think about it. When you alone witness an emergency, you know that you are the only source of aid. If several people are present, however, you might not regard it as your responsibility to help the person in need. Someone else might take care of it. Indeed, this is probably why no one helped poor Kitty Genovese. A lot of people were around, so everyone assumed "somebody else must have called the police."

Several factors influence whether or not someone will intervene in an emergency. One is whether people actually notice the event. When people are in a hurry, they are less likely to notice an emergency (Darley & Batson, 1973). Moreover, when many people are present and doing nothing, a person is less likely to interpret an event as an emergency. This is an example of informational social influence, because in this ambiguous situation people look to others for clues as to what should be done. If everyone else is doing nothing, then maybe there's no emergency after all.

Even if we notice an event and interpret it as an emergency, we must decide that it is our responsibility to do something. In addition to a diffusion of responsibility, people often do a cost-benefit analysis to determine whether helping is worth the cost. Sometimes it is dangerous to be helpful. If you get to this step and decide it is worth helping, you still might not know how to help. If you witness someone having a heart attack and want to help, you might not know CPR. Even if you've passed all the previous hurdles, you may not be able to help after all, but you can still call 911.

Altruism The term **altruism** refers to a selfless concern for and giving of aid to others. Because altruists often expose themselves to greater danger than those who selfishly protect themselves, helping poses risks to personal survival. For this reason, altruism makes no sense from an evolutionary perspective (Dawkins, 1989). So why do humans and other animals sometimes engage in altruistic behavior?

Evolutionary theory offers two explanations for altruistic behavior: kin selection and reciprocal altruism. **Kin selection** is the evolutionary mechanism that prompts individuals to help their close relatives, or kin, so that they will survive to reproduce and pass on related genes to their offspring (Hamilton, 1964). For instance, a dominant macaque monkey will share food with a subordinate monkey only if the two are close relatives (Belisle & Chapais, 2001; Furuichi, 1983). Individuals who help close relatives may be risking their lives, but they are also increasing the chances that, if they do not survive, at least some of their genes will survive in their relatives.

bystander effect
A phenomenon in which the greater the number of bystanders who witness an emergency, the less likely any one of them is to help.

altruism
Selfless attitudes and behavior toward others.

kin selection
The evolutionary favoring of genes that prompt individuals to help their relatives, or kin.

©Ashley Cooper/Corbis Documentary/Getty Images

From an evolutionary point of view, true altruism has no clear survival advantage.

 How can we explain altruistic behavior?

Kin selection is more common in social animals, such as bees. Greenberg (1979) bred bees to have varied degrees of genetic relatedness and then released them near a nest watched by guard bees. Because the nest was crowded, not every bee could get in. Guard bees more often let in the closely related bees than the distantly related bees. There is evidence for kin selection in humans, too. Burnstein and colleagues (Burnstein, Crandall, & Kitayama, 1994) asked people to specify whom they would be most likely to help in life-and-death situations and in non-life-and-death situations. People reported they would be more likely to help a relative in life-and-death situations. In fact, when people are rescuing others from a burning building, they are much more likely to look for relatives first (Sime, 1983).

Another evolutionary explanation for altruistic behavior is **reciprocal altruism**, helping others in the hope that they will help you in the future (Trivers, 1971, 1985). It is easier for humans to survive when group members cooperate, and reciprocal altruism promotes such cooperation. You might help another member of your group if you believe that you might benefit in some way as a result. From an evolutionary perspective, reciprocal altruism should be most common in species that are social, for only animals that live in groups have opportunities to benefit from reciprocal helping.

Some people have argued that these evolutionary mechanisms do not adequately explain all altruistic behavior. After all, what about Wesley Autrey? Some social psychologists argue that in our relations with others we try to maximize our gains and minimize our losses (Thibaut & Kelley, 1959). This is the essence of **social exchange theory**, a nonevolutionary explanation of altruistic behavior that says we help others because such behavior can be rewarding, but we will help only if the rewards will outweigh the costs. How can helping be rewarding? For one thing, helping someone in need relieves our own distress at witnessing suffering. Also, helping someone is an investment in the future, because it is possible that they will help us when we need help. In this sense, social exchange is essentially the same as reciprocal altruism.

reciprocal altruism
The act of helping others in the hope that they will help us in the future.

social exchange theory
The idea that we help others when we understand that the benefits to ourselves are likely to outweigh the costs.

According to social exchange theory, truly selfless altruism does not exist. What about Wesley Autrey? Were his actions representative of selfless altruism? He did say that he didn't want his daughters to see the man die. Perhaps by helping, Autrey was protecting the psychological well-being of his kids (which is kin selection after all). Human and nonhuman primates may have both selfish and nonselfish motives for the helping (de Waal & Suchak, 2010). An example of a selfish motive would be helping a suffering person to ease the guilt of not helping. In nonselfish helping, the helper derives no personal benefit.

Whatever the cause of altruistic behavior, psychological science is uncovering more and more evidence of the benefits of being kind and lending a hand. First, helping feels good, better than indulging ourselves, whether we are talking about sacrifices we make in our most intimate relationships (Kogan et al., 2010) or giving gifts or resources to strangers (Dunn, Aknin, & Norton, 2008). In fact, the joy of giving is seen even in toddlers (Aknin, Hamlin, & Dunn, 2012). A large-scale interview and questionnaire study showed that helping behavior may be beneficial for health—it may help buffer against the effects of stress (Poulin et al., 2013). Specifically, the researchers found an overall connection between stress and mortality in the 5-year period following the study—the more stress, the more likely to be dead 5 years after the study started—with a crucial exception. If people reported that they regularly lent a hand to others, this stress-mortality link was broken.

There are other benefits to being kind. When given the opportunity to think of others—to be generous, as it were—people are more likely to change behavior if they see that the behavior change is for the general good. In one clever but very simple study, Grant and Hoffman (2011) conducted a study on whether such an approach might help medical professionals increase hand washing (one of the major factors in preventing the spread of disease in health care settings). In one bathroom, they put a sign encouraging all employees to wash their hands, as it would help them (the employees themselves) not get sick. In another bathroom, they printed a similar sign, but this one said it would help them prevent others from getting sick. They only changed one word in the sign to change this meaning. They then kept track of how much soap was used in each bathroom, as a measure of hand washing. Surprisingly, more soap was used in the bathroom in which the sign emphasized the effects of hand washing behavior on the health of others, which indicates that concern for others provided a greater motivation for behavior change.

Empathy   C. Daniel Batson (1991) has proposed that true selfless helping occurs only when there is empathy. **Empathy** can be defined as sharing feeling and understanding about another person's situation. According to Batson's **empathy-altruism hypothesis**, people will offer selfless help only when they truly empathize with the victim. Consider the following example: A professor is talking with a student in his office. While pleading with the professor to postpone an upcoming test, the student begins to cry. Reacting to the student's distress, the professor becomes upset as well. The professor decides to help the student by postponing the test. Batson and his colleagues believe that two different motivations may underlie the professor's behavior.

The first motivation Batson calls the *egoistic motivation*. The professor may help the student in order to relieve the professor's own distress. This is not true altruism and would fit with social exchange theory, in which the reward is the reduction of distress. A second motivation, *empathic motivation*, holds that the professor's behavior may spring from an altruistic desire to reduce the distress of the person in need. Unlike the egoistic helper, the empathic helper serves another with the primary goal of helping the student through the crisis.

Challenge Your Assumptions

True or False? People will sometimes risk their lives to help others.
True: People will sometimes put themselves at great risk to help others, without giving their own safety a second thought. These are rare acts of heroism, but they happen and are difficult to explain by current theories of altruistic behavior.

empathy
The ability to share the feelings of others and understand their situations.

empathy-altruism hypothesis
The idea that people help others selflessly only when they feel empathy for them.

In order to understand the brain mechanisms of empathy, Singer and colleagues examined brain activation during a person's real pain experience and when witnessing the pain of a loved one (Singer et al., 2004). They created an experiment to study the response to a loved one's pain in the confines of an fMRI scanner. Singer obtained measures of functional brain activity in the female partner of a couple while the woman herself received a painful stimulus to her hand and then while she witnessed her male partner receiving the same painful stimulus; see the Research Process for this chapter (Figure 6). The actual pain stimulus, which was a mild electric shock delivered by an electrode attached to the hand, activated a well-known pain circuit in the brain, involving the somatosensory cortex, insula, anterior cingulate cortex (ACC), thalamus, and cerebellum. When her partner was experiencing pain, only those structures in the pain circuit that are triggered by the emotional aspect of pain showed activation, most notably the front region of the insula and the ACC. So when a partner experiences pain, people truly do feel it *with* their loved ones. Increasing evidence across various studies now supports the idea that the insula and anterior cingulate are key neural structures involved in empathy (Berhardt & Singer, 2012).

Psychological science has recently turned to understanding other prosocial states underlying prosocial behavior; foremost among them is compassion. **Compassion** is a state of relationship in which one feels kindness toward another who is suffering and one feels motivated to help relieve that suffering. Compassion may motivate helping behavior. Currently, there are several training programs designed to help people develop their compassion, many of them coming from major universities, such as Stanford (see http://ccare.stanford.edu/) and Emory (see https://tibet.emory.edu/cognitively-based-compassion-training/). These programs draw on meditation practices from Buddhism that are designed to develop compassion, but they are accessible to people from any religious background (or no religion). Such compassion training programs appear to increase positive affect and self-reported compassion, support helping behavior, and promote beneficial physiological changes (Condon et al., 2013; Fredrickson et al., 2008; Jazaieri et al., 2012, 2013; Pace et al., 2009; Weng et al., 2013).

compassion
A state of relationship in which one feels kindness toward another who is suffering and one feels motivated to help relieve that suffering.

Liking, Attraction, and Love

What makes one person want to be with another? Is this process different for friends and lovers? What is love, anyway? In this section we will see how psychologists tackle a few questions of the human heart. Let's first examine how we come to like and be attracted to other people, and then we'll take a look at love.

Familiarity, Similarity, and Attraction As we have seen throughout this chapter, research in social psychology shows that merely being exposed to an object, an idea, or a person causes you to like it more (Zajonc, 1968). The more often we see a face, the more we like it.

People with similar ideas, values, and interests are more likely to like one another and share satisfying, long-lasting relationships (Keller, Thiessen, & Young, 1996). For example, researchers randomly assigned male college students to be roommates in a certain dorm at the beginning of the year. Roommates who became real friends had common backgrounds, similar majors, and similar political viewpoints (Newcomb, 1961). People report that they like and want to help others who have similar personalities, attitudes, or beliefs (Wakimoto & Fujihara, 2004; Westmaas & Silver, 2006). Finally, people also tend to be attracted to and partner with people of a level of attractiveness similar to themselves—a phenomenon known as *assortative mating* (Buss, 2004). There is a moderately strong correlation between the personality of one's ideal partner and one's own personality; married couples also often have strongly correlated

Research Process

① Research Question

If empathy really is feeling what another person is feeling, are pain circuits in the brain activated similarly when someone feels pain and when empathizing with a loved one's pain?

② Method

In a quasi-experimental study, Tania Singer and colleagues (2004) used fMRI to measure brain activation in women when they received a mild shock to the hand and while they witnessed their partner receiving the same painful stimulus.

The partner sat next to the fMRI scanner. The woman and her partner placed their right hands on a tilted board, which allowed the woman to see her and her partner's right hand with the help of a mirror. On a large screen the woman saw visual cues that indicated whether she or her partner would get low pain or high pain. When administered, the shock lasted for 2 seconds.

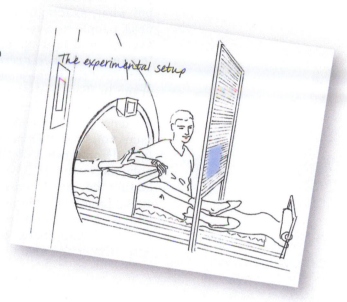

The experimental setup

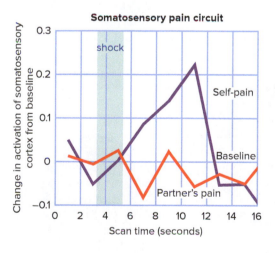

③ Results

A mild shock was administered 3.5 seconds after the scan began, lasting for 2 seconds. The scans showed that self-pain activated all the structures in the pain circuit, while the partner's pain (the empathic pain condition) mainly activated the structures typically involved only in the emotional aspect of pain (anterior cingulate cortex, or ACC, and the insula). The graphs show brain activation for the women as a change from a baseline (pain-free) state.

▼ The similarity in patterns of activation in the ACC across these two conditions suggests that the women empathized with—that is, *felt*—their partner's pain.

▲ The difference in patterns of activation in the somatosensory cortex suggests that the women did not experience the same sensory aspects of pain when their partners received the shock as when they received the shock themselves.

④ Conclusion

Experienced pain activates all pain networks in the brain (emotional and sensory), but empathic pain activates only the emotional pain network. When a loved one experiences pain, people truly do feel their loved one's pain, but that feeling may be more emotional than sensory.

FIGURE 6

FEELING ANOTHER'S PAIN. Empathy for a loved one's pain involves brain circuitry that is activated by real pain.

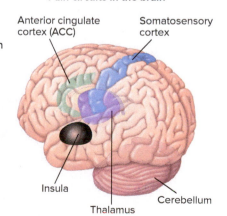

Pain circuits in the brain

Anterior cingulate cortex (ACC)

Somatosensory cortex

Insula

Thalamus

Cerebellum

Source: "Empathy for Pain Involves the Affective but Not Sensory Components of Pain," by T. Singer, B. Seymour, J. O. O'Doherty, H. Kaube, R. J. Dolan, & C. D. Frith, 2004, *Science, 303*, 1157–1162.

ages, levels of intelligence, and imaginativeness (Botwin, Buss, & Shackelford, 1997; Keller et al., 1996).

Physical and Chemical Attractiveness Humans worldwide value physical attractiveness in partners (Buss, 1999; Etcoff, 1999; Miller, 2000), but what, exactly, is considered to be attractive? In research on attractiveness, people rate average and symmetrical faces as more attractive than less average and less symmetrical faces. *Average*, in this case, does not mean "common." Rather, *average* means that the size, location, and shape of each feature of the face—nose, eyes, mouth, cheekbones—are mathematically average in the population. They are neither too big nor too small, neither too far apart nor too close together. Look at the faces in Figure 7. These faces were produced by computer technology that morphed images of several real faces together. The more faces averaged, the higher the attractiveness ratings. People rated the 8-face composite as more attractive than the 4-face composite; the 16-face composite as more attractive than the 8; and the 32-face composite as more attractive than the 16 (Langlois & Roggman, 1990; Langlois, Roggman, & Musselman, 1994). Although standards for beauty vary by culture, average faces are rated as most attractive all over the world (Langlois & Roggman, 1990). Furthermore, infants as young as 6 or 9 months of age also tend to prefer average faces over others, although they

FIGURE 7
RATING PHYSICAL ATTRACTIVENESS. The more faces that are morphed into one image, the more they move toward having average features. As they become more average in features, the faces are perceived as increasing in attractiveness.

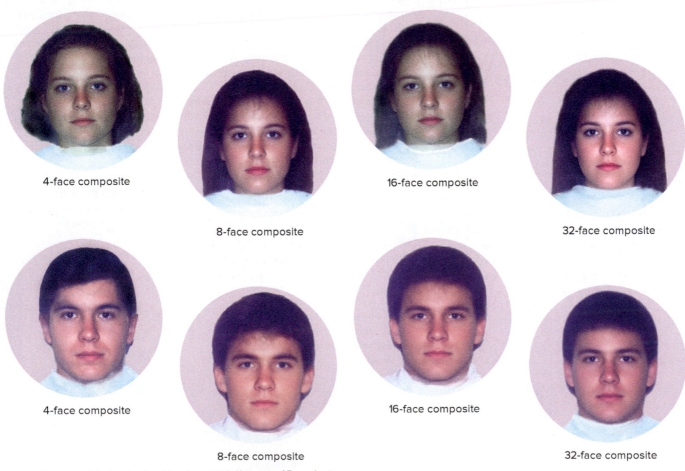

4-face composite

8-face composite

16-face composite

32-face composite

4-face composite

8-face composite

16-face composite

32-face composite

are too young for other people to have had much influence over their face preferences (Hoss & Langlois, 2003).

Averaged faces tend to be more symmetrical, and people seem to prefer symmetry when they rate faces for attractiveness (Etcoff, 1999). Moreover, symmetry is a rough indicator of genetic fitness; that is, symmetrical faces and bodies are signs of fewer genetic mutations (Miller, 2000).

Scent plays a role in attraction, but we are not talking about perfumes. Pheromones—scents produced by animals that have an effect on other members of the same species—are well-established modes of social communication among many animal species. They are full of sexual and organizational messages, but whether they operate or even exist in humans has been a matter of debate (Brennan, 2010).

Apparently, scent matters in humans as well, but not in the way you would think. In a clever experiment, researchers instructed men and women to wear a clean T-shirt to bed for two nights (Thornhill et al., 2003). The shirt had no perfumes and was not washed with deodorant soaps. The T-shirts were returned to the lab and sealed in zippered bags. An independent group of students rated the attractiveness of pictures of the people who had worn the shirts. Another group of students smelled and rated the T-shirts on attractiveness of odor. Men preferred the scent of women in their fertile phase; fertile women preferred the scent of men who were most symmetrical.

In a similar study in which men smelled women's shirts, researchers measured men's testosterone levels in response to the smells. Men released more testosterone when exposed to the scent of ovulating women than when exposed to the scent of nonovulating women (Miller & Maner, 2010).

Sexual Attraction and Mate Selection   What qualities do you look for in a prospective sexual partner? **Sexual strategies theory** suggests that men and women often approach relationships differently (Buss & Schmitt, 1993). In virtually all societies, men and women use both short-term matings (affairs, one-night stands) and long-term matings (marriages, extended companionships). Both are effective ways to increase one's reproductive fitness, but each strategy has strengths and weaknesses. Sex differences in attraction arise because *parental investment* is greater for women than for men (Trivers, 1972). Consequently, men devote a larger portion of their total mating effort to short-term mating than do women (Buss, 1999).

Buss (1999) found that men report wanting an average of 18 different partners throughout their lifetimes, whereas women report wanting only four or five. Men value qualities that may signal fertility and accessibility (e.g., large breasts, wide hips compared to waist, youth), especially in short-term partners. This is less true in evaluating long-term partners. Women, in contrast, value men who can provide resources to support their offspring.

These days, social network sites have begun to play a major role in the dating game. Sites like OkCupid and Tinder make use of people's reliance on their mobile devices and shortened attention spans to make matches. OkCupid matches people on the basis of their responses to questions obtained ahead of time. Possible matches are then sent via email to the member, whose option it is to follow up on the possibility of real-life contact. Tinder translates the speed-dating model to the mobile app atmosphere. The user looks at possible matches on his or her phone (based on some background information but less extensive than OkCupid) and then sends texts. Then an exchange may or may not ensue, after which it is up to the participants to follow up regarding a "real-life" meet-up. Not surprisingly, behavior on these dating sites is often governed by personality, socioeconomical factors, and race, just as is face-to-face interaction. A detailed analysis of over 125,000 OkCupid users revealed that, although people freely interact with members of various races, there is a pattern to use. People are much less likely to cross racial lines when initiating a contact than when responding to one, though experience with interracial communication

Challenge Your Assumptions
True or False? Attractive faces are anything but average.
False: Probably for evolutionary reasons regarding fitness, people the world over tend to find faces that look like the mathematical average of many faces are considered to be the most attractive.

sexual strategies theory
The idea that men and women face different problems when they seek out mates, so they often approach relationships in very different ways.

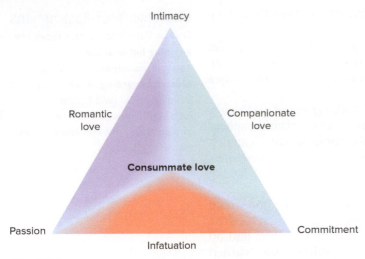

FIGURE 8
STERNBERG'S TRIANGULAR THEORY OF LOVE. In Sternberg's model, all types of love are made up of three components: intimacy, passion, and commitment. Each type of love consists of a different balance of the three components. When all three exist in equal proportions, consummate love exists (Sternberg, 1986).

triangular theory of love
Sternberg's idea that three components (intimacy, passion, and commitment), in various combinations, can explain all the forms of human love.

Connection

Men are more likely than women to be interested in casual sex.

See "Sex: Survival of the Species," in the chapter "Motivation and Emotion" for an evolutionary explanation. (p. 418)

Connection

Attachment is a bidirectional relationship requiring the active participation of infants and caregivers.

See "Early Socioemotional Development," in the chapter "Human Development." (p. 184)

increases the likelihood of such behavior in the future (Lewis, 2013).

Mate selection factors might drive sexual partnerships, but these evolutionary pressures operate outside conscious awareness. Once people mate, it is the love that may develop between two people that keeps them together, but what is love?

Love   As a concept, love is not easy to define. It takes many different forms and means different things to different people at different times in their lives.

Types of Love   Humans love in many different ways. We love our parents, lovers, friends, brothers and sisters, children, dogs, lattes, and music. How do we account for the variations? One well-known theory is Robert Sternberg's **triangular theory of love** (Sternberg, 1986). Sternberg proposed that three components—intimacy, passion, and commitment, in various combinations—can explain all the forms of human love (see Figure 8). *Intimacy* refers to close, connected, and bonded feelings in loving relationships. *Passion* refers to the drives that lead to romance, physical attraction, and sexual consummation, accompanied by physiological changes and arousal. *Commitment* refers to both the decision to love someone—or not—and the decision to commit to love for the long term.

These three components are present in different amounts for different kinds of love. *Companionate love* exists when intimacy and commitment are high and passion is low. In *passionate love*, intimacy and passion are high and commitment is low. *Lust* is characterized by a lot of passion but no intimacy or commitment. In contrast, arranged marriages are all about commitment, at least in the beginning, with no intimacy or passion.

Love as Attachment   Love is also closely connected to a well-known psychological phenomenon: attachment. An important concept in human development, attachment is an affection-based bond between infants and their primary caregivers that protects infants from threats to their survival (Bowlby, 1969). Attachment researchers distinguish among secure, avoidant, and anxious/ambivalent attachment styles (Ainsworth et al., 1978).

The attachment system established when we are infants forms a template for our adult relationships with others, including our intimate partners, according to Cynthia Hazan and Phillip Shaver (1987). Hazan and Shaver argued that the infant-caregiver attachment system underlies the important dynamics and individual differences in adult romantic relationships. By categorizing people's infant-caregiver attachment style based on an adult attachment interview, they found that securely attached adults report that they easily get close to others, readily trust others, and have more satisfying romantic relationships. Anxious/ambivalent adults tend to have less satisfying relationships, are more preoccupied with them, and fear that their partners do not want the intimacy they desire. Avoidant adults are uncomfortable being close to others and have less satisfying relationships (Hazan & Shaver, 1987).

As you can see, we have a partial understanding of how liking, attraction, and love work, but psychological science has yet to explain how these elements come together. Evolutionary psychology offers one integrative framework. In this view, for example, liking and loving both evolved to help ensure survival of the species.

Quick Quiz 4: Social Relations

1. Being exposed to violent media affects which kind of responses in young boys?
   a. the ability to form lasting social relationships
   b. physiological responses while viewing a violent film
   c. a and b
   d. none of the above

2. According to Batson's empathy-altruism hypothesis,
   a. people will offer selfless help only when they truly empathize with the victim.
   b. true altruism exists only in empathic responses to family members.
   c. there is no such thing as true altruism, but there is true empathy.
   d. empathy and altruism are linked only in cases of heroic rescues.

3. What kind of faces do people tend to find more attractive?
   a. faces that have unique features rarely seen in the common population
   b. faces that are arithmetically average
   c. faces in which the eyebrow-to-nose ratio is less than 1
   d. none of the above

4. Adults who tend to have less satisfying relationships, are more preoccupied with them, and fear that their partners do not want the intimacy they desire can be categorized as having what type of attachment style?
   a. securely attached
   b. suppressively attached
   c. avoidant
   d. anxious/ambivalent

Answers can be found at the end of the chapter.

Bringing It All Together

Making Connections in Social Behavior

Analysis of the Jonestown Cult

A tragic event of late 20th-century history illustrates many of the social-psychological concepts discussed in this chapter. It involves a cult and mass suicide. In late November 1978, under the direction of the Reverend Jim Jones on a compound in "Jonestown," Guyana, members of the group People's Temple fed a poison-laced drink to their children and then drank it themselves. More than 900 adults and children died. Most were found lying together, arm in arm.

Most of the members of the People's Temple went willingly to their deaths. Why? After years of indoctrination and isolation from mainstream society, they had been led into complete commitment to Jones and the People's Temple. People's Temple had all the hallmarks of a cult.

A **cult** is an extremist group led by a charismatic, totalitarian leader in which coercive methods are used to prevent members from leaving the group.

If we apply social-psychological theory to an analysis of these events, they become more comprehensible, because we can see that the members of the People's Temple were not very different from us. Four principles of social psychology—persuasion, conformity, obedience, and cognitive dissonance—can shed light on the tragedy of Jonestown (Osherow, 1999).

cult
An extremist group led by a charismatic, totalitarian leader in which coercive methods are used to prevent members from leaving the group.

©Bettmann/Getty Images

Jim Jones

Jim Jones and the People's Temple

Jim Jones founded the People's Temple in Indiana in 1958, preaching a message of brotherhood, racial integration, and freedom from poverty. His group helped feed and employ the poor. Jones presented a public image of a beloved leader who promoted a vision of racial harmony.

Throughout the 1960s, the group grew in size and popularity, but rumors surfaced that Jones used coercive methods to keep people from leaving the People's Temple. In the mid-1970s, after a great deal of bad publicity, Jones and his followers moved to a jungle outpost he called Jonestown, in Guyana, South America. In 1978, U.S. Congressman Leo Ryan heard reports that the People's Temple was holding members against their will, and he led a delegation of government officials, reporters, and concerned relatives to Jonestown to talk with residents about how they liked living there. Two families secretly informed Ryan that they wanted out. As Ryan's party and these two "defector" families tried to board their plane for the United States, Temple gunmen ambushed and killed five people, including Congressman Ryan. This ambush precipitated the mass suicide, an act that Jones and his followers had rehearsed many times. It was their final act of rebellion against the system that they believed forced them into exile.

The Role of Persuasion

Jones was a charismatic figure. He sought out people who needed to hear his message: the urban poor, minorities, the elderly, ex-addicts, and convicts. Potential members of the People's Temple first encountered an almost idyllic scene in which blacks and whites lived, worked, and worshiped together in total harmony. Guests were greeted warmly and invited to share a meal. Jones also gave them miracles. He cured diseases; he made predictions that came true with uncanny frequency. Members were motivated to believe in Jones; they appreciated the racial harmony, sense of purpose, and relief from feelings of worthlessness that the People's Temple provided.

Jones carefully managed his public image. He used letter writing and the political clout of hundreds of cult members to praise him and impress the politicians and reporters who supported the People's Temple, as well as to criticize and intimidate its opponents. Most important, Jones limited the information available to members.

The Role of Conformity and Obedience

Conformity played a role in the People's Temple from the outset. Even getting into the group was not easy. People underwent a strict initiation process, which actually drew members more firmly into the group. As they became increasingly involved in the People's Temple, they committed themselves more strongly to the group, because they were required to donate their property and 25% of their income to the church. Before they entered the meeting room for each service, they wrote self-incriminating letters, which were turned over to the church. If anyone objected, the refusal was interpreted as a "lack of faith" in Jones. All of these rules made the group more important than the individuals, making conformity to the group all the more likely.

As he gradually increased his demands, Jones also exposed cult members to the concept of a "final ritual," mass suicide. Rehearsals of this ritual tested followers and their faith in Jones. In essence, Jones was making use of what social psychologists call the *foot-in-the-door* technique by getting people to agree to a moderate request (i.e., rehearsal). Once cult members had agreed to engage in frequent rehearsals of mass suicide, it became easier for them to go through with the real thing.

The suicides at Jonestown can be viewed as the product of obedience—people complying with the orders of a leader and reacting to the threat of force. In the People's Temple, whatever Jim Jones commanded, the members did. Jones was a forceful authority. By the early 1970s, the members of the People's Temple lived in constant fear of severe punishment—brutal beatings coupled with public humiliation—for committing trivial or even inadvertent offenses. Milgram's experiments show us that the power of authority need not be so explicitly threatening to create compliance with demands. Nor does the consensus of the group need to be coercive, as Asch's experiments on

©Bettmann/Getty Images

These are some of the victims of the mass suicide at Jonestown, Guyana, in 1978. People's Temple leader Jim Jones used his status as an authority figure to persuade, intimidate, and indoctrinate his followers over several years, apparently convincing them that death was the only alternative to being captured and separated from the group.

conformity indicate. However, Jones's power was both threatening and coercive.

Jones used threats to impose the discipline and devotion he demanded, and he took steps to eliminate any behavior that might encourage resistance among his followers. As Solomon Asch found in his experiments on conformity, if just one confederate expresses an opinion different from that of the majority, the rate of conformity drastically declines. This is minority social influence. In the People's Temple, Jones tolerated no dissent, made sure that members had no allegiance more powerful than their loyalty to him, and tried to make the alternative of leaving the church unthinkable. Anyone who dared to dissent was terrorized as a traitor, thereby squelching the possibility of minority social influence.

How did Jones do this? He used informers who reported indiscretions, split families to prevent allegiances, and forced parents to give over their children to the Temple. He thereby created conditions in which kin selection could not promote helping between members. Similarly, Jones worked to dissolve marital bonds by forcing couples into extramarital relations (sometimes with Jones himself). "Families are part of the enemy system," Jones said, because they weakened the individual's dedication to the cause. Not surprisingly, it was very hard to leave the cult. Not being able to defect or escape from the group, people had little choice but to conform.

The Role of Cognitive Dissonance

Cognitive dissonance helps explain why cult members believed Jones to the end and why so few defected. People did not become cult members all at once. Rather, the process of justifying their choice and becoming committed to Jones unfolded slowly over the course of weeks and months, sometimes years. Jones knew what he was doing. Starting the process with harsh acts of initiation is a perfect way to get people to rationalize their otherwise embarrassing behavior. If people don't see the group they are about to join very positively, how can they possibly justify going through such humiliation in order to get in?

Even so, how could members not seek to escape and accept killing themselves and their children so easily? These acts were the product of a situation that made dissent impossible and faith in Jones and the Temple absolute. Once they were isolated from the rest of the world at Jonestown, escape was impossible. When escape is impossible, people rationalize their predicament. The members of the People's Temple reduced their cognitive dissonance by changing their attitude to conform with their behavior. In this case, they told themselves that Jones was great and his message was wonderful. When the time to commit suicide finally arrived, most of the members clearly drank the juice quite willingly and by their own choice, so strong was their belief in Jones and his message.

Chapter Review

GROUP LIVING AND SOCIAL INFLUENCE

- Social psychology is the study of the effects of the real or imagined presence of others on people's thoughts, feelings, and actions.

- We act differently when other people are present than we do when we are alone. Sometimes our performance is improved when we are with other people; sometimes it is hindered. In addition, people adjust their behavior in order to conform to what others are doing or to adhere to the rules of their culture.

- An individual can change the majority opinion of a group, but doing so takes perseverance and consistency.

©StockFinland/E+/Getty Images

- Obedience to authority can and has led to numerous instances of people doing things they otherwise would not, from soldiers in Nazi Germany and Abu Ghraib prison in Iraq to participants in Milgram's studies.

SOCIAL PERCEPTION

- We are constantly drawing conclusions about why people do what they do; that is, we make attributions. Sometimes we say that internal qualities of the person were the cause of a behavior. Other times we see outside forces in the environment as the cause of a person's behavior.

- When forming opinions about others, we use schemas about individuals based on what they are like or are likely to do based simply on the group they belong to. Opinions formed this way are stereotypes. Similarly, a prejudice is an attitude toward a group of people or an individual member of a group based on unfair generalizations about that group. Finally, discrimination is preferential treatment of certain people that is driven by prejudicial attitudes.

- Applying stereotypes, prejudices, and discrimination to people based on their racial-ethnic group affiliations is racism. Racism operates both inside (explicitly) and outside (implicitly) our awareness.

ATTITUDES AND BEHAVIOR

- Psychologists define attitudes as a person's favorable or unfavorable beliefs, feelings, or actions toward an object, an idea, or a person. People's attitudes and behaviors do not always match and are often resistant to change.

- One explanation for why and how people change their attitudes is cognitive dissonance, which is the feeling of discomfort caused by information that differs from one's conception of oneself as a reasonable and sensible person.

- Persuasion is another way in which attitudes can be changed.

SOCIAL RELATIONS

- People hurt other people, help other people, and are attracted to and love other people.

- *Aggression* refers to violent behaviors that are intended to cause psychological and/or physical harm to another being. Aggression stems from a complex interplay of genetic and social forces.

- The more people who witness an accident or a crime, the more likely it is that no one will call for help or intervene. This phenomenon is the bystander effect.

- People also act in prosocial ways to help others in need. In life-and-death situations, kin selection explains why people are most willing to help those who are most closely related to them.

- Relationships that are bound by similarities in personality, attitude, intelligence, and attractiveness tend to last the longest.

- People all over the world rate as most attractive those faces that possess average and symmetrical features. Sexual strategies theory suggests that men and women face different problems when they seek out mates, so they often approach relationships in very different ways.

- Sternberg's triangular theory of love states that all of the different forms of love each consist of different amounts of the three components: intimacy, passion, and commitment. Romantic love, for example, exists when intimacy and passion are present but commitment is absent.

BRINGING IT ALL TOGETHER: MAKING CONNECTIONS IN SOCIAL BEHAVIOR

- The People's Temple was a cult, which is an extremist group led by a charismatic, totalitarian leader who uses coercive methods to prevent members from leaving the group.

- The methods Jim Jones used to ensure his followers' obedience and conformity included persuasion, rigid discipline and punishment of dissent, isolation, separation from family, and forced marital infidelity. Cult members resolved cognitive dissonance brought on by their situation through rationalization, telling themselves that Jones was a great leader with a wonderful message.

Key Terms

aggression
altruism
attitudes
attributions
bystander effect
cognitive dissonance
compassion
conformity
cult
dehumanization
discrimination
empathy

empathy-altruism hypothesis
fundamental attribution error
groupthink
informational social influence
in-group/out-group bias
kin selection
minority social influence
normative social influence
obedience
out-group homogeneity
persuasion
prejudice

prosocial behavior
reciprocal altruism
self-serving bias
sexual strategies theory
social exchange theory
social facilitation
social loafing
social norms
stereotypes
triangular theory of love

Quick Quiz Answers

Quick Quiz 1: 1. c; **2.** d; **3.** a; **4.** c   **Quick Quiz 2: 1.** d; **2.** c; **3.** a; **4.** d; **5.** b
Quick Quiz 3: 1. b; **2.** d; **3.** a   **Quick Quiz 4: 1.** b; **2.** a; **3.** b; **4.** d

15 Psychological Disorders

Chapter Outline

Challenge Your Assumptions

True or False?

- Most people who suffer from mental illness are dangerous. (see page 570)

- Vaccines can cause autism. (see page 574)

- Schizophrenia is a disorder of split personalities. (see page 576).

- What is in your gut can cause depression. (see page 584)

- For some people, technology use is an addiction. (see page 601)

- All the great artists in history can be viewed as psychologically disturbed. (see page 602)

©Cavan Images/Getty Images RF

Langley and Homer Collyer were brothers who lived in a large three-story house in New York City (Frost & Steketee, 2010). In March 1947, police were called because a neighbor reported that one of the brothers had died in the house. The police, however, could not enter through the front door or any other doors or windows on the first floor. All entrances were blocked with household items and appliances—newspapers, boxes, pianos, and car parts, to name but a few examples. When the fire department finally gained entrance on the second and third floors, what they found (after workers spent a total of 3 weeks cleaning out the house) was astonishing: a car, a horse-drawn carriage, 14 grand pianos, a rusted bicycle, even a fake two-headed fetus in formaldehyde. All in all, more than 170 tons (340,000 pounds) of stuff were removed from the house. The entire house was filled from floor to ceiling, and the only way to move around was through tunnels. As it turned out, the booby-trapped boxes the brothers had set up to prevent anyone from coming in had apparently caused Langley's death. Homer, however, was blind and relied on Langley to feed him; and so when Langley died, Homer gradually starved to death. The Collyer brothers were among the first widely publicized compulsive hoarders—people who collect stuff to the point that it interferes with everyday functioning.

Ted Bundy was a handsome, well-educated, and charming man, who also happened to be one of the worst serial killers in U.S. history—murdering between 20 and 100 women, though most likely about 35 (Keppel, 2005; Sullivan, 2009). Between 1974 and 1978, he charmed young female students between the ages of 15 and 25 with a story of being hurt and needing help to carry his books. Once they were in his car, he would often batter them with a baseball bat or crowbar and sometimes have sex with the body.

Artists Vincent van Gogh and Paul Gauguin had an intense argument on December 23, 1888, a Sunday evening in the middle of winter. Over what they argued, we do not know. What we do know is how it ended: van Gogh, in a fit of rage, took a razor and cut off the lower portion of his left ear. He then wrapped the earlobe in a newspaper and gave it to a prostitute named Rachel, telling her to "keep this object carefully" (Runyan, 1981).

That the Collyer brothers, Bundy, and van Gogh each had some kind of disordered behavior is apparent. What is not so easy to agree on, however, is how to define psychological disorder in general and how to specify the concrete criteria for particular disorders. Clearly, these three examples are extreme cases, but behavior varies along a continuum from more to less disordered. In this chapter, we describe many psychological disorders and explain some of what is known about how they develop. As we discuss the causes of these disorders, we will focus on explanations that intertwine the biological with the environmental (Kendler, 2005; Moffitt, Caspi, & Rutter, 2005; Uher & McGuffin, 2010). We will begin by considering what it means for behavior to be disordered and how disorders are diagnosed. At the end of the chapter, we will explore the topic of creativity and psychological disorders and consider whether artists are more likely than the general population to suffer from a psychological disorder.

DEFINING PSYCHOLOGICAL DISORDERS

Creative artists such as Vincent van Gogh are different from most people. So, too, are spelling bee champs, Olympic athletes, and class valedictorians, yet *different* does not mean *disordered*. Does a young child who has more than 5,000 baseball cards and can tell you something about every one of them suffer from a psychological disorder? What about people who wash their hands for 45 minutes 10 times a day? How do psychologists distinguish behavior that is simply different from behavior that is disordered?

Human behavior is complex and highly variable. Certain ways of behaving in the world are shown by more of the population on a regular basis and seem to be well adapted for functioning well in certain environments. These might be behaviors we call *normal*. Less common ways of behaving might be revealed through exceptional talent or might not be well suited for the environment. We might consider these less common behaviors disordered, because they do not function well in the world. It is with this context in mind that we use the term *psychological disorders*.

Over time, understanding of and explanations for psychological disorders have gone through many significant changes. As discussed in the chapter "Introduction to Psychology," the medical model became the prevalent explanation for psychological disorders beginning in the 19th century and has lasted until now. The primary assumption of the medical model is that mental, like physical, illnesses are best diagnosed and treated as medical illnesses. Psychiatry is a branch of medicine, so it is not a coincidence that terms such as *illness*, *diagnosis*, and *therapy* or *treatment* are used in the context of psychological disorders. Borrowing from medicine, in their attempt to understand and treat psychological disorders, psychologists and psychiatrists aim to group them into a smaller set of categories. The classification and diagnosis of psychological disorders is fraught with ambiguity and disagreement. The first attempt to do so in the United States began with the government census of 1840 and simply had one category: "idiocy/insanity" (Greenberg, Shuman, & Meyer, 2004). The first official attempt at diagnosing mental disorders in the United States came in 1952 with the publication of the *Diagnostic and Statistical Manual* (*DSM*). It was not until the third edition in 1980 that diagnoses became grounded in scientific evidence and clinical observations rather than theory. Currently in its fifth edition, the *DSM-5* has continued the tradition of defining disorders based on a combination of scientific evidence and clinical observations (American Psychiatric Association [APA], 2013).

How do psychologists define *mental disorder*? Following a long-standing tradition, the *DSM-5* defines a mental disorder as a **syndrome**—a set of related conditions—of clinically significant disturbances of thoughts, feelings, or behaviors. More specifically, they argue for the "4 Ds" of determining whether something is a mental disorder (APA, 2013). There has to be

disturbance of thought, emotion, or behavior,
dysfunction of biological or developmental processes,
distress or *disability* in everyday life (especially relationships or work), and
deviant thought, emotion, or behavior, but only if also dysfunctional; deviance alone is not enough.

Let's look at each of these a little more closely. Psychological disorders are distinguished by their clinically significant *disturbance* of psychological processes of thought, emotion, and behavior. Mental disorders are distinguished from physical disorders that affect physiological and bodily structures and processes. *Dysfunctional* behavior interferes with everyday functioning, such as

©Art Media/Print Collector/Getty Images

Is the act of cutting one's ear off—as van Gogh did after a violent disagreement with friend and fellow painter Paul Gauguin—necessarily a sign of psychological disorder?

Connection

Early conceptualizations of mental illness blamed demons and spirits. The modern medical model originated in the 1800s in Europe.

See "A Brief History of the Practice of Clinical Psychology" in the chapter "Introduction to Psychology." (p. 11)

syndrome
A group, or cluster of related symptoms that are characteristic of a disorder.

©Mitchell Funk/Getty Images

 Do you think this person has a psychological disorder?

Recall that a behavior must be deviant, distressing to the individual, and dysfunctional to be classified as disordered.

Challenge Your Assumptions

True or False? Most people who suffer from mental illness are dangerous.

False: Most people who suffer from mental illness are not dangerous to others or even themselves.

Connection

Eating disorders—both anorexia and bulimia—and their symptoms are discussed more fully in "Eating Disorders," in the chapter "Motivation and Emotion." (p. 416)

participating in everyday social relationships, holding a regular job, or being productive, and occasionally it can be a risk to oneself or others. *Distressing* behavior leads to discomfort, pain, or anguish, either in the person directly or in others, especially family members. The distressing element is one reason we say a person is "suffering" from a disorder. *Deviant* literally means "different from the norm," or different from what most people do. It is important to point out, as the *DSM-5* does, that deviant behavior can be classified as disordered only if it is also dysfunctional. Albert Einstein was deviant in his intelligence and creativity, but he was not suffering from a psychological disorder. Behaviors that possess only one or even two of these "4 Ds" are not typically classified as disordered. Finally, if a behavior is culturally accepted, it cannot be a disorder, such as hallucinations of shamans in some preliterate cultures.

Most people suffering from psychological disorders do not pose a risk to others, but some do. For instance, people who are sexually attracted to children (pedophiles) and individuals with violent impulse disorder could be a very real danger to others. Others may pose a risk to themselves; for example, people with severe depression are at heightened risk of attempting suicide (APA, 2013).

The *DSM-5* derives from an American perspective of psychological illness. More than previous editions, the *DSM-5* tries to expand beyond the U.S. perspective by aiming to be consistent with international standards for disorder classification and discussing the prevalence rates of certain disorders in different countries. Some disorders are found only in certain cultures. For instance, in some Southeast Asian cultures, certain men suffer from *koro*, the debilitating belief that one's genitals are retracting into one's body. In parts of the Middle East, some people suffer from *zar*—the belief that they are possessed by spirits—and run around in fits of laughter, shouting, and singing (Watters, 2010).

Additionally, some disorders spread from culture to culture (Watters, 2010). For example, in China, anorexia nervosa has been extremely rare; when it was described, the fear of being fat was not a symptom. Sufferers most frequently complained of having bloated stomachs. However, a single widely publicized case of anorexia in 1994 that led to the death of a Hong Kong teenager suddenly made anorexia a much more commonly reported disorder—rates of the disorder had increased dramatically by the late 1990s. Moreover, because the journalists in Hong Kong who were covering the story tended to use the American *DSM* to describe the disorder, with the increase in prevalence also came a change in symptoms. After the publicity surrounding this case, more and more Chinese people with anorexia began to complain mostly of their fear of being fat, not of bloated stomachs. In short, their disorder became more Americanized.

There has always been debate about the best way to approach categorizing psychological disorders. Critics have argued since the 1990s about the somewhat arbitrary designations of the *DSM*, and indeed the *DSM-5* has been met with controversy. Some critics claim the approach of classifying disorders on the basis of shared symptoms, which has long been the *DSM* approach, has resulted in too many categories and may be antiquated (Tavris, 2013). Others have recently argued that the *DSM* ignores biology and that diseases should be classified by shared biological underpinnings (Jabr, 2013). Recent evidence from more than 60,000 people worldwide suggests that five major psychiatric disorders (autism spectrum disorder, attention deficit hyperactivity disorder, bipolar disorder, depression, and schizophrenia) actually have a common genetic cause (Cross-Disorder Group of the Psychiatric Genomics Consortium, 2013). Moreover, recent evidence suggests—as with intelligence—that one general dimension or factor underlies all of the major psychological disorders (Caspi et al., 2014). Such findings imply that mental disorders are not as distinct and different as the *DSM-5* categories would imply.

How common are mental disorders? The answer is that they are surprisingly common (see Figure 1). In a given year, 26% of the U.S. population suffers from a diagnosable disorder. Even though these are nonnormative patterns of behavior, they are not rare. Over the course of an entire lifetime, almost half (46%) of the adults in the United States will suffer from at least one psychological disorder. Similar percentages have been reported in New Zealand and Spain (Moffitt et al., 2010; Serrano-Blanco et al., 2010). In the United States, more than half of those 46% will suffer from two or more disorders (Kessler et al., 2005). The existence of two or more disorders at the same time is called **comorbidity**. Some recent research suggests that fear-based disorders (phobias and panic disorder) may often develop first and predict the onset of other disorders later in life (Kessler et al., 2012).

The *DSM-5* describes 21 major categories of disorder, covering more than 350 distinct disorders. Figure 2 lists the major ones. In this chapter, we examine 10 of the 21 major disorders:

> neurodevelopmental disorders
> schizophrenia
> depressive disorders
> bipolar disorders
> anxiety disorders
> obsessive-compulsive disorder
> posttraumatic stress disorder
> dissociative disorders
> somatic symptom disorders
> personality disorders

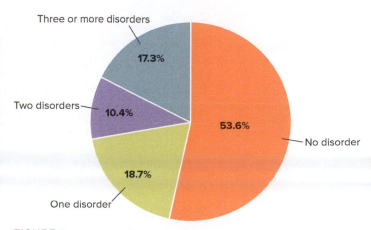

FIGURE 1

PERCENTAGE OF AMERICAN ADULTS WHO WILL EXPERIENCE A PSYCHOLOGICAL DISORDER AT SOME POINT DURING THEIR LIVES. Of the 46% of the population who will suffer a psychological disorder during their lifetime, more than half will suffer from at least two different disorders (Kessler et al., 2005).

Connection

Dementia and Alzheimer's disease are neurocognitive disorders related to age. Other disorders, such as sleep disorders, can occur at any time in a person's life.

See "Late Adulthood," in the chapter "Human Development," (p. 203) and "Disorders of Sleep," in the chapter "Consciousness." (p. 237)

comorbidity
The occurrence of two or more psychological disorders at the same time.

Disorder	Description
Disorders usually first diagnosed in infancy, childhood, or adolescence	Attention deficit hyperactivity disorder; autistic spectrum disorders; learning disorders; conduct and oppositional disorder; separation anxiety disorder; and feeding, tic, and elimination disorders.
Anxiety disorders	Characterized by motor tension, hyperactivity, and apprehensive expectation/thoughts. Include generalized anxiety disorder, panic disorder, phobic disorder, and posttraumatic stress disorder.
Somatic symptom disorders	Occur when psychological symptoms take a physical form even though no physical causes can be found. Include hypochondriasis and conversion disorder.
Factitious disorders	Characterized by the individual's deliberate fabrication of a medical or mental disorder to gain medical attention.
Dissociative disorders	Involve a sudden loss of memory or change of identity.
Delirium, dementia, amnestic, and other cognitive disorders	Disorders involving problems in consciousness and cognition, such as substance-induced delirium or dementia related to Alzheimer's disease.
Mood disorders	Characterized by a primary disturbance in mood; include depressive disorders and bipolar disorder (sometimes called manic depression).
Schizophrenia and other psychotic disorders	Characterized by distorted thoughts and perceptions, odd communication, inappropriate emotion, and other unusual behaviors.
Substance-related disorders	Characterized by abuse or dependence on drugs, such as alcohol, cocaine, and hallucinogens.
Sexual and gender-identity disorders	Consist of three main types of disorders: gender-identity disorders (person is not comfortable with identity as a female or male), paraphilias (person has a preference for unusual sexual acts to stimulate sexual arousal), and sexual dysfunctions (impairments in sexual functioning).
Eating disorders	Include anorexia nervosa and bulimia nervosa (see Chapter 11).
Sleep disorders	Consist of primary sleep disorders, such as insomnia and narcolepsy, and sleep disorders due to a general medical condition, such as sleep apnea (see Chapter 6).
Impulse-control disorders not elsewhere classified	Include kleptomania, pyromania, and compulsive gambling.
Adjustment disorders	Characterized by distressing emotional or behavioral symptoms in response to an identifiable stressor.
Intellectual disability	Low intellectual functioning and an inability to adapt to everyday life (see Chapter 10).
Personality disorders	Develop when personality traits become inflexible and maladaptive.
Other conditions that may be a focus of clinical attention	Include relational problems (with a partner, sibling, and so on), problems related to abuse or neglect (physical abuse of a child, for example), or additional conditions (such as bereavement, academic problems, and religious or spiritual problems).

1. Approximately what percentage of American adults at some point in their life are going to suffer any kind of mental disorder?
   a. 25%
   b. 35%
   c. 45%
   d. 55%

2. Which is the following criteria is NOT part of diagnosis mental disorders?
   a. deviant
   b. dangerous
   c. dysfunctional
   d. disturbing

Answers can be found at the end of the chapter.

NEURODEVELOPMENTAL DISORDERS

Although most clinical diagnoses are reserved for adults (older than 18), a number of disorders are prominent in childhood. The *DSM-5* refers to these as *neurodevelopmental disorders*, which include intellectual disabilities (formerly mental retardation) and learning disabilities. We will discuss two of them: attention deficit hyperactivity disorder (ADHD) and autism spectrum disorder. See Figure 3 for an overview of these two disorders.

Types of Neurodevelopmental Disorders

Jade seldom can work more than a few minutes on any task, whether it is doing homework, reading, or even watching television. At school, she is constantly fidgeting in her chair and blurts out whatever she is thinking. Jade's teacher regularly must ask her to be quiet and stop disrupting others. Her homework

Disorder	Major symptoms	Behaviors
Attention deficit hyperactivity disorder (ADHD)	Inattention	Often fails to give close attention to details or makes careless mistakes, cannot sustain attention, does not listen when spoken to, does not follow through on instructions
	Hyperactivity	Fidgets with hands or feet, leaves seat in classroom when sitting is expected, inappropriate and excessive running or climbing, talks excessively
	Impulsivity	Blurts out answers before question is complete, cannot wait turn, often intrudes or interrupts others
Autism spectrum disorder	Impaired social interaction	Has impaired eye-to-eye gaze and facial expressions, fails to develop peer relationships, lacks sharing interests
	Impaired communication	Has impaired or severely delayed speech; language use is stereotypic or repetitive
	Repetitive and stereotypic behaviors	Shows preoccupation and repetitive interests or behaviors (such as finger or hand flapping), inflexible routines or rituals

FIGURE 3
SYMPTOMS AND BEHAVIORS OF TWO CHILDHOOD DISORDERS. (APA, 2013.)

Challenge Your Assumptions

True or False? Vaccines can cause autism.

False: Not only is there no scientific evidence for this claim, the study on which it was based was fabricated (see "The Nature of Science" in the chapter "Conducting Research in Psychology").

©ZUMA Press/Alamy

People at the high-functioning end of autism spectrum disorder may have independent, productive lives in spite of their social impairments and narrow interests. One such individual is Temple Grandin, who earned a PhD in animal science and became a professor at Colorado State University. A leading animal rights advocate, Grandin has designed humane facilities for livestock and has written and spoken extensively about animal rights.

is full of careless mistakes, even though she usually knows the answers. With these symptoms, psychologists would probably diagnose Jade as suffering from **attention deficit hyperactivity disorder (ADHD)**. To receive the diagnosis of ADHD, the child must have displayed these symptoms before age 12. Between 5% and 10% of American school-age children, 8% of children in the United Kingdom, and 3%–5% of children worldwide meet the diagnostic criteria of ADHD (Alloway, Elliott, & Holmes, 2010; Kessler et al., 2005). Boys are more likely to be diagnosed with ADHD than girls by a ratio of about 2 to 1 (APA, 2013). ADHD begins in childhood, but, for about 30%, the symptoms continue into adulthood (Barbaresi et al., 2013).

Let's consider Antoine, who until age 1 behaved in ways that seemed "normal." At the end of that year, however, subtle signs indicated that his development wasn't typical: He didn't babble or point to objects, he made very little eye contact, and he was hardly speaking at 18 months. When he did speak, he often simply repeated what someone else had said, and later he would say "you" when he meant "I." Moreover, he regularly flapped his hands. Finally, he became very interested in the details and sensory experience of objects. He often would smell and taste toys. Psychologists would diagnose Antoine with **autism spectrum disorder** (**ASD**), formerly known as autism, from *autos*, meaning "self"). Autism spectrum disorder is characterized by severe language and social impairment combined with repetitive habits and inward-focused behaviors.

Evidence suggests that people with autism spectrum disorder are extremely sensitive to sensory stimulation and have trouble integrating multiple sources of sensory information, such as sight, sound, and touch (Iarocci & McDonald, 2006; Reynolds & Lane, 2008). Children with ASD also are more interested in inanimate objects than in people and social activities, and have difficulty with joint attention (Baron-Cohen et al., 2001). **Joint attention** is the ability to make eye contact with others and to look in the same direction as someone else. For example, if a mother points at something she is interested in, a child with ASD is less likely to look in the same direction. Researchers who were not aware of diagnoses and who closely examined eye contact made by children on their first-birthday home videos were able to correctly classify children as having autism spectrum disorder 77% of the time (Osterling & Dawson, 1994). Failure to show evidence of joint attention in early childhood is—or to initiate joint attention with another person—is one of the most reliable behavioral indicators of which children will go on to develop autism (Dawson et al., 2004; Rice, Adamson, Winner, & McGee, 2016). What is more, training programs that enhance children's ability to share attention with others show promise as a treatment for autistic spectrum disorder (Murza, Schwartz, Hahs-Vaughn, & Nye, 2016).

Historically, approximately 5 to 6 children in 1,000 in the United States met the criteria for ASD, but current estimates say that up to 1% of the U.S. population meets the criteria for ASD (APA, 2013). Rates also have increased in other countries, such as Israel (Davidovitch et al., 2013) and India (Mamidala et al., 2013). Some researchers believe the disorder may be overdiagnosed; however, the evidence suggests the rise is mostly due to increased awareness.

Autism encompasses a range of disorders, ranging from severe disability to high functioning. On the high-functioning end of the spectrum, children have impaired social interest and skills and restricted interests, but they may be quite advanced in their speech and have above-average intelligence (APA, 2013). For instance, children on the high-functioning end of the spectrum may engage adults in long-winded and "professorial" discussions on one, rather narrow topic. Because Hans Asperger (1991/1944) first described this type of high-functioning autistic behavior, it became known as Asperger syndrome. The *DSM-5* eliminated Asperger syndrome as a separate diagnostic category, although many people previously diagnosed as such still identify with the term and may call themselves "Aspies."

Causes of Neurodevelopmental Disorders

Neurodevelopmental disorders sometimes stem from genetic factors that may remain latent unless triggered by an environmental condition (Howe, 2010; Larsson, Larsson, & Lichtenstein, 2004). For ADHD, one of the environmental factors is whether the mother smokes while pregnant. However, smoking during pregnancy leads to conduct and impulse problems only if the child has one form of a dopamine gene but not another (Kahn et al., 2003). Neither prenatal smoke exposure alone nor the dopamine genotype alone is significantly associated with increased behavior disorders. One environmental factor, long suspected by many parents to cause ADHD, is excessive sugar consumption (Bussing et al., 2007). Controlled clinical studies, however, do not support a relationship between the amount of sugar consumed and hyperactivity, and this conclusion has held in other countries (Kim & Chang, 2011; Whalen & Henker, 1998).

The causes of autism spectrum disorder are still largely unknown, though a number of factors that increased the risk of autism spectrum disorder have been identified. Low vitamin D levels in utero and early life is more common in children with autism spectrum disorder (Mazahery et al., 2016). Head size is a marker of possible autism spectrum disorder, with a larger head circumference and brain volume in the population of people with autism spectrum disorder than controls (Sacco, Gabriele, & Persico, 2015). In many cases, the brain is smaller than normal at birth but grows much faster during the first few years of life than the brains of nonautistic children (Courchesne, Campbell, & Solso, 2010; Pua, Bowden, & Seal, 2017). The brain of a 5-year-old with autism spectrum disorder is the same size as that of a typical 13-year-old (Blakeslee, 2005). Although we do not yet know which genes are involved, this abnormal rate of brain growth is almost certainly due to genetic influences. In addition, the frontal lobes, where much processing of social information occurs, are less well connected in children with autistic than in nonautistic children (Belmonte et al., 2004). Finally, in children with autism spectrum disorder, the amygdala appears to be larger than in children without the disorder (Bachevalier, 2011; Mosconi et al., 2009; Pua et al., 2017). Differences in amygdala function between people with autism spectrum disorder and those without may be connected to socio-emotional effects of autism (Herrington, Miller, Pandey, & Schultz, 2016).

One theory about the origins of autism spectrum disorder is based on the mirror neurons (Ramachandran & Oberman, 2006; Wadsworth et al., 2016). As we saw in earlier chapters, mirror neurons fire both when a person performs a particular behavior (such as reaching for an object) and when he or she simply watches someone else performing the same behavior. Mirror neurons are thought to be involved in many, if not most, social behaviors, such as observational learning, imitation, and even language learning. Because children with ASD are deficient in these skills, neuroscientists have predicted that mirror neurons malfunction in ASD children; research results show that this is indeed the case (Ramachandran & Oberman, 2006).

Connection

Despite having extensive media attention, research shows conclusively that there is no evidence that vaccines cause autism.

See "The Nature of Science," in the chapter "Conducting Research in Psychology." (p. 37)

Quick Quiz 2: Neurodevelopmental Disorders

1. Jolo is a 5-year-old boy who does not speak, waves his arms around a lot, does not make eye contact, and does not seem to connect with other kids or adults. Jolo may have which disorder?
   a. autistic spectrum disorder
   b. ADHD
   c. childhood depression
   d. theory of mind

2. Kelly fidgets a lot, blurts out what she is thinking, and makes many careless mistakes in her homework, even when she knows the answers. Kelly most likely would be diagnosed with which childhood disorder?
   a. low IQ
   b. autistic spectrum disorder
   c. anxiety disorder
   d. ADHD

Answers can be found at the end of the chapter.

Challenge Your Assumptions

True or False? Schizophrenia is a disorder of split personalities.

False: Schizophrenia and split personality (multiple personality, now known as dissociative disorder) are very different disorders.

positive symptoms (of schizophrenia)
The perceptual experiences associated with schizophrenia, including hallucinations, delusional thinking, and disorganized thought and speech.

hallucinations
Convincing sensory experiences that occur in the absence of an external stimulus.

FIGURE 4
INABILITY TO PERCEIVE FRAGMENTS IN SCHIZOPHRENIA. Perceiving fragments as parts of a whole can be difficult for people with schizophrenia. When normal subjects view fractured images like these in sequence, they identify the object quickly, but individuals with schizophrenia often cannot make that leap swiftly (Javitt & Coyle, 2004).

©Ingram Publishing/Alamy RF

SCHIZOPHRENIA

Some disorders result primarily from disturbances of thought and perception; as a group, these are known as the **psychotic disorders**. They are characterized by an inability to distinguish real from imagined perceptions. One very serious psychotic disorder is **schizophrenia**, which involves profound disturbances in thought and emotion—in particular, impairments in perception, such as hallucinations. Emil Kraepelin, who coined the term *schizophrenia* (literally "split mind") in the 1890s, viewed the disorder as a split from reality, not a split attitude or split personality, as is sometimes mistakenly assumed. According to the National Institute of Mental Health (NIMH, 2007), approximately 1% of the American population is afflicted with this disorder at any given time, making schizophrenia much less common than depression. Genetically, however, if a first-degree relative (a biological parent, sibling, or child) has the disorder, the odds of a person having the disorder rise to 10% (NIMH, 2007).

Major Symptoms of Schizophrenia

For a diagnosis of schizophrenia, at least two of the following symptoms must persist for 1 month. Moreover, at least one of these symptoms must come from the first three (delusions, hallucinations, or disorganized speech; APA, 2013):

- Delusions
- Hallucinations
- Disorganized speech
- Grossly disorganized behavior or catatonic behavior (immobile and unresponsive, though awake)
- Negative symptoms (such as not speaking or being unable to experience emotion)

The symptoms of schizophrenia fall into three major categories: positive, negative, and cognitive. Note that "positive" and "negative" in this context do not mean "good" and "bad" but rather the "presence" and "absence" of behaviors. The bizarre perceptual experiences associated with schizophrenia are known as **positive symptoms**. These include hallucinations, delusional thinking, and disorganized thought and speech. Typically, perception is poorly integrated as well. Look, for instance, at the pictures of watches in Figure 4. People with schizophrenia have trouble putting the fragmented image together and perceiving it as a watch.

Hallucinations are convincing sensory experiences that occur in the absence of an external stimulus. Auditory hallucinations are the most common type of hallucination in schizophrenia, typically taking the form of hearing voices inside one's head in the absence of external auditory stimulation. The following account from a person with schizophrenia describes an auditory hallucination:

> Recently my mind has played tricks on me, creating The People inside my head who sometimes come out to haunt me and torment me. They surround me in rooms, hide behind trees and under the snow outside. They taunt me and scream at me and devise plans to break my spirit. The voices come and go, but The People are always there, always real. ("I Feel I Am Trapped," 1986)

People with schizophrenia experience such voices as real and are convinced that someone is living inside their heads. This is a defining feature of psychosis (Nolen-Hoeksema, 2007). Similar to but distinct from hallucinations,

delusions are false beliefs, often exaggerated claims, that a person holds in spite of evidence to the contrary, such as the idea that one is Jesus Christ.

Other patients experience less flamboyant, but no less disabling, symptoms that are characterized by an absence of what would be considered appropriate behavior. These **negative symptoms** include nonresponsiveness, emotional flatness, immobility or the striking of strange poses (catatonia), reduction of speaking, and inability to complete tasks. Traditionally, negative symptoms have been harder to diagnose and treat than positive symptoms.

People with schizophrenia show **cognitive symptoms**, including problems with working memory, attention, verbal and visual learning and memory, reasoning and problem solving, speed of processing, and disordered speech (Barch, 2005). For example, the speech of a person with schizophrenia often follows grammatical rules, but the content makes little sense. Such utterances are referred to as **word salad**. Similarly, patients sometimes make up new words. In the following example, a woman who believed she was the only female professor at the "University of Smithsonian" (no such place) in England uses new words to produce a word salad.

> I am here from a foreign university . . . and you have to have a "plausity" of all acts of amendment to go through for the children's code . . . and it is no mental disturbance or "putenance." . . . It is an "amorition" law. . . . It is like their "privatilinia" and the children have to have this "accentuative" law so they don't go into the "mortite" law of the church. (Vetter, 1968, p. 306)

Origins of Schizophrenia

Schizophrenia offers a perfect, though tragic, illustration of the dynamic interplay between biology and experience in the development of a psychological disorder. Historically, this explanation has been called the **diathesis-stress model**. *Diathesis* is the Greek word for "predisposition," so the diathesis-stress view is that biological predispositions plus stress or abusive environments together produce psychological disorders. Some researchers describe the diathesis-stress interaction between biological dispositions and environmental forces as a two-stage model (Kandel, 2000a; Lewis & Levitt, 2002). Stage one is the biological-genetic foundation, or disposition, and stage two is an environmental event that occurs at some point after conception, such as maternal infection, chronic stress, or certain drug use (such as marijuana or amphetamines) at particular critical points in development (Fergusson, Horwood, & Ridder, 2005).

Although genetic factors play an important role in the development of schizophrenia, they do not make it inevitable. The heritability rates are 70%–85%, suggesting that the disorder is due largely to genetic influences (Cardno & Gottesman, 2000; Gebicke-Haerter, 2012; Harrison & Owen, 2003; Kandel, 2000a; Lewis & Levitt, 2002; Vyas et al., 2010). Scientists have identified as many as 19 genes that contribute to schizophrenia, but the mechanisms they regulate have only recently been understood by neuroscientists (Harrison & Owen, 2003; Harrison & Weinberger, 2005; Mei & Xiong, 2008; Stefansson et al., 2009). The fact that one identical twin can develop schizophrenia, whereas the other genetically identical twin may not develop it, indicates that genes alone do not cause schizophrenia. Instead, genes can be epigenetically turned on or off by environmental experiences during brain development to produce the disorder (Gebicke-Haerter, 2012; Grossman et al., 2003; Moffitt et al., 2005; Petronis, 2004). Recent research has reported up to 100 genes related to schizophrenia with epigenetic tags (methyl-groups; Gebicke-Haerter, 2012).

The more abuse and neglect (adverse experiences) children experience in their early home lives, the more likely they are to suffer from schizophrenia later (Edwards et al., 2003; Whitfield et al., 2005). Adverse experiences in the form of abuse and neglect often happen during the critical periods of brain growth and

delusions
One of the symptoms of schizophrenia: false beliefs or exaggerations held despite evidence to the contrary, such as the idea that one is a famous person.

negative symptoms (of schizophrenia)
Symptoms that include nonresponsiveness, emotional flatness, immobility, catatonia, problems with speech, and inability to complete tasks.

cognitive symptoms (of schizophrenia)
Problems with working memory, attention, verbal and visual learning and memory, reasoning and problem solving, processing, and speech.

word salad
The speech of people with schizophrenia, which may follow grammatical rules but be nonsensical in terms of content.

diathesis-stress model
An explanation for the origin of psychological disorders as a combination of biological predispositions (diathesis) plus stress or an abusive environment.

FIGURE 5

These MRI images show the brain of a typically developing 3-year-old child who has had a normal amount of cognitive, social, and linguistic stimulation (left) and that of a 3-year-old child who was deprived of regular social, linguistic, tactile, or cognitive stimulation (right). Growth is clearly stunted in the child who suffered from extreme neglect. Additionally, the dark, butterfly-shaped structures (ventricles) are much larger in the child who suffered from extreme neglect. Enlarged ventricles are common in people with schizophrenia (Perry, 2002).

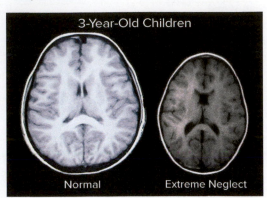

3-Year-Old Children

Normal   Extreme Neglect

©Muammer Mujdat Uzel/Getty Images RF

development (see Figure 5; Perry, 2002). In the child who suffered extreme neglect, notice the much smaller overall brain size as well as the enlarged ventricles (butterfly shapes) in the middle of the brain. These features are two of the major brain abnormalities characteristic of schizophrenia. One of the oldest findings on the brain and schizophrenia is the tendency of people with schizophrenia to have enlarged ventricles (the fluid-filled spaces in the brain; Lieberman et al., 2001).

Although we may not yet know their causes or how exactly they interact with environmental forces, certain biological and brain abnormalities are hallmarks of schizophrenia. In this section, we will consider some of the better-known ones: maternal infection, dysfunctional prefrontal and hippocampus activity, enlarged ventricles, an excess of dopamine activity in the basal ganglia, and a deficiency in the neurotransmitter glutamate.

Maternal Infections and Schizophrenia As first discussed in the chapter "The Biology of Behavior," during fetal development, neural growth can occur at a rate of 250,000 new neurons per minute and peak at approximately *3 million* per minute (Purves & Lichtman, 1985)! Consequently, what happens to both the mother and the fetus is crucial; any kind of disease or toxic substance experienced by the mother may dramatically affect neural growth in the fetus. If a woman contracts an infection during pregnancy, the risk of the child's developing schizophrenia later in life increases dramatically (Boska, 2008; Brown, 2006; Koenig, 2006; Moreno et al., 2011). Prenatal exposure to infections and diseases such as influenza, rubella, toxoplasmosis, and herpes has been linked to increased risk of schizophrenia (Buka et al., 2001; Nielsen, Meyer, & Mortensen, 2016) and deficits in brain development (Moreno et al., 2011; Short et al., 2010). The effect appears not to exist, however, during the first and second trimesters of pregnancy (months 1–6; Selten et al., 2010).

Infection as a risk factor for schizophrenia extended beyond the fetal environment. Using medical records of over 1 million people in Denmark, researchers analyzed the relationship between infection (of any kind) and schizophrenia and found a high degree of overlap between these two disorders (Nielsen, Meyer, & Mortensen, 2016). Men with schizophrenia who have the blood infection of toxoplasmosis experience more severe symptoms than schizophrenic men who do not have taxoplasmosis (Esshili et al., 2016).

Schizophrenia and the Brain Abnormal brain development before birth may be responsible for many of the brain dysfunctions that are characteristic of schizophrenia (Lewis & Levitt, 2002). One mechanism by which maternal infections, for instance, may increase the risk of schizophrenia is by affecting the path neurons take when they migrate during fetal brain growth (Kandel, 2000a; Koenig, 2006). One of the most widely recognized brain abnormalities is a dysfunctional prefrontal cortex and its working memory; in people with schizophrenia, there is evidence of both reduced and excessive activity in that area (Andreasen et al., 1997; Barch, 2005; Goldman-Rakic, 1999; Weinberger et al., 2001; Vyas et al., 2010). Moreover, the genes in the prefrontal cortex that regulate how synapses function are dysfunctional in people with schizophrenia compared to those without the disease (Mirnics et al., 2000). Often the hippocampus is smaller in people with schizophrenia compared to those without the disorder (Barch, 2005; Harrison, 2004). See Figure 6 for an overview of these and other areas of the brain affected by schizophrenia.

Brain problems in schizophrenia may not be simply a function of abnormalities in certain structures but may also stem from problems in the communications among groups of neurons. In people without schizophrenia, neural networks are

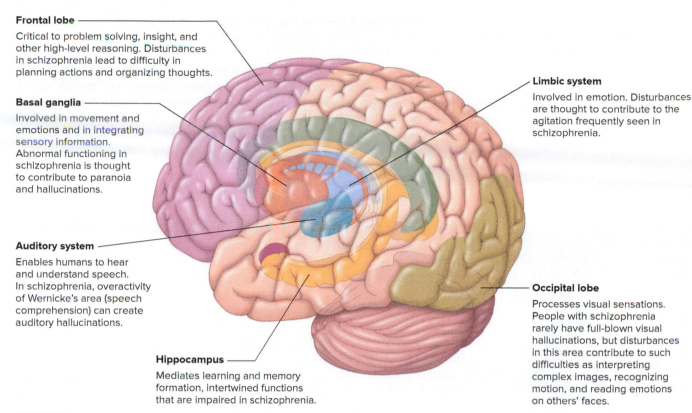

Frontal lobe

Critical to problem solving, insight, and other high-level reasoning. Disturbances in schizophrenia lead to difficulty in planning actions and organizing thoughts.

Basal ganglia

Involved in movement and emotions and in integrating sensory information. Abnormal functioning in schizophrenia is thought to contribute to paranoia and hallucinations.

Auditory system

Enables humans to hear and understand speech. In schizophrenia, overactivity of Wernicke's area (speech comprehension) can create auditory hallucinations.

Hippocampus

Mediates learning and memory formation, intertwined functions that are impaired in schizophrenia.

Limbic system

Involved in emotion. Disturbances are thought to contribute to the agitation frequently seen in schizophrenia.

Occipital lobe

Processes visual sensations. People with schizophrenia rarely have full-blown visual hallucinations, but disturbances in this area contribute to such difficulties as interpreting complex images, recognizing motion, and reading emotions on others' faces.

FIGURE 6

AREAS OF THE BRAIN IMPAIRED BY SCHIZOPHRENIA. The structures highlighted here do not function normally in people with schizophrenia. Limbic system structures not shown here are the hypothalamus, amygdala, and cingulate gyrus (Javitt & Coyle, 2004).

efficiently clustered in close groups and move in and out of orderly and chaotic patterns of firing (Bassett et al., 2008). This process is essential for learning and memory. In people with schizophrenia, however, these networks are less clustered, less efficient, and more disorderly, especially in the frontal lobes (Bassett et al., 2008).

A new area of research as to the neural basis of schizophrenia concerns the developmental process of pruning. As was explained in the chapter "Human Development," pruning is the process by which synapses that are not used or reinforced by experience are selectively eliminated in the process of the early brain development and adolescence. Genetic studies indicate that people who have a gene that is tagged for excessive pruning are more likely to develop schizophrenia (Sekar et al., 2016). This finding might shed light on why there are reduced brain tissue in the prefrontal cortex in people with schizophrenia, as well explain some of the symptoms—too much pruning of brain tissue in areas needed for problem solving and emotion regulation (Ohtani et al., 2014).

One of the most obvious and difficult positive symptom of schizophrenia is hallucinations. What is going on in the brain during a hallucination? Brain imaging studies show that hallucinations activate the brain in ways similar, but not identical, to real external stimulation (Shergill et al., 2000; Shergill et al., 2003; Silbersweig et al., 1995). For example, activity in the auditory cortex of the temporal lobe and the visual cortex of the occipital lobe during visual and auditory hallucinations shows striking similarities to the kind of brain activity that occurs when visual and auditory stimuli are present. The part of the brain involved in interpreting and comprehending speech (Wernicke's area of the left hemisphere) is also activated during hallucinations (Stephane, Barton, & Boutros, 2001). Also noteworthy, however, is the lack of activity in the frontal lobes during the

Connection

During fetal development, the brain is extremely vulnerable to many different kinds of toxins.

See "Nature and Nurture Influences on Fetal Development," in the chapter "Human Development." (p. 169)

hallucination, which suggests that the person is unable to monitor and determine the source of the images or sounds (Shergill et al., 2003).

Neurochemistry of Schizophrenia   For decades, the prevailing view on the neurochemistry of schizophrenia was the *dopamine hypothesis*, which states that people with schizophrenia have an excess of dopamine activity in certain areas of the brain (Javitt & Coyle, 2004; Kegeles et al., 2010). The dopamine hypothesis was based on two findings. First, Nobel laureate Arvid Carlsson discovered that amphetamines stimulate dopamine release and therefore may mimic the hallucinations and delusions of schizophrenia (Javitt & Coyle, 2004). Second, early antipsychotic drugs that block dopamine receptors were somewhat effective at treating positive symptoms.

Challenging Assumptions in the Discovery of Dopamine   Before 1952, no one knew that dopamine is a neurotransmitter. The belief at the time was that dopamine was merely a precursor of epinephrine (Yeragani et al., 2010). Moreover, most scientists were convinced that dopamine had no role to play in brain function (Carlsson, 1987). We now know, partly due to Arvid Carlsson's discoveries, that dopamine not only is involved in controlling our muscle movement and with the basic feelings of reward and pleasure but also is one of the main neurotransmitters involved in the development of schizophrenia.

However, nearly 10 years after Carlsson's groundbreaking work on dopamine, many neuroscientists could not accept that it is a neurotransmitter, because they still believed neurotransmitters had to be electrical rather than chemical (Iversen & Iversen, 2007). Although the first drug treatments for schizophrenia were discovered by others, Carlsson's work helped support the view that schizophrenia is at least partly caused by excessive amounts of dopamine in the brain—a view now known as the dopamine hypothesis (Iversen & Iversen, 2007). Due to the central role that dopamine plays in schizophrenia, Parkinson's disease, and even ADHD, it is fair to say that the field of psychopharmacology would not be the same today without the early pioneering work of Arvid Carlsson.

©Pressens Bild/Henrik Montgomery/AP Photo

Arvid Carlsson

There are, however, some problems with the dopamine hypothesis and schizophrenia. As we discuss in more detail in the next chapter, dopamine-specific medications (major tranquilizers) effectively treat only positive symptoms and even then are not entirely effective. In addition, only a minority of the people who receive the traditional drug treatment find it effective in managing their symptoms (Javitt & Coyle, 2004). When researchers became aware that another set of recreational drugs led to schizophrenia-like symptoms that did not directly involve dopamine, they turned their attention to these drugs. These drugs, PCP ("angel dust") and ketamine (an animal anesthetic, used recreationally as "Vit K" or "Special K"), do not affect dopamine production; instead, they impair the functioning of a different neurotransmitter, glutamate, and one of its receptors, NMDA. Glutamate is a major excitatory neurotransmitter that regulates the release of dopamine. PCP and ketamine block the action of glutamate, thus producing the same kinds of disturbances seen in schizophrenia (Harrison & Owen, 2003; Moghaddam, 2003). Glutamate deficiencies, then, may also explain many of the symptoms of schizophrenia (Javitt & Coyle, 2004). A gene related to glutamate plays a role in prefrontal cortex functioning in schizophrenics (Fallgatter et al., 2010).

These findings stimulated researchers to explore the role of glutamate in schizophrenia more fully. Not only is it crucial in learning, memory, neural processing, and brain development, but it also amplifies certain neural signals, making some stimuli more important than others (Goff & Coyle, 2001; Javitt & Coyle, 2004; Mayer, 2004). This process is crucial to selective attention; that is, focusing attention on some items of information while ignoring others. Thus, dysfunction in glutamate action would explain why people with schizophrenia have trouble with selective attention, cognitive control, and working memory. In fact, brain imaging studies now reveal higher concentrations of glutamate in areas of the brains of people with schizophrenia that are crucial to attention and memory (Gallinat et al., 2016). One emerging view is that schizophrenia involves both dopamine and glutamate abnormalities (Howes, McCutcheon & Stone, 2015; Laruelle, 2014).

Quick Quiz 3: Schizophrenia

1. Which of the following is a negative symptom of schizophrenia?
   a. hallucinations
   b. delusions of grandeur
   c. catatonia
   d. fatigue

2. The heritability rate for schizophrenia is roughly
   a. 100%.
   b. 60%.
   c. 80%.
   d. 25%.

3. Low levels of which neurotransmitter might explain why people with schizophrenia have trouble with selective attention, cognitive control, and working memory?
   a. acetylcholine
   b. glutamate
   c. norepinephrine
   d. GABA

Answers can be found at the end of the chapter.

DEPRESSIVE DISORDERS

If schizophrenia and other psychotic disorders are expressions of thought and perceptual disturbances, then bipolar disorder and depression are expressions of disturbance in mood and emotion. The depressive disorders, bipolar disorders, and anxiety disorder are marked especially by disturbances in emotional behavior that prevent people from functioning effectively in everyday life.

We all feel blue from time to time. Feeling sad after being rejected by a lover or failing an exam presents a normal response to life challenges, as does getting into a funk after a series of hard breaks. Yet being unable to leave your bed for days or failing to eat from a profound sense of despair or disinterest in doing anything—often without direct provocation—is something different altogether, and it may reflect an underlying disorder in psychological health.

According to the *DSM-5*, there are several forms of **depressive disorder**. What most people refer to as "depression" is formally called **major depressive disorder**, a chronic condition characterized by enduring changes in mood, motivation, and sense of self-worth. According to *DSM-5*, to be diagnosed with major depressive disorder, one must have at least five of nine symptoms associated with major depression, which must continue for at least 2 consecutive weeks (APA, 2013):

1. Depressed (sad, listless) mood that stays low all day for several days
2. Reduced interest or pleasure in doing anything
3. Significant change in body weight (indicating dieting or overeating)
4. Sleep disturbances
5. Sluggishness or restlessness
6. Daily fatigue or loss of energy
7. Daily feelings of worthlessness, self-reproach, or excessive guilt
8. Lack of ability to concentrate or think clearly
9. Recurrent thoughts of death or suicidal ideation

Most importantly, symptoms must significantly impact daily functioning, in terms of both social and work-related contexts, and they must be a source of distress, in order to be the basis for a diagnosis of major depressive disorder. Overall, approximately 7% of the American population has major depressive disorder, but the occurrence varies depending on age and sex. The disorder is three times more

depressive disorder
The highest order category of the depressive disorders and subsumes all forms of depression, including major depressive disorder and persistent depressive disorder.

major depressive disorder
A mood disorder characterized by pervasive low mood, lack of motivation, low energy, and feelings of worthlessness and guilt that last for at least 2 consecutive weeks.

likely in 18- to 29-year-olds than in 60+-year-olds. Females experience depression up to two or three times as often as males (teen and up; APA, 2013; Neitzke, 2016).

persistent depressive disorder (PDD)

Previously known as *dysthymia* and involves same symptoms as major depression but at less severe levels.

Other forms of depressive disorder have milder symptoms but last longer. One of these milder forms is **persistent depressive disorder (PDD**, previously called *dysthymia*). Most of the symptoms are the same as in a major depressive disorder, but they are less intense in PDD, though the depressive mood lasts most of the day and most of the time for at least 2 years.

Depression manifests itself differently in different people, but only rarely is it only about feeling blue. Although sadness is the emotion most associated with depression, many find the lack of interest in or ability to *feel* anything (positive or negative) to be the most disabling aspect of living with depression. The Pulitzer Prize–winning novelist William Styron, who went through a major depressive episode in his 60s, offered a poignant account of the experience in his book *Darkness Visible*. For Styron, as for many seriously depressed people, the feelings of despair reached a point at which ending his life seemed to be the only guaranteed source of relief:

> I had not as yet chosen the mode of my departure, but I knew that that step would come next, and soon, as inescapable as nightfall. . . . Late one bitterly cold night, when I knew that I could not possibly get myself through the following day, I sat in the living room of the house bundled up against the chill. . . . I had forced myself to watch the tape of a movie. . . . At one point in the film . . . came a contralto voice, a sudden soaring passage from the Brahms *Alto Rhapsody*.
>
> This sound, which like all music—indeed, like all pleasure— I had been numbly unresponsive to for months, pierced my heart like a dagger, and in a flood of swift recollection I thought of all the joys the house had known; the children who had rushed through its rooms, the festivals, the love and work, the honestly earned slumber, the voices and the nimble commotion. . . . All this I realized was more

©Daniel Grizelj/Getty Images

 What factors and symptoms are needed before everyday blues turn into a diagnosis of major depressive disorder?

than I could ever abandon. . . . I drew upon some last gleam of sanity to perceive the terrifying dimensions of the mortal predicament I had fallen into. I woke up my wife and soon telephone calls were made. The next day I was admitted to the hospital. (1990, pp. 63–67)

The kind of unbearable hopelessness we see in Styron's comments may be one reason that people with depression are at a higher risk of committing suicide than others. Indeed, suicide is a major risk for people with depression, and suicidal thinking is included as a symptom of depression (APA, 2013; Hawton et al., 2013). In fact, having depressive disorder is considered a risk factor for suicide in adolescents and adults (Shain, 2016).

Origins of Depression

Depression is sometimes caused by a stressful or traumatic life event, such as physical or sexual abuse, but not always. For some people, depression just happens, like turning on or off a light switch, and is traceable to biochemical factors. Still others develop depression from a combination of neurochemistry and life circumstance—the diathesis-stress model again (Bukh et al., 2009).

One kind of enduring stress that may play a causal role in depression is a sense of inability to control the circumstances in one's life—especially the aversive ones. When people have numerous stressful experiences over which they feel no control, they eventually give up. **Learned helplessness** is the sense of failure that results from repeated inability to control or escape from overwhelmingly stressful situations. It has been studied extensively in both animal and human models as a model of depression (Maier & Seligman, 2016). In the classic experiments on learned helplessness, an animal is placed in a cage with a metal floor that may deliver a shock. If the animal is repeatedly shocked no matter what it does to try to escape, it will eventually give up (Seligman, 1972). This is called learned helplessness, because the animal eventually learns that no matter what it does to try to escape, it does not make a difference. This giving up in the face of repeated adversity has offered a powerful behavioral model of depression that is consistent with the relationship of extreme stress to the incidence of depression.

Experiencing extreme stress in childhood increases one's risk for depression later in life. Survey researchers studying adverse experiences found that people who reported the most adverse childhood experiences were more likely to be depressed than people who reported no adverse childhood experiences (Anda et al., 2006; Pietrek et al., 2013; Wang et al., 2010), a relationship that holds among European Americans, African Americans, Hispanics, and Asian Americans (Llabre et al., 2017; Youssef et al., 2017). The effects of childhood trauma have lasting impact. A study of hundreds of women and their children and causes of depression reported that women with more adverse childhood experiences were more likely to have postpartum depression, more likely to have a child with a psychological disorder, and likely to have babies with impaired socioemotional skills (McDonnell & Valentino, 2016). Psychological resilience—or the ability to manage and recover from stress well—can reduce the likelihood of depression in people who have experienced severe stress and adverse childhood experiences (Llabre et al., 2017).

Trauma is a unique kind of overwhelming stress that can lead to depression as well as a number of other psychological disorders. Experience in a wartime setting is a well-known trauma, with many consequences for mental health. Nearly 400 female combat veterans completed a large-scale survey on their experiences

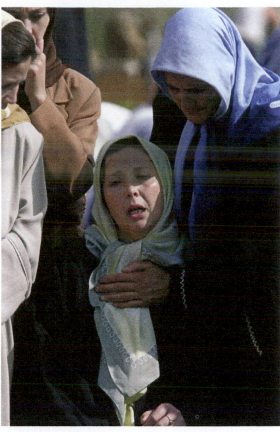

©Philippe Desmazes/AFP/Getty Images

Stressful life events, such as the death of a loved one, can trigger a major depressive episode in people who have a genetic predisposition for depression.

learned helplessness
The sense of powerlessness that arises from the repeated inability to control or escape from stressful situations.

in military combat settings and also answered questions on a number of psychological symptoms. Women reported on their experiences with killing, witnessing killing, feeling in danger, and sexual assault, among other situations. Having experiences any of these was correlated with posttraumatic stress disorder, but experience of sexual assault was the *only* variable that predicted whether a woman was experiencing symptoms of depression (Goldstein et al., 2017).

Many factors have been identified as biological causes and markers of depression. Depression is heritable—data indicate that about 40% of people carry genes that increase their likelihood of developing depressive disorder, which can be triggered by stress—genes related to serotonin transport seen particularly important for depression (Haberstick et al., 2016). Numerous studies point to deficiencies in serotonin in depression, which is why many treatments target serotonergic synapses.

The biology of depression may be observable even at the sub-cellular level. The mitochondria are structures inside cells (in this case, inside neurons) that play a key role in cell metabolism. Several studies report findings of mitochondrial dysfunction in specific brain tissues linked with the occurrence of depression and other psychological disorders, but it is not clear if this is a cause or an effect of the disease (Devaraju & Zakharenko, 2017; Tobe, 2013).

The effects of stressful environments appear to interact with particular biological dispositions and personality traits to produce depression, especially in people who have experienced severe stress, trauma, and abuse (Clark, 2005; Hankin, 2010; Krueger, 1999; Slavich et al., 2010; Uher & McGuffin, 2010). People who are deficient in the neurotransmitters serotonin and neuropeptide Y (NPY) are most susceptible to depression after experiencing extremely stressful situations (Lowry et al., 2008; Morales-Medina, Dumont, & Quirion, 2010; Risch et al., 2009). A meta-analysis of 34 studies found support for an interaction between differences in serotonin genes, adverse experiences, and the development of depression (Uher & McGuffin, 2010). One of the 34 studies in this meta-analysis provides a nice example of the research into the nature-nurture origins of depression; see the "Research Process" for more details (Figure 7). Also, the personality traits of anxiety, neuroticism, and negative emotionality, for instance, are most associated with vulnerability to depression.

In animals, experimental-induced stress kills neurons in the hippocampus, which can lead to symptoms of depression (Jacobs, 2004; Jacobs, van Praag, & Gage, 2000; Kendler, Karkowski, & Prescott, 1999). In humans, stressful events, especially social rejection, start a host of biological reactions, including activating the hypothalamic-pituitary-adrenal (HPA) system, which increases the likelihood of developing depression (Slavich et al., 2010). Indeed, recent evidence suggests that stress is associated with accelerated aging of cells, which in turn is associated with depression (Kiecolt-Glaser & Wilson, 2016; Wolkowitz et al., 2010).

You may recall from the chapter "Stress and Health," the role of the gut-brain axis in health. In recent years, connections have been drawn between intestinal microorganisms (the gut microbiome) and health problems, such as allergies and obesity. There is an intricate balance among these intestinal microbiomes in our bodies, and the state of the balance is both affected by our moods and can affect our moods. If the balance gets upset by diet, illness, or stress, then problems can occur (Martinez, Leone, & Chang, 2017; Mayer et al., 2014). The microbiome of the gut also appears to play a role in autistic spectrum disorder and other psychological disorders (Blázquez & Berin, 2017; Ley et al., 2006; Mulle, Sharp, & Cubells, 2013). As it turns out, these microorganisms in the gut can release substances that affect the immune system and the central nervous system, including depression (Evrensel & Ceylan, 2015). Gut microbes can release serotonin and GABA—two neurotransmitters that have been implicated in depression and other psychological disorders (Barrett et al., 2012; Foster & McVey Neufeld, 2013; Haberstick et al., 2016; Lerner et al., 2016; Mayer et al., 2014).

Challenge Your Assumptions

True or False? What is in your gut can cause depression.

True: The balance of the countless microorganisms in your gut plays an important role in not only immune response but also in long-term emotional states such as depression and anxiety.

Research Process

Research Question

How do genetic and environmental differences interact to affect the development of depression?

Method

Avshalom Caspi and colleagues followed a group of nearly 1,000 people from age 3 until age 26 (Caspi, Sugden, et al., 2003). The investigators measured life events experienced by the participants at different ages. They obtained data on the presence of long and short forms of the serotonin gene in the participants' genotypes. One form (allele) comes from each parent.

Results

They found that people who had inherited two short forms (s/s) of the serotonin gene were more likely to exhibit depressive symptoms following stressful life events than were those who had inherited the long form (l/l). For example, in the graph shown here, we see that if people experience a few major stressful events (no more than two), their risk of having a major depressive episode does not

©hartphotography/Shutterstock.com

increase, regardless of which form of the serotonin gene they carry. But if they experience three or four stressful events, the likelihood that they will have a major depressive episode nearly doubles or triples in those with the short form compared to those with the long form.

Conclusion

Depression is most likely in individuals who carry the short form of the gene *and* experience many severe life stressors. Neither condition by itself is likely to lead to depression.

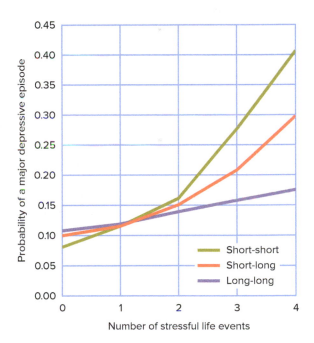

FIGURE 7

GENE-ENVIRONMENT INTERACTION IN THE DEVELOPMENT OF DEPRESSION. Individuals with at least one short allele of the serotonin gene are more likely to experience depression than those with two long alleles. Those with two short forms of the gene are most vulnerable to depression if they experience at least three stressful life events. (Source: "Influence of life stress on depression: Moderation by a polymorphism in the 5-HTT gene," by A. Caspi, K. Sugden, T. E. Moffitt, A. Taylor, I. W. Craig, H. Harrington, . . . Poulton, R., 2003, *Science*, *301*, 386–389.)

BIPOLAR DISORDER

bipolar disorder
A mood disorder characterized by substantial mood fluctuations, cycling between very low (depressive) and very high (manic) moods.

manic episodes
One mood cycle in bipolar disorder, typically involving increased energy, sleeplessness, euphoria, irritability, delusions of grandeur, increased sex drive, and "racing" thoughts that last at least 1 week.

hypomanic episodes
Symptoms of mania (e.g., increased energy, euphoria, racing thoughts) but that are less severe.

People who suffer from **bipolar disorder** experience severe mood fluctuations, cycling between very low (major depressive) and very high (manic or hypomanic) episodes. (At one time, this disorder was called manic depression.) **Manic episodes** typically involve increased energy, sleeplessness, euphoria, irritability, delusions of grandeur, increased sex drive, and "racing" thoughts that last *at least 1 week*. **Hypomanic episodes** are nearly the same symptoms but shorter in duration—they last *at least 4 days* (**APA, 2013**). A useful mnemonic for remembering the symptoms of mania is D-I-G-F-A-S-T (Carlat, 1998):

D = Distractibility
I = Indiscretion
G = Grandiosity
F = Flight of ideas
A = Activity increased
S = Sleep (decreased need for)
T = Talkativeness

The *DSM-5* distinguishes between two kinds of bipolar disorder, depending on the severity of the mania (APA, 2013). Bipolar I is more severe because it involves meeting the criteria for mania (at least 7 days), whereas bipolar II is less severe because it involves meeting the criteria for hypomania (at least 4 days). Recall that *hypo* means "below," so hypomania is not as severe as mania. Thus, the degree of depression is the same in bipolar I and II, but the mania is less severe in bipolar II than in I.

People with either form of bipolar disorder often find the initial onset of the manic phase pleasant, especially compared to the dullness and despair of the depressive phase. Unfortunately, the symptoms quickly become quite unpleasant and frightening. The manic upswing spirals out of control, often leading to frenetic activity, excessive energy, and grandiose thinking, in which sufferers think they have relationships with important people or expertise in areas where they have none. Indiscretion occurs when a person says things that are somewhat inappropriate or gets involved in promiscuous sexual relationships. Figure 8 lists the characteristics and symptoms of depression and bipolar disorder.

Virginia Woolf, the groundbreaking early-20th-century writer, suffered from bipolar disorder. She dealt with bouts of severe depression and frenetic

	Major symptoms	Behaviors
major depressive disorder	Low mood, lack of motivation, low energy, feelings of worthlessness and guilt that last for at least two weeks	Change in eating behavior, intense anxiety or sadness, feeling of being disconnected, and/or inability to take pleasure in enjoyable experiences
bipolar disorder	Extreme swings in mood between depressive and manic episodes	Manic episodes characterized by distractibility, increased activity, euphoria, grandiosity, decreased need for sleep, talkativeness, flight of ideas, and indiscretion

FIGURE 8

MAJOR SYMPTOMS AND BEHAVIORS OF DEPRESSIVE DISORDERS AND BIPOLAR DISORDER. (APA, 2013)

mania, which ultimately led to her suicide in 1941. Virginia's husband, the writer Leonard Woolf, offered revealing descriptions of her condition while manic:

> She talked almost without stopping for two or three days, paying no attention to anyone in the room or anything said to her. For about a day when she was coherent, the sentences meant something, though it was nearly all wildly insane. Then gradually it became completely incoherent, a mere jumble of dissociated words. (quoted in Jamison, 1993, p. 29)

In an even milder but longer-lasting form of bipolar disorder called **cyclothymia**, both the manic and the depressive episodes are less severe than they are in bipolar II disorder—that is, the hypomanic and depressive symptoms never reach the criteria for hypomania and major depression.

cyclothymia
A relatively mild form of bipolar disorder.

Causes of Bipolar Disorder

What causes bipolar disorder? As is true for other psychological disorders, multiple biological and environmental factors appear to interact in ways scientists are only now beginning to understand. The dynamic relationship between the environment and the brain in bipolar disorder may be seen as early as prenatal development. Fetuses exposed to large amounts of alcohol may suffer permanent effects, including increased risks for bipolar disorder as well as depression, schizophrenia, alcoholism, intellectual disability, and drug abuse (Famy, Streissguth, & Unis, 1998; O'Conner & Paley, 2006).

FIGURE 9

THE BIPOLAR BRAIN. PET scan images show the brain of someone with bipolar disorder over the course of 10 days. Blue and green indicate low levels of brain activity, and red and yellow indicate high levels of brain activity. The top and bottom images show the low activity of depression, whereas the middle images show an increased level of brain activity during mania. Note how quickly this person cycled in and then out of the manic phase (10 days).

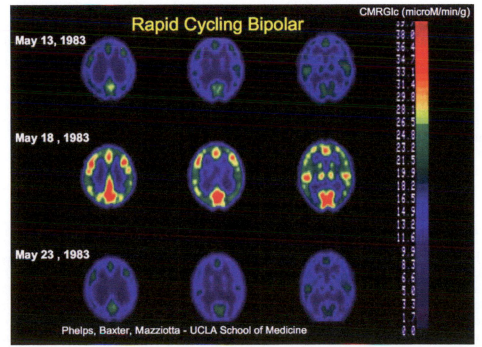

Courtesy of Drs. Phelps, Baxter, Mazziotta, UCLA School of Medicine

The genetics of bipolar disorder are complex. Many variations of genes appear to play a role in the development of the disorder, the specifics of which are only beginning to be understood (Comer, 2007; Luykx et al., 2010; Shastry, 2005). Twin studies also point to a role for genetics in bipolar disorder. If one identical twin develops bipolar disorder, there is a 40%–70% chance that the other twin will also develop the disorder (Müller-Oerlinghausen, Berghöfer, & Bauer, 2002; Shastry, 2005). Even if the chance is 70% that both twins will have the disorder, life events, such as stress and trauma, also play a role in the development of bipolar disorder (Müller-Oerlinghausen et al., 2002; Shastry, 2005).

Abnormalities in the brains of people who suffer from bipolar disorder may be a cause or a result of the biochemical, genetic, and environmental elements that contribute to the disorder. The prefrontal cortex, amygdala, hippocampus, and basal ganglia all may play a role (Müller-Oerlinghausen et al., 2002; Shastry, 2005). Overactivity in many of these regions is evident in the PET scan images displayed in Figure 9, showing up as red areas compared to the blue regions that indicate depressed mood. There may also be problems in the connectivity among the key regions involved in emotional processing, such as the prefrontal cortex and amygdala (Chepenik et al., 2010).

Neurochemistry is also important in bipolar disorder. In both the manic and depressed phases, serotonin levels are low, but low serotonin may be coupled with high levels of norepinephrine in the manic phase and with low levels in the depressed phase (Comer, 2007; Müller-Oerlinghausen et al., 2002). In addition, thyroid hormones, which control metabolism, are sometimes present in either abnormally high or low levels in people with bipolar disorder (Bauer & Whybrow, 2001; Müller-Oerlinghausen et al., 2002).

Quick Quiz 4: Depressive Disorders and Bipolar Disorder

1. Latresha is not hungry, is extremely tired, and doesn't feel like doing much of anything. She often feels that life is just hopeless. These symptoms have been going on for 2 months now. She probably is suffering from which mood disorder?
   a. generalized anxiety disorder
   b. bipolar disorder
   c. major depressive disorder
   d. obsessive-compulsive disorder

2. David went home for Christmas break and found that his mother, who was usually depressed, had just purchased dozens of birdhouses from a local gift store. She'd had each custom-wrapped and was planning to give them to all the extended members of the family and all her neighbors, whom she claimed to love like family. She had spent thousands of dollars. What might be going on with David's mom?
   a. She had won the lottery.
   b. She has bipolar disorder.
   c. She has an overactive hypothalamus.
   d. She is just depressed.

3. Which neurotransmitter is reduced in both the manic and the depressive phases of bipolar disorder?
   a. acetylcholine
   b. dopamine
   c. norepinephrine
   d. serotonin

Answers can be found at the end of the chapter.

ANXIETY DISORDERS

Fear and anxiety are normal reactions to danger or future threat. These emotions create bodily changes—such as increases in heart rate—that support useful responses to danger. For some, however, fear and anxiety can get out of hand, occurring repeatedly in response to imagined threat and sometimes persisting for days. For about 26% of the U.S. population, though, anxious states can interfere with everyday functioning (Kessler et al., 2012). In this section we discuss five of the more common forms of anxiety disorders (see Figure 10).

FIGURE 10
MAJOR SYMPTOMS AND CRITERIA OF SPECIFIC ANXIETY DISORDERS.

Disorder	Major symptoms	Behaviors
Generalized anxiety disorder (GAD)	Pervasive/excessive anxiety lasting at least 6 months	Inability to relax
Panic disorder	Persistent worry about having a panic attack	*Panic attack:* Heart palpitations, trembling, dizziness, intense dread, and fear of dying *Panic disorder:* Prone to panic attacks, concerned about having a panic attack and about embarrassment of having a panic attack
Agoraphobia	Fear of not being able to escape or of help not being available if panic attack should occur in public place	Unwilling to leave home so as to avoid panic attacks
Social phobia	Persistent fear of humiliation in the presence of others	Highly anxious, extremely self-conscious about appearance or behavior or both, possibly housebound
Specific phobias	Undue anxiety response to particular objects or situations	Intense fear or panic when confronted with particular situations or objects or even when thinking about them

 What overarching symptom do all of these disorders share?

Generalized Anxiety Disorder

Generalized anxiety disorder (GAD) is a common anxiety disorder, characterized by a pervasive, excessive, hard-to-control state of anxiety or worry that lasts at least 6 months (APA, 2013). People with GAD may also have trouble with sleep, body restlessness or agitation, difficulty concentrating, or muscle tension. Adults must exhibit at least three of the preceding symptoms to receive a diagnosis of GAD (APA, 2013). GAD affects between 3% and 9% of the U.S. population, although females are twice as likely as males to have GAD (APA, 2013). It is also more common in the United States in people of European descent than in those of non-European descent.

Unlike those suffering from other anxiety disorders, people with GAD often have been anxious throughout their lives and cannot recall when they began to feel that way (Barlow, 2004). In everyday language, we might call such people "worrywarts"—those who worry about anything and everything, often out of proportion to the actual threat. The writer, director, and actor Woody Allen has made a career out of his pervasive tendency to worry. Allen says he uses filmmaking and writing as a creative distraction from his pervasive anxiety (Briggs, 2005). The constant anxiety of GAD can be debilitating, however, preventing many people who suffer from it from being able to work at all.

generalized anxiety disorder (GAD)
A state of pervasive and excessive anxiety lasting at least 6 months.

Panic Disorder

The core of panic disorder is the panic attack. **Panic attacks** involve sudden changes in body and mind, characterized by an overwhelming sense of impending doom, heart palpitations, trembling, sweating, shortness of breath, dizziness, intense dread, nausea, and even a fear of dying. Such attacks are associated with perceptions of threat and can occur for a number of reasons: fear of danger, an inability to escape, fear of embarrassment, or fear of a specific category of objects. Panic attacks usually last about 10 minutes but sometimes come and go over a

panic attacks
An anxiety disorder; associated with perceptions of threat and occurring because of fear of danger, inability to escape, embarrassment, or specific objects, for example.

period of an hour or more. Due to their physiological effects, people undergoing a panic attack may believe they are having a heart attack or are "going crazy."

Panic disorder is defined by frequent panic attacks and pervasive and persistent fear, worry, embarrassment, and concern about having future panic attacks (APA, 2013). The preoccupation with and anxiety over having another attack create an anxious mood, which then increases the likelihood of more worrisome thoughts and, ironically, another attack. Thus, panic disorder creates a positive feedback cycle, wherein anxiety about future attacks hijacks the body's emergency response system and catapults it out of control. To receive a diagnosis of panic disorder, a panic attack must be followed by at least a month of persistent worry over future attacks, along with the development of potentially maladaptive behaviors to avoid attacks (e.g., avoidance of putting oneself in unfamiliar situations).

People who have only occasional panic attacks without intense anxiety or fear about the possibility of future panic attacks do not qualify for the diagnosis of panic disorder. Although about 10% of the U.S. population has experienced a panic attack in the past 12 months (Grant et al., 2006), only about 2%–3% of the population has panic disorder (APA, 2013). In the United States, panic disorder is more common in women than men and less common in older adults. Overall, in Asian, African, and Latin American countries, the rates are very low—less than 1%—and the specific concerns or persistent worries appear to vary by culture (APA, 2013).

Social Phobia (Social Anxiety Disorder)

A **phobia** is a persistent and unreasonable fear of a particular object, situation, or activity (APA, 2013). Some people suffer extreme anxiety when they have to interact with other people, viewing each interaction as a possible opportunity to be scrutinized by others. **Social phobia**, or **social anxiety disorder**, is marked by a pronounced fear of humiliation or embarrassment in the presence of others or severe self-consciousness about one's appearance, behavior, or both. Consider the case of Sarah, who hates going to the grocery store: She would not dare ask anyone working there how to find an item, out of fear that she might look stupid for not being able to find it herself. She doesn't want anyone to know she is anxious about being in the store. She is concerned that her voice might quiver when forced to say the obligatory "hello" to the cashier. This would make her seem really foolish, and everybody would stare at her foolishness.

Fear like Sarah's can be paralyzing, making it very difficult to go out into public situations, even though in most cases the person recognizes that these fears are irrational. Unfortunately, the high degree of anxious arousal produced by social phobia may lead the person to act very nervously and thus, in a self-fulfilling way, exhibit behaviors that do attract other people's attention.

Agoraphobia

Agoraphobia is the most severe of all phobias (Bouton, Mineka, & Barlow, 2001). Contrary to popular belief, the primary "fear" in agoraphobia is not of being out in public. Formally, **agoraphobia** is intense anxiety, fear, and panic about being in places from which escape might be difficult or in which help might not be available, should a panic attack occur, such as in open spaces, in a public market, in line somewhere,

panic disorder
An anxiety disorder characterized by panic attacks and persistent anxiety about having more attacks.

phobia
An anxiety disorder: an ongoing and irrational fear of a particular object, situation, or activity.

social phobia (social anxiety disorder)
An anxiety disorder: fear of humiliation in the presence of others, characterized by intense self-consciousness about appearance or behavior or both.

agoraphobia
An anxiety disorder involving fear of being in places from which escape might be difficult or in which help might not be available, should a panic attack occur.

©Juice Images/Getty Images RF

People with social phobia are extremely self-conscious and fearful of embarrassing themselves in front of others.

outside of the home alone, or in enclosed spaces (e.g., movie theaters; APA, 2013). This fear of being unable to escape keeps people at home, where they feel safe. Panic attacks are associated with agoraphobia in about one-third of all cases.

Specific Phobias

Only a few of us enjoy spiders, snakes, or heights, but most of us feel only mild levels of anxiety about such objects or experiences. Some of us, however, go beyond mild levels of fear. In the United States, up to 9% of the population has a *specific phobia* for a particular object or situation, such as spiders (arachnophobia), heights, flying, enclosed spaces (claustrophobia), doctors and dentists, or snakes (APA, 2013). Specific phobias are marked by an intense and immediate fear, even panic, when confronted with very particular situations or objects; even thinking about those situations or objects may set off the fear reaction. People with specific phobias are not generally anxious people, but they will do almost anything to avoid coming in contact with the feared object or experiencing the feared event or object. Megan Fox, Britney Spears, and Jennifer Aniston all fear flying. Aniston, for instance, feels compelled to perform the same ritual each time she boards a plane (*Jennifer Aniston talks*, 2009), a "good luck" superstition in the face of her fear:

> If I walk onto an airplane, I always have to go on with my right foot first and tap the outside of the plane. I have always done it. For luck. Someone told me to do it and I don't remember when that was. But it's kind of stuck.

©Kathy Hutchins/Shutterstock.com

Actress Jennifer Aniston has spoken publicly about her fear of flying and the ritual she performs before each flight.

Origins of Anxiety Disorders

How do anxiety disorders develop? Like all animals, humans have evolved fear mechanisms to determine whether a situation is safe and whether we need to try to fight or flee (LeDoux, 2000). Additionally, as is true for most complex traits, some people are more genetically disposed to anxiety than others. Anxiety disorders—and most other psychological disorders—result from the interplay between biological and environmental factors. Instead of offering either biological or social theories of disorders, we present integrated nature-nurture (diathesis-stress) explanations.

Three biological factors that make people vulnerable to anxiety disorders are deficiencies in the neurotransmitter GABA, their genetic heritage, and their personalities. Researchers have discovered that people who are prone to anxiety are deficient in receptors for GABA, a major inhibitory neurotransmitter (Charney, 2004; Nikolaus et al., 2010). Deficiencies in GABA lead to excessive activation in certain brain regions, especially the limbic structures associated with fear. Moreover, the fact that major medications for treating anxiety disorders work on GABA receptors is further evidence for GABA's role in anxiety. Genetic heritability estimates for generalized anxiety, panic disorder, and agoraphobia range from 30%–40% (Hettema, Neale, & Kendler, 2001; Maron, Hettema, & Shlik, 2010).

As for personality, people who are high in neuroticism—prone to worry, anxiety, and nervousness—are more likely to develop anxiety disorders (Eysenck, 1982; Hamer & Copeland, 1998). Degree of extraversion may play a role in some anxiety disorders as well. For instance, in panic disorder, people who are more introverted are more likely than those who are extraverted to avoid putting themselves in public situations (Rosellini et al., 2010).

An ambitious study that is changing the way psychologists view the interaction between biology and environment in the development of psychological disorders, including anxiety disorders, is the Adverse Childhood Experiences (ACE) study. For the ACE study, more than 17,000 participants have been interviewed about eight "adverse childhood experiences," including abuse, domestic violence, and serious household dysfunction (meaning that someone in the household abused drugs, had a psychological disorder, or committed criminal acts). Researchers correlated the adverse childhood experiences with health and mental health outcomes in adulthood.

The results were dramatic. The more adverse childhood experience participants reported, the worse the psychological outcomes. For example, someone who reported four or more adverse childhood experiences was two and a half times as likely to suffer from anxiety disorder as someone who reported no adverse childhood experiences (Anda et al., 2006). Perry (2002) found that when children were removed from neglectful home environments at age 1 or 2 and placed in caring foster homes, the size of their brains increased dramatically. If they were removed from the neglectful environment after age 4, however, there was little increase in brain size (circumference). If they were removed after age 5, there was almost no increase (see Figure 11). Generally, for a child's brain size to be anywhere near normal, the child needs regular environmental stimulation by about age 4.

In summary, people who have the bad luck of having a genetic predisposition to anxiety, low levels of GABA, or the personality trait of neuroticism *along with* the experience of chronic stress or abuse are most likely to develop anxiety disorders. Those who have the biological predispositions *or* experience abuse are next most likely to develop these disorders, whereas those who have *neither* biological vulnerability nor chronically stressful experiences are least likely to develop these disorders.

FIGURE 11

EFFECTS OF NEGLECT AND REMOVAL FROM NEGLECTFUL ENVIRONMENTS ON CHILDREN'S BRAIN SIZE. Percentile of head circumference means the percentage of people in the population who have heads that are a particular size or smaller. Thus, 30th percentile means that only 30% of people have that size or smaller. The younger the child is when he or she is removed from a neglectful home, the larger the brain/head size is after 1 year in a nurturing foster home (Perry, 2002).

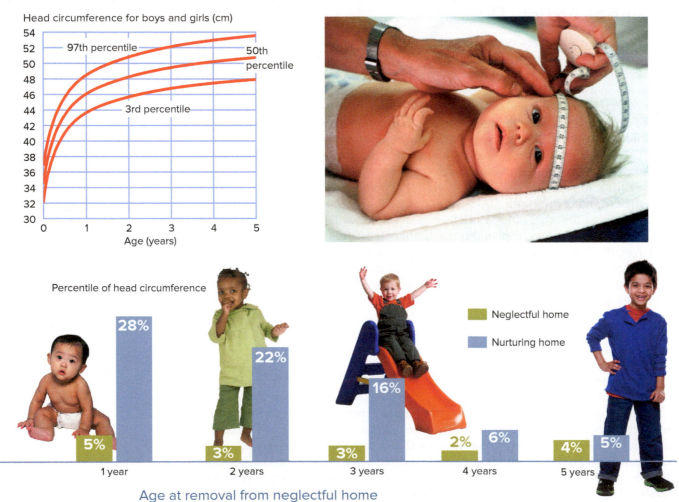

1. The occurrence of two or more disorders at the same time is known as
   a. bipolar disorder.
   b. comorbidity.
   c. dipolarity.
   d. syndrome.

2. Maya is so preoccupied with fears of embarrassing or humiliating herself in public that she avoids going shopping or out for walks in town. What disorder best describes this set of symptoms?
   a. generalized anxiety disorder
   b. specific phobia

   c. panic disorder
   d. social phobia

3. People who are prone to anxiety are deficient in receptors for _____, a major inhibitory neurotransmitter.
   a. GABA
   b. glutamate
   c. serotonin
   d. dopamine

Answers can be found at the end of the chapter.

OBSESSIVE-COMPULSIVE DISORDER

Obsessive-compulsive disorder (OCD) is a disorder that is manifested in both thought and behavior. An **obsession** is an unwanted thought, word, phrase, or image that persistently and repeatedly comes into a person's mind and causes distress. People with OCD have thoughts that they cannot dismiss, especially negative thoughts that most people can disregard (APA, 2013). A **compulsion** is a repetitive behavior performed in response to uncontrollable urges or according to a ritualistic set of rules. In short, obsessions are thought disturbances, whereas compulsions are repetitive behaviors.

Obsessive-compulsive disorder most often involves cleaning, checking, or counting behaviors that interfere with everyday functioning. A man who is obsessed with security might check that the front door is locked 15 or 20 times before being able to drive away; a woman who is obsessed with germs might wash her hands dozens or even hundreds of times throughout the day.

People who suffer from OCD often know that their thoughts are irrational, or at least that their compulsive behaviors are excessive, but they cannot stop themselves. In some cases, compulsive behaviors stem from superstitions. For example, a man might feel the need to tap the wall 65 times before leaving a room for fear that not doing so will mean that his parents will die. He knows rationally that there is no connection between wall tapping and the death of one's parents, but he performs the ritual nevertheless. The 12-month prevalence rate of OCD in the United States is 1.2%, and internationally it is between 1.1% and 1.8% (APA, 2013).

In OCD, too many thoughts are held in awareness, too much importance is ascribed to all thoughts (rational or irrational), and thinking about one's thoughts is excessive (Janeck et al., 2003). Research on cognitive performance in people with OCD reveals a preoccupation with conscious thinking; it is hard for people with this disorder to keep certain ideas or information out of their awareness.

obsessive-compulsive disorder (OCD)
An anxiety disorder in which obsessive thoughts lead to compulsive behaviors.

obsession
An unwanted thought, word, phrase, or image that persistently and repeatedly comes into a person's mind and causes distress.

compulsion
A repetitive behavior performed in response to uncontrollable urges or according to a ritualistic set of rules.

Causes of Obsessive-Compulsive Disorder

Some scientists argue that the brain circuit that connects the caudate, the anterior cingulate cortex (ACC), and the limbic structures (such as the amygdala and hypothalamus) is working overtime in OCD (Aouizerate et al., 2004; Schwartz, 1999a, 1999b). The overactive ACC creates a perpetual feeling that something is wrong, which the limbic system structures translate into anxiety. In turn, anxiety stimulates more intrusive thoughts, which sometimes become compulsive actions. These actions occur as behavioral responses aimed at reducing the tensions or anxiety generated by the situation (from the caudate nucleus). Relief may be experienced, but only briefly, before the anxiety returns. The cycle goes on endlessly, due to the hyperactivity of the brain circuit—which is stuck in the "on" position. So this circuit involving the ACC, caudate nucleus, and limbic structures supports the obsessive thinking and compulsive responding (Fitzgerald et al., 2005; Guehl et al., 2008).

A 2017 study with mice reports a potentially promising new underlying cause of OCD (Ullrich et al., 2017). When researchers manipulated a protein known as SPRED2 in the brains of mice, making it not function properly, the mice behaved in an OCD-like way with excessive and compulsive grooming rituals. This suggests that SPRED2 acts to inhibit compulsive behaviors. This is new research, however, and has not yet been replicated or examined in humans so further confirmation is needed before we can be sure it is a cause of OCD.

As with schizophrenia, infection is a risk factors for OCD. OCD is more common in people who have been infected with toxoplasmosis (Flegr & Horáček, 2016). Another culprit is streptococcal infection (as in "strep throat"), which increases the risk of OCD as well as other psychological disorders according large-scale, population-based studies (Mell, Davis, & Owens, 20005; Singer et al., 2015). Once again, the co-occurrence of various types of infections and the occurrence of a psychological disorder points to a role of the immune system—the system that is control of response to infection—may play a role in brain changes underlying the development of certain psychological problems (Breen et al., 2015).

Quick Quiz 6: Obsessive-Compulsive Disorder

1. Rebecca has to count to seven chews every time she eats. If she is interrupted or loses count, she has to start all over again. This is an example of a(n)
   a. compulsion.
   b. obsession.
   c. anxiety.
   d. panic attack.

2. Joshua is constantly worried about getting sick from the germs everywhere he goes. He can't help but think about the germs, the germs, the germs. This is an example of a(n)
   a. compulsion.
   b. obsession.
   c. anxiety.
   d. panic attack.

Answers can be found at the end of the chapter.

POSTTRAUMATIC STRESS DISORDER

posttraumatic stress disorder (PTSD)

A type of trauma- and stressor-related disorder that involves intrusive and persistent cognitive, emotional, and physiological symptoms triggered by catastrophic or horrifying events.

Posttraumatic stress disorder (PTSD) is one of the trauma- and stressor-related disorders and involves a set of intrusive and persistent cognitive, emotional, and physiological symptoms triggered by exposure to a catastrophic or horrifying event—such as experiences of war, attempted murder, rape, natural disasters, the sudden death of a loved one, or physical or sexual abuse. In order to receive a diagnosis of PTSD, one must have directly experienced a traumatic event or witnessed such an event occurring to others, learned of a violent or accidental extreme trauma (e.g., death or sexual violence) occurring to a loved one, and/or repeatedly been exposed to or reminded of the details of such an event (APA, 2013). People suffering from PTSD experience a number of intrusive symptoms that last for at least 1 month. These may include recurring intrusive thoughts, feelings, or memories of the traumatic event, either while awake or dreaming, as well as *flashbacks*, vivid reactions in which the person feels as if he or she were experiencing the traumatic event all over again. There may be avoidance of situations or stimuli that might trigger the recollection of the event, as well as a number of persistent cognitive symptoms, such as a distorted view of oneself and self-blame associated with the trauma, as well as persistent emotional and physiological reactivity. For instance, people with PTSD are easily startled, may have hair-trigger tempers, and may be reckless or self-destructive.

War veterans are at increased risk not only for PTSD but also for depression, drug abuse, and suicide after returning home. The depth of despair in war-induced PTSD is seen in the following suicide note from an Iraq war veteran who took his own life in June 2013: "All day, every day a screaming agony in every nerve ending in my body. It is nothing short of torture. My mind is a wasteland, filled with visions of incredible horror, unceasing depression, and crippling anxiety" (Cook, 2013). Upwards of 24% of the veterans from Iraq have developed PTSD (Renshaw, 2011; Roehr, 2007; Tanielian & Jaycox, 2008). In fact, the hypothalamic-pituitary axis (HPA), a major neuroendocrine system of the stress response (see Chapter 12), may be dysfunctional in war veterans with PTSD (Golier, Caramanica, & Yehuda, 2012). In fact, an inability to recover from or quiet an hypothalamic-pituitary axis excitation is a key feature of PTSD (Daskalakis et al., 2016).

People of all ages can experience posttraumatic stress symptoms, including children who have experienced a serious trauma, such as extreme physical or sexual abuse (APA, 2013; Nixon et al., 2010). Compared to healthy controls, children with posttraumatic stress symptoms show reduced brain activity in the hippocampus while performing a verbal memory task (Carrion et al., 2010). The hippocampus plays a central role in learning and memory, so these results suggest that posttraumatic stress interferes with learning.

DISSOCIATIVE DISORDERS

Daydreaming and being caught up in a great novel or movie are common, everyday experiences in which we may lose our sense of time, space, and ourselves. **Dissociative disorders** magnify this effect: They produce extreme disruptions or gaps in memory, identity, or consciousness. These disorders lack a clear physical cause, such as brain injury, and often stem from extreme stress, trauma, or abusive experiences, especially during childhood. Although dissociative disorders are often associated with trauma, the *DSM-5* places them in their own category. We focus on the most dramatic dissociative disorder: dissociative identity disorder.

dissociative disorders
Psychological disorders characterized by extreme splits or gaps in memory, identity, or consciousness.

Dissociative Identity Disorder

People with **dissociative identity disorder (DID)** develop at least two distinct personalities, each with a unique set of memories, behaviors, thoughts, and emotions. Consider the case of Eric, 29, who was found wandering around a shopping mall in Daytona Beach, Florida:

> Eric began talking to doctors in two voices: the infantile rhythms of "young Eric," a dim and frightened child, and the measured tones of "older Eric," who told a tale of terror and child abuse. According to "older Eric," after his immigrant German parents died, a harsh stepfather and his mistress took Eric from his native South Carolina to a drug dealer's hideout in a Florida swamp. Eric said he was raped by several gang members and watched his stepfather murder two men. (quoted in Comer, 2007, p. 208)

dissociative identity disorder (DID)
A dissociative disorder in which a person develops at least two distinct personalities, each with its own memories, thoughts, behaviors, and emotions; some psychiatrists question the legitimacy of the disorder.

Eric had 27 distinct personalities, 3 of whom were female. Among these personalities were Dwight, a middle-aged and quiet man; Michael, an arrogant jock; Phillip, an argumentative lawyer; and Jeffrey, a blind, mute, and rather hysterical man.

Eric is a classic example of what used to be called "multiple personality disorder" but is now referred to as dissociative identity disorder. The symptoms of dissociative identity disorder include two or more distinct personality states, amnesia, and self-destructive behaviors. People with dissociative identity disorder may not remember anything about an experience or a particular period of their life and may cut themselves. Up to 70% have attempted suicide. Also somewhat common are fugue states, in which people do not recall anything about how they got to where they are. For instance, they might end up at a beach or nightclub or at home but have no memory of how they came to be there.

Although it may not be diagnosed until adolescence, DID often develops in childhood but may develop at any period of life (APA, 2013; Comer, 2007). Although the sample size was relatively small, one study found that only about 1.5% of people had the disorder during the last 12-month period prior to the survey (APA, 2013). A history of sexual or physical abuse is very common. In another study, more than 90% of people with DID reported being either sexually or physically abused (Ellason, Ross, & Fuchs, 1996).

However, the diagnosis of DID is somewhat controversial, with some psychiatrists claiming the diagnosis is not real but rather is produced unintentionally by therapists themselves (Putnam & McHugh, 2005). Further, there is a lack of solid research on the causes of the disorder. According to a recent review of a decade's worth of published cases of DID, the causes are still not well understood and are controversial, and actual occurrence rates are hard to identify (Boysen & VanBergen, 2013; Brand, Loewenstein, & Speigel, 2013).

Causes of Dissociative Disorders

People who suffer from dissociative disorders have one characteristic in common: They lived through a highly traumatic experience. Many suffered sexual or physical abuse or survived a terrible accident or natural disaster in which a loved one was killed. Most explanations of dissociative disorders view them as a coping strategy gone awry (Putnam, 2006). The experience was so traumatic that the individual disconnects or dissociates the self from the event as a way of having it happen not to "him" or "her" but rather to "someone else." However, not everyone who experiences traumatic events develops a dissociative disorder. Also, some researchers and clinicians argue that DID results from a complex interaction of social–cognitive factors, including problems with attention and memory, disruptions in the sleep-wake cycle, and exposure to trauma or intense stress (Lynn et al., 2012). Other theorists argue that particular personality traits, such as susceptibility to hypnotism, make some people more likely to develop dissociative disorders (Kihlstrom, 2005).

SOMATIC SYMPTOM DISORDERS

somatic symptom disorder
A psychological disorder in which a person complains of multiple physical disorders that cause disruption and that persist for at least 6 months.

Some disorders take bodily or physical form and mimic physical diseases. The general term for these disorders is **somatic symptom disorders**. As you may recall from our discussion of the neuron, *soma* means "body"; hence, the term *somatic* means "bodily." An older term for bodily disorders—hypochondriasis—has now been divided into two related but distinct disorders: somatic symptom disorder and illness anxiety disorder.

Somatic symptom disorder occurs when a person complains of multiple physical disorders that cause distress and disruption of the person's life and that persist for at least 6 months. This disorder has the following two main criteria (APA, 2013):

- One or more distressing somatic symptoms that disrupt daily life
- Excessive thoughts, feelings, or behaviors related to bodily symptoms

Somatic symptom disorder occurs in 5%–7% of the U.S. adult population (APA, 2013).

illness anxiety disorder
Preoccupation with and anxiety about acquiring a serious illness for at least 6 months.

Some people have just the fear of the somatic symptoms and therefore would be diagnosed with **illness anxiety disorder**, *DSM-5* says illness preoccupation must be present for at least 6 months. A person with this disorder will also frequently and excessively check for the symptoms.

With the Internet and easy access to medical information, more and more people are self-diagnosing without evidence of real symptoms and without professional evaluations. People who self-diagnose primarily from information found on the Internet are informally referred to as *cyberchondriacs* (White & Horvitz, 2009).

Quick Quiz 7: PTSD, Dissociative Disorders, and Somatic Symptom Disorders

1. What is one of the most serious and common mental disorders suffered by war veterans?
   a. dissociative disorder
   b. somatic symptom disorder
   c. posttraumatic stress disorder
   d. schizophrenia

2. Which of the following physiological structure is NOT one affected in post-traumatic stress disorder?
   a. parietal lobe
   b. hippocampus
   c. pituitary
   d. hypothalamus

3. _____ produce extreme splits or gaps in memory, identity, or consciousness.

   a. Dissociative disorders
   b. Bipolar disorders
   c. Mood disorders
   d. Cognitive disorders

4. The primary difference between somatic symptom disorder and illness anxiety disorder is
   a. illness anxiety disorder has only somatic symptoms.
   b. illness anxiety disorder does not have somatic symptoms.
   c. only somatic symptom disorder involves persistent concern about bodily symptoms.
   d. only somatic symptom disorder involves anxiety.

Answers can be found at the end of the chapter.

PERSONALITY DISORDERS

As we saw in the chapter "Personality: The Uniqueness of the Individual," personality consists of an individual's unique, long-term behavior patterns. **Personality disorders** are maladaptive and inflexible patterns of cognition, emotion, and behavior that generally develop in late childhood or adolescence and continue into adulthood. There are three distinct clusters of personality disorders: odd-eccentric, dramatic-emotional, and anxious-fearful (see Figure 12). Almost 15% of the general adult population (older than 18) and 20% of the young adult population (ages 18–25) suffer from some form of personality disorder (APA, 2013; Blanco et al., 2008; Lenzenweger et al., 2007).

personality disorders
Patterns of cognition, emotion, and behavior that develop in late childhood or adolescence and are maladaptive and inflexible; they are more stable than clinical disorders.

Odd-Eccentric Personality Disorders

The three major odd-eccentric personality disorders are schizoid, schizotypal, and paranoid (APA, 2013). People with **schizoid personality disorder** do not want close relationships; are emotionally aloof, reclusive, and humorless; and want to live solitary lives. They always choose solitary activities; have little to no interest in sex; lack any close friends; and appear indifferent to praise or criticism from others. Similarly, a person with **schizotypal personality disorder** is isolated and asocial but in addition has very odd thoughts, perceptual distortions, and beliefs. For instance, people with schizotypal personality disorder may believe that stories on TV or in the newspaper were written directly about them. Moreover, the person dresses, acts, and appears in peculiar or eccentric ways. In terms of the symptoms people experience, schizotypal personality disorder seems like a higher functioning version of schizophrenia as well as a personality disorder (Chemerinski et al., 2013).

People with **paranoid personality disorder** are extremely suspicious and mistrustful of other people, in ways that are both unwarranted and not adaptive. They may often test the loyalty of their friends and lovers because they

schizoid personality disorder
An odd-eccentric personality disorder characterized by a desire to avoid close relationships as well as by emotional aloofness, reclusivity, and a lack of humor.

schizotypal personality disorder
An odd-eccentric personality disorder characterized by a desire to live an isolated and asocial life, but also by the presence of odd thoughts and beliefs.

paranoid personality disorder
An odd-eccentric personality disorder characterized by extreme suspicions and mistrust of others in unwarranted and maladaptive ways.

Cluster	Major symptoms	Personality disorders
Odd-eccentric	Lack of interest in social relationships, inappropriate or flat emotion, thought, and coldness	Schizoid
	Isolated, odd, and bizarre thoughts and beliefs	Schizotypal
	Extreme, unwarranted, and maladaptive suspicion	Paranoid
Dramatic-emotional	Wild, exaggerated behaviors, extreme need for attention, suicidal, seductive, unstable relationships, shifting moods	Histrionic
	Shifting moods, dramatic, impulsive, self-injury (e.g., cutting)	Borderline
	Grandiose thoughts and sense of one's importance, exploitative, arrogant, lack of concern for others	Narcissistic
	Impulsive, violent, deceptive, and criminal behavior; no respect for social norms, ruthless	Antisocial
Anxious-fearful	Anxious and worrying, sense of inadequacy, fear of being criticized, nervousness, avoids social interaction	Avoidant
	Pervasive selflessness, need to be cared for, fear of rejection, total dependence on and submission to others	Dependent
	Extreme perfectionism and anxiety over minor disruption of routine, very rigid activities and relationships, pervades most aspects of everyday life	Obsessive-compulsive

FIGURE 12

THREE CLUSTERS OF PERSONALITY DISORDERS AND THEIR MAJOR SYMPTOMS. (APA, 2013)

histrionic personality disorder
A dramatic-emotional personality disorder characterized by the desire to be the center of attention and by dramatic, seductive, flamboyant, and exaggerated behaviors.

borderline personality disorder
A dramatic-emotional personality disorder characterized by out-of-control emotions, fear of being abandoned by others, and vacillation between idealizing and despising people who are close to the person with the disorder.

narcissistic personality disorder
A dramatic-emotional personality disorder characterized by having an extremely positive and arrogant self-image and being extraordinarily self-centered; other symptoms are an exaggerated sense of self-importance and grandiosity.

believe others are trying to harm them. They may be regularly suspicious of their spouses' faithfulness even if there is no evidence they have been unfaithful. If someone does slight or insult them, they often hold a grudge for an unusually long time. For example, if someone with paranoid personality disorder discovers that a colleague has just been promoted to a position she had wanted, she might conclude that the boss does not appreciate her and is actively trying to sabotage her career. When she sees coworkers talking later that day, she might assume that they are talking about her in a disparaging manner.

Dramatic-Emotional Personality Disorders

Another class of personality disorder involves dramatic and emotional disorders, of which there are four (APA, 2013). People with **histrionic personality disorder** want very much to be the center of attention and often behave in very dramatic, seductive, flamboyant, and exaggerated ways. They can also be very emotional, intense, self-centered, and shallow in their emotions and relationships. Those with **borderline personality disorder** have out-of-control emotions, are very afraid of being abandoned by others, and vacillate between idealizing and despising those who are close to them. They are more likely than most to hurt themselves (cutting, burning, or attempting suicide) or suffer from eating disorders or substance abuse. MRI studies show that abnormalities in the processing of emotional information in borderline personality disorders may be linked with overly sensitive amygdala response to negative stimuli in laboratory tests (**Hazlett, 2016**). Individuals with **narcissistic personality disorder** have an extremely positive and arrogant self-image, and most of their time and attention are self-focused. They have an exaggerated sense of self-importance and are grandiose. As a result, they often make unrealistic and unreasonable demands of others and ignore others' needs or wishes. They may be quite successful and climb the career ladder very quickly, but their narcissism often isolates them from others. Narcissistic personality disorder can co-occur with anxiety disorder and substance abuse (Eaton et al., 2016).

Formerly known as "sociopathic" or "psychopathic" personality, **antisocial personality disorder** is marked by extremely impulsive, deceptive, violent, ruthless, and callous behaviors. People with antisocial personality disorder are most likely to engage in criminal, deceptive, and violent behaviors. Although only about 3% of the population has this disorder, between 45% and 75% of male prison inmates are diagnosed with it (Fazel & Danesh, 2002; Hare, 1993). Only about 20% of female prisoners are diagnosed with antisocial personality disorder (Fazel & Danesh, 2002). Do not confuse *antisocial* with *asocial*. Antisocial personality is a serious and potentially dangerous disorder, whereas being asocial simply means being shy and not enjoying social situations.

antisocial personality disorder
Dramatic-emotional personality disorder characterized by extremely impulsive, deceptive, violent, ruthless, and callous behaviors; a serious and potentially dangerous disorder.

Anxious-Fearful Personality Disorders

The third cluster of personality disorders consists of the avoidant, dependent, and obsessive-compulsive personality disorders. Each of these is characterized by persistent high levels of anxiety, nervousness, and fear.

People with **avoidant personality disorder** are so afraid of being criticized that they avoid interacting with others and become socially isolated. They often feel inadequate and have low self-esteem; therefore, they tend to choose professions that allow them to be alone. People with **dependent personality disorder** fear rejection and have a strong need to be cared for. They feel safe only in dependent relationships with others; ironically, however, they tend to drive others away because they are so clingy and demanding. People with **obsessive-compulsive personality disorder (OCPD)** are very rigid in their habits, extremely perfectionistic in how things have to be done, and frequently very rigid list makers and rule followers. This personality disorder is similar to the clinical disorder with the same name but is more general and does not have true obsessions and compulsions. Also, people with OCD know they have a problem, whereas people with OCPD are convinced their way is the right and only way things can be done. In short, OCD is usually focused only on cleanliness or checking, whereas obsessive-compulsive personality disorder is focused on all aspects of a person's life, as illustrated in the following case study of a 32-year-old accountant:

avoidant personality disorder
An anxious-fearful personality disorder characterized by extreme fear of being criticized, low self-esteem, and avoidance of social interaction.

dependent personality disorder
An anxious-fearful personality disorder characterized by fear of being rejected and a strong need to be cared for.

obsessive-compulsive personality disorder (OCPD)
An anxious-fearful personality disorder characterized by rigid habits and extreme perfectionism; more general than obsessive-compulsive disorder.

> For many years he has maintained an almost inviolate schedule. On weekdays he arises at 6:47, has two eggs soft-boiled for 2 minutes, 45 seconds, and is at his desk at 8:15. Lunch is at 12:00, dinner at 6:00, bedtime at 11:00. He has separate Saturday and Sunday schedules, the latter characterized by a methodical and thorough trip through the *New York Times*. Any change in schedule causes him to feel varying degrees of anxiety, annoyance, and a sense that he is doing something wrong and wasting his time. . . . [His] major problems are with women and follow the same repetitive pattern. At first, things go well. Soon, however, he begins to resent the intrusion upon his schedule a woman inevitably causes. This is most strongly illustrated in the bedtime arrangements. He must spray his sinuses, take two aspirin, straighten the apartment, do 35 sit-ups and read two pages of the dictionary. (Spitzer and colleagues, quoted in Nolen-Hoeksema, 2007, pp. 451–452)

Origins of Personality Disorders

Research on murderers has identified a cluster of traits possessed by most of these violent criminals: being male, coming from abusive and neglectful households, having at least one psychological disorder (often antisocial personality disorder), and having suffered some kind of injury to the head or brain (Pincus, 1999, 2001; Strueber, Lueck, & Roth, 2006–2007). The frontal lobes and amygdala of many violent criminals are unusually disordered in size, activity, and function (Raine, 2013; Yang et al., 2009). Just being abused, having a psychological disorder, or suffering a brain injury is not enough. To become antisocial and violent, a person usually has to experience all of these conditions.

Moreover, as a result of suffering head injuries, living in a constant state of fear and abuse, or both, murderers almost always have moderate to severe problems of impulse control, social intelligence, working memory, and attention (Strueber et al., 2006–2007). Recall the principle of neuroplasticity from the chapter "The Biology of Behavior." Research on brain development suggests that living under a constant threat of abuse and stress changes the neural connectivity in the brain, making it less likely to develop many complex synaptic connections, especially in the frontal lobes. Being in a constant state of fear often leads to neural systems that are primed for unusually high levels of anxiety, impulsive behavior, and a state of constant alertness. These are all conditions that might lead to violent or criminal behaviors. Finally, genetics interacts with abusive experience to create personality disorders. Different forms of one particular gene, for instance, when coupled with being abused as a child, make violent and antisocial behavior in adulthood more likely (Caspi et al., 2002).

Connection

Neuroplasticity occurs when neurons and hence brain structure and function change as a result of input from the environment.

See "Brain Plasticity and Neurogenesis," in the chapter "The Biology of Behavior." (p. 105)

Connection

How does the environment shape the expression of our genes?

See "The Environment Can Change Gene Expression: Epigenetics," in the chapter "The Biology of Behavior." (p. 79)

©THE FILM COMPANY/AF archive/Alamy

In the film *Monster*, Charlize Theron portrayed Aileen Wuornos, a prostitute who confessed to killing several men. Abandoned by her parents in childhood, Wuornos later ran away from her grandparents' home and turned to prostitution to support herself. At one of her trials, a psychiatrist testified that she was mentally ill with borderline personality disorder. Nevertheless, she was convicted of murder and later executed.

Psychology in the Real World

Can Internet Use Become an Addiction?

In March 2010, police discovered that a couple in South Korea had starved their 3-month-old daughter due to neglect caused by their constant preoccupation with the online multiplayer fantasy game *Prius Online*. The tragic irony is that in the parents' version of *Prius Online*, they were raising a virtual baby (Greenemeier, 2013)!

As this case demonstrates, some people just can't stay offline. For many people, this in itself may not be a serious problem. In some cases, however, people are online all day; they check their Facebook or Twitter feeds dozens or even hundreds of times a day, and they cannot continue their work or activities around the home without logging on. For them, Internet use has become so intrusive that it adversely affects their professional and personal lives in the real world.

As with all disorders, something becomes a problem once it causes clinically significant disruptions of everyday life. For the first time, the *DSM-5* includes a category called Internet Gaming Disorder, but due to insufficient and inconclusive evidence it is classified as a "Condition for Further Study." Any five of nine criteria must be present during a 12-month period for a diagnosis to be made:

1. Preoccupation with Internet games (not Internet gambling)
2. Withdrawal symptoms when games are taken away (e.g., irritability, sadness, anxiety)
3. Tolerance—that is, more and more time is needed to be satisfied
4. Unsuccessful attempts to stop or control one's habit
5. Loss of interest in previous hobbies and entertainment
6. Continued excessive use despite knowing of their psychological problems
7. Deceives family, friends, and therapists about how much one plays games
8. Use of Internet games to cope or escape from a negative mood
9. Jeopardized or loss of a significant relationship, job, or educational/career opportunity due to Internet gaming activity

Some of these criteria are, in fact, signs of addiction— namely, tolerance, mood regulation, and disruption of relationships, job, or school. Moreover, researchers have suggested that some people do experience behavioral withdrawal symptoms, such as emotions of irritation and anger, when the computer or smartphone is not available (Block, 2008). The Chinese government has labeled compulsive and disruptive Internet use "an addiction" (APA, 2013).

Although there are hundreds of publications on gaming or Internet use disorder, and some evidence does suggest it may be addictive, mental health professionals do not completely agree on whether excessive and dysfunctional Internet use is an addiction, a compulsion, or an impulse disorder (Petry & O'Brien, 2013). Internet dependence is related to increased incidence of depression and lower levels of self-report (Wu et al., 2016), though it is not clear if it Internet dependence causes depression or vice versa. Indeed there is some controversy over whether Internet dependence is a unique disorder or if it is just a sign of underlying pathology, such as depression (Van Ameringen et al., 2016).

Challenge Your Assumptions

True or False? For some people, technology use is an addiction.
False: Technology use does not meet the formal definition of addiction according to the American Psychiatric Association (that requires physiological withdrawal symptoms when stopped). But some people clearly use technology in a compulsive and life-disrupting manner.

In a review of the research from the United States, between 9.8% and 15.2% of high school and college students met the criteria for Internet dependency (M. Moreno et al., 2011). Averages from studies across Europe and Asia report that 12% excessively play computer games, 10% abuse them, and 3% are dependent upon them. In China, prevalence rates for Internet disorder range from 8%–13.5%, with males outnumbering females about 2 to 1 (Wu et al., 2013). For Massively Multiplayer Online Role-Playing Games (MMORPGs), the rates of dysfunctional use were even higher, with 18% experiencing academic, health, or relationship problems (and 8% saying they spend more than 40 hours a week playing video games). Internet addiction is also reported as a major problem in Iran (Ostovar et al., 2016).

Worldwide, more people than ever before are relying on their mobile devices for texting, using social network sites, and perusing the Internet. Some psychologists describe *mobile addiction* as the excessive, impulsive checking and use of a mobile device (e.g., smartphone), especially in potentially dangerous or illegal contexts, such as while driving (Salehan & Negahban, 2013).

Whether these forms of technology dependency meet the criteria for mental disorders remains to be seen, but we know that overuse of such devices may have deleterious effects, such as impaired cognition and task performance while multitasking (Borst, Taatgen, & van Rijn, 2010). As more and more of us engage our time in such multitasking, we are likely to feel the effects of such chronic distraction on a social level.

Bringing It All Together

Making Connections in Psychological Disorders

Creativity and Mental Health

For thousands of years, people have associated "madness" with "genius." Many of the world's most creative people have been touched by more than their fair share of mental instability, if not outright "madness." Perhaps, some have argued, that is just the price of greatness (Ludwig, 1995). Amadeus Mozart, Ludwig von Beethoven, Robert Schumann, Vincent van Gogh, Virginia Woolf, Ernest Hemingway, William Styron, Jackson Pollock, Howard Hughes, Sylvia Plath, Salvador Dalí, and the Nobel Prize–winning mathematician John F. Nash, Jr., are just some of the creative geniuses who have suffered from a psychological disorder. So many creative individuals have experienced some psychological condition that many people think creativity and disorders of the mind are connected. The term *mad genius* reflects this belief. To be clear, however, suffering from psychological disorders is not necessary to be creative. There are, however—at least in art, literature, poetry, and music—higher rates of disorders than in the general population (Ludwig, 1995; Post, 1994).

Challenge Your Assumptions

True or False? All the great artists in history can be viewed as psychologically disturbed.

False: Creative artists are at higher risk for mental illness over the course of their lifetimes, but there are many exceptions to the rule. There is no causal connection between the two.

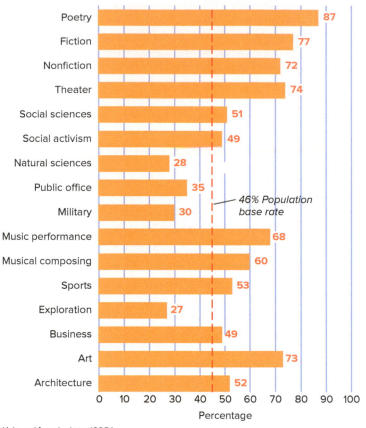

FIGURE 13

LIFETIME RATES OF PSYCHOLOGICAL DISORDERS IN FAMOUS PEOPLE IN 16 PROFESSIONS.

(Adapted from Ludwig, 1995.)

Exploring the connection between psychological disorders and creativity offers an opportunity to look again at the topics discussed in this chapter. We address two questions: (1) What is the evidence that creative people suffer from psychological disorders at a higher rate than the rest of the population? (2) Which disorders are more likely to be linked with creativity?

Evidence for a Relationship between Creativity and Psychological Disorders

To help us answer the first question, we can look at an impressive study of creativity and psychological disorder conducted by Arnold Ludwig. In a biographical study of 1,005 eminent people in 18 professions, Ludwig (1995) examined the lifetime rates of psychological disorder across the professions and over lifetimes. Lifetime rate is the likelihood that a person will suffer a disorder at some point in his or her lifetime. Lifetime rates for any psychiatric illness are remarkably high for people in the arts: 87% of poets, 77% of fiction writers, 74% of actors, 73% of visual artists, 72% of nonfiction writers, 68% of musical performers, and 60% of musical composers (see Figure 13). Compare these figures with the 46% lifetime rate in the general population for any disorder (Kessler et al., 2005). The data from this large-scale study clearly indicate a higher prevalence of disorder in creative artists than in the general population.

Which Disorders Affect Creative Individuals?

Not all disorders are associated with creative ability. There is evidence, however, for a connection between creativity and many of the disorders discussed in this chapter.

Autism Spectrum Disorder and Creativity

Some people with autism spectrum disorder are extremely gifted in one domain, such as music or math, a phenomenon known as savant syndrome (see the chapter "Intelligence, Problem Solving, and Creativity"). Most autistic savants do not produce great works of original genius, because their amazing feats of calculation and recall are not original. However, some savants produce truly creative works of art, usually math analyses, musical compositions, drawings, or paintings (Fitzgerald, 2004). One of the 20th century's greatest mathematicians, Srinivasa Ramanujan, showed clear signs of childhood autism (Fitzgerald, 2004). Composer Wolfgang Amadeus Mozart also may have been such a savant. A contemporary creative savant is Matt Savage (born in 1992), who was diagnosed with autism at the age of 3. He is a professional jazz musician and composer who had recorded three albums by the time he was 14.

Asperger syndrome, or what is now known as high-functioning autism, has been associated with creative ability in science, math, and engineering (Austin, 2005; Baron-Cohen et al., 2001). Baron-Cohen and his colleagues report that engineers, mathematicians, and physical scientists score much higher than nonscientists on measures of high-functioning autism or Asperger syndrome and score higher than social scientists on a nonclinical measure of autism. Children with Asperger are more than twice as likely as normal children to have a father or grandfather who was an engineer (Baron-Cohen et al., 1997, 1998, 2001).

Psychotic Symptoms and Creativity

Having unusual thoughts is common to both creative people and those with schizophrenia. For instance, much of the art of Salvador Dalí, who claimed to be psychotic, consists of bizarre, dreamlike images bordering on the kinds of delusions experienced by people with schizophrenia. John F. Nash, Jr., the mathematician made famous by the book and movie *A Beautiful Mind*, is a creative person who also has schizophrenia (Nasar, 1998). He is creative despite, rather than because of, the psychotic episodes he has experienced; all of his creative work preceded his schizophrenic symptoms and stopped after they began.

It is the milder psychotic symptoms, however, that are most strongly associated with creativity (Fink et al., 2012; Kinney et al., 2000–2001; Nettle & Clegg, 2005; Schuldberg, 2000–2001). Each of the following groups of people manifest unusual thought processes that are milder than those of schizophrenia: first-degree relatives of individuals with schizophrenia, people with schizotypal personality disorder, and those who score high on the normal personality dimension of psychoticism (see the chapter "Personality: The Uniqueness of the Individual"). These people are more likely to have unusual thought processes that develop into creative achievements that other people recognize to be significant (Burch et al., 2006; Fisher et al., 2004). Having

FIGURE 14

BIPOLAR DISORDER AND CREATIVITY IN THE WORK OF ROBERT SCHUMANN. The composer's creative output coincided directly with the highs and lows of his disorder. His most productive years (1840 and 1849) were marked by his most hypomanic periods.

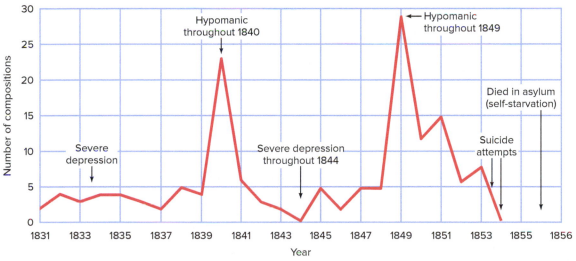

(Adapted from Slater & Meyer, 1959.)

a lot of ideas come to mind quickly can lead to many unusual associations that may be creative, but they may also be so unusual as to be similar to the bizarre associations seen in people with schizophrenia (Carson, Peterson, & Higgins, 2003; Eysenck, 1995; Fink et al., 2012). Recent evidence has uncovered variations in a gene (*neuregulin 1*) that appears to connect psychosis and creativity; it may partially explain why a maladaptive trait such as schizophrenia would continue in the gene pool (Keri, 2009; Venkatasubramanian & Kalmady, 2010).

Connection

Creative thinking requires novelty and connections among ideas.

See "What Is Creativity?" in the chapter "Intelligence, Problem Solving, and Intelligence." (p. 393)

Depression and Creativity

Emotional distress is a familiar companion to creative people. Many highly creative people have suffered from major depression (Ludwig, 1995). Across the 16 professions identified in Figure 13, the lifetime rate of just depression was 30%, with poets (77%), fiction writers (59%), and visual artists (50%) having the highest rates. In addition, poets are 20 times more likely to commit suicide, a key indicator for depression, than most people (Ludwig, 1995). One recent study, in fact, found that social rejection combined with a biological disposition toward depression enhanced participants' artistic creativity (Akinola & Mendes, 2008). In less creative populations, there is often only a weak relationship between depression and creativity (Silvia & Kimbrel, 2010).

Although highly creative artists and writers may have a higher rate of depression than the general population, depressive episodes themselves do not generate much creative output. Recall that a complete lack of motivation is a common symptom of depression, so lower productivity would follow. Still, the experiences one has while depressed might inspire and motivate the creation of works of art as a way of understanding it.

Bipolar Disorder and Creativity

For more than three decades, studies of the relationship between psychological disorders and creativity have devoted more attention to bipolar illness than to any other condition (Andreasen & Glick, 1988; Bowden, 1994; Fodor & Laird, 2004; Jamison, 1993; Ludwig, 1995). Actors (17%), poets (13%), architects (13%), and nonfiction writers (11%) all exceed a 10% lifetime rate of bipolar disorder—10 times the rate in the general population (Ludwig, 1995).

There is a positive relationship between bipolar disorder and creative thought. For instance, some studies show that highly creative people are more likely than noncreative people to have bipolar disorder (Andreasen, 1987, 2006; Jamison, 1993; Jamison et al., 1980; Richards, 1994). Others report the other side of the coin: People with bipolar disorder are likely to be more creative than those without this condition (Fodor & Laird, 2004; Richards, 1994; Richards & Kinney, 1990). Indeed, many creative individuals throughout history have been bipolar (Jamison, 1993).

The manic phase is more likely than the depressive phase to generate creative behavior (Andreasen & Glick, 1988; Jamison et al., 1980). For example, Robert Schumann's creative output spiked with his manic episodes (see Figure 14). Few artists and writers are creative during their depressed phases; rather, they are creatively inspired during the milder form of mania, the hypomanic phase.

Quick Quiz 8: Personality Disorders

1. People with _____ personality disorder are so afraid of being criticized that they stay away from others and become socially isolated.
   a. borderline
   b. avoidant
   c. dependent
   d. psychopathic

2. Individuals with which kind of personality disorder are most likely to commit crimes and end up in jail?
   a. asocial
   b. narcissistic
   c. antisocial
   d. avoidant

Answers can be found at the end of the chapter.

Chapter Review

©Cavan Images/Getty Images RF

DEFINING PSYCHOLOGICAL DISORDERS

- Psychologists agree on four general criteria for a psychological disorder: disruptive, distressing, dysfunctional, and deviant (but only if also dysfunctional).

- A major tool for diagnosing disorders is the *Diagnostic and Statistical Manual (DSM-5)*.

NEURODEVELOPMENTAL DISORDERS

- The most common disorders to affect children are attention deficit hyperactivity disorder (ADHD) and autism spectrum disorder.

- ADHD consists of severe inattention, hyperactivity, and impulsivity.

- Children with autism spectrum disorder (ASD) show very inward-focused behaviors, with severe language and social impairment combined with repetitive habits and behaviors. They also have serious deficits in understanding other people's thoughts, feelings, and intentions.

SCHIZOPHRENIA

- Schizophrenia is a psychotic disorder of profound disturbances in thought, perception, and emotion.

- Positive symptoms of schizophrenia include hallucinations, delusional thinking, and disorganized thought and speech.

- Negative symptoms of schizophrenia include nonresponsiveness, flattened affect, immobility or strange poses, reduction of speaking, and inability to complete tasks.

- Cognitive symptoms of schizophrenia include disordered thinking, including impaired attention and profound difficulty in monitoring conflicting sources of information.

DEPRESSIVE DISORDERS

- People with major depressive disorder experience a pervasive low mood, lack of motivation, low energy, and feelings of worthlessness and guilt.

BIPOLAR DISORDER

- Bipolar disorder involves substantial mood fluctuation between depressive and manic episodes, with bipolar I being more severe and longer-lasting than bipolar II.

ANXIETY DISORDERS

- Anxiety disorders occur when fears and worrying are out of proportion to the situation and interfere with everyday functioning.

- Generalized anxiety disorder, a pervasive state of anxiety lasting at least 6 months, consists of excessive worrying about relatively minor events of daily life.

- Panic disorder is extreme anxiety about having a panic attack.

- Social phobia (social anxiety disorder), a pronounced fear of humiliation in the presence of others, is marked by severe self-consciousness about appearance, behavior, or both.

- Specific phobias involve an intense fear when confronted with particular situations or objects, such as spiders or heights.

OBSESSIVE-COMPULSIVE DISORDER

- Obsessive-compulsive disorder is a disorder of thought (obsession) and behavior (compulsion).

- Obsessions are anxiety-producing thoughts that can preoccupy a person throughout the day and are beyond the person's control.

- Compulsions are repetitive behaviors, which are often rituals that people have developed to control the anxiety created by the obsessions.

POSTTRAUMATIC STRESS DISORDER

- PTSD involves a set of intrusive and persistent cognitive, emotional, and physiological symptoms triggered by exposure to a catastrophic or horrifying event—such as experiences of war, attempted murder, rape, natural disasters, sudden death of a loved one, or physical or sexual abuse.

DISSOCIATIVE DISORDERS

- Dissociative disorders entail the loss of a sense of time and space but also involve extreme gaps in memories, identity, or consciousness.

- People with dissociative identity disorder (DID) develop at least two distinct personalities, each of whom has a unique set of memories, behaviors, thoughts, and emotions. Some experts have reservations about classifying DID as a disorder.

SOMATIC SYMPTOM DISORDERS

- Somatic symptom disorder occurs when a person complains of one or more distressing somatic symptoms that disrupt daily life coupled with excessive thoughts, feelings, or behaviors related to the bodily symptoms.

- Illness anxiety disorder is diagnosed in the absence of somatic symptoms and when the person nevertheless has a preoccupation with and extreme anxiety about acquiring a serious illness.

PERSONALITY DISORDERS

- Personality disorders differ from clinical disorders in being generally a more consistent part of a person's personality than the clinical disorders (e.g., schizophrenia, depression, and bipolar disorder).

- The schizoid personality is very emotionally cold, reclusive, humorless, or uninteresting; someone with schizotypal personality disorder expresses very odd thoughts and behavior, is socially isolated, and has a restricted range of emotions.

- Paranoid personality disorder is marked by extreme suspiciousness and mistrust of other people, in ways that are both unwarranted and not adaptive.

- Those with borderline personality disorder suffer from out-of-control emotions, are very afraid of being abandoned by others, and vacillate between idealizing those close to them and despising them.

- People with dependent personality disorder fear rejection and have such a strong need to be cared for that they form very clingy relationships with others.

- Antisocial personality disorder is marked by extremely impulsive, deceptive, violent, and ruthless behaviors.

BRINGING IT ALL TOGETHER: MAKING CONNECTIONS IN PSYCHOLOGICAL DISORDERS

- Creativity and psychological disorders are related, especially in the arts. Disorders such as depression, bipolar disorder, anxiety disorders, substance abuse, and suicide occur at higher rates in creative artists than in members of other professions and in the general population.

Key Terms

agoraphobia
antisocial personality disorder
attention deficit hyperactivity disorder (ADHD)
autism spectrum disorder (ASD)
avoidant personality disorder
bipolar disorder
borderline personality disorder
cognitive symptoms (of schizophrenia)
comorbidity
compulsion
cyclothymia
delusions
dependent personality disorder
depressive disorder
diathesis-stress model
dissociative disorders

dissociative identity disorder (DID)
generalized anxiety disorder (GAD)
hallucinations
histrionic personality disorder
hypomanic episodes
illness anxiety disorder
joint attention
learned helplessness
major depressive disorder
manic episodes
narcissistic personality disorder
negative symptoms (of schizophrenia)
obsession
obsessive-compulsive disorder (OCD)
obsessive-compulsive personality disorder (OCPD)
panic attacks

panic disorder
paranoid personality disorder
persistent depressive disorder (PDD)
personality disorders
phobia
positive symptoms (of schizophrenia)
posttraumatic stress disorder (PTSD)
psychotic disorders
schizoid personality disorder
schizophrenia
schizotypal personality disorder
social phobia (social anxiety disorder)
somatic symptom disorders
syndrome
word salad

Quick Quiz Answers

Quick Quiz 1: 1. c; **2.** b   **Quick Quiz 2: 1.** a; **2.** d   **Quick Quiz 3: 1.** c; **2.** c; **3.** b   **Quick Quiz 4: 1.** c; **2.** b; **3.** d
Quick Quiz 5: 1. b; **2.** d; **3.** a   **Quick Quiz 6: 1.** a; **2.** b   **Quick Quiz 7: 1.** c; **2.** a; **3.** a; **4.** b   **Quick Quiz 8: 1.** b; **2.** c

16 Treatment of Psychological Disorders

Chapter Outline

Challenge Your Assumptions

True or False?

- Electrical stimulation of neurons by electrical impulse is a brutal practice of the past and is not used in treatment today. (see pp. 616-617)

- Psychedelic drugs like MDMA and psilocybin offer promise in treating PTSD. p. 638

- Fears of specific objects or situations such as spiders or flying cannot be successfully treated with behavioral therapy. p. 624

©Daly and Newton/OJO Images/Getty Images RF

All Ayelet Waldman wanted was to have a normal day—to get out of bed, face the world, be with her family, and go about her job. None of this sounds special, but such days were not common for Ayelet. Everyday felt completely unpredictable—some days she would wake up fine, others she would feel excessively cheerful and energetic. More often than not, however, Ayelet woke up feeling worthless and unable to go on (Waldman, 2017).

Waldman, a successful writer, wife, and mother of four, suffered from bipolar disorder. She lived with unpredictable mood swings that pose serious difficulties for her marriage, family, and work. She rarely woke up and just had a "normal" day. Despite trying what seemed like everything: numerous antidepressant drugs, antipsychotic drugs, psychotherapy combined therapies—she could not find effective, consistent relief.

Then Ayelet read of a new, highly controversial approach: taking very tiny doses of the hallucinogenic drug lysergic acid diethylamide (also known as LSD) for mood regulation once every three days. She had never taken the drug and was not at all interested in using it for recreation or to "trip." This middle-class, working mom did not want to break the law. Yet after reading how it changed the daily lives of those who had tried it after just one treatment, Ayelet decided to find a way to try it. "I did this because I was afraid I was going to kill myself" (Ayelet Waldman, from Williams, 2017).

Day 1 after a microscopic dose, Ayelet felt like something had shifted. She did not feel high—she just had a good day. Then she had another good day, and then another. Nothing in the history of her illness or treatment had provided that. Numerous scientific studies have examined the effects of one or two controlled larger doses of psychedelic drugs in the context of psychotherapy, but microdosing has barely been studied (Tupper et al., 2015). Currently, it is illegal, and much more research is needed. Ayelet's personal experiment with LSD as a treatment for bipolar disorder is one example, however, of the efforts in the growing, though controversial field of *psychedelic medicine*, in which legal, scientific studies have shown significant benefits to targeted application of psychedelic drugs in the treatment of several psychological disorders.

Most people who struggle with psychological disorders never get treatment (Kazdin, 2017). Of those who do, the attempts to find the right treatment seem endless. This is why some turn to unconventional treatments, such as electrical brain stimulation or psychedelic drugs. In this chapter, we will discuss both conventional and unconventional approaches to treating psychological disorders, describe what they involve, and look at what research tells us about how well they work.

We will cover biomedical, psychological, and technology-based approaches to treating disorders. Biomedical approaches include drugs, surgical treatments, and electric stimulation and magnetic treatments. Psychological approaches include psychoanalytic, humanistic, cognitive, and behavior therapies. Technology-based therapies make use of virtual reality, Internet-based treatments, and apps. Combined therapies either use drugs and psychotherapies together or might involved less traditional approaches, such as meditation, with more traditional techniques. Psychedelic medicine fits into this latter category. Although we begin by discussing biomedical treatments and psychological treatments separately for clarity, bear in mind that both kinds of treatment work together in modifying the brain, thought, feeling, and behavior.

BIOMEDICAL TREATMENTS FOR PSYCHOLOGICAL DISORDERS

Mental health professionals rely on four major forms of treatment to help alleviate the symptoms of—and sometimes to cure—psychological disorders: biomedical, psychological, technology-based, and combined therapies (see Figure 1). While most mental health professionals rely on all four, each practitioner works from a perspective based on training, personal interest, and experience. In other words, the same disorder can be treated in different ways depending on the clinician. People seeking treatment should keep in mind these differences in perspective when selecting someone to help, because different clinician backgrounds don't always lead to the same clinical outcome (see "Psychology in the Real World").

Drug Therapies

Numerous pharmaceutical drugs are available for the treatment of psychological disorders. Drugs can be used to treat, but usually not cure, everything from mild anxiety to schizophrenia.

Drug Treatments for Schizophrenia   Today, drug therapies are typically the first choice for schizophrenia. Prior to the 1950s, there were no drugs to treat the disorder. In 1952, the French physician Henri Laborit discovered that a class of drugs, the **phenothiazines**, helped diminish hallucinations, confusion, agitation, and paranoia in people with schizophrenia. He made this discovery by accident, after looking for a way to reduce the shock that sometimes occurs after major surgery (shock results when the body does not receive enough blood, and tissues are therefore deprived of oxygen; *Drug for treating schizophrenia*, 1998).

Phenothiazines block dopamine receptors in the brain. As discussed in the chapter "Psychological Disorders," the prevailing view for decades was that

phenothiazines
Drugs used to treat schizophrenia; help diminish hallucinations, confusion, agitation, and paranoia but also have adverse side effects.

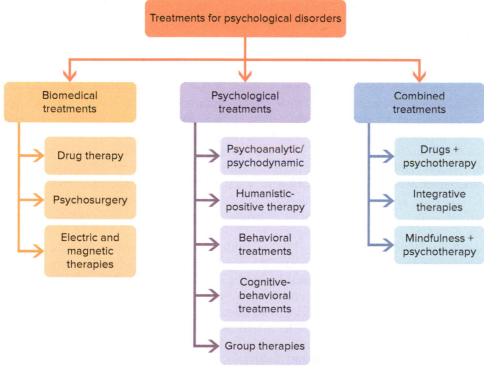

FIGURE 1
SOME MAJOR APPROACHES TO THE TREATMENT OF PSYCHOLOGICAL DISORDERS.

schizophrenia resulted from an excess of dopamine in the brain—a view dubbed the *dopamine hypothesis*. Although the dopamine hypothesis has come into question, the most commonly used drugs for schizophrenia are still those that reduce the availability of dopamine in the brain (Javitt & Coyle, 2004).

The best-known phenothiazine is chlorpromazine (marketed as Thorazine in the United States). Another drug, haloperidol (Haldol), discovered at about the same time, showed similar effects on schizophrenic symptoms. The phenothiazines and haloperidol are known as **traditional antipsychotics**, because they were the first medications used to manage psychotic symptoms. Unfortunately, they have many unpleasant side effects, including fatigue, visual impairments, and a condition called **tardive dyskinesia**, which consists of repetitive, involuntary movements of the jaw, tongue, face, and mouth (such as grimacing and lip smacking) and body tremors. Tardive dyskinesia is particularly problematic, as the effects often continue for months after the drugs have been discontinued (Aquino & Lang, 2014; Trugman, 1998).

Some newer antipsychotic drugs, called **atypical antipsychotics**, also known as second-generation antipsychotics, do not have these side effects and are considered by many physicians as the first line of treatment for schizophrenia. Clozapine (Clozaril), olanzapine (Zyprexa), and risperidone (Risperdal) are examples of atypical antipsychotics. These drugs block a different type of dopamine receptor than the traditional antipsychotics do, which makes them less likely to create tardive dyskinesia, but they do not eliminate this side effect and may not perform much better than the traditional medications (Divac et al., 2016). Unfortunately, even these medications can produce some unpleasant or dangerous side effects, such as major weight gain, increased risk of diabetes, a reduction in the number of certain white blood cells, problems with balance, cardiovascular problems in older patients, and, rarely, increased risk of a particular kind of cancer (Fraser et al., 2015; Javitt & Coyle, 2004; Lieberman et al., 2005; Pasternak et al., 2014; Young, Taylor, and Lawrie, 2015). Figure 2 summarizes some major disorders, their primary drug therapies, and the side effects of each medication.

Drug Treatments for Depressive and Anxiety Disorders Six major categories of drugs are used to treat mood and anxiety disorders: monoamine oxidase (MAO) inhibitors, tricyclic antidepressants, selective serotonin reuptake inhibitors (SSRIs), benzodiazepines, barbiturates, and lithium.

The **monoamine oxidase (MAO) inhibitors** were among the first pharmaceuticals used to treat depression (Burgess, 2009). These drugs reduce the action of the enzyme monoamine oxidase, which breaks down monoamine neurotransmitters (including norepinephrine, epinephrine, dopamine, and serotonin) in the brain. By inhibiting the action of this enzyme, MAO inhibitors allow more of these neurotransmitters to stay active in the synapse for a longer time, which presumably improves mood. Brand names include Marplan, Nardil, and Parnate. Unfortunately, MAO inhibitors interact with many foods and common over-the-counter drugs, such as antihistamines, to produce undesirable, even dangerous, side effects—such as life-threatening increases in blood pressure. Therefore, they are not often prescribed for depression (Fiedorowicz & Swartz, 2004; Yamada & Yasuhara, 2004). A transdermal patch, which allows administration of an MAO inhibitor without its having to enter the digestive tract, may provide some of the benefits of these drugs without the risks caused by their interactions with foods (Pae et al., 2007). Despite these drawbacks, some people with treatment-resistant depression use these medications with some success when other options fail to relieve their symptoms (Larsen, Krogh-Nielsen, & Brøsen, 2016).

Tricyclic antidepressants, such as imipramine and amitriptyline, marketed under the trade names Elavil and Anafranil, are still popular for treating depression. They are also used in chronic pain management, as treatment for attention deficit hyperactivity disorder (ADHD), and as a treatment for bedwetting. These

traditional antipsychotics
Historically, the first medications used to manage psychotic symptoms.

tardive dyskinesia
Repetitive, involuntary movements of jaw, tongue, face, and mouth resulting from the extended use of traditional antipsychotic drugs.

atypical antipsychotics
Newer antipsychotic drugs, which do not create tardive dyskinesia.

monoamine oxidase (MAO) inhibitors
A class of drugs used to treat depression; they slow the breakdown of monoamine neurotransmitters in the brain.

tricyclic antidepressants
Drugs used for treating depression as well as chronic pain and ADHD.

Disorder	Class of drug treatment	Drug name	Side effects
Schizophrenia	Chlorpromazine	Thorazine	Fatigue, visual impairment, tardive dyskinesia
	Haloperidol	Haldol	Fatigue, visual impairment, tardive dyskinesia
	Clozapine	Clozaril	Weight gain, increased risk of diabetes, reduction of white blood cells
	Risperidone	Risperdal	Weight gain, increased risk of diabetes, reduction of white blood cells
Anxiety	SSRIs	Paxil, Prozac Zoloft, Celexa	Agitation, insomnia, nausea, difficulty achieving orgasm; rare cases of increased risk for suicide
	Benzodiazepines	Valium, Librium	Can be addictive
	Barbiturates	Pentobarbital	Slows breathing and heart rate; can lead to overdose
Depression	MAO inhibitors	Nardil, Parnate	Dangerous increases in blood pressure
	Tricyclic antidepressants	Elavil, Anafranil	Dry mouth, weight gain, irritability, confusion, constipation
	SSRIs	Paxil, Prozac Zoloft, Celexa	Agitation, insomnia, nausea, difficulty achieving orgasm; rare cases of increased risk for suicide
	Buspirone	Wellbutrin	Weight loss, dry mouth, headaches
Bipolar disorder	Lithium	Lithobid	Diarrhea, nausea, tremors, kidney failure, cognitive effects, adverse cardiac effects

FIGURE 2

SUMMARY OF MAJOR DRUGS USED TO TREAT PSYCHOLOGICAL DISORDERS. Most of the major psychological disorders can be treated with some form of medication, to varying degrees of effectiveness and with various side effects.

drugs appear to work by blocking the reuptake of serotonin and norepinephrine almost equally, so that more of these neurotransmitters are available in the brain. However, the tricyclics produce unpleasant side effects, such as dry mouth, weight gain, irritability, confusion, and constipation (Zeino, Sisson, & Bjarnason, 2010).

Many of the unpleasant side effects of the tricyclic antidepressants come from their effects on norepinephrine. People with depression have serotonin deficiencies (Delgado et al., 1994; Drevets et al., 1999). Therefore, the development of drugs that target only serotonin offered hope for treatment with fewer side effects. One class of drugs brought to the market in the 1990s, the **selective serotonin reuptake inhibitors (SSRIs)**, make more serotonin available in the synapse. Prozac (fluoxetine), Zoloft (sertraline), Paxil (paroxetine), and Celexa (citalopram) are some of the more widely used SSRIs and are among the most widely prescribed psychotherapeutic drugs in the United States.

Here is how SSRIs work: Serotonin, like all neurotransmitters, is released from the presynaptic neuron into the synapse. It then binds with serotonin-specific receptor sites on the postsynaptic neuron to stimulate the firing of that neuron. Normally, neurotransmitters that do not bind with the postsynaptic neuron either are taken back up into the presynaptic neuron (the reuptake process) or are destroyed by enzymes in the synapse. The SSRIs inhibit the reuptake process, thereby allowing more serotonin to bind with the postsynaptic neuron (Murphy, 2010; see Figure 3). By allowing more serotonin to be used, the SSRIs alleviate some of the symptoms of depression. Serotonin-only drugs do not produce the undesirable side effects that the tricyclics, which affect both serotonin and norepinephrine activity, may produce (Cipriani et al., 2010).

selective serotonin reuptake inhibitors (SSRIs)
Drugs prescribed primarily for depression and some anxiety disorders that work by making more serotonin available in the synapse.

Connection

The neurotransmitter serotonin plays a role in mood, sleep, eating, temperature regulation.

See "Common Neurotransmitters" in "The Biology of Behavior," p. 88.

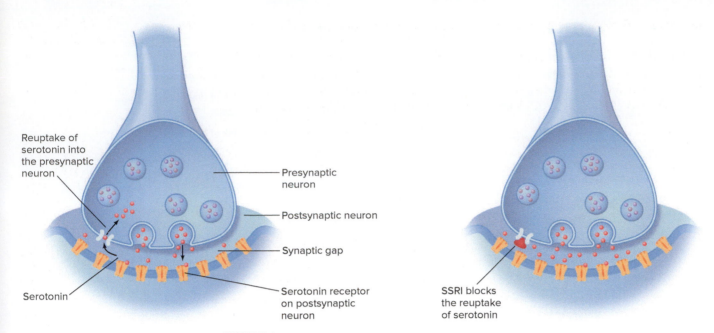

FIGURE 3

EFFECT OF SSRIs ON REUPTAKE OF SEROTONIN. SSRIs increase serotonin levels by blocking the reuptake of serotonin into the presynaptic neuron. As a result, more serotonin stays in the synaptic cleft, where it can bind with receptors on the postsynaptic neuron.

Although SSRIs are prescribed primarily for depression, they are also used to treat certain anxiety disorders, especially OCD, as well as disorders of impulse control, such as compulsive gambling or skin picking (Schumer, Bartley, & Bloch, 2016; Vaswani, Linda, & Ramesh, 2003). In fact, these drugs may be better for impulse disorders than depression. SSRIs, however, can have some side effects, such as agitation, insomnia, nausea, and difficulty in achieving orgasm. This last side effect has led some physicians to prescribe SSRIs to treat premature ejaculation (Waldinger et al., 2004). Another highly publicized but infrequent side effect of SSRI is an increased likelihood of suicide attempt compared to other treatments for depression (Fergusson et al., 2005). The recently publicized cases of teens on SSRIs committing suicide often neglect to report that adolescents are usually in severely depressed states when they are prescribed SSRIs and are therefore more likely to attempt or to commit suicide, no matter the prescription (Wessely & Kerwin, 2004). Widespread antidepressant use may be associated with a decrease in suicide rates worldwide, but the nature of that relationship is a matter of debate (Isacsson et al., 2010).

Two major classes of drugs, the **benzodiazepines** (Valium, Librium) and the **barbiturates**, are prescribed for anxiety. Both have calming effects and can be addictive, but barbiturates have the higher risk of overdose. People with anxiety disorders often take SSRIs as well.

One promising new area of in treatment for some anxiety disorders involves disrupting memory of fear experiences. This approach has been applied to simple phobias and to PTSD, as well. The treatment of simple phobias involves using medications to impair memory for previous fearful experiences with the phobic object. For example, in one study spider phobics were put in a room where a baby tarantula in a jar sat on a table, and were told they would have to touch it soon. This was not true actually, but the possibility of contact was what induced their fear. Later they were exposed to it again. Half of the sample was administered a dose of a drug (propranolol), which can block the reconsolidation of memories. The others received a placebo. Those who received the memory blockers showed

benzodiazepines
A class of anxiety-reducing drugs that can be addictive but are less dangerous than barbiturates.

barbiturates
A class of anxiety-reducing sedatives that can be addictive and carry a risk of overdose.

less fear and more approach behaviors than those who did not, indicating that the memory blocker worked (Soeter & Kindt, 2015). The effects lasted for months following the single administration of the memory-blocking propanolol. Although memory modification raises many ethical concerns, drugs targeting fearful or traumatic memories may help relieve enormous suffering in millions of people if properly applied in the treatment of psychological disorders (Elsey & Kindt, 2016).

We will discuss the drug treatment of anxiety disorders in more detail later in this chapter's "Bringing It All Together" section.

The treatment of bipolar disorder presents many challenges, as the manic episodes have to be regulated, the depressive episodes prevented, and the shifts from one type of episode to the other controlled. Because no one drug can manage all these effects, treatment often consists of a combination of drug therapies. **Lithium** has long been prescribed for its ability to stabilize the mania associated with bipolar disorder. We do not know how lithium works, although it appears to influence many neurotransmitter systems in the brain, including glutamate, the major excitatory neurotransmitter in the brain, which appears to play a substantial role in schizophrenia (Chuang, 2004; Jope, 1999). Taking lithium can be unpleasant and dangerous, because it can cause diarrhea, nausea, tremors, cognitive problems, kidney failure, brain damage, and even adverse cardiac effects (Aichorn et al., 2006). Also, because the amount of lithium required for effective treatment is not very different from the amount that can cause harm, it is difficult to determine the effective dosage. In addition, some people develop tolerance to lithium after years of treatment, making the drug less effective (Post et al., 1998). For these reasons, physicians need to monitor their patients' lithium levels carefully by regularly testing their blood.

Due to toxicity concerns, physicians often favor other drugs to treat the mania phase, including drugs prescribed to prevent convulsions, either alone or in combination with lithium. Currently, the most commonly used drugs for managing mania are the atypical antipsychotics, such as olanzapine (trade name Zyprexa) and valproate (marketed as Depakote or Depacon; Jarema, 2007; Malhi, Adams, & Berk, 2010). These drugs are showing effectiveness in the United States as well as in other countries, such as Russia and South Korea (Kuliko & Komarov, 2013; López-Muñoz et al., 2013). The use of atypical antipsychotics in treating mood disorders in general (e.g., for anxiety, bipolar disorder, and depression) is increasing, partly because the dosage required to be effective is rather low and therefore has fewer side effects (Blier, 2005).

Psychosurgery

Recall from the chapter "Introduction to Psychology" the evidence from very early human history of attempts to cure insanity by trephining, which is drilling a hole in the skull to allow evil spirits to escape. Although current psychological disorders are not usually treated by surgical means, early-20th-century physicians experimented with surgery to disrupt the transmission of brain signals in people suffering from psychosis. In a procedure known as **prefrontal lobotomy**, they severed connections between the prefrontal cortex and the lower portion of the brain. Because the prefrontal cortex is involved in thinking (and, we now know is crucial for working memory and planned action) and the lower areas are more concerned with emotion, they believed the surgery would modify behavior and possibly disengage the disruptive thought patterns involved in hallucinations and confused thinking. Typically, however, prefrontal lobotomies produced profound personality changes, often leaving the patient listless or subject to seizures; some patients were even reduced to a vegetative state (Mashour, Walker, & Martuza, 2005).

Rosemary Kennedy, younger sister to John F. Kennedy, underwent a lobotomy when she was 23 years old to treat her erratic, often violent mood swings. Instead of producing the desired calming effect, the lobotomy left Rosemary

lithium
A salt that is prescribed for its ability to stabilize the mania associated with bipolar disorder.

©Jeffrey Mayer/Getty Images

Actor Robert Downey, Jr., has struggled with symptoms of bipolar disorder and drug abuse for a number of years.

 Can you think of pros and cons to taking medications to treat bipolar disorder?

prefrontal lobotomy
A form of psychosurgery in which the connections between the prefrontal cortex and the lower portion of the brain are severed; no longer in use.

mentally incapacitated. She would stare blankly at walls for hours on end and lost the ability to speak coherently (Lerner, 1996).

After the introduction of the traditional antipsychotic medications, lobotomy fell out of favor. Moreover, the practice was widely regarded as cruel and inhumane. Today a very few, highly constrained forms of brain surgery are occasionally performed, but only as a last resort after other forms of treatment have been unsuccessful (Mashour et al., 2005).

electroconvulsive therapy (ECT) The treatment of last resort for severe depression that involves passing an electrical current through a person's brain in order to induce a seizure.

Electric and Magnetic Therapies

Although brain surgery for psychological disorders is rare, there are other ways to stimulate or decrease brain activation. Bizarre as it seems, electrical current can be used to help ease the suffering caused by certain psychological disorders. The application of electrical current as a medical practice goes back centuries: Apparently, the ancient Romans used electric fish to treat headaches (Abrams, 1997). As we saw in the chapter opening, one of the more innovative applications of electrical stimulation may well hold the key to unlocking the mystery of depression.

Electroconvulsive Therapy The notion of "shock therapy" conjures up images of barbaric torture of psychiatric patients, yet electroconvulsive therapy is still used and can be effective for severe cases of depression in people who have not responded to other therapies (Fink, 2006). **Electroconvulsive therapy (ECT)** involves passing an electrical current through a person's brain in order to induce a seizure. The origins of ECT stem from the observation that people who have seizures become calm afterwards (Abrams, 1997). Physicians thought that ECT could be an effective treatment for schizophrenia, because the induced seizures would calm the patient. Research eventually demonstrated, however, that ECT did not treat the symptoms of schizophrenia effectively at all, and it disappeared as a viable therapy for years. It resurfaced later as a treatment for people with severe cases of depression.

Today, ECT is administered by connecting electrodes to the patient's head and passing an electrical current (ranging from 60 to 140 volts) through the brain for one-third to one-half second. The voltage is not lethal, because it is administered only to the head—indeed, the same voltage to the chest would be lethal. The treatment is called electro*convulsive* because the procedure produces a brief seizure, including bodily convulsions. To minimize the convulsions, patients are given an anesthetic and a muscle relaxant prior to ECT. Standard ECT treatment involves up to 12 sessions over the course of several weeks. Some people report immediate relief of their depressive symptoms after treatment, although scientists do not fully understand how ECT works to relieve them (Nolen-Hoeksema, 2007). The downside to ECT is that it creates some permanent memory loss and other types of cognitive damage, because it actually destroys some brain tissue. Using ECT on one side of the brain rather than both appears to reduce the risk of memory loss (Squire, 1977).

©Will & Deni McIntyre/Science Source

Challenging the assumptions of earlier generations of psychiatrists, more current therapists discovered that ECT is an effective treatment for depression but not schizophrenia.

Repetitive Transcranial Magnetic Stimulation The idea of somehow stimulating or manipulating brain activity with an external application of energy has

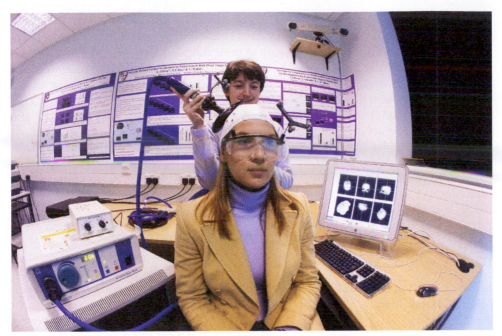

©Simon Fraser/University of Durham/Science Source

Transcranial magnetic stimulation exposes specific areas of the brain to bursts of high-intensity magnetic fields and may be used to treat people with severe depression when other options have failed.

enduring appeal. Some practitioners have tried to find a way to do this without creating more harm. ECT was a good idea in some respects, but as just mentioned, it leaves people with memory damage and other negative effects. In **repetitive transcranial magnetic stimulation (rTMS)**, physicians expose particular brain structures to bursts of high-intensity magnetic fields instead of electricity. Like ECT, repetitive transcranial magnetic stimulation is usually reserved for people with severe depression who have not responded well to other forms of therapy. Although some people experience relief from this therapy, it is not yet clear how much magnetic stimulation is optimal and for what length of time (Fitzgerald et al., 2006; Turner-Shea, Bruno, & Pridmore, 2006). rTMS has also shown preliminary success in treating the negative symptoms of schizophrenia (Brunelin et al., 2010).

rTMS can stimulate the outer layer of the cortex only. A related technology, **transcranial direct current stimulation (tDCS)**, can stimulate subcortical brain structures. While TMS requires involves equipment that must be used in a medical setting, direct transcranial stimulation equipment is smaller and can be used when people are moving—so it is more portable. Transcranial direct current stimulation shows promise in helping people with treatment-resistant OCD. It may work by disrupting circuits in subcortical brain areas that underlying compulsive behavior (Bation et al., 2016). Although this technique is still in its infancy, a major review of several studies shows that tDCS may be helpful not only to OCD, but also depression, schizophrenia, substance abuse, and eating disorders (Kekic et al., 2016).

Deep Brain Stimulation   One of the most promising and exciting new treatments for various psychological disorders involves deep brain stimulation, which entails implanting electrodes into the brain to allow for electrical stimulation of specific brain regions and clusters of neurons. The technique first received attention as a treatment for Parkinson's disease, but as we will discuss in more detail in the next section, it soon showed promise for people with severe depression

repetitive transcranial magnetic stimulation (rTMS)
A treatment for severe depression involving exposure of specific brain structures to bursts of high-intensity magnetic fields instead of electricity.

transcranial direct current stimulation (tDCS)
A method of treatment that can stimulate both cortical and deeper brain structures; unlike rTMS it can be used during movement.

Courtesy of Helen Mayberg

Helen Mayberg

(Drevets et al., 1997; Mayberg, 2003; Shestyuk et al., 2005). Stimulating certain areas of the brain involved in emotion and reward in people with severe depression leads to substantial improvements in their moods.

Deep brain stimulation more recently has shown promise in treating other psychological disorders as well, such as anorexia, obsessive-compulsive disorder, and Alzheimer's disease (Figee et al., 2013; Lipsman et al., 2013; Naesström, Blomstedt, & Bodlund, 2016). For instance, by stimulating the regions of the hippocampus involved in memory formation, deep brain stimulation has helped slow down dementia (Laxton & Lozano, 2012; Lyketsos et al., 2012). The research on effectiveness of deep brain stimulation is limited by the small number of people who have opted to get electrodes implanted deep into the brain (Naesström, Blomstedt, & Bodlund, 2016).

Challenging Assumptions in the Treatment of Severe Depression

In her quest to understand the brain circuitry of depression, psychiatrist and neurologist Helen Mayberg was the first to discover what appears to be a neural switch that activates depression. The path that led Mayberg to discover how a brain region called Brodmann's Area 25 (we'll call it Area 25) may control depression is an interesting story of how scientific discovery depends on challenging assumptions, luck, tenacity, creativity, vision, and hard work.

No one had ever thought about applying deep brain stimulation to depressed brain regions. Mayberg tried it with 12 patients whose severe depression had failed to respond to anything else. She and her colleagues implanted electrodes in Area 25 and delivered voltage to that area from an external stimulator. For 11 of the patients, the depression ceased almost immediately (Mayberg et al., 2005). Shortly after activation of the electrodes, these patients said that they felt "sudden calmness or lightness," "disappearance of the void," or "connectedness."

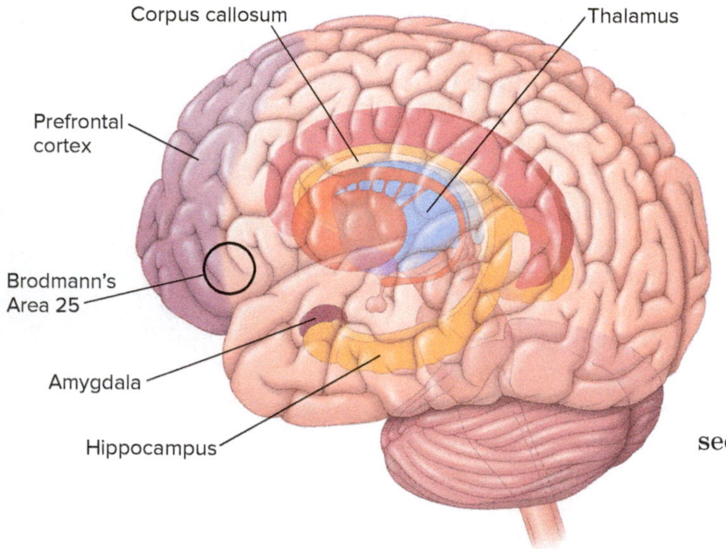

Mayberg and her colleagues had stumbled on a surprising phenomenon: Area 25 was actually *hyperactive* in these depressed patients. Finding overactivation in any brain area of depressed people challenged researchers' and clinicians' assumptions, since many had found that depression was related to underactivity rather than overactivity of certain cortical areas (Shestyuk et al., 2005). Specifically, Mayberg found overactivity in Area 25 located in the prefrontal cortex and surrounded by the limbic system and its emotional and memory centers of the brain (see Figure 4). Mayberg reasoned that if Area 25 plays a key role in sustaining depressive thinking, one should see a reduction in activity in this area after successful treatment for the disorder. This, in fact, is what she and her colleagues found (Goldapple et al., 2004; Kennedy et al., 2001).

Figure 5 illustrates the location of the implanted electrodes and the wearable pacemaker for stimulating them. Note that the treatment involves brain stimulation in the operating room as well as a method for stimulating the implants in daily life. Patients wear an external pacemaker that controls the delivery of electrical stimulation to Area 25.

FIGURE 4

BRODMANN'S AREA 25, THE PREFRONTAL CORTEX, AND THE LIMBIC SYSTEM. Brodmann's Area 25 is located in the cingulate region of the prefrontal cortex, where it is surrounded by the corpus callosum and structures of the limbic system (amygdala, hippocampus, thalamus). The limbic system is important in regulating emotion and motivation.

In the following passage, Mayberg describes what happened when the stimulator was turned on to activate the electrode just implanted in Area 25 in the brain of Deanna, her first treatment case. What follows is Mayberg's account of what Deanna said when, unbeknownst to Deanna, the surgical team had turned on the stimulator:

> "So we turn it on," Mayberg told me later, "and all of a sudden she says to me, 'It's very strange,' she says, 'I know you've been with me in the operating room this whole time. I know you care about me. But it's not that. I don't know what you just did. But I'm looking at you, and it's like I just feel suddenly more connected to you.'"
>
> Mayberg, stunned, signaled with her hand to the others, out of Deanna's view, to turn the stimulator off. "And they turn it off," Mayberg said, "and she goes: 'God, it's just so odd. You just went away again. I guess it wasn't really anything.'"
>
> "It was subtle like a brick," Mayberg told me. "There's no reason for her to say that. Zero. And all through those tapes I have of her, every time she's in the clinic beforehand, she always talks about this disconnect, this closeness and sense of affiliation she misses, that was so agonizingly painful for her to lose. And there it was. It was back in an instant." (Dobbs, 2006a).

Although most people who have had the procedure experience dramatic improvements or complete elimination of their depression, some do not. Large-scale clinical trials are under way in which Mayberg and others are studying the effects of the stimulation of Area 25 on larger groups of people with treatment-resistant depression. Initial findings suggest that deep brain stimulation offers relief for the symptoms of severe depression without impairing cognitive function, and the effects have lasted up to 1 year (Bewernick et al., 2012; Lozano, Mayberg, & Kennedy, 2012; Mayberg, 2009; Rizvi et al., 2009; Schlaepfer, 2013). Moreover, follow-up research has expanded our understanding of the brain regions involved in treating depression with deep brain stimulation. For example, Schlaepfer (2013) has reported evidence that brain regions other than Area 25 involved in treating depression with deep brain stimulation include the medial forebrain bundle and the nucleus accumbens—regions intimately connected to reward and pleasure.

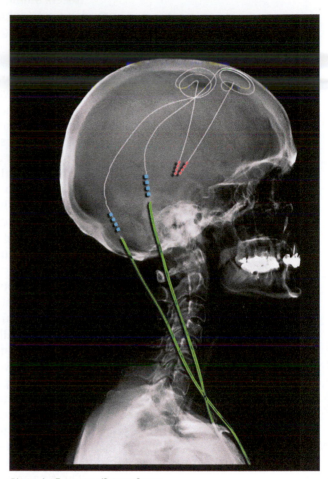

FIGURE 5

DEEP BRAIN ELECTRODES AND STIMULATOR FOR STIMULATION OF AREA 25 IN DEPRESSED PATIENTS. A pacemaker implanted in the person's chest sends electrical impulses to electrodes projecting down into Area 25 of the frontal cortex.

Effectiveness of Biomedical Treatments

Therapies are only as good as they are effective. At the end of each specific form of therapy, we evaluate the current evidence for how effective this type of therapy is.

The SSRIs and tricyclics show comparable effectiveness in the treatment of depression (Kendrick et al., 2006). Both do a reasonable job of regulating depression and are preferable to the MAO inhibitors, given the undesirable, possibly dangerous side effects of the latter. Of the various classes of antidepressants, the SSRIs have the fewest adverse side effects, and people seem to tolerate them better for long-term use (Nemeroff, 2007). Still, these drugs can take up to 4 weeks to have an effect. Presumably, this is how long it takes synapses to produce enough new receptor sites to make use of the increased amounts of serotonin made available by SSRIs.

Initially SSRIs seemed like a great solution for several disorders (depression, anxiety, impulse disorders), but they have turned out to not perform as well as originally hoped. Initial claims for success in a large-scale trial of adolescents done by a pharmaceutical company that sells some of these drugs, was later found to be erroneous on reanalysis. Paroxetine (Paxil) was not found effective to treat depression in adolescents and, in fact, had many negative side effects (Le Noury et al., 2015). Still, these drugs are used widely.

Recent studies, however, suggest that some of the more popular drugs for depression might not be as effective as was once thought. A study by Turner and colleagues (2008) suggests that the medical journals were biased in their publications of findings on the effectiveness of antidepressants. Nearly one-third of all FDA studies—most of which reported negative results on antidepressants—were not published. As a result, for over a decade the impression of the effectiveness of these medications was overestimated (94% versus the more modest and more representative 51%). According to a large-scale meta-analysis, most widely used prescription antidepressants may be no better than placebos for people with mild to moderate depression. For those with severe depression, they are beneficial when compared to placebos (Fournier et al., 2010). The SSRI fluoxetine (Prozac) actually can harm certain kinds of neural growth and block synapse formation (Xu et al., 2010). A large, randomized trial in Romania compared the effectiveness and cost-effectiveness of drug treatment with Prozac and two kinds of psychotherapy (cognitive therapy and rational emotive therapy). They measured depression scores before, twice during, and 6 months after a 14-week treatment course. The psychological therapies were more effective than Prozac, as well as more cost-effective. It is not clear whether the same results would hold in the United States (Sava et al., 2009). Given that over 20% of the U.S. population takes these drugs, some researchers have challenged the assumption that the SSRIs are effective or that their effect comes through their increase in serotonin reception (Greenberg, 2013; Kirsch et al., 2002).

Lithium is still widely used for the treatment of mania. Lithium does appear to have long-term effectiveness in treating bipolar disorder (Berghöfer et al., 2008). The evidence, however, for lithium's effectiveness in treating "acute" phases of mania is weak in spite of its regular use for this purpose in the United States (Reed et al., 2009). Lithium does not appear to be superior to anticonvulsant or antipsychotic medications, or both, in regulating manic episodes. Moreover, these other medications have fewer toxic side effects. Some research indicates that lithium may be most effective in preventing relapse and suicide in people with bipolar disorder, but many providers are not aware of this benefit (Carney & Goodwin, 2005).

The treatment of schizophrenia still presents a huge problem for mental health professionals. Both traditional and atypical antipsychotic drugs work best on the positive symptoms of schizophrenia, such as hallucinations and delusions, but are generally less effective on the negative symptoms, such as flattened affect, as well as on the cognitive confusion that is characteristic of the disorder (Javitt & Coyle, 2004). One atypical antipsychotic, clozapine (Clorazil), does appear to be somewhat effective in treating the negative symptoms, but it also has a potentially serious side effect: diabetes (Javitt & Coyle, 2004). One of the major problems in treating schizophrenia, however, is persuading patients to continue taking the medication. Because of the unpleasant and often dangerous side effects of these drugs, patients often stop taking them. Up to 74% of people using traditional and atypical antipsychotics discontinue treatment (Lieberman et al., 2005; McEvoy et al., 2006). Recent evidence that glutamate may drive the neurotransmitter system in schizophrenia offers hope for the development of more effective, less aversive drug therapies for the disorder (Patil et al., 2007).

ECT is regarded as a treatment of last resort for severely depressed people who have not responded to any other therapy. Although many patients report immediate relief with ECT treatment, its benefits usually last only as long as the treatments are maintained. Also, ECT can have severe side effects, including memory loss and confusion. ECT treatment to one hemisphere of the brain appears to work better than treatment to both hemispheres and creates fewer cognitive side effects (Sackheim et al., 1993). A controlled trial found that ECT and pharmacological therapy for depression were about equally effective in preventing relapse in people with major depressive disorder, but each form of treatment helped only about half the people studied (Kellner et al., 2006).

Deep brain stimulation and other electrical stimulation techniques show promise in treating depression and other disorders, but it is complicated to implement such therapies (Schlaepfer, 2015).

Quick Quiz 1: Biomedical Treatments for Psychological Disorders

1. The antidepressant medications known as the SSRIs work by
   a. inhibiting monoamine oxidase.
   b. decreasing serotonin levels by inhibiting the reuptake of serotonin into the presynaptic neuron.
   c. increasing serotonin levels by inhibiting the reuptake of serotonin into the presynaptic neuron.
   d. reducing the activity of the neurotransmitter glutamate.

2. Your Aunt Julia has been in treatment for years for schizophrenia. She often has jerky spastic movements, which she tells you are from her medication, not the disorder itself. What side effect is she experiencing?
   a. intolerance
   b. reactive dysphoria
   c. tardive dyskinesia
   d. insomnia

3. Electroconvulsive therapy (ECT) is still in limited use for people with which disorder?
   a. schizophrenia
   b. obsessive-compulsive disorder
   c. generalized anxiety disorder
   d. severe disorder

4. Helen Mayberg was surprised to find that brain images of Area 25 showed _____ in people with severe depression and helped devise a way to treat them with deep brain stimulation.
   a. reduced activity
   b. hyperactivity
   c. tumors
   d. reduced blood flow

5. Both traditional and atypical antipsychotic drugs work best on the _____ symptoms of schizophrenia, but they are generally less effective on the _____ symptoms.
   a. negative; positive
   b. positive; negative
   c. cognitive; emotional
   d. emotional; cognitive

Answers can be found at the end of the chapter.

PSYCHOLOGICAL TREATMENTS FOR PSYCHOLOGICAL DISORDERS

A number of psychological therapies have developed alongside the various medications and biologically based techniques for treating psychological disorders. **Psychotherapy** is the use of psychological techniques to modify maladaptive behaviors or thought patterns, or both, and to help patients develop insight into their own behavior. In psychotherapy a therapist and a client work together, or a therapist works with a group of people.

People may engage in psychotherapy for self-development as well as for the treatment of psychological disorders. The types of psychotherapeutic approaches in treating disorders are outlined in Figure 1: psychoanalytic therapy, humanistic/positive therapy, behavior therapies, cognitive treatments, cognitive-behavioral treatments, and group therapy. Each type of psychotherapy has its own explanation of what causes different disorders as well as how they should be treated.

Psychoanalytic Therapy

The oldest and most direct lineage to Freudian therapy is known as *psychoanalytic therapy*. Based on Sigmund Freud's own practices, **psychoanalytic therapy** is the original form of "talk therapy" and is oriented toward major personality change with a focus on uncovering unconscious motives, especially

psychotherapy
The use of psychological techniques to modify maladaptive behaviors or thought patterns, or both, and to help patients develop insight into their own behavior.

psychoanalytic therapy
Based on Freud's ideas, a therapeutic approach oriented toward major personality change with a focus on uncovering unconscious motives, especially through dream interpretation.

through dream interpretation. It tends to require meeting three to five times a week. Currently classical, or Freudian, psychoanalysis is relatively rare. Freudian psychoanalysis, so innovative in its day, is today influential in how it inspires various perspectives in talk therapy, many of which have taken off in very different directions from where Freud started.

Sigmund Freud argued that "dreams are the royal road to the unconscious" (Freud, 1900/1953, p. 608). Freud's two major techniques for interpreting dreams in order to uncover their unconscious content were free association and symbols. In **free association**, the client recounts a dream and then tries to take one image or idea and say whatever comes to mind, regardless of how threatening, disgusting, or troubling it may be. After this has been done with the first image, the process is repeated until the client has made associations with all the recalled dream images. Ideally, somewhere in the chain of free associations is a connection that unlocks the key to the dream. The second technique for interpreting dreams is through *symbols*; that is, dream images are thought of as representing, or being symbolic of, something else. Classic examples of symbols are a snake symbolizing a penis and a cave representing a vagina. If the techniques just described are successful, the patient becomes aware of the disturbing thoughts in his or her unconscious, and the problematic symptoms decrease.

In the process of **transference**, the client unconsciously reacts to someone in a current relationship as though that person were someone from the client's past. While the client is in therapy, that someone is the therapist, but it can be anyone in the person's present life circumstances. For example, a woman whose father was verbally abusive to her might find herself shirking her job responsibilities because she experiences extreme fear when her older male supervisor at work speaks with even a slightly raised voice. The supervisor thinks this is an overreaction, but he does not realize that the woman's response stems from her relating to him as if he were her father. If these reactions occur during a therapy session, as they often do, the therapist can use the transference to help the client understand how her behavior and emotions in current relationships are influenced by her relationship with her father. By working through the unconsciously transferred feelings in the therapeutic setting, a client might be freed from their powerful grip in other settings.

Like transference, defense mechanisms are also central to psychodynamic theory and therapy. Freud and his daughter Anna (who was also a noted psychoanalyst) described many different defense mechanisms, all of which operate unconsciously and involve defending against anxiety and threats to the ego. The most basic one is repression, which involves forcing threatening feelings, ideas, or motives into the unconscious. In psychodynamic therapy, dream interpretation and transference are used to uncover repressed defenses and unconscious wishes.

Some or all of these techniques may lead the client to **catharsis**, the process of releasing intense, often unconscious, emotions in a therapeutic setting.

Humanistic/Positive Therapy

Humanistic/positive therapies seek to help the client reach his or her greatest potential. This field originated as *humanistic psychology*, with work of Carl Rogers (1951), who developed **client-centered therapy**. Client-centered therapy holds that people have mental health problems because there is a gap between who they are and who they would ideally like to be. The therapist must show the client unconditional positive regard—that is, genuine acceptance and empathy for the client, regardless of what he or she has said or done. The goal is to create an atmosphere in which clients can communicate their feelings with certainty that they are being understood rather than judged. If this unconditional positive regard is effective, the client will develop a strong sense of self-worth and the confidence to strive for self-fulfillment.

free association
A psychotherapeutic technique in which the client takes one image or idea from a dream and says whatever comes to mind, regardless of how threatening, disgusting, or troubling it may be.

transference
The process in psychotherapy in which the client reacts to a person in a present relationship as though that person were someone from the client's past.

catharsis
The process of releasing intense, often unconscious emotions in a therapeutic setting.

client-centered therapy
A form of humanistic therapy in which the therapist shows unconditional positive regard for the patient.

©Michael Rougier/Time & Life Pictures/Getty Images

Carl Rogers (far right) leads a group therapy session.

More recently, positive psychology has developed its own form of psychotherapy, generally referred to as *positive psychotherapy* (Rashid, 2008; Seligman, Rashid, & Parks, 2006). This therapy focuses explicitly on increasing a person's happiness, well-being, and positive emotions. Depression, for example, is treated not only by reducing helplessness, sense of worthlessness, and negative emotions but also by actively trying to create a greater sense of well-being and a sense of gratitude. Gratitude training, for instance, involves daily exercises in noticing and finding things in life for which one is grateful and thankful. People who regularly acknowledge what they have to be thankful for have a higher sense of well-being and happiness (Emmons & McCullough, 2003).

Behavior Therapies

In **behavior therapies**, therapists apply the principles of classical and operant conditioning to treat psychological disorders. They focus on changing behavior rather than thoughts, feelings, or motives. The idea is to help clients eliminate undesirable behaviors and increase the frequency of desirable ones.

Behavioral therapists employ the basic principles of operant conditioning through the use of **token economies** to treat maladaptive behaviors. This technique is based on a simple principle: Desirable behaviors are reinforced with a token, such as a small chip or fake coin, which the client can then exchange for privileges. Parents can use this approach with their children—if their room is messy and they clean it, they get a token. The kids can turn in five tokens for candy or a toy. The more this happens, the more likely they are to clean their rooms, or so the logic goes.

In the realm of mental health, the technique was used with some success in the 1950s and 1960s to reduce undesirable psychotic behaviors in patients in mental institutions (Nolen-Hoeksema, 2007). Recent uses include the treatment of substance abuse by people with schizophrenia. Each time the patients did not use drugs, they were rewarded with small amounts of money. Coupled with problem solving and social-skills training, this token system helped control substance abuse in hospitalized patients with schizophrenia, who are generally very hard to treat (Bellack et al., 2006). Also, the use of token economies may encourage socially appropriate behaviors and enhance life skills in children with autism spectrum disorder (Matson & Boisjoli, 2009).

behavior therapies
Therapies that apply the principles of classical and operant conditioning in the treatment of psychological disorders.

token economies
A behavioral technique in which desirable behaviors are reinforced with a token, such as a small chip or fake coin, which can be exchanged for privileges.

FIGURE 6

HIERARCHY OF EXPOSURE TO SPIDERS (THE PHOBIC OBJECT) IN A PATIENT WITH ARACHNOPHOBIA.

1: ©Geoff du Feu/Alamy RF; 3: ©Design Pics/Yuri Arcurs RF; 4: ©Brand X Pictures/Stockbyte/Getty Images RF; 8: ©Will Heap/Getty Images; 9: ©Dirk Freder/Getty Images RF

systematic desensitization
A behavioral therapy technique, often used for phobias, in which the therapist pairs relaxation with gradual exposure to a phobic object, generating a hierarchy of increasing contact with the feared object.

Systematic desensitization is a widely used application of behavior therapy that is especially effective for treating simple phobias (Tyron, 2005). Systematic desensitization pairs relaxation with gradual exposure to a phobic object. First, the therapist generates a hierarchy of increasing contact with the feared object, ranging from mild to extreme. Figure 6 shows a possible hierarchy for a person with arachnophobia (a fear of spiders). In addition to increasing exposure, the therapist helps the client learn relaxation techniques that he or she can use when experiencing anxiety, especially anxiety related to the phobic object. The therapist works to help the client relax and then exposes the client to the phobic stimulus at gradually increasing levels of intensity. The idea to pair two incompatible body responses, relaxation and anxiety, is a clever one. People cannot be both relaxed and anxious at the same time. It works! Systematic desensitization often successfully treats phobias and some other anxiety disorders (Tyron, 2005).

Challenge Your Assumptions

True or False? Fears of specific objects or situations such as spiders or flying cannot be successfully treated with behavioral therapy.
False: Both can be treated successfully with systematic desensitization.

Systematic desensitization involves three levels of exposure to a phobic object: imagined, virtual, and real. In imagined exposure, people simply imagine contact with the phobic object. The next level is virtual reality exposure. At this stage, the individual may be shown photographs or exposed to a virtual reality computer simulation. For instance, one type of virtual reality software allows clients to simulate flying during treatment for flying phobia, as depicted in Figure 7 (Wiederhold & Wiederhold, 2005). The most realistic level of exposure is in vivo exposure, in which the client makes real-life contact with the phobic object.

flooding
Form of in vivo exposure in which the client experiences extreme exposure to the phobic object.

Implosion therapy, or **flooding**, is a form of in vivo exposure in which the client experiences extreme exposure to the phobic object, as when someone who is arachnophobic is asked to hold three hairy tarantulas at once. Flooding, in this sense, is very different from systematic desensitization. Flooding involves heavy exposure to the feared object, whereas systematic desensitization involves gradually making the person less sensitive to the feared object, one step at a time.

Cognitive and Cognitive-Behavioral Treatments

cognitive therapy
Any type of psychotherapy that works to restructure irrational thought patterns.

Any type of psychotherapy that works to restructure irrational thought patterns is known as **cognitive therapy**. Typically, in cognitive therapy the therapist helps the client identify irrational thought patterns and then challenges these thoughts. Cognitive therapy (CT) is structured and problem oriented, with the primary goal of fixing erroneous thought patterns, as we will illustrate with an example shortly. It is also time limited and involves a collaborative effort by the therapist

FIGURE 7
SYSTEMATIC DESENSITIZATION IN THE TREATMENT OF FLYING PHOBIA. Because it is impractical and expensive to do therapy while on an airplane, simulating flying in a virtual reality format is an effective and cost-efficient way of systematically desensitizing people who are afraid of flying.

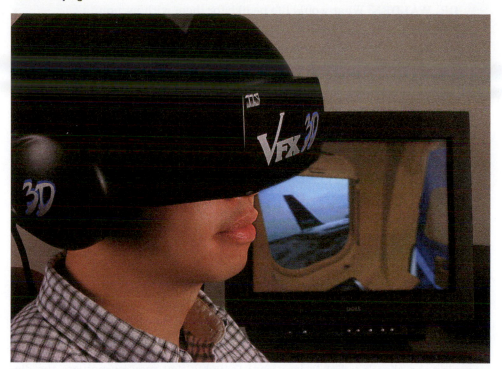

©The Charlotte Observer, Christopher A. Record/AP Photo

and the client. In using cognitive therapy, the therapist relies on what is known as the Socratic method: The therapist poses questions that help the client recognize erroneous logic that may support problematic thinking (Beck & Emery, 1985).

Let's consider the real-life case of Carlos, a 39-year-old man suffering from major depressive disorder. Carlos had tried several medications for his depression and had undergone one voluntary hospitalization, without satisfactory effects. His general practitioner, Dr. Hsu, recommended him for cognitive therapy. Many therapists believe that depressed people perceive events in such a way that they see only potentially adverse outcomes. Cognitive therapy for depression aims to point out the negative bias in such depressive thinking. Consider the following exchange between Carlos and his therapist, Dr. Walden (Gorenstein & Comer, 2002, pp. 54–55):

> **DR. WALDEN:** You say you are a "basket case" and can barely function. What leads you to those conclusions?
>
> **CARLOS:** Well, I've been hospitalized. That's how bad it's been. I just can't believe it.
>
> **DR. WALDEN:** . . . Tell me again what led to the hospitalization.
>
> **CARLOS:** I sort of panicked when the medicine didn't help, and I stopped going to work or anything else. Dr. Hsu figured that as long as I wasn't working, I might as well go into the hospital where I could try different drugs without having to manage all the side effects on my

©Tom M Johnson/Blend Images/Getty Images RF

Cognitive-behavioral therapy focuses on changing a client's way of thinking in order to avoid irrational thoughts. Asking the client to break down problems into steps that can be tackled one at a time illustrates this approach.

own. I also was pretty miserable at the time. I told Dr. Hsu my family might be better off without me.

DR. WALDEN: Do you think they would be better off?

CARLOS: I don't know. I'm not doing them much good.

DR. WALDEN: What would life be like for them without you?

CARLOS: It would be terrible for them. I suppose saying they'd be better off without me is going too far. As bad off as I am, I'm still able to do a few things.

DR. WALDEN: What are you able to do?

CARLOS: Well, I'm not in the hospital anymore. And I don't think I will be back either. . . . I mainly went in because I thought I could get better treatment or whatever. But it didn't pan out, so what would be the point of going back in?

DR. WALDEN: So the fact that you were in the hospital isn't really a sign that you are now or were ever a "basket case," which I take to mean someone who is completely helpless and cannot function.

Notice how Dr. Walden helps Carlos use his own logic to point out errors in the thinking that supports his notion of being worthless. For instance, Dr. Walden helps Carlos see that in spite of being hospitalized for depression, he was neither useless to his family nor totally unable to do things. Carlos came to realize that he really wasn't a "basket case" after all (Gorenstein & Comer, 2002).

Often therapists integrate cognitive techniques for restructuring irrational thoughts with behavioral techniques to shape desirable behaviors in what is known as **cognitive-behavioral therapy (CBT)**. As the name implies, the focus of CBT is to change both thoughts and behavior. CBT entails restructuring thoughts, loosening the client's belief in irrational thoughts that may perpetuate the disorder, and offering incentives for acquiring more adaptive thought and behavior patterns. Cognitive-behavioral therapy is a short-term psychological treatment that has been successfully applied to disorders as varied as depression, phobias, posttraumatic stress disorder (PTSD), obsessive-compulsive disorder, eating disorders, and substance abuse. Think of CBT as a tool for teaching skills that curtail *depressogenic thinking*, or thinking that tends to help generate depressed moods. CBT has revolutionized the treatment of many psychological disorders.

CBT helps clients change the way they evaluate potential emotional threats. To do this, CBT encourages reappraisal, which entails reexamining a situation that was previously seen as stressful. For example, people who are depressed often hold the depressogenic thought that they can't do anything because all tasks seem insurmountable. Through problem solving, clients can learn to adopt a new outlook. For depressed people who think they cannot do anything, the approach would be to list the various steps in a given task and then work on each step until the task is completed. Not only will the client successfully accomplish the task but that accomplishment may also have the further benefit of improving mood. Research on the cognitive processes involved in CBT in relation to treatment effectiveness shows that people who engage in more problem solving during CBT reap more benefits (Chen, Jordan, & Thompson, 2006).

Group Therapy

In **group therapy**, several people who share a common problem all meet regularly with a therapist to help themselves and one another; the therapist acts as a facilitator. Group therapy often follows a structured process, with clear treatment goals such as learning to overcome social anxiety disorder. The group serves as both a source of support and an aid to the therapeutic process by allowing several people with a common problem to listen to, discuss with, and critique

cognitive–behavioral therapy (CBT)
An approach to treating psychological disorders that combines techniques for restructuring irrational thoughts with operant and classical conditioning techniques to shape desirable behaviors.

group therapy
A therapeutic setting in which several people who share a common problem all meet regularly with a therapist to help themselves and one another.

one another. The interactions among participants becomes as much a part of the treatment as people's individual comments. These relationships become real-life contexts in which the various issues play out in front of the group. The presence of other people with the same problem also helps remove feelings of isolation.

Groups can offer less structured therapeutic contexts as well. **Support groups** are meetings of people who share a common situation, be it a disorder, a disease, or an ill family member. They meet regularly to share experiences, usually without programmatic treatment goals. They usually have a facilitator, a regular meeting time, and an open format. Support groups offer a sense of community, a forum for information exchange, and a place to share feelings for people who may have felt isolated by their situation. Support groups are widely available for people with all types of psychological disorders, as well as those living with chronic illnesses, such as diabetes or cancer.

Groups can be categorized in terms of their focus, such as eating disorders, substance abuse, OCD, or bereavement, and may be time-limited or ongoing. Time-limited groups run for a set number of sessions, tend to follow a program of treatment, and usually do not add members after the first few meetings. Ongoing groups, in contrast, welcome new members as they appear. Alcoholics Anonymous (AA) and other substance abuse groups that follow AA's 12-step approach are examples of ongoing groups. Also in this category are "life support groups," in which people who are coping with, say, a spouse with a brain tumor or a son with major depressive disorder can meet and share their feelings about what they are going through.

Psychological treatments have been used not only to alleviate psychological disorders but also to help prevent the development of such disorders. Given the difficulties in treating many psychological disorders and the costs to individuals and society of the large numbers of people suffering from such conditions, prevention programs are an increasing area of effort in psychology and medicine (see the "Preventing Disorders" section later in this chapter). Figure 8

support groups
Meetings of people who share a common situation, be it a disorder, a disease, or coping with an ill family member.

Therapy	Cause of problem	Goal of therapy	Techniques
Psychodynamic	Disorders are symptoms of unconscious and repressed thoughts, feelings, and motives.	Work to uncover repressed and unconscious thoughts, feelings, and motives (defense mechanisms).	Dream interpretation, free association, transference Catharsis
Humanistic	Conditions are blocking personal growth.	Create conditions for optimal growth.	Unconditional positive regard, empathic listening
Behavior	Maladaptive behavior has been reinforced and rewarded.	Change reinforcers and rewards to change maladaptive behavior.	Classical and operant conditioning; token economies; systematic desensitization
Cognitive	Irrational thoughts lead to disordered behaviors.	Change emotions/irrational thoughts.	Critical questioning (Socratic method)
Cognitive–behavioral	Maladaptive behaviors have been reinforced and irrational thoughts have developed.	Change thoughts and behavior.	Restructure thoughts and offer incentives for acquiring more adaptive thoughts and behaviors; reappraisal
Group	Being isolated and unsupported makes disorders worse.	Facilitate support groups and sense of community so person realizes he or she is not alone.	Support groups; 12-step programs

FIGURE 8
CAUSES, GOALS, AND TECHNIQUES OF PSYCHOLOGICAL THERAPIES. Each major psychological perspective has its own theory of what causes psychological disorders, as well as distinct goals and techniques of treatment.

summarizes the psychotherapies discussed in this section and lists what each therapy addresses as the causes of a disorder, as well as the therapy's treatment goals and techniques.

Effectiveness of Psychological Treatments

An increasingly prevalent view is that therapists need to make treatment choices based on the empirical evidence of their efficacy—that is, they need to be **evidence-based therapies** (APA Presidential Task Force, 2006). However, very little research has addressed the issue of which psychotherapies work best for various disorders. Decades ago, a review of the literature on the effectiveness of various types of psychotherapies showed that people who received any kind of therapy were better off on a number of outcomes relevant to mental status than were most people who did not receive therapy (Smith & Glass, 1977). The study revealed no significant differences between behavior therapies and psychodynamic ones. Current meta-analyses of the effectiveness of psychotherapy continue to show that most forms of therapy are effective and few significant differences exist in effectiveness among general psychotherapy, cognitive-behavioral therapy, and psychodynamic therapy (Shedler, 2010). This conclusion is sometimes referred to as the **dodo bird verdict**, after the dodo bird in *Alice in Wonderland* (Luborsky, Singer, & Luborsky, 1975). The dodo bird proclaims, "Everybody has won, and must have prizes." The idea is that psychotherapy tends to work, but which kind of therapy one has appears not to matter too much.

However, this assessment does not mean there are no differences in effectiveness. In some cases, the usefulness of psychotherapy depends on the nature of the disorder being treated and the state of the patient's mental health. Some conditions are more responsive to psychological intervention than others. Personality disorders are best helped with psychodynamic psychotherapy (Shedler, 2010), phobias with behavior therapy (Tyron, 2005), and schizophrenia with drug therapy (Javitt & Coyle, 2004). For instance, people with schizophrenia experience such disordered thinking that it may be very difficult to teach them to work with their feelings and thoughts in order to change their behavior. That said, long-term group therapy appears to improve the basic life skills of people with schizophrenia (Sigman & Hassan, 2006).

People experiencing depressive disorders are much more responsive to psychological approaches than are people suffering from schizophrenic disorders, but the approach needs to be matched up carefully with the disorder. Systematic desensitization, for example, is quite effective for treating a simple phobia but is inappropriate for treating depression. Length of treatment matters as well. As therapy continues, effectiveness declines (Howard et al., 1986; Kopta, 2003). Perhaps the potency of a psychological treatment begins to wear out after a certain point, or maybe only the harder-to-treat cases stay in therapy longer (Barkham et al., 2006).

Cognitive therapy and cognitive–behavioral therapy have shown perhaps the greatest effectiveness of any form of psychotherapy for treating various psychological disorders, but they are especially effective for certain cases of depression and anxiety disorders (Kehle, 2008; Tolin, 2010; Venning et al., 2009). Recent data suggest that cognitive therapy is as effective as antidepressants in treating severe depression (Hollon et al., 2005). In one study, depicted in the "Research Process" for this chapter (Figure 9), experimental groups of individuals diagnosed with depression received either cognitive therapy or drug therapy, while a control group was treated with a placebo. Cognitive therapy was as effective as drug therapy in treating depression, with fewer risks (DeRubeis et al., 2005). In the treatment of obsessive-compulsive disorder, CBT slows metabolism in the caudate nucleus, an area of the brain that is overactive in people suffering from this disorder (Linden, 2006). In short, psychotherapy can change the brain.

Research Process

1 Research Question

Is cognitive therapy as effective as the more expensive antidepressant medication in treating people with depression?

2 Method

Two hundred forty patients with moderate to serious depression participated in a 16-week experimental study. Half of them were randomly assigned to the antidepressant medication condition, and the other half were randomly assigned to either the cognitive therapy or placebo pill condition. The medication group received Paxil (paroxetine) for 16 weeks and no psychotherapy. The cognitive therapy group received individualized cognitive psychotherapy on a regular basis for 16 weeks. Those in the placebo pill condition received the placebo for 8 weeks and Paxil for the final 8 weeks.

©Andrea Morini/Getty Images RF

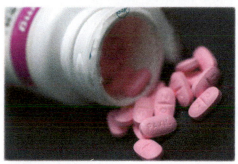

©Joe Raedle/Getty Images

Depression scores were measured twice a week for all 16 weeks using a standard depression questionnaire, the Hamilton Depression Rating Scale. A score of 12 and above is representative of depression. Participants had to have initial scores of 20 or higher to be included in the study.

3 Results

The criterion for the absence of depression was a score lower than 12 on the Hamilton Depression Rating Scale. After 8 weeks, 50% of the medication group, 43% of the cognitive therapy group, and 25% of the placebo group were no longer depressed, as the graph shows. After 16 weeks, 58% of both the medication and cognitive therapy groups were no longer depressed.

4 Conclusion

After 16 weeks of treatment, cognitive therapy and drug therapy were equally effective in treating depression, and both were superior to a placebo condition.

FIGURE 9

COMPARING COGNITIVE THERAPY AND DRUG THERAPY IN THE TREATMENT OF DEPRESSION. Is cognitive therapy as effective as medications in the treatment of major depression? In practice, cognitive therapy and drug therapy are often combined effectively to treat depression.

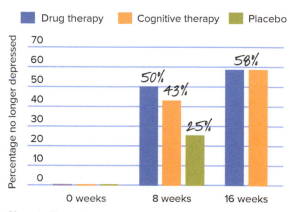

Source: "Cognitive Therapy vs Medications in the Treatment of Moderate to Severe Depression," by R. J. DeRubeis, S. Hollon, J. Amsterdam, R. Shelton, P. Young, R. Salomon, . . . R. Gallop, 2005, *Archives of General Psychiatry, 62,* 409–416.

Behavioral treatments such as systematic desensitization are very effective in treating certain anxiety disorders, especially simple phobias, including performance anxiety and public speaking (Lazarus & Abramovitz, 2004; Tyron, 2005). In vivo exposure appears to offer the most effective treatment of simple phobias, such as snake phobia, but people are more likely to drop out of such therapies than are those undergoing other forms of systematic desensitization (Buchanan & Houlihan, 2008; Choy, Fyer, & Lipsitz, 2007).

Quick Quiz 2: Psychological Treatments for Psychological Disorders

1. José's therapist asks to hear about José's week. José tells him about some difficulty he is having with his wife and how he feels worthless in his marriage. The therapist expresses his empathy and understanding. He tells José he knows what it's like to feel worthless and how uncomfortable that feeling is. What therapeutic approach is José's therapist taking?
   a. humanistic/positive
   b. cognitive–behavioral
   c. cognitive
   d. psychodynamic

2. Which of the following methods is widely used for the effective treatment of simple phobias?
   a. flooding (implosion therapy)
   b. token economies

   c. client-centered therapy
   d. systematic desensitization

3. Often therapists integrate cognitive techniques for restructuring irrational thoughts with behavioral techniques to shape desirable behaviors in what is known as
   a. cognitive–behavioral therapy.
   b. humanistic thought therapy.
   c. psychodynamic therapy.
   d. behavior modification.

Answers can be found at the end of the chapter.

TECHNOLOGY-BASED TREATMENTS FOR PSYCHOLOGICAL DISORDERS

A number of new therapies make use of technology or the Internet to complement current therapies or make psychotherapeutic techniques available to people who might otherwise not have access to therapy or seek it out. These are the **technology-based therapies**.

In **virtual reality therapies**, virtual (digital simulation) environments create therapeutic situations that might be hard to create otherwise. For instance, virtual reality therapy has been used for the treatment of phobias, such as a fear of flying (as we saw in the section on desensitization), or the treatment of PTSD by re-creating a traumatic situation (McLay et al., 2010, 2012; Ready et al., 2010; Riva, 2009). Both of these situations would be either costly or nearly impossible to replicate in real-life therapy (Cukor et al., 2009). Recent research shows virtual reality therapy to also be an effective environment for treatment for social phobia (Bouchard et al., 2016; Gebara et al., 2016; Anderson et al., 2013).

The Internet, apps, and social networks offer online therapeutic environments, as well. The virtual world known as *Second Life* provides a place for people to meet, interact, and develop a social milieu. This online program, which has been downloaded by 15 million users around the world, is a virtual environment where people interact with others in real time. It is mostly used recreationally but increasingly commercially and therapeutically as well (Lisetti et al., 2009). Therapeutically, the participants are patients and therapists, each of whom has an avatar (hence, the name *avatar therapy*). Both people can talk through a headset to give their avatars a voice, or they can chat by text written on screen. Each participant can walk, fly, travel to different locations, and manipulate his or her own facial expressions and body language. As with other online games,

technology-based therapies
Therapies that make use of technology or the Internet to complement current therapies or to make psychotherapeutic techniques available to more people.

virtual reality therapies
Therapies that use virtual (digital simulation) environments to create therapeutic situations that would be hard to create otherwise.

participants encounter other avatars—here the avatars depict both the therapist and people in controlled, lifelike social situations. They interact socially in a virtual environment that feels safer than real life for someone with social phobia.

Therapy apps create a text-based environment for therapeutic conversation between a client (the user) and therapist. Both therapist and client are anonymous to one another. These apps are new and test the boundaries of some legal and ethical ground, as they operate on a 100% anonymity rule (on both sides). Although most therapy operates on conditions of confidentiality between therapist and clients, there is not anonymity. Therapist and client are face to face in real-life therapy. In most states, therapists are legally required to report to authorities (such as child protective services or a hotline) anything that arises in the therapeutic conversation that implies child abuse or neglect. Therapy apps and online virtual rooms are working on resolving those concerns (Ferguson, 2016).

Effectiveness of Technology-Based Therapy

James Herbert at Drexel University is studying the effectiveness of *Second Life* treatment for social phobia (social anxiety disorder) (Yuen et al., 2013). His group offers cognitive–behavioral therapy (CBT) in *Second Life*, in 12 weekly sessions. Through avatars, a client meets with a therapist in a private, secure virtual room. Clients learn new techniques and get opportunities to practice. *Second Life* offers people with social anxiety—who avoid therapy that requires them to get out of the house and go to a new environment—a "safe" form of psychotherapy, because they are not directly observed or exposed to ridicule and embarrassing situations.

Early research on the effectiveness of virtual therapies indicates that it can help people with specific phobias as well as real-life therapy (Morina et al., 2015). A major review of the published studies indicates that virtual therapies are effective in the treatment of many different disorders (Valmaggia et al., 2016), although they may not be quite as effective in treating social anxiety as real-life interventions (Kampmann et al., 2016). Drawbacks to technology-based therapy, however, include its difficulty in ensuring confidentiality and in intervening if patients become an immediate danger to themselves or others.

It is a bit too early to know how well the therapy apps work for treating psychological disorders. Virtual reality treatments, however, do show promise in the treatment of phobias (Monge, Lopez, & Guerrero, 2017).

Quick Quiz 3: Technology-Based Treatments for Psychological Disorders

1. Two disorders that virtual reality therapy is especially well suited for treating are
   a. phobias and trauma.
   b. phobias and schizophrenia.
   c. depression and anxiety.
   d. anti-social personality disorder and narcissism.

2. One of the drawbacks to technology-based therapies is
   a. its expense.
   b. its lack of confidentiality.
   c. its lack of effectiveness.
   d. therapists can only intervene in certain disorders.

Answers can be found at the end of the chapter.

COMBINED APPROACHES

Some approaches combine different types of psychotherapy or combine nontraditional practices with traditional approaches. Sometimes the optimal treatment for a psychological disorder may be to combine drugs with psychotherapy. We will look at several combined approaches: drugs and psychotherapy, integrative therapy, and mindfulness training and psychotherapy.

Drugs and Psychotherapy

Given the dynamic interplay between biological and psychological influences in many psychological disorders, combined treatments might work better than either alone (Ganasen, Ipser, & Stein, 2010). The drugs can modify some of the debilitating effects of a disorder enough that patients can function sufficiently well to learn techniques that might help in changing their problematic thinking and behavior. This approach works best for depressive and anxiety disorders, in which thinking is not severely impaired. A combined therapy to manage depression might employ drugs to help manage the depressive state along with CBT to help clients recognize and control the thought patterns that may push them into depressive states (Cuijpers et al., 2010; Teasdale et al., 2000).

Integrative Therapy

integrative therapy
An eclectic approach in which the therapist draws on different treatment approaches and uses those that seem most appropriate for the situation.

Some therapists take an *eclectic* approach to psychotherapy, which means they draw on numerous techniques in their work with clients. These clinicians are typically trained in many methods and use those that seem most appropriate, given the situation, without loyalty to any particular orientation or treatment. This approach is known as **integrative therapy** (Norcross, Bike, & Evans, 2009; Prochaska & Norcross, 2007). For a client showing symptoms of simple phobia and suffering from depression, behavioral therapy may be best for treating the phobia while cognitive techniques may work better for the depression. Problems of self-esteem might best be treated with a humanistic approach.

The vast majority of clinical psychologists practicing in the United States say they take an integrative-eclectic approach to treating disorders (Norcross, Bike, & Evans, 2009; Norcross, Karpiak, & Lister, 2005). These practitioners share the experience that no one therapeutic approach is effective for all psychological disorders.

Prolonged exposure therapy is an integrative treatment program for people who have posttraumatic stress disorder (PTSD; Foa et al., 2005; Powers et al., 2010). It combines CBT with the imagined exposure form of systematic desensitization and relaxation. For clients with PTSD, this involves a course of individual therapy in which clients directly process traumatic events and thus reduce trauma-induced psychological disturbances. Thus, a person with combat-related PTSD might revisit traumatic war scenes (such as the death of a compatriot) in her mind and engage in cognitive approaches with the therapist to reduce irrational thinking about her role in that event (e.g., she could not have saved him). This technique has been used effectively for the treatment of combat- and rape-related PTSD (Cahill et al., 2006; Foa et al., 2005; Mørkved et al., 2014; Nacash et al., 2007; Powers et al., 2010). Sometimes drugs prescribed for anxiety disorders are used in combination with prolonged exposure therapy to treat PTSD (Rothbaum et al., 2006).

Connection

Mindfulness is heightened awareness of the present moment, whether of events in one's environment or in one's own mind that can be developed through meditation.

See "Full Consciousness" in "Consciousness," p. 219.

Mindfulness Training and Psychotherapy

Some newer therapies integrate the nontraditional practice of mindfulness meditation with psychotherapeutic techniques to treat psychological disorders (Chiesa, Brambilla, & Serretti, 2010; Farb et al., 2010). In mindfulness meditation, the meditator is trained to calm the body and the mind and to notice the thoughts or feelings that might draw his or her attention, without getting pulled around by them and without clinging to them. These skills help people keep thoughts or emotions in perspective. We will explore two combined approaches in this vein: mindfulness-based cognitive therapy and dialectical behavior therapy.

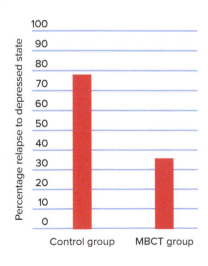

FIGURE **10**

EFFECTIVENESS OF MINDFULNESS-BASED COGNITIVE THERAPY (MBCT) FOR DEPRESSION. When people with depression were treated with mindfulness-based cognitive therapy, they were much less likely to experience a relapse compared to a comparison group of people with depression who received treatment as usual (Teasdale et al., 2000).

John Teasdale and his colleagues pioneered the applications of mindfulness meditation to the treatment of major depressive disorder (Segal, Williams, & Teasdale, 2002; Teasdale et al., 2000). Their approach combines elements of CBT with mindfulness meditation to create a treatment known as **mindfulness-based cognitive therapy (MBCT)**. Both mindfulness meditation and cognitive therapy involve restructuring one's thoughts. Standard cognitive therapy helps depressed people recognize their depressogenic thought patterns and has been very effective in reducing relapse when administered during depressive episodes. Mindfulness meditation develops skills for approaching thoughts nonjudgmentally and enhances people's ability to realize that they are neither bound by their thoughts nor defined by them. To the extent that depression stems from recursive "negative" thought patterns in which the person becomes caught in a feedback loop that is reinforced by repeated episodes of depression, mindfulness meditation might help the patient break out of these loops (Farb et al., 2010; Teasdale et al., 1995).

Meditation-based therapies have been used with some success in the treatment of both positive and negative symptoms of schizophrenia. A general goal in mindfulness meditation is for a person to gain perspective on his or her own thoughts and feelings and, ultimately, change the person's relationships with them. The most common treatment for the positive symptoms of schizophrenia is to try to reduce hallucinations (usually voices) by the use of tranquilizers that ultimately sedate the mind. The downside of such treatment is cognitive dulling—lots of unpleasant side effects. As a result, many people choose not to take their drugs.

But what if people with schizophrenia could learn to live more easily with these symptoms and not be defined and utterly controlled by them? A new approach in the treatment of schizophrenic symptoms focuses on changing the relationship with the voices rather than trying to make them go away. Mindfulness training for schizophrenia takes this novel approach.

A regular regimen of several brief sessions of mindfulness meditation may help people with schizophrenia keep their "voices," or auditory hallucinations, in perspective and not believe them to be real. Initial controlled and case studies indicate that people with schizophrenia experience less distress and improved functioning after such training (Chadwick et al., 2009; Taylor, Harper, & Chadwick, 2009). Another type of meditation, loving-kindness meditation, which helps cultivate a sense of caring for self and others, may offer promise in the treatment of the negative symptoms of schizophrenia (Johnson et al., 2011).

Another combined treatment involving mindfulness is **dialectical behavior therapy (DBT)**, a program developed for the treatment of borderline personality disorder (Linehan, 1993). DBT integrates elements of CBT with exercises aimed at developing mindfulness without meditation. The training, which involves individual as well as group therapy, is designed to help clients develop a nonjudgmental attitude toward their emotions and to accept their current behavior. These skills and attitudes form the cornerstone of personality change, enabling clients to learn how to regulate their own emotions (Linehan et al., 1991).

Effectiveness of Combined Approaches

In spite of the logic for combining drugs with cognitive–behavioral therapy for both the treatment and the prevention of depression (Nolen-Hoeksema, 2007), few studies have systematically examined the relative benefits of drugs, psychotherapy, and the combination of the two. However, a 14-month study of mental health in more than 500 children examined the relative effectiveness of medication, behavior therapy, and the combination of the two approaches in treating a variety of disorders (Edwards, 2002). For ADHD, the combination of drugs and behavior therapy was superior to behavioral intervention and better than medication alone for most outcome measures (Edwards, 2002). Other research has reported that combining psychosocial intervention with atypical antipsychotic medication effectively reduces relapse rates

mindfulness-based cognitive therapy (MBCT)
An approach that combines elements of CBT with mindfulness meditation to help people with depression learn to recognize and restructure negative thought patterns.

dialectical behavior therapy (DBT)
Treatment that integrates elements of CBT with exercises aimed at developing mindfulness without meditation and is used to treat borderline personality disorders.

Psychology in the Real World

How to Choose a Therapist

Nearly 50% of the adult population at some point in their lives will suffer from a psychological disorder, whether it is phobia, depression, anxiety, schizophrenia, or something else (Kessler et al., 2005). However, only a subset of those who need therapy seek it out or receive it (*Mental health*, 2001). Why? One reason has to do with the stigma of "seeing a shrink"—many people do not want their friends, family, or coworkers and bosses to know they are seeing a therapist. There is a stigma attached to the need for mental health treatment (*Mental health*, 2001). Moreover, people often think they have friends and family who can help them so they don't need a therapist. In fact, therapists are trained professionals who have more knowledge, understanding, and training to deal with a whole range of mental health concerns than family and friends. These two forms of help, of course, are not mutually exclusive and should both be sought in unison.

Indeed, research on the effectiveness of treatment shows consistently that treatment is better than no treatment. Suppose that you or a friend or family member is showing signs of difficulty coping or adjusting and would like to find a good therapist. How would you go about doing that?

First, you need to understand the different types of therapists and what they can and cannot do. As briefly described in the chapter "Introduction to Psychology," most therapists fall into the following five groups:

- *Psychiatrists* are medical doctors who specialize in psychiatry. They are typically the only therapists who can prescribe medications. They often treat the most severe psychological disorders.

- *Clinical psychologists* are trained to help people with moderate to severe psychological disorders that interfere with everyday functioning. They assess, diagnose, and treat people with disorders. They are often trained in PhD (doctorate of philosophy) programs but also in PsyD programs (doctorate of psychology). Clinical psychologists often focus on past experiences as the causes of current problems.

- *Counselors* work in social settings and help people adjust to normal work- and family-related difficulties. They focus on the present rather than the past. Counselors are often trained in education departments and receive either a doctorate of education (EdD) or a master's degree in counseling.

- *Social workers* have a master's degree in social work (MSW) and are trained in clinical practice. Once they pass the licensing exam, they are licensed clinical social workers (LCSWs).

- *Marriage and family therapists* (*MFTs*) are people who receive a master's degree in clinical psychology; they have many hours of supervised training and pass the

and increases general functioning in those suffering from schizophrenia for up to 12 months after treatment (Kim et al., 2008).

Clinical research shows that prolonged exposure therapy (an integrative CBT approach) is effective, substantially reducing the symptoms of PTSD over extended periods of up to 18 months after treatment is complete (Foa et al., 1999). Although it has still not been widely adopted by clinicians, prolonged exposure therapy shows substantial benefits compared to no therapy, supportive counseling, and other procedures designed to reduce stress (Cahill et al., 2006).

The advantage of mindfulness-based cognitive therapy (MBCT) compared with standard cognitive therapy is that it works when the person is in a nondepressive state, so it might help prevent relapse. Breakthrough initial work on MBCT showed that it can prevent relapse in people who have had at least three previous depressive episodes. Participants who had recently completed successful drug therapy for their most recent bout of depression were randomly assigned to participate in MBCT or to continue with the treatment they otherwise would have received (treatment as usual), which included seeking help from other sources, such as family or a doctor (Segal, Williams, & Teasdale, 2002). Figure 10 shows that those who practiced MBCT relapsed into depression only about half as often as those who received treatment as usual (Teasdale et al., 2000). More recently, MBCT was shown to be effective in preventing depressive relapse regardless of the number of previous depressive episodes (Geschwind et al., 2012), and in reducing experiences of anxiety and stress in

licensing exam. As the name implies, MFTs specialize in helping couples and families deal with conflict or difficulties.

A therapist's experience is important (Saisan, Smith, & Segal, 2010). You should look for someone who is trained and has experience in the area in which you are having difficulty. For instance, if you are experiencing obsessive-compulsive disorder, your therapist should have experience helping people with this disorder.

Note that these specialists are not qualified to practice therapy just because they have earned their primary degree (e.g., MD, PhD, PsyD, MSW). They must also undergo up to 1,500 hours of supervised training and pass a licensing exam before they can practice therapy. Therefore, at a minimum you want to make sure the therapist you are considering is licensed and in good standing. Each state has a regulatory board that can tell you whether complaints have been filed against a therapist. Some regulatory websites are dedicated to particular kinds of therapists, such as MFTs (see, for example, http://www.amftrb.org/).

In finding a therapist, trusting your gut feeling is important. Relationships with therapists, after all, *are* relationships. Some work and some do not. You have to feel comfortable with and trust your therapist. You should feel comfortable setting up a trial period of perhaps five or six sessions and then determining whether you want to continue. All good therapists will respect your decision to go elsewhere if therapy is not working for you and won't try to make you feel guilty or convince you to stay. If they do, that is a red flag (Saisan et al., 2010).

The approach and orientation of the therapist may matter to you. Some approaches are very short-term and targeted, and others are very long-term and general. You have to decide which is right for you. Two of the more common approaches are cognitive–behavioral therapy (CBT) and psychoanalytic/psychodynamic therapy. Most therapists will take an eclectic or integrative approach, even if they were trained in a particular orientation. Even those trained in a particular orientation, such as psychodynamic or cognitive–behavioral, may use techniques from different orientations if they feel that those will work best for a particular person.

Finally, once you make all of these decisions, you still need to find a therapist who fits your needs. The most common resources for assisting in finding a therapist are your family doctor, your family and friends, lists of providers recommended by your insurance plan, and mental health associations. So ask a doctor or a friend when you are beginning to search for a therapist. Get advice from multiple sources and see whether there is any overlap. Once you have a recommendation, it is wise to speak with the therapist on the phone to get a sense of your comfort level with this person, or try an initial session. You should not feel obligated to continue with someone if you feel the connection is not right.

nonclinical samples (Kaviani, Javaheri, & Hatami, 2011). By restructuring thoughts, MBCT actually restructures synaptic connections involved in learning, memory, and emotion—another example of how experience can restructure the brain.

Borderline personality disorder has long been considered nearly untreatable, but dialectical behavior therapy (DBT) became the first treatment effective in reducing the symptoms (Soler et al., 2009). DBT reduces self-inflicted harmful behaviors, lowers scores on depression questionnaires, decreases dysfunctional patterns associated with substance abuse, and increases the likelihood of staying in treatment (Koerner & Linehan, 2000; Kröger et al., 2006; Linehan, Heard, & Armstrong, 1993). Most important, DBT reduces the risk of suicide attempts—the most disastrous risk associated with borderline personality disorder—much more than does nonbehavioral psychotherapy (Linehan et al., 2006). Not only is DBT effective in treating borderline personality disorder, but it has also been adapted to treat eating disorders, conduct disorders, and domestic violence (Kristeller, Baer, & Quillian-Wolever, 2006; Nelson-Gray et al., 2006; Rathus, Cavuoto, & Passarelli, 2006). In a recent study of a group of people with a variety of diagnoses, participation in a weekly DBT course led to reductions in self-reported anxiety and depression and offered participants an increased sense of hope (Ritschel, Cheavens, & Nelson, 2012).

For all of the variety of treatments available, one of the most challenging aspects of psychological interventions is finding a therapist. "Psychology in the Real World" offers practical information on how to choose a therapist.

Quick Quiz 4: Combined Approaches

1. Dr. Chisholm believes that different disorders require different techniques and strategies for treatment. She is most likely a practitioner of
   a. psychoanalysis.
   b. positive psychotherapy.
   c. mindfulness meditation.
   d. integrative therapy.

2. Combining drugs with psychotherapy works well for which of the following disorders?
   a. mood disorders
   b. anxiety disorders

   c. both a and b
   d. neither a nor b

3. Dialectical behavior therapy (DBT) is a combined treatment program developed for the treatment of
   a. schizophrenia.
   b. borderline personality disorder.
   c. bipolar disorder.
   d. panic disorder

Answers can be found at the end of the chapter.

EMERGING THERAPIES

There are exciting new therapies on the horizon, but they are not yet fully developed and tested for widespread application. In this section, we briefly highlight a few of the more interesting new developments that appear to offer great promise for future treatment.

One new possible treatment involves using light to stimulate neural activity in certain brain regions—a technique generally known as **optogenetics**, a combination of light (hence, the *opto* prefix) stimulation and genetics to manipulate the activity of individual neurons (Deisseroth, 2010). This technique might offer more precise brain stimulation than techniques such as rTMS, tDCS, or deep brain stimulation. Optogenetics was chosen as "Breakthrough of the Decade" by *Science* magazine in 2010. The technique has been used in various mental health–related applications, such as treating obsessive-compulsive disorder and chemical dependency. Researchers have used light to stimulate neurons in the orbitofrontal region of the brain in mice and were able to decrease compulsive behaviors (Burguière et al., 2013). In other researcher, stimulation of neurons in the reward center of the brain (the nucleus accumbens) that are activated by cocaine and, when silenced, greatly decreased the appetite for cocaine (Witten et al., 2010). Optogenetics has also helped our understanding of obsessive-compulsive disorder by helping uncover pathways in the brain (such as those in the striatum) that support compulsive behavior (Burguière et al., 2015), which may allow for carefully targeted treatments (Touriño, Eban-Rothschild, & de Lecea, 2013).

Another potentially exciting future therapy is the regulation of specific genes involved in various mental disorders. A steady stream of recent research has confirmed the role of one particular gene (*neuregulin 1*) in the development of schizophrenia (Law et al., 2006; Mei & Xiong 2008; Yin et al., 2013). Although still in early stages in animals, therapies based on this understanding may be quite beneficial in controlling some of the major symptoms of schizophrenia (Mei & Xiong, 2008; Yin et al., 2013).

Some promising new areas of treatment make use of accidental findings of treatments used for other purposes. Consider the case of Botox, which is used for cosmetic purposes. Botox treatment for wrinkles involves injection of a very small amount of botulism toxin (a naturally occurring paralytic agent) into the facial muscles underlying common wrinkle areas (such as the area between the eyebrows), causing paralysis and relaxing nearby wrinkles. Once the Botox is injected, people frown less. As discussed in the chapter "Motivation and Emotion," there is fairly strong evidence for facial feedback contributing to the experience of emotion, so if you reduce muscle feedback from the face,

optogenetics
A treatment that uses a combination of light stimulation and genetics to manipulate the activity of individual neurons.

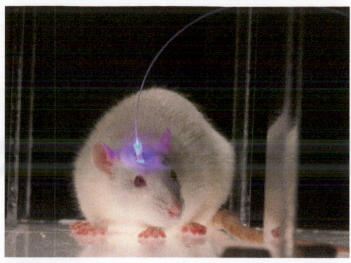

©John B. Carnett/Popular Science via Getty Images

Optogenetics carefully controls electrical impulses to the brain that activate specific neurons. This technique offers promise for the treatment of psychological disorders in humans, such as compulsive disorders.

you reduce the emotional experience (Dimberg & Söderkvist, 2011). A handful of studies have shown that after Botox injections to the glabellar region, people feel less depressed (Davis et al., 2010), because feedback to the brain from the facial muscles involved in certain negative emotions is reduced. There is even evidence for significant improvements in mood for people who have major depressive disorder (Wollmer et al., 2012). Botox may offer an easy new treatment for certain types of depression, but further research is needed to test the long-term effectiveness of this treatment. Botox treatment is not without drawbacks, however, as it can reduce one's ability to read other people's facial expressions, which is likely due to reduced facial mimicry during social interaction (Neal & Chartrand, 2011).

Psychedelic Medicine: A New Hope

A new hope for treatment of psychological disorders is emerging field **psychedelic medicine**, which is defined as the controlled use of psychedelic drugs for the treatment of physical and mental disorders. The roots go back to the mid-20th century. There were numerous studies in the 1950s–1970s, and then a blackout on research that corresponded to rescheduling of these substances (making most illegal and not even allowed for medical use) (Tupper et al., 2015). This area has been revitalized and made much more rigorous in the 21st century.

Before it was illegal, LSD was being used in conjunction with psychotherapy to help people deal with alcoholism, but their work was cut short when the drug became illegal (Krebs & Johansen, 2012). The same can be said of MDMA (chemical name of the street drug ecstasy or "molly"), which showed early promise in psychotherapy due to its ability to enhance emotional experiences and connection. Recently, however, partly motivated by the lack of effective therapies for many disorders, a line of rigorous research on these controlled substances has emerged. Although many more studies are needed, one of the most remarkable things about these various approaches is that psychedelics can have long-lasting, beneficial impact on many disorders after only a single administration or session.

Most psychedelic treatments for psychological disorders are combined therapies, wherein very limited administration of the psychedelic is used to "prime"

psychedelic medicine
The controlled use of psychedelic drugs for the treatment of physical and mental disorders.

the person for certain cognitive and affective conditions, and the therapy offers a communicative structure to work on issues (emotion memories usually) that arise.

The exact format of psychedelic-assisted therapy varies depending on the therapist and the substance used, but usually they are in a comfortable room, with two therapists or a sitter and a therapist. The client/patient is informed about possible effects of drug (or placebo—in the case of research studies). There is a control condition with the placebo administered instead of the actual drug. The client usually guides what happens next, with the therapist(s) as facilitator to any thoughts, feelings, or insights. Usually follow-up sessions are scheduled, but often the drug is administered only in that initial session and/or one follow-up session. Main areas of treatment so far are: posttraumatic stress disorder (PTSD), anxiety, depression, and addiction (Daniel & Haberman, 2017; Tupper et al., 2015).

PTSD: One of the major areas in which psychedelics have been applied is in the treatment of posttraumatic stress disorder (PTSD). Foremost among those used is MDMA, the chemical name for "ecstasy" or "molly," which when combined with psychotherapy can help patients be more at ease with thoughts and memories around the traumatic event that ordinarily create severe anxiety to recall (Mithoefer, Grob, & Brewerton, 2016). MDMA-assisted therapy is emerging as one of the most promising new treatments for PTSD, as smaller scale studies indicate triple the success of treating the disorder compared to treatment as usual (Mithoefer & Mithoefer, 2017). At the time of this writing, the Food and Drug Administration (FDA) has approved advancing MDMA research to Phase III clinical trials, which allows for testing the treatment on large samples of people (Maxmen, 2017). Although MDMA has been associated with severe reactions and death in recreational use, the kind used in these studies is pure and does not pose the dangers of what can occur with some street versions of the drug, which can be tainted with more dangerous substances, such as methamphetamine.

Psilocybin, the active chemical in "magic mushrooms," may help people with PTSD access previously repressed memories of trauma so that they can better heal. In PTSD, it is crucial to the various psychotherapeutic approaches to treatment to relive emotion and recall scenes around trauma. Psilocybin has been shown in fMRI research to activate emotional and memory centers in the brain (Carhart-Harris et al., 2012) as well as dampening perceptions of threat, thereby making it easier for people to relive trauma without excessive stress (Kraehenmann et al., 2016).

Anxiety: Perhaps the most profound work with anxiety and psilocybin is the work around the anxiety of death. Rigorous controlled studies show that a single guided session of psilocybin can significantly increase scores on personality measures and is responsible for spiritual experience and insight into the meaning of life (Griffiths, Richards, Johnson, McCann, & Jesse, 2008; MacLean et al., 2011). When offered to people experiencing anxiety and depression around their impending death from a terminal disease like cancer, it has had similar benefits—alleviating anxiety and depression, helping them find meaning in their lives, and plan the transitions more openly (Griffiths et al., 2016). At a more basic science level, recent neuroscience research in humans shows that psilocybin can modulate systems in the amygdala involved in detection of threat—systems that appear to be overactive (Kraehenmann et al., 2016).

Psilocybin has also been shown to be effective in helping people with treatment-resistance depression (the kind of serious cases where nothing else has helped). One recent study reported that after just two psilocybin-aided

Challenge Your Assumptions

True or False? Psychedelic drugs like psilocybin and MDMA offer promise in treating PTSD.

True: Both psychedelics—especially MDMA—when combined with psychotherapy have showed promise in treating this previously very difficult to treat disorder, by making emotions associated with trauma more accessible to the patient.

therapy sessions (one week apart), people reported significant relief from depressive symptoms that lasted up to 3 months with no adverse side-effects (Carhart-Harris et al., 2016). Much more research is needed here, and the legal issues make widespread availability of such treatments impossible right now.

Addiction: One of the first treatment applications for psychedelics was in dealing with addiction, but promising studies were cut short and cancelled when the substance was made illegal. New work points to success in using psychedelic substances to treat abuse of other substances, such as: LSD and psilocybin for alcoholism, (Krebs & Johansen, 2015), psilocybin for treating both nicotine dependence and alcoholism (Bogenschutz et al., 2015), and the plant hallucinogen ibogaine to treat addiction to the prescription drug oxycontin or heroin withdrawal (Cloutier-Gill et al., 2016).

It might be surprising to think of using one drug to get people off another, but this is not a new strategy in clinical science—the SSRIs have been used for smoking cessation treatment for years. After only 2 to 3 sessions with psilocybin, smokers quit and most have still stayed away from nicotine after more than a year after these sessions. Hallucinogens appear to work for treating addiction because they have the ability to reduce craving, which underlies all addiction. Much more research is needed, but what sets these treatments apart from more conventional drug therapies is that they often work in one or two administrations—long-term use is not necessary or recommended (Johnson, Garcia-Romeu, & Griffiths, 2016).

It is important to also point out that although potentially beneficial, psychedelic therapies, like all therapies, are not without risks. One known risk is these drugs may instigate psychotic disorders in people with personal or family histories of psychosis, so these individuals are typically excluded from such therapy (Krebs & Johansen, 2012; Tupper et al., 2015). Other possible adverse effects are more short-lived and include anxiety, fear, and increased heart rate and blood pressure. Finally, ibogaine can create risk for cardiac problems or death (Belgers et al., 2016).

This being the case, most of these drugs are not habit forming and not harmful. A large-scale survey study of over 100,000 people in the population shows that controlled amounts of psychedelics as a class of therapy have little to no discernible long-term effects on psychological or physical health or suicidal behavior (Johansen & Krebs, 2015). Most of these substances are not known to cause addiction, and with careful monitored application can treat disorders in just 1 or 2 sessions.

Quick Quiz 5: Emerging Therapies

1. Optogenetics has shown promise in the treatment of which of the following disorders?
   a. depression
   b. schizophrenia
   c. obsessive-compulsive disorder
   d. all of the above

2. How does Botox work to improve mood?
   a. by stimulating the brain centers involved in emotion and reward
   b. by paralyzing the facial muscles involved in negative emotions

   c. both a and b
   d. neither a nor b

3. Psychedelics have been used to treat which psychological disorder(s)?
   a. addiction
   b. severe depression
   c. PTSD
   d. all of the above

Answers can be found at the end of the chapter.

PREVENTING DISORDERS

The best and safest form of treatment for psychological disorders is prevention. *Prevention* focuses on identifying risk factors for disorders, targeting at-risk populations, and offering training programs that decrease the likelihood of disorders occurring. Many prevention efforts are under way in this country, but most focus on depression, the number one mental health concern in the United States (Kessler et al., 2005).

Just as a healthy diet and an exercise program can help prevent heart disease, prevention programs train people to behave in ways that help stave off depression and other psychological disorders. Preventing depression in at-risk groups, for instance, has decreased the onset of depression by as much as 25% (Beekman et al., 2010). This rate compares well to the success rate for those who receive therapy. Many prevention programs focus on children, because interventions earlier in life increase the likelihood of making a difference. A recent meta-analysis of more than 30 intervention programs for depression in teens found that shorter interventions and those that involve homework are the most effective (Stice et al., 2009).

Teen depression is a growing problem and the major cause of suicide in young people (Wessely & Kerwin, 2004). In a large-scale study of the risk factors for adolescent depression, Van Voorhees and colleagues (2008) conducted face-to-face interviews of teens in grades 7–12 in the home, obtained parent surveys, and measured depressive symptoms using a questionnaire. They found that several characteristics put teens at risk for a depressive episode: being female, being of a nonwhite race-ethnicity, having low-income status, being in poor health,

©Jeff Greenberg/PhotoEdit

Some people resist seeking mental health treatment.

 Can you think of reasons it is important to offer public education of mental health?

and experiencing parental conflict. Teens who felt a connection among family members, warmth from their parents, and peer acceptance; who did better in school; and who participated in religious activities were less likely to have a depressive episode (Van Voorhees et al., 2008). Research on elementary school children reports similar findings (Dallaire et al., 2008).

In addition to poverty and unemployment, psychosocial factors—especially life stress and a pessimistic outlook on life—increase the risk of depression (Southwick, Vythilingam, & Charney, 2005). For this reason, some intervention programs for teens focus on teaching them skills for dealing with stress, including developing a more optimistic outlook. One after-school program for teens at risk of developing depression is based on CBT. The participants have already experienced mild to moderate symptoms of the disorder; therefore, this program involves retraining in ways of thinking about adversity in life. Clarke and colleagues (1995) reported that compared to those who did not receive the training, those who participated were significantly less likely to become clinically depressed 18 months later.

Another program, the Penn Resiliency Program (PRP), is designed to prevent depression and other psychological disorders by teaching resilience and skills for coping with stress, problem solving (flexibility in the face of adverse or challenging circumstances), and cognitive restructuring (learning to change one's perspective on events). In a meta-analysis of 17 interventions on nearly 2,500 teenagers, Brunwasser and colleagues found that PRP participants had reported fewer depressive symptoms at postintervention and both follow-up assessments compared with youths receiving no intervention (Brunwasser, Gillham, & Kim, 2009). More specifically, in a large-scale study of 697 middle school children, the PRP was administered in weekly 90-minute sessions over a 12-week period (Gillham et al., 2007). PRP significantly reduced depressive symptoms at follow-up compared to a control group and to another intervention, which was not aimed at resiliency, in two of the three schools.

In a similar prevention program, students were assigned to a control group or to an 8-week training program, which consisted of a weekly, 90-minute workshop based on PRP. The group in the training program reported significantly fewer symptoms of anxiety and depression and significantly greater well-being. Although there were no differences between the groups on depressive episodes 6 months later, the students in the training program had increased their ability to achieve an optimistic outlook (Seligman, Schulman, & Tryon, 2007). This is a crucial skill, because depressive thinking is characterized by a tendency to see the negative in any situation. For example, if a glass is filled halfway, someone who is thinking negatively sees the glass as half empty. Helping people look at things differently—in this case, seeing the glass as half full—should help prevent a relapse into depression (Teasdale et al., 2000). Thus, positive outlooks ingrained early in life ought to help prevent a lifetime of depression.

Bringing It All Together

Making Connections in the Treatment of Psychological Disorders

Approaches to the Treatment of OCD and Anxiety Disorders

Obsessive-compulsive disorder and anxiety disorders are diverse groups of conditions. Although they share the core symptoms of fear and anxiety, the *DSM-5* treats them as separate categories. Because they are so diverse, mental health practitioners use a wide variety of treatment strategies to help people with these disorders. Due to their varied symptoms and treatments, these disorders offer a useful context in which to illustrate the application of the treatments discussed in this chapter.

Drug Therapies
Drug therapies play a major role in the management and treatment of obsessive-compulsive disorder and anxiety disorders. The main categories of medication used for treatment are the antidepressants and the antianxiety drugs.

Antidepressants
Many doctors prescribe SSRIs for the treatment of OCD, anxiety disorders, social phobia, posttraumatic stress disorder (PTSD), and panic disorder. People who take SSRIs for these disorders report that these medications help them disengage from the repetitive cycle of anxiety-provoking thoughts that otherwise would snowball into anxiety. As a result, the SSRIs may help change patterns of thinking when combined with the thought restructuring

of CBT and may allow OCD patients to apply cognitive techniques to learn how to think differently. Recent findings that people with OCD who take SSRIs often relapse suggest that combining these drugs with psychological treatments might be more effective than the drugs alone (Catapano et al., 2006). The SSRIs are also considered the first line of treatment for generalized anxiety disorder (Baldwin & Polkinghorn, 2005).

Other antidepressants are prescribed for OCD and anxiety disorders, but much less often. Most tricyclic antidepressants apparently do not work for people with OCD, for example, but do work for certain anxiety disorders. One tricyclic, clomipramine (CMI), however, is most effective on norepinephrine synapses and actually reduces the symptoms of OCD. Because tricyclics have numerous side effects, medical professionals tend to prescribe SSRIs instead (Bleier, Habib, & Flament, 2006).

Antianxiety Medications
Drugs that soothe the agitation of anxiety are used to treat anxiety disorders, especially for people who suffer from panic attacks. Occasionally, physicians prescribe beta-blockers—drugs that block the action of neurotransmitters such as norepinephrine—to quickly calm the aroused sympathetic nervous system. One such drug is

propanolol, which is often used to treat high blood pressure and other cardiovascular conditions. These medications calm the physiological symptoms of anxiety by bringing down heart rate, blood pressure, and breathing rate. The benzodiazepines (for example, Valium) also calm the physiological arousal caused by anxiety and are widely prescribed for social phobia, panic disorder, and generalized anxiety disorder. They can also treat or prevent panic attacks in high-anxiety situations, but they are best used only occasionally. When regular users discontinue benzodiazepine use, they experience withdrawal symptoms, such as insomnia, tremors, increased anxiety, tachycardia (rapid heartbeat), and sweating. Newer antianxiety medications, such as buspirone (used for generalized anxiety disorder), are less likely to create withdrawal symptoms, but they require longer, continuous usage to be effective. The newer selective norepinephrine reuptake inhibitors, as well as SSRIs, are also used in the treatment of anxiety disorders (Dell'Osso et al., 2009).

Psychotherapeutic Treatments

As we have seen, cognitive–behavioral therapy helps people with anxiety disorders identify irrational thoughts and undo thinking patterns that support fear; it also helps them modify their responses to anxiety-provoking situations. CBT effectively treats specific phobias and social phobia in children as well as adults (Hirshfeld-Becker et al., 2010). According to a recent meta-analysis, CBT appears to be superior to other psychotherapeutic approaches in treating anxiety disorders overall (Tolin, 2010).

Group CBT therapy is particularly effective in treating social phobia (Hofman et al., 2006; Tolin, 2010). Such contexts usually involve weekly meetings for about 12 weeks, as well as homework assignments each week. In addition to the normal benefits of CBT for reducing anxious thoughts and behaviors, the social factors involved in a group play a key role in the therapy's effectiveness. Because all the participants have gone through similar situations and can share their experiences, this support helps prevent feelings of isolation and helplessness. Also, group members provide examples of success. If someone in a social phobia group has managed to go to a deli, order a sandwich, and pay the cashier and it went well, this provides an example that simple social transactions really can be done. Other group members might be inspired to try it themselves. Avatar therapy, with virtual reality group CBT, is now being used to treat social phobia as well (Riva, 2009).

Traditional psychodynamic therapies viewed anxiety as the main symptom of what was then commonly called neurosis. Neuroses, according to Freud, most often stemmed from repressed thoughts, feelings, and impulses that usually originated in childhood experiences. Therefore, the main approach of psychodynamic therapies is to uncover the unconscious thoughts, feelings, and impulses that lead to symptoms. Most commonly, this is achieved through dream interpretation, free association, the uncovering of defense mechanisms, and catharsis. Symptom relief requires insight, and insight requires the emotional release of repressed feelings.

We have already discussed the use of systematic desensitization for the treatment of specific phobias. This process couples relaxation training with gradual exposure to the feared object and is very effective for the treatment of specific phobias, such as the fears of animals, flying, and heights (Aitken & Benson, 1984; Wiederhold & Wiederhold, 2005).

Combined and Integrative Therapies and Anxiety

Sometimes medication can help people get "over the hump" of crippling symptoms, so that a nondrug therapy has a chance to work. Such is the case with the combination of either antidepressants or antianxiety medications and CBT or systematic desensitization. Often the course of medication treatment is short term, until the psychotherapeutic training begins to take effect. Alternatively, the medication may be decreased slowly during the course of psychological treatment.

Combining drug therapy and psychotherapy offers hope for treating anxiety disorders, particularly OCD. For example, in a review of the literature on children and teens who suffer from obsessive-compulsive disorder, Kaiser and Bouvard (2009) found that combining drug therapy with CBT was almost always as effective and sometimes more effective than either one alone. Although combined therapies are recommended, a review of the treatment efficacy of combined therapies versus single therapy for anxiety disorders yielded little consistent evidence that combined therapy works better (Black, 2006). In fact, in some cases, drug mechanisms may inhibit the thought processes necessary to make a cognitive or behavior therapy work, as may be the case with combined drug-exposure therapy for anxiety disorders (Otto, McHugh, & Kantak, 2010).

There is evidence that integrative psychotherapeutic approaches offer potential relief from a range of anxiety disorders. As already noted, OCD may be treated with mindfulness meditation practices and cognitive therapy. Mindfulness-based cognitive therapy shows promise in the treatment of generalized anxiety disorder (Evans et al., 2008). Also, dialectical behavior therapy (DBT), which was developed to treat borderline personality disorder, has been used effectively to treat posttraumatic stress disorder (Wagner & Linehan, 2006).

Chapter Review

BIOMEDICAL TREATMENTS FOR PSYCHOLOGICAL DISORDERS

- Both biomedical and psychological approaches are used to treat psychological disorders. Drugs are the most commonly used biomedical treatment.

- Many different drugs are used to treat depression. The older antidepressants include the monoamine oxidase (MAO) inhibitors and the tricyclic antidepressants. The selective serotonin reuptake inhibitors (SSRIs) reduce the reuptake of serotonin at the synapse and create far fewer unpleasant side effects than the older antidepressants.

- Helen Mayberg discovered what may be a neural switch for depression, known as Area 25. Deep brain stimulation of Area 25 can provide sudden relief from depression in people who have failed to respond to any other treatment.

- The SSRIs and tricyclics are equally effective in the treatment of depression. The SSRIs have the fewest adverse side effects and seem to be tolerated better for long-term use.

- Lithium is prescribed to stabilize the mania associated with bipolar disorder. Due to the toxicity of lithium, medical professionals often prescribe other drugs to regulate manic episodes.

- The evidence for lithium's effectiveness in treating bipolar disorder is weak, in spite of its regular use for this purpose in the United States. It does not appear to be superior to less toxic anticonvulsants or antipsychotics in regulating manic episodes.

- Drug therapies for schizophrenia include the traditional antipsychotics, which are rarely prescribed these

©Daly and Newton/Getty Images RF

days due to their adverse side effects, and the atypical antipsychotics. The atypical antipsychotics do not lead to tardive dyskinesia, and they are somewhat better at treating negative symptoms.

- Both traditional and atypical antipsychotic drugs work best on the positive symptoms of schizophrenia. Certain atypical antipsychotic drugs may relieve the negative symptoms.

- Psychosurgery is brain surgery performed to treat psychological disorders. Prefrontal lobotomy was once used to reduce psychotic behavior, but it is now considered an outdated and cruel procedure.

- Electroconvulsive therapy (ECT) involves passing electrical current through the brain to induce a seizure. Because ECT can lead to memory loss, the only currently acceptable clinical application of ECT is for cases of severe depression that fail to respond to any other treatment.

- Although many patients report immediate relief with ECT, usually it is effective only as long as treatments are maintained. Also, the adverse effects of ECT on memory can be fairly severe.

PSYCHOLOGICAL TREATMENTS FOR PSYCHOLOGICAL DISORDERS

- Psychotherapy is the use of psychological techniques to modify maladaptive behaviors or thought patterns, or both, and to develop insight into the client's behavior.

- Psychodynamic therapies aim to uncover unconscious conflicts, motives, or other underlying psychological difficulties. Psychodynamic therapists use several techniques, such as free association, to access the unconscious.

- Humanistic/positive therapies, such as client-centered therapy, help clients realize their full potential. Therapists create an atmosphere in which clients can communicate their feelings with the certainty that they are being understood rather than judged.

- Behavior therapies apply the principles of conditioning to the treatment of disorders. Systematic desensitization, a widely used behavioral method, pairs relaxation with gradual exposure to a phobic object.

- Cognitive therapies work to restructure irrational thought patterns. Often therapists combine cognitive techniques for changing irrational thoughts with behavioral techniques to shape desirable behaviors in what is known as cognitive–behavioral therapy (CBT). CBT is a short-term psychological treatment that has been successfully applied to many disorders.

- Psychotherapy is more effective for certain disorders than for others. CBT may be the most effective form of psychotherapy, especially for certain cases of depression and anxiety disorders.

TECHNOLOGY-BASED TREATMENTS FOR PSYCHOLOGICAL DISORDERS

- A number of newer therapies make use of technology or the Internet to complement current therapies or to make psychotherapeutic techniques available to people who might otherwise not have access to them or seek them out.

- Virtual reality therapies, a subset of which is known as "avatar therapy," use virtual environments (digital simulations) that create therapeutic situations that might be hard to create otherwise.

COMBINED APPROACHES

- Combined treatments are increasingly common in practice. These include methods that combine drugs with psychotherapy and those that combine various forms of psychotherapy with each other. Mindfulness practices have also been added to traditional treatments.

- Many treatments, including CBT, are administered as group therapy. Group contexts serve as both a source of support and an aid to the therapeutic process, allowing several people with similar problems to listen, discuss, and criticize one another.

- In some cases, the most effective treatments for many psychological disorders integrate one form of treatment with another.

EMERGING THERAPIES

- Some therapies, such as optogenetics, gene manipulation, and even Botox, are "not yet ready for prime time" but show promise for the future.

PREVENTING DISORDERS

- Prevention focuses on identifying the risk factors for disorders, targeting at-risk populations, and offering training programs that decrease the likelihood of disorders occurring.

- Many prevention efforts are under way in this country, but most focus on the prevention of depression, the number one mental health concern in the United States.

BRINGING IT ALL TOGETHER: MAKING CONNECTIONS IN THE TREATMENT OF PSYCHOLOGICAL DISORDERS

- Both drug therapy and psychotherapy together are often used to treat obsessive-compulsive disorder (OCD) and anxiety disorder.

Key Terms

atypical antipsychotics
barbiturates
behavior therapies
benzodiazepines
catharsis
client-centered therapy
cognitive–behavioral therapy (CBT)
cognitive therapy
dialectical behavior therapy (DBT)
dodo bird verdict
electroconvulsive therapy (ECT)
evidence-based therapies
flooding
free association

group therapy
integrative therapy
lithium
mindfulness-based cognitive therapy (MBCT)
monoamine oxidase (MAO) inhibitors
optogenetics
phenothiazines
prefrontal lobotomy
psychedelic medicine
psychoanalytic therapy
psychotherapy
repetitive transcranial magnetic stimulation (rTMS)

selective serotonin reuptake inhibitors (SSRIs)
support groups
systematic desensitization
tardive dyskinesia
technology-based therapies
token economies
traditional antipsychotics
transcranial direct current stimulation (tDCS)
transference
tricyclic antidepressants
virtual reality therapies

Quick Quiz Answers

Quick Quiz 1: 1. b; **2.** c; **3.** d; **4.** b; **5.** b   **Quick Quiz 2: 1.** a; **2.** d; **3.** a   **Quick Quiz 3: 1.** a; **2.** a
Quick Quiz 4: 1. d; **2.** c; **3.** b   **Quick Quiz 5: 1.** c; **2.** b; **3.** d

Glossary

absent-mindedness A form of forgetfulness that results from inattention.

absolute threshold The lowest intensity level of a stimulus a person can detect half of the time.

accommodation The process by which the muscles control the shape of the lens to adjust to viewing objects at different distances.

acetylcholine (ACh) A neurotransmitter that controls muscle movement and plays a role in mental processes such as learning, memory, attention, sleeping, and dreaming.

achievement motivation A desire to do things well and overcome obstacles.

acquired immunity Immunity provided by antibodies produced in the body in response to specific antigens.

action potential The impulse of positive charge that runs down an axon.

adaptations Inherited solutions to ancestral problems that have been selected for because they contribute in some way to reproductive success.

adaptive behavior Adjustment to and coping with everyday life.

addiction A condition that results from habitual use or physical and psychological dependence on a substance.

adolescence The transition period between childhood and adulthood.

adrenal glands Endocrine structures that release hormones important in regulating the stress response and emotions.

adrenal-medullary system A major neuroendocrine pathway stimulated during stress, in which the hypothalamus activates the sympathetic nervous system.

affective traits Stable predispositions toward certain types of emotional responses.

afterimages Visual images that remain after removal of or looking away from the stimulus.

aggression Violent behavior that is intended to cause psychological or physical harm, or both, to another being.

agoraphobia An anxiety disorder involving fear of being in places from which escape might be difficult or in which help might not be available, should a panic attack occur.

AIM Three biologically based dimensions of consciousness—activation, input, and mode.

alarm stage The phase of the general adaptation syndrome in which all of the body's resources respond to a perceived threat.

algorithm A step-by-step procedure or formula for solving a problem.

alleles Different forms of a gene.

all-or-none principle The idea that, once the threshold has been crossed, either an action potential fires or it does not.

allostasis The process by which the body achieves stability through physiological change.

alpha waves The pattern of brain activity when one is relaxed and drowsy; slower, higher-energy waves than beta waves.

altruism Selfless attitudes and behavior toward others.

Alzheimer's disease A degenerative disease marked by progressive cognitive decline and characterized by a collection of symptoms, including confusion, memory loss, mood swings, and eventual loss of physical function.

amnesia Memory loss due to brain injury or disease.

amygdala A small, almond-shaped structure located directly in front of the hippocampus; has connections with many important brain regions and is important for processing emotional information, especially that related to fear.

anima According to Jung, the female part of the male personality.

animistic thinking A belief that inanimate objects are alive.

animus According to Jung, the male part of the female personality.

anorexia nervosa An eating disorder in which people cannot maintain 85% of their ideal body weight for their height, have an intense fear of eating, and have a distorted body image.

anterograde amnesia The inability to remember events and experiences that occur after an injury or the onset of a disease.

antigen Any foreign substance that triggers an immune response.

antisocial personality disorder Dramatic-emotional personality disorder characterized by extremely impulsive, deceptive, violent, ruthless, and callous behaviors; a serious and potentially dangerous disorder.

aphasia A deficit in the ability to speak or comprehend language.

appraisal The evaluation of a situation with respect to how relevant it is to one's own welfare; drives the process by which emotions are elicited.

arborization The growth and formation of new dendrites.

archetypes Ancient or archaic images that result from common ancestral experiences.

association A process by which two pieces of information from the environment are repeatedly linked, so that we begin to connect them in our minds.

associative network A chain of associations between related concepts.

asylums Facilities for treating the mentally ill in Europe during the Middle Ages and into the 19th century.

attachment The strong emotional connection that develops early in life between infants and their caregivers.

attention The limited capacity to process information that is under conscious control.

attention deficit hyperactivity disorder (ADHD) A childhood disorder characterized by inability to focus attention for more than a few minutes, to remain still and quiet, to do careful work.

attitudes An individual's favorable or unfavorable beliefs, feelings, or actions toward an object, an idea, or a person.

attributions Inferences made about the causes of other people's behavior.

atypical antipsychotics Newer antipsychotic drugs, which do not create tardive dyskinesia.

auditory nerve The nerve that receives action potentials from the hair cells and transmits auditory information to the brain.

autism spectrum disorder (ASD) A childhood disorder characterized by severe language and social impairment along with repetitive habits and inward-focused behaviors.

automatic processing Encoding of information that occurs with little effort or conscious attention to the task.

autonomic nervous system (ANS) All the nerves of the peripheral nervous system that serve involuntary systems of the body, such as the internal organs and glands.

availability heuristic A device we use to make decisions based on the ease with which estimates come to mind or how available they are to our awareness.

avoidant personality disorder An anxious-fearful personality disorder characterized by extreme fear of being criticized, low self-esteem, and avoidance of social interaction.

awareness Monitoring of information from the environment and from one's own thoughts.

axon A long projection that extends from a neuron's soma; it transmits electrical impulses toward the adjacent neuron and stimulates the release of neurotransmitters.

babbling Sounds made as a result of the infant's experimentation with a complex range of phonemes, which include consonants as well as vowels; starts around 5–6 months of age.

barbiturates A class of anxiety-reducing sedatives that can be addictive and carry a risk of overdose.

basal ganglia A collection of structures surrounding the thalamus; involved in voluntary motor control.

base-rate Is how common is an event or trait in the general population.

basic emotions The set of emotions that are common to all humans; includes anger, disgust, fear, happiness, sadness, and surprise.

basic tendencies The essence of personality: the Big Five personality dimensions, as well as talents, aptitudes, and cognitive abilities.

basilar membrane A membrane that runs through the cochlea; contains the hair cells.

behavior modification The principles of operant conditioning used to change behavior.

behavior therapies Therapies that apply the principles of classical and operant conditioning in the treatment of psychological disorders.

behavioral genetics The scientific study of the role of heredity in behavior.

behavioral measures Measures based on systematic observation of people's actions either in their normal environment or in a laboratory setting.

behavioral neuroscience The study of the links among brain, mind, and behavior.

behavioral thresholds The points at which a person moves from not having a particular response to having one.

behaviorism A school of psychology that proposed that psychology can be a true science only if it examines observable behavior, not ideas, thoughts, feelings, or motives.

benzodiazepines A class of anxiety-reducing drugs that can be addictive but are less dangerous than barbiturates.

beta waves The pattern of brain activity when one is awake; rapid, low-energy waves.

big data Extremely large amount of data captured from online behaviors (especially social media), which are then collected and analyzed for patterns by sophisticated analytic programs.

Big Five (five-factor model) A theory of personality that includes the following five dimensions: openness to experience, conscientiousness, extraversion, agreeableness, and neuroticism (OCEAN).

binocular depth cues Aids to depth perception that rely on input from both eyes.

binocular disparity The difference in retinal images due to the fact that our two eyes are separated by a few inches and is an important cue in depth perception.

biological constraint model A view on learning which proposes that some behaviors are inherently more likely to be learned than others.

biological psychology The study of the relationship between bodily systems and chemicals and how they influence behavior and thought.

biological sex Is the anatomical and physiological characteristics of males and females.

bipolar disorder A mood disorder characterized by substantial mood fluctuations, cycling between very low (depressive) and very high (manic) moods.

blocking The inability to retrieve some information that once was stored.

bodily senses The senses based in the skin, the body, or any membrane surfaces.

borderline personality disorder A dramatic-emotional personality disorder characterized by out-of-control emotions, fear of being abandoned by others, and vacillation between idealizing and despising people who are close to the person with the disorder.

bottom-up processing The idea that perception is a process of building a perceptual experience from smaller pieces.

broad intelligence One of Carroll's three levels of intelligence; includes abilities such as crystallized and fluid intelligence, memory, learning, and processing speed.

broaden-and-build model Fredrickson's model for positive emotions, which posits that they widen our cognitive perspective and help us acquire useful life skills.

Broca's area The area in the left frontal lobe responsible for the ability to produce speech.

bulimia nervosa An eating disorder characterized by binge eating and a perceived lack of control during the eating session.

by-product Is a structure or trait that is not a functional adaptation, but is a offshoot of an adaptation.

bystander effect A phenomenon in which the greater the number of bystanders who witness an emergency, the less likely any one of them is to help.

cardiovascular reactivity (CVR) model The hypothesis that hostility can increase the likelihood of heart disease through at least two different causal routes.

cardiovascular system The heart, the blood, and all the blood vessels.

case study A study design in which a psychologist, often a therapist, observes one person over a long period of time.

catecholamines Chemicals released from the adrenal glands that function as hormones and as neurotransmitters to control ANS activation.

category Consist of perceiving similar features in objects, ideas, or events and treating them as if they are the same.

catharsis The process of releasing intense, often unconscious emotions in a therapeutic setting.

causal inferences Judgments about causation of one thing by another.

cellular immunity The immune response that occurs when T lymphocytes (T cells) fight antigens.

central nervous system (CNS) The part of the nervous system that comprises the brain and spinal cord.

cerebellum A hindbrain structure involved in body movement, balance, coordination, fine-tuning motor skills, and cognitive activities such as learning and language.

cerebral cortex The thin outer layer of the cerebrum, in which much of human thought, planning, perception, and consciousness takes place.

cerebrum Each of the large halves of the brain; covered with convolutions, or folds.

child-directed speech Changes in adult speech patterns—apparently universal—when speaking to young children or infants; characterized by higher pitch, changes in voice volume, use of simpler sentences, emphasis on the here and now, and use of emotion to communicate messages.

chromosome A coiled-up thread of DNA.

chunking Breaking down a list of items to be remembered into a smaller set of meaningful units.

cingulate gyrus A beltlike structure in the middle of the brain; plays an important role in attention and cognitive control.

circadian rhythms The variations in physiological processes that cycle within approximately a 24-hour period, including the sleep–wake cycle.

cis-gendered Is when a person's gender identity is the same (cis) as their sex assigned at birth.

classical conditioning A form of associative learning in which a neutral stimulus becomes associated with a stimulus to which one has an automatic, inborn response.

client-centered therapy A form of humanistic therapy in which the therapist shows unconditional positive regard for the patient.

clinical psychology The treatment of mental, emotional, and behavioral disorders and the promotion of psychological health.

cochlea A bony tube of the inner ear, which is curled like a snail's shell and filled with fluid.

cognition Mental processes involved in acquiring, processing, and storing knowledge.

cognitive dissonance The feeling of discomfort caused by information that is different from a person's conception of himself or herself as a reasonable and sensible person.

cognitive psychology The study of how people perceive, remember, think, speak, and solve problems.

cognitive symptoms (of schizophrenia) Problems with working memory, attention, verbal and visual learning and memory, reasoning and problem solving, processing, and speech.

cognitive therapy Any type of psychotherapy that works to restructure irrational thought patterns.

cognitive–behavioral therapy (CBT) An approach to treating psychological disorders that combines techniques for restructuring irrational thoughts with operant and classical conditioning techniques to shape desirable behaviors.

collective unconscious According to Jung, the form of consciousness that consists of the shared universal experiences of our ancestors—God, mother, life, death, water, earth, aggression, survival—that have been passed down from generation to generation.

collectivism Cultures that tend to be more concerned about the impact of their behavior on their family, friends, and social groups.

coma A state of consciousness in which the eyes are closed and the person is unresponsive and unarousable.

comorbidity The occurrence of two or more psychological disorders at the same time.

compassion A state of relationship in which one feels kindness toward another who is suffering and one feels motivated to help relieve that suffering.

compensation Adler's description of an unconscious reaction people have to cover up their weaknesses and sense of inferiority by striving for superiority.

compulsion A repetitive behavior performed in response to uncontrollable urges or according to a ritualistic set of rules.

concept A mental grouping of objects, events, or people.

concept hierarchy An arrangement of related concepts in a particular way, with some being general and others specific.

concrete operational stage Piaget's third stage of cognitive development, which spans ages 6–11, during which the child can perform mental operations—such as reversing—on real objects or events.

conditioned response (CR) A behavior that an organism learns to perform when presented with the CS.

conditioned stimulus (CS) A previously neutral input that an organism learns to associate with the UCS.

conditioned taste aversion The learned avoidance of a particular taste or food.

conditioning A form of associative learning in which behaviors are triggered by associations with events in the environment.

cones Photoreceptors that are responsible for color vision and are most functional in conditions of bright light.

confirmation bias The tendency to selectively attend to information that supports one's general beliefs while ignoring information or evidence that contradicts one's beliefs.

conformity The tendency of people to adjust their behavior to what others are doing or to adhere to the norms of their culture.

confounding variable The variable whose influence on the dependent variable cannot be separated from the independent variable being examined.

conjunction fallacy An error in logic that occurs when people say the combination of two events is more likely than either event alone.

connectome The map of all neural networks in the human brain; the wiring diagram of the brain.

consciousness An awareness of one's surroundings and of what's in one's mind at a given moment; includes aspects of being awake and aware.

conservation Recognition that when some properties (such as shape) of an object change, other properties (such as volume) remain constant.

consolidation The process of establishing, stabilizing, or solidifying a memory; the second stage of long-term memory formation.

construct validity The degree to which a test measures the concept it claims to measure, such as intelligence.

continuity The Gestalt law that says we see points or lines in such a way that they follow a continuous path.

continuous reinforcement Reinforcement of a behavior every time it occurs.

control group A group of research participants who are treated in exactly the same manner as the experimental group, except that they do not receive the independent variable, or treatment.

conventional level The second level in Kohlberg's theory of moral reasoning, during which the person values caring, trust, and relationships as well as the social order and lawfulness.

convergent thinking problems Problems that have known solutions and require analytic thinking and the use of learned strategies and knowledge to come up with the correct answer.

cooing The first sounds humans make other than crying, consisting almost exclusively of vowels; occurs during the first 6 months of life.

coping The act of dealing with stress or emotions.

cornea The clear, hard covering that protects the lens of the eye.

corpus callosum Nerve fibers that connect the two hemispheres of the brain.

correlation coefficients Statistics that range from –1.0 to +1.0 and assess the strength and direction of association between two variables.

correlational designs Studies that measure two or more variables and their relationship to one another; not designed to show causation.

cortisol A stress hormone produced by the body to ensure that the body gets enough fuel during emotional arousal and stress.

cortical arousal The brain's level of activity at a resting state and its sensitivity to stimulation.

creativity Thinking and/or behavior that is both novel—original and useful—and adaptive.

critical thinking A process by which one analyzes, evaluates, and forms ideas.

crystallized intelligence The kind of knowledge that one gains from experience and learning, education, and practice.

cult An extremist group led by a charismatic, totalitarian leader in which coercive methods are used to prevent members from leaving the group.

cultural test bias The notion that group differences in IQ scores are caused by different cultural and educational backgrounds, not by real differences in intelligence.

cyberbullying The willful and repeated harm inflicted through the medium of electronic text.

cyclothymia A relatively mild form of bipolar disorder.

dark adaptation The process of adjustment to seeing in the dark.

debriefing The explanation of the purposes of a study following data collection.

deductive reasoning Reasoning from general statements of what is known to specific conclusions.

default mode network A brain network that consists of regions of the frontal and parietal lobes that are active when a person is not focused on anything in particular from the outside and becomes less active when a person is focused on a particular stimulus.

defense mechanisms Unconscious strategies the mind uses to protect itself from anxiety by denying and distorting reality in some way.

dehumanization A tendency to portray a group of people as unworthy of human rights and traits—intended to make them feel unworthy.

delta waves Type of brain activity that dominates N3 sleep; higher energy than theta waves.

delusions One of the symptoms of schizophrenia: false beliefs or exaggerations held despite evidence to the contrary, such as the idea that one is a famous person.

demand characteristics Subtle, often unconscious, cues given by experimenters to the participants as to how they should behave in the role of participant.

dementia A loss of mental function, in which many cognitive processes are impaired, such as the ability to remember, reason, solve problems, make decisions, and use language.

dendrites Fingerlike projections from a neuron's soma that receive incoming messages from other neurons.

dependent personality disorder An anxious-fearful personality disorder characterized by fear of being rejected and a strong need to be cared for.

dependent variable In an experiment, the outcome or response to the experimental manipulation.

depressants Substances that decrease or slow down central nervous system activity.

depressive disorder The highest order category of the depressive disorders and subsumes all forms of depression, including major depressive disorder and persistent depressive disorder.

depth perception The ability to see things in three dimensions and to discriminate what is near from what is far.

descriptive designs Study designs in which the researcher defines a problem and variable of interest but makes no prediction and does not control or manipulate anything.

descriptive statistics Measures used to describe and summarize research.

developmental psychology The study of how thought and behavior change and remain stable across the life span.

dialectical behavior therapy (DBT) Treatment that integrates elements of CBT with exercises aimed at developing mindfulness without meditation and is used to treat borderline personality disorders.

diathesis-stress Biological predispositions plus stress or abusive environments together produce psychological disorders.

diathesis-stress model An explanation for the origin of psychological disorders as a combination of biological predispositions (diathesis) plus stress or an abusive environment.

difference threshold The smallest amount of change between two stimuli that a person can detect half of the time.

diffusion tensor imaging A method of brain measurement similar to MRI that provides a measure of white matter rather than grey matter; ideal for examining connections between brain regions, rather than those regions themselves.

discrimination The preferential treatment of certain people, usually driven by prejudicial attitudes.

disorders of consciousness A diagnostic category that encompasses the variety of ways in which wakefulness and awareness might be compromised.

display rules Learned norms or rules, often taught very early, about when it is appropriate to express certain emotions and to whom one should show them.

dissociative disorders Psychological disorders characterized by extreme splits or gaps in memory, identity, or consciousness.

dissociative identity disorder (DID) A dissociative disorder in which a person develops at least two distinct personalities, each with its own memories, thoughts, behaviors, and emotions; some psychiatrists question the legitimacy of the disorder.

divergent thinking problems Problems that have no known solutions and require novel solutions.

DNA (deoxyribonucleic acid) A large molecule that contains genes.

dodo bird verdict The finding that most forms of therapy are effective and few significant differences exist in effectiveness among standard therapies.

dominant alleles Alleles that show their effect even if there is only one allele for that trait in the pair.

dopamine A neurotransmitter released in response to behaviors that feel good or are rewarding to the person or animal; also involved in voluntary motor control.

double-blind studies Studies in which neither the participants nor the researchers administering the treatment know who has been assigned to the experimental or control group.

Down syndrome A chromosomal disorder characterized by mild to profound intellectual disability.

dreams Images, thoughts, and feelings experienced during sleep.

drives The perceived states of tension that occur when our bodies are deficient in some need, creating an urge to relieve the tension.

Duchenne smile A smile that expresses true enjoyment, involving both the muscles that pull up the lip corners diagonally and those that contract the band of muscles encircling the eye.

educational psychology The study of how students learn, the effectiveness of particular teaching techniques, the social psychology of schools, and the psychology of teaching.

effect size A measure of the strength of the relationship between two variables or the extent of an experimental effect.

effortful processing Encoding of information that occurs with careful attention and conscious effort.

ego One of Freud's provinces of the mind; a sense of self; the only part of the mind that is in direct contact with the outside world; operates on the "reality principle."

egocentrism Viewing the world from one's own perspective and not being capable of seeing things from another person's perspective.

electroconvulsive therapy (ECT) The treatment of last resort for severe depression that involves passing an electrical current through a person's brain in order to induce a seizure.

electroencephalography (EEG) A method for measuring brain activity in which the electrical activity of the brain is recorded from electrodes placed on a person's scalp.

embodied cognition The thought processes involved in representing parts of the body and/or reenacting bodily actions in thoughts.

embryo A developing organism from 2 weeks until about 8 weeks after conception.

embryonic stage The second prenatal stage, from 2 weeks to 8 weeks after conception, when all of the major organs form.

emerging adulthood The transitional phase between adolescence and young adulthood; includes ages 18–25 years.

emotion regulation The cognitive and behavioral efforts people make to modify their emotions.

emotional competence The ability to control emotions and know when it is appropriate to express certain emotions.

emotional disclosure A way of coping with stress through writing or talking about the situation.

emotion-focused coping A way of dealing with stress that aims to regulate the experience of distress.

emotional intelligence The ability to recognize emotions in oneself and others, empathic understanding, and skills for regulating emotions in oneself and others.

emotional response The physiological, behavioral/expressive, and subjective changes that occur when emotions are generated.

emotions Brief, acute changes in conscious experience and physiology that occur in response to a personally meaningful situation.

empathy The ability to share the feelings of others and understand their situations.

empathy-altruism hypothesis The idea that people help others selflessly only when they feel empathy for them.

empirical method A method for developing questionnaire items that focuses on including questions that characterize the group the questionnaire is intended to distinguish.

empiricism The view that all knowledge and thoughts come from experience.

enactive learning Learning by doing.

encoding The process by which the brain attends to, takes in, and integrates new information; the first stage of long-term memory formation.

endocannabinoids Natural, marijuana-like substances produced by the body.

endocrine system The system of glands that secrete and regulate hormones in the body.

enzymatic degradation A way of removing excess neurotransmitter from the synapse in which enzymes specific for that neurotransmitter bind with the neurotransmitter and destroy it.

epigenetics The study of changes in the way genes are turned on or off without a change in the sequence of DNA.

epinephrine Also known as adrenaline, a neurotransmitter that arouses bodily systems (such as increasing heart rate).

episodic memory The form of memory that recalls the experiences we have had.

ethics The rules governing the conduct of a person or group in general or in a specific situation—or more simply, standards of right and wrong.

ethology The scientific study of animal behavior.

Eureka insight (insight solution) A sudden solution that comes to mind in a flash.

event-related potential (ERP) A technique that extracts electrical activity from raw EEG data to measure cognitive processes.

evidence-based therapies Treatment choices based on empirical evidence that they produce the desired outcome.

evolution The change over time in the frequency with which specific genes occur within a breeding species.

evolutionary psychology The branch of psychology that studies human behavior by asking what adaptive problems it may have solved for our early ancestors.

exhaustion stage The phase of the general adaptation syndrome when all resources for fighting the threat have been depleted and illness is more likely.

experiment A research design that includes independent and dependent variables and random assignment of participants to control and experimental groups or conditions.

experimental group A group consisting of those participants who will receive the treatment or whatever is predicted to change behavior.

experimenter expectancy effects A result that occurs when the behavior of the participants is influenced by the experimenter's knowledge of who is in the control group and who is in the experimental group.

explicit memory Knowledge that consists of the conscious recall of facts and events; also known as declarative memory.

expressive suppression A response-focused strategy for regulating emotion that involves the deliberate attempt to inhibit the outward manifestation of an emotion.

extinction The weakening and disappearance of a conditioned response in the absence of reinforcement.

extrinsic motivation Motivation that comes from outside the person and usually involves rewards and praises.

fabrication Presenting or publishing scientific results that are made up.

Facial Action Coding System (FACS) A widely used method for measuring all observable muscular movements that are possible in the human face.

facial feedback hypothesis Sensory feedback from the facial musculature during expression affects emotional experience.

false memories Memories for events that never happened but were suggested by someone or something.

falsification Is the changing, altering, or deleting scientific data.

familial-cultural intellectual disability Occurs when environmental deprivation, such as neglect and poor nutrition, is to blame for some cases of milder intellectual disability. Genetics play no role in this form of disability.

feature detectors Neurons in the visual cortex that analyze the retinal image and respond to specific aspects of shapes, such as angles and movements.

fetal alcohol spectrum disorder (FASD) A consequence of prenatal alcohol exposure that causes multiple problems, notably brain damage.

fetal stage The third prenatal stage, which begins with the formation of bone cells 8 weeks after conception and ends at birth.

figure A specific object in front of an unformed background.

fixation The inability to break out of a particular mind-set in order to think about a problem from a fresh perspective.

fixed-interval (FI) schedule A pattern of intermittent reinforcement in which responses are always reinforced after a set period of time has passed.

fixed-ratio (FR) schedule A pattern of intermittent reinforcement in which reinforcement follows a set number of responses.

flashbulb memory Is a detailed snapshot memory for what we were doing when we first heard of a major, public, and emotionally charged event.

flexibility of thought The ability to come up with many different categories of ideas and think of other responses besides the obvious one.

flooding Form of in vivo exposure in which the client experiences extreme exposure to the phobic object.

fluid intelligence Raw mental ability, pattern recognition, and abstract reasoning that can be applied to a problem one has never confronted before.

forensic psychology The field that blends psychology, law, and criminal justice.

forgetting The weakening or loss of memories over time.

forgetting curve A graphic depiction of how recall steadily declines over time.

formal operational stage Piaget's final stage of cognitive development, from age 11 or 12 on through adulthood, when formal logic is possible.

fovea A spot on the back of the retina that contains the highest concentration of cones in the retina; place of clearest vision.

fraternal twins Twins that develop from two different eggs fertilized by two different sperm.

free association A psychotherapeutic technique in which the client takes one image or idea from a dream and says whatever comes to mind, regardless of how threatening, disgusting, or troubling it may be.

frequency The number of times a particular score occurs in a set of data.

functional fixedness A mind-set in which one is blind to unusual uses of common, everyday things or procedures.

functional MRI (fMRI) A brain imaging technique that uses magnetic fields to produce detailed images of activity in areas of the brain and other soft tissues.

functionalism The 19th-century school of psychology that argued it was better to look at why the mind works the way it does than to describe its parts.

fundamental attribution error The tendency to explain others' behavior in dispositional rather than situational terms.

g-factor theory Spearman's theory that intelligence is a single general (g) factor made up of specific components.

GABA (gamma-aminobutyric acid) A major inhibitory neurotransmitter in the brain that tells postsynaptic neurons not to fire; it slows CNS activity and is necessary to regulate and control neural activity.

gate control theory of pain The idea that the spinal cord regulates the experience of pain by the balancing of signals to the brain from small pain nerve fibers and larger non-pain fibers. The pain "gate"opens when more pain signals are sent to the brain than non-pain signals. Pain is blocked when the reverse happens.

gender Refers to the culturally and socially constructed behaviors and roles appropriate to men and women.

gender identity Is the gender one feels oneself to be internally.

gene-by-environment interaction research A method of studying heritability by comparing genetic markers; allows researchers to assess how genetic differences interact with the environment to produce certain behaviors in some people but not in others.

general adaptation syndrome (GAS) As defined by Hans Selye, a generalized, nonspecific set of changes in the body that occur during extreme stress.

general intelligence One of Carroll's three levels of intelligence; very similar to Spearman's concept of "g."

generalized anxiety disorder (GAD) A state of pervasive and excessive anxiety lasting at least 6 months.

generativity A term Erik Erikson used to describe the process in adulthood of creating new ideas, products, or people.

genes Small segments of DNA that contain information for producing proteins.

genetic marker Is a specific location on a gene that can identify an individual.

genius High intelligence combined with creative accomplishments that have a tremendous impact on a given field.

genome All the genetic information in DNA.

genotype The entire genetic makeup of an organism.

germinal stage The first prenatal stage of development, which begins at conception and lasts 2 weeks.

Gestalt psychology A theory of psychology that maintains that we perceive things as wholes rather than as a compilation of parts.

glial cells Central nervous system cells that provide structural support, promote efficient communication between neurons, and serve as scavengers, removing cellular debris.

glucocorticoids Hormones responsible for maintaining the activation of physiological systems during emergencies.

glucose A simple sugar that provides energy for cells throughout the body, including the brain.

glutamate A major excitatory neurotransmitter in the brain that increases the likelihood that a postsynaptic neuron will fire; important in learning, memory, neural processing, and brain development.

graded potentials Small changes in membrane potential that by themselves are insufficient to trigger an action potential.

grammar The entire set of rules for combining symbols and sounds to speak and write a particular language.

gray matter Is the brain tissue composed of neuron cell bodies.

ground The background behind objects or figures.

group therapy A therapeutic setting in which several people who share a common problem all meet regularly with a therapist to help themselves and one another.

groupthink A situation in which the thinking of the group takes over, so much so that group members forgo logic or critical analysis in the service of reaching a decision.

gustatory cortex The cortical region of the brain located in the insula area of the frontal lobe where taste sensations are processed and interpreted.

gut-brain axis The bi-directional pathway between the intestines and the central nervous system, by which changes in the intestinal environment affect the brain and vice versa.

hair cells Inner ear sensory receptors for sound that transduce sound vibrations into neural impulses.

hallucinations Convincing sensory experiences that occur in the absence of an external stimulus.

hallucinogens Substances that create distorted perceptions of reality ranging from mild to extreme.

health behavior approach An explanation for illness or health that focuses on the role of behaviors such as diet, exercise, or substance abuse.

health psychology The study of the role psychological factors play in regard to health and illness.

heritability The extent to which a characteristic is influenced by genetics.

heuristics Mental shortcuts; methods for making complex and uncertain decisions and judgments.

hierarchies Ways of organizing related pieces of information from the most specific feature they have in common to the most general.

highly superior autobiographical memory (HSAM) Occurs when people can recall in considerable detail personal events from almost any day of their adolescent and adult life.

hippocampus A limbic structure that wraps itself around the thalamus; plays a vital role in learning and memory.

histrionic personality disorder A dramatic-emotional personality disorder characterized by the desire to be the center of attention and by dramatic, seductive, flamboyant, and exaggerated behaviors.

homeostasis The process by which all organisms work to maintain physiological equilibrium, or balance around an optimal set point.

hormones Chemicals, secreted by glands, that travel in the bloodstream and carry messages to tissues and organs all over the body.

human development The study of change and continuity in the individual across the life span.

human language A communication system specific to *Homo sapiens*; it is open and symbolic, has rules of grammar, and allows its users to express abstract and distant ideas.

humanistic psychology A theory of psychology that focuses on personal growth and meaning as a way of reaching one's highest potential.

hypersomnia A sleep difficulty characterized by sleeping more than 10 hours a day for 2 weeks or more; includes an urge to nap during inappropriate times.

hypnosis A state characterized by focused attention, suggestibility, absorption, lack of voluntary control over behavior, and suspension of critical faculties; occurs when instructed by someone trained in hypnosis; may be therapeutic.

hypomanic episodes Symptoms of mania (e.g., increased energy, euphoria, racing thoughts) but that are less severe.

hypothalamic-pituitary-adrenal (HPA) axis A major neuroendocrine pathway relevant to the stress response involving the hypothalamus, pituitary gland, and adrenal cortex.

hypothalamus A limbic structure; the master regulator of almost all major drives and motives we have, such as hunger, thirst, temperature, and sexual behavior; also controls the pituitary gland.

hypothesis A specific, informed, and testable prediction of the outcome of a particular set of conditions in a research design.

id One of Freud's provinces of the mind; the seat of impulse and desire; the part of our personality that we do not yet own; it owns or controls us.

ideational fluency The ability to produce many ideas.

identical twins Twins that develop from a single fertilized egg that splits into two independent cells.

illness anxiety disorder Preoccupation with and anxiety about acquiring a serious illness for at least 6 months.

implicit memory A kind of memory made up of knowledge based on previous experience, such as skills that we perform automatically once we have mastered them; resides outside conscious awareness.

imprinting The rapid and innate learning of the characteristics of a caregiver very soon after birth.

in-group/out-group bias A tendency to show positive feelings toward people who belong to the same group as we do, and negative feelings toward those in other groups.

incentive Any external object or event that motivates behavior.

independent variable A property that is manipulated by the experimenter under controlled conditions to determine whether it causes the predicted outcome of an experiment.

individualism Cultures that are more concerned with how their behavior will affect their own personal goals.

individuation The process of a person's personality becoming whole and full.

inductive reasoning Reasoning to general conclusions from specific evidence.

industrial/organizational (I/O) psychology The application of psychological concepts and questions to work settings.

inferential statistics Analyses of data that allow us to test hypotheses and make an inference as to how likely a sample score is to occur in a population.

inferiority complex An unhealthy need to dominate or upstage others as a way of compensating for feelings of deficiency.

informational social influence Conformity to the behavior of others because one views them as a source of knowledge about what one is supposed to do.

insomnia A sleep difficulty characterized by difficulty falling and staying asleep, as well as not feeling rested.

instinctive drift Learned behavior that shifts toward instinctive, unlearned behavior tendencies.

institutional review boards (IRBs) Organizations that evaluate research proposals to make sure research involving humans does not cause undue harm or distress.

insula A small structure inside the cerebrum that plays an important role in the perception of bodily sensations, emotional states, empathy, and addictive behavior.

integrative therapy An eclectic approach in which the therapist draws on different treatment approaches and uses those that seem most appropriate for the situation.

intellectual disability Significant limitations in intellectual functioning as well as in everyday adaptive behavior, which start before age 18.

intelligence A set of cognitive skills that includes abstract thinking, reasoning, problem solving, and the ability to acquire knowledge.

inter-rater reliability A measure of how much agreement there is in ratings when using two or more raters or coders to rate personality or other behaviors.

interference Disruption of memory because other information competes with the information we are trying to recall.

intermittent reinforcement Reinforcement of a behavior—but not after every response.

internal reliability A characteristic of an intelligence test in which questions on a given subtest tend to correlate very highly with other items on the subtest.

interneurons Neurons that communicate only with other neurons.

interviews Occur between two people, one asking questions and the other answering them and the answers are open-ended. Sometimes interview questions are predetermined and sometimes they are spontaneous.

intimacy As defined by Erikson, the ability to fuse one's identity with another's without the fear of losing it.

intrinsic motivation Motivation that comes from within a person and includes the elements of challenge, enjoyment, mastery, and autonomy.

introspection The main method of investigation for structuralists; it involves looking into one's own mind for information about the nature of conscious experience.

ions Chemically charged particles that predominate in bodily fluids; found both inside and outside cells.

iris The muscle that forms the colored part of the eye; it adjusts the pupil to regulate the amount of light that enters the eye.

James-Lange theory of emotion The idea that it is the perception of the physiological changes that accompany emotions that produces the subjective emotional experience.

joint attention The ability to make eye contact with others and to look in the same direction that someone else is looking.

just noticeable difference Is a difference threshold that is the smallest change in a stimulus that can be perceived most of the time.

kin selection The evolutionary favoring of genes that prompt individuals to help their relatives, or kin.

language acquisition device (LAD) An innate, biologically based capacity to acquire language, proposed by Noam Chomsky as part of his nativist view of language.

latent learning Learning that occurs in the absence of reinforcement and is not demonstrated until later, when reinforcement occurs.

latent level Freud's deeper, unconscious level of dreams; their meaning is found at this level.

law of closure The tendency to perceive a whole object in the absence of complete information.

law of effect The consequences of a behavior increase (or decrease) the likelihood that the behavior will be repeated.

learned helplessness The sense of powerlessness that arises from the repeated inability to control or escape from stressful situations.

learning Enduring changes in behavior that occur with experience.

learning curve The rate at which learning occurs over time.

lens The structure that sits behind the pupil; it bends the light rays that enter the eye to focus images on the retina.

levels of processing The concept that the more deeply people encode information, the better they will recall it.

life satisfaction The overall evaluation we make of our lives and an aspect of subjective well-being.

limbic system A connection group of forebrain structures (hypothalamus, amygdala, hippocampus, and cingulate gyrus) that share important functions in emotion memory and motivation and regulate autonomic and endocrine function.

linguistic determinism hypothesis The proposition that our language determines our way of thinking and our perceptions of the world; the view taken by Sapir and Whorf.

lithium A salt that is prescribed for its ability to stabilize the mania associated with bipolar disorder.

long-term memory The part of memory that has the capacity to store a vast amount of information for as little as 30 seconds and as long as a lifetime.

long-term potentiation (LTP) The strengthening of a synaptic connection that results when a synapse of one neuron repeatedly fires and excites another neuron.

longitudinal designs Make observations of the same people over time, ranging from months to decades.

magnetic resonance imaging (MRI) A brain imaging technique that uses magnetic fields to produce detailed images of the structure of the brain and other soft tissues.

major depressive disorder A mood disorder characterized by pervasive low mood, lack of motivation, low energy, and feelings of worthlessness and guilt that last for at least 2 consecutive weeks.

manic episodes One mood cycle in bipolar disorder, typically involving increased energy, sleeplessness, euphoria, irritability, delusions of grandeur, increased sex drive, and "racing" thoughts that last at least 1 week.

manifest level Freud's surface level of dreams, recalled upon waking.

mean The arithmetic average of a series of numbers.

measures The tools and techniques used to assess thought or behavior.

mechanisms Adaptive solutions to problems of survival and reproduction.

mechanoreceptors Receptor cells in the skin that are sensitive to different tactile qualities, such as shape, grooves, vibrations, and movements.

median The score that separates the lower half of scores from the upper half.

meditation Practices that people use to calm the mind, stabilize concentration, focus attention, and enhance awareness of the present moment.

medulla A hindbrain structure that extends directly from the spinal cord; regulates breathing, heart rate, and blood pressure.

memory The ability to take in, solidify, store and use information; also the store of what has been learned and remembered.

menarche The first menstrual period.

mental age The equivalent chronological age a child has reached based on his or her performance on an IQ test.

mental representation A structure in the mind—such as an idea or image—that stands for something else, such as an external object or thing sensed in the past or future, not the present.

mental rotation The process of imagining an object turning in three-dimensional space.

mental set A tendency to continue to use problem-solving strategies that have worked in the past, even if better solutions are available.

meta-analysis A research technique for combining all research results on one question and drawing a conclusion.

metabolic syndrome A group of factors related to body composition, weight, and diet that increase risk of stroke, diabetes, and heart disease.

metacognitive thinking The process that includes the ability first to think and then to reflect on one's own thinking.

microbiome The environment of trillions of various microorganisms living with our bodies, which perform important metabolic and physiological functions.

mindfulness A heightened awareness of the present moment, whether of events in one's environment or in one's own mind.

mindfulness-based cognitive therapy (MBCT) An approach that combines elements of CBT with mindfulness meditation to help people with depression learn to recognize and restructure negative thought patterns.

minimally conscious State in which a patient shows signs of intentional behavior (such as visually tracking a person), but cannot communicate.

minority social influence When a small number of individuals in a larger group shifts majority opinion by presenting a consistent, unwavering message.

mirror neurons Nerve cells that are active when we observe others performing an action as well as when we are performing the same action.

misinformation effect Occurs when information learned after an original event (e.g., crime) is wrong or misleading but gets incorporated into the memory as true.

mnemonic device A method devised to help us remember information, such as a rhyme or an acronym.

mode A statistic that represents the most commonly occurring score or value.

modeling The imitation of behaviors performed by others. A kind of observational learning.

monoamine oxidase (MAO) inhibitors A class of drugs used to treat depression; they slow the breakdown of monoamine neurotransmitters in the brain.

monocular depth cues Aids to depth perception that do not require two eyes.

monogenic The hereditary passing on of traits determined by a single gene.

moods Affective states that operate in the background of consciousness and tend to last longer than most emotions.

moral treatment A 19th-century approach to treating the mentally ill with dignity in a caring environment.

motivation The urge to move toward one's goals; to accomplish tasks.

motor neurons Nerve cells that carry commands for movement from the brain to the muscles of the body.

multiple-factor theory of intelligence The idea that intelligence consists of distinct dimensions and is not just a single factor.

mutation A random change in genetic sequence.

myelin sheath The fatty substance wrapped around some axons, which insulates the axon, making the nerve impulse travel more efficiently.

narcissistic personality disorder A dramatic-emotional personality disorder characterized by having an extremely positive and arrogant self-image and being extraordinarily self-centered; other symptoms are an exaggerated sense of self-importance and grandiosity.

narcolepsy A sleep disorder characterized by excessive daytime sleepiness and weakness in facial and limb muscles.

narrow intelligence One of Carroll's three levels of intelligence; includes many distinct abilities.

nativist view of language The idea that we discover language rather than learn it, that language development is inborn.

natural immunity The form of immunity that is the first response to antigens.

natural selection A feedback process whereby nature favors one design over another because it has an impact on reproduction.

naturalistic observation A study in which the researcher unobtrusively observes and records behavior in the real world.

nature through nurture The position that the environment constantly interacts with biology to shape who we are and what we do.

near infrared spectrometry (NIRS) Uses light rather than magnets to produces images of brain tissue.

needs Inherently biological states of deficiency (cellular or bodily) that compel drives.

negative punishment The removal of a stimulus to decrease behavior.

negative reinforcement The removal of a stimulus after a behavior to increase the frequency of that behavior.

negative symptoms (of schizophrenia) Symptoms that include nonresponsiveness, emotional flatness, immobility, catatonia, problems with speech, and inability to complete tasks.

neural migration The movement of neurons from one part of the fetal brain to their more permanent destination; occurs during months 3–5 of the fetal stage.

neurocultural theory of emotion Ekman's explanation that some aspects of emotion, such as facial expressions and physiological changes associated with emotion, are universal and others, such as emotion regulation, are culturally derived.

neuroendocrine system The hormonal systems involved in emotions and stress.

neurogenesis The development of new neurons.

neurons The cells that process and transmit information in the nervous system.

neuroplasticity The brain's ability to adopt new functions, reorganize itself, or make new neural connections throughout life, as a function of experience.

neuropsychoanalysis The scientific movement, started in the late 1990s, that combined Freudian ideas with neuroscientific methods.

neurotransmitters Chemicals that transmit information between neurons.

neutral stimulus An object or situation that when presented alone does not lead to an automatic (or unconditioned) response.

night terrors A state that occurs when a person walks around, speaks incoherently, and ultimately awakens, terrified, from sleep.

nociceptive pain Pain from skin and/or tissue damage or injury.

node of Ranvier The gap(s) in the myelin sheath across which the action potential jumps.

non-REM The form of sleep with few eye movements, which are slow rather than fast.

non-shared environment Consists of living conditions that individuals do not have in common, such as having different parents, birth-order, schools, and peers.

norepinephrine A neurotransmitter that activates the sympathetic response to stress, increasing heart rate, rate of respiration, and blood pressure in support of rapid action.

normal distribution A bell curve; a plot of how frequent data are that is perfectly symmetrical, with most scores clustering in the middle and only a few scores at the extremes.

normative social influence Conformity to the behavior of others in order to be accepted by them.

norms Involve collecting data on a given test using a large and representative sample (on age, gender, ethnicity, etc.) to determine the average score and amount of variability in that score. This is then used as a standard against which specific samples or individuals can be compared.

obedience A type of social influence in which a person yields to the will of another person, complying with their demands.

object permanence The ability to realize that objects still exist when they are not being sensed.

observational learning Learning influenced by watching the behavior of others.

obsession An unwanted thought, word, phrase, or image that persistently and repeatedly comes into a person's mind and causes distress.

obsessive-compulsive disorder (OCD) An anxiety disorder in which obsessive thoughts lead to compulsive behaviors.

obsessive-compulsive personality disorder (OCPD) An anxious-fearful personality disorder characterized by rigid habits and extreme perfectionism; more general than obsessive-compulsive disorder.

olfactory bulb A forebrain structure that sends information either directly to the smell-processing areas in the cortex or indirectly to the cortex by way of the thalamus.

olfactory sensory neurons The sensory receptors for smell that reside high up inside the nose.

one-word utterances Single words (such as "mama," "dada," "more," or "no!") occur around 12 months of age.

operant conditioning The process of changing behavior by manipulating the consequences of that behavior.

opponent-process theory The theory that color vision results from cones linked together in three pairs of opposing colors, so that activation of one member of the pair inhibits activity in the other.

optic chiasm The point at which strands of the optic nerve from half of each eye cross over to the opposite side of the brain.

optic nerve The structure composed of the axons of ganglion cells from the retina that carry visual information from the eye to the brain.

optogenetics A treatment that uses a combination of light stimulation and genetics to manipulate the activity of individual neurons.

originality The ability to come up with unusual and novel ideas.

out-group homogeneity The tendency to see all members of an out-group as the same.

pain A complex emotional and sensory experience associated with actual or potential tissue damage.

panic attacks An anxiety disorder; associated with perceptions of threat and occurring because of fear of danger, inability to escape, embarrassment, or specific objects, for example.

panic disorder An anxiety disorder characterized by panic attacks and persistent anxiety about having more attacks.

papillae Textured structures on the surface of the tongue; contain thousands of taste buds.

paranoid personality disorder An odd-eccentric personality disorder characterized by extreme suspicions and mistrust of others in unwarranted and maladaptive ways.

parasympathetic nervous system The branch of the autonomic nervous system that usually relaxes or returns the body to a less active, restful state.

perceived organizational support Employees' beliefs about how much the organization appreciates and supports their contributions and well-being.

perception A psychological process: the act of organizing and interpreting sensory experience.

perceptual constancy The ability of the brain to preserve perception of objects in spite of changes in retinal image when an object changes in position or distance from the viewer.

perceptual set The effect of frame of mind on perception; a tendency to perceive stimuli in a certain manner.

peripheral nervous system The part of the nervous system that comprises all the nerve cells in the body outside the central nervous system.

persistent depressive disorder (PDD) Previously known as *dysthymia* and involves same symptoms as major depression but at less severe levels.

personal unconscious According to Jung, the form of consciousness that consists of all our repressed and hidden thoughts, feelings, and motives.

personality The unique and relatively enduring set of behaviors, feelings, thoughts, and motives that characterize an individual.

personality disorders Patterns of cognition, emotion, and behavior that develop in late childhood or adolescence and are maladaptive and inflexible; they are more stable than clinical disorders.

personality psychology The study of what makes people unique and the consistencies in people's behavior across time and situations.

personality questionnaires Self-report instruments on which respondents indicate the extent to which they agree or disagree with a series of statements as they apply to their personality.

persuasion The act of attempting to change the opinions, beliefs, or choices of others by explanation or argument.

phantom limb pain Occurs when a person who has lost an arm or leg continues to feel pain in the lost limb.

phenothiazines Drugs used to treat schizophrenia; help diminish hallucinations, confusion, agitation, and paranoia but also have adverse side effects.

phenotype An organism's observed characteristics.

phobia An anxiety disorder: an ongoing and irrational fear of a particular object, situation, or activity.

photoreceptors Cells in the retina (called rods and cones) that convert light energy into nerve energy.

physiological measures Measures of bodily responses, such as blood pressure or heart rate, used to determine changes in psychological state.

physiological reactivity approach An explanation for the causal role of stress-related bodily changes in illness.

pituitary gland The master endocrine gland of the body; controls the release of hormones from glands throughout the body.

placebo A substance or treatment that appears identical to the actual treatment but lacks the active substance.

plagiarism Is when someone presents words or ideas of other people as their own.

polygenic The process by which many genes interact to create a single characteristic.

pons A hindbrain structure that serves as a bridge between lower brain regions and higher midbrain and forebrain activity.

population The entire group a researcher is interested in—for example, all humans, all adolescents, all boys, all girls, all college students.

positive psychology A scientific approach to studying, understanding, and promoting healthy and positive psychological functioning.

positive punishment The addition of a stimulus that decreases behavior.

positive reinforcement The presentation or addition of a stimulus after a behavior occurs that increases how often that behavior will occur.

positive symptoms (of schizophrenia) The perceptual experiences associated with schizophrenia, including hallucinations, delusional thinking, and disorganized thought and speech.

positron emission tomography (PET) A brain imaging technique that measures blood flow to active areas in the brain.

postconventional level The third level in Kohlberg's theory of moral reasoning, in which the person recognizes universal moral rules that may trump unjust or immoral local rules.

posttraumatic stress disorder (PTSD) A type of trauma- and stressor-related disorder that involves intrusive and persistent cognitive, emotional, and physiological symptoms triggered by catastrophic or horrifying events.

preconventional level The first level in Kohlberg's theory of moral reasoning, focusing on avoiding punishment or maximizing rewards.

predictive validity The degree to which intelligence test scores are positively related to real-world outcomes, such as school achievement or job success, and thus have predictive value.

prefrontal cortex The frontmost region of the frontal lobes; plays an important role in attention, appropriate social behavior, impulse control, and working memory.

prefrontal lobotomy A form of psychosurgery in which the connections between the prefrontal cortex and the lower portion of the brain are severed; no longer in use.

prejudice A biased attitude toward a group of people or an individual member of a group based on unfair generalizations about what members of that group are like.

prenatal programming The process by which events in the womb alter the development of physical and psychological health.

preoperational stage The second major stage of cognitive development (ages 2–5), which begins with the emergence of symbolic thought.

primary appraisal A quick assessment of the meaning of a given environmental event for the individual.

primary reinforcers Innate, unlearned reinforcers that satisfy biological needs (such as food, water, or sex).

priming A kind of implicit memory that arises when recall is improved by earlier exposure to the same or similar stimuli.

proactive interference Disruption of memory because previously learned information interferes with the learning of new information.

problem-focused coping A way of dealing with stress that aims to change the situation that is creating stress.

procedural memory A kind of memory made up of implicit knowledge for almost any behavior or physical skill we have learned.

prodigy A young person who is extremely gifted and precocious in one area and at least average in intelligence.

projection A defense mechanism in which people deny particular ideas, feelings, or impulses and project them onto others.

projective tests Personality assessments in which the participant is presented with a vague stimulus or situation and asked to interpret it or tell a story about what he or she sees.

prosocial behavior Action that is beneficial to others.

protolanguage Very rudimentary language; also known as pre-language; used by earlier species of *Homo*.

prototypes The best-fitting examples of a category.

proximity A Gestalt law that says we tend to group objects together that are near one another.

pruning The degradation of synapses and dying off of neurons that are not strengthened by experience.

pseudoscience Claims presented as scientific that are not supported by evidence obtained with the scientific method.

psychedelic medicine The controlled use of psychedelic drugs for the treatment of physical and mental disorders.

psychoactive drugs Naturally occurring or synthesized substances that, when ingested or otherwise taken into the body, reliably produce qualitative changes in conscious experience.

psychoanalysis A clinically based approach to understanding and treating psychological disorders; assumes that the unconscious mind is the most powerful force behind thought and behavior.

psychoanalytic therapy Based on Freud's ideas, a therapeutic approach oriented toward major personality change with a focus on uncovering unconscious motives, especially through dream interpretation.

psychology The scientific study of thought and behavior.

psychoneuroimmunology (PNI) The science of how psychological factors relate to changes in the immune system.

psychophysics The study of how people experience physical stimuli such as light, sound waves, and touch.

psychosomatic theory The idea that emotional factors can lead to the occurrence or worsening of illness.

psychotherapy The use of psychological techniques to modify maladaptive behaviors or thought patterns, or both, and to help patients develop insight into their own behavior.

psychotic disorders Psychological disorders of thought and perception, characterized by inability to distinguish between real and imagined perceptions.

puberty The period when sexual maturation begins; it marks the beginning of adolescence.

punishment A stimulus that decreases the frequency of a behavior.

pupil The opening in the iris through which light enters the eye.

qualitative research Research that involves data gathered from open-ended and unstructured answers rather than quantitative or numeric answers.

quantitative intelligence Is the ability to reason and solve problems by carrying out mathematical operations and using logic.

quantitative research Research that collects information using any kind of numeric and quantifiable scale and often has limited response options.

quantitative trait loci (QTL) approach A technique in behavioral genetics that looks for the location on genes that might be associated with particular behaviors.

quasi-experimental design A research method similar to an experimental design except that it makes use of naturally occurring groups rather than randomly assigning subjects to groups.

random assignment The method used to assign participants to different research conditions, so that all participants have the same chance of being in any specific group.

rapid eye movements (REM) Quick movements of the eye that occur during sleep, thought to mark phases of dreaming.

rational (face valid) method A method for developing questionnaire items that involves using reason or theory to come up with a question.

rationalism The view that using logic and reason is the way to understand how the world works.

reaction formation A defense mechanism that occurs when an unpleasant idea, feeling, or impulse is turned into its opposite.

reaction range For a given trait, such as IQ, the genetically determined range of responses by an individual to his or her environment.

reappraisal An emotion regulation strategy in which one reevaluates an event, so that a different emotion results.

reasoning The process of drawing inferences or conclusions from principles and evidence.

recessive alleles Alleles that show their effects only when both alleles are the same.

reciprocal altruism The act of helping others in the hope that they will help us in the future.

reconsolidation Occurs when a reactivation of a memory weakens the original memory and a new consolidation happens, but this time resulting a slightly different memory.

recovered memory A memory from a real event that was encoded, stored, but not retrieved for a long period of time until some later event brings it suddenly to consciousness.

reflexes Inborn and involuntary behaviors—such as coughing, swallowing, sneezing, or vomiting—that are elicited by very specific stimuli.

refractory period The span of time, after an action potential has been generated, when the neuron is returning to its resting state and the neuron cannot generate an action potential.

rehearsal The process of repeatedly practicing material, so that it enters long-term memory.

reinforcer An internal or external event that increases the frequency of a behavior.

reliability The consistency of a measurement, such as an intelligence test.

repetitive transcranial magnetic stimulation (rTMS) A treatment for severe depression involving exposure of specific brain structures to bursts of high-intensity magnetic fields instead of electricity.

replication The repetition of a study to confirm the results; essential to the scientific process.

representative sample A research sample that accurately reflects the population of people one is studying.

representativeness heuristic A strategy we use to estimate the probability of one event based on how typical it is of another event.

repression The unconscious act of keeping threatening thoughts, feelings, or impulses out of consciousness.

research designs Plans of action for how to conduct a scientific study.

resistance stage In the general adaptation syndrome, extended effort by the body to deal with a threat.

resting potential The difference in electrical charge between the inside and outside of the axon when the neuron is at rest.

reticular activating system A bundle of nerves in the brainstem that are involved in wakefulness and the transition between wakefulness and sleep.

reticular formation A network of nerve fibers that runs up through both the hindbrain and the midbrain; it is crucial to waking up and falling asleep.

retina The thin layer of nerve tissue that lines the back of the eye.

retrieval The recovery of information stored in memory; the fourth stage of long-term memory.

retroactive interference Disruption of memory because new experiences or information causes people to forget previously learned experiences or information.

retrograde amnesia An inability to recall events or experiences that happened before the onset of a disease or injury.

reuptake A way of removing excess neurotransmitter from the synapse, in which excess neurotransmitter is returned to the sending, or presynaptic, neuron for storage in vesicles and future use.

rods Photoreceptors that function in low illumination and play a key role in night vision; responsive to dark and light contrast.

Rorschach Inkblot Test A projective test in which the participant is asked to respond to a series of ambiguous inkblots.

samples Subsets of the population studied in a research project.

sampling Is the procedure researchers use to obtain participants from a population.

savant syndrome A very rare condition in which people with serious mental handicaps also show isolated areas of ability or brilliance.

schedules of reinforcement Patterns of intermittent reinforcement distinguished by whether reinforcement occurs after a set number of responses or after a certain amount of time has passed since the last reinforcement.

schemas Mental frameworks that develop from our experiences with particular people, objects, or events.

schizoid personality disorder An odd-eccentric personality disorder characterized by a desire to avoid close relationships as well as by emotional aloofness, reclusivity, and a lack of humor.

schizophrenia A psychotic disorder characterized by significant disturbances in thought and emotion, specifically problems with perception, including hallucinations.

schizotypal personality disorder An odd-eccentric personality disorder characterized by a desire to live an isolated and asocial life, but also by the presence of odd thoughts and beliefs.

scientific method The procedures by which scientists conduct research, consisting of five basic processes: observation, prediction, testing, interpretation, and communication.

scientific thinking A process using the cognitive skills required to generate, test, and revise theories.

secondary (conditioned) reinforcers Reinforcers that are learned by association, usually via classical conditioning (such as money, grades, and peer approval).

secondary appraisal Self-assessment of the resources available to cope with stress.

securely attached An attachment style characterized by infants who will gradually explore new situations when the caregiver leaves and initiate contact when the caregiver returns after separation.

selective attention The ability to focus awareness on specific features in the environment while ignoring others.

selective serotonin reuptake inhibitors (SSRIs) Drugs prescribed primarily for depression and some anxiety disorders that work by making more serotonin available in the synapse.

self-actualization The inherent drive to realize one's full potential.

self-conscious emotions Types of emotion that require a sense of self and the ability to reflect on actions; they occur as a function of meeting expectations (or not) and abiding (or not) by society's rules.

self-fulfilling prophecy A statement that affects events to cause the prediction to become true.

self-reports Written or oral accounts of a person's thoughts, feelings, or actions.

self-serving bias The tendency to make situational attributions for our failures but dispositional attributions for our successes.

semantic memory A form of memory that recalls facts and general knowledge, such as what we learn in school.

semicircular canals A structure of the inner ear involved in maintaining balance.

sensation A physical process: the stimulation of our sense organs by features of the outer world.

sensorimotor stage Piaget's first stage of cognitive development (ages 0–2), when infants learn about the world by using their senses and by moving their bodies.

sensory adaptation The process by which our sensitivity diminishes when an object constantly stimulates our senses.

sensory memory The part of memory that holds information in its original sensory form for a very brief period of time, usually about half a second or less.

sensory neurons Nerve cells that receive incoming sensory information from the sense organs (eye, ear, skin, tongue, nose).

sensory threshold Refers to how much of a stimulus is required for it to be perceived.

sentence phase The stage when children begin speaking in fully grammatical sentences; usually age 2½ to 3.

separation anxiety The distress reaction shown by babies when they are separated from their primary caregiver (typically shown at around 9 months of age).

serial position effect The tendency to have better recall for items in a list according to their position in the list.

serotonin A neurotransmitter with wide-ranging effects; involved in dreaming and in controlling emotional states, especially anger, anxiety, and depression.

set point The ideal fixed setting of a particular physiological system, such as internal body temperature.

sexual behavior Actions that produce arousal and increase the likelihood of orgasm.

sexual orientation Sexual orientation refers to a person's inherent romantic, emotional and sexual attraction to other people—whether same sex, opposite sex, or both.

sexual selection Operates when members of the opposite sex find certain traits attractive or appealing and therefore over long periods of times these traits become more common in the population.

sexual strategies theory The idea that men and women face different problems when they seek out mates, so they often approach relationships in very different ways.

shadow According to Jung, the dark and morally objectionable part of ourselves.

shamans Medicine men or women who treat people with mental problems by driving out their demons with elaborate rituals, such as exorcisms, incantations, and prayers.

shaping The reinforcement of successive approximations of a desired behavior.

shared environment Consists of living conditions that individuals have in common, such as having the same parents, schools, and peers.

short-term memory The part of memory that temporarily (for 2 to 30 seconds) stores a limited amount of information before it is either transferred to long-term storage or forgotten.

signal detection theory The viewpoint that both stimulus intensity and decision-making processes are involved in the detection of a stimulus.

similarity A Gestalt law that says we tend to group like objects together in visual perception.

single-blind studies Studies in which participants do not know the experimental condition (group) to which they have been assigned.

Skinner box A simple chamber in which a small animal can move around, with a food dispenser and a response lever to trigger food delivery.

sleep apnea A chronic disorder in which there are pauses in breathing during sleep, which shifts sleep from deep to light, often resulting in poor sleep quality and daytime sleepiness.

sleepwalking A sleep difficulty characterized by activities occurring during non-REM sleep that usually occur when one is awake, such as walking and eating.

social desirability bias The tendency toward favorable self-presentation that could lead to inaccurate self-reports.

social exchange theory The idea that we help others when we understand that the benefits to ourselves are likely to outweigh the costs.

social facilitation A phenomenon in which the presence of others improves one's performance.

social learning theory The kind of learning that occurs when we model the behavior of others.

social loafing A phenomenon in which the presence of others causes one to relax one's standards and slack off.

social norms Rules about acceptable behavior imposed by the cultural context in which one lives.

social phobia (social anxiety disorder) An anxiety disorder: fear of humiliation in the presence of others, characterized by intense self-consciousness about appearance or behavior or both.

social psychology The study of how living among others influences thought, feeling, and behavior.

social referencing The ability to make use of social and emotional information from another person—especially a caregiver—in an uncertain situation.

softwiring In contrast to hardwiring, biological systems—genes, brain structures, brain cells—are inherited but open to modification from the environment.

soma The cell body of the neuron.

somatic nervous system Nerve cells of the peripheral nervous system that serve the skeletal muscles. Somatic nerves transmit from the central nervous system (CNS) to the skeletal muscles and sensory information from the skeletal muscles back to the CNS.

somatic symptom disorder A psychological disorder in which a person complains of multiple physical disorders that cause disruption and that persist for at least 6 months.

somatosensory cortex A strip of the parietal lobe involved in the processing and perception of sensory information from the body, especially temperature, touch, pressure, and pain.

spatial intelligence Is defined as ability or mental skill to solve spatial problems such as navigating, and visualizing objects from different angles.

spermarche The first ejaculation.

spontaneous recovery The sudden reappearance of an extinguished response.

sports psychology The study of psychological factors in sports and exercise.

stagnation A situation in which an adult becomes more self-focused than oriented toward others and does not contribute in a productive way to society or family.

standard deviation A statistical measure of how much scores in a sample vary around the mean.

statistics The collection, analysis, interpretation, and presentation of numerical data.

stereotypes Schemas of how people are likely to behave based simply on groups to which they belong; they are oversimplified perspectives of people based solely on their group membership.

stimulants Substances that activate the nervous system.

stimulus discrimination The restriction of a CR (such as salivation) to only the exact CS to which it was conditioned.

stimulus generalization Extension of the association between UCS and CS to include a broad array of similar stimuli.

storage The retention of memory over time; the third stage of long-term memory formation.

stress A response elicited when a situation overwhelms a person's perceived ability to meet the demands of the situation.

stressors Events that trigger a stress response.

striving for superiority According to Adler, the major drive behind all behavior, whereby humans naturally strive to overcome their inherent inferiorities or deficiencies, both physical and psychological.

Stroop effect A delay in reaction time when the colors of words on a test and their meaning differ.

structuralism The 19th-century school of psychology that argued that breaking down experience into its elemental parts offers the best way to understand thought and behavior.

subjective experience of emotion The changes in the quality of our conscious experience that occur during emotional responses.

subjective well-being The state that consists of life satisfaction, domain satisfactions, and positive and negative affect.

sublimation A defense mechanism that involves expressing a socially unacceptable impulse in a socially acceptable way.

successful intelligence According to Sternberg, an integrated set of abilities needed to attain success in life.

suggestibility A problem with memory that occurs when memories are implanted in our minds based

on leading questions, comments, or suggestions by someone else or some other source.

superego One of Freud's provinces of the mind; the part of the self that monitors and controls behavior; "stands over us" and evaluates actions in terms of right and wrong; our conscience.

support groups Meetings of people who share a common situation, be it a disorder, a disease, or coping with an ill family member.

sustained attention The ability to maintain focused awareness on a target or an idea.

sympathetic nervous system The branch of the autonomic nervous system that activates bodily systems in times of emergency.

synapse The junction between an axon and the adjacent neuron, where information is transmitted from one neuron to another.

synaptic vesicles Tiny sacs in the terminal buttons that contain neurotransmitters.

synaptogenesis The formation of entirely new synapses or connections with other neurons.

syndrome A group, or cluster of related symptoms that are characteristic of a disorder.

synesthesia An unusual sensory experience in which a person experiences sensations in one sense when a different sense is stimulated.

syntax The rules for arranging words and symbols to form sentences or parts of sentences in a particular language.

systematic desensitization A behavioral therapy technique, often used for phobias, in which the therapist pairs relaxation with gradual exposure to a phobic object, generating a hierarchy of increasing contact with the feared object.

t-test A statistic that compares two means to see whether they could come from the same population.

tardive dyskinesia Repetitive, involuntary movements of jaw, tongue, face, and mouth resulting from the extended use of traditional antipsychotic drugs.

taste buds Structures inside the papillae of the tongue that contain the taste receptor cells.

taste receptor cells Sensory receptors for taste that reside in the taste buds.

technology-based therapies Therapies that make use of technology or the Internet to complement current therapies or to make psychotherapeutic techniques available to more people.

telomerase An enzyme that adds DNA sequences to telomeres.

temperament The biologically based tendency to behave in particular ways from very early in life.

teratogens Substances that can disrupt normal prenatal development and cause lifelong deficits.

terminal button A little knob at the end of the axon that contains tiny sacs of neurotransmitters.

test bias A characteristic of a test that produces different outcomes for different groups.

test fairness A judgment about how test results are applied to different groups based on values and philosophical inclinations.

test-retest reliability The consistency of scores on a test over time.

thalamus A forebrain structure that receives information from the senses and relays it to the cerebral cortex for processing.

theory A set of related assumptions from which scientists can make testable predictions.

theory of mind Ideas and knowledge about how other people's minds work.

theta waves A pattern of brain activity during N1 sleep; slower, lower-energy waves than alpha waves.

thinking outside the box An approach to problem solving that requires breaking free of self-imposed conceptual constraints and thinking about a problem differently in order to solve it.

three-stage model of memory The classification of memories based on duration as sensory, short-term, and long-term.

timbre Is the quality or "color" of a particular sound and is a result of the sound's complexity or number of sound frequencies.

token economies A behavioral technique in which desirable behaviors are reinforced with a token, such as a small chip or fake coin, which can be exchanged for privileges.

tolerance The need to consume increasing amounts of a drug to get the desired effect.

top-down processing Perception of the whole based on our experience and expectations, which guide our perception of smaller, elemental features of a stimulus.

traditional antipsychotics Historically, the first medications used to manage psychotic symptoms.

trait A disposition to behave consistently in a particular way.

transcranial direct current stimulation (tDCS) A method of treatment that can stimulate both cortical and deeper brain structures; unlike rTMS it can be used during movement.

transcranial direct current stimulation (tDCS) Electrical stimulation of the brain.

transduction The conversion of physical into neural information.

transference The process in psychotherapy in which the client reacts to a person in a present relationship as though that person were someone from the client's past.

transgender identity Occurs when one identifies with the opposite gender one was assigned at birth.

triangular theory of love Sternberg's idea that three components (intimacy, passion, and commitment), in various combinations, can explain all the forms of human love.

triarchic theory of intelligence Sternberg's three-part model of intelligence, including analytic, creative, and practical intelligence.

trichromatic color theory The theory that all color that we experience results from a mixing of three colors of light (red, green, and blue).

tricyclic antidepressants Drugs used for treating depression as well as chronic pain and ADHD.

twin-adoption studies Research into hereditary influence on twins, both identical and fraternal, who were raised apart (adopted) and who were raised together.

two-word utterances Phrases children put together, starting around 18 months, such as "my ball," "mo wawa," or "go way."

tympanic membrane The eardrum.

Type A Behavior Pattern (TABP) A way of responding to challenge or stress, characterized by hostility, impatience, competitiveness, and time urgency.

unconditional positive regard The acceptance of another person regardless of his or her behavior.

unconditioned response (UCR) The natural, automatic, inborn, and involuntary reaction to a stimulus.

unconditioned stimulus (UCS) The environmental input that always produces the same unlearned, involuntary response.

unconscious One of Freud's three levels of consciousness; it contains all the drives, urges, or instincts that are outside awareness but nonetheless motivate most of our speech, thoughts, feelings, or actions.

universal Common to all human beings and seen in cultures all over the world.

validity The degree to which a test accurately measures what it purports to measure, such as intelligence, and not something else, and the degree to which it predicts real-world outcomes.

variable A characteristic that changes, or "varies," such as age, gender, weight, intelligence, anxiety, and extraversion.

variable-interval (VI) schedule A pattern of intermittent reinforcement in which responses are reinforced after time periods of different duration have passed.

variable-ratio (VR) schedule A pattern of intermittent reinforcement in which the number of responses needed for reinforcement changes.

vegetative state A state of minimal consciousness in which the eyes might be open, but the person is otherwise unresponsive.

verbal intelligence Is the ability to solve problems and analyze information using language-based reasoning.

virtual reality therapies Therapies that use virtual (digital simulation) environments to create therapeutic situations that would be hard to create otherwise.

visual acuity The ability to see clearly.

visual imagery Visual representations created by the brain after the original stimulus is no longer present.

wakefulness The degree of alertness reflecting whether a person is awake or asleep.

Weber's law The finding that the size of a just noticeable difference is a constant fraction of the intensity of the stimulus.

Wernicke's area The area deep in the left temporal lobe responsible for the ability to speak in meaningful sentences and to comprehend the meaning of speech.

white matter Brain tissue made up of white myelinated axons.

withdrawal symptoms The adverse effects people with physical dependence experience if they stop using a drug.

word salad The speech of people with schizophrenia, which may follow grammatical rules but be nonsensical in terms of content.

working memory The part of memory required to attend to and solve a problem at hand.

Yerkes-Dodson law The principle that moderate levels of arousal lead to optimal performance.

young adulthood The development stage that usually happens by the mid-20s, when people complete the key developmental tasks of emerging adulthood.

zone of proximal development The distance between what a child can learn alone and what that child can learn assisted by someone else, usually an adult.

zygote The single cell that results when a sperm fertilizes an egg.

References

AAA Newsroom. (2015). http://newsroom.aaa .com/2015/03/distraction-teen-crashes-even -worse-thought/

Aamodt, M. G. (2010). *Industrial/organizational psychology: An applied approach* (6th ed.). Belmont, CA: Wadsworth.

Abbate-Daga, G., Gramaglia, C., Amianto, F., Marzola, E., & Fassino, S. (2010). Attachment insecurity, personality, and body dissatisfaction in eating disorders. *Journal of Nervous and Mental Disease, 198,* 520–524.

Aberg, M. A. I., Pedersen, N. L., Torén K., Svartengrenf, M., Backstrand, B., Johnsson, T., ... Kuhn, H. G. (2009). Cardiovascular fitness is associated with cognition in young adulthood. *Proceedings of the National Academy of Sciences, 106,* 20906–20911. doi: 10.1073/pnas.0905307106

Abraham, A. (2013). The world according to me: Personal relevance and the medial prefrontal cortex. *Frontiers in Human Neuroscience, 7,* 341. doi: 10.3389/fnhum.2013.00341

Abrams, R. (1997). *Electroconvulsive therapy* (3rd ed.). New York, NY: Oxford University Press.

Ackerman, D. (1990). *A natural history of the senses.* New York, NY: Vintage Books.

Adam, T. C., & Epel, E. S. (2007). Stress, eating and the reward system. *Physiology & Behavior, 91,* 449–458.

Adams, L., & Szaluta, J. (1996). *Psycho-analysis and the humanities.* Philadelphia, PA: Brunner/Mazel.

Adamson, L., & Bakeman, R. (1985). Affect and attention: Infants observed with mothers and peers. *Child Development, 56,* 582–593.

Ader, R., & Cohen, N. (1975). Behaviorally conditioned immunosuppression. *Psychosomatic Medicine, 37,* 333–340.

Adler, A. (1931). *What life should mean to you.* New York, NY: Capricorn Books.

Adler, A. (1956). *The individual psychology of Alfred Adler: A systematic presentation in selections from his writings* (H. L. Ansbacher & R. R. Ansbacher, Eds.). New York, NY: Norton.

Adler, J. (2012). Erasing painful memories. *Scientific American, 306,* 56–61.

Adler, J. (Ed.). (2004). *Forensic psychology: Concepts, debates and practice.* Cullupton, England: Willan.

Adler, R. F., & Benbunan-Fich, R. (2015). The effects of task difficulty and multitasking on performance. *Interacting with Computers, 27*(4), 430-439. doi:10.1093/iwc/iwu005

Adolphs, R., Cahill, L., Schul, R., & Babinsky, R. (1997). Impaired declarative memory for emotional material following bilateral amygdala damage in humans. *Learning and Memory, 4,* 291–300.

Adolphs, R., Gosselin, F., Buchanan, T. W., Tranel, D., Schyns, P., & Damasio, A. R. (2005). A mechanism for impaired fear recognition after amygdala damage. *Nature, 433,* 68–72.

Adolphs, R., Tranel, D., & Buchanan, T. W. (2005). Amygdala damage impairs emotional

memory for gist but not details of complex stimuli. *Nature Neuroscience, 8,* 512–518.

Adolphs, R., Tranel, D., & Damasio, A. R. (1998, June 4). The human amygdala in social judgment. *Nature, 393,* 470–474.

Adolphs, R., Tranel, D., Damasio, H., & Damasio, A. R. (1994, December 15). Impaired recognition of emotion in facial expressions following bilateral damage to the human amygdala. *Nature, 372,* 669–672.

Aichorn, W., Huber, R., Stuppaeck, C., & Whitworth, A. B. (2006). Cardiomyopathy after long-term treatment with lithium—more than a coincidence? *Journal of Psychopharmacology, 20,* 589–591.

Ainsworth, M. D. S., Blehar, M. C., Waters, E., & Wall, S. (1978). *Patterns of attachment: A psychological study of the strange situation.* Hillsdale, NJ: Erlbaum.

Aitken, J. R., & Benson, J. W. (1984). The use of relaxation/desensitization in treating anxiety associated with flying. *Aviation Space and Environmental Medicine, 55,* 196–199.

Akaike, A. (2006). Preclinical evidence of neuroprotection by cholinesterase inhibitors. *Alzheimer Disease and Associated Disorders, 20*(Suppl. 1), S8–S11.

Akinola, M., & Mendes, W. B. (2008). The dark side of creativity: Biological vulnerability and negative emotions lead to greater artistic creativity. *Personality and Social Psychological Bulletin, 34,* 1677–1686.

Aknin, L. B., Hamlin, J. K., & Dunn, E. W. (2012). Giving leads to happiness in young children. *PLoS ONE, 7,* e39211. doi: 10.1371 /journal.pone.0039211

Alam, M., Barrett, K. C., Hodapp, R. M., & Arndt, K. A. (2008). Botulinum toxin and the facial feedback hypothesis: Can looking better make you feel happier? *Journal of the American Academy of Dermatology, 58,* 1061–1072.

Al-Atiyyat, N. M. H. (2009). Cultural diversity and cancer pain. *Journal of Hospice & Palliative Nursing, 11,* 154–164.

Alberini, C. M., & Chen, D. Y. (2012). Memory enhancement: Consolidation, reconsolidation and insulin-like growth factor 2. *Trends in Neurosciences, 35,* 274–283. doi: 10.1016/j.tins.2011.12.007

Albert, D. J. (1966). The effects of polarizing currents on the consolidation of learning. *Neuropsychologia, 4,* 65–77.

Aldington, S., Harwood, M., Cox, B., Weatherall, M., . . . Beasley, R. (2008). Cannabis use and risk of lung cancer: A case-control study. *European Respiratory Journal, 31,* 280–286.

Aleksic, V., & Ivanovic, M. (2016). Psychometric evaluation of the reliability of IPVIS-OS multiple intelligences assessment instrument for early adolescents. *Journal of Educational Sciences and Psychology, 6,* 21–34.

Alem, S., Perry, C. J., Zhu, X., Loukola, O. J., Ingraham, T., Sóvik, E., & Chittka, L. (2016).

Associative mechanisms allow for social learning and cultural transmission of string pulling in an insect. *PLOS Biology,* 1–28. Available at http://doi .org/10.1371/journal.pbio.1002564

Alex, C., Lindgren, M., Shapiro, P. A., McKinley, P. S., Brondolo, E. N., Myers, M. M., ... Sloan, R. P. (2013). Aerobic exercise and strength training effects on cardiovascular sympathetic function in healthy adults: A randomized controlled trial. *Psychosomatic Medicine, 75*(4), 375–381.

Alladi, S., Bak, T. H., Mekala, S., Rajan, A., Chaudhuri, J. R., Mioshi, E., ... Kaul, S. (2016). Impact of bilingualism on cognitive outcome after stroke. *Stroke, 47*(1), 258–261. Available at http:// doi.org/10.1161/STROKEAHA.115.010418

Allemand, M., Zimprich, D., & Hendriks, A. A. J. (2008). Age differences in five personality domains across the life span. *Developmental Psychology, 44,* 758–770.

Allen, D. G., Shore, L. M., & Griffeth, R. W. (2003). The role of perceived organizational support and supportive human resource practices in the turnover process. *Journal of Management, 29,* 99–118.

Allen, L., & Gorski, R. (2007). *Sex differences in the bed nucleus of the stria terminalis of the human brain* [e-book]. Cambridge, MA: MIT Press.

Allergan, Inc. (2013). MEDICATION GUIDE BOTOX® Cosmetic (onabotulinumtoxinA) for injection.

Allison, D. B., Heshka, S., Neale, M. C., Lykken, D. T., & Heymsfield, S. B. (1994). A genetic analysis of relative weight among 4,020 twin pairs, with an emphasis on sex effects. *Health Psychology, 13,* 362–365.

Alloway, T., Elliott, J., & Holmes, J. (2010). The prevalence of ADHD-like symptoms in a community sample. *Journal of Attention Disorders, 14,* 52–56. doi: 10.1177/1087054709356197

Allport, G. W. (1937). *Personality: A psychological interpretation.* New York, NY: Holt, Rinehart & Winston.

Allport, G. W. (1954). *The nature of prejudice.* Cambridge, MA: Addison-Wesley.

Allport, G. W., & Odbert, H. W. (1936). Trait-names: A psycho-lexical study. *Psychological Monographs, 47,* 1–171.

Alt, K. W., Jeunesse, C., Buritrago-Tellez, C. H., Wächter, R., Boes, E., & Pichler, S. L. (1997, May 22). Evidence for stone-age cranial surgery. *Nature, 387,* 360.

Altman, J., & Das, G. D. (1966). Autoradiographic and histological studies of postnatal neurogenesis. I. A longitudinal investigation of the kinetics, migration and transformation of cells incorporating tritiated thymidine in neonate rats, with special reference to postnatal neurogenesis in some brain regions. *Journal of Comparative Neurology, 126,* 337–389.

Alves, J., Perelman, J., Soto-Rojas, V., Richter, M., Rimpela, A., Loureiro, I. ... Lorant, V. (2016). The role of parental smoking on adolescent smoking and its social patterning: A cross-sectional survey in six European cities. *Journal of Public Health*, published first online at doi: 10.1093/pubmed/fdw040.

Alzheimer's Association. (2008). *What is Alzheimer's?* Retrieved March 10, 2008, from http://www.alz.org/alzheimers_disease_what_is_alzheimers.asp#plaques

Alzheimer's Association. (2016). *2016 Alzheimer's disease facts and figures, 9*(2). Retrieved October 24, 2016, from http://dx.doi.org/10.1016/j.jalz.2016.03.001

Amabile, T. M. (1996). *Creativity in context.* Boulder, CO: Westview.

Amabile, T. M., & Khaire, M. (2008, October). Creativity and the role of the leader. *Harvard Business Review*, 1–11.

Amabile, T. M., & Kramer, S. J. (2007, May). Inner work life: Understanding the subtext of business performance. *Harvard Business Review*, 1–13.

Amabile, T. M., Hill, K. G., Hennessey, B. A., & Tighe, E. M. (1994). The Work Preference Inventory—Assessing intrinsic and extrinsic motivational orientations. *Journal of Personality and Social Psychology, 66*, 950–967.

Amaral, D. G. (2000). The functional organization of perception and movement. In E. R. Kandal, J. H. Schwartz, & T. M. Jessell (Eds.), *Principles of neuroscience* (4th ed) (pp. 337–348). New York: McGraw-Hill.

Amedi, A., Merabet, L. B., Bermpohl, F., & Pascual-Leone, A. (2005). The occipital cortex in the blind. *Current Directions in Psychological Science, 14*, 306–311.

American Heart Association. (2005). *Heart disease and stroke statistics—2005 update.* Dallas, TX: Author.

American Psychiatric Association (APA). (2013). *Diagnostic and statistical manual of mental disorders* (5th ed.). Washington, DC: Author.

Amichai-Hamburger, Y., & Vinitzky, G. (2010). Social network use and personality. *Computers in Human Behavior, 26*, 1289–1295.

Amin, V., & Lhila, A. (2016). Decomposing racial differences in adolescent smoking in the U.S. *Economics & Human Biology, 22*, 161–176. Retrieved from http://doi.org/10.1016/j.ehb.2016.05.001

Ammar, A., Blanchette, A., Sale, D., LaForest, D., Palumbo, T., Swift, A., ... & Commissaris, R. L. (2016). Texting, drugs and driving: A "triple threat" to driving safety? *Journal of Ergonomics, 6*(2), e1000154–e1000154.

Anacker, C., Cattaneo, A., Musaelyan, K., Zunszain, P. A., Horowitz, M., Molteni, R., ... Pariante, C. M. (2013). Role for the kinase SGK1 in stress, depression, and glucocorticoid effects on hippocampal neurogenesis. *Proceedings of the National Academy of Sciences, 110*, 8708–8713.

Anda, R. F., Felitti, V. J., Bremner, J. D., Walker, J. D., Whitfield, C., Perry, B. D., ... Giles, W. H. (2006). The enduring effects of abuse and related adverse experiences in childhood: A convergence of evidence from neurobiology and epidemiology. *European Archives of Psychiatry and Clinical Neuroscience, 256*, 174–186.

Anderson, C. A., Shibuya, A., Ihori, N., Swing, E. L., Bushman, B. J., Sakamoto, A., ... Saleem, M. (2010). Violent video game effects on aggression, empathy, and prosocial behavior in Eastern and Western countries. *Psychological Bulletin, 136*, 151–173.

Anderson, C., & Horne, J. A. (2013). Driving drowsy also worsens driver distraction. *Sleep Medicine, 14*(5), 466–468. Retrieved from http://dx.doi.org/10.1016/j.sleep.2012.11.014

Anderson, P. L., Price, M., Edwards, S. M., Obassaju, M. A., Schmerts, S. K., Zimand, E., & Calamaras, M. R. (2013). Virtual reality exposure therapy for social anxiety disorder: A randomized controlled trial. *Journal of Consulting and Clinical Psychology.* doi: 10.1037/a0033559

Andersson, M. A., & Christakis, N. A. (2016). Desire for weight loss, weight-related social contact, and body mass outcomes. *Obesity.* doi: 10.1002/oby.21512

Andrade, F. C. D., Raffaelli, M., Teran-Garcia, M., Jerman, J. A., Garcia, C. A., & Up Amigos 2009 Study Group. (2012). Weight status misperception among Mexican young adults. *Body Image, 9*, 184–188.

Andreasen, N. C. (1987). Creativity and psychological disorder: Prevalence rates in writers and their first-degree relatives. *American Journal of Psychiatry, 144*, 1288–1292.

Andreasen, N. C. (2006). *The creative brain.* New York, NY: Penguin.

Andreasen, N. C., & Glick, I. D. (1988). Bipolar affective disorder and creativity: Implications and clinical management. *Comprehensive Psychiatry, 29*, 207–216.

Andreasen, N. C., O'Leary, D. S., Flaum, M., Nopoulos, P., Watkins, G. L., ... Ponto, L. L. B. (1997). Hypofrontality in schizophrenia: Distributed dysfunctional circuits in neuroleptic-naïve patients. *The Lancet, 349*, 1730–1734.

Anokhin, P. K. (2013). *Biology and neurophysiology of the conditioned reflex and its role in adaptive behavior: International series of monographs in cerebrovisceral and behavioral physiology and conditioned reflexes* (Vol. 3). Elsevier.

Anothaisintawee, T., Reutrakul, S., Van Cauter, E., & Thakkinstian, A. (2016). Sleep disturbances compared to traditional risk factors for diabetes development: Systematic review and meta-analysis. *Sleep Medicine Reviews, 30*, 11–24. doi: 10.1016/j.smrv.2015.10.002

Anselmi, P., Vianello, M., Voci, A., & Robusto, E. (2013). Implicit sexual attitude of heterosexual, gay and bisexual individuals: Disentangling the contribution of specific associations to the overall measure. *PLoS ONE, 8*, e78990. doi: 10.1371/journal.pone.0078990

Anson, K., & Ponsford, J. (2006). Coping and emotional adjustment following traumatic brain injury. *Journal of Head Trauma Rehabilitation, 21*, 248–259.

Anthonisen, N. R., Skeans, M. A., Wise, R. A., Manfreda, J., Kanner, R. E., & Connett, J. E. (Lung Health Study Research Group). (2005). The effects of a smoking cessation intervention on 14.5-year mortality: A randomized clinical trial. *Annals of Internal Medicine, 142*, 233–239.

Aouizerate, B., Guehl, D., Cuny, E., Rougier, A., Bioulac, B., Tignol, J., & Burbaud, P. (2004). Pathophysiology of obsessive-compulsive disorder: A necessary link between phenomenology, neuropsychology, imagery and physiology. *Progress in Neurobiology, 72*, 195–221.

APA Presidential Task Force on Evidence-Based Practice, US. (2006). Evidence-based practice in psychology. *American Psychologist, 61*, 271–285.

Apsche, J. (1993). *Probing the mind of a serial killer.* Morrisville, PA: International Information Associates.

Aquino, C. C. H., & Lang, A. E. (2014). Tardive dyskinesia syndromes: Current concepts. *Parkinsonism & Related Disorders, 20*, S113–S117.

Arbib, M., Liebal, K., & Pika, S. (2008). Primate vocalization, gesture, and the evolution of human language. *Current Anthropology, 49*, 1053–1063. doi: 10.1086/593015

Arden, R., Trzaskowski, M., Garfield, V., & Plomin, R. (2014). Genes influence young children's human figure drawings and their association with intelligence a decade later. *Psychological Science, 25*(10), 1843–1850. Available at https://doi.org/10.1177/0956797614540686

Argyle, M. (2001). *The psychology of happiness* (2nd ed.). New York, NY: Routledge.

Arling, G. L., & Harlow, H. F. (1967). Effects of social deprivation on maternal behavior of rhesus monkeys. *Journal of Comparative and Physiological Psychology, 64*, 371–377.

Aramagan, Esref. (n.d.). Retrieved October 23, 2007 from http://www.esrefarmagan.com/bio.html

Armenta, C. N., Fritz, M. M., & Lyubomirsky, S. (2016). Functions of positive emotions: Gratitude as a motivator of self-improvement and positive change. *Emotion Review.* doi: 10.1177/1754073916669596

Armstrong, T. (2009). *Multiple intelligences in the classroom* (3rd ed.). Alexandria, VA: ASCD.

Arnett, J. J. (2004). *Emerging adulthood: The winding road from the late teens to the twenties.* New York, NY: Oxford University Press.

Arnett, J. J. (2006). Emerging adulthood: Understanding the new way of coming of age. In J. J. Arnett and J. L. Tanner (Eds.), *Emerging adults in America: Coming of age in the 21st century* (pp. 3–19). Washington, DC: American Psychological Association.

Arnold, M. B. (1960). *Emotion and personality: Vol. 1. Psychological aspects.* New York, NY: Columbia University Press.

Aron, E. N., & Aron, A. (1997). Sensory-processing sensitivity and its relation to introversion and emotionality. *Journal of Personality and Social Psychology, 73*(2), 345–368. Retrieved from https://doi.org/10.1037/0022-3514.73.2.345

Aron, E. N., Aron, A., & Jagiellowicz, J. (2011). Sensory processing sensitivity. *Personality and Social Psychology Review.* Retrieved from https://doi.org/10.1177/1088868311434213

Arseneault, L., Cannon, M., Witton, J., & Murray, R. M. (2004). Causal association between cannabis and psychosis: Examination of the evidence. *British Journal of Psychiatry, 184*, 110–117.

Arseneault, L., Moffitt, T. E., Caspi, A., Taylor, A., Rijsdijk, F., Jaffee, S. R., ... Measelle, J. (2003). Strong genetic effects on cross-situational antisocial behaviour among 5-year-old children according to mothers, teachers, examiner-observers, and twins' self-reports. *Journal of Child Psychology and Psychiatry, 44*, 832–848.

Artola, A. (2008). Diabetes-, stress- and ageing-related changes in synaptic plasticity in hippocampus and neocortex—The same metaplastic process? *European Journal of Pharmacology, 585*, 153–162.

Asher, L., Friel, M., Griffin, K., & Collins, L. M. (2016). Mood and personality interact to determine cognitive biases in pigs. *Biology Letters, 12*(11), 20160402+. Available at http://doi.org/10.1098/rsbl.2016.0402

Ashkenazi, S., Black, J. M., Abrams, D. A., Hoeft, F., & Menon, V. (2013). Neurobiological underpinnings of math and reading learning disabilities. *Journal of Learning Disabilities, 46*, 549–569. doi: 10.1177/0022219413483174

Ashley, N. T., & Demas, G. E. (2017). Neuroendocrine-immune circuits, phenotypes, and interactions. *Hormones and Behavior, 87*, 25–34. Available at http://dx.doi.org/10.1016/j.yhbeh.2016.10.004

Askgaard, G., Grønbæk, M., Kjær, M. S., Tjønneland, A., & Tolstrup, J. S. (2015). Alcohol drinking pattern and risk of alcoholic liver cirrhosis: A prospective cohort study. *Journal of Hepatology, 62*(5), 1061–1067. Available at http://dx.doi.org/10.1016/j.jhep.2014.12.005

Asperger, H. (1991). "Autistic psychopathy" in childhood (U. Frith, Trans.). In U. Frith (Ed.), *Autism and Asperger syndrome* (pp. 37–62). New York, NY: Cambridge University Press. (Original work published 1944).

Assouline, M., & Meir, E. I. (1987). Meta-analysis of the relationship between congruence and well-being measures. *Journal of Vocational Behavior, 31*, 319–332.

Asthana, S., & Oostvogels, R. (2001). The social construction of male 'homosexuality' in India: Implications for HIV transmission and prevention. *Social Science & Medicine, 52*(5), 707–721.

Athanasopoulos, P., Bylund, E., Montero-Melis, G., Damjanovic, L., Schartner, A., Kibbe, A., ... Thierry, G. (2015). Two languages, two minds: Flexible cognitive processing driven by language of operation. *Psychological Science*, 1–9. Available at http://doi.org/10.1177/0956797614567509

Atkin, A. J., Sharp, S. J., Corder, K., & Van Sluijs, E. M. F. (2014). Prevalence and correlates of screen time in youth: An international perspective. *American Journal of Preventive Medicine, 47*(6), 803–807. Available at http://doi.org/10.1016/j.amepre.2014.07.043

Atkinson, J. W. (1964). *An introduction to motivation*. New York, NY: Van Nostrand.

Atkinson, R. C., & Shiffrin, R. M. (1971). The control of short-term memory. *Scientific American, 225*, 82–90.

Augur, H. (2016). Who are you? Big data tackles personality, behavior and psychology. Retrieved online June 29, 2016 at http://dataconomy.com/big-data-tackles-personality-behavior-psychology/

Austin (Tex.) Police Department. (1966). Austin, TX Police Department Records of the Charles Whitman mass murder case. Austin History Center, Austin Public Library.

Austin, E. J. (2005). Personality correlates of the broader autism phenotype as assessed by the Autism Spectrum Quotient (AQ). *Personality and Individual Differences, 38*, 451–460.

Austin, M., Hadzi-Pavlovic, D., Leader, L., Saint, K., & Parker, G. (2004). Maternal trait anxiety, depression, and life-event stress in pregnancy: Relationships with infant temperament. *Early Human Development, 81*, 183–190.

Azadfar, P., Akbari, L., Sheibani-Nia, S., Noroozian, M., Assarzadegan, F., & Houshmand, M. (2014). Analysis of APP gene in early onset Alzheimer's disease patients. *Neurobiology of Aging, 35*(3). doi: 10.1016/j.neurobiolaging.2013.10.062

Azizian, A., & Polich, J. (2007). Evidence for attentional gradient in the serial position memory curve from event-related potentials. *Journal of Cognitive Neuroscience, 19*, 2071–2081.

Baan, R., Straif, K., Grosse, Y., Secretan, B., El Ghissassi, F., Boucard, V., ... Cogliano, B. (2007). Carcinogenicity of alcoholic beverages. *The Lancet Oncology, 8*, 292–293.

Baars, B. J. (1997). In the theatre of consciousness: Global workspace theory, a rigorous scientific theory of consciousness. *Journal of Consciousness Studies, 4*, 292–309.

Babson, K. A., Feldner, M. T., & Badour, C. L. (2010). Cognitive behavioral therapy for sleep disorders. *Psychiatric Clinics of North America, 33*, 629–640.

Bachevalier, J. (2011). The amygdala in autism spectrum disorders. In E. Hollander, A. Kolevzon, & J. T. Coyle (Eds.), *Textbook of autism spectrum disorders* (pp. 363–374). Arlington, VA: American Psychiatric Publishing.

Bachorowski, J. (1999). Vocal expression and perception of emotion. *Current Directions in Psychological Science, 8*, 53–57.

Bachorowski, J., & Owren, M. J. (2001). Not all laughs are alike: Voiced but not unvoiced laughter readily elicits positive affect. *Psychological Science, 12*, 252–257.

Baddeley, A. D. (1998). The central executive: A concept and some misconceptions. *Journal of the International Neuropsychological Society, 4*, 523–526.

Baddeley, A. D. (2003). Working memory: Looking back and looking forward. *Nature Reviews Neuroscience, 4*, 829–839.

Baddeley, A. D. (2007). *Working memory, thought, and action*. New York, NY: Oxford University Press.

Baek, J., & Bullock, L. M. (2014). Cyberbullying: A cross-cultural perspective. *Emotional & Behavioural Difficulties, 19*(2), 226–238. Available at http://doi.org/10.1080/13632752.2013.849028

Baer, R. A., Smith, G. T., Hopkins, J., Krietemeyer, J., & Toney, L. (2006). Using self-report assessment methods to explore facets of mindfulness. *Assessment, 13*, 27–45.

Bagwell, C. L., Newcomb, A. F., & Bukowski, W. M. (1998). Preadolescent friendship and rejection as predictors of adult adjustment. *Child Development, 69*, 140–153.

Bahremand, M., Alikhani, M., Zakiei, A., Janjani, P., & Aghaei, A. (2016). Emotion risk-factor in patients with cardiac diseases: The role of cognitive emotion regulation strategies, positive affect and negative affect (A case-control study). *Global Journal of Health Science, 8*(1), 173. doi: 10.5539/gjhs.v8n1p173

Baier, B., Karnath, H., Dieterich, M., Birklein, F., Heinze, C., & Müller, N. G. (2010). Keeping memory clear and stable—The contribution of human basal ganglia and prefrontal cortex to working memory. *Journal of Neuroscience, 30*, 9788–9792. doi: 10.1523/JNEUROSCI.1513–10.2010

Bailey, J. M., Dunne, M. P., & Martin, N. G. (2000). Genetic and environment effects on sexual orientation and its correlates in an Australian twin sample. *Journal of Personality and Social Psychology, 78*, 524–536.

Bailey, J. M., Kirk, K. M., Zhu, G., Dunne, M. P., & Martin, N. G. (2000). Do individual differences in sociosexuality represent genetic or environmentally contingent strategies? Evidence from the Australian twin registry. *Journal of Personality and Social Psychology, 78*, 537–545.

Bailey, J. M., Vasey, P. L., Diamond, L. M., Breedlove, S. M., Vilain, E., & Epprecht, M. (2016). Sexual orientation, controversy, and science. *Psychological Science in the Public Interest, 17*(2), 45–101. Available at http://doi.org/10.1177/1529100616637616

Bailey, J. M., & Zucker, K. J. (1995). Childhood sex-typed behavior and sexual orientation: A conceptual analysis and quantitative review. *Developmental Psychology, 31*, 43–55.

Bailey, M. T., & Coe, C. L. (1999). Maternal separation disrupts the integrity of the intestinal microflora in infant rhesus monkeys. *Dev. Psychobiol. 35*, 146–155. doi: 10.1002/(SICI)1098-2302(199909)35:2<146::AID-DEV7>3.0.CO;2-G

Bailey, N. W., & Zuk, M. (2009). Same-sex sexual behavior and evolution. *Trends in Ecology & Evolution, 24*, 439–446.

Baillargeon, R., & DeVos, J. (1991). Object permanence in young infants: Further evidence. *Child Development, 62*, 1227–1246.

Baird, B. M., Lucas, R. E., & Donnellan, M. B. (2010). Life satisfaction across the lifespan: Findings from two nationally representative panel studies. *Social Indicators Research, 99*(2), 183–203. Available at https://doi.org/10.1007/s11205-010-9584-9

Baird, J. C., Wagner, M., & Fuld, K. (1990). A simple but powerful theory of the moon illusion. *Journal of Experimental Psychology: Human Perception and Performance, 16*, 675–677.

Bak, T. H., Nissan, J. J., Allerhand, M. M., & Deary, I. J. (2014). Does bilingualism influence cognitive aging? *Annals of Neurology, 75*(6), 959–963. Available at http://doi.org/10.1002/ana.24158

Baldwin, D. S., & Polkinghorn, C. (2005). Evidence-based pharmacotherapy of generalized anxiety disorder. *International Journal of Neuropsychopharmacology, 8*, 293–302.

Ball, K., Crawford, D., & Kenardy, J. (2004). Longitudinal relationships among overweight, life satisfaction, and aspirations in young women. *Obesity Research, 12*, 1019–1030.

Ballanyi, K., Panaitescu, B., & Ruangkittisakul, A. (2010). Control of breathing by "Nerve Glue." *Science Signaling, 3*(147), pe41. doi: 10.1126/scisignal.3147pe41

Ballesta, S., Reymond, G., Pozzobon, M., & Duhamel, J-R. (2016). Effects of MDMA Injections on the behavior of socially-housed long-tailed Macaques (*Macaca fascicularis*). *PLoS ONE, 11*(2): e0147136. doi:10.1371/journal.pone.0147136

Balsis, S., Carpenter, B., & Storandt, M. (2005). Personality change precedes clinical diagnosis of dementia of the Alzheimer type. *The Journals of Gerontology: Series B: Psychological Sciences and Social Sciences, 60B*, P98–P101.

Baltes, P. B., & Smith, J. (2008). The fascination of wisdom: Its nature, ontogeny, and function. *Perspectives on Psychological Science, 3*, 56–64.

Baltes, P. B., Reuter-Lorenz, & Rösler, F. (Eds.) (2006). *Lifespan development and the brain: The perspective of bio-cultural co-construction*. New York, NY: Cambridge University Press.

Banaji, M. R., & Greenwald, A. G. (1995). Implicit gender stereotyping in judgments of fame. *Journal of Personality and Social Psychology, 68*, 181–198.

Banducci, S. E., Ward, N., Gaspar, J. G., Schab, K. R., Crowell, J. A., Kaczmarski, H., & Kramer, A. F. (2016). The effects of cell phone and text message conversations on simulated street crossing. *Human Factors: The Journal of the Human Factors and Ergonomics Society, 58*(1), 150–162. doi: 10.1177/0018720815609501

Bandura, A. (1969). *Principles of behavior modification*. New York, NY: Holt, Rinehart & Winston.

Bandura, A. (1986). *Social foundations of thought and action: A social cognitive theory*. Englewood Cliffs, NJ: Prentice-Hall.

Bandura, A. (1997). *Self-efficacy: The exercise of control*. New York, NY: Freeman.

Bandura, A., Ross, D., & Ross, S. A. (1961). Transmission of aggression through imitation of aggressive models. *Journal of Abnormal and Social Psychology, 63*, 575–582.

Bandura, A., Ross, D., & Ross, S. A. (1963). Vicarious reinforcement and imitative learning. *Journal of Abnormal and Social Psychology, 67*, 601–608.

Banks, M. S., & Salapatek, P. (1983). Infant visual perception. In P. H. Mussen (Ed.), *Handbook of child psychology* (4th ed., Vol. 2). New York, NY: Wiley.

Bansal, R., Peterson, B. S., Gingrich, J., Hao, X., Odgerel, Z., Warner, V., ... & Sourander, A. (2016). Serotonin signaling modulates the effects of familial risk for depression on cortical thickness. *Psychiatry Research: Neuroimaging, 248*, 83–93. http://dx.doi.org/10.1016/j.pscychresns.2016.01.004

Barac, R., & Bialystok, E. (2012). Bilingual effects on cognitive and linguistic development: Role of language, cultural background, and education. *Child Development, 83*(2), 413–422.

Baran, B., Pace-Schott, E. F., Ericson, C., & Spencer, R. M. C. (2012). Processing of emotional reactivity and emotional memory over sleep. *Journal of Neuroscience, 32*, 1035–1042. doi: 10.1523/JNEUROSCI.2532-11.2012

Barbaresi, W. J., Colligan, R. C., Weaver, A. L., Voigt, R. G., Killian, J. M., & Katusic, S. K. (2013, March 4). Mortality, ADHD, and psychosocial adversity in adults with childhood ADHD: A prospective study. *Pediatrics*. doi: 10.1542/peds.2012-2354

Barbazanges, A., Piazza, P. V., Le Moal, M., & Maccari, S. (1996). Maternal glucocorticoid secretion mediates long-term effects of prenatal stress. *Journal of Neuroscience, 16*, 3943–3949.

Barber, L. K., Munz, D. C., Bagsby, P. G., & Powell, E. D. (2010). Sleep consistency and sufficiency: Are both necessary for less psychological strain? *Stress and Health, 26*(3), 186–193.

Barbour, K. A., Edenfield, T. M., & Blumenthal, J. A. (2007). Exercise as a treatment for depression and other psychiatric disorders. *Journal of Cardiopulmonary Rehabilitation and Prevention, 27*, 359–367.

Barch, D. M. (2005). The cognitive neuroscience of schizophrenia. *Annual Review of Clinical Psychology, 1*, 321–353.

Bargh, J. A. (1997). The automaticity of everyday life. In R. S. Wyer, Jr. (Ed.), *The automaticity of everyday life: Advances in social cognition* (pp. 1–61). Mahwah, NJ: Erlbaum.

Barkham, M., Connell, J., Stiles, W. B., Miles, J. N. V., Margison, F., Evans, C., & Mellor-Clark, J. (2006). Dose-effect relations and responsive regulation of treatment duration: The good enough level. *Journal of Consulting and Clinical Psychology, 74*, 160–167.

Barlow, D. H. (2004). Psychological treatments. *American Psychologist, 59*, 869–878.

Baron, A., & Galizio, M. (2006). The distinction between positive and negative reinforcement: Use with care. *Behavior Analyst, 296*, 141–151.

Bar-On, R. (2004). The Bar-On Emotional Quotient Inventory (EQ-i): Rationale, description, and

summary. In G. Geher (Ed.), *Measuring emotional intelligence: Common ground and controversy* (pp. 111–142). Hauppauge, NY: Nova Science.

Baron-Cohen, S. (Ed.) (1997). *The maladapted mind: Classic readings in evolutionary psychopathology*. East Sussex, UK: Psychology Press.

Baron-Cohen, S., Bolton, P., Wheelwright, S., Scahill, V., Short, L., Mead, G., & Smith, A. (1998). Autism occurs more often in families of physicists, engineers, and mathematicians. *Autism, 2*, 296–301.

Baron-Cohen, S., Wheelwright, S., Skinner, R., Martin, J., & Clubley, E. (2001). The Autism-Spectrum Quotient (AQ): Evidence from Asperger syndrome/high-functioning autism, males and females, scientists and mathematicians. *Journal of Autism & Developmental Disorders, 31*, 5–17.

Baron-Cohen, S., Wheelwright, S., Stott, C., Bolton, P., & Goodyer, I. (1997). Is there a link between engineering and autism? *Autism, 1*, 101–109.

Barr, C. L., Kroft, J., Feng, Y., Wigg, K., Roberts, W., Malone, M., ... Kennedy, J. L. (2002). The norepinephrine transporter gene and attention-deficit hyperactivity disorder. *American Journal of Medical Genetics, 114*, 255–259.

Barrés, R., Yan, J., Egan, B., Treebak, J. T., Rasmussen, M., Fritz, T., Caidahl, K., Krook, A., O'Gorman, D. J., & Zierath, J. R. (2012). Acute exercise remodels promoter methylation in human skeletal muscle. *Cell Metabolism, 15*, 405–411. doi: 10.1016/j.cmet.2012.01.001

Barrett, E., Ross, R. P., O'Toole, P. W., Fitzgerald, G. F., & Stanton, C. (2012). Gamma-aminobutyric acid production by culturable bacteria from the human intestine. *Journal of Applied Microbiology, 113*(2), 411–417. Available at http://doi.org/10.1111/j.1365-2672.2012.05344.x

Barrett, L. F., Lane, R. D., Sechrest, L., & Schwartz, G. E. (2000). Sex differences in emotional awareness. *Personality and Social Psychology Bulletin, 26*, 1027–1035.

Barrett, L. F., Ochsner, K. N., & Gross, J. J. (2007). On the automaticity of emotion. In J. Bargh (Ed.), *Social psychology and the unconscious: The automaticity of higher mental processes* (pp. 173–217). New York, NY: Psychology Press.

Barrett-Cheetham, E., Williams, L. A., & Bednall, T. C. (2016). A differentiated approach to the link between positive emotion, motivation, and eudaimonic well-being. *The Journal of Positive Psychology*, 1–14. doi: 10.1080/17439760.2016.1152502

Bartels, M., Rietveld, M. J., van Baal, G. C., & Boomsma, D. I. (2002). Genetic and environmental influences on the development of intelligence. *Behavior Genetics, 32*, 237–249.

Barth, J., Schumacher, M., & Herrmann-Lingen, C. (2004). Depression as a risk factor for mortality in patients with coronary heart disease: A meta-analysis. *Psychosomatic Medicine, 66*, 802–813.

Bartholow, B. D., Bushman, B. J., & Sestir, M. A. (2006). Chronic violent video game exposure and desensitization to violence: Behavioral and event-related brain potential data. *Journal of Experimental Social Psychology, 42*, 532–539.

Baş, G. (2016). The effect of multiple intelligences theory-based education on academic achievement: A meta-analytic review. *Educational Sciences: Theory & Practice, 16*(6), 1833–1864. Available at http://doi.org/10.12738/estp.2016.6.0015

Basak, C., Boot, W. R., Voss, M. W., & Kramer, A. F. (2008). Can training in a real-time strategy video game attenuate cognitive decline in older adults? *Psychology and Aging, 23*, 765–777.

Basbaum A. L., & Jessell, T. M. (2000). The perception of pain. In E. R. Kandel, J. H. Schwartz, & T. M. Jessell (Eds.), *Principles of neural science* (4th ed., pp. 472–491). New York, NY: McGraw-Hill.

Bassett, E. B., Verchinski, B. A., Mattay, V. S., Weinberger, D. R., & Meyer-Lindenberg, A. (2008). Hierarchical organization of human cortical networks in health and schizophrenia. *Journal of Neuroscience, 28*, 9239–9248.

Basson, R. (2000). The female sexual response: A different model. *Journal of Sex & Marital Therapy, 26*, 51–65.

Basten, U., Hilger, K., & Fiebach, C. J. (2015). Where smart brains are different: A quantitative meta-analysis of functional and structural brain imaging studies on intelligence. *Intelligence, 51*, 10–27. Available at http://doi.org/10.1016/j.intell.2015.04.009

Batey, M., & Furnham, A. (2008). Creativity, intelligence, and personality: A critical review of the scattered literature. *Genetic, Social, and General Psychology Monographs, 132*, 355–429.

Batey, M., Furnham, A., & Safiullina, X. (2010). Intelligence, general knowledge and personality as predictors of creativity. *Learning and Individual Differences, 20*(5), 532–535. doi: 10.1016/j.lindif.2010.04.008

Bation, R., Poulet, E., Haesebaert, F., Saoud, M., & Brunelin, J. (2016). Transcranial direct current stimulation in treatment-resistant obsessive-compulsive disorder: An open-label pilot study. *Progress in Neuro-Psychopharmacology and Biological Psychiatry, 65*, 153–157. Available at http://dx.doi.org/10.1016/j.pnpbp.2015.10.001

Batson, C. D. (1991). *The altruism question: Toward a social psychological answer*. Hillsdale, NJ: Erlbaum.

Bauer, E., & Bauer, P. (1996). *Bears: Biology, ecology and conservation*. Minneapolis, MN: Voyageur Press.

Bauer, F., Korpert, K., Neuberger, M., Raber, A., & Schwetz, F. (1991). Risk factors for hearing loss at different frequencies in a population of 47388 noise-exposed workers. *Journal of Acoustic Society of America, 6*, 3086–3098.

Bauer, M., & Whybrow, P. C. (2001). Thyroid hormone, neural tissue and mood modulation. *World Journal of Biological Psychiatry, 2*, 57–67.

Baumeister, J. C., Papa, G., & Foroni, F. (2016). Deeper than skin deep— The effect of botulinum toxin-A on emotion processing. *Toxicon, 118*, 86–90. Available at http://dx.doi.org/10.1016/j.toxicon.2016.04.044

Baumeister, R. F., & Leary, M. (1995). The need to belong: Desire for interpersonal attachments as a fundamental human motivation. *Psychological Bulletin, 117*, 497–529.

Baumeister, R. F., & Masicampo, E. J. (2010). Conscious thought is for facilitating social and cultural interactions: How mental simulations serve the animal-culture interface. *Psychological Review, 117*, 945–971.

Baumeister, R. F., Masicampo, E. J., & Vohs, K. D. (2011). Do conscious thoughts cause behavior? *Annual Review of Psychology, 62*, 331–361.

Baumrind, D. (1964). Some thoughts on ethics of research: After reading Milgram's "Behavioral study of obedience." *American Psychologist, 19*, 421–423.

Bavelier, D., Tomann, A., Hutton, C., Mitchell, T., Corina, D., ... & Liu, G. (2000). Visual attention to the periphery is enhanced in congenitally deaf individuals. *Journal of Neuroscience, 20*, 1–6.

Beadle-Brown, J., Murphy, G., & Wing, L. (2006). The Camberwell cohort 25 years on: Characteristics and changes in skills over time. *Journal of Applied*

Research in Intellectual Disabilities, 19(4), 317–329. doi: 10.1111/j.1468-3148.2006.00289.x

Beauchamp, G. K., & Mennella, J. A. (2009). Early flavor learning and its impact on later feeding behavior. *Journal of Pediatric Gastroenterology & Nutrition, 48,* S25–S30. doi: 10.1097/MPG.0b013e31819774a5

Beck, A. T., & Emery, G. (1985). *Anxiety disorders and phobias.* New York, NY: Basic Books.

Beck, K. H., & Watters, S. (2016). Characteristics of college students who text while driving: Do their perceptions of a significant other influence their decisions? *Transportation Research Part F: Traffic Psychology and Behaviour, 37,* 119–128. Retrieved from http://dx.doi.org/10.1016/j.trf.2015.12.017

Beekman, A. T. F., Smit, F., Stek, M. L., Reynolds, C. F., & Cuijpers, P. C. (2010). Preventing depression in high-risk groups. *Current Opinion in Psychiatry, 23,* 8–11.

Beeman, M. J., & Bowden, E. M. (2000). The right hemisphere maintains solution-related activation for yet-to-be solved insight problems. *Memory & Cognition, 28,* 1231–1241.

Beever, T. G., & Chiarello, R. J. (2009). Cerebral dominance in musicians and non-musicians. *Science, 185,* 537–539.

Beghetto, R. A., & Kaufman, J. C. (2007). Toward a broader conception of creativity: A case for mini-creativity. *Psychology of Aesthetics, Creativity, and the Arts, 1,* 73–79.

Begley, S. (2007). *Train your mind, change your brain.* New York, NY: Ballantine Books.

Belgers, M., Leenaars, M., Homberg, J. R., Ritskes-Hoitinga, M., Schellekens, A. F. A., & Hooijmans, C. R. (2016). Ibogaine and addiction in the animal model, a systematic review and meta-analysis. *Translational Psychiatry, 6*(5), e826. doi: 10.1038/tp.2016.71

Belin-Rauscent, A., Daniel, M. L., Puaud, M., Jupp, B., Sawiak, S., Howett, D., … & Everitt, B. J. (2016). From impulses to maladaptive actions: The insula is a neurobiological gate for the development of compulsive behavior. *Molecular Psychiatry, 21*(4), 491–499. doi: 10.1038/mp.2015.140

Belisle, P., & Chapais, B. (2001). Tolerated co-feeding in relation to degree of kinship in Japanese macaques. *Behaviour, 138,* 487–509.

Bellack, A. S., Bennett, M. E., Gearon, J. S., Brown, C. H., & Yang, Y. (2006). A randomized clinical trial of a new behavioral treatment for drug abuse in people with severe and persistent mental illness. *Archives of General Psychiatry, 63,* 426–432.

Bellander, M., Berggren, R., Mårtensson, J., Brehmer, Y., Wenger, E., Li, T. Q., … Lövdén, M. (2016). Behavioral correlates of changes in hippocampal gray matter structure during acquisition of foreign vocabulary. *NeuroImage, 131,* 205–213. Available at http://doi.org/10.1016/j.neuroimage.2015.10.020

Bellesi, M. (2015). Sleep and oligodendrocyte functions. *Current Sleep Medicine Reports, 1,* 20–26. doi:10.1007/s40675-014-0008-2

Bellesi, M., Pfister-Genskow, M., Maret, S., Keles, S., Tononi, G., & Cirelli, C. (2013). Effects of sleep and wake on oligodendrocytes and their precursors. *Journal of Neuroscience, 33,* 14288–14300. doi: http://dx.doi.org/10.1523/JNEUROSCI.5102-12.2013

Bellur, S., Nowak, K. L., & Hull, K. S. (2015). Make it our time: In class multitaskers have lower academic performance. *Computers in Human Behavior, 53*(2015), 63–70. Available at http://doi.org/10.1016/j.chb.2015.06.027

Belmonte, M. K., Allen, G., Beckel-Mitchener, A., Boulanger, L. M., Carper, R. A., & Webb, S. J. (2004). Autism and abnormal development of brain connectivity. *Journal of Neuroscience, 24,* 9228–9231.

Bem, D. J. (2011). Feeling the future: Experimental evidence for anomalous retroactive influences on cognition and affect. *Journal of Personality and Social Psychology, 100*(3), 407–425. doi:10.1037/a0021524

Bem, D. J., & Horonton, C. (1994). Does psi exist? Replicable evidence for an anomalous process of information transfer. *Psychological Bulletin, 115,* 4–18.

Bem, D. J., Palmer, J., & Broughton, R. S. (2001). Updating the Ganzfeld database: A victim of its own success? *Journal of Parapsychology, 65*(3), 207–218.

Bender, A., Jox, R.J., Grill, E., Straube, A., & Lulé, D. (2015). Persistent vegetative state and minimally conscious state: A systematic review and meta-analysis of diagnostic procedures. *Deutsches Ärzteblatt International, 112,* 235–242.

Benet-Martinez, V., & Oishi, S. (2008). Culture and personality. In O. P. John, R. W. Robins, & L. A. Pervin (Eds.), *Handbook of personality: Theory and research* (pp. 542–567). New York, NY: Guilford Press.

Benjamin, J., Li, L., Patterson, C., Greenburg, B. D., Murphy, D. L., & Hamer, D. H. (1996). Population and familial association between the D4 dopamine receptor gene and measures of novelty seeking. *Nature Genetics, 12,* 81–84.

Benjamin, L. T., Jr. (2007). *A brief history of modern psychology.* Malden, MA: Blackwell.

Benner, E. J., Luciano, D., Jo, R., Abdi, K., Paez-Gonzalez, P., Sheng, H., … Kuo, C. T. (2013). Protective astrogenesis from the SVZ niche after injury is controlled by Notch modulator Thbs4. *Nature, 497,* 369–374. doi: 10.1038/nature12069

Bennett, C. M., & Baird, A. A. (2006). Anatomical changes in the emerging adult brain: A voxel-based morphometry study. *Human Brain Mapping, 27,* 766–777.

Bennett, E. L., Diamond, M. C., Krech, D., & Rosenzweig, M. R. (1964). Chemical and anatomical plasticity of brain. *Science, 146,* 610–619.

Bennett, P. J., Sekuler, R., & Sekuler, A. B. (2007). The effects of aging on motion detection and direction identification. *Vision Research, 47,* 799–809.

Bercich, R. A., Wang, Z., Mei, H., Hammer, L. H., Seburn, K. L., Hargrove, L. J., & Irazoqui, P. P. (2016). Enhancing the versatility of wireless biopotential acquisition for myoelectric prosthetic control. *Journal of Neural Engineering, 13*(4), 046012. doi: 10.1088/1741-2560/13/4/046012

Berenbaum, S. A., & Beltz, A. M. (2011). Sexual differentiation of human behavior: Effects of prenatal and pubertal organizational hormones. *Frontiers in Neuroendocrinology, 32,* 183–200. doi: 10.1016/j.yfme.2011.03001

Berenbaum, S. A., Korman, K., & Leveroni, C. (1995). Early hormones and sex differences in cognitive abilities. *Learning and Individual Differences, 7,* 303–321.

Berghöfer, A., Alda, M., Adli, M., Baethge, C., Bauer, M., Bschor, T., … Pfennig, A. (2008). Long-term effectiveness of lithium in bipolar disorder: A multicenter investigation of patients with typical and atypical features. *Journal of Clinical Psychiatry, 69,* 1860–1868. doi: 10.4088/JCP.v69n1203

Berhardt, B. C., & Singer, T. (2012). The neural basis of empathy. *Annual Review of Neuroscience, 35,* 1–23. doi: 10.1146/annurev-neuro-062111-150536

Berkman, L. F., & Glass, T. (2000). Social integration, social networks, social support and health. In L. F. Berkman & I. Kawachi (Eds.), *Social epidemiology* (pp. 137–173). New York, NY: Oxford University Press.

Berlin, K. L., Means, M. K., & Edinger, J. D. (2011). Nightmare reduction in a Vietnam veteran using imagery rehearsal therapy. *Journal of Clinical Sleep Medicine, 6,* 487–488.

Berlyne, D. (1960). *Conflict, arousal, and curiosity.* New York, NY: McGraw-Hill.

Berna, C., Leknes, S., Holmes, E. A., Edwards, R. R., Goodwin, G., & Tracey, I. (2010). Induction of depressed mood disrupts emotion regulation neurocircuitry and enhances pain unpleasantness. *Biological Psychiatry, 67,* 1083–1090.

Bernardi, R. E., & Spanagel, R. (2013). The clockΔ19 mutation in mice fails to alter the primary and secondary reinforcing properties of nicotine. *Drug and Alcohol Dependence.* doi: http://dx.doi.org/10.1016/j.drugalcdep.2013.08.024

Bernat, J. (2006). Chronic disorders of consciousness. *The Lancet, 367,* 1181–1192.

Bernier, R., & Dawson, G. (2009). The role of mirror neuron dysfunction in autism. In J. A. Pineda (Ed.), *Mirror neuron systems: The role of mirroring processes in social cognition* (pp. 261–286). Totowa, NJ: Humana Press.

Bernstein, H. G., Steiner, J., Guest, P. C., Dobrowolny, H., & Bogerts, B. (2015). Glial cells as key players in schizophrenia pathology: Recent insights and concepts of therapy. *Schizophrenia Research, 161,* 4–18. Available at http://dx.doi.org/10.1016/j.schres.2014.03.035

Berridge, K. C. (2004). Motivation concepts in behavioral neuroscience. *Physiology and Behavior, 81,* 179–209.

Berry, C. M., Ones, D. S., & Sackett, P. R. (2007). Interpersonal deviance, organizational deviance, and their common correlates: A review and meta-analysis. *Journal of Applied Psychology, 92,* 410–424.

Bersani, F. S., Lindqvist, D., Mellon, S. H., Epel, E. S., Yehuda, R., Flory, J., … Coy, M. (2016). Association of dimensional psychological health measures with telomere length in male war veterans. *Journal of Affective Disorders, 190,* 537–542. Available at http://dx.doi.org/10.1016/j.jad.2015.10.037

Berthoud, H. R. (2002). Multiple neural systems controlling food intake and body weight. *Neuroscience and Biobehavioral Reviews, 26,* 393–428.

Bewernick, B. H., Kayser, S., Sturm, V., & Schlaepfer, T. E. (2012). Long-term effects of nucleus accumbens deep brain stimulation in treatment-resistant depression: Evidence for sustained efficacy. *Neuropsychopharmacology, 37*(9), 1975–1985.

Bexton, W. H., Heron, W., & Scott, T. H. (1954). Effects of decreased variation in the sensory environment. *Canadian Journal of Psychology, 8,* 70–76.

Bhattacharya, A., Derecki, N. C., Lovenberg, T. W., & Drevets, W. C. (2016). Role of neuroimmunological factors in the pathophysiology of mood disorders. *Psychopharmacology, 233*(9), 1623–1636. doi: 10.1007/s00213-016-4214-0

Bhattecharjee, Y. (2013, April 26). The mind of a con man. *New York Times Magazine.* Retrieved on May 23, 2015, at http://www.nytimes.com/2013/04/28/magazine/diederik-stapels-audacious-academic-fraud.html?pagewanted=all&_r=0

Bherer, L., Erickson, K. I., & Liu-Ambrose, T. (2013). A review of the effects of physical activity and exercise on cognitive and brain functions in older adults. *Journal of Aging Research.* doi: 10.1155/2013/657508

Bialystok, E., Barac, R., Blaye, A., & Poulin-Dubois, D. (2010). Word mapping and executive functioning in young monolingual and bilingual children. *Journal of Cognition and Development, 11*(4), 485–508. doi: 10.1080/15248372.2010.516420

Bialystok, E., & Craik, F. I. M. (2010). Cognitive and linguistic processing in the bilingual mind. *Current Directions in Psychological Science, 19,* 19–23.

Bialystok, E., Craik, F. I. M., & Ryan, J. (2006). Executive control in a modified antisaccade task: Effects of aging and bilingualism. *Journal of Experimental Psychology: Learning, Memory, & Cognition, 32,* 1341–1354.

Bickerton, D. (1995). *Language and human behavior.* Seattle: University of Washington Press.

Binder, E., Droste, S. K., Ohl, F., & Reul, J. M. (2004). Regular voluntary exercise reduces anxiety-related behavior and impulsiveness in mice. *Behavioural Brain Research, 155,* 197–206.

Birch, L. L., & Fisher, J. A. (1996). The role of experience in the development of children's eating behavior. In E. D. Capaldi (Ed.), *Why we eat what we eat: The psychology of eating* (pp. 113–141). Washington, DC: American Psychological Association.

Birch, L. L., & Marlin, D. W. (1982). I don't like it; I never tried it: Effects of exposure on two-year-old children's food preferences. *Appetite, 3,* 353–360.

Birdsall, S. M., Birdsall, T. C., & Tims, L. A. (2016). *Current Oncology Report, 18,* 40. doi:10.1007/s11912-016-0530-0

Birdsong, D. (2005). Interpreting age effects in second language acquisition. In J. F. Kroll & A. M. B. de Groot (Eds.), *Handbook of bilingualism: Psycholinguistic approaches* (pp. 109–127). New York, NY: Oxford University Press.

Birdsong, D. (2006). Age and second language acquisition and processing: A selective overview. *Language Learning, 56,* 9–49.

Birks, J. (2009). Cholinesterase inhibitors for Alzheimer's disease (review). *Cochrine Library, 1,* CD005593.

Bishop, S. J. (2007). Neurocognitive mechanisms of anxiety: An integrative account. *Trends in Cognitive Sciences, 11,* 307–316.

Bjork, R. A. (2001, March). How to succeed in college: Learn how to learn. *American Psychological Society Observer, 14,* 3, 9.

Black, D. W. (2006). Efficacy of combined pharmacotherapy and psychotherapy versus monotherapy in the treatment of anxiety disorders. *CNS Spectrums, 11,* 29–33.

Blais, A., Gidengil, E., Fourneir, P., Nevitte, N., Everit, J., & Kim, J. (2010). Political judgments, perceptions of facts, and partisan effects. *Electoral Studies, 29,* 1–12.

Blakeslee, S. (2005, February 8). Focus narrows in search for autism's cause. *The New York Times.* Retrieved from http://www.nytimes.com

Blakeslee, S., & Blakeslee, M. (2007). *The body has a mind of its own.* New York, NY: Random House.

Blalock, D. V., Kashdan, T. B., & Farmer, A. S. (2016). Trait and daily emotion regulation in social anxiety disorder. *Cognitive Therapy and Research, 40*(3), 416–425. doi: 10.1007/s10608-015-9739-8

Blanchard, R. (2004). Quantitative and theoretical analyses of the relation between older brothers and homosexuality in men. *Journal of Theoretical*

Biology, 230(2), 173–187. http://doi.org/10.1016/j.jtbi.2004.04.021

Blanco, C., Okuda, M., Wright, C., Hasin, D., Grant, B., Liu, S., & Olfson, M. (2008). Mental health of college students and their non-college-attending peers: Results from the National Epidemiologic Study on Alcohol and Related Conditions. *Archives of General Psychiatry, 65,* 1429–1437. doi: 10.1001/archpsyc.65.12.1429

Blank, H., & Launay, C. (2014). How to protect eyewitness memory against the misinformation effect: A meta-analysis of post-warning studies. *Journal of Applied Research in Memory and Cognition, 3*(2), 77–88. Available at http://doi.org/10.1016/j.jarmac.2014.03.005

Blask, D. E. (2009). Melatonin, sleep disturbance and cancer risk. *Sleep Medicine Reviews, 13,* 257–264. doi:10.1016/j.smrv.2008.07.007

Blass, T. (2004). *The man who shocked the world: The life and legacy of Stanley Milgram.* New York, NY: Basic Books.

Blázquez, A. B., & Berin, M. C. (2017). Microbiome and food allergy. *Translational Research, 179,* 199–203. Available at http://dx.doi.org/10.1016/j.trsl.2016.09.003

Bleidorn, W., Klimstra, T. A., Denissen, J. A., Rentfrow, P. J., Potter, J., & Gosling, S. D. (2013). Personality maturation around the world: A cross-cultural examination of social-investment theory. *Psychological Science, 24*(12), 2530–2540. doi: 10.1177/0956797613498396

Bleier, P., Habib, R., & Flament, M. F. (2006). Pharmacotherapies in the management of obsessive-compulsive disorder. *Canadian Journal of Psychiatry, 51,* 417–430.

Blier, P. (2005). Atypical antipsychotics for mood and anxiety disorders: Safe and effective adjuncts? *Review of Psychiatry and Neuroscience, 30,* 232–233.

Bloch, C., Kaiser, A., Kuenzli, E., Zappatore, D., Haller, S., Franceschini, R., ... Nitsch, C. (2009). The age of second language acquisition determines the variability in activation elicited by narration in three languages in Broca's and Wernicke's area. *Neuropsychologia, 47*(3), 625–633. Available at http://doi.org/10.1016/j.neuropsychologia.2008.11.009

Block, J. J. (2008). Issues for *DSM-V:* Internet addiction. *American Journal of Psychiatry, 165,* 306–307.

Block, J., Block, J. H., & Keyes, S. (1988). Longitudinally foretelling drug usage in adolescence: Early childhood personality and environmental precursors. *Child Development, 59,* 336–355.

Blonigen, D. M., Hicks, B. M., Krueger, R. F., Patrick, C. J., & Iacono, W. G. (2006). Continuity and change in psychopathic traits as measured via normal-range personality: A longitudinal-biometric study. *Journal of Abnormal Psychology, 115,* 85–95.

Bocchieri Riccardi, L. (2007). Psychological well-being and relationship changes in women after gastric bypass surgery. *Dissertation Abstracts International: Section B: The Sciences and Engineering, 67*(7-B), 4091.

Boettger, M. K., Grossman, D., & Bär, K.-J. (2013). Thresholds and perception of cold pain, heat pain, and the thermal grill illusion in patients with major depressive disorder. *Psychosomatic Medicine, 75,* 281–287. doi: 10.1097/PSY.ob013e3182881a9c

Bogenschutz, M. P., Forcehimes, A. A., Pommy, J. A., Wilcox, C. E., Barbosa, P. C. R., & Strassman, R. J. (2015). Psilocybin-assisted treatment for alcohol dependence:

A proof-of-concept study. *Journal of Psychopharmacology, 29*(3), 289–299. doi: 10.1177/0269881114565144

Bollen, E., & Wojciechowski, F. L. (2004). Anorexia nervosa subtypes and the Big Five personality factors. *European Eating Disorders Review, 12,* 117–121.

Bollinger, J., Rubens, M. T., Zanto, T. P., & Gazzaley, A. (2010). Expectation-driven changes in cortical functional connectivity influence working memory and long-term memory performance. *The Journal of Neuroscience, 30,* 14399–14410. Available at http://dx.doi.org/10.1523/JNEUROSCI.1547-10.2010

Bolour, S., & Braunstein, G. (2005). Testosterone therapy in women: A review. *International Journal of Impotence Research, 17,* 399–408.

Bond, R., & Smith, P. B. (1996). Culture and conformity: A meta-analysis of studies using Asch's (1952b, 1956) line judgment task. *Psychological Bulletin, 119,* 111–137.

Bonnet, M., Decety, J., Jeannerod, M., & Requin, J. (1997). Mental simulation of an action modulates the excitability of spinal reflex pathways in man. *Cognitive Brain Research, 5,* 221–228.

Boroditsky, L. (2001). Does language shape thought? Mandarin and English speakers' conceptions of time. *Cognitive Psychology, 43,* 1–22. doi: 10.1006/cogp.2001.0748

Boroditsky, L. (2011a). How language shapes thought? *Scientific American, 304,* 62–65.

Boroditsky, L. (2011b). How languages construct time. *Space, Time and Number in the Brain,* 333–341. Available at http://doi.org/10.1016/B978-0-12-385948-8.00020-7

Borst, J. P., Taatgen, N. A., & van Rijn, H. (2010). The problem state: A cognitive bottleneck in multitasking. *Journal of Experimental Psychology. Learning, Memory, and Cognition, 36*(2), 363–382. doi: 10.1037/a0018106

Boska, P. (2008). Maternal infection during pregnancy and schizophrenia. *Journal of Psychiatry and Neuroscience, 33,* 183–185.

Botvinick, M. M., Cohen, J. D., & Carter, C. S. (2004). Conflict monitoring and anterior cingulate cortex: An update. *Trends in Cognitive Sciences, 8,* 539–546.

Botwin, M., Buss, D. M., & Shackelford, T. K. (1997). Personality and mate preferences: Five factors in mate selection and marital satisfaction. *Journal of Personality and Social Psychology, 65,* 107–136.

Bouchard, S., Dumoulin, S., Robillard, G., Guitard, T., Klinger, É., Forget, H., ... & Roucaut, F. X. (2016). Virtual reality compared with in vivo exposure in the treatment of social anxiety disorder: A three-arm randomised controlled trial. *The British Journal of Psychiatry,* bjp-bp. doi: 10.1192/bjp.bp.116.184234

Bouchard, T. J., Jr., & Loehlin, J. C. (2001). Genes, evolution, and personality. *Behavioral Genetics, 31,* 243–273.

Bouchard, T. J., Jr., & McGue, M. (1981). Familial studies of intelligence: A review. *Science, 212,* 1055–1059.

Bould, H., De Stavola, B., Magnusson, C., Micali, N., Dal, H., Evans, J., ... & Lewis, G. (2016). The influence of school on whether girls develop eating disorders. *International Journal of Epidemiology, 45*(2), 480–488. doi: 10.1093/ije/dyw037

Boulianne, S. (2015). Online news, civic awareness, and engagement in civic and political life. *New Media & Society*, 1461444815616222. doi: 10.1177/1461444815616222

Bourgeois, S., & Johnson, A. (2004). Preparing for dying: Meaningful practices in palliative care. *Omega: Journal of Death and Dying, 49*, 99–107.

Bouton, M. E., Mineka, S., & Barlow, D. H. (2001). A modern learning theory perspective on the etiology of panic disorder. *Psychological Review, 108*, 4–32.

Bowden, C. L. (1994). Bipolar disorder and creativity. In M. P. Shaw & M. A. Runco (Eds.), *Creativity and affect* (pp. 73–86). Norwood, NJ: Ablex.

Bowden, E. M., & Jung-Beeman, M. (2003). Aha! Insight experience correlates with solution activation in the right hemisphere. *Psychonomic Bulletin & Review, 10*, 730–737.

Bowden, E. M., Jung-Beeman, M., Fleck, J., & Kounios, J. (2005). New approaches to demystifying insight. *Trends in Cognitive Sciences, 9*, 322–328.

Bower, B. (2005, December 10). The Piraha challenge: An Amazonian tribe takes grammar to a strange place. *Science News, 168*(24). Retrieved from http://www.sciencenews.org

Bowlby, J. (1969). *Attachment and loss: Vol. 1. Attachment.* New York, NY: Basic Books.

Bowlby, J. (1973). *Attachment and loss: Vol. 2. Separation, anxiety, and anger.* New York, NY: Basic Books.

Bowlby, J. (1980). *Attachment and loss: Vol. 3. Loss, sadness, and depression.* New York, NY: Basic Books.

Bowman, L. L., Levine, L. E., Waite, B. M., & Gendron, M. (2010). Can students really multitask? An experimental study of instant messaging while reading. *Computers and Education, 54*, 927–931.

Boyack, K. W., Klavans, R., & Börner, K. (2005). Mapping the backbone of science. *Scientometrics, 64*, 351–374.

Boyd, D. (2007). Why youth (heart) social network sites: The role of networked publics in teenage social life. In D. Buckingham (Ed.), *MacArthur Foundation Series on Digital Learning—Youth, Identity, and Digital Media Volume* (pp. 1–26). Cambridge, MA: MIT Press.

Boysen, G. A., & VanBergen, A. (2013). A review of published research on adult dissociative identity disorder: 2000–2010. *Journal of Nervous and Mental Diseases, 201*, 5–11.

Braback, L., Hjern, A., & Rasmussen, F. (2004). Trends is asthma rhinitis and eczema among Swedish conscripts from farming and non-farming environments: A nationwide study over three decades. *Clinical & Experimental Allergy, 34*, 38–43. doi: 10.1111/j.1365-2222.2004.01841.x

Bradberry, C. W. (2007). Cocaine sensitization and dopamine mediation of cue effects in rodents, monkeys, and humans: Areas of agreement, disagreement, and implications for addiction. *Psychopharmacology, 191*, 705–717.

Bradley, R. M. (1972). Development of the taste bud and gustatory papillae in human fetuses. In J. F. Bosma (Ed.), *The third symposium on oral sensation and perception: The mouth of the infant.* Springfield, IL: Thomas.

Bradshaw, J., Steiner, A. M., Gengoux, G., & Koegel, L. K. (2015). Feasibility and effectiveness of very early intervention for infants at-risk for autism spectrum disorder: A systematic review. *Journal of Autism and Developmental Disorders, 45*, 778–794. doi: 10.1007/s10803-014-2235-2

Brand, B. L., Loewenstein, R. J., & Speigel, D. (2013). Patients with DID are found and researched more widely than Boysen and VanBergen recognized. *Journal of Nervous and Mental Disease, 201*, 440.

Brand, G., & Millot, J.-L. (2001). Sex differences in human olfaction: Between evidence and enigma. *Quarterly Journal of Experimental Psychology B: Comparative and Physiological Psychology, 54B*, 259–270.

Brandtzæg, P. B., Lüders, M., & Skjetne, J. H. (2010). Too many Facebook "friends"? Content sharing and sociability versus the need for privacy in social network sites. *International Journal of Human-Computer Interaction, 26*, 1006–1030.

Brant, A. M., Haberstick, B. C., Corley, R. P., Wadsworth, S. J., DeFries, J. C., & Hewitt, J. K. (2009). The developmental etiology of high IQ. *Behavioral Genetics, 39*, 393–405. doi: 10.1007/s10519-009-9268-x

Brant, A. M., Munakata, Y., Boomsma, D. I., DeFries, J. C., Haworth, C. A., Keller, M. C., ... Hewitt, J. K. (2013). The nature and nurture of high IQ: An extended sensitive period for intellectual development. *Psychological Science, 24*(8), 1487–1495.

Brasil-Neto, J. P. (2012). Learning, memory, and transcranial direct current stimulation. *Frontiers in Psychiatry, 3*, 1–4. doi: 10.3389/fpsyt.2012.00080

Braver, T. S., & Barch, D. M. (2002). A theory of cognitive control, aging, cognition, and neuromodulation. *Neuroscience and Biobehavioral Reviews, 26*, 809–817.

Breen, M. S., Maihofer, A. X., Glatt, S. J., Tylee, D. S., Chandler, S. D., Tsuang, M. T., ... & Woelk, C. H. (2015). Gene networks specific for innate immunity define post-traumatic stress disorder. *Molecular Psychiatry, 20*(12), 1538–1545. doi: 10.1038/mp.2015.9

Breiter, H. C., Etcoff, N. L., Whalen, P. J., Kennedy, W. A., Rauch, S. L., Buckner, R. L., ... Rosen, B. R. (1996). Response and habituation of the human amygdala during visual processing of facial expressions. *Neuron, 17*, 875–887.

Breland, K., & Breland, M. (1961). The misbehavior of organisms. *American Psychologist, 16*, 681–684.

Brennan, P. A. (2010). On the scent of sexual attraction. *BMC Biology, 8*, 71–74.

Brenner, J. (2013, September 18). Pew Internet: Mobile. Pew Internet and American Life Project. Retrieved November 18, 2013, from http://pewinternet.org/Commentary/2012/February/Pew-Internet-Mobile.aspx

Breugelmans, S. M., Poortinga, Y. H., Ambadar, Z., Setiadi, B., Vaca, J. B., ... Widiyanto, B. (2005). Body sensations associated with emotions in Rarámuri Indians, rural Javanese, and three student samples. *Emotion, 5*, 166–174.

Brewer, M. B., & Caporael, L. R. (2006). An evolutionary perspective on social identity: Revisiting groups. In M. Schaller, D. T. Kenrick, & J. A. Simpson (Eds.), *Evolution and social psychology* (pp. 143–161). New York, NY: Psychology Press.

Brewerton, T. D., & Duncan, A. E. (2016). Associations between attention deficit hyperactivity disorder and eating disorders by gender: Results from the National Comorbidity Survey Replication. *European Eating Disorders Review, 24*(6), 536–540. doi:10.1002/erv.2468

Bridges, K. (1932). Emotional development in infancy. *Child Development, 3*, 324–341.

Briggs, C. (2005). Allen uses films to avoid anxiety. *BBC News-Online*. Retrieved July 3, 2008, from http://news.bbc.co.uk/2/hi/entertainment/4539493.stm

Brivic, S. (1980). *Joyce between Freud and Jung.* Port Washington, NY: Kennikat Press.

Broadbent, D. E. (1954). The role of auditory localization in attention and memory span. *Journal of Experimental Psychology, 44*, 51–55.

Brockman, R., Ciarrochi, J., Parker, P., & Kashdan, T. (2016). Emotion regulation strategies in daily life: Mindfulness, cognitive reappraisal and emotion suppression. *Cognitive Behaviour Therapy*, 1–23. Available at http://dx.doi.org/10.1080/16506073.2016.1218926

Broderick, M., & Guilleminault, C. (2016). Emerging treatments for narcolepsy. In *Narcolepsy* (pp. 357–368). New York, NY: Springer International Publishing.

Broekman, B. F. P., Chan, Y.-H., Chong, Y.-S., Quek, S.-C., Fung, D., Low, Y.-L. ... Saw, S.-M. (2009). The influence of birth size on intelligence in healthy children. *Pediatrics, 123*, e1011–e1016.

Broude, G., & Greene, S. (1980). Cross-cultural codes on 20 sexual attitudes and practices. In H. Barry & A. Schlegel (Eds.), *Cross-cultural samples and codes* (pp. 313–333). Pittsburgh, PA: University of Pittsburgh Press.

Brown, A. S. (2006). Prenatal infection as a risk factor for schizophrenia. *Schizophrenia Bulletin, 32*, 200–202.

Brown, K. W., & Ryan, R. M. (2003). The benefits of being present: Mindfulness and its role in psychological well-being. *Journal of Personality and Social Psychology, 84*, 822–848.

Brown, K. W., Goodman, R. J., Ryan, R. M., & Anālayo, B. (2016). Mindfulness enhances episodic memory performance: Evidence from a multimethod investigation. *PLoS ONE 11*: e0153309. doi:10.1371/journal.pone.0153309

Brown, R., & Kulik, J. (1977). Flashbulb memories. *Cognition, 5*, 73–99.

Brown, R. T., Reynolds, C. R., & Whitaker, J. S. (1999). Bias in mental testing since Jensen's "Bias in Mental Testing." *School Psychology Quarterly, 14*, 208–238.

Brown, T. S., & Wallace, P. (1980). *Physiological psychology.* New York, NY: Academic Press.

Bruder, C. E. G., Piotrowski, A., Gijsbers, A., Andersson, A., Erickson, S., de Stahl, T. D. ... Dumanski, J. P. (2008). Phenotypically concordant and discordant monozygotic twins display differ DNA copy-number-variation profiles. *American Journal of Human Genetics, 82*, 763–771. doi: 10.1016/j.ajhg.2007.12.011

Brunelin, J., Poulet, E., Bor, J., Rivet, A., Eche, J., d'Amato, T., & Saoud, M. (2010). Transcranial magnetic stimulation (rTMS) and negative symptoms of schizophrenia. *Annales Médico-Psychologiques, 168*, 422–427.

Bruner, J. S., & Minturn, A. L. (1955). Perceptual identification and perceptual organization. *Journal of General Psychology, 53*, 2128.

Brunetti, M., Babiloni, C., Ferretti, A., Del Gratta, C., Merla, A., Olivetti, M., ... Romani, G. L. (2008). Hypothalamus, sexual arousal and psychosexual identity in human males: A functional magnetic resonance imaging study. *European Journal of Neuroscience, 27*, 2922–2927.

Brunwasser, S. M., Gillham, J. E., & Kim, E. S. (2009). A meta-analytic review of Penn Resiliency Program's effect on depressive symptoms.

Journal of Consulting and Clinical Psychology, 77, 1042–1054.

Bryans, W. A. (1959). Mitotic activity in the brain of the adult white rat. *Anatomical Record, 133*, 65–71.

Brymer, E., & Mackenzie, S. H. (2017). Psychology and the extreme sport experience. In *Extreme sports medicine* (pp. 3–13). Springer International Publishing.

Buchanan, J., & Houlihan, D. (2008). The use of in vivo desensitization for the treatment of a specific phobia of earthworms. *Clinical Case Studies, 7*, 12–24. doi: 10.1177/1534650107300863

Buchanan, T. W., Denburg, N. L., Tranel, D., & Adolphs, R. (2001). Verbal and nonverbal emotional memory following unilateral amygdala damage. *Learning & Memory, 8*, 326–335. doi: 10.1101/lm.40101

Buck, L. B. (2000). Smell and taste: The chemical senses. In E. R. Kandel, J. H. Schwartz, & T. M. Jessell (Eds.), *Principles of neural science* (4th ed., pp. 625–647). New York, NY: McGraw-Hill.

Buckley, C. (2007, January 3). Man is rescued by stranger on subway tracks. *The New York Times.* Retrieved from http://www.nytimes.com

Buka, S. L., Tsuang, M. T., Torrey, E. F., Klebanoff, M. A., Bernstein, D., & Yolken, R. H. (2001). Maternal infections and subsequent psychosis among offspring. *Archives of General Psychiatry, 58*, 1032–1037.

Bukh, J., Bock, C., Vinberg, M., Werge, T., Gether, U., & Kessing, L. (2009). Interaction between genetic polymorphisms and stressful life events in first episode depression. *Journal of Affective Disorders, 119*(1–3), 107–115. doi: 10.1016/j.jad.2009.02.023

Bukowski, W. M., & Sippola, L. K. (2001). Groups, individuals, and victimization: A view of the peer system. In J. Juvonen & S. Graham (Eds.), *Peer harassment in school: The plight of the vulnerable and victimized* (pp. 355–377). New York: Guilford.

Bulik, C. M., Kleiman, S. C., & Yilmaz, Z. (2016). Genetic epidemiology of eating disorders. *Current Opinion in Psychiatry, 29*(6), 383–388. doi: 10.1097/YCO.0000000000000275

Bulkeley, K. (1997). *An introduction to the psychology of dreaming.* Westport, CT: Praeger.

Bullivant, S. B., Sellergren, S. A., Stern, K., Spencer, N. A., Jacob, S., Mennella, J. A., & McClintock, M. K. (2004). Women's sexual experience during the menstrual cycle: Identification of the sexual phase by noninvasive measurement of luteinizing hormone. *Journal of Sex Research, 41*, 82–93.

Burch, G., Pavelis, C., Hemsley, D. R., & Corr, P. J. (2006). Schizotypy and creativity in visual artists. *British Journal of Psychology, 97*, 177–190.

Burd, L., Roberts, D., Olson, M., & Odendaal, H. (2007). Ethanol and the placenta: A review. *Journal of Maternal-Fetal and Neonatal Medicine, 20*, 361–375.

Burger, J. M. (2009). Replicating Milgram: Would people still obey today? *American Psychologist, 64*, 1–11. doi: 10.1037/a0010932

Burger, J. M. (2014). Situational features in Milgram's experiment that kept his participants shocking. *Journal of Social Issues, 70*(3), 489–500. doi: 10.1111/josi.12073

Burgess, W. (2009). *The depression answer book.* Naperville, IL: Sourcebooks.

Burguière, E., Monteiro, P., Mallet, L., Feng, G., & Graybiel, A. M. (2015). Striatal circuits, habits, and implications for obsessive–compulsive

disorder. *Current Opinion in Neurobiology, 30*, 59–65. http://dx.doi.org/10.1016/j.conb.2014.08.008

Burnett, G. B., Moll, J., Frith, C., & Blakemore, S.-J. (2008). Development during adolescence of the neural processing of social emotion. *Journal of Cognitive Neuroscience, 21*, 1736–1750.

Burnstein, E., Crandall, C., & Kitayama, S. (1994). Some neo-Darwinian decision rules for altruism: Weighing cues for inclusive fitness as a function of the biological importance of the decision. *Journal of Personality and Social Psychology, 67*, 773–789.

Burt, K. B., & Masten, A. S. (2010). Development in the transition to adulthood: Vulnerabilities and opportunities. In J. E. Grant & M. N. Potenza (Eds.), *Young adult mental health* (pp. 5–18). New York, NY: Oxford University Press.

Burton, C. M., & King, L. A. (2009). The health benefits of writing about positive experiences: The role of broadened cognition. *Psychology & Health, 24*, 867–879.

Bushman, B. J., & Anderson, C. A. (2001). Media violence and the American public: Scientific facts versus media misinformation. *American Psychologist, 56*, 477–489.

Buss, D. M. (1989). Sex differences in human mate preferences: Evolutionary hypotheses tested in 37 cultures. *Behavioral and Brain Sciences, 12*, 1–49.

Buss, D. M. (1991). Evolutionary personality psychology. *Annual Review of Psychology, 42*, 459–491.

Buss, D. M. (1999). *Evolutionary psychology: The new science of the mind.* New York, NY: Allyn & Bacon.

Buss, D. M. (2003). *The evolution of desire: Strategies of human mating* (Rev. ed.). New York, NY: Basic Books.

Buss, D. M. (2004). Sex differences in human mate preferences. In H. T. Reis & C. E. Rusbult (Eds.), *Close relationships: Key readings* (pp. 135–151). Philadelphia: Taylor & Francis.

Buss, D. M. (2011). Personality and the adaptive landscape: The role of individual differences in creating and solving social adaptive problems. In D. M. Buss & P. Hawley (Eds.), *The evolution of personality and individual differences* (pp. 29–57). New York, NY: Oxford University Press.

Buss, D. M., & Greiling, H. (1999). Adaptive individual differences. *Journal of Personality, 67*, 209–243.

Buss, D. M., & Hawley, P. H. (Eds.). (2011). *The evolution of personality and individual differences.* New York, NY: Oxford University Press.

Buss, D. M., & Schmitt, D. P. (1993). Sexual strategies theory: An evolutionary perspective on human mating. *Psychological Review, 100*, 204–232.

Bussey, K., & Bandura, A. (1999). Social cognitive theory of gender development and differentiation. *Psychological Review, 106*, 676–713. Available at http://dx.doi.org/10.1037/0033-295X.106.4.676

Bussing, R., Gary, F. A., Mills, T. L., & Wilson Garvan, C. (2007). Cultural variations in parental health beliefs, knowledge, and information sources related to attention-deficit/hyperactivity disorder. *Journal of Family Issues, 28*, 291–318. doi: 10.1177/0192513X06296117

Buxton, O. M., Cain, S. W., O'Connor, S. P., Porter, J. H., Duffy, J. F., Wang, W., Czeisler, C. A., & Shea, S. A. (2012). Adverse metabolic consequences in humans of prolonged sleep restriction combined with circadian disruption. *Science Translational Medicine, 4*, 129ra43. doi: 10.1126/scitranslmed.3003200

Cacioppo, J. T., Fowler, J. H., & Christakis, N. A. (2009). Alone in the crowd: The structure and spread

of loneliness in a large social network. *Journal of Personality and Social Psychology, 97*, 977–991.

Cahill, S. P., Foa, E. B., Hembree, E. A., Marshall, R. D., & Nacash, N. (2006). Dissemination of exposure therapy in the treatment of posttraumatic stress disorder. *Journal of Traumatic Stress, 19*, 597–610.

Cai, D., Pearce, K., Chen, S., & Glanzman, D. L. (2012). Reconsolidation of long-term memory in aplysia. *Current Biology, 22*(19), 1783–1788. Available at http://doi.org/10.1016/j.cub.2012.07.038

Cain, M. S., Leonard, J. A., Gabrieli, J. D. E., & Finn, A. S. (2016). Media multitasking in adolescence. *Psychonomic Bulletin & Review.* Available at http://doi.org/10.3758/s13423-016-1036-3

Caird, J. K., Johnston, K. A., Willness, C. R., Asbridge, M., & Steel, P. (2014). A meta-analysis of the effects of texting on driving. *Accident Analysis and Prevention, 7*, 311–314. Retrieved from http://dx.doi.org/10.1016/j.aap.2014.06.005

Caird, J. K., Willness, C. R., Steel, P., & Scialfa, C. (2008). A meta-analysis of the effects of cell phones on driver performance. *Accident Analysis and Prevention, 40*, 1282–1293.

Calkins, M. W. (1898). Short studies in memory and in association from the Wellesley College Psychological Laboratory. I.: A study of immediate and delayed recall of the concrete and of the verbal. *Psychological Review, 5*, 451–456.

Calvert, S. L., Rideout, V. J., Woolard, J. L., Barr, R. F., & Strouse, G. A. (2005). Age, ethnicity, and socioeconomic patterns in early computer use. *American Behavioral Scientist, 48*, 590–607.

Cameron, J. D., Cyr, M., & Doucet, E. (2010). Increased meal frequency does not promote greater weight loss in subjects who were prescribed an 8-week equi-energetic energy restricted diet. *British Journal of Nutrition, 103*, 1098–1101. doi: 10.1017/S0007114509992984

Campbell, A. (2008). Attachment, aggression and affiliation: The role of oxytocin in female social behavior. *Biological Psychology, 77*, 1–10.

Campbell, F. A., & Ramey, C. T. (1995). Cognitive and school outcomes for high-risk African-American students at middle adolescence: Positive effects of early intervention. *American Educational Research Journal, 32*, 743–772.

Campbell, F. A., Ramey, C. T., Pungello, E. P., Sparling, J., & Miller-Johnson, S. (2002). Early childhood education: Young adult outcomes from the Abecedarian Project. *Applied Developmental Science, 6*, 42–57.

Campbell, J. A., Walker, R. J., & Egede, L. E. (2016). Associations between adverse childhood experiences, high-risk behaviors, and morbidity in adulthood. *American Journal of Preventive Medicine, 50*(3), 344–352. Available at http://dx.doi.org/10.1016/j.amepre.2015.07.022

Camperio Ciani, A. S., Capiluppi, C., Veronese, A., & Sartori, G. (2007). The adaptive value of personality differences revealed by small island population dynamics. *European Journal of Personality, 21*, 3–22.

Campos, J. J., & Stenberg, C. (1981). Perception, appraisal, and emotion: The onset of social referencing. In M. E. Lamb & L. R. Sherrod (Eds.), *Infant social cognition: Empirical and theoretical considerations* (pp. 273–314). Hillsdale, NJ: Erlbaum.

Camras, L. A., Oster, H., Bakeman, R., Meng, Z., Ujiie, T., & Campos, J. J. (2007). Do infants show distinct negative facial expressions for fear and anger? Emotional expression in 11-month-old European American, Chinese, and Japanese infants. *Infancy, 11*, 131–155.

Cannon, S., Lawry, K., Brudell, M., Rees, R., Wenke, R., & Bisset, L. (2016). Appetite for change: A multidisciplinary team approach to behavioral modification for weight management in a community health group setting. *Eating and Weight Disorders–Studies on Anorexia, Bulimia and Obesity*, 1–8. doi:10.1007/s40519-016-0274-8

Cannon, W. B. (1927). The James-Lange theory of emotion: A critical examination and an alternative theory. *American Journal of Psychology, 39*, 10–124.

Cannon, W. B. (1929). *Bodily changes in pain, hunger, fear, and rage: An account of recent researches into the function of emotional excitement.* New York, NY: Appleton.

Cannon, W. B. (1939). *The wisdom of the body.* New York, NY: Norton.

Cannon, W. B., & Washburn, A. L. (1912). An explanation of hunger. *American Journal of Physiology, 29*, 441–454.

Canter, R. R., & Hirsch, J. (1955). An experimental comparison of several psychological scales of weight. *American Journal of Psychology, 68*, 645–649.

Cappuccio, F. P., D'Elia, L., Strazzullo, P., & Miller, M. A. (2010). Sleep duration and all-cause mortality: A systematic review and meta-analysis of prospective studies. *Sleep, 33*, 585–592.

Capri, M., Salvioli, S., Sevini, F., Valensin, S., Celani, L., Monti, D., … Franceschi, C. (2006). The genetics of human longevity. *Annals of the New York Academy of Sciences, 1067*, 252–263.

Carabottia, M., Sciroccoa, A., Masellib, M. A., & Severia, C. (2015). The gut-brain axis: Interactions between enteric microbiota, central and enteric nervous systems. *Ann Gastroenterol, 28*(1), 1–7.

Cardno, A. G., & Gottesman, I. I. (2000). Twin studies of schizophrenia: From bow-and-arrow concordances to Star Wars Mx and functional genomics [Review]. *American Journal of Medical Genetics, 97*, 12–17.

Carew, T. J., & Kandel, E. R. (1973). Acquisition and retention of long-term habituation in Aplysia: Correlation of behavioral and cellular processes. *Science, 182*, 1158–1160.

Carey, B. (2008, December 4). H. M., an unforgettable amnesiac, dies at 82. *The New York Times.* Retrieved from http://www.nytimes.com

Carhart-Harris, R. L., Bolstridge, M., Rucker, J., Day, C. M., Erritzoe, D., Kaelen, M., … & Taylor, D. (2016). Psilocybin with psychological support for treatment-resistant depression: An open-label feasibility study. *The Lancet Psychiatry, 3*(7), 619 627. Available at http://dx.doi.org/10.1016/S2215-0366(16)30065-7

Carhart-Harris, R. L., Leech, R., Williams, T. M., Erritzoe, D., Abbasi, N., Bargiotas, T., … & Wise, R. G. (2012). Implications for psychedelic-assisted psychotherapy: Functional magnetic resonance imaging study with psilocybin. *The British Journal of Psychiatry, 200*(3), 238–244. doi: 10.1192/bjp.bp.111.103309

Carhart-Harrisa, R., Muthukumaraswamy, S., Roseman, L., Kaelena, M., … Nutt, D. J. (2016). Neural correlates of the LSD experience revealed by multimodal neuroimaging. *Proceedings of the National Academy of Sciences, 113*, 4853–4858. doi:10.1073/pnas.1518377113

Carlat, D. J. (1998). The psychiatric review of symptoms: A screening tool for family physicians. *American Family Physician, 58*, 1617–1624.

Carless, S. A. (1999). Career assessment: Holland's vocational interests, personality characteristics, and abilities. *Journal of Career Assessment, 7*, 125–144.

Carlo, G., Knight, G. P., Roesch, S. C., Opal, D., & Davis, A. (2014). Personality across cultures: A critical analysis of Big Five research and current directions. In F. L. Leong, L. Comas-Díaz, G. C. Nagayama Hall, V. C. McLoyd, & J. E. Trimble (Eds.), *APA handbook of multicultural psychology, Vol. 1: Theory and research* (pp. 285–298). Washington, DC: American Psychological Association. doi: 10.1037/14189-015

Carlozzi, N. E., Downing, N. R., McCormack, M. K., Schilling, S. G., Perlmutter, J. S., Hahn, E. A., & … Nance, M. A. (2016). New measures to capture end of life concerns in Huntington disease: Meaning and purpose and concern with death and dying from HDQLIFE (a patient reported outcomes measurement system). *Quality of Life Research: An International Journal of Quality of Life Aspects of Treatment, Care & Rehabilitation, 25*(10), 2403–2415. doi:10.1007/s11136-016-1354-y

Carlsson, A. (1987). Perspectives on the discovery of central monoaminergic neurotransmission. *Annual Review of Neuroscience, 10*, 19–40.

Carlsson, I., Wendt, P., & Risberg, J. (2000). On the neurobiology of creativity: Differences in frontal activity between high and low creative subjects. *Neuropsychologia, 38*, 873–885.

Carnagey, N. L., Anderson, C. A., & Bushman, B. J. (2007). The effect of video game violence on physiological desensitization to real-life violence. *Journal of Experimental Social Psychology, 43*, 489–496.

Carney, S. M., & Goodwin, G. M. (2005). Lithium—A continuing story in the treatment of bipolar disorder. *Acta Psychiatrica Scandinavica, 111*(Suppl. 426), 7–12.

Carotenuto, M., Esposito, M., Cortese, S., Laino, D., & Verrotti, A. (2016). Children with developmental dyslexia showed greater sleep disturbances than controls, including problems initiating and maintaining sleep. *Acta Pædiatrica* (no volume or page number), online only at: http://onlinelibrary.wiley.com/doi/10.1111/apa.13472/abstract. doi:10.1111/apa.13472

Carrion, V. G., Hass, B. W., Garrett, A., Song, S., & Rice, A. L. (2010). Reduced hippocampal activity in youth with post-traumatic stress symptoms: An fMRI study. *Journal of Pediatric Psychology, 35*, 559–569.

Carroll, J. B. (1993). *Human cognitive abilities.* New York, NY: Cambridge University Press.

Carroll, J. E., Cole, S. W., Seeman, T. E., Breen, E. C., Witarama, T., Arevalo, J. M. G., Ma, J., & Irwin, M. R. (2016). Partial sleep deprivation activates the DNA damage response (DDR) and the senescence-associated secretory phenotype (SASP) in aged adult humans. *Brain, Behavior, and Immunity, 51*, 223–229. doi: 10.1016/j.bbi.2015.08.024

Carroll, J. L., & Rest, J. (1981, December). Development in moral judgment as indicated by rejection of lower-stage statements. *Journal of Research in Personality, 15*(4), 538–544.

Carson, S. H., Peterson, J. B., & Higgins, D. M. (2003). Decreased latent inhibition is associated with increased creative achievement in high-functioning individuals. *Journal of Personality and Social Psychology, 85*, 499–506.

Carstensen, L. L. (2006). The influence of a sense of time on human development. *Science, 312*, 1913–1915.

Carter, C. S., Mintun, M., Nichols, T. N., & Cohen, J. D. (1997). Anterior cingulate gyrus dysfunction and selective attention deficits in schizophrenia: [15O] H$_2$O PET study during single-trial Stroop task performance. *American Journal of Psychiatry, 154*, 1670–1675.

Carty, C. L., Kooperberg, C., Liu, J., Herndon, M., Assimes, T., Hou, L., … Reiner, A. P. (2015). Leukocyte telomere length and risks of incident coronary heart disease and mortality in a racially diverse population of postmenopausal women. *Arteriosclerosis, Thrombosis, and Vascular Biology, 35*(10), 2225–2231. doi: 10.1161/ATVBAHA.115.305838

Caruso, E. M., Mead, N. L., & Balcetis, E. (2009). Political partisanship influences perception of biracial candidates' skin tone. *Proceedings of the National Academy of Sciences, 106*, 20168–20173.

Carver, C. S., Scheier, M. F., & Segerstrom, S. C. (2010). Optimism. *Clinical Psychology Review, 30*, 879–889.

Caselli, R. J., Dueck, A. C., Locke, D. E., Henslin, B. R., Johnson, T. A., Woodruff, B. K., & … Geda, Y. E. (2016). Impact of personality on cognitive aging: A prospective cohort study. *Journal of The International Neuropsychological Society, 22*, 765–776. doi:10.1017/S1355617716000527

Casey, B. J., Davidson, M., & Rosen, B. (2002). Functional magnetic imaging: Basic principles of and application to developmental science. *Developmental Science, 5*, 301–309.

Caspi, A. (2000). The child is father of the man: Personality continuities from childhood to adulthood. *Journal of Personality and Social Psychology, 78*, 158–172.

Caspi, A., Elder, G. H., & Bem, D. H. (1988). Moving away from the world: Life-course patterns of shy children. *Developmental Psychology, 24*, 824–831.

Caspi, A., Houts, R. M., Belsky, D. W., Goldman-Mellor, S. J., Harrington, H., Israel, S., … Moffitt, T. E. (2014). The p-factor: One general psychopathology factor in the structure of psychiatric disorders? *Clinical Psychological Science, 2*, 119–137. doi: 10.1177/2167702613497473

Caspi, A., McClay, J., Moffitt, T. E., Mill, J., Martin, J., … Craig, I. W. (2002). Role of genotype in the cycle of violence in maltreated children. *Science, 297*, 851–853.

Caspi, A., Roberts, B. W., & Shiner, R. L. (2003). Personality development: Stability and change. *Annual Review of Psychology, 56*, 453–484.

Caspi, A., Sugden, K., Moffitt, T. E., Taylor, A., Craig, I. W., Harrington, H., … Poulton, R. (2003). Influence of life stress on depression: Moderation by a polymorphism in the 5-HTT gene. *Science, 301*, 386–389.

Cassidy, T. (2006). *Birth: The surprising history of how we are born.* New York, NY: Atlantic Monthly Press.

Castelli, D. M., Hillman, C. H., Buck, S. M., & Erwin, H. (2007). Physical fitness and academic achievement in third- and fifth-grade students. *Journal of Sport & Exercise Psychology, 29*, 239–252.

Castles, A., McLean, G. M. T., Bavin, E., Bretherton, L., Carlin, J., Prior, M., … Reilly, S. (2013). Computer use and letter knowledge in preschool children: A population-based study. *Journal of Paediatrics and Child Health, 49*, 193–198. doi: 10.1111/jpc.12126

Catalino, L. I., & Fredrickson, B. L. (2011). A Tuesday in the life of a flourisher: The role of positive emotional reactivity in optimal mental health. *Emotion, 11*, 938–950.

Catapano, F., Perris, F., Masella, M., Rossano, F., Cigliano, M., Magliano, L., ... Maj, M. (2006). Obsessive-compulsive disorder: A 3-year prospective follow-up study of patients treated with serotonin reuptake inhibitors. *Journal of Psychiatric Research, 40,* 502–510.

Cattaneo, A., & Riva, M. A. (2016). Stress-induced mechanisms in mental illness: A role for glucocorticoid signalling. *The Journal of steroid Biochemistry and Molecular Biology, 160,* 169–174. Available at http://dx.doi.org/10.1016/j.jsbmb.2015.07.021

Cavallero, C., & Foulkes, D. (Eds.). (1993). *Dreaming as cognition.* New York, NY: Harvester-Wheatsheaf.

Cawthon, R. M., Smith, K. R., O'Brien, E., Siv-atchenko, A., & Kerber, R. A. (2003). Association between telomere length in blood and mortality in people aged 60 years or older. *The Lancet, 361*(9355), 393–395. Available at http://dx.doi.org/10.1016/S0140-6736(03)12384-7

Cazala, F., Vienney, N., & Stoléru, S. (2015). The cortical sensory representation of genitalia in women and men: A systematic review. *Socioaffective Neuroscience & Psychology, 5.* doi: 10.3402/snp.v5.26428

CBS News. (2007, January 3). Bystander pulls off daring subway rescue. Retrieved from http://www.cbsnews.com/stories/2007/01/03/national/main2324961.shtml?source=search_story

Ceci, S. J., & Williams, W. M. (2007). *Why aren't more women in science? Top researchers debate the evidence.* Washington, DC: American Psychological Association.

Ceci, S. J., & Williams, W. M. (2010). *The mathematics of sex: How biology and society conspire to limit talented women and girls.* New York, NY: Oxford University Press.

Cecil, C. A. M., et al. (2017). Disentangling the mental health impact of childhood abuse and neglect. *Child Abuse & Neglect, 63,* 106–119. Available at http://dx.doi.org/10.1016/j.chiabu.2016.11.024

Centers for Disease Control and Prevention (CDC). (2001). *Cigarette-smoking related mortality.* Retrieved March 26, 2007, from http://www.cdc.gov/tobacco/research_data/health_consequences/mortali.htm

Centers for Disease Control and Prevention (CDC). (2005). *Sexual behavior and selected health measures: Men and women 15–44 years of age, United States, 2002.* Retrieved March 12, 2008, from http://www.cdc.gov/nchs/data/ad/ad362.pdf

Centers for Disease Control and Prevention (CDC). (2015). Keeping it off. Available at http://www.cdc.gov/healthyweight/losing_weight/keepingitoff.html

Centers for Disease Control and Prevention (CDC). (2016). Cigarette Smoking Among Adults—United States, 2005–2015. *Morbidity and Mortality Weekly Report, 65*(44), 1205–11.

Centers for Disease Control and Prevention (CDC). (2017, July 21). *Alcohol use in pregnancy.* Retrieved June 28, 2017, from https://www.cdc.gov/ncbddd/fasd/alcohol-use.html

Chadwick, P., Hughes, S., Russell, D., Russell, I., & Dagnan, D. (2009). Mindfulness groups for distressing voices and paranoia: A replication and randomized feasibility trial. *Behavioral and Cognitive Psychotherapy, 37,* 403–412.

Chaffee, J. (1999). *The thinker's guide to college success* (2nd ed.). Boston, MA: Houghton Mifflin.

Chaline, E. R. (2010). The construction, maintenance, and evolution of gay SM sexualities and sexual identities: A preliminary description

of gay SM sexual identity practices. *Sexualities, 13*(3), 338–356. Available at http://doi.org/10.1177/1363460709363323

Chalmers, D. (2007). The hard problem of consciousness. *The Blackwell companion to consciousness,* 225–235.

Chan, C., Brandone, A., & Tardif, T. (2009). Culture, context, or behavioral control?: English- and Mandarin-speaking mothers' use of nouns and verbs in joint book reading. *Journal of Cross-Cultural Psychology, 40,* 584–602. doi: 10.1177/0022022109335184

Chance, P. (1986). *Thinking in the classroom: A survey of programs.* New York, NY: Teachers College, Columbia University.

Chandra, A., Martinez, G. M., Mosher, W. D., Abma, J. C., & Jones, J. (2005). Fertility, family planning, and reproductive health of U.S. women: Data from the 2002 National Survey of Family Growth. National Center for Health Statistics. *Vital Health Statistics, 23,* 1–160.

Chandra, A., Mosher, W. D., Copen, C., & Slonean, C. (2011). Sexual behavior, sexual attraction, and sexual identity in the United States: Data from 2006–2008 National Survey of Family Growth. *National Health Statistics Reports, 36,* 1–36. Retrieved September 5, 2013, from http://ns1.isminc.com/documents/research/general/TeenSexualBehavior.pdf

Chandra, P. S., Satyanarayana, V. A., Satishchandra, P., Satish, K. S., & Kumar, M. (2009). Do men and women with HIV differ in their quality of life? A study from South India. *AIDS and Behavior, 13*(1), 110–117.

Chang, E. C. (1998). Dispositional optimism and primary and secondary appraisal of a stressor: Controlling for confounding influences and relations to coping and psychological and physical adjustment. *Journal of Personality and Social Psychology, 74,* 1109–1120.

Chaplin, T. M., & Aldao, A. (2013). Gender differences in emotion expression in children: A meta-analytic review. *Psychological Bulletin, 139*(4), 735–765. Available at http://dx.doi.org/10.1037/a0030737

Chapman, B. P., & Moynihan, J. (2009). The brain-skin connection: Role of psychosocial factors and neuropeptides in psoriasis. *Expert Review of Clinical Immunology, 5,* 623–627.

Chappell, M., & Humphreys, M. S. (1994). An auto-associative neural network for sparse representations: Analysis and application to models of recognition and cued recall. *Psychological Review, 101,* 103–128.

Chaput, J. P., Després, J. P., & Tremblay, A. (2007). Short sleep duration is associated with reduced leptin levels and increased adiposity: Results from the Québec Family Study. *Obesity, 15,* 253–261.

Chaput, J. P., & Tremblay, A. (2012). Adequate sleep to improve the treatment of obesity. *Canadian Medical Association Journal, 184,* 1975–1976.

Charil, A., Laplante, D. P., Vaillancourt, C., & King, S. (2010). Prenatal stress and brain development. *Brain Research Reviews, 65,* 56–79.

Charmorro-Premuzic, T., & Steinmetz, C. (2013). The perfect hire. *Scientific American Mind, 24,* 43–47.

Charney, D. S. (2004). Psychological mechanisms of resilience and vulnerability: Implications for successful adaptation to extreme stress. *American Journal of Psychiatry, 161,* 195–216.

Charsar, B. A., Urban, M. W., & Lepore, A. C. (2016). Harnessing the power of cell transplantation to target respiratory dysfunction following spinal

cord injury. *Experimental Neurology.* Online ahead of print. Available at http://dx.doi.org/10.1016/j.expneurol.2016.08.009

Chartrand, T. L., & Dalton, A. N. (2009). Mimicry: Its ubiquity, importance, and functionality. In T. L. Chartrand & A. N. Dalton (Eds.). *Oxford handbook of human action* (pp. 458–483). New York, NY: Oxford University Press.

Chatterjee, A., Strauss, M. E., Smyth, K. A., & Whitehouse, P. J. (1992). Personality changes in Alzheimer's disease. *Archives of Neurology, 49,* 486–491.

Chaudhari, N., & Roper, S. D. (2010). The cell biology of taste. *Journal of Cell Biology, 190,* 285–296.

Cheah, C. S. L., & Nelson, L. (2004). The role of acculturation in the emerging adulthood of aboriginal college students. *International Journal of Behavioral Development, 28,* 494–507.

Chechik, G., Meilijson, I., & Ruppin, E. (1999). Neuronal regulation: A mechanism for synaptic pruning during brain maturation. *Neural Computation, 11,* 2151–2170.

Cheetham, C. E. J., Hammond, M. S. L., Edwards, C. J., & Finnerty, G. T. (2007). Sensory experience alters cortical connectivity and synaptic function site specifically. *Journal of Neuroscience, 27,* 3456–3465.

Chemerinski, E., Triebwasser, J., Roussos, P., & Siever, L. J. (2013). Schizotypal personality disorder. *Journal of Personality Disorders, 27*(5), 652–679. doi: 10.1521/pedi_2012_26_053

Chen, S. Y., Jordan, C., & Thompson, S. (2006). The effect of cognitive behavioral therapy (CBT) on depression: The role of problem-solving appraisal. *Research on Social Work Practice, 16,* 500–510.

Chen, Y., & Knight, Z. A. (2016). Making sense of the sensory regulation of hunger neurons. *Bioessays, 38*(4), 316–324. doi:10.1002/bies.201500167

Chen, Y., Lin, Y. C., Kuo, T. W., & Knight, Z. A. (2015). Sensory detection of food rapidly modulates arcuate feeding circuits. *Cell, 160*(5), 829–841. Available at http://dx.doi.org/10.1016/j.cell.2015.01.033

Chepenik, L. G., Raffo, M., Hampson, M., Lacadie, C., Wang, F., Jones, M. M., ... Blumberg, H. P. (2010). Functional connectivity between ventral prefrontal cortex and amygdala at low frequency in the resting state in bipolar disorder. *Psychiatry Research: Neuroimaging, 182,* 207–210.

Chérif, L., Ayadi, H., Khemekhem, S., Moalla, Y., & Ghribi, F. (2014). Risk factors for youth problematic Internet use: A cross-sectional study. *Adolescent Psychiatry, 4*(2), 122.

Chess, S., & Thomas, A. (1996). *Temperament: Theory and research.* New York, NY: Brunner/Mazel.

Cheyne, J., Carriere, J., & Smilek, D. (2006). Absent-mindedness: Lapses of conscious awareness and everyday cognitive failures. *Consciousness and Cognition: An International Journal, 15,* 578–592. doi: 10.1016/j.concog.2005.11.009

Chia, E., Wang, J. J., Rochtchina, E., Cumming, R. R., Newall, P., & Mitchell, P. (2007). Hearing impairment and health-related quality of life: The Blue Mountains Hearing Study. *Ear & Hearing, 28,* 187–195.

Chiesa, A., Brambilla, P., & Serretti, A. (2010). Functional neural correlates of mindfulness meditations in comparison with psychotherapy, pharmacotherapy and placebo effect. Is there a link? *Acta Neuropsychiatrica, 22,* 104–117. doi: 10.1111/j.1601-5215.2010.00460.x

Chohra, A., & Madani, K. (2016, September). Biological regulation and psychological mechanisms models of adaptive decision-making behaviors: Drives, emotions, and personality. In *International Conference on Computational Collective Intelligence* (pp. 412–422). Springer International Publishing. doi: 10.1007/978 -3-319-45243-2_38

Choi, A. Y., Israel, T., & Maeda, H. (2017). Development and evaluation of the Internalized Racism in Asian Americans Scale (IRAAS). *Journal of Counseling Psychology, 64*(1), 52–64. Available at http://dx.doi.org/10.1037/cou0000183

Choi, I., Nisbett, R. E., & Norenzayan, A. (1999). Causal attribution across cultures: Variation and universality. *Psychological Bulletin, 125,* 47–65.

Chomsky, N. (1972). *Language and mind* (2nd ed.). New York, NY: Harcourt Brace Jovanovich.

Chomsky, N. (1986). *Knowledge of language: Its nature, origins, and use.* New York, NY: Praeger.

Chomsky, N. (2000). *New horizons in the study of language and the mind.* Cambridge, England: Cambridge University Press.

Chow, T. W., & Cummings, J. L. (1999). Frontal-subcortical circuits. In B. L. Miller & J. L. Cummings (Eds.), *The human frontal lobes: Functions and disorders* (pp. 3–26). New York, NY: Guilford Press.

Chowdhury, M., & Benson, B. A. (2011). Use of differential reinforcement to reduce behavior problems in adults with intellectual disabilities: A methodological review. *Research in Developmental Disabilities, 324*(2), 383–394.

Choy, Y., Fyer, A. J., & Lipsitz, J. D. (2007). Treatment of specific phobia in adults. *Clinical Psychology Review, 27*(3), 266–286. Advance online publication. doi: 10.1016/j.cpr.2006.10.002

Christakis, N. A., & Fowler, J. H. (2007). The spread of obesity in a large social network over 32 years. *New England Journal of Medicine, 357,* 370–379.

Christakis, N. A., & Fowler, J. H. (2008). The collective dynamics of smoking in a large social network. *New England Journal of Medicine, 358,* 2249–2258.

Christakis, N. A., & Fowler, J. H. (2009). *Connected: The surprising power of our social networks and how they shape our lives.* New York, NY: Little, Brown.

Christakis, N. A., & Fowler, J. H. (2010). Social network sensors for early detection of contagious outbreaks. *PLoS ONE, 5*(1–8), e12948. doi: 10.1371 /journal.pone.0012948

Christensen, K., Herskind, A. M., & Vaupel, J. W. (2006). Why Danes are smug: Comparative study of life satisfaction in the European Union. *British Medical Journal, 333,* 1289–1291.

Chuang, D. M. (2004). Lithium protection from glutamate excitotoxicity: Therapeutic implications. *Clinical Neuroscience Research, 4,* 243–252.

Cicchetti, D. (2001). How a child builds a brain. In W. W. Hartup & R. A. Weinberg (Eds.), *Child psychology in retrospect and prospect.* Mahwah, NJ: Erlbaum.

Cipriani, A., La Ferla, T., Furukawa, T. A., Signoretti, A., Nakagawa, A., Churchill, R., ... Barbui, C. (2010). Sertraline versus other antidepressive agents for depression [Review]. *Cochrane Database of Systematic Reviews,* Issue 4.

Clancy, P. M. (1985). The acquisition of Japanese. In D. Slobin (Ed.), *The cross-linguistic study of language acquisition: Vol. 1. The data.* Hillsdale, NJ: Erlbaum.

Clapp, W. C., Rubens, M. T., Sabharwal, J., & Gazzaley, A. (2011). Deficit in switching between functional brain networks underlies the impact of multitasking on working memory in older adults. *PNAS, 108*(17), 7212–7217. Available at http://doi .org/10.1073/pnas.1015297108

Clark, A. S., & Schneider, M. L. (1997). Effects of prenatal stress on behavior in adolescent rhesus monkey. *Annals of the New York Academy of Sciences, 807,* 490–491.

Clark, L. A. (2005). Temperament as a unifying basis for personality and psychopathology. *Journal of Abnormal Psychology, 114,* 505–521.

Clark, L., Bosworth, H., Welsh-Bohmer, K., Dawson, D., & Siegler, I. (2000). Relation between informant-rated personality and clinician-rated depression in patients with memory disorders. *Neuropsychiatry, Neuropsychology, & Behavioral Neurology, 13,* 39–47.

Clark, R. D., III, & Hatfield, E. (1989). Gender differences in willingness to engage in casual sex. *Journal of Psychology and Human Sexuality, 2,* 39–55.

Clark, R. D., III, & Hatfield, E. (2003). Love in the afternoon. *Psychological Inquiry, 14,* 227–231.

Clark, R. P., & Berris, C. E. (2005). Botulinum toxin: A treatment for facial asymmetry caused by facial nerve paralysis. *Plastic and Reconstructive Surgery, 115*(2), 573-574. doi: 10.1097/01. PRS.0000150149.74749.55

Clark, W. R., & Grunstein, M. (2000). *Are we hardwired? The role of genes in human behavior.* New York, NY: Oxford University Press.

Clarke, G. N., Hawkins, W., Murphy, M., Sheeber, L. B., Lewinsohn, P. M., & Seeley, J. R. (1995). Targeted prevention of unipolar depressive disorder in an at-risk sample of high school adolescents: A randomized trial of group cognitive intervention. *Journal of the American Academy of Child & Adolescent Psychiatry, 34,* 312–321.

Clarkson, J., & Herbison, A. E. (2016). Hypothalamic control of the male neonatal testosterone surge. *Philosophical Transactions of the Royal Society B-Biological Sciences, 371.* Retrieved online October 10, 2016. Published online at doi: 10.1098 /rstb.2015.0115

Classen, C. (2012). *The deepest sense: A cultural history of touch.* Urbana, IL: University of Illinois Press.

Clay, Z., Archbold, J., & Zuberbühler, K. (2015). Functional flexibility in wild bonobo vocal behaviour. *PeerJ, 3,* e1124. doi 10.7717/peerj.1124

Cleeremans, A. (2011). The radical plasticity thesis: How the brain learns to be conscious. *Frontiers in Psychology, 2,* Article 86. doi: 10.3389/ fpsyg.2011.00086 online only

Cloutier-Gill, L., Wood, E., Millar, T., Ferris, C., & Eugenia Socias, M. (2016). Remission of severe opioid use disorder with ibogaine: A case report. *Journal of Psychoactive Drugs, 48*(3), 214–217. doi: 10.1080/02791072.2016.1180467

Code of Federal Regulations. (2002). 45 C.F.R, Part VI, Section 689 (pp. 237–242). Retrieved online on January 29, 2017 at https://www.nsf.gov/oig/_pdf /cfr/45-CFR-689.pdf

Coe, C. L., & Lubach, G. R. (2008). Fetal programming: Prenatal origins of health and illness. *Current Directions in Psychological Science, 17,* 36–41.

Cohen, J. (2010, April 2). Boxed about the ears, ape language research still standing. *Science, 328,* 38–39.

Cohen, J. D. (2005). The vulcanization of the human brain. *Journal of Economic Perspectives, 19,* 3–24.

Cohen, K. M. (2002). Relationship among childhood sex-atypical behavior, spatial ability, handedness, and sexual orientation in men. *Archives of Sexual Behavior, 31,* 129–143.

Cohen, S. (2004). Social relationships and health. *American Psychologist, 59,* 676–684.

Cohen, S., Alper, C. M., Doyle, W. J., Adler, N., Treanor, J. J., & Turner, R. B. (2008). Objective and subjective socioeconomic status and susceptibility to the common cold. *Health Psychology, 27,* 268–274.

Cohen, S., Doyle, W. J., Turner, R. B., Alper, C. M., & Skoner, D. P. (2003). Sociability and susceptibility to the common cold. *Psychological Science, 14,* 389–395.

Cohen, S., Janicki-Deverts, D., Doyle, W. J., Miller, G. E., Frank, E., Rabin, B. S., & Turner, R. S. (2012). Chronic stress, glucocorticoid receptor resistance, inflammation, and disease risk. *Proceedings of the National Academy of Sciences* (PNAS), *109,*5995–5999. doi: 10.1073/pnas.1118355109

Cohen, S., Tyrrell, D. A. J., & Smith, A. P. (1993). Negative life events, perceived stress, negative affect, and susceptibility to the common cold. *Journal of Personality and Social Psychology, 64,* 131–140.

Cohen, S., & Wills, T. A. (1985). Stress, social support, and the buffering hypothesis. *Psychological Bulletin, 98,* 310–357.

Colcombe, S. J., Erickson, K. I., Scalf, P. E., Kim, J. S., Praskash, R., McAuley, E., ... Kramer, A. F. (2006). Aerobic exercise training increases brain volume in aging humans. *Journal of Gerontology, 61,* 1166–1170.

Colcombe, S. J., & Kramer, A. F. (2003). Fitness effects on the cognitive function of older adults: A meta-analytic study. *Psychological Science, 14,* 125–130.

Cole, S. W. (2009). Social regulation of human gene expression. *Current Directions in Psychological Science, 18,* 132–137.

Cole, S. W. (2010). Elevating the perspective on human stress genomics. *Psychoneuroendocrinology, 35,* 955–962.

Cole, S. W., Arevaloa, J. M. G., Takahashia, R., Sloan, E. K., Lutgendorf, S. K., Sood, A. K., ... Seeman, T. E. (2010). Computational identification of gene–social environment interaction at the human IL6 locus. *Proceedings of the National Academy of Sciences, 107,* 5681–5686.

Cole, S. W., Hawkley, L. C., Arevalo, J. M., Sung, C. Y., Rose, R. M., & Cacioppo, J. T. (2007). Social regulation of gene expression in human leukocytes. *Genome Biology, 8,* R189.1–R189.13.

Collignon, O., Girard, S., Gosselin, F., Saint-Amour, D., Lepore, F., & Lassonde, M. (2010). Women process multisensory emotion expressions more efficiently than men. *Neuropsychologia, 48,* 220–225.

Collins, A., & Loftus, E. F. (1975). A spreading activation theory of semantic processing. *Psychological Review, 82,* 407–428.

Collinson, S. L., Meyyappan, A., & Rosenfeld, J. V. (2009). Injury and recovery: Severe traumatic brain injury. *Brain Injury, 23,* 71–76. doi: 10.1080/02699050802649647

Colom, R., Haier, R., Head, K., Álvarez-Linera, J., Quiroga, M., Shih, P., & Jung, R. E. (2009). Gray matter correlates of fluid, crystallized, and spatial intelligence: Testing the P-FIT model. *Intelligence, 37*(2), 124–135.

Comer, R. J. (2007). *Abnormal psychology* (6th ed.). New York, NY: Worth.

Comery, T. A., Stamoudis, C. X., Irwin, S. A., & Greenough, W. T. (1996). Increased density of multiple-head dendritic spines on medium-sized spiny neurons of the striatum in rats reared in a complex environment. *Neurobiology of Learning and Memory, 66,* 93–96.

Compton, W. M., Han, B., Hughes, A., Jones, C. M., & Blanco, C. (2016). Use of marijuana for medical purposes among adults in the United States. *Journal of the American Medical Association.* Published online December 19, 2016. doi:10.1001/jama.2016.18900

Condon, P., Desbordes, G., Miller, W. B., & DeSteno, D. (2013). Meditation increases compassionate responses to suffering. *Psychological Science, 24*(10), 2125–2127. doi: 10.1177/0956797613485603

Conduct Problems Prevention Research Group. (1999a). Initial impact of the Fast Track prevention trial for conduct problems: I. The high-risk sample. *Journal of Consulting and Clinical Psychology, 67,* 631–647.

Conduct Problems Prevention Research Group. (1999b). Initial impact of the Fast Track prevention trial for conduct problems: II. Classroom effects. *Journal of Consulting and Clinical Psychology, 67,* 648–657.

Conel, J. L. (1939). *The cortex of the newborn.* Cambridge, MA: Harvard University Press.

Conron, K. J., Scott, G., Stowell, G. S., & Landers, S. (2012). Transgender health in Massachusetts: Results from a household probability sample of adults. *American Journal of Public Health, 102,* 118–122. doi: 10.2105/AJPH.2011.300315

Conte, F., Carobbi, G., Errico, B. M., & Ficca, G. (2012). The effects of pre-sleep learning on sleep continuity, stability, and organization in elderly individuals. *Frontiers in Neurology, 3,* 1–9. doi: 10.3389/fneur.2012.00109

Conway, A. R., Skitka, L. J., Hemmerich, J. A., & Kershaw, T. C. (2009). Flashbulb memory for 11 September 2001. *Applied Cognitive Psychology, 23,* 605–623. Available at http://dx.doi.org/10.1002/acp.1497

Cook, A., Johnson, C., & Bradley-Johnson, S. (2015). White noise to decrease problem behaviors in the classroom for a child with attention deficit hyperactivity disorder (ADHD). *Child & Family Behavior Therapy, 37,* 38–50. Available at http://dx.doi.org/10.1080/07317107.2015.1000234

Cook, C. C. (2013, July 6). Soldier's suicide note goes viral; family demands better for veterans. *CNN News,* retrieved July 6, 2013, from http://www.cnn.com/2013/07/06/us/soldier-suicide-note/index.html?hpt=hp_t2

Corkin, S. (1984). Lasting consequences of bilateral medial temporal lobectomy: Clinical course and experimental findings in H. M. *Seminars in Neurology.* Available at http://doi.org/10.1055/s-2008-1041556

Costa, P. T. (1996). Work and personality: Use of the NEO–PI–R in industrial/organizational psychology. *Applied Psychology: An International Review, 45,* 225–241.

Costa, P. T., & McCrae, R. R. (1976). Age differences in personality structure: A cluster analytic approach. *Journal of Gerontology, 31,* 564–570.

Costa, P. T., & McCrae, R. R. (1992). *NEO PI-R professional manual.* Odessa, FL: Psychological Assessment Resources.

Costa, P. T., Herbst, J. H., McCrae, R. R., & Siegler, I. C. (2000). Personality at midlife: Stability, intrinsic maturation, and response to life events. *Assessment, 7,* 365–378.

Cote, J., Clobert, J., Brodin, T., Fogarty, S., & Sih, A. (2014). Personality traits and spatial ecology in nonhuman animals. In P. J. Rentfrow (Ed.), *Geographical psychology: Exploring the interaction of environment and behavior* (pp. 89–112). Washington, DC: American Psychological Association. doi: 10.1037/14272-006

Cotman, C. W., Berchtold, N. C., & Christie, L. A. (2007). Exercise builds brain health: Key roles of growth factor cascades and inflammation. *Trends in Neurosciences, 30,* 464–472.

Couch, D., & Liamputtong, P. (2008). Online dating and mating: The use of Internet to meet sexual partners. *Qualitative Health Research, 18,* 268–279.

Coudé, G., Festante, F., Cilia, A., Loiacono, V., Bimbi, M., Fogassi, L., & Ferrari, P. F. (2016). Mirror neurons of ventral premotor cortex are modulated by social cues provided by others' gaze. *The Journal of Neuroscience, 36*(11), 3145–3156. doi: http://dx.doi.org/10.1523/JNEUROSCI.3220-15.2016

Courage, M. L., Bakhtiar, A., Fitzpatrick, C., Kenny, S., & Brandeau, K. (2015). Growing up multitasking: The costs and benefits for cognitive development. *Developmental Review, 35,* 5–41. doi: 10.1016/j.dr.2014.12.002

Courchesne, E., Campbell, K., & Solso, S. (2010). Brain growth across the life span in autism: Age-specific changes in anatomical pathology. *Brain Research.* doi: 10.1016/j.brainres.2010.09.101

Courtiol, E., & Wilson, D. A. (2016). Neural representation of odor-guided behavior in the rat olfactory thalamus. *The Journal of Neuroscience, 36,* no. 22 (2016): 5946–5960. doi: http://dx.doi.org/10.1523/JNEUROSCI.0533-16.2016

Cowan, N. (2008). What is the difference between long-term, short-term, and working memory? *Neuron, 61*(1): 6–9. doi: 10.1016/j.neuron.2008.12.023

Cox, S. R., Bak, T. H., Allerhand, M., Redmond, P., Starr, J. M., Deary, I. J., & MacPherson, S. E. (2016). Bilingualism, social cognition and executive functions: A tale of chickens and eggs. *Neuropsychologia, 91,* 299–306. Available at http://doi.org/10.1016/j.neuropsychologia.2016.08.029

Craft, M. A., Davis, G. C., & Paulson, R. M. (2012). Expressive writing in early breast cancer survivors. *Journal of Advanced Nursing, 69,* 305–315. doi: 10.1111/j.1365-2648.2012.06008.x

Craik, F. I., Govoni, R., Naveh-Benjamin, M., & Anderson, N. D. (1996). The effects of divided attention on encoding and retrieval processes in human memory. *Journal of Experimental Psychology: General, 125*(2), 159–180.

Craik, F. I. M. (1979). The structure and organization of memory. *Annual Review of Psychology, 30,* 63–102.

Craik, F. I. M., & Lockhart, R. S. (1972). Levels of processing: A framework for memory research. *Journal of Verbal Learning and Verbal Behavior, 11,* 671–684.

Craik, F. I. M., & Tulving, E. (1975). Depth of processing and the retention of words in episodic memory. *Journal of Experimental Psychology: General, 104,* 268–294.

Crain, S., Crain, M. A., & Crain, S. M. (2013). Emotional and physical distress relief using a novel endorphinergic formulation. *Journal of Behavioral and Brain Science, 3,* 441–453.

Crandall, C. S. (1988). Social contagion of binge eating. *Journal of Personality and Social Psychology, 55*(4), 588–598.

Crandall, S. R., & Connors, B. W. (2016). Diverse ensembles of inhibitory interneurons. *Neuron, 90*(1), 4–6. Available at http://dx.doi.org/10.1016/j.neuron.2016.03.022

Crawford, S. E., & Alaggia, R. (2008). The best of both worlds? Family influences on mixed race youth identity development. *Qualitative Social Work, 7,* 81–98.

Crews, F. (1998). *Unauthorized Freud: Doubters confront a legend.* New York, NY: Viking.

Crook, T. H., Youngjohn, J. R., Larrabee, G. J., & Salama, M. (1992). Aging and everyday memory: A cross-cultural study. *Neuropsychology, 6,* 123–136.

Cropley, J. E., Eaton, S. A., Aiken, A., Young, P. E., Giannoulatou, E., Ho, J. W., … & Langley, K. G. (2016). Male-lineage transmission of an acquired metabolic phenotype induced by grand-paternal obesity. *Molecular Metabolism, 5,* 699–708. Available at http://dx.doi.org/10.1016/j.molmet.2016.06.008

Cross, S. E., & Markus, H. (1999). The cultural constitution of personality. In L. A. Pervin & O. P. John (Eds.), *Handbook of personality theory and research* (pp. 378–396). New York, NY: Guilford Press.

Cross-Disorder Group of the Psychiatric Genomics Consortium. (2013, April 20–26). Identification of risk loci with shared effects on five major psychiatric disorders: A genome-wide analysis. *The Lancet, 381,* 1371–1379. Retrieved from http://dx.doi.org/10.1016/S0140-6736(12)62129-1

Crouch, R., Wilson, A., & Newbury, J. (2011). A systematic review of the effectiveness of primary health education or intervention programs in improving rural women's knowledge of heart disease risk factors and changing lifestyle behaviours. *International Journal of Evidence-Based Healthcare, 9*(3), 236–245.

Crow, S. J., Peterson, C. B., Swanson, S. A., Raymond, N. C., Specker, S., Eckert, E. D., & Mitchell, J. E. (2009). Increased mortality in bulimia nervosa and other eating disorders. *American Journal of Psychiatry, 166,* 1342–1346.

Crump, T. (2001). *A brief history of science.* New York, NY: Carroll & Graf.

Cruwys, T., Platow, M. J., Rieger, E., Byrne, D. G., & Haslam, S. A. (2016). The social psychology of disordered eating: The situated identity enactment model. *European Review of Social Psychology, 27*(1), 160–195. doi: 10.1080/10463283.2016.1229891

Crystal, J. D., Maxwell, K. W., & Hohmann, A. G. (2003). Cannabinoid modulation of sensitivity to time. *Behavioural Brain Research, 144,* 57–66.

Csikszentmihalyi, M. (1990). *Flow: The psychology of optimal experience.* New York, NY: HarperPerennial.

Csikszentmihalyi, M. (1996). *Creativity: Flow and the psychology of discovery and invention.* New York, NY: HarperCollins.

Cuijpers, P., van Straten, A., Hollon, S., & Andersson, G. (2010). The contribution of active medication to combined treatments of psychotherapy and pharmacotherapy for adult depression: A meta-analysis. *Acta Psychiatrica Scandinavica, 121,* 415–423. doi: 10.1111/j.1600-0447.2009.01513.x

Cukor, J., Spitalnick, J., Difede, J., Rizzo, A., & Rothbaum, B. O. (2009). Emerging treatments for PTSD. *Clinical Psychology Review, 29,* 715–726.

Culvers, J. (2010, April 17). 7 Tips for improving the effectiveness of your diet. Retrieved from http://ezinearticles.com/?7-Tips-For-Improving-the-Effectiveness-of-Your-Diet&id=4128679

Cummings, J. H., Bingham, S. A., Heaton, K. W., & Eastwood, M. A. (1992). Fecal weight, colon cancer risk, and dietary intake of nonstarch polysaccharides (dietary fiber). *Gastroenterology, 103,* 1783–1789.

Cummings, W. C., & Thompson, P. O. (1971). Underwater sounds from the blue whale, *Balenoptera musculus. Journal of the American Acoustical Society, 50,* 1193. doi: 10.1121/1.1912752

Cunningham, W. A., & Zelazo, P. D. (2006). Attitudes and evaluations: A social cognitive neuroscience perspective. *Trends in Cognitive Sciences, 11*, 97–104.

Curley, J. P., Jensen, C. L., Mashoodh, R., & Champagne, F. A. (2011). Social influences on neurobiology and behavior: Epigenetic effect during development. *Psychoneuroendocrinology.* doi: 10.1016/j.psyneuen.2010.06.005

Currais, A., Quehenberger, O., Armando, A. M., Daugherty, D., Maher, P., & Schubert, D. (2016). Amyloid proteotoxicity initiates an inflammatory response blocked by cannabinoids. *Aging and Mechanisms of Disease, 2*, 16012. doi:10.1038/npjamd.2016.12

Curtiss, S. (1977). *Genie: A psycholinguistic study of a modern-day wild child.* New York, NY: Academic Press.

Cusack, C. L., Swahari, V., Hampton, H. W., Ramsey, J., & Deshmukh, M. (2013). Distinct pathways mediate axon degeneration during apoptosis and axon-specific pruning. *Nature Communications, 4.* Available at http://dx.doi .org/10.1038/ncomms2910 L3-0.1038/ncomms2910

Cussler, E. C., Going, S. B., Houtkooper, L. B., Stanford, V. A., Blew, R. M., Flint-Wagner, H. G., ... Lohman, T. G. (2005). Exercise frequency and calcium intake predict 4-year bone changes in postmenopausal women. *Osteoporosis International, 16*, 2129–2141.

Cutting, A. L., & Dunn, J. (2002). The cost of understanding other people: Social cognition predicts young children's sensitivity to criticism. *Journal of Child Psychology and Psychiatry, 43*, 849–860.

Cytowic, R. E. (1989). *Synaesthesia: A union of the senses.* New York, NY: Springer-Verlag.

Czech, C., & Adessi, C. (2004). Disease modifying therapeutic strategies in Alzheimer's disease targeting the amyloid cascade. *Current Neuropharmacology, 2*, 295–307.

D'Anglejan, A. (1979). Solving problems in deductive reasoning: Three experimental studies of adult second language learners. *Working Papers on Bilingualism, No. 17.*

D'Ausilio, R. (2008, September 10). What motivates your employees? Intrinsic vs. extrinsic rewards. Retrieved from http://www.tmcnet.com/channels /performance-management/articles/39417 -what-motivates-employees-intrinsic-vs-extrinsic- rewards.htm

Dabbs, J. M., Jr., Carr, T. S., & Frady, R. L. (1995). Testosterone, crime, and misbehavior among 692 male prison inmates. *Personality and Individual Differences, 18*, 627–633.

Dabbs, J. M., Jr., & Hargrove, M. F. (1997). Age, testosterone, and behavior among female prison inmates. *Psychosomatic Medicine, 59*, 477–480.

Daee, A., Robinson, P., Lawson, M., Turpin, J. A., Gregory, B., & Tobias, J. D. (2002). Psychologic and physiologic effects of dieting in adolescents. *Southern Medical Journal, 95*, 1032–1041.

Dale, P. S., Dionne, G., Eley, T. C., & Plomin, R. (2000). Lexical and grammatical development: A behavioural genetic perspective. *Journal of Child Language, 27*, 619–642.

Dallaire, D. H., Cole, D. A., Smith, T. M., Ciesla, J. A., LaGrange, B., Jacquez, F. M., ... Folmer, A. S. (2008). Predicting children's depressive symptoms from community and individual risk factors. *Journal of Youth and Adolescence, 37*, 830–846.

Dallman, M. F., Pecoraro, N. C., & la Fleur, S. E. (2005). Chronic stress and comfort foods: Self-medication and abdominal obesity. *Brain, Behavior, and Immunity, 19*, 275–280.

Damasio, A. R. (2000). *The feeling of what happens: Body and emotion in the making of consciousness.* Chicago, IL: Harcourt.

Daniel, J., & Haberman, M. (2017). Clinical potential of psilocybin as a treatment for mental health conditions. *Mental Health Clinician, 7*(1), 24–28. doi: http://dx.doi.org/10.9740/mhc.2017.01.024

Danziger, N., Prkachin, K. M., & Willer, J-C. (2006). Is pain the price of empathy? The perception of others' pain in patients with congenital insensitivity to pain. *Brain, 129*, 2494–2507.

Darley, J. M., & Batson, C. D. (1973). "From Jerusalem to Jericho": A study of situational and dispositional variables in helping behavior. *Journal of Personality and Social Psychology, 27*, 100–108.

Darley, J. M., & Latané, B. (1968). Bystander intervention in emergencies: Diffusion of responsibility. *Journal of Personality and Social Psychology, 8*, 377–383.

Darwin, C. (1859). *The origin of species.* London: Murray (reprinted in 1964 by Harvard University Press).

Darwin, C. (1998). *The expression of the emotions in man and animals.* New York, NY: Oxford University Press. (Original work published 1872)

Dasgupta, N., McGhee, D. E., Greenwald, A. G., & Banaji, M. R. (2000). Automatic preference for white Americans: Eliminating the familiarity explanation. *Journal of Experimental Social Psychology, 36*, 316–328.

Daskalakis, N. P., McGill, M. A., Lehrner, A., & Yehuda, R. (2016). Endocrine aspects of PTSD: Hypothalamic-pituitary-adrenal (HPA) axis and beyond. *Comprehensive Guide to Post-Traumatic Stress Disorders*, 245–260. doi: 10.1007/978-3-319-08359-9_130

Davidovitch, M., Hemo, B., Manning-Courtney, P., & Fombonne, E. (2013). Prevalence and incidence of autism spectrum disorder in an Israeli population. *Journal of Autism and Developmental Disorders, 43*, 785–793.

Davidson, R. J. (1994). On emotion, mood, and related affective constructs. In P. Ekman & R. J. Davidson (Eds.), *The nature of emotion: Fundamental questions* (pp. 51–55). New York, NY: Oxford University Press.

Davidson, R. J. (2001). Toward a biology of personality and emotion. *Annals of the New York Academy of Sciences, 935*, 191–207.

Davidson, R. J. (2004). What does the pre-frontal cortex "do" in affect?: Perspectives on frontal EEG asymmetry research. *Biological Psychology, 67*, 219–233.

Davidson, R. J., Ekman, P., Saron, C., Senulis, J., & Friesen, W. V. (1990). Approach-withdrawal and cerebral asymmetry: Emotional expression and brain physiology I. *Journal of Personality and Social Psychology, 58*, 330–341.

Davidson, R. J., Kabat-Zinn, J., Schumacher, J., Rosenkranz, M., Muller, D., Santorelli, S. F., . . . Sheridan, J. F. (2003). Alterations in brain and immune function produced by mindfulness meditation. *Psychosomatic Medicine, 65*, 564–570.

Davis, E. M., & Fingerman, K. L. (2015). Digital dating: Online profile content of older and younger adults. *J Gerontol B Psychol Sci Soc Sci*, 1–8. Available at http://doi.org/10.1093/geronb/gbv042

Davis, J. I., Senghas, A., Brandt, F., & Ochsner, K. N. (2010). The effects of BOTOX injections on emotional experience. *Emotion, 10*(3), 433–40. doi: 10.1037/a0018690

Davis, T. S., Wark, H. A. C., Hutchinson, D. T., Warren, D. J., O'Neill, K., Scheinblum, T., ... & Greger, B. (2016). Restoring motor control and sensory feedback in people with upper extremity amputations using arrays of 96 microelectrodes implanted in the median and ulnar nerves. *Journal of Neural Engineering, 13*(3), 036001. doi: 10.1088/1741-2560/13/3/036001

Dawkins, R. (1989). *The selfish gene* (new ed.). New York, NY: Oxford University Press.

Dawson, G., Toth, K., Abbott, R., Osterling, J., Munson, J., Estes, A., & Liaw, J. (2004). Early social attention impairments in autism: Social orienting, joint attention, and attention to distress. *Developmental Psychology, 40*(2), 271. doi: 10.1037/0012-1649.40.2.271

De Bruijn, G. J., Spaans, P., Jansen, B., & Van't Riet, J. (2016). Testing the effects of a message framing intervention on intentions towards hearing loss prevention in adolescents. *Health Education Research, 31*(2), 161–170. Available at http://doi .org/10.1093/her/cyw006

de Celis, M. F. R., Bornstein, S. R., Androutsellis-Theotokis, A., Andoniadou, C. L., Licinio, J., Wong, M. L., & Ehrhart-Bornstein, M. (2016). The effects of stress on brain and adrenal stem cells. *Molecular psychiatry, 21*(5), 590–593. doi:10.1038/mp.2015.23

De Fruyt, F., & Murvielde, I. (1999). RAISEC types and Big Five traits as predictors of employment status and nature of employment. *Personnel Psychology, 52*, 701–727.

de Graaf-Peters, V. B., & Hadders-Algra, M. (2006). Ontogeny of the human central nervous system: What is happening when? *Early Human Development, 82*, 257–266.

De Lisi, R., & Wolford, J. L. (2002). Improving children's mental rotation accuracy with computer game playing. *Journal of Genetic Psychology, 163*, 272–282.

de Moor, Costa, P. T., Terracciano, A., Krueger, R. F., de Geus, E. J. C., Toshiko, T., ... Boomsma, D. I. (2012). Meta-analysis of genome-wide association studies for personality. *Molecular Psychiatry, 17*(3), 337–349. Available at http://doi .org/10.1038/mp.2010.128

De Neys, W., Vartanian, O., & Goel, V. (2008). Smarter than we think: When our brains detect that we are biased. *Psychological Science, 19*, 483–489.

de Vivo, L., Bellesi, M., Bushong, E. A., Ellisman, M. H., Tononi, G., & Cirelli, C. (2017). *Science, 355*(6324), 507–510 doi: 10.1126/science.aah5982

de Vries, D. A., & Kühne, R. (2015). Facebook and self-perception: Individual susceptibility to negative social comparison on Facebook. *Personality and Individual Differences, 86*, 217–221. Available at http://doi.org/10.1016/j.paid.2015.05.029

de Waal, F. B. M., & Suchak, M. (2010). Prosocial primates: Selfish and unselfish motivations. *Philosophical Transactions of the Royal Society of London B, 365*, 2711–2722.

de Win, M. M. L., Reneman, L., Reitsma, J. B., den Heeten, G. J., Booij, J., & van den Brink, W. (2004). Mood disorders and serotonin transporter density in ecstasy users—The influence of long-term abstention, dose, and gender. *Psychopharmacology, 173*, 376–382.

de Zilva, D., Newell, B. R., & Mitchell, C. J. (2016). Multiple context mere exposure: Examining the limits of liking. *The Quarterly Journal of Experimental Psychology, 69*(3), 521–534. doi: 10.1080/17470218.2015.1057188

Deacon, T. (1997). *Symbolic species: Co-evolution of language and the brain.* New York, NY: Norton.

Deary, I. J., Graham, T., Wilson, V., Starr, J. M., & Whalley, L. J. (2003). Population sex differences in IQ at age 11: The Scottish mental survey 1932. *Intelligence, 31,* 533–542.

"Debbie Reynolds dead at 84; son says stress over Carrie Fisher's death 'was too much'." (2016). http://www.syracuse.com/celebrity-news/index.ssf/2016/12/debbie_reynolds_dead_at_84_son_says_stress_over_carrie_fishers_death_was_too_muc.html

Debes, R. (2010). Which empathy? Limitations in the mirrored "understanding" of emotion. *Synthese, 175,* 219–239.

DeCasper, A. J., & Fifer, W. (1980). Of human bonding: Newborns prefer their mothers' voices. *Science, 208,* 1174–1176.

DeCasper, A. J., & Spence, M. J. (1986). Pre-natal maternal speech influences newborns' perception of speech sounds. *Infant Behavior & Development, 9,* 133–150.

Deci, E. L., & Ryan, R. M. (1985). *Intrinsic motivation and self-determination in human behavior.* New York, NY: Plenum.

Declerck, C. H., Boone, C., & Kiyonari, T. (2010). Oxytocin and cooperation under conditions of uncertainty: The modulating role of incentives and social information. *Hormones and Behavior, 57,* 368–374.

Dedoncker, J., Brunoni, A. R., Baeken, C., & Vanderhasselt, M. (2016). The effect of the interval-between-sessions on prefrontal transcranial direct current stimulation (tDCS) on cognitive outcomes: A systematic review and meta-analysis. *Journal of Neural Transmission, 123*(10), 1159–1172. doi:10.1007/s00702-016-1558-x

DeDonno, M. A., Rivera-Torres, K., Monis, A., & Fagan, J. F. (2014). The influence of a time limit and bilingualism on Scholastic Assessment Test performance. *North American Journal of Psychology, 16,* 211–223.

Deisseroth, K. (2010). Optogenetics. *Nature Methods, 8,* 26–29. doi: 10.1038/nmeth.f.324

DeKeyser, R., & Larson-Hall, J. (2005). What does the critical period really mean? In J. F. Kroll & A. M. B. DeGroot (Eds.), *Handbook of bilingualism: Psycholinguistic approaches* (pp. 88–108). New York, NY: Oxford University Press.

Delgado, M. K., Wanner, K. J., & McDonald, C. (2016). Adolescent cellphone use while driving: An overview of the literature and promising future directions for prevention. *Media and Communication, 4*(3), 79. doi: 10.17645/mac.v4i3.536

Delgado, P. L., Price, L. H., Miller, H. L., Salomon, R. M., Aghajanian, G. K., Heninger, G. R., & Charney, D. S. (1994). Serotonin and the neurobiology of depression—Effects of tryptophan depletion in drug-free depressed patients. *Archives of General Psychiatry, 51,* 865–874.

DeLisi, M., Umphress, Z. R., & Vaughn, M. G. (2009). The criminology of the amygdala. *Criminal Justice and Behavior, 36,* 1241–1252.

Dell'Osso, B., Buoli, M., Baldwin, D. S., & Altamura, A. C. (2009). Serotonin norepinephrine reuptake inhibitors (SNRIs) in anxiety disorders: A comprehensive review of their clinical efficacy. *Human Psychopharmacology: Clinical & Experimental, 25,* 17–29.

DeLongis, A., Folkman, S., & Lazarus, R. S. (1988). The impact of daily stress on health and mood: Psychological and social resources as mediators. *Journal of Personality and Social Psychology, 54,* 486–495.

Dement, W. (1999). *The promise of sleep.* New York, NY: Delacorte Press.

Demir, E., & Dickson, B. J. (2005). Fruitless splicing specifies male courtship behavior in *Drosophila. Cell, 121,* 785–794.

Denizet, M., Cotter, L., Lledo, P. M., & Lazarini, F. (2016). Sensory deprivation increases phagocytosis of adult-born neurons by activated microglia in the olfactory bulb. *Brain, Behavior, and Immunity.* Online ahead of print. Available at http://dx.doi.org/10.1016/j.bbi.2016.09.015

Denny, C. A., Kheirbek, M. A., Alba, E. L., Tanaka, K. F., Brachman, R. A., Laughman, K. B., ... Hen, R. (2014). Hippocampal memory traces are differentially modulated by experience, time, and adult neurogenesis. *Neuron, 83*(1), 189–201. http://doi.org/10.1016/j.neuron.2014.05.018

Deoni, S. C. L., Dean, D. C., III, Piryatinsky, I., O'Muircheartaigh, J., Waskiewicz, N., Lehman, K., Han, M., & Dirks, H. (2013). Breastfeeding and early white matter development: A cross-sectional study. *NeuroImage, 82,* 77–86. doi: 10.1016/j.neuroimage.2013.05.090

Derbyshire, S. W. G., Whalley, M. G., Stenger, A., & Oakley, D. A. (2004). Cerebral activation during hypnotically induced and imagined pain. *NeuroImage, 23,* 392–401.

Derry, G. (1999). *What science is and how it works.* Princeton, NJ: Princeton University Press.

Derryberry, D., & Tucker, D. M. (1994). Motivating the focus of attention. In P. M. Niedenthal & S. Kitayama (Eds.), *The heart's eye: Emotional influences in perception and attention* (pp. 167–196). San Diego, CA: Academic Press.

DeRubeis, R. J., Hollon, S., Amsterdam, J., Shelton, R., Young, P., Salomon, R., ... Gallop, R. (2005). Cognitive therapy vs medications in the treatment of moderate to severe depression. *Archives of General Psychiatry, 62*(4), 409–416.

Devaraju, P., & Zakharenko, S. S. (2017). Mitochondria in complex psychiatric disorders: Lessons from mouse models of 22q11.2 deletion syndrome. *Bioessays.* doi: 10.1002/bies.201600177

Devilbiss, D. M., & Berridge, C. W. (2008). Cognition-enhancing doses of methylphenidate preferentially increase prefrontal cortex neuronal responsivity. *Biological Psychiatry, 64,* 626–635.

Devine, P. (1989). Stereotypes and prejudice: Their automatic and controlled components. *Journal of Personality and Social Psychology, 56,* 5–18.

DeWall, C. N., MacDonald, G., Webster, G. D., Masten, C. L., Baumeister, R. F., Powell, C., ... Eisenberger, N. I. (2010). Acetaminophen reduces social pain: Behavioral and neural evidence. *Psychological Science, 21,* 931–937.

DeWall, C., Masten, C. L., Powell, C., Combs, D., Schurtz, D. R., & Eisenberger, N. I. (2012). Do neural responses to rejection depend on attachment style? An fMRI study. *Social Cognitive and Affective Neuroscience, 7*(2), 184–192. doi: 10.1093/scan/nsq107

DeYoung, C., Shamosh, N., Green, A., Braver, T., & Gray, J. (2009). Intellect as distinct from openness: Differences revealed by fMRI of working memory. *Journal of Personality and Social Psychology, 97,* 883–892.

Dhabhar, F. S. (2009). Enhancing versus suppressive effects of stress on immune function: Implications for immuno-protection and immunopathology. *Neuroimmunomodulation, 16,* 300–317.

Dhabhar, F. S. (2013). Psychological stress and immunoprotection versus immunopathology in the skin. *Clinics in Dermatology, 31,* 18–30. Retrieved from http://dx.doi.org/10.1016/j.clindermatol.2011.11.003

Diamond, L. M. (2003). Was it a phase? Young women's relinquishment of lesbian/bisexual identities over a 5-year period. *Journal of Personality and Social Psychology, 84*(2), 352–364. Available at http://doi.org/10.1037/0022-3514.84.2.352

Diamond, L. M. (2008). Female bisexuality from adolescence to adulthood: Results from a 10-year longitudinal study. *Developmental Psychology, 44,* 5–14.

Dias, R. G., & Ressler, K. J. (2013). Parental olfactory experience influences behavior and neural structure in subsequent generations. *Nature Neuroscience.* doi: 10.1038/nn.3594. Advanced online publication retrieved December 24, 2013, from http://www.fpamed.com/wp-content/uploads/2013/12/olefactory-gene.pdf

Dick, A. S., Bernal, B., & Tremblay, P. (2013). The language connectome: New pathways, new concepts. *The Neuroscientist: A Review Journal Bringing Neurobiology, Neurology and Psychiatry, 20*(December 2013), 453–467. Retrieved from http://doi.org/10.1177/1073858413513502

Dickinson, A., Jones, M., & Milne, E. (2016). Measuring neural excitation and inhibition in autism: Different approaches, different findings and different interpretations. *Brain Research, 1648,* 277–289. Available at http://dx.doi.org/10.1016/j.brainres.2016.07.011

Diener, E., & Seligman, M. E. P. (2004). Beyond money toward an economy of well-being. *Psychological Science, 5,* 1–31.

Diener, E., Suh, E. M., Lucas, R. E., & Smith, H. L. (1999). Subjective well-being: Three decades of progress. *Psychological Bulletin, 125,* 276–302.

Dietrich, K., Succop, P., Berger, O., & Hammond, P. (1991). Lead exposure and the cognitive development of urban preschool children: The Cincinnati Lead Study cohort at age 4 years. *Neurotoxicology and Teratology, 13*(2), 203–211.

Digman, J. M. (1990). Personality structure: Emergence of the Five-Factor Model. *Annual Review in Psychology, 41,* 417–440.

Dimberg, U., & Söderkvist, S. (2011). The voluntary facial action technique: A method to test the facial feedback hypothesis. *Journal of Nonverbal Behavior, 35,* 17–33.

Dinan, T. G., & Cryan, J. F. (2012). Regulation of the stress response by the gut microbiota: Implications for psychoneuroendocrinology. *Psychoneuroendocrinology, 37*(9), 1369–1378. Available at http://doi.org/10.1016/j.psyneuen.2012.03.007

Dindar, M., & Akbulut, Y. (2016). Effects of multitasking on retention and topic interest. *Learning and Instruction, 41,* 94–105. Available at http://doi.org/10.1016/j.learninstruc.2015.10.005

Dingemanse, N. J., Both, C., Drent, P. J., Van Oers, K., & Van Noordwijk, A. J. (2002). Repeatability and heritability of exploratory behaviour in great tits from the wild. *Animal Behaviour, 64,* 929–938.

Dinn, W. M., Aycicegi, A., & Harris, C. L. (2004). Cigarette smoking in a student sample: Neurocognitive and clinical correlates. *Addictive Behaviors, 29,* 107–126.

DiPietro, J. A. (2012). Maternal stress in pregnancy: Considerations for fetal development. *Journal of Adolescent Health, 51*(Suppl. 2), S3–S8. doi: 10.1016/j.jadohealth.2012.04.008

DiPietro, J. A., Hodgson, D. M., Costigan, K. A., & Johnson, T. R. B. (1996). Fetal antecedents of infant temperament. *Child Development, 67*, 2568–2583.

Distracted Driving. (2013, May 23). Retrieved October 17, 2013, from http://www.cdc.gov /motorvehiclesafety/distracted_driving/

Divac, N., Prostran, M., Jakovcevski, I., & Cerovac, N. (2014). Second-generation antipsychotics and extrapyramidal adverse effects. *BioMed Research International, 2014.* doi: 10.1155/2014/656370

Dobbs, D. (2006a, April 2). A depression switch? *New York Times Magazine.* Retrieved from http:// www.nytimes.com

Dockray, S., & Steptoe, A. (2010). Positive affect and psychobiological processes. *Neuroscience and Biobehavioral Reviews, 35*, 69–75.

Doctorate Recipients. (2016). Table 16: Doctorate recipients, by sex and subfield of study: 2014. https://www.nsf.gov/statistics/2016/nsf16300/

Doetsch, F., & Scharff, C. (2001). Challenges for brain repair: Insights from adult neurogenesis in birds and mammals. *Brain, Behavior & Evolution, 58*, 306–322.

Dolcos, F., LaBar, K. S., & Cabeza, R. (2005). Remembering one year later: Role of the amygdala and the temporal lobe memory system in retrieving emotional memories. *Proceedings of the National Academy of Sciences, 102*, 2626–2631.

Dolinoy, D., & Jirtle, R. L. (2008). Environmental epigenomics in human health and disease. *Environmental and Molecular Mutagenesis, 49*, 4–8.

Dolinski, D., Grzyb, T., Folwarczny, M., Grzybala, P., Krzyszycha, K., Martynowska, K., & Trojanowski, J. (2017). Would you deliver an electric shock in 2015? Obedience in the experimental paradigm developed by Stanley Milgram in the 50 years following the original studies. *Social Psychological and Personality Science*, published online at 10.1177/1948550617693060

Doll, R., Peto, R., Boreham, J., & Sutherland, I. (2004). Mortality in relation to smoking: 50 years' observations on male British doctors. *British Medical Journal, 328*, 1519–1528.

Domhoff, G. W. (2001). A new neurocognitive theory of dreams. *Dreaming, 11*, 13–33.

Dominguez, J. M., & Hull, E. M. (2005). Dopamine, the medial preoptic area, and male sexual behavior. *Physiology & Behavior, 86*, 356–368.

Dong, J. Y., Zhang, Y.-H., Wang, P., & Qin, L.-Q. (2012). Meta-analysis of dietary glycemic load and glycemic index in relation to risk of coronary heart disease. *American Journal of Cardiology, 109*, 1608–1613.

Dorethy, M., Fiebert, M., & Warren, C. (2014). Examining social networking site behaviors: Photo sharing and impression management on Facebook. *International Review of Social Sciences and Humanities, 6*(2), 111–116. Retrieved October 20, 2016 from http://irssh.com/yahoo_site_admin/assets /docs/10_IRSSH-723-V6N2.39115416.pdf

Doron, J., & Martinent, G. (2016). Appraisal, coping, emotion, and performance during elite fencing matches: A random coefficient regression model approach. *Scandinavian Journal of Medicine & Science in Sports.* doi: 10.1111/sms.12711

Doty, R. L., Applebaum, S., Zusho, H., & Settle, R. G. (1985). Sex differences in odor identification ability: A cross-cultural analysis. *Neuropsychologia, 23*, 667–672.

Drevets, W. C., Frank, E., Price, J. C., Kupfer, D. J., Holt, D., Greer, P. J., ... Mathis, C. (1999). PET imaging of serotonin 1A receptor binding in depression. *Biological Psychiatry, 46*, 1375–1387.

Drevets, W. C., Price, J. L., Simpson, J. R., Todd, R. D., Reich, T., Vannier, M., & Raichle, M. (1997). Subgenual prefrontal cortex abnormalities in mood disorders. *Nature, 386*, 824–827.

Drug for treating schizophrenia identified. (1998). Retrieved from http://www.pbs.org/wgbh/ aso/databank/entries/dh52dr.html

Dubai, Y. (2004). The neurobiology of consolidations, or, How stable is the engram? *Annual Review of Psychology, 55*, 51–86.

Dube, A. R., & Kamath, J. (2013). Social constructions of male sexual identity: Translational limitations of western 'homosexuality' in an Indian male patient. *Journal of Gay & Lesbian Mental Health, 17*(3), 352–360. doi: 10.1080/19359705.2013.767154

Duckworth, A., & Quinn, P. D. (2009). Development and validation of the Short Grit Scale (GRIT–S). *Journal of Personality Assessment, 91*(2), 166–174.

Duckworth, A. L., Peterson, C., Matthews, M. D., & Kelly, D. R. (2007). Grit: Perseverance and passion for long-term goals. *Journal of Personality and Social Psychology, 92*(6), 1087–1101. doi: 10.1037/0022-3514.92.6.1087

Duckworth, R. A. (2010). Evolution of personality: Developmental constraints on behavioral flexibility. *The Auk, 127*(4), 752–758.

Due, P., Holstein, B. E., Ito, H., & Groth, M. V. (1991). Diet and health behavior in Danish children aged 11–15 years. *Tandlaegernes Tidsskr, 6*(8), 232–237.

Dumay, N. (2016). Sleep not just protects memories against forgetting, it also makes them more accessible. *Cortex, 74*, 289–296. Available at http:// doi.org/10.1016/j.cortex.2015.06.007

Dunbar, R. I. M. (1996). *Grooming, gossip and the evolution of language.* London, England: Faber & Faber.

Dunbar, R. I. M. (2001). Brains on two legs: Group size and the evolution of intelligence. In F. B. M. deWaal (Ed.), *Tree of origin: What primate behavior can tell us about human social evolution* (pp. 173–191). Cambridge, MA: Harvard University Press.

Duncan, J., Seitz, R. J., Koldny, J., Bor, D., Herzog, H., Ahmed, A., ... Emslie, H. (2000, July 21). A neural basis for general intelligence. *Science, 289*, 457–460.

Duncan, S. C., Duncan, T. E., & Strycker, L. A. (2006). Alcohol use from ages 9 to 16: A cohort-sequential latent growth model. *Drug and Alcohol Dependence, 81*, 71–81.

Duncker, K. (1945). On problem-solving. *Psychological Monographs, 58*, ix. (Whole No. 270).

Dunn, E. W., Aknin, L. B., & Norton, M. I. (2008). Spending money on others promotes happiness. *Science, 319*, 1687–1688.

Durante, D., & Dunson, D. B. (2016). Bayesian inference and testing of group differences in brain networks. *Bayesian Analysis, 0*(0), 1–30. Available at https://doi.org/10.1214/16-BA1030

Durlak, J. A., Taylor, R. D., Kawashima, K., Pachan, M. K., DuPre, E. P., Celio, C. I., ... Weissberg, R. P. (2007). Effects of positive youth development programs on school, family, and community systems. *American Journal of Community Psychology, 39*, 269–286.

Dye, M. W. G., & Bavelier, D. (2004). Playing video games enhances visual attention in children. *Journal of Vision, 4*, 40A.

Eagly, A. H., & Chaiken, S. (1998). Attitude structure and function. In D. T. Gilbert, S. T. Fiske, & G. Lindzey (Eds.), *The handbook of social psychology* (4th ed., Vol. 1, pp. 269–322). New York, NY: McGraw-Hill.

Eapen, B. C., Murphy, D. P., & Cifu, D. X. (2016). Neuroprosthetics in amputee and brain injury rehabilitation. *Experimental Neurology.* Available at http://dx.doi.org/10.1016/j.expneurol.2016.08.004

Eaton, N. R., Rodriguez-Seijas, C., Krueger, R. F., Campbell, W. K., Grant, B. F., & Hasin, D. S. (2016). Narcissistic personality disorder and the structure of common mental disorders. *Journal of Personality Disorders*, 1–13. doi: 10.1521/ pedi_2016_30_260

Ebbeling, C. B., Leidig, M. M., Feldman, H. A., Lovesky, M. M., & Ludwig, D. S. (2007). Effects of a low-glycemic load vs. low-fat diet in obese young adults: A randomized trial. *Joural of the American Medical Association, 297*(19), 2092–2102. doi: 10.1001/jama.297.19.2092

Ebstein, R. P. (2006). The molecular genetic architecture of human personality: Beyond self-report questionnaires. *Molecular Psychiatry, 11*, 427–445.

Ebstein, R. P., Israel, S., Chew, S. H., Zhong, S., & Knafo, A. (2010). Genetics of human social behavior. *Neuron, 65*, 831–844.

Ebstein, R. P., Novick, O., Umansky, R., Priel, B., Osher, Y., Blaine, D., ... Belmaker, R. H. (1996). Dopamine *D4* receptor *D4DR* exon III polymorphism associated with the human personality trait of novelty seeking. *Nature Genetics, 12*, 78–80.

Edelman, S., Lemon, J., Bell, D. R., & Kidman, A. D. (1999). Effects of group CBT on the survival time of patients with metastatic breast cancer. *Psychooncology, 8*, 474–481.

Eder, P., & Eisenberger, R. (2008). Perceived organizational support: Reducing the negative influence of coworker withdrawal behavior. *Journal of Management, 34*, 55–68.

Edmonds, C. V., Lockwood, G. A., & Cunningham, A. J. (1999). Psychological response to long-term therapy: A randomized trial with metastatic breast cancer patients. *Psychooncology, 8*, 74–91.

Edwards, J. H. (2002). Evidenced-based treatment for child ADHD: "Real-world" practice implications. *Journal of Mental Health Counseling, 24*, 126–139.

Edwards, V. J., Holden, G. W., Felitti, V. J., & Anda, R. F. (2003). Relationship between multiple forms of childhood maltreatment and adult mental health in community respondents: Results from the adverse childhood experiences study. *American Journal of Psychiatry, 160*, 1453–1460.

Eftekhar, A., Fullwood, C., & Morris, N. (2014). Capturing personality from Facebook photos and photo-related activities: How much exposure do you need? *Computers in Human Behavior, 37*, 162–170. Available at http://doi.org/10.1016/j.chb.2014.04.048

Ehsani, J., Li, K., & Simons-Morton, B. (2015). Teenage drivers portable electronic device use while driving. *The National Academies of Sciences, Engineering Medicine*, 219–225.

Eichenbaum, H. (2010). Memory systems. *WIREs Cognitive Science, 1*, 478–490.

Eisenberger, N. I., Jarcho, J. M., Lieberman, M. D., & Naliboff, B. D. (2006). An experimental study of shared sensitivity to physical pain and social rejection. *Pain, 126*, 132–138.

Eisenberger, N. I. (2013). The pain of social disconnection: Examining the shared neural underpinnings of physical and social pain. *Nature Reviews Neuroscience.* Advance online publication at doi: 10.1038/nrn3231

Eisenberger, R., & Cameron, J. (1996). Detrimental effects of reward: Reality or myth? *American Psychologist, 51*, 1153–1166.

Eisenberger, R., Rhoades, L., & Cameron, J. (1999). Does pay for performance increase or decrease perceived self-determination and intrinsic motivation? *Journal of Personality and Social Psychology, 77*, 1026–1040.

Eisenberger, R., Shanock, L., & Williams, K. D. (2003). Rewards, intrinsic motivation and creativity: A case study of methodological and conceptual isolation. *Creativity Research Journal, 15*, 121–130.

Eisenberger, R., Stinglhamber, F., Vandenberghe, C., Sucharski, I., & Rhoades, L. (2002). Perceived supervisor support: Contributions to perceived organizational support and employee retention. *Journal of Applied Psychology, 87*, 565–573.

Ekman, P. (1972). Universals and cultural differences in facial expressions of emotion. In J. Cole (Ed.), *Nebraska Symposium on Motivation 1971, Vol. 19* (pp. 207–283). Lincoln: University of Nebraska Press.

Ekman, P. (1973). Cross-cultural studies of facial expression. In *Darwin and facial expression: A century of research in review* (pp. 169–222). New York, NY: Academic Press.

Ekman, P. (1984). Expression and the nature of emotion. In K. R. Scherer & P. Ekman (Eds.), *Approaches to emotion* (pp. 319–343). Hillsdale, NJ: Erlbaum.

Ekman, P. (1992). An argument for basic emotions. *Cognition & Emotion, 6*, 169–200.

Ekman, P. (2003). *Emotions revealed*. New York, NY: Holt.

Ekman, P., Davidson, R. J., & Friesen, W. V. (1990). The Duchenne smile: Emotional expression and brain physiology II. *Journal of Personality and Social Psychology, 58*, 342–353.

Ekman, P., & Friesen, W. V. (1969). The repertoire of nonverbal behavior—Categories, origins, usage, and coding. *Semiotica, 1*, 49–98.

Ekman, P., & Friesen, W. V. (1971). Constants across cultures in the face and emotion. *Journal of Personality and Social Psychology, 17*, 124–129.

Ekman, P., & Friesen, W. V. (1978). *The Facial Action Coding System*. Palo Alto, CA: Consulting Psychologists Press.

Ekman, P., Friesen, W. V., & Hager, J. (2002). *The facial action coding system* (2nd ed.). Salt Lake City, UT: Research Nexus.

Ekman, P., Friesen, W. V., O'Sullivan, M., Chan, A., Diacoyanni-Tarlatzis, I., ... Heider, K. (1987). Universals and cultural differences in the judgments of facial expressions of emotion. *Journal of Personality and Social Psychology, 53*, 712–717.

Ekman, P., Levenson, R. W., & Friesen, W. V. (1983). Autonomic nervous system activity distinguishes among emotions. *Science, 221*(4616), 1208–1210. doi: 10.1126/science.6612338

Ekman, P., & O'Sullivan, M. (1991). Who can catch a liar? *American Psychologist, 46*, 913–920.

Ekman, P., & O'Sullivan, M. (2006). From flawed self-assessment to blatant whoppers: The utility of voluntary and involuntary behavior in detecting deception. *Behavioral Sciences & The Law, 24*(5), 673–686. doi: 10.1002/bsl.729

Ekman, P., O'Sullivan, M., & Frank, M. G. (1999). A few can catch a liar. *Psychological Science, 10*, 263–266.

Ekman, P., & Rosenberg, E. L. (Eds.). (2005). *What the face reveals: Basic and applied studies of spontaneous facial expression using the Facial Action Coding System (FACS)* (2nd ed.). New York, NY: Oxford University Press.

Ekman, P., Sorenson, E. R., & Friesen, W. V. (1969). Pan-cultural elements in facial displays of emotion. *Science, 164*, 86–88.

Elaut, E., Buysse, A., De Sutter, P., Gerris, J., De Cuypere, G., & T'Sjoen, G. (2016). Cycle-related changes in mood, sexual desire, and sexual activity in oral contraception-using and nonhormonal-contraception-using couples. *Journal of Sex Research, 53*(1), 125–136. doi:10.1080/00224499.2014.976780

Elbert, T., Pantev, C., Wienbruch, C., Rockstroh, B., & Taub, E. (1995). Increased cortical representation of the fingers of the left hand in string players. *Science, 270*, 305–307.

Ellason, J. W., Ross, C. A., & Fuchs, D. L. (1996). Lifetime Axis I and Axis II comorbidity and childhood trauma history in dissociative identity disorder. *Psychiatry, 59*, 255–266.

Ellickson, P. L., Orlando, M., Tucker, J. S., & Klein, D. J. (2004). From adolescence to young adulthood: Racial/ethnic disparities in smoking. *American Journal of Public Health, 94*, 293–299.

Ellickson, P. L., Tucker, J. S., & Klein, D. J. (2001). Sex differences in predictors of adolescent smoking cessation. *Health Psychology, 20*, 186–195.

Ellis, E., & Ames, M. A. (1987). Neurohormonal functioning and sexual orientation: A theory of heterosexuality-homosexuality. *Psychological Bulletin, 101*, 233–258.

Ellsworth, P. C., & Scherer, K. R. (2003). Appraisal processes in emotion. In R. J. Davidson, K. R. Scherer, & H. Goldsmith (Eds.), *Handbook of affective sciences* (pp. 572–595). New York, NY: Oxford University Press.

Elman, J. L., Bates, E. A., Johnson, M. H., Karmiloff-Smith, A., Parisi, D., & Plunkett, K. (1996). *Rethinking innateness: A connectionist perspective on development*. Cambridge, MA: MIT Press.

Elms, A. (1993). *Uncovering lives: The uneasy alliance between biography and psychology*. New York, NY: Oxford University Press.

Elsey, J., & Kindt, M. (2016). Manipulating human memory through reconsolidation: Ethical implications of a new therapeutic approach. *AJOB Neuroscience, 7*(4), 225–236. doi: 10.1080/21507740.2016.1218377

Emery, R. A. (2006). Holland codes, careers, and college majors. Retrieved from http://www.hollandcodes.com/support-files/su-careers-majors-and-model.pdf

Emmons, R. A., & McCullough, M. E. (2003). Counting blessings versus burdens: An experimental investigation of gratitude and subjective well-being in daily life. *Journal of Personality and Social Psychology, 84*, 377–389. doi: 10.1037/0022-3514.84.2.377

Empana, J. P., Sykes, D. H., Luc, G., Juhan-Vague, I., Arveiler, D., Ferrieres, J., ... Ducimetiere, P. (2005). Contributions of depressive mood and circulating inflammatory markers to coronary heart disease in healthy European men: The Prospective Epidemiological Study of Myocardial Infarction (PRIME). *Circulation, 111*, 2299–2305.

Emsell, L., Van Hecke, W., & Tournier, J. D. (2016). Introduction to diffusion tensor imaging. In *Diffusion Tensor Imaging* (pp. 7–19). New York: Springer.

Engel, A. K., Debener, S., & Kranczioch, C. (2006, August). Coming to attention. *Scientific American Mind, 17*, 46–53.

Engelberg, J. K., Hill, L. L., Rybar, J., & Styer, T. (2015). Distracted driving behaviors related to cell phone use among middle-aged adults. *Journal of Transport and Health, 2*, 434–440. doi: 10.1016/j.jth.2015.05.002

Enzinger, C., Fazekas, F., Matthews, P. M., Ropele, S., Schmidt, H., Smith, S., & Schmidt, R. (2005). Risk factors for progression of brain atrophy in aging: Six-year follow-up of normal subjects. *Neurology, 64*, 1704–1711.

Epel, E. S., Blackburn, E. H., Lin, J., Dhabhar, F. S., Adler, N. E., & Morrow, J. D. (2004). Accelerated telomere shortening in response to life stress. *Proceedings of the National Academy of Sciences, 101*, 17312–17315. doi: 10.1073/pnas.0407162101

Epel, E. S., McEwen, B., Seeman, T., Matthews, K., Castellazzo, G., Brownell, K. D., ... Ickovics, J. R. (2000). Stress and body shape: Stress-induced cortisol secretion is consistently greater among women with central fat. *Psychosomatic Medicine, 62*, 623–632.

Erdelyi, M. (2010). The ups and downs of memory. *American Psychologist, 65*, 623–633. doi: 10.1037/a0020440

Erikson, E. H. (1968). *Identity: Youth and crisis*. New York, NY: Norton.

Erikson, E. H. (1982). *The life-cycle completed: A review*. New York, NY: Norton.

Eriksson, P. S., Perfilieva, E., Bjork-Eriksson, T., Alborn, A. M., Nordborg, C., Peterson, D. A., & Gage, F. H. (1998). Neurogenesis in the adult human hippocampus. *Nature Medicine, 4*, 1313–1317.

Eroglu, C., & Barres, B. A. (2010, November 11). Regulation of synaptic connectivity by glia. *Nature, 468*, 223–231.

Esshili, A., Thabet, S., Jemli, A., Trifa, F., Mechri, A., Zaafrane, F., ... & Jrad, B. B. H. (2016). Toxoplasma gondii infection in schizophrenia and associated clinical features. *Psychiatry Research, 245*, 327–332. Available at http://dx.doi.org/10.1016/j.psychres.2016.08.056

Etcoff, N. (1999). *Survival of the prettiest*. New York, NY: Anchor Books.

Etkin, A., Egner, T., & Kalish, R. (2011). Emotional processing in anterior cingulate and medial prefrontal cortex. *Trends in Cognitive Science, 15*, 85–93.

Evans, L. M., Akiskal, H. S., Greenwood, T. A., Nievergelt, C. M., Keck, P. E., McElroy, S. L., ... Kelso, J. R. (2007). Suggestive linkage of a chromosomal locus on 18p11 to cyclothymic temperament in bipolar disorder families. *American Journal of Medical Genetics, 147B*, 326–332.

Evans, S., Ferrando, S., Findler, M., Stowell, C., Smart, C., & Haglin, D. (2008). Mindfulness-based cognitive therapy for generalized anxiety disorder. *Journal of Anxiety Disorders, 22*, 716–721.

Everett, D. L. (2005). Cultural constraints on grammar and cognition in Piraha: Another look at the design features of human language. *Current Anthropology, 46*, 621–646.

Evrensel, A., & Ceylan, M. E. (2015). The gut-brain axis: The missing link in depression. *Clinical Psychopharmacology and Neuroscience, 13*(3), 239. Available at https://doi.org/10.9758/cpn.2015.13.3.239

Exaptations. (2006). Retrieved November 28, 2007, from http://evolution.berkeley.edu/evosite/evo101/IIIE5cExaptations.shtml

Exelmans, L., Custers, K., & Van den Bulck, J. (2015). Violent video games and delinquent behavior in adolescents: A risk factor perspective. *Aggressive Behavior, 41*, 267–279. doi: 10.1002/ab.21587

Exner, J. E., Jr. (1974). *The Rorschach: A comprehensive system.* New York, NY: Wiley.

Extraordinary people—The boy who sees without eyes. (2007, May 7). [Video file]. From the 2003 television series *Extraordinary People.* Retrieved from http://www.youtube.com/watch?v=qLziFMF4DHA

Eysenck, H. J. (1947). *Dimensions of personality.* London, England: Routledge & Kegan Paul.

Eysenck, H. J. (1980). *The causes and effects of smoking.* London, England: Temple Smith.

Eysenck, H. J. (1982). *Personality, genetics, and behavior: Selected papers.* New York, NY: Praeger.

Eysenck, H. J. (1990). Biological dimensions of personality. In L. A. Pervin (Ed.), *Handbook of personality: Theory and research* (pp. 244–276). New York, NY: Guilford Press.

Eysenck, H. J. (1995). *Genius: The natural history of creativity.* Cambridge, England: Cambridge University Press.

Eysenck, H. J. (1997). Personality and experimental psychology: The unification of psychology and the possibility of a paradigm. *Journal of Personality and Social Psychology, 73,* 1224–1237.

Facione, P. A. (1990). *Critical thinking: A statement of expert consensus for purposes of educational assessment and instruction—The Delphi report.* Millbrae: California Academic Press.

Faigman, D. L., Fienberg, S. E., & Stern, P. C. (2003). The limits of the polygraph. *Issues in Science and Technology, 20,* no. 1. (Fall 2003).

Faith, M. A., Fiala, S. E., Cavell, T. A., & Hughes, J. N. (2011). Mentoring highly aggressive children: Pre–post changes in mentors' attitudes, personality, and attachment tendencies. *Journal of Primary Prevention, 32*(5–6), 253–270. doi: 10.1007/s10935-011-0254-8

Falk, E. B., Spunt, R. P., & Lieberman, M. D. (2012). Ascribing beliefs to ingroup and outgroup political candidates: Neural correlates of perspective-taking, issue importance and days until the election. *Phil. Trans. R. Soc. B, 367*(1589), 731–743. doi:10.1098/rstb.2011.0302

Fallgatter, A. J., Ehlis, A.-C., Herrmann, M. J., Hohoff, C., Reif, A., Freitag, C. M., & Deckert, J. (2010). DTNBP1 (dysbindin) gene variants modulate prefrontal brain function in schizophrenic patients—Support for the glutamate hypothesis of schizophrenias. *Genes, Brain and Behavior, 9,* 489–497.

Famous people with the gift of dyslexia. (2013, April 2). Retrieved January 7, 2014, from Davis Dyslexia Association International, Dyslexia the Gift web site: http://www.dyslexia.com/famous.htm

Famy, C., Streissguth, A. P., & Unis, A. S. (1998). Psychological disorder in adults with fetal alcohol syndrome or fetal alcohol effects. *Journal of Pediatric Psychology, 155,* 552–554.

Fancher, R. E. (1985). *The intelligence men: Makers of the IQ controversy.* New York, NY: Norton.

Fancher, R. E. (1996). *Pioneers of psychology* (3rd ed.). New York, NY: Norton.

Fantz, R. L. (1963). Pattern vision in newborn infants. *Science, 140,* 296–297.

Farb, N., Anderson, A., Mayberg, H., Bean, J., McKeon, D., & Segal, Z. (2010). Minding one's emotions: Mindfulness training alters the neural expression of sadness. *Emotion, 10,* 25–33. doi: 10.1037/a0017151

Farber, N. B., & Olney, J. W. (2003). Drugs of abuse that cause developing neurons to commit suicide. *Developmental Brain Research, 147,* 37–45.

Fardouly, J., Diedrichs, P. C., Vartanian, L. R., & Halliwell, E. (2015). Social comparisons on social media: The impact of Facebook on young women's body image concerns and mood. *Body Image, 13,* 38–45. Available at http://doi.org/10.1016/j.bodyim.2014.12.002

Fazel, S., & Danesh, J. (2002). Serious mental disorder in 23,000 prisoners: A systematic review of 62 surveys. *The Lancet, 359,* 545–550.

Feinberg, M., Willer, R., & Keltner, D. (2012). Flustered and faithful: Embarrassment as a signal of prosociality. *Journal of Personality and Social Psychology, 102,* 81–97. doi: 10.1037/a0025403

Feist, G. J. (1993). A structural model of scientific eminence. *Psychological Science, 4,* 366–371.

Feist, G. J. (1998). A meta-analysis of the impact of personality on scientific and artistic creativity. *Personality and Social Psychological Review, 2,* 290–309.

Feist, G. J. (1999). Personality in scientific and artistic creativity. In R. J. Sternberg (Ed.), *Handbook of human creativity* (pp. 273–296). Cambridge, England: Cambridge University Press.

Feist, G. J. (2004). Creativity and the frontal lobes. *Bulletin of Psychology and the Arts, 5,* 21–28.

Feist, G. J. (2006b). *The psychology of science and the origins of the scientific mind.* New Haven, CT: Yale University Press.

Feist, G. J. (2016). Intrinsic and extrinsic science: A dialectic of scientific fame. *Perspectives on Psychological Science, 11,* 893–895.

Feist, G. J., & Barron, F. X. (2003). Predicting creativity from early to late adulthood: Intellect, potential and personality. *Journal of Research in Personality, 37,* 62–88.

Feist, G. J., Bodner, T. E., Jacobs, J. F., Miles, M., & Tan, V. (1995). Integrating top-down and bottom-up structural models of subjective well-being: A longitudinal investigation. *Journal of Personality and Social Psychology, 68,* 138–150.

Feist, J., Feist, G. J., & Roberts, T. A. (2013). *Theories of personality* (8th ed.). New York, NY: McGraw-Hill.

Feldman, D. H. (2004). Child prodigies: A distinctive form of giftedness. In R. J. Sternberg (Ed.), *Definition and conceptions of giftedness* (pp. 133–144). Thousand Oaks, CA: Corwin Press.

Feldman-Barrett, L., Tugade, M. M., & Engle, R. W. (2004). Individual differences in working memory capacity and dual-process theories of mind. *Psychological Bulletin, 130,* 553–573.

Felt, L. J., & Robb, M. B. (2016). *Technology addiction: Concern, controversy, and finding balance.* San Francisco, CA: Common Sense Media.

Feng, X., Shaw, D. S., Kovacs, M., Lane, T., O'Rourke, F. E., & Alarcon, J. H. (2008). Emotion regulation in preschoolers: The roles of behavioral inhibition, maternal affective behavior, and maternal depression. *Journal of Child Psychology and Psychiatry, 49,* 132–141.

Feng, Z., Hu, W., Hu, Y., & Teng, M. (2006). Acrolein is a major cigarette-related lung cancer agent: Preferential binding at *p53* mutational hotspots and inhibition of DNA repair. *Proceedings of the National Academy of Sciences, 103,* 15404–15409.

Fenson, L., Dale, P., Reznick, J. S., Bates, E., Thal, D. J., & Pethick, S. (1994). Variability in early communicative development. *Monographs of the Society for Research in Child Development, 59* (5, Serial No. 242).

Ferguson, C. (2016, December 19). Breakdown: Inside the messy world of anonymous therapy app Talkspace. *The Verge.* Retrieved online from http://www.theverge.com/2016/12/19/14004442/talkspace-therapy-app-reviews-patient-safety-privacy-liability-online

Ferguson, C. J., & Kilburn, J. (2009). The public health risks of media violence: A meta-analytic review. *Journal of Pediatrics, 154,* 759–763.

Ferguson, C. J., & Kilburn, J. (2010). Much ado about nothing: The misestimation and overinterpretation of violent video game effects in Eastern and Western nations: Comment on Anderson et al. (2010). *Psychological Bulletin, 136,* 174–178.

Fergusson, D., Doucette, S., Glass, K. C., Shapiro, S., Healy, D., ... Hebert, P. (2005). Association between suicide attempts and selective serotonin reuptake inhibitors: Systematic review of randomized controlled trials. *British Medical Journal, 330,* 396–402.

Fergusson, L., Horwood, J., & Ridder, E. M. (2005). Tests of causal linkages between cannabis use and psychotic symptoms. *Addiction, 100,* 354–366.

Fernald, A. (1992). Human maternal vocalizations to infants as biologically relevant signals: An evolutionary perspective. In J. Barkow, L. Cosmides, & J. Toody (Eds.), *The adapted mind: Evolutionary psychology and the generation of culture* (pp. 391–428). New York, NY: Oxford University Press.

Fernald, A., & Morikawa, H. (1993). Common themes and cultural variations in Japanese and American mothers' speech to infants. *Child Development, 64,* 637–656.

Fernandes, M. A., & Moscovitch, M. (2000). Divided attention and memory: Evidence of substantial interference effects at retrieval and encoding. *Journal of Experimental Psychology: General, 129*(2), 155–176.

Fernandes, M. A., Wammes, J. D., Priselac, S., & Moscovitch, M. (2016). Interfering with free recall of words: Detrimental effects of phonological competition. *Neuropsychologia, 90,* 59–71. doi: 10.1016/j.neuropsychologia.2016.05.009

Ferrucci, R., Mamell, F., Guidi, I., Mrakic-Sposta, I., Vergari, M., Marceglia, S., ... Priori, A. (2008). Transcranial direct current stimulation improves recognition memory in Alzheimer disease. *Neurology, 71,* 493–498.

Ferster, C. B., & Skinner, B. F. (1957). *Schedules of reinforcement.* Englewood Cliffs, NJ: Prentice-Hall.

Festinger, L. (1957). *A theory of cognitive dissonance.* Stanford, CA: Stanford University.

Festl, R., & Quandt, T. (2016). The role of online communication in long-term cyberbullying involvement among girls and boys. *Journal of Youth and Adolescence, 45*(9), 1931–1945. Available at http://doi.org/10.1007/s10964-016-0552-9

Fiedorowicz, J., & Swartz, K. (2004). The role of monoamine oxidase inhibitors in current psychiatric practice. *Journal of Psychiatric Practice, 10,* 239–248.

Field, T. M., Hernandez-Reif, M., Diego, M., Feijo, L., Vera, Y., & Gil, K. (2004). Massage therapy by parents improves early growth and development. *Infant Behavior and Development, 27,* 435–442.

Field, T. M., Schanberg, S. M., Scafidi, F., Bauer, C. R., Vega-Lahr, N., Garcia, R., ... Kuhn, C. M. (1986). Tactile/kinesthetic stimulation effects on preterm neonates. *Pediatrics, 77,* 654–658.

Fields, H. L. (2005). *Pain: Mechanisms and management.* New York, NY: McGraw-Hill.

Fields, H. L. (2009, September/October). The psychology of pain. *Scientific American Mind,* 42–49.

Fields, R. D. (2005). Making memories stick. *Scientific American, 292,* 75–81.

Fields, R. D. (2008). White matter matters. *Scientific American, 298,* 54–61.

Figee, M., Luigjes, J., Smolders, R., Valencia-Alfonso, C. E., Van Wingen, G., De Kwaasteniet, B., ... & Levar, N. (2013). Deep brain stimulation restores frontostriatal network activity in obsessive-compulsive disorder. *Nature neuroscience, 16*(4), 386–387. doi:10.1038/nn.3344

Filimon, F., Nelson, J. D., Hagler, D. J., & Sereno, M. I. (2007). Human cortical representations for reaching: Mirror neurons for execution, observation, and imagery. *NeuroImage, 37,* 1315–1328.

Finger, S. (1994). *Origins of neuroscience: A history of explorations into brain function.* New York, NY: Oxford University Press.

Fink, A., Slamar-Halbedl, M., Unterrainer, H. F., & Weiss, E. M. (2012). Creativity: Genius, madness, or a combination of both? *Psychology of Aesthetics, Creativity, and the Arts, 6,* 11–18. doi: 10.1037/a0024874

Fink, M. (2006). ECT in therapy-resistant mania: Does it have a place? *Bipolar Disorders, 8,* 307–309.

Finke, R. A., Ward, T. B., & Smith, S. M. (1992). *Creative cognition: Theory, research and applications.* Cambridge, MA: MIT Press.

Fischer, A. H., & Manstead, A. S. R. (2000). Gender differences in emotion across cultures. In A. H. Fischer (Ed.), *Emotion and gender: Social psychological perspectives* (pp. 91–97). London, England: Cambridge University Press.

Fischer, D. B., Boes, A. D., Demertzi, A., Evrad, H. C., Laureys, S., Edlow, B., ...Pascual-Leone, A. (2016). A human brain network derived from coma-causing brainstem lesions. *Neurology,* Published online before print November 4, 2016. doi: http://dx .doi.org/10.1212/WNL.0000000000003404

Fischer, G. G. (2004). Should I order an EEG? An overview of electroencephalography in the hospital setting at Gundersen Lutheran Medical Center. *Gundersen Lutheran Medical Journal, 3,* 26–29.

Fisher, J. E., Mohanty, A., Herrington, J. D., Koven, N. S., Miller, G. A., & Heller, W. (2004). Neuropsychological evidence for dimensional schizotypy: Implications for creativity and psychopathology. *Journal of Research in Personality, 38,* 24–31.

Fitch, G. A., Soccolich, S. A., Guo, F., McClafferty, J., Fang, Y., Olson, R. L., Perez, M. A., Hanowski, R. J., Hankey, J. M., & Dingus, T. A. (2013, April). *The impact of hand-held and hands-free cell phone use on driving performance and safety-critical event risk.* (Report No. DOT HS 811 757). Washington, DC: National Highway Traffic Safety Administration.

Fitzgerald, K. D., Welsh, R. C., Gehrig, W. J., Abelson, J. L., Himle, J. A., Liberzon, I., & Taylor, S. F. (2005). Error-related hyperactivity of the anterior cingulate cortex in obsessive-compulsive disorder. *Biological Psychiatry, 57,* 287–294.

Fitzgerald, M. (2004). *Autism and creativity.* Hove, England: Brunner-Routledge.

Fitzgerald, P. B., Benitez, J., de Castella, A. R., Daskalakis, Z. J., & Kulkarni, J. (2006). Naturalistic study of the use of transcranial magnetic stimulation in the treatment of depressive

relapse. *Australian and New Zealand Journal of Psychiatry, 40,* 764–768.

Flaherty, M. (2005). Gender differences in mental rotation ability in three cultures: Ireland, Ecuador and Japan. *Psychologia: An International Journal of Psychology in the Orient, 48,* 31–38.

Flammer, E., & Bongartz, W. (2003). On the efficacy of hypnosis: A meta-analytic study. *Contemporary Hypnosis, 20,* 179–197.

Flegal, K. M., Carroll, M. D., Ogden, C. L., & Curtin, L. R. (2010). Prevalence and trends in obesity among U.S. adults, 1999–2008. *Jama, 303*(3), 235–241. doi: 10.1001/jama.2009.2014

Flege, J. E. (1999). Age of learning and second language speech. In D. Birdsong (Ed.), *Second language acquisition and the critical period hypothesis* (pp. 101–131). Mahwah, NJ: Erlbaum.

Flege, J. E., Munro, M. J., & MacKay, I. R. A. (1995a). Effects of age of second-language learning on the production of English consonants. *Speech Communication, 16,* 1–26.

Flege, J. E., Munro, M. J., & MacKay, I. R. A. (1995b). Factors affecting strength of perceived foreign accent in a second language. *Journal of the Acoustical Society of America, 97,* 2540–2551.

Flegr, J., & Horáček, J. (2017). Toxoplasma-infected subjects report an obsessive-compulsive disorder diagnosis more often and score higher in obsessive-compulsive inventory. *European Psychiatry, 40,* 82–87. Available at http://dx.doi .org/10.1016/j.eurpsy.2016.09.001

Fleischer, J., Breer, H., & Strotmann, J. (2009). Mammalian olfactory receptors. *Frontiers in Cellular Neuroscience, 3,* 1–10.

Flora, S. R., & Polenick, C. A. (2013). Effects of sugar consumption on human behavior and performance. *The Psychological Record, 63,* 513–524.

Foa, E. B., Dancu, C. V., Hembree, E. A., Jaycox, L. H., Meadows, E. A., & Street, G. P. (1999). A comparison of exposure therapy, stress inoculation training, and their combination for reducing posttraumatic stress disorder in female assault victims. *Journal of Consulting and Clinical Psychology, 67,* 194–200.

Foa, E. B., Hembree, E. A., Cahill, S. P., Rauch, S. A., Riggs, D. S., Feeny, N. C., & Yadin, E. (2005). Randomized trial of prolonged exposure for PTSD with and without cognitive restructuring: Outcome at academic and community clinics. *Journal of Consulting and Clinical Psychology, 73,* 953–964.

Fodor, E. M., & Laird, B. A. (2004). Therapeutic intervention, bipolar inclination, and literary creativity. *Creativity Research Journal, 16,* 149–161.

Foerde, K., Knowlton, B., & Poldrack, R. (2006). Modulation of competing memory systems by distraction. *Proceedings of the National Academy of Sciences, 103,* 11778–11783.

Fogassi, L., & Ferrari, P. F. (2006). Mirror neurons and the evolution of embodied language. *Current Directions in Psychological Science, 16,* 136–141.

Foley, K. E. (2016). Ideas in movement: The next wave of brain-computer interfaces. *Nature Medicine, 22*(1), 2–5. doi:10.1038/nm0116-2

Folkman, S. (1997). Positive psychological states and coping with severe stress. *Social Science and Medicine, 45,* 1207–1221.

Folkman, S., & Moskowitz, J. T. (2000). Positive affect and the other side of coping. *American Psychologist, 55,* 647–654.

Folley, B. S., & Park, S. (2005). Verbal creativity and schizotypal personality in relation to prefrontal hemispheric laterality: A behavioral and

near-infrared optical imaging study. *Schizophrenia Research, 80,* 271–282.

Fong-Torres, B. (2010, April 25). Tom Petty: "Go after what you love." An interview. *Parade Magazine.*

Fonteille, V., & Stoléru, S. (2011). The cerebral correlates of sexual desire: Functional neuroimaging approach, *Sexologies, 20,* 142–148. Available at http://dx.doi.org/10.1016/j .sexol.2010.03.011

Ford, B. Q., & Mauss, I. B. (2015). Culture and emotion regulation. *Current Opinion in Psychology, 3,* 1–5. Available at http://dx.doi.org/10.1016/j .copsyc.2014.12.004

Ford, C., & Beach, F. (1951). *Patterns of sexual behavior.* New York, NY: Harper & Row.

Ford, D. (2008). Intelligence testing and cultural diversity: The need for alternative instruments, policies, and procedures. In J. L. VanTessa-Baska (Ed.), *Alternative assessments with gifted and talented students* (pp. 107–128). Waco, TX: Prufrock Press.

Ford, E. S., Cunningham, T. J., Giles, W. H., & Croft, J. B. (2015). Trends in insomnia and excessive daytime sleepiness among U.S. adults from 2002 to 2012. *Sleep Medicine, 16*(3), 372–378. Retrieved from http://dx.doi.org/10.1016/j .sleep.2014.12.008

Forgas, J. P. (2016). Can sadness be good for you? *Australian Psychologist.* doi: 10.1111/ap.12232

Forgeard, M., Winner. E., Norton, A., & Schlaug, G. (2008). Practicing a musical instrument in childhood is associated with enhanced verbal ability and nonverbal reasoning. *PLoS One, 3,* e3566.

Fossum, I. N., Nordnes, L. T., Storemark, S. S., Bjorvatn, B., & Pallesen, S. (2014). The association between use of electronic media in bed before going to sleep and insomnia symptoms, daytime sleepiness, morningness, and chronotype. *Behavioral Sleep Medicine, 12,* 343–357. doi: 10.1080/15402002.2013.819468

Foster, J. A., & McVey Neufeld, K. A. (2013). Gut-brain axis: How the microbiome influences anxiety and depression. *Trends in Neurosciences, 36*(5), 305–312. Available at http://doi.org/10.1016 /j.tins.2013.01.005

Fothergill, E., Guo, J., Howard, L., Kerns, J. C. Knuth, N. D. Brychta R., ... Hall, K. D. (2016). Persistent metabolic adaptation 6 years after "The Biggest Loser" competition. *Obesity, 24,* 1612–1619. doi: 10.1002/oby.21538

Foulkes, D. (1996). Dream research: 1953–1993. *Sleep: Journal of Sleep Research & Sleep Medicine, 19,* 609–624.

Fournier, J. C., DeRubeis, R. J., Hollon, S. D., Dimidjian, S., Amsterdam, J. D., Shelton, R. C., & Fawcett, I. (2010). Antidepressant drug effects and depression severity: Patient-level meta-analysis. *Journal of the American Medical Association, 303,* 47–53.

Fouts, R. S. (1997). *Next of kin: My conversations with chimpanzees.* New York, NY: Avon.

Fouts, R. S., Fouts, D. H., & Schoenfeld, D. (1984). Sign language conversational interaction between chimpanzees. *Sign Language Studies, 42,* 1–12.

Fowler, J. H., & Christakis, N. A. (2010). Cooperative behavior cascades in human social networks. *Proceedings of the National Academy of Sciences, 107,* 5334–5338.

Fraga, M. F., Ballestar, E., Paz, M. F., Ropero, S., Setien, F. Ballestar, M. L., ... Esteller, M. (2005). Epigenetic differences arise during the lifetime of monozygotic twins. *Proceedings of the*

National Academy of Sciences, 102, 10604–10609. doi: 10.1073/pnas.0500398102

Franco, O. H., de Laet, C., Peeters, A., Jonker, J., Mackenbach, J., & Nusselder, W. (2005). Effects of physical activity on life expectancy with cardiovascular disease. *Archives of Internal Medicine, 165,* 2355–2360.

Frank, M. G., & Ekman, P. (1997). The ability to detect deceit generalizes across different types of high stakes lies. *Journal of Personality and Social Psychology, 72,* 1429–1439.

Fraser, L. A., Liu, K., Naylor, K. L., Hwang, Y. J., Dixon, S. N., Shariff, S. Z., & Garg, A. X. (2015). Falls and fractures with atypical antipsychotic medication use: A population-based cohort study. *JAMA Internal Medicine, 175*(3), 450–452. doi: 10.1001/jamainternmed.2014.6930

Fratiglioni, L., Winblad, B., & von Strauss, E. (2007). Prevention of Alzheimer's disease and dementia. Major findings from the Kungsholmen Project. *Physiology & Behavior, 92,* 98–104.

Fredrickson, B. L. (1998). What good are positive emotions? *Review of General Psychology, 2,* 300–319.

Fredrickson, B. L. (2001). The role of positive emotions in positive psychology: The broaden-and-build theory of positive emotions. *American Psychologist, 56,* 218–226.

Fredrickson, B. L. (2016). The eudaimonics of positive emotions. In *Handbook of eudaimonic well-being* (pp. 183–190). Springer International Publishing. doi: 10.1007/978-3-319-42445-3_12

Fredrickson, B. L., Cohn, M. A., Coffey, K. A., Pek, J., & Finkel, S. M. (2008). Open hearts build lives: Positive emotions, induced through loving-kindness meditation, build consequential personal resources. *Journal of Personality and Social Psychology, 95*(5), 1045. doi: 10.1037/a0013262

Fredrickson, B. L., & Levenson, R. W. (1998). Positive emotions speed recovery from the cardiovascular sequelae of negative emotions. *Cognition & Emotion, 12,* 191–220.

Fredrickson, B. L., & Losada, M. F. (2005). Positive affect and the complex dynamics of human flourishing. *American Psychologist, 60*(7), 678–686. doi: 10.1037/0003-066X.60.7.678.

Fredrickson, B. L., Tugade, M. M., Waugh, C. E., & Larkin, G. R. (2003). What good are positive emotions in crises? A prospective study of resilience and emotions following the terrorist attacks on the United States on September 11th, 2001. *Journal of Personality and Social Psychology, 84,* 365–376.

Freeman, H., Brosnan, S., Hopper, L., Lambeth, S., Schapiro, S., & Gosling, S. (2013). Developing a comprehensive and comparative questionnaire for measuring personality in chimpanzees using a simultaneous top-down/bottom-up design. *American Journal of Primatology, 75,* 1042–1053.

Fregni, F., Boggio, P. S., Nitsche, M., Bermpohl, F., Antal, A., Feredoes, E., ... Pascual-Leone, A. (2005). Anodal transcranial direct current stimulation of the prefrontal motor cortex enhances working memory. *Brain Research, 166,* 23–30. doi: 10.1007/s00221-005-2334-6

French, S. E., Seidman, E., Allen, L., & Aber, J. L. (2006). The development of ethnic identity during adolescence. *Developmental Psychology, 42,* 1–10.

French-Belgian Collaborative Group. (1982). Ischemic heart disease and psychological patterns: Prevalence and incidence studies in Belgium and France. *Advances in Cardiology, 29,* 25–31.

Freud, A. (1946). *The ego and the mechanisms of defense.* New York, NY: International Universities Press.

Freud, S. (1953). The interpretation of dreams. In J. Strachey (Ed. & Trans.), *The standard edition of the complete works of Sigmund Freud* (Vols. 4 & 5). London, England: Hogarth Press. (Original work published 1900)

Freud, S. (1959). *Inhibitions, symptoms, and anxiety.* In J. Strachey (Ed. & Trans.), *Standard edition of the complete works of Sigmund Freud* (Vol. 20). London, England: Hogarth Press. (Original work published 1926.)

Freud, S. (1960). *Psychopathology of everyday life.* In J. Strachey (Ed. & Trans.), *Standard edition of the complete works of Sigmund Freud* (Vol. 6). London, England: Hogarth Press. (Original work published 1901)

Freud, S. (1964). *New introductory lectures on psychoanalysis.* In J. Strachey (Ed. & Trans.), *The standard edition of the complete works of Sigmund Freud* (Vol. 22). London, England: Hogarth Press. (Original work published 1933)

Freund, A., & Ritter, J. (2009). Midlife crisis: A debate. *Gerontology, 55,* 582–591. doi: 10.1159/000227322

Fridlund, A. J., Beck, H. P., Goldie, W. D., & Irons, G. (2012). Little Albert: A neurologically impaired child. *History of Psychology. 15,* 302–327. doi: 10.1037/a0026720

Friedman, J. M., & Halaas, J. L. (1998). Leptin and the regulation of body weight in mammals. *Nature, 395,* 763–770. doi: 10.1038/27376

Friesen, W. V. (1972). *Cultural differences in facial expressions in a social situation: An experimental test of the concept of display rules.* Unpublished doctoral dissertation, University of California, San Francisco.

Frijda, N. H. (1986). *The emotions.* Cambridge, England: Cambridge University Press.

Frith, U., & Frith, C. (2010). The social brain: Allowing humans to boldly go where no other species has been. *Philosophical Translations of the Royal Society B: Biological Sciences, 365,* 165–176.

Frokjaer, V. B., Vinberg, M., Erritzoe, D., Svarer, C., Baare, W., Budtz-Joergensen, E., ... Knudsen, G. M. (2009). High familial risk for mood disorder is associated with low dorsolateral prefrontal cortex serotonin transporter binding. *NeuroImage, 46,* 360–366.

Frost, R. O., & Steketee, G. (2010). *Stuff: Compulsive hoarding and the meaning of things.* Boston, MA: Houghton Mifflin.

Fuhrman, O., Mccormick, K., Chen, E., Jiang, H., Shu, D., Mao, S., & Boroditsky, L. (2011). How linguistic and cultural forces shape conceptions of time: English and Mandarin time in 3D. *Cognitive Science, 35*(7), 1305–1328. Available at http://doi.org/10.1111/j.1551-6709.2011.01193.x

Fuller, J. L., & Thompson, W. R. (1960). *Behavior genetics.* New York, NY: Wiley.

Furnham, A., & Bachtiar, V. (2008). Personality and intelligence as predictors of creativity. *Personality and Individual Differences, 45,* 613–617.

Furuichi, T. (1983). Interindividual distance and influence of dominance on feeding in a natural Japanese macaque troop. *Primates, 24,* 445–455.

Furumoto, L. (1981). Mary Whiton Calkins (1863–1930). *Psychology of Women Quarterly, 5,* 55–68. doi: 10.1111/j.1471-6402.1981.tb01033.x

Fuster, J. M. (1999). Cognitive functions of the frontal lobes. In B. L. Miller & J. L. Cummings (Eds.), *The human frontal lobes: Functions and disorders* (pp. 187–195). New York, NY: Guilford Press.

Fuster, J. M. (2002). Frontal lobe and cognitive development. *Journal of Neurocytology, 31,* 373–385.

Gage, F. H. (2002). Neurogenesis in the adult brain. *Journal of Neuroscience, 22,* 612–613.

Gage, F. H., Kemperman, G., & Song, H. (Eds.). (2008). *Adult neurogenesis.* Cold Spring Harbor, NY: Cold Spring Harbor Laboratory Press.

Galak, J., LeBoeuf, R. A., Nelson, L. D., & Simmons, J. P. (2012). Correcting the past: Failures to replicate psi. *Journal of Personality and Social Psychology, 103*(6), 933–948. doi:10.1037/a0029709

Galanter, E. (1962). Contemporary psychophysics. In R. Brown (Ed.), *New directions in psychology* (pp. 87–157). New York, NY: Holt, Rinehart & Winston.

Gale, A. (1983). Electroencephalographic studies of extraversion-introversion: A case study in the psychophysiology of individual differences. *Personality and Individual Differences, 4,* 371–380.

Galin, D. (1994). The structure of awareness: Contemporary applications of William James' forgotten concept of "The Fringe." *Journal of Mind and Behavior, 15,* 375–402.

Gallagher, A. M., & Kaufman, J. C. (2005). *Gender differences in mathematics: An integrative psychological approach.* New York, NY: Cambridge University Press.

Gallagher, M., & Lopez, S. (2007). Curiosity and well-being. *Journal of Positive Psychology, 2*(4), 236–248.

Gallagher, R. M., & Rosenthal, L. J. (2008). Chronic pain and opiates: Balancing pain control and risks in long-term opioid treatment. *Archives of Physical Medicine and Rehabilitation, 89*(Suppl. 1), S77–S82.

Gallinat, J., McMahon, K., Kühn, S., Schubert, F., & Schaefer, M. (2016). Cross-sectional study of glutamate in the anterior cingulate and hippocampus in schizophrenia. *Schizophrenia Bulletin, 42*(2), 425–433. doi: https://doi.org/10.1093/schbul/sbv124

Ganasen, K., Ipser, J., & Stein, D. (2010). Augmentation of cognitive behavioral therapy with pharmacotherapy. *Psychiatric Clinics of North America, 33,* 687–699. doi: 10.1016/j.psc.2010.04.008

Ganepy, J- F., Watson, K. K., Du, E., Xie, D. L., Erb, J., Amasino, D., & Platt, M. L. (2015). Social learning in humans and other animals., *Frontiers in Neuroscience, 8,* 152–199.

Ganis, G., Thompson, W., & Kosslyn, S. (2009). Visual mental imagery: More than "seeing with the mind's eye." In J. R. Brockmole (Ed.), *The visual world in memory* (pp. 215–249). New York, NY: Psychology Press.

Garcia, J., Kimeldorf, D. J., & Koelling, R. A. (1955). A conditioned aversion towards saccharin resulting from exposure to gamma radiation. *Science, 122,* 157–159.

Garcia, J., & Koelling, R. A. (1966). The relation of cue to consequence in avoidance learning. *Psychonomic Science, 4,* 123–124.

Garcia, J., McGowan, B. K., & Green, K. F. (1972). Biological constraints on conditioning. In A. H. Black & W. F. Prokasy (Eds.), *Classical conditioning II: Current research and theory* (pp. 3–27). New York, NY: Appleton-Century-Crofts.

Garcia-Bailo, B., Toguri, C., Eny, K. M., & El-Sohemy, A. (2009). Genetic variation in taste and its influence on food selection. *OMICS: A Journal of Integrative Biology, 13,* 69–80.

García-Cabezas, M. Á., & Barbas, H. (2016). Anterior cingulate pathways may affect emotions through orbitofrontal cortex. *Cerebral Cortex.* doi: 10.1093/cercor/bhw284

Garcia-Rizo, C., Fernandez-Egea, E., Miller, B. J., Oliveira, C., Justicia, A., Griffith, J. K., ... Kirkpatrick, B. (2013). Abnormal glucose tolerance, white blood cell count, and telomere length in newly diagnosed, antidepressant-naive patients with depression. *Brain, Behavior, and Immunity, 28,* 49–53. Available at http://dx.doi.org/10.1016/j.bbi.2012.11.009

Garcia-Sierra, A., Rivera-Gaxiola, M., Percaccio, C. R., Conboy, B. T., Romo, H., Klarman, L., ... Kuhl, P. K. (2011). Bilingual language learning: An ERP study relating early brain responses to speech, language input, and later word production. *Journal of Phonetics, 39*(4), 546–557. Available at http://doi.org/10.1016/j.wocn.2011.07.002

Gardner, H. (1980). *Artful scribbles: The significance of children's drawings.* New York, NY: Basic Books.

Gardner, H. (1983). *Frames of mind: The theory of multiple intelligences.* New York, NY: Basic Books.

Gardner, H. (1987). *The mind's new science: A history of the cognitive revolution.* New York, NY: Basic Books.

Gardner, H. (1993). *Frames of mind: The theory of multiple intelligences* (2nd ed.). New York, NY: Basic Books.

Gardner, H. (1999). *Intelligence reframed: Multiple intelligences for the 21st century.* New York, NY: Basic Books.

Gardner, R. A., Gardner, B. T., & Van Cantfort, T. E. (Eds.). (1989). *Teaching sign language to chimpanzees.* Albany, NY: SUNY Press.

Garland, S. N., Zhou, E. S., Gonzalez, B. D., & Rodriguez, N. (2016). The quest for mindful sleep: A critical synthesis of the impact of mindfulness-based interventions for insomnia. *Current Sleep Medicine Reports.* e-pub ahead of print: doi: 10.1007/s40675-016-0050-3

Garrett, R. K., & Danziger, J. N. (2008). IM = Interruption management? Instant messaging and disruption in the workplace. *Journal of Computer-Mediated Communication, 13,* 23–42.

Garrett, R. K., Weeks, B. E., & Neo, R. L. (2016). Driving a wedge between evidence and beliefs: How online ideological news exposure promotes political misperceptions. *Journal of Computer-Mediated Communication, 21*(5), 33–1348. doi: 10.1111/jcc4.12164

Gates, G. (2011). How many people are lesbian, gay, bisexual and transgender? Retrieved on October 12, 2016 at http://williamsinstitute.law.ucla.edu/wp-content/uploads/Gates-How-Many-People-LGBT-Apr-2011.pdf

Gates, M. F., & Allee, W. C. (1933). Conditioned behavior of isolated and grouped cockroaches on a simple maze. *Journal of Comparative Psychology, 15,* 331–358.

Gathercole, V. C. M., & Hoff, E. (2007). Input and the acquisition of language: Three questions. In E. Hoff & M. Shatz (Eds.), *The handbook of language development* (pp. 107–127). Oxford, England: Blackwell.

Gazdzinski, S., Durazzo, T. C., & Meyerhoff, D. J. (2005). Temporal dynamics and determinants of whole brain tissue volume changes during recovery from alcohol dependence. *Drug and Alcohol Dependence, 78,* 263–273.

Geary, D., & DeSoto, M. C. (2001). Sex differences in spatial abilities among adults in the United States and China. *Evolution and Cognition, 7,* 172–177.

Gebara, C. M., Barros-Neto, T. P. D., Gertsenchtein, L., & Lotufo-Neto, F. (2016). Virtual reality exposure using three-dimensional images for the treatment of social phobia. *Revista Brasileira de Psiquiatria, 38*(1), 24–29. doi: 10.1590/1516-4446-2014-1560

Gebicke-Haerter, P. J. (2012). Epigenetics of schizophrenia. *Pharmacopsychiatry, 45*(Suppl. 1), S42–S48.

Geerlings, S. W., Beekman, A., Deeg, D., Twisk, J., & van Tilburg, W. (2002). Duration and severity of depression predict mortality in older adults in the community. *Psychological Medicine, 32,* 609–618.

Georges, E. (1995). A cultural and historical perspective on confession. In J. W. Pennebaker (Ed.), *Emotion, disclosure, and health* (pp. 11–22). Washington, DC: American Psychological Association.

Georgiadis, J. R., Kortekaas, R., Kuipers, R., Nieuwenburg, A., Pruim, J., Simone Reinders, A. A. T., & Holstege, G. (2006). Regional cerebral blood flow changes associated with clitorally induced orgasm in healthy women. *European Journal of Neuroscience, 24,* 3305–3316.

Gerber, M., Endes, K., Brand, S., Herrmann, C., Colledge, F., Donath, L., ... Zahner, L. (2017). In 6- to 8-year-old children, hair cortisol is associated with body mass index and somatic complaints, but not with stress, health-related quality of life, blood pressure, retinal vessel diameters, and cardiorespiratory fitness. *Psychoneuroendocrinology, 76,* 1–10. Available at http://dx.doi.org/10.1016/j.psyneuen.2016.11.008

Gershberg, F. B., & Shimamura, A. P. (1995). The role of the frontal lobes in the use of organizational strategies in free recall. *Neuropsychologia, 13,* 1305–1333.

Gervain, J., Vines, B. W., Chen, L. M., Seo, R. J., Hensch, T. K., Werker, J. F., & Young, A. H. (2013). Valproate reopens critical-period learning of absolute pitch. *Frontiers in Systems Neuroscience, 7*(December), 1–11. http://doi.org/10.3389/fnsys.2013.00102

Geschwind, N., Peeters, F., Huibers, M., van Os, J., & Wichers, M. (2012). Efficacy of mindfulness-based cognitive therapy in relation to prior history of depression: Randomised controlled trial. *British Journal of Psychiatry, 201,* 320–325. doi: 10.1192/bjp.bp.111.104851

Getzmann, S., Golob, E. J., & Wascher, E. (2016). Focused and divided attention in a simulated cocktail-party situation: ERP evidence from younger and older adults. *Neurobiology of Aging, 41,* 138–149.

Gibson, E., & Walk, R. (1960). The visual cliff. *Scientific American, 202,* 64–71.

Gibson, J. J. (1950). *The perception of the visual world.* Boston, MA: Houghton Mifflin.

Gibson, J. J. (1966). *The senses considered as perceptual systems.* Boston, MA: Houghton Mifflin.

Gibson, L. E., & Hensley, C. (2013). The social construction of sexuality in prison. *The Prison Journal, 93*(3), 355–370. Available at http://doi.org/10.1177/0032885513490503

Giedd, J. N., Blumenthal, J., Jeffries, N. O., Castellanos, F. X., Liu, H., Zijdenbos, A., Paus, T., Evans, A. C., & Rapoport, J. L. (1999). Brain development during childhood and adolescence: A longitudinal MRI study. *Nature Neuroscience, 2,* 861–863.

Giles, G. E., Mahoney, C. R., Brunye, T. T., Gardony, A. L., Taylor, H. A., & Kanarek, R. B. (2012). Differential cognitive effects of energy drink ingredients: Caffeine, taurine, and glucose. *Pharmacology, Biochemistry, and Behavior, 102,* 569–577.

Gillespie, N. A., Cloninger, C. R., Heath, A. C., & Martin, N. G. (2003). The genetic and environmental relationship between Cloninger's dimensions of temperament and character. *Personality and Individual Differences, 35,* 1931–1946.

Gillham, J. E., Reivich, K. J., Freres, D. R., Chaplin, T. M., Shatté, A. J., Samuels, B., ... Martin, E. P. (2007). School-based prevention of depressive symptoms: A randomized controlled study of the effectiveness and specificity of the Penn Resiliency Program. *Journal of Consulting and Clinical Psychology, 75,* 9–19.

Giltay, E. J., Geleijnse, J. M., Zitman, F. G., Hoekstra, T., & Schouten, E. G. (2004). Dispositional optimism and all-cause andcardiovascular mortality in a prospective cohort of elderly Dutch men and women. *Archives of General Psychiatry, 61,* 1126–1135.

Giuliani, N. R., Drabant, E. M., & Gross, J. J. (2010). Anterior cingulate cortex volume and emotion regulation: Is bigger better? *Biological Psychology, 86,* 379–382.

Givón, T. (2002). The visual information-processing system as an evolutionary precursor of human language. In T. Givón & B. F. Malle (Eds.), *The evolution of language out of pre-language* (pp. 3–50). Amsterdam, Netherlands: John Benjamins.

Gjerde, P. F., & Cardilla, K. (2009). Developmental implications of openness to experience in preschool children: Gender differences in young adulthood. *Developmental Psychology, 45,* 1455–1464.

Glaser, R., & Kiecolt-Glaser, J. K. (2005). Stress-induced immune dysfunction: Implications for health. *Nature Reviews Immunology, 4,* 243–251.

Glasper, E. R., Leuner, B., & Gould, E. (2008). Adult neurogenesis finds its niche. *Nature Neuroscience, 11,* 708–731.

Glassman, A., & Shapiro, P. (1998). Depression and the course of coronary artery disease. *American Journal of Psychiatry, 155,* 4–11.

Gneezy, U., Meier, S., & Rey-Biel, P. (2011). When and why incentives (don't) work to modify behavior. *Journal of Economic Perspectives, 25,* 1–21.

Goel, V., & Vartanian, O. (2005). Dissociating the roles of right ventral lateral and dorsal lateral prefrontal cortex in generation and maintenance of hypotheses in set-shift problems. *Cerebral Cortex, 15,* 1170–1177.

Goff, D. C., & Coyle, J. T. (2001). The merging role of glutamate in the pathophysiology and treatment of schizophrenia. *American Journal of Psychiatry, 158,* 1367–1377.

Goglin, S. E., Farzaneh-Far, R., Epel, E. S., Lin, J., Blackburn, E. H., & Whooley, M. A. (2016). Change in leukocyte telomere length predicts mortality in patients with stable coronary heart disease from the Heart and Soul Study. *PloS ONE, 11*(10), e0160748.

Goldapple, K., Segal, Z., Garson, C., Lau, M., Bieling, P., Kennedy, S., & Mayberg, H. (2004). Modulation of cortical-limbic pathways in major depression. *Archives of General Psychiatry, 61,* 34–41.

Goldfield, B. A. (2000). Nouns before verbs in comprehension vs. production: The view from pragmatics. *Journal of Child Language, 27,* 501–520.

Goldin, P., McRae, K., Ramel, W., & Gross, J. J. (2008). The neural bases of emotion regulation: Reappraisal and suppression of negative emotion. *Biological Psychiatry, 63,* 577–586.

Goldman-Rakic, P. S. (1999). The physiological approach: Functional architecture of working memory and disordered cognition in schizophrenia. *Biological Psychiatry, 46,* 650–661.

Goldsmith, T. H. (2006). What birds see. *Scientific American, 295,* 69–75.

Goldstein, E. B. (2007). *Sensation and perception* (7th ed.). Belmont, CA: Thomson-Wadsworth.

Goldstein, L. A., Dinh, J., Donalson, R., Hebenstreit, C. L., & Maguen, S. (2017). Impact of military trauma exposures on posttraumatic stress and depression in female veterans. *Psychiatry Research.* Available at http://linkinghub.elsevier.com/retrieve/pii/S0165178116311787

Goldstein, T., Bridge, J., & Brent, D. (2008). Sleep disturbance preceding completed suicide in adolescents. *Journal of Consulting and Clinical Psychology, 76*(1), 84–91.

Goleman, D. P. (1995). *Emotional intelligence: Why it can matter more than IQ for character, health and lifelong achievement.* New York, NY: Bantam Books.

Golier, J. A., Caramanica, K., & Yehuda, R. (2012). Neuroendocrine response to CRF stimulation in veterans with and without PTSD in consideration of war zone era. *Psychoneuroendocrinology, 37,* 350–357. doi: 10.1016/j.psyneuen.2011.07.004

Gonzalez, V., & Mark, G. (2004). "Constant, constant, multi-tasking craziness": Managing multiple working spheres. *Proceedings of ACM CHI'04,* 113–120.

Goodwin, P., McGill, B., & Chandra A. (2009). *Who marries and when? Age at first marriage in the United States, 2002.* NCHS data brief No. 19. Hyattsville, MD: National Center for Health Statistics.

Goodwin, P. J. (2004). Support groups in breast cancer: When a negative result is positive. *Journal of Clinical Oncology, 22,* 4244–4246.

Goodwin, P. J., Leszcz, M., Ennis, M., Koopmans, J., Vincent, L., Guther, H., … Hunter, J. (2001). The effect of group psychosocial support on survival in metastatic breast cancer. *New England Journal of Medicine, 345,* 1719–1726.

Gopnik, A. (2009). *The philosophical baby.* New York, NY: Farrar, Straus & Giroux.

Gopnik, A., Meltzoff, A. N., & Kuhl, P. K. (1999). *The scientist in the crib: Minds, brains, and how children learn.* New York, NY: Morrow.

Gordon, P. (2004). Numerical cognition without words: Evidence from Amazonia. *Science, 306,* 496–499.

Gorenstein, E. E., & Comer, R. J. (2002). *Case Studies in Abnormal Psychology.* New York: Worth.

Görlach, M. G., Kohlmann, S., Shedden-Mora, M., Rief, W., & Westermann, S. (2016). Expressive suppression of emotions and overeating in individuals with overweight and obesity. *European Eating Disorders Review.* doi: 10.1002/erv.2452

Goshen, I. (2014). The optogenetic revolution in memory research. *Trends in Neurosciences, 37*(9), 511–522. http://doi.org/10.1016/j.tins.2014.06.002

Gosling, S. D., & John, O. P. (1999). Personality dimensions in non-human animals: A cross-species review. *Current Directions in Psychological Science, 8,* 69–75.

Gotink, R. A., Meijboom, R., Vernooij, M. W., Smits, M., & Hunink, M. G. M. (2016). 8-week mindfulness based stress reduction induces brain changes similar to traditional long-term meditation practice—A systematic review. *Brain and Cognition, 108,* 32–41. doi: 10.1016/j.bandc.2016.07.001

Goto, H. (1971). Auditory perception by normal Japanese adults of the sounds "l" and "r." *Neuropsychologia, 9,* 317–323.

Gottfredson, L. (1997). Mainstream science on intelligence: An editorial with 52 signatories, history, and bibliography. *Intelligence, 24,* 13–23.

Gottlieb, G. (1991). Experiential canalization of behavioral development: Theory. *Developmental Psychology, 27*(1), 4–13. doi: 10.1037/0012-1649.27.1.4

Gottlieb, N. H., & Green, L. W. (1984). Life events, social network, life-style, and health: An analysis of the 1979 National Survey of Personal Health Practices and Consequences. *Health Education Quarterly, 11,* 91–105.

Gottschalk, S. (2010). The presentation of avatars in Second Life: Self and interaction in social virtual spaces. *Symbolic Interaction, 33,* 501–525.

Gough, H. G., & Bradley, P. (1996). *California psychological inventory manual* (3rd ed.). Palo Alto, CA: Consulting Psychologists Press.

Gould, E., Vail, N., Wagers, M., & Gross, C. G. (2001). Adult-generated hippocampal and neocortical neurons in macaques have a transient existence. *Proceedings of the National Academy of Sciences, 98,* 10910–10917.

Gould, S. J. (1981). *The mismeasure of man.* New York, NY: Norton.

Gould, S. J., & Vrba, E. S. (1982). Exaptation: A missing term in the science of form. *Paleobiology, 8,* 4–15.

Gow, A., Whiteman, M., Pattie, A., Whalley, L., Starr, J., & Deary, I. (2005). Lifetime intellectual function and satisfaction with life in old age: Longitudinal cohort study. *British Medical Journal, 331*(7509), 141–142. doi: 10.1136/bmj.38531.675660.F7

Graff, J., & Mansury, I. M. (2008). Epigenetic codes in cognition and behavior. *Behavioural Brain Research, 192,* 70–87.

Grafman, J., Schwab, K., Warden, D., Pridgeon, A., Brown, H. R., & Salazar, A. M. (1996). Frontal lobe injuries, violence, and aggression: A report of a Vietnam head injury study. *Neurology, 46,* 1231–1238.

Graham, S., & Lowery, B. S. (2004). Priming unconscious racial stereotypes about adolescent offenders. *Law and Human Behavior, 28,* 483–504.

Graner, J., Oakes, T. R., French, L. M., & Riedy, G. (2013). Functional MRI in the investigation of blast-related traumatic brain injury. *Frontiers in Neurology, 4 MAR*(March), 1–18. Available at http://doi.org/10.3389/fneur.2013.00016

Grant, A. M., & Hoffman, D. A. (2011). It's not all about me: Motivating hand hygiene among health care professionals by focusing on patients. *Psychological Science, 22,* 1494–1499. doi: 10.1177/0956797611419172

Grant, B. F., Hasin, D. S., Stinson, F. S., Dawson, D. A., Goldstein, R. B., Smith, S., … Saha, T. D. (2006). The epidemiology of *DSM-IV-TR* panic disorder and agoraphobia in the United States: Results from the National Epidemiologic Survey on Alcohol and Related Conditions. *Journal of Clinical Psychiatry, 67,* 363–374.

Grant, J. A., Courtemanche, J., Duerden, E. G., Duncan, G. H., & Rainville, P. (2010). Cortical thickness and pain sensitivity in Zen meditators. *Emotion, 10,* 43–53.

Gray, J. A. (1970). The psychophysiological basis of introversion-extraversion. *Behaviour Research and Therapy, 8,* 249–266.

Gray, J. A. (1987). Perspectives on anxiety and impulsivity: A commentary. *Journal of Research in Personality, 21,* 493–509.

Gray, J. L., & Thompson, P. (2004). Neurobiology of intelligence: Science and ethics. *Nature Reviews: Neuroscience, 5,* 471–482.

Graziano, M. S. (2016). Ethological action maps: A paradigm shift for the motor cortex. *Trends in Cognitive Sciences, 20*(2), 121–132. Available at http://dx.doi.org/10.1016/j.tics.2015.10.008

Green, D., & Swets, J. (1974). *Signal detection theory and psychophysics.* Melbourne, FL: Krieger.

Green, V. A., & Cillessen, A. H. N. (2008). Achievement versus maintenance of control in six-year-old children's interactions with peers: An observational study. *Educational Psychology, 28,* 161–180.

Greenberg, G. (2013, September 3). The psychiatric drug crisis. *The New Yorker.* Retrieved September 15, 2013, from http://www.newyorker.com/online/blogs/elements/2013/09/psychiatry-prozac-ssri-mental-health-theory-discredited.html?utm_source=ny&utm_campaign=generalsocial&utm_medium=facebook&mobify=0

Greenberg, L. (1979). Genetic component of bee odor in kin recognition. *Science, 206,* 1095–1097.

Greenberg, M. T., & Kusché, C. A. (1998). *Promoting alternative thinking strategies.* Boulder: University of Colorado, Institute of Behavioral Sciences.

Greenberg, S., Shuman, D. W., & Meyer, R. G. (2004). Unmasking forensic diagnosis. *International Journal of Law and Psychiatry, 27,* 1–15. doi: 10.1016/j.ijlp.2004.01.001.PMID 15019764

Greenemeier, L. (2013, June). Real world. *Scientific American, 308,* 24.

Greengross, G., Martin, R. A., & Miller, G. (2012). Personality traits, intelligence, humor styles, and humor production ability of professional stand-up comedians compared to college students. *Psychology of Aesthetics, Creativity, and the Arts, 6,* 74–82. doi: 10.1037/a0025774

Greenough, W. T., Volkmar, F. R., & Juraska, J. M. (1973). Effects of rearing complexity on dendritic branching in fronto-lateral and temporal cortex of the rat. *Experimental Neurology, 41,* 371–378.

Greenwald, A. G. (2009, March). Interview by ScienceWatch [Web]. Retrieved from http://sciencewatch.com/inter/aut/2009/09-mar/09marGreen/

Greenwald, A. G., McGhee, D. E., & Schwartz, J. L. K. (1998). Measuring individual differences in implicit cognition: The implicit association test. *Journal of Personality and Social Psychology, 74,* 1464–1480.

Greenwald, A. G., Poehlman, T., Uhlmann, E., & Banaji, M. R. (2009). Understanding and using the Implicit Association Test: III. Meta-analysis of predictive validity. *Journal of Personality and Social Psychology, 97,* 17–41. doi: 10.1037/a0015575

Gregori, M., Taylor, M., Salvati, E., Fe, F., Mancini, S. Balducci, C., … Allsop, D. (2016). Retro-inverso peptide inhibitor nanoparticles as potent inhibitors of aggregation of the Alzheimer's Aβ peptide. *Nanomedicine: Nanotechnology, Biology, and Medicine.* Retrieved October 24, 2106, from http://dx.doi.org/10.1016/j.nano.2016.10.006

Gregory, R. J. (2007). *Psychological testing* (5th ed.). New York, NY: Allyn & Bacon.

Griffin, I. C., & Nobre, A. C. (2003). Orienting attention to locations in internal representations. *Journal of Cognitive Neuroscience, 15,* 1176–1194.

Available at http://dx.doi.org/10.1162/089892903322598139

Griffiths, R. R., Johnson, M. W., Carducci, M. A., Umbricht, A., Richards, W. A., Richards, B. D., ... & Klinedinst, M. A. (2016). Psilocybin produces substantial and sustained decreases in depression and anxiety in patients with life-threatening cancer: A randomized double-blind trial. *Journal of Psychopharmacology*, *30*(12), 1181–1197. doi: 10.1177/0269881116675513

Griffiths, R. R., Johnson, M. W., Richards, W. A., Richards, B. D., McCann, U., & Jesse, R. (2011). Psilocybin occasioned mystical-type experiences: Immediate and persisting dose-related effects. *Psychopharmacology*, *218*(4), 649–665.

Griffiths, R. R., Richards, W. A., Johnson, M. W., McCann, U. D., & Jesse, R. (2008). Mystical-type experiences occasioned by psilocybin mediate the attribution of personal meaning and spiritual significance 14 months later. *Journal of Psychopharmacology*, *22*(6), 621–632. doi: 10.1177/0269881108094300

Griffiths, R. R., Richards, W. A., McCann, U., & Jesse, R. (2006). Psilocybin can occasion mystical-type experiences having substantial and sustained personal meaning and spiritual significance. *Psychopharmacology*, *187*, 268–283.

Grigorenko, E. (2000). Heritability and intelligence. In R. J. Sternberg (Ed.), *Handbook of intelligence* (pp. 53–91). New York, NY: Cambridge University Press.

Grolnick, W. S., McMenamy, J. M., & Kurowski, C. O. (2006). Emotional self-regulation in infancy and toddlerhood. In L. Balter & C. S. Tamis-LeMonda (Eds.), *Child psychology: A handbook of contemporary issues* (2nd ed., pp. 3–25). New York, NY: Psychology Press.

Groome, L., Mooney, D., Holland, S., Smith, Y., Atterbury, J., & Dykman, R. (2000). Temporal pattern and spectral complexity as stimulus parameters for eliciting a cardiac orienting reflex in human fetuses. *Perception and Psychophysics*, *62*(2), 313–320.

Gross, C. G. (2000). Neurogenesis in the adult brain: Death of a dogma. *Nature Reviews Neuroscience*, *1*, 67–73.

Gross, J. J. (1998). The emerging field of emotion regulation: An integrative review. *Review of General Psychology*, *2*, 271–299.

Gross, J. J. (2002). Emotion regulation: Affective, cognitive, and social consequences. *Psychophysiology*, *39*, 281–291. doi: 10.1017/S0048577201393198

Gross, J. J., & Levenson, R. W. (1993). Emotional suppression—Physiology, self-report, and expressive behavior. *Journal of Personality and Social Psychology*, *64*, 970–986.

Gross, J. J., & Levenson, R. W. (1997). Hiding feelings: The acute effects of inhibiting positive and negative emotions. *Journal of Abnormal Psychology*, *106*, 95–103.

Gross, J. J., Richards, J. M., & John, O. P. (2006). Emotion regulation in everyday life. In D. K. Snyder, J. A. Simpson, & J. N. Hughes (Eds.), *Emotion regulation in families: Pathways to dysfunction and health* (pp. 13–35). Washington, DC: American Psychological Association.

Grossberg, S., & Vladusich, T. (2010). How do children learn to follow gaze, share joint attention, imitate their teachers, and use tools during social interactions? *Neural Networks*, *23*, 940–965.

Grossman, A. W., Churchill, J. D., McKinney, B. C., Kodish, I. M., Otte, S. L., & Greenough, W. T. (2003). Experience effects on brain development: Possible contributions to psychopathology. *Journal of Child Psychology and Psychiatry*, *44*, 33–63.

Grossman, P., Kappos, L., Gensicke, H., D'Souza, M., Mohr, D. C., Penner, I. K., & Steiner, C. (2010). MS quality of life, depression, and fatigue improve after mindfulness training. *Neurology*, *75*, 1141–1149.

Grossman, T., Striano, T., & Friederici, A. D. (2006). Crossmodal integration of emotional information from face and voice in the infant brain. *Developmental Science*, *9*, 309–315.

Guarnaccia, V., Dill, C. A., Sabatino, S., & Southwick, S. (2001). Scoring accuracy using the comprehensive system for the Rorschach. *Journal of Personality Assessment*, *77*, 464–474.

Guarraci, F. A., & Benson, A. (2005). "Coffee, tea and me": Moderate doses of caffeine affect sexual behavior in female rats. *Pharmacology, Biochemistry and Behavior*, *82*, 522–530.

Guastella, A. J., & Hickie, I. B. (2016). Oxytocin treatment, circuitry, and autism: A critical review of the literature placing oxytocin into the autism context. *Biological psychiatry*, *79*(3), 234–242. http://dx.doi.org/10.1016/j.biopsych.2015.06.028

Guehl, D., Benazzouz, A., Aouizerate, B., Cuny, E., Rotgé, J.-Y., ... Rougier, A. (2008). Neuronal correlates of obsessions in the caudate nucleus. *Biological Psychiatry*, *63*, 557–562.

Guilford, J. P. (1967). *The nature of human intelligence*. New York, NY: McGraw-Hill.

Guillem, K., & Peoples, L. (2010). Progressive and lasting amplification of accumbal nicotine-seeking neural signals. *Journal of Neuroscience*, *30*, 276–286.

Guilleminault, C., Kirisoglu, C., Bao, G., Arias, V., Chan, A., & Li, K. K. (2005). Adult chronic sleepwalking and its treatment based on polysomnography. *Brain*, *128*, 1062–1069.

Guiraud, A., deLorgeril, M., Zeghichi, S., Laporte, F., Salen, P., ... Saks, V. (2008). Interactions of ethanol drinking with n-3 fatty acids in rats: Potential consequences for the cardiovascular system. *British Journal of Nutrition*, 1–8. Advance online publication. Retrieved July 10, 2008. doi: 10.1017/S0007114508981472

Gunderson, E., Moline, J., & Catalano, P. (1997). Risks of developing noise-induced hearing loss in employees of urban music clubs. *American Journal of Industrial Medicine*, *31*, 75–79.

Güngör, D., Bornstein, M. H., De Leersnyder, J., Cote, L., Ceulemans, E., & Mesquita, B. (2013). Acculturation of personality: A three-culture study of Japanese, Japanese Americans, and European Americans. *Journal of Cross Cultural Psychology*, *44*, 701–718. doi: 10.1177/0022022112470749

Gupta, S., Agarwal, A., Banerjee, J., & Alvarez, J. G. (2007). The role of oxidative stress in spontaneous abortion and recurrent pregnancy loss: A systematic review. *Obstetrical, Gynecological Survey*, *62*, 335–347.

Gutteling, B. M., de Weerth, C., Willemsen-Swinkels, S. H. N., Huizink, A. C., Mulder, E. J. H., Visser, G. H. A., & Buitelaar, J. K. (2005). The effects of prenatal stress on temperament and problem behavior of 27-month-old toddlers. *European Child and Adolescent Psychiatry*, *14*, 41–51.

Haberstick, B. C., Boardman, J. D., Wagner, B., Smolen, A., Hewitt, J. K., Killeya-Jones, L. A., ... & Siegler, I. C. (2016). Depression, stressful life events, and the impact of variation in the serotonin transporter: Findings from the National Longitudinal Study of Adolescent to Adult Health (Add Health). *PloS ONE*, *11*(3), e0148373. Available at http://dx.doi.org/10.1371/journal.pone.0148373

Hadad, C. (2015, October 13). Why some 13-year-olds check social media 100 times a day. Retrieved online October 14, 2015 at http://www.cnn.com/2015/10/05/health/being-13-teens-social-media-study/

Hafetz, J. S., Jacobsohn, L. S., García-España, J., Curry, A. E., & Winston, F. K. (2010). Adolescent drivers' perceptions of the advantages and disadvantages of abstention from in-vehicle cell phone use. *Accident Analysis and Prevention*, *42*(6), 1570–1576. doi: 10.1016/j.aap.2010.03.015

Haidt, J., & Keltner, D. (1999): Culture and facial expression: Open-ended methods find more expressions and a gradient of recognition. *Cognition & Emotion*, *13*, 225–266.

Haier, R. J., Jung, R. E., Yeo, R. A., Head, K., & Alkire, M. T. (2004). Structural brain variation and general intelligence. *NeuroImage*, *23*, 425–433.

Hakuta, K., Bialystok, E., & Wiley, E. (2003). Critical evidence: A test of the critical-period hypothesis for second-language acquisition. *Psychological Science*, *14*, 31–38.

Hale, B., Seiser, L., & McGuire, E. J. (2005). Mental imagery. In J. Taylor & J. Wilson (Eds.), *Applying sport psychology: Four perspectives* (pp. 117–135). Champaign, IL: Human Kinetics.

Halevi-Katz, D. N., Yaakobi, E., Putter-Katz, H. (2015). Exposure to music and noise-induced hearing loss (NIHL) among professional pop/rock/jazz musicians. *Noise Health*, *17*, 158–164. Available at http://www.noiseandhealth.org/text.asp?2015/17/76/158/155848

Hall, J. A., & Matsumoto, D. (2004). Gender difference in the judgment of multiple emotions from facial expression. *Emotion*, *4*, 201–206.

Hall, K., & Brosnan, S. F. (2016). A comparative perspective on the evolution of moral behavior. In *The evolution of morality* (pp. 157–176). Springer International Publishing. doi: 10.1007/978-3-319-19671-8_8

Halpern, D. (2004). A cognitive-process taxonomy for sex differences in cognitive abilities. *Current Directions in Psychological Science*, *13*, 135–139.

Halpern, J. H., Pope, H. G., Sherwood, A. R., Barry, S., Hudson, J. I., & Yurgelun-Todd, D. (2004). Residual neuropsychological effects of illicit 3,4-methylenedioxymethamphet-amine (MDMA) in individuals with minimal exposure to other drugs. *Drug and Alcohol Dependence*, *75*, 135–147.

Hamann, S., Herman, R. A., Nolan, C. L., & Wallen, K. (2004). Men and women differ in amygdala response to visual sexual stimuli. *Nature Neuroscience*, *7*, 411–416.

Hamer, D., & Copeland, P. (1998). *Living with our genes*. New York, NY: Anchor Books.

Hamilton, W. D. (1964). The genetical evolution of social behaviour I and II. *Journal of Theoretical Biology*, *7*, 1–16, 17–52.

Hammer, A. L., & Macdaid, G. P. (1992). *Career report manual*. Palo Alto, CA: Consulting Psychologists Press.

Hampton, W. H., Unger, A., Von Der Heide, R. J., & Olson, I. R. (2016). Neural connections foster social connections: A diffusion-weighted imaging study of social networks. *Social Cognitive and Affective Neuroscience*, nsv153. 721–727. doi: 10.1093/scan/nsv153

Han, J. (2004). Acupuncture and endorphins. *Neuroscience Letters*, *361*, 258–261.

Hanafin, J. (2014). Multiple intelligences theory, action research, and teacher professional development: The Irish MI Project. *Australian Journal of Teacher Education*, *39*(4), 126–141. Available at http://doi.org/10.14221/ajte.2014v39n4.8

Haney, C., Banks, W. C., & Zimbardo, P. G. (1973). Interpersonal dynamics in a simulated prison. *International Journal of Criminology and Penology, 1*, 69–97.

Hankin, B. L. (2010). Personality and depressive symptoms: Stress generation and cognitive vulnerabilities to depression in a prospective daily diary study. *Journal of Clinical and Social Psychology, 29*, 369–401.

Hannigan, T. P. (1995). Body odor: The international student and cross-cultural communication. *Culture & Psychology, 1*, 497–503.

Hansen, R., Gartlehner, G., Webb, A. P., Morgan, L. C., Moore, C. G., & Jonas, D. E. (2008). Efficacy and safety of donepezil, galantamine, and rivastigmine for the treatment of Alzheimer's disease: A systematic review and meta-analysis. *Journal of Clinical Interventions in Aging, 3*, 211–225.

Hansen, R. A., Gartiehner, G., Lohr, K. N., & Daufer, D. (2007). Functional outcomes of drug treatment in Alzheimer's disease: A systematic review and meta-analysis. *Drugs & Aging, 24*(2), 155–167.

Harackiewicz, J. M., & Sansone, C. (1991). Goals and intrinsic motivation: You can get there from here. In M. L. Maehr & P. R. Pintrich (Eds.), *Advances in motivation and achievement: Goals and self-regulatory processes* (Vol. 7, pp. 21–49). Greenwich, CT: JAI Press.

Hare, R. D. (1993). *Without conscience: The disturbing world of the psychopaths among us.* New York, NY: Pocket Books.

Hargittai, E. (2008). Whose space? Differences among users and non-users of social network sites. *Journal of Computer-Mediated Communication, 13*, 276–297.

Hargrave, G. E., & Hiatt, D. (1989). Use of the California Psychological Inventory in law enforcement officer selection. *Journal of Personality Assessment, 53*, 267–277.

Hargrove, L. J., Simon, A. M., Lipschutz, R., Finucane, S. B., & Kuiken, T. A. (2013). Non-weight-bearing neural control of a powered transfemoral prothesis. *Journal of NeuroEngineering and Rehabilitation, 10*, 62. Retrieved from http://www.jneuroengrehab.com/content/10/1/62

Harkins, S. G. (1987). Social loafing and social facilitation. *Journal of Experimental Social Psychology, 23*, 1–18.

Harlow, H. (1958). The nature of love. *American Psychologist, 13*, 573–685.

Harmon, D. (2006). Free-radical theory of aging: An update. *Annals of the New York Academy of Sciences, 1067*, 10–21.

Harmon-Jones, E. (2003). Clarifying the emotive functions of asymmetrical frontal cortical activity. *Psychophysiology, 40*, 838–848.

Harris Interactive. (2008). Cell phone usage continues to increase. Retrieved October 18, 2013, from http://www.harrisinteractive.com/vault/Harris-Interactive-Poll-Research-Cell-Phone-Usage-Continues-to-Increase-2008-04.pdf

Harris, J. R. (1998). *The nurture assumption: Why children turn out the way they do.* New York, NY: Free Press.

Harris, M. B. (1974). Mediators between frustration and aggression in a field experiment. *Journal of Experimental Social Psychology, 10*, 561–571.

Harris, S., Kaplan, J. T., Curiel, A., Bookheimer, S. Y., Iacoboni, M., & Cohen, M. S. (2009). The neural correlates of religious and nonreligious belief. *PLoS One, 4*, e0007272. doi: 10.1371/journal.pone.0007272

Harris, S., Sheth, S. A., & Cohen, M. S. (2008). Functional neuroimaging of belief, disbelief, and uncertainty. *Annuals of Neurology, 63*, 141–147.

Harrison, P. J. (2004). The hippocampus in schizophrenia: A review of the neuropathological evidence and its pathophysiological implications. *Psychopharmacology, 174*, 151–162.

Harrison, P. J., & Owen, M. (2003). Genes for schizophrenia? Recent findings and their pathophysiological implications. *The Lancet, 361*, 417–419.

Harrison, P. J., & Weinberger, D. R. (2005). Schizophrenia genes, gene expression, and neuropathology: On the matter of their convergence. *Molecular Psychiatry, 10*, 40–68.

Hart, B., & Risley, T. R. (1992). American parenting of language-learning children: Persisting differences in family-child interactions observed in natural home environments. *Developmental Psychology, 28*(6), 1096–1105. doi: 10.1037/0012-1649.28.6.1096

Hart, B., & Risley, T. R. (1995). *Meaningful differences in the everyday experience of young American children.* Baltimore, MD: Paul H. Brooks.

Hartmann, P., Reuter, M., & Nyborga, H. (2006). The relationship between date of birth and individual differences in personality and general intelligence: A large-scale study. *Personality and Individual Differences, 40*, 1349–1362. doi:10.1016/j.paid.2005.11.017

Hartshorne, J. K., & Germine, L. T. (2015). When does cognitive functioning peak? The asynchronous rise and fall of different cognitive abilities across the life span. *Psychological Science, 26*(4), 433–443. Available at http://doi.org/10.1177/0956797614567339

Hasher, L., & Zacks, R. T. (1979). Automatic and effortful processes in memory. *Journal of Experimental Psychology: General, 108*, 356–388.

Haslam, S. A., & Reicher, S. D. (2012). Contesting the "nature" of conformity: What Milgram and Zimbardo's studies really show. *PLoS Biol, 10*, e1001426. doi: 10.1371/journal.pbio.1001426

Hauser, M. D., Chomsky, N., & Fitch, W. T. (2002). The faculty of language: What is it, who has it, and how did it evolve? *Science, 298*, 1569–1579.

Havard, A. (2016). Questions about the validity of the binge or heavy drinking criterion have implications for more than just treatment evaluation. *Addiction, 11*, 1733–1734.

Havas, D. A., Glenberg, A. M., Gutowski, K. A., Lucarelli, M. J., & Davidson, R. J. (2010). Cosmetic use of botulinum toxin-A affects processing of emotional language. *Psychological Science, 21*, 895–900.

Hawton, K., Comabella, C., Haw, C., & Saunders, K. (2013). Risk factors for suicide in individuals with depression: A systematic review. *Journal of Affective Disorders, 147*, 17–28.

Hayes, B. D., Klein-Schwartz, W., & Doyon, S. (2008). Toxicity of buprenorphine overdoses in children. *Pediatrics, 121*, 782–786.

Hayes, M., Van Stolk-Cooke, K., & Muench, F. (2015). Understanding Facebook use and the psychological affects of use across generations. *Computers in Human Behavior, 49*, 507–511. Available at http://doi.org/10.1016/j.chb.2015.03.040

Haynes, S. G., Levine, S., Scotch, N., Feinleib, M., & Kannel, W. B. (1978). The relationship of psychosocial factors to coronary heart disease in the Framingham Study. I. Methods and risk factors. *American Journal of Epidemiology, 107*, 362–383.

Hazan, C., & Shaver, P. (1987). Romantic love conceptualized as an attachment process. *Journal of Personality and Social Psychology, 52*, 511–524.

Hazlett, E. A. (2016). Neural substrates of emotion-processing abnormalities in borderline personality disorder. *Biological Psychiatry, 79*(2), 74–75. Available at http://dx.doi.org/10.1016/j.biopsych.2015.10.008

Headey, B. (2008). Life goals matter to happiness: A revision of set-point theory. *Social Indicators Research, 86*, 213–231.

Health and Human Services. (2004). *New surgeon general's report expands the list of diseases caused by smoking.* Retrieved August 19, 2008, from http://www.hhs.gov/news/press/2004pres/20040527a.html

Heath, R. G. (1975). Brain function and behavior. *Journal of Nervous and Mental Disease, 160*, 159–175.

Hebb, D. O. (1949). *The organization of behavior: A neuropsychological theory.* New York, NY: Wiley.

Hedden, T., & Gabrieli, J. D. E. (2004). Insights into the ageing mind: A view from cognitive neuroscience. *Nature Reviews Neuroscience, 5*, 87–96.

Hedges, L., & Nowell, A. (1995). Sex differences in mental test scores, variability, and numbers of high-scoring individuals. *Science, 269*, 41–45.

Hegelson, V. S., & Taylor, S. E. (1993). Social comparisons and adjustment among cardiac patients. *Journal of Applied Social Psychology, 23*, 1171–1195.

Heider, F. (1958). *The psychology of interpersonal relations.* New York, NY: Wiley.

Hennenlotter, A., Dresel, C., Castrop, F., Ceballos Baumann, A. O., Wohlschläger, A. M., & Haslinger, B. (2009). The link between facial feedback and neural activity within central circuitries of emotion—New insights from *Botulinum* toxin–induced denervation of frown muscles. *Cerebral Cortex, 19*, 537–542.

Henriques-Calado, J., Duarte-Silva, M. E., & Ferreira, A. S. (2016). Personality traits in women with Alzheimer's disease: Comparisons with control groups with the NEO-FFI. *Personality and Individual Differences, 101*, 341–347. doi:10.1016/j.paid.2016.06.024

Herdener, M., Esposito, F., di Salle, F., Boller, C., Hilti, C. C., Habermeyer, B., … Cattapan-Ludewig, K. (2010). Musical training induces functional plasticity in human hippocampus. *Journal of Neuroscience, 30*(4), 1377–1384. doi: 10.1523/JNEUROSCI.4513-09.2010

Hering, E. (1878). *Zur Lehre vom Lichtsinn.* Vienna, Austria: Gerold.

Herrington, J. D., Heller, W., Mohanty, A., Engels, A. S, Banich, M. T., Webb, A. G., & Miller, G. A. (2010). Localization of asymmetric brain function in emotion and depression. *Psychophysiology, 47*, 442–454.

Herrington, J. D., Miller, J. S., Pandey, J., & Schultz, R. T. (2016). Anxiety and social deficits have distinct relationships with amygdala function in autism spectrum disorder. *Social Cognitive and Affective Neuroscience, 11*(6), 907–914. doi: https://doi.org/10.1093/scan/nsw015

Herrnstein, R. J., & Murray, C. (1994). *The bell curve: Intelligence and class structure in American life.* New York, NY: Free Press.

Herz, R. (2004). A naturalistic analysis of autobiographical memories triggered by olfactory visual and auditory stimuli. *Chemical Senses, 29*, 217–224.

Hesse, E., & Main, M. (2006). Frightened, threatening, and dissociative parental behavior in low-risk samples: Description, discussion, and interpretations. *Development and Psychopathology, 18,* 309–343.

Hettema, J. M., Neale, M. C., & Kendler, K. S. (2001). A review and meta-analysis of the genetic epidemiology of anxiety disorders. *American Journal of Psychiatry, 158,* 1568–1578.

Heylens, G., De Cuypere G., & Zucker, K. J., Schelfaut, C., Elaut, E., Bossche, H. V. ... T'Sjoen, G. (2012). Gender identity disorder in twins: A review of the case report literature. *Journal of Sex Medicine, 9,* 751–757.

Hidi, S. (2016). Revisiting the role of rewards in motivation and learning: Implications of neuroscientific research. *Educational Psychology Review, 28*(1), 61–93. doi: 10.1007/s10648-015-9307-5

Hien, D. A., & Miele, G. M. (2003). Emotion-focused coping as a mediator of maternal cocaine abuse and antisocial behavior. *Psychology of Addictive Behaviors, 17,* 49–55.

Hilgard, E. (1965). *Hypnotic susceptibility.* New York, NY: Harcourt, Brace, & World.

Hilgard, E. (1977). *Divided consciousness: Multiple controls in human thought and action.* New York, NY: Wiley.

Hillman, C. H., Buck, S. M., Themanson, J. R., Pontifex, M. B., & Castelli, D. M. (2009). Aerobic fitness and cognitive development: Event-related brain potential and task performance indices of executive control in preadolescent children. *Developmental Psychology, 45,* 114–129.

Hillman, C. H., Erickson, K. I., & Kramer, A. F. (2008). Be smart, exercise your heart: Exercise effects on brain and cognition. *Nature Reviews Neuroscience, 9,* 58–65.

Hines, L. M., & Rimm, E. B. (2001). Moderate alcohol consumption and coronary heart disease: A review. *Postgraduate Medical Journal, 77,* 747–752.

Hines, M. (2010). Sex-related variation in human behavior and the brain. *Trends in Cognitive Sciences, 14*(10), 448–456. doi: 10.1016/j.tics.2010.07.005

Hines, M., Fane, B., Pasterski, V., Matthews, G., Conway, G., & Brook, C. (2003). Spatial abilities following prenatal androgen abnormality: Targeting and mental rotations performance in individuals with congenital adrenal hyperplasia. *Psychoneuroendocrinology, 28,* 1010–1026. doi: 10.1016/S0306-4530(02)00121-X

Hirsch, C. (2013). Ginkgo biloba extract did not reduce risk for Alzheimer disease in elderly patients with memory complaints. *Annals of Internal Medicine, 158* (2), JC7.

Hirshfeld-Becker, D. R., Masek, B., Henin, A., Blakely, L. R., Pollock-Wurman, R. A., McQuade, J., ... Biederman, J. (2010). Cognitive behavioral therapy for 4- to 7-year-old children with anxiety disorders: A randomized clinical trial. *Journal of Consulting and Clinical Psychology, 78,* 498–510.

Hirst, W., Phelps, E. A., Meksin, R., Vaidya, C. J., Johnson, M. K., Mitchell, K. J., ... Olsson, A. (2015). A ten-year follow-up of a study of memory for the attack of September 11, 2001: Flashbulb memories and memories for flashbulb events. *Journal of Experimental Psychology General, 144*(3), 604–623. Available at http://doi.org/10.1037/xge0000055

Hitchman, S. C., & Fong, G. T. (2011). Gender empowerment and female-to-male smoking prevalence ratios. *Bulletin of the World Health Organization, 89*(3), 195–202. doi: 10.2471/BLT.10.079905

Ho, Y.-C, Cheung, M.-C, & Chan, A. S. (2003). Music training improves verbal but not visual memory: Cross-sectional and longitudinal explorations in children. *Neuropsychology, 17,* 439–450.

Hobaiter, C., & Byrne, R. W. (2014). The meanings of chimpanzee gestures. *Current Biology, 24*(14), 1596–1600. Available at http://doi.org/10.1016/j.cub.2014.05.066

Hobaiter, C., Poisot, T., Zuberbühler, K., Hoppitt, W., & Gruber, T. (2014). Social network analysis shows direct evidence for social transmission of tool use in wild chimpanzees. *PLoS Biology, 12*(9). Available at http://doi.org/10.1371/journal.pbio.1001960

Hobson, H. M., & Bishop, D. V. (2016). Mu suppression–a good measure of the human mirror neuron system? *Cortex.* E-pub ahead of print. Available at http://dx.doi.org/10.1016/j.cortex.2016.03.019

Hobson, J. A. (2001). *The dream drugstore: Chemically altered states of consciousness.* Cambridge, MA: MIT Press.

Hobson, J. A. (2002). *Dreaming: An introduction to the science of sleep.* New York, NY: Oxford University Press.

Hochberg, L. R., Bacher, D., Jarosiewicz, B., Masse, N. Y., Simeral, J. D., Vogel, J., ... Donoghue, J. P. (2012). Reach and grasp by people with tetraplegia using a neurally controlled robotic arm. *Nature, 485,* 372–375. doi: 10.1038/nature11076

Hodgetts, W., Szarko, R., & Rieger, J. (2009). What is the influence of background noise and exercise on the listening levels of iPod users? *International Journal of Audiology, 48,* 825–832.

Hoff, E. (2006). How social contexts support and shape language development. *Developmental Review, 26,* 55–88.

Hoff, E., Core, C., Place, S., Rumiche, R., Senor, M., & Parra, M. (2012). Dual language exposure and early bilingual development. *Journal of Child Language, 39,* 1–27. doi: 10.1017/S0305000910000759

Hoffmann, H., Kessler, H., Eppel, T., Rukavina, S., & Traue, H. C. (2010). Expression intensity, gender and facial emotion recognition: Women recognize only subtle facial emotions better than men. *Acta Psychologica, 135,* 278–283.

Hofman, S. G., Schulz, S. M., Meuret, A. F., Moscovitch, D. A., & Suvak, M. (2006). Sudden gains during therapy of social phobia. *Journal of Consulting and Clinical Psychology, 74,* 687–697.

Hofstede, G. (2001). *Culture's consequences: Comparing values, behaviors, institutions, and organizations across nations* (2nd ed.). Thousand Oaks, CA: Sage.

Hogan, M. J., Parker, J. D. A., Wiener, J., Watters, C., Wood, L. M., & Oke, A. (2010). Academic success in adolescence: Relationships among verbal IQ, social support and emotional intelligence. *Australian Journal of Psychology, 62,* 30–41.

Hogan, T. P. (2007). *Psychological testing: A practical introduction* (2nd ed.). New York, NY: John Wiley.

Hohmann, A. G., Suplita, R. L., Bolton, N. M., Neely, M. H., Fegley, D., Mangieri, R., . . . Piomelli, D. (2005). An endocannabinoid mechanism for stress-induced analgesia. *Nature, 435,* 1108–1112.

Holden, C. (1980). Identical twins reared apart. *Science, 207,* 1323–1328.

Holder, M., Coleman, B., & Wallace, J. (2010). Spirituality, religiousness, and happiness in children aged 8–12 years. *Journal of Happiness Studies, 11,* 131–150.

Holland, J. L. (1985). *Making vocational choices: A theory of vocational personalities and work environments.* Englewood Cliffs, NJ: Prentice Hall.

Hollon, S. D., DeRubeis, R. J., Shelton, R. C., Amsterdam, J. D., Salomon, R. M., O'Reardon, J. P., ... Gallop, R. (2005). Prevention of relapse following cognitive therapy vs. medications in moderate to severe depression. *Archives of General Psychiatry, 62,* 417–422.

Holmes, J., Gathercole, S. E., & Dunning, D. L. (2009). Adaptive training leads to sustained enhancement of poor working memory in children. *Developmental Science, 12,* F9–F15.

Holmes, T. H., & Rahe, R. H. (1967). The social readjustment rating scale. *Journal of Psychosomatic Research, 11,* 211–218.

Holstege, G., Georgiadis, J., Paans, A., Meiners, L., van der Graaf, F., & Reinders, A. (2003). Brain activation during human male ejaculation. *Journal of Neuroscience, 23* (27), 9185–9193.

Hölzel, B. K., Carmody, J., Vangel, M., Congleton, C., Yerramsetti, S. M., Gard, T., & Lazar, S. (2010). Mindfulness practice leads to increases in regional brain gray matter density. *Psychiatry Research: Neuroimaging, 191,* 36–43. doi: 10.1016/j.pscychresns.2010.08.006

Hopfield, J. J. (1982). Neural networks and physical systems with emergent collective computational abilities. *Proceedings of the National Academy of Sciences, 79,* 2554–2558.

Hopper, L., Price, S., Freeman, H., Lambeth, S., Schapiro, S., & Kendal, R. (2013). Influence of personality, age, sex, and estrous state on chimpanzee problem-solving success. *Animal Cognition.* doi: 10.1007/s10071-013-0715-y

Hopson, J. L. (1998, September/October). Fetal psychology. *Psychology Today, 31,* 44. Retrieved from http://www.leaderu.com/orgs/tul/psychtoday9809.html

Horn, J. L., & Cattell, R. B. (1966). Refinement and test of the theory of fluid and crystallized general intelligences. *Journal of Educational Psychology, 57,* 253–270.

Horney, K. (1945). *Our inner conflicts: A constructive theory of neurosis.* New York, NY: Norton.

Horney, K. (1950). *Neurosis and human growth: The struggle toward self-realization.* New York, NY: Norton.

Horváth, K., Myers, K., Foster, R., & Plunkett, K. (2015). Napping facilitates word learning in early lexical development. *Journal of Sleep Research, 24,* 503–509. doi: 10.1111/jsr.12306

Hosking, S., Young, K., & Regan, M. (2006). The effects of text messaging on young novice driver performance: Monash University Accident Research Centre, Report No. 246. Retrieved from http://www.monash.edu.au/muarc/reports/muarc246. pdf

Hoss, R. A., & Langlois, J. H. (2003). Infants prefer attractive faces. In O. Pascalis & A. Slater (Eds.), *The development of face processing in infancy and early childhood: Current perspectives* (pp. 27–38). New York, NY: Nova Science.

Hotson, G., McMullen, D. P., Fifer, M. S., Johannes, M. S., Katyal, K. D., Para, M. P., ... & Crone, N. E. (2016). Individual finger control of a modular prosthetic limb using high-density electrocorticography in a human subject. *Journal of Neural Engineering, 13*(2), 026017 .doi: 10.1088/1741-2560/13/2/026017

Hötting, K., & Röder, B. (2013). Beneficial effects of physical exercise on neuroplasticity and cognition. *Neuroscience and Biobehavioral Reviews, 37*(9 Pt B), 2243–2257.

Houlihan, A. E., Gibbons, F. X., Gerrard, M., Yeh, H., & Reimer, R. A. (2008). The impact of early sexual onset on the self-concept and subsequent risky behavior of African American adolescents. *Journal of Early Adolescence, 28,* 70–91.

Howard, B. V., Manson, J. E., Stefanick, M. L., Beresford, S. A., Frank, G., Jones, B., ... Prentice, R. (2006). Low-fat dietary pattern and weight change over 7 years: The Women's Health Initiative Dietary Modification Trial. *Journal of the American Medical Association, 295,* 39–49.

Howard, K. I., Kopta, S. M., Krause, M. S., & Orlinsky, D. E. (1986). The dose-effect relationship in psychotherapy. *American Psychologist, 41,* 159–164.

Howard, M. A., & Marczinski, C. A. (2010). Acute effects of a glucose energy drink on behavioral control. *Experimental Clinical Psychopharmacology, 18,* 553–561.

Howe, D. (2010). ADHD and its comorbidity: An example of gene-environment interaction and its implications for child and family social work. *Child & Family Social Work, 15,* 265–275. doi: 10.1111/j.1365-2206.2009.00666.x

Howes, C., & Matheson, C. C. (1992). Sequences in the development of competent play with peers: Social and social pretend play. *Developmental Psychology, 28,* 961–974.

Howes, O., McCutcheon, R., & Stone, J. (2015). Glutamate and dopamine in schizophrenia: An update for the 21st century. *Journal of psychopharmacology, 29*(2), 97-115. doi: 10.1177/0269881114563634

Hu, T., Zhang, D., & Ran, G. (2016). Self-serving attributional bias among Chinese adolescents. *Personality and Individual Differences, 91,* 80–83. Available at http://dx.doi.org/10.1016/j.paid.2015.10.008 0191-8869/

Huang, A. L., Chen, X., Hoon, M. A., Chandrashekar, J., Guo, W., Tranker, D., . . . Zucker, C. S. (2006). The cells and logic for mammalian sour taste detection. *Nature, 442,* 934–938. doi: 10.1038/nature05084

Huang, H., Coleman, S., Bridge, J. A., Yonkers, K., & Katon, W. (2013). A meta-analysis of the relationship between antidepressant use in pregnancy and the risk of preterm birth and low birth weight. *General Hospital Psychiatry.* Prepublication available online at http://dx.doi.org/10.1016/j.genhosppsych.2013.08.002

Huang, Y. J., Zhang, Z-F., Tashkin, D. P., Feng, B., Straif, K., and Hashibe, M. (2015). An epidemiologic review of marijuana and cancer: An update. *Cancer Epidemiology Biomarkers Preview, 24,* 15–31. doi:10.1158/1055-9965.EPI-14-1026

Hubbard, E. M., & Ramachandran, V. S. (2005). Neurocognitive mechanisms of synesthesia. *Neuron, 48,* 509–520.

Hubel, D., & Wiesel, T. (1962). Receptive fields, binocular interaction and functional architecture in the cat's visual cortex. *Journal of Physiology of London, 160,* 106–154.

Hubel, D., & Wiesel, T. (1979). Brain mechanisms of vision. *Scientific American, 241,* 130–144.

Hudson, W. (1960). Pictorial depth perception in subcultural groups in Africa. *Journal of Social Psychology, 52,* 183–208.

Huesmann, L. R., Moise-Titus, J., & Podolski, C. (2003). Longitudinal relations between children's exposure to TV violence and their aggressive and violent behavior in young adulthood: 1977–1992. *Developmental Psychology, 39,* 201–221.

Huff, D. (1954). *How to lie with statistics.* New York, NY: Norton.

Hughes, D. J., Furnham, A., & Batey, M. (2013). The structure and personality predictors of self-rated creativity. *Thinking Skills and Creativity, 9,* 76–84. doi: 10.1016/j.tsc.2012.10.001

Hull, C. L. (1943). *Principles of behavior: An introduction to behavior theory.* New York, NY: Appleton-Century.

Hunter, J. E., & Schmidt, F. L. (2000). Racial and gender bias in ability and achievement tests: Resolving the apparent paradox. *Psychology, Public Policy and Law, 6,* 151–158.

Hurley, D. (2013, November 3). Jumper cables for the mind. *The New York Times Magazine,* 50–53.

Huston, A. C., Wright, J. C., Marquis J., & Green S. B. (1999). How young children spend their time: Television and other activities. *Developmental Psychology, 35,* 912–925.

Hutchinson, S., Lee, L. H., Gaab, N., & Schlaug, G. (2003). Cerebellar volume of musicians. *Cerebral Cortex, 13,* 943–949.

Huttenlocher, J., Vasilyeva, M., Cymerman, E., & Levine, S. (2002). Language input at home and at school: Relation to child syntax. *Cognitive Psychology, 45,* 337–374.

Hyde, J. S. (1990). Meta-analysis and the psychology of gender differences. *Signs: Journal of Women in Culture & Society, 16,* 53–73.

Hyde, J. S. (2005). The genetics of sexual orientation. In J. S. Hyde (Ed.), *Biological substrates of human sexuality* (pp. 9–20). Washington, DC: American Psychological Association.

Hyde, K. L., Lerch, J., Norton, A., Forgeard, M., Winner, E., Evans, A. C., & Schlaug, G. (2009). Musical training shapes structural brain development. *Journal of Neuroscience, 29,* 3019–3025.

Hyde, T. S., & Jenkins, J. J. (1973). Recall for words as a function of semantic, graphic, and syntactic orienting tasks. *Journal of Verbal Learning and Verbal Behavior, 12,* 471–480.

Hyman, S. E. (2005). Neurotransmitters. *Current Biology, 15,* R154–R158.

Hysek, C. M., Schmid, Y., Simmler, L. D., Domes, G., Heinrichs, M., Eisenegger, C., Preller, K. H., Quednow, B. B., & Liechti, M. E. (2013). MDMA enhances emotional empathy and prosocial behavior. *Social Cognitive and Affective Neuroscience, 9,* 1645–1652. doi:10.1093/scan/nst161

I Feel I Am Trapped. (1986, March 16). *New York Times.*

Iacoboni, M., & Mazziotta, J. C. (2007). Mirror neuron system: Basic findings and clinical applications. *Annals of Neurology, 62,* 213–218.

Iarocci, G., & McDonald, J. (2006). Sensory integration and the perceptual experience of persons with autism. *Journal of Autism and Developmental Disorders, 36,* 77–90.

Iber, C., Ancoli-Israel, S., Chesson, A., & Quan, S. F. (2007). *The AASM Manual for the Scoring of Sleep and Associated Events: Rules, Terminology and Technical Specifications.* Westchester: American Academy of Sleep Medicine.

Ijichi, C., Collins, L. M., & Elwood, R. W. (2013). Pain expression is linked to personality in horses. *Applied Animal Behaviour Science.* doi: 10.1016/j.applanim.2013.12.007

Ilieva, I., Boland, J., & Farah, M. J. (2013). Objective and subjective cognitive enhancing effects of mixed amphetamine salts in healthy people. *Neuropharmacology, 64,* 496–505. doi: 10.1016/j.neuropharm.2012.07.021

Ilieva, I. P., Hook, C. J., & Farah, M. J. (2015). Prescription stimulants' effects on healthy inhibitory control, working memory, and episodic memory: A meta-analysis. *Journal of Cognitive Neuroscience, 27,* 1069–1089. doi: 10.1162/jocn_a_00776

Inagaki, T. K., & Eisenberger, N. I. (2013). Shared neural mechanisms underlying social warmth and physical warmth. *Psychological Science, XX,* 1–9. Online ahead of print, published on September 18, 2013. doi: 10.1177/0956797613492773

Inagaki, T. K., Ray, L. A., Irwin, M. R., Way, B. M., & Eisenberger, N. I. (2016). Opioids and social bonding: Naltrexone reduces feelings of social connection. *Social Cognitive and Affective Neuroscience,* nsw006. doi: 10.1093/scan/nsw006

Ingvalson, E. M., Holt, L. L., & McClelland, J. L. (2011). Can native Japanese listeners learn to differentiate /r–l/ on the basis of F3 onset frequency? *Bilingualism: Language and Cognition, 15*(2), 434–435. Available at http://doi.org/10.1017/S1366728912000041

Ironson, G., O'Cleirigh, C., Leserman, J., Stuetzle, R., Fordiani, J., Fletcher, M., & Schneiderman, N. (2013). Gender-specific effects of an augmented written emotional disclosure intervention on posttraumatic, depressive, and HIV-disease-related outcomes: A randomized, controlled trial. *Journal of Consulting and Clinical Psychology, 81,* 284–298. doi: http://dx.doi.org/10.1037/a0030814

Isacsson, G., Rich, C., Jureidini, J., & Raven, M. (2010). The increased use of antidepressants has contributed to the world-wide reduction in suicide rates. *British Journal of Psychiatry, 196,* 429–433.

Isen, A. M., Daubman, K. A., & Nowicki, G. P. (1987). Positive affect facilitates creative problem solving. *Journal of Personality and Social Psychology, 52,* 1122–1131.

Isfort, R. W., & Gerich, M. E. (2016). High hope for medical marijuana in digestive disorders. *American Journal of Gastroenterology, 111,* 159–160. doi:10.1038/ajg.2016.3

Itri, J., Michel, S., Waschek, J., & Colwell, C. (2004). Circadian rhythm in inhibitory synaptic transmission in the mouse suprachiasmatic nucleus. *Journal of Neurophysiology, 92*(1), 311–319.

Iuculano, T., Rosenberg-Lee, M., Supekar, K., Lynch, C. J., Khouzam, A., Phillips, J., Uddin, L. Q., & Menon, V. (2014). Brain organization underlying superior mathematical abilities in children with autism. *Biological Psychiatry, 75,* 223–230. doi: 10.1016/j.biopsych.2013.06.018

Ivcevic, Z., & Ambady, N. (2012). Personality impressions from identity claims on Facebook. *Psychology of Popular Media Culture, 1*(1), 38–45. Available at http://doi.org/10.1037/a0027329

Iversen, S. D., & Iversen, L. L. (2007). Dopamine: 50 years in perspective. *Trends in Neurosciences, 30,* 188–193.

Izard, C. E. (1969). The emotions and emotion constructs in personality and culture research. In R. B. Cattell (Ed.), *Handbook of modern personality theory.* Chicago, IL: Aldine Press.

Izard, C. E., Trentacosta, C. J., King, K. A., & Mostow, A. J. (2004). An emotion-based prevention program for Head Start children. *Early Education & Development, 15,* 407–422.

Jaber, R., Mzayek, F., Madhivanan, P., Khader, Y., & Maziak, W. (2016). Predictors of cigarette smoking progression among a school-based sample of adolescents in Irbib, Jordan: A longitudinal study (2008–2011). *Nicotine & Tobacco Research, 18,* 403–409. doi: 10.1093/ntr/ntv100

Jablensky, A., & Woodbury, M. A. (1995). Dementia praecox and manic-depressive insanity in 1908: A grade of Membership analysis of the Kraepelinian dichotomy. *European Archives of Psychiatry and Clinical Neuroscience, 245,* 202–209.

Jabr, F. (2013, April 30). New DSM-5 ignores biology of mental Illness. *Scientific American*. Retrieved from http://www.scientificamerican.com/article.cfm?id=new-dsm5-ignores-biology-mental-illness

Jackson, K. M. (2008). Heavy episodic drinking: Determining the predictive utility of five or more drinks. *Psychology of Addictive Behaviors, 22*, 68–77.

Jackson, L. A., von Eye, A., Biocca, F. A., Barbatsis, G., Zhao, Y., & Fitzgerald, H. E. (2006). Does home Internet use influence the academic performance of low-income children? *Developmental Psychology, 42*, 429–435.

Jackson, T., Gao, X., & Chen, H. (2014). Differences in neural activation to depictions of physical exercise and sedentary activity: An fMRI study of overweight and lean Chinese women. *International Journal of Obesity*, advance online publication.

Jacobous, J., Bava, S., Cohen-Zion, M., Mahmood, O., & Tapert, S. F. (2010). Functional consequences of marijuana use in adolescents. *Pharmacology Biochemistry and Behavior, 92*(4), 559–565. http://doi.org/10.1016/j.pbb.2009.04.001

Jacobs, B. L. (2004). Depression: The brain finally gets into the act. *Current Directions in Psychological Science, 13*, 103–106.

Jacobs, B. L., van Praag, H., & Gage, F. H. (2000). Adult brain neurogenesis and psychiatry: A novel theory of depression. *Molecular Psychiatry, 5*, 262–269.

Jacobs, D. R., Jr., Adachi, H., Mulder, I., Kromhout, D., Menotti, A., Nissinen, A., & Blackburn, H. (1999). Cigarette smoking and mortality risk: Twenty-five-year follow-up of the Seven Countries Study. *Archives of Internal Medicine, 159*, 733–740.

Jacobs, G. H., & Nathans, J. (2009). The evolution of primate color vision. *Scientific American, 300*, 56–63.

Jacobs, T. L., Epel, E. S., Lin, J., Blackburn, E. H., Wolkowitz, O. M., Bridwell, D. A., ... Saron, C. D. (2010). Intensive meditation training, immune cell telomerase activity, and psychological mediators. *Psychoneuroendocrinology*. Published online ahead of print. doi: 10.1016/j.psyneuen.2010.09.010

Jacobsen, L. K., Krystal, J. H., Mencl, E., Westerveld, M., Frost, S. J., & Pugh, K. R. (2005). Effects of smoking and smoking abstinence on cognition in adolescent tobacco smokers. *Biological Psychiatry, 57*, 56–66.

Jacobson, S., & Jacobson, J. (2000). *Teratogenic insult and neurobehavioral function in infancy and childhood*. Mahwah, NJ: Erlbaum.

Jacoby, L. L., Hessels, S., & Bopp, K. (2001). Proactive and retroactive effects in memory performance: Dissociating recollection and accessibility bias. In H. Roediger, J. S. Nairne, I. Neath, & A. M. Suprenant (Eds.), *The nature of remembering: Essays in honor of Robert G. Crowder* (pp. 35–54). Washington, DC: American Psychological Association.

Jagiellowicz, J., Xu, X., Aron, A., Aron, E., Cao, G., Feng, T., & Weng, X. (2011). The trait of sensory processing sensitivity and neural responses to changes in visual scenes. *Social Cognitive and Affective Neuroscience, 6*(1), 38–47. Retrieved from https://doi.org/10.1093/scan/nsq001

James, T., Strunk, J., Arndt, J., & Duarte, A. (2016). Age-related deficits in selective attention during encoding increase demands on episodic reconstruction during context retrieval: An ERP study. *Neuropsychologia, 86*, 66–79. doi:10.1016/j.neuropsychologia.2016.04.009

James, W. (1884). What is an emotion? *Mind, 9*, 188–205.

Jameson, K. A. (2009). Human potential for tetrachromacy. *Glimpse, 2.3*(autumn), 82–91. Retrieved October 25, 2016 from http://aris.ss.uci.edu/~kjameson/Jameson2009GlimpsejournalTetrachromacyAndSupplement.pdf

Jameson, K. A., Winkler, A. D., Goldfarb, K., Media, B., & Monica, S. (2016). Art, interpersonal comparisons of color experience, and potential tetrachromacy. *Invited Proceedings paper for the 2016 IS&T International Symposium on Electronic Imaging (EI 2016)*. Technical Session on Human Vision and Electronic Imaging.

Jamison, K. R. (1993). *Touched with fire: Manic-depressive illness and the artistic temperament*. New York, NY: Free Press.

Jamison, K. R., Gerner, R. H., Hammen, C., & Padesky, C. (1980). Clouds and silver linings: Positive experiences associated with primary affective disorders. *American Journal of Psychiatry, 137*, 198–202.

Jan, J. E., Reiter, R. J., Bax, M. C. O., Ribary, U., Freeman, R. D., & Wasdell, M. B. (2010). Long-term sleep disturbances in children: A cause of neuronal loss. *European Journal of Pediatric Neurology, 14*, 380–390.

Janeck, A. S., Calamari, J. E., Riemann, B. C., & Heffelfinger, S. K. (2003). Too much thinking about thinking? Metacognitive differences in obsessive-compulsive disorder. *Journal of Anxiety Disorders, 17*, 181–195.

Janis, I. L. (1983). *Groupthink* (2nd ed., rev.). Boston, MA: Houghton Mifflin.

Jarema, M. (2007). Atypical antipsychotics in the treatment of mood disorders. *Current Opinion in Psychiatry, 21*, 23–29.

Jauk, E., Benedek, M., Dunst, B., & Neubauer, A. C. (2013). The relationship between intelligence and creativity: New support for the threshold hypothesis by means of empirical breakpoint detection. *Intelligence, 41*(4), 212–221. doi: 10.1016/j.intell.2013.03.003

Javitt, D. C., & Coyle, J. T. (2004). Decoding schizophrenia. *Scientific American, 290*, 48–55.

Jazaieri, H., Jinpa, T., McGonigal, K., Rosenberg, E. L., Finkelstein, J., Simon-Thomas, E., ... Goldin, P. (2012). Enhancing compassion: A randomized controlled trial of a compassion cultivation training program. *Journal of Happiness Studies*. doi: 10.1007/s10902-012-9373-z

Jazaieri, H., McGonigal, K., Jinpa, T., Doty, J. R., Gross, J. J., & Goldin, P. (2013). A randomized controlled trial of compassion cultivation training: Effects on mindfulness, affect, and emotion regulation. *Motivation & Emotion*. Published online ahead of print. doi: 10.1007/s11031-013-9368-z

Jenkins, W. M., Merzenich, M. M., Ochs, M. T., Allard, T., & Guic-Roble, E. (1990). Functional reorganization of primary somatosensory cortex in adult owl monkeys after behaviorally controlled tactile stimulation. *Journal of Neurophysiology, 63*, 82–104.

Jennifer Aniston talks about her flying ritual. (2009). Retrieved from http://www.imnotobsessed.com/2009/09/30/jennifer-aniston-talks-about-her-flying-ritual

Jensen, A. R. (1969). How much can we boost IQ and scholastic achievement? *Harvard Educational Review, 39*, 1–23.

Jeong, Y. J., Aldwin, C. M., Igarashi, H., & Spiro III, A. (2016). Do hassles and uplifts trajectories predict mortality? Longitudinal findings from the VA Normative Aging Study. *Journal of Behavioral Medicine, 39*(3), 408–419. doi: 10.1007/s10865-015-9703-9

Jerison, H. J. (2000). The evolution of intelligence. In R. J. Sternberg (Ed.), *The handbook of intelligence* (pp. 216–244). New York, NY: Cambridge University Press.

Ji, D., & Wilson, M. A. (2007). Coordinated memory replay in the visual cortex and hippocampus during sleep. *Nature Neuroscience, 10*, 100–107.

Jiang, W., Zhao, F., Guderley, N., & Manchaiah, V. (2016). Daily music exposure dose and hearing problems using personal listening devices in adolescents and young adults: A systematic review. *International Journal of Audiology, 55*(4), 197–205. Available at http://doi.org/10.3109/14992027.2015.1122237

Jimenez, R. T., Garcia, G. E., & Pearson, P. D. (1994). *The metacognitive strategies of Latina/o students who read Spanish and English*. Center for the Study of Reading, Technical Report No. 601. Urbana-Champaign, IL: College of Education.

Jobsis, F. F. (1977). Noninvasive, infrared monitoring of cerebral and myocardial oxygen sufficiency and circulatory parameters. *Science, 198*, 1264–1267. doi: 10.1126/science.929199

Johansen, J. P., Cain, C. K., Ostroff, L. E., & LeDoux, J. E. (2011). Molecular mechanisms of fear learning and memory. *Cell, 147*, 509–524.

Johansen, P. Ø., & Krebs, T. S. (2015). Psychedelics not linked to mental health problems or suicidal behavior: A population study. *Journal of Psychopharmacology, 29*(3), 270–279. doi: 10.1177/0269881114568039

Johansson, A. E. E., Petrisko, M. A., & Chasens, E. R. (2016). Adolescent sleep and the impact of technology use before sleep on daytime function. *Journal of Pediatric Nursing*. Online ahead of print: http://www.sciencedirect.com/science/article/pii/S0882596316300355

Johansson, S. (2013). The talking Neanderthals: What do fossils, genetics, and archeology say? *Biolinguistics, 7*, 35–74.

John, O. P., & Srivastava, S. (1999). The Big Five trait taxonomy: History, measurement, and theoretical perspectives. In L. A. Pervin & O. P. John (Eds.), *Handbook of personality theory and research* (pp. 102–138). New York, NY: Guilford Press.

Johnson, D. P., Penn, D. L., Fredrickson, B. L., Kring, A. M., Meyer, P. S. Catalino, L. I., & Brantley, M. (2011). A pilot study of loving-kindness meditation for the negative symptoms of schizophrenia. *Schizophrenia Research, 129*, 137–140. doi: 10.1016/j.schres.2011.02.015

Johnson, K. J., Waugh, C. E., & Fredrickson, B. L. (2010). Smile to see the forest: Facially expressed positive emotions broaden cognition. *Cognition & Emotion, 24*, 299–321. doi: 10.1080/02699930903384667

Johnson, M. W., Garcia-Romeu, A., & Griffiths, R. R. (2016). Long-term follow-up of psilocybin-facilitated smoking cessation. *The American Journal of Drug and Alcohol Abuse*, 1–6. doi: 10.3109/00952990.2016.1170135

Johnson, R. E., Fudala, P. J., & Payne, R. (2005). Buprenorphine: Considerations for pain management. *Journal of Pain and Symptom Management, 29*, 297–326.

Jokela, M. (2009). Personality predicts migration within and between U.S. states. *Journal of Research in Personality, 43*, 79–83. doi: 10.1016/j.jrp.2008.09.005

Jokela, M., Hintsa, T., Hintsanen, M., & Keltikangas-Jarvinen, L. (2010). Adult temperament and childbearing over the life course. *European Journal of Personality, 24,* 151–166.

Jones, D. K., Knösche, T. R., & Turner, R. (2012). White matter integrity, fiber count, and other fallacies: The do's and don'ts of diffusion MRI. *NeuroImage, 73,* 239–254. doi: /10.1016/j.neuroimage.2012.06.08

Jope, R. S. (1999). Anti-bipolar therapy: Mechanism of action of lithium. *Molecular Psychiatry, 4,* 117–128.

Jordahl, T., & Lohman, B. J. (2009). A bioecological analysis of risk and protective factors associated with early sexual intercourse of young adolescents. *Children and Youth Services Review, 31,* 1272–1282.

Josefsson, K., Jokela, M., Cloninger, C., Hintsanen, M., Salo, J., Hintsa, T., ... Keltikangas-Järvinen, L. (2013). Maturity and change in personality: Developmental trends of temperament and character in adulthood. *Development and Psychopathology, 25*(3), 713–727. doi: 10.1017/S0954579413000126

Joy, S. P. (2012). Origins of originality: Innovation motivation and intelligence in poetry and comics. *Empirical Studies of the Arts, 30*(2), 195–213. doi: 10.2190/EM.30.2.f

Judd, T. (2014). Making sense of multitasking: The role of Facebook. *Computers & Education, 70,* 194–202. Retrieved from http://dx.doi.org/10.1016/j.compedu.2013.08.013

Juliano, L. M., & Griffiths, R. R. (2004). A critical review of caffeine withdrawal: Empirical validation of symptoms and signs, incidence, severity, and associated features. *Psychopharmacology, 176,* 1–29.

Junco, R. (2012). In-class multitasking and academic performance. *Computers in Human Behavior, 28,* 2236–2243. Retrieved from http://dx.doi.org/10.1016/j.chb.2012.06.031

Jung, C. G. (1931/1960). The stages of life. In H. Read, M. Fordham, & G. Adler (Eds.) & R. F. C. Hull (Trans.), *The collected works of C. G. Jung* (Vol. 8). New York, NY: Pantheon.

Jung, C. G. (1964). The role of the unconscious. In *Collected works* (Vol. 10, Trans. R. F. C. Hull). New York, NY: Bollingen Foundation. (Originally published 1918.)

Jung, R. E., & Haier, R. J. (2007). The parieto-frontal integration theory (P-FIT) of intelligence: Converging neuroimaging evidence. *The Behavioral and Brain Sciences, 30*(2), 135–154 (discussion 154–187).

Jung, R. E., Gasparovic, C., Chavez, R. S., Flores, R. A., Smith, S. M., Caprihan, A., & Yeo, R. A. (2009). Biochemical support for the "threshold" theory of creativity: A magnetic resonance spectroscopy study. *Journal of Neuroscience, 29,* 5319–5325.

Jung, R. E., Mead, B. S., Carrasco, J., & Flores, R. A. (2013). The structure of creative cognition in the human brain. *Frontiers in Human Neuroscience, 7*(July), 330. Available at http://doi.org/10.3389/fnhum.2013.00330

Jung, R. E., Segall, J. M., Jeremy Bockholt, H., Flores, R. A., Smith, S. M., Chavez, R. S., & Haier, R. J. (2010). Neuroanatomy of creativity. *Human Brain Mapping, 31*(3), 398–409. Available at http://doi.org/10.1002/hbm.20874

Jung, Y.-H., Kang, D.-H., Jang, J. H., Park, H. Y., Byun, M. S., Kwon, S. J., ... Kwon, J. S. (2010). The effects of mind-body training on stress reduction, positive affect, and plasma catecholamines. *Neuroscience Letters, 479,* 138–142.

Jusczyk, P. W. (1997). *The discovery of spoken language.* Cambridge, MA: MIT Press.

Jussim, L., & Harber, K. D. (2005). Teacher expectations and self-fulfilling prophecies: Knowns and unknowns, resolved and unresolved controversies. *Personality and Social Psychology Review, 9,* 131–155.

Just, M. A., Keller, T. A., & Cynkar, J. (2008). A decrease in brain activation associated with driving when listening to someone speak. *Brain Research, 1205,* 70–80.

Juster, R.-P., McEwen, B. S., & Lupien, S. J. (2010). Allostatic load biomarkers of chronic stress and impact on health and cognition. *Neuroscience and Biobehavioral Reviews, 35,* 2–16.

Kabat-Zinn, J. (1990). *Full catastrophe living.* New York, NY: Delta.

Kabat-Zinn, J., Lipworth, L., & Burney, R. (1985). The clinical use of mindfulness meditation for the self-regulation of chronic pain. *Journal of Behavioral Medicine, 8,* 163–190.

Kabat-Zinn, J., Massion, A. O., Kristeller, J., Peterson, L. G., Fletcher, K. E., Pbert, L., ... Santorelli, S. F. (1992). Effectiveness of a meditation-based stress reduction program in the treatment of anxiety disorders. *American Journal of Psychiatry, 149,* 936–943.

Kabat-Zinn, J., Wheeler, E., Light, T., Skillings, A., Scharf, M. J., Cropley, T. G., ... Bernhard, J. D. (1998). Influence of a mindfulness meditation-based stress reduction intervention on rates of clearing in patients with moderate to severe psoriasis undergoing phototherapy (UVB) and photochemotherapy (PUVA). *Psychosomatic Medicine, 60,* 625–632.

Kadosh, R. C., & Elliot, P. (2013). Brain stimulation has a long history. *Nature, 500,* 529.

Kagan, J. (2003). Biology, context, and developmental inquiry. *Annual Review of Psychology, 54,* 1–23.

Kahan, T. L. (2001). Consciousness in dreaming. A metacognitive approach. In T. Bulkeley (Ed.), *Dreams: A reader on religious, cultural, and psychological dimensions of dreaming* (pp. 333–360). New York, NY: Palgrave Macmillan.

Kahan, T. L., & LaBerge, S. (1994). Lucid dreaming as metacognitions: Implications for cognitive science. *Consciousness and Cognition, 3,* 246–264.

Kahn, R. S., Khoury, J., Nichols, W. C., & Lanphear, B. P. (2003). Role of dopamine transporter genotype and maternal prenatal smoking in childhood hyperactive-impulsive, inattentive, and oppositional behaviors. *Journal of Pediatrics, 143,* 104–110.

Kahneman, D. (2002). Autobiography—Nobel Prize for 2002 in Economics. Retrieved from http://nobelprize.org/nobel_prizes/economics/laureates/2002/kahneman.html

Kahneman, D., & Tversky, A. (1972). Subjective probability: A judgment of representativeness. *Cognitive Psychology, 3,* 430–454.

Kahneman, D., & Tversky, A. (1979). Prospect theory: An analysis of decision under risk. *Econometrica, 47,* 263–292.

Kahn-Greene, E. T., Killgore, D. B., Kamimori, G. H., Balkin, T. J., & Killgore, W. D. S. (2007). The effects of sleep deprivation on symptoms of psychopathology in healthy adults. *Sleep Medicine, 8,* 215–221.

Kaiser, B., & Bouvard, M. (2009). Obsessive-compulsive disorder in children and adolescents: Efficacy of combined treatment. *Clinical Neuropsychiatry: Journal of Treatment Evaluation, 6,* 94–100.

Kalat, J. W. (2007). *Biological psychology* (9th ed). Belmont, CA: Wadsworth.

Kales, A., Kales, J. D., Soldatos, C. R., Caldwell, A. B., Charney, D. S., & Martin, E. D. (1980). Nightmares: Clinical characteristics and personality patterns. *American Journal of Psychiatry, 137,* 1197–1201.

Kaliman, P., Parrizas, M., Lalanza, J. F., Camins, A., Escorihuela, R. M., & Pallas, M. (2011). Neurophysiological and epigenetic effects of physical exercise on the aging process. *Ageing Research Reviews, 10,* 475–486. doi: 10.1016/j.arr.2011.05.002

Kam, C. M., Greenberg, M. T., & Kusché, C. A. (2004). Sustained effects of the PATHS curriculum on the social and psychological adjustment of children in special education. *Journal of Emotional and Behavioral Disorders, 12,* 66–78.

Kaminsky, Z., Petronis, A., Wang, S.-C., Levine, B., Ghaffar, O., Floden, D., & Feinstein, A. (2008). Epigenetics of personality traits: An illustrative study of identical twins discordant for risk-taking behavior. *Twin Research and Human Genetics, 11,* 1–11.

Kammrath, L. K., Mendoza-Denton, R., & Mischel, W. (2005). Incorporating *if ... then ...* personality signatures in person perception: Beyond the person-situation dichotomy. *Journal of Personality and Social Psychology, 88,* 605–618.

Kampmann, I. L., Emmelkamp, P. M., Hartanto, D., Brinkman, W. P., Zijlstra, B. J., & Morina, N. (2016). Exposure to virtual social interactions in the treatment of social anxiety disorder: A randomized controlled trial. *Behaviour Research and Therapy, 77,* 147–156. Available at http://dx.doi.org/10.1016/j.brat.2015.12.016

Kanayama, G., Rogowska, J., Pope, H. G., Gruber, S. A., & Yurgelun-Todd, D. A. (2004). Spatial working memory in heavy cannabis users: A functional magnetic resonance imaging study. *Psychopharmacology, 176,* 239–247.

Kandel, E. R. (2000a). Disorders of thought and volition: Schizophrenia. In E. R. Kandel, J. H. Schwartz, & T. M. Jessell (Eds.), *Principles of neural science* (4th ed., pp. 1188–1208). New York, NY: McGraw-Hill.

Kandel, E. R. (2000b). Nerve cells and behavior. In E. R. Kandel, J. M. Schwartz, & T. M. Jessell (Eds.), *Principles of neural science* (4th ed., pp. 19–35). New York, NY: McGraw-Hill.

Kandel, E. R. (2001). The molecular biology of memory storage: A dialogue between genes and synapses. *Science, 294,* 1030–1038.

Kandel, E. R. (2006). *In search of memory: The emergence of a new science of mind.* New York, NY: Norton.

Kandel, E. R., Kupfermann, I., & Iversen, S. (2000). Learning and memory. In E. R. Kandel, J. H. Schwartz, & T. M. Jessell (Eds.), *Principles of neural science* (4th ed., pp. 1227–1246). New York, NY: McGraw-Hill.

Kanner, A. D., Coyne, J. C., Schaefer, C., & Lazarus, R. S. (1981). Comparison of two modes of stress measurement: Daily hassles and uplifts versus major life events. *Journal of Behavioral Medicine, 4,* 1–39.

Kanwisher, N. (2000). Domain specificity in face perception. *Nature Neuroscience, 3,* 759.

Kaplan, R. L., Van Damme, I., Levine, L. J., & Loftus, E. F. (2015). Emotion and false memory. *Emotion Review, 8,* 8–13. Available at http://doi.org/10.1177/1754073915601228

Karama, S., Lecours, A. R., Leroux, J.-M., Bourgouin, P., Beaudoin, G., Joubert, S., ... Beauregard, M. (2002). Areas of brain activation in males and females during viewing of erotic film excerpts. *Human Brain Mapping, 16*, 1–13.

Karatsoreos, I. A., & McEwen, B. S. (2011). Psychobiological allostasis: Resistance, resilience and vulnerability. *Trends in Cognitive Sciences, 15*, 576–584, ISSN 1364-6613. Retrieved from http://dx.doi.org/10.1016/j.tics.2011.10.005

Karfopoulou, E., Anastasiou, C. A., Avgeraki, E., Kosmidis, M. H., & Yannakoulia, M. (2016). The role of social support in weight loss maintenance: Results from the MedWeight study. *Journal of Behavioral Medicine, 39*(3), 511–518. doi:10.1007/s10865-016-9717-y

Karns, C. M., Dow, M. W., & Neville, H. J. (2012). Altered cross-modal processing in the primary auditory cortex of congenitally deaf adults: A visual-somatosensory fMRI study with a double-flash illusion. *The Journal of Neuroscience, 32*(28), 9626–9638. Available at http://doi.org/10.1523/JNEUROSCI.6488-11.2012

Karpinski, A. C., Kirschner, P., Ozer, I., & Ochwo, P. (2013). An exploration of social networking site use, multitasking, and academic performance among United States and European university students. *Computers in Human Behavior, 29*, 1182–1192. doi: 10.1016/j.chb.2012.10.011

Karwowski, M., & Gralewski, J. (2013). Threshold hypothesis: Fact or artifact? *Thinking Skills and Creativity, 8*, 25–33. doi: 10.1016/j.tsc.2012.05.003

Kaufman, A. S. (1979). *Intelligent testing with the WISC-R*. New York, NY: Wiley.

Kaufman, A. S., & Kaufman, N. L. (1983). *K-ABC interpretive manual*. Circle Pines, MN: American Guidance Service. (2nd ed., 2004, KABC-II).

Kaufman, J. C., & Plucker, J. A. (2011). Intelligence and creativity. In R. J. Sternberg, & S. B. Kaufman (Eds.), *The Cambridge handbook of intelligence* (pp. 771–783). Cambridge: Cambridge University Press.

Kaufman, S. B. (2013). *Ungifted: Intelligence redefined*. New York, NY: Basic Books.

Kaufman, S. B., Kozbelt, A., Silvia, P., Kaufman, J. C., Ramesh, S., & Feist, G. J. (2016). Who finds Bill Gates sexy? Creative mate preferences as a function of cognitive ability, personality, and creative achievement. *Journal of Creative Behavior, 50*, 294–307.

Kaul, P., Passafiume, J., Sargent, R. C., & O'Hara, B. F. (2010). Meditation acutely improves psychomotor vigilance, and may decrease sleep need. *Behavioral and Brain Functions, 6*, ArtID47. doi: 10.1186/1744-9081-6-47

Kaviani, H., Javaheri, F., & Hatami, N. (2011). Mindfulness-based cognitive therapy (MBCT) reduces depression and anxiety induced by real stressful setting in non-clinical population. *International Journal of Psychology and Psychology Therapy, 11*, 285–296.

Kawamura, Y., & Kare, M. R. (1987). *Umami: A basic taste*. New York, NY: Marcel Dekker.

Kaye, L., Malone, S., & Wall, H. (2016). Emojis: Insights, affordances and possibilities for psychological science. *Trends in Cognitive Sciences*. Available at http://dx.doi.org/10.1016/j.tics.2016.10.007

Kazdin, A. E. (2017). Addressing the treatment gap: A key challenge for extending evidence-based psychosocial interventions. *Behaviour Research and Therapy, 88*, 7–18. Available at http://dx.doi.org/10.1016/j.brat.2016.06.004

Kazemi, A., Ehsanpour, S., & Nekoei-Zahraei, N. S. (2012). A randomized trial to promote health

belief and to reduce environmental tobacco smoke exposure in pregnant women. *Health Education Research, 27*, 151–159. doi: 10.1093/her/cyr102

Keeler, R. F. (1983). Naturally occurring teratogens from plants. In R. F. Keeler & A. T. Tu (Eds.), *Handbook of natural toxins: Vol. 1. Plant and fungal toxins* (pp. 161–191). New York, NY: Marcel Dekker.

Keenan, R. M., Jenkins, A. J., Cone, E. J., & Henningfield, J. E. (1994). Smoked and IV nicotine, cocaine and heroin have similar abuse liability. *Journal of Addictive Diseases, 13*, 259–269.

Kegeles, L. S., Abi-Dargham, A., Frankle, W. G., Gil, R., Cooper, T. B., Slifstein, M., ... Laruelle, M. (2010). Increased synaptic dopamine function in associative regions of the striatum in schizophrenia. *Archives in General Psychiatry, 67*, 231–239.

Kehle, S. (2008). The effectiveness of cognitive behavioral therapy for generalized anxiety disorder in a frontline service setting. *Cognitive Behaviour Therapy, 37*, 1–7. doi: 10.1080/16506070802190262

Kekic, M., Boysen, E., Campbell, I. C., & Schmidt, U. (2016). A systematic review of the clinical efficacy of transcranial direct current stimulation (tDCS) in psychiatric disorders. *Journal of Psychiatric Research, 74*, 70–86. Available at http://dx.doi.org/10.1016/j.jpsychires.2015.12.018

Kell, H. J., Lubinski, D., & Benbow, C. P. (2013). Who rises to the top? Early indicators. *Psychological Science, 24*(5), 648–59. http://doi.org/10.1177/0956797612457784

Keller, A., Litzelman, K., Wisk, L. E., Maddox, T., Cheng, E. R., Creswell, P. D., & Witt, P. (2012). Does the perception that stress affects health matter? The association with health and mortality. *Health Psychology, 31*, 677. doi: 10.1037/a0026743

Keller, M. C., Thiessen, D., & Young, R. K. (1996). Mate assortment in dating and married couples. *Personality and Individual Differences, 21*, 217–221.

Kelley, H. H., & Michela, J. L. (1980). Attribution theory and research. *Annual Review of Psychology, 31*, 457–501.

Kelley, M. E., Wan, C. R., Broussard, B., Crisafio, A., Cristofaro, S., Johnson, S., Reed, T. A., Amar, P., Kaslow, N. J., Walker, E. F., & Compton, M. T. (2016). Marijuana use in the immediate 5-year premorbid period is associated with increased risk of onset of schizophrenia and related psychotic disorders. *Schizophrenia Research, 171*, 62–67. doi: 10.1016/j.schres.2016.01.015

Kellman, P. J., & Arterberry, M. E. (2006). Infant visual perception. In D. Kuhn & R. Siegler (Eds.), *Handbook of child psychology: Vol. 2. Cognition, perception, and language* (6th ed., 109–160). Hoboken, NJ: Wiley.

Kellner, C. H., Knapp, R. G., Petrides, G., Rummans, T. A., Husain, M. M., Rasmussen, K., ... Fink, M. (2006). Continuation electro-convulsive therapy vs. pharmacotherapy for relapse prevention in major depression. *Archives of General Psychiatry, 63*, 1337–1344.

Keltner, D. (1995). Signs of appeasement: Evidence of distinct displays of embarrassment, amusement, and shame. *Journal of Personality and Social Psychology, 68*, 441–454.

Kempermann, G. (2006). Adult neurogenesis. In P. B. Baltes, P. A. Reuter-Lorenz, & F. Rösler (Eds.), *Lifespan development and the brain: The perspective of biocultural co-constructivism* (pp. 82–107). New York, NY: Cambridge University Press.

Kempermann, G., & Gage, F. H. (1999). Experience-dependent regulation of adult hippocampal neurogenesis: Effects of long-term stimulation and stimulus withdrawal. *Hippocampus, 9*, 321–332.

Kendler, K. S. (2005). "A gene for ... ": The nature of gene action in psychiatric disorders. *American Journal of Psychiatry, 162*, 1243–1252.

Kendler, K. S., Karkowski, L. M., & Prescott, C. A. (1999). Causal relationship between stressful life events and the onset of major depression. *American Journal of Psychiatry, 156*, 837–841.

Kendler, K. S., Kuhn, J. W., Vittum, J., Prescott, C. A., & Riley, B. (2005). The interaction of stressful life events and a serotonin transporter polymorphism in the prediction of episodes of major depression. *Archives of General Psychiatry, 62*, 529–535.

Kendler, K. S., Ohlsson, H., Maes, H. H., Sundquist, K., Lichtenstein, P., & Sundquist, J. (2015). A population-based Swedish twin and sibling study of cannabis, stimulant and sedative abuse in men. *Drug and Alcohol Dependence, 149*, 49–54. doi: 10.1016/j.drugalcdep.2015.01.016

Kendrick, T., Peveler, R., Logworth, L., Baldwin, D., Moore, M., Chatwin, J., ... Thompson, C. (2006). Cost-effectiveness and cost-utility of tricyclic antidepressants, selective serotonin reuptake inhibitors and lofepramine: Randomized controlled trial. *British Journal of Psychiatry, 188*, 337–345.

Kennedy, J. M., & Juricevic, I. (2006). Blind man draws using diminution in three dimensions. *Psychonomic Bulletin & Review, 13*, 506–509.

Kennedy, S. H., Evans, K. R., Krüger, S., Mayberg, H. S., Meyer, J. H., McCann, S., ... Vaccarino, F. J. (2001). Changes in regional brain glucose metabolism measured with positron emission tomography after paroxetine treatment of major depression. *American Journal of Psychiatry, 158*, 899–905.

Kenrick, D. T., Griskevicius, V., Neuberg, S. L., & Schaller, M. (2010). Renovating the pyramid of needs: Contemporary extensions built upon ancient foundations. *Perspective on Psychological Science, 5*, 292–314. doi: 10.1177/1745691610369469

Kensinger, E. A., Garoff-Eaton, R. J., & Schacter, D. L. (2007). How negative emotion enhances the visual specificity of a memory. *Journal of Cognitive Neuroscience, 19*, 1872–1887.

Keppel, R. (2005). *The riverman: Ted Bundy and I hunt for the Green River killer*. New York, NY: Pocket Books.

Keri, S. (2009). Genes for psychosis and creativity: A promoter polymorphism of the *neuregulin 1* gene is related to creativity in people with high intellectual achievement. *Psychological Science, 20*, 1070–1073. doi: 10.1111/j.1467-9280.2009.02398.x

Kerig, P., & Wenar, C. (2006). *Developmental psychology: From infancy through adolescence* (5th ed.). New York, NY: McGraw-Hill.

Kessler, R. C., Avenevoli, S., McLaughlin, K. A., Greif Green, J., Lakoma, M. D., Pine, D. S., ... Reis Merikangas, K. (2012). Lifetime comorbidity of *DSMIV* disorders in the U.S. National Comorbidity Survey Replication Adolescent Supplement (NCSA). *Psychological Medicine, 42*, 1997–2010. doi: 10.1017/S0033291712000025

Kessler, R. C., Berglund, P., Demler, O., Jin, R., Merikangas, K. R., & Walters, E. E. (2005). Lifetime prevalence and age-of-onset distributions of *DSM-IV* disorders in the National Comorbidity Survey replication. *Archives of General Psychiatry, 62*, 593–602.

Key Learning Community. (n.d.). Retrieved July 13, 2007, from http://www.ncrel.org/sdrs/areas /issues/methods/assment/as7key.htm

Keyes, C. L. M. (2002). The mental health continuum: From languishing to flourishing in life. *Journal of Health and Social Behavior, 43,* 207–222.

Keyes, C. L. M., & Lopez, S. J. (2002). Toward a science of mental health: Positive directions in diagnosis and interventions. In C. R. Snyder & S. J. Lopez (Eds.), *Handbook of positive psychology* (pp. 45–59). Oxford, England: Oxford University Press.

Khandaker, G. M., Dibben, G. R. M., & Jones, P. B. (2012). Prenatal maternal influenza and schizophrenia in offspring: What does this tell us about fetal programming of chronic disease? *Journal of Pediatric Infectious Diseases, 7,* 61–68. doi: 10.3233/JPI-120346

Khatami, M. (2009). Inflammation, aging, and cancer: Tumoricidal versus tumorigenesis of immunity. *Cell Biochemistry Biophysiology, 55,* 55–79.

Kiecolt-Glaser, J. K., & Wilson, S. J. (2016). Psychiatric disorders, morbidity, and mortality: Tracing mechanistic pathways to accelerated aging. *Psychosomatic Medicine, 78*(7), 772–775. doi: 10.1097/ PSY.0000000000000373

Kiecolt-Glaser, J. K., Marucha, P. T., Malarkey, W. B., Mercado, A. M., & Glaser, R. (1995). Slowing of wound healing by psychological stress. *The Lancet, 346,* 1194–1196.

Kihlstrom, J. F. (2005). Dissociative disorders. *Annual Review of Clinical Psychology, 1,* 227–253.

Kim, B., Lee, S., Choi, T., Suh, S., Kim, Y., Yook, K., & Lee, E. H. (2008). Effectiveness of a combined therapy of long-acting injectable risperidone and psychosocial intervention for relapse prevention in patients with schizophrenia. *Clinical Psychopharmacology and Neuroscience, 6,* 31–37.

Kim, D. A., Benjamin, E. J., Fowler, J. H., & Christakis, N. A. (2016). Social connectedness is associated with fibrinogen level in a human social network. *Proceedings of the Royal Society B, 283,* published on. doi: 10.1098/rspb.2016.0958

Kim, H. K. (2005). Can only intelligent people be creative? A meta-analysis. *Journal of Secondary Gifted Education, 16,* 57–66.

Kim, J., & Lee, J. E. (2011). The Facebook paths to happiness: Effects of the number of Facebook friends and self-presentation on subjective well-being. *Cyberpsychology, Behavior and Social Networking, 6,* 359–364.

Kim, K. H. S., Relkin, N. R., Lee, K. M., & Hirsch, J. (1997). Distinct cortical areas associated with native and second languages. *Nature, 388,* 171–174.

Kim, S.-E., Ko, I.-G., Kim, B.-K., Shin, M.-S., Cho, S., Kim, C.-J., ... Jee, Y.-S. (2010). Treadmill exercise prevents aging-induced failure of memory through an increase in neurogenesis and suppression of apoptosis in rat hippocampus. *Experimental Gerontology, 45,* 357–365.

Kim, Y. (2011). The contribution of social network sites to exposure to political difference: The relationships among SNSs, online political messaging, and exposure to cross-cutting perspectives. *Computers in Human Behavior, 27,* 971–977. Available at http://dx.doi.org/10.1016/j.chb.2010.12.001

Kim, Y., & Chang, H. (2011). Correlation between attention deficit hyperactivity disorder and sugar consumption, quality of diet, and dietary behavior in school children. *Nutrition Research and Practice, 5,* 236–245. doi: 10.4162/nrp.2011.5.3.236

Kimball, J. (2003). *Joyce and the early Freudians.* Gainesville: University Press of Florida.

Kimura, D. (2007). "Underrepresentation" or misinterpretation? In S. J. Ceci & W. M. Williams (Eds.), *Why aren't more women in science?: Top researchers debate the evidence* (pp. 39–46). Washington, DC: American Psychological Association.

Kincses, T. Z., Antal, A., Nitsche, M. A., Bartfai, O., & Paulus, W. (2004). Facilitation of probabilistic classification learning by transcranial direct current stimulation of the prefrontal cortex in the human. *Neuropsychologia, 42*(1), 113–117.

King, D. E., Mainous, A. G., III, & Geesey, M. E. (2008). Adopting moderate alcohol consumption in middle age: Subsequent cardiovascular events. *American Journal of Medicine, 121,* 201–206.

King, L. A., & Hicks, J. A. (2012). Positive affect and meaning in life: The intersection of hedonism and eudaimonia. In P. P. Wong (Ed.), *The human quest for meaning: Theories, research, and applications* (2nd ed., pp. 125–141). New York, NY: Routledge/Taylor & Francis Group.

Kingery, K. M., Narad, M., Garner, A. A., Antonini, T. N., Tamm, L., & Epstein, J. N. (2015). Extended visual glances away from the roadway are associated with ADHD- and texting-related driving performance deficits in adolescents. *Journal of Abnormal Child Psychology, 43*(6), 1175–1186. doi: 10.1007/s10802-014-9954-x

Kinney, D. K., Richards, R., Lowing, P. A., LeBlanc, D., Zimbalist, M. E., & Harlan, P. (2000–2001). Creativity in offspring of schizophrenic and control parents: An adoption study. *Creativity Research Journal, 13,* 17–26.

Kinnish, K. K., Strassberg, D. S., & Turner, C. W. (2005). Sex differences in the flexibility of sexual orientation: A multidimensional retrospective assessment. *Archives of Sexual Behavior, 34,* 173–183. doi: org/10.1007/s10508-005-1795-9

Kinsey, A. C., Pomeroy, W. B., & Martin, C. E. (1948). *Sexual behavior in the human male.* Philadelphia, PA: Saunders.

Kinsey, A. C., Pomeroy, W. B., Martin, C. E., & Gebhard, P. H. (1953). *Sexual behavior in the human female.* Philadelphia, PA: Saunders.

Kirkham, T. C. (2005). Endocannabinoids in the regulation of appetite and body weight. *Behavioral Pharmacology, 16,* 297–313.

Kirkpatrick, L. A. (2005). *Attachment, evolution, and the psychology of religion.* New York, NY: Guilford Press.

Kirk-Sanchez, N. J., & McGough, E. L. (2013). Physical exercise and cognitive performance in the elderly: Current perspectives. *Clinical Interventions in Aging, 9,* 51–62. Retrieved from http:// dx.doi.org/10.2147/CIA.S39506

Kirsch, I., Moore, T. J., Scoboria, A., & Nicholls, S. S. (2002). The emperor's new drugs: An analysis of antidepressant medication data submitted to the U.S. Food and Drug Administration. *Prevention & Treatment, 5,* ArtID23. Retrieved from http://www .journals.apa.org/prevention/volume5/pre0050023a .html

Kirsh, S. J. (2006). Cartoon violence and aggression in youth. *Aggression and Violent Behavior, 11,* 547–557.

Kisilevsky, B. S., Muir, D. W., & Low, J. A. (1992). Maturation of human fetal responses to vibroacoustic stimulation. *Child Development, 63,* 1497–1508.

Klauer, S. G., Guo, F., Simons-Morton, B. G., Ouimet, M. C., Lee, S. E., & Dingus, T. A. (2014). Distracted driving and risk of road crashes among novice and experienced drivers. *New England Journal of Medicine, 370*(1), 54–59. doi: 10.1056/ NEJMsa1204142

Klein, D. A., & Miller, A. L. (2011). Dialectical behavior therapy for suicidal adolescents with borderline personality disorder. *Child and Adolescent Psychiatric Clinics of North America, 20*(2), 205–216.

Klein, H. S. (2004). *A population history of the United States.* New York, NY: Cambridge University Press.

Klein, R. A., Ratliff, K. A., Vianello, M., Adams, R. B., Bahnik, S., Bernstein, M. J. ... Nosek, B. A. (2014). Investigating variation in replicability: A "many labs" research project. *Social Psychology, 45,* 142–152. doi: 10.1027/1864-9335/a000178

Klein, R. G. (1999). *The human career: Human biological and cultural origins* (2nd ed.). Chicago, IL: University of Chicago Press.

Klink, D., & Den Heijer, M. (2014). Genetic aspects of gender identity development and gender dysphoria. In B. C. Kreukels, T. D. Steensma, A. C. de Vries, B. C. Kreukels, T. D. Steensma, & A. C. de Vries (Eds.), *Gender dysphoria and disorders of sex development: Progress in care and knowledge* (pp. 25–51). New York, NY: Springer Science + Business Media. doi:10.1007/978-1-4614-7441-8_2

Kloosterman, K. (2009, August 13). *Teaching the blind to see through sound.* Retrieved from http:// www.israel21c.org/

Klopfer, P. H. (1958). Influence of social interaction on learning rates in birds. *Science, 128,* 903.

Klucharev, V., Hytonen, K., Rijpkema, M., Smidts, A., & Fernandez, G. (2009). Reinforcement learning signal predicts social conformity. *Neuron, 61,* 140–151.

Klüver, H., & Bucy, P. (1939). Preliminary analysis of functioning of the temporal lobes in monkeys. *Archives of Neurology and Psychiatry, 42,* 979–1000.

Knox, R. (2007, April 26). *Kids' use of earbuds worries hearing experts.* Retrieved from http://www .npr.org/templates/story/story.php?storyId=9797364

Kobayashi, M., Saito, S., Kobayakawa, T., Deguchi, Y., & Costanzo, R. M. (2006). Cross-cultural comparison of data using the odor stick identification test for Japanese (OSIT-J). *Chemical Senses, 31,* 335–342.

Koch, C., Massimini, M., Boly, M., & Tononi, G. (2016). Neural correlates of consciousness: Progress and problems. *Nature Reviews Neuroscience, 17*(5), 307–321. doi: 10.1038/nrn.2016.22

Koelega, H. S. (1992). Extraversion and vigilance performance: Thirty years of inconsistencies. *Psychological Bulletin, 112,* 239–258.

Koenig, J. I. (2006). Schizophrenia: A unique translational opportunity in behavioral neuroendocrinology. *Hormones and Behavior, 50,* 602–611.

Koerner, K., & Linehan, M. M. (2000). Research on dialectical behavior therapy for patients with borderline personality disorder. *Psychiatric Clinics of North America, 23,* 151–167.

Kogan, A., Impett, E. A., Oveis, C., Hui, B., Gordon, A. M., & Keltner, D. (2010). When giving feels good: The intrinsic benefits of sacrifice in romantic relationships for the communally motivated. *Psychological Science, 21,* 1918–1924. doi: 10.1177/0956797610388815

Koh, J. S., Kang, H., Choi, S. W., & Kim, H. O. (2002). Cigarette smoking associated with premature facial wrinkling: Image analysis of facial skin replicas. *International Journal of Dermatology, 41,* 21–27.

Kohlberg, L. (1981). *Essays on moral development: Vol. I. The philosophy of moral development.* New York, NY: Harper & Row.

Kohn, P. M., Lafreniere, K., & Gurevich, M. (1991). Hassles, health, and personality. *Journal of Personality and Social Psychology, 61,* 478–482.

Kokko, K., Pulkkinen, L., & Mesiäinen, P. (2009). Timing of parenthood in relation to other life transitions and adult social functioning. *International Journal of Behavioral Development, 33,* 356–365.

Kolb, B., & Whishaw, I. Q. (2003). *Fundamentals of human neuropsychology* (5th ed.). New York, NY: Worth.

Komaroff, A. L. (2017). The microbiome and risk for obesity and diabetes. *Journal of the American Medical Association, 317*(4), 355–356. doi: 10.1001/jama.2016.20099

Kometer, M., Schmidt, A., Bachmann, R., Studerus, E., Seifritz, E., & Vollenweider, F. X. (2012). Psilocybin biases facial recognition, goal-directed behavior, and mood state toward positive relative to negative emotions through different serotonergic subreceptors. *Biological Psychiatry, 72*(11), 898–906. doi: 10.1016/j.biopsych.2012.04.005

Komisaruk, B. R., & Whipple, B. (2005). Functional MRI of the brain during orgasm in women. *Annual Review of Sex Research, 16*(February), 62–86. Available at http://doi.org/10.1080/10532528.2005.10559829

Kondziella, D., Friberg, C. K., Frokjaer, V. G., Fabricius, M., & Møller, K. (2016). Preserved consciousness in vegetative and minimal conscious states: Systematic review and meta-analysis. *Journal of Neurology, Neurosurgery, & Psychiatry, 87,* 485–492. doi:10.1136/jnnp-2015-310958

Kopell, B. H., Rezai, A. R., Chang, J. W., & Vitek, J. L. (2006). Anatomy and physiology of the basal ganglia: Implications for deep brain stimulation in Parkinson's disease. *Movement Disorders, 21,* S238–S246.

Kopta, S. M. (2003). The dose-effect relationship in psychotherapy: A defining achievement for Dr. Kenneth Howard. *Journal of Clinical Psychology, 59,* 727–733.

Korkeila, M., Kaprio, J., Rissanen, A., Koshenvuo, M., & Sorensen, T. L. (1998). Predictors of major weight gain in adult Finns: Stress, life satisfaction and personality traits. *International Journal of Obesity Related Metabolic Disorders, 22*(10), 949–957.

Kornell, N., & Bjork, R. A. (2007). The promise and perils of self-regulated study. *Psychonomic Bulletin & Review, 14,* 219–224.

Kornell, N., Castel, A., Eich, T., & Bjork, R. (2010). Spacing as the friend of both memory and induction in young and older adults. *Psychology and Aging, 25,* 498–503. doi: 10.1037/a0017807

Kornhaber, M. L., Fierros, E., & Veenema, S. (2004). *Multiple intelligences: Best ideas from research and practice.* Boston, MA: Pearson.

Kosinski, M., Stillwell, D., & Graepel, T. (2013). Private traits and attributes are predictable from digital records of human behavior. *Proceedings of the National Academy of Sciences of the United States of America, 110*(15), 5802–5805. doi: 10.1073/pnas.1218772110

Koslowski, B. (1996). *Theory and evidence: The development of scientific reasoning.* Cambridge, MA: MIT Press.

Kosslyn, S. M. (2002, July 15). What shape are a German shepherd's ears?: A talk with Stephen Kosslyn. *Edge.* Retrieved from http://www.edge.org/3rd_culture/kosslyn/kosslyn_index.html

Kosslyn, S. M. (2005). Mental images and the brain. *Cognitive Neuropsychology, 22,* 333–347.

Kosslyn, S. M., Van Kleeck, M. H., & Kirby, K. N. (1990). A neurologically plausible model of individual differences in visual mental imagery. In P. J. Hampson, D. F. Marks, & J. T. E. Richardson (Eds.), *Imagery: Current developments* (pp. 39–77). Florence, KY: Taylor & Frances/Routledge.

Kottke, J. L., & Sharafinski, C. E. (1988). Measuring perceived supervisory and organizational support. *Educational and Psychological Measurement, 48,* 1075–1079.

Kounios, J., & Beeman, M. (2015). *The Eureka factor: Aha moments, creative insight, and the brain.* New York, NY: Random House.

Kounios, J., Frymiare, J. L., Bowden, E. M., Fleck, J. I., Subramaniam, K., Parrish, T. B., & Jung-Beeman, M. (2006). The prepared mind: Neural activity prior to problem presentation predicts subsequent solution by sudden insight. *Psychological Science, 17,* 882–890.

Kovács, A. M. (2009). Early bilingualism enhances mechanisms of false-belief reasoning. *Developmental Science, 12,* 48–54.

Kovács, A. M., & Mehler, J. (2009). Flexible learning of multiple speech structures in bilingual infants. *Science, 325,* 611–612. doi: 10.1126/science.1173947

Kraaj, V., van der Veek, S. M. C., Garnefski, N., Schroevers, M., Witlox, R., & Maes, S. (2008). Coping, goal adjustment, and psychological well-being in HIV-infected men who have sex with men. *AIDS Patient Care and STDs, 22,* 395–402.

Kraehenmann, R., Schmidt, A., Friston, K., Preller, K. H., Seifritz, E., & Vollenweider, F. X. (2016). The mixed serotonin receptor agonist psilocybin reduces threat-induced modulation of amygdala connectivity. *NeuroImage: Clinical, 11,* 53–60. Available at http://dx.doi.org/10.1016/j.nicl.2015.08.009

Krakauer, J. (1996). *Into thin air.* New York, NY: Anchor Books.

Kramarik, A. (2006). *Akiane: Her life, her art, her poetry.* Nashville, TN: W Publishing Group.

Kramer, A. D. I., Guillory, J. E., & Hancock, J. T. (2014). Experimental evidence of massive-scale emotional contagion through social networks. *PNAS.* Retrieved from www.pnas.org/cgi/doi/10.1073/pnas.1320040111

Kranczioch, C., Debener, S., Schwarzbach, J., Goebel, R., & Engel, A. K. (2005). Neural correlates of conscious perception in the attentional blink. *NeuroImage, 24,* 704–714.

Krebs, T. S., & Johansen, P. Ø. (2012). Lysergic acid diethylamide (LSD) for alcoholism: Meta-analysis of randomized controlled trials. *Journal of Psychopharmacology, 26*(7), 994–1002. doi: 10.1177/0269881112439253

Kremer, S., Bult, J. H., Mojet, J., & Kroeze, J. H. (2007). Food perception with age and its relationship to pleasantness. *Chemical Senses, 32,* 591–602.

Kreukels, B. P. C., & Guillamon, A. (2016). Neuroimaging studies in people with gender incongruence. *International Review of Psychiatry, 28*(1), 120–128. doi:10.3109/09540261.2015.1113163

Kringelbach, M. L., & Berridge, K. C. (2015). Motivation and pleasure in the brain. In W. Hofmann & L. F. Nordgren (Eds.), *The psychology of desire* (pp. 129–146). New York: Guilford Press.

Kristeller, J. L., Baer, R. A., & Quillian-Wolever, R. (2006). Mindfulness-based approaches to eating disorders. In R. A. Baer (Ed.), *Mindfulness-based treatment approaches: Clinician's guide to evidence base and applications* (pp. 75–91). San Diego, CA: Elsevier Academic Press.

Kristjansson, A. L., Sigfusdottir, I. D., James, J. E., Allegrante, J. P., & Helgason, A. R. (2010). Perceived parental reactions and peer respect as predictors of adolescent cigarette smoking and alcohol use. *Addictive Behaviors, 35,* 256–259.

Kristof-Brown, A. L., Zimmerman, R. D., & Johnson, E. C. (2005). Consequences of individuals' fit at work: A meta-analysis of person-job, person-organization, person-group, and person-supervisor fit. *Personnel Psychology, 58,* 281–342.

Kroeber, A. L. (1948). *Anthropology.* New York, NY: Harcourt Brace Jovanovich.

Kroes, M. C. W., Tendolkar, I., van Wingen, G. A., van Waarde, J. A., Strange, B. A., Fernández, G., ... Fernández, G. (2014). An electroconvulsive therapy procedure impairs reconsolidation of episodic memories in humans. *Nature Neuroscience, 17*(2), 204–6. Available at https://doi.org/10.1038/nn.3609

Kröger, C., Schweiger, U., Sipos, V., Arnold, R., Kahl, K. G., Schunert, T., ... Reinecker, H. (2006). Effectiveness of dialectical behavior therapy for borderline personality disorder in an inpatient setting. *Behaviour Research and Therapy, 44,* 1211–1217.

Krueger, R. F. (1999). Personality traits in late adolescence predict mental disorders in early adulthood: A prospective-epidemiological study. *Journal of Personality, 67,* 39–65.

Krueger, R. F., & Johnson, W. (2008). Behavioral genetics and personality: A new look at the integration of nature and nurture. In O. P. John, R. W. Robins, & L. A. Pervin (Eds.), *Handbook of personality: Theory and research* (pp. 287–310). New York, NY: Guilford Press.

Krummel, D., Seligson F., & Guthrie, H. (1996). Hyperactivity: Is candy causal? *Critical Review of Food Science and Nutrition, 36,* 31–47.

Krystal, A. D. (2005). The effect of insomnia definitions, terminology, and classifications on clinical practice. *Journal of American Geriatrics Society, 53,* S255–S263.

Kteily, N., & Bruneau, E. (2017). Backlash: The politics and real-world consequences of minority group dehumanization. *Personality and Social Psychology Bulletin, 43*(1), 87–104. doi: 10.1177/0146167216675334

Kteily, N., Bruneau, E., Waytz, A., & Cotterill, S. (2015). The ascent of man: Theoretical and empirical evidence for blatant dehumanization. *Journal of Personality and Social Psychology, 109,* 901–931. doi: 10.1037/pspp0000048

Kübler-Ross, E. (1969). *On death and dying.* New York, NY: Macmillan.

Kubota, M., Nakazaki, S., Hirai, S., Saeki, N., Yamaura, A., & Kusaka, T. (2001). Alcohol consumption and frontal lobe shrinkage: Study of 1432 non-alcoholic subjects. *Journal of Neurology, Neurosurgery, and Psychiatry, 71,* 104–106.

Kubzansky, L. D., Sparrow, D., Vokonas, P., & Kawachi, I. (2001). Is the glass half empty or half full? A prospective study of optimism and coronary heart disease in the Normative Aging Study. *Psychosomatic Medicine, 63,* 910–916.

Kuhl, P. K., Conboy, B. T., Coffey-Corina, S., Padden, D., Rivera-Gaxiola, M., & Nelson, T. (2008). Phonetic learning as a pathway to language: New data and native language magnet theory expanded (NLM-e). *Philosophical Transactions of the Royal Society B-Biological Sciences, 363,* 979–1000.

Kuhl, P. K., & Meltzoff, A. N. (1997). Evolution, nativism, and learning in the development of language and speech. In M. Gopnik (Ed.), *The* inheritance and innateness of grammars (pp. 7–44). New York, NY: Oxford University Press.

Kuhl, P. K., Stevens, E., & Hayashi, A. (2006). Infants show a facilitation effect for native language phonetic perception between 6 and 12 months. *Developmental Science, 9*, F13–F21.

Kuhl, P. K., Stevens, E., Hayashi, A., Deguchi, T., Kiritani, S., & Iverson, P. (2006). Infants show a facilitation effect for native language phonetic perception between 6 and 12 months. *Developmental Science, 9*(2). Available at http://doi .org/10.1111/j.1467-7687.2006.00468.x

Kuhn, D. (1993). Connecting scientific and informal reasoning. *Merrill-Palmer Quarterly, 39*, 74–103.

Kuhn, D., Amsel, E., & O'Loughlin, M. (1988). *The development of scientific thinking skills.* Orlando, FL: Academic Press.

Kuhn, D., & Pearsall, S. (2000). Developmental origins of scientific thinking. *Journal of cognition and development, 1*, 113–129.

Kulikov, A., & Komarov, I. (2013). Cost-effectiveness of atypical antipsychotics as treatment for patients with bipolar disorder (episodes of mania): A comparison between quetiapine, aripiprazole, olanzapine, risperidone and ziprasidone in the Russian health care. *Value in Health, 16*, A61–A62. doi: 10.1016 /j.jval.2013.03.1583

Kunkel, C. (2009). Schooling built on multiple intelligences. *School Administrator, 66*, 24–25.

Kuo, L. E., Kitlinska, J. B., Tilan, J. U., Li, L., Baker, S. B., Johnson, M. D., … Zukowska, Z. (2007). Neuropeptide Y acts directly in the periphery on fat tissue and mediates stress-induced obesity and metabolic syndrome. *Nature Medicine, 13*, 803–811.

Kurson, R. (2007). *Crashing through: The true story of risk, adventure and the man who dared to see.* New York, NY: Random House.

Kusché, C. A., & Greenberg, M. T. (1994). *The PATHS curriculum.* Seattle, WA: Developmental Research and Programs.

Kwon, Y., & Lawson, A. E. (2000). Linking brain growth with the development of scientific reasoning ability and conceptual change during adolescence. *Journal of Research in Science Teaching, 37*, 44–62.

La Precious, H., Ware, C., Mason, J., McGuire, E., Lewis, D. W., Pagano, L., & Alley, W. (2009, May 2). *The distracted teenage driver.* Paper presented at Pediatric Academic Societies Annual Meeting, Baltimore, MD.

LaBerge, S. (1985). *Lucid dreaming.* Los Angeles, CA: Tarcher.

Labonte, B., Yerko, V., Gross, J., Mechawar, N., Meany, M. J., Szyf, M., & Ruecki, G. (2012). Differential glucocorticoid receptor exon 1_B, 1_C, and 1_H expression and methylation in suicide completers with a history of childhood abuse. *Biological Psychiatry, 72*, 41–48.

Ladenbauer, J., Külzow, N., Passmann, S., Antonenko, D., Grittner, U., Tamm, S., & Flöel, A. (2016). Brain stimulation during an afternoon nap boosts slow oscillatory activity and memory consolidation in older adults. *Neuroimage, 142*311–142323. doi:10.1016/j.neuroimage.2016.06.057

LaFrance, M., Hecht, M. A., & Paluk, B. L. (2003). The contingent smile: A meta-analysis of sex differences in smiling. *Psychological Bulletin, 129*, 305–334.

LaFreniere, P., & MacDonald, K. (2013). A postgenomic view of behavioral development and adaptation to the environment. *Developmental Review, 33*, 89–109. Available at http://dx.doi .org/10.1016/j.dr.2013.01.002

Lagopoulos, J. (2007). Functional MRI: An overview. *Acta Neuropsychiatrica, 19*, 64–65.

Lamb, R. J., Morral, A. R., Kirby, K. C., Iguchi, M. Y., & Galbicka, G. (2004). Shaping smoking cessation using percentile schedules. *Drug and Alcohol Dependence, 76*, 247–259.

Lametti, D. R., & Watkins, K. E. (2016). Cognitive neuroscience: The neural basis of motor learning by observing. *Current Biology, 26*(7), R288–R290. Available at http://dx.doi.org/10.1016/j .cub.2016.02.045

Lamp, R., & Krohn, E. (2001). A longitudinal predictive validity investigation of the SB:FE and K-ABC with at-risk children. *Journal of Psychoeducational Assessment, 19*, 334–349.

Lanciano, T., Curci, A., & Semin, G. R. (2010). The emotional and reconstructive determinants of emotional memories: An experimental approach to flash-bulb memory investigation. *Memory, 18*, 473–485.

Landry, R. G. (1973). The relationship of second language learning and verbal creativity. *Modern Language Journal, 57*, 110–113.

Lang, E., Berbaum, K., Faintuch, S., Hatsiopoulou, O., Halsey, N., Li, X., Berbaum, M., … Baum, J. (2006). Adjunctive self-hypnotic relaxation for outpatient medical procedures: A prospective randomized trial with women undergoing large core breast biopsy. *Pain, 126*, 155–164.

Lang, P. J., & Bradley, M. M. (2010). Emotion and the motivational brain. *Biological Psychology, 84*, 437–450.

Lange, C. (1992). *The emotions* (I. A. Haupt, Trans.). Baltimore, MD: Williams & Wilkins. (Original work published 1885)

Lange, P. G. (2008). Publicly private and privately public: Social networking on YouTube. *Journal of Computer-Mediated Communication, 13*, 361–380.

Langlois, J. H., & Roggman, L. A. (1990). Attractive faces are only average. *Psychological Science, 1*, 115–121.

Langlois, J. H., Roggman, L. A., & Musselman, L. (1994). What is average and what is not average about attractive faces? *Psychological Science, 5*, 214–220.

Lapsley, D. K. (2006). Moral stage theory. In M. Killen & J. G. Smetana (Eds.), *Handbook of moral development* (pp. 37–66). Mahwah, NJ: Erlbaum.

Larsen, J. K., Krogh-Nielsen, L., & Brösen, K. (2016). The monoamine oxidase inhibitor isocarboxazid is a relevant treatment option in treatment-resistant depression-experience-based strategies in Danish psychiatry. *Health Care: Current Reviews, 1–4.* doi: 10.4172/2375-4273.1000168

Larson, L., Wu, T., Bailey, D., Gasser, C., Bonitz, V., & Borgen, F. (2010). The role of personality in the selection of a major: With and without vocational self-efficacy and interests. *Journal of Vocational Behavior, 76*, 211–222.

Larsson, J., Larsson, H., & Lichtenstein, P. (2004). Genetic and environmental contributions to stability and change of ADHD symptoms between 8 and 13 years of age: A longitudinal twin study. *Journal of American Academy of Child and Adolescent Psychiatry, 43*, 1267–1275.

Laruelle, M. (2014). Schizophrenia: From dopaminergic to glutamatergic interventions. *Current Opinion in Pharmacology, 14*, 97–102. Available at http://dx.doi.org/10.1016/j.coph.2014.01.001

Lasagabaster, D. (2000). The effects of three bilingual education models on linguistic creativity. *International Review of Applied Linguistics in Language Teaching, 38*, 213–228.

Laschet, J., Kurcewicz, I., Minier, F., Trottier, S., Khallou-Laschet, J., Louvel, J., … Pumain, R. (2007). Dysfunction of GABA-sub(A) receptor glycolysis-dependent modulation in human partial epilepsy. *Proceedings of the National Academy of Sciences, 104*(9), 3472–3477. doi: 10.1073/ pnas.0606451104

Laumann, E., Paik, A., Glasser, D., Kang, J., Wang, T., Levinson, B., … Gingell, C. (2006). A cross-national study of subjective sexual well-being among older women and men: Findings from the global study of sexual attitudes and behaviors. *Archives of Sexual Behavior, 35*(2), 145–161. doi: 10.1007/s10508-005-9005-3

Laureys, S. (2007). Eyes open, brain shut. *Scientific American, 296*, 84–89.

Lauzon, N. M., Bechard, M., Ahmad, T., & Laviolette, S. R. (2013). Supra-normal stimulation of dopamine D_1 receptors in the prelimbic cortex blocks behavioral expression of both aversive and rewarding associative memories through a cyclic-AMP-dependent signaling pathway. *Neuropharmacology, 67*, 104–114. doi: 10.1016/j .neuropharm.2012.10.029

Lavelli, M., & Fogel, A. (2005). Developmental changes in the relationship between the infant's attention and emotion during early face-to-face communication: The 2-month transition. *Developmental Psychology, 41*, 265–280.

Lavie, N., Hirst, A., De Fockert, J. W., & Viding, E. (2004). Load theory of selective attention and cognitive control. *Journal of Experimental Psychology: General, 133*, 339–354.

Law, A. J., Lipska, B. K., Weickert, C. S., Hyde, T. M., Straub, R. E., Hahimoto, R., … Weinberger, D. R. (2006). Neuregulin 1 transcripts are differentially expressed in schizophrenia and regulated by 5' SNPs associated with the disease. *Proceedings of the National Academy of Sciences USA, 103*, 6747–6752.

Lawless, H. T., Schlake, S., Smythe, J., Lim, J., Yang, H., Chapman, K., & Bolton, B. (2004). Metallic taste and retronasal smell. *Chemical Senses, 29*, 25–33. doi: 10.1093/chemse/bjh003

Laxton, A. W., & Lozano, A. M. (2012). Deep brain stimulation for the treatment of Alzheimer disease and dementia. *World Neurosurgery, S28.e1–S28.e8.* doi: 10.1016/j.wneu.2012.06.028

Lazar, S. W., Kerr, C., Wasserman, R. H., Gray, J. R., Greve, D., Treadway, M. T., … Fischl, B. (2005). Meditation experience is associated with increased cortical thickness. *NeuroReport, 216*, 1893–1897.

Lazarus, A. A., & Abramovitz, A. (2004). A multimodal behavioral approach to performance anxiety. *Journal of Clinical Psychology, 60*, 831–840.

Lazarus, R. S. (1983). The costs and benefits of denial. In *The denial of stress* (S. Breznitz, Ed.), pp. 1–30. New York, NY: International Universities Press.

Lazarus, R. S. (1991). *Emotion and adaptation.* New York, NY: Oxford University Press.

Lazarus, R. S., & Folkman, S. (1984). *Stress, appraisal, and coping.* New York, NY: Springer.

Lazarus, R. S., Kanner, A. A., & Folkman, S. (1980). Emotions: A cognitive-phenomenological analysis. In R. Plutchik & H. Kellerman (Eds.), *Emotion: Theory, research, and experience: Vol. 1. Theories of emotion* (pp. 189–217). New York, NY: Academic Press.

Le Bars, P. L., Katz, M. M., Berman, N., Itil, T. M., Freedman, A. M., & Schatzberg, A. F. (1997). A placebo-controlled, double-blind, randomized trial of an extract of ginkgo biloba for dementia. *Journal of the American Medical Association, 278*, 1327–1332.

Le Noury, J., Nardo, J. M., Healy, D., Jureidini, J., Raven, M., Tufanaru, C., & Abi-Jaoude, E. (2015). Restoring Study 329: Efficacy and harms of paroxetine and imipramine in treatment of major depression in adolescence. *BJM, 351*, h4320. doi: https://doi.org/10.1136/bmj.h4320

Leary, M. R. (2007). Motivational and emotional aspects of the self. *Annual Review of Psychology, 58*, 317–344.

Leary, M. R., Kowalski, R. M., Smith, L., & Phillips, S. (2003). Teasing, rejection, and violence: Case studies of the school shootings. *Aggressive Behavior, 29*, 202–214.

Leary, M. R., Twenge, J. M., & Quinlivan, E. (2006). Interpersonal rejection as a determinant of anger and aggression. *Personality and Social Psychology Review, 10*, 111–132.

Ledbetter, S. (2015, October 13). This haunted world. Retrieved online June 23, 2016 at https://blogs.chapman.edu/wilkinson/2015/10/13/this-haunted-world/

LeDoux, J. (1996). *The emotional brain: The mysterious underpinnings of emotional life.* New York, NY: Simon & Schuster.

LeDoux, J. (2000). Emotion circuits in the brain. *Annual Review of Neuroscience, 23*, 155–184.

Lee, C., & Chiou, W. (2013). Keep logging in! Experimental evidence showing the relation of affiliation needs to the idea of online social networking. *Cyberpsychology, Behavior, and Social Networking, 16*(6), 419–422.

Lee, C., Therriault, D., & Linderholm, T. (2012). On the cognitive benefits of cultural experience: Exploring the relationship between studying abroad and creative thinking. *Applied Cognitive Psychology, 26*(5), 768–778.

Lee, C. S., & Therriault, D. J. (2011). The cognitive underpinnings of creative thought: A latent variable analysis exploring the roles of intelligence and working memory in three creative thinking processes. *Intelligence, 41*, 306–320. doi: 10.106/j.intell2013.04.008

Lee, E., Ahn, J., & Kim, Y. J. (2014). Personality traits and self-presentation at Facebook. *Personality and Individual Differences, 69*, 162–167. Available at http://doi.org/10.1016/j.paid.2014.05.020

Lee, H., Macbeth, A. H., Pagani, J. H., & Young, S. W. (2009). Oxytocin: The great facilitator of life. *Progress in Neurobiology, 88*, 127–151.

Lee, K. A. (2006). Sleep dysfunction in women and its management. *Current Treatment Options in Neurology, 8*, 376–386.

Lee, M. L., Howard, M. E., Horrey, Y. S. J., Liangd, Y., Anderson, C., Shreeve, M. S., O'Brien, S., and Czeisler, C.A.(2016). High risk of near-crash driving events following night-shift work. *Proceedings of the National Academy of Sciences 113*, 176–181. doi: /10.1073/pnas.1510383112

Leitner, J. B., Hehman, E., Ayduk, O., & Mendoza-Denton, R. (2016). Racial bias is associated with ingroup death rate for blacks and whites: Insights from Project Implicit. *Social Science & Medicine, 170*, 220–227. Available at http://dx.doi.org.libaccess.sjlibrary.org/10.1016/j.socscimed.2016.10.007

Lemay, E. P., Jr., & Ashmore, R. D. (2004). Reactions to perceived categorization by others during the transition to college: Internalization and self-verification processes. *Group Processes & Intergroup Relations, 7*, 173–187.

Lenhart, A. (2015). Teens, social media and technology overview 2015: Smartphones facilitate shifts in communication landscape for teens. *Pew Research Center*, (April), 1–47. Available at http://doi.org/10.1016/j.chb.2015.08.026

Lenhart, A., Anderson, M., & Smith, A. (2015). Teens, technology, and romantic relationships: Appendix A: Lesbian, gay, bisexual, and transgender teens. Retrieved February 10, 2017 at http://www.pewinternet.org/2015/10/01/lesbian-gay-bisexual-and-transgender-teens/

Lenneberg, E. (1967). *The biological foundations of language.* New York, NY: Wiley.

Lennie, P. (2000). Colorvision. In E. R. Kandel, J. H. Schwartz, & T. M. Jessell (Eds.), *Principles of neural science* (4th ed., pp. 572–589). New York, NY: McGraw-Hill.

Lenzenweger, M. F., Lane, M. C., Loranger, A. W., & Kessler, R. C. (2007). *DSM-IV* personality disorders in the National Comorbidity Survey Replication. *Biological Psychiatry, 15*, 553–564.

Lepage, J.-F., & Théoret, H. (2007). The mirror neuron system: Grasping others' actions from birth? *Developmental Science, 10*, 513–523.

LePort, A. K. R., Stark, S. M., McGaugh, J. L., & Stark, C. E. L. (2016). Highly superior autobiographical memory: Quality and quantity of retention over time. *Frontiers in Psychology, 6*(JAN), 1–10. Available at http://doi.org/10.3389/fpsyg.2015.02017

Lerner, L. (1996). *The Kennedy women: The saga of an American family.* New York, NY: Random House.

Lerner, M. S., Niciu, M. J., Ballard, E. D., Park, M., Park, L. T., Nugent, A., & Zarate, C. A. (2016). Glutamate and GABA systems in the pathophysiology of major depression and antidepressant response to ketamine. *Biological Psychiatry.* Available at http://dx.doi.org/10.1016/j.biopsych.2016.05.005

Lesch, K. P., Bengel, D., Heils, A., Sabol, S. Z., Greenburg, B. D., Petri, S., … Murphy, D. L. (1996). Association of anxiety-related traits with a polymorphism in the serotonin transporter gene regulatory region. *Science, 274*, 1527–1531. doi: 10.1126/science.274.5292.1527

Lethbridge-Cejku, M., & Vickerie, J. (2005). Summary health statistics for U.S. adults: National Health Interview Survey, 2003. National Center for Health Statistics, *Vital Health Statistics, 10*.

Letzring, T. D., Edmonds, G. W., & Hampson, S. E. (2014). Personality change at mid-life is associated with changes in self-rated health: Evidence from the Hawaii personality and health cohort. *Personality and Individual Differences, 58*, 60–64. doi: 10.1016/j.paid.2013.10.002

Leuner, B., Glasper, E. R., & Gould, E. (2010). Sexual experience promotes adult neurogenesis in the hippocampus despite an initial elevation in stress hormones. *PLoS ONE, 5*, 1–8. doi: 10.1371/journal.pone.0011597

Leuner, B., & Gould, E. (2010). Structural plasticity and hippocampal function. *Annual Review of Psychology, 61*, 111–140.

LeVay, S. (1991). A difference in hypothalamic structure between heterosexual and homosexual men. *Science, 253*, 1034–1037.

Levenson, R. W. (1988). Emotion and the autonomic nervous system: A prospectus for research on autonomic specificity. In H. Wagner (Ed.), *Social psychophysiology and emotion: Theory and clinical applications* (pp. 17–42). London, England: Wiley.

Levenson, R. W. (2003). Blood, sweat, and fears: The autonomic architecture of emotion. *Annals of the New York Academy of Sciences, 1000*, 348–366.

Levenson, R. W., Carstensen, L. L., & Gottman, J. M. (1994). The influence of age and gender on affect, physiology, and their interactions: A study of long-term marriages. *Journal of Personality and Social Psychology, 67*, 56–68.

Levenson, R. W., Ekman, P., & Friesen, W. V. (1990). Voluntary facial action generates emotion-specific autonomic nervous system activity. *Psychophysiology, 27*, 363–384.

Levenson, R. W., Ekman, P., Heider, K., & Friesen, W. V. (1992). Emotion and autonomic nervous system activity in the Minangkabau of West Sumatra. *Journal of Personality and Social Psychology, 62*, 972–988.

Levine, L. E., Waite, B. M., & Bowman, L. L. (2012). Mobile media use, multitasking and distractibility. *International Journal of Cyber Behavior, Psychology and Learning, 2*(3), 15–29. Available at http://doi.org/10.4018/ijcbpl.2012070102

Levy, B. J., Kuhl, B. A., & Wagner, A. D. (2010). The functional neuroimaging of forgetting. In S. Della Sala (Ed.), *Current Issues in Memory: Forgetting* (pp. 135–163). New York: Psychology Press.

Levy, D. M., Wobbrock, J. O., Kaszniak, A. W., & Ostergren, M. (2012). The effects of mindfulness meditation training on multitasking in a high-stress information environment. *Proceedings of Graphics Interface (GI '12)*, Toronto, Ontario, May 28–30, 2012, 45–52.

Lewis, D., & Levitt, P. (2002). Schizophrenia as a disorder of neurodevelopment. *Annual Review of Neuroscience, 25*, 409–432. doi: 10.1146/annurev.neuro.25.11270.142754

Lewis, G. D., Farrell, L., Wood, M. J., Martinovic, M., Arany, Z., Rowe, G. C., … Gerszten, R. E. (2010). Metabolic signatures of exercise in human plasma. *Science Translational Medicine, 2*, 33–37.

Lewis, K. (2013). The limits of racial prejudice. *Proceedings of the National Academy of the Sciences, 110*, 18814–18819. doi: 10.1073/pnas.1308501110

Ley, R. E., Turnbaugh, P. J., Klein, S., & Gordon, J. I. (2006). Microbial ecology: Human gut microbes associated with obesity. *Nature, 444*(7122), 1022–1023. doi:10.1038/4441022a

Li, H., & Chen, G. (2016). In vivo reprogramming for CNS repair: Regenerating neurons from endogenous glial cells. *Neuron, 91*, 728–738. Available at http://dx.doi.org/10.1016/j.neuron.2016.08.004

Li, H., Liang, A., Guan, F., Fan, R., Chi, L., & Yang, B. (2013). Regular treadmill running improves spatial learning and memory performance in young mice through increased hippocampal neurogenesis and decreased stress. *Brain Research, 1531*, 1–8. Retrieved from http://dx.doi.org/10.1016/j.brainres.2013.07.041

Li, P., Legault, J., & Litcofsky, K. A. (2014). Neuroplasticity as a function of second language learning: Anatomical changes in the human brain. *Cortex: A Journal Devoted to the Study of the Nervous System and Behavior, 58*, 301–324. doi: 10.1016/j.cortex.2014.05.001

Lidz, J., & Gleitman, L. R. (2004). Argument structure and the child's contribution to language learning. *Trends in Cognitive Sciences, 8*, 157–161.

Lieberman, J. A., Chakos, M., Wu, H., Alvir, J., Hoffman, E., Robinson, D., & Bilder, R. (2001). Longitudinal study of brain morphology in first episodes of schizophrenia. *Biological Psychiatry, 49*, 487–499.

Lieberman, J. A., Stroup, T. S., McEvoy, J. P., Swartz, M. S., Rosenheck, R. A., Perkins, D. O., ... Hsiao, J. K. (2005). Effectiveness of anti-psychotic drugs in patients with chronic schizophrenia. *New England Journal of Medicine, 353*, 1209–1223.

Liebert, R. M., & Baron, R. A. (1972). Some immediate effects of televised violence on children's behavior. *Developmental Psychology, 6*, 469–475.

Liehr, P., Marcus, M. T., Carroll, D., Granmayeh, L. K., Cron, S. G., & Pennebaker, J. W. (2010). Linguistic analysis to assess the effect of a mindfulness intervention on self-change for adults in substance use recovery. *Substance Abuse, 31*, 79–85.

Lihoreau, M., Brepson, L., & Rivault, C. (2009). The weight of the clan: Even in insects, social isolation can induce a behavioural syndrome. *Behavioural Processes, 82*, 81–84.

Lin, J., Epel, E., & Blackburn, E. (2012). Telomeres and lifestyle factors: Roles in cellular aging. *Mutation Research, 730*, 85–89. doi: 10.1016/j.mrfmmm.2011.08.003

Lin, K., & Lu, H. (2011). Why people use social networking sites: An empirical study integrating network externalities and motivation theory. *Computers in Human Behavior, 27*, 1152–1161.

Lin, L. Y., Sidani, J. E., Shensa, A., Radovic, A., Miller, E., Colditz, J. B., ... Primack, B. A. (2016). Association between social media use and depression among U.S. young adults. *Depression and Anxiety, 33*(4), 323–331. Available at http://doi.org/10.1002/da.22466

Linden, D. E. J. (2006). How psychotherapy changes the brain—The contribution of functional neuroimaging. *Molecular Psychiatry, 11*, 528–538.

Lindgren, K. P., Kaysen, D., Werntz, A. J., Gasser, M. L., & Teachman, B. A. (2013). Wounds that can't be seen: Implicit trauma associations predict posttraumatic stress disorder symptoms. *Journal of Behavior Therapy and Experimental Psychiatry, 44*, 368–375. Available at http://dx.doi.org/10.1016/j.jbtep.2013.03.003

Lindsay, D. S., Hagen, L., Read, J. D., Wade, K. A., & Garry, M. (2004). True photographs and false memories. *Psychological Science, 15*, 149–154.

Linehan, M. M. (1993). *Skills training manual of treating borderline personality disorder.* New York, NY: Guilford Press.

Linehan, M. M., Armstrong, H. E., Suarez, A., Allmon, D., & Heard, H. L. (1991). Cognitive-behavioral treatment of chronically parasuicidal borderline patients. *Archives of General Psychiatry, 48*, 1060–1064.

Linehan, M. M., Comtois, K. A., Murray, A. M., Brown, M. Z., Gallop, R. J., Heard, H. L., ... Lindenboim, N. (2006). Two-year randomized controlled trial and follow-up of dialectical behavior therapy vs. therapy by experts for suicidal behaviors and borderline personality disorder. *Archives of General Psychiatry, 63*, 757–766.

Linehan, M. M., Heard, H. L., & Armstrong, H. E. (1993). Naturalistic follow-up of a behavioral treatment for chronically parasuicidal borderline patients. *Archives of General Psychiatry, 50*, 971–974.

Lipkus, I. M., Barefoot, J. C., Williams, R. B., & Siegler, I. C. (1994). Personality measures as predictors of smoking initiation and cessation in the UNC alumni heart study. *Health Psychology, 13*, 149–155.

Lippa, R. (1994). *Introduction to social psychology.* Pacific Grove, CA: Brooks/Cole.

Lipsman, N., Woodside, D. B., Giacobbe, P., Hamani, C., Carter, J. C., Norwood, S. J., Sutandar, K., Staab, R., Elias, G., Lyman, C. H.,

Smith, G. S., & Lozano, A. M. (2013). Subcallosal cingulate deep brain stimulation for treatment-refractory anorexia nervosa: A phase 1 pilot trial. *The Lancet, 381*, 1361–1370.

Lisetti, C., Pozzo, E., Lucas, M., Hernandez, F., Selverman, W., Kurtines, B., & Pasztor, A. (2009). *Second Life*, bio-sensors, and exposure therapy for anxiety disorders. *Annual Review of CyberTherapy and Telemedicine, 7*, 19–21.

Litt, E., (2013). Understanding social network site users' privacy tool use. *Computers in Human Behavior, 29*, 1649–1656. Available at http://dx.doi.org/10.1016/j.chb.2013.01.049

Litwin, H., Schwartz, E., & Damri, N. (2010). Cognitive stimulation leisure activity and subsequent cognitive function: A SHARE-based analysis. *The Gerontologist.* Retrieved October 22, 2016 from http://gerontologist.oxfordjournals.org/content/early/2016/04/26/geront.gnw084.short. doi: 10.1093/geront/gnw084

Liu, H., Elliott, S., & Umberson, D. (2009). Marriage in young adulthood. In J. E. Grant & M. N. Potenza (Eds.), *Young adult mental health* (pp. 169–280). New York, NY: Oxford University Press.

Liu, S., Wilson, J. G., Jiang, F., Griswold, M., Correa, A., & Mei, H. (2016). Multi-variant study of obesity risk genes in African Americans: The Jackson Heart Study. *Gene, 593*(2), 315–321. Available at http://dx.doi.org/10.1016/j.gene.2016.08.041

Liu, T., Xu, C., Rota, M., Cai, H., Zhang, C., Shi, M., Yuan, R., Weng, H., Meng, X., Kwong, J. S. W., & Sun, X. (2016). Sleep duration and risk of all-cause mortality: A flexible, non-linear, meta-regression of 40 prospective cohort studies. *Sleep Medicine Reviews.* Available online March 3, 2016. Retrieved from http://dx.doi.org/10.1016/j.smrv.2016.02.005

Liu, Y., Wang, H., Weng, S., Su, W., Wang, X., Guo, Y., & ... Shi, T. (2015). Occupational hearing loss among Chinese municipal solid waste landfill workers: A cross-sectional study. *Plos ONE, 10*(6), e0128719. doi:10.1371/journal.pone.0128719

Ljungberg, J. K., Hansson, P., Andrés, P., Josefsson, M., & Nilsson, L. G. (2013). A longitudinal study of memory advantages in bilinguals. *PLoS ONE, 8*(9). Available at http://doi.org/10.1371/journal.pone.0073029

Llabre, M. M., Scneiderman, N., Gallo, L. C., Arguelles, W., Daviglus, M. L., Franklyn Gonzalez, I. I., ... & Penedo, F. J. (2017). Childhood trauma and adult risk factors and disease in Hispanics/Latinos in the U.S.: Results from the Hispanic Community Health Study/Study of Latinos (HCHS/SOL) sociocultural ancillary study. *Psychosomatic Medicine.* doi: 10.1097/PSY.0000000000000394

Locke, J. (1959). *An essay concerning human understanding: Vol. 1.* New York, NY: Dover. (Original work published 1690)

Lockhart, R. S., & Craik, F. I. M. (1990). Levels of processing: A retrospective commentary on a framework for memory research. *Canadian Journal of Psychology, 44*, 77–112.

Lodi-Smith, J., Geise, A., Roberts, B., & Robins, R. (2009). Narrating personality change. *Journal of Personality and Social Psychology, 96*, 679–689.

Loehlin, J. C., McCrae, R. R., Costa, P. T., & John, O. P. (1998). Heritabilities of common and measure specific components of the Big Five personality factors. *Journal of Research in Personality, 32*, 431–453.

Loeser, J. D., & Melzack, R. (1999). Pain: An overview. *The Lancet, 353*, 1607–1609.

Loftus, E. (1996). *Eyewitness testimony.* Cambridge, MA: Harvard University Press.

Loftus, E. (2003). Make-believe memories. *American Psychologist, 58*, 864–873.

Loftus, E. F. (1974). Leading questions and the eyewitness report. *Cognitive Psychology, 7*, 560–572.

Loftus, E. F. (1997). Creating false memories. *Scientific American, 277*, 70–75.

Loftus, E. F. (2005). Planting misinformation in the human mind: A 30-year investigation of the malleability of memory. *Learning and Memory, 12*, 361–366.

Loftus, E. F., & Pickrell, J. E. (1995). The formation of false memories. *Psychiatric Annuals, 25*, 720–725.

Long, M. (1990). Maturational constraints on language development. *Studies in Second Language Acquisition, 12*, 251–285.

Looi, C. Y., Duta, M., Brem, A.-K., Huber, S., Nuerk, H.-C., & Cohen Kadosh, R. (2016). Combining brain stimulation and video game to promote long-term transfer of learning and cognitive enhancement. *Scientific Reports, 6*(August 2015), 22003. Available at http://doi.org/10.1038/srep22003

López-Muñoz, F., Shen, W. W., Pae, C., Moreno, R., Rubio, G., Molina, J. D., Noriega, C., Pérez-Nieto, M. A., Huelves, L., & Álamo, C. (2013). Trends in scientific literature on atypical antipsychotics in South Korea: A bibliometric study. *Psychiatry Investigation, 10*, 8–16. doi: 10.4306/pi.2013.10.1.8

Lorenc, Z. P., Kenkel, J. M., Fagien, S., Hirmand, H., Nestor, M. S., Sclafani, A. P., Sykes, J. M., & Waldorf, H. A. (2013). A review of OnabotulinumtoxinA (Botox). *Aesthetic Surgery Journal, 33*, 9S–12S. doi: 10.1177/1090820X12474629

Lorenz, K. (1935). Der Kumpan in der Umwelt des Vogels. *Journal of Ornithology, 83*, 137–215.

Lorenz, K. (1937). The companion in the bird's world. *Auk, 54*, 245–273.

Lovaas, O. I. (1987). Behavioral treatment and normal educational and intellectual functioning in young autistic children. *Journal of Consulting and Clinical Psychology, 55*, 3–9.

Lovell, B., & Wetherell, M. A. (2011). The cost of caregiving: Endocrine and immune implications in elderly and non elderly caregivers. *Neuroscience & Biobehavioral Reviews, 35*, 1342–1352.

Lovett, R. (2005, September 24). Coffee: The demon drink? *New Scientist.* Retrieved online on March 14, 2014 at http://www.newscientist.com/article/mg18725181.700-coffee-the-demon-drink.html

Lowry, C. A., Hale, M. W, Evans, A. K., Keerkens, J., Staub, D. R., Gasser, P. J., & Shekhar, A. (2008). Serotonergic systems, anxiety, and affective disorder focus on the dorsomedial part of the dorsal raphe nucleus. *Annals of the New York Academy of Sciences, 1148*, 86–94.

Lozano, A. M., Mayberg, H. S., & Kennedy, S. H. (2012). Response-deep brain stimulation and depression. *Journal of Neurosurgery, 116*(2), 313.

Lubinski, D., & Benbow, C. P. (2006). Study of mathematically precocious youth after 35 years: Uncovering antecedents for the development of math-science expertise. *Perspectives on Psychological Science, 1*, 316–345.

Lubinski, D., Benbow, C. P., & Kell, H. J. (2014). Life paths and accomplishments of mathematically precocious males and females four decades later. *Psychological Science, 25*(12), 2217–2232. Available at http://doi.org/10.1177/0956797615575525

Luborsky, L., Singer, B., & Luborsky, L. (1975). Comparative studies of psychotherapy. *Archives of General Psychiatry, 32*, 995–1008.

Luchins, A. S., & Luchins, E. H. (1970). *Wertheimer's seminars revisited: Problem solving and thinking.* Albany, NY: SUNY Press.

Ludwig, A. M. (1995). *The price of greatness.* New York, NY: Guilford Press.

Luecken, L. J., Hagan, M. J., Wolchik, S. A., Sandler, I. N., & Tein, J. Y. (2016). A longitudinal study of the effects of child-reported maternal warmth on cortisol stress response 15 years after parental divorce. *Psychosomatic Medicine, 78*(2), 163–170. doi: 10.1097/PSY.0000000000000251

Lundy, B. L., & Drouin, M. (2016). From social anxiety to interpersonal connectedness: Relationship building within face-to-face, phone, and instant messaging mediums. *Computers in Human Behavior, 54*, 271–277. doi: 10.1016/j.chb.2015.08.004

Lupis, S. B., Lerman, M., & Wolf, J. M. (2014). Anger responses to psychosocial stress predict heart rate and cortisol stress responses in men but not women. *Psychoneuroendocrinology, 49*, 84–95. Available at http://dx.doi.org/10.1016/j.psyneuen.2014.07.004

Lutman, M. E., & Spencer, H. S. (1991). Occupational noise and demographic factors in hearing. *Acta Otolaryngologica, Suppl. 476*, 74–84.

Lutz, A., Slagter, H. A., Rawlings, N. B., Francis, A. D., Greischar, L. L., & Davidson, R. J. (2009). Mental training enhances attentional stability: Neural and behavioral evidence. *Journal of Neuroscience, 29*, 13418–13427.

Luykx, J. J., Boks, M. P. M., Terwindt, A. P. R., Bakker, S., Kahn, R. S., & Ophoff, R. A. (2010). The involvement of GSK3β in bipolar disorder: Integrating evidence from multiple types of genetic studies. *European Neuropsychopharmacology, 20*, 357–368.

Lyketsos, C. G., Targum, S. D., Pendergrass, J. C., & Lozano, A. M. (2012). Deep brain stimulation: A novel strategy for treating Alzheimer's disease. *Innovations in Clinical Neuroscience, 9*(11–12), 10.

Lynn, R. (2006). *Race differences in intelligence: An evolutionary analysis.* Augusta, GA: National Summit.

Lynn, S. J., Evans, J., Laurence, J., & Lilienfeld, S. O. (2015). What do people believe about memory? Implications for the science and pseudoscience of clinical practice. *The Canadian Journal of Psychiatry / La Revue Canadienne de Psychiatrie, 60*(12), 541–545.

Lynn, S. J., Lilienfeld, S. O., Merckelbach, H., Giesbrecht, T., & van der Kloet, D. (2012). Dissociation and dissociative disorders: Challenging conventional wisdom. *Current Directions in Psychological Science, 21*, 48–53. doi: 10.1177/0963721411429457

Lyons, D. E. (2009). The rational continuum of human imitation. In J. A. Pineda (Ed.), *Mirror neuron systems: The role of mirroring processes in social cognition* (pp. 77–103). Totowa, NJ: Humana Press.

Lyons, D. M., Buckmaster, P. S., Lee, A. G., Wu, C., Mitra, R., Duffey, L. M., ... Schatzberg, A. F. (2010). Stress coping stimulates hippocampal neurogenesis in adult monkeys. *Proceedings of the National Academy of Sciences, 107*, 14823–14827.

Ma, X., Edgecombe, G. D., Hou, X., Goral, T., & Strausfeld, N. J. (2015). Preservational pathways of corresponding brains of a Cambrian Euarthropod. *Current Biology, 25*(22), 2969–2975. Available at http://doi.org/10.1016/j.cub.2015.09.063

Maas, J. (1998). *Power sleep.* New York, NY: Villard.

Macaskill, M. (2008, February 10). Blind taught to "see" like a bat. *The Sunday Times.* Retrieved from http://www.timesonline.co.uk

Maccoby, E. E. (2000). Perspectives on gender development. *International Journal of Behavioral Development, 24*, 398–406.

Maccoby, E. E., & Jacklin, C. N. (1974). *The psychology of sex differences.* Stanford, CA: Stanford University Press.

Maccoby, E. E., & Jacklin, C. N. (1987). Gender segregation in childhood. In H. Reese (Ed.), *Advances in child behavior and development.* New York, NY: Academic Press.

MacDonald, G., & Leary, M. R. (2005). Why does social exclusion hurt? The relationship between social and physical pain. *Psychological Bulletin, 131*, 202–223.

MacDonald, G., Kingsbury, R., & Shaw, S. (2005). *Adding insult to injury: Social pain theory and response to social exclusion.* New York, NY: Psychology Press.

MacDonald, K. (1995). Evolution, the five factor model, and levels of personality. *Journal of Personality, 63*, 525–567.

MacKinnon, D. W. (1970). Creativity: A multifaceted phenomenon. In J. Roslansky (Ed.), *Creativity* (pp. 19–32). Amsterdam, Netherlands: North-Holland.

MacLane, C. N., & Walmsley, P. T. (2010). Reducing counterproductive work behavior through employee selection. *Human Resource Management Review, 20*, 62–72.

MacLean, K. A., Ferrer, E., Aichele, S., Bridwell, D. A., King, B. G., Jacobs, T. L., ... Saron, C. D. (2010). Intensive meditation training leads to improvements in perceptual discrimination and sustained attention. *Psychological Science, 21*, 829–839.

MacLean, K. A., Johnson, M. W., & Griffiths, R. R. (2011). Mystical experiences occasioned by the hallucinogen psilocybin lead to increases in the personality domain of openness. *Journal of Psychopharmacology, 25*(11), 1453–1461. doi: 10.1177/0269881111420188

Macmillan, M. (2000). *An odd kind of fame: Stories of Phineas Gage.* Cambridge, MA: MIT Press.

MacWhinney, B. (1999). *The emergence of language.* Mahwah, NJ: Erlbaum.

Maddi, S. R., Matthews, M. D., Kelly, D. R., Villarreal, B., & White, M. (2012). The role of hardiness and grit in predicting performance and retention of USMA cadets. *Military Psychology, 24*(1), 19–28. doi: 10.1080/08995605.2012.639672

Madigan, S., & O'Hara, R. (1992). Short-term memory at the turn of the century: Mary Whiton Calkins's memory research. *American Psychologist, 47*, 170–174.

Maes, H. M. M., Neale, M. C., & Eaves, L. J. (1997). Genetic and environmental factors in relative body weight and human adiposity. *Behavior Genetics, 27*, 325–351.

Maestripieri, D., Higley, J. D., Lindell, S. G., Newman, T. K., McCormack, K. M., & Sanchez, M. M. (2006). Early maternal rejection affects the development of monoaminergic systems and adult abusive parenting in rhesus macaques (*Macaca mulatto*). *Behavioral Neuroscience, 120*, 1017–1024.

Maguire, E. A., Woollett, K., & Spiers, H. J. (2006). London taxi drivers and bus drivers: A structural MRI and neuropsychological analysis. *Hippocampus, 16*, 1091–1101.

Maier, N. R. F. (1931). Reasoning in humans: II. The solution of a problem and its appearance. *Journal of Comparative and Physiological Psychology, 12*, 181–194.

Maier, S. F., & Seligman, M. E. (2016). Learned helplessness at fifty: Insights from neuroscience. *Psychological Review, 123*(4), 349. Available at http://dx.doi.org/10.1037/rev0000033

Main, M., & Hesse, E. (1990). Lack of resolution of mourning in adulthood and its relationship to infant disorganization: Some speculations regarding causal mechanisms. In M. Greenberg, D. Cicchetti, & E. M. Cummings (Eds.), *Attachment in the preschool years* (pp. 161–184). Chicago, IL: University of Chicago Press.

Mainieri, A. G., Heim, S., Straube, B., Binkofski, F., & Kircher, T. (2013). Differential role of the mentalizing and the mirror neuron system in the imitation of communicative gestures. *NeuroImage, 81*, 294–305. Available at http://dx.doi.org/10.1016/j.neuroimage.2013.05.021

Majid, A., & Levinson, S. C. (2011). The senses in language and culture. *Senses and Society, 6*, 5–18.

Malanchini, M., Tosto, M. G., Garfield, V., Dirik, A., Czerwik, A., Arden, R., & ... Kovas, Y. (2016). Preschool drawing and school mathematics: The nature of the association. *Child Development, 87*(3), 929–943. doi:10.1111/cdev.12520

Malhi, G. S., Adams, D., & Berk, M. (2010). The pharmacological treatment of bipolar disorder in primary care. *Medical Journal of Australia, 193*, S24–S30.

Malik, S. Z., & Shahid, S. (2016). Effect of emotional intelligence on academic performance among business students in Pakistan. *Bulletin of Education and Research, 38*(1).

Malkinson, T. S., & Bartolomeo, P. (2016). *Human attention networks and their dysfunctions after brain damage.* New York: Springer, pp. 39–59. doi: 10.1007/978-1-4939-3435-5_4 39–59

Mallick, H. N., Tandon, S., Jagannathan, N. R., Gulia, K. K., & Kumar, V. M. (2007). Brain areas activated after ejaculation in healthy young human subjects. *Indian Journal of Physiology and Pharmacology, 51*, 81–85.

Mamidala, M. P., Polinedi, A., Kumar, P., Rajesh, N., Vallamkonda, O. R., Udani, V., Singhal, N., & Rajesh, V. (2013). Prenatal, perinatal and neonatal risk factors of autism spectrum disorder: A comprehensive epidemiological assessment from India. *Research in Developmental Disabilities, 34*, 3004–3013. doi: 10.1016/j.bbr.2011.03.031

Mangels, J. A., Gershberg, F. B., Shimamura, A. P., & Knight, R. T. (1996). Impaired retrieval from remote memory in patients with frontal lobe damage. *Neuropsychology, 10*, 32–41.

Mangialasche, F., Solomon, A., Winblad, B., Mecocci, P., & Kivipelto, M. (2010). Alzheimer's disease: Clinical trials and drug development. *Lancet Neurology, 9*, 702–716.

Manjoo, F. (2016, June 7). In the fight for transgender equality, winning hearts and minds online. *New York Times* online. Retrieved November 15, 2016 at http://www.nytimes.com/2016/06/09/technology/in-the-fight-for-transgender-equality-winning-hearts-and-minds-online.html?ribbon-ad-idx=3&rref=technology&module=Ribbon&version=origin®ion=Header&action=click&contentCollection=Technology&pgtype=article&_r=1

Manley, M. H., Diamond, L. M., & Anders, S. M. Van. (2015). Polyamory, monoamory, and sexual fluidity: A longitudinal study of identity and sexual trajectories. *Psychology of Sexual Orientation and Gender Diversity, 2*(2), 168–180. Available at http://doi.org/10.1037/sgd0000098

Mann, S., & Cadman, R. (2014). Does being bored make us more creative? (*Creativity Research Journal Online*) *Journal Creativity Research Journal, 26*(2), 1040–419. Available at http://doi.org/10.1080/10400419.2014.901073

Mann, T., Tomiyama, A. J., Westling, E., Lew, A.-M., Samuels, B., & Chatman, J. (2007). Medicare's search for effective obesity treatments: Diets are not the answer. *American Psychologist, 62,* 220–233.

Mantler, T. (2013). A systematic review of smoking youths' perceptions of addiction and health risks associated with smoking: Utilizing the framework of the health belief model. *Addiction Research & Theory, 21,* 306–317. Retrieved from http://search.proquest.com/docview/1411060670?accountid=14505

Mantua, J., Baran, B., & Spencer, R. M. (2016). Sleep benefits consolidation of visuo-motor adaptation learning in older adults. *Experimental Brain Research, 234*(2), 587–595. doi: 10.1007/s00221-015-4490-7

Marais, L., Stein, D. J., & Daniels, W. M. U. (2009). Exercise increases BDNF levels in the striatum and decreases depressive-like behavior in chronically stressed rats. *Metabolic Brain Disease, 24,* 587–597.

Marchetto, N. M., Glynn, R. A., Ferry, M. L., Ostojic, M., Wolff, S. M., Yao, R., & Haussmann, M. F. (2016). Prenatal stress and newborn telomere length. *American Journal of Obstetrics and Gynecology.* Available at http://dx.doi.org/10.1016/j.ajog.2016.01.177

Marcia, J. E. (1966). Development and validation of ego-identity status. *Journal of Personality and Social Psychology, 3,* 551–558. doi: 10.1037/h0023281

Marcus, B., Machilek, F., & Schütz, A. (2006). Personality in cyberspace: Personal web sites as media for personality expressions and impressions. *Journal of Personality and Social Psychology, 90,* 1014–1031.

Marek, G. J., & Aghajanian, G. K. (1996). LSD and the phenethylamine hallucinogen DOI are potent partial agonists at 5-HT2A receptors on interneurons in the rat piriform cortex. *Journal of Pharmacology and Experimental Therapeutics, 278,* 1373–1382.

Marijuana research. (2004, December 8). [Editorial]. *Scientific American, 291,* 8.

Marin, O. (2012). Interneuron dysfunction in psychiatric disorders. *Nature Reviews Neuroscience, 13,* 107–120. doi: 10.1038/nrn3155

Marioni, R. E., Harris, S. E., Shah, S., McRae, A. F., von Zglinicki, T., Martin-Ruiz, C., … Deary, I. J. (2016). The epigenetic clock and telomere length are independently associated with chronological age and mortality. *International journal of epidemiology, 45*(2), 424-432. doi: 10.1093/ije/dyw041

Mark, G., Gudith, D., & Klocke, U. (2008). The cost of interrupted work: More speed and stress. *CHI '08: Proceeding of the twenty-sixth annual SIGCHI conference on human factors in computing systems.* New York, NY: ACM.

Marks, R. A. (2006). *The superlative, sensitive shark.* Retrieved from http://www.pbs.org/kqed/oceanadventures/episodes/sharks/indepth-senses.html

Markus, H., & Kitayama, S. (1991). Culture and the self: Implications for cognition, emotion, and motivation. *Psychological Review, 98,* 224–253.

Maron, E., Hettema, J. M., & Shlik, J. (2010). Advances in molecular genetics of panic disorder. *Molecular Psychiatry, 15,* 681–701.

Marsh, A. A., Yu, H. H., Pine, D. S., & Blair, R. J. R. (2010). Oxytocin improves specific recognition of positive facial expressions. *Psychopharmacology, 209,* 225–232.

Marshall, L., Molle, M., Hallschmid, M., & Born, J. (2004). Transcranial direct current stimulation during sleep improves declarative memory. *Journal of Neuroscience, 24*(44), 9985–9992.

Martin, C. C., DiDonato, M., Clary, L., Fabes, R., Kreiger, T., Palermo, F., & Hanish, L. (2012). Preschool children with gender normative and gender non-normative peer preferences: Psychosocial and Environmental Correlates. *Archives of Sexual Behavior, 41*(4), 831–847.

Martin, G., & Pear, J. J. (2015). *Behavior modification: What it is and how to do it.* Hove, UK: Psychology Press.

Martindale, C. (1999). Biological bases of creativity. In R. J. Sternberg (Ed.), *Handbook of creativity* (pp. 137–152). Cambridge, England: Cambridge University Press.

Martindale, C. (2005, October 2). One face, one neuron. *Scientific American, 293,* 22–23.

Martinez, G., Daniels, K., & Chandra, A. (2012, April 12). *Fertility of Men and Women aged 15–44 years in the United States: National Survey of Family Growth, 2006–2010.* Retrieved November 16, 2013, from http://www.cdc.gov/nchs/data/nhsr/nhsr051.pdf

Martinez, K. B., Leone, V., & Chang, E. B. (2017). Western diets, gut dysbiosis, and metabolic diseases: Are they linked? *Gut Microbes.* doi: 10.1080/19490976.2016.1270811

Maschi, S., Clavenna, A., Campi, R., Schiavetti, B., Bernat, M., & Bonati, M. (2008). Neonatal outcome following pregnancy exposure to antidepressants: A prospective controlled cohort study. *BJOG—An International Journal of Obstetrics and Gynaecology, 115,* 283–289.

Mash, E. J., & Wolf, D. A. (2010). *Abnormal child psychology* (4th ed.). Belmont, CA: Wadsworth.

Mashour, G. A., Walker, E. E., & Martuza, R. L. (2005). Psychosurgery: Past, present, and future. *Brain Research Reviews, 48,* 409–419.

Masling, J. M., & Bornstein, R. F. (2005). *Scoring the Rorschach: Retrospect and prospect.* Mahwah, NJ: Erlbaum.

Maslow, A. (1968). *Toward a psychology of being* (2nd ed.). New York, NY: Van Nostrand.

Maslow, A. (1970). *Motivation and personality* (2nd ed.). New York, NY: Harper & Row.

Mason, J. W. (1971). A re-evaluation of the concept of "non-specificity" in stress theory. *Journal of Psychiatric Research, 8,* 323–333.

Mason, J. W. (1975). A historical view of the stress field. *Journal of Human Stress, 1,* 6–12.

Masten, C. L., Eisenberger, N. I., Borofsky, L. A., Pfeifer, J. H., McNealy, K., Mazziotta, J. C., & Dapretto, M. (2009). Neural correlates of social exclusion during adolescence: Understanding the distress of peer rejection. *Social cognitive and affective neuroscience, 4*(2), 143-157. doi:10.1093/scan/nsp007

Masters, W. H., & Johnson, V. E. (1966). *The human sexual response.* Boston, MA: Little & Brown.

Masuda, A., & Wendell, J. W. (2010). Mindfulness mediates the relation between disordered eating–related cognitions and psychological distress. *Eating Behaviors, 11,* 293–296.

Masuda, T., & Nisbett, R. E. (2001). Attending holistically versus analytically: Comparing the context sensitivity of Japanese and Americans. *Journal of Personality and Social Psychology, 81,* 922–934.

Mateo, Y., Budygin, E. A., John, C. E., & Jones, S. R. (2004). Role of serotonin in cocaine effects in mice with reduced dopamine transporter function. *Proceedings of the National Academy of Sciences, 101,* 372–377.

Mathias, J. L., & Wheaton, P. (2007). Changes in attention and information-processing speed following severe traumatic brain injury: A meta-analytic review. *Neuropsychology, 21,* 212–223.

Mathiesen, B. B., Förster, P. L. V., & Svendsen, H. A. (2004). Affect regulation and loss of initiative in a case of orbitofrontal injury. *Neuropsychoanalysis, 6,* 47–62.

Mathur, M. B., Epel, E., Kind, S., Desai, M., Parks, C. G., Sandler, D. P., & Khazeni, N. (2016). Perceived stress and telomere length: A systematic review, meta-analysis, and methodologic considerations for advancing the field. *Brain, Behavior, and Immunity, 54,* 158–169. Available at http://dx.doi.org/10.1016/j.bbi.2016.02.002

Maticka-Tyndale, E., Harold, E. S., & Opperman, M. (2003). Casual sex among Australian schoolies. *Journal of Sex Research, 40,* 158–169.

Matson, J. L., & Boisjoli, J. A. (2009). The token economy for children with intellectual disability and/or autism: A review. *Research in Developmental Disabilities, 30,* 240–248.

Matson, J. L., Turygin, N. C., Beighley, J., Rieske, R., Tureck, K., & Matson, M. L. (2012). Applied behavior analysis in autism spectrum disorders: Recent developments, strengths, and pitfalls. *Research in Autism Spectrum Disorders, 6,* 144–150. Retrieved from http://dx.doi.org/10.1016/j.rasd.2011.03.014

Matsumoto, D., & Juang, L. (2004). *Culture and psychology* (3rd ed.). Belmont, CA: Thomson-Wadsworth.

Matsumoto, D., & Willingham, B. (2006). The thrill of victory and the agony of defeat: Spontaneous expressions of medal winners of the 2004 Athens Olympic Games. *Journal of Personality and Social Psychology, 91,* 568–581.

Matsumoto, D., Yoo, S. H., & Fontaine, J. (2008). Mapping expressive differences around the world: The relationship between emotional display rules and individualism versus collectivism. *Journal of Cross-Cultural Psychology, 39,* 55–74. doi: 10.1177/0022022107311854

Matthews, K. A., Glass, D. C., Rosenman, R. H., & Bortner, R. W. (1977). Competitive drive, Pattern A, and coronary heart disease: A further analysis of some data from the Western Collaborative Group Study. *Journal of Chronic Diseases, 30,* 489–498.

Mauss, I. B., Levenson, R. W., McCarter, L., Wilhelm, F. H., & Gross, J. J. (2005). The tie that binds? Coherence among emotion experience, behavior, and physiology. *Emotion, 5,* 175–190.

Max, J. E., Levin, H. S., Schachar, R. J., Landis, J., Saunders, A. E., Ewing-Cobbs, L., … Dennis, M. (2006). Predictors of personality change due to traumatic brain injury in children and adolescents six to twenty-four months after injury. *Journal of Neuropsychiatry and Clinical Neurosciences, 18,* 21–32. doi: 10.1176/appi.neuropsych.18.1.21

Max, J. E., Robertson, B. A. M., & Lansing, A. E. (2001). The phenomenology of personality change due to traumatic brain injury in children and adolescents. *Journal of Neuropsychiatry and Clinical Neurosciences, 13,* 161–170.

Maximova, K., McGrath, J. J., Barnett, T., O'Loughlin, J., Paradis, G., & Lambert, M. (2008). Do you see what I see? Weight status misperception and exposure to obesity among children and adolescents. *International Journal of Obesity, 32,* 1008–1015.

Maxmen, A. (2017). Psychedelic compound in ecstasy moves closer to approval to treat PTSD. *Nature News* (28 April 2017) | doi:10.1038/nature.2017.21917

May, P. A., & Gossage, J. P. (2001). Estimating the prevalence of fetal alcohol syndrome. A summary. *Alcohol Research & Health, 25,* 159–167.

Mayberg, H. S. (1997). Limbic-cortical dysregulation: A proposed model of depression. *Journal of Neuropsychiatry and Clinical Neuroscience, 9,* 471–481.

Mayberg, H. S. (2003). Modulating dysfunctional limbic-cortical circuits in depression: Towards development of brain-based algorithms for diagnosis and optimized treatment. *British Medical Bulletin, 65,* 193–207.

Mayberg, H. S. (2009). Targeted electrode-based modulation of neural circuits for depression. *Journal of Clinical Investigation, 119,* 717–725.

Mayberg, H. S., Lozano, A. M., Voon, V., McNeely, H. E., Seminowicz, D., ... Hamani, C. (2005). Deep brain stimulation for treatment-resistant depression. *Neuron, 45,* 651–660.

Mayer, E. A., Knight, R., Mazmanian, S. K., Cryan, J. F., & Tillisch, K. (2014). Gut microbes and the brain: Paradigm shift in neuroscience. *The Journal of Neuroscience: The Official Journal of the Society for Neuroscience, 34*(46), 15490–15496. Available at http://doi.org/10.1523/JNEUROSCI.3299-14.2014

Mayer, J. D., Salovey, P., Caruso, D. R., & Sitarenios, G. (2003). Measuring emotional intelligence with MSCEIT V.2.0. *Emotion, 3,* 97–105.

Mayer, M. (2004). Structure and function of glutamate receptors in the brain. *Annals of the New York Academy of Sciences, 1038,* 125–130.

Mazahery, H., Camargo, C. A., Conlon, C., Beck, K. L., Kruger, M. C., & von Hurst, P. R. (2016). Vitamin D and autism spectrum disorder: A literature review. *Nutrients, 8*(4), 236. doi:10.3390/nu8040236

Mazza, S., Gerbier, E., Gustin, M.-P., Kasikci, Z., Koenig, O., Toppino, T. C., & Magnin, M. (2016). Relearn faster and retain longer: Along with practice, sleep makes perfect. *Psychological Science,* 1–10. Available at http://doi.org/10.1177/0956797616659930

McArdle, J. J., & Prindle, J. J. (2008). A latent change score analysis of a randomized clinical trial in reasoning training. *Psychology and Aging, 23,* 702–719.

McCabe, C., & Rolls, E. T. (2007). Umami: A delicious flavor formed by convergence of taste and olfactory pathways in the human brain. *European Journal of Neuroscience, 25,* 1855–1864.

McCarthy, J. (2016, May 19). Americans' support for gay marriage high, at 61%. Retrieved November 12, 2016. Published online at http://www.gallup.com/poll/191645/americans-support-gay-marriage-remains-high.aspx

McCarthy, M. M., & Nugent, B. M. (2015). At the frontier of epigenetics of brain sex differences. *Frontiers in Behavioral Neuroscience, 9,* 221. doi: 10.3389/fnbeh.2015.0022

McCarthy, N. (2016, December 9). Most Americans believe fake news headlines. *Statista: The Statistics Portal.* Retrieved January 20, 2017 at https://www.statista.com/chart/7153/most-americans-believe-fake-news-headlines/

McClelland, D. C. (1985). How motives, skills, and values determine what people do. *American Psychologist, 40,* 812–825.

McClelland, J. L. (1988). Connectionist models and psychological evidence. *Journal of Memory and Language, 27,* 107–123.

McClelland, J. L., Fiez, J. A., & McCandliss, B. D. (2002). Teaching the /r/-/l/ discrimination to Japanese adults: Behavioral and neural aspects.

Physiology and Behavior, 77(4–5), 657–662. Available at http://doi.org/10.1016/S0031-9384(02)00916-2

McClelland, J. L., & Rogers, T. (2003). The parallel distributed processing approach to semantic knowledge. *Nature Reviews Neuroscience, 44,* 310–322.

McClelland, J. L., & Rumelhart, D. (1985). Distributed memory and the representation of general and specific information. *Journal of Experimental Psychology: General, 114,* 159–188.

McClung, C. (2015). Circadian rhythms in mood disorders. In C. S. Colwell (Ed.), *Circadian Medicine.* Hoboken, NJ: John Wiley & Sons. doi: 10.1002/9781118467831.ch17

McCrae, R. R. (2002). NEO-PI-R data from 36 cultures: Further intercultural comparisons. In R. R. McCrae & J. Allik (Eds.), *The Five-Factor Model of personality across cultures* (pp. 105–125). New York, NY: Kluwer Academic/Plenum.

McCrae, R. R., & Allik, J. (Eds.). (2002). *The Five-Factor Model of personality across cultures.* New York, NY: Kluwer Academic/Plenum.

McCrae, R. R., & Costa, P. T. (1996). Toward a new generation of personality theories: Theoretical contexts for the Five-Factor Model. In J. S. Wiggins (Ed.), *The Five-Factor Model of personality: Theoretical perspectives* (pp. 51–87). New York, NY: Guilford Press.

McCrae, R. R., & Costa, P. T. (1997). Personality trait structure as a human universal. *American Psychologist, 52,* 509–516.

McCrae, R. R., & Costa, P. T. (1999). A five-factor theory of personality. In L. A. Pervin & O. P. John (Eds.), *Handbook of personality theory and research* (pp. 139–153). New York, NY: Guilford Press.

McCrae, R. R., & Costa, P. T. (2003). *Personality in adulthood: A five-factor theory perspective* (2nd ed.). New York, NY: Guilford.

McCrae, R. R., & Costa, P. T., Jr. (2008). The five-factor theory of personality. In O. P. John, R. W. Robins, & L. A. Pervin (Eds.), *Handbook of personality: Theory and research* (pp. 159–181). New York, NY: Guilford Press.

McCrae, R. R., Terracciano, A., De Fruyt, F., De Bolle, M., Gelfand, M. J., & Costa, P. T., Jr. (2010). The validity and structure of culture-level personality scores: Data from ratings of young adolescents. *Journal of Personality, 78,* 815–838.

McDaniel, M. A. (2005). Big-brained people are smarter: A meta-analysis of the relationship between in vivo brain volume and intelligence. *Intelligence, 33*(4), 337–346. doi: 10.1016/j.intell.2004.11.005

McDonald, C. C., & Sommers, M. S. (2015). Teen drivers' perceptions of inattention and cell phone use while driving. *Traffic Injury Prevention, 16,* S52–S58. doi: 10.1080/15389588.2015.1062886

McDonnell, C. G., & Valentino, K. (2016). Intergenerational effects of childhood trauma: Evaluating pathways among maternal ACEs, perinatal depressive symptoms, and infant outcomes. *Child Maltreatment, 21*(4), 317–326. doi: 10.1177/1077559516659556

McEvoy, J. P., Lieberman, J. A., Stroup, T. S., Davis, S. M., Meltzer, H. Y., Rosenheck, R. A., ... Hsiao, J. K. (2006). Effectiveness of clozapine versus olanzapine, quetiapine, and risperidone in patients with chronic schizophrenia who did not respond to prior atypical antipsychotic treatment. *American Journal of Psychiatry, 163,* 600–610. doi: 10.1176/appi.ajp.163.4.600

McEwen, B. S. (2005). Glucocorticoids, depression, and mood disorders: Structural remodeling in the brain. *Metabolism, 54,* 20–23.

McEwen, B. S. (2016). In pursuit of resilience: Stress, epigenetics, and brain plasticity. *Annals of*

the New York Academy of Sciences. doi: 10.1111/nyas.13020

McEwen, B. S., De Kloet, E. R., & Rostene, W. (1986). Adrenal steroid receptors and actions in the nervous system. *Physiological Review, 66,* 1121–1188.

McGaugh, J. L. (2000). Memory—A century of consolidation. *Science, 287,* 248–251.

McGaugh, J. L. (Ed.). (2016). *Emotions and bodily responses: A psychophysiological approach.* Academic Press.

McGenney, B. E. (2012). Cannabinoids and hallucinogens for headache. *Headache, 53,* 447–458. doi: 10.1111/head.12025

McGowan, P. O. (2012). Epigenetic clues to the biological embedding of early life adversity. *Biological Psychiatry, 72,* 4–5. doi: 10.1016/j.biopsych.2012.04.017

McKinley, M., Cairns, M., Denton, D., Egan, G., Mathai, M., Uschakov, A., ... Oldfield, B. J. (2004). Physiological and pathophysiological influences on thirst. *Physiology & Behavior, 81*(5), 795–803. doi: 10.1016/j.physbeh.2004.04.055

McLay, R. N., Graap, K., Spira, J., Perlman, K., Johnston, S., Rothbaum, B. O., ... Rizzo, A. (2012). Development and testing of virtual reality exposure therapy for post-traumatic stress disorder in active duty service members who served in Iraq and Afghanistan. *Military Medicine, 177,* 635–642.

McLay, R. N., McBrien, C., Wiederhold, M. D., & Wiederhold, B. K. (2010). Exposure therapy with and without virtual reality to treat PTSD while in combat theater: A parallel case series. *Cyberpsychology, Behavior, and Social Networking, 13,* 37–42. doi: 10.1089/cyber.2009.0346

McTiernan, A. (2005). Obesity and cancer: The risks, science, and potential management strategies. *Oncology (Williston Park), 19,* 871–881.

Meaney, M. J. (2010). Epigenetics and the biological definition of gene [H11003] environment interactions. *Child Development, 81,* 41–79.

Mechelli, A., Crinion, J. T., Noppeney, U., O'Doherty, J., Ashburner, J., Frackowiak, R. S., & Price, C. J. (2004). Neurolinguistics: Structural plasticity in the bilingual brain. *Nature, 431,* 757. doi: 10.1038/431757a

Mechtcheriakov, S., Brenneis, B., Koppel-Staetter, F., Schocke, M., & Marksteiner, J. (2007). A widespread distinct pattern of cerebral atrophy in patients with alcohol addiction revealed by voxel-based morphometry. *Journal of Neurology, Neurosurgery, and Psychiatry, 78,* 610–614.

Medina, A. E., & Krahe, T. E. (2008). Neocortical plasticity deficits in fetal alcohol spectrum disorders: Lessons from barrel and visual cortex. *Journal of Neuroscience Research, 86,* 256–263.

Mednick, S. A., & Mednick, M. T. (1967). *Remote Associates Test: Experimenter's manual.* Boston, MA: Houghton Mifflin.

Medvec, V., Madey, S., & Gilovich, T. (1995, October). When less is more: Counterfactual thinking and satisfaction among Olympic medalists. *Journal of Personality and Social Psychology, 69*(4), 603–610.

Mehta, M. A., Sahakian, B. J., & Robbins, T. W. (2001). Comparative psychopharmacology of methylphenidate and related drugs in human volunteers, patients with ADHD, and experimental animals. In M. V. Solanto, A. F. T Arnsten, & F. X. Castellanos (Eds.), *Stimulant drugs and ADHD: Basic and clinical neuroscience* (pp. 303–311). New York, NY: Oxford University Press.

Mei, L., & Xiong, W.-C. (2008). Neuregulin 1 in neural development, synaptic plasticity and schizophrenia. *Nature Reviews Neuroscience, 9,* 437–452.

Melis, A. P., & Semmann, D. (2010). How is human cooperation different? *Philosophical Transactions of the Royal Society of London B, 365,* 2663–2674.

Mell, J. C., Howard, S. M., & Miller, B. L. (2003). Art and the brain: The influence of frontotemporal dementia on an accomplished artist. *Neurology, 60,* 1707–1710.

Mell, L. K., Davis, R. L., & Owens, D. (2005). Association between streptococcal infection and obsessive-compulsive disorder, Tourette's syndrome, and tic disorder. *Pediatrics, 116*(1), 56–60. doi: 10.1542/peds.2004-2058

Meltzoff, A. N., & Moore, M. K. (1977). Imitation of facial and manual gestures by human neonates. *Science, 198,* 75–78.

Meltzoff, A. N., & Moore, M. K. (1983). Newborn infants imitate adult facial gestures. *Child Development, 54,* 702–709.

Melzack, R., & Wall, P. D. (1965). Pain mechanisms: A new theory. *Science, 150,* 971–979.

Melzack, R., & Wall, P. D. (1988). *The challenge of pain* (rev. ed.). New York, NY: Penguin.

Memory Pill Helps the Brain Like Prescription Glasses Help the Eyes. (January 13, 2013). *San Francisco Chronicle.*

Mendelsohn, A., Furman, O., & Dudai, Y. (2010). Signatures of memory: Brain coactivations during retrieval distinguish correct from incorrect recollection. *Frontiers in Behavioral Neuroscience, 4,* 1–12.

Mennella, J. A., & Beauchamp, G. K. (1996). The early development of human flavor preferences. In E. D. Capaldi (Ed.), *Why we eat what we eat: The psychology of eating* (pp. 83–112). Washington, DC: APA Books.

Mennella, J. A., Johnson, A., & Beauchamp, G. K. (1995). Garlic ingestion by pregnant women alters the odor of amniotic fluid. *Chemical Senses, 20,* 207–209.

Mental health: A report of the surgeon general. (2001). Retrieved from http://www.surgeongeneral .gov/library/mentalhealth/home.html

Merskey, H., & Bogduk, N. (1994). *Classification of chronic pain.* Seattle, WA: International Association for the Study of Pain Press.

Merten, J. (2005). Culture, gender and the recognition of the basic emotions. *Psychologia, 48,* 306–316.

Meunier, M., & Bachevalier, J. (2002). Comparison of emotional responses in monkeys with rhinal cortex or amygdala lesions. *Emotion, 2,* 147–161.

Meyer, D. E., & Kieras, D. E. (1997). A computational theory of executive cognitive processes and multiple-task performance: Part 1. Basic mechanisms. *Psychological Review, 104,* 3–65.

Meyer-Bahlburg, H. F. L., Dolezal, C., Baker, W. W., & New, M. I. (2008). Sexual orientation in women with classical or non-classical congenital adrenal hyperplasia as a function of degree of prenatal androgen excess. *Archives of Sexual Behavior, 37,* 85–99.

Miao, C. F., Lund, D. J., & Evan, K. R. (2009). Reexamining the influence of career stages on salesperson motivation: A cognitive and affective perspective. *Journal of Personal Selling and Sales Management, 29,* 243–255.

Michael, J. (1975). Positive and negative reinforcement, a distinction that is no longer necessary; or a better way to talk about bad things. *Behaviorism, 3,* 33–45.

Michikyan, M., Subrahmanyam, K., & Dennis, J. (2014). Can you tell who I am? Neuroticism, extraversion, and online self-presentation among young adults. *Computers in Human Behavior, 33,* 179–183. Available at http://doi.org/10.1016/j.chb.2014.01.010

Miczek, K. A., de Almeida, R. M. M., Kravitz, E. A., & Rissman, E. F. (2007). Neurobiology of escalated aggression and violence. *Journal of Neuroscience, 27,* 11803–11806.

Miething, A., Rostila, M., Edling, C., & Rydgren, J. (2016). The influence of social network characteristics on peer clustering in smoking: A two-wave panel study of 19- and 23-year-old Swedes. *PLoS ONE, 11*(10), e0164611. Available at http://dx.doi.org/10.1371/journal.pone.0164611

Mifflin, K., Chorney, J., & Dick, B. (2016). Attention and working memory in female adolescents with chronic pain and pain-free female adolescents: A preliminary pilot study. *The Clinical Journal of Pain, 32*(7), 609–616. doi: 10.1097/AJP.0000000000000239

Mikolajczak, M., & Luminet, O. (2008). Trait emotional intelligence and the cognitive appraisal of stressful events: An exploratory study. *Personality and Individual Differences, 44,* 1445–1453.

Milgram, S. (1963). Behavioral study of obedience. *Journal of Abnormal and Social Psychology, 67,* 371–378.

Milgram, S. (1974). *Obedience to authority: An experimental view.* New York, NY: Harper.

Mill, J., & Petronis, A. (2008). Pre- and perinatal environmental risks for attention-deficit hyperactivity disorder (ADHD): The potential role of epigenetic processes in mediating susceptibility. *Journal of Child Psychology and Psychiatry, 49,* 1020–1030.

Miller, A. H., Capuron, L., & Raison, C. L. (2005). Immunologic influences on emotion regulation. *Clinical Neuroscience Research, 4,* 325–333.

Miller, B. L., & Cummings, J. L. (Eds.). (1999). *The human frontal lobes: Functions and disorders.* New York, NY: Guilford Press.

Miller, G. A. (1956). The magical number seven, plus or minus two: Some limits on our capacity for processing information. *Psychological Review, 63,* 81–97.

Miller, G. E., & Chen, E. (2013). The biological residue of childhood poverty. *Child Development Perspectives, 7,* 67–73. doi: 10.1111/cdep.12021

Miller, G. E., Chen, E., & Parker, K. J. (2011). Psychological stress in childhood and susceptibility to the chronic diseases of aging: Moving toward a model of behavioral and biological mechanisms. *Psychological Bulletin, 137*(6), 959. Available at http://dx.doi.org/10.1037/a0024768

Miller, G. F. (2000). *The mating mind: How sexual choice shaped the evolution of human nature.* New York, NY: Doubleday.

Miller, G. F., & Penke, L. (2007). The evolution of human intelligence and the coefficient of additive genetic variance in human brain size. *Intelligence, 35,* 97–114. doi: 10.1016/j.intell.2006.08.008

Miller, L. A., & Tippett, L. J. (1996). Effects of focal brain lesions on visual problem-solving. *Neuropsychologia, 34,* 387–398.

Miller, S. L., & Maner, J. K. (2010). Scent of a woman: Men's testosterone responses to olfactory ovulation cues. *Psychological Science, 21,* 276–283.

Millstein, R. A., Celano, C. M., Beale, E. E., Beach, S. R., Suarez, L., Belcher, A. M., ... Huffman, J. C. (2016). The effects of optimism and gratitude on adherence, functioning and mental health following an acute coronary syndrome. *General Hospital Psychiatry, 43,* 17–22. Available at http://dx.doi.org/10.1016/j.genhosppsych.2016.08.006

Milner, B. (1962). Les troubles de la mémoire accompagnant des lésions hippocampiques bilatérales. In *Physiologie de l'hippocampe* (pp. 257–272). Paris, France: Centre National de la Recherche Scientifique. English translation: P. M. Milner & S. Glickman (Eds.). (1965). *Cognitive processes and the brain: An enduring problem in psychology. Selected readings* (pp. 97–111). Princeton, NJ: Van Nostrand.

Milner, B., Corkin, S., & Teuber, H. L. (1968). Further analysis of the hippocampal amnesic syndrome: 14-year follow-up study of H. M. *Neuropsychologia, 6,* 215–234.

Mirescu, C., & Gould, E. (2006). Stress and adult neurogenesis. *Hippocampus, 16,* 233–238.

Mirescu, C., Peters, J. D., Noiman, L., & Gould, E. (2006). Sleep deprivation inhibits adult neurogenesis in the hippocampus by elevating glucocorticoids. *Proceedings of the National Academy of Sciences, 103,* 19170–19175. doi: 10.1073/pnas.0608644103

Mirnics, K., Middleton, F. A., Marquez, A., Lewis, D. A., & Levitt, P. (2000). Molecular characterization of schizophrenia viewed by microarray analysis of gene expression in prefrontal cortex. *Neuron, 28,* 53–67.

Mischel, W. (2009). From personality and assessment (1968) to personality science, 2009. *Journal of Research in Personality, 43,* 282–290.

Mischel, W. (2015). *The Marshmallow Test: Why Self-Control Is the Engine of Success.* New York: Little Brown & Co.

Mischel, W., Ayduk, O., Berman, M. G., Casey, B. J., Gotlib, I. H., Jonides, J., ... Shoda, Y. (2011). "Willpower" over the life span: Decomposing self-regulation. *Social Cognitive and Affective Neuroscience, 6*(2), 252–256. Available at https://doi .org/10.1093/scan/nsq081

Mischel, W., & Ebbesen, E. B. (1970). Attention in delay of gratification. *Journal of Personality and Social Psychology, 16*(2), 329–337. Available at https://doi.org/10.1037/h0029815

Mischel, W., Ebbesen, E. B., & Zeiss, A. R. (1972). Cognitive and attentional mechanisms in delay of gratification. *Journal of Personality and Social Psychology, 21*(2), 204–218. Available at https://doi.org/10.1037/h0032198

Mischel, W., & Shoda, Y. (1995). A cognitive-affective system theory of personality: Reconceptualizing situations, dispositions, dynamics, and invariance in personality structure. *Psychological Review, 102,* 246–268.

Mischel, W., & Shoda, Y. (1999). Integrating dispositions and processing dynamics within a unified theory of personality: The cognitive-affective personality system. In L. A. Pervin & O. P. John (Eds.), *Handbook of personality: Theory and research* (pp. 197–218). New York, NY: Guilford Press.

Mischel, W., Shoda, Y., & Rodriguez, M. L. (1989). Delay of gratification in children, *Science, 244,* 933–938.

Mithoefer, M., & Mithoefer, A. (2017). MDMA-assisted psychotherapy for PTSD: Lessons from phase 2 clinical trials , 3rd International meeting of Psychedelic Science, Oakland, CA, April 22, 2017.

Mithoefer, M. C., Grob, C. S., & Brewerton, T. D. (2016). Novel psychopharmacological therapies for psychiatric disorders: Psilocybin and MDMA. *The Lancet Psychiatry, 3*(5), 481–488. Available at http:// dx.doi.org/10.1016/S2215-0366(15)00576-3

Miyake, A., Friedman, N. P., Emerson, M. J., Witzki, A. H., & Howerter, A. (2000). The unity and diversity of executive functions and their contributions to complex "frontal lobe" tasks: A latent variable approach. *Cognitive Psychology, 41,* 49–100.

Miyashita, T., Kubik, S., Lewandowski, G., & Guzowski, J. F. (2008). Networks of neurons, networks of genes: An integrated view of memory consolidation. *Neurobiology of Learning and Memory, 89,* 269–284.

Mizuno, S., Mihara, T., Miyaoka, T., Inagaki, T., & Horiguchi, J. (2005, March). CSF iron, ferritin and transferrin levels in restless legs syndrome. *Journal of Sleep Research, 14*(1), 43–47.

Modi, K. K., Rangasamy, S. B., Dasarathi, S., Roy, A., & Pahan, K. (2016). Cinnamon converts poor learning mice to good learners: Implications for memory improvement. *Journal of Neuroimmune Pharmacology,* 1–15. Available at http://doi.org/10.1007/s11481-016-9693-6

Moffitt, T. E., Brammer, G. L., Caspi, A., Fawcett, J. P., Raleigh, M., Yuwiler, A., & Silva, P. (1998). Whole blood serotonin relates to violence in an epidemiological study. *Biological Psychiatry, 43,* 446–457.

Moffitt, T. E., Caspi, A., & Rutter, M. (2005). Strategy for investigating interactions between measured genes and measured environments. *Archives of General Psychiatry, 62,* 473–481.

Moffitt, T. E., Caspi, A., Taylor, A., Kokaua, T. J., Milne, B. J., Polanczyk, G., & Poulton, R. (2010). How common are common mental disorders? Evidence that lifetime prevalence rates are doubled by prospective *versus* retrospective ascertainment. *Psychological Medicine, 40,* 899–909. doi: 10.1017/S0033291709991036

Moghaddam, B. (2003). Bringing order to the glutamate chaos in schizophrenia. *Neuron, 40,* 881–884.

Moisala, M., Salmela, V., Hietajärvi, L., Salo, E., Carlson, S., Salonen, O., Lonka, K. Hakkarainen, K., Salmela-Aro, K., & Alho, K. Media multitasking is associated with distractibility and increased prefrontal activity in adolescents and young adults. *NeuroImage, 134,* 113–121. doi: 10.1016/j.neuroimage.2016.04.011

Moller, J., Hallqvist, J., Diderichsen, F., Theorell, T., Reuterwall, C., & Ahblom, A. (1999). Do episodes of anger trigger myocardial infarction? A case-crossover analysis in the Stockholm Heart Epidemiology Program (SHEEP). *Psychosomatic Medicine, 61,* 842–849.

Moloney, R. D., Desbonnet, L., Clarke, G., Dinan, T. G., & Cryan, J. F. (2014). The microbiome: Stress, health and disease. *Mammalian Genome, 25*(1–2), 49–74. Available at http://doi.org/10.1007/s00335-013-9488-5

Mommersteeg, P. M., Schoemaker, R. G., Naudé, P. J., Eisel, U. L., Garrelds, I. M., Schalkwijk, C. G., … Denollet, J. (2016). Depression and markers of inflammation as predictors of all-cause mortality in heart failure. *Brain, Behavior, and Immunity.* Available at http://dx.doi.org/10.1016/j.bbi.2016.03.012

Monge, J. P., López, G., & Guerrero, L. A. (2017). Supporting phobia treatment with virtual reality: Systematic desensitization using oculus rift. In *Advances in Human Factors and Ergonomics in Healthcare* (pp. 391–401). Springer International Publishing.

Monk, T. H., Folkarc, S., & Wedderburn, A. I. (1996). Maintaining safety and high performance on shiftwork. *Applied Ergonomics, 27*(1), 17–23.

Montague, D. P. F., & Walker-Andrews, A. S. (2001). Peekaboo: A new look at infants perception of emotion. *Developmental Psychology, 37,* 826–838.

Montgomery, G. H., DuHamel, K. N., & Redd, W. H. (2000). A meta-analysis of hypnotically induced analgesia: How effective is hypnosis? *International Journal of Clinical and Experimental Hypnosis, 48,* 138–153.

Montiel-Castro, A. J., González-Cervantes, R. M., Bravo-Ruiseco, G., & Pacheco-López, G. (2013). The microbiota-gut-brain axis: Neurobehavioral correlates, health and sociality. *Frontiers in Integrative Neuroscience, 7*(October), 70. Available at http://doi.org/10.3389/fnint.2013.00070

Moody, E. W., Sunsay, C., & Bouton, M. E. (2006). Priming and trial spacing in extinction: Effects on extinction performance, spontaneous recovery, and reinstatement in appetitive conditioning. *Quarterly Journal of Experimental Psychology, 59,* 809–829.

Moore, E. S., Ward, R. E., Wetherill, L. F., Rogers, J. L., Autti-Rämö, I., Fagerlund, A., … Foroud, T. (2007). Unique facial features distinguish fetal alcohol syndrome patients and controls in diverse ethnic populations. *Alcoholism: Clinical and Experimental Research, 31,* 1707–1713. doi: 10.1111/j.1530-0277.2007.00472.x

Moore, R. Y., & Eichler, V. B. (1972). Loss of a circadian adrenal corticosterone rhythm following suprachiasmatic lesions in the rat. *Brain Research, 42,* 201–206.

Morales-Medina, J. C., Dumont, Y., & Quirion, R. (2010). A possible role of neuropeptide Y in depression and stress. *Brain Research, 1314,* 194–205.

Moran, E. M., Snelson, C., & Elison-Bowers, P. (2010). Image and video disclosure of substance use on social media websites. *Computers in Human Behavior, 26,* 1405–1411.

Morawetz, C., Bode, S., Baudewig, J., Kirilina, E., & Heekeren, H. R. (2016). Changes in effective connectivity between dorsal and ventral prefrontal regions moderate emotion regulation. *Cerebral Cortex, 26*(5), 1923–1937. doi: 10.1093/cercor/bhv005

Moray, N. (1959). Attention in dichotic listening: Affective cues and the influence of instructions. *Quarterly Journal of Experimental Psychology, 11,* 56–60.

Morello, G., Imperatore, R., Palomba, L., Finelli, C., Labruna, G., Pasanisi, F., … & Di Marzo, V. (2016). Orexin-A represses satiety-inducing POMC neurons and contributes to obesity via stimulation of endocannabinoid signaling. *Proceedings of the National Academy of Sciences,* 201521304. doi: 10.1073/pnas.1521304113

Moreno, J. L., Kurita, M., Holloway, T., López, J., Cadagan, R., Martínez-Sobrido, L., … & González-Maeso, J. (2011). Maternal influenza viral infection causes schizophrenia-like alterations of 5-HT2A and mGlu2 receptors in the adult offspring. *Journal of Neuroscience, 31*(5), 1863–1872. doi: https://doi.org/10.1523/JNEUROSCI.4230-10.2011

Morgenstern, N. A., Lombardi, G., & Schinder, A. F. (2008). Newborn granule cells in the ageing dentate gyrus. *Journal of Physiology, 586,* 3751–3757.

Morina, N., Ijntema, H., Meyerbröker, K., & Emmelkamp, P. M. (2015). Can virtual reality exposure therapy gains be generalized to real-life? A meta-analysis of studies applying behavioral assessments. *Behaviour Research and Therapy, 74,* 18–24. Available at http://dx.doi.org/10.1016/j.brat.2015.08.010

Mörkved, N., Hartmann, K., Aarsheim, L. M., Holen, D., Milde, A. M., Bomyea, J., & Thorp, S. R. (2014). A comparison of narrative exposure therapy and prolonged exposure therapy for PTSD. *Clinical Psychology Review, 34*(6),

453–467. Available at http://dx.doi.org/10.1016/j.cpr.2014.06.005

Morris, M. W., & Peng, K. (1994). Culture and cause: American and Chinese attributions for social and physical events. *Journal of Personality and Social Psychology, 67,* 949–971.

Morris, N. M., Udry, J. R., Khandawood, F., & Dawood, M. Y. (1987). Marital sex frequency and midcycle female testosterone. *Archives of Sexual Behavior, 16,* 27–37.

Morris, P. L., Robinson, R. G., Raphael, B., & Hopwood, M. J. (1996). Lesion location and post-stroke depression. *Journal of Neuropsychiatry and Clinical Neurosciences, 8,* 399–403.

Morrison, R. S., Maroney-Galin, C., Kralovec, P. D., & Meier, D. E. (2005). The growth of palliative care programs in United States hospitals. *Journal of Palliative Medicine, 8*(6), 1127–1134.

Morton, F., Lee, P. C., Buchanan-Smith, H. M., Brosnan, S. F., Thierry, B., Paukner, A., … Weiss, A. (2013). Personality structure in brown capuchin monkeys (*Sapajus apella*): Comparisons with chimpanzees (*Pan troglodytes*), orangutans (*Pongo spp.*), and rhesus macaques (*Macaca mulatta*). *Journal of Comparative Psychology, 127*(3), 282–298. doi: 10.1037/a0031723

Moruzzi, G., & Magoun, H. W. (1949). Brain stem reticular formation and activation of the EEG. *Electroencephalography and Clinical Neurophysiology, 1,* 455–473.

Mosconi, M., Cody-Hazlett, H., Poe, M., Gerig, G., Gimpel-Smith, R., & Piven, J. (2009). Longitudinal study of amygdala volume and joint attention in 2- to 4-year-old children with autism. *Archives of General Psychiatry, 66,* 509–516. doi: 10.1001/archgenpsychiatry.2009.19

Moscovici, S. (1985). Social influence and conformity. In G. Lindzey & E. Aronson (Eds.), *The handbook of social psychology* (3rd ed., Vol. 2, pp. 347–412). New York, NY: Random House.

Moscovitch, M. (2010). Memory consolidation: Past, present and future. *Journal of Neurology, Neurosurgery, and Psychiatry, 81,* e2. doi: 10.1136/jnnp.2010.217554.4

Moser, D., Anderer, P., Gruber, G., Parapatics, S., Loretz, E., Boeck, M., … Dorffner, G. (2009). Sleep classification according to AASM and Rechtschaffen & Kales: Effects on sleep scoring parameters. *Sleep, 32,* 139–149. doi: 10.1016/j.molmet.2016.00

Moses-Kolko, E. L., Bogen, D., Perel, J., Bregard, A., Uhl, K., … Levin, B. (2005). Neonatal signs after late in utero exposure to serotonin reuptake inhibitors: Literature review and implications for clinical applications. *Journal of the American Medical Association, 293,* 2372–2383.

Moskowitz, J. (2003). Positive affect predicts lower risk of AIDS mortality. *Psychosomatic Medicine, 65,* 620–626.

Moskowitz, J., Folkman, S., Collette, L., & Vittinghoff, E. (1996). Coping and mood during AIDS related caregiving and bereavement. *Annals of Behavioral Medicine, 18,* 49–57.

Moss, M. (2013). *Salt, sugar, fat: How the food giants hooked us.* New York, NY: Random House.

Motluk, A. (2005, January 29). Senses special: The art of seeing without sight. *New Scientist, 2484,* 37. Available at http://www.newscientist.com

Mount, M. K., Barrick, M. R., Scullen, S. M., & Rounds, J. (2005). Higher-order dimensions of the Big Five personality traits and the Big Six vocational interest types. *Personnel Psychology, 58,* 447–478.

Mrazek, M. D., Franklin, M. S., Phillips, D. T., Baird, B., & Schooler, J. W. (2013). Mindfulness training improves working memory capacity and GRE performance while reducing mind wandering. *Psychological Science, 24*(5), 776–781. doi: 10.1177/0956797612459659

Mueller, N. T., Bakacs, E., Combellick, J., Grigoryan, Z., & Dominguez-Bello M. G. (2015). The infant microbiome development: Mom matters. *Trends in Molecular Medicine, 21*, 109–117. doi: 10.1016/j.molmed.2014.12.002

Mühlberger, A., Wieser, M. J., Gerdes, A. B. M., Frey, M. C. M., Weyers, P., & Pauli, P. (2011). Stop looking angry and smile, please: Start and stop of the very same facial expression differentially activate threat- and reward-related brain networks. *SCAN, 6*, 321–329.

Mukamal, K. J., & Ding, E. L. (2016). Pinpointing the health effects of alcohol. *British Medical Journal, 353*, i3043. doi: 10.1136/bmj.i3043 (Published online June 14, 2016).

Mulle, J. G., Sharp, W. G., & Cubells, J. F. (2013). The gut microbiome: A new frontier in autism research. *Current Psychiatry Reports, 15*(2), 1–9. doi: 10.1007/s11920-012-0337-0

Müller-Oerlinghausen, B., Berghöfer, A., & Bauer, M. (2002). Bipolar disorder. *The Lancet, 359*, 241–247.

Mummert, M. E. (2016). Psychological stress as a determinant of skin barrier function: Immunological pathways and therapeutic opportunities. In *Skin Stress Response Pathways* (pp. 433–447). Springer International Publishing. doi: 10.1007/978-3-319-43157-4_21

Munro, G. D., Lasane, T. P., & Leary, S. P. (2010). Political partisan prejudice: Selective distortion and weighting of evaluative categories in college admissions applications. *Journal of Applied Social Psychology, 40*, 2434–2462.

Munsinger, H. (1975). The adopted child's IQ: A critical review. *Psychological Bulletin, 82*, 623–659.

Müri, R. M. (2016). Cortical control of facial expression. *Journal of Comparative Neurology, 524*(8), 1578–1585. doi: 10.1002/cne.23908

Murphy, G., & Greene, C. M. (2015). High perceptual load causes inattentional blindness and deafness in drivers. *Visual Cognition, 23*, 810–814. doi: 10.1080/13506285.2015.1093245

Murphy, M. C., Nau, A. C., Fisher, C., Kim, S. G., Schuman, J. S., & Chan, K. C. (2016). Top-down influence on the visual cortex of the blind during sensory substitution. *NeuroImage, 125*, 932–940. Available at http://dx.doi.org/10.1016/j.neuroimage.2015.11.021

Murphy, S. E. (2010). Using functional neuroimaging to investigate the mechanisms of action of selective serotonin reuptake inhibitors (SSRIs). *Current Pharmaceutical Design, 16*, 1990–1997.

Murray, H. A. (1938/1962). *Explorations in personality*. New York, NY: Science Editions.

Murray, J. (2009). *Top 10 weight loss tips: Physical activity and healthy eating habits are key to losing weight*. Retrieved from http://weight-loss-methods.suite101.com/article.cfm/top_10_weight_loss_tips

Murza, K. A., Schwartz, J. B., Hahs-Vaughn, D. L., & Nye, C. (2016). Joint attention interventions for children with autism spectrum disorder: A systematic review and meta-analysis. *International Journal of Language & Communication Disorders, 51*(3), 236–251. doi: 10.1111/1460-6984.12212

Muscanell, N. L., & Guadagno, R. E. (2012). Make new friends or keep the old: Gender and personality differences in social networking use. *Computers in Human Behavior, 28*, 107–112.

Muthukumaraswamy, S. D., Carhart-Harris, R. L., Moran, R. J., Brookes, M. J., Williams, T. M., Errtizoe, D., ... Nutt, D. J. (2013). Broadband cortical desynchronization underlies the human psychedelic state. *Journal of Neuroscience, 33*, 15171–15183. doi: 10.1523/JNEUROSCI.2063-13.2013

Myers, I. B. (1962). *Myers-Briggs Type Indicator manual*. Princeton, NJ: Educational Testing Service.

Nabavi, S., Fox, R., Proulx, C. D., Lin, J. Y., Tsien, R. Y., & Malinow, R. (2014). Engineering a memory with LTD and LTP. *Nature, 511*(7509), 348–352. Available at http://doi.org/10.1038/nature13294

Nabi, H., Shipley, M. J., Vahtera, J., Hall, M., Korkeila, J., Marmot, M., ... Singh-Manoux, A. (2010). Effects of depressive symptoms and coronary heart disease and their interactive associations on mortality in middle-aged adults: The Whitehall II cohort study. *Heart, 11*, 1645–1650.

Nacash, N., Foa, E. B., Fostick, L., Polliack, M., Dinstein, Y., ... Tzur, D. (2007). Prolonged exposure therapy for chronic combat-related PTSD: A case report on five veterans. *CNS Spectrums, 12*, 690–695.

Nadarajah, B., & Parnavelas, J. (2002). Modes of neuronal migration in the developing cerebral cortex. *Nature Reviews Neuroscience, 3*, 423–432.

Nader, K., Schafe, G. E., & Le Doux, J. E. (2000). Fear memories require protein synthesis in the amygdala for reconsolidation after retrieval. *Nature, 406*(6797), 722–726. Available at http://doi.org/10.1038/35021052

Nadkarni, A., & Hofmann, S. (2012). Why do people use Facebook? *Personality and Individual Differences, 52*, 243–249.

Naesström, M., Blomstedt, P., & Bodlund, O. (2016). A systematic review of psychiatric indications for deep brain stimulation, with focus on major depressive and obsessive-compulsive disorder. *Nordic Journal of Psychiatry, 70*(7), 483–491. doi: 10.3109/08039488.2016.1162846

Nakajima, K., Takeoka, M., Mori, M., Hashimoto, S., Sakurai, A., Nose, H., ... Taniguchi, S. (2010). Exercise effects on methylation of *ASC* gene. *International Journal of Sports Medicine, 31*, 671–675. doi: 10.1055/s-0029-1246140

Naqvi, N. H., Rudrauf, D., Damasio, H., & Bechara, A. (2007). Damage to the insula disrupts addiction to cigarette smoking. *Science, 315*, 531–534.

Nasar, S. (1998). *A beautiful mind*. New York, NY: Touchstone.

Nash, M. R., Hulsey, T. L., Sexton, M. C., Harralson, T. L., Lambert, W., & Lynch, G. V. (1993). *Adult psychopathology associated with a history of childhood sexual abuse: A psychoanalytic perspective*. Washington, DC: American Psychological Association.

National Center for Health Statistics. Health, United States. (2015). *With special feature on racial and ethnic health disparities*. Hyattsville, MD. 2016.

National Center for Statistics and Analysis. (2016, August). 2015 motor vehicle crashes: Overview. (Traffic Safety Facts Research Note. Report No. DOT HS 812 318). Washington, DC: National Highway Traffic Safety Administration.

National Eye Institute. (2002). *Vision problems in the U.S.: Prevalence of adult vision impairment and age-related eye disease in America, 2002.*

Retrieved January 20, 2007, from http://www.nei.nih.gov/eyedata/pdf/VPUS.pdf

National Health & Nutrition Examination Survey, 2005–2006. Published online. Retrieved November 16, 2016 at https://wwwn.cdc.gov/nchs/nhanes/search/nhanes05_06.aspx

National Heart, Lung, and Blood Institute (NHLBI). (2012). https://www.nhlbi.nih.gov/health/health-topics/topics/sleepapnea

National Highway Traffic Safety Administration (NHTSA). (2014). http://www.nhtsa.gov/About+NHTSA/Press+Releases/2015/2014-traffic-deaths-drop-but-2015-trending-higher

National Highway Traffic Safety Administration (NHTSA). (2015). Retrieved January 23, 2017. http://www.nhtsa.gov/About+NHTSA/Press+Releases/2015/2014-traffic-deaths-drop-but-2015-trending-higher

National Human Genome Research Institute. (2010). *A brief guide to genomics*. Retrieved from http://www.genome.gov/18016863

National Institute of Mental Health (NIMH). (2007). *Schizophrenia*. Washington, DC: NIMH Publication #06-3517.

National Institute on Alcohol Abuse and Alcoholism. (2005). *Heavy episodic consumption of alcohol*. Retrieved April 4, 2008, from http://www.collegedrinkingprevention.gov/NIAAACollegeMaterials/TaskForce/HeavyEpisodic_00.aspx

National Institute on Deafness and Other Communication Disorders. (2008). *Quick statistics*. Bethesda, MD: U.S. Department of Health and Human Services. Retrieved from http://www.nidcd.nih.gov/health/statistics/quick.htm

National Sleep Foundation. (2008). *2008 Sleep in America poll*. Retrieved April 2, 2008, from http://www.sleepfoundation.org/site/c.huIXKjM0IxF/b.3933533/

Nauta, W. J. H., & Feirtag, M. (1979). The organization of the brain. *Scientific American, 241*, 88–111.

NCHS. (2000). *Data file documentation, National Health Interview Survey, 1998*. Hyattsville, MD: National Center for Health Statistics.

Neal, D. T., & Chartrand, T. L. (2011). Embodied emotion perception. *Social Cognition and Personality Science, 2*, 673–678.

Neisser, U., Boodoo, G., Bouchard, T. J., Boykin, A. W., Brody, N., ... Ceci, S. J. (1996). Intelligence: Knowns and unknowns. *American Psychologist, 51*, 77–101.

Neitzke, A. B. (2016). An illness of power: Gender and the social causes of depression. *Culture, Medicine, and Psychiatry, 40*(1), 59–73. doi: 10.1007/s11013-015-9466-3

Nelson-Gray, R. O., Keane, S. P., Hurst, R. M., Mitchell, J. T., Warburton, J. B., ... Chok, J. T. (2006). A modified DBT skills training program for oppositional defiant adolescents: Promising preliminary findings. *Behaviour Research and Therapy, 44*, 1811–1820.

Nemeroff, C. B. (2007). The burden of severe depression: A review of diagnostic challenges and treatment alternatives. *Journal of Psychiatric Research, 41*, 189–206.

Nesbit, S. M., Conger, J. C., & Conger, A. J. (2007). A quantitative review of the relationship between anger and aggressive driving. *Aggression and Violent Behavior, 12*, 156–176.

Nettle, D. (2006). The evolution of personality variation in humans and other animals. *American Psychologist, 61*, 622–631.

Nettle, D. (2011). Evolutionary perspectives on the Five-Factor Model of personality. In D. M. Buss & P. H. Hawley (Eds.), *The evolution of personality and individual differences* (pp. 5–28). New York, NY: Oxford University Press.

Nettle, D., & Clegg, H. (2005). Schizotypy, creativity, and mating success in humans. *Proceedings of the Royal Society (B)*. doi: 10.1098/rspb.2005.3349

Neuberg, S. L., & Cottrell, C. A. (2006). Evolutionary bases of prejudices. In M. Schaller, J. A. Simpson, & D. T. Kenrick (Eds.), *Evolution and social psychology* (pp. 163–187). New York, NY: Psychology Press.

Neuberg, S. L., Kenrick, D. T., & Schaller, M. (2011). Human threat management systems: Self-protection and disease avoidance. *Neuroscience and Biobehavioral Reviews, 35*, 1042–1051.

Neugebauer, R., Hoek, H. W., & Susser, E. (1999). Prenatal exposure to wartime famine and development of antisocial personality disorder in early adulthood. *Journal of the American Medical Association, 282*, 455–462.

Newcomb, T. M. (1961). *The acquaintance process.* Oxford, England: Holt, Rinehart & Winston.

Newcombe, N. S., & Uttal, D. H. (2006). Whorf versus Socrates, round 10. *Trends in Cognitive Sciences, 10*, 394–396.

Newport, E. L. (2003). Language development, critical periods in. In L. Nadel (Ed.), *Encyclopedia of cognitive science* (Vol. 2, pp. 733–740). London, England: Nature Group Press.

Ngun, T. C., & Vilain, E. (2014). The biological basis of human sexual orientation: Is there a role for epigenetics? *Advances in Genetics, 86*, 167–184.

Nickerson, C., Schwarz, N., Diener, E., & Kahneman, D. (2003). Zeroing in on the dark side of the American dream: A closer look at the negative consequences of the goal for financial success. *Psychological Science, 14*, 531–536.

Nicklaus, S. (2016). The role of food experiences during early childhood in food pleasure learning. *Appetite, 104*, 3–9. Available at http://dx.doi.org/10.1016/j.appet.2015.08.022

Nicoll, R. A., & Alger, B. E. (2004). The brain's own marijuana. *Scientific American, 291*, 69–75.

Nielsen, P. R., Meyer, U., & Mortensen, P. B. (2016). Individual and combined effects of maternal anemia and prenatal infection on risk for schizophrenia in offspring. *Schizophrenia Research, 172*(1), 35–40. Available at http://dx.doi.org/10.1016/j.schres.2016.02.025

Nieman, D. C., Custer, W. F., Butterworth, D. E., Utter, A. C., & Henson, D. A. (2000). Psychological response to exercise and/or energy restriction in obese women. *Journal of Psychosomatic Research, 48*(1), 23–29.

Nikkelen, S. C., Vossen, H. M., & Valkenburg, P. M. (2015). Children's television viewing and ADHD-related behaviors: Evidence from the Netherlands. *Journal of Children And Media, 9*(4), 399–418. doi:10.1080/17482798.2015.1088872

Nikolaus, S., Antke, C., Beu, M., & Muller, H. W. (2010). Cortical GABA, striatal dopamine and midbrain serotonin as the key players in compulsive and anxiety disorders—Results from in vivo imaging studies. *Reviews in the Neurosciences, 21*, 119–139.

Nilsson, L. G. (2003). Memory function in normal aging. *Acta Neurologica Scandinavica Supplementum, 179*, 7–13.

NIOSH. (1998). Criteria for a recommended standard. Retrieved online November 10, 2016, at http://www.cdc.gov/niosh/docs/98-126/pdfs/98-126.pdf

Niraula, A., Sheridan, J. F., & Godbout, J. P. (2017). Microglia priming with aging and stress. *Neuropsychopharmacology, 42*(1), 318–333. doi: 10.1038/npp.2016.185

Nisbett, R. E., Peng, K., Choi, I., & Norenzayan, A. (2001). Culture and systems of thought: Holistic versus analytic cognition. *Psychological Review, 108*, 291–301.

Nisbett, R. E., & Wilson, T. D. (1977). Telling more than we can know: Verbal reports on mental processes. *Psychological Review, 84*, 231–259.

Nishida, A., Hisaoka, K., Zensho, H., Uchitomi, Y., Morinobu, S., & Yamawaki, S. (2002). Antidepressant drugs and cytokines in mood disorders. *International Immunopharmacology, 2*, 1619–1626.

Nishimura, E., Granter, S. R., & Fisher, D. E. (2005). Mechanisms of hair graying: Incomplete melanocyte stem cell maintenance in the niche. *Science, 307*, 720–724.

Nishino, S., Sato, M., Matsumura, M., & Kanbayashi, T. (2015). Narcolepsy–cataplexy syndrome and symptomatic hypersomnia. In *Sleep medicine* (pp. 205–221). New York, NY: Springer.

Nithianantharajah, J., & Hannan, A. (2006). Enriched environments, experience dependent plasticity and disorders of the nervous system. *Nature Reviews Neuroscience, 7*, 697–709.

Nixon, R. D. V., Ellis, A. A., Nehmy, T. J., & Ball, S.-A. (2010). Screening and predicting posttraumatic stress and depression in children following single-incident trauma. *Journal of Clinical Child & Adolescent Psychology, 39*, 588–596.

Nock, M. K., Park, J. M., Finn, C. T., Deliberto, T. L., Dour, H. J., & Banaji, M. R. (2010). Measuring the suicidal mind: Implicit cognition predicts suicidal behavior. *Psychological Science, 21*, 511–517.

Noda, H., Iso, H., Toyoshima, H., Date, C., Yamamoto, A., ... Kikuchi, S. (2005). Walking and sports participation and mortality from coronary heart disease and stroke. *Journal of the American College of Cardiology, 46*, 1761–1767.

Nolen-Hoeksema, S. (2007). *Abnormal psychology* (4th ed.). New York, NY: McGraw-Hill.

Nolte, C., & Yollin, P. (2006, April 19). Officials salute city's majestic rise from rubble of '06—and the survivors. *San Francisco Chronicle*, pp. A1, A12.

Norcross, J. C., Bike, D., & Evans, K. (2009). The therapist's therapist: A replication and extension 20 years later. *Psychotherapy: Theory, Research, Practice, Training, 46*, 32–41. doi: 10.1037/a0015140

Norcross, J. C., Karpiak, C. P., & Lister, K. M. (2005). What's an integrationist? A study of self-identified integrative and (occasionally) eclectic psychologists. *Journal of Clinical Psychology, 61*, 1587–1594.

Norcross, J. C., Sayette, M. A., Mayne, T. J., Karg, R. S., & Turkson, M. A. (1998). Selecting a doctoral program in professional psychology: Some comparisons among PhD counseling, PhD clinical, and PsyD clinical psychology programs. *Professional Psychology: Research and Practice, 29*, 609–614.

Norden, D. M., & Godbout, J. P. (2013). Microglia of the aged brain: Primed to be activated and resistant to regulation. *Neuropathology and Applied Neurobiology, 39*(1), 19–34. Available at http://doi.org/10.1111/j.1365-2990.2012.01306.x

Norenzayan, A., & Nisbett, R. E. (2000). Culture and causal cognition. *Current Directions in Psychological Science, 9*, 132–135.

Nottebohm, F. (1985). Neuronal replacement in adulthood. *Annals of the New York Academy of Sciences, 457*, 143–161.

Nouchi, R., Taki, Y., Takeuchi, H., Sekiguchi, A., Hashizume, H., Nozawa, T., ... Kawashima, R. (2014). Four weeks of combination exercise training improved executive functions, episodic memory, and processing speed in healthy elderly people: Evidence from a randomized controlled trial. *Age, 36*(2), 787–799. Available at https://doi.org/10.1007/s11357-013-9588-x

Novak, M. A. (2003). Self-injurious behavior in rhesus monkeys: New insights into its etiology, physiology, and treatment. *American Journal of Primatology, 59*, 3–19.

Nowak, M. A., & Sigmund, K. (2005, October 27). Evolution of indirect reciprocity. *Nature, 437*, 1291–1298.

Nuechterlein, K., & Parasuraman, R. (1983). Visual sustained attention: Image degradation produces rapid sensitivity decrement over time. *Science, 220*, 327–329.

Nugent, B. M., Wright, C. L., Shetty, A. C., Hodes, G. E., Lenz, K. M., Mahurkar, A., ... McCarthy, M. M. (2015). Brain feminization requires active repression of masculinization via DNA methylation. *Nature Neuroscience, 18*(5), 690–697. doi:10.1038/nn.3988

Nugent, N. R., Goldberg, A., & Uddin, M. (2016). Topical review: The emerging field of epigenetics: Informing models of pediatric trauma and physical health. *Journal of Pediatric Psychology, 41*(1), 55–64. doi: 10.1093/jpepsy/jsv018

Nusbaum, E. C., & Silvia, P. J. (2011). Are intelligence and creativity really so different? Fluid intelligence, executive processes, and strategy use in divergent thinking. *Intelligence, 39*(1), 36–45. doi: 10.1016/j.intell.2010.11.002

Nutt, A. E., (2015). *Becoming Nicole: The transformation of an American family.* New York, NY: Random House.

Oaten, M., Stevenson, R. J., & Case, T. I. (2009). Disgust as a disease-avoidance mechanism. *Psychological Bulletin, 135*, 303–321. doi: 10.1037/a001482

Oatley, K., & Johnson-Laird, P. N. (2011). Basic emotions in social relationships, reasoning, and psychological illnesses. *Emotion Review, 3*, 424–433.

Oberlander, T. F. (2012). Fetal serotonin signaling: Setting pathways for early childhood development and behavior. *Journal of Adolescent Health, 51*, S9–S16. doi: 10.1016/j.jadohealth.2012.04.009

Oberman, L. M., & Ramachandran, V. S. (2007). The simulating social mind: The role of mirror neuron system and simulation in the social and communicative deficits of autism spectrum disorders. *Psychological Bulletin, 133*, 310–327.

O'Cleirigh, C., Ironson, G., Fletcher, M. A., & Schneiderman, N. (2008). Written emotional disclosure and processing of trauma are associated with protected health status and immunity in people living with HIV /AIDS. *British Journal of Health Psychology, 13*, 81–84.

O'Connor, K. (2016). Hans Eysenck and the Individual Differences Paradigm in the clinical setting. *Personality and Individual Differences, 103*, 99–104. Retrieved from http://doi.org/10.1016/j .paid.2016.03.052

O'Conner, M. J., & Paley, B. (2006). The relationship of prenatal alcohol exposure and the postnatal environment of child depressive symptoms. *Journal of Pediatric Psychology, 31*, 50–64.

O'Connor, S. S., Whitehill, J. M., King, K. M., Kernic, M. A., Boyle, L. N., Bresnahan, B. W., ... & Ebel, B. E. (2013). Compulsive cell phone use and history of motor vehicle crash. *Journal of Adolescent Health, 53*(4), 512–519. Retrieved from http://dx.doi.org/10.1016/j.jadohealth.2013.05.015

O'Craven, K. M., & Kanwisher, N. N. (2000). Mental imagery of faces and places activates corresponding stimulus-specific brain regions. *Journal of Cognitive Neuroscience, 12,* 1013–1023. doi: 10.1162/08989290051137549

Oehen, P., Traber, R., Widmer, V., & Schnyder, U. (2013). A randomized, controlled pilot study of MDMA (±3,4-methylenedioxymethamphetamine)-assisted psychotherapy for treatment of resistant, chronic post-traumatic stress disorder (PTSD). *Journal of Psychopharmacology, 27,* 40–52. doi: 10.1177/0269881112464827

Ogden, C. L., Lamb, M. M., Carroll, M. D., & Flegal, K. M. (2010). *Obesity and socioeconomic status in adults: United States 1988–1994 and 2005–2008.* NCHS data brief no. 50. Hyattsville, MD: National Center for Health Statistics.

Öhman, A. (2002). Automaticity and the amygdala: Nonconscious responses to emotional faces. *Current Directions in Psychological Science, 11,* 62–66.

Ohnishi, T., Matsuda, H., Asada, T., Aruga, M., Hirakata, M., Nishikawa, M., ... Imabayashi, E. (2001). Functional anatomy of musical perception in musicians. *Cerebral Cortex, 11,* 754–760. doi: 10.1093/cercor/11.8.754

Ohtani, T., Levitt, J. J., Nestor, P. G., Kawashima, T., Asami, T., Shenton, M. E., ... & McCarley, R. W. (2014). Prefrontal cortex volume deficit in schizophrenia: A new look using 3T MRI with manual parcellation. *Schizophrenia Research, 152*(1), 184–190. Available at http://dx.doi.org/10.1016/j.schres.2013.10.026

Oitzl, M. S., Champagne, D. L., van der Veen, R., & de Kloet, E. R. (2010). Brain development under stress: Hypotheses of glucocorticoid actions revisited. *Neuroscience & Biobehavioral Reviews, 34,* 853–866.

Olds, J., & Milner, P. (1954). Positive reinforcement produced by electrical stimulation of septal area and other regions of rat brain. *Journal of Comparative and Physiological Psychology, 47,* 419–427.

Oliveira, B. S., Zunzunegui, M. V., Quinlan, J., Fahmi, H., Tu, M. T., & Guerra, R. O. (2016). Systematic review of the association between chronic social stress and telomere length: A life course perspective. *Ageing research reviews, 26,* 37–52. Available at http://dx.doi.org/10.1016/j.arr.2015.12.006

Oliver, M. B., & Hyde, J. S. (1993). Gender differences in sexuality: A meta-analysis. *Psychological Bulletin, 114,* 29–51.

Olson, J. M., & Zanna, M. P. (1993). Attitudes and attitude change. *Annual Review of Psychology, 44,* 117–154.

Olulade, O. A., Jamal, N. I., Koo, D. S., Perfetti, C. A., LaSasso, C., & Eden, G. F. (2016). Neuroanatomical evidence in support of the bilingual advantage theory. *Cerebral Cortex, 26*(7), 3196–3204. http://doi.org/10.1093/cercor/bhv152

Omark, D., Omark, M., & Edelman, M. (1973). Formation of dominance hierarchies in young children. In T. R. Williams (Ed.), *Physical anthropology.* The Hague, Netherlands: Mouton.

Ong, E. Y. L., Ang, R. P., Ho, J. C. M., Lim, J. C. Y., Goh, D. H., Lee, C. S., & Chua, A. Y. K. (2011). Narcissism, extraversion and adolescents' self-presentation on Facebook. *Personality and Individual Differences, 50*(2), 180–185. Available at http://doi.org/10.1016/j.paid.2010.09.022

Ong, J. C., Shapiro, S. L., & Manber, R. (2008). Combining mindfulness meditation with cognitive-behavior therapy for insomnia: A treatment-development study. *Behavior Therapy, 39,* 171–182.

Onodera, A. (2003). Changes in self-concept in the transition to parenthood. *Japanese Journal of Developmental Psychology, 14,* 180–190.

Ophir, E., Nass, C. I., & Wagner, A. D. (2009). Cognitive control in media multi-taskers. *Proceedings of the National Academy of Sciences, 106,* 15583–15587.

Oppezzo, M., & Schwartz, D. L. (2014). Give your ideas some legs: The positive effect of walking on creative thinking. *Journal of Experimental Psychology. Learning, Memory, and Cognition, 40*(4), 1142–1152. Available at http://doi.org/10.1037/a0036577

Orne, M. T. (1959). The nature of hypnosis: Artifact and essence. *Journal of Abnormal and Social Psychology, 58,* 277–299.

Orr, E. S., Sisic, M., Ross, C., Simmering, M. G., Arseneault, J. M., & Orr, R. (2009). The influence of shyness on the use of Facebook in an undergraduate sample. *Cyberpsychology & Behavior, 12*(3), 337–340. doi:10.1089/cpb.2008.0214

Ortigosa, A., Carro, R. M., & Quiroga, J. (2014). Predicting user personality by mining social interactions in Facebook. *Journal of Computer & System Sciences, 80*(1), 57–71. doi: 10.1016/j.jcss.2013.03.008

Oscar-Berman, M., & Marinkovic, K. (2003). Alcoholism and the brain: An overview. *Alcohol Research & Health, 27,* 125–133.

Osherow, N. (1999). Making sense of the nonsensical: An analysis of Jonestown. In E. Aronson (Ed.), *Readings about the social animal* (8th ed., pp. 71–88). New York, NY: Worth/Freeman.

Osorio, D., & Vorobyev, M. (2005). Photoreceptor spectral sensitivities in terrestrial animals: Adaptations for luminance and colour vision. *Proceedings. Biological Sciences/The Royal Society, 272*(1574), 1745–1752. Available at http://doi.org/10.1098/rspb.2005.3156

Oster, H. (2005). The repertoire of infant facial expressions: An ontogenetic perspective. In J. Nadel & D. Muir (Eds.), *Emotional development* (pp. 261–292). New York, NY: Oxford University Press.

Osterling, J., & Dawson, G. (1994). Early recognition of children with autism: A study of first birthday home videotapes. *Journal of Autism and Developmental Disorders, 24,* 247–257.

Ostovar, S., Allahyar, N., Aminpoor, H., Moafian, F., Nor, M. B. M., & Griffiths, M. D. (2016). Internet addiction and its psychosocial risks (depression, anxiety, stress and loneliness) among Iranian adolescents and young adults: A structural equation model in a cross-sectional study. *International Journal of Mental Health and Addiction, 14*(3), 257–267. doi: 10.1007/s11469-015-9628-0

Ostry, D. J., Darainy, M., Mattar, A. A. G., Wong, J., & Gribble, P. L. (2010). Somatosensory plasticity and motor learning. *Journal of Neuroscience, 30,* 5384–5393.

Ottersen, O. P. (2010). How hardwired is the brain? Technological advances provide new insight into brain malleability and neurotransmission. *Nutrition Reviews, 68,* S60–S64. doi: 10.1111/j.1753-4887.2010.00350.x

Otto, M. W., McHugh, R. K., & Kantak, K. M. (2010). Combined pharmacotherapy and cognitive-behavioral therapy for anxiety disorders: Medication effects, glucocorticoids, and attenuated treatment outcomes. *Clinical Psychology: Science and Practice, 17,* 91–103.

Ouellet, M.-C., & Morin, C. M. (2006). Fatigue following traumatic brain injury: Frequency, characteristics, and associated factors. *Rehabilitation Psychology, 51,* 140–149.

Ouellet, M.-C., Beaulieu-Bonneau, S., & Morin, C. M. (2006). Insomnia in patients with traumatic brain injury: Frequency, characteristics, and risk factors. *Journal of Head Trauma Rehabilitation, 21,* 199–212.

Owen, A. M. (2013). Detecting consciousness: A unique role for neuroimaging. *Annual Review of Psychology, 64,* 109–133.

Owen, A. M., Coleman, M. R., Boly, M., Davis, M., Laureys, S., & Pickard, J. D. (2006). Detecting awareness in the vegetative state. *Science, 313,* 1402.

Oyama, S. (1976). A sensitive period for the acquisition of a nonnative phonological system. *Journal of Psycholinguistic Research, 5,* 261–283.

Özgüven, N., & Mucan, B. (2013). The relationship between personality traits and social media use. *Social Behavior & Personality: An International Journal, 41*(3), 517–528.

Pace, T. W., Negi, L. T., Adame, D. D., Cole, S. P., Sivilli, T. I., Brown, T. D., Issa, M. J., & Raison, C. L. (2009). Effect of compassion meditation on neuroendocrine, innate immune and behavioral responses to psychosocial stress. *Psychoneuroendocrinology, 34,* 87–98.

Pae, C.-U., Lim, H.-K., Han, C., Neena, A., Lee, C., & Patkar, A. A. (2007). Selegiline transdermal system: Current awareness and promise. *Progress in Neuro-Psychopharmacology & Biological Psychiatry, 31,* 1153–1163.

Page, T. F., Pelham, W. E., III, Fabiano, G. A., Greiner, A. R., Gnagy, E. M., Hart, K. C., ... & Pelham, W. E., Jr. (2016). Comparative cost analysis of sequential, adaptive, behavioral, pharmacological, and combined treatments for childhood ADHD. *Journal of Clinical Child & Adolescent Psychology,* 1–12. doi: 10.1080/15374416.2015.1055859

Pan, B. A., Rowe, M. L., Singer, J. D., & Snow, C. E. (2005). Maternal correlates of growth in toddler vocabulary production in low-income families. *Child Development, 76,* 763–946.

Panagopoulou, E., Montgomery, A., & Tarlatzis, B. (2010). Experimental emotional disclosure in women undergoing infertility treatment: Are drop outs better off? *Social Science & Medicine, 69,* 678–681.

Panjwani, N., Chaplin, T. M., Sinha, R., & Mayes, L. C. (2016). Gender differences in emotion expression in low-income adolescents under stress. *Journal of Nonverbal Behavior, 40*(2), 117–132. doi: 10.1007/s10919-015-0224-6

Panksepp, J. (1998). *Affective neuroscience: The foundations of human and animal emotions.* Oxford, England: Oxford University Press.

Panksepp, J. (2000). Emotions as natural kinds within the mammalian brain. In M. Lewis & J. M. Haviland-Jones (Eds.), *Handbook of emotions* (2nd ed., pp. 137–156). New York, NY: Guilford Press.

Pantev, C., Engelien, A., Candia, V., & Elbert, T. (2001). Representational cortex in musicians: Plastic alterations in response to musical practice. In R. J. Zatorre & I. Peretz (Eds.), *The biological foundations of music: Annals of the New York Academy of Sciences* (pp. 300–314). New York, NY: New York Academy of Sciences.

Papadakaki, M., Tzamalouka, G., Gnardellis, C., Lajunen, T. J., & Chliaoutakis, J. (2016). Driving performance while using a mobile phone: A simulation study of Greek professional drivers. *Transportation Research Part F, 38,* 164–170. doi: 10.1016/j.trf2016.02.006

Papagno, C., Pisoni, A., Mattavelli, G., Casarotti, A., Comi, A., Fumagalli, F., ... & Bello, L. (2016). Specific disgust processing in the left insula: New evidence from direct electrical stimulation. *Neuropsychologia, 84,* 29–35. Available at http://dx.doi.org/10.1016/j.neuropsychologia.2016.01.036

Parasuraman, R. (1998). *The attentive brain.* Cambridge, MA: MIT Press.

Paris, R., & Helson, R. (2002). Early mothering experience and personality change. *Journal of Family Psychology, 16,* 172–185.

Park, G., Yaden, D. B., Schwartz, H. A., Kern, M. L., Eichstaedt, J. C., Kosinski, M., ... Seligman, M. E. (2016). Women are warmer but no less assertive than men: Gender and language on Facebook. *PLOS ONE, 11,* e0155885. doi:10.1371/journal.pone.0155885

Park, I. (2015). The role of affect spin in the relationships between proactive personality, career indecision, and career maturity. *Frontiers in Psychology, 6,* 1754. Retrieved October 24, 2016 at http://dx.doi.org/10.3389/fpsyg.2015.01754

Parker, E. S., Cahill, L., & McGaugh, J. L. (2006). A case of unusual autobiographical remembering. *Neurocase, 12,* 35–49.

Parker, S. T., & McKinney, M. L. (1999). *Origins of intelligence: The evolution of cognitive development in monkeys, apes, and humans.* Baltimore, MD: Johns Hopkins University Press.

Parks, E. J., & McCrory, M. A. (2005). When to eat and how often? *American Journal of Nutrition, 81,* 3–4.

Parrott, A. C. (2013). Human psychobiology of MDMA or 'Ecstasy': An overview of 25 years of empirical research. *Human Psychopharmacology: Clinical and Experimental, 28*(4), 289–307. doi: 10.1002/hup.2318

Partanen, E., Kujala, T., Näätänen, R., Liitola, A., Sambeth, A., & Huotilainen, M. (2013). Learning-induced neural plasticity of speech processing before birth. *Proceedings of the National Academy of Sciences of the United States of America, 110*(37), 15145–15150. Available at http://doi.org/10.1073/pnas.1302159110

Pascual-Leone, A. (2001). The brain that plays music and is changed by it. *Annals of the New York Academy of Sciences, 930,* 315–329.

Passer, M. W., & Smith, B. D. (1998). *Psychology: Science and understanding.* New York, NY: McGraw-Hill.

Pasternak, B., Svanström, H., Ranthe, M. F., Melbye, M., & Hviid, A. (2014). Atypical antipsychotics olanzapine, quetiapine, and risperidone and risk of acute major cardiovascular events in young and middle-aged adults: A nationwide register-based cohort study in Denmark. *CNS Drugs, 28*(10), 963–973. doi: 10.1007/s40263-014-0176-0

Pasterski, V., Zucker, K. J., Hindmarsh, P. C., Hughes, I. A., Acerini, C., Spencer, D., ... Hines, M. (2015). Increased cross-gender identification independent of gender role behavior in girls with congenital adrenal hyperplasia: Results from a standardized assessment of 4- to 11-year-old children. *Archives of Sexual Behavior, 44*(5), 1363–1375. doi:10.1007/s10508-014-0385-0

Patihis, L., Frenda, S. J., LePort, A. K. R., Petersen, N., Nichols, R. M., Stark, C. E. L., McGaugh, J. L., & Loftus, E. F. (2013). False memories in highly superior autobiographical memory individuals. *PNAS Early Edition.* Retrieved from http://www.pnas.org/cgi/doi/10.1073/pnas.1314373110

Patil, S. T., Zhang, L., Martenyi, F., Lowe, S. L., Jackson, K. A., Andreev, B. V., ... Schoepp, D. (2007). Activation of mGlu2/3 receptors as a new approach to treat schizophrenia: A randomized Phase 2 clinical trial. *Nature Medicine, 13,* 1102–1107. doi: 10.1038/nm1632

Patterson, C. J. (2008). *Child development.* New York, NY: McGraw-Hill.

Patterson, D. R. (2004). Treating pain with hypnosis. *Current Directions in Psychological Science, 13,* 252–255.

Paul, E. S., Harding, E. J., & Mendl, M. (2005). Measuring emotional processes in animals: The utility of a cognitive approach. *Neuroscience and Biobehavioral Reviews, 29,* 469–491.

Paulesu, E., Frith, C. D., & Frackowiak, R. S. J. (1993). The neural correlates of the verbal component of working memory. *Nature, 362,* 342–345.

Paulozzi, L. J. (2006). Opioid analgesia involvement in drug abuse deaths in American metropolitan areas. *American Journal of Public Health, 96,* 1755–1757.

Paus, T., Keshavan, M., & Giedd, J. N. (2008). Why do many psychiatric disorders emerge during adolescence? *Nature Reviews Neuroscience, 9,* 947–957.

Pavlov, I. P. (1906). The scientific investigation of the psychical faculties or processes in the higher animals. *Science, 24,* 613–619.

Pavlov, I. P. (1928). *Lectures on conditioned reflexes: Twenty-five years of objective study of the higher nervous activity (behaviour) of animals* (W. H. Gantt, Trans.). New York, NY: Liveright.

Pawluski, J. L., Lambert, K. G., & Kinsley, C. H. (2016). Neuroplasticity in the maternal hippocampus: Relation to cognition and effects of repeated stress. *Hormones and Behavior, 77,* 86–97. Available at http://dx.doi.org/10.1016/j.yhbeh.2015.06.004

Payne, J. D., & Kensinger, E. A. (2010). Sleep's role in the consolidation of emotional episodic memories. *Current Directions in Psychological Science, 19*(5), 290–295. doi: 10.1177/0963721410383978

Payne, J. D., & Nadel, L. (2004). Sleep, dreams, and memory consolidation: The role of the stress hormone cortisol. *Learning & Memory, 11*(6), 671–678. doi: 10.1101/lm.77104

Payne, J. D., Tucker, M. A., Ellenbogen, J. M., Wamsley, E. J., Walker, M. P., Schacter, D. L., & Stickgold, R. (2012). Memory for semantically related and unrelated declarative information: The benefit of sleep, the cost of wake. *PLoS ONE, 7*(3), 1–7. Available at http://doi.org/10.1371/journal.pone.0033079

Pearson, J. D., Morrell, C. H., Gordon-Salant, S., Brant, L. J., Metter, E. J., Klein, L., & Fozard, J. L. (1995). Gender differences in a longitudinal study of age-associated hearing loss. *Journal of the Acoustical Society of America, 97,* 1197–1205. doi: 10.1121/1.412231

Pedersen, D. M., & Wheeler, J. (1983). The Müller–Lyer illusion among Navajos. *Journal of Social Psychology, 121,* 3–6.

Peigneux, P., Laureys, S., Fuchs, S., Collette, F., Perrin, F., Reggers, J., ... Maquet, P. (2004). Are spatial memories strengthened in the human hippocampus during slow wave sleep? *Neuron, 44,* 535–545. doi: 10.1016/j.neuron.2004.10.007

Pelham, W. E., Jr., Fabiano, G. A., Waxmonsky, J. G., Greiner, A., Gnagy, E. M., Pelham, W. E., III, ... Murphy, S. A. (2016). Treatment sequencing for childhood ADHD: A multiple-randomization study of adaptive medication and behavioral interventions. *Journal of Clinical Child & Adolescent Psychology, 45,* 396–415. doi: 10.1080/15374416.2015.1105138

Pellicer-Chenoll, M., Garcia-Masso, X., Morales, J., Serra-Ano, P., Solana-Tramunt, M., Gonzalez, L.-M., & Toca-Herrera, J.-L. (2015). Physical activity, physical fitness and academic achievement in adolescents: A self-organizing maps approach. *Health Education Research, 30*(3), 436–448. Available at http://doi.org/10.1093/her/cyv016

Penfield, W., & Milner, B. (1958). Memory deficit produced by bilateral lesions in the hippocampal zone. *Archives of Neurology & Psychiatry (Chicago), 79,* 475–497.

Peng, Y., Gillis-Smith, S., Jin, H., Tränkner, D., Ryba, N. J. P., & Zuker, C. S. (2015). Sweet and bitter taste in the brain of awake behaving animals. *Nature, 527*(7579), 512–515. Available at http://doi.org/10.1038/nature15763

Pennebaker, J. W. (1995). *Emotion, disclosure, and health.* Washington, DC: American Psychological Association.

Pennebaker, J. W., Kiecolt-Glaser, J. K., & Glaser, R. (1988). Disclosure of traumas and immune function: Implications for psychotherapy. *Journal of Consulting and Clinical Psychology, 56,* 239–245.

Peper, J. S., Schnack, H. G., Brouwer, R. M., Van Baal, G. C. M., ... Pol, H. E. H. (2009). Heritability of regional and global brain structure at the onset of puberty: A magnetic resonance imaging study in 9-year-old twin pairs. *Human Brain Mapping, 30,* 2184–2196.

Pepperberg, I. M. (2016). Animal language studies: What happened? *Psychonomic Bulletin & Review,* published online, July 2016. doi:10.3758/s13423-016-1101-y

Pereira, A. C., Huddleston, D. E., Brickman, A. M., Sosunov, A. A., Hen, R., McKhann, G. M., ... Small, S. A. (2007). An *in vivo* correlate of exercise induced neurogenesis in the adult dentate gyrus. *Proceedings of the National Academy of Sciences, 104,* 5638–5643.

Perez, M., Ohrt, T. K., & Hoek, H. W. (2016). Prevalence and treatment of eating disorders among Hispanics/Latino Americans in the United States. *Current Opinion in Psychiatry, 29*(6), 378–382. doi: 10.1097/YCO.0000000000000277

Perrin, F., Maquet, P., Peigneux, P., Ruby, P., Degueldre, C., Balteau, E., ... & Laureys, S. (2005). Neural mechanisms involved in the detection of our first name: A combined ERPs and PET study. *Neuropsychologia, 43*(1), 12–19. doi:10.1016/j.neuropsychologia.2004.07.002

Perrin, J. S., Leonard, G., Perron, M., Pike, G. B., Pitiot, A., Richer, L., ... Paus, T. (2009). Sex differences in the growth of white matter during adolescence. *NeuroImage, 45,* 1055–1066.

Perry, B. D. (2002). Childhood experience and the expression of genetic potential: What childhood neglect tells us about nature and nurture. *Brain and Mind, 3,* 79–100.

Perry, C. J., Baciadonna, L., & Chittka, L. (2016). Unexpected rewards induce dopamine-dependent positive emotion–like state changes in bumblebees. *Science, 353*(6307), 1529–1531. doi: 10.1126/science.aaf4454

Perry, R., & Zeki, S. (2000). The neurology of saccades and covert shifts in spatial attention: An event-related fMRI study. *Brain, 123,* 2273–2288.

Persky, H., Dreisbach, L., Miller, W. R., O'Brien, C. P., Khan, M. A., Lief, H. I., ... Strauss, D. (1982). The relation of plasma androgen levels to sexual behaviors and attitudes of women. *Psychosomatic Medicine, 44,* 305–319.

Persky, H., Lief, H. I., Strauss, D., Miller, W. R., & O'Brien, C. P. (1978). Plasma testosterone level and sexual behavior of couples. *Archives of Sexual Behavior, 7,* 157–173.

Perszyk, D. R., & Waxman, S. R. (2016). Listening to the calls of the wild: The role of experience in linking language and cognition in young infants. *Cognition, 153,* 175–181. Available at http://doi.org/10.1016/j.cognition.2016.05.004

Pessoa, L. (2008). On the relationship between emotion and cognition. *Nature Reviews Neuroscience, 9,* 148–158.

Peters, R. M., Hackeman, E., & Goldreich, D. (2009). Diminutive digits discern delicate details: Fingertip size and the sex difference in tactile spatial acuity. *Journal of Neuroscience, 29,* 15756–15761.

Petersen, J. L., & Hyde, J. S. (2010). A meta-analytic review of research on gender differences in sexuality, 1993–2007. *Psychological Bulletin, 136,* 21–38. doi: 10.1037/a0017504

Petronis, A. (2004). Schizophrenia, neurodevelopment, and epigenetics. In M. S. Keshavan, J. L. Kennedy, & R. M. Murray (Eds.), *Neurodevelopment and schizophrenia* (pp. 174–190). New York, NY: Cambridge University Press.

Petry, N. M., & O'Brien, C. P. (2013). Internet gaming disorder and the DSM-5. *Addiction, 108,* 1186–1187. doi: 10.1111/add.12162

Petzinger, G. M., Fisher, B. E., McEwen, S., Beeler, J. A., Walsh, J. P., & Jakowec, M. W. (2013). Exercise-enhanced neuroplasticity targeting motor and cognitive circuitry in Parkinson's disease. *The Lancet Neurology, 12*(7), 716–726. doi: 10.1016/S1474-4422(13)70123-6

Pevsner-Fischer, M., Blacher, E., Tatirovsky, E., Ben-Dov, I. Z., & Elinav, E. (2017). The gut microbiome and hypertension. *Current Opinion in Nephrology and Hypertension, 26*(1), 1–8. doi: 10.1097/MNH.0000000000000293

Pew Research Center. (2016). 15% of American adults have used online dating sites or mobile dating apps. *Pew Research.* Retrieved October 23, 2016 from http://www.pewinternet.com/2016/02/11/15 -percent-of-american-adults-have-used-online -dating-sites-or-mobile-dating-apps/

Phan, K. L., Wager, T., Taylor, S. F., & Liberzon, I. (2002). Functional neuroanatomy of emotion: A meta-analysis of emotion activation studies in PET and fMRI. *NeuroImage, 16,* 331–348.

Phelps, E. A. (2006). Emotion and cognition: Insights from the study of the human amygdala. *Annual Review of Psychology, 57,* 27–53.

Phelps, E. A., & LeDoux, J. E. (2005). Contributions of the amygdala to emotional processing: From animal models to human behavior. *Neuron, 48,* 175–187.

Phelps, E. A., & Sharot, T. (2008). How (and why) emotion enhances the subjective sense of recollection. *Current Directions in Psychological Science, 17,* 147–152.

Piaget, J. (1954). *The construction of reality in the child.* New York, NY: Basic Books.

Piaget, J. (1972b). Intellectual evolution from adolescence to adulthood. *Human Development, 15,* 1–12.

Piaget, J., & Inhelder, B. (1967). *The child's conception of space.* New York, NY: Norton.

Pickrell, J. K., & Reich, D. (2014). Toward a new history and geography of human genes informed by ancient DNA. *Trends in Genetics, 30*(9), 377–389. Available at http://doi.org/10.1016/j .tig.2014.07.007

Pietrek, C., Elbert, T., Weierstall, R., Müller, O., & Rockstroh, B. (2013). Childhood adversities in relation to psychiatric disorders. *Psychiatry Research, 206,* 103–110. doi: 10.1016 /j.psychres.2012.11.003

Pietschnig, J., Penke, L., Wicherts, J. M., Zeiler, M., & Voracek, M. (2015). Meta-analysis of associations between human brain volume and intelligence differences: How strong are they and what do they mean? *Neuroscience and Biobehavioral Reviews, 57,* 411–432. Available at http://doi .org/10.1016/j.neubiorev.2015.09.017

Pincus, J. H. (1999). Aggression, criminality, and the frontal lobes. In B. L. Miller & J. L. Cummings (Eds.), *The human frontal lobes: Functions and disorders* (pp. 547–556). New York, NY: Guilford Press.

Pincus, J. H. (2001). *Base instincts: What makes killers kill?* New York, NY: Norton.

Pinker, S. (1994). *The language instinct: How the mind creates language.* New York, NY: HarperPerennial.

Pinker, S. (2002). *The blank slate.* New York, NY: Viking.

Pinker, S. (2004, Fall). Why nature and nurture won't go away. *Daedalus,* 1–13.

Pinsker, H. M., Hening, W. A., Carew, T. J., & Kandel, E. R. (1973). Long-term sensitization of a defensive withdrawal reflex in *Aplysia. Science, 182,* 1039–1042.

Pitel, A. L., Segobin, S. H., Ritz, L., Eustache, F., & Beaunieux, H. (2015). Thalamic abnormalities are a cardinal feature of alcohol-related brain dysfunction. *Neuroscience and Biobehavioral Reviews, 54,* 38–45. doi: 10.1016/j .neubiorev.2014.07.023

Pittman, R. K., Sanders, K. M., Zusman, R. M., Healy, A. R., Cheema, F., Lasko, N. B., Cahill, L., & Orr, S. P. (2002). Pilot study of secondary prevention of posttraumatic stress disorder with propranolol. *Biological Psychiatry, 51,* 189–142.

"Pizzagate" shooting suspect: "The intel on this wasn't 100 percent." (2016, December 8). *CBSNEWS.* Retrieved online January 1, 2017, at http://www.cbsnews.com/news/pizzagate-shoot-ing-suspect-edgar-maddison-welch-intel-wasnt-100-percent/

Platsidou, M. (2010). Trait emotional intelligence of Greek special education teachers in relation to burnout and job satisfaction. *School Psychology International, 31,* 60–76.

Platts-Mills, T. A. E. (2015). The allergy epidemics: 1870–2010. *Journal of Allergy and Clinical Immunology, 136,* 3–13. doi: 10.1016.j.jaci.2015.03.048

Pliatsikas, C., & Luk, G. (2016). Executive control in bilinguals: A concise review on fMRI studies. *Bilingualism: Language and Cognition, 53*(9), 1689–1699. http://doi.org/10.1017 /CBO9781107415324.004

Pliner, P. (1982). The effects of mere exposure on liking for edible substances. *Appetite, 3,* 283–290.

Plomin, R., & Caspi, A. (1999). Behavioral genetics and personality. In L. A. Pervin & O. P. John (Eds.), *Handbook of personality theory and research* (pp. 251–276). New York, NY: Guilford Press.

Plomin, R., & Petrill, S. A. (1997). Genetics and intelligence: What's new? *Intelligence, 24,* 53–77.

Plomin, R., DeFries, J. C., Knopik, V. S., & Neiderhiser, J. M. (2013). *Behavioral genetics* (6th edition). New York: Worth Publishers.

Plucker, J. A., Beghetto, R. A., & Dow, G. T. (2004). Why isn't creativity more important to educational psychologists? Potentials, pitfalls, and future directions in creativity research. *Educational Psychologist, 39,* 83–96.

Plunkett, K. (1997). Theories of early language acquisition. *Trends in Cognitive Sciences, 1,* 146–153.

Poeppel, D., Emmorey, K., Hickok, G., & Pylkkänen, L. (2012). Towards a new neurobiology of language. *Journal of Neuroscience, 32*(41), 14125–14131. Available at http://doi.org/10.1523 /JNEUROSCI.3244-12.2012

Poeppl, T. B., Langguth, B., Rupprecht, R., Laird, A. R., & Eickhoff, S. B. (2016). A neural circuit encoding sexual preference in humans. *Neuroscience and Biobehavioral Reviews, 68,* 530–536. Available at http://doi.org/10.1016/j .neubiorev.2016.06.025

Poeppl, T. B., Langguth, B., Rupprecht, R., Safton, A., Bzdok, D., Laird, A. R., & Eickhoff, S. B. (2016). The neural basis of sex differences in sexual behavior: A quantitative meta-analysis. *Frontiers in Neuroendocrinology.* Published online. Retrieved November 13, 2016 at http://dx.doi.org/10.1016/j .yfrne.2016.10.001

Pohlmeyer, E. A., Oby, E. R., Perreault, E. J., Solla, S. A., Kilgore, K. L., Kirsch, R. F., & Miller, L. E. (2009). Toward the restoration of hand use to a paralyzed monkey: Brain-controlled functional electrical stimulation of forearm muscles. *PLoS ONE, 4,* e5924. doi: 10.1371/journal.pone.0005924

Polderman, T. J. C., Benyamin, B., de Leeuw, C. A., Sullivan, P. F., van Bochoven, A., Visscher, P. M., & Posthuma, D. (2015). Meta-analysis of the heritability of human traits based on fifty years of twin studies. *Nature Genetics, 47*(7), 702–709.

Pollan, M. (2013, May 15). Some of my best friends are germs. *New York Times Magazine.* Retrieved online January 20, 2017 at http://www.nytimes .com/2013/05/19/magazine/say-hello-to-the-100-trillion -bacteria-that-make-up-your-microbiome.html

Popper, K. (1965). *Conjectures and refutations: The growth of scientific knowledge.* New York, NY: Harper.

Porfeli, E. J., & Skorikov, V. B. (2010). Specific and diversive career exploration during late adolescence. *Journal of Career Assessment, 18,* 46–58.

Posner, M. I., & Rothbart, M. K. (2007). Research on attention networks as a model for the integration of psychological science. *Annual Review of Psychology, 58,* 1–23.

Post, F. (1994). Creativity and psychopathology: A study of 291 world-famous men. *British Journal of Psychiatry, 165,* 22–34.

Post, R. M., Frye, M. A., Denicoff, K. D., Leverich, G. S., Kimbrell, T. A., & Dunn, R. T. (1998). Beyond lithium in the treatment of bipolar illness. *Neuropsychopharmacology, 19,* 206–219.

Poulin, M. J., Brown, S. L., Dillard, A. J., & Smith, D. M. (2013). Giving to others and the association between stress and mortality. *American Journal of Public Health, 103,* 1649–1655. doi: 10.2105/AJPH.2012.300876

Powell, L. H., Kazlauskaite, R., Shima, C., & Appelhans, B. M. (2010). Lifestyle in France and the United States: An American perspective. *Journal of the American Dietetic Association, 10,* 845–847.

Powell, R. A., Digdon, N., Harris, B., & Smithson, C. (2014). Correcting the record on Watson, Rayner, and Little Albert: Albert Barger as "Psychology's lost boy." *American Psychologist, 69*(6), 600. Available at http://dx.doi.org/10.1037/a0036854

Powers, M., Halpern, J., Ferenschak, M., Gillihan, S., & Foa, E. (2010). A meta-analytic review of prolonged exposure for posttraumatic stress disorder. *Clinical Psychology Review, 30,* 635–641. doi: 10.1016/j.cpr.2010.04.007

Prahbu, V., Sutton, C., & Sauser, W. (2008). Creativity and certain personality traits: Understanding the mediating effect of intrinsic motivation. *Creativity Research Journal, 20,* 53–66.

Preckel, F., Holling, H., & Wiese, M. (2006). Relationship of intelligence and creativity in gifted and non-gifted students: An investigation of threshold theory. *Personality and Individual Differences, 40,* 159–170.

Premack, D. (1971). Language in chimpanzees? *Science, 172,* 808–822.

Price, J. (2008). *The woman who can't forget: A memoir.* New York, NY: Free Press.

Priori, A., Beradelli, A., Rona, S., Accornero, N., & Manfredi, M. (1998). Polarization of the human motor cortex through the scalp. *Neuroreport, 9,* 2257–2260. doi: 10.1097/00001756-199807130-00020

Prochaska, J. O., & Norcross, J. C. (2007). *Systems of psychotherapy* (6th ed.). Belmont, CA: Wadsworth.

Profet, M. (1992). Pregnancy sickness as adaptation: A deterrent to maternal ingestion of teratogens. In J. Barkow, L. Cosmides, & J. Tooby (Eds.), *The adapted mind* (pp. 327–365). New York, NY: Oxford University Press.

Przulj, D., McRobbie, H., & Hajek, P. (2016). Effects of nicotine-free e-cigarettes on urges to smoke and cigarette withdrawal symptoms: A randomised cross-over study. *Journal of Addiction Research & Therapy, 7,* 1. doi: 10.4172/2155-6105.1000259

Ptito, M., & Desgent, S. (2006). Sensory input–based adaptation and brain architecture. In P. B. Baltes, P. A. Reuter-Lorenz, & F. Rösler (Eds.), *Lifespan development and the brain: The perspective of biocultural coconstructivism* (pp. 111–133). New York, NY: Cambridge University Press.

Pua, E. P. K., Bowden, S. C., & Seal, M. L. (2017). Autism spectrum disorders: Neuroimaging findings from systematic reviews. *Research in Autism Spectrum Disorders, 34,* 28–33. Available at http://dx.doi.org/10.1016/j.rasd.2016.11.005

Pugh, M. J. V., & Hart, D. (1999). Identity development and peer group participation. In J. A. McLellan & M. J. V. Pugh (Eds.), *The role of peer groups in adolescent social identity: Exploring the importance of stability and change* (pp. 55–70). San Francisco, CA: Jossey-Bass.

Pulver, C. A., & Kelly, K. R. (2008). Incremental validity of the Myers-Briggs Type Indicator in predicting academic major selection of undecided university students. *Journal of Career Assessment, 16,* 441–455.

Purves, D., & Lichtman, J. W. (1985). *Principles of neural development.* Sunderland, MA: Sinauer.

Putnam, F., & McHugh, P. (2005). Issue 3: Is multiple personality disorder a valid diagnosis? In R. P. Halgin (Ed.), *Taking sides: Clashing views on controversial issues in abnormal psychology* (3rd ed., pp. 42–53). New York, NY: McGraw-Hill.

Putnam, F. W. (2006). Dissociative disorders. In D. Cicchetti & D. J. Cohen (Eds.), *Developmental psychopathology: Vol. 3. Risk, disorder, and adaptation* (pp. 657–695). Hoboken, NJ: John Wiley.

Qin, X. A., Koutstaal, W., & Engel, S. A. (2014). The hard-won benefits of familiarity in visual search: Naturally familiar brand logos are found faster. *Attention, Perception, & Psychophysics, 76*(4), 914-930. doi: 10.3758/s13414-014-0623-5

Qiu, J., Li, H., Jou, J., Liu, J., Yeujia, L., Feng, T., ... Zhang, Q. (2010). Neural correlates of the "aha" experiences: Evidence from an fMRI study of insight problem solving. *Cortex, 46,* 397–403.

Quach, D., Mano, K. E. J., & Alexander, K. (2016). A randomized controlled trial examining the effect of mindfulness meditation on working memory capacity in adolescents. *Journal of Adolescent Health, 58,* 489–496. doi: 10.1016/j.jadohealth.2015.09.024

Quillian, M. (1968). Semantic memory. In M. Minsky (Ed.). *Semantic information processing* (pp. 227–270). Cambridge, MA: MIT Press.

Quirin, M., Meyer, F., Cacioppo, J., Heise, N., Kuhl, J., Kustermann, E., ... Cacciopo, J. T. (2013). Neural correlates of social motivation: An fMRI study on power versus affiliation. *International Journal of Psychophysiology, 88,* 289–295.

Quiroga, R. Q., Reddy, L., Kreiman, G., Koch, C., & Fried, I. (2005). Invariant visual representation by single neurons in the human brain. *Nature, 435,* 1102–1107.

Raffaele, P. (2006, November). Speaking Bonobo. *Smithsonian.* Retrieved from http://www.smithsonianmagazine.com

Rahman, Q. (2005). The neurodevelopment of human sexual orientation. *Neuroscience and Biobehavioral Reviews, 29,* 1057–1066.

Rahn, E. J., & Hohmann, A. G. (2009). Cannabinoids as pharmacotherapies for neuropathic pain: From the bench to the bedside. *Neurotherapeutics, 6,* 713–737.

Raichle, M. E., MacLeod, A. M., Snyder, A. Z., Powers, W. J., Gusnard, D. A., & Shulman, G. L. (2001). A default mode of brain function. *Proceedings of the National Academy of Sciences of the United States of America, 98*(2), 676–82. Available at http://doi.org/10.1073/pnas.98.2.676

Raichle, M. E., & Snyder, A. Z. (2007). A default mode of brain function: A brief history of an evolving idea. *Neuroimage, 37,* 1083–1090 [discussion 1097–1089].

Raij, T. T., Numminen, J., Närvänen, S., Hiltunen, J., & Hari, R. (2005). Brain correlates of subjective reality of physically and psychologically induced pain. *Proceedings of the National Academy of Sciences, 102,* 2147–2151.

Raine, A. (2013). *The anatomy of violence: The biological roots of crime.* New York, NY: Pantheon.

Raleigh, M. J., McGuire, M. T., Brammer, G. L., Pollack, D. B., & Yuwiler, A. (1991). Serotonergic mechanisms promote dominance in adult male vervet monkeys. *Brain Research, 559,* 181–190.

Ramachandran, V. S., & Hubbard, E. M. (2003, May). Hearing colors, tasting shapes. *Scientific American, 288,* 52–59.

Ramachandran, V. S., & Oberman, L. M. (2006). Broken mirrors: A theory of autism. *Scientific American, 295,* 63–69.

Ramanathan, L., Gulyani, S., Nienhuis, R., & Siegel, J. M. (2002). Sleep deprivation decreases superoxide dismutase activity in rat hippocampus and brainstem. *NeuroReport, 13,* 1387–1390.

Ransdell, S. (2010). Online activity, motivation, and reasoning among adult learners. *Computers in Human Behavior, 26,* 70–73. doi: 10.1016/j.chb.2009.09.002

Rao, V., Spiro, J. R., Handel, S., & Onyike, C. U. (2008). Clinical correlates of personality changes associated with traumatic brain injury. *Journal of Neuropsychiatry and Clinical Neurosciences, 20,* 118–119.

Rapoport, J., Chavez, A., Greenstein, D., Addington, A., & Gogtay, N. (2009). Autism spectrum disorders and childhood-onset schizophrenia: Clinical and biological contributions to a relation revisited. *Journal of the American Academy of Child & Adolescent Psychiatry, 48*(1), 10–18. doi: 10.1097/CHI.0b013e31818b1c63

Rashid, T. (2008). Positive psychotherapy. In S. J. Lopez (Ed.), *Positive psychology: Exploring the best in people, Vol. 4: Pursuing human flourishing* (pp. 188–217). Westport, CT: Praeger/Greenwood.

Rath, J., Wurnig, M., Fischmeister, F., Klinger, N., Hollinger, I., Geissler, A., ... & Beisteiner, R. (2016). Between- and within-site variability of fMRI localizations. *Human Brain Mapping, 37,* 2151–2160. doi: 10.1002/hbm.23162

Rathus, J. H., Cavuoto, N., & Passarelli, V. (2006). Dialectical behavior therapy (DBT): A mindfulness-based treatment for intimate partner violence. In R. A. Baer (Ed.), *Mindfulness-based treatment approaches: Clinician's guide to evidence base and applications* (pp. 333–358). San Diego, CA: Elsevier Academic Press.

Ravizza, S. M., Uitvlugt, M. G., & Hazeltine, E. (2016). Where to start? Bottom-up attention improves working memory by determining encoding order. *Journal of Experimental Psychology: Human Perception and Performance, 42*(12), 1959–1968. Available at http://doi.org/10.1037/xhp0000275

Rawl, S. M., Skinner, C. S., Perkins, S. M., Springston, J., Wang, H.-L., Russell, K. M., ... Champion, V. (2012). Computer-delivered tailored intervention improves colon cancer screening knowledge and health beliefs of African-Americans. *Health Education Research, 27,* 868–885. doi: 10.1093/her/cys094

Rayan, A., & Ahmad, M. (2016). Effectiveness of mindfulness-based interventions on quality of life and positive reappraisal coping among parents of children with autism spectrum disorder. *Research in Developmental Disabilities, 55,* 185–196. Available at http://dx.doi.org/10.1016/j.ridd.2016.04.002

Raymaekers, L., Smeets, T., Peters, M., & Merckelbach, H. (2010). Autobiographical memory specificity among people with recovered memories of childhood sexual abuse. *Journal of Behavior Therapy and Experimental Psychiatry, 41,* 338–344. doi: 10.1016/j.jbtep.2010.03.004

Raz, A., Fan, J., & Posner, M. I. (2005). Hypnotic suggestion reduces conflict in the human brain. *Proceedings of the National Academy of Sciences, 102,* 9978–9983.

Raz, A., & Shapiro, T. (2002). Hypnosis and neuroscience. *Archives of General Psychiatry, 59,* 85–90.

Raz, N. (2000). Aging of the brain and its impact on cognitive performance: Integration of structural and functional findings. In F. I. M. Craik & T. A. Salthouse (Eds.), *The handbook of aging and cognition* (pp. 1–90). Mahwah, NJ: Erlbaum.

Read, J. C. A. (2015). The place of human psychophysics in modern neuroscience. *Neuroscience, 296,* 116–129. Retrieved from http://doi.org/10.1016/j.neuroscience.2014.05.036

Ready, D. J., Gerardi, R. J., Backscheider, A. G., Mascaro, N., & Rothbaum, B. O. (2010). Comparing virtual reality exposure therapy to present-centered therapy with 11 U. S. Vietnam veterans with PTSD. *Cyberpsychology, Behavior, and Social Networking, 13,* 49–54. doi: 10.1089/cyber.2009.0239

Realo, A., Allik, J., & Vadi, M. (1997). The hierarchical structure of collectivism. *Journal of Research in Personality, 31,* 93–116.

Reed, C., Novick, D., Gonzalez-Pinto, A., Bertsch, J., & Haro, J. (2009). Observational study designs for bipolar disorder—What can they tell us about treatment in acute mania? *Progress in Neuro-Psychopharmacology & Biological Psychiatry, 33,* 715–721. doi: 10.1016/j.pnpbp.2009.03.024

Reed, D. E., Zhang, Y., Beyak, M. J., Lourenssen, S., Blennerhassett, M. G., Paterson, W. G., & Vanner, S. J. (2016). Stress increases descending inhibition in mouse and human colon. *Neurogastroenterology & Motility.* doi: 10.1111/nmo.12755

Reed, G. M., Kemeny, M. E., Taylor, S. E., Wang, H. Y. J., & Visscher, B. R. (1994). Realistic acceptance as a predictor of decreased survival time in gay men with AIDS. *Health Psychology, 13,* 299–307.

Reese, P. P., Kessler, J. B., Doshi, J. A., Friedman, J., Mussell, A. S., Carney, C., ... Lawnicki, V. (2016). Two randomized controlled pilot trials of social forces to improve statin adherence among patients with diabetes. *Journal of General Internal Medicine, 31*(4), 402–410. doi: 10.1007/s11606-015-3540-y

Refinetti, R. (2006). *Circadian physiology* (2nd ed.). Boca Raton, FL: CRC Press.

Regan, P. C. (2016). Sexual instinct and sexual drive. *The Wiley Blackwell Encyclopedia of Gender and Sexuality Studies.* Retrieved November 12, 2016, published online at doi: 10.1002/9781118663219.wbegss301

Regier, T., & Kay, P. (2009). Language, thought, and color: Whorf was half right. *Trends in Cognitive Sciences, 13,* 439–446.

Regier, T., Kay, P., Gilbert, A., & Ivry, R. (2010). Language and thought: Which side are you on, anyway? In B. C. Malt & P. Wolff (Eds.), *Words and the mind: How words capture human experience* (pp. 165–182). New York, NY: Oxford University Press.

Reichert, C. F., Maire, M., Schmidt, C., & Cajochen, C. (2016). Sleep-wake regulation and its impact on working memory performance: The role of adenosine. *Biology, 5*(1), 11. doi:10.3390/biology5010011

Reilly, D., & Neumann, D. L. (2013). Gender-role differences in spatial ability: A meta-analytic review. *Sex Roles, 68*(9–10), 521–535. doi: 10.1007/s11199-013-0269-0

Reimagining the tragic mulatto. (2010, March 2). [Radio broadcast transcript]. Retrieved from http://www.npr.org/templates/transcript/transcript.php?storyId=124244813

Renaud, S., & de Lorgeril, M. (1992). Wine, alcohol, platelets, and the French paradox for coronary heart disease. *The Lancet, 339,* 1523–1526.

Renshaw, K. D. (2011). Working with the new generation of service members/veterans from Operations Enduring and Iraqi Freedom. *Cognitive and Behavioral Practice, 18,* 82–84. doi: 10.1016/j.cbpra.2010.03.003

Rentfrow, P. J., & Gosling, S. D. (2003) The do re mi's of everyday life: The structure and personality correlates of music preferences. *Journal of Personality and Social Psychology, 84,* 1236–1256.

Research Misconduct. (n.d.). Retrieved on January 29, 2017 at http://www.apa.org/research/responsible/misconduct/

Retz, W., Reif, A., Freitag, C., Retz-Junginger, P., & Rösler, M. (2010). Association of a functional variant of neuronal nitric oxide synthase gene with self-reported impulsiveness, venturesomeness and empathy in male offenders. *Journal of Neural Transmission, 117,* 321–324.

Rexrode, K. M., Buring, J. E., & Manson, J. E. (2001). Abdominal and total adiposity and risk of coronary heart disease in men. *International Journal of Obesity, 25,* 1047–1056.

Rexrode, K. M., Carey, V. J., Hennekens, C. H., Walters, E. E., Colditz, G. A., Stampfer, M. J., ... Manson, J. E. (1998). Abdominal adiposity and coronary heart disease in women. *Journal of the American Medical Association, 280,* 1843–1848. doi: 10.1001/jama.280.21.1843

Reynolds, C. R. (2000). Why is psychometric research on bias in mental testing so often ignored? *Psychology, Public Policy, and Law, 6,* 144–150.

Reynolds, S., & Lane, S. J. (2008). Diagnostic validity of sensory over-responsivity: A review of the literature and case reports. *Journal of Autism & Developmental Disorders, 38,* 516–529.

Rhoades, G. K., Stanley, S. M., & Markman, H. J. (2009). The pre-engagement cohabitation effect: A replication and extension of previous findings. *Journal of Family Psychology, 23,* 107–111.

Ricciardelli, L. A. (1992). Creativity and bilingualism. *Journal of Creative Behavior, 26,* 242–254.

Rice, C. E., Adamson, L. B., Winner, E., & McGee, G. G. (2016). A cross-sectional study of shared attention by children with autism and typically developing children in an inclusive preschool setting. *Topics in Language Disorders, 36*(3), 245–265. doi: 10.1097/TLD.0000000000000099

Rice, F., Jones, I., & Thapar, A. (2007). The impact of gestational stress and prenatal growth on emotional problems in offspring: A review. *Acta Psychiatrica Scandinavica, 115*(3), 171–183.

Rice, M. L. (1989). Children's language acquisition. *American Psychologist, 44,* 149–156.

Rice, W. R., Friberg, U., & Gavrilets, S. (2012). Homosexuality as a consequence of epigenetically canalized sexual development. *Quarterly Review of Biology, 87,* 343–368.

Richards, J. E., Reynolds, G. D., & Courage, M. L. (2010). The neural basis of infant attention. *Current Directions in Psychological Science, 19,* 41–46.

Richards, R. L., & Kinney, D. K. (1990). Mood swings and creativity. *Creativity Research Journal, 3,* 202–217.

Richardson, J. D., Huddy, W. P., & Morgan, S. M. (2008). The hostile media effect, biased assimilation, and perceptions of a presidential debate. *Journal of Applied Social Psychology, 38,* 1255–1270. doi: 10.1111/j.1559-1816.2008.00347.x

Riddle, J. P., Smith, H. E., & Jones, C. J. (2016). Does written emotional disclosure improve the psychological and physical health of caregivers? A systematic review and meta-analysis. *Behaviour Research and Therapy, 80,* 23–32. Available at http://dx.doi.org/10.1016/j.brat.2016.03.004

Rideout, V. (2016). Measuring time spent with media: The Common Sense census of media use by U.S. 8- to 18-year-olds. *Journal of Children and Media, 10*(1), 138–144. Available at http://doi.org/10.1080/17482798.2016.1129808

Ridley, M. (2003). *Nature via nurture: Genes, experience, and what makes us human.* New York, NY: HarperCollins.

Rieger, G., Linsenmeier, J. A. W., Gygax, L., & Bailey, J. M. (2008). Sexual orientation and childhood gender nonconformity: Evidence from home videos. *Developmental Psychology, 44*(1), 46–58. Available at http://doi.org/doi 10.1037/0012-1649.44.1.46

Ries, M., & Marks, W. (2005). Selective attention deficits following severe closed head injury: The role of inhibitory processes. *Neuropsychology, 19,* 476–481.

Rinpoche, S. (1992). *The Tibetan book of living and dying.* New York, NY: HarperCollins.

Risch, N., Herrell, R., Lehner, T., Liang, K.-Y., Eaves, L., Hoh, J., ... Mirerikangas, K. R. (2009). Interaction between the serotonin transporter gene (*5-HTTLPR*), stressful life events, and risk of depression: A meta-analysis. *Journal of the American Medical Association, 301,* 2462–2471.

Ritschel, L. A., Cheavens, J. S., & Nelson, J. (2012). Dialectical behavior therapy in an intensive outpatient program with a mixed-diagnostic sample. *Journal of Clinical Psychology, 68,* 221–235.

Riva, G. (2009). Virtual reality: An experiential tool for clinical psychology. *British Journal of Guidance & Counselling, 37,* 337–345. doi: 10.1080/03069880902957056

Rizvi, S., Kennedy, S. H., McNeely, H., Giacobbe, P., Mayberg, H. S., & Lozano, A. M. (2009). Functional outcome after 12 months of deep brain stimulation for treatment resistant major depressive disorder. *European Neuropsychopharmacology, 19,* S388–S389.

Rizzolatti, G., & Arbib, M. A. (1998). Language within our grasp. *Trends in Neuroscience, 21,* 188–194.

Rizzolatti, G., & Craighero, L. (2004). The mirror-neuron system. *Annual Review of Neuroscience, 27,* 169–192.

Rizzolatti, G., Fadiga, L., Gallese, V., & Fogassi, L. (1996). Premotor cortex and the recognition of motor actions. *Brain Research: Cognitive Brain Research, 3,* 131–141.

Roberts, B. W., & Mroczek, D. (2008). Personality trait change in adulthood. *Current Directions in Psychological Science, 17,* 31–35.

Roberts, B. W., Walton, K. E., & Viechtbauer, W. (2006). Patterns of mean-level change in personality traits across the life course: A meta-analysis of longitudinal studies. *Psychological Bulletin, 132,* 1–25.

Robertson, I. (2003). The absent mind: Attention and error. *The Psychologist, 16,* 476–479.

Robinson, D. N. (1995). *An intellectual history of psychology* (3rd ed.). Madison: University of Wisconsin Press.

Robinson, L. A., & Klesges, R. C. (1997). Ethnic and gender differences in risk factors for smoking onset. *Health Psychology, 16*(6), 499. Available at http://dx.doi.org/10.1037/0278-6133.16.6.499

Rock, C. L., Flatt, S. W., Pakiz, B., Barkai, H. S., Heath, D. D., & Krumhar, K. C. (2016). Randomized clinical trial of portion-controlled prepackaged foods to promote weight loss. *Obesity, 24*(6), 1230–1237. doi:10.1002/oby.21481

Röder, B. (2006). Blindness: A source and case of neuronal plasticity. In P. B. Baltes, P. A. Reuter-Lorenz, & F. Rösler (Eds.), *Lifespan development and the brain* (pp. 134–157). New York, NY: Cambridge University Press.

Rodrigues, A., Loureiro, M., & Caramelli, P. (2010). Musical training, neuroplasticity and cognition. *Dementia & Neuropsychologia, 4*(4), 277–286.

Roehr, B. (2007). High rate of PTSD in returning Iraq War veterans. *Medscape Medical News.* Retrieved July 5, 2008, from http://www.medscape.com/viewarticle/565407

Roehrs, T., Zorick, F. J., & Roth, T. (2000). Transient and short-term insomnias. In M. H. Kryger, T. Roth, & W. C. Dement (Eds.), *Principles and practice of sleep medicine.* Philadelphia, PA: Saunders.

Rogelberg, S. G., & Gill, P. M. (2006). The growth of industrial and organizational psychology: Quick facts. Retrieved December 6, 2007, from http://www.siop.org/tip/backissues/july04/05rogelberg.aspx

Rogers, C. R. (1951). *Client-centered counseling.* Boston, MA: Houghton Mifflin.

Rogers, C. R. (1959). A theory of therapy, personality, and interpersonal relationships, as developed in the client-centered framework. In S. Koch (Ed.), *Psychology: A study of a science* (Vol. 3). New York, NY: McGraw-Hill.

Rogers, C. R. (1980). *A way of being.* Boston, MA: Houghton Mifflin.

Roid, G. H., & Pomplun, M. (2005). Interpreting the Stanford-Binet Intelligence Scales, fifth edition.

In D. P. Flanagan & P. L. Harrison (Eds.), *Contemporary intellectual assessment: Theories, tests, and issues* (pp. 325–343). New York, NY: Guilford Press.

Rolland, J. P. (2002). Cross-cultural generalizability of the Five-Factor Model of personality. In R. R. McCrae & J. Allik (Eds.), *The Five-Factor Model of personality across cultures* (pp. 7–28). New York, NY: Kluwer Academic/Plenum.

Rolls, E. T. (2004). The functions of the orbitofrontal cortex. *Brain and Cognition, 55*, 11–29.

Rolls, E. T. (2015). Limbic systems for emotion and for memory, but no single limbic system. *Cortex, 62*, 119–157. Available at http://dx.doi.org/10.1016/j.cortex.2013.12.005

Romain, J. (2008). Grand larceny in the first grade: Traumatic brain injury in the school-aged years. In J. N. Apps, R. F. Newby, & L. W. Roberts (Eds.), *Pediatric neuropsychology case studies: From the exceptional to the commonplace* (pp. 23–31). New York, NY: Springer Science.

Ronn, T., Volkov, P., Davega, C., Dayeh, T., Hall, E., Olsson, A. H., ... Ling, C. (2013). A six months exercise intervention influences the genome-wide DNA methylation pattern in human adipose tissue. *Plos Genetics, 9*, e1003572. doi: 10.1371/journal.pgen.1003572

Rosch, E. (1973). Natural categories. *Cognitive Psychology, 4*, 328–350.

Rosch, E. (1975). Cognitive representations of semantic categories. *Journal of Experimental Psychology: General, 104*, 192–223.

Rose, A. J., Vegiopoulos, A., & Herzig, S. (2010). Role of glucocorticoids and the glucocorticoid receptor in metabolism: Insights from genetic manipulations. *Journal of Steroid Biochemistry & Molecular Biology, 122*, 10–20.

Rose, N. (2016). Reading the human brain: How the mind became legible. *Body & Society, 22*, 140–177. doi: 10.1177/1357034X15623363

Rose, N. S., Craik, F. I. M., & Buchsbaum, B. R. (2015). Levels of processing in working memory: Differential involvement of frontotemporal networks. *Journal of Cognitive Neuroscience, 27*, 522–532. doi: 10.1162/jocn_a_00738

Rosellini, A. J., Lawrence, A. E., Meyer, J. F., & Brown, T. A. (2010). The effects of extraverted temperament on agoraphobia in panic disorder. *Journal of Abnormal Psychology, 119*, 420–426.

Roseman, I. J. (1984). Cognitive determinants of emotion: A structural theory. *Review of Personality & Social Psychology, 5*, 11–36.

Rosen, L. D., Carrier, L. M., & Cheever, N. A. (2012). Facebook and texting made me do it: Media-induced task-switching while studying. *Computers in Human Behavior, 29*, 948–958. doi: 10.1016/j.chb.2012.12.001

Rosen, L. D., Cheever, N. A., Cummings, C., & Felt, J. (2007). The impact of emotionality and self-disclosure on online dating versus traditional dating. *Computers in Human Behavior, 24*, 2124–2157.

Rosenberg, E. L. (1998). Levels of analysis and the organization of affect. *Review of General Psychology, 2*, 247–270.

Rosenberg, E. L., & Ekman, P. (1994). Coherence between expressive and experiential systems in emotion. *Cognition & Emotion, 8*, 201–229.

Rosenberg, E. L., & Ekman, P. (2000). Emotion: Methods of study. In A. Kasdan (Ed.), *Encyclopedia of psychology* (pp. 171–175). Washington, DC: American Psychological Association and Oxford University Press.

Rosenberg, E. L., Ekman, P., Jiang, W., Coleman, R. E., Hanson, M., O'Connor, C., ...

Blumenthal, J. A. (2001). Linkages between facial expressions of anger and transient myocardial ischemia in men with coronary artery disease. *Emotion, 1*, 107–115. doi: 10.1037/1528-3542.1.2.107

Rosenberger, P. H., Ickovics, J. R., Epel, E., Nadler, E., Jokl, P., Fulkerson, J. P., ... Dhabhar, F. (2009). Surgery stress-induced immune cell redistribution profiles predict short-term and long-term postsurgical recovery. A prospective study. *Journal of Bone and Joint Surgery, 91*, 2783–2794.

Rosenblum, L. (2010). *See what I am saying.* New York, NY: Norton.

Rosenman, R. H., Brand, J. H., Jenkins, C. D., Friedman, M., Straus, R., & Wurm, M. (1975). Coronary heart disease in the Western Collaborative Group Study: Final follow-up experience of 8.5 years. *Journal of the American Medical Association, 233*, 872–877.

Rosenman, R. H., Friedman, M., Straus, R., Wurm, M., Kositchek, R., Hahn, W., & Werthessen, N. T. (1964). A predictive study of coronary artery disease. *Journal of the American Medical Association, 189*, 113–124.

Rosenquist, J. N., Murabito, J., Fowler, J. H., & Christakis, N. A. (2010). The spread of alcohol consumption behavior in a large social network. *Annals of Internal Medicine, 152*, 426–433.

Rosenthal, R. (1976). *Experimenter effects in behavioral research, enlarged edition.* New York, NY: Irvington.

Rosenthal, R. (1986). Meta-analytic procedures and the nature of replication: The debate. *Journal of Parapsychology, 50*(4), 315–336.

Rosenthal, R. (1994). On being one's own case study: Experimenter effects in behavioral research—30 years later. In W. Shadish & S. Fuller (Eds.), *The social psychology of science* (pp. 214–229). New York, NY: Guilford Press.

Rosenthal, R., & Fode, K. L. (1963). The effect of experimenter bias on the performance of the albino rat. *Behavioral Science, 8*, 183–189.

Rosenthal, R., & Rubin, D. B. (1978). Interpersonal expectancy effects: The first 345 studies. *The Behavioral and Brain Sciences, 3*, 377–386.

Rosenzweig, M. R., & Bennett, E. L. (1969). Effects of differential environments on brain weights and enzyme activities in gerbils, rats and mice. *Developmental Psychobiology, 2*, 87–95.

Rosenzweig, M. R., Krech, D., Bennett, E. L., & Diamond, M. C. (1962). Effects of environmental complexity and training on brain chemistry and anatomy: A replication and extension. *Journal of Comparative and Physiological Psychology, 55*, 429–437.

Roso-Bas, F., Jiménez, A. P., & García-Buades, E. (2016). Emotional variables, dropout and academic performance in Spanish nursing students. *Nurse education today, 37*, 53–58. Available at http://dx.doi.org/10.1016/j.nedt.2015.11.021

Ross, L. (1977). The intuitive psychologist and his shortcomings: Distortions in the attribution process. In L. Berkowitz (Ed.), *Advances in experimental social psychology* (Vol. 10, pp. 173–220). New York, NY: Academic Press.

Rossetto, A., Megighian, M., Scorzeto, C., & Montecucco, C. (2013). Botulinum neurotoxins. *Toxicon, 67*, 31–36.

Rothbaum, B. O., Cahill, S. P., Foa, E. B., Davidson, J. R. T., Compton, J., Connor, K. M., ... Hahn, C.-G. (2006). Augmentation of sertraline with prolonged exposure in the treatment of posttraumatic stress disorder. *Journal of Traumatic Stress, 19*, 625–638. doi: 10.1002/jts.20170

Rothenberg, D. (2005). *Why birds sing: A journey through the mystery of bird song.* New York, NY: Basic Books.

Rouder, J. N., & Morey, R. D. (2011). A Bayes factor meta-analysis of Bem's ESP claim. *Psychonomic Bulletin & Review, 18*(4), 682–689. doi:10.3758/s13423-011-0088-7

Rowe, G., Hirsch, J. B., & Anderson, A. K. (2007). Positive affect increases the breadth of attentional selection. *Proceedings of the National Academy of Sciences, 104*, 383–388.

Rowland, N. E., Li, B.-H., & Morien, A. (1996). Brain mechanisms and the physiology of feeding. In E. D. Capaldi (Ed.), *Why we eat what we eat: The psychology of eating* (pp. 173–204). Washington, DC: American Psychological Association.

Roy, M., Pichè, M., Chen, J.-I., Peretz, I., & Rainville, P. (2009). Cerebral and spinal modulation of pain by emotions. *Proceedings of the National Academy of Sciences, 106*, 20900–20905.

Rozin, P. (1996). Sociocultural influences on human food selection. In E. D. Capaldi (Ed.), *Why we eat what we eat: The psychology of eating* (pp. 233–263). Washington, DC: American Psychological Association.

Rozin, P., & Fallon, A. E. (1987). Perspectives on disgust. *Psychological Review, 94*, 23–41.

Ruan, J. (2004). Bilingual Chinese/English first-graders developing metacognition about writing. *Literacy, 38*, 106–112.

Ruff, H. (1999). Population-based data and the development of individual children: The case of low to moderate lead levels and intelligence. *Journal of Developmental & Behavioral Pediatrics, 20*(1), 42–49.

Rumbaugh, D. M., Beran, M. J., & Savage-Rumbaugh, S. (2003). Language. In D. Maestripieri (Ed.), *Primate psychology* (pp. 395–423). Cambridge, MA: Harvard University Press.

Rumelhart, D. E. (1990). Brain style computation: Learning and generalization. In S. F. Zornetzer, J. L. Davis, & C. Lau (Eds.), *An introduction to neural and electronic networks* (pp. 405–420). New York, NY: Academic Press.

Runyan, W. M. (1981). Why did Van Gogh cut off his ear? The problem of alternative explanations in psychobiography. *Journal of Personality and Social Psychology, 40*, 1070–1077.

Runyan, W. M. (1982). *Life histories and psychobiography.* New York, NY: Oxford University Press.

Rushton, W. A. H. (1961). Rhodopsin measurement and dark adaptation in a subject deficient in cone vision. *Journal of Physiology, 156*, 193–205.

Russo, F. (2016, January/February). Debate is growing about how to meet the needs of transgender kids. *Scientific American Mind, 27*, 27–35.

Rutter, M. (2002). Nature, nurture, and development: From evangelism through science toward policy and practice. *Child Development, 73*, 1–21.

Rutter, M. (2006). *Genes and behavior: Nature-nurture interplay explained.* Malden, MA: Blackwell.

Ruysschaert, L., Warreyn, P., Wiersema, J. R., Oostra, A., & Roeyers, H. (2014). Exploring the role of neural mirroring in children with autism spectrum disorder. *Autism Research, 7*, 197–206. doi: 10.1002/aur.1339

Ruzgis, P. M., & Grigorenko, E. L. (1994). Cultural meaning systems, intelligence and personality. In R. J. Sternberg & P. Ruzgis (Eds.), *Personality and intelligence* (pp. 248–270). New York, NY: Cambridge University Press.

Ryan, G., Baerwald, J., & McGlone, G. (2008). Cognitive mediational deficits and the role of coping styles in pedophile and ephebophile Roman Catholic clergy. *Journal of Clinical Psychology, 64,* 1–16.

Ryan, R. M., Huta, V., & Deci, E. L. (2008). Living well: A self-determination theory perspective on eudaimonia. *Journal of Happiness Studies, 9,* 139–170.

Ryan, T., & Xenos, S. (2011). Who uses Facebook? An investigation into the relationship between the Big Five, shyness, narcissism, loneliness, and Facebook usage. *Computers in Human Behavior, 27*(5), 1658–1664. doi: 10.1016/j.chb.2011.02.004

Rymer, R. (1993). *Genie: A scientific tragedy.* New York, NY: HarperPerennial.

Saarimäki, H., Gotsopoulos, A., Jääskeläinen, I. P., Lampinen, J., Vuilleumier, P., Hari, R., ... & Nummenmaa, L. (2016). Discrete neural signatures of basic emotions. *Cerebral Cortex, 26*(6), 2563–2573. doi: 10.1093/cercor/bhv086

Saarni, C. (1984). An observational study of children's attempts to monitor their expressive behavior. *Child Development, 55,* 1504–1513.

Saarni, C. (1999). *The development of emotional competence.* New York, NY: Guilford Press.

Sabbagh, L. (2006, August/September). The teen brain, hard at work: No, really. *Scientific American Mind, 17,* 21–25.

Sacco, R., Gabriele, S., & Persico, A. M. (2015). Head circumference and brain size in autism spectrum disorder: A systematic review and meta-analysis. *Psychiatry Research: Neuroimaging, 234*(2), 239–251. Available at http://dx.doi .org/10.1016/j.pscychresns.2015.08.016

Sacco, R. L., Elkind, M., Boden-Albala, B., Lin, I.-F., Kargman, D. E., Hause, W. A., ... Paik, M. C. (1999). The protective effect of moderate alcohol consumption on ischemic stroke. *Journal of the American Medical Association, 281,* 53–60. doi: 10.1001/jama.281.1.53

Sackeim, H. A., Greenberg, M. S., Weiman, A. L., Gur, R. C., Hungerbuhler, J. P., & Geschwind, N. (1982). Hemispheric asymmetry in the expression of positive and negative emotions: Neurologic evidence. *Archives in Neurology, 39,* 210–218.

Sackeim, H. A., Prudic, J., Devanand, D. P., Kiersky, J. E., Fitzsimons, L., Moody, B. J., ... & Settembrino, J. M. (1993). Effects of stimulus intensity and electrode placement on the efficacy and cognitive effects of electroconvulsive therapy. *New England Journal of Medicine, 328*(12), 839–846.

Sadlo, G. (2016). Towards a neurobiological understanding of reduced self-awareness during flow: An occupational science perspective. In *Flow experience* (pp. 375–388). Springer International Publishing. doi: 10.1007/978-3-319-28634-1_22

Sagui, S. J., & Levens, S. M. (2016). Cognitive reappraisal ability buffers against the indirect effects of perceived stress reactivity on Type 2 diabetes. *Health Psychology.* doi: 10.1037/hea0000359

Sahdra, B. K., MacLean, K. A., Ferrer, E., Shaver, P. R., Rosenberg, E. L., Jacobs, T. L., ... Saron, C. D. (2011). Enhanced response inhibition during intensive meditation training predicts improvements in self-reported adaptive socio-emotional functioning. *Emotion, 11,* 299–312.

Saisan, J., Smith, M., & Segal, J. (2010, May). *Psychotherapy and counseling: Finding a therapist and getting the most out of therapy.* Retrieved September 10, 2010, from http://www.helpguide.org/ mental/psychotherapy_therapist_counseling.htm

Sakai, K. (2005). Language acquisition and brain development. *Science, 310,* 815–819.

Salehan, M., & Negahban, A. (2013). Social networking on smartphones: When mobile phones become addictive. *Computers in Human Behavior, 29*(6), 2632–2639.

Salman, M. S., & Tsai, P. (2016). The role of the pediatric cerebellum in motor functions, cognition, and behavior: A clinical perspective. *Neuroimaging Clinics of North America, 26*(3), 317–329. Available at http://dx.doi.org/10.1016/j.nic.2016.03.003

Salmerón, J., Manson, J. E., Stampfer, M. J., Colditz, G. A., Wing, A. L., & Willett, W. C. (1997). Dietary fiber, glycemic load, and risk of non-insulin-dependent diabetes mellitus in women. *Journal of the American Medical Association, 277,* 472–477. doi: 10.1001/jama.1997.03540300040031

Salovey, P., & Mayer, J. D. (1990). Emotional intelligence. *Imagination, Cognition, and Personality, 9,* 185–211.

Salthouse, T. A. (2000). Steps toward the explanation of adult differences in cognition. In T. J. Perfect & E. A. Maylor (Eds.), *Models of cognitive aging* (pp. 19–49). Oxford, England: Oxford University Press.

Salvucci, D. D., & Taatgen, N. A. (2008). Threaded cognition: An integrated theory of concurrent multitasking. *Psychological Review, 115,* 101–130. doi: 10.1037/0033-295X.115.1.101

Sana, F., Weston, T., & Cepeda, N. J. (2013). Laptop multitasking hinders classroom learning for both users and nearby peers. *Computers and Education, 62,* 24–31. Available at http://doi .org/10.1016/j.compedu.2012.10.003

Sanbonmatsu, D. M., Strayer, D. L., Biondi, F., Behrends, A. A., & Moore, S. M. (2015). Cell-phone use diminishes self-awareness of impaired driving. *Psychonomic Bulletin & Review, 23,* 617–623.

Sanders, L. (2009). Single brain cells selectively fire in response to specific thoughts: Thinking about her face activates "Halle Berry" neuron. *Science News, 176,* 9. doi: 10.1002/scin.5591761107

Santangelo, V., & Macaluso, E. (2013). Visual salience improves spatial working memory via enhanced parieto-temporal functional connectivity. *The Journal of Neuroscience, 33,* 4110–4117. Available at http://dx.doi.org/10.1523/ JNEUROSCI.4138-12.2013

Santos, L. E., Beckman, D., & Ferreira, S. T. (2016). Microglial dysfunction connects depression and Alzheimer's disease. *Brain, Behavior, and Immunity, 55,* 151–165. Available at http://dx.doi .org/10.1016/j.bbi.2015.11.011

Santrock, J. W. (2010). *A topical approach to life-span development* (5th ed.). New York, NY: McGraw-Hill.

Sapolsky, R. (1998). *Why zebras don't get ulcers: An updated guide to stress, stress-related disease and coping.* New York, NY: Freeman.

Saraswat, A., Weinand, J. D., & Safer, J. D. (2015). Evidence supporting the biologic nature of gender identity. *Endocrine Practice, 21,* 199–204. doi: 10.4158/EP14351.RA

Sarlio-Lähteenkorva, S. (2001). Weight loss and quality of life among obese people. *Social Indicators Research, 54*(3), 329–354.

Sasaki, S., Ozaki, K., Yamagata, S., Takahashi, Y., Shikishima, C., Kornacki, T., ... & Ando, J. (2016). Genetic and environmental influences on traits of gender identity disorder: A study of Japanese twins across developmental stages. *Archives of Sexual Behavior, 45,* 1681–1695. doi: 10.1007 /s10508-016-0821-4

Sauter, D. A., Eisner, F., Ekman, P., & Scott, S. K. (2010). Cross-cultural recognition of basic emotions through nonverbal emotional vocalizations. *Proceedings of the National Academy of Sciences, 107,* 2408–2412.

Sava, F. A., Yates, B. T., Lupu, V., Szentagotai, A., & David, D. (2009). Cost-effectiveness and cost-utility of cognitive therapy, rational emotive behavioral therapy, and fluoxetine (Prozac) in treating depression: A randomized clinical trial. *Journal of Clinical Psychology, 65,* 36–52.

Savicki, V., Downing-Burnette, R., Heller, L., Binder, F., & Suntinger, W. (2004). Contrasts, changes, and correlates in actual and potential intercultural adjustment. *International Journal of Intercultural Relations, 28*(3–4), 311–329. doi: 10.1016/j.ijintrel.2004.06.001

Savin-Williams, R. C., & Vrangalova, Z. (2013). Mostly heterosexual as a distinct sexual orientation group: A systematic review of the empirical evidence. *Developmental Review, 33,* 58–88. doi: 10.1016/j.dr.2013.01.001

Sawyer, R. K. (2006). *Explaining creativity: The science of human innovation.* New York, NY: Oxford University Press.

Scarr, S. (1981). *Race, social class, and individual differences in I.Q.* Hillsdale, NJ: Erlbaum.

Schaal, B., Marlier, L., & Soussignan, R. (2000). Human fetuses learn odors from their pregnant mother's diet. *Chemical Senses, 25,* 729–737.

Schacter, D. L. (2001). *The seven sins of memory.* Boston, MA: Houghton Mifflin.

Schacter, D. L., & Loftus, E. F. (2013). Memory and law: What can cognitive neuroscience contribute? *Nature Neuroscience, 16*(2), 119–123. Available at http://doi.org/10.1038/nn.3294

Schaefer, E. J., Gleason, J. A., & Dansinger, M. L. (2005). The effects of low-fat, high-carbohydrate diets on plasma lipoproteins, weight loss, and heart disease risk reduction. *Current Atherosclerosis Reports, 7,* 421–427.

Schaie, K. W. (1996). *Intellectual development in adulthood: The Seattle Longitudinal Study.* New York, NY: Cambridge University Press.

Schein, E., & Bernstein, P. (2007). *Identical strangers: A memoir of twins separated and re-united.* New York, NY: Random House.

Schellenberg, E. G. (2004). Music lessons enhance IQ. *Psychological Science, 15,* 511–514.

Schellenberg, E. G. (2006). Long-term positive associations between music lessons and IQ. *Journal of Educational Psychology, 98,* 457–468.

Schellenberg, E. G. (2011). Examining the association between music lessons and intelligence. *British Journal of Psychology, 102*(3), 283–302. doi: 10.1111/j.2044-8295.2010.02000.x

Schellenberg, E. G. (2016). Music training and nonmusical abilities. In S. Hallam, I. Cross, M. Thaut, S. Hallam, I. Cross, M. Thaut (Eds.), *The Oxford handbook of music psychology,* 2nd ed. (pp. 415–429). New York, NY: Oxford University Press.

Scherer, K. R., Banse, R., & Wallbott, H. G. (2001). Emotion inferences from vocal expression correlate across languages and cultures. *Journal of Cross-Cultural Psychology, 32,* 76–92.

Scherer, K. R., Banse, R., Wallbott, H. G., & Goldbeck, T. (1991). Vocal cues in emotion coding and decoding. *Motivation and Emotion, 15,* 123–148.

Scherer, K. R., Dan, E., & Flykt, A. (2006). What determines a feeling's position in affective space? A case for appraisal. *Cognition & Emotion, 20,* 92–113.

Schienle, A., Schäfer, A., & Vaitl, D. (2008). Individual differences in disgust imagery: A functional magnetic resonance imaging study. *NeuroReport, 19,* 527–530.

Schindler, E. A. D., Gottschalk, C. H., Weil, M. J., Shapiro, R. E., Wright, D. A., & Sewell, R. A. (2015) Indoleamine hallucinogens in cluster headache: Results of the clusterbusters medication use survey, *Journal of Psychoactive Drugs, 47*, 372–381. doi: 10.1080/02791072.2015.1107664

Schlaepfer, T. E. (2013). Neuromodulation of reward circuits with deep brain stimulation in treatment resistant depression. *Biological Psychiatry, 73*, 143s.

Schlaepfer, T. E. (2015). Deep brain stimulation for major depression-steps on a long and winding road. *Biological Psychiatry, 78*(4), 218–219. Available at http://dx.doi.org/10.1016/j.biopsych.2015.06.020

Schlaug, G., Jäncke, L., Huang, Y., Staiger, J. F., & Steinmetz H. (1995). Increased corpus callosum size in musicians. *Neuropsychologia, 33*, 1047–1055.

Schmand, B., Eikelenboom, P., & van Gool, W. A. (2011). Value of neuropsychological tests, neuroimaging, and biomarkers for diagnosing Alzheimer's disease in younger and older age cohorts. *Journal of the American Geriatrics Society, 59*(9), 1705–1710. doi: 10.1111/j.1532-5415.2011.03539.x

Schmand, B., Smit, J., Lindeboom, J., Smits, C., Hooijer, C., Jonker, C., & Deelman, B. (1997). Low education is a genuine risk factor for accelerated memory decline and dementia. *Journal of Clinical Epidemiology, 50*, 1025–1033.

Schmid, L. C., Mittag, M., Poll, S., Steffen, J., Wagner, J., Geis, H. R., … & Fuhrmann, M. (2016). Dysfunction of somatostatin-positive interneurons associated with memory deficits in an Alzheimer's disease model. *Neuron, 92*(1), 114–125. Available at http://dx.doi.org/10.1016/j.neuron.2016.08.034

Schmidt, M. E., & Vandewater, E. A. (2008). Media and attention, cognition, and school achievement. *The Future of Children, 18*, 63–85.

Schmithorst, V. J., Holland, S. K., & Dardzinski, B. J. (2008). Developmental differences in white matter architecture between boys and girls. *Human Brain Mapping, 29*, 696–710.

Schmitt, D. (2003). Universal sex differences in the desire for sexual variety: Tests from 52 nations, 6 continents, and 13 islands. *Journal of Social and Personality Psychology, 85*, 85–104. doi: 10.1037/0022-3514.85.1.85

Schnakers, C., Vanhaudenhuyse, A., Giacino, J., Ventura, M., Boly, M., Majerus, S., Moonen, G., & Laureys, S. (2009). Diagnostic accuracy of the vegetative and minimally conscious state: Clinical consensus versus standardized neurobehavioral assessment. *BMC Neurology, 9*, 35–39. doi:10.1186/1471-2377-9-35

Schneider, J. A., Arvanitakis, Z., Bang, W., & Bennett, D. A. (2007). Mixed brain pathologies account for most dementia cases in community-dwelling older persons. *Neurology, 69*, 2197–2204.

Schneider, S. M. (2016). Income inequality and subjective well-being: Trends, challenges, and research directions. *Journal of Happiness Studies, 17*(4), 1719–1739. doi: 10.1007/s10902-015-9655-3

Schoenfeld, M. A., Neuer, G., Tempelmann, C., Schüßler, K., Noesselt, T., Hopf, J. M., & Heinze, H. J. (2004). Functional magnetic resonance tomography correlates of taste perception in the human primary taste cortex. *Neuroscience, 127*(2), 347–353. Available at http://doi.org/10.1016/j.neuroscience.2004.05.024

Schreiner, T., & Rasch, B. (2016). The beneficial role of memory reactivation for language learning during sleep: A review. *Brain & Language.* E-pub ahead of print. doi: 10.1016/j.bandl.2016.02.005

Schuldberg, D. (2000–2001). Six subclinical spectrum traits in normal creativity. *Creativity Research Journal, 13*, 5–16.

Schuler, J. L. H., & O' Brien, W. H. (1997). Cardiovascular recovery from stress and hypertension risk factors: A meta-analytic review. *Psychophysiology, 34*, 649–659.

Schulkin, J. (Ed.). (2005). *Allostasis, homeostasis, and the costs of physiological adaptation.* New York, NY: Cambridge University Press.

Schulte-Rüther, M., Otte, E., Adigüzel, K., Firk, C., Herpertz-Dahlmann, B., Koch, I., & Konrad, K. (2016). Intact mirror mechanisms for automatic facial emotions in children and adolescents with autism spectrum disorder. *Autism Research.* doi: 10.1002/aur.1654

Schultz, W. T. (2005). *Handbook of psychobiography.* New York, NY: Oxford University Press.

Schumer, M. C., Bartley, C. A., & Bloch, M. H. (2016). Systematic review of pharmacological and behavioral treatments for skin picking disorder. *Journal of Clinical Psychopharmacology, 36*(2), 147–152. doi: 10.1097/JCP.0000000000000462

Schuppli, C., Meulman, E. J. M., Forss, S. I. F., Aprilinayati, F., van Noordwijk, M. A., & van Schaik, C. P. (2016). Observational social learning and socially induced practice of routine skills in immature wild orang-utans. *Animal Behaviour, 119*, 87e98. doi.org/10.1016/j.anbehav.2016.06.014

Schutte, N. S., Malouff, J. M., Thorsteinsson, E. B., Bhullar, N., & Rooke, S. E. (2007). A meta-analytic investigation of the relationship between emotional intelligence and health. *Personality and Individual Differences, 42*, 921–933.

Schwartz, G. M., Izard, C. E., & Ansul, S. E. (1985). The 5-month-old's ability to discriminate facial expressions of emotion. *Infant Behavior and Development, 8*, 65–77.

Schwartz, H. A., & Ungar, L. H. (2015). Data-driven content analysis of social media: A systematic overview of automated methods. *The ANNALS of the American Academy of Political and Social Science, 659*, 78–94. doi: 10.1177/0002716215569197

Schwartz, J. H. (2000). Neurotransmitters. In E. R. Kandel, J. M. Schwartz, & T. M. Jessell (Eds.), *Principles of neural science* (4th ed., pp. 280–297). New York, NY: McGraw-Hill.

Schwartz, J. M. (1999a). First steps toward a theory of mental force: PET imaging of systematic cerebral changes after psychological treatment of obsessive-compulsive disorder. In S. R. Hameroff, A. W. Kaszniak, & D. J. Chalmers (Eds.), *Toward a science of consciousness III: The third Tucson discussions and debates.* Boston, MA: MIT Press.

Schwartz, J. M. (1999b). A role for volition and attention in the generation of new brain circuitry: Toward a neurobiology of mental force. *Journal of Consciousness Studies, 6*, 115–142.

Schwerdtfeger, A. (2007). Individual differences in auditory, pain, and motor stimulation. *Journal of Individual Differences, 28*, 165–177.

Scott, J. (2000). Rational choice theory. In G. Browning, A. Halcli, & F. Webster (Eds.), *Understanding contemporary society: Theories of the present* (pp. 126–138). New York, NY: Sage.

Scruggs, J. L., Schmidt, D., & Deutch, A. Y. (2003). The hallucinogen 1-[2,5-dimethoxy-4-iodophenyl]-2-aminopropane (DOI) increases cortical extracellular glutamate levels in rats. *Neuroscience Letters, 346*, 137–140.

Scully, J. A., Tosi, H., & Banning, K. (2000). Life event checklists: Reevaluating the Social Readjustment Rating Scale after 30 years. *Educational and Psychological Measurement, 60*, 864–876.

Sebastian, C., Viding, E., Williams, K. D., & Blakemore, S. (2010). Social brain development and the affective consequences of ostracism in adolescence. *Brain and Cognition, 72*, 134–145.

Segal, N. (1999). *Entwined lives: Twins and what they tell us about human nature.* New York, NY: Plume.

Segal, Z. V., Williams, J. M. G., & Teasdale, J. D. (2002). *Mindfulness-based cognitive therapy for depression.* New York, NY: Guilford Press.

Seifert, K. L., Hoffnung, R. J., & Hoffnung, M. (2000). *Lifespan development* (2nd ed.). Boston, MA: Houghton Mifflin.

Sekar, A., Bialas, A. R., de Rivera, H., Davis, A., Hammond, T. R., Kamitaki, N., … & Genovese, G. (2016). Schizophrenia risk from complex variation of complement component 4. *Nature, 530*(7589), 177–183. doi: 10.1038/nature16549

Seligman, M. (2003). Positive psychology: Fundamental assumptions. *The Psychologist, 16*, 126–127.

Seligman, M. E. P. (1972). Learned helplessness. *Annual Review of Medicine, 23*(1), 407–412. doi: 10.1146/annurev.me.23.020172.002203

Seligman, M. E. P., & Csikszentmihalyi, M. (2000). Positive psychology: An introduction. *American Psychologist, 55*, 5–14. doi: 10.1037/0003-066X.55.1.5

Seligman, M. E. P., & Hager, J. L. (Eds.). (1972). *The biological boundaries of learning.* New York, NY: Appleton.

Seligman, M. E. P., Rashid, R., & Parks, A. C. (2006). Positive psychotherapy. *American Psychologist, 61*, 774–788.

Seligman, M. E. P., Schulman, P., & Tryon, A. M. (2007). Group prevention of depression and anxiety symptoms. *Behaviour Research and Therapy, 45*, 1111–1126.

Selkoe, D. (2002). Alzheimer's disease is a synaptic failure. *Science, 298*(5594), 789–791.

Selten, J. P., Frissen, A., Lensvelt-Mulder, G., & Morgan, V. A. (2010). Schizophrenia and the 1957 pandemic of influenza: Meta-analysis. *Schizophrenia Bulletin, 36*, 219–228. doi: 10.1093/schbul/sbp147

Selye, H. (1946). The general adaptation syndrome and diseases of adaptation. *Journal of Clinical Endocrinology, 6*, 117–230.

Selye, H. (1976). *The stress of life.* New York, NY: McGraw-Hill.

Sen, A. N., Gopinath, S. P., & Robertson, C. S. (2016). Clinical application of near-infrared spectroscopy in patients with traumatic brain injury: A review of the progress of the field. *Neurophotonics, 3*, 031409–031409. doi: 10.1117/1.NPh.3.3.031409

Sen, B., & Swaminathan, S. (2007). Maternal prenatal substance use and behavior problems among children in the U.S. *Journal of Mental Health Policy and Economics, 10*, 189–206.

Sergerstrom, S. C., & Sephton, S. E. (2010). Optimistic expectancies and cell-mediated immunity: The role of positive affect. *Psychological Science, 21*, 448–455. doi: 10.1177/095679761036206

Serpell, R. (1982). Measures of perception, skills, and intelligence. In W. W. Hartup (Ed.), *Review of child development research* (Vol. 6, pp. 392–440). Chicago, IL: University of Chicago Press.

Serrano-Blanco, A., Palao D. J., Luciano, J. V., Pinto-Meza, A., Lujan, L., Fernandez, A., … Haro, J. M. (2010). Prevalence of mental disorders in primary care: Results from the Diagnosis and Treatment of Mental Disorders in Primary Care Study (DASMAP). *Social Psychiatry and*

Psychiatric Epidemiology, 45, 201–210. doi: 10.1007/s00127-009-0056-y

Sessa, B. (2016). MDMA and PTSD treatment. PTSD: From novel pathophysiology to innovative therapeutics. *Neuroscience Letters.* doi:10.1016/j.neulet.2016.07.004 (E-pub ahead of print)

Shadish, W. R., Cook, T. D., & Campbell, D. T. (2002). *Experimental and quasi-experimental designs for generalized causal inference.* Boston: Houghton Mifflin.

Shain, B. (2016). Suicide and suicide attempts in adolescents. *Pediatrics,* e20161420. doi: 10.1542/peds.2016-1420

Shank, D. B., & Cotten, S. R. (2014). Does technology empower urban youth? The relationship of technology use to self-efficacy. *Computers & Education, 70,* 184–193.

Shargorodsky, J., Curhan, S. G., Curhan, G. C., & Eavey, R. (2010). Change in prevalence of hearing loss in U.S. adolescents. *Journal of the American Medical Association, 304,* 772–778.

Shastry, B. S. (2005). Bipolar disorder: An update. *Neurochemistry International, 46,* 273–279.

Shaw, P., Greenstein, D., Lerch, J., Clasen, L., Lenroot, R., Gogtay, N., ... Giedd, J. (2006). Intellectual ability and cortical development in children and adolescents. *Nature, 440,* 676–679.

Shedler, J. (2010). The efficacy of psychodynamic psychotherapy. *American Psychologist, 65,* 98–109.

Shekelle, R. B., Hulley, S. B., Neston, J. D., Billings, J. H., Borboni, N. O., ... Gerace, T. A. (1985). The MRFIT behavior pattern study: Type A behavior and incidence of coronary heart disease. *American Journal of Epidemiology, 122,* 559–570.

Shen, H., Sabaliauskas, N., Sherpa, A., Fenton, A. A., Stelzer, A., Aoki, C., & Smith, S. S. (2010). A critical role for 4β GABAA receptors in shaping learning deficits at puberty in mice. *Science, 327,* 1515–1518.

Shepard, M. (1995). Kraepelin and modern psychiatry. *European Archives of Psychiatry and Clinical Neuroscience, 245,* 189–195.

Shepard, R., & Metzler, J. (1971). Mental rotation of three-dimensional objects. *Science, 171,* 701–703.

Shergill, S. S., Brammer, M. J., Fukuda, R., Williams, S. C. R., Murray, R. M., & McGuire, P. K. (2003). Engagement of brain areas implicated in processing inner speech in people with auditory hallucinations. *British Journal of Psychiatry, 182,* 525–531.

Shergill, S. S., Brammer, M. J., Williams, S. C. R., Murray, R. M., & McGuire, P. K. (2000). Mapping auditory hallucinations in schizophrenia using functional magnetic resonance imaging. *Archives of General Psychiatry, 57,* 1033–1038.

Shermer, M. (1997). *Why people believe weird things: Pseudoscience, superstition, and other confusions of our time.* New York, NY: W. H. Freeman.

Shermer, M. (2011). *The believing brain: From ghosts and gods to politics and conspiracies—How we construct beliefs and reinforce them as truths.* New York, NY: St. Martin's Griffin.

Shestyuk, A. Y., Deldin, P. J., Brand, J. E., & Deveney, C. M. (2005). Reduced sustained brain activity during processing of positive emotional stimuli in major depression. *Biological Psychiatry, 57,* 1089–1096.

Shiell, M. M., Champoux, F., & Zatorre, R. J. (2016). The right hemisphere planum temporale supports enhanced visual motion detection ability in deaf people: Evidence from cortical thickness. *Neural Plasticity, 2016.* Retrieved from http://dx.doi.org/10.1155/2016/7217630

Shin, J., Lee, S. H., Shin, S. M., Kim, M. H., Park, S. G., & Park, B. (2016). Prescribing patterns of the four most commonly used sedatives in endoscopic examination in Korea: Propofol, midazolam, diazepam, and lorazepam. *Regulatory Toxicology and Pharmacology, 71,* 565–570. doi: 10.1016/j.yrtph.2015.01.007

Shomaker, L. B., & Furman, W. (2009). Interpersonal influences on late adolescent girls' and boys' disordered eating. *Eating Behaviors, 10,* 97–106.

Shore, L. M., & Wayne, S. J. (1993). Commitment and employee behavior: Comparison of affective commitment and continuance commitment with perceived organizational support. *Journal of Applied Psychology, 78,* 774–780.

Short, S. J., Lubach, G. R., Karasin, A. I., Olsen, C. W., Styner, M., Knickmeyer, R. C., ... Coe, C. L. (2010). Maternal influenza infection during pregnancy impacts postnatal brain development in the rhesus monkey. *Biological Psychiatry, 67,* 965–973.

Siegel, J. T., & Thomson, A. L. (2016). Positive emotion infusions of elevation and gratitude: Increasing help-seeking intentions among people with heightened levels of depressive symptomatology. *The Journal of Positive Psychology,* 1–16. doi: 10.1080/17439760.2016.1221125

Siegman, A. W., Anderson, R., Herbst, J., Boyle, S., & Wilkinson, J. (1992). Dimensions of anger-hostility and cardiovascular reactivity in provoked and angered men. *Journal of Behavioral Medicine, 15,* 257–272.

Sigman, M., & Hassan, S. (2006). Benefits of long-term group therapy to individuals suffering schizophrenia: A prospective 7-year study. *Bulletin of the Menninger Clinic, 70,* 273–282.

Sigurdsson, T., Doyere, V., Cain, C. K., & LeDoux, J. E. (2007). Long-term potentiation in the amygdala: A cellular mechanism of fear learning and memory. *Neuropharmacology, 52,* 215–227.

Silbersweig, D. A., Stern, E., Frith, C., Cahill, C., Holmes, A., Grootoonk, S., ... Frackowiak, R. S. J. (1995). A functional neuroanatomy of hallucinations in schizophrenia. *Nature, 378,* 176–179. doi: 10.1038/378176a0

Silverman, I., Choi, J., & Peters, M. (2007). The hunter-gatherer theory of sex differences in spatial abilities: Data from 40 countries. *Archives of Sexual Behavior, 36,* 261–268. doi: 10.1007/s10508-006-9168-6

Silverstein, S. M., Menditto, A. A., & Stuve, P. (2001). Shaping attention span: An operant conditioning procedure to improve neurocognition and functioning in schizophrenia. *Schizophrenia Bulletin, 27,* 247–257.

Silvia, P. J. (2006). *Exploring the psychology of interest.* New York, NY: Oxford University Press.

Sime, J. D. (1983). Affiliative behavior during escape to building exits. *Journal of Environmental Psychology, 3,* 21–41.

Simmons, S. M., Hicks, A., & Caird, J. K. (2016). Safety-critical event risk associated with cell phone tasks as measured in naturalistic driving studies: A systematic review and meta-analysis. *Accident Analysis and Prevention, 87,* 161–169. Retrieved from http://dx.doi.org/10.1016/j.aap.2015.11.015

Simmons, V. N., Heckman, B. W., Fink, A. C., Small, B. J., & Brandon, T. H. (2013). Efficacy of an experiential, dissonance-based smoking intervention for college students delivered via the internet. *Journal of Consulting and Clinical Psychology, 81,* 810–820. Available at http://dx.doi.org/10.1037/a0032952

Simner, J., Sagiv, N., Mulvenna, C., Tsakanikos, E., Witherby, S., Fraser, C., ... Ward, J. (2006). Synesthesia: The prevalence of atypical cross-modal experiences. *Perception, 35,* 1024–1033.

Simon, H. A. (1978). Information-processing theory of human problem solving. In W. K. Estes (Ed.), *Handbook of learning and cognitive processes: Vol. 5. Human information processing* (pp. 271–295). Hillsdale, NJ: Erlbaum.

Simon, K. N., Werchan, D., Goldstein, M. R., Sweeney, L., Bootzin, R. R., Nadel, L., & Gómez, R. L. (2016). Sleep confers a benefit for retention of statistical language learning in 6.5 month old infants. *Brain and Language.* Retrieved from http://dx.doi.org/10.1016/j.bandl.2016.05.002

Simonds, J., Kieras, J. E., Rueda, M. R., & Rothbart, M. K. (2007). Effortful control, executive attention, and emotional regulation in 7–10-year-old children. *Cognitive Development, 22,* 474–488.

Simons, D. J., & Chabris, C. F. (1999). Gorillas in our midst: Sustained inattentional blindness for dynamic events. *Perception, 28,* 1059–1074.

Simons, D. J., Boot, W. R., Charness, N., Gathercole, S. E., Chabris, C. F., Hambrick, D. Z., & Stine-Morrow, E. A. L. (2016). Do "brain-training" programs work? *Psychological Science in the Public Interest, 17*(3), 103–186. Available at http://doi.org/10.1177/1529100616661983

Simons, M., & Nave, K. A. (2016). Oligodendro-cytes: Myelination and axonal support. *Cold Spring Harbor Perspectives in Biology, 8*(1), a020479. doi: 10.1101/cshperspect.a020479

Simon-Thomas, E. R., Keltner, D. J., Sauter, D., Sinicropi-Yao, L., & Abramson, A. (2009). The voice conveys specific emotions: Evidence from vocal burst displays. *Emotion, 9,* 838–846.

Simonton, D. K. (1999). *Origins of genius.* New York, NY: Oxford University Press.

Simpson, K. (2001). The role of testosterone in aggression. *McGill Journal of Medicine, 6,* 32–40.

Simpson, K. A., & Bloom, S. R. (2010). Appetite and hedonism: Gut hormones and the brain. *Endocrinology Metabolism Clinics of North America, 39,* 729–743.

Singer, H. S., Mascaro-Blanco, A., Alvarez, K., Morris-Berry, C., Kawikova, I., Ben-Pazi, H., ... & Cunningham, M. W. (2015). Neuronal antibody biomarkers for Sydenham's chorea identify a new group of children with chronic recurrent episodic acute exacerbations of tic and obsessive compulsive symptoms following a streptococcal infection. *PloS ONE, 10*(3), e0120499. doi: 10.1371/journal.pone.0120499

Singer, T., Seymour, B., O'Doherty, J. O., Kaube, H., Dolan, R. J., & Frith, C. D. (2004). Empathy for pain involves the affective but not sensory components of pain. *Science, 303,* 1157–1162.

Sirignono, S. W., & Lachman, M. E. (1985). Personality change during the transition to parenthood: The role of perceived infant temperament. *Developmental Psychology, 21,* 558–567.

Skinner, B. F. (1938). *The behavior of organisms.* New York, NY: Appleton.

Skinner, B. F. (1953). *Science and human behavior.* New York, NY: Free Press.

Skinner, B. F. (1957). *Verbal behavior.* New York, NY: Appleton-Century-Crofts.

Skinner, B. F. (1971). *Beyond freedom and dignity.* New York, NY: Knopf.

Skinner, B. F. (1990). Can psychology be a science of mind? *American Psychologist, 45,* 1206–1210.

Skoe, E., & Kraus, N. (2012). A little goes a long way: How the adult brain is shaped by musical training in childhood. *Journal of Neuroscience, 32*(34), 11507–11510. doi: 10.1523/JNEUROSCI.1949-12.2012

Slamecka, N. J., & McElree, B. (1983). Normal forgetting of verbal lists as a function of their degree of learning. *Journal of Experimental Psychology: Learning, Memory, & Cognition, 9*, 384–397.

Slater, E., & Meyer, A. (1959). Contributions to a pathography of the musicians: Robert Schumann. *Confinia Psychiatrica, 2*, 65–94.

Slavich, G. M., O'Donovan, A., Epel, E., & Kemeny, M. (2010). Black sheep get the blues: A psychobiological model of social rejection and depression. *Neurosciences and Biobehavioral Reviews, 35*, 39–45. doi: 10.1016/j.neubiorev.2010.01.003

Sloan, P., Arsenault, L., & Hilsenroth, M. (2002). *Use of the Rorschach in the assessment of war-related stress in military personnel.* Ashland, OH: Hogrefe & Huber.

Slutske, W. E., Moffitt, T., Poulton, R., & Caspi, A. (2012). Undercontrolled temperament at age 3 predicts disordered gambling at age 32: A longitudinal study of a complete birth cohort. *Psychological Science, 23*, 510–516. doi: 10.1177/0956797611429708

Smallwood, P. M., Olveczky, B. P., Williams, G. L., Jacobs, G. H., Reese, B. E., Meister, M., & Nathans, J. (2003). Genetically engineered mice with an additional class of cone photoreceptors: Implications for the evolution of color vision. *Proceedings of the National Academy of Sciences, 100*, 11706–11711. doi: 10.1073/pnas.1934712100

Smith, A. D., Fildes, A., Cooke, L., Herle, M., Shakeshaft, N., Plomin, R., & Llewellyn, C. (2016). Genetic and environmental influences on food preferences in adolescence. *The American Journal of Clinical Nutrition, 104*(2), 446–453. doi: 10.3945/ ajcn.116.133983

Smith, B. C., Armelie, A. P., Boarts, J. M., Brazil, M., & Delahanty, D. L. (2016). PTSD, depression, and substance use in relation to suicidality risk among traumatized minority lesbian, gay, and bisexual youth. *Archives of Suicide Research, 20*, 80–93. doi: 10.1080/13811118.2015.1004484

Smith, C. A., & Ellsworth, P. C. (1987). Patterns of appraisal and emotion related to taking an exam. *Journal of Personality and Social Psychology, 52*, 475–488.

Smith, E. M., & Blalock, J. E. (1988). A molecular basis for interactions between the immune and neuroendocrine systems. *International Journal of Neuroscience, 38*, 355–364.

Smith, H. R., Comella, C., & Högl, B. (2008). *Sleep medicine.* Cambridge, United Kingdom: Cambridge University Press.

Smith, M., & Glass, G. (1977). Meta-analysis of psychotherapy outcome studies. *American Psychologist, 32*, 752–760.

Smith, N., Young, A., & Lee, C. (2004). Optimism, health-related hardiness and well-being among older Australian women. *Journal of Health Psychology, 9*, 741–752.

Smith, S. M., Nichols, T. E., Vidaurre, D., Winkler, A. M. Behrens, T. E. J., Glasser, M. F. ... Miller, K. L. (2015). A positive-negative mode of population covariation links brain connectivity, demographics and behavior. *Nature Neuroscience: Brief Communications, 18*, 1565–1567. doi: 10.1038/nn.4125

Smyth, J. M. (1998). Written emotional expression, effect sizes, outcome types, and moderating variables. *Journal of Consulting & Clinical Psychology, 66*, 174–184.

Snarey, J. R. (1985). Cross-cultural universality of social-moral development: A critical review of Kohlbergian research. *Psychological Bulletin, 97*, 202–232.

Snyderman, M., & Rothman, S. (1987). Survey of expert opinion on intelligence and aptitude testing. *American Psychologist, 42*, 137–144.

Soderstrom, N. C., Kerr, T. K., & Bjork, R. A. (2016). The critical importance of retrieval—and spacing—for learning. *Psychological Science, 27*(2), 223–230. Available at http://doi.org/10.1177/0956797615617778

Soeter, M., & Kindt, M. (2010). Dissociating response systems: Erasing fear from memory. *Neurobiology of Learning and Memory, 94*, 30–41.

Soeter, M., & Kindt, M. (2015). An abrupt transformation of phobic behavior after a post-retrieval amnesic agent. *Biological Psychiatry, 78*(12), 880–886. Available at http://doi.org/10.1016/j.biopsych.2015.04.006

Solan, T. D., & Lindow, S. W. (2014). Mercury exposure in pregnancy: A review. *Journal of Perinatal Medicine, 42*, 725–729.

Soler, J., Pascual, J. C., Tiana, T., Cebria, A., Barrachina, J., Campins, M. J., ... Pérez, V. (2009). Dialectical behaviour therapy skills training compared to standard group therapy in borderline personality disorder: A 3-month randomized controlled clinical trial. *Behaviour Research and Therapy, 47*, 353–358.

Solms, M. (2000). Dreaming and REM sleep are controlled by different brain mechanisms. *Behavioral and Brain Sciences, 23*, 843–850.

Solms, M. (2004). Freud returns. *Scientific American, 290*(5), 82–88.

Solms, M., & Turnbull, O. (2002). *The brain and the inner world: An introduction to the neuroscience of subjective experience.* New York, NY: Other Press.

Song, S. (2006, March 27). Mind over medicine. *Time, 167*, 13.

Soorya, L. V., Carpenter, L. A., & Romanczyk, R. G. (2011). In E. Hollander, A. Kolevzon, & J. T. Coyle (Eds.). *Textbook of autism spectrum disorders* (pp. 525–535). Arlington, VA, US: American Psychiatric Publishing, Inc.

Sorce, J. F., Emde, R. N., Campos, J., & Klinnert, M. D. (1985). Maternal emotional signaling: Its effect on the visual cliff behavior of 1-year-olds. *Developmental Psychology, 21*, 195–200.

Southwick, S. M., Vythilingam, M., & Charney, D. S. (2005). The psychobiology of depression and resilience to stress: Implications for prevention and treatment. *Annual Review of Clinical Psychology, 1*, 255–291.

Sowell, E. R., Thompson, P. M., Tessner, K. D., & Toga, A. W. (2001). Mapping continued brain growth and gray matter density reduction in dorsal frontal cortex: Inverse relationships during postadolescent brain maturation. *Journal of Neuroscience, 21*, 8619–8829.

Spack, N. (2014, April). How I help transgender teens become who they want to be. TED talk, retrieved from https://www.ted.com/talks/norman_spack_how_i_help_transgender_teens_become_who_they_want_to_be/transcript?language=en

Spalding, K. L., Arner, E., Westermark, P. O., Bernard, S., Buchholz, B. A., ... Bergmann, O. (2008, June 5). Dynamics of fat cell turnover in humans. *Nature, 453*, 783–787. doi: 10.1038/nature06902

Spartano, N. L., Himali, J. J., Beiser, A. S., Lewis, G. D., DeCarli, C., Vasan, R. S., &

Seshadri, S. (2016). Midlife exercise, blood pressure, heart rate, and fitness relate to brain volume 2 decades later. *Neurology, 86*, 1313–1319. doi: http://dx.doi.org/10.1212/WNL.0000000000002415

Spearman, C. (1904). "General intelligence," objectively determined and measured. *American Journal of Psychology, 15*, 201–292.

Spearman, C. (1923). *The nature of "intelligence" and the principles of cognition.* London, England: Macmillan.

Spector, F., & Maurer, D. (2009). Synesthesia: A new approach to understanding the development of perception. *Developmental Psychology, 45*, 175–189.

Speisman, R. B., Kumar, A., Rani, A., Pastoriza, J. M., Severance, J. E., Foster, T. C., & Ormerod, B. K. (2013). Environmental enrichment restores neurogenesis and rapid acquisition in aged rats. *Neurobiology of Aging, 34*, 263–274. Retrieved from http://dx.doi.org/10.1016/j.neurobiolaging.2012.05.023

Spelke, E. (2008). Effects of music instruction on developing cognitive systems at the foundations of mathematics and science. *Learning, Arts and the Brain: The Dana Consortium Report on Arts and Cognition.* New York, NY: Dana Press.

Spencer, J. P. (2010). The impact of fruit flavonoids on memory and cognition. *British Journal of Nutrition, 104*(Supp), S40–S47.

Spencer, S. M., & Patrick, J. H. (2009). Social support and personal mastery as protective resources during emerging adulthood. *Journal of Adult Development, 16*, 191–198.

Sperry, R. W., Gazzaniga, M. S., & Bogen, J. E. (1969). Interhemispheric relationships: The neocortical commissures: Syndromes of hemisphere disconnection. In P. J. Vinken & G. W. Bruyn (Eds.), *Handbook of Clinical Neurology* (pp. 273–290). Amsterdam, Netherlands: North-Holland.

Spiegel, D., Bloom, J. R., Kraemer, H. C., & Gottheil, E. (1989). Effect of psychosocial treatment on survival of patients with metastatic breast cancer. *The Lancet, 8668*, 88–91.

Spinrad, T. L., Eisenberg, N., Cumberland, A., Fabes, R. A., Valiente, C., ... Shepard, S. A. (2006). Relation of emotion-related regulation to children's social competence: A longitudinal study. *Emotion, 6*, 498–510.

Sproesser, G., Schupp, H. T., & Renner, B. (2014). The bright side of stress-induced eating: Eating more when stressed but less when pleased. *Psychological Science, 25*, 58–65, first published on October 28, 2013. doi: 10.1177/0956797613494849

Squeglia, L. M., & Gray, K. M. (2016). Alcohol and drug use and the developing brain. *Current Psychiatry Reports, 18*(5). http://doi.org/10.1007/s11920-016-0689-y

Squire, L. (1987). *Memory and brain.* New York, NY: Oxford University Press.

Squire, L. R. (1977). ECT and memory loss. *American Journal of Psychiatry, 134*, 997–1001.

Squire, L. R. (2009). The legacy of patient H.M. for neuroscience. *Neuron, 61*, 6–9. doi: 10.1016/j.neuron.2008.12.023

Srivastava, S. K., & Pant, N. (2016). Emotional intelligence and academic achievement among graduate students. *International Journal of Research in Social Sciences, 6*(6), 22–30.

Stafford, T., & Grimes, A. (2012). Memory enhances the mere exposure effect. *Psychology and Marketing, 29*, 995–1003. doi: 0.1002/mar.20581

Staggs, G. D., Larson, L. M., & Borgen, F. H. (2007). Convergence of personality and interests: Meta-analysis of the multidimensional personality questionnaire and the strong interest inventory. *Journal of Career Assessment, 15*, 423–445.

Stanko-Kaczmarek, M., & Kaczmarek, L. D. (2016). Effects of tactile sensations during finger painting on mindfulness, emotions, and scope of attention. *Creativity Research Journal, 28*(3), 283–288. doi: 10.1080/10400419.2016.1189769

Stanley, J. (1996). In the beginning: The study of mathematically precocious youth. In C. P. Benbow & D. Lubinski (Eds.), *Intellectual talent* (pp. 225–235). Baltimore, MD: Johns Hopkins University Press.

Stanton, A. L., Danoff-Burg, S., Sworowski, L. A., Rodriguez-Hanley, A., Kirk, S. B., & Austenfeld, J. L. (2002). Randomized, controlled trial of written emotional expression and benefit finding in breast cancer patients. *Journal of Clinical Oncology, 20*, 4160–4168.

Starr, C., & Taggart, R. (2004). *Biology: The unity and diversity of life* (10th ed.). Belmont, CA: Thomson-Brooks Cole.

Steen, R. G. (2010). Retractions in the scientific literature: Is the incidence of research fraud increasing? *Journal of Medical Ethics, 37*, 249–253.

Steen, R. G., Casadevall, A., & Fang, F. C. (2013). Why has the number of scientific retractions increased? *PLOS ONE, 8*, e68397.

Steensma, T. D., Kreukels, B. P. C., de Vries, A. L. C., & Cohen-Kettenis, P. T. (2013). Gender identity development in adolescence. *Hormones and Behavior, 64*(2), 288–297. Available at http://doi.org/10.1016/j.yhbeh.2013.02.020

Steensma, T. D., McGuire, J. K., Kreukels, B. C., Beekman, A. J., & Cohen-Kettenis, P. T. (2013). Factors associated with desistence and persistence of childhood gender dysphoria: A quantitative follow-up study. *Journal of the American Academy of Child & Adolescent Psychiatry, 52*(6), 582–590. doi:10.1016/j.jaac.2013.03.016

Steers, M. L. N., Wickham, R. E., & Acitelli, L. K. (2014). Seeing everyone else's highlight reels: How Facebook usage is linked to depressive symptoms. *Journal of Social and Clinical Psychology, 33*(8), 701–731. doi: 10.1521/jscp.2014.33.8.701

Stefansson, H., Ophoff, R. A., Steinberg, S., Andreassen, O. A., Chicon, S., Rujescu, D., ... Collier, D. A. (2009). Common variants conferring risks of schizophrenia. *Nature, 460*, 744–747.

Steinberg, L. (2005). Cognitive and affective development in adolescence. *Trends in Cognitive Science, 9*, 69–74.

Steinberg, L. (2010). *Adolescence* (9th ed.). New York, NY: McGraw-Hill.

Steiner, B., Wolf, S., & Kempermann, G. (2006). Adult neurogenesis and neurodegenerative disease. *Regenerative Medicine, 1*, 15–28.

Steinhausen, H., & Spohr, H. (1998). Long-term outcome of children with fetal alcohol syndrome: Psychopathology, behavior, and intelligence. *Alcoholism: Clinical and Experimental Research, 22*(2), 334–338.

Stellar, E. (1954). The physiology of motivation. *Psychological Review, 61*, 5–22.

Stelmack, R. M., & Geen, R. G. (1992). The psychophysiology of extraversion. In A. Gale & M. W. Eysenck (Eds.), *Handbook of individual differences: Biological perspectives* (pp. 227–254). Chichester, UK: Wiley.

Stenberg, C. R., Campos, J. J., & Emde, R. (1983). The facial expression of anger in seven-month-old infants. *Child Development, 54*, 178–184.

Stepanski, L. M. (2006). At day's close: Night in times past. *Journal of Popular Culture, 39*, 1111–1113. doi: 10.1111/j.1540-5931.2006.00347.x

Stephane, M., Barton, S., & Boutros, N. N. (2001). Auditory verbal hallucinations and dysfunction of the neural substrates of speech. *Schizophrenia Research, 50*, 61–78.

Stephens, T. (2007). How a Swiss invention hooked the world. Available at http://www.swissinfo.ch/eng/how-a-swiss-invention-hooked-the-world/5653568

Sterling, P., & Eyer, J. (1988). Allostasis: A new paradigm to explain arousal pathology. In S. Fisher & H. S. Reason (Eds.), *Handbook of life stress, cognition and health* (pp. 629–649). New York, NY: John Wiley.

Stern, S. A., & Alberini, C. M. (2013). Mechanisms of memory enhancement. *Wiley Interdisciplinary Reviews: Systems Biology and Medicine, 5*, 37–53. doi: 10.1002/wsbm.1196

Sternberg, R. J. (1985). *Beyond IQ: A triarchic theory of human intelligence.* New York, NY: Cambridge University Press.

Sternberg, R. J. (1988). *The triarchic mind: A new theory of human intelligence.* New York, NY: Viking Press.

Sternberg, R. J. (1998). Principles of teaching for successful intelligence. *Educational Psychologist, 55*, 65–72.

Sternberg, R. J. (2000). The concept of intelligence. In. R. J. Sternberg (Ed.), *The handbook of intelligence* (pp. 3–15). Cambridge, England: Cambridge University Press.

Sternberg, R. J. (2003). A broad view of intelligence: A theory of successful intelligence. *Consulting Psychology Journal: Practice and Research, 55*, 139–154.

Sternberg, R. J. (2006a). *Cognitive psychology* (4th ed.). Belmont, CA: Thomson-Wadsworth.

Sternberg, R. J. (2006b). The Rainbow Project: Enhancing the SAT through assessments of analytical, practical, and creative skills. *Intelligence, 34*, 321–350.

Sternberg, R. J. (Ed.). (2004). *Definitions and conceptions of giftedness.* Thousand Oaks, CA: Corwin Press.

Sternberg, R. J., & Detterman, D. K. (Eds.). (1986). *What is intelligence? Contemporary viewpoints on its nature and definition.* Norwood, NJ: Ablex.

Sternberg, R. J., Grigorenko, E. L., & Kidd, K. K. (2005). Intelligence, race, and genetics. *American Psychologist, 60*, 46–59.

Stevens, J. S., & Hamann, S. (2012). Sex differences in brain activation to emotional stimuli: A meta-analysis of neuroimaging studies. *Neuropsychologia, 50*(7), 1578–1593. doi: 10.1016/j.neuropsychologia.2012.03.011

Stevens, S. B., & Morris, T. L. (2007). College dating and social anxiety: Using the Internet as a means of connecting to others. *CyberPsychology & Behavior, 10*, 680–688.

Stewart, J. H. (2005). Hypnosis in contemporary medicine. *Mayo Clinic Proceedings, 80*, 511–524.

Stewart, R. A., Rule, A. C., & Giordano, D. A. (2007). The effect of fine motor skill activities on kindergarten attention. *Early Childhood Education Journal, 35*, 103–109.

Stewart, V. M. (1973). Tests of the "carpentered world" hypothesis by race and environment in America and Zambia. *International Journal of Psychology, 8*, 83–94.

Stice, E., Shaw, H., Bohon, C., Marti, C. N., & Rhode, P. (2009). A meta-analytic review of depression prevention programs for children and adolescents: Factors that predict magnitude of intervention effects. *Journal of Consulting and Clinical Psychology, 77*, 486–503.

Stickgold, R. (2005). Sleep-dependent memory consolidation. *Nature, 437*, 1272–1278.

Stickgold, R., & Walker, M. P. (2007). Sleep-dependent memory consolidation and reconsolidation. *Sleep Medicine, 8*, 331–343.

Stiles, J. (2008). *The fundamentals of brain development: Integrating nature and nurture.* Cambridge, MA: Harvard University Press.

Stockwell, T., Zhao, J., Panwar, S., Roemer, A., Naimi, T., & Chikritzhs, T. (2016). Do "moderate" drinkers have reduced mortality risk? A systematic review and meta-analysis of alcohol consumption and all-cause mortality. *Journal of Studies on Alcohol and Drugs, 77*(2), 185–198. doi: http://dx.doi.org/10.15288/jsad.2016.77.185

Stoléru, S., Fonteille, V., Cornélis, C., Joyal, C., & Moulier, V. (2012). Functional neuroimaging studies of sexual arousal and orgasm in healthy men and women: A review and meta-analysis. *Neuroscience and Biobehavioral Reviews, 36*(6), 1481–1509. Available at http://doi.org/10.1016/j.neubiorev.2012.03.006

Strack, F., Martin, L. L., & Stepper, S. (1988). Inhibiting and facilitating conditions of the human smile: A nonobtrusive test of the facial feedback hypothesis. *Journal of Personality and Social Psychology, 54*, 768–777.

Strange, B. A., & Dolan, R. J. (2006). Anterior medial temporal lobe in human cognition: Memory for fear and the unexpected. *Neuropsychiatry, 11*, 198–218.

Strassman, R. J. (1984). Adverse reactions to psychedelic drugs. A review of the literature. *Journal of Nervous and Mental Disease, 172*, 577–595.

Strauss, M. E., Pasupathi, M., & Chatterjee, A. (1993). Concordance between observers in descriptions of personality change in Alzheimer's disease. *Psychology and Aging, 8*, 475–480.

Strayer, D. L., Drews, F. A., & Couch, D. J. (2006). A comparison of the cell-phone driver and the drunk driver. *Human Factors, 48*, 381–391.

Streissguth, A., Barr, H., Sampson, P., Darby, B., & Martin, D. (1989). IQ at age 4 in relation to maternal alcohol use and smoking during pregnancy. *Developmental Psychology, 25*(1), 3–11.

Striedter, G. (2005). *Principles of brain evolution.* Sunderland, MA: Sinauer.

Strombach, T., Strang, S., Park, S. Q., & Kenning, P. (2016). Common and distinctive approaches to motivation in different disciplines. *Progress in Brain Research, 229*, 3–23. http://dx.doi.org/10.1016/bs.pbr.2016.06.007

Stroodley, C. J., & Schmahmann, J. D. (2009). Functional topography in the human cerebellum: A meta-analysis of neuroimaging studies. *Neuro-Image, 44*, 489–501.

Stroop, J. R. (1935). Studies of interference in serial-verbal reaction. *Journal of Experimental Psychology, 18*, 643–662.

Strueber, D., Lueck, M., & Roth, G. (2006–2007). The violent brain. *Scientific American Mind, 17*, 20–27.

Stuss, D. T., & Knight, R. T. (Ed.). (2002). *Principles of frontal lobe function.* New York: Oxford University Press.

Styles, E. A. (2006). *The psychology of attention* (2nd ed.). Hove, England: Psychology Press.

Suarez, E. C., Bates, M. P., & Harralson, T. L. (1998). The relation of hostility to lipids and lipoproteins in women: Evidence for the role of antagonistic hostility. *Annals of Behavioral Medicine, 20,* 59–63.

Suarez, E. C., Harlan, E., Peoples, M. C., & Williams, R. B., Jr. (1993). Cardiovascular reactivity and emotional responses in women: The role of hostility and harassment. *Health Psychology, 12,* 459–468.

Suarez, E. C., & Williams, R. B., Jr. (1989). Situational determinants of cardiovascular and emotional reactivity in high and low hostile men. *Psychosomatic Medicine, 51,* 404–418.

Subrahmanyam, K., & Greenfield, P. (2008). Online communication and adolescent relationships. *The Future of Children, 18,* 119–146.

Suchotzki, K., Verschuere, B., Van Bockstaele, B., Ben-Shakhar, G., & Crombez, G. (2017, February 9). Lying takes time: A meta-analysis on reaction time measures of deception. *Psychological Bulletin.* Advance online publication. Available at http://dx.doi.org/10.1037/bul0000087

Sudo, N., Chida, Y., Aiba, Y., Sonoda, J., Oyama, N., Yu, X. N., … Koga, Y. (2004). Postnatal microbial colonization programs the hypothalamic–pituitary–adrenal system for stress response in mice. *The Journal of Physiology, 558*(1), 263–275. doi: 10.1113/jphysiol.2004.063388

Sulaiman, A. H., Seluakumaran, K., & Husain, R. (2013). Hearing risk associated with the usage of personal listening devices among urban high school students in Malaysia. *Public Health, 127,* 710–715.

Sullivan, E. V., Harris, R. A., & Pfefferbaum, A. (2010). Alcohol's effects on brain and behavior. *Alcohol Research & Health, 33,* 127–143.

Sullivan, K., Zaitchik, D., & Tager-Flusberg, H. (1994). Preschoolers can attribute second-order beliefs. *Developmental Psychology, 30,* 395–402.

Sullivan, K. M. (2009). *The Bundy murders: A comprehensive history.* Jefferson, NC: McFarland.

Sundquist, J., Ohlsson, H., Winkleby, M. A., Sundquist, K., & Crump, C. (2016). School achievement and risk of eating disorders in a Swedish national cohort. *Journal of the American Academy of Child & Adolescent Psychiatry, 55*(1), 41–46. Available at http://dx.doi.org/10.1016/j.jaac.2015.09.021

Suomi, S. (2005). Genetic and environmental factors influencing the expression of impulsive aggression and serotonergic functioning in rhesus monkeys. In R. E. Tremblay, W. W. Hartup, & J. Archer (Eds.), *Developmental origins of aggression* (pp. 63–82). New York, NY: Guilford Press.

Susskind, J. M., Lee, D. H., Cusi, A., Feiman, R., Grabski, W., & Anderson, A. K. (2008). Expressing fear enhances sensory acquisition. *Nature Neuroscience, 11,* 843–850.

Sweatt, J. D. (2010, May 7). Epigenetics and cognitive aging. *Science, 328,* 701–702. doi: 10.1126/science.1189968

Swets, J. A. (1964). *Signal detection and recognition by human observers.* New York, NY: Wiley.

Syed, M., & Azmitia, M. (2010). Narrative and ethnic identity exploration: A longitudinal account of emerging adults' ethnicity-related experiences. *Developmental Psychology, 46,* 208–219.

Syed, M., & Seiffge-Krenke, I. (2013). Personality development from adolescence to emerging

adulthood: Linking trajectories of ego development to the family context and identity formation. *Journal of Personality and Social Psychology, 104*(2), 371–84. Available at https://doi.org/10.1037/a0030070

Szaflarski, J. P., Schmithorst, V. J., Altaye, M., Byars, A. W., Ret, J., Plante, E., & Holland, S. K. (2006). A longitudinal functional magnetic resonance imaging study of language development in children 5 to 11 years old. *Annals of Neurology, 59,* 796–807. doi: 10.1002/ana.20817

Takahashi, Y., Yamagata, S., Kijima, N., Shigemasu, K., Ono, Y., & Ando, J. (2007). Continuity and change in behavioral inhibition and activation systems: A longitudinal behavioral genetic study. *Personality and Individual Differences, 43*(6), 1616–1625.

Takeuchi, H., Taki, Y., Sassa, Y., Hashizume, H., Sekiguchi, A., Fukushima, A., & Kawashima, R. (2010). White matter structures associated with creativity: Evidence from diffusion tensor imaging. *NeuroImage, 51,* 11–18.

Talati, A., Bao, Y., Kaufman, J., Shen, L., Schaefer, C. A., & Brown, A. S. (2013). Maternal smoking during pregnancy and bipolar disorder in offspring. *American Journal of Psychiatry, 170,* 1178–1185. doi: 10.1176/appi.ajp.2013.12121500

Talmi, D., Grady, C. L., Goshen-Gottstein, Y., & Moscovitch, M. (2005). Neuroimaging the serial position curve: A test of single-store versus dual-store models. *Psychological Science, 16,* 717–723.

Tambs, K., Hoffman, H. J., Borchgrevink, H. M., Holmen, J., & Engdahl, B. (2006). Hearing loss induced by occupational and impulse noise: Results on threshold shifts by frequencies, age and gender from the NordTrøndelag Hearing Loss Study. *International Journal of Audiology, 45,* 309–317.

Tamin, R. M., Borokhovski, E., Pickup, D., Bernard, R. M., & El Saadi, L. (2015). *Tablets for teaching and learning: A systematic review and meta-analysis.* Burnaby, British Columbia: Commonwealth of Learning.

Tammet, D. (2006). *Born on a blue day: A memoir.* New York, NY: Free Press.

Tan, A., Ma, W., Vira, A., Marwha, D., & Eliot, L. (2016). The hippocampus is not sexually-dimorphic: Meta-analysis of structural MRI volumes. *NeuroImage, 124,* 350. doi: 10.1016/j.neuroimage.2015.08.050

Tang, Z., & Orwin, R. G. (2009). Marijuana initiation among American youth and its risks as dynamic processes: Prospective findings from a national longitudinal study. *Substance Use & Misuse, 44,* 195–211.

Tangney, J. P., Stuewig, J., & Mashek, D. J. (2007). Moral emotions and moral behavior. *Annual Review of Psychology, 58,* 345–372.

Tanielian, T., & Jaycox, L. H. (Eds.). (2008). *Invisible wounds of war: Psychological and cognitive injuries, their consequences, and services to assist recovery.* Santa Monica, CA: Rand Corp.

Tardif, T., Gelman, S., & Xu, F. (1999). Putting the "noun bias" in context: A comparison of English and Mandarin. *Developmental Psychology, 70,* 620–635.

Tare, M., & Gelman, S. A. (2010). Can you say it another way? Cognitive factors in bilingual children's pragmatic language skills. *Journal of Cognition and Development, 11*(2), 137–158. doi: 10.1080/15248371003699951

Tarmann, A. (2002, May/June). Out of the closet and onto the Census long form. *Population Today, 30,* 1, 6.

Tarrasch, R., Berman, Z., & Friedmann, N. (2016). Mindful reading: Mindfulness meditation

helps keep readers with dyslexia and ADHD on the lexical track. *Frontiers in Psychology,* published online, May 10, 2016. doi: 10.3389/fpsyg.2016.00578

Tartter, V. C. 1980. Happy talk: Perceptual and acoustic effects of smiling on speech. *Percept. Psychophys., 27*(1), 24–27. doi: 10.3758/BF03199901

Tarver, J., Daley, D., & Sayal, K. (2014). Beyond symptom control for attention-deficit hyperactivity disorder (ADHD): What can parents do to improve outcomes? *Child: Care, Health and Development, 41,* 1–14. doi: 10.1111/cch.12159

Tashkin, D. (2006, May 23). *Marijuana smoking not linked to lung cancer.* Paper presented at the annual meeting of the American Thoracic Society, San Diego, CA.

Tashkin, D. R., Baldwin, G. C., Sarafian, T., Dubinett, S., & Roth, M. D. (2002). Respiratory and immunologic consequences of marijuana smoking. *Journal of Clinical Pharmacology, 42,* S71–S81.

Tau, B., Launay, J., & Dunbar, R. I. (2016). Silent disco: Dancing in synchrony leads to elevated pain thresholds and social closeness. *Evolution and Human Behavior, 37*(5), 343–349. Available at http://dx.doi.org/10.1016/j.evolhumbehav.2016.02.004

Tavris, C. (2013, May 18). How psychiatry went crazy. *The Wall Street Journal,* C5.

Taylor, C. B., Kass, A. E., Trockel, M., Cunning, D., Weisman, H., Bailey, J., … & Wilfley, D. E. (2016). Reducing eating disorder onset in a very high risk sample with significant comorbid depression: A randomized controlled trial. *Journal of Consulting and Clinical Psychology, 84*(5), 402–414. Available at http://dx.doi.org/10.1037/ccp0000077

Taylor, K. N., Harper, S., & Chadwick, P. (2009). Impact of mindfulness on cognition and affect in voice hearing: Evidence from two case studies. *Behavioral and Cognitive Psychotherapy, 37,* 397–402.

Taylor, O. D. (2015). The cultural influence of adolescent prescription drug abuse. *Journal of Human Behavior in the Social Environment, 25*(4), 304–311. http://dx.doi.org/10.1080/10911359.2014.969124

Taylor, S. E. (1989). *Positive illusions: Creative self-deception and the healthy mind.* New York, NY: Basic Books.

Taylor, W. C., Kimbro, R. T., Evans-Hudnall, G., Haughton, L., & Barnes, A. S. (2015). Sedentary behavior, body mass index, and weight loss maintenance among African American women. *Ethnicity & Disease, 25*(1), 38–45.

Teasdale, J. D., Segal, Z., Williams, M. G., Ridgeway, V. A., Soulsby, J. M., & Lau, M. A. (2000). Prevention of relapse/recurrence in major depression by mindfulness-based cognitive therapy. *Journal of Consulting and Clinical Psychology, 68,* 615–623.

Tellegen, A. (2000). *Manual for the multidimensional personality questionnaire.* Minneapolis: University of Minnesota Press.

Tellegen, A., Ben-Porath, Y. S., McNulty, J. L., Arbisi, P. A., Graham, J. R., & Kaemmer, B. (2003). *The MMPI-2 Restructured Clinical Scales: Development, validation, and interpretation.* Minneapolis: University of Minnesota Press.

Tellegen, A., Lykken, D. T., Bouchard, T. J., Wilcox, K. J., Segal, N. L., & Rich, S. (1988). Personality similarity in twins reared apart and together. *Journal of Personality and Social Psychology, 54,* 1031–1039.

ten Brinke, L. F., Bolandzadeh, N., Nagamatsu, L. S., Hsu, C. L., Davis, J. C., Miran-Khan, K., & Liu-Ambrose, T. (2015). Aerobic exercise increases hippocampal volume in older women with probable mild cognitive impairment: A 6-month randomised controlled trial. *British Journal of Sports Medicine, 49,* 248–254. doi: 10.1136/bjsports-2013-093184

Teo, K., Lear, S., Islam, S., Mony, P., Dehghan, M., Li, W., ... Yusuf, S. (2013). Prevalence of a healthy lifestyle among individuals with cardiovascular disease in high-, middle- and low-income countries: The Prospective Urban Rural Epidemiology (PURE) Study. *Journal of the American Medical Association, 309*(15), 1613–1621. doi: 10.1001/jama.2013.3519

Terrace, H. S. (1987). *Nim: A chimpanzee who learned sign language.* New York, NY: Columbia University Press.

Thagard, P. (2005). *Mind: An introduction to cognitive science* (2nd ed.). Cambridge, MA: MIT Press.

Thapar, A., Langley, K., Asherson, P., & Gill, M. (2007). Gene-environment interplay in attention-deficit hyperactivity disorder and the importance of a developmental perspective. *British Journal of Psychiatry, 190,* 1–3.

The odds of dying from . . . (2010). National Safety Council. Retrieved from http://www.nsc.org/news_resources/injury_and_death_statistics/pages/theoddsofdyingfrom.aspx

The peculiar institution. (2002). [Editorial]. *Scientific American, 286,* 8.

Thibaut, J. W., & Kelley, H. H. (1959). *The social psychology of groups.* New York, NY: Wiley.

Thomas, A., & Chess, S. (1977). *Temperament and development.* New York, NY: Brunner/ Mazel.

Thompson, R. F., & Madigan, S. A. (2005). *Memory: The key to consciousness.* Washington, DC: Joseph Henry Press.

Thompson, W. L., & Kosslyn, S. M. (2000). Neural systems activated during visual mental imagery. In A. W. Toga & J. C. Mazziotta (Eds.), *Brain mapping: The systems* (pp. 535–560). San Diego, CA: Academic Press.

Thompson-Cannino, J., Cotton, R., & Torneo, E. (2009). *Picking cotton: A memoir of injustice and redemption.* New York, NY: St. Martin's Griffin.

Thorndike, E. L. (1905). *Elements of psychology.* New York, NY: Seiler.

Thornhill, R., Gangestad, S. W., Miller, R., Scheyd, G., McCollough, J. K., & Franklin, M. (2003). Major histocompatibility complex genes, symmetry, and body scent attractiveness in men and women. *Behavioral Ecology, 14,* 668–678.

Thornton, L. M., Welch, E., Munn-Chernoff, M. A., Lichtenstein, P., & Bulik, C. M. (2016). Anorexia nervosa, major depression, and suicide attempts: Shared genetic factors. In *Suicide and life-threatening behavior.* doi: 10.1111/sltb.12235

Thune, I., & Furberg, A. S. (2001). Physical activity and cancer risk: Dose-response and cancer, all sites and site specific. *Medicine and Science in Sports and Exercise, 33,* S530–S550.

Tielbeek, J. J., Linnér, R. K., Beers, K., Posthuma, D., Popma, A., & Polderman, T. C. (2016). Meta-analysis of the serotonin transporter promoter variant (5-HTTLPR) in relation to adverse environment and antisocial behavior. *American Journal of Medical Genetics Part B: Neuropsychiatric Genetics, 171*(5), 748–760. doi:10.1002/ajmg.b.32442

Titman, N. (2014, December 16). How many people in the United Kingdom are nonbinary? *Practical Androgyny.* Retrieved on October 7, 2016 at http://practicalandrogyny.com/2014/12/16/how-many-people-in-the-uk-are-nonbinary/

Tobe, E. H. (2013). Mitochondrial dysfunction, oxidative stress, and major depressive disorder. *Neuropsychiatric Disease and Treatment, 9,* 567–573. doi: 10.2147/NDT.S44282

Tobias, S., & Everson, H. T. (2002). *Knowing what you know and what you don't: Further research on metacognitive knowledge monitoring.* New York, NY: College Entrance Examination Board.

Tobin, D. J. (2004). Biology of hair pigmentation. In B. Forslind, M. Lindberg, and L. Norlen (Eds.), *Skin, hair, nails: Structure and function* (pp. 319–363). New York, NY: Marcel Dekker.

Tolin, D. F. (2010). Is cognitive-behavioral therapy more effective than other therapies? A meta-analytic review. *Clinical Psychology Review, 30,* 710–720.

Tolman, E. C., & Honzik, C. H. (1930). Introduction and removal of reward, and maze performance in rats. *University of California Publications in Psychology, 4,* 257–275.

Tomasello, M., & Hermann, E. (2010). Ape and human cognition: What's the difference? *Current Directions in Psychological Science, 19,* 3–8.

Tomiyama, A., O'Donovan, A., Lin, J., Puterman, E., Lazaro, A., Chan, J., ... Epel, E. (2012). Does cellular aging relate to patterns of allostasis? An examination of basal and stress reactive HPA axis activity and telomere length. *Physiology & Behavior, 106*(1), 40–45. doi: 10.1016/j.physbeh.2011.11.016

Tomkins, S. S. (1962). *Affect, imagery, consciousness: Vol. 1. The positive affects.* New York, NY: Springer.

Tomkins, S. S. (1981). The quest for primary motives: Biography and autobiography of an idea. *Journal of Personality and Social Psychology, 41,* 306–329.

Tomson, S. N., Narayan, M., Allen, G. I., & Eagleman, D. M. (2013). Neural networks of colored sequence synesthesia. *Journal of Neuroscience, 33,* 14098–14106. doi: 10.1523/JNEUROSCI.5131-12-2013

Tong, E. M. W., Ellsworth, P. C., & Bishop, G. D. (2009). An S-shaped relationship between changes in appraisal and changes in emotions. *Emotion, 9,* 821–837.

Tooby, J., & Cosmides, L. (1990). The past explains the present: Emotional adaptations and the structure of ancestral environments. *Ethology and Sociobiology, 11,* 375–424.

Tooby, J., & Cosmides, L. (1992). The psychological foundations of culture. In J. H. Barkow, L. Cosmides, & J. Tooby (Eds.), *The adapted mind: Evolutionary psychology and the generation of culture* (pp. 19–136). New York, NY: Oxford University Press.

Touriño, C., Evan-Rothschild, A., & de Lecea, L. (2013). Optogenetics in psychiatric diseases. *Current Opinion in Neurobiology, 23,* 430–435 doi: 10.1016/j.conb.2013.03.007

Toussaint, N., de Roon, M., van Campen, J. P. C. M., Kremer, S., & Boesveldt, S. (2015). Loss of olfactory function and nutritional status in vital older adults and geriatric patients. *Chemical Senses, 40*(3), 197–203. http://doi.org/10.1093/chemse/bju113

Townsend, J. M., Wasserman, T. H., & Rosenthal, A. (2015). Gender difference in emotional reactions and sexual coercion in casual sexual relations: An evolutionary perspective. *Personality and Individual Differences, 85,* 41–49. Available at http://doi.org/10.1016/j.paid.2015.04.03

Townsend, S. S. M., Markus, H. R., & Bergsieker, H. B. (2009). My choice, your categories: The denial of multiracial identities. *Journal of Social Issues, 65,* 185–204.

Toyota, Y., Ikeda, M., Shinagawa, S., Matsumoto, T., Matsumoto, N., Hokoishi, K., ... Tanabe, H. (2007). Comparison of behavioral and psychological symptoms in early-onset and late-onset Alzheimer's disease. *International Journal of Geriatric Psychiatry, 22*(9), 896–901. doi: 10.1002/gps.1760

Tracy, J. L., & Matsumoto, D. M. (2008). The spontaneous display of pride and shame: Evidence for biologically innate nonverbal displays. *Proceedings of the National Academy of Science, 105,* 11655–11660.

Tracy, J. L., & Robins, R. W. (2007). Emerging insights into the nature and function of pride. *Current Directions in Psychological Science, 16,* 147–150.

Tracy, J. L., & Robins, R. W. (2008). The nonverbal expression of pride: Evidence for cross-cultural recognition. *Journal of Personality and Social Psychology, 94,* 516–530.

Tracy, J. L., Shariff, A. F., Zhao, W., & Henrich, J. (2013). Cross-cultural evidence that the nonverbal expression of pride is an automatic status signal. *Journal of Experimental Psychology: General, 142,* 163–180. doi: 10.1037/a0028412

Transcripts of "Secrets of the Wild Child." (1997). Retrieved from http://www.pbs.org/wgbh/nova/transcripts/2112gchild.html

Treffert, D. A. (2006). *Extraordinary people: Understanding savant syndrome* (Updated version). Lincoln, NE: iUniverse.

Treffert, D. A., & Christensen, D. D. (2005). Inside the mind of a savant. *Scientific American, 293,* 108–113.

Treisman, A. (1964). Verbal cues, language and meaning in selective attention. *American Journal of Psychology, 77,* 206–209.

Tremblay, K., & Ross, B. (2007). Effects of age and age-related hearing loss on the brain. *Journal of Communication Disorders, 40,* 305–312.

Tremblay, P., & Dick, A. S. (2016). Broca and Wernicke are dead, or moving past the classic model of language neurobiology. *Brain and Language, 162,* 60–71. Available at http://dx.doi.org/10.1016/j.bandl.2016.08.004

Trentacosta, C. J., & Izard, C. E. (2007). Kindergarten children's emotion competence as a predictor of their academic competence in first grade. *Emotion, 7,* 77–88.

Trepte, S., & Reinecke, L. (2013). The reciprocal effects of social network site use and the disposition for self-disclosure: A longitudinal study. *Computers in Human Behavior, 29,* 1102–1112. Available at http://dx.doi.org/10.1016/j.chb.2012.10.002

Trezza, V., Cuomo, V., & Vanderschuren, L. J. M. J. (2008). Cannabis and the developing brain: Insights from behavior. *European Journal of Pharmacology, 585*(2–3), 441–452. http://doi.org/10.1016/j.ejphar.2008.01.058

Triandis, H. C. (1993). Collectivism and individualism as cultural syndromes. *Cross-Cultural Research: The Journal of Comparative Social Science, 27,* 155–180. Available at http://dx.doi.org/10.1177/106939719302700301

Triandis, H. C. (1996). The psychological measurement of cultural syndromes. *American Psychologist, 51*(4), 407–415. Available at http://doi.org/10.1037/0003-066X.51.4.407

Triplett, N. (1898). The dynamogenic factors in pacemaking and competition. *American Journal of Psychology, 9,* 507–533.

Trivers, R. L. (1971). The evolution of reciprocal altruism. *Quarterly Review of Biology, 46,* 35–57.

Trivers, R. L. (1972). Parental investment and sexual selection. In B. Campbell (Ed.), *Sexual selection and the descent of man, 1871–1971* (pp. 136–179). Chicago, IL: Aldine.

Trivers, R. L. (1985). *Social evolution*. Menlo Park, CA: Benjamin/Cummings.

Troisi, A. (2003). Psychopathology. In D. Maestripieri (Ed.), *Primate psychology* (pp. 451–470). Cambridge, MA: Harvard University Press.

Tronick, E., Morelli, G. A., & Ivey, P. K. (1992). The Efe forager infant and toddler's pattern of social relationships: Multiple and simultaneous. *Developmental Psychology, 28*, 568–577.

Trucking stats and FAQ's. (n.d.). Retrieved January 20, 2007, from http://www.geocities.com/TheTropics/1608/stats.htm

True, M., Pisani, L., & Oumar, F. (2001). Infant-mother attachment among the Dogon of Mali. *Child Development, 72*, 1451–1466.

Trugman, J. M. (1998). Tardive dyskinesia: Diagnosis, pathogenesis, and management. *Neurologist, 4*, 180–187.

Tsai, J., & Chentsova-Dutton, Y. (2003). Variation among European Americans in emotional facial expression. *Journal of Cross-Cultural Psychology, 34*, 650–657.

Tsai, J. L., Chentsova-Dutton, Y., Friere-Bebeau, L., & Przymus, D. E. (2002). Emotional expression and physiology in European Americans and Hmong Americans. *Emotion, 2*, 380–397.

Tsai, J. L., Levenson, R. W., & Carstensen, L. L. (2000). Autonomic, expressive, and subjective responses to emotional films in older and younger Chinese American and European American adults. *Psychology and Aging, 15*, 684–693.

Tsakiris, M., Hesse, M. D., Boy, C., Haggard, P., & Fink, G. R. (2007). Neural signatures of body ownership: A sensory network for bodily self-consciousness. *Cerebral Cortex, 17*, 2235–2244.

Tseng, W. S. (1973). The development of psychiatric concepts in traditional Chinese medicine. *Archives of General Psychiatry, 29*, 569–575.

Tsikerdekis, M. (2013). The effects of perceived anonymity and anonymity states on conformity and groupthink in online communities: A Wikipedia study. *Journal of the American Society for Information Science and Technology, 64*(5), 1001–1015. doi: 10.1002/asi.22795

Tucci, S., & Akey, J. M. (2016). Population genetics: A map of human wanderlust. *Nature, 538*, 179–180.

Tucker-Drob, E. M., Rhemtulla, M., Harden, K., Turkheimer, E., & Fask, D. (2011). Emergence of a gene × socioeconomic status interaction on infant mental ability between 10 months and 2 years. *Psychological Science, 22*(1), 125–133. doi: 10.1177/0956797610392926

Tugade, M. M., & Fredrickson, B. L. (2004). Resilient individuals use positive emotions to bounce back from negative emotional experiences. *Journal of Personality and Social Psychology, 86*, 320–333.

Tully, K., & Bolshakov, V. (2010). Emotional enhancement of memory: How norepinephrine enables synaptic plasticity. *Molecular Brain, 3*, 15. doi: 10.1186/1756-6606-3-15

Tully, P. J., & Cosh, S. M. (2013). Generalized anxiety disorder prevalence and comorbidity with depression in coronary heart disease: A meta-analysis. *Journal of Health Psychology, 18*, 1601–1616. doi: 10.1177/1359105312467390

Tulving, E. (1972). Episodic and semantic memory. In E. Tulving & W. Donaldson (Eds.), *Organization of memory* (pp. 381–403). New York, NY: Academic Press.

Tulving, E. (1985). How many memory systems are there? *American Psychologist, 40*, 385–398.

Tupper, K. W., Wood, E., Yensen, R., & Johnson, M. W. (2015). Psychedelic medicine: A re-emerging therapeutic paradigm. *Canadian Medical Association Journal, 187*(14), 1054–1059. doi: 10.1503/cmaj.141124

Turati, C., Natale, E., Bolognini, N., Senna, I., Picozzi, M., Longhi, E., & Cassia, V. M. (2013). The early development of human mirror mechanisms: Evidence from electromyographic recordings at 3 and 6 months. *Developmental Science, 16*, 793–800.

Turel, O., & Bechara, A. (2017). Effects of motor impulsivity and sleep quality on swearing, interpersonally deviant and disadvantageous behaviors on online social networking sites. *Personality and Individual Differences, 108*, 91–97. Available at http://dx.doi.org/10.1016/j.paid.2016.12.005

Turkheimer, E., & Gottesman, I. (1991). Individual differences and the canalization of human behavior. *Developmental Psychology, 27*, 18–22.

Turner, E. H., Matthews, A. M., Linardatos, E., Tell, R. A., & Rosenthal, R. (2008). Selective publication of antidepressant trials and its influence on apparent efficacy. *New England Journal of Medicine, 358*, 252–260.

Turner-Shea, Y., Bruno, R., & Pridmore, S. (2006). Daily and spaced treatment with transcranial magnetic stimulation in major depression: A pilot study. *Australian and New Zealand Journal of Psychiatry, 40*, 759–763.

Tversky, A., & Kahneman, D. (1974). Judgment under uncertainty: Heuristics and biases. *Science, 185*, 1124–1131.

Tversky, A., & Kahneman, D. (1983). Extensional versus intuitive reasoning: The conjunction fallacy in probability judgment. *Psychological Review, 90*, 293–315.

Tyron, W. W. (2005). Possible mechanisms for why desensitization and exposure therapy work. *Clinical Psychology Review, 25*, 67–95.

U.S. Census Bureau. (2009a). *Current population survey*. Retrieved from http://www.census.gov/population/socdemo/hh-fam/ms2.xls

U.S. Census Bureau. (2009b). *Table 4: Annual estimates of the two or more races resident population by sex and age for the United States: April 1, 2000 to July 1, 2008* [Data file]. Retrieved from http://www.census.gov/popest/national/asrh/NC-EST2008/NC-EST2008-04-TOM.csv

U.S. Department of Health and Human Services. (2006). *The health consequences of involuntary exposure to tobacco smoke: A report of the surgeon general—Executive summary*. Retrieved from http://www.surgeongeneral.gov/library/secondhandsmoke/report/executivesummary.pdf

U.S. Senate. (2004). *Report of the Select Committee on Intelligence on the U.S. intelligence community's prewar intelligence assessments on Iraq*. Retrieved from http://www.gpoaccess.gov/serialset/creports/iraq.html

Udry, J. R., Morris, N. M., & Waller, L. (1973). Effect of contraceptive pills on sexual activity in the luteal phase of the human menstrual cycle. *Archives of Sexual Behavior, 2*, 205–214.

Uher, J. (2008). Comparative personality research: Methodological approaches. *European Journal of Personality* [serial online], *22*(5), 427–455.

Uher, R., & McGuffin, P. (2010). The moderation by the serotonin transporter gene of environmental adversity in the etiology of depression: 2009 update. *Molecular Psychiatry, 15*, 18–22.

Uhlhaas, P. J., Roux, F., Singer, W., Haenschel, C., Sireteanu, R., & Rodriguez, E. (2009). The development of neural synchrony reflects late maturation and restructuring functional networks in humans. *Proceedings of the National Academy of Sciences, 106*, 9866–9871.

Uhlhaas, P. J., & Singer, W. (2010). Abnormal neural oscillations and synchrony in schizophrenia. *Nature Reviews Neuroscience, 11*, 100–113.

Ullrich, M., Weber, M., Post, A. M., Popp, S., Grein, J., Zechner, M., ... Shuh, K. (2017). OCD-like behavior is caused by dysfunction of thalamo-amygdala circuits and upregulated TrkB/ERK-MAPK signaling as a result of SPRED2 deficiency. *Molecular Psychiatry*, doi: 10.1038/mp.2016.232

University of Cambridge. (2011, February 10). Extra testosterone reduces your empathy, researchers find. *ScienceDaily*. Retrieved from http://www.sciencedaily.com/releases/2011/02/110209105556.htm

Utoyama, M., Akieda-Asai, S., Koda, S., Nunoi, H., & Date, Y. (2016). Role of the neural pathway from hindbrain to hypothalamus in the regulation of energy homeostasis in rats. *Neuroscience letters, 614*, 83–88. Available at http://dx.doi.org/10.1016/j.neulet.2016.01.005

Utz, K. S., Dimova, V., Oppenländer, K., & Kerkhoff, G. (2010). Electrified minds: Transcranial direct current stimulation (tDCS) and galvanic vestibular stimulation (GVS) as methods of non-invasive brain stimulation in neuropsychology—A review of current data and future implications. *Neuropsychologia, 48*, 2789–810. doi: 10.1016/j.neuropsychologia.2010.06.002

Utz, S., Tanis, M., & Vermeulen, I. (2012). It is all about being popular: The effects of need for popularity on social network site use. *Cyberpsychology, Behavior, and Social Networking, 15*(1), 37–42. doi: 10.1089/cyber.2010.0651

Uylings, H. B. M. (2006). Development of the human cortex and the concept of "critical" or "sensitive" periods. *Language Learning, 56*, 59–90.

Vaccarino, V., & Bremner, J. D. (2016). Behavioral, emotional and neurobiological determinants of coronary heart disease risk in women. *Neuroscience & Biobehavioral Reviews*. Available at http://dx.doi.org/10.1016/j.neubiorev.2016.04.023

Valente, M., Placid, F., Oliveira, A. J., Bigagli, A., Morghen, I., Proietti, R., & Gigli, G. L. (2002). Sleep organization pattern as a prognostic marker at the sub-acute stage of post-traumatic coma. *Clinical Neurophysiology, 113*, 1798–1805.

Valenzuela, M. J., Matthews, F. E., Brayne, C., Ince, P., Halliday, G., Kril, J. J., ... Sachdev, P. S. (2012). Multiple biological pathways link cognitive lifestyle to protection from dementia. *Biological Psychiatry, 71*, 783–791. doi: 10.1016/j.biopsych.2011.07.036

Valkenburg, P. M., & Peter, J. (2007b). Who visits online dating sites? Exploring some characteristics of online daters. *CyberPsychology & Behavior, 10*, 849–852.

Valmaggia, L. R., Latif, L., Kempton, M. J., & Rus-Calafell, M. (2016). Virtual reality in the psychological treatment for mental health problems: An systematic review of recent evidence. *Psychiatry Research, 236*, 189–195. Available at http://dx.doi.org/10.1016/j.psychres.2016.01.015

Valois, R. F., Zullig, K. J., Huebner, E. S., & Drane, J. W. (2003). Dieting behaviors, weight perceptions, and life satisfaction among public high school adolescents. *Eating Disorders, 11*, 271–288.

Van Ameringen, M., Simpson, W., Patterson, B., Turna, J., & Khalesi, Z. (2016). Internet addiction or psychopathology in disguise? Results from a survey of college-aged internet users. *European Neuropsychopharmacology, 26,* S700–S701. Available at http://dx.doi.org/10.1016/S0924-977X(16)31834-X

Van Cappellen, P., Toth-Gauthier, M., Saroglou, V., & Fredrickson, B. L. (2016). Religion and well-being: The mediating role of positive emotions. *Journal of Happiness Studies, 17*(2), 485–505. doi: 10.1007/s10902-014-9605-5

van den Elsen, L. W., Poyntz, H. C., Weyrich, L. S., Young, W., & Forbes-Blom, E. E. (2017). Embracing the gut microbiota: The new frontier for inflammatory and infectious diseases. *Clinical & Translational Immunology, 6*(1), e125. doi: 10.1038/cti.2016.91

van der Schuur, W. A., Baumgartner, S. E., Sumter, S. R., & Valkenburg, P. M. (2015). The consequences of media multitasking for youth: A review. *Computers in Human Behavior, 53,* 204–215. Available at http://doi.org/10.1016/j.chb.2015.06.035

Van Gerven, P., Van Boxtel, M., Meijer, W., Willems, D., & Jolles, J. (2007). On the relative role of inhibition in age-related working memory decline. *Aging, Neuropsychology, and Cognition, 14,* 95–107. doi: 10.1080/138255891007038

van IJzendoorn, M., & Juffer, F. (2005). Adoption is a successful natural intervention enhancing adopted children's IQ and school performance. *Current Directions in Psychological Science, 14,* 326–330.

van IJzendoorn, M., & Sagi, A. (1999). Cross-cultural patterns of attachment: Universal and contextual dimensions. In J. Cassidy & P. Shaver (Eds.), *Handbook of attachment* (pp. 265–286). New York, NY: Guilford Press.

van Leeuwen, T. M., den Ouden, H. M., & Hagoort, P. (2011). Effective connectivity determines the nature of subjective experience in grapheme-color synesthesia. *Journal of Neuroscience, 31*(27), 9879–9884. doi: 10.1523/JNEUROSCI.0569-11.2011

van Praag, H., Kempermann, G., & Gage, F. H. (1999). Running increases cell proliferation and neurogenesis in the adult mouse dentate gyrus. *Nature Neuroscience, 2,* 266–270.

Van Voorhees, B. W., Paunesku, D., Kuwabara, S. A., Basu, A., Gollan, J., Hankin, B. L., & Reinecke, M. (2008). Protective and vulnerability factors predicting new-onset depressive episode in a representative of U.S. adolescents. *Journal of Adolescent Health, 42,* 605–616. doi: 10.1016/j.jadohealth.2007.11.135

van Vugt, M. K., & Jha, A. P. (2011). Investigating the impact of mindfulness meditation training on working memory: A mathematical modeling approach. *Cognitive, Affective & Behavioral Neuroscience, 11,* 344–353. doi: 10.3758/s13415-011-0048-8

Vanhaudenhuyse, A., Boly, M., Balteau, E., Schnakers, C., Moonen, G., Luxen, A., ... Faymonville, M. E. (2009). Pain and non-pain processing during hypnosis: A thulium-YAG event-related fMRI study. *NeuroImage, 47,* 1047–1054.

Vaquero, L., Hartmann, K., Ripollés, P., Rojo, N., Sierpowska, J., François, C., ... Altenmüller, E. (2016). Structural neuroplasticity in expert pianists depends on the age of musical training onset. *Neuroimage, 126,* 106–119. doi:10.1016/j.neuroimage.2015.11.008

Vaswani, M., Linda, F. K., & Ramesh, S. (2003). Role of selective serotonin reuptake inhibitors in psychiatric disorders: A comprehensive review. *Progress in Neuro-Psychopharmacology and Biological Psychiatry, 2,* 85–102.

Vaughan, W. (2009). Painless deprivation. *Science, 324*(5930), 1014.

Veith, I. (1965). *Hysteria: The history of a disease.* Chicago, IL: University of Chicago Press.

Veliz, P., McCabe, S. E., & Boyd, C. J. (2016). Extreme binge drinking among adolescent athletes: A cause for concern? *The American Journal on Addictions, 25,* 37–40. doi: 10.1111/ajad.12323

Vellas, B., Coley, N., Ouseet, P.-J., Bartigues, J.-F., Dubois, B., Grandjean, H., ... Andrieu, S. (2012). Long-term use of standardised ginkgo biloba extract for the prevention of Alzheimer's disease (GuidAge): A randomised placebo-controlled trial. *The Lancet Neurology, 11,* 851–859.

Venkatasubramanian, G., & Kalmady, S. V. (2010). Creativity, psychosis, and human evolution: The exemplar case of *neuregulin 1* gene. *Indian Journal of Psychiatry, 52,* 282.

Venning, A., Kettler, L., Eliott, J., & Wilson, A. (2009). The effectiveness of cognitive-behavioural therapy with hopeful elements to prevent the development of depression in young people: A systematic review. *International Journal of Evidence-Based Healthcare, 7,* 15–33. doi: 10.1111/j.1744-1609.2009.00122.x

Ventura-Bort, C., Löw, A., Wendt, J., Moltó, J., Poy, R., Dolcos, F., ... & Weymar, M. (2016). Binding neutral information to emotional contexts: Brain dynamics of long-term recognition memory. *Cognitive, Affective, & Behavioral Neuroscience, 16*(2), 234–247. doi: 10.3758/s13415-015-0385-0

Verburg-van Kemenade, B. L., Cohen, N., & Chadzinska, M. (2016). Neuroendocrine-immune interaction: Evolutionarily conserved mechanisms that maintain allostasis in an ever-changing environment. *Developmental & Comparative Immunology.* Available at http://dx.doi.org/10.1016/j.dci.2016.05.015

Verkhratsky, A., Rodriguez, J. J., & Parpura, V. (2012). Neuro transmitters and integration in neuronal-astroglial networks. *Neurochemistry Research, 37,* 2326–2338. doi: 10.1007/s11064-012-0765-6

Verquer, M. L., Beehr, T. A., & Wagner, S. H. (2003). A meta-analysis of relations between person-organization fit and work attitudes. *Journal of Vocational Behavior, 63,* 473–489.

Vetter, H. J. (1968). New-word coinage in the psychopathological context. *Psychiatric Quarterly, 42,* 298–312.

Vik, F. N., Bjørnarå, H. B., Overby, N. C., Lien, N., Androutsos, O., Maes, L., ... Bere, E. (2013). Associations between eating meals, watching TV while eating meals and weight status among children, ages 10–12 years in eight European countries: The ENERGY cross-sectional study. *The International Journal of Behavioral Nutrition and Physical Activity, 10,* 58. Available at http://doi.org/10.1186/1479-5868-10-58

Villemure, C., & Schweinhardt, P. (2010). Supraspinal pain processing: Distinct roles of emotion and attention. *The Neuroscientist, 16,* 276–284.

Vinson, G. A., Connelly, B. S., & Ones, D. S. (2007). Relationships between personality and organization switching: Implications for utility estimates. *International Journal of Selection and Assessment, 15,* 118–133.

Virginia Tech Transportation Institute. (July 29, 2009). *New data from Virginia Tech Transportation Institute provides insight into cell phone use and driving distraction.* Retrieved January 23, 2017. www.vtnews.vt.edu/articles/2009/07/2009-571.html

Virués-Ortega, J. (2010). Applied behavior analytic intervention for autism in early childhood: Meta-analysis, meta-regression and dose-response meta-analysis of multiple outcomes. *Clinical Psychology Review, 30,* 387–399.

Vo, M., Lau, J., & Rubinstein, M. (2016). Eating disorders in adolescent and young adult males: Presenting characteristics. *Journal of Adolescent Health.* Available at http://dx.doi.org/10.1016/j.jadohealth.2016.04.005

Vogel, E. A., Rose, J. P., Okdie, B. M., Eckles, K., & Franz, B. (2015). Who compares and despairs? The effect of social comparison orientation on social media use and its outcomes. *Personality and Individual Differences, 86,* 249–256. Available at http://doi.org/10.1016/j.paid.2015.06.026

Vogt Weisenhorn, D. M., Giesert, F., & Wurst, W. (2016). Diversity matters–heterogeneity of dopaminergic neurons in the ventral mesencephalon and its relation to Parkinson's disease. *Journal of Neurochemistry.* doi: 10.1111/jnc.13670

Von dem Hagen, E. A. H., Beaver, J. D., Ewbank, M. P., Keane, J., Passamonti, L., Lawrence, A. D., & Calder, A. J. (2009). Leaving a bad taste in your mouth but not in my insula. *Social Cognitive and Affective Neurosciences, 4,* 379–386.

Vyas, N. S., Patel, N. H., Nijran, K. S., Al-Nahhas, A., & Puri, B. K. (2010). Insights into schizophrenia using positron emission tomography: Building the evidence and refining the focus. *British Journal of Psychiatry, 197,* 3–4.

Vygotsky, L. S. (1978). *Mind and society: The development of higher psychological processes.* Cambridge, MA: Harvard University Press.

Wadlinger, H. A., & Isaacowitz, D. M. (2006). Positive mood broadens visual attention to positive stimuli. *Motivation & Emotion, 30,* 89–101.

Wadsworth, H. M., Maximo, J. O., Lemelman, A. R., Clayton, K., Sivaraman, S., Deshpande, H. D., ... & Kana, R. K. (2017). The action imitation network and motor imitation in children and adolescents with autism. *Neuroscience, 343,* 147–156. Available at http://dx.doi.org/10.1016/j.neuroscience.2016.12.001

Wagner, A. W., & Linehan, M. M. (2006). Applications of dialectical behavior therapy to posttraumatic stress disorder and related problems. In V. M. Folette & J. I. Ruzek (Eds.), *Cognitive-behavioral therapies for trauma* (2nd ed., pp. 117–145). New York, NY: Guilford Press.

Wagner, T. D., & Ochsner, K. N. (2005). Sex differences in the emotional brain. *NeuroReport, 16,* 85–87.

Wahlbeck, K., Forsen, T., Osmond, C., Barker, D. J. P., & Erikkson, J. G. (2001). Association of schizophrenia with low maternal body mass index, small size at birth, and thinness during childhood. *Archives of General Psychiatry, 58,* 48–55.

Wai, J., Lubinski, D., & Benbow, C. (2009). Spatial ability for STEM domains: Aligning over 50 years of cumulative psychological knowledge solidifies its importance. *Journal of Educational Psychology, 101,* 817–835.

Waite, L. J., Laumann, E. O., Das, A., & Schumm, L. P. (2009). Sexuality: Measures of partnerships, practices, attitudes, and problems in the National Social Life, Health, and Aging Study. *Journal of Gerontology: Social Sciences, 64B*(S1), i56–i66. doi: 10.1093/geronb/gbp038

Wakimoto, S., & Fujihara, T. (2004). The correlation between intimacy and objective similarity in interpersonal relationships. *Social Behavior and Personality, 32,* 95–102.

Waldinger, M. D., Zwinderman, A. H., Schweitzer, D. H., & Olivier, B. (2004). Relevance of methodological design for the interpretation of efficacy of drug treatment of premature ejaculation: A systematic review and meta-analysis. *International Journal of Impotence Research, 16,* 369–381.

Waldman, A. (2017). *A really good day: How micro-dosing made a mega difference in my mood, my marriage, and my life*. New York, NY: Knopf.

Walhovd, K. B., Fjell, A. M., Brown, T. T., Kuperman, J. M., Chung, Y., Hagler, D. R., … Dale, A. M. (2012). Long-term influence of normal variation in neonatal characteristics on human brain development. *Proceedings of the National Academy of Sciences of the United States of America, 109*(49), 20089–20094. doi: 10.1073/pnas.1208180109

Walhovd, K. B., Westerhausen, R., de Lange, A.-M. G., Bråthen, A. C. S., Grydeland, H., Engvig, A., & Fjell, A. M. (2016). Premises of plasticity—And the loneliness of the medial temporal lobe. *NeuroImage, 131*, 48–54. doi: 10.1016/j.neuroimage.2015.10.060

Walker, M., Thornton, L., De Choudhury, M., Teevan, J., Bulik, C. M., Levinson, C. A., & Zerwas, S. (2015). Facebook use and disordered eating in college-aged women. *Journal of Adolescent Health, 57*(2), 157–163. Available at http://doi.org/10.1016/j.jadohealth.2015.04.026

Walker, M. P., & Stickgold, R. (2006). Sleep, memory and plasticity. *Annual Review of Psychology, 57*, 139–166. doi: 10.1146/annurev.psych.56091103.070307

Walker, R. W., Skowronski, J. J., & Thompson, C. P. (2003). Life is pleasant—And memory helps to keep it that way. *Review of General Psychology, 7*, 203–210.

Wallace, B. A. (2006). *The attention revolution: Unlocking the power of the focused mind*. Boston, MA: Wisdom.

Wallas, G. (1926). *The art of thought*. New York, NY: Harcourt & Brace.

Wallhagen, M. I., Strawbridge, W. J., Cohen, R. D., & Kaplan, G. A. (1997). An increasing prevalence of hearing impairment and associated risk factors over three decades of Alameda County Study. *American Journal of Public Health, 87*, 440–442.

Wallien, M. C., & Cohen-Kettenis, P. T. (2008). Psychosexual outcome of gender-dysphoric children. *Journal of the American Academy of Child & Adolescent Psychiatry, 47*(12), 1413–1423. doi:10.1097/CHI.0b013e31818956b9

Walsh, S. P., White, K. M., & Young, R. M. (2009). The phone connection: A qualitative exploration of how belongingness and social identification relate to mobile phone use amongst Australian youth. *Journal of Community and Applied Social Psychology, 19*, 225–240. doi: 10.1002./casp.983

Wamsley, E. J., Tucker, M., Payne, J. D., Benavides, J. A., & Stickgold, R. (2010). Dreaming of a learning task is associated with enhanced sleep-dependent memory consolidation. *Current Biology, 20*, 850–855. doi: 10.1016/j.cub.2010.03.027

Wang, D. (2017). A study of the relationship between narcissism, extraversion, drive for entertainment, and narcissistic behavior on social networking sites. *Computers in Human Behavior, 66*, 138–148. Available at http://dx.doi.org/10.1016/j.chb.2016.09.036

Wang, J.-L., Jackson, L. A., Gaskin, J., & Wang, H.-Z. (2014). The effects of social networking site (SNS) use on college students' friendship and well-being. *Computers in Human Behavior, 37*, 229–236. Available at http://doi.org/10.1016/j.chb.2014.04.051

Wang, S., Zhang, Z., Guo, Y., Teng, G., & Chen, B. (2008). Hippocampal neurogenesis and behavioural studies on adult ischemic rat response to chronic mild stress. *Behavioural Brain Research, 189*, 9–16.

Wang, S., Zhou, M., Chen, T., Yang, X., Chen, G., Wang, M., & Gong, Q. (2016). Grit and the brain: Spontaneous activity of the dorsomedial prefrontal cortex mediates the relationship between the trait grit and academic performance. *Social Cognitive and Affective Neuroscience*, nsw145. doi: 10.1093/scan/nsw145

Wang, Z., Inslicht, S. S., Metzler, T. J., Henn-Haase, C., McCaslin, S. E., Tong, H., … Marmar, C. R. (2010). A prospective study of predictors of depression symptoms in police. *Psychiatry Research, 175*, 211–216.

Ward, J. (2013). Synesthesia. *Annual Review of Psychology, 64*, 49–75. doi: 10.1146/annurev-psych-113011-143840

Ware, M. A. (2016). Cannabis and cancer: Toward a new understanding. *Current Oncology, 23*(Suppl 2), S5–S6. http://doi.org/10.3747/co.23.3185

Warga, C. (1987). Pain's gatekeeper. *Psychology Today, 21*, 50–59.

Wason, P. C. (1960). On the failure to eliminate hypotheses in a conceptual task. *Quarterly Journal of Experimental Psychology, 12*, 129–140.

Wasserman, J. D., & Tulsky, D. S. (2005). A history of intelligence assessment. In D. P. Flanagan & P. L. Harrison (Eds.), *Contemporary intellectual assessment: Theories, tests, and issues* (pp. 3–38). New York, NY: Guilford Press.

Watanabe, T., Ito, M., Miyake, F., Ogawa, R., Tamura, M., & Namba, F. (2016). Measuring brain tissue oxygen saturation in term infants using new portable NIRS. *Pediatrics International*. doi: 10.1111/ped.13099

Watanabe, Y., Arase, S., Nagaoka, N., Kawai, M., & Matsumoto, S. (2016). Chronic psychological stress disrupted the composition of the murine colonic microbiota and accelerated a murine model of inflammatory bowel disease. *PloS ONE, 11*(3), e0150559. doi: 10.1371/journal.pone.0150559

Waterhouse, J. J., Atkinson, G. G., Edwards, B. B., & Reilly, T. T. (2007). The role of a short post-lunch nap in improving cognitive, motor, and sprint performance in participants with partial sleep deprivation. *Journal of Sports Sciences, 25*, 1557–1566.

Waterland, R., & Jirtle, R. L. (2003). Transposable elements: Targets for early nutritional effects on epigenetic gene regulation. *Molecular and Cellular Biology, 23*, 5293–5300.

Watkins, L. R., & Maier, S. F. (2003). When good pain turns bad. *Current Directions in Psychological Science, 12*, 232–236.

Watling, C. N., Armstrong, K. M., Smith, S. S., & Obst, P. L. (2016). Crash risk perception of sleepy driving and its comparisons with drink driving and speeding: Which behavior is perceived as the riskiest? *Traffic Injury and Prevention, 17*, 400–405. doi: 10.1080/15389588.2015.1096350

Watson, G. L., Arcona, A. P., & Antonuccio, D. O. (2015). The ADHD drug abuse crisis on American college campuses. *Ethical Human Psychology and Psychiatry, 17*(1), 5–21. http://dx.doi.org/10.1891/1559-4343.17.1.5

Watson, J. B. (1925). *Behaviorism*. New York, NY: Norton.

Watson, J. B., & Rayner, R. (1920). Conditioned emotional reactions. *Journal of Experimental Psychology, 3*, 1–14.

Watson, J. M., & Strayer, D. L. (2010). Supertaskers: Profiles in extraordinary multitasking ability. *Psychonomic Bulletin & Review, 17*, 479–485. doi: 10.3758/PBR.17.4.479

Watters, E. (2010). *Crazy like us: The globalization of the American psyche*. New York, NY: Free Press.

Waxenberg, S. E., Drellich, M. G., & Sutherland, A. M. (1959). The role of hormones in human behavior: I. Changes in female sexuality after adrenalectomy. *Journal of Clinical Endocrinology and Metabolism, 19*, 193–202.

Waxman, J., Van Lieshout, R. J., Saigal, S., Boyle, M. H., & Schmidt, L. A. (2013). Still cautious: Personality characteristics of extremely low birth weight adults in their early 30s. *Personality and Individual Differences, 55*(8), 967–971. doi: 10.1016/j.paid.2013.08.003

Way, B. M., Taylor, S. E., & Eisenberger, N. I. (2009). Variation in the i-opioid receptor gene (OPRM1) is associated with dispositional and neural sensitivity to social rejection. *Proceedings of the National Academy of Sciences, 106*, 15079–15084.

Weathers, S. B. (2000). *Left for dead: My journey home from Everest*. New York, NY: Villard Books (Kindle edition).

Weaver, D. (1998). The suprachiasmatic nucleus: A 25-year retrospective. *Journal of Biological Rhythms, 13*, 100–112.

Webb, H., Jirotka, M., Stahl, B. C., Housley, W., Edwards, A., Williams, M., … & Burnap, P. (2016). Digital wildfires: Hyper-connectivity, havoc and a global ethos to govern social media. *ACM SIGCAS Computers and Society, 45*(3), 193–201. Available at http://dx.doi.org/10.1145/2874239.2874267

Webb, L., Stegall, S., Mirabile, S., Zeman, J., Shields, A., & Perry-Parrish, C. (2016). The management and expression of pride: Age and gender effects across adolescence. *Journal of Adolescence, 52*, 1–11. Available at http://dx.doi.org/10.1016/j.adolescence.2016.06.009

Weber, J., & Wahl, J. (2006). Neurological aspects of trephinations from Neolithic times. *International Journal of Osteoarchaeology, 16*, 536–545.

Wechsler, D. (1944). *Measurement of adult intelligence* (3rd ed.). Baltimore, MD: Williams & Wilkins.

Wechsler, D. (1958). *The measurement and appraisal of adult intelligence* (4th ed.). Baltimore, MD: Williams & Wilkins.

Wechsler, H. L., Lee, J. E., & Kuo, M. (2002). Trends in college binge drinking during a period of increased prevention efforts. *Journal of American College Health, 50*, 203–217.

Weeks, J. C., & Hasher, L. (2016). Divided attention reduces resistance to distraction at encoding but not retrieval. *Psychonomic Bulletin & Review*. Available at http://doi.org/10.3758/s13423-016-1210-7

Weil, A., & Rosen, W. (1998). *From chocolate to morphine*. Boston, MA: Houghton Mifflin.

Weiland, B. J., Thayer, R. E., Depue, B. E., Sabbineni, A., Bryan, A. D., & Hutchison, K. E. (2015). Daily marijuana use is not associated with brain morphometric measures in adolescents or adults. *The Journal of Neuroscience, 35*, 1505–1512. doi:10.1523/JNEUROSCI.2946-14.2015

Weinberg, R. A. (1989). Intelligence and IQ: Issues and great debates. *American Psychologist, 44*, 98–104.

Weinberg, R. S., & Gould, D. (2007). *Foundations of sport and exercise psychology* (4th ed.). Champaign, IL: Human Kinetics.

Weinberger, D. R., Egan, M. F., Bertolino, A., Callicott, J. H., Mattay, V. S., Lipska, B. K., … Goldberg, T. E. (2001). Prefrontal neurons and the genetics of schizophrenia. *Biological Psychiatry, 50*, 825–844.

Weinberger, M., Hiner, S. L., & Tierney, W. M. (1987). In support of hassles as a measure of stress in predicting health outcomes. *Journal of Behavioral Medicine, 10*, 19–31.

Weinstein, T. A., Capitanio, J. P., & Gosling, S. D. (2008). Personality in animals. In O. P. John, R. W. Robins, & L. A. Pervin (Eds.), *Handbook of personality: Theory and research* (pp. 328–348). New York, NY: Guilford Press.

Weisinger, R. S., Denton, D. A., McKinley, M. J., Miselis, R. R., Park, R. G., & Simpson, J. B. (1993). Forebrain lesions that disrupt water homeostasis do not eliminate the sodium appetite of sodium deficiency in sheep. *Brain Research, 628*(1), 166–178. Available at http://dx.doi .org/10.1016/0006-8993(93)90952-J

Weissman, M. M., Wickramaratne, P., Gameroff, M. J., Warner, V., Pilowsky, D., Kohad, R. G., ... & Talati, A. (2016). Offspring of depressed parents: 30 years later. *American Journal of Psychiatry.* doi: 10.1176/appi.ajp.2016.15101327

Weitzman, E. D., Fukushima, D., Nogeire, C., Roffwarg, H., Gallagher, T. F., & Hellman, L. (1971). Twenty-four hour pattern of the episodic secretion of cortisol in normal subjects. *Journal of Clinical Endocrinology and Metabolism, 33,* 14–22.

Weller, J. A., Shackleford, C., Dieckmann, N., & Slovic, P. (2013). Possession attachment predicts cell phone use while driving. *Health Psychology, 32*(4), 379. doi: 10.1037/a0029265

Wellisch, D. K., & Cohen, M. (2011). In the midnight hour: Cancer and nightmares. A review of theories and interventions in psycho-oncology. *Palliative and Supportive Care, 9,* 191–200. doi: 20111478-9515/11

Wells, T. S., Seelig, A. D., Ryan, M. A., Jones, J. M., Hooper, T. I., Jacobson, I. G., & Boyko, E. J. (2015). Hearing loss associated with U.S. military combat deployment. *Noise Health, 17,* 34–42.

Wenden, A. L. (1998). Metacognitive knowledge and language learning. *Applied Linguistics, 19,* 515–537.

Weng, H. Y., Fox, A. S., Shackman, A. J., Stodola, D. E., Caldwell, J. Z. K., Olson, M. C., Rogers, G. M., & Davidson, R. J. (2013). Compassion training alters altruism and neural responses to suffering. *Psychological Science, 24,* 1171–1180. doi: 10.1177/0956797612469537

Wenger, E., & Lövdén, M. (2016). The learning hippocampus: Education and experience-dependent plasticity. *Mind, Brain, and Education, 10,* 171–183. doi: 10.1111/mbe.12112

Wermke, M., Sorg, C., Wohlschläger, A. M., & Drzezga, A. (2008, February 26). A new integrative model of cerebral activation, deactivation and default mode function in Alzheimer's disease. *European Journal of Nuclear Medicine and Molecular Imaging.*Advance online publication. doi: 10.1007/ s00259-007-0698-5

Werner, N. E., Cades, D. M., & Boehm-Davis, D. A. (2015). Multitasking and interrupted task performance: From theory to application. In L. D. Rosen, N. A. Cheever, L. M. Carrier, L. D. Rosen, N. A. Cheever, L. M. Carrier (Eds.), *The Wiley handbook of psychology, technology and society* (pp. 436–452). Wiley-Blackwell.

Wertheimer, M. (1959). *Productive thinking.* New York, NY: Harper.

Wessely, S., & Kerwin, R. (2004). Suicide risk and the SSRIs. *Journal of the American Medical Association, 292,* 379–381.

Westen, D., Blagov, P. S., Harenski, K., Kilts, C., & Hamann, S. (2006). Neural bases of motivated reasoning: An fMRI study of emotional constraints on partisan political judgment in the 2004 U.S. presidential election. *Journal of Cognitive Neuroscience, 18,* 1947–1958.

Westen, D., Gabbard, G. O., & Ortigo, K. M. (2008). Psychoanalytic approaches to personality. In O. P. John, R. W. Robins, & L. A. Pervin (Eds.), *Handbook of personality: Theory and research* (pp. 61–113). New York, NY: Guilford Press.

Westlye, L. T., Walhovd, K. B., Dale, A. M., Bjornerud, A., Due-Tonnessen, P., Engvig, A., ... Fjell, A. M. (2010). Life-span changes of the human brain white matter: Diffusion tensor imaging (DTI) and volumetry. *Cerebral Cortex, 20,* 2055–2068.

Westmaas, J. L., & Silver, R. C. (2006). The role of perceived similarity in supportive responses to victims of negative life events. *Personality and Social Psychology Bulletin, 32,* 1537–1546.

Weston, D. (1998). The scientific legacy of Sigmund Freud: Toward a psychodynamically informed psychological science. *Psychological Bulletin, 124,* 333–371.

Wethington, E. (2000). Expecting stress: Americans and the "midlife crisis." *Motivation & Emotion, 24,* 85–103.

Whalen, C. K., & Henker, B. (1998). Attention-deficit/hyperactivity disorder. In T. H. Ollendick & M. Hersen (Eds.), *Handbook of child psychopathology* (pp. 181–212). New York, NY: Plenum Press.

What causes Down syndrome? (2011). National Down Syndrome Society. Retrieved July 20, 2007, from http://www.ndss.org/index.php?option=com _content&view=article&id=60&Itemid=77

What people do and do not believe. (2009, December 15). Retrieved October 11, 2013, from www .harrisinteractive.com/vault/ Harris_Poll_2009_15_15.pdf

Whipps, J. M., Lewis, K., & Cooke, R. C. (1988). Mycoparasitism and plant disease control. In N. M. Burge (Ed.), *Fungi in biological control systems* (pp. 161–187). Manchester, UK: Manchester University Press.

White, A. M. (2003, Spring). What happened? Alcohol, memory blackouts, and the brain. *Alcohol Research & Health,* 186–196.

White, P. (2006). A background to acupuncture and its use in chronic painful musculoskeletal conditions. *Journal of the Royal Society of Health, 126,* 219–227.

White, R. (1964). *The abnormal personality.* New York, NY: Ronald Press.

White, R. W., & Horvitz, E. (2000). Cyberchondria: Studies of the escalation of medical concerns in Web search. *ACM Transactions on Information Systems (TOIS), 27.* Retrieved from http://doi.acm .org/10.1145/1629096.1629101

Whitfield, C. L., Dube, S. R., Felitti, V. J., & Anda, R. E. (2005). Adverse childhood experiences and hallucinations. *Child Abuse and Neglect, 29,* 797–810.

Whiting, B., & Edwards, C. (1988). *Children of different worlds: The formation of social behavior.* Cambridge, MA: Harvard University Press.

Whitlock, J. R., Heynen, A. J., Shuler, M. G., & Bear, M. F. (2006). Learning induces long-term potentiation in the hippocampus. *Science, 313,* 1093–1097.

Whitty, M. T., Doodson, J., Creese, S., & Hodges, D. (2017). A picture tells a thousand words: What Facebook and Twitter images convey about our personality. *Personality and Individual Differences,* 10–14. Available at https://doi .org/10.1016/j.paid.2016.12.050

Whorf, B. L. (1956). *Language, thought, and reality: Selected writings of Benjamin Lee Whorf* (J. B. Carroll, Ed.). Cambridge, MA: MIT Press.

Wickelgren, I. (2009, September/October). I do not feel your pain. *Scientific American Mind,* 51–57.

Wickens, T. D. (2002). *Elementary signal detection theory.* New York: NY: Oxford University Press.

Wieczorek, J., Blazejczyk , K., & Morita, T. (2016) Changes in melatonin secretion in tourists after rapid movement to another lighting zone without transition of time zone. *Chronobiology International, 33,* 220–233. doi: 10.3109/07420528.2015.1130050

Wiederhold, B. K., & Wiederhold, M. D. (2005). Specific phobias and social phobia. In B. K. Wiederhold & M. D. Wiederhold (Eds.), *Virtual reality therapy for anxiety disorders: Advances in evaluation and treatment* (pp. 125–138). Washington, DC: American Psychological Association.

Wilensky, A., Schafe, G., Kristensen, M., & LeDoux, J. (2006). Rethinking the fear circuit: The central nucleus of the amygdala is required for the acquisition, consolidation, and expression of Pavlovian fear conditioning. *Journal of Neuroscience, 26*(48), 12387–12396.

Wiley, C. (1997). What motivates employees according to over 40 years of motivation surveys. *International Journal of Manpower, 18*(3), 263–280.

Wilkening, F., & Sodian, B. (2005). Scientific reasoning in young children: An introduction. *Swiss Journal of Psychology, 64,* 137–139.

Wille, B., De Fruyt, F., & Feys, M. (2010). Vocational interests and Big Five traits as predictors of job instability. *Journal of Vocational Behavior, 76,* 547–558.

Williams, A. (2017). How LSD saved one woman's marriage. *The New York Times,* January 7, 2017. Available at https://www.nytimes.com/2017/01/07 /style/microdosing-lsd-ayelet-waldman-michael -chabon-marriage.html

Williams, G., Cai, X. J., Elliot, J. C., & Harrold, J. A. (2004). Anabolic neuropeptides. *Physiology and Behavior, 81,* 211–222.

Williams, K. D., & Zudro, L. (2001). Ostracism: On being ignored, excluded, and rejected. In M. R. Leary (Ed.), *Interpersonal rejection* (pp. 21–53). New York, NY: Oxford University Press.

Williams, R., Briggs, R., & Coleman, P. (1995). Career-rated personality changes associated with senile dementia. *International Journal of Geriatric Psychiatry, 10,* 231–236.

Williams, R. B., Jr., Haney, T. L., Lee, K. L., Kong, Y., Blumenthal, J. A., & Whalen, R. (1980). Type A behavior, hostility, coronary atherosclerosis. *Psychosomatic Medicine, 42,* 539–549.

Willis, S. L., Tennstedt, S. L., Marsiske, M., Ball, K., Elias, J., Koepke, K. M., ... for the ACTIVE Study Group. (2006). Long-term effects of cognitive training on everyday functional outcomes in older adults. *Journal of the American Medical Association, 295,* 2805–2814.

Wilson, T. D., Reinhard, D. A., Westgate, E. C., Gilbert, D. T., Ellerbeck, N., Hahn, C., & ... Shaked, A. (2014). Just think: The challenges of the disengaged mind. *Science, 345*(6192), 75–77. doi: 10.1126/science.1250830

Wimmer, H., & Perner, J. (1983). Beliefs about beliefs: Representation and constraining function of wrong beliefs in young children's understanding of deception. *Cognition, 13,* 103–128.

Winawer, J., Witthoft, N., Frank, M. C., Wu, L., Wade, A. R., & Boroditsky, L. (2007). Russian blues reveal effect of language on color discrimination. *Proceedings of the National Academy of Sciences, 104,* 7780–7785.

Windy, B., & Cleeremans, A. (2015). Consciousness as a graded and an all-or-none phenomenon: A conceptual analysis. *Consciousness and Cognition, 35,* 185–191. doi: org/10.1016/j.concog.2015.03.002

Wing, R., & Jeffery, R. (1999). Benefits of recruiting participants with friends and increasing social support for weight loss and maintenance. *Journal of Consulting and Clinical Psychology, 67,* 132–138.

Winward, J. L., Hanson, K. L., Tapert, S. F., & Brown, S. A. (2014). Heavy alcohol use, marijuana use, and concomitant use by adolescents are associated with unique and shared cognitive decrements. *Journal of the International*

Neuropsychological Society, 20(8), 784–795. doi:10.1017/S1355617714000666

Witelson, S. F., Kigar, D. L., Scamvougeras, A., Kideckel, D. M., Buck, B., Stanchev, P. L., Bronskill, M., & Black, S. (2008). Corpus callosum anatomy in right-handed homosexual and heterosexual men. Archives of Sexual Behavior, 37, 857–863.

Witkin, H. A., & Asch, S. E. (1948). Studies in space orientation. IV. Further experiments on perception of the upright with displaced visual fields. Journal of Experimental Psychology, 38, 762–782.

Witte, K., & Allen, M. (2000). A meta-analysis of fear appeals: Implications for effective public health campaigns. Health Education & Behavior, 27, 591–615.

Witten, I. B., Lin, S.-C., Brodsky, M., Prakash, R., Diester, I., Anikeeva, P., ... Deisseroth, K. (2010). Cholinergic interneurons control local circuit activity and cocaine conditioning. Science, 330, 1677–1681.

Wixted, J. T., & Cai, D. J. (2014). Memory consolidation. In K. Ochsner & S. Kosslyn (Eds.), Oxford handbook of cognitive neuroscience (pp. 1–59). New York: Oxford University Press.

Wölfling, K., Flor, H., & Grüsser, S. M. (2008). Psychophysiological responses to drug-associated stimuli in chronic heavy cannabis use. European Journal of Neuroscience, 27, 976–983.

Wolkowitz, O. M., Epel, E. S., Reus, V. I., & Mellon, S. H. (2010). Depression gets old fast: Do stress and depression accelerate cell aging? Depression and Anxiety, 27(4), 327–338. doi: 10.1002/da.20686

Wollmer, M. A., Boer, C., Kalak, N., Beck, J., ... Kruger, T. H. C. (2012). Facing depression with Botulinum toxin: A randomized controlled trial. Journal of Psychiatric Research, 46, 574–581.

Wong, C. C. Y., Caspi, A., Williams, B., Craig, I. W., Houts, R., Ambler, A., ... Mill, J. (2010). A longitudinal study of epigenetic variation in twins. Epigenetics, 5, 1–11.

Wood, A., Rychlowska, M., Korb, S., & Niedenthal, P. (2016). Fashioning the face: Sensorimotor simulation contributes to facial expression recognition. Trends in Cognitive Sciences, 20(3), 227–240. Available at http://dx.doi.org/10.1016/j.tics.2015.12.010

Wood, J. J., Ehrenreich-May, J., Alessandri, M., Fujii, C., Renno, P., Laugeson, E., ... & Murphy, T. K. (2015). Cognitive behavioral therapy for early adolescents with autism spectrum disorders and clinical anxiety: A randomized, controlled trial. Behavior Therapy, 46(1), 7–19. http://dx.doi.org/10.1016/j.beth.2014.01.002

Woodley of Menie, M. A., te Nijenhuis, J., Fernandes, H. F., & Metzen, D. (2016). Small to medium magnitude Jensen effects on brain volume: A meta-analytic test of the processing volume theory of general intelligence. Learning and Individual Differences, 51, 215–219. doi:10.1016/j.lindif.2016.09.007

Work-related hearing loss. (2001). National Institute for Occupational Safety and Health, NIOSH, Publication No. 2001-103. Retrieved from http://www.cdc.gov/niosh/docs/2001-103/

Wouters-Adriaens, M., & Westerterp, K. (2006). Basal metabolic rate as a proxy for overnight energy expenditure: The effect of age. British Journal of Nutrition, 95, 1166–1170.

Wright, J. S., & Panksepp, J. (2012). An evolutionary framework to understand foraging, wanting, and desire: The neuropsychology of the SEEKING system. Neuropsychoanalysis, 14(1), 5–39.

Wu, H., Luo, Y., & Feng, C. (2016). Neural signatures of social conformity: A coordinate-based activation likelihood estimation meta-analysis of functional brain imaging studies. Neuroscience &

Biobehavioral Reviews, 71, 101–111. Available at http://dx.doi.org/10.1016/j.neubiorev.2016.08.038

Wu, M., Kujawa, A., Lu, L. H., Fitzgerald, D. A., Klumpp, H., Fitzgerald, K. D., ... & Phan, K. L. (2016). Age-related changes in amygdala–frontal connectivity during emotional face processing from childhood into young adulthood. Human Brain Mapping. doi: 10.1002/hbm.23129

Wu, X., Chen, X., Han, J., Meng, H., ... Luo, J. (2013). Prevalence and factors of addictive Internet use among adolescents in Wuhan, China: Interactions of parental relationship with age and hyperactivity-impulsivity. PLoS ONE, 8, e61782. doi: 10.1371/journal.pone.0061782

Wu, X. S., Zhang, Z. H., Zhao, F., Wang, W. J., Li, Y. F., Bi, L., ... & Gong, F. F. (2016). Prevalence of Internet addiction and its association with social support and other related factors among adolescents in China. Journal of Adolescence, 52, 103–111. Available at http://dx.doi.org/10.1016/j.adolescence.2016.07.012

Wurtz, R. H., & Kandel, E. R. (2000a). Central visual pathways. In E. R. Kandel, J. H. Schwartz, & T. M. Jessell (2000). Principles of neural science (4th ed., pp. 523–545). New York, NY: McGraw-Hill.

Wurtz, R. H., & Kandel, E. R. (2000b). Perception of motion, depth, and form. In E. R. Kandel, J. H. Schwartz, & T. M. Jessell (Eds.), Principles of neural science (4th ed., pp. 548–571). New York, NY: McGraw-Hill.

Xia, M., Huang, R., Guo, V., Southall, N., Ming-Hsuang, C., Inglese, J., ... Nirenberg, M. (2009). Identification of compounds that potentiate CREB signaling as possible enhancers of long-term memory. Proceedings of the National Academy of Sciences, 106, 2412–2417. doi: 10.1073/pnas.0813020106

Xiang, J., Shen, H., & Li, J. (2009). Need-pressure trials of borderline personality disorder in Thematic Apperception Test. Chinese Mental Health Journal, 23, 340–344.

Xiao, Q., Signorello, L. B., Brinton, L. A., Cohen, S. S., Blot, W. J., & Matthews, C. E. (2016). Sleep duration and breast cancer risk among black and white women. Sleep Medicine 20, 25–29. doi: /10.1016/j.sleep.2015.11.010

Xie, L., Kang, H., Xu, Q., Chen, M. J., Liao, Y., Thiyagarajan, M., ... Nedergaard, M. (2013). Sleep drives metabolite clearance from the adult brain. Science, 342, 373–377. doi: 10.1126/science.1241224

Xu, F., & Garcia, V. (2008). Intuitive statistics by 8-month-old infants. Proceedings of the National Academy of Sciences, 105, 5012–5015.

Xu, F., Luk, C., Richard, M. P., Zaidi, W., Farkas, S., Getz, A., ... Syed, N. I. (2010). Antidepressant fluoxetine suppresses neuronal growth from both vertebrate and invertebrate neurons and perturbs synapse formation between Lymnaea neurons. European Journal of Neuroscience, 31, 994–1005.

Yaemsiri, S., Slining, M. M., & Agarwal, S. K. T. I. (2011). Perceived weight status, overweight diagnosis, and weight control among U.S. adults: The NHANES 2003–2008 Study. International Journal of Obesity, 35, 1063–1070. doi: 10.1038/ijo.2010.229

Yamada, M., & Yasuhara, H. (2004). Clinical pharmacology of MAO inhibitors: Safety and future. NeuroToxicology, 25, 215–221.

Yanagisawa, K., Masui, K., Furutani, K., Nomura, M., Ura, M., & Yoshida, H. (2011). Does higher general trust serve as a psychosocial buffer against social pain? An NIRS study of social exclusion. Social Neuroscience, 6, 190–197. doi: 10.1080/17470919.2010.506139

Yang, Y., Raine, A., Han, C.-B., Schug, R. A., Toga, A. W., & Narr, K. L. (2010). Reduced

hippocampal and parahippocampal volumes in murderers with schizophrenia. Psychiatry Research: Neuroimaging, 182, 9–13.

Yang, Y., Raine, A., Narr, K. L., Colletti, P., & Toga, A. W. (2009). Localization of deformations within the amygdala in individuals with psychopathy. Archives of General Psychiatry, 66, 966–994. doi: 10.1001.archgenpsychiatry.2009.110

Yannis, G., Laiou, A., Papantoniou, P., & Gkartzonikas, C. (2016). Simulation of texting impact on young drivers' behavior and safety on motorways. Transportation Research Part F: Traffic Psychology and Behaviour, 41(Part A), 10–18. doi: 10.1016/j.trf.2016.06.003

Yao, Y., Kelly, M. T., Sajikumar, S., Serrano, P., Tian, D., Bergold, P. J., ... Sacktor, T. C. (2008). PKM maintains late long-term potentiation by N-ethylmaleimmide-sensitive factor/GluR2-dependent trafficking of postsynaptic AMPA receptors. Journal of Neuroscience, 28, 7820–7827. doi: 10.1523/JNEUROSCI.0223-08.2008

Yates, D. (2016). Synaptogenesis: A synaptic bridge. Nature Reviews Neuroscience, 17(3), 135. doi: 10.1038/nrn.2016.12

Ybarra, M. L., & Mitchell, K. J. (2008). How risky are social networking sites? A comparison of places online where youth sexual solicitation and harassment occurs. Pediatrics, 121, e350–e357. doi: 10.1542/peds.2007.0693

Yeragani, V. K., Tancer, M., Chokka, P., & Baker, G. B. (2010). Arvid Carlsson, and the story of dopamine. Indian Journal of Psychiatry, 52, 87–88. Retrieved from http://www.indianjpsychiatry.org/text.asp?2010/52/1/87/58907

Yerkes, R. M., & Dodson, J. D. (1908). The relation of strength of stimulus to rapidity of habit-formation. Journal of Comparative Neurology and Psychology, 18, 459–482.

Yin, D.-M., Chen, Y.-J., Lu, Y.-S., Bean, J. C., Sathyamurthy, A., Shen, C., ... Mei, L. (2013). Reversal of behavioral deficits and synaptic dysfunction in mice overexpressing neuregulin 1. Neuron, 78, 644–657. doi: 10.1016/j.neuron2013.03.028

Yin, J. C. P., Del Vecchio, M., Zhou, H., & Tully, T. (1995). CREB as a memory modulator: Induced expression of a dCREB2 activator isoform enhances long-term memory in Drosophila. Cell, 81, 107–115.

Yoder, A. M., Widen, S. C., & Russell, J. A. (2016). The word disgust may refer to more than one emotion. Emotion, 16(3), 301–308. Retrieved from http://search.proquest.com/docview/1735911568?accountid=14505

Yoemans, N. D. (2011). The ulcer sleuths: The search for the cause of peptic ulcers. Journal of Gastroenterology and Hepatology, 26(Suppl. s1), 35–41.

Yoon, J., & Thye, S. (2000). Supervisor support in the work place: Legitimacy and positive affectivity. Journal of Social Psychology, 140, 295–316.

Young, L. C., Zaun, B. J., & VanderWerf, E. A. (2008). Successful same-sex pairing in Laysan albatross. Biology Letters, 4, 323–325.

Young, S., Taylor, M., & Lawrie, S. M. (2015). "First do no harm." A systematic review of the prevalence and management of antipsychotic adverse effects. Journal of Psychopharmacology 29.4, 353-362. doi: 10.1177/0269881114562090

Youssef, N. A., Belew, D., Hao, G., Wang, X., Treiber, F. A., Stefanek, M., ... & Su, S. (2017). Racial/ethnic differences in the association of childhood adversities with depression and the role of resilience. Journal of Affective Disorders, 208, 577–581. Available at http://dx.doi.org/10.1016/j.jad.2016.10.024

Youyou, W., Kosinski, M., & Stillwell, D. (2015). Computer-based personality judgments are more accurate than those made by humans. *Proceedings of the National Academy of Sciences, 112*(4), 1036–1040. Available at http://doi.org/10.1073/pnas.1418680112

Yu, A. Y., Tian, S. W., Vogel, D., & Kwok, R. C.-H. (2010). Can learning be virtually boosted? An investigation of online social networking impacts. *Computers & Education, 55*, 1494–1503.

Yuen, E. K., Herbert, J. D., Forman, E. M., Goetter, E. M., Comer, R., & Bradley, J. (2013). Treatment of social anxiety disorder using online virtual environments in *Second Life. Behavior Therapy, 44*, 51–61.

Yushkevich, P. A., Amaral, R. C., Augustinack, J. C., Bender, A. R., Bernstein, J. D., Boccardi, M., & ... Zeineh, M. M. (2015). Quantitative comparison of 21 protocols for labeling hippocampal subfields and parahippocampal subregions in in vivo MRI: Towards a harmonized segmentation protocol. *Neuroimage, 111*, 526–541. doi:10.1016/j.neuroimage.2015.01.004

Zajonc, R. B. (1965). Social facilitation. *Science, 149*, 269–274.

Zajonc, R. B. (1968). Attitudinal effects of mere exposure. *Journal of Personality and Social Psychology, 9*, 1–27.

Zak, P. J., Stanton, A. A., & Ahmadi, S. (2007). Oxytocin increases generosity in humans. *PLoS ONE, 2*, 1–5.

Zaki, J., Wager, T. D., Singer, T., Keysers, C., & Gazzola, V. (2016). The anatomy of suffering: Understanding the relationship between nociceptive and empathic pain. *Trends in Cognitive Sciences, 20*(4), 249–259. Available at http://doi.org/10.1016/j.tics.2016.02.003

Zarka, P. (2011). Astronomy and astrology. *Proceedings of the International Astronomical Union, 5*, 420–425. doi:10.1017/S1743921311002602

Zeidan, F., Martucci, K. T., Kraft, R. A., Gordon, N. S., McHaffie, J. G., & Coghill, R. C. (2011). Brain mechanisms supporting the modulation of pain by mindfulness meditation. *Journal of Neuroscience, 31*, 5540–5548.

Zeino, Z., Sisson, G., & Bjarnason, I. (2010). Adverse effects of drugs on small intestine and colon. *Best Practice & Research Clinical Gastroenterology, 24*, 133–141.

Zelaya, C. E., Lucas, J. W., & Hoffman, H. J. (2015). Self-reported hearing trouble in adults aged 18 and over: United States, 2014. *NCHS Data Brief* (214), 1–8. Retrieved from http://ovidsp.ovid.com/ovidweb.cgi?T=JS&PAGE=reference&D=medl&NEWS=N&AN=26462204

Zhang, L. (2010). Do thinking styles contribute to metacognition beyond self-rated abilities? *Educational Psychology, 30*, 481–494. doi:10.1080/01443411003659986

Zhang, R., Wang, Y. Q., & Su, B. (2008). Molecular evolution of a primate-specific microRNA family. *Molecular Biology and Evolution, 25*(7), 1493–1502. Available at http://doi.org/10.1093/molbev/msn094

Zhang, Y., Jin, X., Shen, X., Zhang, J., & Hoff, E. (2008). Correlates of early language development in Chinese children. *International Journal of Behavioral Development, 32*, 145–151. doi: 10.1177/0165025407087213

Zhao, Y., Montoro, R., Igartua, K., & Thombs, B. D. (2010). Suicidal ideation and attempt among adolescents reporting "unsure" sexual identity or heterosexual identity plus same-sex attraction or behavior: Forgotten groups? *Journal of the American Academy of Child & Adolescent Psychiatry, 49*(2), 104–113. doi: 10.1097/00004583-201002000-00004

Zhou, J. N., Hofman, M. A., Gooren, L. J., & Swaab, D. F. (1995). A sex difference in the human brain and its relation to transsexuality. *Nature, 378*, 68–70.

Zhou, R., We, C., Patrick Rau, P.-L., & Zhang, W. (2009). Young driving learners' intention to use a handheld or hands-free mobile phone when driving. *Transportation Research Part F: Traffic and Behaviour, 12*, 208–217. doi: 10.1016/j.trf.2008.11.003

Zhu, B., Chen, C., Loftus, E. F., He, Q., Chen, C., Lei, X., ... Dong, Q. (2012). Brief exposure to misinformation can lead to long-term false memories. *Applied Cognitive Psychology, 26*(2), 301–307. Available at http://doi.org/10.1002/acp.1825

Zhu, B., Chen, C., Loftus, E. F., Lin, C., He, Q., Chen, C., & ... Dong, Q. (2010a). Individual differences in false memory from misinformation: *Cognitive factors. Memory, 18*(5), 543–555. doi: 10.1080/09658211.2010.487051

Zhu, B., Chen, C., Loftus, E. F., Lin, C., He, Q., Chen, C., & ... Dong, Q. (2010b). Individual differences in false memory from misinformation: Personality characteristics and their interactions with cognitive abilities. *Personality and Individual Differences, 48*(8), 889–894. doi: 10.1016/j.paid.2010.02.016

Ziegler, G., Dahnke, R., Winkler, A. D., & Gaser, C. (2013). Partial least squares correlation of multivariate cognitive abilities and local brain structure in children and adolescents. *NeuroImage, 82*, 284–294.

Zigler, E. F., Finn-Stevenson, M., & Hall, N. W. (2002). *The first three years and beyond.* New Haven, CT: Yale University Press.

Zimbardo, P. (2007). *The Lucifer effect: Understanding how good people turn evil.* New York, NY: Random House.

Zimmer, C. (2005, March 1). Looking for personality in animals, of all people. *The New York Times.* Retrieved from http://www.nytimes.com

Zimmer, C. (2015, March 5). Is most of our DNA garbage? Retrieved October 25, 2016 at *New York Times Magazine*, published online at http://www.nytimes.com/2015/03/08/magazine/is-most-of-our-dna-garbage.html?_r=0

Zimmer-Gembeck, M. J., & Collins, W. A. (2008). Gender, mature appearance, alcohol use, and dating as correlates of sexual partner accumulation from ages 16–26 years. *Journal of Adolescent Health, 42*, 564–572.

Zimmerman, C. (2007). The development of scientific thinking skills in elementary and middle school. *Developmental Review, 27*, 172–223.

Zimmermann, J., & Neyer, F. J. (2013). Do we become a different person when hitting the road? Personality development of sojourners. *Journal of Personality and Social Psychology, 105*(3), 515–530. doi: 10.1037/a0033019

Zullig, K., Pun, S., & Huebner, E. (2007). Life satisfaction, dieting behavior, and weight perceptions among college students. *Applied Research in Quality of Life, 2*(1), 17–31.

Name Index

Karnath, H., 279, 280
Karns, C. M., 148
Karpiak, C. P., 632
Karpinski, A. C., 70
Karwowski, M., 401
Kashdan, T., 467
Kashdan, T. B., 430
Kasikci, Z., 263, 264
Kaslow, N. J., 251
Kass, A. E., 418
Kaszniak, A. W., 227
Katon, W., 170
Katusic, S. K., 574
Katyal, K. D., 102
Katz, M. M., 279
Kaube, H., 150, 444, 556, 557
Kaufman, A. S., 375, 376, 377
Kaufman, J., 169
Kaufman, J. C., 388, 394, 401, 506
Kaufman, N. L., 376, 377
Kaufman, S. B., 368, 506
Kaul, P., 237
Kaul, S., 363
Kaviani, H., 634
Kawachi, I., 469
Kawamura, Y., 154
Kawashima, R., 290, 395, 397
Kawashima, T., 579
Kawikova, I., 594
Kay, P., 346
Kaye, L., 439
Kaysen, D., 545
Kayser, S., 619
Kazdin, A. E., 610
Kazemi, A., 487
Kazlauskaite, R., 481
Keane, J., 445
Keane, S. P., 635
Keck, P. E., 79
Keeler, R. F., 169
Keenan, R. M., 248
Keerkens, J., 584
Kegeles, L. S., 580
Kehle, S., 628
Kekic, M., 617
Keles, S., 233, 234
Kell, H. J., 382
Keller, A., 487
Keller, M. C., 177, 385, 556, 558
Keller, T. A., 222
Kelley, H. H., 536, 554
Kelley, M. E., 251
Kellman, P. J., 173
Kellner, C. H., 621
Kelly, D. R., 470
Kelly, K. R., 518
Kelly, M. T., 278
Kelso, J. R., 79
Keltikangas-Järvinen, L., 201, 521
Keltner, D., 433, 439, 440, 555
Kemeny, M., 584
Kemeny, M. E., 469
Kempermann, G., 108, 203, 205, 327
Kempton, M. J., 631
Kenardy, J., 451
Kendal, R., 513
Kendler, K. S., 91, 246, 568, 584, 591
Kendrick, T., 619
Kenkel, J. M. Fagien, S., 442
Kennedy, J. L., 91
Kennedy, J. M., 115, 116
Kennedy, S., 618
Kennedy, S. H., 618, 619
Kennedy, W. A., 443
Kenning, P., 407
Kenny, S., 224
Kenrick, D. T., 410, 411, 430
Kensinger, E. A., 240, 263, 264
Kerber, R. A., 471
Keri, S., 604
Kerig, P., 381
Kerkhoff, G., 283
Kern, M. L., 70

Kernic, M. A., 30, 223
Kerns, J. C., 415
Kerr, C., 227
Kerr, T. K., 292
Kershaw, T. C., 265
Kerwin, R., 614, 640
Keshavan, M., 193, 194
Kessing, L., 583
Kessler, H., 447
Kessler, R. C., 571, 574, 588, 597, 602, 634, 640
Kettler, L., 628
Key Learning Community, 374
Keyes, C. L. M., 451, 452
Keyes, S., 521
Keysers, C., 150, 444
Khader, Y., 328
Khaire, M., 427, 428
Khalesi, Z., 601
Khallou-Laschet, J., 91
Khan, M. A., 420
Khandaker, G. M., 170
Khandawood, F., 420
Khatami, M., 464
Khazeni, N., 471
Kheirbek, M. A., 280
Khemekhem, S., 208
Khoury, J., 575
Khouzam, A., 383
Kibbe, A., 334
Kidd, K. K., 387
Kideckel, D. M., 423
Kidman, A. D., 468
Kiecolt-Glaser, J. K., 476, 584
Kieras, D. E., 224
Kieras, J. E., 188
Kiersky, J. E., 620
Kigar, D. L., 423
Kihlstrom, J. F., 596
Kijima, N., 521
Kikuchi, S., 482
Kilburn, J., 551
Kilgore, K. L., 102
Killeya-Jones, L. A., 584
Killgore, D. B., 236
Killgore, W. D. S., 236
Killian, J. M., 574
Kilts, C., 501
Kim, B., 633
Kim, B.-K., 483
Kim, C.-J., 483
Kim, D. A., 4
Kim, E. S., 640
Kim, H. K., 401
Kim, H. O., 248
Kim, J., 126, 425
Kim, J. S., 205
Kim, K. H. S., 361, 362, 363
Kim, M. H., 246
Kim, S., 203
Kim, S. G., 106, 117
Kim, S.-E., 483
Kim, Y., 542, 575, 633
Kim, Y. J., 520
Kimball, J., 498
Kimbrell, T. A., 615
Kimbro, R. T., 416
Kimeldorf, D. J., 314, 315, 474
Kimura, D., 351
Kincses, T. Z., 283
Kind, S., 471
Kindt, M., 278, 285, 615
King, B. G., 227
King, D. E., 246
King, K. A., 449
King, K. M., 30, 223
King, L., 81, 84, 89, 95, 134, 146
King, L. A., 451, 467
King, S., 464
Kingery, K. M., 223
Kingsbury, R., 541
Kinney, D. K., 603, 604
Kinnish, K. K., 424
Kinsey, A. C., 48, 421

Kinsley, C. H., 105
Kirby, K. C., 309
Kirby, K. N., 349
Kircher, T., 85
Kirilina, E., 444
Kirisoglu, C., 237
Kiritani, S., 336
Kirk, K. M., 420, 423
Kirk, S. B., 467
Kirkham, T. C., 412
Kirkpatrick, B., 471
Kirkpatrick, L. A., 184
Kirk-Sanchez, N. J., 483
Kirsch, I., 620
Kirsch, R. F., 102
Kirschner, P., 70
Kirsh, S. J., 551
Kisilevsky, B. S., 168
Kitayama, S., 157, 554
Kitlinska, J. B., 482
Kiyonari, T., 445
Kjær, M. S., 481
Klahr, D., 192
Klarman, L., 362
Klauer, S. G., 222
Klavans, R., 6
Klebanoff, M. A., 578
Kleiman, S. C., 418
Klein, D. A., 309
Klein, D. J., 329
Klein, H. S., 198
Klein, L., 202
Klein, R. A., 42
Klein, R. G., 93
Klein, S., 584
Klein-Schwartz, W., 247
Kleitman, N., 230
Klesges, R. C., 329
Klimstra, T. A., 511
Klinedinst, M. A., 638
Klinger, É., 630
Klinger, N., 110
Klink, D., 199
Klinnert, M. D., 187, 437
Klocke, U., 224
Kloosterman, K., 122
Klopfer, P. H., 529
Klucharev, V., 532
Klumpp, H., 98, 601
Klüver, H., 98
Knafo, A., 445
Knapp, R. G., 621
Knickmeyer, R. C., 578
Knight, G. P., 511
Knight, R., 584
Knight, R. T., 99, 281
Knight, Z. A., 412
Knopik, V. S., 77, 79, 80
Knösche, T. R., 111
Knowlton, B., 5, 225
Knox, R., 147
Knudsen, G. M., 91
Knuth, N. D., 415
Ko, I.-G., 483
Kobayakawa, T., 157
Kobayashi, M., 157
Koch, C., 96, 132
Koch, I., 326
Koda, S., 97
Kodish, I. M., 577
Koegel, L. K., 309
Koelega, H. S., 124
Koelling, R. A., 314, 315, 316, 474
Koenig, J. I., 170, 578
Koenig, O., 263, 264
Koepke, K. M., 203, 210
Koerner, K., 635
Koga, Y., 480
Kogan, A., 555
Koh, J. S., 248
Kohad, R. G., 91
Kohlberg, L., 182–183
Kohn, P. M., 459

Kokaua, T. J., 571
Kokko, K., 201
Kolb, B., 101
Koldny, J., 384
Komaroff, A. L., 479
Komarov, I., 615
Kometer, M., 252
Komisaruk, B. R., 419
Kondziella, D., 217, 218
Kong, Y., 478
Konrad, K., 326
Koo, D. S., 362
Kooperberg, C., 471
Koopmans, J., 468
Kopell, B. H., 99
Koppel-staetter, F., 245
Kopta, S. M., 628
Korb, S., 442
Korkeila, J., 479
Korkeila, M., 451
Korman, K., 351
Kornacki, T., 164
Kornell, N., 260, 292, 293
Kornhaber, M. L., 373, 374
Korpert, K., 147
Kortekaas, R., 419, 429
Koshenvuo, M., 451
Kosinski, M., 70, 517, 519, 520
Koslowski, B., 39, 353
Kosmidis, M. H., 416
Kosslyn, S. M., 349
Kottke, J. L., 428
Kounios, J., 98, 307
Koutstaal, W., 547
Kovács, A. M., 363
Kovacs, M., 188
Kovas, Y., 377
Koven, N. S., 603
Kowalski, R. M., 425
Kozbelt, A., 506
Kraaj, V., 466
Kraehenmann, R., 638
Kraemer, H. C., 468
Kraft, R. A., 226
Krahe, T. E., 170
Krakauer, J., 406
Kralovec, P. D., 206
Kramarik, A., 381
Kramer, A. D. I., 71
Kramer, A. F., 204, 205, 209, 210, 223, 327, 483
Kramer, S. J., 428
Kranczioch, C., 215
Kraus, N., 176
Krause, M. S., 628
Kravitz, E. A., 550
Krebs, T. S., 637, 639
Krech, D., 326
Kreiger, T., 199
Kreiman, G., 132
Kremer, S., 202
Kreukels, B. C., 196
Kreukels, B. P. C., 199, 424
Krietemeyer, J., 226
Kril, J. J., 483
Kring, A. M., 633
Kringelbach, M. L., 90
Kristeller, J., 485
Kristeller, J. L., 219, 635
Kristensen, M., 443
Kristjansson, A. L., 195
Kristof-Brown, A. L., 518, 519
Kroeber, A. L., 158
Kroes, M. C. W., 285
Kroeze, J. H., 202
Kroft, J., 91
Kröger, C., 635
Krogh-Nielsen, L., 612
Krohn, E., 378
Kromhout, D., 481
Krook, A., 483
Krueger, R. F., 509, 510, 521, 584, 599
Kruger, M. C., 575
Krüger, S., 618

Stampfer, M. J., 415, 482
Stanchev, P. L., 423
Stanford, V. A., 482
Stanko-Kaczmarek, M., 431
Stanley, J., 381
Stanley, S. M., 201
Stanton, A. A., 445
Stanton, A. L., 467
Stanton, C., 584
Stanwell-Smith, R., 480
Stark, C. E. L., 274, 287
Stark, S. M., 274
Starr, C., 78
Starr, J., 378
Starr, J. M., 363, 388
Staub, D. R., 584
Steel, P., 30, 222, 223
Steen, R. G., 66
Steensma, T. D., 196, 424
Steers, M. L. N., 543
Stefanek, M., 583
Stefanick, M. L., 414
Stefansson, H., 577
Steffen, J., 85
Stein, D., 632
Stein, D. J., 483
Steinberg, L., 194, 195
Steinberg, S., 577
Steiner, A. M., 309
Steiner, B., 205
Steiner, C., 485
Steiner, J., 83
Steinhausen, H., 386
Steinmetz, C., 518
Steinmetz, H., 176
Stek, M. L., 640
Steketee, G., 568
Stellar, E., 411
Stelmack, R. M., 124
Stelzer, A., 193
Stenberg, C. R., 187
Stenger, A., 242
Stepanski, L. M., 237
Stephane, M., 579
Stephens, T., 391
Stepper, S., 441
Steptoe, A., 469
Sterling, P., 463
Stern, E., 579
Stern, K., 420
Stern, P. C., 538
Stern, S. A., 278
Stern, W., 375
Sternberg, R. J., 349, 352, 363, 368,
    372, 387, 389, 560
Stevens, E., 336, 337
Stevens, J. S., 448
Stevens, S. B., 31
Stevenson, R. J., 429, 430
Stewart, J. H., 240, 241
Stewart, R. A., 172
Stewart, V. M., 156
Stice, E., 640
Stickgold, R., 235, 260, 264
Stiles, J., 176
Stiles, W. B., 628
Stillwell, D., 517, 519, 520
Stine-Morrow, E. A. L., 209, 210
Stinglhamber, F., 428
Stinson, F. S., 590
Stockwell, T., 481
Stodola, D. E., 556
Stoléru, S., 98, 101, 419
Stone, J., 581
Storandt, M., 523
Storemark, S. S., 236
Stowell, C., 642
Stowell, G. S., 199
Strachan, D. P., 480
Strack, F., 441
Straif, K., 251, 481
Strang, S., 407
Strange, B. A., 264, 285

Strassberg, D. S., 424
Strassman, R. J., 252, 639
Straub, R. E., 636
Straube, A., 218
Straube, B., 85
Straus, R., 477
Strausfeld, N. J., 93
Strauss, D., 420
Strauss, M. E., 523
Strawbridge, W. J., 202
Strayer, D. L., 30, 71, 208, 225
Strazzullo, P., 233
Street, G. P., 634
Streissguth, A., 381, 386
Streissguth, A. P., 587
Striano, T., 187
Striedter, G., 93
Strombach, T., 407
Stroodley, C. J., 96
Stroop, J. R., 241
Strotmann, J., 153
Stroup, T. S., 612, 620
Strouse, G. A., 207
Strueber, D., 550, 600
Strunk, J., 286
Strycker, L. A., 196
Studerus, E., 252
Stuetzle, R., 467
Stuewig, J., 432, 433
Stuppaeck, C., 615
Sturm, V., 619
Stuss, D. T., 99
Stuve, P., 309
Styer, T., 71
Styles, E. A., 219, 220
Styner, M., 578
Styron, W., 582–583
Su, S., 583
Su, W., 202
Suarez, A., 633
Suarez, E. C., 478
Suarez, L., 469
Subrahmanyam, K., 30, 520
Subramaniam, K., 98
Succop, P., 381, 386
Suchak, M., 555
Sucharski, I., 428
Suchotzki, K., 538
Sudo, N., 480
Sugden, K., 91, 585
Suh, E. M., 450, 451
Suh, S., 633
Sulaiman, A. H., 147
Sullivan, E. V., 245
Sullivan, K., 182
Sullivan, P. F., 509
Sumter, S. R., 266
Sun, X., 233
Sundquist, J., 246, 418
Sundquist, K., 246, 418
Sung, C. Y., 464
Sunsay, C., 303
Suntinger, W., 522
Suomi, S., 91
Supekar, K., 383
Suplita, R. L., 251
Susser, E., 169
Susskind, J. M., 447
Sutandar, K., 618
Sutherland, A. M., 420
Sutherland, I., 248, 481
Sutton, C., 399
Suvak, M., 642
Svanström, H., 612
Svarer, C., 91
Svartengrenf, M., 144, 200
Svendsen, H. A., 523
Swaab, D. F., 199
Swahari, V., 173
Swaminathan, S., 170
Swanson, S. A., 417
Swartz, K., 612
Swartz, M. S., 612, 620

Sweatt, J. D., 80
Sweeney, L., 234
Swets, J. A., 125
Swift, A., 223
Swing, E. L., 551
Sworowski, L. A., 467
Syed, M., 196, 199
Syed, N. I., 620
Sykes, D. H., 479
Sykes, J. M., 442
Szabo, Yvette, 6–7
Szaflarski, J. P., 342, 343
Szaluta, J., 498
Szarko, R., 147
Szentagotai, A., 620
Szyf, M., 476

T

Taatgen, N. A., 224, 225, 601
Tager-Flusberg, H., 182
Taggart, R., 78
Takahashi, Y., 164, 521
Takahashia, R., 464
Takeuchi, H., 290, 395, 397
Taki, Y., 290, 395, 397
Talati, A., 91, 169
Talmi, D., 272
Tambs, K., 147
Tamin, R. M., 56
Tamm, L., 223
Tamm, S., 283
Tammet, D., 275, 383
Tamura, M., 111, 479
Tan, A., 56
Tan, V., 459
Tanabe, J., 291
Tanaka, K. F., 280
Tandon, S., 419
Tang, Z., 196
Tangney, J. P., 432, 433
Tanis, M., 425
Tapert, S. F., 251
Tardif, T., 337
Tare, M., 363
Tarlatzis, B., 467
Tarmann, A., 421
Tarrasch, R., 226
Tartter, V. C., 440
Tarver, J., 311
Tashkin, D. P., 251
Tashkin, D. R., 251
Tatirovsky, E., 479
Tau, B., 528, 529
Taub, E., 176
Tavris, C., 571
Taylor, A., 91, 510, 571, 585
Taylor, C. B., 418
Taylor, D., 639
Taylor, H. A., 279
Taylor, K. N., 633
Taylor, M., 205
Taylor, O. D., 249
Taylor, R. D., 449
Taylor, S. E., 469, 528
Taylor, S. F., 444, 594
Taylor, W. C., 416
te Nijenhuis, J., 383, 384
Teachman, B. A., 545
Teasdale, D. J. D., 226, 632, 633, 634, 641
Teevan, J., 209
Tein, J. Y., 476
Tell, R. A., 620
Tellegen, A., 509, 517, 518
Tempelmann, C., 154
ten Brinke, L. F., 290
Tendolkar, I., 285
Teng, G., 464
Teng, M., 248
Tennstedt, S. L., 203, 210
Teo, K., 483
Terman, L., 375

Terracciano, A., 509, 511
Terrace, H. S., 345
Terwindt, A. P. R., 588
Tessner, K. D., 193
Teuber, H. L., 276
Thabet, S., 578
Thagard, P., 349
Thakkinstian, A., 235
Thal, D. J., 336
Thapar, A., 56, 79, 510
Thayer, R. E., 251
Themanson, J. R., 175
Theorell, T., 478
Théoret, H., 187, 324
Therriault, D., 522
Therriault, D. J., 397
Thibaut, J. W., 554
Thierry, B., 512
Thierry, G., 334
Thiessen, D., 556, 558
Thiyagarajan, M., 233, 234
Thomas, A., 184
Thombs, B. D., 195
Thompson, C., 619
Thompson, C. P., 266
Thompson, P., 384
Thompson, P. M., 193
Thompson, P. O., 145
Thompson, R. F., 260, 269, 270,
    272, 281
Thompson, S., 626
Thompson, W. L., 349
Thompson, W. R., 79
Thompson-Cannino, J., 258, 286
Thomson, A. L., 432
Thorndike, E. L., 304
Thornhill, R., 559
Thornton, L., 209
Thornton, L. M., 418
Thorp, S. R., 632
Thorsteinsson, E. B., 449
Thune, I., 482
Thye, S., 428
Tian, D., 278
Tian, S. W., 425
Tiana, J., 635
Tielbeek, J. J., 509
Tierney, W. M., 459
Tighe, E. M., 427
Tignol, J., 593
Tilan, J. U., 482
Tillisch, K., 584
Tims, L. A., 251
Tippett, L. J., 397
Titman, N., 199
Tjønneland, A., 481
Tobe, E. H., 584
Tobias, J. D., 413
Tobias, S., 363
Tobin, D. J., 471
Toca-Herrera, J.-L., 207
Todd, R. D., 618
Toga, A. W., 193, 550, 580, 600
Toguri, C., 154
Tolin, D. F., 628, 642
Tolman, E. C., 318
Tolstrup, J. S., 481
Tomann, A., 106
Tomasello, M., 343
Tomiyama, A., 471
Tomiyama, A. J., 415
Tomkins, S. S., 429, 437, 441
Tomson, S. N., 155
Toney, L., 226
Tong, E. M. W., 435
Tong, H., 583
Tononi, G., 96, 233, 234, 235
Tooby, J., 18, 24, 25, 431
Toppino, T. C., 263, 264
Torén K., 144, 200
Torneo, E., 258, 286
Torrey, E. F., 578
Toshiko, T., 509

Walker-Andrews, A. S., 187
Wall, H., 439
Wall, P., 151
Wall, S., 185, 560
Wallace, B. A., 226
Wallace, J., 451
Wallace, P., 411
Wallas, G., 394
Wallbott, H. G., 440
Wallen, K., 98
Waller, L., 420
Wallhagen, M. I., 202
Wallien, M. C., 196
Walmsley, P. T., 519
Walsh, J. P., 205
Walsh, S. P., 30
Walters, E. E., 482, 571, 574, 602, 634, 640
Walton, K. E., 521, 522
Wammes, J. D., 286
Wamsley, E. J., 235, 260, 264
Wan, C. R., 251
Wang, D., 543
Wang, F., 588
Wang, H., 202
Wang, H. Y. J., 469
Wang, H.-L., 487
Wang, H.-Z., 209
Wang, J. J., 202
Wang, J.-L., 209
Wang, M., 470
Wang, P., 415
Wang, S., 464, 470
Wang, S.-C., 80
Wang, W., 235
Wang, X., 202, 583
Wang, Z., 102, 583
Wanner, K. J., 71, 223
Warburton, J. B., 635
Ward, J., 155, 156
Ward, N., 223
Ward, R. E., 170
Ward, T. B., 397
Warden, D., 550
Ware, C., 208
Ware, M. A., 251
Warga, C., 152
Wark, H. A. C., 102
Warner, V., 91
Warren, C., 209
Warren, D. J., 102
Warreyn, P., 326
Waschek, J., 230
Wascher, E., 220
Wasdell, M. B., 234
Washburn, A. L., 411
Waskiewicz, N., 84
Wason, P. C., 353
Wasserman, J. D., 375
Wasserman, R. H., 227
Wasserman, T. H., 420
Watanabe, T., 111, 479
Waterhouse, J. J., 230
Waterland, R., 170
Waters, E., 185, 560
Watkins, G. L., 578
Watkins, K. E., 84
Watkins, L. R., 149
Watling, C. N., 236
Watson, G. L., 249
Watson, J. B., 303
Watson, J. M., 225
Watson, K. K., 324
Watters, C., 448, 449
Watters, E., 570
Watters, S., 223
Waugh, C. E., 432, 470
Waxenberg, S. E., 420
Waxman, J., 101
Waxman, S. R., 336, 347
Waxmonsky, J. G., 311
Way, B. M., 528
Wayne, S. J., 428

Waytz, A., 540
We, C., 30
Weatherall, M., 251
Weathers, S. B., 406
Weaver, A. L., 574
Weaver, D., 230
Webb, A. G., 444
Webb, A. P., 278
Webb, H., 433, 532
Webb, S. J., 575
Weber, J., 11
Weber, M., 594
Webster, G. D., 528
Wechsler, D., 375
Wechsler, H. L., 245, 246
Wedderburn, A. I., 230
Weeks, B. E., 547
Weeks, J. C., 286
Weickert, C. S., 636
Weierstall, R., 583
Weil, A., 156, 243, 247, 248, 249, 252
Weil, M. J., 252
Weiland, B. J., 251
Weiman, A. L., 444
Weinand, J. D., 199
Weinberg, R. A., 385
Weinberg, R. S., 10
Weinberger, D. R., 577, 578, 579, 636
Weinberger, M., 459
Weinstein, T. A., 512–513
Weisinger, R. S., 407
Weisman, H., 418
Weiss, A., 512
Weiss, E. M., 603, 604
Weissberg, R. P., 449
Weissman, M. M., 91
Weiten, W., 130
Weitzman, E. D., 240
Welch, E., 418
Weller, J. A., 223
Wellisch, D. K., 237, 238
Wells, T. S., 147
Welsh, R. C., 594
Welsh-Bohmer, K., 523
Wenar, C., 381
Wendell, J. W., 485
Wenden, A. L., 363
Wendt, J., 101
Wendt, P., 395, 397
Weng, H. Y., 556
Weng, S., 202
Weng, X., 124
Weng , H., 233
Wenger, E., 322–323, 362
Wenke, R., 306
Werchan, D., 234
Werge, T., 583
Werker, J. F., 198, 203
Wermke, M., 204
Werner, N. E., 5
Werntz, A. J., 545
Wertheimer, M., 350
Wessely, S., 614, 640
Westen, D., 501
Westerhausen, R., 323
Westermark, P. O., 414
Westerterp, K., 235
Westerveld, M., 329
Westgate, E. C., 528
Westling, E., 415
Westlye, L. T., 175
Westmaas, J. L., 556
Weston, D., 498
Weston, T., 266
Wetherell, M. A., 462
Wetherill, L. F., 170
Wethington, E., 203
Weyers, P., 443, 444
Weyman, M. T., 91
Weyrich, L. S., 479
Whalen, C. K., 575
Whalen, P. J., 443
Whalen, R., 478

Whalley, L., 378
Whalley, L. J., 388
Whalley, M. G., 242
What causes Down syndrome?, 381
What people do and do not believe, 42
Wheaton, P., 253
Wheeler, E., 226, 485
Wheeler, J., 156
Wheelwright, S., 574, 603
Whipple, B., 419
Whipps, J. M., 479
Whishaw, I. Q., 101
Whitaker, J. S., 379
White, A. M., 91
White, K. M., 30
White, M., 470
White, P., 151
White, R., 394
White, R. W., 597
Whitehill, J. M., 30, 223
Whitehouse, P. J., 523
Whiteman, M., 378
Whitfield, C., 583, 592
Whitfield, C. L., 577
Whiting, B., 190
Whitlock, J. R., 276
Whitty, M. T., 520
Whitworth, A. B., 615
Whooley, M. A., 471
Whorf, B. L., 345
Whybrow, P. C., 588
Wichers, M., 634
Wicherts, J. M., 383, 384
Wickelgren, I., 157
Wickens, T. D., 125
Wickham, R. E., 543
Wickramaratne, P., 91
Widen, S. C., 447
Widiyanto, B., 441
Widmer, V., 249
Wieczorek, J., 230
Wiederhold, B. K., 624, 630, 642
Wiederhold, M. D., 624, 630, 642
Wienbruch, C., 176
Wiener, J., 448, 449
Wiersema, J. R., 326
Wiese, M., 401
Wiesel, T., 130
Wieser, M. J., 443, 444
Wigg, K., 91
Wilcox, C. E., 639
Wilcox, K. J., 509
Wilensky, A., 443
Wiley, C., 426
Wiley, E., 361
Wilfley, D. E., 418
Wilhelm, F. H., 431
Wilkening, F., 192
Wilkinson, J., 478
Wille, B., 519
Willems, D., 290
Willemsen-Swinkels, S. H. N., 171
Willer, J-C., 150
Willer, R., 433
Willett, W. C., 415
Williams, A., 610
Williams, B., 80
Williams, G., 411, 412
Williams, G. L., 136
Williams, J. M. G., 632, 634
Williams, K. D., 194, 425, 444, 528, 541
Williams, L. A., 451
Williams, M., 433, 532
Williams, M. G., 226, 632, 633, 634, 641
Williams, R., 523
Williams, R. B., 329
Williams, R. B., Jr., 478
Williams, S. C. R., 579, 580
Williams, T. M., 91, 638
Williams, W. M., 351, 388
Willingham, B., 446
Willis, S. L., 203, 210
Willness, C. R., 30, 222, 223

Wills, T. A., 468, 477
Wilson, A., 483, 628
Wilson, D. A., 97
Wilson, J. G., 414
Wilson, M. A., 281
Wilson, S. J., 584
Wilson, T. D., 60, 528
Wilson, V., 388
Wilson Garvan, C., 575
Wimmer, H., 182
Winawer, J., 347, 348
Winblad, B., 204, 278
Windy, B., 216
Wing, A. L., 415
Wing, L., 310
Wing, R., 416
Winkleby, M. A., 418
Winkler, A. D., 134, 383
Winkler, A. M., 384
Winner, E., 176, 177, 574
Winston, F. K., 30
Winward, J. L., 251
Wise, R. A., 309, 329
Wise, R. G., 638
Wisk, L. E., 487
Witarama, T., 235
Witelson, S. F., 423
Witherby, S., 155
Witkin, H. A., 531
Witlox, R., 466
Witt, P., 487
Witte, K., 549
Witten, I. B., 636
Witthoft, N., 347, 348
Witton, J., 251
Witzki, A. H., 280, 444
Wixted, J. T., 263
Wobbrock, J. O., 227
Woelk, C. H., 594
Wohlschläger, A. M., 204, 441
Wojciechowski, F. L., 418
Wolchik, S. A., 476
Wolf, D. A., 381
Wolf, J. M., 440
Wolf, S., 205
Wolff, S. M., 471
Wölfling, K., 251
Wolford, J. L., 207
Wolkowitz, O. M., 471, 584
Wollmer, M. A., 442, 637
Wong, C. C. Y., 80
Wong, J., 149
Wong, M. L., 464
Wood, A., 442
Wood, E., 610, 637, 638, 639
Wood, J. J., 306
Wood, L. M., 448, 449
Wood, M. J., 482
Woodbury, M. A., 13
Woodley of Menie, M. A., 383, 384
Woodruff, B. K., 290
Woodside, D. B., 618
Woolard, J. L., 207
Woolf, L., 587
Woollett, K., 98
Work-related hearing loss, 202
Wouters-Adriaens, M., 235
Wright, C., 597
Wright, C. L., 166
Wright, D. A., 252
Wright, J. C., 207
Wright, J. S., 501
Wu, C., 464
Wu, H., 532, 578
Wu, L., 347, 348
Wu, M., 98, 601
Wu, T., 518
Wu, X., 601
Wurm, M., 477
Wurnig, M., 110
Wurst, W., 96
Wurtz, R. H., 101, 129, 131

Subject Index

ASL (American Sign Language), 343–345
Asperger's syndrome, 603
association, 261, 298, 299
associative network, 261, 261f
assortative mating, 556
assumptions, challenging, 544–545
asthma, 479
astrology, 42, 43
asylums, 13
Atkinson's model of success, 426
atmospheric perspective, 138, 138f
attachment, 184–186, 560
attachment theory, 184–185
attention, 219
  in cell-phone use while driving, 222–223
  distracted driving, 222–223
  in encoding, 286
  frontal lobes and, 99
  learning and, 292
  meditation and, 226
  memory and, 262–263, 269f, 271f, 273f
  in multitasking, 208
  multitasking, 224–225
  selective, 220–221, 253
  sustained, 222–223, 224f
  technology use and, 208
attention deficit hyperactivity disorder (ADHD)
  Adderall and, 249
  brain activity, 575
  combined therapies for, 633
  drug treatments for, 612
  environmental factors, 575
  norepinephrine and, 91
  overview of, 573–574, 573f
attentional disorders, 311
attitudes
  changes in, 547–549, 548f
  components of, 546
  definition of, 546
  nature and nurture of, 546–547
attraction, 556, 558–559, 558f
attributions, 536–538
atypical antipsychotics, 612
auditory canal, 146, 146f
auditory cortex, 101, 106, 153f, 279, 579, 579f
auditory nerve, 146f, 147
Australopithecus, 94f
autism, 479f
  Asperger's syndrome, 603
  creativity and, 603
  neural synchrony in, 193
  operant conditioning and, 309–310
  savant syndrome and, 382
  vaccines and, 39f
autism spectrum disorder
  causes of, 575
  head size as marker, 575
  mirror neurons, 575
  overview of, 573f, 574, 574f
autobiographical memory recall, 266, 287
automatic processing, 260
autonomic nervous system (ANS).
  See also sympathetic nervous system
  emotional response and, 436–437
  immune system and, 473
  stress and, 459–460, 461f
  structure of, 81, 81f
Autrey, Wesley, 552
availability heuristic, 356–358
avatar, 31
avatar therapy, 630–631, 642
averages, 52
avoidant personality disorder, 599
awareness, 215, 216–219, 217f
axons, 83, 84f, 87f, 92, 277f

B

B lymphocytes, 475
babbling, 336–337
BAC (blood alcohol concentration), 244, 245f
backward conditioning, 301
bad stress, 486–487
Baddeley's model of working memory, 271f
Bandura, Albert, 319, 319f
Bantu people, 157, 157f
barbiturates, 246, 614
Bartlett, Frederick, 18
basal ganglia, 97f, 98–99, 116f, 323, 579f
baseline state, 463
base-rates, 356
basic anxiety, 500–501, 500f
basic emotions, 430, 431f
basic hostility, 500–501, 500f
basic tendencies, 505
basilar membrane, 146, 146f
A Beautiful Mind, 603
Bedlam, 13
behavior
  behavioral thresholds, 493–494
  change of, 547–549, 548f
  counterproductive work, 519
  evolution of, 23–26, 23f
  four Ds of mental disorders, 569–570
  genes and, 77–80
  genetics and, 79–80, 508–510, 509f
  observation of, 45–48, 515–516
  prosocial, 552–556
  sexual, 48, 48f
  Type A Behavior Pattern, 477–479, 478f
behavior change, 547–549, 548f
behavior modification, 311, 329. *See also* operant conditioning
behavior therapies, 623–624
behavioral adaptation, 25–26, 25f
behavioral geneticists, 508
behavioral genetics, 18
  complexity of, 79
  epigenetics and, 79–80
  personality, 508–510, 509f
  polygenic influence, 79
  principles of, 79–80
  research, 80
  twin-adoption studies, 79
behavioral measures, 59f, 60–61
behavioral neuroscience, 8–9, 18
behavioral thresholds, 493–494
behaviorism, 16–17
behaviorism-learning perspective, 20, 22f
Bell, Alexander Graham, 15
bell curve, 62f, 379, 380f. *See also* normal distribution
The Bell Curve (Herrnstein and Murray), 387
belongingness, 425
beneficence, 67
Benzedrine, 249
benzodiazepines, 246, 614, 642
beta waves, 230
beta-blockers, 641
bias
  assumptions about objectivity, 5
  confirmation, 353
  experimenter expectancy effects, 54
  fundamental attribution error, 537
  in-group/out-group, 540–541
  implicit, 544
  in IQ tests, 378–379
  self-serving, 537–538
  social desirability, 60
big data, 56–57
Big Five model, 505, 505f
bilingualism, 361–363, 363f
binge drinking, 245–246
binocular depth cues, 137

binocular disparity, 137
biological constraint model, 317
biological psychology, 8–9
biological sciences, 38, 38f
biological theories
  on dreams, 239
  of personality, 507–508
bipolar cells, 128f
bipolar disorder, 586–588
  brain and, 587f, 588
  causes of, 587–588
  creativity and, 603f, 604
  drug treatment of, 613f, 615, 620
  symptoms of, 586, 586f
  treatments for, 610
biracial people, 200
birds, color vision, 134, 134f
birds, neurogenesis in, 107
birth order, 499
birth weight, 386
bisexuality. *See* sexual orientation
blind spot, 128, 128f
blindness
  brain reorganization in, 106, 106f, 115
  color, 135–136, 136f
  painting and, 76, 76f, 115–117, 115f, 116f
  perception and, 116–117
blocking, 290
blood alcohol concentration (BAC), 244, 245f
blood sugar, in digestion, 411
BMI (body mass index), 413, 413f
Bobo doll studies, 319–321, 320f, 322f, 551
bodily senses, 148–149. *See also specific senses*
bodily-kinesthetic intelligence, 372, 373f
body image, 413
body mass index (BMI), 413, 413f
body temperature, 228, 230, 230f, 408, 408f
Bolt, Usain, 432f
borderline personality disorder, 598, 600f, 633, 635
Botox
  emotion and, 441, 442
  new areas of treatment, 636–637
Braille, 117
brain. *See also specific brain structures*
  activity and creativity, 396
  in adolescence, 192–194, 194f
  aggression and, 98, 550
  alcohol and, 245, 245f
  alcohol use and, 245, 245f
  Armagan story, 115–117, 116f
  of arthropod, 93f
  bipolar disorder and, 587f, 588
  blindness or deafness and, 106
  in central nervous system, 81f
  cerebral cortex, 96, 99–101, 99f, 103–104
  cerebral hemispheres, 101, 103, 105f, 338, 395, 396
  in childhood, 173–175, 175f, 578, 578f
  consciousness, 218
  creativity and, 394–397
  depression and, 584, 617–618, 618f
  development, in infancy and childhood, 168f
  development in adolescence, 192–194
  development in middle adulthood, 202–203
  development of in infancy and toddlerhood, 173–175
  in early adulthood, 198
  effects of neglect in children, 592f

electrical stimulation to enhance memory, 284, 284f
  emotions and, 442–445, 443f
  empathy and, 556
  environmental influences on, 22, 173–175, 175f
  evolution of, 93–95, 94f
  exercise and, 483
  forebrain, 95, 95f, 96–97
  glutamate and, 91
  hearing and, 147–148
  hindbrain, 95, 95f, 96, 97
  imaging of, 109–111, 110f
  in infancy, 173–175, 175f
  intelligence and, 193–194, 194f, 383–384, 384f
  language acquisition and, 341, 343f
  language and, 336
  language development and, 338f
  in late adulthood, 203, 209–210
  learning and, 105–106, 234–235, 325f
  limbic system, 97–99, 97f
  long-term memory, 281–282, 282f
  measurement of, 109–111
  measurement techniques, 109–111, 110f
  meditation and, 227–228, 227f
  memory and, 267f, 275–284, 280f
  midbrain, 95, 95f, 96
  in middle adulthood, 202
  mind and, 22
  musical training and, 176–177, 176f, 203, 326
  myelination in, 175, 175f, 193
  myelination of, 175f
  pain and, 150–151, 151f
  painting and, 115–117, 116f
  personality and, 507–508
  plasticity and neurogenesis, 105–106, 105f, 204–205
  prenatal development, 166–169, 167f–168f
  regions involved in imagining and perceiving faces and places, 112, 112f
  regions of, 95–101, 97f, 103–104, 105f
  schizophrenia and, 578–580, 578f, 579f
  second-language learning and, 361–363, 363f
  sensory memory and, 279
  sexual activity and, 419–420
  sexual orientation and, 423
  short-term memory, 280
  sleep and, 230–232, 232f
  smell and, 153, 153f
  social pain and, 528–529, 541, 541f
  stimulation of and memory, 282–284, 284f
  stress and, 464
  structure of, 95f
  structure of in mammals, 95f
  structures of in humans, 95f
  synaptic change during learning, 326
  taste and, 154–155
  technology and development of, 207–208, 209–210
  vision and, 127–130, 130f
  visual field, 104f
  visual imagery and, 350
  working memory, 280
brain games, 209–210
brain injury, 253
  aggression and, 550
  consciousness and, 217, 253
  frontal lobes, 100, 100f
  memory and, 258, 267, 267f
  memory loss and, 290–291
  personality change after, 100, 443, 523
  personality disorders and, 600
  sleeping and dreaming and, 253

FR (fixed ratio) schedule, 312, 313*f*
Fragile X syndrome, 381
Franklin, Ben, 283
fraternal twins, 55, 199, 342. *See also*
    twin-adoption studies
free association, 496, 622
free radicals, 235
frequency, 62, 145, 148*f*
Freud, Sigmund, 13*f*, 495–498, 501,
    621–622
friending, 31
frontal lobes, 100*f*
    in adolescence, 193
    alcohol and, 245*f*
    alcohol use and, 245*f*
    creativity and, 395
    location and function of,
        99–100, 99*f*
    location of, 116*f*
    pain and, 151*f*
    schizophrenia and, 579*f*
full consciousness, 219
functional fixedness, 392–393
functional MRI (fMRI), 103, 109–110,
    110*f*, 112, 112*f*, 218
functionalism, 16
fundamental attribution error, 537
fusiform face area (FFA), 112, 112*f*

G

GABA (gamma-aminobutyric acid),
    90, 90*f*, 91, 237, 591
GAD (generalized anxiety disorder),
    589, 589*f*
Gage, Fred "Rusty," 107–108
Gage, Phineas, brain injury of, 100,
    100*f*, 107, 443–444
ganglion cells, 127, 128*f*
Garcia, John, 314, 314*f*
Gardner's multiple intelligences,
    372–373, 373*f*, 374
GAS (general adaptation syndrome),
    462–463, 462*f*, 473
gate control theory of pain, 151
Gauguin, Paul, 568
Gemütlichkeit, 334
gender differences
    in adolescent brain
        development, 193
    in age of first marriage, 201, 201*f*
    in age-related hearing loss, 202,
        202*f*
    in drive for casual sex,
        420–421, 422
    in emotion, 447–448
    in insomnia, 237
    in intelligence, 388, 388*f*
    in mental rotation tasks, 350–351
    in pain thresholds, 157–159
    in parenthood, 201, 201*f*
    in peer interactions, 190
    in personality development,
        190–191
    in puberty, 191–192, 192*f*
    in sexual attraction and mate
        selection, 559
    in sexual response cycle,
        418–419, 419*f*
    in social network influences, 468
    spatial ability and, 351
    in tactile sensitivity, 149
    in tobacco use, 329
gender identity, 195, 199, 199*f*, 421
gender role identification, 351
gene-by-environment interaction
    research, 55, 79
general adaptation syndrome, 473
general adaptation syndrome (GAS),
    462–463, 462*f*
general intelligence, 369–370, 371. *See
    also* intelligence
generalized anxiety disorder (GAD),
    589, 589*f*

generativity, 203
genes. *See also* heritability
    behavior and, 77–80
    chance mutations, 24
    environment and, 79–80
    epigenetics, 79–80
    expression of, 79–80
    genetic markers, 79, 508
    in the human genome, 77
    identical twins, 164
    long-term memory and, 279
    neurodevelopmental
        disorders, 575
    polygenic transmission by, 79
    research on regulation of, 636
    role of, 77
    structures and mechanisms of,
        77–78, 78*f*
genetic influences
    on aggression, 550
    on anxiety disorders, 591
    on attitudes, 546
    on bipolar disorder, 587–588
    on depression, 585, 585*f*
    environmental forces and, 22
    on intelligence, 384–385,
        385*f*, 386*f*
    on language acquisition, 342
    on obesity, 414
    on personality, 507–510, 507*f*, 509*f*
    on schizophrenia, 577, 578
    on sexual orientation, 423
    on stress, 464
    twin-adoption studies and, 80
genetic markers, 79, 508
genius, 394–395, 399–401
genome, 77, 78*f*
genotype, 77, 164
genotypes, identical twins, 164
Genovese, Kitty, 552–553, 553*f*
germinal stage, 165
Gestalt laws of grouping, 139*f*,
    141–143, 142*f*, 143*f*
Gestalt psychology, 17–18
g-factor theory of intelligence, 370
ghrelin, 411, 412*f*
giftedness, 381–383, 382*f*
ginkgo biloba, 279
glial cells, 83
global workspace theory, 215, 216
glucocorticoids, 461
glucose, 411
glutamate
    functions of, 88, 90, 90*f*, 91
    LSD and, 252
    schizophrenia and, 580, 620
gonads, 191
good stress, 486, 487
Goodall, Jane, 46*f*
Gould, Elizabeth, 108
graded potentials, 88
grammar, 335, 341
Grandin, Temple, 574*f*
graphs, misleading, 65, 65*f*
grasping reflex, 172
gratitude training, 623
gray matter, 111, 174, 175*f*
Greeks, ancient, 12
group behavior. *See* social behavior
group therapy, 626–628, 642
groupthink, 531–532
gustatory cortex, 153*f*, 154
gut-brain axis, 479–480, 479*f*

H

habituation, 298
hair cells, 146, 146*f*, 147, 148*f*
Hall, G. Stanley, 15–16
Halle Berry neurons, 132, 132*f*
hallucinations, 243, 576, 579
hallucinogenic mushrooms, 252
hallucinogens, 639
    LSD, 244*f*, 252

marijuana, 244*f*, 250–251
    psilocybin, 252
haloperidol (Haldol), 612
hammer, 146*f*
happiness
    basic needs and, 450–451
    bodily sensations of, 441*f*
    facial expression of, 439*f*
    higher needs and, 450–451
    meaning in life and, 451, 470
    oxytocin and, 445
    positive emotions, 469–470
    world happiness map, 450, 450*f*
Hassles and Uplifts Scale, 459
Head Start, 387, 449
health, changing beliefs about, 487
health behavior approach, 472,
    479–480
health psychology, 10, 31, 472
hearing
    absolute thresholds in, 124*f*
    auditory cortex and, 101
    brain and, 148
    ear and, 146–148, 146*f*, 148*f*
    in middle adulthood, 202, 202*f*
    physics of sound, 144–145, 145*f*
    prenatal, 167*f*, 168–169
    psychology of, 144–145
    psychophysics of, 144–145
    signal detection theory, 125
hearing loss, 147
heart disease. *See* cardiovascular
    disease
Hebb, Donald, 276
Heinz dilemma, 182–183
Helmholtz, Hermann von, 15
hemispheres, cerebral. *See* cerebral
    hemispheres
herbal medications for memory,
    278–279
heritability, 79, 80. *See also* genes;
    genetic influences
heroes, 552
heroin, 247
heterosexuality, 195. *See also* sexual
    orientation
heuristics, 356–358
hierarchies, 261
hierarchy of needs, 410–411,
    410*f*, 411*f*
highly superior autobiographical
    memory (HSAM), 274, 275
hindbrain, 95, 95*f*, 96, 97
hippocampus, 105
    alcohol and, 245, 245*f*
    alcohol use and, 245*f*
    depression and, 618*f*
    emotion and, 443, 443*f*
    exercise and, 483
    functions of, 97–98
    learning and, 323
    location of, 97*f*
    memory and, 258, 264, 267*f*, 276,
        280, 280*f*, 281*f*, 282*f*
    neural growth in, 107–108
    pain and, 151*f*
    post-traumatic stress disorder
        and, 595
    schizophrenia and, 578, 579*f*
    sleep and, 235
    stress and, 464
Hippocrates, 12
Hispanics. *See* race-ethnicity
histrionic personality disorder, 598
hit, 125, 125*f*
Hitzig, Eduard, 99
Hobson's A-I-M model, 239, 239*f*
homeostasis, 408, 408*f*, 463
Homo erectus, 94*f*
Homo neanderthalensis. *See*
    Neanderthals
Homo sapiens, 94, 94*f*
homophobia, 497

homosexuality, 195. *See also* sexual
    orientation
hormones. *See also* specific
    hormones
    aggression and, 550–551
    in endocrine system, 113
    functions of, 113
    hunger and, 411–412, 412*f*
    sex, 113, 191, 351, 420, 550–551
    stress, 460–464, 461*f*
hospice, 206
hostile aggression, 550, 551
hostility
    aggression vs., 550
    basic, 500–501, 500*f*
    heart disease and, 477–479, 478*f*
    overview of, 503–504, 504*f*
HPA axis. *See* hypothalamic-pituitary-
    adrenal (HPA) axis
Huichol tribe of Mexico, 158
human behavior
    evolution of, 23–26
    perspectives on, 20–23, 22*f*
human development, 164
    cognitive, in adolescence,
        192–194, 194*f*
    cognitive, in infancy and
        childhood, 171–180, 174*f*–177*f*,
        183*f*, 207
    cognitive, in infancy and
        childhood, 175–182
    death and dying, 206
    in early adulthood, 197–201,
        198*f*, 201*f*
    of emotions, 187
    fetal development, 165–171
    of language, 336–339, 338*f*
    in late adulthood, 203–206, 204*f*,
        205*f*, 210
    in middle adulthood, 202–203,
        202*f*, 209–210
    of moral reasoning, 182–183, 183*f*
    personality, in adolescence,
        196–197, 196*f*
    personality, in early
        adulthood, 201
    personality, in infancy, 184
    personality, in late adulthood, 206
    personality, in middle adulthood,
        202–203
    physical, in adolescence,
        191–192, 192*f*
    physical, in infancy and
        childhood, 171–175
    physical, in infancy and
        childhood, 167–171,
        167*f*–171*f*, 175*f*
    prenatal, 165–166, 165*f*, 166*f*
    of sleep over the life span,
        232–233, 232*f*
    social, in adolescence,
        194–196, 196*f*
    socioemotional, in infants and
        children, 184–191, 207–208
    technology, influence of, 207–210
    technology and, 207–210,
        208*f*, 209*f*
    of vision, 132
human genome, 81
human language, 335. *See also*
    language
human perception, psychophysics
    of, 14–16
human rationality, 358–359
human research, ethics in, 66–68
humane treatment, 69
humanistic psychology, 17,
    501–503
humanistic-positive psychological
    theories
    Maslow on, 502
    Rogers on, 502–503
    summary of, 495*f*
    in treatment, 622–623

three mountains task, 179–180, 180*f*
three-dimensional movies, 137, 137*f*
three-stage model of memory, 268, 269*f*
thresholds, in action potentials, 92
thrill-seeking behavior, 509
thyroid gland, 111*f*, 113, 114*f*
thyroid hormones, bipolar disorder and, 588
timbre, 145
timeline of psychology, 19*f*
Tinder, 559
tip-of-the-tongue phenomenon, 218, 290
Titchener, Edward, 16
TMS (transcranial magnetic stimulation), 616–617, 617*f*
tobacco use, 248
  cognitive dissonance and, 547, 548*f*
  health effects of, 481
  nicotine, 91, 248, 481
  in pregnancy, 170
  reasons for, 327–329, 328*f*
  secondhand smoke, 481
  social networks and, 542
toddlerhood
  brain development in, 173–175
  cognitive development in, 175–182
  motor development in, 171–172, 172*f*
  physical development in, 171–175
  sensory development in, 172–173
token economies, 623
tolerable stress, 487
tolerance, 243
tongue, 154
top-down processing, 157
touch, 124*f*, 149, 186–187
touch therapy, 186–187, 187*f*
toxic stress, 487
toxoplasmosis, 594
tracts, 111
traditional antipsychotics, 612
trait theories, 495*f*, 504–505, 505*f*
traits, 493
  in personality, 493, 495*f*, 504–505, 505*f*
  polygenic transmission of, 79
transcranial direct current stimulation (tDCS), 210, 283, 283*f*, 617
transcranial magnetic stimulation (TMS), 616–617, 617*f*
transduction, 123
transference, 622
transgender identity, 195–196, 199, 199*f*
trauma
  depression and, 583–584
  memory and, 264–265, 265*f*
treatment of disorders
  of anxiety disorders, 641–642
  behavioral treatments, 623–624
  biological treatment effectiveness, 619–621
  choosing a therapist, 634–635
  cognitive treatments, 624–626
  combined approach effectiveness, 633–635, 633*f*
  combined drug therapy and psychotherapy, 632
  combined mindfulness training and psychotherapy, 633–635

drug therapies, 612–615, 613*f*, 614*f*, 619–621, 628
electric and magnetic therapies, 616–618, 617*f*, 619*f*, 620–621
group therapies, 626–628, 642
humanistic-positive therapies, 622–623
integrative therapies, 632
major approaches, 611*f*
prevention of disorders, 640–641
psychoanalytic/psychodynamic therapies, 621–622
psychological treatment effectiveness, 628–630
psychosurgery, 615–616
technology-based therapies, 630–631
treatments, 628–630
trephination, 11, 11*f*
triangular theory of love, 560, 560*f*
triarchic theory of intelligence, 372
trichromatic, 133, 134*f*
trichromatic color theory, 135, 135*f*
tricyclic antidepressants, 612–613, 641
triplet puzzle, 353–354
trisomy-21, 380–381
Trump, Donald, 540
t-test, 63–64
Tversky, Amos, 358–359, 359*f*
twin-adoption studies, 164
  behavioral genetics, 79
  on bipolar disorder, 588
  eating disorders, 418
  epigenetics and, 80
  fraternal twins, 55
  hypothetical situations from, 55*f*
  identical twins, 55, 164
  on intelligence, 384, 385*f*
  on language acquisition, 342
  overview of, 54–56
  on personality traits, 509, 509*f*
  on schizophrenia, 577
  on sexual orientation, 423
twins, fraternal, 55, 199, 342
twins, identical, 164, 199, 342
Twitter, 542
two-string problem, 390, 390*f*, 392–393
two-word utterances, 337
tympanic membrane, 146, 146*f*
Type A Behavior Pattern (TABP), 477–479, 478*f*

U

ultrasonic sounds, 145
ultraviolet light, 134
Ulysses (Joyce), 394
umami, 154
unconditional positive regard, 503
unconditioned response (UCR), 300–301, 302*f*
unconditioned stimulus (UCS), 300–302, 302*f*
unconscious, 496, 501
Underwood, Ben, 122
universal, definition of, 437
universal grammar, 341, 346
Urbanmyths.com, 355

V

vaccines, 39*f*, 475
validity, 40, 378

Valium, 246
Van Gogh, Vincent, 568, 569
variable interval (VI) schedule, 313, 313*f*
variable ratio (VR) schedule, 312–313, 313*f*
variables, 44
vegetative state, 217–218, 217*f*
verbal intelligence, 369
verbal representation, 351–352, 352*f*
verbal representation of thought, 351–352
vestibular cortex, 153*f*
veterans, PTSD in. *See* posttraumatic stress disorder (PTSD)
VI (variable interval) schedule, 313, 313*f*
Vicodin, 246
video games, 207, 210, 551–552
violence, 443. *See also* aggression
  sensitivity to, 552
  in video games, 551–552
virtual reality exposure, 624, 625*f*
virtual reality therapies, 630–631
viruses, as teratogens, 170
vision, 124, 127
  absolute thresholds in, 124*f*
  brain and, 127–130, 130*f*
  color, 128*f*, 133–136, 133*f*, 136*f*
  cultural variation in, 156–157, 157*f*, 159*f*
  deficiencies in, 135–136
  depth perception, 137–140, 138*f*, 156–157, 157*f*
  eye and, 127, 128*f*
  Gestalt laws of grouping, 139*f*, 141–143, 142*f*, 143*f*
  infant development of, 172–173, 173*f*, 174*f*
  motion perception, 136–137
  neurons and, 130–132, 131*f*
  night, 124
  patterns and wholes, 141–143
  perception of color, 133–136
  perceptual constancy in, 140–141, 141*f*
  prenatal development of, 169
  size and shape perception, 140–141
  visual cortex and, 101
  visual representation, 349–351, 350*f*
  visual stimuli, sensing, 127–133
visual acuity, 127, 173
visual cliff, 173, 174*f*
visual cortex, 101, 116–117, 116*f*, 153*f*, 279
visual field, 103, 104*f*
visual imagery, 349, 397, 397*f*
visual pathways, 127–130, 130*f*
visual representation of thought, 349–351
visual stimuli, 127–133
visuospatial sketch pad, 271, 271*f*, 274*f*, 280*f*
visuospatial sketchpad, 270, 271
vividness, 357
vocabulary, 339–340, 339*f*
vocal expression, emotions and, 440, 447
voltage-dependent channels, 86
VR (variable ratio) schedule, 312–313, 313*f*

W

WAIS (Wechsler Adult Intelligence Scale), 365, 366*f*–367*f*, 377, 378
Wakefield, Andrew, 39
wakefulness, 216–219, 217*f*
Waldman, Ayelet, 610
water jar problems, 389, 390*f*, 391
Watson, John, 16–17, 303, 303*f*
wavelengths, 133–134, 134*f*
Weathers, Beck, 406–407
Weber, Ernst, 15
Weber's law, 126
Wechsler Adult Intelligence Scale (WAIS), 365, 366*f*–367*f*, 376*f* 377, 378
Wechsler Intelligence Scale for Children (WISC), 375, 376*f* 377, 377*f*
weight, properties of, 15
weight loss, 415–416, 451
well-being, 450–452
Wernicke, Carl, 103
Wernicke's area, 103, 103*f*, 280*f*, 336, 343*f*
Wertheimer, Max, 17
white matter, 111, 174, 175*f*
wholes, perception of, 141–143
Whorf-Sapir hypothesis, 346–347
wilderness survival, 406–407
Willie Horton advertisements, 549
WISC (Wechsler Intelligence Scale for Children), 375, 377, 377*f*
wisdom, 204, 206
witch hunts, 12*f*, 13
withdrawal symptoms, 243
women and girls. *See also* gender differences
  menarche in, 191
  as psychologists, 16
  sexual response cycle in, 418–419, 419*f*
  testosterone in, 420
  thinness and obesity in, 413–414, 417*f*
Woolf, Virginia, 586–587
word salad, 393–394, 577
working memory, 269–272, 271*f*, 280, 280*f*, 377, 377*f*. *See also* short-term memory
workplace. *See also* industrial/organizational (I/O) psychology
  career identity, 198
  employee motivation models, 426–429, 429*f*
  hearing loss in, 147, 202
  personality and, 518–519
work-related hearing loss, 202
world happiness map, 450*f*
writing, as coping strategy, 467
Wundt, Wilhelm, 15, 15*f*, 16
Wuornos, Aileen, 600*f*

Y

Yap people, 157–158
Yerkes-Dodson law, 409, 409*f*
young adulthood, 200–201, 201*f*, 208–209, 209*f*

Z

Zoloft, 170, 613
zone of proximal development, 181
zygote, 165, 165*f*